Real-Time Data Analysis Exercises

Up-to-date macro data is a great way to engage in and understand the usefulness of macro variables and their impact on the economy. Real-Time Data Analysis exercises communicate directly with the Federal Reserve Bank of St. Louis's FRED site, so every time FRED posts new data, students see new data.

End-of-chapter exercises accompanied by the Real-Time Data Analysis icon 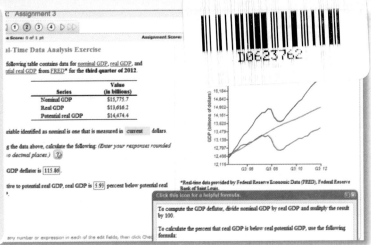 include Real-Time Data versions in **MyEconLab**.

Select in-text figures labeled **MyEconLab** Real-Time Data update in the electronic version of the text using FRED data.

Current News Exercises

Posted weekly, we find the latest microeconomic and macroeconomic news stories, post them, and write auto-graded multi-part exercises that illustrate the economic way of thinking about the news.

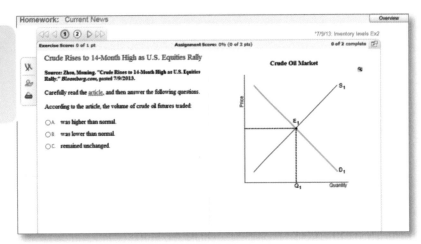

Interactive Homework Exercises

Participate in a fun and engaging activity that helps promote active learning and mastery of important economic concepts.

Pearson's experiments program is flexible and easy for instructors and students to use. For a complete list of available experiments, visit *www.myeconlab.com*.

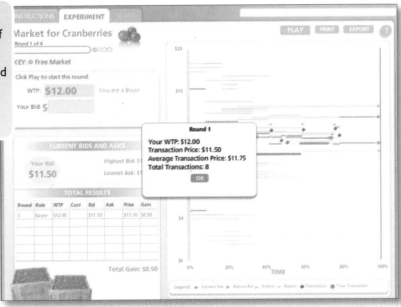

Managerial Economics and Strategy

THE PEARSON SERIES IN ECONOMICS

Abel/Bernanke/Croushore
Macroeconomics*

Bade/Parkin
Foundations of Economics*

Berck/Helfand
The Economics of the Environment

Bierman/Fernandez
Game Theory with Economic Applications

Blanchard
Macroeconomics*

Blau/Ferber/Winkler
The Economics of Women, Men, and Work

Boardman/Greenberg/ Vining/ Weimer
Cost-Benefit Analysis

Boyer
Principles of Transportation Economics

Branson
Macroeconomic Theory and Policy

Brock/Adams
The Structure of American Industry

Bruce
Public Finance and the American Economy

Carlton/Perloff
Modern Industrial Organization

Case/Fair/Oster
Principles of Economics*

Caves/Frankel/Jones
World Trade and Payments: An Introduction

Chapman
Environmental Economics: Theory, Application, and Policy

Cooter/Ulen
Law & Economics

Downs
An Economic Theory of Democracy

Ehrenberg/Smith
Modern Labor Economics

Farnham
Economics for Managers

Folland/Goodman/Stano
The Economics of Health and Health Care

Fort
Sports Economics

Froyen
Macroeconomics

Fusfeld
The Age of the Economist

Gerber
International Economics*

González-Rivera
Forecasting for Economics and Business

Gordon
Macroeconomics*

Greene
Econometric Analysis

Gregory
Essentials of Economics

Gregory/Stuart
Russian and Soviet Economic Performance and Structure

Hartwick/Olewiler
The Economics of Natural Resource Use

Heilbroner/Milberg
The Making of the Economic Society

Heyne/Boettke/Prychitko
The Economic Way of Thinking

Hoffman/Averett
Women and the Economy: Family, Work, and Pay

Holt
Markets, Games, and Strategic Behavior

Hubbard/O'Brien
Economics*

Money, Banking, and the Financial System*

Hubbard/O'Brien/Rafferty
Macroeconomics*

Hughes/Cain
American Economic History

Husted/Melvin
International Economics

Jehle/Reny
Advanced Microeconomic Theory

Johnson-Lans
A Health Economics Primer

Keat/Young/Erfle
Managerial Economics

Klein
Mathematical Methods for Economics

Krugman/Obstfeld/Melitz
International Economics: Theory & Policy*

Laidler
The Demand for Money

Leeds/von Allmen
The Economics of Sports

Leeds/von Allmen/Schiming
Economics*

Lipsey/Ragan/Storer
Economics*

Lynn
Economic Development: Theory and Practice for a Divided World

Miller
Economics Today*
Understanding Modern Economics

Miller/Benjamin
The Economics of Macro Issues

Miller/Benjamin/North
The Economics of Public Issues

Mills/Hamilton
Urban Economics

Mishkin
The Economics of Money, Banking, and Financial Markets*

The Economics of Money, Banking, and Financial Markets, Business School Edition*

Macroeconomics: Policy and Practice*

Murray
Econometrics: A Modern Introduction

Nafziger
The Economics of Developing Countries

O'Sullivan/Sheffrin/Perez
Economics: Principles, Applications and Tools*

Parkin
Economics*

Perloff
Microeconomics*

Microeconomics: Theory and Applications with Calculus*

Perloff/Brander
Managerial Economics and Strategy*

Phelps
Health Economics

Pindyck/Rubinfeld
Microeconomics*

Riddell/Shackelford/Stamos/ Schneider
Economics: A Tool for Critically Understanding Society

Ritter/Silber/Udell
Principles of Money, Banking & Financial Markets*

Roberts
The Choice: A Fable of Free Trade and Protection

Rohlf
Introduction to Economic Reasoning

Ruffin/Gregory
Principles of Economics

Sargent
Rational Expectations and Inflation

Sawyer/Sprinkle
International Economics

Scherer
Industry Structure, Strategy, and Public Policy

Schiller
The Economics of Poverty and Discrimination

Sherman
Market Regulation

Silberberg
Principles of Microeconomics

Stock/Watson
Introduction to Econometrics

Studenmund
Using Econometrics: A Practical Guide

Tietenberg/Lewis
Environmental and Natural Resource Economics

Environmental Economics and Policy

Todaro/Smith
Economic Development

Waldman
Microeconomics

Waldman/Jensen
Industrial Organization: Theory and Practice

Walters/Walters/Appel/ Callahan/Centanni/Maex/ O'Neill
Econversations: Today's Students Discuss Today's Issues

Weil
Economic Growth

Williamson
Macroeconomics

Managerial Economics and Strategy

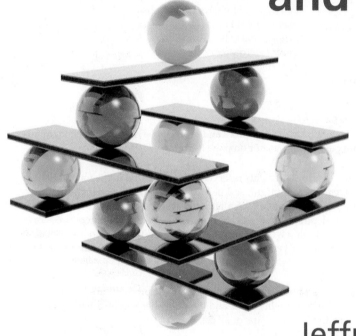

Jeffrey M. Perloff
University of California, Berkeley

James A. Brander
Sauder School of Business,
University of British Columbia

PEARSON

Boston   Columbus   Indianapolis   New York   San Francisco   Upper Saddle River
Amsterdam   Cape Town   Dubai   London   Madrid   Milan   Munich   Paris   Montreal   Toronto
Delhi   Mexico City   Sao Paulo   Sydney   Hong Kong   Seoul   Singapore   Taipei   Tokyo

For Jackie, Lisa, Barbara, and Cathy

Editor-in-Chief: Donna Battista
Executive Acquisitions Editor: Adrienne D'Ambrosio
Editorial Project Manager: Sarah Dumouchelle
Editorial Assistant: Elissa Senra-Sargent
Executive Marketing Manager: Lori DeShazo
Managing Editor: Jeff Holcomb
Senior Production Project Manager: Meredith Gertz
Senior Procurement Specialist: Carol Melville
Art Director: Jonathan Boylan
Cover Designer: John Christiana
Cover Image: Artisilense/Shutterstock
Image Manager: Rachel Youdelman
Photo Research: Integra Software Services, Ltd.
Associate Project Manager—Text Permissions: Samantha Blair Graham

Text Permissions Research: Electronic Publishing Services
Director of Media: Susan Schoenberg
Content Leads, MyEconLab: Noel Lotz and Courtney Kamauf
Executive Media Producer: Melissa Honig
Project Management and Text Design: Gillian Hall, The Aardvark Group
Composition and Illustrations: Laserwords Maine
Copyeditor: Rebecca Greenberg
Proofreader: Holly McLean-Aldis
Indexer: John Lewis
Printer/Binder: RR Donnelley
Cover Printer: Lehigh Phoenix
Text Font: Palatino

Credits and acknowledgments borrowed from other sources and reproduced, with permission, in this textbook appear on the appropriate page within text or on page E-51.

Many of the designations by manufacturers and sellers to distinguish their products are claimed as trademarks. Where those designations appear in this book, and the publisher was aware of a trademark claim, the designations have been printed in initial caps or all caps.

Library of Congress Cataloging-in-Publication Data

Perloff, Jeffrey M.
    Managerial economics and strategy/Jeffrey Perloff, James Brander. — First edition.
        pages cm
    Includes bibliographical references and index.
    ISBN 978-0-321-56644-7
    1. Managerial economics. I. Brander, James A. II. Title.
    HD30.22.P436 2014
    338.5024′658 — dc23

2013022387

10 9 8 7 6 5 4 3 2 1

www.pearsonhighered.com

ISBN 10: 0-321-56644-0
ISBN 13: 978-0-321-56644-7

Brief Contents

Contents

Preface

Successful managers make extensive use of economic tools when making important decisions. They use these tools to produce at minimum cost, to choose an output level to maximize profit, and for many other managerial decisions including:

- Whether to offer buy-one-get-one-free deals
- How much to advertise
- Whether to sell various goods as a bundle
- What strategies to use to compete with rival firms
- How to design compensation contracts to provide appropriate incentives for employees
- How to structure an international supply chain to take advantage of cross-country differences in production costs

We illustrate how to apply economic theory using actual business examples and real data. Our experience teaching managerial economics at the Wharton School (University of Pennsylvania) and the Sauder School of Business (University of British Columbia) as well as teaching a wide variety of students at the Massachusetts Institute of Technology; Queen's University; and the University of California, Berkeley, has convinced us that students prefer our emphasis on real-world issues and examples from actual markets.

Main Innovations

This book differs from other managerial economics texts in three main ways.

- It places greater emphasis than other texts on *modern theories* that are increasingly useful to managers in areas such as industrial organization, transaction cost theory, game theory, contract theory, and behavioral economics.
- It makes more extensive use of real-world business examples to illustrate how to use economic theory in making business decisions.
- It employs a *problem-based* approach to demonstrate how to apply economic theory to specific business decisions.

Modern Theories for Business Decisions

This book has all the standard economic theory, of course. However, what sets it apart is its emphasis on modern theories that are particularly useful for managers.

Industrial Organization. How do managers differentiate their products to increase their profits? When do mergers pay off? When should a firm take (legal) actions to prevent entry of rivals? What effects do government price regulations have on firms' behavior? These and many other questions are addressed by industrial organization theories.

Transaction Cost Theory. Why do some firms produce inputs while others buy them from a market? Why are some firms vertically integrated whiles others are not? We use transaction cost theory to address questions such as these, particularly in Chapter 7.

Game Theory. Should the manager of a radio station schedule commercial breaks at the same time as rival firms? What strategy should a manager use when bidding in an auction for raw materials? The major issue facing many managers is deciding what strategies to use in competing with rivals. This book goes well beyond other managerial economics texts by making significant use of game theory in Chapters 12–14 to examine such topics as oligopoly quantity and price setting, entry and exit decisions, entry deterrence, and strategic trade policy. Game theory provides a way of thinking about strategies and it provides methods to choose strategies that maximize profits. Unlike most microeconomic and managerial economics books, our applications of game theory are devoted almost exclusively to actual business problems.

Contract Theory. What kind of a contract should a manager offer a worker to induce the employee to work hard? How do managers avoid moral hazard problems so they aren't taken advantage of by people who have superior information? We use modern contract theory to show how to write contracts to avoid or minimize such problems.

Behavioral Economics. Should a manager allow workers to opt in or opt out of a retirement system? How can the manager of a motion picture firm take advantage of movie reviews? We address questions such as these using behavioral economics— one of the hottest new areas of economic theory—which uses psychological research and theory to explain why people deviate from rational behavior. These theories are particularly relevant for managers, but sadly they have been largely ignored by most economists until recently.

Real-World Business Examples

We demonstrate that economics is practical and useful to managers by examining real markets and actual business decisions. We do so in two ways. In our presentation of the basic theory, we use real-world data and examples. Second, we examine many real-world problems in our various application features.

To illustrate important economic concepts, we use graphs and calculations based on actual markets and real data. Students learn the basic model of supply and demand using estimated supply and demand curves for avocados, and they practice estimating demand curves using real data such as from the Portland Fish Exchange. They study how imported oil limits pricing by U.S. oil producers using real estimated supply and demand curves, derive cost curves from Japanese beer manufacturers using actual estimated production functions, and analyze oligopoly strategies using estimated demand curves and cost and profit data from the real-world rivalries between United Airlines and American Airlines and between Coke and Pepsi.

Problem-Based Learning

Managers have to solve business problems daily. We use a problem-solving approach to demonstrate how economic theory can help mangers make good decisions. In each chapter, we solve problems using a step-by-step approach to model good problem-solving techniques. At the end of the chapter, we have an extensive set of questions. Some of these require the student to solve problems similar to the solved problems in the chapter, while others ask the student to use the tools of the chapter to answer questions about applications within the chapter or new real-world problems. We also provide exercises asking students to use spreadsheets to apply the theory they have learned to real-world problems.

Features

This book has more features dedicated to showing students how to apply theory to real-world problems than do rival texts.

Managerial Implications. Managerial Implications sections contain simple bottom-line statements of economic principles that managers can use to make key managerial decisions. For example, we describe how managers can assess whether they are maximizing profit by using data to estimate demand elasticities. We also show how they can structure discounts to maximize profits, promote customer loyalty, design auctions, prevent gray markets, and use important insights from game theory to improve managerial decisions.

Mini-Cases. Over a hundred Mini-Cases apply economic theory to interesting and important managerial problems. For example, Mini-Cases demonstrate how price increases on iTunes affect music downloads (using actual data), how to estimate Blackberry's production function using real-world data, why some top-end designers limit the number of designer bags customers can buy, how "poison pills" at Yahoo! affected shareholders, how Pfizer used limit pricing to slow entry of rivals, why advertisers pay so much for Superbowl commercials, and how managers of auto manufacturing firms react to tariffs and other regulations.

Q&As. After the introductory chapter, each chapter provides three to five Q&As (Questions & Answers). Each Q&A poses a qualitative or quantitative problem and then uses a step-by-step approach to solve the problem. Most of the 55 Q&As focus on important managerial issues such as how a cost-minimizing firm would adjust to changing factor prices, how a manager prices bundles of goods to maximize profits, how to determine Intel's and AMD's profit-maximizing quantities and prices using their estimated demand curves and marginal costs, and how to allocate production across plants internationally.

Managerial Problems and Managerial Solutions. After the introductory chapter, each chapter starts with a Managerial Problem that motivates the chapter by posing real-world managerial questions that can be answered using the economic principles and methods developed in the chapter. At the end of each chapter, we answer these questions in the Managerial Solution. Thus, each pair of these features combines the essence of a Mini-Case and a Q&A.

End-of-Chapter Questions. Starting with Chapter 2, each chapter ends with an extensive set of questions, many of which are based on real-world problems. Each Q&A has at least one associated end-of-chapter question that references the Q&A and allows the student to answer a similar problem, and many of the questions are related to Mini-Cases that appear in the book. The answers to selected end-of-chapter problems appear at the end of the book, and all of the end-of-chapter questions are available in MyEconLab for self-assessment, homework, or testing.

Spreadsheet Exercises. In addition to the verbal, graphical, and mathematical exercises, each chapter has two end-of-chapter spreadsheet exercises. These exercises demonstrate how managers can use a spreadsheet to apply the economic methods described in the chapter. They address important managerial issues such a choosing the profit-maximizing level of advertising or designing compensation contracts to effectively motivate employees. Students can complete the spreadsheet exercises in MyEconLab, which includes additional spreadsheet exercises.

Using Calculus. Calculus presentations of the theory appear at the appropriate points in the text in a Using Calculus feature. In contrast, most other books relegate calculus to appendices, mix calculus in with other material where it cannot easily be skipped, or avoid calculus entirely. We have a few appendices, but most of our calculus material is in Using Calculus sections, which are clearly identified and structured as discrete treatments. Therefore this book may be conveniently used both by courses that use calculus and those that do not. Some end-of-chapter questions are designed to use calculus and are clearly indicated.

Alternative Organizations

Because instructors differ in the order in which they cover material and in the range of topics covered, this text has been designed for maximum flexibility. The most common approach to teaching managerial economics is to follow the sequence of the chapters in the order presented. However, many variations are possible. For example, some instructors choose to address empirical methods (Chapter 3) first. Some instructors skip consumer theory (Chapter 4), which they can safely do without causing problems in later chapters.

Chapter 7, Firm Organization and Market Structure, provides an overview of the key issues that are discussed in later chapters, such as types of firms, profit maximization and its alternatives, conflicts between managers and owners (and other "agency" issues), and the structure of markets. We think that presenting this material early in the course is ideal, but all of this material except for the section on profit maximization can be covered later.

Because our treatment of game theory is divided into two chapters (Chapters 12 and 13), instructors can conveniently choose how much game theory to present. Later chapters that reference game theory do so in such a way that the game theoretical material can be easily skipped. Although Chapter 11 on oligopoly and monopolistic competition precedes the game theory chapters, a course could cover the game theory chapters first (with only minor explanations by the instructor). And a common variant is to present Chapter 14 on uncertainty earlier in the course.

The last chapter, Global Business (17), should be very valuable for instructors who take an international perspective. To promote this viewpoint, every chapter contains examples of dealing with firms based in a variety of countries in addition to the United States.

MyEconLab

MyEconLab's powerful assessment and tutorial system works hand-in-hand with this book.

Features for Students

MyEconLab puts students in control of their learning through a collection of testing, practice, and study tools. Students can study on their own, or they can complete assignments created by their instructor. In MyEconLab's structured environment, students practice what they learn, test their understanding, and pursue a personalized study plan generated from their performance on sample tests and quizzes. In Homework or Study Plan mode, students have access to a wealth of tutorial features, including the following:

▶ Instant feedback on exercises taken directly from the text helps students understand and apply the concepts.

▶ Links to the eText version of this textbook allow the student to quickly revisit a concept or an explanation.

▶ Enhanced Pearson eText, available within the online course materials and offline via an iPad/Android app, allows instructors and students to highlight, bookmark, and take notes.

▶ Learning aids help students analyze a problem in small steps, much the same way an instructor would do during office hours.

▶ Temporary Access for students who are awaiting financial aid provides a 14-day grace period of temporary access.

Experiments in MyEconLab

Experiments are a fun and engaging way to promote active learning and mastery of important economic concepts. Pearson's Experiment program is flexible and easy for instructors and students to use.

▶ Single-player experiments allow students to play against virtual players from anywhere at any time they have an Internet connection.

▶ Multiplayer experiments allow instructors to assign and manage a real-time experiment with their classes.

▶ Pre- and post-questions for each experiment are available for assignment in MyEconLab.

For a complete list of available experiments, visit **www.myeconlab.com**.

Features for Instructors

MyEconLab includes comprehensive homework, quiz, text, and tutorial options, where instructors can manage all assessment needs in one program.

▶ All of the end-of-chapter questions are available for assignment and auto-grading.

▶ Test Item File questions are available for assignment or testing.

▶ The Custom Exercise Builder allows instructors the flexibility of creating their own problems for assignments.

- ▶ The powerful Gradebook records each student's performance and time spent on the tests, study plan, and homework and can generate reports by student or by chapter.
- ▶ Advanced Communication Tools enable students and instructors to communicate through email, discussion board, chat, and ClassLive.
- ▶ Customization options provide new and enhanced ways to share documents, add content, and rename menu items.
- ▶ A prebuilt course option provides a turn-key method for instructors to create a MyEconLab course that includes assignments by chapter.

Supplements

A full range of supplementary materials to support teaching and learning accompanies this book.

- ▶ The *Online Instructor's Manual* by Souren Soumbatiants of Franklin University has many useful and creative teaching ideas. It also offers additional discussion questions, and provides solutions for all the end-of-chapter questions in the text.
- ▶ The *Online Test Bank* by Todd Fitch of the University of California, Berkeley, features problems of varying levels of complexity, suitable for homework assignments and exams. Many of these multiple-choice questions draw on current events.
- ▶ The *Computerized Test Bank* reproduces the Test Bank material in the TestGen software, which is available for Windows and Macintosh. With TestGen, instructors can easily edit existing questions, add questions, generate tests, and print the tests in a variety of formats.
- ▶ The *Online PowerPoint Presentation* by Nelson Altamirano of National University contains text figures and tables, as well as lecture notes. These slides allow instructors to walk through examples from the text during in-class presentations.

These teaching resources are available online for download at the Instructor Resource Center, **www.pearsonhighered.com/perloff**, and on the catalog page for *Managerial Economics and Strategy*.

Acknowledgments

Our greatest debt is to our very patient students at MIT; the University of British Columbia; the University of California, Berkeley; and the University of Pennsylvania for tolerantly dealing with our various approaches to teaching them economics. We appreciate their many helpful (and usually polite) suggestions.

We also owe a great debt to our editors, Adrienne D'Ambrosio and Jane Tufts. Adrienne D'Ambrosio, Executive Acquisitions Editor, was involved in every stage in designing the book, writing the book, testing it, and developing supplemental materials. Jane Tufts, our developmental editor, reviewed each chapter of this book for content, pedagogy, and presentation. By showing us how to present the material as clearly and thoroughly as possible, she greatly strengthened this text.

Our other major debt is to Satyajit Ghosh, University of Scranton, for doing most of the work on the spreadsheet exercises in the chapters and in MyEconLab. We benefitted greatly from his creative ideas about using spreadsheets to teach managerial economics.

We thank our teaching colleagues who provided many helpful comments and from whom we have shamelessly borrowed ideas. We particularly thank Tom Davidoff, Stephen Meyer, Nate Schiff, Ratna Shrestha, Mariano Tappata, and James Vercammen for using early versions of the textbook and for making a wide range of helpful contributions. We are also grateful to our colleagues Jen Baggs, Dennis Carlton, Jean-Etienne de Bettignes, Keith Head, Larry Karp, John Ries, Tom Ross, Leo Simon, Chloe Tergiman, and Ralph Winter for many helpful comments. We thank Evan Flater, Kai Rong Gan, Guojun He, Joyce Lam, WeiYi Shen, and Louisa Yeung for their valuable work as research assistants on the book.

We are very grateful to the many reviewers who spent untold hours reading and commenting on our original proposal and several versions of each chapter. Many of the best ideas in this book are due to them.

We'd especially like to thank Kristen Collett-Schmitt, Matthew Roelofs, and Adam Slawski for carefully reviewing the accuracy of the entire manuscript multiple times and for providing very helpful comments. We thank all the following reviewers, all of whom provided valuable comments at various stages:

Laurel Adams, *Northern Illinois University*

James C. W. Ahiakpor, *California State University, East Bay*

Nelson Altamirano, *National University*

Ariel Belasen, *Southern Illinois University, Edwardsville*

Bruce C. Brown, *California State Polytechnic University, Pomona*

Donald Bumpass, *Sam Houston State University*

James H. Cardon, *Brigham Young University*

Jihui Chen, *Illinois State University*

Ron Cheung, *Oberlin College*

Abdur Chowdhury, *Marquette University*

George Clarke, *Texas A&M International University*

Kristen Collett-Schmitt, *University of Notre Dame*

Douglas Davis, *Virginia Commonwealth University*

Christopher S. Decker, *University of Nebraska, Omaha*

Craig A. Depken, II, *University of North Carolina, Charlotte*

Jed DeVaro, *California State University, East Bay*

David Ely, *San Diego State University*

Asim Erdilek, *Case Western Reserve University*

Satyajit Ghosh, *University of Scranton*

Rajeev Goel, *Illinois State University*

Abbas P. Grammy, *California State University, Bakersfield*

Clifford Hawley, *West Virginia University*

Matthew John Higgins, *Georgia Institute of Technology*

Jack Hou, *California State University, Long Beach*

Timothy James, *Arizona State University*

Peter Daniel Jubinski, *St. Joseph's University*

Chulho Jung, *Ohio University*

Barry Keating, *University of Notre Dame*

Tom K. Lee, *California State University, Northridge*

Dale Lehman, *Alaska Pacific University*

Vincent J. Marra Jr., *University of Delaware*

Sheila J. Moore, *California Lutheran University*

Thomas Patrick, *The College of New Jersey*

Anita Alves Pena, *Colorado State University*

Troy Quast, *Sam Houston State University*

Barry Ritchey, *Anderson University*

Matthew R. Roelofs, *Western Washington University*

Amit Sen, *Xavier University*

Stephanie Shayne, *Husson University*

Adam Slawski, *Pennsylvania State University*

Caroline Swartz, *University of North Carolina, Charlotte*

Scott Templeton, *Clemson University*

Keith Willett, *Oklahoma State University*

Douglas Wills, *University of Washington, Tacoma*

Mark L. Wilson, *Troy University*

David Wong, *California State University, Fullerton*

It was a pleasure to work with the excellent staff at Pearson, who were incredibly helpful in producing this book. Meredith Gertz did a wonderful job of supervising the production process, assembling the extended publishing team, and managing the design of the handsome interior. Gillian Hall and the rest of the team at The Aardvark Group Publishing Services, including our copyeditor, Rebecca Greenberg, have our sincere gratitude for designing the book and keeping the project on track and on schedule. Ted Smykal did a wonderful job drawing most of the cartoons. Sarah Dumouchelle helped edit, arranged for the supplements, and was helpful in many other ways. We also want to acknowledge, with appreciation, the efforts of Melissa Honig, Courtney Kamauf, and Noel Lotz in developing MyEconLab, the online assessment and tutorial system for the book.

Finally, we thank our wives, Jackie Persons and Barbara Spencer, for their great patience and support during the nearly endless writing process. We apologize for misusing their names—and those of our other relatives and friends—in the book!

J. M. P.
J. A. B.

Introduction

1

An Economist's Theory of Reincarnation: If you're good, you come back on a higher level. Cats come back as dogs, dogs come back as horses, and people—if they've been very good like George Washington—come back as money.

If all the food, clothing, entertainment, and other goods and services we wanted were freely available, no one would study economics, and we would not need managers. However, most of the good things in life are scarce. We cannot have everything we want. Consumers cannot consume everything but must make choices about what to purchase. Similarly, managers of firms cannot produce everything and must make careful choices about what to produce, how much to produce, and how to produce it. Studying such choices is the main subject matter of economics. **Economics** is the study of decision making in the presence of scarcity.[1]

Managerial economics is the application of economic analysis to managerial decision making. Managerial economics concentrates on how managers make economic decisions by allocating the scarce resources at their disposal. To make good decisions, a manager must understand the behavior of other decision makers, such as consumers, workers, other managers, and governments. In this book, we examine decision making by such participants in the economy, and we show how managers can use this understanding to be successful.

Main Topics	1. **Managerial Decision Making:** Economic analysis helps managers develop strategies to achieve a firm's objective—such as maximizing profit—in the presence of scarcity.
In this chapter, we examine two main topics:	2. **Economic Models:** Managers use models based on economic theories to help make predictions about consumer and firm behavior, and as an aid to managerial decision making.

1.1 Managerial Decision Making

A firm's managers allocate the limited resources available to them to achieve the firm's objectives. The objectives vary for different managers within a firm. A production manager's objective is normally to achieve a production target at the lowest possible cost. A marketing manager must allocate an advertising budget to promote the product most effectively. Human resource managers design compensation systems

---

[1]Many dictionaries define economics as the study of the production, distribution, and consumption of goods and services. However, professional economists think of economics as applying more broadly, including any decisions made subject to scarcity.

to encourage employees to work hard. The firm's top manager must coordinate and direct all these activities.

Each of these tasks is constrained by resource scarcity. At any moment in time, a production manager has to use the existing factory and a marketing manager has a limited marketing budget. Such resource limitations can change over time but managers always face constraints.

Profit

Most private sector firms want to maximize *profit*, which is the difference between revenue and cost. The job of the senior manager in a firm, usually called the *chief executive officer* (CEO), is to focus on the *bottom line*: maximizing profit.

The CEO orders the production manager to minimize the cost of producing the particular good or service, asks the market research manager to determine how many units can be sold at any given price, and so forth. Minimizing cost helps the firm to maximize profit, but the CEO must also decide how much output to produce and what price to charge. It is the job of the CEO (and other senior executives) to ensure that all managerial functions are coordinated so that the firm makes as much profit as possible. It would be a major coordination failure if the marketing department set up a system of pricing and advertising based on selling 8,000 units a year, while the production department managed to produce only 2,000 units.

The CEO is also often concerned with how a firm is positioned in a market relative to its rivals. Senior executives at Coca-Cola and Pepsi spend a lot of time worrying about each other's actions. Managers in such situations have a natural tendency to view business rivalries like sporting events, with a winner and a loser. However, it is critical to the success of any firm that the CEO focus on maximizing the firm's profit rather than beating a rival.

Trade-Offs

People and firms face trade-offs because they can't have everything. Managers must focus on the trade-offs that directly or indirectly affect profits. Evaluating trade-offs often involves *marginal* reasoning: considering the effect of a small change. Key trade-offs include:

▶ **How to produce:** To produce a given level of output, a firm must use more of one input if it uses less of another input. Car manufacturers choose between metal and plastic for many parts, which affects the car's weight, cost, and safety.

▶ **What prices to charge:** Some firms, such as farms, have little or no control over the prices at which their goods are sold and must sell at the price determined in the market. However, many other firms set their prices. When a manager of such a firm sets the price of a product, the manager must consider whether raising the price by a dollar increases the profit margin on each unit sold by enough to offset the loss from selling fewer units. Consumers, given their limited budgets, buy fewer units of a product when its price rises. Thus, ultimately, the manager's pricing decision is constrained by the scarcity under which consumers make decisions.

Other Decision Makers

It is important for managers of a firm to understand how decisions made by consumers, workers, managers of other firms, and governments constrain their firm. Consumers purchase products subject to their limited budgets. Workers decide on which jobs to take and how much to work given their scarce time and limits on their abilities. Rivals may introduce new, superior products or cut the prices of existing products. Governments around the world may tax, subsidize, or regulate products.

Thus, managers must understand how others make decisions. Most economic analysis is based on the assumption that decision makers are maximizers: they do the best they can with their limited resources. However, economists also consider some contexts in which economic decision makers do not successfully maximize for a variety of psychological reasons—a topic referred to as *behavioral economics*.

Interactions between economic decision makers take place primarily in markets. A **market** is an exchange mechanism that allows buyers to trade with sellers. A market may be a town square where people go to trade food and clothing, or it may be an international telecommunications network over which people buy and sell financial securities. When we talk about a single market, we refer to trade in a single good or group of goods that are closely related, such as soft drinks, movies, novels, or automobiles. The primary participants in a market are firms that supply the product and consumers who buy it, but government policies such as taxes also play an important role in the operation of markets.

Strategy

When interacting with a small number of rival firms, a manager uses a strategy—a battle plan that specifies the *actions* or *moves* that the manager will make to maximize the firm's profit. A CEO's strategy might involve choosing the level of output, the price, or advertising now and possibly in the future. In setting its production levels and price, Pepsi's managers must consider what choices Coca-Cola's managers will make. One tool that is helpful in understanding and developing such strategies is *game theory*, which we use in several chapters.

1.2 Economic Models

Economists use economic models to explain how managers and other decision makers make decisions and to explain the resulting market outcomes. A **model** is a description of the relationship between two or more variables. Models are used in many fields. For example, astronomers use models to describe and predict the movement of comets and meteors, medical researchers use models to describe and predict the effect of medications on diseases, and meteorologists use models to predict weather.

Business economists construct models dealing with economic variables and use such models to describe and predict how a change in one variable will affect another. Such models are useful to managers in predicting the effects of their decisions and in understanding the decisions of others. Models allow managers to consider hypothetical situations—to use a *what-if analysis*—such as "What would happen if we raised our prices by 10%?" or "Would profit rise if we phased out one of our product lines?" Models help managers predict answers to what-if questions and to use those answers to make good decisions.

Mini-Case

Using an Income Threshold Model in China

According to an *income threshold model,* no one who has an income level below a particular threshold buys a particular consumer durable, such as a refrigerator or car. The theory also holds that almost everyone whose income is above that threshold buys the product.

If this theory is correct, we predict that, as most people's incomes rise above the threshold in emergent economies, consumer durable purchases will increase from near zero to large numbers virtually overnight. This prediction is consistent with evidence from Malaysia, where the income threshold for buying a car is about $4,000.

In China, incomes have risen rapidly and now exceed the threshold levels for many types of durable goods. As a result, many experts correctly predicted that the greatest consumer durable goods sales boom in history would take place there. Anticipating this boom, many companies have greatly increased their investments in durable goods manufacturing plants in China. Annual foreign direct investments have gone from $916 million a year in 1983 to $116 billion in 2011. In expectation of this growth potential, even traditional political opponents of the People's Republic—Taiwan, South Korea, and Russia—are investing in China.

One of the most desirable durable goods is a car. Li Rifu, a 46-year-old Chinese farmer and watch repairman, thought that buying a car would improve the odds that his 22- and 24-year-old sons would find girlfriends, marry, and produce grandchildren. Soon after Mr. Li purchased his Geely King Kong for the equivalent of $9,000, both sons met girlfriends, and his older son got married. Four-fifths of all new cars sold in China are bought by first-time customers. An influx of first-time buyers was responsible for China's ninefold increase in car sales from 2000 to 2009. By 2010, China became the second largest producer of automobiles in the world, trailing only Germany. In addition, foreign automobile companies built Chinese plants. For example, Ford invested $600 million in its Chongqing factory in 2012.[2]

Simplifying Assumptions

Everything should be made as simple as possible, but not simpler. —Albert Einstein

A model is a simplification of reality. The objective in building a model is to include the essential issues, while leaving aside the many complications that might distract us or disguise those essential elements. For example, the income threshold model focuses on only the relationship between income and purchases of durable goods. Prices, multiple car purchases by a single consumer, and other factors that might affect durable goods purchases are left out of the model. Despite these simplifications, the model—if correct—gives managers a good general idea of how the automobile market is likely to evolve in countries such as China.

We have described the income threshold model in words, but we could have presented it using graphs or mathematics. Representing economic models using mathematical formulas in spreadsheets has become very important in managerial decision making. Regardless of how the model is described, an economic model is a simplification of reality that contains only its most important features. Without simplifications, it is difficult to make predictions because the real world is too complex to analyze fully.

---

[2]The sources for Mini-Cases are available at the back of the book.

Economists make many *assumptions* to simplify their models. When using the income threshold model to explain car purchasing behavior in China, we *assume* that factors other than income, such as the color of cars, do not have an important effect on the decision to buy cars. Therefore, we ignore the color of cars that are sold in China in describing the relationship between income and the number of cars consumers want. If this assumption is correct, by ignoring color, we make our analysis of the auto market simpler without losing important details. If we're wrong and these ignored issues are important, our predictions may be inaccurate. Part of the skill in using economic models lies in selecting a model that is appropriate for the task at hand.

Testing Theories

Blore's Razor: When given a choice between two theories, take the one that is funnier.

Economic *theory* refers to the development and use of a model to test *hypotheses*, which are proposed explanations for some phenomenon. A useful theory or hypothesis is one that leads to clear, testable predictions. A theory that says "If the price of a product rises, the quantity demanded of that product falls" provides a clear prediction. A theory that says "Human behavior depends on tastes, and tastes change randomly at random intervals" is not very useful because it does not lead to testable predictions and provides little explanation of the choices people make.

Economists test theories by checking whether the theory's predictions are correct. If a prediction does not come true, they might reject the theory—or at least reduce their confidence in the theory. Economists use a model until it is refuted by evidence or until a better model is developed for a particular use.

A good model makes sharp, clear predictions that are consistent with reality. Some very simple models make sharp or precise predictions that are incorrect. Some more realistic and therefore more complex models make ambiguous predictions, allowing for any possible outcome, so they are untestable. Neither incorrect models nor untestable models are helpful. The skill in model building lies in developing a model that is simple enough to make clear predictions but is realistic enough to be accurate. Any model is only an approximation of reality. A good model is one that is a close enough approximation to be useful.

Although economists agree on the methods they use to develop and apply testable models, they often disagree on the specific content of those models. One model might present a logically consistent argument that prices will go up next quarter. Another, using a different but equally logical theory, may contend that prices will fall next quarter. If the economists are reasonable, they will agree that pure logic alone cannot resolve their dispute. Indeed, they will agree that they'll have to use empirical evidence—facts about the real world—to find out which prediction is correct. One goal of this book is to teach managers how to think like economists so that they can build, apply, and test economic models to deal with important managerial problems.

Positive and Normative Statements

Economic analysis sometimes leads to predictions that seem undesirable or cynical. For instance, an economist doing market research for a producer of soft drinks might predict that "if we double the amount of sugar in this soft drink we will significantly increase sales to children." An economist making such a statement is not seeking to undermine the health of children by inducing them to consume excessive amounts of sugar. The economist is only making a scientific prediction about the relationship between cause and effect: more sugar in soft drinks is appealing to children.

Such a scientific prediction is known as a **positive statement**: a testable hypothesis about matters of fact such as cause-and-effect relationships. *Positive* does not mean that we are certain about the truth of our statement; it indicates only that we can test the truth of the statement.

An economist may test the hypothesis that the quantity of soft drinks demanded decreases as the price increases. Some may conclude from that study that "The government should tax soft drinks so that people will not consume so much sugar." Such a statement is a value judgment. It may be based on the view that people *should* be protected from their own unwise choices, so the government *should* intervene.

This judgment is *not* a scientific prediction. It is a **normative statement**: a belief about whether something is good or bad. A normative statement cannot be tested because a value judgment cannot be refuted by evidence. A normative statement concerns what somebody believes *should* happen; a positive statement concerns what *is* or what *will* happen. Normative statements are sometimes called *prescriptive* statements because they prescribe a course of action, while positive statements are sometimes called *descriptive* statements because they describe reality. Although a normative conclusion can be drawn without first conducting a positive analysis, a policy debate will be better informed if a positive analysis is conducted first.[3]

Good economists and managers emphasize positive analysis. This emphasis has implications for what we study and even for our use of language. For example, many economists stress that they study people's *wants* rather than their *needs*. Although people need certain minimum levels of food, shelter, and clothing to survive, most people in developed economies have enough money to buy goods well in excess of the minimum levels necessary to maintain life. Consequently, in wealthy countries, calling something a "need" is often a value judgment. You almost certainly have been told by some elder that "you *need* a college education." That person was probably making a value judgment—"you *should* go to college"—rather than a scientific prediction that you will suffer terrible economic deprivation if you do not go to college. We can't test such value judgments, but we can test a (positive) hypothesis such as "Graduating from college or university increases lifetime income."

SUMMARY

1. **Managerial Decision Making.** Economic analysis helps managers develop strategies to pursue their objectives effectively in the presence of scarcity. Various managers within a firm face different objectives and different constraints, but the overriding objective in most private-sector firms is to maximize profits. Making decisions subject to constraints implies making trade-offs. To make good managerial decisions, managers must understand how consumers, workers, other managers, and governments will act. Economic theories normally (but not always) assume that all decision makers attempt to maximize their well-being given the constraints they face.

2. **Economic Models.** Managers use models based on economic theories to help make predictions and decisions, which they use to run their firms. A good model is simple to use and makes clear, testable predictions that are supported by evidence. Economists use models to construct *positive* hypotheses such as causal statements linking changes in one variable, such as income, to its effects, such as purchases of automobiles. These positive propositions can be tested. In contrast, *normative* statements, which are value judgments, cannot be tested.

---

[3]Some argue that, as (social) scientists, we economists should present only positive analyses. Others argue that we shouldn't give up our right to make value judgments just like the next person (who happens to be biased, prejudiced, and pigheaded, unlike us).

Supply and Demand

2

Talk is cheap because supply exceeds demand.

Burning fossil fuels such as gasoline, coal, and heating oil releases gases containing carbon into the atmosphere.[1] These "greenhouse" gases are widely believed to contribute to global warming. To reduce this problem and raise tax revenues, many environmentalists and political leaders have proposed levying a *carbon tax* on the carbon content in fossil fuels.[2]

When governments impose carbon taxes on gasoline, managers of firms that sell gasoline need to think about how much of the tax they have to absorb and how much they can pass through to firms and consumers who buy gasoline. Similarly, managers of firms that purchase gasoline must consider how any pass-through charges will affect their costs of shipping, air travel, heating, and production. This pass-through analysis is critical in making short-run managerial decisions concerning how much to produce, whether to operate or shut down, and how to set prices and make long-run decisions such as whether to undertake capital investments.

The first broad-based carbon taxes on fuels containing carbon (such as gasoline) were implemented in Finland and Sweden at the beginning of the 1990s. Various other European countries soon followed suit. However, strong opposition to carbon taxes has limited adoption in the United States and Canada. The first North American carbon tax was not introduced

until 2006 in Boulder, Colorado, where it was applied to only electricity generation. In 2007 and 2008, the Canadian provinces of Quebec and British Columbia became the first provinces or states in North America to impose a broad-based carbon tax. Australia adopted a carbon tax in 2012. During the 2012–2013 U.S. federal government budget negotiations, several Congressional leaders called for carbon taxes to help balance the budget.

Such carbon taxes harm some industries and help others. The tax hurts owners and managers of gasoline retailing firms, who need to consider whether they can stay in business in the face of a significant carbon tax. Shippers and

---

[1]Each chapter from Chapter 2 on begins with a Managerial Problem that contains a specific question, which is answered at the end of the chapter using the theories presented in the chapter. Sources for the Managerial Problems, Mini-Cases, and Managerial Implications appear at the back of the book.

[2]Their political opponents object, claiming that fears about global warming are exaggerated and warning of large price increases from such taxes.

manufacturers that use substantial amounts of fuel in production, as well as other firms, would also see their costs of operating rise.

Although a carbon tax harms some firms and industries, it creates opportunities for others. For example, wind power, which is an alternative to fossil fuels in generating electricity, would become much more attractive. Anticipating greater opportunities in this market in the future, Google invested nearly $1 billion in wind and other renewable energy as of 2012. In 2013, Warren Buffett acquired two utility-scale solar plants in Southern California for between $2 and $2.5 billion. DONG Energy A/S and Iberdrola (IBE) SA's Scottish Power unit announced that they would invest £1.6 billion ($2.6 billion) to build a large wind farm off northwest England by 2014.

Motor vehicle sector managers would need to consider whether to change their product mix in response to a carbon tax, perhaps focusing more on fuel-efficient vehicles. Even without a carbon tax, recent increases in gasoline prices have induced consumers to switch from sport utility vehicles (SUVs) to smaller cars. A carbon tax would favor fuel-efficient vehicles even more.

At the end of this chapter, we will return to this topic and answer a question of critical importance to managers in the motor vehicle industry and in other industries affected by gasoline prices: What will be the effect of imposing a carbon tax on the price of gasoline?

To analyze the price and other effects of carbon taxes, managers use an economic tool called the *supply-and-demand model*. Managers who are able to anticipate and act on the implications of the supply-and-demand model by responding quickly to changes in economic conditions, such as tax changes, make more profitable decisions.

The supply-and-demand model provides a good description of many markets and applies particularly well to markets in which there are many buyers and many sellers, as in most agricultural markets, much of the construction industry, many retail markets (such as gasoline retailing), and several other major sectors of the economy. In markets where this model is applicable, it allows us to make clear, testable predictions about the effects of new taxes or other shocks on prices and other market outcomes.

Main Topics

In this chapter, we examine six main topics

1. **Demand:** The quantity of a good or service that consumers demand depends on price and other factors such as consumer incomes and the prices of related goods.

2. **Supply:** The quantity of a good or service that firms supply depends on price and other factors such as the cost of inputs and the level of technological sophistication used in production.

3. **Market Equilibrium:** The interaction between consumers' demand and producers' supply determines the market price and quantity of a good or service that is bought and sold.

4. **Shocks to the Equilibrium:** Changes in a factor that affect demand (such as consumer income) or supply (such as the price of inputs) alter the market price and quantity sold of a good or service.

5. **Effects of Government Interventions:** Government policy may also affect the equilibrium by shifting the demand curve or the supply curve, restricting price or quantity, or using taxes to create a gap between the price consumers pay and the price firms receive.

6. **When to Use the Supply-and-Demand Model:** The supply-and-demand model applies very well to highly competitive markets, which are typically markets with many buyers and sellers.

2.1 Demand

Consumers decide whether to buy a particular good or service and, if so, how much to buy based on its price and on other factors, including their incomes, the prices of other goods, their tastes, and the information they have about the product. Government regulations and other policies also affect buying decisions. Before concentrating on the role of price in determining quantity demanded, let's look briefly at some other factors.

Income plays a major role in determining what and how much to purchase. People who suddenly inherit great wealth might be more likely to purchase expensive Rolex watches or other luxury items and would probably be less likely to buy inexpensive Timex watches and various items targeted toward lower-income consumers. More broadly, when a consumer's income rises, that consumer will often buy more of many goods.

The *price of a related good* might also affect consumers' buying decisions. Related goods can be either *substitutes* or *complements*. A substitute good is a good that might be used or consumed instead of the good in question. Before deciding to go to a movie, a consumer might consider the prices of potential substitutes such as streaming a movie purchased online or going to a sporting event or a concert. Streaming movies, sporting events, and concerts compete with movie theaters for the consumer's entertainment dollar. If sporting events are too expensive, many consumers might choose to see movies instead. Different brands of essentially the same good are often very close substitutes. Before buying a pair of Levi's jeans, a customer might check the prices of other brands and substitute one of those brands for Levi's if its price is sufficiently attractive.

A complement is a good that is used with the good under consideration. Digital audio players such as the iPod application (app) for the iPhone and online audio recordings are complements because consumers obtain recordings online and then download them to audio players to listen to them. A decline in the price of digital audio players would affect the demand for online music. As consumers respond to the decline in the price of audio players by purchasing more such devices, they would also be more inclined to purchase and download online music. Thus, sellers of online music would experience an increase in demand for their product arising from the price decline of a complementary good (audio players).

Consumers' *tastes* are important in determining their demand for a good or service. Consumers do not purchase foods they dislike or clothes they view as unfashionable or uncomfortable. The importance of fashion illustrates how changing tastes affect consumer demand. Clothing items that have gone out of fashion can often be found languishing in discount sections of clothing stores even though they might have been readily purchased at high prices a couple of years (or even a few weeks) earlier when they were in fashion. Firms devote significant resources to trying to change consumer tastes through advertising.

Similarly, *information* about the effects of a good has an impact on consumer decisions. In recent years, as positive health outcomes have been linked to various food items, demand for these healthy foods (such as soy products and high-fiber breads) has typically risen when the information became well known.

Government rules and regulations affect demand. If a city government bans the use of skateboards on its streets, demand for skateboards in that city falls. Governments might also restrict sales to particular groups of consumers. For example, many political jurisdictions do not allow children to buy tobacco products, which reduces the quantity of cigarettes consumed.

Other factors might also affect the demand for specific goods. For example, consumers are more likely to use Facebook if most of their friends use Facebook. This *network* effect arises from the benefits of being part of a network and from the potential costs of being outside the network.

Although many factors influence demand, economists focus most on how a good's *own* price affects the quantity demanded. The relationship between price and quantity demanded plays a critical role in determining the market price and quantity in supply-and-demand analysis. To determine how a change in price affects the quantity demanded, economists ask what happens to quantity when price changes and other factors affecting demand such as income and tastes are held constant.

The Demand Curve

The amount of a good that consumers are *willing* to buy at a given price, holding constant the other factors that influence purchases, is the **quantity demanded**. The quantity demanded of a good or service can exceed the quantity *actually* sold. For example, as a promotion, a local store might sell DVDs for $2 each today only. At that low price, you might want to buy 25 DVDs, but the store might run out of stock before you can select the DVDs you want. Or the store might limit each consumer to a maximum of, for example, 10 DVDs. The quantity you demand is 25; it is the amount you *want*, even though the amount you *actually buy* might be only 10.

Using a diagram, we can show the relationship between price and the quantity demanded. A **demand curve** shows the quantity demanded at each possible price, holding constant the other factors that influence purchases. Figure 2.1 shows the estimated monthly demand curve, D^1, for avocados in the United States.[3] Although this demand curve is a straight line, demand curves may also be smooth curves or wavy lines. By convention, the vertical axis of the graph measures the price, p, per unit of the good. Here the price of avocados is measured in dollars per pound (abbreviated "lb"). The horizontal axis measures the quantity, Q, of the good, which is usually expressed in some *physical measure per time period*. Here, the quantity of avocados is measured in millions of pounds (lbs) per month.

The demand curve hits the vertical axis at $4, indicating that no quantity is demanded when the price is $4 per lb or higher. The demand curve hits the horizontal quantity axis at 160 million lbs, the quantity of avocados that consumers would want if the price were zero. To find out what quantity is demanded at a price between zero and $4, we pick that price—say, $2—on the vertical axis, draw a horizontal line across until we hit the demand curve, and then draw a vertical line down to the horizontal quantity axis. As the figure shows, the quantity demanded at a price of $2 per lb is 80 million lbs per month.

One of the most important things to know about the graph of a demand curve is what is *not* shown. All relevant economic variables that are not explicitly

---

[3]To obtain our estimated supply and demand curves, we used estimates from Carman (2007), which we updated with more recent (2012) data from the California Avocado Commission and supplemented with information from other sources. The numbers have been rounded so that the figures use whole numbers.

FIGURE 2.1 A Demand Curve

The estimated demand curve, D^1, for avocados shows the relationship between the quantity demanded per month and the price per lb. The downward slope of this demand curve shows that, holding other factors that influence demand constant, consumers demand fewer avocados when the price is high and more when the price is low. That is, a change in price causes a *movement along the demand curve*.

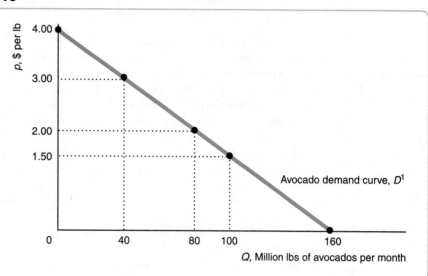

shown on the demand curve graph—income, prices of other goods (such as other fruits or vegetables), tastes, information, and so on—are held constant. Thus, the demand curve shows how quantity varies with price but not how quantity varies with income, the price of substitute goods, tastes, information, or other variables.

Effects of a Price Change on the Quantity Demanded. One of the most important results in economics is the **Law of Demand**: consumers demand more of a good if its price is lower, holding constant income, the prices of other goods, tastes, and other factors that influence the amount they want to consume. According to the Law of Demand, *demand curves slope downward,* as in Figure 2.1.

A downward-sloping demand curve illustrates that consumers demand a larger quantity of this good when its price is lowered and a smaller quantity when its price is raised. What happens to the quantity of avocados demanded if the price of avocados drops and all other variables remain constant? If the price of avocados falls from $2.00 per lb to $1.50 per lb in Figure 2.1, the quantity consumers want to buy increases from 80 million lbs to 100 million lbs.[4] Similarly, if the price increases from $2 to $3, the quantity consumers demand decreases from 80 to 40.

These changes in the quantity demanded in response to changes in price are *movements along the demand curve*. Thus, the demand curve is a concise summary of the answer to the question "What happens to the quantity demanded as the price changes, when all other factors are held constant?"

Although we generally expect demand curves to slope down as does the one for avocados, a vertical or horizontal demand curve is possible. We can think of horizontal and vertical demand curves as being extreme cases of downward-sloping demand. The Law of Demand rules out demand curves that have an upward slope.

The Law of Demand is an empirical claim—a claim about what actually happens. It is not a claim about general theoretical principles. It is theoretically possible that

---

[4]From now on, we will not state the relevant physical and time period measures unless they are particularly relevant. We refer to *quantity* rather than specific units per time period such as "million lbs per month" and *price* rather than "dollars per lb." Thus, we say that the price is $2 (with the "per lb" understood) and the quantity as 80 (with the "millions of lbs per month" understood).

a demand curve could slope upward. However, the available empirical evidence strongly supports the Law of Demand.

Effects of Other Factors on Demand. A demand curve shows the effects of price changes when all other factors that affect demand are held constant. But we are often interested in how other factors affect demand. For example, we might be interested in the effect of changes in income on the amount demanded. How would we illustrate the effect of income changes on demand? One approach is to draw the demand curve in a three-dimensional diagram with the price of avocados on one axis, income on a second axis, and the quantity of avocados on the third axis. But just thinking about drawing such a diagram is hard enough, and actually drawing it without sophisticated graphing software is impossible for many of us.

Economists use a simpler approach to show the effect of factors other than a good's own price on demand. A change in any relevant factor other than the price of the good causes a *shift of the demand curve* rather than a *movement along the demand curve*. These shifts can be readily illustrated in suitable diagrams.

The price of substitute goods affects the quantity of avocados demanded. Many consumers view tomatoes as a substitute for avocados. If the price of tomatoes rises, consumers are more inclined to use more avocados instead, and the demand for avocados rises. The original, estimated avocado demand curve in Figure 2.1 is based on an average price of tomatoes of $0.80 per lb. Figure 2.2 shows how the avocado demand curve shifts *outward* or *to the right* from the original demand curve D^1 to a new demand curve D^2 if the price of tomatoes increases by 55¢ to $1.35 per lb. On the new demand curve, D^2, more avocados are demanded at any given price than on D^1 because tomatoes, a substitute good, have become more expensive. At a price of $2 per lb, the quantity of avocados demanded goes from 80 million lbs on D^1, before the increase in the price of tomatoes, to 91 million lbs on D^2, after the increase.

Similarly, consumers tend to buy more avocados as their incomes rise. Thus, if income rises, the demand curve for avocados shifts to the right, indicating that consumers demand more avocados at any given price.

FIGURE 2.2 A Shift of the Demand Curve

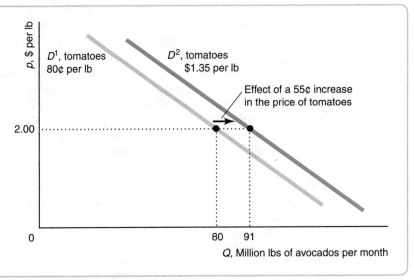

The demand curve for avocados shifts to the right from D^1 to D^2 as the price of tomatoes, a substitute, increases by 55¢ per lb. As a result of the increase in the price of tomatoes, more avocados are demanded at any given price.

In addition, changes in other factors that affect demand, such as information, can shift a demand curve. Reinstein and Snyder (2005) found that movie reviews affect the demand for some types of movies. Holding price constant, they determined that if a film received two-thumbs-up reviews on the then extremely popular Siskel and Ebert movie-review television program the opening weekend demand curve shifted to the right by 25% for a drama, but the demand curve did not significantly shift for an action film or a comedy.

To properly analyze the effects of a change in some variable on the quantity demanded, we must distinguish between a *movement along a demand curve* and a *shift of a demand curve*. A change in the *good's own price* causes a *movement along a demand curve*. A change in *any other relevant factor besides the good's own price* causes a *shift of the demand curve*.

The Demand Function

The demand curve shows the relationship between the quantity demanded and a good's own price, holding other relevant factors constant at some particular levels. We illustrate the effect of a change in one of these other relevant factors by shifting the demand curve. We can represent the same information—information about how price, income, and other variables affect quantity demanded—using a mathematical relationship called the *demand function*. The demand function shows the effect of *all* the relevant factors on the quantity demanded. If the factors that affect the amount of avocados demanded include the price of avocados, the price of tomatoes, and income, the demand function, D, can be written as

$$Q = D(p, p_t, Y) \qquad (2.1)$$

where Q is the quantity of avocados demanded, p is the price of avocados, p_t is the price of tomatoes, and Y is the income of consumers. This expression says that the quantity of avocados demanded varies with the price of avocados, the price of tomatoes (which is a substitute product), and the income of consumers. We ignore other factors that are not explicitly listed in the demand function because we assume that they are irrelevant (such as the price of laptop computers) or are held constant (such as the prices of other related goods, tastes, and information).

Equation 2.1 is a general functional form—it does not specify a particular form for the relationship between quantity, Q, and the explanatory variables, p, p_t, and Y. The estimated demand function that corresponds to the demand curve D^1 in Figures 2.1 and 2.2 has a specific (linear) form. If we measure quantity in millions of lbs per month, avocado and tomato prices in dollars per lb, and average monthly income in dollars, the demand function is

$$Q = 104 - 40p + 20p_t + 0.01Y. \qquad (2.2)$$

When we draw the demand curve D^1 in Figures 2.1 and 2.2, we hold p_t and Y at specific values. The price per lb for tomatoes is $0.80, and average income is $4,000 per month. If we substitute these values for p_t and Y in Equation 2.2, we can rewrite the quantity demanded as a function of only the price of avocados:

$$\begin{aligned} Q &= 104 - 40p + 20p_t + 0.01Y \\ &= 104 - 40p + (20 \times 0.80) + (0.01 \times 4{,}000) \\ &= 160 - 40p. \qquad (2.3) \end{aligned}$$

The demand function in Equation 2.3 corresponds to the straight-line demand curve D^1 in Figure 2.1 with particular fixed values for the price of tomatoes and for income. The constant term, 160, in Equation 2.3 is the quantity demanded (in millions of lbs per month) if the price is zero. Setting the price equal to zero in Equation 2.3, we find that the quantity demanded is $Q = 160 - (40 \times 0) = 160$. Figure 2.1 shows that $Q = 160$ where D^1 hits the quantity axis—where price is zero.

Equation 2.3 also shows us how quantity demanded varies with a change in price: a movement *along* the demand curve. If the price falls from p_1 to p_2, the change in price, Δp, equals $p_2 - p_1$. (The Δ symbol, the Greek letter delta, means "change in" the variable following the delta, so Δp means "change in price.") If the price of avocados falls from $p_1 = \$2$ to $p_2 = \$1.50$, then $\Delta p = \$1.50 - \$2 = -\$0.50$. Quantity demanded changes from $Q_1 = 80$ at a price of $2 to $Q_2 = 100$ at a price of $1.50, so $\Delta Q = Q_2 - Q_1 = 100 - 80 = 20$ million lbs per month.

More generally, the quantity demanded at p_1 is $Q_1 = D(p_1)$, and the quantity demanded at p_2 is $Q_2 = D(p_2)$. The change in the quantity demanded, $\Delta Q = Q_2 - Q_1$, in response to the price change (using Equation 2.3) is

$$
\begin{aligned}
\Delta Q &= Q_2 - Q_1 \\
&= D(p_2) - D(p_1) \\
&= (160 - 40p_2) - (160 - 40p_1) \\
&= -40(p_2 - p_1) \\
&= -40\Delta p.
\end{aligned}
$$

Thus, the change in the quantity demanded, ΔQ, is -40 times the change in the price, Δp.

For example, if $\Delta p = -\$0.50$, then $\Delta Q = -40\Delta p = -40(-0.50) = 20$ million lbs. The change in quantity demanded is positive when the price falls, as in this example. This effect is consistent with the Law of Demand. We can see that a 50¢ decrease in price causes a 20 million lb per month increase in quantity demanded. Similarly, raising the price would cause the quantity demanded to fall.

Using Calculus

Deriving the Slope of a Demand Curve

We can determine how the quantity changes as the price increases using calculus. Given the demand function for avocados is $Q = 160 - 40p$, the derivative of the demand function with respect to price is $dQ/dp = -40$. Therefore, the slope of the demand curve in Figure 2.1, dp/dQ, is also negative, which is consistent with the Law of Demand.

Summing Demand Curves

The overall demand for avocados is composed of the demand of many individual consumers. If we know the demand curve for each of two consumers, how do we determine the total demand curve for the two consumers combined? The total quantity demanded *at a given price* is the sum of the quantity each consumer demands at that price.

We can use individual demand curves to determine the total demand of several consumers. Suppose that the demand curve for Consumer 1 is

$$Q_1 = D^1(p)$$

and the demand curve for Consumer 2 is

$$Q_2 = D^2(p).$$

At price p, Consumer 1 demands Q_1 units, Consumer 2 demands Q_2 units, and the total quantity demanded by both consumers is the sum of these two quantities:

$$Q = Q_1 + Q_2 = D^1(p) + D^2(p).$$

We can generalize this approach to look at the total demand for three, four, or more consumers, or we can apply it to groups of consumers rather than just to individuals. It makes sense to add the quantities demanded only when all consumers face the same price. Adding the quantity Consumer 1 demands at one price to the quantity Consumer 2 demands at another price would not be meaningful for this purpose—the result would not show us a point on the combined demand curve.

Mini-Case

Aggregating the Demand for Broadband Service

We illustrate how to combine individual demand curves to get a total demand curve graphically using estimated demand curves of broadband (high-speed) Internet service (Duffy-Deno, 2003). The figure shows the demand curve for small firms (1–19 employees), the demand curve for larger firms, and the total demand curve for all firms, which is the horizontal sum of the other two demand curves.

At the current average rate of 40¢ per kilobyte per second (Kbps), the quantity demanded by small firms is $Q_s = 10$ (in millions of Kbps) and the quantity demanded by larger firms is $Q_l = 11.5$. Thus, the total quantity demanded at that price is $Q = Q_s + Q_l = 10 + 11.5 = 21.5$.

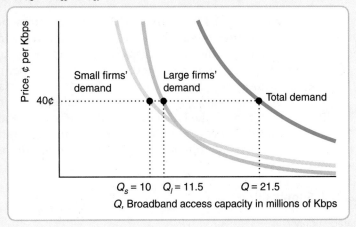

2.2 Supply

Knowing how much consumers want is not enough by itself to tell us what price and quantity will be observed in a market. To determine the market price and quantity, we also need to know how much firms want to supply at any given price. Firms determine how much of a good to supply on the basis of the price of that good and on other factors, including the costs of producing the good. Usually, we expect firms to supply more at a higher price. Before concentrating on the role of price in determining supply, we describe the role of some other factors.

Costs of production (how much the firm pays for factors of production such as labor, fuel, and machinery) affect how much of a product firms want to sell. As a firm's cost falls, it is usually willing to supply more, holding price and other factors constant. Conversely, a cost increase will often reduce a firm's willingness to produce. If the firm's cost exceeds what it can earn from selling the good, the firm will produce nothing. Thus, factors that affect costs also affect supply. If a *technological advance* allows a firm to produce its good at lower cost, the firm supplies more of that good at any given price, holding other factors constant.

Government rules and regulations can also affect supply directly without working through costs. For example, in some parts of the world, retailers may not sell most goods and services on particular days of religious significance. Supply on those days is constrained by government policy to be zero.

The Supply Curve

The **quantity supplied** is the amount of a good that firms *want* to sell at a given price, holding constant other factors that influence firms' supply decisions, such as costs and government actions. We can show the relationship between price and the quantity supplied graphically. A **supply curve** shows the quantity supplied at each possible price, holding constant the other factors that influence firms' supply decisions. Figure 2.3 shows the estimated supply curve, S^1, for avocados. As with the demand curve, the price on the vertical axis is measured in dollars per physical unit (dollars per lb), and the quantity on the horizontal axis is measured in physical units per time period (millions of lbs per month). Because we hold fixed other variables that may affect supply, the supply curve concisely answers the question "What happens to the quantity supplied as the price changes, holding all other relevant factors constant?"

Effects of Price on Supply. We illustrate how price affects the quantity supplied using the supply curve for avocados in Figure 2.3. The supply curve is upward sloping. As the price increases, firms supply more. If the price is $2 per lb, the quantity supplied by the market is 80 million lbs per month. If the price rises to $3, the quantity supplied rises to 95 million lbs. An increase in the price of avocados causes a *movement along the supply curve*, resulting in more avocados being supplied.

Although the Law of Demand requires that the demand curve slope downward, there is *no* corresponding "Law of Supply" stating that the supply curve slopes upward. We observe supply curves that are vertical, horizontal, or downward

FIGURE 2.3 A Supply Curve

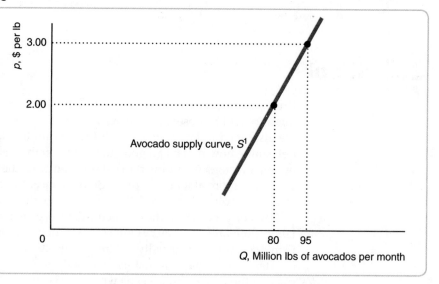

The estimated supply curve, S^1, for avocados shows the relationship between the quantity supplied per month and the price per lb, holding constant cost and other factors that influence supply. The upward slope of this supply curve indicates that firms supply more of this good when its price is high and less when the price is low. An increase in the price of avocados causes firms to supply a larger quantity of avocados; any change in price results in a movement *along the supply curve.*

sloping in particular situations. However, supply curves are commonly upward sloping. Accordingly, if we lack specific information about the slope, we usually draw upward-sloping supply curves. Along an upward-sloping supply curve, a higher price leads to more output being offered for sale, holding other factors constant.

Effects of Other Variables on Supply. A change in a relevant variable other than the good's own price causes the entire *supply curve to shift*. Suppose the price of fertilizer used to produce avocados increases by 55¢ from 40¢ to 95¢ per lb of fertilizer mix. This increase in the price of a key factor of production causes the cost of avocado production to rise. Because it is now more expensive to produce avocados, the supply curve shifts *inward* or *to the left*, from S^1 to S^2 in Figure 2.4. That is, firms want to supply fewer avocados at any given price than before the fertilizer-based cost increase. At a price of $2 per lb for avocados, the quantity supplied falls from 80 million lbs on S^1 to 69 million on S^2 (after the cost increase).

Again, it is important to distinguish between a *movement along a supply curve* and a *shift of the supply curve*. When the price of avocados changes, the change in the quantity supplied reflects a *movement along the supply curve*. When costs or other variables that affect supply change, the entire *supply curve shifts*.

The Supply Function

We can write the relationship between the quantity supplied and price and other factors as a mathematical relationship called the *supply function*. Using a general functional form, we can write the avocado supply function, S, as

$$Q = S(p, p_f), \tag{2.4}$$

where Q is the quantity of avocados supplied, p is the price of avocados, and p_f is the price of fertilizer. The supply function, Equation 2.4, might also incorporate other factors such as wages, transportation costs, and the state of technology, but by leaving them out, we are implicitly holding them constant.

FIGURE 2.4 A Shift of a Supply Curve

A 55¢ per lb increase in the price of fertilizer, which is used to produce avocados, causes the supply curve for avocados to shift left from S^1 to S^2. At the price of avocados of $2 per lb, the quantity supplied falls from 80 on S^1 to 69 on S^2.

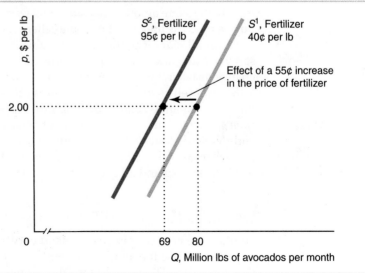

Our estimated supply function for avocados is

$$Q = 58 + 15p - 20p_f, \tag{2.5}$$

where Q is the quantity in millions of lbs per month, p is the price of avocados in dollars per lb, and p_f is the price of fertilizer in dollars per lb of fertilizer mix. If we hold the fertilizer price fixed at 40¢ per lb, we can rewrite the supply function in Equation 2.5 as solely a function of the avocado price. Substituting $p_f = \$0.40$ into Equation 2.5, we find that

$$Q = 58 + 15p - (20 \times 0.40) = 50 + 15p. \tag{2.6}$$

What happens to the quantity supplied if the price of avocados increases by $\Delta p = p_2 - p_1$? As the price increases from p_1 to p_2, the quantity supplied goes from Q_1 to Q_2, so the change in quantity supplied is

$$\Delta Q = Q_2 - Q_1 = (50 + 15p_2) - (50 + 15p_1) = 15(p_2 - p_1) = 15\Delta p.$$

Thus, a \$1 increase in price ($\Delta p = 1$) causes the quantity supplied to increase by $\Delta Q = 15$ million lbs per month. This change in the quantity of avocados supplied as p increases is a *movement along the supply curve*.

Summing Supply Curves

The total supply curve shows the total quantity produced by all suppliers at each possible price. In the avocado case, for example, the overall market quantity supplied at any given price is the sum of the quantity supplied by Californian producers, the quantity supplied by Mexican producers, and the quantity supplied by producers elsewhere.

2.3 Market Equilibrium

The supply and demand curves jointly determine the price and quantity at which a good or service is bought and sold. The demand curve shows the quantities consumers want to buy at various prices, and the supply curve shows the quantities firms want to sell at various prices. Unless the price is set so that consumers want to buy exactly the same amount that suppliers want to sell, either some consumers cannot buy as much as they want or some sellers cannot sell as much as they want.

When all market participants are able to buy or sell as much as they want, we say that the market is in **equilibrium**: a situation in which no participant wants to change its behavior. A price at which consumers can buy as much as they want and sellers can sell as much as they want is called an *equilibrium price*. At this price the quantity demanded equals the quantity supplied. This quantity is called the *equilibrium quantity*. Thus, if the government does not intervene in the market, the supply-and-demand model is in equilibrium when the *market clears* in the sense that buyers and sellers are both able to buy or sell as much as they want at the market price—no one is frustrated and all goods that are supplied to the market are sold.

Using a Graph to Determine the Equilibrium

To illustrate how supply and demand curves determine the equilibrium price and quantity, we use the avocado example. Figure 2.5 shows the supply curve, S, and demand curve, D, for avocados. The supply and demand curves intersect at point

FIGURE 2.5 Market Equilibrium

The intersection of the supply curve, S, and the demand curve, D, for avocados determines the market equilibrium point, e, where $p = \$2$ per lb and $Q = 80$ million lbs per month. At the lower price of $p = \$1.60$, the quantity supplied is only 74, whereas the quantity demanded is 96, so there is excess demand of 22. At $p = \$2.40$, a price higher than the equilibrium price, there is excess supply of 22 because the quantity demanded, 64, is less than the quantity supplied, 86. When there is excess demand or supply, market forces drive the price back to the equilibrium price of $2.

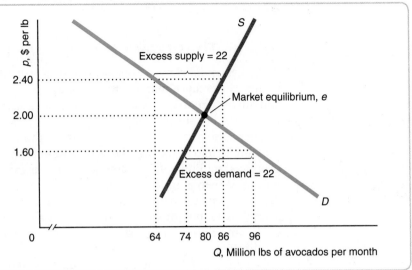

e, the market equilibrium. The equilibrium price is $2 per lb, and the equilibrium quantity is 80 million lbs per month, which is the quantity firms want to sell *and* the quantity consumers want to buy.

Using Algebra to Determine the Equilibrium

We can determine the equilibrium mathematically, using algebraic representations of the supply and demand curves. We use these two equations to solve for the equilibrium price at which the quantity demanded equals the quantity supplied (the equilibrium quantity). The demand curve, Equation 2.3, shows the relationship between the quantity demanded, Q_d, and the price:[5]

$$Q_d = 160 - 40p.$$

The supply curve, Equation 2.6, tells us the relationship between the quantity supplied, Q_s, and the price:

$$Q_s = 50 + 15p.$$

We want to find the equilibrium price, p, at which $Q_d = Q_s = Q$. Thus we set the right sides of these two equations equal, $50 + 15p = 160 - 40p$, and solve for the price.

Adding $40p$ to both sides of this expression and subtracting 50 from both sides, we find that $55p = 110$. Dividing both sides of this last expression by 55, we learn that the equilibrium price is $p = \$2$. We can determine the equilibrium quantity by substituting this p into either the supply equation or the demand equation. Using the demand equation, we find that the equilibrium quantity is

$$\begin{aligned} Q &= 160 - (40 \times 2) \\ &= 160 - 80 \\ &= 80 \end{aligned}$$

[5]Usually, we use Q to represent both the quantity demanded and the quantity supplied. However, for clarity in this discussion, we use Q_d and Q_s.

million lbs per month. We can obtain the same quantity by using the supply curve equation: $Q = 50 + (15 \times 2) = 80$.

Forces That Drive the Market to Equilibrium

A market equilibrium is not just an abstract concept or a theoretical possibility. Economic forces cause markets to adjust to the equilibrium. At the equilibrium, price and quantity remain stable until the market is affected by some new event that shifts the demand or supply curve.

Remarkably, an equilibrium occurs without any explicit coordination between consumers and firms. In a competitive market such as that for most agricultural products, millions of consumers and thousands of firms make their buying and selling decisions independently. Yet each firm can sell the quantity it wants at the market price and each consumer can buy the quantity he or she wants at that price. It is as though an unseen market force like an *invisible hand* (a phrase coined by Adam Smith in 1776) directs people to coordinate their activities to achieve equilibrium.

What forces cause the market to move to equilibrium? If the price is not at the equilibrium level, consumers or firms have an incentive to change their behavior in a way that will drive the price to the equilibrium level, as we now illustrate.

If the price were initially lower than the equilibrium price, consumers would want to buy more than suppliers want to sell. If the price of avocados is $1.60 in Figure 2.5, firms are willing to supply 74 million lbs per month but consumers demand 96 million lbs. At this price, the market is in *disequilibrium*: the quantity demanded is not equal to the quantity supplied. There is **excess demand**—the amount by which the quantity demanded exceeds the quantity supplied at a specified price. If the price is $1.60 per lb, there is excess demand of 22 (= 96 − 74) million lbs per month.

Some consumers are lucky enough to buy the avocados at $1.60 per lb. Other consumers cannot find anyone who is willing to sell them avocados at that price. What can they do? Some frustrated consumers may offer to pay suppliers more than $1.60 per lb. Alternatively, suppliers, noticing these disappointed consumers, might raise their prices. Such actions by consumers and producers cause the market price to rise. As the price rises, the quantity that firms want to supply increases and the quantity that consumers want to buy decreases. This upward pressure on price continues until it reaches the equilibrium price, $2, where there is no excess demand.

If, instead, the price is initially above the equilibrium level, suppliers want to sell more than consumers want to buy. For example, at a price of $2.40, suppliers want to sell 86 million lbs per month but consumers want to buy only 64 million lbs, as Figure 2.5 shows. There is an **excess supply**—the amount by which the quantity supplied is greater than the quantity demanded at a specified price—of 22 (= 86 − 64) million lbs at a price of $2.40. Not all firms can sell as much as they want. Rather than allow their unsold avocados to spoil, firms lower the price to attract additional customers. As long as the price remains above the equilibrium price, some firms have unsold avocados and want to lower the price further. The price falls until it reaches the equilibrium level, $2, where there is no excess supply and hence no pressure to lower the price further.

Not all markets reach equilibrium through the independent actions of many buyers or sellers. In institutionalized or formal markets, such as the Chicago Mercantile Exchange—where agricultural commodities, financial instruments, energy, and metals are traded—buyers and sellers meet at a single location (or on a single Web site).

Often in these markets certain individuals or firms, sometimes referred to as *market makers*, act to adjust the price and bring the market into equilibrium very quickly.

In summary, at any price other than the equilibrium price, either consumers or suppliers are unable to trade as much as they want. These disappointed market participants act to change the price, driving the price to the equilibrium level. The equilibrium price is called the *market clearing price* because there are no frustrated buyers and sellers at this price—the market eliminates or clears any excess demand or excess supply.

2.4 Shocks to the Equilibrium

Once equilibrium is achieved, it can persist indefinitely because no one applies pressure to change the price. The equilibrium changes only if a shock occurs that shifts the demand curve or the supply curve. These curves shift if one of the variables we were holding constant changes. If tastes, income, government policies, or costs of production change, the demand curve or the supply curve or both may shift, and the equilibrium changes.

Effects of a Shift in the Demand Curve

Suppose that the price of fresh tomatoes increases by 55¢ per lb, so consumers substitute avocados for tomatoes. As a result, the demand curve for avocados shifts outward from D^1 to D^2 in panel a of Figure 2.6. At any given price, consumers want more avocados than they did before the price of tomatoes rose. In particular, at the original equilibrium price of avocados of \$2, consumers now want to buy 91 million lbs of avocados per month. At that price, however, suppliers still want to sell only 80 million lbs. As a result, there is excess demand of 11 million lbs. Market pressures drive the price up until it reaches a new equilibrium at \$2.20. At that price, firms want to sell 83 million lbs and consumers want to buy 83 million lbs, the new equilibrium quantity. Thus, the equilibrium moves from e_1 to e_2 as a result of the increase in the price of tomatoes. Both the equilibrium price and the equilibrium quantity of avocados rise as a result of the outward shift of the avocado demand curve. Here the increase in the price of tomatoes causes a *shift of the demand curve*, which in turn causes a *movement along the supply curve*.

Effects of a Shift in the Supply Curve

Now suppose that the price of tomatoes stays constant at its original level but the price of fertilizer mix rises by 55¢ per lb. It is now more expensive to produce avocados because the price of an important input, fertilizer, has increased. As a result, the supply curve for avocados shifts to the left from S^1 to S^2 in panel b of Figure 2.6. At any given price, producers want to supply fewer avocados than they did before the price of fertilizer increased. At the original equilibrium price of avocados of \$2 per lb, consumers still want 80 million lbs, but producers are now willing to supply only 69 million lbs, so there is excess demand of 11 million lbs. Market pressure forces the price of avocados up until it reaches a new equilibrium at e_2, where the equilibrium price is \$2.20 and the equilibrium quantity is 72. The increase in the price of fertilizer causes the equilibrium price to rise but the equilibrium quantity to fall. Here a *shift of the supply curve* results in a *movement along the demand curve*.

FIGURE 2.6 **Equilibrium Effects of a Shift of a Demand or Supply Curve**

(a) A 55¢ per lb increase in the price of tomatoes causes the demand curve for avocados to shift outward from D^1 to D^2. At the original equilibrium (e_1) price of $2, excess demand is 11 million lbs per month. Market pressures drive the price up until it reaches $2.20 at the new equilibrium, e_2. (b) An increase in the price of fertilizer by 55¢ per lb causes producers' costs to rise, so they supply fewer avocados at every price. The supply curve for avocados shifts to the left from S_1 to S_2, driving the market equilibrium from e_1 to e_2, where the new equilibrium price is $2.20.

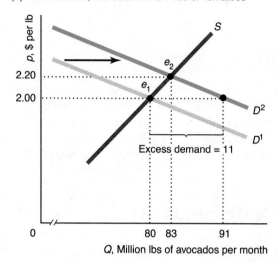

(a) Effect of a 55¢ Increase in the Price of Tomatoes

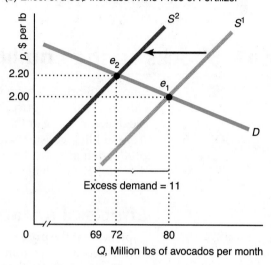

(b) Effect of a 55¢ Increase in the Price of Fertilizer

Q&A 2.1

Using algebra, determine how the equilibrium price and quantity of avocados change from the initial levels, $p = \$2$ and $Q = 80$, if the price of fresh tomatoes increases from its original price of $p_t = 80$¢ by 55¢ to $1.35.

Answer

1. *Show how the demand and supply functions change due to the increase in the price of tomatoes.* In the demand function, Equation 2.2, the quantity demanded depends on the price of tomatoes, p_t, and income, Y, we set income at its original value, 4,000 to obtain:

$$Q = 104 - 40p + 20p_t + 0.01Y$$
$$= 104 - 40p + 20p_t + (0.01 \times 4{,}000)$$
$$= 144 - 40p + 20p_t.$$

(As a check of this equation, when we substitute the original $p_t = \$0.80$ into this equation we get $Q = 160 - 40p$, which is the original demand function, Equation 2.3, that depends on only the price of avocados.) Inserting the new price of tomatoes, $1.35, into this equation, we obtain the new demand equation

$$Q = 144 - 40p + (20 \times 1.35) = 171 - 40p.$$

Thus, an increase in the price of tomatoes shifts the intercept of the demand curve, causing the demand curve to shift away from the origin. The supply function does not depend on the price of tomatoes, so the supply function remains the same as in Equation 2.6:

$$Q = 50 + 15p.$$

2. *Equate the supply and demand functions to determine the new equilibrium.* The equilibrium price is determined by equating the right sides of these supply and demand equations:

$$50 + 15p = 171 - 40p.$$

Solving this equation for p, we find that the equilibrium price of avocados is $p = \$2.20$. We calculate the equilibrium quantity by substituting this price into the supply or demand functions: $Q = 50 + (15 \times 2.20) = 171 - (40 \times 2.20) = 83$.

3. *Show how the equilibrium price and quantity of avocados changes by subtracting the original values from the new ones.* The change in the equilibrium price is $\Delta p = \$2.20 - \$2 = \$0.20$. The change in the equilibrium quantity is $\Delta Q = 83 - 80 = 3$. These changes are illustrated in panel a of Figure 2.6.

In summary, a change in an underlying factor, such as the price of a substitute or the price of an input, shifts the demand curve or the supply curve. As a result of a shift in the demand or supply curve, the equilibrium changes. To describe the effect of this change, we compare the original equilibrium price and quantity to the new equilibrium values.

Managerial Implication

Taking Advantage of Future Shocks

A manager with foresight can take advantage of shocks that will adversely affect rivals in the future. In some industries, such as furniture manufacturing, an increase in the cost of fuel (say due to a new carbon tax) hurts some firms and helps others. A higher fuel price would reduce international outsourcing that relies on shipping.

For example, when the cost of ocean shipping increased precipitously in 2008 due to high oil costs, many U.S. firms substantially increased their domestic production. The cost of shipping a 40-foot container from Shanghai to the United States rose to $8,000 by 2008 from $3,000 earlier in the decade. (However, the rate fell back to $2,308 in 2011 and to $1,667 in 2012.)

According to the Canadian investment bank CIBC World Markets, this increase in shipping costs depressed trade significantly. It caused the foreign supply curve to shift to the left, which in turn caused the total U.S. supply curve (the horizontal sum of the domestic and foreign supply curves) to shift to the left, so that the price of imported furniture in the United States rose. La-Z-Boy, a U.S. domestic furniture manufacturer, benefited from these higher shipping costs. As a La-Z-Boy spokesman observed about the effects of higher shipping costs, "There's just a handful of us left, but it has become easier for us domestic folks to compete."

Before making business decisions, managers of La-Z-Boy and other domestic firms that face significant foreign competition should use the supply-and-demand model to predict the effects of shocks. For example, if domestic manufacturers expect a new carbon tax to raise fuel costs, they know that the resulting shift of the foreign supply curve for their product will increase the market price, so that they should consider increasing their production capacity.

Effects of Shifts in Both Supply and Demand Curves

Some events cause both the supply curve and the demand curve to shift. If both shift, then the qualitative effect on the equilibrium price and quantity may be difficult to predict, even if we know the direction in which each curve shifts. Changes in the equilibrium price and quantity depend on exactly how much the curves shift, as the following Mini-Case and Q&A illustrate.

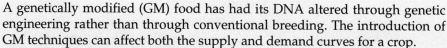

Mini-Case

Genetically Modified Foods

A genetically modified (GM) food has had its DNA altered through genetic engineering rather than through conventional breeding. The introduction of GM techniques can affect both the supply and demand curves for a crop.

The first commercial GM food was Calgene's Flavr Savr tomato that resisted rotting, which the company claimed could stay on the vine longer to ripen to full flavor. It was first marketed in 1994 without any special labeling. Other common GM crops include canola, corn, cotton, rice, soybean, and sugar cane. Using GM seeds, farmers can produce more output at a given cost. As of 2012, GM food crops, which are mostly herbicide-resistant varieties of corn (maize), soybean, and canola oilseed, were grown in 29 countries but over 40% of the acreage was in the United States. In 2012, the share of GE crops in the United States was 88% for corn, 93% for soybean, and 94% for cotton.

Some scientists and consumer groups have raised safety concerns about GM crops. In the European Union (EU), Australia, and several other countries, governments have required labeling of GM products. Although Japan has not approved the cultivation of GM crops, it is the nation with the greatest GM food consumption and does not require labeling. According to some polls, 70% of consumers in Europe object to GM foods. Fears cause some consumers to refuse to buy a GM crop (or the entire crop if GM products cannot be distinguished). In some countries, certain GM foods have been banned. In 2008, the EU was forced to end its de facto ban on GM crop imports when the World Trade Organization ruled that the ban lacked scientific merit and hence violated international trade rules. As of 2013, most of the EU still banned planting most GM crops. Consumers in other countries, such as the United States, are less concerned about GM foods.

In yet other countries, consumers may not even be aware of the use of GM seeds. In 2008, Vietnam announced that it was going to start using GM soybean, corn, and cotton seeds to lower food prices and reduce imports. A study found that one-third of crops sampled in Vietnam in 2010 were genetically modified.

Q&A 2.2

When they became available, StarLink and other GM corn seeds caused the supply curve for the corn used for animal feed to shift to the right. If consumer concerns cause the demand curve for corn to shift to the left, how will the before-GM equilibrium compare to the after-GM equilibrium? Consider the possibility that the demand curve may shift only slightly in some countries but substantially in others.

Answer

1. *Determine the original equilibrium.* The original equilibrium, e_1, occurs where the before-GM supply curve, S^1, intersects the before-GM demand curve, D^1, at price p_1 and quantity Q_1. Both panels a and b of the figure show the same equilibrium.

2. *Determine the new equilibrium.* When GM seeds are introduced, the new supply curve, S^2, lies to the right of S^1 in both panels. In panel a, the new demand curve, D^2, lies only slightly to the left of D^1, while in panel b, D^3 lies substantially to the left of D^1. In panel a, the new equilibrium e_2 is determined by the intersection of S^2 and D^2. In panel b, the new equilibrium e_3 reflects the intersection of D^3 and S^3 (which is the same as S^2 in panel a).

3. *Compare the before-GM equilibrium to the after-GM equilibrium.* In both panels, the equilibrium price falls from p_1 to either p_2 or p_3. The equilibrium quantity rises from Q_1 to Q_2 in panel a, but falls from Q_1 to Q_3 in panel b.

4. *Comment.* When both curves shift, we cannot predict the direction of change of both the equilibrium price and quantity without knowing how much each curve shifts. Obviously whether growers in a country decide to adopt GM seeds depends crucially on consumerresistance to these new products.

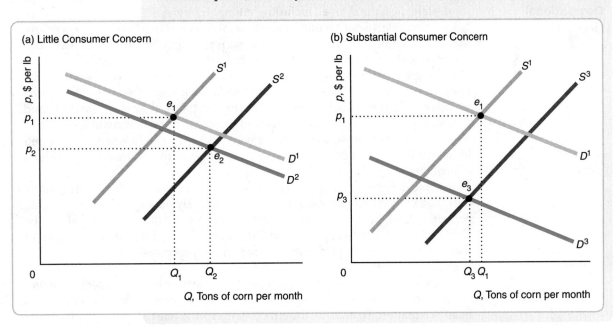

2.5 Effects of Government Interventions

Often governments are responsible for changes in market equilibrium. We examine three types of government policies. First, some government actions shift the supply curve, the demand curve, or both curves, which causes the equilibrium to change. Second, the government may use price controls that cause the quantity demanded to differ from the quantity supplied. Third, the government may tax or subsidize a good, which results in a gap between the price consumers pay and that which sellers receive.

Policies That Shift Curves

Government policies may cause demand or supply curves to shift. Many governments limit who can buy goods. For example, many governments forbid selling cigarettes or alcohol to young people, which decreases the quantity demanded for those goods at each price and thereby shifts their demand curves to the left. Similarly, a government may restrict the amount of foreign products that can be imported, which decreases the quantity supplied of imported goods at each price and shifts the importing country's supply curve to the left. Or, the government could start buying a good, which increases the quantity demanded at each price for the good and shifts the demand curve to the right.

Many occupations are licensed in the United States. In those occupations, working without a license is illegal. More than 800 occupations are licensed at the local, state, or federal level, including animal trainers, dietitians and nutritionists, doctors, electricians, embalmers, funeral directors, hair dressers, librarians, nurses, psychologists, real estate brokers, respiratory therapists, salespeople, teachers, and tree trimmers (but not economists).

During the early 1950s, fewer than 5% of U.S. workers were in occupations covered by licensing laws at the state level. Since then, the share of licensed workers has grown, reaching nearly 18% by the 1980s, at least 20% in 2000, and 29% in 2008. Licensing is more common in occupations that require extensive education: More than 40% of workers with post-college education are required to have a license compared to only 15% of those with less than a high school education.

In some occupations to get licensed one must pass a test, which is frequently designed by licensed members of the occupation. By making the exam difficult, current workers can limit entry. For example, only 42% of people taking the California State Bar Examination in 2011 and in 2012 passed it, although all of them had law degrees. (The national rate for lawyers passing state bar exams in February 2011 was higher, but still only 60%.)

To the degree that testing is objective, licensing may raise the average quality of the workforce. However, its primary effect is to restrict the number of workers in an occupation. To analyze the effects of licensing, one can use a graph similar to panel b of Figure 2.6, where the wage is on the vertical axis and the number of workers per year is on the horizontal axis. Licensing shifts the occupational supply curve to the left, reducing the equilibrium quantity of workers and raising the wage. Kleiner and Krueger (2013) found that licensing raises occupational wages by 18%.

Price Controls

Government policies that directly control the price of a good may alter the market outcome even though they do not affect the demand or supply curves of the good. Such a policy may lead to excess supply or excess demand if the price the government sets differs from the unregulated equilibrium price. We illustrate this result with two types of price control programs. When the government sets a *price ceiling* at $\bar{p}$, the price at which goods are sold may be no higher than $\bar{p}$. When the government sets a *price floor* at $\underline{p}$, the price at which goods are sold may not fall below $\underline{p}$.

Price Ceilings. Price ceilings have no effect if they are set above the equilibrium price that would be observed in the absence of the price controls. If the government says that firms may charge no more than $\bar{p} = \$6$ per gallon of gas and firms are actually charging $p = \$4$, the government's price control policy is irrelevant. However, if the unregulated equilibrium price, p, would be above the price ceiling $\bar{p}$, the price that is actually observed in the market is the price ceiling. For example, if the equilibrium price of gas would be $4 and a price ceiling of $3 is imposed, then the ceiling price of $3 is charged.

Currently, Canada and many European countries set price ceilings on pharmaceuticals. The United States used price ceilings during both world wars, the Korean War, and in 1971–1973 during the Nixon administration, among other times. Hawaii limited the price of wholesale gasoline from 2005–2006. In the aftermath of Hurricane Katrina and the run up in gasoline prices in 2006–2007, and following reports of high oil company profits in 2008, many legislators called for price controls on gasoline, but no legislation was passed.

The U.S. experience with gasoline illustrates the effects of price controls. In the 1970s, the Organization of Petroleum Exporting Countries (OPEC) reduced supplies of crude oil (which is converted into gasoline) to Western countries. As a result, the total supply curve for gasoline in the United States shifted to the left from S^1 to S^2 in Figure 2.7. Because of this shift, the equilibrium price of gasoline would have risen substantially, from p_1 to p_2. In an attempt to protect consumers by keeping gasoline prices from rising, the U.S. government set price ceilings on gasoline in 1973 and 1979.

FIGURE 2.7 Price Ceiling on Gasoline

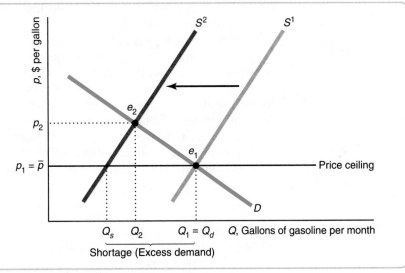

Restrictions on crude oil production (the major input in producing gasoline) cause the supply curve of gasoline to shift from S^1 to S^2. In an unregulated market, the equilibrium price would increase to p_2 and the equilibrium quantity would fall to Q_2. Suppose that the government imposes a price control so that gasoline stations may not charge a price above the price ceiling, $p_1 = \bar{p}$. At this price, producers are willing to supply only Q_s, which is less than the amount $Q_1 = Q_d$ that consumers want to buy. The result is excessive demand, or a shortage of gasoline of $Q_d - Q_s$.

The government told gas stations that they could charge no more than $\bar{p} = p_1$. Figure 2.7 shows the price ceiling as a solid horizontal line extending from the price axis at $\bar{p}$. The price control is binding because $p_2 > \bar{p}$. The observed price is the price ceiling. At $\bar{p}$, consumers *want* to buy $Q_d = Q_1$ gallons of gasoline, which is the equilibrium quantity they bought before OPEC acted. However, firms supply only Q_s gallons, which is determined by the intersection of the price control line with S^2. As a result of the binding price control, there is excess demand of $Q_d - Q_s$.

Were it not for the price controls, market forces would drive up the market price to p_2, the price at which the excess demand would be eliminated. The government price ceiling prevents this adjustment from occurring. As a result, an enforced price ceiling causes a **shortage**: a persistent excess demand.

At the time of the controls, some government officials argued that the shortages were caused by OPEC's cutting off its supply of oil to the United States, but that's not true. Without the price controls, the new equilibrium would be e_2. In this equilibrium, the price, p_2, is much higher than before, p_1; however, there is no shortage. Moreover, without controls, the quantity sold, Q_2, is greater than the quantity sold under the control program, Q_s.

With a binding price ceiling, the supply-and-demand model predicts an *equilibrium with a shortage*. In this equilibrium, the quantity demanded does not equal the quantity supplied. The reason that we call this situation an equilibrium, even though a shortage exists, is that buyers and sellers who abide by the law do not change their behavior. Without the price controls, consumers facing a shortage would try to get more output by offering to pay more, or firms would raise prices. With effective government price controls, both firms and consumers know that they can't drive up the price, so they live with the shortage.

What happens? Some lucky consumers get to buy Q_s units at the low price of $\bar{p}$. Other potential customers are disappointed: They would like to buy at that price, but they cannot find anyone willing to sell gas to them. In addition, consumers spend a lot of time waiting in line—a pure waste that adds considerably to the cost of such government interventions.

What determines which consumers are lucky enough to find goods to buy at the low price when there are price controls? With enforced price controls, sellers use criteria other than price to allocate the scarce commodity. Firms may supply their friends, long-term customers, or people of a certain race, gender, age, or religion. They may sell their goods on a first-come, first-served basis. Or they may limit everyone to only a few gallons.

Another possibility is that firms and customers will try to evade the price controls. A consumer could go to a gas station owner and say, "Let's not tell anyone, but I'll pay you twice the price the government sets if you'll sell me as much gas as I want." If enough customers and gas station owners behaved that way, no shortage would occur. A study of 92 major U.S. cities during the 1973 gasoline price controls found no gasoline lines in 52 of them. However, in cities such as Chicago, Hartford, New York, Portland, and Tucson, potential customers waited in line at the pump for an hour or more.[6] Deacon and Sonstelie (1989) estimated that for every dollar consumers saved due to the 1979 gasoline price controls, they lost $1.16 in waiting time and other factors.

---

[6]See MyEconLab Chapter Resources, Chapter 2, "Gas Lines," for a discussion of the effects of the 1973 and 1979 gasoline price controls.

Mini-Case

Disastrous Price Controls

Robert G. Mugabe, who has ruled Zimbabwe with an iron fist for nearly three decades, has used price controls to try to stay in power by currying favor among the poor.[7] In 2001, he imposed price controls on many basic commodities, including food, soap, and cement, which led to shortages of these goods and a thriving *black*, or *parallel, market* in which the controls were ignored developed. Prices on the black market were two or three times higher than the controlled prices.

He imposed more extreme controls in 2007. A government edict cut the prices of 26 essential items by up to 70%, and a subsequent edict imposed price controls on a much wider range of goods. Gangs of price inspectors patrolled shops and factories, imposing arbitrary price reductions. State-run newspapers exhorted citizens to turn in store owners whose prices exceeded the limits.

The Zimbabwean police reported that they arrested at least 4,000 businesspeople for not complying with the price controls. The government took over the nation's slaughterhouses after meat disappeared from stores, but in a typical week, butchers killed and dressed only 32 cows for the entire city of Bulawayo, which consists of 676,000 people.

Ordinary citizens initially greeted the price cuts with euphoria because they had been unable to buy even basic necessities because of hyperinflation and past price controls. Yet most ordinary citizens were unable to obtain much food because most of the cut-rate merchandise was snapped up by the police, soldiers, and members of Mr. Mugabe's governing party, who were tipped off prior to the price inspectors' rounds.

Manufacturing slowed to a crawl because firms could not buy raw materials and because the prices firms received were less than their costs of production. Businesses laid off workers or reduced their hours, impoverishing the 15% or 20% of adult Zimbabweans who still had jobs. The 2007 price controls on manufacturing crippled this sector, forcing manufacturers to sell goods at roughly half of what it cost to produce them. By mid-2008, the output by Zimbabwe's manufacturing sector had fallen 27% compared to the previous year. As a consequence, Zimbabweans died from starvation. Although we have no exact figures, according to the World Food Program, over five million Zimbabweans faced starvation in 2008.

Aid shipped into the country from international relief agencies and the two million Zimbabweans who fled abroad helped keep some people alive. In 2008, the World Food Program made an urgent appeal for $140 million in donations to feed Zimbabweans, stating that drought and political upheaval would soon exhaust the organization's stockpiles. Thankfully, the price controls were lifted in 2009.

Price Floors. Governments also commonly use price floors. One of the most important examples of a price floor is a minimum wage in a labor market. A minimum wage law forbids employers from paying less than the minimum wage, $\underline{w}$.

---

[7]Mr. Mugabe justified price controls as a means to deal with profiteering businesses that he said were part of a Western conspiracy to re-impose colonial rule. Actually, they were a vain attempt to slow the hyperinflation that resulted from his printing Zimbabwean money rapidly. Prices increased several billion times in 2008, and the government printed currency with a face value of 100 trillion Zimbabwe dollars.

Minimum wage laws date from 1894 in New Zealand, 1909 in the United Kingdom, and 1912 in Massachusetts. The Fair Labor Standards Act of 1938 set a federal U.S. minimum wage of 25¢ per hour. The U.S. federal minimum hourly wage rose to $7.25 in 2009 and remained at that level through early 2013, but 19 states have higher state minimum wages. (State and federal minimum wages are listed at **www.dol.gov**). The minimum wage in Canada differs across provinces, ranging from C$9.50 to C$11.00 (where C$ stands for Canadian dollars) in 2012. See **www.fedee.com/minwage.html** for minimum wages in European countries. If the minimum wage is *binding*—that is, if it exceeds the equilibrium wage, w^*—it creates *unemployment*: a persistent excess supply of labor.

We illustrate the effect of a minimum wage law in a labor market in which everyone is paid the same wage. Figure 2.8 shows the supply and demand curves for labor services (hours worked). Firms buy hours of labor service by hiring workers. The quantity measure on the horizontal axis is hours worked per year, and the price measure on the vertical axis is the wage per hour.

With no government intervention, the market equilibrium is e, where the wage is w^* and the number of hours worked is L^*. The minimum wage creates a price floor, a horizontal line, at $\underline{w}$. At that wage, the quantity demanded falls to L_d and the quantity supplied rises to L_s. As a result, there is an excess supply of labor of $L_s - L_d$. The minimum wage prevents market forces from eliminating this excess supply, so it leads to an equilibrium with unemployment.

The original 1938 U.S. minimum wage law, which was set much higher than the equilibrium wage in Puerto Rico, caused substantial unemployment there. It is ironic that a law designed to help workers by raising their wages may harm some of them by causing them to become unemployed. A minimum wage law benefits only those workers who remain employed.[8]

FIGURE 2.8 Minimum Wage: A Price Floor

In the absence of a minimum wage, the equilibrium wage is w^* and the equilibrium number of hours worked is L^*. A minimum wage, $\underline{w}$, set above w^*, leads to unemployment—persistent excess supply—because the quantity demanded, L_d, is less than the quantity supplied, L_s.

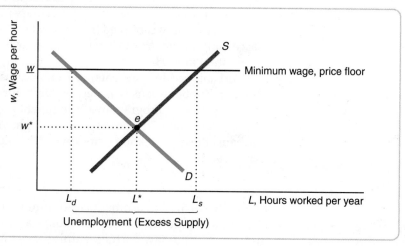

---

[8]The minimum wage could raise the wage enough that total wage payments, wL, rise despite the fall in demand for labor services. If the workers could share the unemployment—everybody works fewer hours than he or she wants—all workers could benefit from the minimum wage. Card and Krueger (1995) have argued, based on alternatives to the simple supply-and-demand model, that minimum wage laws raise wages in some markets (such as fast foods) without significantly reducing employment. In contrast, Neumark and Wascher (2008) conclude, based on an extensive review of minimum wage research, that increases in the minimum wage often have negative effects on employment.

Why Supply Need Not Equal Demand. The price ceiling and price floor examples show that the quantity supplied does not necessarily equal the quantity demanded in a supply-and-demand model. The quantity supplied need not equal the quantity demanded because of the way we define these two concepts. The quantity supplied is the amount sellers *want to sell* at a given price, holding other factors that affect supply, such as the price of inputs, constant. The quantity demanded is the quantity that buyers *want to buy* at a given price, if other factors that affect demand are held constant. The quantity that sellers want to sell and the quantity that buyers want to buy at a given price need not equal the *actual* quantity that is bought and sold.

When the government imposes a binding price ceiling of $\bar{p}$ on gasoline, the quantity demanded is greater than the quantity supplied. Despite the lack of equality between the quantity supplied and the quantity demanded, the supply-and-demand model is useful in analyzing this market because it predicts the excess demand that is actually observed.

We could have defined the quantity supplied and the quantity demanded so that they must be equal. If we were to define the quantity supplied as the amount firms *actually* sell at a given price and the quantity demanded as the amount consumers *actually* buy, supply must equal demand in all markets because the quantity demanded and the quantity supplied are *defined* to be the same quantity.

This distinction is important because many people, including politicians and newspaper reporters, are confused on this point. Someone insisting that "demand *must* equal supply" must be defining supply and demand as the *actual* quantities sold.

Because we define the quantities supplied and demanded in terms of people's *wants* and not *actual* quantities bought and sold, the statement that "supply equals demand" is a theory, not merely a definition. This theory says that the price and quantity in a market are determined by the intersection of the supply curve and the demand curve, and the market clears *if the government does not intervene*. However, the theory also tells us that government intervention can prevent market-clearing. For example, the supply-and-demand model predicts that excess demand will arise if the government imposes a price ceiling below the market-clearing price or excess supply if the government imposes a price floor above the market-clearing price.

Sales Taxes

Governments frequently impose sales taxes on goods, such as the carbon tax discussed at the beginning of the chapter. Sales taxes typically raise the price that consumers pay for a good and lower the price that firms receive for it.

A common sales tax is the *specific tax*, where a specified dollar amount, t, is collected per unit of output. For example, the federal government collects $t = 18.4$¢ on each gallon of gas sold in the United States.[9]

In this section, we examine three questions about the effects of a specific tax:

1. What effect does a specific tax have on equilibrium prices and quantity?
2. Do the equilibrium price and quantity depend on whether the tax is assessed on consumers or on producers?
3. Is it true, as many people claim, that taxes are fully *passed through* to consumers? That is, do consumers pay the entire tax imposed on suppliers (or on consumers)?

---

[9]The other major sales tax is an *ad valorem tax*, where the government collects a percentage of the price that consumers pay. The analysis of ad valorem taxes is similar to the analysis of specific taxes.

Equilibrium Effects of a Specific Tax. To answer these three questions, we must extend the standard supply-and-demand analysis to take taxes into account. We can illustrate the effect of a specific tax on the avocado market equilibrium.

Suppose that the government collects a specific tax of $t = \$0.55$ per lb of avocados from sellers at the time of sale. If consumers pay p, suppliers receive $p - t = p - \$0.55$, and the government keeps $t = \$0.55$.

Before the tax, the intersection of the before-tax avocado demand curve D and the before-tax avocado supply curve S^1 in panel a of Figure 2.9 determines the before-tax equilibrium, e_1, where the equilibrium price is $p_1 = \$2$, and the equilibrium quantity is $Q_1 = 80$. After the tax, firms only keep $\$1.45$ out of the $\$2$ they receive, so they are not willing to supply as many avocados as before the tax. For firms to be willing to sell 80 units after the tax, the firms would have to receive $\$2.55$ before the tax so that they could keep $\$2$. As a result, the after-tax supply curve, S^2, is $t = \$0.55$ above the original supply curve S^1 at every quantity, as the figure shows.

The after-tax equilibrium e_2 is determined by the intersection of S^2 and the demand curve D, where consumers pay $p_2 = \$2.15$, firms receive $p_2 - t = p_2 - \$0.55 = \$1.60$, and $Q_2 = 74$. Thus, the answer to our first question is that the specific tax causes the equilibrium price consumers pay to rise, the equilibrium quantity that firms receive to fall, and the equilibrium quantity to fall. Although the consumers and producers are worse off because of the tax, the government acquires new tax revenue of $\$0.55$ per lb $\times$ 74 million lbs per year $= \$40.7$ million per month.

The Same Equilibrium No Matter Who Is Taxed. Does it matter whether the specific tax is collected from firms or consumers? No: The market outcome is the same regardless of who is taxed.

The amount consumers pay, $p + t$, is the price that firms receive, p, plus the tax, t, that the government collects. Thus, if the final price that consumers pay including the tax is $\$2$, the price that suppliers receive is only $\$1.45$. Consequently, the demand curve as seen by firms shifts downward by $\$0.55$ from D^1 to D^2 in panel b of Figure 2.9. The new equilibrium e_2 occurs where D^2 intersects the supply curve S. The equilibrium quantity, Q_2, is 74. The equilibrium price, p_2, is $\$1.60$, the price firms receive. Consumers pay $p_2 + \$0.55 = \$2.15$. Thus, the market outcome is the same as in panel a where the tax is collected from firms.[10]

Pass-Through. Many people believe that if a tax is imposed on firms they simply raise their price by the amount of the tax—that the tax is fully passed through to consumers. This belief is not true in general. Full pass-through can occur, but partial pass-through is more common. As we just showed for the avocado market in panel a of Figure 2.9, the price consumers pay rises from $\$2$ to $\$2.15$ after a 55¢ specific tax is imposed on firms. Thus, the firms shift only 15¢ of the 55¢ tax to consumers. The firms absorb 40¢ of the tax, because the price that firms receive falls from $\$2$ to $\$1.60$. Thus, the fraction of the tax that consumers pay is $15/55 = 3/11$ and the fraction that firms absorb is $40/55 = 8/11$. As panel b shows, the allocation of the tax is the same if it is collected from consumers rather than firms. However, as the following Q&A shows, the degree of the pass-through depends on the shapes of the supply and demand curves.

---

[10]This analysis assumes that there is no administrative cost to collecting a tax. If collecting a tax from consumers required more resources than collecting taxes from sellers, then the overall economic impact of a tax on consumers differs from the impact of a tax on sellers.

FIGURE 2.9 Effect of a 55¢ Specific Tax on the Avocado Market Collected from Producers

(a) A specific tax of $t = \$0.55$ per lb collected from producers shifts the before-tax avocado supply from S^1 to the after-tax supply curve, S^2. The tax causes the equilibrium to shift from e_1 (the intersection of S^1 and D) to e_2 (intersection of S^2 and D). The equilibrium price, which consumers pay, increases from $2 to $2.15, while the price firms receive falls from $2 to $1.60 (= $2.15 − $0.55).

(b) A specific tax collected from consumers shifts the before-tax avocado demand curve from D^1 to the after-tax demand curve, D^2. Consequently, the equilibrium shifts from e_1 (intersection of D^1 and S) to e_2 (intersection of D^2 with S). The new prices and quantity are the same as those when the tax is collected from firms.

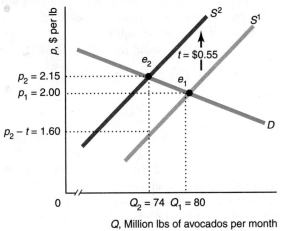

(a) Tax Collected from Firms

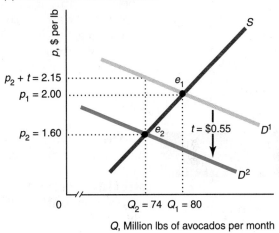

(b) Tax Collected from Consumers

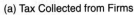

Q&A 2.3

If the supply curve is vertical and demand is linear and downward sloping, what is the effect of a $1 specific tax collected from consumers on equilibrium price and quantity, and what share of the tax is paid for by consumers? Why?

Answer

1. *Determine the equilibrium in the absence of a tax.* The supply curve, S in the graph, is vertical at Q_1 indicating that suppliers will supply Q_1 to the market at any price. The before-tax, downward-sloping linear demand curve, D^1, intersects S at the before-tax equilibrium, e_1, where the price is p_1 and the quantity is Q_1.

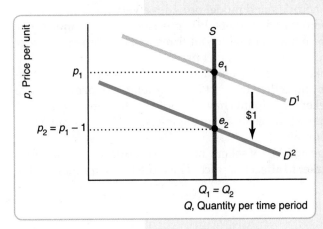

2. *Show how the tax shifts the demand curve and determine the new equilibrium.* A specific tax of $1 shifts the before-tax demand curve downward by $1 to D^2. The intersection of D^2 and S determines the after-tax equilibrium, e_2, where the price firms receive is $p_2 = p_1 - 1$, the price consumers pay after tax is $p_1 = p_2 + 1$, and the quantity is $Q_2 = Q_1$.

3. *Compare the before- and after-tax equilibria.* The specific tax doesn't affect the equilibrium quantity or the tax-inclusive price that consumers pay, but it lowers the price that firms receive by the full amount of the tax. Thus, there is no pass-through of the tax to consumers. Thus,

even though the tax is collected from consumers, consumers pay the same price whether the tax is imposed or not because the price received by firms falls by the amount of the tax.

4. *Explain why.* The reason firms must absorb the entire tax is that, because the supply curve is vertical, the firms sell the same quantity no matter the price. Consumers will not buy that quantity unless their after-tax price is the same as the before-tax price. Therefore, the final price to consumers cannot change and firms must absorb the tax: There is no pass-through. For example, suppose that firms at a farmers' market have a fixed amount of melons that will spoil if they are not sold on this day. The firms sell the melons for the most they can get (p_2 in the figure) because if they do not sell the melons, they are worthless. Consequently, the farmers must absorb the entire tax or be left with unsold melons.

Managerial Implication

Cost Pass-Through

Managers should use pass-through analysis to predict the effect on their price and quantity from not just a new tax but from *any per unit increase in costs*. That is, if the cost of producing avocados rises 55¢ per lb because of an increase in the cost of labor or other factor of production, rather than because of a tax, the same analysis as in panel a of Figure 2.9 would apply, so a manager would know that only 15¢ of this cost increase could be passed through to consumers.

2.6 When to Use the Supply-and-Demand Model

As we have seen, the supply-and-demand model can help us to understand and predict real-world events in many markets. As with many models, the supply-and-demand model need not be perfect to be useful. It is much like a map. A map can leave out many details and still be very valuable—indeed, maps are useful in large part because they simplify reality. Similarly, the supply-and-demand model gains much of its power from its simplicity. The main practical question concerns whether the model is close enough to reality to yield useful predictions and conclusions. We have learned that the supply-and-demand model provides a very good description of actual events in highly competitive markets. It is precisely accurate in *perfectly competitive* markets, which are markets in which all firms and consumers are *price takers*: no market participant can affect the market price.

Perfectly competitive markets have five characteristics that result in price taking by firms: (1) many buyers and sellers transact in a market, (2) all firms produce identical products, (3) all market participants have full information about price and product characteristics, (4) transaction costs are negligible, and (5) firms can easily enter and exit the market over time.

In a market with a very large number of sellers, no single producer or consumer is a large enough part of the market to affect the price. The more firms in a market, the less any one firm's output affects total market output and hence the market price. If one of the many thousands of wheat farmers stops selling wheat, the price of wheat will not change. Similarly, no individual buyer of wheat can cause price to change through a change in buying patterns.

If consumers believe all firms produce identical products, consumers do not prefer one firm's good to another's. Thus, if one firm raised its price, consumers would all buy from the other firm.

If consumers know the prices all firms charge and one firm raises its price, that firm's customers will buy from other firms. If consumers have less information about product quality than a firm, the firm can take advantage of consumers by selling them inferior-quality goods or by charging a much higher price than that charged by other firms. In such a market, the observed price may be higher than that predicted by the supply-and-demand model, the market may not exist at all (consumers and firms cannot reach agreements), or different firms may charge different prices for the same good.

If it is cheap and easy for a buyer to find a seller and make a trade, and if one firm raises its price, consumers can easily arrange to buy from another firm. That is, perfectly competitive markets typically have very low **transaction costs**: the expenses, over and above the price of the product, of finding a trading partner and making a trade for the product. These costs include the time and money spent gathering information on quality and finding someone with whom to trade. The costs of traveling and the value of the consumer's time are transaction costs. Other transaction costs may include the costs of writing and enforcing a contract, such as the cost of a lawyer's time. If transaction costs are very high, no trades at all might occur. In less extreme cases individual trades may occur, but at a variety of prices.

The ability of firms to enter and exit a market freely leads to a large number of firms in a market and promotes price taking. Suppose a firm could raise its price and make a higher profit. If other firms could not enter the market, this firm would not be a price taker. However, if other firms can quickly and easily enter the market, the higher profit will encourage entry until the price is driven back to the original level.

In markets without these characteristics, firms may not be price takers. For example, if there is only one seller of a good or service—a *monopoly*—that seller is a *price setter* and can affect the market price. Because demand curves slope downward, a monopoly can increase the price it receives by reducing the amount of a good it supplies. Firms are also price setters in an *oligopoly*—a market with only a small number of firms. In markets with price setters, the market price is usually higher than that predicted by the supply-and-demand model. That does not make the model wrong. It means only that the supply-and-demand model might not be the right tool to analyze markets with a small number of buyers and/or sellers. In such markets, we use other models.

As a practical matter, it is rare that we would find a market that fully and completely satisfies all the conditions needed for perfect competition. The practical issue concerns whether the market is "competitive enough" for the supply-and-demand model to be useful in the sense that it accurately describes the market and can be used to predict the effects of changes to the equilibrium. Experience has shown that the supply-and-demand model is reliable in a wide range of markets, such as those for agriculture, financial products, labor, construction, many services, real estate, wholesale trade, and retail trade.

Managerial Solution

Carbon Taxes

We conclude our analysis of the supply-and-demand model by returning to the managerial problem posed in the introduction of this chapter: What will be the effect of imposing a carbon tax on the price of gasoline?

The primary targets of carbon taxes are fossil fuels such as oil, natural gas, and coal. These fuels release carbon-based pollutants—including greenhouse gases that contribute to global warming—into the environment. Typically, a carbon tax is a specific tax on the amount of carbon produced by consuming fuels or other products. Currently, the carbon tax in Sweden is $150 per ton of carbon. Because the amount of carbon in a gallon or liter of gasoline is fixed, effectively, a carbon tax is a specific tax on gasoline. Consequently, we can analyze the impact of a carbon tax on gasoline in the same way that we analyzed the effect of a specific tax on avocados.

A good manager considers the short-run and long-run price effects of a tax, which are likely to differ. As we've already seen, the degree to which a tax is passed through to consumers depends on the shapes of the demand and supply curves. Typically, short-run supply and demand curves differ from the long-run curves.

In particular, the long-run supply curve of gasoline differs substantially from the short-run curve. In the long-run, the supply curve is upward sloping, as in our typical figure. However, the U.S. short-run supply curve of gasoline is very close to vertical. The U.S. refinery capacity has fallen over the last quarter century. Currently the 149 U.S. refineries can process a maximum of only 17.3 million barrels of crude oil per day, compared to 1981 when 324 refineries could process 18.6 million barrels per day. Refineries operate at almost full capacity during the summer, when the gasoline demand curve shifts to the right because families take long car trips during their vacations. Consequently, refineries cannot increase their output in the short run, and the supply curve for gasoline is nearly vertical at the maximum capacity, $\overline{Q}$. That is, even if the price of gasoline rises, producers sell no more gasoline than $\overline{Q}$.

From empirical studies, we know that the U.S. federal gasoline specific tax of $t = 18.4¢$ per gallon is shared roughly equally between gasoline companies and

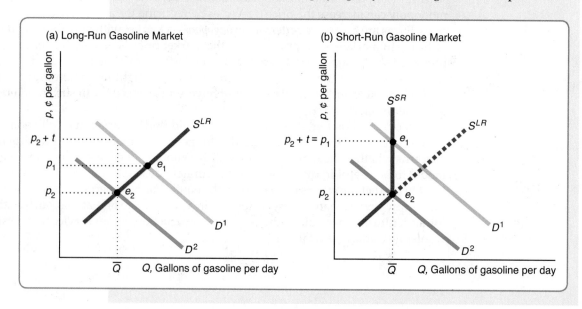

(a) Long-Run Gasoline Market

(b) Short-Run Gasoline Market

consumers in the long run. However, based on what we learned from Q&A 2.3, we expect that most of the tax will fall on firms that sell gasoline in the short run.

We contrast the long-run and short-run effects of a carbon tax in the figure. In both panels, the carbon tax is equivalent to a specific gasoline tax of t per gallon. If this tax is collected from consumers, the before-tax demand curve D^1 shifts down by t to the after-tax demand curve D^2. Also in both panels, the equilibrium shifts from e_1—the intersection of D^1 and the relevant supply curve—to e_2—the intersection of D^2 and the relevant supply curve (though these equilibrium points are not the same across the two panels).

Panel a shows the effect of the tax in the long run, where the long-run supply curve is upward sloping. The price that firms receive falls from p_1 to p_2, and the price that consumers pay rises from p_1 to $p_2 + t$. As the figure illustrates, the tax is roughly equally shared by consumers and firms in the long run.

In the short run in panel b, the upward-sloping short-run supply curve becomes vertical at full capacity, $\overline{Q}$. The price that consumers pay, p_1, is the same before the tax and after the tax. That is, the price that gasoline firms receive, p_2, falls by the full amount of the tax.

Manufacturing and other firms that ship goods are consumers of gasoline. They can expect to absorb relatively little of a carbon tax when it is first imposed, but half of the tax in the long run.[11]

---

[11]An alternative approach to using a carbon tax to control pollution is for the government to restrict emissions directly. Each firm is given a fixed number of emission permits, where each permit allows the owner to release a given quantity of emissions. A market-based variant allows firms to buy or sell these emission permits in a market. The resulting price of an emission permit acts much like a tax on emissions. See Chapter 16.

SUMMARY

1. **Demand.** The quantity of a good or service demanded by consumers depends on the price of a good, the price of goods that are substitutes and complements, consumers' incomes, the information they have about the good, their tastes, government regulations, and other factors. The *Law of Demand*—which is based on observation—says that *demand curves slope downward*: the higher the price, the less quantity of the good demanded, holding constant other factors that affect demand. A change in price causes a *movement along the demand curve*. A change in income, tastes, or another factor that affects demand other than price causes a *shift of the demand curve*. To get a total demand curve, we horizontally sum the demand curves of individuals or other subgroups of consumers. That is, we add the quantities demanded by each individual at a given price to get the total quantity demanded.

2. **Supply.** The quantity of a good or service supplied by firms depends on the price, costs of inputs, the state of technology, government regulations, and other factors. The market supply curve usually but not always slopes upward. A change in price causes a *movement along the supply curve*. A change in the price of an input or in technology causes a *shift of the supply curve*. The total supply curve is the horizontal sum of the supply curves for individual firms.

3. **Market Equilibrium.** Equilibrium arises when no market participant has an incentive to change its behavior. In an unregulated supply-and-demand model, the market equilibrium is a point: a price and a quantity. The market equilibrium is determined by the intersection of the supply curve and demand curve. At the equilibrium price, the market for the good clears in the sense that the quantity of the good demanded by consumers exactly

equals the quantity of the good that suppliers supply to the market, which is the equilibrium quantity. The actions of buyers and sellers put pressure on price and quantity to move toward equilibrium levels if the market price is initially too low or too high.

4. **Shocks to the Equilibrium.** A change in an underlying factor other than a good's own price causes a shift of the supply curve or the demand curve, which alters the equilibrium. For example, if the price of coffee rises, we would expect the demand for tea, a substitute, to shift outward, putting upward pressure on the price of tea and leading to an increase in the quantity of tea sold.

5. **Effects of Government Interventions.** Some government policies—such as restrictions on who can buy a product—cause a shift in the supply or demand curves, thereby altering the equilibrium. Other government policies, such as price controls, can cause the quantity supplied to be greater or

less than the quantity demanded, leading to persistent excesses or shortages. A specific tax, a type of sales tax, typically lowers the equilibrium quantity, raises the price paid by consumers, and lowers the price received by sellers, so firms are unable to pass the entire tax through to consumers.

6. **When to Use the Supply-and-Demand Model.** The supply-and-demand model is a powerful tool used to explain what happens in a market and to make predictions about what will happen if an underlying factor changes. This model accurately predicts what occurs in some markets but not others. The supply-and-demand model performs best in explaining and predicting the behavior of markets with many buyers and sellers, with identical or at least very similar products provided by different producers, with free entry and exit by producers, with full information about price and other market characteristics, and with low transaction costs.

QUESTIONS

All exercises is available on MyEconLab; * = *answer at the back of this book.*

1. Demand

*1.1. Does an increase in average income cause a shift of the demand curve for avocados or a movement along the demand curve? Explain briefly.

1.2. Given the estimated demand function Equation 2.2 for avocados, $Q = 104 - 40p + 20p_t + 0.01Y$, use algebra (or calculus) to show how the demand curve shifts as per capita income, Y, increases by $1,000 a year. Illustrate this shift in a diagram.

1.3. Assume that both the U.S. and Canadian demand curves for lumber are linear. The Canadian demand curve lies inside the U.S. curve (the Canadian demand curve hits the axes at a lower price and a lower quantity than the U.S. curve). Draw the individual country demand curves and the aggregate demand curve for the two countries. Explain the relationship between the country and aggregate demand curves in words.

*1.4. The demand curve for a truckload of firewood for college students in a small town is $Q_c = 400 - p$. It is sometimes convenient to rewrite a demand curve equation with price on the left side. We refer to such a relationship as the *inverse demand function*. Therefore, the inverse demand curve for college students is $p = 400 - Q_c$. The demand curve for other town residents is $Q_r = 400 - 2p$.

a. What is the inverse demand curve for other town residents?

b. At a price of $300, will any firewood be sold to college students? What about other town residents? At what price is the quantity demanded by other town residents zero?

c. Draw the total demand curve, which aggregates the demand curves for college students and other residents.

2. Supply

2.1. Use Equation 2.5, the estimated supply function for avocados, $Q = 58 + 15p - 20p_f$, to determine how much the supply curve for avocados shifts if the price of fertilizer rises by $1.10 per lb. Illustrate this shift in a diagram.

*2.2. Explain why a change in the price of fertilizer causes a shift in the supply curve for avocados rather than a movement along the supply curve for avocados.

*2.3. Holding the price of fertilizer constant, by how much would the price of avocados need to rise to cause an increase of 60 million lbs per month in the quantity of avocados supplied?

2.4. The total U.S. supply curve for frozen orange juice is the sum of the supply curve from Florida and the imported supply curve from Brazil. In a diagram, show the relationship between these three supply curves and explain it in words.

3. Market Equilibrium

*3.1. A large number of firms are capable of producing chocolate-covered cockroaches. The linear, upward-sloping supply curve starts on the price axis at $6 per box. A few hardy consumers are willing to buy this product (possibly to use as gag gifts). Their linear, downward-sloping demand curve hits the price axis at $4 per box. Draw the supply and demand curves. Does an equilibrium occur at a positive price and quantity? Explain your answer.

3.2. The demand curve is $Q = 100 - p$, and the supply curve is $Q = 20 + 3p$. What are the equilibrium price and quantity?

3.3. Using the supply and demand functions for avocados in the chapter, derive the demand and supply curves if $p_t = \$0.80$, $Y = \$4,000$, and $p_f = \$0.95$. What is the equilibrium price and quantity of avocados?

4. Shocks to the Equilibrium

4.1. Using supply-and-demand diagrams, illustrate and explain the effect of an outward shift in the demand curve on price and quantity if
   a. The supply curve is horizontal.
   b. The supply curve is vertical.
   c. The supply curve is upward sloping.

4.2. Use supply-and-demand diagrams to illustrate the qualitative effect of the following possible shocks on the U.S. avocado market.
   a. A new study shows significant health benefits from eating avocados.
   b. Trade barriers that restricted avocado imports from Mexico are eliminated ("Free Trade Party Dip," *Los Angeles Times*, February 6, 2007).
   c. A recession causes a decline in per capita income.
   d. Genetically modified avocado plants that allow for much greater output or yield without increasing cost are introduced into the market.

*4.3. The United States is increasingly *outsourcing* jobs to India: having the work done in India rather than in the United States. For example, the Indian firm Tata Consultancy Services, which provides information technology services, increased its work force by 70,000 workers in 2010 and expected to add 60,000 more in 2011 ("Outsourcing Firm Hiring 60,000 Workers in India," *San Francisco Chronicle*, June 16, 2011). As a result of increased outsourcing, wages of some groups of Indian skilled workers have increased substantially over the years. Use a supply-and-demand diagram to explain this outcome.

4.4. In Q&A 2.1, if the price of tomatoes rises to $1.80 per lb, what are the new equilibrium price and quantity for avocados?

4.5. According to Borjas (2003), immigration into the United States increased the labor supply of working men by 11.0% from 1980 to 2000 and reduced the wage of the average native U.S. worker by 3.2%. Draw a supply-and-demand diagram and label the axes to illustrate what happened.

4.6. Given that the U.S. supply of frozen orange juice comes mainly from Florida and Brazil, what effect would a freeze that damages oranges in Florida have on the price and quantity of frozen orange juice sold in the United States? What effect would the freeze have on the price of grapefruit juice? Use supply-and-demand diagrams in your answer.

4.7. Ethanol, a fuel, is made from corn. Ethanol production increased 15.4 times from 1990 to 2011 (**www .ethanolrfa.org**, January 2013). What effect did this increased use of corn for producing ethanol have on the price of corn and the consumption of corn as food? Illustrate using a supply-and-demand diagram.

4.8. The major BP oil spill in the Gulf of Mexico substantially reduced the harvest of shrimp and other seafood in the Gulf, but had limited impact on the prices that U.S. consumers paid in 2010 (Emmeline Zhao, "Impact on Seafood Prices Is Limited," *Wall Street Journal*, June 20, 2010). The reason was that the United States imports about 83% of its seafood and only 2% of domestic supplies come from the Gulf. Use a supply-and-demand diagram to illustrate what happened.

4.9. Increasingly, instead of advertising in newspapers, individuals and firms use Web sites that offer free or inexpensive classified ads, such as **ClassifiedAds .com**, **Craigslist.org**, **Realtor.com**, **Jobs.com**, **Monster.com**, and portals like Google and Yahoo. Using a supply-and-demand model, explain what will happen to the equilibrium levels of newspaper advertising as the use of the Internet grows. Will the growth of the Internet affect the supply curve, the demand curve, or both? Why?

*4.10. Humans who consume beef products made from diseased animal parts can develop mad cow disease (bovine spongiform encephalopathy, or BSE, a new variant of Creutzfeldt-Jakob disease), a deadly affliction that slowly eats holes in sufferers' brains. The first U.S. case, in a cow imported from Canada, was reported in December 2003. As soon as the United States revealed the discovery of the single mad cow, more than 40 countries slapped an embargo on U.S. beef, causing beef supply curves to shift to the left in those importing countries. At least initially, a few U.S. consumers stopped eating beef, causing the demand curve in the United States to shift slightly to the left. (Schlenker and Villas-Boas, 2009, found that U.S. consumers regained confidence and resumed their earlier levels of beef buying within three months.) In the first few weeks after the U.S. ban, the quantity of beef sold in Japan fell substantially, and the price rose. In contrast, in January 2004, three weeks after the first discovery, the U.S. price fell by about 15% and the quantity sold increased by 43% over the last week in October 2003. Use supply-and-demand diagrams to explain these events.

4.11. In the previous question, you were asked to illustrate why the mad cow disease announcement initially caused the U.S. equilibrium price of beef to fall and the quantity to rise. Show that if the supply and demand curves had shifted in the same directions as above but to greater or lesser degrees, the equilibrium quantity might have fallen. Could the equilibrium price have risen? (*Hint*: See Q&A 2.2.)

*4.12. Increases in the price of petroleum affect the demand curve for aluminum. Petroleum-based chemicals (petrochemicals) are the main raw material used for plastic. Plastics are used to make many products, including beverage containers, auto parts, and construction materials. An alternative to plastic in these (and other) uses is aluminum. Thus, plastic and aluminum are substitutes. An increase in petroleum prices increases the cost of petrochemicals. Petroleum prices also affect the supply curve for aluminum. Increases in petroleum prices tend to raise energy prices, including electricity prices. Electricity is a very important input in producing aluminum. Therefore, increasing petroleum prices tend to increase the cost of electricity. In a supply-and-demand diagram, show how an increase in petroleum prices affects the demand curve and supply curve for aluminum. If the price of petroleum rises, would the price of aluminum rise, fall, remain unchanged, or is the result indeterminate? Would the quantity of aluminum sold rise, fall, remain unchanged, or is the result indeterminate? Explain your answers.

5. Effects of Government Interventions

5.1. Use a supply-and-demand diagram to show the effects of occupational licensing on the equilibrium wage and number of workers in an occupation as described in the Mini-Case "Occupational Licensing."

*5.2. After Katrina, a major hurricane, damaged many U.S. gasoline refineries in 2005, the price of gasoline shot up around the country. The Federal Trade Commission announced that it would investigate price gouging—charging "too much"—and several members of Congress called for price controls on gasoline. What would have been the likely effect of such a law had it been passed?

5.3. Usury laws place a ceiling on interest rates that lenders such as banks can charge borrowers. Why would we expect low-income households in states with usury laws to have significantly lower levels of consumer credit (loans) than comparable households in states without usury laws? (*Hint*: The interest rate is the price of a loan, and the amount of the loan is the quantity measure.)

5.4. Some cities impose rent control laws, which are price controls or limits on the price of rental accommodations (apartments, houses, and mobile homes). As of 2011, New York City alone had approximately one million apartments under rent control. Show the effect of a rent control law on the equilibrium rental price and the quantity of New York City apartments. Show the amount of excess demand on your supply-and-demand diagram.

5.5. If the minimum wage raises the market wage, w, but hours worked, L, fall as a result, total wage payments, wL, may rise or fall. Use supply and demand curves to show that either outcome is possible depending on the shapes (slopes) of the supply and demand curves. (*Hint*: With the wage on the vertical axis and hours worked, L, on the horizontal axis, wage payments equal the area of the box with a height of the equilibrium wage and length of the equilibrium hours worked.)

5.6. Use the demand function and the supply function for the avocado market to determine how the equilibrium price and quantity change when a 55¢ per lb specific tax is imposed on this market, as illustrated in Figure 2.9.

5.7. Worried about excessive drinking among young people, the British government increased the tax on beer by 42% from 2008 to 2012. Does a specific tax substantially reduce the equilibrium quantity of alcohol? Answer in terms of the slopes of the demand and supply curves.

5.8. If the government collects a $1 specific tax, what share of the tax is paid by consumers and firms in each of the following cases? Explain why. (*Hint*: See Q&A 2.3. Depending on the shape of the curves, it may be easier to assume that the tax is collected from consumers or from firms.)
   a. The demand curve is vertical at quantity Q and the supply curve is upward sloping.
   b. The demand curve is horizontal at price p and the supply curve is upward sloping.

c. The demand curve is downward sloping and the supply curve is horizontal at price p.

5.9. Quebec, Canada, offers a per-child subsidy on day care for young children that lowers the price to $7 per child as of 2011 (at a cost of about $10,000 per child per year). (*Hint*: A subsidy is a negative tax.)

    a. What is the effect of this subsidy on the equilibrium price and quantity?

    b. Show the incidence of the subsidy on day care providers and parents using a supply-and-demand diagram.

6. When to Use the Supply-and-Demand Model

6.1. List as many industries as you can for which the supply-and-demand model is likely to be appropriate.

7. Managerial Problem

7.1. During the spring and summer of 2008 when gasoline prices were rising quickly, politicians in several countries proposed a moratorium on some or all gasoline taxes to help consumers. In the United States, John McCain, the Republican candidate for president, proposed suspending the federal gasoline tax of 18.4¢ for the summer when demand tends to be high. (Hillary Clinton, while an active candidate for the Democratic nomination for the president, also pushed this plan.) In the United Kingdom, Prime Minister Gordon Brown proposed delaying a two pence per liter rise in a fuel tax until the fall. How would these short-run policies have affected the prices consumers pay in these countries if the policies had been enacted?

8. Spreadsheet Exercises[12]

8.1. Suppose that the market for video games is competitive with demand function $Q_d = 130 - 4p + 2Y + 3p_m - 2p_c$, where Q_d is the quantity demanded, p is the market price, Y is the monthly budget that an average consumer has available for entertainment, p_m is the average price of a movie, and p_c is the price of a controller that is required to play these games.

    a. Given that $Y = \$100$, $p_m = \$30$, and $p_c = \$30$, use Excel to calculate quantity demanded for $p = \$10$ to $p = \$80$ in $5 increments. Use Excel's charting tool to draw the demand curve.

    b. Now, Y increases to $120. Recalculate the demand schedule in part a. Use Excel's charting tool to draw the new demand curve in the same diagram.

    c. Let $Y = \$100$ and $p_c = \$30$ again, but let p_m increase to $40. Recalculate the demand schedule in part a. Use Excel's charting tool to draw the graph of the new demand curve.

    d. Let $Y = \$100$, $p_m = \$30$, and p_c increases to $40. Recalculate the demand schedule in part a and use Excel to draw the new demand curve.

8.2. In Smalltown, Pennsylvania, the demand function for men's haircuts is $Q_d = 500 - 30p + 0.08Y$, where Q_d is quantity demanded per month, p the price of a haircut, and Y the average monthly income in the town. The supply function for men's haircuts is $Q_s = 100 + 20p - 20w$, where Q_s is the quantity supplied and w the average hourly wage of barbers.

    a. If $Y = \$5000$ and $w = \$10$, use Excel to calculate quantity demanded and quantity supplied for $p = \$5$, 10, 15, 20, 25, and 30. Calculate excess demand for each price. (Note that an excess supply is negative excess demand). Determine the equilibrium price and quantity. Use Excel's charting tool to draw the demand and supply curves.

    b. Assume that Y increases to $6,875 and w increases to $15. Use Excel to recalculate quantity demanded, quantity supplied, and excess demand for $p = \$5$, 10, 15, 20, 25, and 30. Determine the new equilibrium price and quantity. Use Excel to draw the new demand and supply curves. How can you explain the change in equilibrium?

---

[12]The spreadsheet exercises, which appear at the end of each chapter from Chapter 2 on, are based on the work of Satyajit Ghosh in cooperation with the authors. The answers are available on MyEconLab.

3 Empirical Methods for Demand Analysis

98% of all statistics are made up.

From the time Apple launched iTunes in mid-2003 through early 2009, it charged 99¢ for each song on its U.S. site. Despite having sold over nine billion songs by early 2009, Apple was under pressure from many sides to change the price. Music producers wanted Apple to charge more. In the United Kingdom, **Amazon.com**, iTunes's chief rival, announced that it was launching a price war for MP3 music downloads. Should iTunes raise or lower its price? In April 2009, Apple changed to a new U.S. pricing scheme: 69¢ a song for the older catalog, 99¢ for most new songs, and $1.29 for the most popular tracks.

Before the managers of iTunes changed the price, they wanted to predict the likely effect of the price change. Because Apple had always charged a single price, the managers could not use experience with past price variations to estimate the likely consumer response to a price hike. Rather than run a potentially costly experiment of trying different possible prices to see how the quantity demanded would change, iTunes managers could ask a focus group consisting of a random sample of music buyers how they would react to a price hike. After collecting their responses, the managers could analyze the data to predict the likely effects of a price change. How could the managers use the data to estimate the demand curve facing iTunes? How could the managers determine if a price increase would be likely to raise revenue, even though the quantity demanded would fall?

Managers commonly use data to estimate economic relationships, such as the relationship between price and quantity shown by a demand curve, or to examine whether a particular economic theory applies in their markets. Data-based analysis of economic relationships is often referred to as *empirical* analysis. This chapter discusses empirical methods that can be used to analyze economic relationships, focusing particularly on the empirical analysis of demand.

In Chapter 2, we focused on market demand curves in highly competitive markets, such as most agricultural markets. In highly competitive markets with many firms selling identical products, each individual firm is a *price taker*. In such markets, no one firm can significantly influence the market price. Any firm that tried to raise its price above the market equilibrium price would lose all of its sales. However, many firms, such as Apple, operate in markets that are not as competitive. Such firms are *price setters* that can raise their prices without losing all their sales. In the market for music downloads, Apple is a price setter.

A price-setting firm is concerned about the demand curve facing the firm rather than a market demand curve. In particular, the manager of a price-setting firm often wants to know how responsive its quantity demanded is to changes in its price or in other variables that affect demand. For example, in deciding whether to raise the price of iTunes songs by 30¢, an Apple manager would want to know how the number of iTunes downloads would fall in response to a 30¢ increase in price. This responsiveness can be measured empirically using the *price elasticity of demand*.

A manager might also wish to estimate the entire demand function to decide how to set the firm's optimal price, plan an advertising campaign, or choose how large a plant to build. In Chapter 2, we used estimated demand (and supply) functions to determine the equilibrium price and to analyze the effects of government policies on the market. This chapter describes how to estimate demand functions using *regression analysis*, which is an empirical method used to estimate a mathematical relationship between a dependent variable, such as quantity demanded, and explanatory variables, such as price and income.

Further, managers often wish to use data to forecast the future value of an important economic quantity such as future sales. This chapter describes major forecasting methods, focusing particularly on the role of regression analysis in forecasting.

Main Topics	
In this chapter, we examine five main topics	1. **Elasticity:** An elasticity measures the responsiveness of one variable, such as quantity demanded, to a change in another variable, such as price.
	2. **Regression Analysis:** Regression analysis is a method used to estimate a mathematical relationship between a dependent variable, such as quantity demanded, and explanatory variables, such as price and income.
	3. **Properties and Statistical Significance of Estimated Coefficients:** A regression analysis provides information that can be used to assess how much confidence can be placed in the coefficients of an estimated regression relationship, allowing us to infer whether one variable has a meaningful influence on another.
	4. **Regression Specification:** For a regression analysis to be reliable, the specification—the number and identity of explanatory variables and the functional form of the mathematical relationship (such as linear or quadratic)—must be chosen appropriately.
	5. **Forecasting:** Future values of important variables such as sales or revenues can be predicted using regression analysis.

3.1 Elasticity

Managers commonly summarize the responsiveness of one variable—such as the quantity demanded—to a change in another—such as price—using a measure called an **elasticity**, which is the percentage change in one variable divided by the associated percentage change in the other variable. In particular, a manager can use the elasticity of demand to determine how the quantity demanded varies with price.

The Price Elasticity of Demand

In making critical decisions about pricing, a manager needs to know how a change in price affects the quantity sold. The **price elasticity of demand** (or simply the *elasticity of demand* or the *demand elasticity*) is the percentage change in quantity demanded, Q, divided by the percentage change in price, p. That is, the price elasticity of demand (which we represent by ε, the Greek letter epsilon) is

$$\varepsilon = \frac{\text{percentage change in quantity demanded}}{\text{percentage change in price}} = \frac{\Delta Q/Q}{\Delta p/p}. \tag{3.1}$$

The symbol Δ (the Greek letter delta) indicates a change, so ΔQ is the change in the quantity demanded; $\Delta Q/Q$ is the percentage change in the quantity demanded; Δp is the change in price; and $\Delta p/p$ is the percentage change in price. According to Equation 3.1, if a 1% increase in the price of a product results in a 3% decrease in the quantity demanded of that product, the elasticity of demand is $\varepsilon = -3\%/1\% = -3$.

The elasticity of demand is a pure number: it is not measured in any particular units like dollars or pounds (lbs.). A useful way to think about elasticity is to consider the effect of a 1% change. If the price elasticity of demand is –2, a 1% decrease in price would cause quantity demanded to increase by 2%.

Arc Elasticity. Very often, a manager has observed the quantity demanded at two different prices. The manager can use this information to calculate an *arc price elasticity of demand*, which is a price elasticity of demand calculated using two distinct price-quantity pairs.

Suppose the manager observes that the quantity of avocados demanded was 76 million pounds per month at a price of $2.10 per pound, but rose to 84 million pounds when the price fell to $1.90. To use Equation 3.1, the manager needs to determine the percentage change in quantity, $\Delta Q/Q$, and the percentage change in price, $\Delta p/p$.

The change in the quantity demanded as the price falls is $\Delta Q = 84 - 76 = 8$ million pounds. To determine the percentage change in quantity, we need to divide this change by a quantity, Q. Do we use the initial quantity, 76, the final quantity, 84, or something else? When calculating a percentage change, this choice of the base quantity makes a difference. If we use the initial quantity as the base, then the percentage change in quantity is $8/76 \approx 10.5\%$ (where $\approx$ means "approximately equal to"). If we use the final quantity as the base, the percentage change is $8/84 \approx 9.5\%$.

Another approach is to use the average quantity as the base. The average quantity is $(76 + 84)/2 = 80$, so the associated percentage change is $8/80 = 10\%$. Many analysts use the average quantity because the elasticity is the same regardless of whether we start at a quantity of 76 and move to 84 or start at 84 and move to 76. If, instead, the manager consistently uses the initial quantity as the base, or consistently uses the final quantity as the base, then the percentage change would vary depending on the direction of movement.

The percentage change in price can also be calculated by using the average price as the base. The price change is $1.90 - $2.10 = -$0.20. The average price is $($1.90 + $2.10)/2 = $2.00. Thus, the percentage change in price is $-$0.20/$2.00 = -10\%. The elasticity is the percentage change in quantity divided by the percentage change in price or $10\%/(-10\%) = -1$.

An **arc price elasticity** is an elasticity that uses the average price and average quantity as the denominator for percentage calculations. Using Equation 3.1, this arc price elasticity is

$$\varepsilon = \frac{\text{percentage change in quantity demanded}}{\text{percentage change in price}} = \frac{\Delta Q / \overline{Q}}{\Delta p / \overline{p}}, \qquad (3.2)$$

where the bars over Q and p indicate average values.

Managerial Implication

Changing Prices to Calculate an Arc Elasticity

One of the easiest and most straightforward ways for a manager to determine the elasticity of demand for a firm's product is to conduct an experiment. If the firm is a *price setter* and can vary the price of its product—as Apple, Toyota, Kraft Foods, and many other firms can—the manager can change the price and observe how the quantity sold varies. Armed with two observations—the quantity sold at the original price and the quantity sold at the new price—the manager can calculate an arc elasticity. Depending on the size of the calculated elasticity, the manager may continue to sell at the new price or revert back to the original price. It is often possible to obtain very useful information from an experiment in a few or even just one small submarket—in one country, in one city, or even in one supermarket. Managers of price-setting firms should consider using such experiments to assess the effect of price changes on quantity sold.

Q&A 3.1

In the first week after Apple's iTunes raised its price on its most popular songs from 99¢ to $1.29, the quantity demanded of Akon's "Beautiful" fell approximately 9.4% to 52,760 units from the 57,941 units sold in the previous week.[1] What is the arc elasticity of demand for "Beautiful" based on the average price and quantity?

Answer *Use Equation 3.2 to calculate the arc elasticity.* The change in the price is $\Delta p = \$0.30 = \$1.29 - \$0.99$, and the change in quantity is $\Delta Q = -5,181 = 57,941 - 52,760$. The average price is $\overline{p} = \$1.14 = (\$0.99 + \$1.29)/2$, and the average quantity is $\overline{Q} = 55,350.5 = (52,760 + 57,941)/2$. Plugging these values into Equation 3.2, we find that the arc price elasticity of demand for this song is

$$\varepsilon = \frac{\Delta Q / \overline{Q}}{\Delta p / \overline{p}} = \frac{-5,181/55,350.5}{0.30/1.14} \approx \frac{0.094}{0.263} \approx -0.36.$$

When price rose by 26.3%, the quantity demanded fell by 9.4%, so the arc elasticity of demand was $\varepsilon = -0.36$. Based on this elasticity, a 1% rise in price would cause the quantity demanded to fall by roughly one-third of a percent.

Point Elasticity. An arc elasticity is based on a discrete change between two distinct price-quantity combinations on a demand curve. If we let the distance between these two points become infinitesimally small, we are effectively evaluating the elasticity at a single point. We call an elasticity evaluated at a specific price-quantity combination a *point elasticity*.

---

[1]Glenn Peoples, "iTunes Price Change: Sales Down, Revenue Up in Week 1," *Billboard*, April 15, 2009.

If a manager knows only two specific price-quantity points on a demand curve, then the manager's best summary of how quantity demanded responds to price changes is the arc elasticity of demand for the movement between these two points. If, on the other hand, the manager has information about the entire demand curve, it is possible to calculate the point elasticity of demand at any point on the demand curve. The point elasticity indicates the effect on the quantity demanded arising from a very small change in price.

To calculate a point elasticity, we first rewrite the price elasticity formula, Equation 3.1, as

$$\varepsilon = \frac{\Delta Q/Q}{\Delta p/p} = \frac{\Delta Q}{\Delta p}\frac{p}{Q} \tag{3.3}$$

where we are evaluating the elasticity at the point (Q, p) and $\Delta Q/\Delta p$ is the ratio of the change in quantity to the change in price.

Holding other variables that affect demand fixed, we can use Equation 3.3 to calculate the elasticity of demand for a general linear demand curve. The mathematical form of a linear demand curve is given by

$$Q = a + bp \tag{3.4}$$

where a and b are parameters or coefficients. We assume that a is a positive constant and b is a negative constant. The parameter a is the quantity that is demanded if the price is zero. The parameter b shows how much the quantity demanded falls if the price is increased by one unit (such as a dollar). As we showed in Chapter 2, if the price changes from p_1 to p_2, then

$$\Delta Q = Q_2 - Q_1 = (a + bp_2) - (a + bp_1) = b(p_2 - p_1) = b\Delta p, \tag{3.5}$$

so if $\Delta p = 1$, the change in the quantity demanded, $\Delta Q = b$, is negative.

Rearranging Equation 3.5, we see that $\Delta Q/\Delta p = b$. Thus, the elasticity of demand for a linear demand curve is

$$\varepsilon = \frac{\Delta Q}{\Delta p}\frac{p}{Q} = b\frac{p}{Q}. \tag{3.6}$$

As we discussed in Chapter 2, our estimated linear demand curve for avocados is

$$Q = 160 - 40p,$$

where Q is the quantity of avocados in millions of pounds and p is the price in dollars per pound. For this specific linear demand equation, $a = 160$ and $b = -40$. Substituting these values into Equation 3.6, we find that the point elasticity of demand for avocados is

$$\varepsilon = -40\frac{p}{Q}. \tag{3.7}$$

Equation 3.7 allows us to determine the elasticity of demand at any point (any price-quantity combination) on the demand curve. In particular, we can find the point elasticity of demand at $p = \$2.40$, where the quantity demanded is $Q = 160 - (40 \times 2.40) = 64$, by substituting these values into Equation 3.7:

$$\varepsilon = b\frac{p}{Q} = -40\frac{2.40}{64} = -1.5.$$

We previously used the estimated demand function for avocados to calculate the arc elasticity of demand for a price change from $1.90 to $2.10. That elasticity was −1, which is different from the point elasticity of −1.5 just calculated. Although these two elasticities are different, neither is incorrect. Both are appropriate measures—they are just measuring different elasticities. The arc elasticity correctly measures the elasticity associated with a discrete change from a price of $1.90 to a price of $2.10, while the point elasticity correctly measures the elasticity at a price of $2.40. Both elasticity measures are useful. To keep our discussion as short and clear as possible, the subsequent analysis will deal just with point elasticities unless explicitly stated otherwise.

Using Calculus

The Point Elasticity of Demand

As the change in price becomes very small, $\Delta p \to 0$, the ratio $\Delta Q/\Delta p$ converges to the derivative dQ/dp. Thus, the point elasticity of demand in Equation 3.3 may be written as

$$\varepsilon = \frac{dQ}{dp}\frac{p}{Q}. \tag{3.8}$$

Q&A 3.2

Use calculus to show that the elasticity of demand is a constant ε at all prices if the demand function is exponential, $Q = Ap^\varepsilon$. Given that the estimated demand function for broadband service for large firms is $Q = 16p^{-0.296}$ (based on Duffy-Deno, 2003), what is the (constant) elasticity of demand?

Answer

1. *Differentiate the demand function with respect to price to determine* dQ/dp, *and substitute that expression into the definition of the elasticity of demand.* Differentiating the demand function $Q = Ap^\varepsilon$, we find that $dQ/dp = \varepsilon Ap^{\varepsilon-1}$. Substituting that expression into the point elasticity definition, Equation 3.8, we learn that the elasticity is

$$\frac{dQ}{dp}\frac{p}{Q} = \varepsilon Ap^{\varepsilon-1}\frac{p}{Q} = \varepsilon Ap^{\varepsilon-1}\frac{p}{Ap^\varepsilon} = \varepsilon.$$

Because the elasticity is a constant that does not depend on a particular value of p or Q, it is the same at every point along the demand curve.

2. *Use the rule just derived to determine the demand elasticity for broadband service—the elasticity is the exponent on price in the demand formula.* The elasticity of demand, ε, for broadband services for large firms is –0.296 (the exponent on the price in the demand equation).

Elasticity Along the Demand Curve

Whether the elasticity of demand is the same at every price along the demand curve or varies depends on the shape of the demand curve. The only type of demand curve where the elasticity of demand is the same at every price has the functional form $Q = Ap^\varepsilon$, which is called the *constant-elasticity demand* form. Along a constant-elasticity demand curve, the elasticity of demand is the same at every price and is equal to the exponent ε, as Q&A 3.2 demonstrates. The constant A for a constant-elasticity demand curve varies with the type of units used to measure the quantity demanded. For example, A is 2,000 times bigger if quantity demanded is measured in pounds rather than in tons, because there are 2,000 pounds in a ton.

We now turn to three types of linear demand curves: horizontal demand curves, vertical demand curves, and downward-sloping demand curves, which are neither horizontal nor vertical. Except for constant-elasticity demand curves, the elasticity of demand varies with price along downward-sloping demand curves. In particular, the elasticity of demand is different at every point along a downward-sloping linear demand curve.

Horizontal and vertical demand curves are linear, but they have the same price elasticity at every point. Horizontal and vertical demand curves are therefore also special cases of the constant-elasticity demand curve. If the demand curve is horizontal, $\varepsilon = -\infty$ at every point; if the demand curve is vertical, $\varepsilon = 0$ at every point.

Downward-Sloping Linear Demand Curves. We can show that the elasticity of demand is different at every point along a downward-sloping linear demand curve. According to Equation 3.6, the elasticity of demand on a linear demand curve is $\varepsilon = b(p/Q)$. Although b is a constant, the price-quantity ratio, p/Q, varies as we move along the demand curve, so the elasticity must also vary. The elasticity of demand is a more negative number the higher the price and hence the smaller the quantity. A 1% increase in price causes a larger percentage fall in quantity near the top (left) of the demand curve than near the bottom (right).

We use the linear avocado demand curve in Figure 3.1 to illustrate how the elasticity varies with price. At the lower right corner of Figure 3.1, where the avocado demand curve hits the quantity axis ($p = 0$ and $Q = 160$), the elasticity of demand for avocados, Equation 3.7, is $\varepsilon = -40(p/Q) = -40(0/160) = 0$. Where the price is zero, a 1% increase in price does not raise the price—if zero changes by 1% it is still zero. As price does not change, quantity does not change either. At a point where the elasticity of demand is zero, the demand curve is said to be *perfectly inelastic*.

FIGURE 3.1 The Elasticity of Demand Varies Along the Linear Avocado Demand Curve

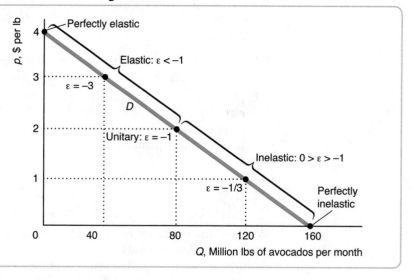

With a linear demand curve, such as the avocado demand curve, the higher the price, the more elastic the demand curve (ε is larger in absolute value: it becomes a more negative number as we move up the demand curve). The demand curve is perfectly inelastic ($\varepsilon = 0$) where the demand curve hits the horizontal axis, is perfectly elastic where the demand curve hits the vertical axis, and has unitary elasticity at the midpoint of the demand curve.

For quantities between the midpoint of the linear demand curve and the lower end where $p = 0$, the demand elasticity lies between zero and negative one: $0 > \varepsilon > -1$. A point along the demand curve where the elasticity is between 0 and -1 is *inelastic* (but not perfectly inelastic): A 1% increase in price leads to a fall in quantity of less than 1%. For example, when the avocado price is $1 so that the quantity demandedis 120, the elasticity of demand is $\varepsilon = -40(1/120) = -\frac{1}{3}$, so a 1% increase in price causes quantity to fall by a third.

Rearranging the elasticity formula in Equation 3.1, the percentage change in Q is ε times the percentage change in price: $\Delta Q/Q = \varepsilon(\Delta p/p)$. If the elasticity ε lies between 0 and -1, the percentage change in quantity is smaller than the percentage change in price. Thus, demand is inelastic in the sense that it changes little in response to a price change. As a physical analogy, if you try to stretch a rope, it stretches only slightly. The change in the price is the force pulling at demand, just as your effort provides the force pulling at the rope. If the quantity demanded does not change much in response to this force, the demand curve is called inelastic.

At the midpoint of the linear demand curve, a 1% increase in price causes a 1% fall in quantity, so the elasticity equals –1, which is called *unitary elasticity*.[2] At prices higher than at the midpoint of the demand curve ($2 on the avocado demand curve), the elasticity of demand is less than negative one, $\varepsilon < -1$. That is, the elasticity is a more negative number because it is larger in absolute value. In this range, the demand curve is called *elastic*. A physical analogy is a rubber band that stretches substantially when you pull on it. A 1% increase in price causes a more than 1% fall in quantity. Figure 3.1 shows that the avocado demand elasticity is –3 where the price is $3 and 40 million lbs are demanded: a 1% increase in price causes a 3% drop in quantity.

Where the demand curve hits the price axis at $p = \$4$ and $Q = 0$, the elasticity of demand is $\varepsilon = -b(4/0)$. As Q approaches zero, the elasticity becomes a larger and larger negative number that approaches negative infinity, $-\infty$. The demand curve is *perfectly elastic* at the point where $Q = 0$. Because quantity is zero at $p = 4$, if we lower the price even slightly so that the quantity demanded becomes positive, there is an infinite percentage increase in the quantity demanded.

Horizontal Demand Curves. Horizontal demand curves have constant elasticity (as do vertical demand curves). The demand curve that is horizontal at p^* in panel a of Figure 3.2 shows that people are willing to buy as much as firms want to sell at any price less than or equal to p^*. If the price increases even slightly above p^*, however, demand falls to zero. Thus, a small increase in price causes an infinite drop in quantity, so the demand curve is perfectly elastic.[3]

A horizontal demand curve is an extreme case of a linear demand curve: it is the flattest possible linear demand curve. Unlike downward-sloping linear demand curves, a horizontal demand curve does not have the property that the elasticity

---

[2]At the midpoint of a general linear demand curve, $Q = a/2$ and $p = -a/(2b)$, so, using Equation 3.6, $\varepsilon = bp/Q = -b(a/[2b])/(a/2) = -1$.

[3]Using the constant-elasticity demand function, as ε becomes a very large negative number, the demand curve becomes increasingly flat and approaches a horizontal line.

FIGURE 3.2 **Vertical and Horizontal Demand Curves**

(a) A horizontal demand curve is perfectly elastic at p^*. (b) A vertical demand curve is perfectly inelastic at every price. (c) The demand curve for insulin of an individual who is diabetic is perfectly inelastic below p^* and perfectly elastic at p^*, which is the maximum price the individual can afford to pay.

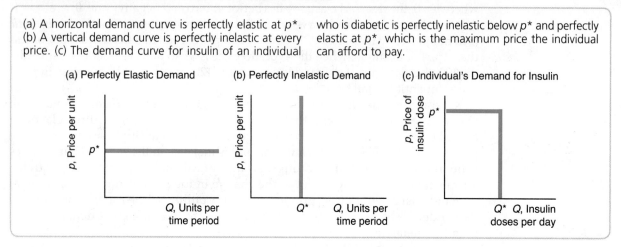

changes along the demand curve. For a horizontal demand curve, the elasticity is negative infinity at every point.

Why would a good's demand curve be horizontal? One reason is that consumers view this good as identical to another good and do not care which one they buy. If consumers view Delicious apples grown in Washington and Delicious apples grown in Oregon as identical, they won't buy Washington apples if these sell for more than apples from Oregon. Similarly, they won't buy Oregon apples if their price is higher than that of Washington apples. If the two prices are equal, consumers do not care which type of Delicious apple they buy. Thus, the demand curve for Oregon apples is horizontal at the price of Washington apples.

Vertical Demand Curves. A vertical demand curve, as in panel b in Figure 3.2, is perfectly inelastic everywhere. Such a demand curve is an extreme case of a linear demand curve—the opposite extreme from the horizontal demand curve. A vertical demand curve has an infinite (vertical) slope. A vertical demand function is also a special case of the constant-elasticity demand function. If ε takes on the value 0, then the demand function is $Q = Ap^0 = A$, so the demand curve is a vertical line at quantity A. If the price goes up, the quantity demanded is unchanged, so $\Delta Q = 0$. The elasticity of demand as given by Equation 3.1 must be zero: $(\Delta Q / \Delta p)(p/Q) = (0/\Delta p)(p/Q) = 0$.

A demand curve is vertical for *essential goods*—goods that people feel they must have and will pay anything to get. Because Jerry has diabetes, his demand curve for insulin could be vertical at a day's dose, Q^*. Panel c of Figure 3.2 assumes that there is a maximum feasible price of p^* and illustrates that demand is unchanged at Q^* for all possible prices less than p^*.

Other Demand Elasticities

In addition to the price elasticity of demand, we can also use elasticities to summarize how quantity demanded changes in response to changes in variables other than the good's price. Two such elasticities are the income elasticity of demand and the cross-price elasticity of demand.

The **income elasticity of demand** is the percentage change in the quantity demanded divided by the percentage change in income, Y:

$$\frac{\text{percentage change in quantity demanded}}{\text{percentage change in income}} = \frac{\Delta Q/Q}{\Delta Y/Y} = \frac{\Delta Q}{\Delta Y}\frac{Y}{Q}.$$

We say a good is **normal** if the quantity demanded increases as income rises. That is, a normal good has a positive income elasticity of demand. Goods like avocados or music downloads are normal goods: people buy more of them when their incomes rise. Conversely, a good is **inferior** if the quantity demanded falls as income rises. Inferior goods have negative income elasticities. For many college students, Kraft Macaroni & Cheese (food in a box) is an inferior good—they buy it when their incomes are low but switch to more appealing and expensive foods when their incomes rise.

The **cross-price elasticity of demand** is the percentage change in the quantity demanded divided by the percentage change in the price of another good, p_o:

$$\frac{\text{percentage change in quantity demanded}}{\text{percentage change in other price}} = \frac{\Delta Q/Q}{\Delta p_o/p_o} = \frac{\Delta Q}{\Delta p_o}\frac{p_o}{Q}.$$

When the cross-price elasticity is negative, people buy less of the good if the price of the other good rises. Such goods are called *complements*. For example, if people insist on having cream in their coffee then, as the price of cream rises, they consume less coffee. The cross-price elasticity of coffee demanded with respect to the price of cream is negative. If, alternatively, the cross-price elasticity is positive, the goods are called *substitutes*. As the price of one good rises, people buy more of the substitute good. For example, as avocados and tomatoes are substitutes, the quantity of avocados demanded increases if the price of tomatoes rises (Chapter 2).

Mini-Case **Substitution May Save Endangered Species**	One reason that many species—including tigers, rhinoceroses, green turtles, geckos, sea horses, pipefish, and sea cucumbers—are endangered, threatened, or vulnerable to extinction is that certain of their body parts are used as aphrodisiacs in traditional Chinese medicine. Is it possible that consumers will switch from such potions to Viagra, a less expensive and almost certainly more effective alternative treatment, and thereby help save these endangered species? We cannot directly calculate the cross-price elasticity of demand between Viagra and the price of body parts of endangered species because their trade is illicit and not reported. However, harp seal and hooded seal genitalia, which are used as aphrodisiacs in Asia, may be legally traded. Before 1998, Viagra was unavailable (effectively, it had an infinite price—one could not pay a high enough price to obtain it). When it became available in Canada at about C\$15 to C\$20 per pill, the demand for seal sex organs fell and the demand curve shifted substantially to the left. According to von Hippel and von Hippel (2002, 2004), 30,000 to 50,000 seal organs were sold in the years just before 1998. In 1998, only 20,000 organs were sold. By 1999–2000 (and thereafter), virtually none were sold. A survey of older Chinese males confirms that, after the introduction of Viagra, they were much more likely to use a Western medicine than traditional Chinese medicines for erectile dysfunction, but not for other medical problems (von Hippel et al., 2005).

This evidence suggests a strong willingness to substitute Viagra for seal organs at current prices and, thus, that the cross-price elasticity between the price of seal organs and Viagra is positive. Thus, Viagra can perhaps save more than marriages.

Demand Elasticities over Time

The shape of a demand curve depends on the time period under consideration. Often one can substitute between products in the long run but not in the short run. When gasoline prices nearly doubled in 2008, most Western consumers did not greatly alter the amount of gasoline that they demanded in the short run. Someone who drove 27 miles to and from work every day in a recently purchased Ford Explorer could not easily reduce the amount of gasoline purchased. However, in the long run, this person could buy a smaller vehicle, get a job closer to home, join a car pool, or reduce the amount of gasoline purchased in other ways.

A survey of hundreds of estimates of gasoline demand elasticities across many countries (Espey, 1998) found that the average estimate of the short-run elasticity was –0.26, and the long-run elasticity was –0.58. Thus, a 1% increase in price lowers the quantity demanded by only 0.26% in the short run but by more than twice as much, 0.58%, in the long run. Bento et al. (2009) estimated a long-run U.S. elasticity of only –0.35. Apparently, U.S. gasoline demand is less elastic than in Canada (Nicol, 2003) and a number of other countries.

Other Elasticities

The relationship between any two related variables can be summarized by an elasticity. In addition to the various demand elasticities that we've mentioned, other elasticities are also important. For example, just as we might measure the price elasticity of demand, we might also measure the price elasticity of supply—which indicates the percentage increase in quantity supplied arising from a 1% increase in price. A manager might be very interested in the elasticity of cost with respect to output, which shows the percentage increase in cost arising from a 1% increase in output. Or, during labor negotiations, a manager might cite the elasticity of output with respect to labor, which would show the percentage increase in output arising from a 1% increase in labor input, holding other inputs constant.

Estimating Demand Elasticities

Price, income, and cross-price demand elasticities are important managerial tools. Managers can use them to predict how the quantity demanded will respond to changes in consumer income, the product's own price, or the price of a related good. Managers use this information to set prices, as in the iTunes example, and in many other ways.

Managers use data to calculate or estimate elasticities. For example, Q&A 3.1 shows how a manager can observe the quantity effect of a change in price to determine the elasticity of demand for iTunes downloads of Akon's "Beautiful." Such a before-and-after price change calculation uses data from before the price change and after the price change to calculate an arc elasticity. By comparing quantities just before and just after a price change, managers can be reasonably sure that other variables that might affect the quantity demanded, such as income, have not changed appreciably.

Managers at iTunes could do such calculations for many songs and obtain an estimate of how the iTunes price change affected overall sales. Such information could then be used for further decision making within iTunes—such as decisions about how quickly to expand and upgrade server capacity or about whether to charge different prices for various songs.

However, it may not always be feasible or desirable for a manager to calculate a before-and-after arc elasticity. A manager often wants an estimate of the demand elasticity before actually making a price change, so as to avoid a potentially expensive mistake. Similarly, a manager may fear a reaction by a rival firm in response to a pricing experiment. Also, a manager wants to know the effect on demand of many possible price changes rather than focusing on just one price change. The manager can use such information to select the best possible price rather than just choose between two particular prices. In effect, the manager would like an estimate of the entire demand curve. Regression analysis is an empirical technique that can be used to estimate an entire demand curve in addition to estimating other important economic relationships.

Mini-Case

Turning Off the Faucet

During droughts, consumers demand more water than the local water utility can supply. The managers of the water utility have to reduce consumption, which they usually do by imposing quotas on consumers. But, should managers consider the alternative of raising the price to reduce consumption? Is that approach feasible, or will households pay "virtually anything" for water?

Many water utility managers and political leaders think that water usage is nearly perfectly inelastic (not sensitive to price). When water is plentiful, public water utilities typically supply water at a price below the cost of providing an extra unit of water to help the poor (and others), figuring that it doesn't greatly affect usage.

Nataraj (2007) used a natural experiment to determine the sensitivity of the quantity of water demanded to price. Like many cities, Santa Cruz, California, sells water using increasing block pricing. Initially, the city charged 65¢ per unit (100 cubic feet) for the first 8 units of water and $1.55 for each extra unit. However, after a drought, it raised its rates and added a third block, charging 69¢ per unit for the first 8 units, $1.64 per unit for units 9–39, and $3.14 per unit for 40 or more units.

Nataraj concluded that the nearly 100% increase in price for 40 or more units led to a 15% to 25% decrease in consumption among heavy users. This result shows that the demand for water is inelastic, but not perfectly inelastic. By substantially raising prices, a government can cut water demand by heavy users significantly, but less than in proportion to the price change.

3.2 Regression Analysis

Regression analysis is a statistical technique used to estimate the mathematical relationship between a *dependent variable*, such as quantity demanded, and one or more *explanatory variables*, such as price and income. The **dependent variable** is the variable whose variation is to be explained. The **explanatory variables** are the factors that are thought to affect the value of the dependent variable.

We focus on using regression analysis to estimate demand functions. However, regression analysis is a powerful tool that is also used to estimate many other relationships of interest to managers. For example, it is possible to estimate the relationships between cost and output or between wages and productivity using regressions. The use of regression analysis and related statistical methods in economics and business is called *econometrics*.

A Demand Function Example

To illustrate the use of regression, we estimate a demand function, where the dependent variable is the quantity demanded. In general, a demand function may include a number of explanatory variables. However, we initially focus on the case in which there is only *one explanatory variable*, the price. We assume that other factors that might affect the quantity demanded, such as income and prices of related goods, remain constant during the relevant period. A demand function with price as the only explanatory variable defines a demand curve.

We also assume initially that the demand function curve is *linear*. That is, the true relationship between the quantity demanded and the price is a straight line, as in Figure 3.1.

The Demand Function and the Inverse Demand Function. There are two ways to write the relationship between the quantity demanded and the price. Quantity is a function of price in a *demand function*, while price is a function of quantity in an *inverse demand function*. An example of a linear demand function with only one explanatory variable is Equation 3.4: $Q = a + bp$.

We can use algebra to rearrange this linear demand equation so that the price is on the left side and the quantity is on the right side. By subtracting a from both sides to obtain $Q - a = bp$, dividing both sides of the equation by b to obtain $(1/b)Q - a/b = p$, and rearranging the terms in the equation, we obtain

$$p = -\frac{a}{b} + \frac{1}{b}Q = g + hQ, \tag{3.9}$$

where $g = -a/b > 0$ and $h = 1/b < 0$, because b is negative. This equation, with p on the left side, is called the *inverse demand function*. If a demand function is a linear function of p, as in Equation 3.4, then the inverse demand function, Equation 3.9, is a linear function of Q with constant coefficients g and h.

The inverse demand function and the demand function contain exactly the same information. Both versions of the demand relationship yield the same straight line when plotted on a diagram and both versions are commonly used. Indeed, many people ignore the distinction between the inverse and direct forms and use the term *demand function* (or *demand curve*) to describe both.

However, when doing regression analysis it is necessary to be clear about which version of the demand function we are estimating. In regression analysis, we put the dependent variable on the left side of the equation and the explanatory variable on the right side.

For example, Bill, the manager of the only lawn care firm in town, surveys customers about how many lawn treatments they will buy at various prices. He views the price as the explanatory variable and the quantity as the dependent variable, so he uses the survey to estimate a demand curve. If instead his survey asked how much customers were willing to pay for various numbers of lawn treatments, he would estimate the inverse demand equation.

Random Errors. For illustrative purposes, we have so far treated the estimated avocado demand curve, $Q = 160 - 40p$, as if it is precisely correct. The demand curve tells us that if price is \$2, then the quantity demanded is 80 (million pounds), and if price falls to \$1.80, then quantity demanded must rise to 88. The real world is not that precise. When we look at actual data, we might see that in a month when price was \$2, quantity demanded was slightly less than 80, while in a month when price was \$1.80 quantity demanded was slightly more than 88. In practical terms, an estimated demand curve is only an estimate; it does not necessarily match actual data perfectly. The imperfection in our estimate arises because we can never hold constant all the possible nonprice factors that affect demand.

For example, if New York experiences unusually warm weather in a particular month, New Yorkers might increase their demand for foods used in salads, including avocados. Many other factors, including random changes in consumer tastes, might also play a role. The data may contain errors. For instance, one month someone may have failed to record a large avocado shipment so that it never showed up in the official data. There are many reasons aside from price changes why the data might exhibit month to month changes in quantity demanded.

If these other factors that affect demand are observed, such as consumers' income, we can include these variables as explanatory variables when we estimate our demand function. However, there are many other factors that are not observed or measured and hence that we cannot include explicitly. When we estimate a demand curve using regression analysis, we capture the effect of these unobserved variables by adding a *random error term, e,* to the demand equation:

$$Q = a + bp + e. \tag{3.10}$$

The **random error term** captures the effects of unobserved influences on the dependent variable that are not included as explanatory variables. The error is called *random* because these factors that might affect demand are unpredictable or even unknowable from the manager's point of view.

Regression analysis seeks to estimate the underlying straight line showing the true effect of price on the quantity demanded by estimating a and b in Equation 3.4 while taking account of the random error term. If we could somehow hold e constant at zero, we could obtain various combinations of Q and p and trace out the straight line given by Equation 3.4, $Q = a + bp$. However, if e does not equal zero, then the observed Q is not on this line. For example, if e takes on a positive value for one month, corresponding to some positive random effect on demand, then the actual Q is larger than the value implied by the linear demand curve $Q = a + bp$.

Mini-Case	The Portland Fish Exchange of Portland, Maine, can be used to illustrate the application of regression analysis to demand estimation. At the Exchange, fishing boats
The Portland Fish Exchange	unload thousands of pounds of cod and many other types of fish on a daily basis. The fish are weighed and put on display in the Exchange's 22,000-square-foot refrigerated warehouse. Buyers inspect the quality of the day's catch. At noon, an auction is held in a room overlooking the fish in the warehouse. Fleece-clad buyers representing fish dealers and restaurants sit facing a screen, an auctioneer, and representatives of the sellers. Bid information is posted on the screen at the

front of the room. Thousands of pounds of fish are sold rapidly.

The quantity of fish delivered each day, Q, varies due to fluctuations in weather and other factors. Because fish spoils rapidly, all the fish must be sold immediately. Therefore, the daily auction price for cod adjusts to induce buyers to demand the amount of cod available on that particular day. Thus, the price-quantity combination for cod on any particular day represents a point on the cod demand curve.

For each day it operates, the Portland Fish Exchange reports the quantity (in pounds) of each particular type of fish sold and the price for that type of fish. For example, on June 12, 2011, 5,913 pounds of cod were sold at $1.46 per pound. A collection of such observations provides a data set that can be used for demand analysis using regression.

Here, quantity is the explanatory variable. Whatever quantity is brought to market is sold that day. Price adjusts to insure that the amount of fish available is demanded by the buyers. As price is "explained by" the quantity brought to market, we can estimate an inverse demand curve.

Regression Analysis Using Microsoft Excel. We illustrate how to estimate a linear regression based on data from the Portland Fish Exchange using Microsoft Excel. Table 3.1 shows a data set (or *sample*) based on reports published online by the Portland Fish Exchange. Each data point is a pair of numbers: the price (dollars per pound) and the quantity of cod (thousands of pounds) bought on a particular day. Our analysis uses eight daily observations. We have ordered the data from the smallest quantity to the largest to make the table easy to read.

Figure 3.3 shows the data points in this sample. Estimating this linear regression is equivalent to drawing a straight line through these data points such that the data points are as close as possible to the line. To fit this line through the quantity-price observations for cod, we estimate the linear inverse demand curve, Equation 3.9, with an error term attached:

$$p = g + hQ + e. \tag{3.11}$$

TABLE 3.1 Data Used to Estimate the Portland Fish Exchange Cod Demand Curve

Price, dollars per pound	Quantity, thousand pounds per day
1.90	1.5
1.35	2.2
1.25	4.4
1.20	5.9
0.95	6.5
0.85	7.0
0.73	8.8
0.25	10.1

FIGURE 3.3 Observed Price-Quantity Data Points for the Portland Fish Exchange

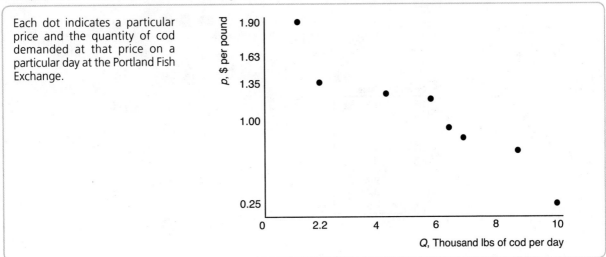

Each dot indicates a particular price and the quantity of cod demanded at that price on a particular day at the Portland Fish Exchange.

The error term, e, captures random fluctuations in factors other than quantity that affect the price on a given day, such as random variations in the number of buyers who show up from day to day.[4] We expect that the error term averages zero in large samples.[5]

In Equation 3.11, g and h are the true coefficients, which describe the actual relationship between price and quantity along the cod inverse demand function. The regression provides us with estimates of these coefficients, $\hat{g}$ and $\hat{h}$, which we can use to predict the expected price, $\hat{p}$, for a given quantity:

$$\hat{p} = \hat{g} + \hat{h}Q. \tag{3.12}$$

One way to estimate $\hat{g}$ and $\hat{h}$ is to use the Microsoft Excel Trendline option for scatterplots.[6]

1. Enter the quantity data in column A and the price data in column B.

2. Select the data, click on the *Insert* tab, and select the *Scatter* option in the Chart area of the Toolbar. A menu of scatterplot types will appear, as the following screenshot shows.

---

[4]The cod supply curve each day is vertical at Q and is largely determined by weather and government regulations on fishing. Because the quantity is determined independent of the price, it is said to be *exogenous*. As a result, we can use quantity to help explain the movement of the dependent variable, price, in our regression equation. Where the supply curve intersects the demand curve determines the equilibrium price for that day. Thus, the fluctuations in the quantity—shifts in the vertical supply curve—trace out the demand curve. The dependent variable, price, is *endogenous*: it is determined inside the system by quantity and by the unobserved variables incorporated in the error term. If quantity and price are simultaneously determined—that is, both are endogenous variables—the demand curve should be estimated using different techniques than those we discuss here.

[5]We use a small data set in this and later examples to keep the presentation short and clear. In practice, regression analysis would normally involve many more observations. Although some studies use only 30 or 40 observations, most regression studies would normally involve hundreds or even thousands of observations, depending on the availability of data.

[6]The following screenshots and detailed instructions are for the Windows version of Excel, but the Macintosh version is similar. Helpful instructions can be found in the Excel Help facility.

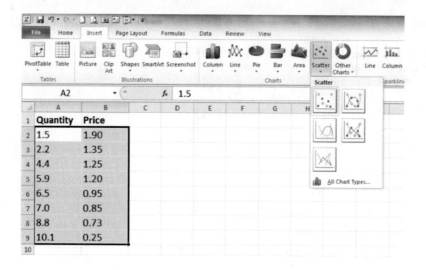

3. Select the first scatterplot type, which is "Scatter with markers only."

4. Select the *Layout* option under the *Chart Tools* tab.

5. Click *Trendline*, then click *More Trendline Options* if nececessary. The Format Trendline dialog should display, as shown in the following screenshot. In this dialog select the options *Linear, Automatic, Display Equation,* and *Display R-squared value*, then click *Close*. The estimated regression line appears in the diagram.

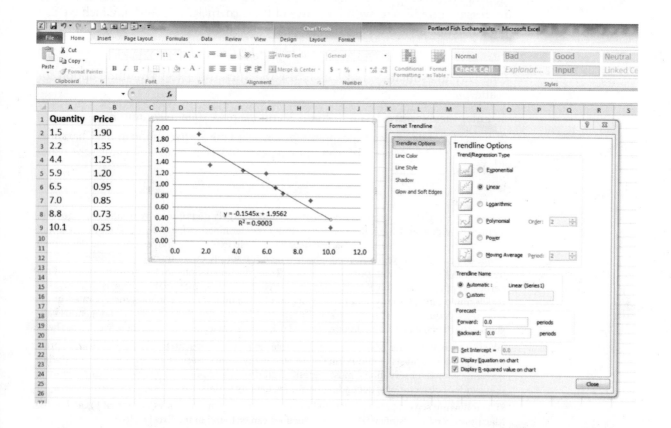

By default, Excel refers to the variable on the vertical axis as y (which is our p) and the variable on the horizontal axis as x (which is our Q). Rounding the coefficient estimates to two decimal places, we obtain the estimated inverse demand curve

$$\hat{p} = 1.96 - 0.15Q, \tag{3.13}$$

where $\hat{g} = 1.96$ and $\hat{h} = -0.15$ are the estimated coefficients.

The estimated inverse demand curve hits the price axis at $\hat{g} = 1.96$, where the price is high enough to drive the quantity demanded to zero. The estimated coefficient $\hat{h} = -0.15$ is the slope of the inverse demand curve. As the quantity increases by one unit (that is, by 1,000 pounds), the estimated change in price needed to induce buyers to purchase this larger quantity is $\hat{h} = -\$0.15 = -15\cent$.[7]

Ordinary Least Squares Regression.

How does the regression routine in Excel estimate the parameters $\hat{g}$ and $\hat{h}$? The objective of the regression procedure is to select a regression line that *fits* the data well in the sense that the line is as close as possible to all the observed points.

As Figure 3.4 shows, it would be impossible to draw a single straight line that fits the data perfectly by going through all eight points. Figure 3.4 shows that there are differences between the actual prices and the prices predicted by the regression line. The second data point from the left ($p = \$1.35$ and $Q = 2.2$) has the largest gap between the actual and predicted prices. The predicted price, given by Equation 3.13, for $Q = 2.2$ is $\hat{p} = 1.96 - 0.15Q = 1.96 - (0.15 \times 2.2) = 1.63$.

The gap between the actual value of the dependent variable (price) and the predicted value is called a *residual*. For this observation, the residual is $\$1.35 - \$1.63 = -\$0.28$, indicating that the actual price is $28\cent$ below the estimated price.

The objective of a regression method is to fit the line to the data such that the residuals are collectively small in some sense. However, there are different criteria that might be used to measure the quality of the fit, leading to different regression methods.

The most commonly used regression method is *ordinary least squares* (OLS). Excel uses this method in its scatterplot Trendline option. The OLS regression method fits the line to minimize the sum of the squared residuals. If $\hat{e}_1$ is the residual for the first data point, $\hat{e}_2$ is the residual for the second data point, and so on, then OLS minimizes the sum $\hat{e}_1^2 + \hat{e}_2^2 + \ldots + \hat{e}_8^2$.[8]

---

[7]The price is $\hat{p}_1 = \hat{g} + \hat{h}Q$ when quantity is Q and $\hat{p}_2 = \hat{g} + \hat{h}(Q + 1)$ when quantity is $Q + 1$. Thus, the change in price is $p_2 - p_1 = (\hat{g} + \hat{h}[Q + 1]) - (\hat{g} + \hat{h}Q) = \hat{h}$. Similarly, using calculus, $d\hat{p}/dQ = \hat{h}$.

[8]If we have a regression equation of the form $Y = a + bX + e$, the formulas used by spreadsheets and statistical programs to determine the OLS parameters are:

$$\hat{b} = \frac{\sum_{i=1}^{n}(X_i - \overline{X})(Y_i - \overline{Y})}{\sum_{i=1}^{n}(X_i - \overline{X})^2}, \text{ and } \hat{a} = \overline{Y} - \hat{b}\,\overline{X},$$

where the observations are indexed by i, there are n observations, a bar above a variable indicates the average value of that variable, and the symbol $\sum_{i=1}^{n}$ indicates that the following expression should be summed from observation 1 through observation n.

FIGURE 3.4 An Estimated Demand Curve for Cod at the Portland Fish Exchange

The dots show the actual quantity-price pair data points. The line is the estimated regression line of the linear relationship between the price and the quantity: $\hat{p} = \hat{g} + \hat{h}Q$ $= 1.96 - 0.15Q$. The gap between the actual price, p, at a given quantity and the estimated price, $\hat{p}$, is the residual for Day i, $\hat{e}_i = p_i - \hat{p}_i$. The figure shows the residual for the second day, where $Q = 2.2$, the observed price is $p_2 = \$1.35$, and the estimated price is $\hat{p}_2 = \$1.63$, so the residual is $\hat{e}_2 = -\$0.28 = \$1.35 - \$1.63$.

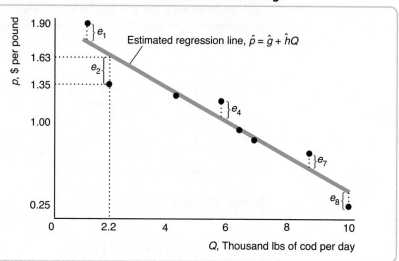

Multivariate Regression

A regression with two or more explanatory variables is called a **multivariate regression** or *multiple regression*. In our cod example, if the price consumers are willing to pay for a given quantity increases with income, Y, then we would estimate an inverse demand function that incorporates both quantity and income as explanatory variables as

$$p = g + hQ + iY + e, \tag{3.14}$$

where g, h, and i are coefficients to be estimated, and e is a random error.

Using OLS, we would estimate the regression line:

$$\hat{p} = \hat{g} + \hat{h}Q + \hat{i}Y,$$

where $\hat{g}$, $\hat{h}$, and $\hat{i}$ are the estimated coefficients and $\hat{p}$ is the *predicted value* of p for any given levels of Q and Y. The objective of an OLS multivariate regression is to fit the data so that the sum of squared residuals is as small as possible, where the residual for any data point is the difference between actual price, p, and predicted price, $\hat{p}$.

A multivariate regression is able to isolate the effects of each explanatory variable holding the other explanatory variables constant. If we use our estimated avocado demand function from Equation 2.2 and hold the price of tomatoes fixed at the base level of $0.80 per lb, the estimated industry demand function is

$$\hat{Q} = 120 - 40p + 0.01Y,$$

where quantity is measured in millions of lbs per month, price is measured in dollars per lb, and Y represents average monthly income in dollars. According to this estimated equation, if average income rises by $200 per month and the price of avocados stays constant, then the estimated quantity would rise by $0.01 \times 200 = 2$ million lbs per month. The regression equation allows us to estimate the effect of changing only one variable, like income, while holding other explanatory variables constant.

Similarly, if income remains constant and the price increases by 5¢ (=$0.05) per lb, then the estimated quantity demanded changes by $40 \times 0.05 = 2$ million lbs per month.

Q&A 3.3

Suppose the estimated demand function for avocados is given by $\hat{Q} = 120 - 40p + 0.01Y$. The manager of a trucking company that specializes in avocado transport wishes to use this estimated demand curve to predict the quantity of avocados demanded at price of $2.70 and an income level of $6,000. What is the predicted quantity? If the actual quantity turns out to be 76 (million lbs) what is the residual? Why would the predicted quantity differ from the actual quantity?

Answer *Use the estimated demand function to determine the predicted quantity.* The predicted quantity is $\hat{Q} = 120 - 40(2.70) + 0.01(6000)Y = 72$. If the actual quantity is 76, then the residual is $76 - 72 = 4$. The actual quantity differs from the predicted quantity because of the random error reflecting other variables not explicitly included in the regression equation.

Goodness of Fit and the R^2 Statistic

Because an estimated regression line rarely goes through all the data points, managers want some measure of how well the estimated regression line fits the data. One measure of the *goodness of fit* of the regression line to the data is the R^2 (R-squared) statistic. The R^2 *statistic* is the share of the dependent variable's variation that is "explained by the regression"—that is, accounted for by the explanatory variables in the estimated regression equation. The highest possible value for R^2 is 1, which indicates that 100% of the variation in the dependent variable is explained by the regression. Such an outcome occurs if the dependent variable lies on the regression line for every observation.

If some observations do not lie on the regression line, as in Figure 3.4, then the R^2 is less than 1. The variation in the dependent variable that is not explained by the regression line is due to the error term in the regression. Given that the regression includes a constant term, the lowest possible value for R^2 is zero, where the estimated regression explains none of the variation in the dependent variable. The R^2 is zero if we try to fit a line through a cloud of points with no obvious slope. Thus, the R^2 statistic must lie between 0 and 1.

For example, Mai owns bakeries in two different small towns, where she faces no competition. She wants to know how many fewer pies she will sell if she raises her price, so she runs experiments in each town. At each bakery, she sets a new price each week for 14 consecutive weeks, so that she observes 14 weekly price-quantity combinations for each town. She then runs a regression to estimate the weekly demand curve, $Q = a + bp$, Equation 3.4, in each town, where we expect that a is positive and b is negative.

Figure 3.5 illustrates these two regressions based on different data sets. In panel a, all the data points are very close to the estimated demand curve. That is, almost all of the variation in the number of pies demanded is explained by the regression. The R^2 statistic is 0.98, which is very close to 1, indicating that the regression line provides very good predictions of the amount demanded at any given price. (As the

FIGURE 3.5 Two Estimated Apple Pie Demand Curves with Different R^2 Statistics

Mai, a bakery owner, changes the price of apple pie every Friday for 14 weeks to determine the weekly demand curve for apple pie. The observed price-quantity data points lie close to the estimated demand curve in panel a where $R^2 = 0.98$. In panel b, where $R^2 = 0.54$, the data points are more widely scattered around the estimated demand curve.

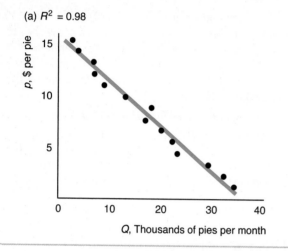

(a) $R^2 = 0.98$

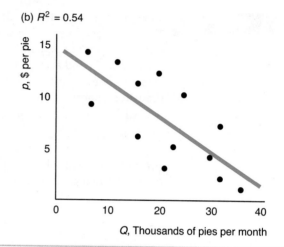

(b) $R^2 = 0.54$

Portland cod regression screenshot illustrates, Excel's Trendline includes an option to calculate the R^2.)

In contrast, the regression line in panel b does not fit the data as well. There are some very large divergences between data points and the predicted values on the regression line due to large random errors, and the R^2 statistic is only 0.54. Thus, Mai is more confident that she can predict the effect of a price change in the first town than in the second.

Managerial Implication

Focus Groups

A recent survey of North American males found 42% were overweight, 34% were critically obese, and 8% ate the survey. —Banksy

Managers interested in estimating market demand curves often can obtain data from published sources, as in our Portland Fish Exchange example. However, if Mai, the baker, wants to estimate the demand function for her firm, she must collect the relevant data herself. To estimate her firm's demand curve, she needs information about how many units customers would demand at various prices.

Mai can hire a specialized marketing firm to recruit and question a *focus group*, which consists of a number of her actual or potential consumers. Members of the group are asked how many pies per week they would want to buy at various prices. Alternatively, the marketing firm might conduct an online or written survey of potential customers designed to elicit similar information, which can be used to estimate a demand curve. Mai should use a focus group if it's the least costly method of learning about the demand curve she faces.

3.3 Properties and Statistical Significance of Estimated Coefficients

Mai is particularly concerned about how close the estimated coefficients of the demand Equation 3.4, $\hat{a}$ and $\hat{b}$, are to the true values. She cares because they determine how reliably she can predict the reduction in the number of pies she sells if she raises her price.

We now discuss the properties of these estimated coefficients and describe statistics that indicate the degree of confidence we can place in these estimated coefficients. These statistics can be obtained using most regression software, including the regression tools in Excel.

Repeated Samples

The intuition underlying statistical measures of confidence and significance is based on repeated samples. For example, Mai could use another focus group to generate an additional sample of data. She could then run a new regression and compare the regression for the first sample to that from this new focus group. If the results from the second sample were similar to those from the first, she would be more confident in the results. If, on the other hand, the results of the second sample were very different from those of the first, she might have significant doubts about whether the estimated demand parameters $\hat{a}$ and $\hat{b}$ from either focus group were close to the true values.

Often it is costly, difficult, or impossible to gather repeated samples to assess the reliability of regression estimates. However, we can do something similar—we can divide a large data set into two subsamples and treat each subsample like a separate experiment. We can use each subsample to calculate regression parameter estimates. For that matter, we can take many random subsamples of the data set and generate estimates for each subsample. We can then assess whether the different parameter estimates for the different subsamples tend to be similar or widely dispersed.

Although the process of running regressions on random subsets of the data and building up a set of parameter estimates is sometimes used, it may be unnecessary. Given certain (usually reasonable) assumptions, we can use statistical formulas to determine how much we would expect the parameter estimates to vary across samples. The nature of this potential variation allows us to assess how much confidence to place in particular regression results.

Desirable Properties for Estimated Coefficients

We would like our regression estimation method to have two properties. First, we would like the estimation technique to be *unbiased* in the sense that the estimated coefficients are not systematically lower or systematically higher than the true coefficients. An estimation method is **unbiased** if it produces an estimated coefficient, $\hat{b}$, that equals the true coefficient, b, on average. The ordinary least squares regression method is unbiased under mild conditions.[9]

---

[9]One important condition for OLS estimation to be unbiased is that the equation be properly specified so that all relevant explanatory variables are included and the functional form is appropriate.

The second property we would like an estimation technique to have is that the estimates should not vary greatly if we repeat the analysis many times using other samples. If we have two proposed unbiased estimation methods, we prefer the method that yields estimates that are consistently closer to the true values rather than a method that produces widely dispersed estimates in repeated samples. An important theoretical result in statistics is that under a wide range of conditions, the ordinary least squares estimation method produces estimates that vary less than other relevant unbiased estimation methods.

For each estimated coefficient, the regression program calculates a standard error. The *standard error* is a measure of how much each estimated coefficient would vary if we reestimated the same underlying true demand relation with many different random samples of observations. The smaller the standard error of an estimated coefficient, the smaller the expected variation in the estimates obtained from different samples. A small standard error means that the various estimated coefficients would be tightly bunched around the true coefficient. If the standard error is large, the estimated coefficients are imprecise indicators of the true values.

A Focus Group Example

Consumers are statistics. Customers are people. —Stanley Marcus (early president of Neiman Marcus)

To illustrate these ideas, suppose that Toyota has asked us to conduct a focus group to predict how the number of Toyota Camry vehicles demanded would change if the price changes. We arrange a focus group of 50 prospective car buyers to illustrate how Toyota could answer this question. We ask members of the group if they would be willing to buy a Camry at various prices. As a result, for each of eight prices ranging from $5,000 to $40,000, we have information on how many Camry vehicles would be demanded by this group.

We estimate a linear demand curve of the form $Q = a + bp + e$ and obtain standard errors to assess the reliability of the estimated parameters. The Excel Trendline does not provide standard errors. However, they are provided by another tool available in Excel for running regressions, the LINEST (for *line esti*mate) function.[10] To use this tool:

1. Enter the data in an Excel spreadsheet as in the following screenshot on the left, putting the quantity in Column A and the price (in thousands of dollars) in Column B.

2. As the left screenshot shows, enter =**LINEST(A2:A9,B2:B9,,TRUE)** in cell A12. After pressing ENTER, you should see –1.4381 in cell A12. This number, the estimated value of b, is the estimated slope of the regression line.

3. Select cells A12 through B14. With Windows Excel, press F2, then CTRL+SHIFT +ENTER.[11] With Mac Excel, press CTRL+U, then COMMAND+ENTER.

4. Format cells A12 through B14 to display three decimal places and right-align the numbers, yielding the output shown in the screenshot on the right.

---

[10]LINEST uses ordinary least squares to estimate the regression line. The Windows version of Excel also has a simpler method for running OLS regressions, which we describe in the appendix to this chapter.

[11]CTRL+SHIFT+ENTER means that you press the Ctrl, Shift, and Enter keys simultaneously.

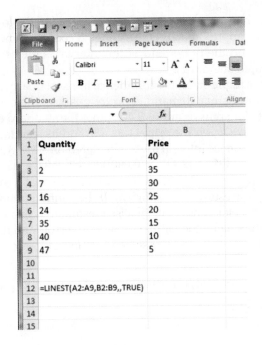
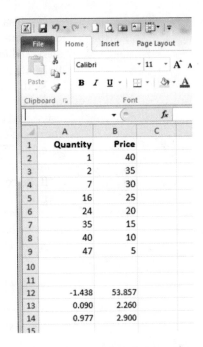

The estimated value of a, rounded to three decimal places, is in cell B12. The estimated demand curve is therefore $\hat{Q} = 53.857 - 1.438p$. The corresponding estimated standard errors are in the cells immediately underneath the coefficient estimates. The estimate of b is -1.438 (cell A12), and its estimated standard error is 0.090 (cell A13). The estimate for a is 53.857 (cell B12), and its estimated standard error is 2.260 (cell B13).

Cell A14 shows that the R^2 is 0.977, which is close to the maximum possible value. This high R^2 indicates that the regression line explains almost all the variation in the observed quantity.[12]

This estimated demand curve can be used to estimate the quantity demanded for any price. According to our estimated demand function, if the price is 27 ($27,000), we expect the focus group consumers to buy $\hat{Q} = 53.857 - (1.438 \times 27) = 15.031$ Camrys. We would round this estimate to 15 cars, given that cars are sold in discrete units. However, if this focus group represented a large group, perhaps a thousand times larger (50,000 consumers), the quantity demanded estimate would be 15,031 vehicles.

Confidence Intervals

We know that an estimated coefficient is not likely to exactly equal the true value. Therefore, it is useful to construct a *confidence interval*, which provides a range of likely values for the true value of a coefficient, centered on the estimated coefficient. For example, a 95% confidence interval is a range of coefficient values such that there is a 95% probability that the true value of the coefficient lies in the specified interval.

The length of a confidence interval depends on the estimated standard error of the coefficient and the number of *degrees of freedom*, which is the number of observations minus the number of coefficients estimated. In our Camry example, there are eight observations and we estimate two coefficients, so there are six degrees of freedom.

---

[12]Cell B14 shows the standard error of the estimated dependent variable.

If the sample has more than 30 degrees of freedom, the lower end of a 95% confidence interval is (approximately) the estimated coefficient minus twice its estimated standard error, and the upper end of the interval is the estimated coefficient plus twice its estimated standard error.

With smaller sample sizes, the confidence interval is larger.[13] With the six degrees of freedom of the Camry demand curve regression, the confidence interval is the estimated coefficient plus or minus 2.447 times the standard error. In this regression, the slope coefficient, $\hat{b}$, on the price is −1.438 and its standard error is 0.090. Therefore, the 95% confidence interval for $\hat{b}$ is centered on −1.438 and goes approximately from −1.658 (= −1.438 − [2.447 × 0.090]) to −1.218 (= −1.438 + [2.447 × 0.090]).

If the confidence interval is small, then we are reasonably sure that the true parameter lies close to the estimated coefficient. If the confidence interval is large, then we believe that parameter is not very precisely estimated. Typically, the more observations we have, the smaller the estimated standard errors and the tighter the confidence interval. Thus, having a larger data set tends to increase our confidence in our results.

Hypothesis Testing and Statistical Significance

There are two possible outcomes: if the result confirms the hypothesis, then you've made a measurement. If the result is contrary to the hypothesis, then you've made a discovery. —Enrico Fermi

A manager can use estimated coefficients and standard errors to test important hypotheses. Very often, the crucial issue for a manager is to determine whether a certain variable really influences another. For example, suppose a firm's manager runs a regression where the demand for the firm's product is a function of the product's price and the prices charged by several possible rivals. If the true coefficient on a rival's price is zero, then the potential rival's product is not in the same market as the manager's product, and the manager can ignore that firm when making decisions. Thus, the manager wants to formally test the *null* hypothesis that the rival's coefficient is equal to zero.

One approach is to determine whether the 95% confidence interval for that coefficient includes zero. If the entire confidence interval for the coefficient on a rival's price contains only positive values, the manager can be 95% confident that the explanatory variable has a positive effect: the higher the rival's prices, the greater the demand for the manager's product.

Equivalently, the manager can test the *null hypothesis* that the coefficient is zero using a *t*-statistic. The LINEST function does not report *t*-statistics automatically, but they are easily calculated. The *t*-statistic equals the estimated coefficient divided by its estimated standard error. That is, the *t*-statistic measures whether the estimated coefficient is large relative to the standard error. In the Camry example, the *t*-statistic for the constant or intercept coefficient is 53.857/2.260 ≈ 23.8, and the *t*-statistic on the price coefficient is −1.438/0.090 ≈ −16.0.

If the absolute value of the *t*-statistic is larger than a *critical value*, then we know that the confidence interval does not include zero, so we reject the null hypothesis that the coefficient is zero. For samples with more than 30 observations, this critical value is about 2, while in our Camry example it is 2.447.

That is, our rule is that we reject the null hypothesis at a 95% level of confidence if the absolute value of the *t*-statistic exceeds the critical value. An equivalent statement

---

[13]The relevant number can be found in a *t*-statistic distribution table.

is that, given a *t*-statistic with a magnitude exceeding the critical value, we will be wrong less than 5% of the time if we reject the hypothesis that the explanatory variable has no effect. The chance that we are wrong when we use a test statistic to reject the null hypothesis is often referred to as the *significance level* of the hypothesis test. Thus in a large sample, if the *t*-statistic is greater than about 2, we reject the null hypothesis that the proposed explanatory variable has no effect at the 5% significance level or 95% confidence level. Rather than use this rather convoluted formal statement, many analysts say simply that the explanatory variable is "statistically significant" or "statistically significantly different from zero."

3.4 Regression Specification

An approximate answer to the right problem is worth a good deal more than an exact answer to an approximate problem. —John Tukey

The first step in a regression analysis is to select a regression equation. We must determine the **regression specification**, which includes the choice of the dependent variable, the explanatory variables, and the functional relationship between them (such as linear, quadratic, or exponential). For example, in the Camry demand curve regression, the dependent variable is the quantity of Camrys demanded, the only explanatory variable is price, measured in thousands of dollars, and the functional relationship between the variables is linear: $Q = a + bp + e$.

A regression analysis is valid only if the regression equation is correctly specified. In particular, the specification should include the appropriate explanatory variables, it must closely approximate the true functional form, and the underlying assumptions about the error term should be correct.

Selecting Explanatory Variables

When selecting variables to include in a regression, we must take care in choosing which explanatory variables to include. The explanatory variables should include all the observable variables that are likely to have a meaningful effect on the dependent variable. We use our understanding of causal relationships, including those that derive from economic theory, to select explanatory variables. In the Camry focus group example, we used our knowledge of demand theory to conclude that the price was likely to affect the quantity demanded.

Mini-Case

Determinants of CEO Compensation

It is unfortunate we can't buy many business executives for what they are worth and sell them for what they think they are worth. —Malcolm Forbes

Human resources managers often use regression studies to determine if their employees are paid comparably with other firms.[14] Similarly, during the major economic crisis of 2007–2009 the very high compensation that chief executive officers (CEOs) of major corporations received were a source of much controversy, and many large banks and other corporations were under pressure to provide evidence to justify their payments. We use multivariate regression to analyze the determinants of CEO compensation. We use economic theory and

---

[14]Another use is in union negotiations. One of us was retained by a large firm to perform a regression analysis to determine how their unionized employees' wages compared to wages of comparable unionized and nonunionized workers in other firms. The firm used this study to bargain with its union.

previous studies to choose the variables that we believe are important determinants of CEO compensation. Then, we test whether these variables belong in the equation.

In our regression analysis, we use data from Standard & Poor's Compustat database on CEO compensation for the 1992–2010 period for corporations in the S&P 500, which is Standard & Poor's list of the 500 largest publicly traded U.S. corporations. We have over 6,200 observations in our data set, where the dependent variable in each observation is the CEO's annual compensation in a particular S&P 500 corporation in a particular year, along with the values of the proposed explanatory variables. Well over half of this compensation was in the form of stock options, which give the holder the right to buy stock in the company at an attractive price far below the market value. The rest consisted primarily of salary and bonuses.

In our multivariate regression, the dependent variable, Y, is CEO compensation in thousands of dollars. We expect the compensation to be greater for CEOs who manage large firms because that requires more work and responsibility. We use two measures of firm size: assets, A (in $ billions), which are related to the firm's capital input, and employees, L (thousands of workers). Presumably a CEO is paid more when the company does well. One measure of a company's success is shareholders' average return over the previous three years, S. This return includes dividends, which are direct payments to shareholders, and capital gains, which are increases in the value of the shares of the shareholders. A CEO may also be worth more to a firm as the CEO's experience, X (the number of years that the CEO has held this job), rises.

We use ordinary least squares to estimate a multivariable regression equation that relates a CEO's salary to these explanatory variables:

$$Y = a + bA + cL + dS + fX + e,$$

where a is a constant and the other coefficients show how much a one unit increase in the corresponding explanatory variable affects CEO compensation. For example, one extra unit (thousand) of employees raises the CEO salary by c. The estimated compensation as a function of the explanatory variables is $\hat{Y} = -377 + 3.86A + 2.27L + 4.51S + 36.1X$, as the following table of regression results shows.

CEO Compensation Regression Results

Explanatory Variable	Coefficient	Standard Error	t-Statistic
Constant	−377	462	−0.82
Assets ($billions), A	3.87	0.70	5.52*
Employees (000s), L	2.26	0.51	4.48*
Shareholder return, S	4.51	1.42	3.17*
Experience (years), X	36.10	8.49	4.25*

* indicates that we can reject the null hypothesis that the coefficient is zero at the 5% significance level.

Based on these t-statistics, we reject the null hypothesis that the coefficients on our four variables are zero at the 5% significance level. Each of these four *t*-statistics is larger than 2. For example, the *t*-statistic on the total assets coefficient is 5.52, which is substantially larger than 2. Thus, we conclude that these variables belong in our specification.

The estimated effect of increasing total assets by $1 billion is to increase the CEO's compensation by $3,870 ($3.87 thousand). If average annual shareholder return over three years increases by one percentage point (say, rising from 8% to 9% per year), a CEO's compensation is higher by $4.51 thousand.

Although these variables are *statistically significantly different than zero*, not all of them are *economically significant*. That is, they do not have a large impact on CEO compensation. For example, the effect of the company's financial performance—shareholders' average return—on CEO salary is relatively small. Most S&P 500 companies have equity values of several billion dollars or more. An increase in shareholder return of one percentage point would apply to the overall equity value and would therefore imply additional returns to shareholders of tens of millions of dollars. However, the difference in CEO salary would be only a small amount (from a CEO's point of view) of less than $5,000 per year. Thus, although the shareholder return variable is statistically significant, it is not very important to a CEO's compensation.

Q&A 3.4

In the Mini-Case just considered, what is the estimated effect of more employees on CEO compensation? Is this effect statistically significant?

Answer

1. *Use the regression coefficient in the estimated CEO compensation function to identify the estimated effect of more employees.* The regression table in the CEO compensation Mini-Case shows that if a firm's workforce increases by 1,000 employees, the CEO's compensation is estimated to rise by about $2.26 thousand per year.

2. *Use the t-statistic shown in the regression table to assess statistical significance.* The t-statistic for the employees is 4.48. The asterisk in the table indicates that this coefficient is significantly different from zero at the 5% significance level, which is the normal standard applied to infer that a coefficient is statistically significant. Thus, we can say that the number of employees is estimated to have a statistically significant effect on CEO compensation.

Correlation and Causation. When selecting explanatory variables, it is important to distinguish between correlation and causation. Two variables, X and Y, are said to be *correlated* if they move together. The quantity demanded and price are negatively correlated: when price goes up, quantity goes down. This correlation is *causal* as changes in price directly affect the quantity demanded.

However, correlation does not necessarily imply causation. For example, sales of gasoline and the incidence of sunburn have a strong positive correlation in U.S. data. Both are relatively high in the summer months of July and August and low in winter months.

Does this correlation mean that a sunburn somehow increases a consumer's demand for gasoline? Should we use the incidence of sunburn as an explanatory variable for gasoline demand? The answer to both these questions is no. The correlation between gasoline sales and sunburn is caused mainly by a third variable, sunshine. During sunny summer months people drive more, in part because they take more vacations that involve driving. They also spend more time in the sun and are therefore more likely to get sunburned. If our gasoline demand regression equation included the incidence of sunburn as an explanatory variable, we would find a high R^2 statistic and a statistically significant positive coefficient on sunburn. However, these results would be *spurious*. Any interpretation that getting sunburned increases the demand for gasoline would be incorrect.

Thus, it is critical that we do not include explanatory variables that have only a spurious relationship to the dependent variable in a regression equation. In estimating gasoline demand we would include price and income as explanatory variables, and we might include sunshine hours or temperature, but we would not include sunburn incidence as an explanatory variable.

If there is a causal relationship between two variables, it is important that we treat the causal variable as the explanatory variable. Suppose that a store selling umbrellas collects weekly data on rainfall and on umbrella sales. It would be incorrect to run a regression with umbrella sales as the explanatory variable and rainfall as the dependent variable. While such a regression would likely yield a statistically significant coefficient on umbrella sales, it makes no sense to think of umbrella sales as affecting rainfall.[15] Because rainfall increases the demand for umbrellas, rainfall should be the explanatory variable and the demand for umbrellas should be the dependent variable.

Omitted Variables. Often, a manager has an otherwise appropriately specified regression but lacks information about one or more potential explanatory variables. Because these variables are not included in the regression specification, they are called *omitted variables*. If a key explanatory variable is missing, then the resulting coefficient estimates and hypothesis tests may be unreliable.

Suppose Jacob and Santiago are managers in the same firm. Jacob wants to estimate the effect of price on quantity demanded and therefore experiments with the price over some time interval, starting with a low price and trying successively higher prices as time proceeds. Santiago, on the other hand, is interested in the effect of advertising on demand and—without telling Jacob—varies the advertising level over the same time interval, starting with a low advertising level and moving to a high level as time passes. Because the higher prices offset the increased advertising activity, the quantity demanded stays fairly stable.

[15]Of course, many people believe that the failure to carry an umbrella causes rain.

Because Jacob does not know about the advertising experiment, after he regresses quantity on price, he is amazed to discover that price increases have no effect on demand. Clearly a regression of quantity demanded on price alone would be highly misleading in this situation, leading Jacob to an incorrect conclusion about the firm's demand curve. If only the price increase occurred, the quantity demanded would have fallen. In this example, it is important to include both price and advertising as explanatory variables.

Functional Form

So far, we have assumed that our regression equations were linear. However, we cannot assume that demand curves or other economic relationships are always linear.

Choosing the correct functional form may be difficult. One useful step, especially if there is only one explanatory variable, is to plot the data and the estimated regression line for each functional form under consideration. We illustrate this approach with an advertising example. A large food manufacturing firm sells its products in many cities throughout the country. To determine the importance of advertising, it holds its price constant across cities but varies the number of commercials per week on local television in each city.[16]

Figure 3.6 shows the relationship between the quantity demanded and advertising, holding price and other relevant explanatory variables constant. Both panels contain the same data points. The vertical axis shows the quantity demanded per family per week, and the horizontal axis is the number of commercials per week on local television.

The two panels have different estimated regression lines based on different functional form specifications. Panel a shows an estimated linear regression, which is based on the assumption that the relationship between the quantity demanded and advertising is linear: $Q = a + bA + e$, where Q is quantity demanded, A is a

FIGURE 3.6 The Effect of Advertising on Demand

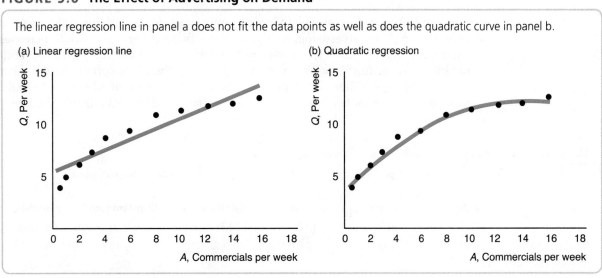

The linear regression line in panel a does not fit the data points as well as does the quadratic curve in panel b.

(a) Linear regression line   (b) Quadratic regression

---

[16]For example, Campbell Soup Company has conducted these types of experiments (Eastlack and Rao, 1989).

measure of the amount of advertising, e is a random error term, and a and b are the parameters to be estimated.

Panel b shows an estimate based on a quadratic regression specification:

$$Q = a + bA + cA^2 + e.$$

The only difference between this specification and the linear specification is that we have added an extra term, the coefficient c times the advertising index squared: cA^2. If $c \neq 0$, the plot of the relationship between Q and A is a curve. If $c = 0$, this extra quadratic term drops out and the equation reverts to a linear form. Therefore, the test of whether c is statistically significantly different from zero can be used as a test of whether the quadratic form is better than the linear form.

Table 3.2 shows OLS estimates of both the linear and quadratic specifications. The estimation of the linear specification does not look bad when considered by itself. The coefficient on advertising is statistically significantly different from zero, and the R^2 is 0.85, which implies that the line "explains" most of the variation in quantity. However, the data points in panel a of Figure 3.6 are not randomly distributed around the regression line. Instead, they are first below the line, then above the line, and then below the line again. This pattern of residuals signals that the linear model is not the proper specification.

The estimated quadratic specification fits the data much better than the linear model: $R^2 = 0.99$. All the coefficients are statistically significantly different from zero. In particular, $\hat{c}$, the estimated coefficient on A^2, is statistically significant, so we reject the linear specification.

The data points appear randomly distributed around the quadratic regression curve in panel b of Figure 3.6. Because the quadratic functional form allows for a curved relationship between quantity and advertising, it captures two important phenomena that the linear specification misses. First, at high levels of advertising intensity, it becomes increasingly difficult to generate more demand, as virtually all potential consumers have purchased the product. The market becomes saturated: no more consumers can be convinced to buy the product. This saturation effect is captured by the declining slope of the regression line in panel b. The linear specification misses this effect.

Second, the linear form overstates the amount of demand that would occur at very low levels of advertising. If advertising activity is very low, small increases have a large payoff—an effect that is captured by the quadratic functional form but not by the linear functional form. A manager using the linear form to assess what would happen at either very high levels or very low levels of advertising would make a serious mistake. And even at intermediate levels of advertising, the linear

TABLE 3.2 Regressions of Quantity on Advertising

	Linear Specification			Quadratic Specification		
	Coefficient	Standard Error	t-Statistic	Coefficient	Standard Error	t-Statistic
Constant	5.43	0.54	10.05*	3.95	0.30	13.18*
Advertising, A	0.53	0.06	8.47*	1.20	0.10	12.18*
Advertising, A^2				−0.04	0.01	−7.05*

*indicates that we can reject the null hypothesis that the coefficient is zero at the 5% significance level.

regression model would consistently understate demand, albeit by only a modest amount.

Although we have focused on linear and quadratic functional forms, there are many other possible functional forms that might be relevant in some circumstances. Selecting among possible functional forms is an important part of regression analysis. In this example, we were able to formally test whether to use a quadratic functional form or a linear functional form in the regression specification. However, it is not always possible to compare functional forms in this way, and it may be necessary to use advanced statistical techniques covered in statistics or econometrics courses to assist in making decisions about functional form specification.

Managerial Implication

Experiments

If your result needs a statistician then you should design a better experiment.
—Ernest Rutherford (Nobel Prize-winning chemist and physicist)

Given the challenges in obtaining data and producing a regression that is properly specified, many firms turn to controlled experiments. For example, a firm can vary its price and observe how consumers react. Unfortunately, firms cannot control all important elements of an experiment as is done in a chemistry or physics lab. As a result, firms often use regressions to hold constant some variables that they could not control explicitly and to analyze their results.

In 1988, the credit card company Capital One was founded with the plan to apply experimental methods to all aspects of its business.[17] For example, if the company wanted to know whether a credit card solicitation would be more successful if mailed in a blue envelope or in a white one, it ran an experiment. By 2000, Capital One was running more than 60,000 tests per year.

Similarly, Harrah's Entertainment relies on randomized tests of various hypotheses to design its marketing. It might send an attractive hotel offer for a Tuesday night to a randomly selected group of customers, and compare the response for that *test* group to other customers who serve as a *control* group.

The Internet now allows many firms to run very low-cost experiments involving tens of thousands of customers. During the 2012 U.S. presidential election, the Obama campaign ran experiments on each type of e-mail fundraising solicitation it used. Google ran about 12,000 randomized experiments in 2009 alone. Google has posted on its website illustrations of how a firm can run randomized experiments on the effectiveness of advertising while controlling for geographic or other differences. In an associated article, Google illustrates one such experiment and the linear regression models they used to analyze it and the hypothesis tests they conducted.[18] Managers should take advantage of the low cost of Internet experiments.

---

[17]The following examples are from Jim Manzi, "What Social Science Does—and Doesn't—Know," **www.city-journal.org/2010/20_3_social-science.html**, Manzi (2012), and Jon Vaver and Jim Koehler, "Measuring Ad Effectiveness Using Geo Experiments," **services.google.com/fh/files/blogs/geo_experiments_final_version.pdf**.

[18]See **services.google.com/fh/files/blogs/geo_experiments_final_version.pdf**.

3.5 Forecasting

Predictions about the future are often referred to as *forecasts*. Managers frequently seek forecasts of important variables related to demand such as sales or revenues. Large banks and other financial institutions commonly make forecasts regarding macroeconomic variables such as interest rates, gross domestic product, unemployment, and inflation. Governments make forecasts of revenues, expenditures, and budget balances, among other things, and we are all familiar with weather forecasts.

There are many different methods of forecasting. We concentrate on two commonly used regression-based methods of forecasting: extrapolation and theory-based econometric forecasting.[19]

Extrapolation

Extrapolation seeks to forecast a variable of interest, like revenue or sales, as a function of time. Extrapolation starts with a series of observations collected over time, referred to as a *time series*. For example, a firm might have monthly sales data for a new product for several years and be interested in projecting future sales based on this historical data. In extrapolation, the time series is *smoothed* in some way to reveal the underlying pattern, and this pattern is then extended or extrapolated into the future to forecast future sales. This type of forecasting is called *pure* time-series analysis because it seeks to forecast future values of some variable, like sales, purely on the basis of past values of that variable and the passage of time.

Trends. Most of us automatically use our eyes to fit a trend line when we look at a plot of data points over time. We now use a regression technique to plot such a trend line formally.

Figure 3.7 shows the quarterly revenue (= price times quantity) for Heinz, which is famous for its most important product, ketchup.[20] The figure plots the quarterly data from the first quarter of 2005 through the fourth quarter of 2011.

Heinz could estimate its revenue, R (in millions of dollars), as a linear function of time, t, which equals 1 in the first quarter of 2005, 2 in the second quarter, and follows this pattern through 28 in the last quarter. The linear regression equation is $R = a + bt + e$, where e is the error term and a and b are the coefficients to be estimated. The estimated trend line is $R = 2{,}089 + 27.66t$, where the coefficient on the time trend is statistically significant. This line is plotted in Figure 3.7. Based on this regression, Heinz could forecast its sales in the first quarter of 2014, which is quarter

---

[19]An alternative approach is to rely on subjective judgments. One judgment-based approach is the *Delphi technique*. A group of experts are asked to make initial forecasts, which are then made known to the group, and the reasoning behind them is discussed. The experts then make new forecasts, and the process is repeated until broad consensus is reached or until the differences in opinion have converged as much as reasonably possible. The resulting forecasts reflect the collective judgment of the group.

[20]The data are from Heinz's annual reports. For financial reporting Heinz defines its quarters as the three-month periods ending in April, July, October, and January. We refer to the quarter ending in April as the first quarter, the quarter ending in July as the second quarter, and so forth. These data refer to worldwide revenues, about half of which come from North America.

FIGURE 3.7 Heinz's Quarterly Revenue: 2005–2012

Each point shows Heinz's revenue in millions of dollars for a particular quarter. A regression is used to fit a trend line through these points. The dashed portion of the line indicates a forecast. The red point at the end of the trend line shows the forecast revenue for the first quarter of 2014.

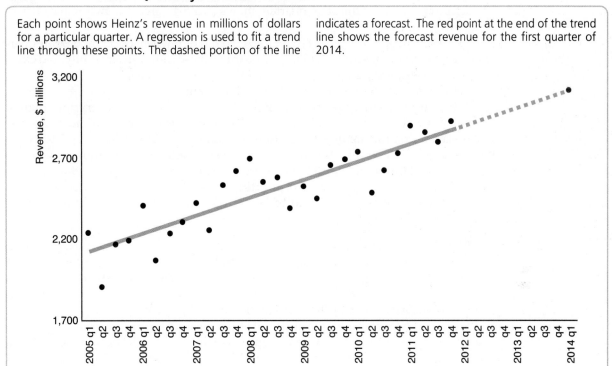

Source: Heinz's Annual Reports.

37, as 2089 + (27.66 × 37) ≈ \$3,112 million (\$3.112 billion), which is the red point at the right end of the trend line. Of course, the further into the future we forecast, the less reliable is the forecast.[21]

Seasonal Variation. If we look at the trend line through the data in Figure 3.7, we notice a distinct pattern of the observations around the trend line. If this variation were purely random, there would not be much we can do about it except to note that our forecasts have potential random errors associated with them. However, because this pattern looks systematic, we may be able to adjust for it. The revenue in the first quarter (late winter and early spring) tends to be above the trend line, while the second quarter tends to be below the trend line, and so forth. It appears that there is a *seasonal* variation in demand for Heinz's products.

In making forecasts, we should adjust for these seasonal effects. We can add variables to our regression that capture the seasonal effects. These variables, often called *seasonal dummy variables*, are variables that equal one in the relevant season and zero otherwise. For example, the first quarter dummy variable is one in the first quarter of the year and zero in the other quarters. We include these indicator variables for

---

[21]Some academics argue that the managers of the U.S. Social Security Administration have made inaccurate forecasts, so that the system will go bankrupt (if nothing is done) earlier than the managers forecast: **www.nytimes.com/2013/01/06/opinion/sunday/social-security-its-worse-than-you-think.html?_r=0.**

only three quarters. The fourth quarter is then interpreted as the base case, and the coefficient on each of the other quarters shows us the difference between that quarter and the base case.

We estimate $R = a + bt + c_1D_1 + c_2D_2 + c_3D_3 + e$, where D_1, D_2, and D_3 are quarterly dummy variables for the first three quarters: those ending in April, July, and October. The new estimated equation is $R = 2{,}094 + 27.97t + 93.8D_1 - 125.3D_2 - 8.60D_3$, where all the coefficients are statistically significant.

Our failure to include the seasonal dummy variables in our original regression may have led to a biased estimate. Based on this new regression model, the forecast value for the quarter ending in January of 2014 is $2094 + (27.97 \times 37) + (93.8 \times 1) - (125.3 \times 0) - (8.60 \times 0) = \$3{,}223$ million. This adjusted forecast is about \$111 million (about 3.5%) more than our previous forecast that ignored seasonal effects. Properly incorporating seasonal effects allows us to adjust for the fact that revenues tend to be higher in the first quarter than in other quarters.

Nonlinear Trends. Although Heinz's revenue follows a linear trend, not all time trends are linear. For example, the market penetration of new products is often nonlinear. After it is first introduced, a new product's market share often grows slowly, as it takes a while for consumers to become familiar with the product. At some point, a successful product *takes off* and sales grow very rapidly. Then, when the product eventually approaches market saturation, sales grow slowly in line with underlying population or real income growth. Ultimately, if the product is displaced by other products, its sales will fall sharply. For example, sales of iPod units followed this pattern.

Theory-Based Econometric Forecasting

Revenue is determined in large part by the consumers' demand curve. We know that the demand is affected by variables such as income, population, and advertising. Yet our forecast based on extrapolation (pure time-series analysis) ignored these structural (causal) variables. The role of such variables may be implicit in an extrapolation. For example, one reason why revenue may have grown smoothly over time is that population increased smoothly over this time period.

As a first approximation, extrapolation is often useful, especially if seasonal effects are properly addressed. However, the problem with such forecasts is that they are not based on a causal understanding of how the variable of interest is actually determined. As a result, it is difficult for the forecaster to understand the underlying causal structure that determines revenue and to anticipate the effects of changes in causal variables such as income or population. If we are interested in underlying economic structure, a different approach is needed.

An alternative forecasting approach uses economic theory, such as a demand framework, to derive the causal relationships between economic variables. For example, in forecasting Heinz's sales or revenue, we could estimate the effect of changes in income on demand for Heinz's products and then take the expected pattern of income growth into account in forecasting sales.

Forecasts based on a regression specification that incorporates underlying causal factors is called *causal econometric forecasting* or *theory-based econometric forecasting*. Such forecasting methods incorporate both extrapolation and estimation of causal or explanatory economic relationships. Thus to forecast sales, we might use both previous values of sales and time as explanatory variables, and we would also use causal variables such as income. That is, with theory-based (causal) econometric forecasting, we predict the dependent variable based on the underlying causal factors—not just on the time-series pattern of the dependent variable.

We use these estimates to make *conditional forecasts*, where our forecast is based on specified values for the explanatory variables. For example, a manager might make one conditional forecast of sales based on the assumption that income will be 5% higher next quarter than this quarter and another conditional forecast based on the assumption that income next quarter will be the same as this quarter.

In our extrapolation analysis, we assumed that Heinz's revenue would grow steadily over time. However, there are underlying causal or structural factors that might affect its revenue. We would expect Heinz's revenue to deviate from the trend line if a rival entered or exited the business, if Heinz added a new major product to its product line or acquired another large company, if the cost of transportation or ingredients changed dramatically, or if the country went into a major recession. Heinz could regress its revenue on these economic factors. It could then use that regression to make forecasts that are conditional on how it expects these other factors to evolve over time.

Forecasting using theory-based econometric modeling is more difficult than employing extrapolation. However, it often provides a better chance of identifying sudden deviations from a simple trend line, and it may contribute more to a firm's understanding of the underlying business interactions.

Managerial Solution

Estimating the Effect of an iTunes Price Change

How could Apple use a focus group to estimate the demand curve for iTunes to determine if raising its price would raise or lower its revenue? To answer this question, we asked a focus group of 20 Canadian college students in 2008 how many popular tracks they downloaded from iTunes when the price was 99¢ and how many they would have downloaded at various other prices assuming that their incomes and the prices of other goods remained constant. The responses were:

Price, $ per song	Quantity, Songs per year
1.49	441
1.29	493
1.19	502
1.09	536
0.99	615
0.89	643
0.79	740
0.69	757
0.49	810

The iTunes managers would first estimate a linear demand curve of song downloads on price, obtaining demand coefficient estimates, the R^2 statistic, and standard errors, and then calculate the t-statistics (dividing each coefficient by its standard error).

Based on these results, the estimated linear demand curve is $\hat{Q} = 1,024 - 413p$, where $\hat{Q}$ is the estimated number of downloads per year and price p is in dollars per song. The price coefficient is -413, which means that a $1 increase in price would reduce estimated quantity demanded by 413 downloads. Converting this result to cents, a 1¢ increase in price would reduce estimated quantity demanded by 4.13 downloads per year. The t-statistic is -12.6, so this coefficient is significantly different from zero. The R^2 statistic is 0.96, indicating that the regression line fits the data closely.

Apple's manager could use such an estimated demand curve to determine how revenue, R, which is price times quantity ($R = p \times Q$), varies with price. Panel a of Figure 3.8 shows the estimated iTunes demand curve. At $p = 99¢$, 615 songs were downloaded by the focus group according to this estimated demand curve. The corresponding revenue is the rectangle consisting of areas $A + B$. The height of this rectangle is the price, $p = 99¢$. The length of the rectangle is the quantity of songs downloaded, $Q = 615$, so the area of the rectangle equals $R = p \times Q = \$0.99 \times 615 \approx \$609$.

If the price were increased to $1.24, the quantity demanded would drop to 512. The corresponding revenue would be the rectangle $= A + C$, where the height is $1.24 and the length is 512. According to the focus group's responses, Apple would lose revenue equal to area B but gain area C. Area B shows how much Apple loses from selling 103 ($= 615 - 512$) fewer units at the original price. Area C is the extra amount it makes on the 512 units it does sell, because it sells each song by $0.25 ($= \$1.24 - \$0.99$) more than it did originally.

An increase in price has two offsetting effects on revenue. Revenue tends to fall because the price increase causes fewer units to be sold. However, revenue tends to rise because a higher price is collected on every unit that is sold. Because these two effects have opposite effects on revenue, management would not know in general whether a particular price increase would raise or lower revenue.

However, because we have estimated the demand curve, we can calculate the size of these two effects and determine the net effect of a price increase on iTunes's revenue. The lost revenue from fewer sales is area B, which is $102. The revenue gain due to the higher price on the units sold is area C, which is $128. Therefore, revenue increases by $26 ($= \$128 - \$102$).

Panel b corresponds to panel a. Its horizontal axis measures quantity as in panel a, but its vertical axis measures revenue (rather than price as in panel a). Panel b shows the revenue curve, which relates revenue to the quantity sold.[22] At the original price of 99¢, where $Q = 615$, the revenue curve shows that revenue is $609, consistent with panel a. This curve shows that the revenue curve reaches its maximum at $1.24.

Given that the cost to Apple of selling an extra song is probably very close to zero, it seems that Apple would like to maximize its revenue. If the general population has similar tastes to the focus group, then Apple's revenue would increase if it raised its price to $1.24 per song.[23]

---

[22]Because the estimated demand curve is $Q = 1,024 - 413p$, the corresponding inverse demand curve is $p \approx 2.48 - 0.00242Q$. Thus, the revenue function is $R = p \times Q \approx 2.48Q - 0.00242Q^2$.
[23]See the Mini-Case "Available for a Song" in Chapter 10 for a larger-scale, more detailed study of Apple's pricing.

FIGURE 3.8 iTunes Focus Group Demand and Revenue Curves

Based on a focus group's responses, we estimate the iTunes demand curve and calculate a revenue (= price × quantity) curve. (a) According to the estimated demand curve, if the price were 99¢, the focus group would download 615 songs per year and revenue would be areas $A + B = \$507 + \$102 = \$609 = p \times Q$ = $0.99× 615. At a price of $1.24, the songs demanded would fall to 512, and the revenue would be areas $A + C = \$507 + \$128 = \$635 = p \times Q = \$1.24 \times 512$. (b) According to the corresponding revenue curve, revenue is greatest for this focus group at $p = \$1.24$, where $R = \$635$.

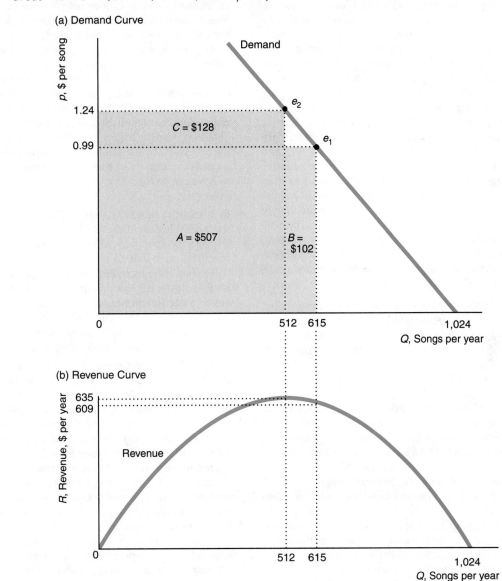

(a) Demand Curve

(b) Revenue Curve

SUMMARY

1. Elasticity. An elasticity shows how responsive one variable is to changes in another variable. The price elasticity of demand, ε, summarizes how much the quantity demanded changes when the price changes. The responsiveness of quantity is related to the shape of a demand curve at a particular point or over a particular interval. Specifically, the price elasticity of demand is the percentage change in the quantity demanded divided by an associated percentage change in price. For example, a 1% increase in price causes the quantity demanded to fall by ε%. Downward-sloping demand curves have a negative elasticity.

The demand curve is perfectly inelastic if $\varepsilon = 0$, is inelastic if ε is between 0 and -1, has unitary elasticity if $\varepsilon = -1$, is elastic if $\varepsilon < -1$, and becomes perfectly elastic as ε approaches negative infinity. The quantity demanded varies less than in proportion to a 1% change in the price if the demand curve is inelastic, but varies more than in proportion if the demand curve is elastic. The elasticity of demand varies along a downward-sloping linear demand curve. A vertical demand curve is perfectly inelastic and a horizontal demand curve is perfectly elastic.

2. Regression Analysis. Regression analysis fits an economic relationship to data. It explains variations in a dependent variable, such as the quantity demanded, using explanatory variables, such as price and income. A linear regression with just one explanatory variable corresponds to putting the dependent variable on the vertical axis, the explanatory variable on the horizontal axis, plotting the data points, and drawing the "best possible" straight line through these points. One method used to find a suitable estimated relationship is ordinary least squares (OLS), which chooses parameter estimates or "draws the regression line" such that the sum of squared deviations of the data points from the regression line is as small as possible. To help assess the fit of the regression line to the data, statistical packages report the R^2 statistic, which is the fraction of the actual variation in the dependent variable explained by the estimated regression equation.

3. Properties and Statistical Significance of Estimated Coefficients. A good estimation method should yield coefficient estimates that are unbiased—that would average out to the true value in repeated samples. It is also desirable that an estimation method does not produce very different coefficient estimates in different random samples. Regression software produces statistics that can be used to assess how much confidence to place in regression coefficient estimates. Standard errors tell us how much we might expect coefficient estimates to differ from their true values. A t-statistic allows us to test whether an estimated regression coefficient is different from zero. We obtain a t-statistic for each coefficient by dividing the coefficient by its standard error. If the t-statistic exceeds a critical value that is approximately equal to 2, we can be confident that the coefficient differs from zero.

4. Regression Specification. Regression analysis is reliable only if the equation to be estimated is properly specified. One important aspect of specification is that all relevant explanatory variables should be included. A second specification issue is that a regression equation must have an appropriate functional form. Excluding relevant explanatory variables, including inappropriate explanatory variables, or using the wrong functional form can lead to misleading results.

5. Forecasting. One method of forecasting is to extrapolate a time series into the future. As a first step in extrapolation, a manager can regress the variable to be forecast, such as sales, on a time-trend variable. Next, using the estimated trend line, a manager can forecast the future value by substituting future times into the estimated regression equation. When extrapolating, it is often necessary to adjust for seasonal or other patterns. A second method of forecasting uses causal economic relationships, where economic variables are used as explanatory variables instead of or in addition to a time trend. Here, forecasting the dependent variable may require the manager to use expected values of the explanatory variables.

QUESTIONS

*All exercises are available on MyEconLab; * = answer at the back of this book; C = use of calculus may be necessary.*

1. Elasticity

1.1. The U.S. Tobacco Settlement between the major tobacco companies and 46 states caused the price of cigarettes to jump 45¢ (21%) in November 1998. Levy and Meara (2005) found only a 2.65% drop in prenatal smoking 15 months later. What is the elasticity of demand for this group?

1.2. When Apple raised the price of iTunes from 99¢ to $1.29, GS Boyz's "Stanky Legg" sales dropped from 22,686 units to 19,692 units (Glenn Peoples, "iTunes Price Change: Sales Down, Revenue Up in Week 1," *Billboard*, April 15, 2009). What was the song's arc elasticity of demand? (*Hint*: See Q&A 3.1.)

*1.3. The demand curve for a good is $Q = 100 - 2p$. What is the elasticity at the point $p = 10$ and $Q = 80$?

1.4. Luchansky and Monks (2009) estimated that the U.S. demand curve for ethanol is $Q = p^{-0.504}p_g^{1.269}v^{2.226}$, where Q is the quantity of ethanol, p is the price of ethanol, p_g is the price of gasoline, and v is the number of registered vehicles. What is the elasticity of demand for ethanol? (*Hint*: See Q&A 3.2.) **C**

1.5. The demand curve for a good is $Q = 1,000 - 2p^2$. What is the elasticity at the point $p = 10$ and $Q = 800$? **C**

1.6. What section of a straight-line demand curve is elastic?

*1.7. According to Duffy-Deno (2003), when the price of broadband access capacity (the amount of information one can send over an Internet connection) increases 10%, commercial customers buy about 3.8% less capacity. What is the elasticity of demand for broadband access capacity for these firms? Is demand at the current price inelastic?

1.8. Suppose that the demand curve for wheat in each country is inelastic up to some "choke" price p^*—a price so high that nothing is bought—so that the demand curve is vertical at Q^* at prices below p^* and horizontal at p^*. If p^* and Q^* vary across countries, what does the world's demand curve look like? Discuss how the elasticity of demand varies with price along the world's demand curve.

*1.9. Calculate the price and cross-price elasticities of demand for coconut oil. The coconut oil demand function (Buschena and Perloff, 1991) is

$$Q = 1,200 - 9.5p + 16.2p_p + 0.2Y,$$

where Q is the quantity of coconut oil demanded in thousands of metric tons per year, p is the price of coconut oil in cents per pound, p_p is the price of palm oil in cents per pound, and Y is the income of consumers. Assume that p is initially 45¢ per pound, p_p is 31¢ per pound, and Q is 1,275 thousand metric tons per year.

1.10. Using the coconut oil demand function from Question 1.9, calculate the income elasticity of demand for coconut oil. (If you do not have all the numbers necessary to calculate numerical answers, write your answers in terms of variables.)

1.11. The Mini-Case "Substitution May Save Endangered Species" describes how the equilibrium changed in the market for seal genitalia (used as an aphrodisiac in Asia) when Viagra was introduced. Use a supply-and-demand diagram to illustrate what happened. Is it possible for a positive quantity to be demanded at various prices, yet nothing is sold in the market?

1.12. Nataraj (2007) found that a 100% increase in the price of water for heavy users in Santa Cruz, California, caused the quantity of water they demanded to fall by an average of 20% (Mini-Case "Turning Off the Faucet"). Before the increase, heavy users initially paid $1.55 per unit, but afterward they paid $3.14 per unit. What can you say about the elasticity of demand? In percentage terms, how much did their water expenditure (price times quantity)—which is the water company's revenue—change?

2. Regression Analysis

2.1. At the Portland Fish Exchange, each day some amount of cod is brought to market. Supply is perfectly inelastic at that amount. How much cod is caught and brought to market varies day to day. Assuming the demand curve does not vary over time, use the supply-demand framework to illustrate how the price is determined on different days. Explain how this process allows us to identify different points on the demand curve.

2.2. Suppose that a restaurant uses a focus group of regular customers to determine how many customers would buy a proposed new menu item at various prices. Can this information be used to estimate an inverse demand curve? A demand curve? Explain briefly. Would it be possible to use a focus group to generate data that could be used to estimate a demand function including both price and income as explanatory variables?

*2.3. The estimated demand curve for popsicles on a particular beach on a sunny summer day is given by $Q = 130 - 3.5p$, where p is measured in dollars. What is the predicted quantity if $p = \$2.00$. If the actual quantity demanded is 129, what is the residual? Suggest at least two unobserved variables incorporated in the random error. (*Hint*: See Q&A 3.3.)

2.4. A producer of outdoor clothing used a focus group to obtain information about the demand for fleece jackets with built-in, battery-operated warming panels. At prices of $100, $90, $80, $70, $60, and $50, the focus group demanded 23, 31, 40, 44, 48, and 60 jackets, respectively. Use the Excel Trendline option to estimate a linear demand function and to determine the associated R^2 statistic. (*Hint*: Put price in the first column. Price will appear on the horizontal axis in this case.)

3. Properties and Statistical Significance of Estimated Coefficients

3.1. Using the data in Table 3.1, estimate the cod demand function if we use only the first seven observations.

3.2. How sensitive are your regression results in Exercise 3.1 to small changes in the data? In particular, how do your regression results change if

    a. The quantity in the first row of Table 3.1 were 2.0 instead of 1.5?

    b. The quantity in the second row of Table 3.1 were 2.7 instead of 2.2?

*3.3. In the Camry focus group analysis in this chapter, we used a regression to estimate the demand for Camrys. Using that equation, how many fewer Camrys would the focus group buy if the price were increased by $1,000? How many Camrys would we expect the focus group to purchase if the price is $20,000? What is the elasticity of demand if the price is $20,000?

3.4. Using the data in Question 2.4, determine the standard error and t-statistic for the price coefficient. Is price statistically significantly different from zero at the 0.05 level of significance? (*Hint*: Use Excel's LINEST tool or, if you have the Windows version, the Regression tool.)

4. Regression Specification

4.1. According to the regression results for CEO compensation, is the effect of experience on CEO compensation statistically significant? Is it economically significant? Explain. (*Hint*: See Q&A 3.4.)

4.2. Suppose that you believe that the demand curve is a constant-elasticity demand curve: $Q = Ap^\varepsilon$, where A is a positive constant and ε is the constant elasticity of demand. You have some data and want to estimate the constant-elasticity demand curve $Q = Ap^\varepsilon u$, where A is a positive constant, ε is the constant elasticity of demand, and u is an error term. Take logarithms of both sides of this equation and show that you get an equation that is linear in logarithmic terms (called a log-linear equation). Explain how you can estimate this equation in Excel or other programs using the OLS techniques that we have discussed.

*4.3. You work for a firm producing fitness equipment. You have been told that the demand curve for the firm's main product—a multistation home gym—is linear. You have been provided with price and quantity data obtained from focus groups and have been asked to run a regression of revenue on price. Should you use a linear functional form—with revenue as a linear function of price—or something else? Explain.

5. Forecasting

5.1. Heinz makes most of its money from ketchup and prepared, packaged foods that are substitutes for fresh foods. From Figure 3.7, we see that its revenue tends to be low in the second quarter (May, June, and July). Can you provide a possible reason for this pattern? (*Hint*: Fresh fruits and vegetables are substitutes for many of Heinz's prepared foods, and ketchup is commonly used on foods prepared at outdoor cookouts.)

5.2. As reported in the chapter, quarterly revenue for Heinz is estimated as $R = 2{,}094 + 27.97t + 93.8D_1 - 125.3D_2 - 8.60D_3$. What does this estimation tell us about second quarter revenues for Heinz? If, as a consultant, you were asked to suggest ways of smoothing quarter-to-quarter revenues for Heinz, what would you suggest?

5.3. Some companies, such as Heinz, can reliably forecast revenues using pure time-series analysis (that is, by extrapolation of prior data, accounting for seasonal effects). Other companies, such as FedEx (which makes money by shipping packages), or Sony (which sells consumer electronics), find that they cannot rely on pure time-series analysis for reliable forecasting. They are strongly affected by recessions and need to use theory-based methods, including such explanatory variables as income in their forecasting models. Why are they different from Heinz?

6. Managerial Problem

6.1. In the Managerial Solution, we estimated a focus group's demand curve for iTunes downloads. The estimated coefficient on price was −413, and the t-statistic was −12.8.

  a. Using these values, what is the standard error of this estimated coefficient?

  b. Suppose we had another focus group sample, ran a regression on that sample, and obtained the same coefficient on price but with a standard error 10 times as large. What can you say about the statistical significance of the price coefficient in this second sample?

*6.2. Using Excel or another program, estimate the linear OLS demand regression for the iTunes focus group data in the Managerial Solution. What is the R^2? What are the coefficient estimates, the standard errors, and the t-statistics for each coefficient? Using a 95% confidence criterion, would you reject the hypothesis that the price coefficient is zero? (You can compare most of your answers to those in the Managerial Solution.)

7. Spreadsheet Exercises

7.1. The marketing department of Acme Inc. has estimated the following demand function for its popular carpet deodorizer, Freshbreeze: $Q = 100 − 5p$, where Q is the quantity of an 8-ounce box (sold in thousand units) and p the price of an 8-ounce box. Using Excel, calculate the point price elasticity of demand, ε, for price, $p = 1, 2, 3, \ldots , 19$. Describe the pattern of price elasticity of demand that you have calculated along the demand curve.

7.2. The ice cream store Cool Stuff sells exotic ice creams, including Tropical Cream and Green Mango. Cool Stuff has been varying the prices of these two flavors over the past 12 weeks and has recorded the sales data. The table shows the quantity sold of Tropical Cream, Q, given the price of a half-gallon of Tropical Cream, p, and the price of the other flavor, Green Mango, p_o. Use these data to estimate the demand function for Tropical Cream. Are the coefficients on the two prices statistically significantly different from zero at the 5% significance level? What is the R^2?

Q	p	p_o
84	8.5	5.25
82	9	6
85	8.75	6
83	9.25	6.5
82	9.5	6.25
84	9.25	6.25
87	8.25	5.25
81	10	7
82	10	7.25
79	10.5	7.25
82	9.5	6.75
78	10.25	7.25

Appendix 3 The Excel Regression Tool

The Regression tool available in the Windows version of Microsoft Excel is easier to use than the LINEST function.[24] We demonstrate its use in Excel 2010 for the Camry focus group example analyzed in Section 3.3.

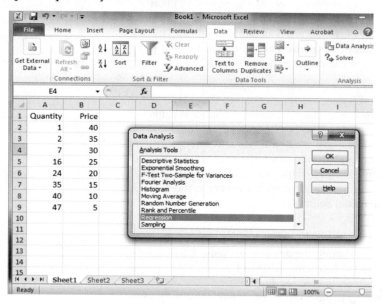

1. As shown in the screenshot, enter the data in an Excel spreadsheet.
2. Click on the *Data* tab, then on the *Data Analysis* icon at the upper right of the spreadsheet.[25] The Data Analysis dialog displays as shown. Select the *Regression* tool and click *OK*.
3. In the Regression dialog that displays, fill in the *Input Y Range* field (the dependent variable) by selecting cells A1 through A9 or by typing **A1:A9** into the box.
4. Fill in the *Input X Range* field (the explanatory variables) by selecting the cells containing the prices or by typing **B1:B9**.
5. Select the *Labels* box. Click the *Output Range* button, enter **A12** in the associated box, and then click *OK*.

Excel displays the regression results. This regression output includes the R^2, which is (approximately) 0.98. It also shows that the estimated regression line is $Q = 53.86 - 1.438p$. Based on the associated t-statistics, we conclude that the coefficients on the constant term (the intercept) and on p are statistically significant at the 0.05 level.

---

[24]The Mac version of Excel (from 2008 onward) has LINEST but does not have the Regression tool. However, similar tools are available from third parties for use with Excel, such as StatPlus, which is available free of charge at **www.analystsoft.com/en/products/statplusmacle**.

[25]If you do not see the *Data Analysis* icon, the Analysis Toolpak is not installed in your version of Excel. See Excel *Help* for installation instructions.

Consumer Choice

4

If this is coffee, please bring me some tea; but if this is tea, please bring me some coffee. —Abraham Lincoln

Managerial Problem

Paying Employees to Relocate

When Google wants to transfer an employee from its Washington, D.C., office to its London branch, it has to decide how much compensation to offer the worker to move. International firms are increasingly relocating workers throughout their home countries and internationally. For example, KPMG, an international accounting and consulting firm, has a goal of having 25% to 30% of its professional staff gain international experience at some point. In 2010, about 5,000 of its 120,000 global employees were on foreign assignment.

As you might expect, workers are not always enthusiastic about being relocated. In a survey by Runzheimer International, 79% of relocation managers responded that they confronted resistance from employees who were asked to relocate to high-cost locations. A survey of some of their employees found that 81% objected to moving because of fear of a lowered standard of living.

One possible approach to enticing employees to relocate is for the firm to assess the goods and services consumed by employees in the original location and then pay those employees enough to allow them to consume essentially the same items in the new location. According to a survey by Mercer, 79% of international firms reported that they provided their workers with enough income abroad to maintain their home lifestyle.

However, economists who advise on compensation packages point out that such an approach will typically overcompensate employees by paying them more than they need to obtain the same level of economic well-being they have in the original city. How can a firm's human resources (HR) manager use consumer theory to optimally compensate employees who are transferred to other cities?

Economists use the theory of consumer choice to analyze consumers' decisions and to derive demand curves. To answer questions about individual consumer choice (or any kind of individual decision making) we need a model of individual behavior. The standard economic model of consumer behavior is based on the following premises or assumptions.

▶ Individual *tastes* or *preferences* determine the pleasure or satisfaction people derive from the goods and services they consume.

▶ Consumers face *constraints* or limits on their choices, particularly because their budgets limit how much they can buy.

▶ Consumers seek to *maximize* the level of satisfaction they obtain from consumption, subject to the constraints they face. People seek to "do the best with what they have."

Consumers spend their money on the bundles of products that give them the most pleasure or satisfaction. Someone who likes music and does not have much of a sweet tooth might spend a lot of money on concerts and relatively little on sweet desserts. By contrast, a consumer who loves chocolate and has little interest in music might spend a significant amount on gourmet chocolate and never go to a concert.

Consumers must make choices about which goods to buy. Limits on the amount they can spend (called "budget constraints") prevent them from buying everything that catches their fancy. Other constraints such as legal restrictions on items such as alcohol and recreational drugs may also restrain their choices. Therefore, consumers buy the bundles of goods they like best subject to their budget constraints and subject to legal or other relevant constraints.

In economic analysis designed to explain behavior, economists assume that *the consumer is the boss* (sometimes referred to as *consumer sovereignty*). If Jason gets pleasure from smoking, an economist does not confuse the economic analysis of Jason's choices by interjecting his or her own personal judgment that smoking is undesirable. Economists accept the consumer's tastes and seek to predict the resulting behavior. Accepting each consumer's tastes is not the same as condoning the resulting behaviors. An economist might reasonably believe that smoking should be avoided. However, if the economist wants to know whether Jason will smoke more next year if the price of cigarettes decreases by 10%, any prediction is unlikely to be correct if the economist says, "He should not smoke; therefore, we predict he will stop smoking next year." A prediction based on Jason's actual tastes is more likely to be correct: "Given that Jason likes cigarettes, he is likely to smoke more next year if the price of cigarettes falls."

Main Topics

In this chapter, we examine six main topics

1. **Consumer Preferences:** We use three properties of preferences to predict which combinations or bundles of goods an individual prefers to other combinations.

2. **Utility:** We summarize a consumer's preferences using a *utility* function, which assigns to each possible bundle of goods a numerical value, *utility*, that reflects the consumer's relative ranking of these bundles.

3. **The Budget Constraint:** Prices and consumers' limited budgets constrain how much they can buy and determine the rate at which a consumer can substitute one good for another.

4. **Constrained Consumer Choice:** Consumers maximize their utility from consuming various possible bundles of goods given their available budgets.

5. **Deriving Demand Curves:** We use consumer theory to derive demand curves and show how a change in price causes a movement along a demand curve.

6. **Behavioral Economics:** Experiments indicate that people sometimes deviate from rational, maximizing behavior.

4.1 Consumer Preferences

I have forced myself to contradict myself in order to avoid conforming to my own taste. —Marcel Duchamp, Dada artist

We start our analysis of consumer behavior by examining consumer preferences. Once we know about consumers' preferences, we will combine that knowledge with information about the constraints consumers face to answer many questions of interest, such as the managerial problem posed at the beginning of this chapter.

A consumer faces choices involving many goods. Would ice cream or cake make a better dessert? Is it better to rent a large apartment or rent a single room and use the savings to pay for trips and concerts? In short, a consumer must allocate his or her available budget to buy a *bundle* (also called a *market basket* or combination) of goods.

How do consumers choose the bundles of goods they buy? One possibility is that consumers behave randomly and blindly choose one good or another without any thought. However, consumers appear to make systematic choices. For example, most consumers buy very similar items each time they visit a grocery store. A consumer typically ignores most items and buys a few particular items repeatedly. A consumer who likes apple juice and dislikes orange juice repeatedly buys apple juice and rarely if ever buys orange juice. In contrast, a consumer who chose randomly would be as likely to buy apple juice as orange juice. By observing a consumer's consistent purchase of apple juice rather than orange juice, we can reject the hypothesis of random choices.

To explain consumer behavior, economists assume that consumers have a set of tastes or preferences that they use to guide them in choosing between goods. These tastes differ substantially among individuals. For example, three out of four European men prefer colored underwear, while three out of four American men prefer white underwear.[1] Let's start by specifying the underlying assumptions in the economist's model of consumer behavior.

Properties of Consumer Preferences

Do not do unto others as you would that they should do unto you. Their tastes may not be the same. —George Bernard Shaw

Economists make three critical assumptions about the properties of consumers' preferences. For brevity, these properties are referred to as *completeness, transitivity,* and *more is better* (or, alternatively, as *nonsatiation*).

Completeness. The completeness property holds that, when facing a choice between any two bundles of goods, a consumer can rank them so that one and only one of the following three relationships is true.

1. The consumer prefers the first bundle to the second.
2. The consumer prefers the second bundle to the first.
3. The consumer likes the two bundles equally and therefore is indifferent between the two bundles.

---

[1]L. M. Boyd, "The Grab Bag," *San Francisco Examiner*, September 11, 1994, p. 5.

This property rules out the possibility that the consumer cannot decide on his or her preferences. Indifference is allowed, but indecision is not.

Transitivity.

We assume that preferences are transitive. More specifically, we say that if a consumer *weakly prefers* Bundle *a* to Bundle *b*—likes *a* at least as much as *b*—and weakly prefers Bundle *b* to Bundle *c*, the consumer also weakly prefers Bundle *a* to Bundle *c*.

Transitivity of weak preference implies that indifference is also transitive: If a consumer is indifferent between Bundle *a* and Bundle *b*, and is indifferent between Bundle *b* and Bundle *c*, then the consumer must also be indifferent between Bundle *a* and Bundle *c*. Strict preference must also be transitive: If *a* is strictly preferred to *b* and *b* is strictly preferred to *c*, it follows that *a* must be strictly preferred to *c*. Also, if *a* is preferred to *b* and the consumer is indifferent between *b* and *c*, then the consumer must also prefer *a* to *c*.

Transitivity is a necessary condition for what most people view as *rational behavior*. Suppose Amy told you she would prefer a scoop of ice cream to a piece of cake but would prefer a piece of cake to a chocolate bar, and then added that she would prefer a chocolate bar to a scoop of ice cream. She might reasonably be accused of being irrational or inconsistent. At the very least, it would be difficult to know which dessert to serve her.

More Is Better.

The more-is-better property holds that, all else being the same, more of a good is better than less. This property is really just a statement of what we mean by a **good**: a commodity for which more is preferred to less, at least at some levels of consumption. In contrast, a **bad** is something for which less is preferred to more, as with pollution (which we study in Chapter 16). Because managers primarily care about goods, we will concentrate on them.

The more-is-better property is not essential for the following analysis of consumer preferences—our most important results would hold even without this property. These results would, if properly interpreted, apply to bads and to items about which we do not care about one way or the other, as well as for goods. However, the more-is-better assumption greatly simplifies the analysis.

Not surprisingly, studies based on data from many nations find that richer people are happier on average than poorer people (Helliwell et al., 2012). But, do people become satiated? Can people be so rich that they can buy everything they want and additional income does not increase their feelings of well-being? Using recent data from many countries, Stevenson and Wolfers (2008) found no evidence of a satiation point beyond which wealthier countries or wealthier individuals have no further increases in subjective well-being. Moreover, they found a clear positive relationship between average levels of self-reported feelings of happiness or satisfaction and income per capita within and across countries.

Less scientific, but perhaps more compelling, is a survey of wealthy U.S. citizens who were asked, "How much wealth do you need to live comfortably?" On average, those with a net worth of over $1 million said that they needed $2.4 million to live comfortably, those with at least $5 million in net worth said that they need $10.4 million, and those with at least $10 million wanted $18.1 million. Apparently, most people never have enough.

Preference Maps

Surprisingly, with just these three properties, we can say a lot about consumer preferences. One of the simplest ways to summarize information about a consumer's preferences is to create a graphical interpretation—sometimes called a *preference map*. For graphical simplicity, we concentrate on choices between only two goods, but the model can be generalized algebraically to handle any number of goods.

Each semester, Lisa, who lives for fast food, decides how many pizzas and burritos to eat. The various bundles of pizzas and burritos she might consume are shown in panel a of Figure 4.1, with (individual-size) pizzas per semester on the horizontal axis and burritos per semester on the vertical axis.

FIGURE 4.1 Bundles of Pizzas and Burritos That Lisa Might Consume

Pizzas per semester are on the horizontal axis, and burritos per semester are on the vertical axis. (a) Lisa prefers more to less, so she prefers Bundle e to any bundle in area B, including d. Similarly, she prefers any bundle in area A, including f, to e. (b) The indifference curve, I^1, shows a set of bundles (including c, e, and a) among which she is indifferent: She likes all three bundles on this curve equally. (c) The three indifference curves, I^1, I^2, and I^3, are part of Lisa's preference map, which summarizes her preferences.

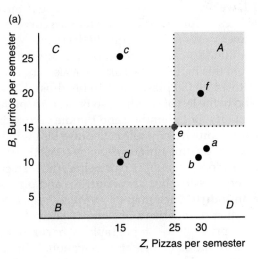

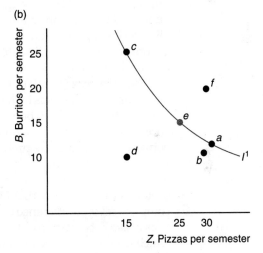

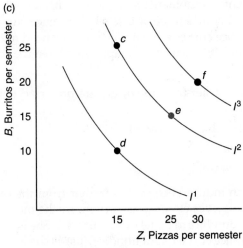

At Bundle e, for example, Lisa consumes 25 pizzas and 15 burritos per semester. By the more-is-better property, Lisa prefers all the bundles that lie above and to the right (area A) to Bundle e because they contain at least as much or more of both pizzas and burritos as Bundle e. Thus, she prefers Bundle f (30 pizzas and 20 burritos) in that region.

By using the more-is-better property, we know that Lisa prefers e to all the bundles that lie in area B, below and to the left of e, such as Bundle d (15 pizzas and 10 burritos). All the bundles in area B contain fewer pizzas or fewer burritos or fewer of both than does Bundle e.

From panel a, we do not know whether Lisa prefers Bundle e to bundles such as b (30 pizzas and 10 burritos) in area D, which is the region below and to the right of e, or c (15 pizzas and 25 burritos) in area C, which is the region above and to the left of Bundle e. We can't use the more-is-better property to determine which bundle is preferred because each of these bundles contains more of one good and less of the other than e does. To be able to state with certainty whether Lisa prefers particular bundles in areas C or D to Bundle e, we have to know more about her tastes for pizza and burritos.

Preferences and Indifference Curves. Suppose we asked Lisa to identify all the bundles that give her the same amount of pleasure she gets from consuming Bundle e. In panel b of Figure 4.1, we use her answers to draw curve I^1 through all bundles she likes as much as she likes e. Curve I^1 is an **indifference curve**: the set of all bundles of goods that a consumer views as being equally desirable.

Indifference curve I^1 includes Bundles c, e, and a, so Lisa is indifferent about consuming Bundles c, e, and a. From this indifference curve, we also know that Lisa prefers e (25 pizzas and 15 burritos) to b (30 pizzas and 10 burritos). How do we know that? Bundle b lies below and to the left of Bundle a, so Bundle a is preferred to Bundle b by the more-is-better property. Both Bundle a and Bundle e are on indifference curve I^1, so Lisa likes Bundle e as much as Bundle a. Because Lisa is indifferent between e and a and she prefers a to b, she must prefer e to b by transitivity.

If we asked Lisa many, many questions, we could, in principle, draw an entire set of indifference curves through every possible bundle of burritos and pizzas. Lisa's preferences are summarized in an **indifference map** or *preference map*, which is a complete set of indifference curves that summarize a consumer's tastes. It is referred to as a *map* because it uses the same principle as a topographical or contour map, in which each line shows all points with the same height or elevation. With an indifference map, each line shows points (combinations of goods) with the same utility or well-being. Panel c of Figure 4.1 shows three of Lisa's indifference curves: I^1, I^2, and I^3. In this figure, the indifference curves are parallel, but they need not be.

We can demonstrate that all indifference curve maps must have the following four properties.

1. Bundles on indifference curves farther from the origin are preferred to those on indifference curves closer to the origin.
2. An indifference curve goes through every possible bundle.
3. Indifference curves cannot cross.
4. Indifference curves slope downward.

First, we show that bundles on indifference curves farther from the origin are preferred to those on indifference curves closer to the origin. By the more-is-better property, Lisa prefers Bundle f to Bundle e in panel c of Figure 4.1. She is indifferent among all the bundles on indifference curve I^3 and Bundle f, just as she is indifferent among all the bundles, such as Bundle c, on indifference curve I^2, and Bundle e. By the move-is-better property, she prefers Bundle f to Bundle e, which she likes as much as Bundle c, so she also prefers Bundle f to Bundle c. By this type of reasoning, she prefers all bundles on I^3 to all bundles on I^2.

Second, we show that an indifference curve goes through every possible bundle. This property is a consequence of the completeness assumption: The consumer can compare any bundle to another. Compared to a given bundle, some bundles are preferred to it, some are enjoyed equally, and some are inferior to it. Connecting the bundles that give the same well-being produces an indifference curve that includes the given bundle.

Third, we show that indifference curves cannot cross. If two indifference curves did cross, the bundle at the point of intersection would be on both indifference curves. But a given bundle cannot be on two indifference curves. Suppose that two indifference curves crossed at Bundle e as in panel a of Figure 4.2. Because Bundles e and a lie on the same indifference curve I^1, Lisa is indifferent between e and a. Similarly, she is indifferent between e and b because both are on I^2. By transitivity, if Lisa is indifferent between e and a and she is indifferent between e and b, she must be indifferent between a and b. But that's impossible! Bundle b is above and to the right of bundle a, which means it contains more of both goods. Thus, Lisa *must* prefer b to a by the more-is-better property. Because preferences are transitive and consumers prefer more to less, indifference curves cannot cross.

Finally, we show that indifference curves must be downward sloping. Suppose to the contrary that an indifference curve sloped upward, as in panel b of Figure 4.2. The consumer is indifferent between Bundles a and b because both lie on the same indifference curve, I. But the consumer must prefer b to a by the more-is-better property: Bundle a lies below and to the left of Bundle b. Because of this contradiction—the consumer cannot both be indifferent between a and b and strictly prefer b to a—indifference curves cannot be upward sloping. For example, if Lisa views pizza and burritos as goods, she cannot be indifferent between a bundle of one pizza and one burrito and another bundle with two of each.

FIGURE 4.2 Impossible Indifference Curves

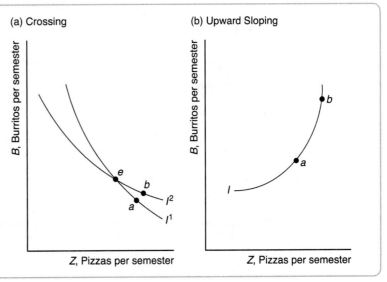

(a) Suppose that the indifference curves cross at Bundle e. Lisa is indifferent between e and a on indifference curve I^1 and between e and b on I^2. If Lisa is indifferent between e and a and she is indifferent between e and b, she must be indifferent between a and b by transitivity. But b has more of both pizzas and burritos than a, so she *must* prefer a to b. Because of this contradiction, indifference curves cannot cross. (b) Suppose that indifference curve I slopes upward. The consumer is indifferent between b and a because they lie on I but prefers b to a by the more-is-better assumption. Because of this contradiction, indifference curves cannot be upward sloping.

(a) Crossing

(b) Upward Sloping

B, Burritos per semester

Z, Pizzas per semester

Willingness to Substitute Between Goods. Lisa is willing to make some trade-offs between goods. The downward slope of her indifference curves shows that Lisa is willing to give up some burritos for more pizza or vice versa. She is indifferent between Bundles *a* and *b* on her indifference curve *I* in panel a of Figure 4.3. If she initially has Bundle *a* (eight burritos and three pizzas), she could get to Bundle *b* (five burritos and four pizzas) by trading three burritos for one more pizza. She is indifferent as to whether she makes this trade or not.

Lisa's willingness to trade one good for another is measured by her **marginal rate of substitution** (*MRS*). The *MRS* shows the rate at which a consumer can substitute one good for another while remaining on the same indifference curve. Graphically, the *MRS* is the slope of the indifference curve.[2] If pizza is on the horizontal axis, Lisa's marginal rate of substitution of burritos for pizza is

$$MRS = \frac{\Delta B}{\Delta Z}$$

where ΔB is the number of burritos Lisa will give up to get ΔZ more pizzas while staying on the same indifference curve. Roughly speaking, we can say that the *MRS* is the amount of one good a consumer will sacrifice to obtain one more unit of

FIGURE 4.3 Marginal Rate of Substitution

(a) At Bundle *a*, Lisa is willing to give up three burritos for one more pizza; at *b*, she is willing to give up only two burritos to obtain another pizza. That is, the relatively more burritos she has, the more she is willing to trade for another pizza. (b) An indifference curve of this shape is unlikely to be observed. Lisa would be willing to give up

more burritos to get one more pizza, the fewer the burritos she has. Moving from Bundle *c* to *b*, she will trade one pizza for three burritos, whereas moving from *b* to *a*, she will trade one pizza for two burritos, even though she now has relatively more burritos to pizzas.

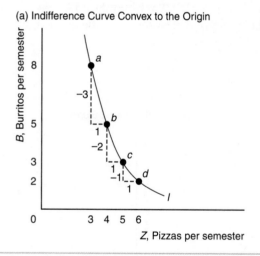

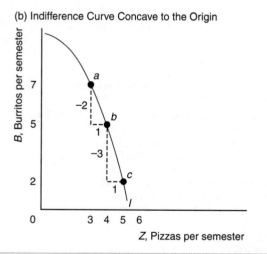

[2]The *slope* of a straight line is "the rise over the run": how much we move along the vertical axis (rise) as we move along the horizontal axis (run). The slope of an indifference curve at a point is the limit of the rise over the run as the change along the horizontal axis (the "run") gets very small. The slope of an indifference curve at a particular point is the same as the slope of a straight line that is tangent to the indifference curve at that point.

We are out of tickets for Swan Lake.
Do you want tickets for Wrestlemania?

another good while staying on the same indifference curve. If ΔZ is 1, then the associated value of ΔB is the *MRS*. Thus if Lisa is willing to give up 3 burritos ($\Delta B = -3$) to get 1 more pizza ($\Delta Z = 1$), then the *MRS* is $-\frac{3}{1} = -3$. We can illustrate why the *MRS* is negative by moving from Bundle a to Bundle b in panel a of Figure 4.3. The negative sign shows that Lisa is willing to give up some of one good to get more of the other: Her indifference curve slopes downward.

In specifying the *MRS*, we must be clear about which good is on the horizontal axis. Because pizza is on the horizontal axis in our figure, the *MRS* of "burritos for pizza" is -3, which is the slope of the indifference curve. If we were to switch axes so that burritos were on the horizontal axis, we could calculate the *MRS* of "pizza for burritos," which measures how much pizza Lisa would give up to get one more burrito while staying on the same indifference curve. In this case, the *MRS* of pizza

for burritos would be $\Delta Z / \Delta B$, which is $-\frac{1}{3}$. From Lisa's point of view, one pizza is worth 3 burritos (the *MRS* of burritos for pizza is -3) or, equivalently, 1 burrito is worth about $\frac{1}{3}$ of a pizza (the *MRS* of pizza for burritos is $-\frac{1}{3}$).

Curvature of Indifference Curves. The indifference curves we have used so far, such as I in panel a of Figure 4.3, are *convex* to the origin of the graph: That is, the indifference curves are "bowed in" toward the origin.

Because the indifference curve in panel a is convex, when Lisa has a large amount of burritos, B, she is willing to give up more of that good to get one more pizza, Z, than she would if she had only a small number of burritos. Starting at point a in panel a of Figure 4.3, Lisa is willing to give up three burritos to obtain one more pizza. At b, she is willing to trade only two burritos for a pizza. At c, she is even less willing to trade; she will give up only one burrito for another pizza. This willingness to trade fewer burritos for one more pizza as we move down and to the right along the indifference curve reflects a *diminishing marginal rate of substitution*.

An indifference curve doesn't have to be convex, but casual observation suggests that most people's indifference curves over most pairs of products are convex. It is unlikely, for example, that Lisa's indifference curves would be *concave*, as in panel b of Figure 4.3. If her indifference curve were concave, Lisa would be willing to give up more burritos to get one more pizza when she has fewer burritos. In panel b, she trades one pizza for three burritos moving from Bundle c to b, and she trades one pizza for only two burritos moving from b to a, even though her ratio of burritos to pizza is greater.

Two extreme types of indifference curves are plausible: straight-line indifference curves and right-angle indifference curves. Straight-line indifference curves reflect **perfect substitutes**, which are goods that are essentially equivalent from the consumer's point of view. The consumer is completely indifferent between the two goods. For example, if Bill cannot taste any difference between Coca-Cola and Pepsi-Cola, he views them as perfect substitutes: He is indifferent between one

FIGURE 4.4 Perfect Substitutes, Perfect Complements, Imperfect Substitutes

(a) Bill views Coke and Pepsi as perfect substitutes. His indifference curves are straight, parallel lines with a marginal rate of substitution (slope) of −1. Bill is willing to exchange one can of Coke for one can of Pepsi. (b) Cathy likes pie à la mode but does not like pie or ice cream by itself: She views ice cream and pie as perfect complements. She will not substitute between the two; she consumes them only in equal quantities. (c) Lisa views burritos and pizza as imperfect substitutes. Her indifference curve lies between the extreme cases of perfect substitutes and perfect complements.

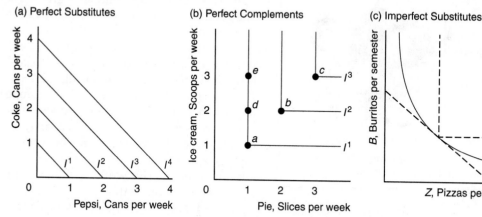
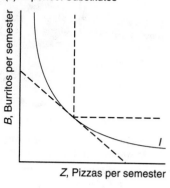

additional can of Coke and one additional can of Pepsi. His indifference curves for these two goods are straight, parallel lines with a slope of −1 everywhere along the curve, as in panel a of Figure 4.4. Thus, Bill's marginal rate of substitution is −1 at every point along these indifference curves.

The slope of indifference curves of perfect substitutes need not always be −1; it can be any constant rate. For example, Helen knows from reading the labels that Clorox bleach is twice as strong as a generic brand, but otherwise no different. As a result, she is indifferent between one cup of Clorox and two cups of the generic bleach. If the generic bleach is on the vertical axis, the slope of her indifference curve is −2.[3]

The other extreme case is **perfect complements**: goods that an individual wants to consume only in fixed proportions. Cathy doesn't like pie by itself or vanilla ice cream by itself, but she loves pie à la mode (a slice of pie with a scoop of vanilla ice cream on top). Her indifference curves have right angles in panel b of Figure 4.4. Bundle a consists of one piece of pie and one scoop of ice cream, combining to make one serving of pie à la mode. If she gets an additional scoop of ice cream but no pie to go with it (Bundle d) she remains on the same indifference curve: the extra scoop of ice cream by itself provides no additional benefit to Cathy. Adding a third scoop of ice cream (shown as Bundle e) is also a matter of indifference to Cathy. She gets no extra benefit and remains on the same indifference curve. Similarly, if Cathy has only one scoop of ice cream, additional pieces of pie beyond the first leave her on the same indifference curve.

With preferences like this, Cathy consumes only bundles like a, b, and c, in which pie and ice cream are in equal proportions. She would never want to pay for any additional ice cream that was not matched by a piece of pie, and she would never

---

[3]Sometimes it is difficult to guess which goods are close substitutes. According to Harper's Index 1994, flowers, perfume, and fire extinguishers rank 1, 2, and 3 among "appropriate" Mother's Day gifts. Few would guess that perfume and fire extinguishers are substitutes.

want to pay for a piece of pie without a scoop of ice cream to go with it. She will only consume ice cream and pie in equal proportions.

With a bundle like a, b, or c, she will not substitute a piece of pie for an extra scoop of ice cream. For example, if she were at b, she would be unwilling to give up an extra slice of pie to get, say, two extra scoops of ice cream, as at point e. Indeed, she wouldn't give up the slice of pie even for a virtually unlimited amount of extra ice cream because the extra ice cream is worthless to her.

The standard-shaped, convex indifference curve in panel c of Figure 4.4 lies between these two extreme examples. Convex indifference curves show that a consumer views two goods as imperfect substitutes.

4.2 Utility

Underlying our model of consumer behavior is the belief that consumers can compare various bundles of goods and decide which gives them the greatest pleasure or satisfaction. It is possible to summarize a consumer's preferences by assigning a numerical value to each possible bundle to reflect the consumer's relative ranking of these bundles.

Following Jeremy Bentham, John Stuart Mill, and other nineteenth-century British economist-philosophers, economists apply the term **utility** to this set of numerical values that reflect the relative rankings of various bundles of goods. The statement that "Lorna prefers Bundle x to Bundle y" is equivalent to the statement that "consuming Bundle x gives Lorna more utility than consuming Bundle y." For example, Lorna prefers x to y if Bundle x gives Lorna a utility level of 10 and Bundle y gives her a utility level of 8.

Utility Functions

If we knew the **utility function**—the relationship between utility measures and every possible bundle of goods—we could summarize the information in indifference maps succinctly. Lisa's utility function, $U(B, Z)$, tells us how much utility she gets from B burritos and Z pizzas. Given that her utility function reflects her preferences, if Lisa prefers Bundle 1, (B_1, Z_1), to Bundle 2, (B_2, Z_2), then the utility she gets from the first bundle exceeds that from the second bundle: $U(B_1, Z_1) > U(B_2, Z_2)$.

For example, suppose that the utility, U, that Lisa gets from burritos and pizzas is

$$U = \sqrt{BZ}.$$

From this function, we know that the more she consumes of either good, the greater the utility she receives. Using this function, we can determine whether Lisa would be happier if she had Bundle x with 9 burritos and 16 pizzas or Bundle y with 13 of each. The utility she gets from x is $12 (= \sqrt{9 \times 16})$. The utility she gets from y is $13 (= \sqrt{13 \times 13})$. Therefore, she prefers y to x.

The utility function is a concept that economists use to help them think about consumer behavior; utility functions do not exist in any fundamental sense. If you asked your mother what her utility function is, she would be puzzled—unless, of course, she is an economist. But if you asked her enough questions about choices of bundles of goods, you could construct a function that accurately summarizes her preferences. For example, by questioning people, Rousseas and Hart (1951) constructed indifference curves between eggs and bacon, and MacCrimmon and Toda

(1969) constructed indifference curves between French pastries and money (which can be used to buy all other goods).

Typically, consumers can easily answer questions about whether they prefer one bundle to another, such as "Do you prefer a bundle with one scoop of ice cream and two pieces of cake to another bundle with two scoops of ice cream and one piece of cake?" But they have difficulty answering questions about how much more they prefer one bundle to another because they don't have a measure to describe how their pleasure from two goods or bundles differs. Therefore, we may know a consumer's rank-ordering of bundles even if we do not have a good idea of how much that consumer prefers one bundle to another.

Ordinal and Cardinal Utility

The term *ordinal* is used to describe a measure that contains information only about rankings or orderings. For example, a movie critic might give a movie between one and four stars. However, a 4-star movie is not necessarily "twice as good" as a 2-star movie or four times as good as a 1-star movie. All we can say is that the critic likes the 4-star movie better than the 2-star movie, which in turn is preferred to the 1-star movie: We really know only the critic's relative rankings. Thus, movie rankings are an ordinal measure, even though numbers (the number of stars) might be used to represent the rankings. With utility, if we know only a consumer's relative rankings of bundles, our measure of utility is *ordinal*.

A *cardinal* measure is based on absolute numerical comparisons, as with length or weight. Cardinal measures contain more information than ordinal measures. For example, money is a cardinal measure. If Sofia has $100 and Hu has $50, we know not only that Sofia has more money than Hu (an ordinal comparison), but that she has precisely twice as much as Hu (a cardinal comparison). Economists sometimes treat utility as a cardinal measure, allowing for statements like "Bundle *A* is twice as good as Bundle *B*," instead of just saying that Bundle *A* is preferred to Bundle *B*.

Most of our discussion of consumer choice in this chapter holds if utility has only ordinal properties. If utility is an ordinal measure, we should not put any weight on the absolute difference between the utility associated with one bundle and another. We care only about the relative utility or ranking of the two bundles.

Marginal Utility

Using Lisa's utility function over burritos and pizza, we can show how her utility changes if she gets to consume more of one of the goods. Suppose that Lisa has the utility function in Figure 4.5. The curve in panel a shows how Lisa's utility rises as she consumes more pizzas while we hold her consumption of burritos fixed at 10. Because pizza is a *good*, Lisa's utility rises as she consumes more pizza.

If her consumption of pizzas increases from $Z = 4$ to 5, $\Delta Z = 5 - 4 = 1$, and her utility increases from $U = 230$ to 250, $\Delta U = 250 - 230 = 20$. The extra utility ($\Delta U$) that she gets from consuming one more unit of a good ($\Delta Z = 1$) is the **marginal utility** from that good. Thus, marginal utility is the slope of the utility function as we hold the quantity of the other good constant.

$$MU_Z = \frac{\Delta U}{\Delta Z}.$$

FIGURE 4.5 Utility and Marginal Utility

As Lisa consumes more pizza, holding her consumption of burritos constant at 10, her total utility, U, increases and her marginal utility of pizza, MU_Z, decreases (though it remains positive). (a) If she increases her consumption of pizza from 4 to 5 per semester while holding her consumption of burritos fixed at 10, her utility increases from 230 to 250. Her marginal utility is the extra utility she gets, $\Delta U = 250 - 230 = 20$ from an extra pizza, $\Delta Z = 1$, which is $MU_Z = \Delta U / \Delta Z = 20/1 = 20$. (b) At $Z = 5$, the height of Lisa's marginal utility curve is 20.

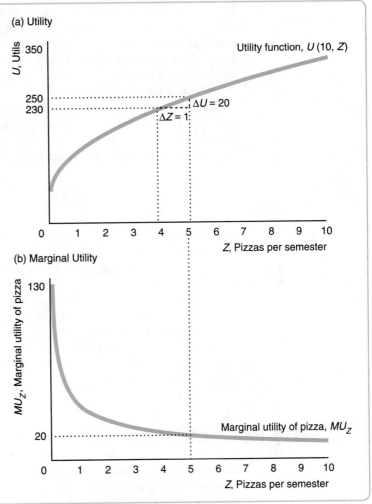

(a) Utility

(b) Marginal Utility

Lisa's marginal utility from increasing her consumption of pizza from 4 to 5 is

$$MU_Z = \frac{\Delta U}{\Delta Z} = \frac{20}{1} = 20.$$

Panel b in Figure 4.5 shows that Lisa's marginal utility from consuming one more pizza varies with the number of pizzas she consumes, holding her consumption of burritos constant. Her marginal utility of pizza curve falls as her consumption of pizza increases, but the marginal utility remains positive: Each extra pizza gives Lisa pleasure, but it gives her less pleasure relative to other goods than did the previous pizza.

Using Calculus

Marginal Utility

The marginal utility from a particular good is the partial derivative of the utility function with respect to that good, which measures how utility changes as we change one good while holding consumption of other goods constant. Thus, if Lisa's utility function is $U(B, Z)$, her marginal utility from Z is the partial derivative of U with respect to Z: $MU_Z = \partial U(B, Z)/\partial Z$.

Marginal Rates of Substitution

Earlier we learned that the marginal rate of substitution (*MRS*) is the slope of the indifference curve. The marginal rate of substitution can also be expressed using marginal utilities. If Lisa has 10 burritos and 4 pizzas in a semester and gets one more pizza, her utility rises. That extra utility is the marginal utility from the last pizza, MU_Z. Similarly, if she receives one extra burrito instead, her marginal utility from the last burrito is MU_B.

Suppose that Lisa trades from one bundle on an indifference curve to another by giving up some burritos to gain more pizza. She gains marginal utility from the extra pizza but loses marginal utility from fewer burritos. We can show that the marginal rate of substitution can be written in terms of the marginal utilities:

$$MRS = \frac{\Delta B}{\Delta Z} = -\frac{MU_Z}{MU_B}. \tag{4.1}$$

Equation 4.1 tells us that the *MRS*, which is the slope of the indifference curve at a particular bundle, depends on the negative of the ratio of the marginal utility of pizza to the marginal utility of burritos. (We derive Equation 4.1 using calculus in Appendix 4A.)

An example illustrates the logic underlying Equation 4.1. Suppose that Lisa gains one unit of utility (one *util*) if she eats one more burrito, $MU_B = 1$, and two utils if she has one more pizza, $MU_Z = 2$. That is, one more pizza gives her as much extra pleasure as two burritos. Thus, her utility stays the same—she stays on the same indifference curve—if she exchanges two burritos for one pizza, so her $MRS = -MU_Z/MU_B = -2$.

4.3 The Budget Constraint

Knowing an individual's preferences is only the first step in analyzing that person's consumption behavior. Consumers maximize their well-being subject to constraints. The most important constraint most of us face in deciding what to consume is our personal budget constraint.

If we cannot save and borrow, our budget is the income we receive in a given period. If we can save and borrow, we can save money early in life to consume later, such as when we retire, or we can borrow money when we are young and repay those sums later in life. Savings are, in effect, a good that consumers can buy. For simplicity, we assume that each consumer has a fixed amount of money to spend now, so we can use the terms *budget* and *income* interchangeably.

For graphical simplicity, we assume that consumers spend their money on only two goods. If Lisa spends all her budget, *Y*, on pizza and burritos, then her budget constraint is

$$p_B B + p_Z Z = Y, \tag{4.2}$$

where $p_B B$ is the amount she spends on burritos and $p_Z Z$ is the amount she spends on pizzas. Equation 4.2 shows that her expenditures on burritos and pizza use up her entire budget.

How many burritos can Lisa buy? Subtracting $p_Z Z$ from both sides of Equation 4.2 and dividing both sides by p_B, we determine the number of burritos she can purchase to be

$$B = \frac{Y}{p_B} - \frac{p_Z}{p_B}Z. \tag{4.3}$$

According to Equation 4.3, Lisa can afford to buy more burritos only if

▶ her income (Y) increases,

▶ the price of burritos (p_B) or pizza (p_Z) falls, or

▶ she purchases fewer pizzas (Z).

For example, if Lisa has one more dollar of income (Y), she can buy $1/p_B$ more burritos.

If $p_Z = \$1$, $p_B = \$2$, and $Y = \$50$, Equation 4.3 is

$$B = \frac{\$50}{\$2} - \frac{\$1}{\$2}Z = 25 - \tfrac{1}{2}Z. \tag{4.4}$$

As Equation 4.4 shows, every two pizzas cost Lisa one burrito. How many burritos can she buy if she spends all her money on burritos? She can buy 25 burritos: By setting $Z = 0$ in Equation 4.3, we find that $B = Y/p_B = \$50/\$2 = 25$. Similarly, if she spends all her money on pizza, she can buy 50 of them: Setting $B = 0$, we can solve for $Z = Y/p_Z = \$50/\$1 = 50$.

Instead of spending all her money on pizza or all on burritos, she can buy some of each. Table 4.1 shows four possible bundles she could buy. For example, she can buy 20 burritos and 10 pizzas with $50.

Equation 4.4 is plotted in Figure 4.6. This line is called a **budget line** or *budget constraint*: the bundles of goods that can be bought if the entire budget is spent on those goods at given prices. This budget line shows the combinations of burritos and pizzas that Lisa can buy if she spends all of her $50 on these two goods. The four bundles in Table 4.1 are labeled on this line.

Lisa could, of course, buy any bundle that cost less than $50. The **opportunity set** is all the bundles a consumer can buy, including all the bundles inside the budget constraint and on the budget constraint (all those bundles of positive Z and B such that $p_B B + p_Z Z \leq Y$). Lisa's opportunity set is the shaded area in Figure 4.6. She could buy 10 burritos and 15 pieces of pizza for $35, which falls inside the constraint. Unless she wants to spend the other $15 on some other good, though, she might as

TABLE 4.1 Allocations of a $50 Budget Between Burritos and Pizza

Bundle	Burritos, $2 each	Pizza, $1 each
a	25	0
b	20	10
c	10	30
d	0	50

FIGURE 4.6 Budget Line

If $Y = \$50$, $p_Z = \$1$, and $p_B = \$2$, Lisa can buy any bundle in the opportunity set, the shaded area, including points on the *budget line*, L^1, $B = Y/p_B - (p_Z/p_B)Z = \$50/\$2 - (\$1/\$2)Z$. If Lisa buys one more unit of Z, she must reduce her consumption of B by $-(p_Z/p_B) = -\frac{1}{2}$ to stay within her budget. Thus, the slope, $\Delta B/\Delta Z$, of her budget line, which is also called the marginal rate of transformation (*MRT*), is $-(p_Z/p_B) = -\frac{1}{2}$.

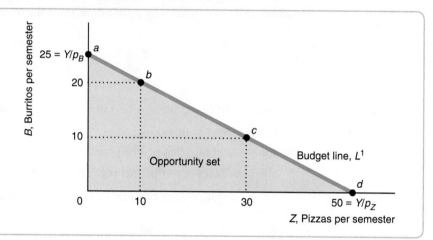

well spend all of it on the food she loves and pick a bundle on the budget constraint rather than inside it.[4]

Slope of the Budget Line

The slope of the budget line is determined by the relative prices of the two goods. According to the budget line, Equation 4.3, $B = Y/p_B - (p_Z/p_B)Z$, so every extra unit of Z that Lisa purchases reduces B by $-p_Z/p_B$. That is, the slope of the budget line is $\Delta B/\Delta Z = -p_Z/p_B$. Thus, the slope of the budget line depends on only the relative prices.

Lisa faces prices of $p_Z = \$1$ and $p_B = \$2$, so the slope of her budget line is $-p_Z/p_B = -\$1/\$2 = -\frac{1}{2}$. For example, if we reduce the number of pizzas from 10 at point b in Figure 4.6 to 0 at point a, the number of burritos that Lisa can buy rises from 20 at point b to 25 at point a, so $\Delta B/\Delta Z = (25 - 20)/(0 - 10) = 5/(-10) = -\frac{1}{2}$.

The slope of the budget line is called the **marginal rate of transformation** (*MRT*): the trade-off the market imposes on the consumer in terms of the amount of one good the consumer must give up to purchase more of the other good:

$$MRT = \frac{\Delta B}{\Delta Z} = -\frac{p_Z}{p_B}. \tag{4.5}$$

Because Lisa's $MRT = -\frac{1}{2}$, she can "trade" an extra pizza for half a burrito or, equivalently, she has to give up two pizzas to obtain an extra burrito.

---

[4]The budget line in Figure 4.6 is a smooth, continuous line, which implies that Lisa can buy fractional numbers of burritos and pizzas. Is that true? Will a restaurant sell you a half of a burrito? Maybe not. Why then don't we draw the budget line and opportunity set as discrete points (bundles) of whole numbers of burritos and pizzas instead of a continuous line? One reason is that Lisa can buy a burrito at a *rate* of one-half per time period. If Lisa buys one burrito every other week, she buys an average of one-half burrito every week. Thus, it is plausible that she could purchase fractional amounts over a particular time period.

Using Calculus

The Marginal Rate of Transformation

By differentiating the budget constraint, Equation 4.3, $B = Y/p_B - (p_Z/p_B)Z$, with respect to Z, we confirm that the slope of the budget constraint, or marginal rate of transformation, is $MRT = dB/dZ = -p_Z/p_B$, as in Equation 4.5.

Effects of a Change in Price on the Opportunity Set

If the price of pizza doubles but the price of burritos remains unchanged, the budget line swings in toward the origin in panel a of Figure 4.7. If Lisa spends all her money on burritos, she can buy as many burritos as before, so the budget line still hits the burrito axis at 25. If she spends all her money on pizza, however, she can now buy only half as many pizzas as before, so the budget line intercepts the pizza axis at 25 instead of at 50.

The new budget line is steeper and lies inside the original one. As the price of pizza increases, the slope of the budget line, MRT, changes. The original line, L^1, at the original prices, $MRT = -\frac{1}{2}$, shows that Lisa could trade half a burrito for one pizza or two pizzas for one burrito. The new line, L^2, $MRT = p_Z/p_B = -\$2/\$2 = -1$, indicates that she can now trade one burrito for one pizza, due to the increase in the price of pizza.

Unless Lisa only wants to eat burritos, she is unambiguously worse off due to this increase in the price of pizza because she can no longer afford the combinations of pizza and burritos in the shaded "Loss" area.

A decrease in the price of pizza would have the opposite effect: The budget line would rotate outward, pivoting around the intercept on the burrito axis. As a result, Lisa's opportunity set would increase.

FIGURE 4.7 Changes in the Budget Line

(a) If the price of pizza increases from $1 to $2 a slice, Lisa's budget line rotates from L^1 to L^2 around the intercept on the burrito axis. The slope or MRT of the original budget line, L^1, is $-\frac{1}{2}$, while the MRT of the new budget line L^2 is -1. The shaded area shows the combinations of pizza and burritos that Lisa can no longer afford. (b) If Lisa's budget doubles from $50 to $100 and prices don't change, her new budget line moves from L^1 to L^3. This shift is parallel: Both budget lines have the same slope or MRT of $-\frac{1}{2}$. The new opportunity set is larger by the shaded area.

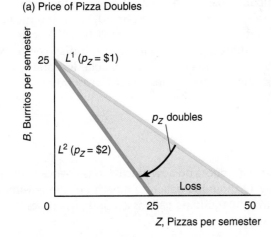

(a) Price of Pizza Doubles

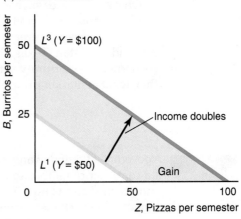

(b) Income Doubles

Effects of a Change in Income on the Opportunity Set

If the consumer's income increases, the consumer can buy more of all goods. Suppose that Lisa's income increases by $50 per semester to $Y = \$100$. Her budget line shifts outward—away from the origin—and is parallel to the original constraint in panel b of Figure 4.7. Why is the new constraint parallel to the original one? The intercept of the budget line on the burrito axis is Y/p_B, and the intercept on the pizza axis is Y/p_Z. Thus, holding prices constant, the intercepts shift outward in proportion to the change in income. Originally, if she spent all her money on pizza, Lisa could buy $50 = \$50/\$1$ pizzas; now she can buy $100 = \$100/\$1$. Similarly, the burrito axis intercept goes from $25 = \$50/\$2$ to $50 = \$100/\$2$. Initially, if she consumed 25 burritos, Lisa could not consume any pizza; now if she consumes 25 burritos she can also consume 50 pizzas.

A change in income affects only the position and not the slope of the budget line, because the slope is determined solely by the relative prices of pizza and burritos. A decrease in the prices of both pizzas and burritos in the same proportion has the same effect as an increase in income, as the next Q&A shows.

Q&A 4.1

Is Lisa better off if her income doubles or if the prices of both the goods she buys fall by half?

Answer *Show that Lisa's budget line and her opportunity set are the same with either change.* As panel b of Figure 4.7 shows, if her income doubles, her budget line has a parallel shift outward. The new intercepts at $50 = 2Y/p_B = (2 \times 50)/2$ on the burrito axis and $100 = 2Y/p_Z = (2 \times 50)/1$ on the pizza axis are double the original values. If the prices fall by half, her budget line is the same as if her income doubles. The intercept on the burrito axis is $50 = Y/(p_B/2) = 50/(2/2)$, and the intercept on the pizza axis is $100 = Y/(p_Z/2) = 50/(1/2)$. Therefore, Lisa is equally well off if her income doubles *or* if prices fall by half.

Mini-Case

Rationing

During emergencies, governments frequently ration food, gas, and other staples rather than let their prices rise, as the United States and the United Kingdom did during World War II. Cuban citizens receive a ration book that limits their purchases of staples such as rice, legumes, potatoes, bread, eggs, and meat.

Water rationing is common during droughts. During 2010–2013, water quotas were imposed in areas of California, Egypt, Honduras, India, Kenya, New Zealand, Pakistan, Texas, the U.S. Midwest, and Venezuela. Rationing affects consumers' opportunity sets because they cannot necessarily buy as much as they want at market prices.

Q&A 4.2

A government rations water, setting a quota on how much a consumer can purchase. If a consumer can afford to buy 12 thousand gallons a month but the government restricts purchases to no more than 10 thousand gallons a month, how does the consumer's opportunity set change?

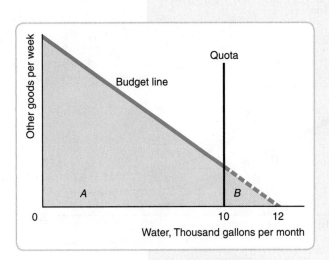

Answer

1. *Draw the original opportunity set using a budget line between water and all other goods.* In the graph, the consumer can afford to buy up to 12 thousand gallons of water a week if not constrained. The opportunity set, areas A and B, is bounded by the axes and the budget line.

2. *Add a line to the figure showing the quota, and determine the new opportunity set:* A vertical line at 10 thousand on the water axis indicates the quota.

    The new opportunity set, area A, is bounded by the axes, the budget line, and the quota line.

3. *Compare the two opportunity sets:* Because of the rationing, the consumer loses part of the original opportunity set: the triangle B to the right of the 10 thousand gallons line. The consumer has fewer opportunities because of rationing.

4.4 Constrained Consumer Choice

My problem lies in reconciling my gross habits with my net income. —Errol Flynn

Were it not for the budget constraint, consumers who prefer more to less would consume unlimited amounts of all goods. Well, they can't have it all! Instead, consumers maximize their well-being subject to their budget constraints. Now, we have to determine the bundle of goods that maximizes well-being subject to the budget constraint.

The Consumer's Optimal Bundle

Given information about Lisa's preferences (as summarized by her indifference curves) and how much she can spend (as summarized by her budget line), we can determine Lisa's optimal bundle. Her optimal bundle is the bundle out of all the bundles that she can afford that gives her the most pleasure. Here, we use graphical techniques to find her optimal bundle.

We first show that Lisa's optimal bundle must be on the budget line in Figure 4.8. Bundles that lie on indifference curves above the constraint, such as those on I^3, are not in her opportunity set. Although Lisa prefers Bundle f on indifference curve I^3 to e on I^2, she cannot afford to purchase f. Even though Lisa could buy a bundle inside the budget line, she does not want to do so, because more is better than less: For any bundle inside the constraint (such as d on I^1), another bundle on the constraint has more of at least one of the two goods, and hence she prefers that bundle. Therefore, the optimal bundle must lie on the budget line.

We can also show that bundles that lie on indifference curves that cross the budget line (such as I^1, which crosses the constraint at a and c) are less desirable than certain other bundles on the constraint. Only some of the bundles on indifference curve I^1

FIGURE 4.8 Consumer Maximization, Interior Solution

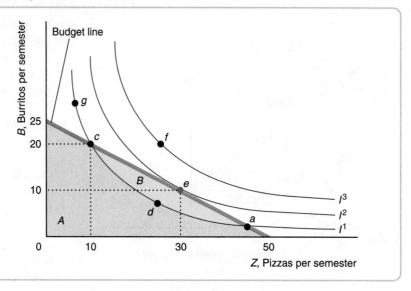

Lisa's optimal bundle is *e* (10 burritos and 30 pizzas) on indifference curve *I²*. Indifference curve *I²* is tangent to her budget line at *e*. Bundle *e* is the bundle on the highest indifference curve (highest utility) that she can afford. Any bundle that is preferred to *e* (such as points on indifference curve *I³*) lies outside of the opportunity set so she cannot afford them. Bundles inside the opportunity set, such as *d*, are less desirable than *e* because they represent less of one or both goods.

lie within the opportunity set: Bundles *a* and *c* and all the points on *I¹* between them, such as *d*, can be purchased. Because *I¹* crosses the budget line, the bundles between *a* and *c* on *I¹* lie strictly inside the constraint, so bundles in the opportunity set (area *A* + *B*) are preferable to these bundles on *I¹* and are affordable. By the more-is-better property, Lisa prefers *e* to *d* because *e* has more of both pizza and burritos than *d*. By transitivity, *e* is preferred to *a*, *c*, and all the other points on *I¹*—even those, like *g*, that Lisa can't afford. Because indifference curve *I¹* crosses the budget line, area *B* contains at least one bundle that is preferred to—lies above and to the right of—at least one bundle on the indifference curve.

Thus, the optimal bundle—the *consumer's optimum*—must lie on the budget line and be on an indifference curve that does not cross it. If Lisa is consuming this bundle, she has no incentive to change her behavior by substituting one good for another.

So far, we've shown that the optimal bundle must lie on an indifference curve that touches the budget line but does not cross it. This condition can hold in two ways. The first is an *interior solution*, in which the optimal bundle has positive quantities of both goods and lies between the ends of the budget line. The other possibility, called a *corner solution*, occurs when the optimal bundle is at one end of the budget line, where the budget line forms a corner with one of the axes.

Interior Solutions. In Figure 4.8, Bundle *e* on indifference curve *I²* is the optimum bundle. It is in the interior of the budget line away from the corners. Lisa prefers consuming a balanced diet, *e*, of 10 burritos and 30 pizzas, to eating only one type of food or the other.

For the indifference curve *I²* to touch the budget line but not cross it, it must be *tangent* to the budget line at point *e*. At the point of tangency, the budget line and the indifference curve have the same slope at the point *e* where they touch. The slope of the indifference curve, the marginal rate of substitution, measures the rate at which Lisa is *willing* to trade burritos for pizza: $MRS = -MU_Z/MU_B$, Equation 4.1. The slope of the budget line, the marginal rate of transformation, measures the rate at which Lisa *can* trade her money for burritos or pizza in the market: $MRT = -p_Z/p_B$, Equation 4.5. Thus, Lisa's utility is maximized at the bundle where the rate at which she is willing to trade burritos for pizza equals the rate at which she can trade:

$$MRS = -\frac{MU_Z}{MU_B} = -\frac{p_Z}{p_B} = MRT. \qquad (4.6)$$

(Appendix 4B uses calculus to derive Equation 4.6.)

Rearranging terms, this condition is equivalent to

$$\frac{MU_Z}{p_Z} = \frac{MU_B}{p_B}. \qquad (4.7)$$

Equation 4.7 says that the marginal utility of pizza divided by the price of a pizza (the amount of extra utility from pizza per dollar spent on pizza), MU_Z/p_Z, equals the marginal utility of burritos divided by the price of a burrito, MU_B/p_B. Thus, Lisa's utility is maximized if the last dollar she spends on pizza gets her as much extra utility as the last dollar she spends on burritos. If the last dollar spent on pizza gave Lisa more extra utility than the last dollar spent on burritos, Lisa could increase her happiness by spending more on pizza and less on burritos. Her cousin Spenser is a different story.

Q&A 4.3

Nate's utility function over raspberry jelly, J, and peanut butter, N, is $U = JN$. Nate's marginal utility from jelly is $MU_J = N$, and his marginal utility from peanut butter is $MU_N = J$.[5] The raspberry jelly Nate buys is $5 per jar and peanut butter is $10 per jar. Nate has a budget of $100 to allocate to these two items. If Nate maximizes his utility, how much of each good will he consume?

Answer

1. *Derive Nate's budget line by setting his expenditure equal to his available budget.* The expenditure on each item is its price times the amount consumed, so Nate's budget, 100, equals the sum of the expenditures on these items two goods: $100 = 5J + 10N$.

2. *Use Equation 4.7 to find the relationship between N and J.* Equation 4.7 states that Nate maximizes his utility if he equalizes his marginal utility per dollar across jelly and peanut butter: $MU_J/5 = MU_N/10$. That is, $N/5 = J/10$ or $N = J/2$.

3. *Substitute this utility-maximizing condition into the budget equation to determine J and N.* Substituting this optimality condition into the budget constraint, we learn that $100 = 5J + 10N = 5J + 10(J/2) = 10J$. Solving this expression for J, we find that $J = 10$.

4. *Substitute the solution for J into the budget line to solve for N.* Substituting $J = 10$ into the budget constraint, we learn that $100 = 5J + 10N = 50 + 10N$, or $50 = 10N$, or $N = 5$. Thus, Nate's utility-maximizing bundle is $J = 10$ and $N = 5$.

---

[5]The marginal utility with respect to J, MU_J, is $\partial U/\partial J = \partial(JN)/\partial J = N$. Similarly, $MU_N = \partial(JN)/\partial N = J$.

FIGURE 4.9 Consumer Maximization, Corner Solution

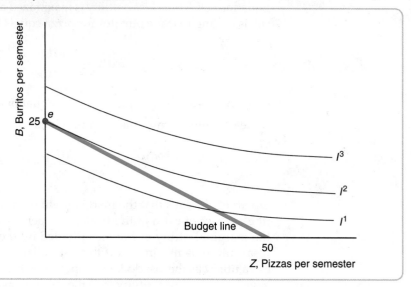

Spenser's indifference curves are flatter than Lisa's indifference curves in Figure 4.8. That is, he is willing to give up more pizzas for one more burrito than is Lisa. Spenser's optimal bundle occurs at a corner of the opportunity set at Bundle e: 25 burritos and 0 pizzas.

Corner Solutions. Some consumers choose to buy only one of the two goods: a corner solution. They so prefer one good to another that they only purchase the preferred good.

Spenser's indifference curves in Figure 4.9 are flatter than Lisa's in Figure 4.8. That is, he is willing to trade more pizza for an extra burrito than is Lisa. Spenser's optimal Bundle e, where he buys 25 burritos and no pizza, lies on an indifference curve that touches the budget line only once, at the upper-left corner. It is on the highest indifference curve that touches the budget line.

Mini-Case	Are you reading this book electronically? E-books are appearing everywhere in the English-speaking world. Thanks to the popularity of the Kindle, iPad, and other e-book readers, in 2012, e-books accounted for 25% of trade books (and 33% of fiction books) sold in the United States and 13% in the United Kingdom. E-books sold well in Australia and Canada as well. In contrast, in Germany, only about 1% of books sold are e-books.

Why Americans Buy More E-Books Than Do Germans

Why are e-books more successful in the United States than in Germany? Jürgen Harth of the German Publishers and Booksellers Association attributed the difference to tastes or what he called a "cultural issue." More than others, Germans love printed books—after all, the modern printing press was invented in Germany. As Harth said, "On just about every corner there's a bookshop. That's the big difference between Germany and the United States."

An alternative explanation concerns government regulations and taxes that affect prices in Germany. Even if Germans and Americans have the same tastes, Americans are more likely to buy e-books because they are less expensive than printed books in the United States but e-books are more expensive than printed books in Germany.

Unlike in the United States, where publishers and booksellers can choose what prices to set, Germany regulates book prices. To protect small booksellers, its fixed-price system requires all booksellers to charge the same price, for new printed books. In addition, although e-books can sell for slightly lower prices, they are subject to a 19% tax rather than to the 7% tax that applies to printed books.[6]

Q&A 4.4

Must we appeal to differences in tastes to explain why Germans and Americans read different types of books, or can taxes and price differences explain this difference? Suppose that Max, a German, and Bob, an American, are avid readers with identical incomes and tastes. Both are indifferent between reading a novel in a traditional book or using an e-reader. Therefore, traditional books and e-books are perfect substitutes and the indifference curves for both Max and Bob have a slope of −1. Assume that the pretax price of e-books is less than for printed books in both Germany and the United States, but that the after-tax price of e-books is higher than for printed books in Germany only. Use an indifference-curve/budget-line analysis to explain why Max would be less inclined to buy e-books than Bob.

Answer

1. *Describe their indifference curves.* Both Max and Bob view e-books and printed books as substitutes, and both have an indifference curve for buying books that is a straight line with a slope of −1, as the figure shows.

2. *Describe the slopes of their budget line.* With printed books on the vertical axis, Max faces a budget line, L^M, that is relatively steep—steeper than his indifference curve—because the German taxes make e-books relatively expensive. Bob has a budget line that is flatter than his indifference curve.

3. *Use an indifference curve and a budget line to show why Max and Bob make different choices.* As the figure shows, Bob maximizes his utility by spending his entire book budget on e-books. He chooses the Bundle e_B, where his indifference curve I hits his budget line L^B on the e-book axis. In contrast, Max spends his entire book budget on printed books, at point e_M.

If Bob and Max viewed the two types of books as imperfect substitutes and had the usual convex indifference curves, they would each buy a mix of e-books and printed books. However, because of the relatively lower price of e-books in the United States, Bob would buy relatively more e-books.

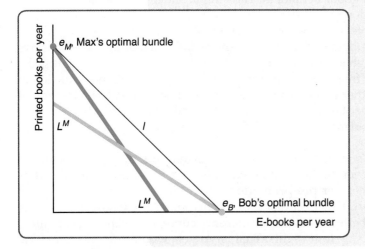

Promotions

Managers often use promotions to induce consumers to purchase more units. Two of the most frequently used promotions are *buy one, get one free* (BOGOF) and *buy one, get the second one at half price*. Such deals create kinks in the consumer's budget line. Consequently, whether a consumer responds to such offers depends on their tastes (the shape of their indifference curves).

Buy One, Get One Free Promotion. In a BOGOF promotion, a customer gets a free unit of the product after buying one unit (or some other number of units) at the regular price. For example, a supermarket might offer a fifth fruit drink for

free if the customer buys four at the regular price. Promotions of this type are often used for items like CDs, restaurant meals, movie tickets, and other relatively inexpensive consumer products. A 2013 search of Google for "buy one get one free" found 10.8 million websites. Remarkably, even a realty company, Michael Crews Development, has tried to sell homes using a BOGOF promotion, providing a second $400,000 house to the buyer of a first house at $1.6 million or more.

In 2013, the Four Seasons Resort in the Seychelles Islands offered one free night at its five-star hotel to customers who pay for three nights at the normal rate. The effect of such promotions on purchasing behavior can be illustrated using indifference curves and budget lines. Before the promotion was announced, Angela and Betty were separately planning to stay at the hotel for two nights each this month. Each has the same income and allocates the same budget to her vacation.

Figure 4.10 shows that Angela takes advantage of the promotion and Betty does not because their tastes differ. Both panels of the figure show the same budget lines. The horizontal axis shows the nights spent at the hotel per month and the vertical axis measures all other goods per month. Their initial budget line before the promotion, L^1, is a standard downward sloping line, where the slope depends on the ratio of the full price of a hotel room to the price of other goods.

The new BOGOF budget line, L^2, is the same as the initial budget line for stays of fewer than three nights. However, if Angela or Betty pays for three nights, she gets an extra night for free. That is, she can get a fourth night with no reduction in her consumption of other goods. Therefore, her new budget line has a horizontal segment one night wide starting at three nights. For additional nights (beyond four) she would pay the regular price, so L^2 resumes its same downward slope for stays exceeding four nights.

In panel a, Angela's indifference curve I^1 is tangent to L^1 at point x, which is located at two nights on the horizontal axis. Because I^1 is the highest indifference curve that touches her pre-promotion budget line, she chooses to spend two nights at the resort. However, her indifference curve I^1 cuts the new budget line L^2, so she can do better. A higher indifference curve, I^2, touches L^2 at point y, where she chooses to stay four nights. That is, Angela would prefer to purchase three nights and get an extra night for free with the promotion than pay for and stay only two nights.

Betty's indifference curves in panel b differ from Angela's. Again, we assume that initially Betty chooses to stay two nights at Bundle x where her indifference

FIGURE 4.10 BOGOF Promotion

Angela and Betty are separately deciding how many nights to stay at the resort. Without the promotion, Angela or Betty's initial budget line is L^1. With the BOGOF promotion where if either stays three nights, she gets the fourth night for free, the new budget line is L^2. (a) Without the promotion, Angela's indifference curve I^1 is tangent to L^1 at point x, so she chooses to spend two nights at the resort. With the BOGOF promotion, Angela prefers to purchase three nights and get an extra night for free with the promotion than pay for and stay only two nights: Because her indifference curve I^1 cuts the new budget line L^2, there's a higher indifference curve, I^2, that touches L^2 at point y, where she chooses to stay four nights. (b) Without the promotion, Betty chooses to stay two nights at x where her indifference curve I^3 is tangent to L^1. Because I^3 does not cut the new budget line L^2, no higher indifference curve can touch L^2, so Betty stays only two nights, at x, and does not take advantage of the BOGOF promotion.

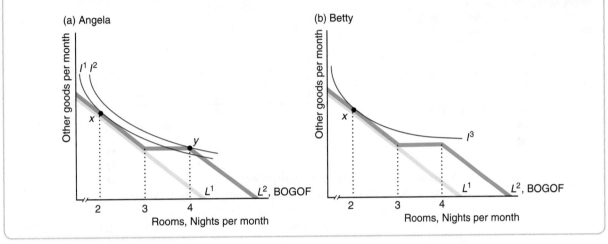

curve I^3 is tangent to L^1. Because I^3 is flatter than Angela's I^1 in panel a (Betty is willing to give up fewer other goods for another night at the resort than is Angela), I^3 does not cut the new budget line L^2. Thus, no higher indifference curve can touch L^2, so Betty stays only two nights, at x, and does not take advantage of the promotion

BOGOF Versus a Half-Price Promotion.
As we've just seen, whether the hotel's BOGOF promotion induces consumers to buy extra units depends on the consumers' tastes: Only a customer whose pre-promotion indifference curve crosses the new budget line will participate in the promotion. Consequently, another promotion may be more effective than BOGOF if a manager can design a promotion such that consumers' indifference curves *must* cross the new budget line so that consumers will definitely participate.

As an alternative to the BOGOF promotion ("the fourth night free if you pay for three nights"), the resort could offer a *half-price* promotion in which, after staying two nights at full price, the next two nights are half the usual price. The resort earns the same revenue from either promotion if someone stays four nights.

Figure 4.11 reproduces the information in Betty's panel b from the Figure 4.10 and adds a new half-price promotion constraint, L^3. The original, no-promotion budget line, L^1, is a light-blue line. The BOGOF budget line, L^2, is a dark-blue dashed line. The half-price budget line, L^3, is a dark-blue solid line. For stays of more than two nights up to four nights, the price of a room is cut in half, so the slope of L^3 is half as steep as it is for the first two full-price nights. For stays of more than four nights, the full-price is charged, so the slope of L^3 for more than four nights is the same as on L^1 and L^2.

FIGURE 4.11   Half-Price Versus BOGOF Promotions

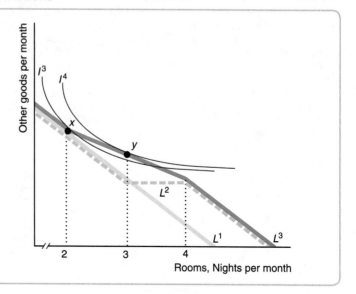

The resort's BOGOF promotion, which provides a fourth night free if one pays for three nights, creates a kink in the budget line L^2. With the half-price promotion, budget line L^3, the third and fourth nights are half price to a customer who pays full price for the first two nights, hence L^3 is half as steep at L^1 from two to four nights. Before either promotion is announced, Betty planned to stay two nights, Bundle x, where her indifference curve I^3 is tangent to the original budget line L^1. Because Betty's original indifference curve, I^3 does not cross L^2, she will not take advantage of the BOGOF promotion. However, because I^3 crosses the half-price promotion budget line L^3, Betty takes advantage of the promotion. Betty's optimal bundle is y, where she stays three nights, which is located where her indifference curve I^4 is tangent to the half-price promotion line L^3.

Although Betty's original indifference curve I^3 does not cross the BOGOF budget line L^2, it *must* cross the L^3 budget line of the half-price promotion. We know that I^3 crosses L^2 because the original indifference curve I^3 is tangent to L^1 at x, while L^3 is half as steeply sloped as L^1 at x, so it cannot be tangent to I^3 and must cut I^3. Because I^3 crosses L^3, we know that Betty has a higher indifference curve that touches L^3. Betty chooses to stay three nights, where her higher indifference curve I^4 is tangent to L^3 at y.

Managerial Implication

Designing Promotions

When deciding whether to use either BOGOF or half-price promotions, a manager should take costs into account. For example, offering such a promotion is more likely to pay if a hotel has excess capacity so that the cost of providing a room for an extra night's stay is very low. The manager also needs to determine whether its customers are more like Angela or more like Betty. To design an effective promotion, a manager should use experiments to learn about customers' preferences. For example, a manager could offer each promotion for a short period of time and keep track of how many customers respond to each promotion, how many nights they choose to stay, and by how much the promotion increased the firm's profit.

4.5 Deriving Demand Curves

We use consumer theory to show how much the quantity demanded of a good falls as its price rises. An individual chooses an optimal bundle of goods by picking the point on the highest indifference curve that touches the budget line. A change in a price causes the budget line to rotate, so that the consumer chooses a new optimal bundle. By varying one price and holding other prices and income constant, we determine how the quantity demanded changes as the price changes, which is the information we need to draw the demand curve.

We derive a demand curve using the information about tastes from indifference curves. To illustrate how to construct a demand curve, we estimated a set of indifference curves between recorded music—primarily tracks or songs purchased from iTunes, Amazon, Rhapsody, or other similar sources—and live music (at clubs, concerts, and so forth) using data for British young people (ages 14–24). Of these young people, college students spend about £18 per quarter on live music and £12 per quarter on music tracks for a total budget of £30 for music.[7]

Panel a of Figure 4.12 shows three of the estimated indifference curves for a typical British college student, whom we call Jack.[8] These indifference curves are convex to the origin: Jack views live music and tracks as imperfect substitutes. We can construct Jack's demand curve for music tracks by holding his budget, his tastes, and the price of live music constant at their initial levels and varying the price of tracks.

The vertical axis in panel a measures the amount of live music that Jack consumes each quarter, and the horizontal axis measures the number of tracks he buys per quarter. Jack spends $Y = £30$ per year on live music and tracks. We set the price of live music, p_m, at £1 by choosing the units appropriately (so the units do not correspond to a concert or visit to a club). The price of tracks, p_t, is £0.5 per track. Jack can buy 30 ($= Y/p_m = 30/1$) units of live music if he spends all his money on that, or up to 60 ($= Y/p_t = 30/0.5$) tracks if he buys only tracks. The slope of his budget line, L^3, is $-p_t/p_m = -0.5/1 = -0.5$. Given budget line L^3, Jack consumes 18 units of live music per quarter and 24 tracks per quarter, Bundle e_3, which is determined by the tangency of indifference curve I^3 and budget line L^3.

Now suppose that the price of tracks doubles to £1 per track while the price of live music and his budget remain constant. If he were to spend all his money on live music, he could buy the same 30 units as before, so the intercept on the vertical axis of L^2 is the same as for L^3. However, if he were to spend all his money on tracks, he could buy only half as much as before (30 instead of 60 tracks), so L^2 hits the horizontal axis half as far from the origin as L^3. As a result, L^2 has twice as steep a slope, $-p_t/p_m = -1/1 = -1$, as does L^3. The slope is steeper because the price of tracks has fallen relative to the price of live music.

Because tracks are now relatively more expensive, Jack buys relatively fewer of them. He chooses Bundle e_2, where his indifference curve I^2 is tangent to L^2. He now buys only 12 tracks per quarter (compared to 24 at e_3.)[9]

If the price of a track doubles again to £2, Jack consumes Bundle e_1, 6 tracks per quarter. The higher the price of tracks, the less happy Jack is because he consumes less music on the same budget: He is on indifference curve I^1, which is lower than I^2 or I^3.

We can use the information in panel a to draw Jack's demand curve for tracks, D^1, in panel b. Corresponding to each possible price of a track on the vertical axis of panel b, we record on the horizontal axis the number of tracks that Jack chooses in panel a.

---

[7]Data on total expenditures are from *The Student Experience Report, 2007*, **www.unite-students.com**, while budget allocations between live and recorded music are from the 2008 survey into the *Music Experience and Behaviour in Young People* produced by the British Music Rights and the University of Hertfordshire.

[8]The estimated utility function is $U = M^{0.6}T^{0.4}$, where M is the units of live music and T is the number of tracks.

[9]The figure shows that he buys the same amount of live music, 18 units, when the price of tracks rises. This property is due to the particular utility function (a Cobb-Douglas) that we use in this example. With most other utility functions, the quantity of live music would change.

FIGURE 4.12 Deriving an Individual's Demand Curve

If the price of recorded songs—tracks of music—rises, holding constant the price of live music (at £1 per unit), the music budget (at £30 per quarter), and tastes, the typical British college student, Jack, buys fewer tracks. This figure is based on our estimate of the typical student's utility function. (a) On budget line L^3, the price of a track is £0.5. Jack's indifference curve I^3 is tangent to L^3 at Bundle e_3, where he buys 18 units of live music and 24 tracks per quarter. If the price of a track doubles to £1, the new budget line is L^2, and Jack reduces the number of tracks he demands to 12 per quarter. If the price doubles again, to £2, Jack buys only 6 tracks. (b) By varying the price of a track, we trace out Jack's demand curve, D_1. The tracks price-quantity combinations E_1, E_2, and E_3 on the demand curve for tracks in panel b correspond to optimal Bundles e_1, e_2, and e_3 in panel a.

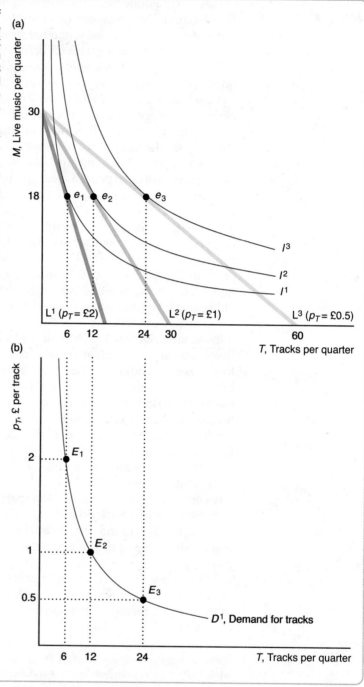

Points E_1, E_2, and E_3 on the demand curve in panel b correspond to Bundles e_1, e_2, and e_3 in panel a. Both e_1 and E_1 show that when the price of a track is £2, Jack demands 6 tracks per quarter. When the price falls to £1, Jack increases his consumption to 12 tracks, point E_2. The demand curve, D^1, is downward sloping as predicted by the Law of Demand.

4.6 Behavioral Economics

So far, we have assumed that consumers are rational, maximizing individuals. A new field of study, **behavioral economics**, adds insights from psychology and empirical research on human cognitive and emotional biases to the rational economic model to better predict economic decision making.[10] We discuss three applications of behavioral economics in this section: tests of transitivity, the endowment effect, and salience. Later in this book, we examine the psychology of decision making in networks (Chapter 9), strategic interactions (Chapter 13), and under uncertainty (Chapter 14).

Tests of Transitivity

In our presentation of the basic consumer choice model at the beginning of this chapter, we assumed that consumers make transitive choices. But do consumers actually make transitive choices?

A number of studies of both humans and animals show that preferences usually are transitive and hence consistent with our assumption. However, some situations can induce intransitive choices. Weinstein (1968) used an experiment to determine how frequently people give intransitive responses. None of the subjects knew the purpose of the experiment. They were given choices between ten goods, offered in pairs, in every possible combination, and were told that each good had a value of $3. Weinstein found that 93.5% of the responses of adults—people over 18 years old—were transitive. However, only 79.2% of children aged 9–12 gave transitive responses.

Based on these results, one might conclude that it is appropriate to assume that adults exhibit transitivity for most economic decisions. On the other hand, one might modify the theory when applying it to children or when novel goods are introduced.

Economists normally argue that rational people should be allowed to make their own consumption choices so as to maximize their well-being. However, some might conclude that children's lack of transitivity or rationality provides one justification for political and economic restrictions and protections placed on young people.

Endowment Effects

Experiments show that people have a tendency to stick with the bundle of goods that they currently possess. One important reason for this tendency is called the **endowment effect**, which occurs when people place a higher value on a good if they own it than they do if they are considering buying it.

We normally assume that an individual can buy or sell goods at the market price. Rather than rely on income to buy some mix of two goods, an individual who was *endowed* with several units of one good could sell some and use that money to buy units of another good.

We assume that a consumer's endowment does not affect the indifference curve map. In a classic buying and selling experiment, Kahneman et al. (1990) challenged this

---

[10]The introductory chapter of Camerer et al. (2004) and DellaVigna (2009) are excellent surveys of the major papers in this field and heavily influenced the following discussion.

assumption. In an undergraduate law and economics class at Cornell University, 44 students were divided randomly into two groups. Members of one group were given coffee mugs that were available at the student store for $6. Those students *endowed* with a mug were told that they could sell it and were asked the minimum price that they would accept for the mug. The subjects in the other group, who did not receive a mug, were asked how much they would pay to buy the mug. Given the standard assumptions of our model and that the subjects were chosen randomly, we would expect no difference between the selling and buying prices. However, the median selling price was $5.75 and the median buying price was $2.25. Sellers wanted more than twice what buyers would pay. This type of experiment has been repeated many times with many variations and consistently demonstrates an endowment effect.

However, some economists believe that this result has to do with the experimental design. Plott and Zeiler (2005) argued that if you take adequate care to train the subjects in the procedures and make sure they understand them, we no longer find this result. List (2003) examined the actual behavior of sports memorabilia collectors and found that amateurs who do not trade frequently exhibited an endowment effect, unlike professionals or amateurs who traded a lot. Thus, experience may reduce or even eliminate the endowment effect, and people who buy goods for resale may be less likely to become attached to these goods.

Others accept the results and have considered how to modify the standard model to reflect the endowment effect (Knetsch, 1992). One implication of these experimental results is that people will only trade away from their endowments if prices change substantially. This resistance to trade could be captured by having a kink in the indifference curve at the endowment bundle. (We showed indifference curves with a kink at a 90° angle in panel b of Figure 4.4.) These indifference curves could have an angle greater than 90°, and the indifference curve could be curved at points other than at the kink. If the indifference curve has a kink, the consumer does not shift to a new bundle in response to a small price change, but may shift if the price change is large.

Mini-Case

**How You Ask the
Question Matters**

One practical implication of the endowment effect is that consumers' behavior may differ depending on how a choice is posed. Many workers are offered the choice of enrolling in their firm's voluntary tax-deferred retirement (pension) plan, called a 401(k) plan. The firm can pose the choice in two ways: It can automatically sign up employees for the program and let them opt out if they want, or it can tell employees that to participate in the program they must sign up (opt in) to participate.

These two approaches might seem identical, but the behaviors they lead to are not. Madrian and Shea (2001, 2002) found that well over twice as many workers participate if they are automatically enrolled (but may opt out) than if they must opt in: 86% versus 37%. In short, inertia matters.

Because of this type of evidence, federal law was changed in 2006 and 2007 to make it easier for employers to enroll their employees in their 401(k) plans automatically. According to Aon Hewitt, the share of large firms that automatically enroll new hires in 401(k) plans was 67% in 2012, up from 58% in 2007. Participation in defined-contribution retirement plans in large companies rose from 67% in 2005 to 76% in 2010, due to the increased use of automatic enrollment.

Salience

We often use economic theories based on the assumption that decision makers are aware of all relevant information. In this chapter, we assume that consumers know their own income, relevant prices, and their own tastes, and hence they make informed decisions.

Behavioral economists and psychologists have demonstrated that people are more likely to consider information if it is presented in a way that grabs their attention or if it takes relatively little thought or calculation to understand. Economists use the term *salience*, in the sense of *striking* or *obvious*, to describe this idea. For example, *tax salience* is awareness of a tax.

If a store's posted price includes the sales tax, consumers observe a change in the price as the tax rises. On the other hand, if a store posts the pretax price and collects the tax at the cash register, consumers are less likely to note that the post-tax price has increased when the tax rate increases. Chetty et al. (2007) compared consumers' response to a rise in an *ad valorem* sales tax on beer (called an *excise tax*) that is included in the posted price to an increase in a general *ad valorem* sales tax, which is collected at the cash register but not reflected in the posted price. An increase in either tax has the same effect on the final price, so an increase in either tax should have the same effect on purchases if consumers pay attention to both taxes.[11] However, a 10% increase in the posted price, which includes the excise tax, reduces beer consumption by 9%, whereas a 10% increase in the price due to a rise in the sales tax that is not posted reduces consumption by only 2%. Chetty et al., also conducted an experiment where they posted tax-inclusive prices for 750 products in a grocery store and found that demand for these products fell by about 8% relative to control products in that store and comparable products at nearby stores.

One explanation for the lack of an effect of a tax on consumer behavior is consumer ignorance. For example, Furnham (2005) found that even at the age of 14 or 15, young people do not fully understand the nature and purpose of taxes. Similarly, unless the tax-inclusive price is posted, many consumers ignore or forget about taxes.

An alternative explanation for ignoring taxes is **bounded rationality**: people have a limited capacity to anticipate, solve complex problems, or enumerate all options. To avoid having to perform hundreds of calculations when making purchasing decisions at a grocery store, many people chose not to calculate the tax-inclusive price. However, when post-tax price information is made available to them without the need to do calculations, consumers make use of it. One way to modify the standard model to incorporate bounded rationality is to assume that people incur a cost to making calculations—such as the time taken or the mental strain—and that deciding whether to incur this cost is part of their rational decision-making process.

People incur this calculation cost only if they think the gain from a better choice of goods exceeds the cost. More people pay attention to a tax when the tax rate is high or when their demand for the good is elastic (they are sensitive to price). Similarly, some people are more likely to pay attention to taxes when making large, one-time purchases—such as for a computer or car—rather than small, repeated purchases—such as for a bar of soap.

---

[11]The final price consumers pay is $p^* = p(1 + \beta)(1 + \alpha)$, where p is the pretax price, α is the general sales tax, and β is the excise tax on beer.

Thus inattention due to bounded rationality is rational—consumers are doing the best they can in view of their limited powers of calculation. In contrast, inattention due to lack of salience is not rational. People would do better if they paid attention to less obvious information, but they just don't bother.

Managerial Implication

Simplifying Consumer Choices

Today's consumers are often overwhelmed by choices. Cable TV subscribers must select from many possible channels, most of which the consumer has never seen. Because consumers have bounded rationality, most consumers dislike considering all the possibilities and making decisions. To avoid making decisions, many consumers do not buy these services and goods even though they would greatly benefit from making these purchases.

To avoid this problem, good managers make decision-making easier for consumers. For example, they may offer default bundles so that consumers don't have to make a large number of difficult decisions. Cable TV companies package groups of channels by content. Instead of choosing between possibly hundreds of individual channels, a consumer can opt for the sports package or the movie package. Instead of thinking through each option, the customer can make a much easier decision such as "I like sports" or "I like movies" and is more likely to make a purchase.

Managerial Solution

Paying Employees to Relocate

We conclude our analysis of consumer theory by returning to the managerial problem posed in the introduction of this chapter: How can a firm's human resources manager use consumer theory to optimally compensate employees who are transferred to other cities?

Relocation managers collect information about the cost of living in various cities around the world from government sources (U.S. Defense Department, U.S. Government Services Administration, U.S. Office of Personnel Management, U.S. State Department), publications (*Money Magazine*, *Monthly Labor Review*), websites (**bankrate.com**, **bestplaces.net**, **citymayors.com**, **homefair.com**, **moving.com**), and data and human resources consulting firms (such as EIU Data Services, Mercer Consulting, and Runzheimer International).[12] From this information, managers know that it is more expensive to buy the same bundle of goods in one city than another and that the relative prices of goods differ across cities.

As we noted in the Managerial Problem, most firms say they pay their employees enough in their new city to buy the same bundle of goods as in their original city. We want to investigate whether such firms are paying employees more than they have to for them to relocate. We illustrate our reasoning using an employee who cares about only two goods.

Alexx's firm wants to transfer him from its Seattle office to its London office, where he will face different prices and cost of living. Alexx, who doesn't care

---

[12]The University of Michigan's library maintains an excellent list of cost-of-living sources, **www.lib.umich.edu/govdocs/steccpi.html**, for comparisons of both U.S. and international cities. See **cgi.money.cnn.com/tools/costofliving/costofliving.html** or **www.bankrate.com/calculators/mortgages/moving-cost-of-living-calculator.aspx?ec_id=m1025821** for calculators that compare U.S. cities' cost of living. An international calculator is available at **www.numbeo.com**.

whether he lives in Seattle or London, spends his money on housing and entertainment. Like most firms, his employer will pay him an after-tax salary in British pounds such that he can buy the same bundle of goods in London that he is currently buying in Seattle. Will Alexx benefit by moving to London? Could his employer have induced him to relocate for less money?

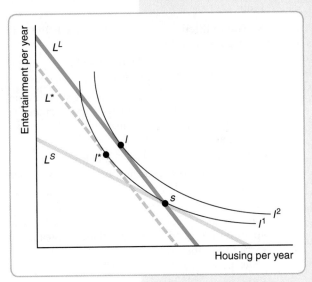

Alexx's optimal bundle, s, in Seattle is determined by the tangency of his indifference curve I^1 and his Seattle budget line L^S in the figure. It cost 53% more to live in London than Seattle on average in 2011. If the prices of all goods are exactly 53% higher in London than in Seattle, the relative costs of housing and entertainment is the same in both cities. In that case, if his firm raises Alexx's income by 53%, his budget line does not change and he buys the same bundle, s, and his level of utility is unchanged.

However, relative prices are not the same in both cities. Controlling for quality, housing is relatively more expensive and entertainment—concerts, theater, museums, zoos—is relatively less expensive in London than in Seattle. Thus, if Alexx's firm adjusts his income so that Alexx can buy the same bundle, s, in London as he did in Seattle, his new budget line in London, L^L, must go through s but have a different slope. Because entertainment is relatively less expensive than housing in London compared to Seattle, if Alexx spends all his money on entertainment, he can buy more in London than in Seattle. Similarly, if he spends all his money on housing, he can buy less housing in London than in Seattle. As a result, L^L hits the vertical axis at a higher point than the L^S line and cuts the L^S line at Bundle s.

Alexx's new optimal bundle, l, is determined by the tangency of I^2 and L^L. Thus, because relative prices are different in London and Seattle, Alexx is better off with the transfer after receiving the firm's 53% higher salary. He was on I^1 and is now on I^2. Alexx could buy his original bundle, s, but chooses to substitute toward entertainment, which is relatively inexpensive in London, thereby raising his utility.

Consequently, his firm could have induced him to move with less compensation. If the firm lowers his income, the London budget line he faces will be closer to the origin but will have the same slope as L^L. The firm can lower his income until his lower-income London budget line, $L*$, is tangent to his Seattle indifference curve, I^1, at Bundle $l*$. Alexx still substitutes toward the relatively less expensive entertainment in London, but he is only as well off as he was in Seattle (he remains on the same indifference curve as when he lived in Seattle). Thus, his firm can induce Alexx to transfer to London for less than what the firm would have to pay so that Alexx could buy his original Seattle consumption bundle in London.

SUMMARY

Consumers maximize their utility (well-being) subject to constraints based on their income and the prices of goods.

1. **Consumer Preferences.** To predict consumers' responses to changes in constraints, economists use a theory about individuals' preferences. One way of summarizing a consumer's preferences is with a family of indifference curves. An indifference curve consists of all bundles of goods that give the consumer a particular level of utility. On the basis of observations of consumers' behavior, economists assume that consumers' preferences have three properties: completeness, transitivity, and more is better (nonsatiation). Given these three assumptions, indifference curves have the following properties:

   - Consumers get more utility or satisfaction from bundles on indifference curves that are farther from the origin.

   - There is an indifference curve through any given bundle.

   - Indifference curves cannot cross.

   - Indifference curves slope downward.

2. **Utility.** Economists use the term *utility* to describe the set of numerical values that reflect the relative rankings of bundles of goods. By comparing the utility a consumer gets from each of two bundles, we know that the consumer prefers the bundle with the higher utility. The marginal utility, *MU*, from a good is the extra utility a person gets from consuming one more unit of that good, holding the consumption of all other goods constant. The rate at which a consumer is willing to substitute Good 1 for Good 2, the marginal rate of substitution, *MRS*, depends on the relative amounts of marginal utility the consumer gets from each of the two goods.

3. **The Budget Constraint.** The amount of goods consumers can buy at given prices is limited by their income. As a result, the greater a consumer's income or the lower the prices of goods, the more the consumer can buy. The consumer has a larger opportunity set. The marginal rate of transformation (*MRT*) shows how much of one good the consumer must give up in trade for one more unit of another good. The *MRT* depends on the relative prices of the two goods.

4. **Constrained Consumer Choice.** Each person picks an affordable bundle of goods that maximizes his or her utility. If an individual consumes both Good 1 and Good 2 (an interior solution), the individual's utility is maximized when the following four equivalent conditions hold:

   - The indifference curve for Goods 1 and 2 is tangent to the budget line.

   - The consumer buys the bundle of goods that is on the highest obtainable indifference curve.

   - The consumer's marginal rate of substitution (the slope of the indifference curve) equals the marginal rate of transformation (the slope of the budget line).

   - The last dollar spent on Good 1 gives the consumer as much extra utility as the last dollar spent on Good 2.

   Sometimes, consumers choose to buy only one of the two goods (corner solutions). The last dollar spent on the good that is purchased gives more extra utility than would spending a dollar on the other good, which the consumer chooses not to buy.

5. **Deriving Demand Curves.** Individual demand curves can be derived by using the information about preferences contained in a consumer's indifference curve map. By varying the price of one good while holding other prices and income constant, we find how the quantity demanded varies as its own price changes, which is the information we need to draw the good's demand curve. Consumers' preferences, which are captured by the indifference curves, determine the shape of the demand curve.

6. **Behavioral Economics.** Using insights from psychology and empirical research on human cognition and emotional biases, economists are starting to modify the rational economic model to better predict economic decision making. Some decision makers, particularly children, fail to make transitive choices in certain circumstances. Some consumers exhibit an endowment effect: They place a higher value on a good if they own it than they do if they are considering buying it. Consequently, they are less sensitive to price changes and hence less likely to trade than would be predicted by the standard economic model. Consumers are more inclined to take into account information that is readily available to them (salient), while ignoring other information.

QUESTIONS

*All exercises are available on MyEconLab; * = answer at the back of this book.*

1. Consumer Preferences

1.1. Give as many reasons as you can why we believe that economists assume that the more-is-better property holds and explain how these explanations relate to the results in the Mini-Case "You Can't Have Too Much Money."

*1.2. Arthur spends his income on bread and chocolate. He views chocolate as a good but is neutral about bread, in that he doesn't care if he consumes it or not. Draw his indifference curve map.

1.3. Show that an indifference curve

    a. Cannot be thick (cannot have positive thickness, rather than being just a line).

    b. Cannot bend backward (forming a "hook" at the end).

1.4. Which of the following pairs of goods are complements and which are substitutes? Are the goods that are substitutes likely to be perfect substitutes for some or all consumers?

    a. A popular novel and a gossip magazine

    b. A camera and film

    c. A pair of sunglasses and a stick of butter

    d. A Panasonic Blu-ray player and a Samsung Blu-ray player

1.5. Give as many reasons as you can why we believe that indifference curves are convex to the origin.

2. Utility

*2.1. William eats hot dogs only with mustard and consumes mustard only with hot dogs. He puts one unit of mustard on each hot dog he eats. Show his preference map. What is his utility function?

2.2. If Mia views two cups of tea as a perfect substitute for one cup of coffee and vice versa, what is her marginal rate of substitution between tea and coffee?

2.3. Lorna consumes cans of anchovies, A, and boxes of biscuits, B. Each of her indifference curves reflects strictly diminishing marginal rates of substitution. If $A = 2$ and $B = 2$, her marginal rate of substitution between cans of anchovies and boxes of biscuits equals $-1(= MU_A/MU_B)$. Will she prefer a bundle with three cans of anchovies and a box of biscuits to a bundle with two of each? Why?

*2.4. Andy purchases only two goods, apples (a) and kumquats (k). He has an income of $40 and can buy apples at $2 per pound and kumquats at $4 per pound. His utility function is $U(a, k) = 3a + 5k$. That is, his constant marginal utility for apples is 3 and his constant marginal utility for kumquats is 5. What bundle of apples and kumquats should Andy purchase to maximize his utility? Why?

3. The Budget Constraint

3.1. Yuka consumes mangos and oranges. She is given four mangos and three oranges. She can buy or sell mangos for $2 each. Similarly, she can buy or sell an orange for $1. If Yuka has no other source of income, draw her budget line and write the equation.

3.2. If the budget line is $Y = 500 = p_B B + p_Z Z = 5B + 10Z$, what is the marginal rate of transformation, MRT, between B (burritos) and Z (pizza)?

3.3. Change Q&A 4.1 so that Lisa's budget and the price of pizza double, but the price of burritos remains constant. Show how her budget constraint and opportunity set changes. Is Lisa necessarily better off than before these changes? (*Hint*: What happens to the intercepts of the budget line?)

*3.4. Dale goes to the opera and ice hockey games. Draw a budget line for Dale. If the government imposes a 25% income tax on her, what happens to her budget line and opportunity set? (*Hint*: See Q&A 4.2.)

3.5. Alexander spends all his money on chocolate bars and songs that he downloads. The price of a chocolate bar and of a song is $1 each. His parents give him an allowance of $50 and four chocolate bars each month. Draw his opportunity set, assuming that he cannot sell the chocolate bars to his friends. How does the oppurtunity set change if he can sell the chocolate bars at the market price?

4. Constrained Consumer Choice

4.1. Linda loves buying shoes and going out to dance. Her utility function for pairs of shoes, S, and the number of times she goes dancing per month, T, is $U(S, T) = 2ST$, so $MU_S = 2T$ and $MU_T = 2S$. It costs Linda $50 to buy a new pair of shoes or to spend an evening out dancing. Assume that she has $500 to spend on clothing and dancing. (*Hint*: See Q&A 4.3.)

    a. What is the equation for her budget line? Draw it (with T on the vertical axis), and label the slope and intercepts.

b. What is Linda's marginal rate of substitution? Explain.

c. Use math to solve for her optimal bundle. Show how to determine this bundle in a diagram using indifference curves and a budget line.

*4.2. Nadia likes spare ribs, R, and fried chicken, C. Her utility function is $U = 10R^2C$. Her marginal utilities are $MU_R = 20RC$ and $MU_C = 10R^2$. Her weekly income is $90, which she spends on only ribs and chicken.

a. If she pays $10 for a slab of ribs and $5 for a chicken, what is her optimal consumption bundle? Show her budget line, indifference curve, and optimal bundle, e_1, in a diagram.

b. Suppose the price of chicken doubles to $10. How does her optimal consumption of chicken and ribs change? Show her new budget line and optimal bundle, e_2, in your diagram.

4.3. Lucas chooses between water and all other goods. If he spends all his money on water, he can buy 15 thousand gallons per week. At current prices, his optimal bundle is e_1, where he buys both types of goods. Show e_1 in a diagram. During a drought, the government limits the number of gallons per week that he may purchase to 10 thousand. Using diagrams, discuss under which conditions his new optimal bundle, e_2, will be the same as e_1. If the two bundles differ, can you state where e_2 must be located relative to e_1?

*4.4. Gasoline is typically less expensive in the United States than across the border in Canada, but now suppose that U.S. gasoline price rises above that in Canada due to a change in taxes. How would the gasoline-purchasing behavior of a person who lives equally close to gas stations in both countries change? Answer using an indifference curve and budget line diagram.

4.5. Suppose we change Q&A 4.4 so that Max and Bob have indifference curves that are convex to the origin. Use a figure to discuss how the different slopes of their budget lines affect the choices they make. Can you make any unambiguous statements about how many total books each can buy? Can you make an unambiguous statement if you know that Bob's budget line goes through Max's optimal bundle?

4.6. Ralph usually buys one pizza and two colas from the local pizzeria. The pizzeria announces a special: All pizzas after the first one are half-price. Show the original and new budget line. What can you say about the bundle Ralph will choose when faced with the new constraint?

4.7. Until 2012, California, Texas, and Pennsylvania required firms to collect sales taxes for online sales if the chain had a physical presence (a "brick" store as opposed to a "click" store) in those states. Thus, those states collected taxes on Best Buy's online sales, because it had stores in each of those states, but they did not collect taxes from Amazon.com because it did not have physical locations in those states. Starting in 2012, Amazon had to pay taxes in these states. After the tax was imposed on Amazon, Best Buy had a 4% to 6% increase in its online sales in those states relative to the rest of the chain (**www.bizjournals.com/twincities/news/2013/01/11/best-buys-online-sales-up-in-states.html**). Use an indifference-curve/budget-line diagram to show why Best Buy's sales rose after taxes were imposed on Amazon. (*Hint:* Start by drawing a typical consumer's indifference curve between buying a good from Amazon or from Best Buy.)

4.8. The local swimming pool charges nonmembers $10 per visit. If you join the pool, you can swim for $5 per visit but you have to pay an annual fee of F. Use an indifference curve diagram to find the value of F such that you are indifferent between joining and not joining. Suppose that the pool charged you exactly that value of F. Would you go to the pool more or fewer times than if you did not join? For simplicity, assume that the price of all other goods is $1.

4.9. Based on panel a in Figure 4.10, show that Angela would accept the BOGOF promotion or the half-price promotion. Show that she may choose to stay either three or four nights with the half-price promotion depending on the exact shape of her indifference curves.

5. Deriving Demand Curves

5.1. Some of the largest import tariffs (taxes on only imported goods) are on shoes. Strangely, the tariff is higher on cheaper shoes. The highest U.S. tariff, 67%, is on a pair of $3 canvas sneakers, while the tariff on $12 sneakers is 37%, and that on $300 Italian leather imports is 0%. (Adam Davidson, "U.S. Tariffs on Shoes Favor Well-Heeled Buyers," National Public Radio, June 12, 2007, **www.npr.org/templates/story/story.php?storyId=10991519**.) Laura buys either inexpensive, canvas sneakers ($3 before the tariff) or more expensive gym shoes ($12 before the tariff) for her many children. Use an indifference curve and budget line figure to show how imposing these unequal tariffs affects the bundle of shoes that she buys compared to what she would have bought in the absence of tariffs. Can you confidently predict whether she'll buy relatively more expensive gym shoes after the tariff? Why or why not?

5.2. Draw diagrams similar to Figure 4.12 but with different shape indifference curves to show that as the price of tracks rises, the amount of live music Jack will buy may rise or fall.

5.3. Derive and plot Olivia's demand curve for pie if she eats pie only à la mode and does not eat either pie or ice cream alone (pie and ice cream are complements).

5.4. According to **towerswatson.com**, at large employers, 48% of employees earning between $10,000 and $24,999 a year participated in a voluntary retirement savings program, compared to 91% who earned more than $100,000. We can view savings as a good. In a figure, plot savings versus all other goods. Show why a person is more likely to "buy" some savings (put money in a retirement account) as the person's income rises.

6. Behavioral Economics

6.1. Illustrate the logic of the endowment effect using a kinked indifference curve. Let the angle be greater than 90°. Suppose that the prices change, so the slope of the budget line through the endowment changes. Use the diagram to explain why an individual whose endowment point is at the kink will only trade from the endowment point if the price change is substantial.

*6.2. Why would a consumer's demand for a product change when the product price is quoted inclusive of taxes rather than before tax? Do you think fewer people would apply for a job if the salary were quoted after deducting income tax rather than in pretax form?

7. Managerial Problem

7.1. In the Managerial Problem, suppose that entertainment is relatively more expensive in London than in Seattle so that the L^L budget line cuts the L^S budget line from below rather than from above as in the figure in the Managerial Solution. Show that the conclusion that Alexx is better off after his move if his

new income allows him to buy bundle s still holds. Explain the logic behind the following statement: "The analysis holds as long as the relative prices differ in the two cities. Whether both prices, one price, or neither price in London is higher than in Seattle is irrelevant to the analysis."

8. Spreadsheet Exercises

8.1. Lucy has just been promoted to a managerial position and given a new office. She is very fond of small Persian carpets and Native American paintings and wants to get some carpets and paintings for her office. Her utility function for carpets (x) and paintings (y) is given by

$$U(x, y) = \sqrt{xy}.$$

Using Excel's charting tool, draw an indifference curve for $U = 4$ and another one for $U = 6$, where both indifference curves contain 1, 2, 4, and 8 carpets on a graph with carpets on the horizontal axis and paintings on the vertical axis.

8.2. As described in Exercise 8.1, Lucy wants carpets and paintings for her office. Her company has given her a budget of $7,200 for this purpose. Persian carpets of the size that she wants can be purchased for $900 each and paintings from a local Native American artist cost $400 each.

a. Using Excel's charting tool, draw Lucy's budget constraint if her budget is $5,000. Use 0, 1, 2, 3, 4, and 5 carpets as possible quantities. Put carpets on the horizontal axis and paintings on the vertical axis.

b. Combining the information in the previous exercise with this exercise, use Excel to illustrate Lucy's utility-maximizing solution given that her budget is $5,000, the price of a carpet is $1,000, and the price of a painting is $500.

Appendix 4A   The Marginal Rate of Substitution

We can derive Equation 4.1 using calculus. Lisa's utility function is $U(B, Z)$. Along an indifference curve, we hold utility fixed at $\overline{U} = U(B, Z)$. If we increase Z, we would have to lower B to keep her on the same indifference curve. Let $B(Z)$ be the implicit function that shows how much B it takes to keep Lisa's utility at $\overline{U}$ given that she consumes Z. Thus, we can write her indifference curve as $\overline{U} = U(B(Z), Z)$, which is solely a function of Z.

We want to know how much B must change if we increase Z, dB/dZ, given that we require her utility to remain constant by staying on the original indifference curve. To answer this question, we differentiate $\overline{U} = U(B(Z), Z)$ with respect to Z and set this derivative to zero because $\overline{U}$ is constant along an indifference curve.

$$\frac{d\overline{U}}{dZ} = 0 = \frac{\partial U(B(Z),Z)}{\partial B}\frac{dB}{dZ} + \frac{\partial U(B(Z),Z)}{\partial Z} = MU_B\frac{dB}{dZ} + MU_Z.$$

The partial derivatives show how utility changes as we change either B or Z holding the other constant. We know that $d\overline{U}/dZ = 0$ because $\overline{U}$ is a constant along the indifference curve. Rearranging terms in this expression, we obtain Equation 4.1 (where dB/dZ replaces $\Delta B/\Delta Z$): $MRS = dB/dZ = -MU_Z/MU_B$.

For example, the Cobb-Douglas utility function (named after its inventors) is $U = B^a Z^{1-a}$. The marginal utilities are $MU_B = aB^{a-1}Z^{1-a} = aU/B$ and $MU_Z = (1-a)B^a Z^{-a} = (1-a)U/Z$. Thus,

$$MRS = -\frac{MU_Z}{MU_B} = -\frac{(1-a)U/Z}{aU/B} = \frac{(1-a)}{a}\frac{B}{Z}. \tag{4A.1}$$

Appendix 4B   The Consumer Optimum

We can derive Equation 4.6 using calculus. Lisa's objective is to maximize her utility, $U(B, Z)$, subject to (s.t.) a budget constraint:

$$\max_{B, Z} U(B,Z)$$
$$\text{s.t.} \quad Y = p_B B + p_Z Z, \tag{4B.1}$$

where B is the number of burritos she buys at price p_B, Z is the number of pizzas she buys at price p_Z, Y is her income, and $Y = p_B B + p_Z Z$ is her budget constraint. This mathematical statement of her problem shows that her *choice variables* are B and Z, which appear under the "max" term in the equation.

Because we cannot directly solve a constrained maximization problem, we want to convert Equation 4B.1 into an unconstrained problem by substituting the budget constraint into the utility function. Using algebra, we rearrange her budget constraint so that B is a function of Z: $B(Z) = (Y - p_Z Z)/p_B$. Substituting this expression for $B(Z)$ into the utility function, we rewrite her problem as

$$\max_{Z} \; U(B(Z), Z) = U\left(\frac{Y - p_z Z}{p_B}, Z\right). \tag{4B.2}$$

Because Equation 4B.2 is unconstrained, we can use standard maximization techniques to solve it. We derive the first-order condition by setting the derivative of Lisa's utility function with respect to Z equal to zero:

$$\frac{dU}{dZ} = \frac{\partial U}{\partial B}\frac{dB}{dZ} + \frac{\partial U}{\partial Z} = \left(-\frac{p_z}{p_B}\right)\frac{\partial U}{\partial B} + \frac{\partial U}{\partial Z} = \left(-\frac{p_z}{p_B}\right)MU_B + MU_Z = 0, \tag{4B.3}$$

where $MU_B(B, Z) = \partial U(B, Z)/\partial B$. Rearranging the terms in Equation 4B.3, we obtain the condition in Equation 4.6 that her utility is maximized if the slope of the indifference curve, MRS, equals the slope of the budget line, MRT:

$$MRS = -\frac{MU_Z}{MU_B} = -\frac{p_z}{p_B} = MRT. \tag{4B.4}$$

If the utility function is Cobb-Douglas, the MRS is given by Equation 4A.1, so Equation 4B.4 becomes

$$MRS = -\frac{MU_Z}{MU_B} = -\frac{(1-a)}{a}\frac{B}{Z} = -\frac{p_z}{p_B},$$

or

$$(1 - a)p_z Z = a p_B B. \tag{4B.5}$$

Rearranging the budget constraint, $p_z Z = Y - p_B B$. Substituting $Y - p_B B$ for $p_z Z$ in Equation 4B.5, we obtain $(1 - a)(Y - p_B B) = a p_B B$. Thus, $B = aY/p_B$. Similarly, by substituting $p_B B = Y - p_z Z$ in Equation 4B.5, we find that $Z = (1 - a)/p_z$.

5 Production

Hard work never killed anybody, but why take a chance? —Charlie McCarthy

John Nelson, American Licorice Company's Union City plant manager, invested $10 million in new labor-saving equipment, such as an automated drying machine. This new equipment allowed the company to cut its labor force from 450 to 240 workers.

The factory produces 150,000 pounds of Red Vines licorice a day and about a tenth as much black licorice. The manufacturing process starts by combining flour and corn syrup (for red licorice) or molasses (for black licorice) to form a slurry in giant vats. The temperature is raised to 200° for several hours. Flavors are introduced and a dye is added for red licorice. Next the mixture is drained from the vats into barrels and cooled overnight, after which it is extruded through a machine to form long strands. Other machines punch an air hole through the center of the strands, after which the strands are twisted and cut. Then, the strands are dried in preparation for packaging.

Food manufacturers are usually less affected by recessions than are firms in other industries. Nonetheless during major economic downturns, the demand curve for licorice may shift to the left, and Mr. Nelson must consider whether to reduce production by laying off some of his workers. He needs to decide how many workers to lay off. To make this decision, he faces a managerial problem: How much will the output produced per worker rise or fall with each additional layoff?

This chapter looks at an important set of decisions that managers, such as those of American Licorice, have to face. First, the firm must decide how to produce licorice. American Licorice now uses relatively more machines and fewer workers than in the past. Second, if a firm wants to expand its output, it must decide how to do that in both the short run and the long run. In the short run, American Licorice can expand output by hiring extra workers or extending the workweek (more shifts per day or more workdays per week) and using extra materials. To expand output even more, American Licorice would have to install more equipment and eventually build a new plant, all of which take time. Third, given its ability to change its output level, a firm must determine how large to grow. American Licorice determines how much to invest based on its expectations about future demand and costs.

Firms and the managers who run them perform the fundamental economic function of producing output—the goods and services that consumers want. The main lesson of this chapter is that firms are not black boxes that mysteriously transform inputs (such as labor, capital, and materials) into outputs. Economic theory explains how firms make decisions about production processes, the types of inputs to use, and the volume of output to produce.

Main Topics

In this chapter, we examine five main topics

1. **Production Functions:** A production function summarizes how a firm converts inputs into outputs using one of possibly many available technologies.

2. **Short-Run Production:** In the short run, only some inputs can be varied, so the firm changes its output by adjusting its variable inputs.

3. **Long-Run Production:** In the long run, all factors of production can be varied and the firm has more flexibility than in the short run in how it produces and how it changes its output level.

4. **Returns to Scale:** How the ratio of output to input varies with the size of the firm is an important factor in determining the size of a firm.

5. **Productivity and Technological Change:** Technological progress increases productivity: the amount of output that can be produced with a given amount of inputs.

5.1 Production Functions

A firm uses a *technology* or *production process* to transform *inputs* or *factors of production* into *outputs*. Firms use many types of inputs. Most of these inputs can be grouped into three broad categories:

▶ **Capital (K).** Services provided by long-lived inputs such as land, buildings (such as factories and stores), and equipment (such as machines and trucks)

▶ **Labor (L).** Human services such as those provided by managers, skilled workers (such as architects, economists, engineers, and plumbers), and less-skilled workers (such as custodians, construction laborers, and assembly-line workers)

▶ **Materials (M).** Natural resources and raw goods (e.g., oil, water, and wheat) and processed products (e.g., aluminum, plastic, paper, and steel)

The output can be a *service*, such as an automobile tune-up by a mechanic, or a *physical product*, such as a computer chip or a potato chip.

Firms can transform inputs into outputs in many different ways. Companies that manufacture candy differ in the skills of their workforce and the amount of equipment they use. While all employ a chef, a manager, and some relatively unskilled workers, many candy firms also use skilled technicians and modern equipment. In small candy companies, the relatively unskilled workers shape the candy, decorate it, package it, and box it by hand. In slightly larger firms, relatively unskilled workers may use conveyor belts and other equipment that was invented decades ago. In modern, large-scale plants, the relatively unskilled laborers work with robots and other state-of-the-art machines, which are maintained by skilled technicians. Before deciding which production process to use, a firm needs to consider its various options.

The various ways in which inputs can be transformed into output are summarized in the **production function**: the relationship between the quantities of inputs used and the *maximum* quantity of output that can be produced, given current knowledge about technology and organization. The production function for a firm that uses only labor and capital is

$$q = f(L, K), \tag{5.1}$$

where q units of output (such as wrapped candy bars) are produced using L units of labor services (such as hours of work by assembly-line workers) and K units of capital (such as the number of conveyor belts).

The production function shows only the *maximum* amount of output that can be produced from given levels of labor and capital, because the production function includes only efficient production processes. A firm engages in **efficient production** (achieves *technological efficiency*) if it cannot produce its current level of output with fewer inputs, given existing knowledge about technology and the organization of production. A profit-maximizing firm is not interested in production processes that are inefficient and waste inputs: Firms do not want to use two workers to do a job that can be done as well by one worker.

A firm can more easily adjust its inputs in the long run than in the short run. Typically, a firm can vary the amount of materials and of relatively unskilled labor it uses comparatively quickly. However, it needs more time to find and hire skilled workers, order new equipment, or build a new manufacturing plant.

The more time a firm has to adjust its inputs, the more factors of production it can alter. The **short run** is a period of time so brief that at least one factor of production cannot be varied practically. A factor that cannot be varied practically in the short run is called a **fixed input**. In contrast, a **variable input** is a factor of production whose quantity can be changed readily by the firm during the relevant time period. The **long run** is a lengthy enough period of time that all relevant inputs can be varied. In the long run, there are no fixed inputs—all factors of production are variable inputs.

Suppose that a painting company's customers all want the paint job on their homes to be finished by the end of the day. The firm could complete these projects on time if it had one fewer job. To complete all the jobs, it needs to use more inputs. Even if it wanted to do so, the firm does not have time to buy or rent an extra truck and buy another compressor to run a power sprayer; these inputs are fixed in the short run. To get the work done that afternoon, the firm uses the company's one truck to pick up and drop off temporary workers, each equipped with only a brush and paint, at the last job. In the long run, however, the firm can adjust all its inputs. If the firm wants to paint more houses every day, it hires more full-time workers, gets a second truck, purchases more compressors to run the power sprayers, and uses a computer to keep track of all its projects.

How long it takes for all inputs to be variable depends on the factors a firm uses. For a janitorial service whose only major input is workers, the short run is a brief period of time. In contrast, an automobile manufacturer may need several years to build a new manufacturing plant or to design and construct a new type of machine. A pistachio farmer needs the better part of a decade before newly planted trees yield a substantial crop of nuts.

For many firms, materials and often labor are variable inputs over a month. However, labor is not always a variable input. Finding additional highly skilled workers may take substantial time. Similarly, capital may be a variable or fixed input. A firm can rent small capital assets (such as trucks or office furniture) quickly, but it may take the firm years to obtain larger capital assets (buildings and large, specialized pieces of equipment).

To illustrate the greater flexibility that a firm has in the long run than in the short run, we examine the production function in Equation 5.1, in which output is a function of only labor and capital. We look first at the short-run and then at the long-run production processes.

5.2 Short-Run Production

The short run is a period in which there is at least one fixed input. Focusing on a production process in which capital and labor are the only inputs, we assume that capital is the fixed input and that labor is variable. The firm can therefore increase output only by increasing the amount of labor it uses. In the short run, the firm's production function, Equation 5.1, becomes

$$q = f(L, \overline{K}),\tag{5.2}$$

where q is output, L is the amount of labor, and $\overline{K}$ is the firm's fixed amount of capital.

To illustrate the short-run production process, we consider a firm that assembles computers for a manufacturing firm that supplies it with the necessary parts, such as computer chips and disk drives. If the assembly firm wants to increase its output in the short run, it cannot do so by increasing its capital (eight workbenches fully equipped with tools, electronic probes, and other equipment for testing computers). However, it can increase output in the short run by hiring extra workers or paying current workers extra to work overtime.

The Total Product Function

The exact relationship between *output* or *total product* and *labor* can be illustrated by using a particular function, Equation 5.2, a table, or a figure. Table 5.1 shows the relationship between output and labor when a firm's capital is fixed. The first column lists the fixed amount of capital: eight fully equipped workbenches. The second column shows how much of the variable input, labor, the firm uses. In this example, the labor input is measured by the number of workers, as all work the same number of hours. Total output—the number of computers assembled in a day—is listed in the third column. As the number of workers increases, total output first increases and then decreases.

With zero workers, no computers are assembled. One worker with access to the firm's equipment assembles five computers in a day. As the number of workers increases, so does output: 1 worker assembles 5 computers in a day, 2 workers assemble 18, 3 workers assemble 36, and so forth. The maximum number of computers that can be assembled with the capital on hand, however, is limited to 110 per day. That maximum can be produced with 10 or 11 workers. If the firm were to use 12 or more workers, the workers would get in each other's way and production would be lower than with 11 workers. The dashed line in the table indicates that a firm would not use more than 11 workers, because it would be inefficient to do so. We can show how extra workers affect the total product by using two additional concepts: the marginal product of labor and the average product of labor.

TABLE 5.1 Total Product, Marginal Product, and Average Product of Labor with Fixed Capital

Capital, $\overline{K}$	Labor, L	Output, Total Product of Labor q	Marginal Product of Labor, $MP_L = \Delta q/\Delta L$	Average Product of Labor, $AP_L = q/L$
8	0	0		
8	1	5	5	5
8	2	18	13	9
8	3	36	18	12
8	4	56	20	14
8	5	75	19	15
8	6	90	15	15
8	7	98	8	14
8	8	104	6	13
8	9	108	4	12
8	10	110	2	11
8	11	110	0	10
8	12	108	−2	9
8	13	104	−4	8

Labor is measured in workers per day. Capital is fixed at eight fully equipped workbenches.

The Marginal Product of Labor

Before deciding whether to employ more labor, a manager wants to determine how much an extra unit of labor, $\Delta L = 1$, will increase output, Δq. That is, the manager wants to know the **marginal product of labor** (MP_L): the change in total output resulting from using an extra unit of labor, holding other factors (capital) constant. If output changes by Δq when the amount of labor increases by ΔL, the change in output per unit of labor is

$$MP_L = \frac{\Delta q}{\Delta L}.$$

As Table 5.1 shows, if the number of workers increases from 1 to 2, $\Delta L = 1$, output rises by $\Delta q = 13 = 18 - 5$, so the marginal product of labor is 13.

Using Calculus

Calculating the Marginal Product of Labor

The short-run production function, $q = f(L, \overline{K})$ can be written as solely a function of L because capital is fixed: $q = g(L)$. The calculus definition of the marginal product of labor is the derivative of this production function with respect to labor: $MP_L = dg(L)/dL$.

In the long run, when both labor and capital are free to vary, the marginal product of labor is the partial derivative of the production function, Equation 5.1, $q = f(L, K)$, with respect to labor:

$$MP_L = \frac{\partial q}{\partial L} = \frac{\partial f(L,K)}{\partial L}.$$

We use the symbol $\partial q/\partial L$ instead of dq/dL to represent a partial derivative.[1] We use partial derivatives when a function has more than one explanatory variable. Here, q is a function of both labor, L, and capital, K. To obtain a partial derivative with respect to one variable, say L, we differentiate as usual where we treat the other variables (here just K) as constants.

Q&A 5.1

For a linear production function $q = f(L, K) = 2L + K$ and a multiplicative production function $q = LK$, what are the short-run production functions given that capital is fixed at $\bar{K} = 100$? What are the marginal products of labor for these short-run production functions?

Answer

1. *Obtain the short-run production functions by setting* $\bar{K} = 100$. The short-run linear production function is $q = 2L + 100$ and the short-run multiplicative function is $q = L \times 100 = 100L$.

2. *Determine the marginal products of labor by differentiating the short-run production functions with respect to labor.* The marginal product of labor is $MP_L = d(2L + 100)/dL = 2$ for the short-run linear production function and $MP_L = d(100L)/dL = 100$ for the short-run multiplicative production function.

The Average Product of Labor

Before hiring extra workers, a manager may also want to know whether output will rise in proportion to this extra labor. To answer this question, the firm determines how extra labor affects the **average product of labor** (AP_L): the ratio of output to the amount of labor used to produce that output,

$$AP_L = \frac{q}{L}.$$

Table 5.1 shows that 9 workers can assemble 108 computers a day, so the average product of labor for 9 workers is $12 (= 108/9)$ computers a day. Ten workers can assemble 110 computers in a day, so the average product of labor for 10 workers is $11 (= 110/10)$ computers. Thus, increasing the labor force from 9 to 10 workers lowers the average product per worker.

Graphing the Product Curves

Figure 5.1 and Table 5.1 show how output (total product), the average product of labor, and the marginal product of labor vary with the number of workers. (The figures are smooth curves because the firm can hire a "fraction of a worker" by

---

[1]Above, we defined the marginal product as the extra output due to a discrete change in labor, such as an additional worker or an extra hour of work. In contrast, the calculus definition of the marginal product—the partial derivative—is the rate of change of output with respect to the labor for a very small (infinitesimal) change in labor As a result, the numerical calculation of marginal products can differ slightly if derivatives rather than discrete changes are used.

employing a worker for a fraction of a day.) The curve in panel a of Figure 5.1 shows how a change in labor affects the *total product*, which is the amount of output that can be produced by a given amount of labor. Output rises with labor until it reaches its maximum of 110 computers at 11 workers, point *B*; with extra workers, the number of computers assembled falls.

Panel b of the figure shows how the average product of labor and marginal product of labor vary with the number of workers. We can line up the figures in panels a and b vertically because the units along the horizontal axes of both figures,

FIGURE 5.1 Production Relationships with Variable Labor

(a) The total product of labor curve shows how many computers, *q*, can be assembled with eight fully equipped workbenches and a varying number of workers, *L*, who work eight-hour days (see columns 2 and 3 in Table 5.1). Where extra workers reduce the number of computers assembled (beyond point *B*), the total product curve is a dashed line, which indicates that such production is inefficient and is thus not part of the production function. The slope of the line from the origin to point *A* is the average product of labor for six workers. (b) Where the marginal product of labor ($MP_L = \Delta q/\Delta L$, column 4 of Table 5.1) curve is above the average product of labor ($AP_L = q/L$, column 5 of Table 5.1) curve, the AP_L must rise. Similarly, if the MP_L curve is below the AP_L curve, the AP_L must fall. Thus, the MP_L curve intersects the AP_L curve at the peak of the AP_L curve, point *b*, where the firm uses 6 workers.

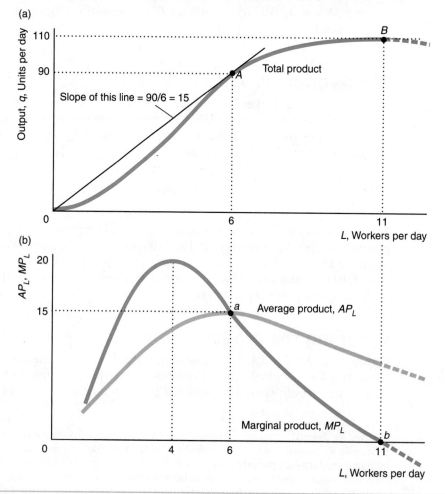

the number of workers per day, are the same. The vertical axes differ, however. The vertical axis is total product in panel a and the average or marginal product of labor—a measure of output per unit of labor—in panel b.

The Effect of Extra Labor.

In most production processes, the average product of labor first rises and then falls as labor increases. One reason the AP_L curve initially rises in Figure 5.1 is that it helps to have more than two hands when assembling a computer. One worker holds a part in place while another one bolts it down. As a result, output increases more than in proportion to labor, so the average product of labor rises. Doubling the number of workers from one to two more than doubles the output from 5 to 18 and causes the average product of labor to rise from 5 to 9, as Table 5.1 shows.

Similarly, output may initially rise more than in proportion to labor because of greater specialization of activities. With greater specialization, workers are assigned to tasks at which they are particularly adept, and time is saved by not having workers move from task to task.

As the number of workers rises further, however, output may not increase by as much per worker because workers might have to wait to use a particular piece of equipment or get in each other's way. In Figure 5.1, as the number of workers exceeds 6, total output increases less than in proportion to labor, so the average product falls.

If more than 11 workers are used, the total product curve falls with each extra worker as the crowding of workers gets worse. Because that much labor is not efficient, that section of the curve is drawn with a dashed line to indicate that it is not part of the production function, which includes only efficient combinations of labor and capital. Similarly, the dashed portions of the average and marginal product curves are irrelevant because no firm would hire additional workers if doing so meant that output would fall.

Relationships Among Product Curves.

The three curves are geometrically related. First we use panel b to illustrate the relationship between the average and marginal product of labor curves. Then we use panels a and b to show the relationship between the total product of labor curve and the other two curves.

An extra hour of work increases the average product of labor if the marginal product of labor exceeds the average product. Similarly, if an extra hour of work generates less extra output than the average, the average product falls. Therefore, the average product rises with extra labor if the marginal product curve is above the average product curve, and the average product falls if the marginal product is below the average product curve. Consequently, the average product curve reaches its peak, point a in panel b of Figure 5.1, where the marginal product and average product are equal: where the curves cross.

The geometric relationship between the total product curve and the average and marginal product curves is illustrated in panels a and b of Figure 5.1. We can determine the average product of labor using the total product of labor curve. The average product of labor for L workers equals the slope of a straight line from the origin to a point on the total product of labor curve for L workers in panel a. The slope of this line equals output divided by the number of workers, which is the definition of the average product of labor. For example, the slope of the straight line drawn from the origin to point A ($L = 6, q = 90$) is 15, which equals the "rise" of $q = 90$ divided by the "run" of $L = 6$. As panel b shows, the average product of labor for 6 workers at point a is 15.

The marginal product of labor also has a geometric relationship to the total product curve. The slope of the total product curve at a given point equals the marginal product of labor. That is, the marginal product of labor equals the slope of a straight line that is tangent to the total output curve at a given point. For example, at point B in panel a where there are 11 workers, the line tangent to the total product curve is flat so the marginal product of labor is zero (point b in panel b): A little extra labor has no effect on output. The total product curve is upward sloping when there are fewer than 11 workers, so the marginal product of labor is positive. If the firm is foolish enough to hire more than 11 workers, the total product curve slopes downward (dashed line), so the MP_L is negative: Extra workers lower output.

When there are 6 workers, the average product of labor equals the marginal product of labor. The reason is that the line from the origin to point A in panel a is tangent to the total product curve, so the slope of that line, 15, is the marginal product of labor and the average product of labor at point a in panel b, which is the peak of the AP_L curve.

The Law of Diminishing Marginal Returns

Next to *supply equals demand*, the most commonly used economic phrase claims that there are **diminishing marginal returns**: If a firm keeps increasing an input, holding all other inputs and technology constant, the corresponding increases in output will eventually become smaller (diminish). As most observed production functions have this property, this pattern is often called the *law of diminishing marginal returns*. This law determines the shape of the marginal product of labor curves: if only one input is increased, *the marginal product of that input will diminish eventually*.

In Table 5.1, if the firm goes from 1 to 2 workers, the marginal product of labor of the second worker is 13. If 1 or 2 more workers are used, the marginal product rises: The marginal product for the third worker is 18, and the marginal product for the fourth worker is 20. However, if the firm increases the number of workers beyond 4, the marginal product falls: The marginal product of a fifth worker is 19, and that of the sixth worker is 15. Beyond 4 workers, each extra worker adds less and less extra output, so the total product of labor curve rises by smaller increments. At 11 workers, the marginal product is zero. This diminishing return to extra labor might be due to crowding, as workers get in each other's way. As the amount of labor used grows large enough, the marginal product curve approaches zero and the total product curve becomes nearly flat.

Instead of referring to the *law of diminishing marginal returns*, some people talk about the *law of diminishing returns*—leaving out the word *marginal*. Making this change invites confusion as it is not clear if the phrase refers to marginal returns or total returns. If as labor increases the marginal returns fall but remain positive, the total return rises. In panel b of Figure 5.1, marginal returns start to diminish when the labor input exceeds 4 but total returns rise, as panel 1 shows, until the labor input exceeds 11, where the marginal returns become negative.

A second common misinterpretation of this law is to claim that marginal products must fall as we increase an input without requiring that technology and other inputs stay constant. If we increase labor while simultaneously increasing other factors or adopting superior technologies, the marginal product of labor can continue to rise.

Mini-Case

Malthus and the Green Revolution

In 1798, Thomas Malthus—a clergyman and professor of political economy—predicted that (unchecked) population would grow more rapidly than food production because the quantity of land was fixed. The problem, he believed, was that the fixed amount of land would lead to a diminishing marginal product of labor, so output would rise less than in proportion to the increase in farm workers, possibly leading to widespread starvation and other "natural" checks on population such as disease and violent conflict. Brander and Taylor (1998) argue that such a disaster might have occurred on Easter Island about 500 years ago.

Today the earth supports a population about seven times as large as when Malthus made his predictions. Why haven't most of us starved to death? The answer is that a typical agricultural worker produces vastly more food today than was possible when Malthus was alive. The output of a U.S. farm worker today is more than double that of an average worker just 50 years ago. We do not see diminishing marginal returns to labor because the production function has changed due to substantial technological progress in agriculture and because farmers make greater use of other inputs such as fertilizers and capital.

Two hundred years ago, most of the world's population had to work in agriculture to feed themselves. Today, less than 2% of the U.S. population works in agriculture. Over the last century, food production grew substantially faster than the population in most developed countries. For example, since World War II, the U.S. population doubled but U.S. food production tripled.

Of course, the risk of starvation is more severe in low-income countries than in the United States. Fortunately, agricultural production in these nations increased dramatically during the second half of the twentieth century, saving an estimated *billion* lives. This increased production was due to a set of innovations called the *Green Revolution*, which included development of drought- and insect-resistant crop varieties, improved irrigation, better use of fertilizer and pesticides, and improved equipment.

Perhaps the most important single contributor to the Green Revolution was U.S. agronomist Norman Borlaug, who won the Nobel Peace Prize in 1970. However, as he noted in his Nobel Prize speech, superior science is not the complete answer to preventing starvation. A sound economic system and a stable political environment are also needed.

Economic and political failures such as the breakdown of economic production and distribution systems due to wars have caused per capita food production to fall, resulting in widespread starvation and malnutrition in sub-Saharan Africa. According to the United Nations Food and Agriculture Organization, about 27% of the population of sub-Saharan Africa suffer from significant undernourishment along with more than 17% of the population in South Asia (India, Pakistan, Bangladesh, and nearby countries)—harming over 500 million people in these two regions alone.

5.3 Long-Run Production

We started our analysis of production functions by looking at a short-run production function in which one input, capital, was fixed, and the other, labor, was variable. In the long run, however, both of these inputs are variable. With both factors variable, a firm can usually produce a given level of output by using a great deal of labor and very little capital, a great deal of capital and very little labor, or moderate amounts of both. That is, the firm can substitute one input for another while continuing to produce the same level of output, in much the same way that a consumer can maintain a given level of utility by substituting one good for another.

Typically, a firm can produce in a number of different ways, some of which require more labor than others. For example, a lumberyard can produce 200 planks an hour with 10 workers using hand saws, with 4 workers using handheld power saws, or with 2 workers using bench power saws.

We illustrate a firm's ability to substitute between inputs in Table 5.2, which shows the amount of output per day the firm produces with various combinations of labor per day and capital per day. The labor inputs are along the top of the table, and the capital inputs are in the first column. The table shows four combinations of labor and capital that the firm can use to produce 24 units of output (in bold numbers): The firm may employ (a) 1 worker and 6 units of capital, (b) 2 workers and 3 units of capital, (c) 3 workers and 2 units of capital, or (d) 6 workers and 1 unit of capital.

Isoquants

These four combinations of labor and capital are labeled a, b, c, and d on the "$q = 24$" curve in Figure 5.2. We call such a curve an **isoquant**, which is a curve that shows the efficient combinations of labor and capital that can produce the same (*iso*) level of output (*quantity*). The isoquant shows the smallest amounts of inputs that will produce a given amount of output. That is, if a firm reduced either input, it could not produce as much output. If the production function is $q = f(L, K)$, then the equation for an isoquant where output is held constant at $\bar{q}$ is

$$\bar{q} = f(L, K).$$

An isoquant shows the flexibility that a firm has in producing a given level of output. Figure 5.2 shows three isoquants corresponding to three levels of output. These isoquants are smooth curves because the firm can use fractional units of each input.

TABLE 5.2 Output Produced with Two Variable Inputs

				Labor, L		
Capital, K	1	2	3	4	5	6
1	10	14	17	20	22	**24**
2	14	20	**24**	28	32	35
3	17	**24**	30	35	39	42
4	20	28	35	40	45	49
5	22	32	39	45	50	55
6	**24**	35	42	49	55	60

FIGURE 5.2 A Family of Isoquants

These isoquants show the combinations of labor and capital that produce 14, 24, or 35 units of output, q. Isoquants farther from the origin correspond to higher levels of output. Points a, b, c, and d are various combinations of labor and capital the firm can use to produce $q = 24$ units of output. If the firm holds capital constant at 2 and increases labor from 1 (point e on the $q = 14$ isoquant) to 3 (c), its output increases to $q = 24$ isoquant. If the firm then increases labor to 6 (f), its output rises to $q = 35$.

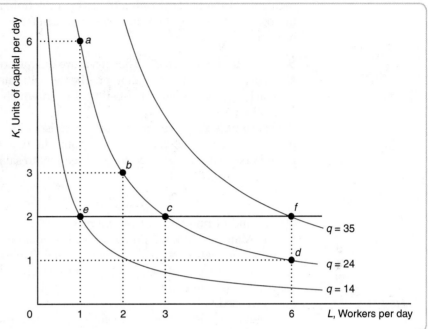

We can use these isoquants to illustrate what happens in the short run when capital is fixed and only labor varies. As Table 5.2 shows, if capital is constant at 2 units, 1 worker produces 14 units of output (point e in Figure 5.2), 3 workers produce 24 units (point c), and 6 workers produce 35 units (point f). Thus, if the firm holds one factor constant and varies another factor, it moves from one isoquant to another. In contrast, if the firm increases one input while lowering the other appropriately, the firm stays on a single isoquant.

Properties of Isoquants. Isoquants have most of the same properties as indifference curves. The biggest difference between indifference curves and isoquants is that an isoquant holds quantity constant, whereas an indifference curve holds utility constant. We now discuss three major properties of isoquants. Most of these properties result from firms producing efficiently.

First, *the farther an isoquant is from the origin, the greater the level of output.* That is, the more inputs a firm uses, the more output it gets if it produces efficiently. At point e in Figure 5.2, the firm is producing 14 units of output with 1 worker and 2 units of capital. If the firm holds capital constant and adds 2 more workers, it produces at point c. Point c must be on an isoquant with a higher level of output—here, 24 units—if the firm is producing efficiently and not wasting the extra labor.

Second, *isoquants do not cross.* Such intersections are inconsistent with the requirement that the firm always produces efficiently. For example, if the $q = 15$ and $q = 20$ isoquants crossed, the firm could produce at either output level with the same combination of labor and capital. The firm must be producing inefficiently if it produces $q = 15$ when it could produce $q = 20$. So that labor-capital combination should not lie on the $q = 15$ isoquant, which should include only efficient combinations of inputs. Thus, efficiency requires that isoquants do not cross.

Third, *isoquants slope downward.* If an isoquant sloped upward, the firm could produce the same level of output with relatively few inputs or relatively many inputs. Producing with relatively many inputs would be inefficient. Consequently, because isoquants show only efficient production, an upward-sloping isoquant is impossible. Virtually the same argument can be used to show that isoquants must be thin.

Shapes of Isoquants. The curvature of an isoquant shows how readily a firm can substitute one input for another. The two extreme cases are production processes in which inputs are perfect substitutes or in which they cannot be substituted for each other.

If the inputs are perfect substitutes, each isoquant is a straight line. Suppose either potatoes from Maine, x, or potatoes from Idaho, y, both of which are measured in pounds per day, can be used to produce potato salad, q, measured in pounds. The production function is

$$q = x + y.$$

One pound of potato salad can be produced by using 1 pound of Idaho potatoes and no Maine potatoes, 1 pound of Maine potatoes and no Idaho potatoes, or any combination that adds up to 1 pound in total. Panel a of Figure 5.3 shows the $q = 1$, 2, and 3 isoquants. These isoquants are straight lines with a slope of -1 because we need to use an extra pound of Maine potatoes for every pound fewer of Idaho potatoes used.[2]

Sometimes it is impossible to substitute one input for the other: Inputs must be used in fixed proportions. Such a production function is called a *fixed-proportions production function*. For example, the inputs needed to produce 12-ounce boxes of

FIGURE 5.3 Substitutability of Inputs

(a) If inputs are perfect substitutes, each isoquant is a straight line. (b) If the inputs cannot be substituted at all, the isoquants are right angles (the dashed lines show that the isoquants would be right angles if we included inefficient production). (c) Typical isoquants lie between the extreme cases of straight lines and right angles. Along a curved isoquant, the ability to substitute one input for another varies.

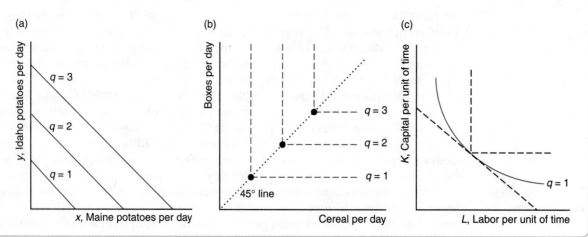

---

[2]The isoquant for $\bar{q} = 1$ pound of potato salad is $1 = x + y$, or $y = 1 - x$. This equation shows that the isoquant is a straight line with a slope of -1.

cereal are cereal (in 12-ounce units per day) and cardboard boxes (boxes per day). If the firm has one unit of cereal and one box, it can produce one box of cereal. If it has one unit of cereal and two boxes, it can still make only one box of cereal. Thus, in panel b, the only efficient points of production are the large dots along the 45° line.[3] Dashed lines show that the isoquants would be right angles if isoquants could include inefficient production processes.

Other production processes allow imperfect substitution between inputs. These processes have isoquants that are convex to the origin (so the middle of the isoquant is closer to the origin than it would be if the isoquant were a straight line). They do not have the same slope at every point, unlike the straight-line isoquants. Most isoquants are smooth, slope downward, curve away from the origin, and lie between the extreme cases of straight lines (perfect substitutes) and right angles (fixed proportions), as panel c illustrates.

Mini-Case

A Semiconductor Isoquant

We can show why isoquants curve away from the origin by deriving an isoquant for semiconductor integrated circuits (ICs, or "chips")—the "brains" of computers and other electronic devices. Semiconductor manufacturers buy silicon wafers and then use labor and capital to produce the chips.

A chip consists of multiple layers of silicon wafers. A key step in the production process is to line up these layers. Three alternative alignment technologies are available, using different combinations of labor and capital. In the least capital-intensive technology, employees use machines called *aligners*, which require workers to look through microscopes and line up the layers by hand. A worker using an aligner can produce 25 ten-layer chips per day.

A second, more capital-intensive technology uses machines called *steppers*. The stepper aligns the layers automatically. This technology requires less labor: A single worker can produce 50 ten-layer chips per day.

A third, even more capital-intensive technology combines steppers with wafer-handling equipment, which further reduces the amount of labor needed. A single worker can produce 100 ten-layer chips per day. In the diagram the vertical axis measures the amount of capital used. An aligner represents less capital than a basic stepper, which in turn is less capital than a stepper with wafer-handling capabilities.

All three technologies use labor and capital in fixed proportions. To produce 200 chips takes 8 workers and 8 aligners, 3 workers and 6 basic steppers, or 1 worker and 4 steppers with wafer-handling capabilities. The accompanying graph shows the three right-angle isoquants corresponding to each of these three technologies.

Some plants employ a combination of these technologies, so that some workers use one type of machine while others use different types. By doing so, the plant can produce using intermediate combinations of labor and capital, as the solid-line, kinked isoquant illustrates. The firm does *not* use a combination of the aligner and the wafer-handling stepper technologies because those combinations

---

[3]This fixed-proportions production function is the minimum of g and b, $q = \min(g, b)$, where g is the number of 12-ounce measures of cereal, b is the number of boxes used in a day, and the min function means "the minimum number of g or b." For example, if g is 4 and b is 3, q is 3.

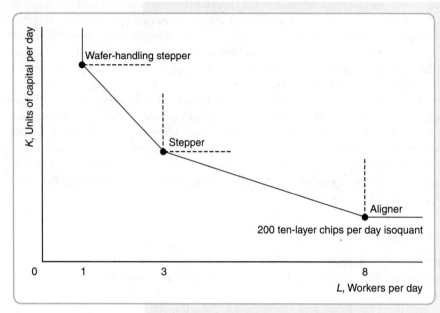

are less efficient than using the basic stepper: The line connecting the aligner and wafer-handling stepper technologies is farther from the origin than the lines between those technologies and the basic stepper technology.

New processes are constantly being invented. As they are introduced, the isoquant will have more and more kinks (one for each new process) and will begin to resemble the smooth, convex isoquants we've been drawing.

Substituting Inputs

The slope of an isoquant shows the ability of a firm to replace one input with another while holding output constant. Figure 5.4 illustrates this substitution using an estimated isoquant for a U.S. printing firm, which uses labor, L, and capital, K, to print its output, q.[4] The isoquant shows various combinations of L and K that the firm can use to produce 10 units of output.

The firm can produce 10 units of output using the combination of inputs at a or b. At point a, the firm uses 2 workers and 16 units of capital. The firm could produce the same amount of output using $\Delta K = -6$ fewer units of capital if it used one more worker, $\Delta L = 1$, point b. If we drew a straight line from a to b, its slope would be $\Delta K / \Delta L = -6$. Thus, this slope tells us how many fewer units of capital (6) the firm can use if it hires one more worker.[5]

The slope of an isoquant is called the *marginal rate of technical substitution (MRTS)*:

$$MRTS = \frac{\text{change in capital}}{\text{change in labor}} = \frac{\Delta K}{\Delta L}.$$

The **marginal rate of technical substitution** tells us how many units of capital the firm can replace with an extra unit of labor while holding output constant. Because isoquants slope downward, the $MRTS$ is negative. That is, the firm can produce a given level of output by substituting more capital for less labor (or vice versa).

---

[4]This isoquant for $\bar{q} = 10$ is based on the estimated production function $q = 2.35L^{0.5}K^{0.4}$ (Hsieh, 1995), where the unit of labor, L, is a worker-day. Because capital, K, includes various types of machines, and output, q, reflects different types of printed matter, their units cannot be described by any common terms. This production function is an example of a Cobb-Douglas production function.

[5]The slope of the isoquant at a point equals the slope of a straight line that is tangent to the isoquant at that point. Thus, the straight line between two nearby points on an isoquant has nearly the same slope as that of the isoquant.

FIGURE 5.4 How the Marginal Rate of Technical Substitution Varies Along an Isoquant

Moving from point *a* to *b*, a U.S. printing firm (Hsieh, 1995) can produce the same amount of output, $q = 10$, using six fewer units of capital, $\Delta K = -6$, if it uses one more worker, $\Delta L = 1$. Thus, its $MRTS = \Delta K/\Delta L = -6$. Moving from point *b* to *c*, its $MRTS$ is -3. If it adds yet another worker, moving from *c* to *d*, its $MRTS$ is -2. Finally, if it moves from *d* to *e*, its $MRTS$ is -1. Thus, because the isoquant is convex to the origin, it exhibits a diminishing marginal rate of technical substitution. That is, each extra worker allows the firm to reduce capital by a smaller amount as the ratio of capital to labor falls.

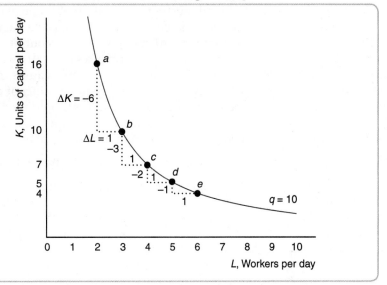

Substitutability of Inputs Varies Along an Isoquant. The *MRTS* varies along a curved isoquant, as in Figure 5.4. If the firm is initially at point *a* and it hires one more worker, the firm can give up 6 units of capital and yet remain on the same isoquant (at point *b*), so the *MRTS* is −6. If the firm hires another worker, the firm can reduce its capital by 3 units and stay on the same isoquant, moving from point *b* to *c*, so the *MRTS* is −3. This decline in the *MRTS* (in absolute value) along an isoquant as the firm increases labor illustrates a *diminishing MRTS*. The more labor and less capital the firm has, the harder it is to replace remaining capital with labor and the flatter the isoquant becomes.

In the special case in which isoquants are straight lines, isoquants do not exhibit diminishing marginal rates of technical substitution because neither input becomes more valuable in the production process: The inputs remain perfect substitutes. Q&A 5.2 illustrates this result.

Q&A 5.2

A manufacturer produces a container of potato salad using one pound of Idaho potatoes, one pound of Maine potatoes, or one pound of a mixture of the two types of potatoes. Does the marginal rate of technical substitution vary along the isoquant? What is the *MRTS* at each point along the isoquant?

Answer

1. *Determine the shape of the isoquant.* As panel a of Figure 5.3 illustrates, the potato salad isoquants are straight lines because the two types of potatoes are perfect substitutes.

2. *On the basis of the shape, conclude whether the MRTS is constant along the isoquant.* Because the isoquant is a straight line, the slope is the same at every point, so the *MRTS* is constant.

3. *Determine the MRTS at each point.* Earlier, we showed that the slope of this isoquant was −1, so the *MRTS* is −1 at each point along the isoquant. That is, because the two inputs are perfect substitutes, 1 pound of Idaho potatoes can be replaced by 1 pound of Maine potatoes.

Substitutability of Inputs and Marginal Products.   The marginal rate of technical substitution is equal to the ratio of marginal products. Because the marginal product of labor, $MP_L = \Delta q/\Delta L$, is the increase in output per extra unit of labor, if the firm hires ΔL more workers, its output increases by $MP_L \times \Delta L$. For example, if the MP_L is 2 and the firm hires one extra worker, its output rises by 2 units.

A decrease in capital alone causes output to fall by $MP_K \times \Delta K$, where $MP_K = \Delta q/\Delta K$ is the marginal product of capital—the output the firm loses from decreasing capital by one unit, holding all other factors fixed. To keep output constant, $\Delta q = 0$, this fall in output from reducing capital must exactly equal the increase in output from increasing labor:

$$(MP_L \times \Delta L) + (MP_K \times \Delta K) = 0.$$

Rearranging these terms, we find that

$$-\frac{MP_L}{MP_K} = \frac{\Delta K}{\Delta L} = MRTS. \tag{5.3}$$

Thus the ratio of marginal products equals the $MRTS$ (in absolute value).

We can use Equation 5.3 to explain why marginal rates of technical substitution diminish as we move to the right along the isoquant in Figure 5.4. As we replace capital with labor (move down and to the right along the isoquant), the marginal product of capital increases—when there are few pieces of equipment per worker, each remaining piece is more useful—and the marginal product of labor falls, so the $MRTS = -MP_L/MP_K$ falls in absolute value.

Cobb-Douglas Production Functions.   We can illustrate how to determine the $MRTS$ for a particular production function, the Cobb-Douglas production function. It is named after its inventors, Charles W. Cobb, a mathematician, and Paul H. Douglas, an economist and U.S. Senator. Through empirical studies, economists have found that the production processes in a very large number of industries can be accurately summarized by the Cobb-Douglas production function, which is

$$q = AL^\alpha K^\beta, \tag{5.4}$$

where A, α, and β are all positive constants.

We used regression analysis to estimate the production function for the BlackBerry smartphone, which was the first major smartphone.[6] The estimated Cobb-Douglas production function is $Q = 2.83L^{1.52}K^{0.82}$. That is, $A = 2.83$, $\alpha = 1.52$, and $\beta = 0.82$.

The constants α and β determine the relationships between the marginal and average products of labor and capital (as we show in the following section, Using Calculus). The marginal product of labor is α times the average product of labor, $AP_L = q/L$. That is, $MP_L = \alpha q/L = \alpha AP_L$. By dividing both sides of the expression by AP_L, we find that α equals the ratio of the marginal product of labor to the average product of labor: $\alpha = MP_L/AP_L$. Similarly, the marginal product of capital is $MP_K = \beta q/K = \beta AP_K$, and $\beta = MP_K/AP_K$.

---

[6]The data are from the annual and quarterly reports from 1999 through 2009 of Research In Motion (renamed BlackBerry in 2013), the company that manufactures BlackBerry phones.

The marginal rate of technical substitution along an isoquant that holds output fixed at $\bar{q}$ is

$$MRTS = -\frac{MP_L}{MP_K} = -\frac{\alpha\bar{q}/L}{\beta\bar{q}/K} = -\frac{\alpha}{\beta}\frac{K}{L}. \tag{5.5}$$

For example, given the BlackBerry's production function, $Q = 2.83L^{1.52}K^{0.82}$, its $MP_L = \alpha AP_L = 1.52AP_L$, and its $MRTS = -(1.52/0.82)K/L \approx -1.85K/L$. The $MRTS$ tells the firm's managers the rate at which they can substitute capital for labor without reducing output.

Using Calculus

Cobb-Douglas Marginal Products

To obtain the marginal product of labor for the Cobb-Douglas production function, Equation 5.4, $q = AL^{\alpha}K^{\beta}$, we partially differentiate the production function with respect to labor, holding capital fixed:

$$MP_L = \frac{\partial q}{\partial L} = \alpha AL^{\alpha-1}K^{\beta} = \alpha\frac{AL^{\alpha}K^{\beta}}{L} = \alpha\frac{q}{L}.$$

We obtain the last equality by substituting $q = AL^{\alpha}K^{\beta}$. Similarly, we can derive the marginal product of capital by partially differentiating the production function with respect to K:

$$MP_K = \frac{\partial q}{\partial K} = \beta AL^{\alpha}K^{\beta-1} = \beta\frac{AL^{\alpha}K^{\beta}}{K} = \beta\frac{q}{K}.$$

5.4 Returns to Scale

So far, we have examined the effects of increasing one input while holding the other input constant (shifting from one isoquant to another) or decreasing the other input by an offsetting amount (moving along an isoquant). We now turn to the question of *how much output changes if a firm increases all its inputs proportionately.* The answer helps a firm determine its *scale* or size in the long run.

In the long run, a firm can increase its output by building a second plant and staffing it with the same number of workers as in the first one. Whether the firm chooses to do so depends in part on whether its output increases less than in proportion, in proportion, or more than in proportion to its inputs.

Constant, Increasing, and Decreasing Returns to Scale

If, when all inputs are increased by a certain proportion, output increases by that same proportion, the production function is said to exhibit **constant returns to scale** (*CRS*). A firm's production process, $q = f(L, K)$, has constant returns to scale if, when the firm doubles its inputs—by, for example, building an identical second plant and using the same amount of labor and equipment as in the first plant—it doubles its output:

$$f(2L, 2K) = 2f(L, K) = 2q.$$

We can check whether the potato salad production function has constant returns to scale. If a firm uses x_1 pounds of Idaho potatoes and y_1 pounds of Maine potatoes, it produces $q_1 = x_1 + y_1$ pounds of potato salad. If it doubles both inputs, using $x_2 = 2x_1$ Idaho and $y_2 = 2y_1$ Maine potatoes, it doubles its output:

$$q_2 = x_2 + y_2 = 2x_1 + 2y_1 = 2(x_1 + y_1) = 2q_1.$$

Thus, the potato salad production function exhibits constant returns to scale.

This'll save a lot of time!

If output rises more than in proportion to an equal proportional increase in all inputs, the production function is said to exhibit **increasing returns to scale** (*IRS*). A technology exhibits increasing returns to scale if doubling inputs more than doubles the output:

$$f(2L, 2K) > 2f(L, K) = 2q.$$

Why might a production function have increasing returns to scale? One reason is that, although it could build a copy of its original small factory and double its output, the firm might be able to more than double its output by building a single large plant, thereby allowing for greater specialization of labor or capital. In the two smaller plants, workers have to perform many unrelated tasks such as operating, maintaining, and fixing the machines they use. In the large plant, some workers may specialize in maintaining and fixing machines, thereby increasing efficiency. Similarly, a firm may use specialized equipment in a large plant but not in a small one.

If output rises less than in proportion to an equal proportional increase in all inputs, the production function exhibits **decreasing returns to scale** (*DRS*). A technology exhibits decreasing returns to scale if doubling inputs causes output to rise less than in proportion:

$$f(2L, 2K) < 2f(L, K) = 2q.$$

One reason for decreasing returns to scale is that the difficulty of organizing, coordinating, and integrating activities increases with firm size. An owner may be able to manage one plant well but may have trouble running two plants. In some sense, the decreasing returns to scale stemming from the owner's difficulties in running a larger firm may reflect our failure to take into account some factor such as management skills in our production function. If a firm increases various inputs but does not increase the management input in proportion, the "decreasing returns to scale" may occur because one of the inputs to production, management skills, is fixed. Another reason is that large teams of workers may not function as well as small teams, in which each individual takes greater personal responsibility.

Q&A 5.3

Under what conditions does a Cobb-Douglas production function, Equation 5.4, $q = AL^{\alpha}K^{\beta}$, exhibit decreasing, constant, or increasing returns to scale?

Answer

1. *Show how output changes if both inputs are doubled.* If the firm initially uses L and K amounts of inputs it produces $q_1 = AL^{\alpha}K^{\beta}$. After the firm doubles the amount of both labor and capital it uses, it produces

$$q_2 = A(2L)^{\alpha}(2K)^{\beta} = 2^{\alpha+\beta}AL^{\alpha}K^{\beta} = 2^{\alpha+\beta}q_1. \qquad (5.6)$$

That is, q_2 is $2^{\alpha+\beta}$ times q_1. If we define $\gamma = \alpha + \beta$, then Equation 5.6 tells us that

$$q_2 = 2^{\gamma}q_1. \qquad (5.7)$$

Thus, if the inputs double, output increases by 2^{γ}.

2. *Give a rule for determining the returns to scale.* If $\gamma = 1$, we know from Equation 5.7 that $q_2 = 2^1 q_1 = 2q_1$. That is, output doubles when the inputs double, so the Cobb-Douglas production function has constant returns to scale. If $\gamma < 1$, then $q_2 = 2^{\gamma}q_1 < 2q_1$ because $2^{\gamma} < 2$ if $\gamma < 1$. That is, when input doubles, output increases less than in proportion, so this Cobb-Douglas production function exhibits decreasing returns to scale. Finally, the Cobb-Douglas production function has increasing returns to scale if $\gamma > 1$ so that $q_2 > 2q_1$. Thus, the rule for determining returns to scale for a Cobb-Douglas production function is that the returns to scale are decreasing if $\gamma < 1$, constant if $\gamma = 1$, and increasing if $\gamma > 1$.

Comment: One interpretation of γ is that, as all inputs increase by 1%, output increases by γ%. Thus, for example, if $\gamma = 1$, a 1% increase in all inputs increases output by 1%.

Mini-Case

Returns to Scale in U.S. Manufacturing

Increasing, constant, and decreasing returns to scale are commonly observed. The table shows estimates of Cobb-Douglas production functions and returns to scale for various U.S. manufacturing industries (based on Hsieh, 1995).

	Labor, α	Capital, β	Returns to Scale, $\gamma = \alpha + \beta$
Decreasing Returns to Scale			
Tobacco products	0.18	0.33	0.51
Food and kindred products	0.43	0.48	0.91
Transportation equipment	0.44	0.48	0.92
Constant Returns to Scale			
Apparel and other textile products	0.70	0.31	1.01
Furniture and fixtures	0.62	0.40	1.02
Electronics and other electric equipment	0.49	0.53	1.02
Increasing Returns to Scale			
Paper and allied products	0.44	0.65	1.09
Petroleum and coal products	0.30	0.88	1.18
Primary metal	0.51	0.73	1.24

The table shows that the estimated returns to scale measure γ for a tobacco firm is $\gamma = 0.51$: A 1% increase in the inputs causes output to rise by 0.51%. Because output rises less than in proportion to the inputs, the tobacco production function exhibits decreasing returns to scale. In contrast, firms that manufacture primary metals have increasing returns to scale production functions, in which a 1% increase in all inputs causes output to rise by 1.24%.

The accompanying graphs use isoquants to illustrate the returns to scale for the electronics, tobacco, and primary metal firms. We measure the units of labor, capital, and output so that, for all three firms, 100 units of labor and 100 units of capital produce 100 units of output on the $q = 100$ isoquant in the three panels. For the constant returns to scale electronics firm, panel a, if both labor and capital are doubled from 100 to 200 units, output doubles to 200 ($= 100 \times 2^1$, multiplying the original output by the rate of increase using Equation 5.7).

That same doubling of inputs causes output to rise to only 142 ($\approx 100 \times 2^{0.51}$) for the tobacco firm, panel b. Because output rises less than in proportion to inputs, the production function has decreasing returns to scale. If the primary metal firm doubles its inputs, panel c, its output more than doubles, to 236 ($\approx 100 \times 2^{1.24}$), so the production function has increasing returns to scale.

These graphs illustrate that the spacing of the isoquant determines the returns to scale. The closer together the $q = 100$ and $q = 200$ isoquants, the greater the returns to scale.

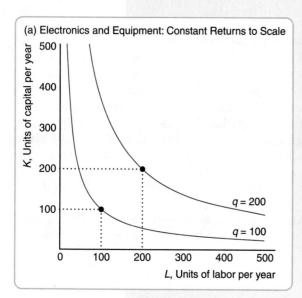

(a) Electronics and Equipment: Constant Returns to Scale

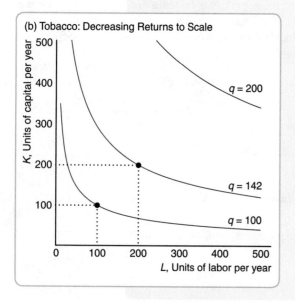

(b) Tobacco: Decreasing Returns to Scale

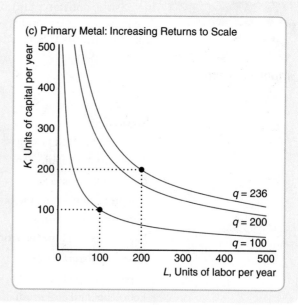

(c) Primary Metal: Increasing Returns to Scale

Varying Returns to Scale

When the production function is Cobb-Douglas, the returns to scale are the same at all levels of output. However, in other industries, a production function's returns to scale may vary as the output level changes. A firm might, for example, have increasing returns to scale at low levels of output, constant returns to scale for some range of output, and decreasing returns to scale at higher levels of output.

Many production functions have increasing returns to scale for small amounts of output, constant returns for moderate amounts of output, and decreasing returns for large amounts of output. When a firm is small, increasing labor and capital allows for gains from cooperation between workers and greater specialization of workers and equipment—*returns to specialization*—so there are increasing returns to scale. As the firm grows, returns to scale are eventually exhausted. There are no more returns to specialization, so the production process has constant returns to scale. If the firm continues to grow, the owner starts having difficulty managing everyone, so the firm suffers from decreasing returns to scale.

We show such a pattern in Figure 5.5. Again, the spacing of the isoquants reflects the returns to scale. Initially, the firm has one worker and one piece of equipment, point a, and produces 1 unit of output on the $q = 1$ isoquant. If the firm doubles its inputs, it produces at b, where $L = 2$ and $K = 2$, which lies on the dashed line through the origin and point a. Output more than doubles to $q = 3$, so the production function exhibits increasing returns to scale in this range. Another doubling of inputs to c causes output to double to 6 units, so the production function has constant returns to scale in this range. Another doubling of inputs to d causes output to increase by only a third, to $q = 8$, so the production function has decreasing returns to scale in this range.

FIGURE 5.5 Varying Scale Economies

The production function that corresponds to these isoquants exhibits varying returns to scale. Initially, the firm uses one worker and one unit of capital, point a. Point b has double the amount of labor and capital as does a. Similarly, c has double the inputs of b, and d has double the inputs of c. All these points lie along the dashed 45° line. The first time the inputs are doubled, a to b, output more than doubles from $q = 1$ to $q = 3$, so the production function has increasing returns to scale. The next doubling, b to c, causes a proportionate increase in output, constant returns to scale. At the last doubling, from c to d, the production function exhibits decreasing returns to scale.

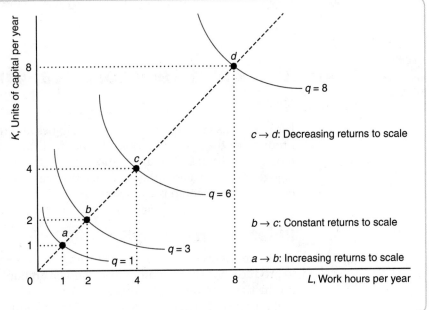

Managerial Implication

Small Is Beautiful

The industrial revolution of the late eighteenth century took advantage of economies of scale to revolutionize production. Since then, the pursuit of scale economies has driven firms to become larger and larger in most industries. However, a number of recent inventions may cause savvy managers to reverse this trend. Entrepreneurs and managers should consider whether new technologies make small-scale production economically attractive.

One of the most striking of these inventions is three-dimensional (3D) printing, which may greatly reduce the advantages of long production runs. An employee gives instructions (essentially a blueprint) to a 3D printer, presses *Print*, and the machine builds the object from the ground up, either by depositing material from a nozzle, or by selectively solidifying a thin layer of plastic or metal dust using drops of glue or a tightly focused beam. The final product can be a machine part, a bicycle frame, or a work of art.

This technology changes the relative positions of isoquants, potentially reducing dramatically the extent of increasing returns to scale and allowing small entrepreneurs to compete effectively with larger firms. It may also allow greater customization at little additional cost.

Currently these machines work only with certain plastics, resins, and metals, and have a precision of around a tenth of a millimeter. Costs have fallen to the point where manufacturing using 3D printers is cost effective, and new uses seem virtually unlimited. For example, in 2012, scientists at the University of Glasgow demonstrated that 3D printing can be used to create existing and new chemical compounds and, in 2013, a Dutch architect announced plans for the first 3D printed building. Moreover, 3D printing may lead to increased innovation and specialization. Any shape that you can design on a computer can be printed.

Managers should use this technology to experiment. Managers can produce small initial runs to determine the size of the market and consumers' acceptance of the product. Based on information from early adopters, managers can determine if the market warrants further production and quickly modify designs to meet end-users' desires.

5.5 Productivity and Technological Change

Progress was all right. Only it went on too long. —James Thurber

Because firms may use different technologies and different methods of organizing production, the amount of output that one firm produces from a given amount of inputs may differ from that produced by another firm. Further, after a positive technological or managerial innovation, a firm can produce more from a given amount of inputs than it could previously.

Relative Productivity

Firms are not necessarily equally *productive*, in the sense that one firm might be able to produce more than another from a given amount of inputs. A firm may be more productive than others if its manager knows a better way to organize production or if it is the only firm with access to a new invention. Union-mandated work rules, government regulations, or other institutional restrictions that affect only some firms might also lower the relative productivity of those firms.

Differences in productivity across markets may be due to differences in the degree of competition. In competitive markets, in which many firms can enter and exit the market easily, less productive firms lose money and are driven out of business, so the firms that are actually producing are equally productive. In a less competitive oligopoly market, with few firms and no possibility of entry by new firms, a less productive firm may be able to survive, so firms with varying levels of productivity are observed.

Mini-Case

U.S. Electric Generation Efficiency

Prior to the mid-1990s, over 90% of the electricity was produced and sold to consumers by investor-owned utility monopolies that were subject to government regulation of the prices they charged. Beginning in the mid-1990s, some states mandated that electric production be *restructured*. In such a state, the utility monopoly was forced to sell its electric generation plants to several other firms. These new firms sell the electricity they generate to the utility monopoly, which delivers the electricity to final consumers. Because they expected these new electric generator firms to compete with each other, state legislators hoped that this increased competition would result in greater production efficiency.

Fabrizio, Rose, and Wolfram (2007) found that, in anticipation of greater competition, the generation plant operators in states that had restructured had reduced their labor and nonfuel expenses by 3% to 5% (holding output constant) relative to investor-owned utility monopoly plants in states that did not restructure. When compared to plants run by government-owned or cooperatively owned utility monopolies that were not exposed to restructuring incentives, these gains were even greater: 6% in labor and 13% in nonfuel expenses.

Innovation

In its production process, a firm tries to use the best available technological and managerial knowledge. An advance in knowledge that allows more output to be produced with the same level of inputs is called **technological progress**. The invention of new products is a form of technological innovation. The use of robotic arms increases the number of automobiles produced with a given amount of labor and raw materials. Better *management or organization of the production process* similarly allows the firm to produce more output from given levels of inputs.

Technological Progress. A technological innovation changes the production process. Last year a firm produced

$$q_1 = f(L, K)$$

units of output using L units of labor services and K units of capital service. Due to a new invention that the firm uses, this year's production function differs from last year's, so the firm produces 10% more output with the same inputs:

$$q_2 = 1.1f(L, K).$$

Flath (2011) estimated the annual rate of technical innovation in Japanese manufacturing firms to be 0.91% for electric copper, 0.87% for medicine, 0.33% for steel pipes and tubes, 0.19% for cement, and 0.08% for beer.

This type of technological progress reflects *neutral technical change*, in which more output is produced using the same ratio of inputs. However, technological progress may be *nonneutral*. Rather than increasing output for a given mix of inputs, technological progress could be *capital saving*, where the firm can produce the same level of output as before using less capital and the same amount of other inputs. The American Licorice Company's automated drying machinery in the Managerial Problem is an example of labor-saving technological progress.

Alternatively, technological progress may be *labor saving*. Basker (2012) found that the introduction of barcode scanners in grocery stores increased the average product of labor by 4.5% on average across stores. Amazon bought Kiva Systems in 2012 with the intention of using its robots to move items in Amazon's warehouses, partially replacing workers. Other robots help doctors perform surgery quicker and reduce patients' recovery times.

Organizational Change.

Organizational changes may also alter the production function and increase the amount of output produced by a given amount of inputs. In the early 1900s, Henry Ford revolutionized mass production of automobiles through two organizational innovations. First, he introduced interchangeable parts, which cut the time required to install parts because workers no longer had to file or machine individually made parts to get them to fit.

Second, Ford introduced a conveyor belt and an assembly line to his production process. Before this change, workers walked around the car, and each worker performed many assembly activities. In Ford's plant, each worker specialized in a single activity such as attaching the right rear fender to the chassis. A conveyor belt moved the car at a constant speed from worker to worker along the assembly line. Because his workers gained proficiency from specializing in only a few activities and because the conveyor belts reduced the number of movements workers had to make, Ford could produce more automobiles with the same number of workers. These innovations reduced the ratio of labor to capital used. In 1908, the Ford Model T sold for $850, when rival vehicles sold for $2,000. By the early 1920s, Ford had increased production from fewer than a thousand cars per year to two million per year.

Mini-Case	In 2009, the automotive world was stunned when India's new Tata Motors started selling the Nano, its tiny, fuel-efficient four-passenger car. With a base price of less than $2,500, it is by far the world's least expensive car. The next cheapest car in India, the Maruti 800, sold for about $4,800.
Tata Nano's Technical and Organizational Innovations	The Nano's dramatically lower price is not the result of amazing new inventions; it is due to organizational innovations that led to simplifications and the use of less expensive materials and procedures. Although Tata Motors filed for 34 patents related to the design of the Nano (compared to the roughly 280 patents awarded to General Motors annually), most of these patents are for mundane items such as the two-cylinder engine's balance shaft and the configuration of the transmission gears.
	Instead of relying on innovations, Tata reorganized both production and distribution to lower costs. It reduced manufacturing costs at every stage of the process with a no-frills design, decreased vehicle weight, and made other major production improvements.

The Nano has a single windshield wiper, one side-view mirror, no power steering, a simplified door-opening lever, three nuts on the wheels instead of the customary four, and a trunk that does not open from the outside—it is accessed by folding down the rear seats. The Nano has smaller overall dimensions than the Maruti, but about 20% more seating capacity because of design decisions, such as putting the wheels at the extreme edges of the car. The Nano is much lighter than comparable models due to the reduced amount of steel, the use of lightweight steel, and the use of aluminum in the engine. The ribbed roof structure is not only a style element but also a strength structure, which is necessary because the design uses thin-gauge sheet metal. Because the engine is in the rear, the driveshaft doesn't need complex joints as in a front-engine car with front-wheel drive. To cut costs further, the company reduced the number of tools needed to make the components and thereby increased the life of the dies used by three times the norm. In consultation with their suppliers, Tata's engineers determined how many useful parts the design required, which helped them identify functions that could be integrated in parts.

Tata's plant can produce 250,000 Nanos per year and benefits from economies of scale. However, Tata's major organizational innovation was its open distribution and remote assembly. The Nano's modular design enables an experienced mechanic to assemble the car in a workshop. Therefore, Tata Motors can distribute a complete knock-down (CKD) kit to be assembled and serviced by local assembly hubs and entrepreneurs closer to consumers. The cost of transporting these kits, produced at a central manufacturing plant, is charged directly to the customer. This approach is expected to speed up the distribution process, particularly in the more remote locations of India. The car has been a great success, selling more than 8,500 cars in May 2012.

Managerial Solution **Labor Productivity During Recessions**	During a recession, a manager of the American Licorice Company has to reduce output and decides to lay off workers. Will the firm's labor productivity—average product of labor—go up and improve the firm's situation or go down and harm it? Layoffs have the positive effect of freeing up machines to be used by remaining workers. However, if layoffs force the remaining workers to perform a wide variety of tasks, the firm will lose the benefits from specialization. When there are many workers, the advantage of freeing up machines is important and increased multitasking is unlikely to be a problem. When there are only a few workers, freeing up more machines does not help much (some machines might stand idle some of the time), while multitasking becomes a more serious problem. Holding capital constant, a change in the number of workers affects a firm's average product of labor. Labor productivity could rise or fall. For example, in panel b of Figure 5.1, the average product of labor rises up to 15 workers per day

and then falls as the number of workers increases. The average product of labor falls if the firm has 6 or fewer workers and lays 1 off, but rises if the firm initially has 7 to 11 workers and lays off a worker.

For some production functions, layoffs always raise labor productivity because the AP_L curve is downward sloping everywhere. For such a production function, the positive effect of freeing up capital always dominates any negative effect of layoffs on average product. For example, layoffs raise the AP_L for any Cobb-Douglas production function, $q = AL^{\alpha}K^{\beta}$, where α is less than one.[7] All the estimated production functions listed in the "Returns to Scale in U.S. Manufacturing" Mini-Case have this property.

Let's return to our licorice manufacturer. According to Hsieh (1995), the Cobb-Douglas production function for food and kindred product plants is $q = AL^{0.43}K^{0.48}$, so $\alpha = 0.43$ is less than one and the AP_L curve slopes downward at every quantity. We can illustrate how much the AP_L rises with a layoff for this particular production function. If $A = 1$ and $L = K = 10$ initially, then the firm's output is $q = 10^{0.43} \times 10^{0.48} \approx 8.13$, and its average product of labor is $AP_L = q/L \approx 8.13/10 = 0.813$. If the number of workers is reduced by one, then output falls to $q = 9^{0.43} \times 10^{0.48} \approx 7.77$, and the average product of labor rises to $AP_L \approx 7.77/9 \approx 0.863$. That is, a 10% reduction in labor causes output to *fall* by 4.4%, but causes the average product of labor to *rise* by 6.2%. The firm's output falls less than 10% because each remaining worker is more productive.

Until recently, most large Japanese firms did not lay off workers during downturns. Thus, in contrast to U.S. firms, their average product of labor fell during recessions because their output fell while labor remained constant. Similarly, European firms have 30% less employment volatility over time than do U.S. firms, at least in part because European firms that fire workers are subject to a tax (Veracierto, 2008). Consequently, with other factors held constant in the short run, recessions might be more damaging to the profit of a Japanese or European firm than to the profit of a comparable U.S. firm. However, retaining *good* workers over short-run downturns might be a good long-run policy.

SUMMARY

1. **Production Functions.** A production function summarizes how a firm combines inputs such as labor, capital, and materials to produce output using the current state of knowledge about technology and management. A production function shows how much output can be produced efficiently from various levels of inputs. A firm produces efficiently if it cannot produce its current level of output with less of any one input, holding other inputs constant.

2. **Short-Run Production.** A firm can vary all its inputs in the long run but only some of them in the short run. In the short run, a firm cannot adjust the quantity of some inputs, such as capital. The firm varies its output in the short run by adjusting its variable inputs, such as labor. If all factors are fixed except labor, and a firm that was using very little labor increases its use of labor, its output may rise more than in proportion to the increase in labor because of greater specialization of workers.

---

[7]For this Cobb-Douglas production function, the average product of labor is $AP_L = q/L = AL^{\alpha}K^{\beta}/L = AL^{\alpha-1}K^{\beta}$. By partially differentiating this expression with respect to labor, we find that the change in the AP_L as the amount of labor rises is $\partial AP_L/\partial L = (\alpha - 1)AL^{\alpha-2}K^{\beta}$, which is negative if $\alpha < 1$. Thus, as labor falls, the average product of labor rises.

Eventually, however, as more workers are hired, the workers get in each other's way or must wait to share equipment, so output increases by smaller and smaller amounts. This latter phenomenon is described by the law of diminishing marginal returns: The marginal product of an input—the extra output from the last unit of input—eventually decreases as more of that input is used, holding other inputs fixed.

3. **Long-Run Production.** In the long run, when all inputs are variable, firms can substitute between inputs. An isoquant shows the combinations of inputs that can produce a given level of output. The marginal rate of technical substitution is the absolute value of the slope of the isoquant and indicates how easily the firm can substitute one factor of production for another. Usually, the more of one input the firm uses, the more difficult it is to substitute that input for another input. That is, there are diminishing marginal rates of technical substitution as the firm uses more of one input.

4. **Returns to Scale.** When a firm increases all inputs in proportion and its output increases by the same proportion, the production process is said to exhibit constant returns to scale. If output increases less than in proportion to the increase in inputs, the production process has decreasing returns to scale; if it increases more than in proportion, it has increasing returns to scale. All three types of returns to scale are commonly seen in actual industries. Many production processes exhibit first increasing, then constant, and finally decreasing returns to scale as the size of the firm increases.

5. **Productivity and Technological Change.** Even if all firms in an industry produce efficiently given what they know and the institutional and other constraints they face, some firms may be more productive than others, producing more output from a given bundle of inputs. More productive firms may have access to managerial or technical innovations not available to its rivals. Technological progress allows a firm to produce a given level of output using less inputs than it did previously. Technological progress changes the production function.

QUESTIONS

*All exercises are available on MyEconLab; * = answer at the back of this book.*

1. Production Functions

1.1. What are the main types of capital, labor, and materials used to produce licorice?

*1.2. Suppose that for the production function $q = f(L, K)$, if $L = 3$ and $K = 5$ then $q = 10$. Is it possible that $L = 3$ and $K = 6$ also yields $q = 10$ for this production function? Why or why not?

1.3. Consider Boeing (a producer of jet aircraft), General Mills (a producer of breakfast cereals), and Wacky Jack's (which claims to be the largest U.S. provider of singing telegrams). For which of these firms is the *short run* the longest period of time? For which is the long run the shortest? Explain.

2. Short-Run Production

*2.1. If each extra worker produces an extra unit of output, how do the total product of labor, average product of labor, and marginal product of labor vary with labor? Plot these curves in a graph similar to Figure 5.1.

2.2. Each extra worker produces an extra unit of output up to six workers. As more workers are added, no additional output is produced. Draw the total product of labor, average product of labor, and marginal product of labor curves in a graph similar to Figure 5.1.

*2.3. Suppose that the production function is $q = L^{0.75}K^{0.25}$. (*Hint*: See Q&A 5.1.)

   a. What is the average product of labor, holding capital fixed at $\overline{K}$?

   b. What is the marginal product of labor?

   c. How is the marginal product of labor related to the average product of labor?

2.4. In the short run, a firm cannot vary its capital, $K = 2$, but can vary its labor, L. It produces output q. Explain why the firm will or will not experience diminishing marginal returns to labor in the short run if its production function is

   a. $q = 10L + K$.

   b. $q = L^{0.5}K^{0.5}$.

2.5. Based on the information in the Mini-Case "Malthus and the Green Revolution," how did the average product of labor in food production change over time?

3. Long-Run Production

3.1. Why must isoquants be thin?

3.2. According to Card (2009), (a) workers with less than a high school education are perfect substitutes for those with a high school education, (b) "high school equivalent" and "college equivalent" workers are imperfect substitutes, and (c) within education groups, immigrants and natives are imperfect substitutes. For each of these comparisons, draw the isoquants for a production function that uses two types of workers. For example, in part (a), production is a function of workers with a high school diploma and workers with less education.

*3.3. To produce a recorded DVD, $q = 1$, a firm uses one blank disk, $D = 1$, and the services of a recording machine, $M = 1$, for one hour. (*Hint*: See Q&A 5.2.)

   a. Draw the isoquants for this production function and explain its shape.

   b. What is the *MRTS* at each point along the isoquant corresponding to $q = 100$?

   c. Draw the total product, average product, and marginal product of labor curves (you will probably want to use two diagrams) for this production function.

3.4. The production function at Ginko's Copy Shop is $q = 1,000 \times \min(L, 3K)$, where q is the number of copies per hour, L is the number of workers, and K is the number of copy machines. As an example, if $L = 4$ and $K = 1$, then the minimum of L and $3K$, $\min(L, 3K) = 3$, and $q = 3,000$.

   a. Draw the isoquants for this production function.

   b. Draw the total product, average product, and marginal product of labor curves for this production function for some fixed level of capital.

3.5. Using the figure in the Mini-Case "A Semiconductor Isoquant," show that as the firm employs additional fixed-proportion technologies, the firm's overall isoquant approaches a smooth curve similar to that in panel c of Figure 5.3.

*3.6. A laundry cleans white clothes using the production function $q = B + 2G$, where B is the number of cups of Clorox bleach, G is the number of cups of a generic bleach that is half as potent, and q is the basketfuls of clothes that are cleaned. Draw an isoquant for one basketful of clothes. What is the marginal product of B? What is the marginal rate of technical substitution at each point on an isoquant?

*3.7. At $L = 4$, $K = 4$, the marginal product of labor is 2 and the marginal product of capital is 3. What is the marginal rate of technical substitution (*MRTS*)?

4. Returns to Scale

4.1. To speed relief to isolated South Asian communities that were devastated by the December 2004 tsunami, the U.S. government doubled the number of helicopters from 45 to 90 in early 2005. Navy admiral Thomas Fargo, head of the U.S. Pacific Command, was asked if doubling the number of helicopters would "produce twice as much [relief]." He predicted, "Maybe pretty close to twice as much." (Vicky O'Hara, *All Things Considered*, National Public Radio, January 4, 2005, **www.npr.org/dmg/dmg.php?prgCode=ATC&showDate=04-Jan-2005&segNum=10&NPRMediaPref=WM&getAd=1**.) Identify the outputs and inputs and describe the production process. Is the admiral discussing a production process with nearly constant returns to scale, or is he referring to another property of the production process?

*4.2. The production function for the automotive and parts industry is $q = L^{0.27}K^{0.16}M^{0.61}$, where M is energy and materials (based on Klein, 2003). What kind of returns to scale does this production function exhibit? What is the marginal product of materials?

4.3. Under what conditions do the following production functions exhibit decreasing, constant, or increasing returns to scale? (*Hint*: See Q&A 5.3.)

   a. $q = L + K$.

   b. $q = L + L^{\alpha}K^{\beta} + K$.

4.4. A production function has the property that $f(xL, xK) = x^2 f(L, K)$ for any positive value of x. What kind of returns to scale does this production function exhibit? If the firm doubles L and K, show that the marginal product of labor and the marginal product of capital also double.

*4.5. Show in a diagram that a production function can have diminishing marginal returns to a factor and constant returns to scale.

4.6. Is it possible that a firm's production function exhibits increasing returns to scale while exhibiting diminishing marginal productivity of each of its inputs? To answer this question, calculate the marginal productivities of capital and labor for the production of electronics and equipment, tobacco, and primary metal using the information listed in the "Returns to Scale in U.S. Manufacturing" Mini-Case.

*4.7. The BlackBerry production function indicated in the text is $Q = 2.83L^{1.52}K^{0.82}$. Epple et al. (2010) estimate that the production function for U.S. housing is $q = 1.38L^{0.144}M^{0.856}$, where L is land and M is an aggregate of all other mobile, nonland factors, which we call materials. Haskel and Sadun (2012) estimate the production function for U.K. supermarkets is $Q = L^{0.23}K^{0.10}M^{0.66}$, where L is labor, K is capital, and M is materials. What kind of returns to scale do these production functions exhibit?

4.8. Michelle's business produces ceramic cups using labor, clay, and a kiln. She produces cups using a fixed proportion of labor and clay, but regardless of how many cups she produces, she uses only one kiln. She can manufacture 25 cups a day with one worker and 35 with two workers. Does her production process illustrate *decreasing returns to scale* or a *diminishing marginal product of labor*? What is the likely explanation for why output doesn't increase proportionately with the number of workers?

4.9. Does it follow that because we observe that the average product of labor is higher for Firm 1 than for Firm 2, Firm 1 is more productive in the sense that it can produce more output from a given amount of inputs? Why?

5. Productivity and Technological Change

*5.1. Firm 1 and Firm 2 use the same type of production function, but Firm 1 is only 90% as productive as Firm 2. That is, the production function of Firm 2 is $q_2 = f(L, K)$, and the production function of Firm 1 is $q_1 = 0.9f(L, K)$. At a particular level of inputs, how does the marginal product of labor differ between the firms?

5.2. In a manufacturing plant, workers use a specialized machine to produce belts. A new machine is invented that is laborsaving. With the new machine, the firm can use fewer workers and still produce the same number of belts as it did using the old machine. In the long run, both labor and capital (the machine) are variable. From what you know, what is the effect of this invention on the AP_L, MP_L, and returns to scale? If you require more information to answer this question, specify what you need to know.

5.3. Until the mid-eighteenth century when spinning became mechanized, cotton was an expensive and relatively unimportant textile (Virginia Postrel, "What Separates Rich Nations from Poor Nations?" *New York Times*, January 1, 2004). Where it used to take a hand-spinner 50,000 hours to hand-spin 100 pounds of cotton, an operator of a 1760s-era hand-operated cotton mule-spinning machine could produce 100 pounds of stronger thread in 300 hours. When the self-acting mule spinner automated the process after 1825, the time dropped to 135 hours, and cotton became an inexpensive, common cloth. In a figure, show how these technological changes affected isoquants. Explain briefly.

6. Managerial Problem

6.1. If a firm lays off workers during a recession, how will the firm's marginal product of labor change? (*Hint*: See Figure 5.1.)

*6.2. During recessions, U.S. firms lay off a larger proportion of their workers than Japanese firms do. (It has been claimed that Japanese firms continue to produce at high levels and store the output or sell it at relatively low prices during the recession.) Assuming that the production function remains unchanged over a period that is long enough to include many recessions and expansions, would you expect the average product of labor to be higher in Japan or the United States? Why?

7. Spreadsheet Exercises

7.1. Labor, L, and capital, K, are the only inputs in each of the following production functions:

a. $q_1 = (L + K)^2$.
b. $q_2 = (\sqrt{L} + \sqrt{K})^2$.
c. $q_3 = (20 + \sqrt{L} + \sqrt{K})^2$.

For each production function, use a spreadsheet to find the output associated with the following output combinations: $L = 2, K = 2$; $L = 4, K = 4$; and $L = 8, K = 8$. Determine whether each production function exhibits increasing returns to scale, decreasing returns to scale, constant returns to scale, or variable returns to scale over this range.

7.2. The Green Revolution (see the Mini-Case "Malthus and the Green Revolution") was based in part on extensive experimentation. The following data illustrates the relationship between nitrogen fertilizer (in pounds of nitrogen) and the output of a particular type of wheat (in bushels). Each observation is based on one acre of land and all other relevant inputs to production (such as water, labor, and capital) are held constant. The fertilizer levels are 20, 40, 60, 80, 100, 120, 140, and 160, and the associated output levels are 47, 86, 107, 131, 136, 148, 149, and 142.

a. Use Excel to estimate the short-run production function showing the relationship between fertilizer input and output. (*Hint*: As described in Chapter 3, use the Trendline option to regress output on fertilizer input. Try a linear function and try a quadratic function and determine which function fits the data better.)

b. Does fertilizer exhibit the law of diminishing marginal returns? What is the largest amount of fertilizer that should ever be used, even if it is free?

6 Costs

An economist is a person who, when invited to give a talk at a banquet, tells the audience there's no such thing as a free lunch.

A manager of a semiconductor manufacturing firm, who can choose from many different production technologies, must determine whether the firm should use the same technology in its foreign plant that it uses in its domestic plant. U.S. semiconductor manufacturing firms have been moving much of their production abroad since 1961, when Fairchild Semiconductor built a plant in Hong Kong. According to the Semiconductor Industry Association, world-wide semiconductor billings from the Americas dropped from 66% in 1976, to 34% in 1998, and to 18% by April 2013. Firms are moving their production abroad because of lower taxes, lower labor costs, and capital grant benefits. Capital grants are funds provided by a foreign government to firms to induce them to produce in that country. Such grants can reduce the cost of owning and operating an overseas semiconductor fabrication facility by as much as 25% compared to the costs of a U.S.-based plant.

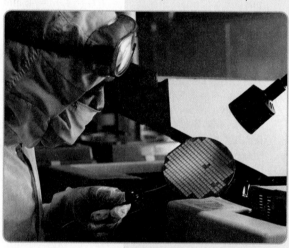

The semiconductor manufacturer can produce a chip using sophisticated equipment and relatively few workers or many workers and less complex equipment. In the United States, firms use a relatively capital-intensive technology, because doing so minimizes their cost of producing a given level of output. Will that same technology be cost minimizing if they move their production abroad?

A firm uses a two-step procedure to determine the most efficient way to produce a certain amount of output. First, the firm determines which production processes are *technically efficient* so that it can produce the desired level of output without any wasted or unnecessary inputs. As we saw in Chapter 5, the firm uses engineering and other information to determine its production function, which summarizes the many technically efficient production processes available. A firm's production function shows the maximum output that can be produced with any specified combination of *inputs* or *factors of production*, such as labor, capital, energy, and materials.

The firm's second step is to pick from these technically efficient production processes the one that is also **economically efficient**, minimizing the cost of producing a specified output level.[1] To determine which process minimizes its cost

---

[1]Similarly, economically efficient production implies that the quantity of output is maximized for any given level of cost.

of production, the firm uses information about the production function and the cost of inputs.

Managers and economists need to understand the relationship between costs of inputs and production to determine the least costly way to produce. By minimizing the cost of producing a given level of output, a firm can increase its profit.

Main Topics

In this chapter, we examine five main topics

1. **The Nature of Costs:** When considering the cost of a proposed action, a good manager takes account of foregone alternative opportunities.
2. **Short-Run Costs:** To minimize costs in the short run, the firm adjusts its variable factors of production (such as labor), but cannot adjust its fixed factors (such as capital).
3. **Long-Run Costs:** In the long run, all inputs are variable because the firm has the time to adjust all its factors of production.
4. **The Learning Curve:** A firm might be able to lower its costs of production over time as its workers and managers learn from experience about how best to produce a particular product.
5. **The Costs of Producing Multiple Goods:** If the firm produces several goods simultaneously, the cost of each may depend on the quantities of all the goods produced.

6.1 The Nature of Costs

Too caustic? To hell with the costs, we'll make the picture anyway. —Samuel Goldwyn

Making sound managerial decisions about investment and production requires information about the associated costs. Some cost information is provided in legally required financial accounting statements. However, such statements do not provide sufficient cost information for good decision making. Financial accounting statements correctly measure costs for tax purposes and to meet other legal requirements, but good managerial decisions require a different perspective on costs.

To produce a particular amount of output, a firm incurs costs for the required inputs such as labor, capital, energy, and materials. A firm's manager (or accountant) determines the cost of labor, energy, and materials by multiplying the price of the factor times the number of units used. If workers earn $20 per hour and the firm hires 100 hours of labor per day, then the firm's cost of labor is $20 \times 100 = \$2,000$ per day. The manager can easily calculate these *explicit costs*, which are its direct, out-of-pocket payments for inputs to its production process during a given time period. While calculating explicit costs is straightforward, some costs are implicit in that they reflect only a foregone opportunity rather than explicit, current expenditure. Properly taking account of foregone opportunities requires particularly careful attention when dealing with durable capital goods, as past expenditures for an input may be irrelevant to current cost calculations if that input has no current, alternative use.

Opportunity Costs

A fundamental principle of managerial decision making is that managers should focus on *opportunity costs*. The **opportunity cost** of a resource is the value of the best alternative use of that resource. Explicit costs are opportunity costs. If a firm purchases an input in a market and uses that input immediately, the input's opportunity cost is the amount the firm pays for it, the market price. After all, if the firm did not use the input in its production process, its best alternative would be to sell it to someone else at the market price. The concept of an opportunity cost becomes particularly useful when the firm uses an input that it cannot purchase in a market or that was purchased in a market in the past.

A key example of such an opportunity cost is the value of a manager's time. For example, Maoyong owns and manages a firm. He pays himself only a small monthly salary of $1,000 because he also receives the firm's profit. However, Maoyong could work for another firm and earn $11,000 a month. Thus, the opportunity cost of his time is $11,000—from his best alternative use of his time—not the $1,000 he actually pays himself.

A financial statement may not include such an opportunity cost, but Maoyong needs to take account of this opportunity cost to make decisions that maximize his profit. Suppose that the explicit cost of operating his firm is $40,000, including the rent for work space, the cost of materials, the wage payments to an employee, and the $1,000 a month he pays himself. The full, opportunity cost of the firm is $50,000, which includes the extra $10,000 in opportunity cost for Maoyong's time beyond the $1,000 that he already pays himself. If his firm's revenue is $49,000 per month and he considers only his explicit costs of $40,000, it appears that his firm makes a profit of $9,000. In contrast, if he takes account of the full opportunity cost of $50,000, his firm incurs a loss of $1,000.

Another example of an opportunity cost is captured in the well-known phrase "There's no such thing as a free lunch." Suppose your parents come to town and offer to take you to lunch. Although they pay the explicit cost—the restaurant's tab—for the lunch, you still incur the opportunity cost of your time. No doubt the best alternative use of your time is studying this textbook, but you could also consider working at a job for a wage or watching television as possible alternatives. In considering whether to accept the "free" lunch, you need to compare this true opportunity cost against the benefit of dining with your parents.

Mini-Case

The Opportunity Cost of an MBA

During major economic downturns, do applications to MBA programs fall, hold steady, or take off like tech stocks during the first Internet bubble? Knowledge of opportunity costs helps us answer this question.

The biggest cost of attending an MBA program is often the opportunity cost of giving up a well-paying job. Someone who leaves a job paying $6,000 per month to attend an MBA program is, in effect, incurring a $6,000 per month opportunity cost, in addition to the tuition and cost of textbooks (though this one is well worth the money).

Thus, it is not surprising that MBA applications rise in bad economic times when outside opportunities decline. People thinking of going back to school face a reduced opportunity cost of entering an MBA program if they think they might be laid off or might not be promoted during an economic downturn. As Stacey Kole, deputy dean for the MBA program at the University of Chicago Graduate School of Business, observed, "When there's a go-go economy, fewer people decide to go back to school. When things go south the opportunity cost of leaving work is lower."

In 2008, when U.S. unemployment rose sharply and the economy was in poor shape, the number of people seeking admission to MBA programs rose sharply. The number of applicants to MBA programs for the class of 2008–2009 increased over the previous year by 79% in the United States, 77% in the United Kingdom, and 69% in other European programs. Applicants increased substantially for 2009–2010 as well in Canada and Europe. However, as economic conditions improved, global applications fell in 2011 and were relatively unchanged in 2012.

Q&A 6.1

Meredith's firm has sent her to a conference for managers and paid her registration fee. Included in the registration fee is free admission to a class on how to price derivative securities, such as options. She is considering attending, but her most attractive alternative opportunity is to attend a talk at the same time by Warren Buffett on his investment strategies. She would be willing to pay $100 to hear his talk, and the cost of a ticket is $40. Given that attending either talk involves no other costs, what is Meredith's opportunity cost of attending the derivatives talk?

Answer *To determine her opportunity cost, determine the benefit that Meredith would forego by attending the derivatives class.* Because she incurs no additional fee to attend the derivatives talk, Meredith's opportunity cost is the foregone benefit of hearing the Buffett speech. Because she values hearing the Buffett speech at $100, but only has to pay $40, her net benefit from hearing that talk is $60 (= $100 − $40). Thus, her opportunity cost of attending the derivatives talk is $60.

Costs of Durable Inputs

Determining the opportunity cost of capital such as land, buildings, or equipment is more complex than calculating the cost of inputs that are bought and used in the same period such as labor services, energy, or materials. Capital is a **durable good**: a product that is usable for a long period, perhaps for many years. Two problems may arise in measuring the cost of a firm's capital. The first is how to allocate the initial purchase cost over time. The second is what to do if the value of the capital changes over time.

We can avoid these two measurement problems if capital is rented instead of purchased. For example, suppose a firm can rent a small pick-up truck for $400 a month or buy it outright for $20,000. If the firm rents the truck, the rental payment is the relevant opportunity cost per month. The truck is rented month by month, so the firm does not have to worry about how to allocate the purchase cost of a truck over time. Moreover, the rental rate would adjust if the cost of trucks changes over time. Thus, if the firm can rent capital for short periods of time, it calculates the cost of this capital in the same way that it calculates the cost of nondurable inputs such as labor services or materials.

The firm faces a more complicated problem in determining the opportunity cost of the truck if it purchases the truck. The firm's accountant may *expense* the truck's purchase price by treating the full $20,000 as a cost when the truck is purchased, or the accountant may *amortize* the cost by spreading the $20,000 over the life of the truck, following rules set by an accounting organization or by a relevant government authority such as the Internal Revenue Service (IRS).

A manager who wants to make sound decisions about operating the truck does not expense or amortize the truck using such rules. The firm's opportunity cost of using the truck is the amount that the firm would earn if it rented the truck to others. Thus, even though the firm owns the truck, the manager should view the opportunity cost of this capital good as a rent per time period. If the value of an older truck is less than that of a newer one, the rental rate for the truck falls over time.

If no rental market for trucks exists, we must determine the opportunity cost in another way. Suppose that the firm has two choices: It can choose not to buy the truck and keep the truck's purchase price of $20,000, or it can use the truck for a year and sell it for $17,000 at the end of the year. If the firm did not purchase the truck it would deposit the $20,000 in a bank account that pays, for example, 2% per year, earning $400 in interest and therefore having $20,400 at the end of the year. Thus, the opportunity cost of capital of using the truck for a year is $20,400 − $17,000 = $3,400.[2] This $3,400 opportunity cost equals the depreciation of the truck of $3,000 (= $20,000 − $17,000) plus the $400 in foregone interest that the firm could have earned over the year if the firm had invested the $20,000.

The value of trucks, machines, and other equipment declines over time, leading to declining rental values and therefore to declining opportunity costs. In contrast, the value of some land, buildings, and other forms of capital may rise over time. To maximize its economic profit, a firm must properly measure the opportunity cost of a piece of capital even if its value rises over time. If a beauty parlor buys a building when similar buildings in that area rent for $1,000 per month, then the opportunity cost of using the building is $1,000 a month. If land values rise causing rents in the area to rise to $2,000 per month, the beauty parlor's opportunity cost of its building rises to $2,000 per month.

Sunk Costs

An opportunity cost is not always easy to observe but should always be taken into account in deciding how much to produce. In contrast, a **sunk cost**—a past expenditure that cannot be recovered—though easily observed is not relevant to a manager when deciding how much to produce now. If an expenditure is sunk, it is not an opportunity cost. Nonetheless, a sunk cost paid for a specialized input should still be deducted from income before paying taxes even if that cost is sunk, and must therefore appear in financial accounts.

If a firm buys a forklift for $25,000 and can resell it for the same price, then the expenditure is not sunk, and the opportunity cost of using the forklift is $25,000. If instead the firm buys a specialized piece of equipment for $25,000 and cannot resell it, then the original expenditure is a sunk cost—it cannot be recovered. Because this equipment has no alternative use—it cannot be resold—its opportunity cost is zero, and hence should not be included in the firm's current cost calculations. If the specialized equipment that originally cost $25,000 can be resold for $10,000, then only $15,000 of the original expenditure is sunk, and the opportunity cost is $10,000.

---

[2]The firm would also pay for gasoline, insurance, and other operating costs, but these items would all be expensed as operating costs and would not appear in the firm's accounts as capital costs.

Managerial Implication

Ignoring Sunk Costs

A manager should ignore sunk costs when making current decisions. To see why, consider a firm that paid $300,000 for a parcel of land for which the market value has fallen to $200,000, which is the land's current opportunity cost. The $100,000 difference between the $300,000 purchase price and the current market value of $200,000 is a sunk cost that has already been incurred and cannot be recovered. The land is worth $240,000 to the firm if it builds a plant on this parcel. Is it worth carrying out production on this land or should the land be sold for its market value of $200,000? A manager who uses the original purchase price in the decision-making process would falsely conclude that using the land for production will result in a $60,000 loss: the value to using the land of $240,000 minus the purchase price of $300,000. Instead, the firm should use the land because it is worth $40,000 more as a production facility than the firm's next best alternative of selling the land for $200,000. Thus, the firm should use the land's opportunity cost in making its decisions and ignore the land's sunk cost. In short, "there's no use crying over spilt milk."

6.2 Short-Run Costs

When making short-run and long-run production and investment decisions, managers must take the relevant costs into account. As noted in Chapter 5, the short run is the period over which some inputs, such as labor, can be varied while other inputs, such as capital, are fixed. In contrast, in the long run, the firm can vary all its inputs. For simplicity in our graphs, we concentrate on firms that use only two inputs, labor and capital. We focus on the case in which labor is the only variable input in the short run, and both labor and capital are variable in the long run. However, we can generalize our analysis to examine a firm that uses any number of inputs.

We start by examining various measures of cost and cost curves that can be used to analyze costs in both the short run and the long run. Then we show how the shapes of the short-run cost curves are related to the firm's production function.

Common Measures of Cost

All firms use the same basic cost measures for making both short-run and long-run decisions. The measures should be based on inputs' opportunity costs.

Fixed Cost, Variable Cost, and Total Cost. A **fixed cost (F)** is a cost that does not vary with the level of output. Fixed costs, which include expenditures on land, office space, production facilities, and other *overhead* expenses, cannot be avoided by reducing output and must be incurred as long as the firm stays in business.

Fixed costs are often sunk costs, but not always. For example, a restaurant rents space for $2,000 per month on a month-to-month lease. This rent does not vary with the number of meals served (its output level), so it is a fixed cost. Because the restaurant has already paid this month's rent, this fixed cost is a sunk cost: the restaurant cannot get the $2,000 back even if it goes out of business. Next month, if the restaurant stays open, it will have to pay the fixed, $2,000 rent. If the restaurant has a month-to-month rental agreement, this fixed cost of $2,000 is an *avoidable cost*, not a

Fixed   *Variable*

sunk cost. The restaurant can shut down, cancel its rental agreement, and avoid paying this fixed cost. Therefore, in planning for next month, the restaurant should treat the $2,000 rent as a fixed cost but not as a sunk cost. Thus, the fixed cost of $2,000 per month is a fixed cost in both the short run (this month) and in the long run. However, it is a sunk cost only in the short run.

A **variable cost (VC)** is a cost that changes as the quantity of output changes. Variable costs are the costs of *variable inputs*, which are inputs that the firm can adjust to alter its output level, such as labor and materials.

A firm's **cost (or total cost)**, C, is the sum of a firm's variable cost and fixed cost:

$$C = VC + F.$$

Because variable costs change as the output level changes, so does total cost. For example, in Table 6.1, if the fixed cost is $F = \$48$ and the firm produces 5 units of output, its variable cost is $VC = \$100$, so its total cost is $C = \$148$.

Average Cost. Firms use three average cost measures corresponding to fixed, variable, and total costs. The **average fixed cost (AFC)** is the fixed cost divided by the units of output produced: $AFC = F/q$. The average fixed cost falls as output rises because the fixed cost is spread over more units. The average fixed cost falls from $48 for 1 unit of output to $4 for 12 units of output in Table 6.1.

The **average variable cost (AVC)**, or variable cost per unit of output, is the variable cost divided by the units of output produced: $AVC = VC/q$. Because the variable

TABLE 6.1 How Cost Varies with Output

Output, q	Fixed Cost, F	Variable Cost, VC	Total Cost, C	Marginal Cost, MC	Average Fixed Cost, $AFC = F/q$	Average Variable Cost, $AVC = VC/q$	Average Cost, $AC = C/q$
0	48	0	48				
1	48	25	73	25	48	25	73
2	48	46	94	21	24	23	47
3	48	66	114	20	16	22	38
4	48	82	130	16	12	20.5	32.5
5	48	100	148	18	9.6	20	29.6
6	48	120	168	20	8	20	28
7	48	141	189	21	6.9	20.1	27
8	48	168	216	27	6	21	27
9	48	198	246	30	5.3	22	27.3
10	48	230	278	32	4.8	23	27.8
11	48	272	320	42	4.4	24.7	29.1
12	48	321	369	49	4.0	26.8	30.8

cost increases with output, the average variable cost may either increase or decrease as output rises. In Table 6.1, the average variable cost is $25 at 1 unit, falls until it reaches a minimum of $20 at 6 units, and then rises.

The **average cost (AC)**—or *average total cost*—is the total cost divided by the units of output produced: $AC = C/q$. Because total cost is $C = VC + F$, if we divide both sides of the equation by q, we find that average cost is the sum of the average fixed cost and the average variable cost:

$$AC = \frac{C}{q} = \frac{F}{q} + \frac{VC}{q} = AFC + AVC.$$

In Table 6.1, because AFC falls with output and AVC eventually rises with output, average cost falls until output is 8 units and then rises.

Marginal Cost. A firm's **marginal cost (MC)** is the amount by which a firm's cost changes if the firm produces one more unit of output. The marginal cost is

$$MC = \frac{\Delta C}{\Delta q}$$

where ΔC is the change in cost when the change in output, Δq, is 1 unit in Table 6.1. If the firm increases its output from 2 to 3 units ($\Delta q = 1$), its total cost rises from $94 to $114 so $\Delta C = \$20$. Thus its marginal cost is $\Delta C/\Delta q = \$20$.

Because only variable cost changes with output, marginal cost also equals the change in variable cost from a one-unit increase in output:

$$MC = \frac{\Delta VC}{\Delta q}.$$

As the firm increases output from 2 to 3 units, its variable cost increases by $\Delta VC = \$20 = \$66 - \$46$, so its marginal cost is $MC = \Delta VC/\Delta q = \$20$. A firm takes account of its marginal cost curve to decide whether it pays to change its output level.

Using Calculus

Calculating Marginal Cost

Using calculus, we may alternatively define the marginal cost as $MC = dC/dq$, which is the rate of change of cost as we make an infinitesimally small change in output. Because $C = VC + F$, it follows that $MC = dVC/dq + dF/dq = dVC/dq$, because fixed costs do not change as output changes: $dF/dq = 0$.

For example, suppose that the variable cost is $VC = 4q + 6q^2$ and the fixed cost is $F = 10$, so the total cost is $C = VC + F = 4q + 6q^2 + 10$. Using the variable cost, the marginal cost is $dVC/dq = d(4q + 6q^2)/dq = 4 + 12q$. We get the same expression for marginal cost if we use the total cost: $dC/dq = d(4q + 6q^2 + 10)/dq = 4 + 12q$.

Cost Curves

We illustrate the relationship between output and the various cost measures in Figure 6.1. Panel a shows the variable cost, fixed cost, and total cost curves that correspond to Table 6.1. The fixed cost, which does not vary with output, is a horizontal line at $48. The variable cost curve is zero at zero units of output and rises with

FIGURE 6.1 Cost Curves

(a) Because the total cost differs from the variable cost by the fixed cost, F, of $48, the total cost curve, C, is parallel to the variable cost curve, VC. (b) The marginal cost curve, MC, cuts the average variable cost, AVC, and average cost, AC, curves at their minimums. The height of the AC curve at point a equals the slope of the line from the origin to the cost curve at A. The height of the AVC at b equals the slope of the line from the origin to the variable cost curve at B. The height of the marginal cost is the slope of either the C or VC curve at that quantity.

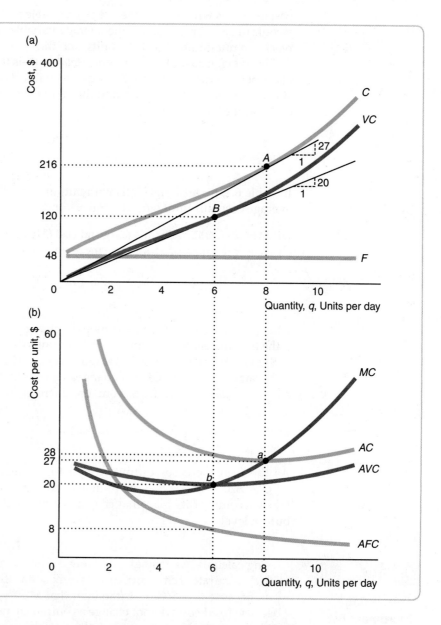

output. The total cost curve, which is the vertical sum of the variable cost curve and the fixed cost line, is $48 higher than the variable cost curve at every output level, so the variable cost and total cost curves are parallel.

Panel b shows the average fixed cost, average variable cost, average cost, and marginal cost curves. The average fixed cost curve falls as output increases. It approaches zero as output gets large because the fixed cost is spread over many units of output. The average cost curve is the vertical sum of the average fixed cost and average variable cost curves. For example, at 6 units of output, the average variable cost is 20 and the average fixed cost is 8, so the average (total) cost is 28.

The relationships between the average and marginal cost curves and the total cost curve are similar to those between the average and marginal product curves and the total product curve (as discussed in Chapter 5). The average cost at a particular output level is the slope of a line from the origin to the corresponding point on the total cost curve. The slope of that line is the rise (the cost at that output level) divided by the run (the output level), which is the definition of the average cost. In panel a, the slope of the line from the origin to point A is the average cost for 8 units of output. The height of the cost curve at A is 216, so the slope is $216/8 = 27$, which is the height of the average cost curve at the corresponding point a in panel b.

Similarly, the average variable cost is the slope of a line from the origin to a point on the variable cost curve. The slope of the dashed line from the origin to B in panel a is 20 (the height of the variable cost curve, 120, divided by the number of units of output, 6), which is also the height of the average variable cost curve at 6 units of output, point b in panel b.

The marginal cost is the slope of either the cost curve or the variable cost curve at a given output level. Because the total cost and variable cost curves are parallel, they have the same slope at any given output. The difference between total cost and variable cost is fixed cost, which does not affect marginal cost.

The thin black line from the origin is tangent to the cost curve at A in panel a. Thus, the slope of the thin black line equals both the average cost and the marginal cost at point a (8 units of output). This equality occurs at the corresponding point a in panel b, where the marginal cost curve intersects the average cost.

Where the marginal cost curve is below the average cost, the average cost curve declines with output. Because the average cost of 47 for 2 units is greater than the marginal cost of the third unit, 20, the average cost for 3 units falls to 38.[3] Where the marginal cost is above the average cost, the average cost curve rises with output. At 8 units, the marginal cost equals the average cost (at point a in panel b, the minimum point of the average cost curve), so the average is unchanging.

Because the dashed line from the origin is tangent to the variable cost curve at B in panel a, the marginal cost equals the average variable cost at the corresponding point b in panel b. Again, where marginal cost is above average variable cost, the average variable cost curve rises with output; where marginal cost is below average variable cost, the average variable cost curve falls with output. Because the average cost curve is above the average variable cost curve everywhere and the marginal cost curve is rising where it crosses both average curves, the minimum of the average variable cost curve, b, is at a lower output level than the minimum of the average cost curve, a.

Production Functions and the Shapes of Cost Curves

The production function determines the shape of a firm's cost curves. The production function shows the amount of inputs needed to produce a given level of output (Chapter 5). The firm calculates its variable cost by multiplying the quantity of each input by its price and summing the costs of the variable inputs.

In this section, we focus on cost curves in the short run. If a firm produces output using capital and labor, and its capital is fixed in the short run, the firm's variable cost is its cost of labor. Its labor cost is the wage per hour, w, times the number of hours of labor, L, employed by the firm: $VC = wL$.

In the short run, when the firm's capital is fixed, the only way the firm can increase its output is to use more labor. If the firm increases its labor enough, it reaches the

---

[3]From Table 6.1, we know that the average cost of the first two units is 47. If we add a third unit with a marginal cost of 20, the new average can be calculated by adding the average values of the first two units plus the marginal cost of the third unit and dividing by 3: $(47 + 47 + 20)/3 = 38$. Thus, if we add a marginal cost that is less than the old average cost, the new average cost must fall.

point of *diminishing marginal returns to labor*, at which each extra worker increases output by a smaller amount. We can use this information about the relationship between labor and output—the production function—to determine the shape of the variable cost curve and its related curves.

The Variable Cost Curve.

If input prices are constant, the firm's production function determines the shape of the variable cost curve. We illustrate this relationship in Figure 6.2. The firm faces a constant input price for labor, the wage, of $10 per hour.

The total product of labor curve in Figure 6.2 shows the firm's short-run production function relationship between output and labor when capital is held fixed. At point *a*, the firm uses 5 hours of labor to produce 1 unit of output. At point *b*, it takes 20 hours of labor to produce 5 units of output. Here, output increases more than in proportion to labor: Output rises 5 times when labor increases 4 times. In contrast, as the firm moves from *b* to *c*, output increases less than in proportion. Output doubles to 10 as a result of increasing labor from 20 to 46—an increase of 2.3 times. The movement from *c* to *d* results in even a smaller increase in output relative to labor. This flattening of the total product curve at higher levels of labor reflects diminishing marginal returns to labor.

This curve shows both the production relation of output to labor and the variable cost relation of output to cost. Because each hour of work costs the firm $10, we can relabel the horizontal axis in Figure 6.2 to show the firm's variable cost, its cost of labor. To produce 5 units of output takes 20 hours of labor, so the firm's variable cost

FIGURE 6.2 Variable Cost and Total Product

The firm's short-run variable cost curve and its total product curve have the same shape. The total product curve uses the horizontal axis measuring hours of work. The variable cost curve uses the horizontal axis measuring labor cost, which is the only variable cost.

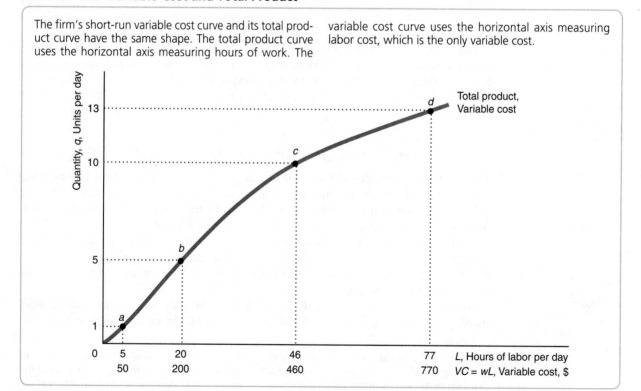

is $200. By using the variable cost labels on the horizontal axis, the total product of labor curve becomes the variable cost curve.

As output increases, the variable cost increases more than proportionally due to the diminishing marginal returns. Because the production function determines the shape of the variable cost curve, it also determines the shape of the marginal, average variable, and average cost curves. We now examine the shape of each of these cost curves in detail, because when making decisions, managers rely more on these per-unit cost measures than on total variable cost.

The Marginal Cost Curve. The marginal cost is the change in variable cost as output increases by one unit: $MC = \Delta VC / \Delta q$. In the short run, capital is fixed, so the only way the firm can produce more output is to use extra labor. The extra labor required to produce one more unit of output is $\Delta L / \Delta q$. The extra labor costs the firm w per unit, so the firm's cost rises by $w(\Delta L / \Delta q)$. As a result, the firm's marginal cost is

$$MC = \frac{\Delta VC}{\Delta q} = w\frac{\Delta L}{\Delta q}.$$

The marginal cost equals the wage times the extra labor necessary to produce one more unit of output. To increase output by one unit from 5 to 6 units takes 4 extra hours of work in Figure 6.2. If the wage is $10 per hour, the marginal cost is $40.

How do we know how much extra labor we need to produce one more unit of output? That information comes from the production function. The marginal product of labor—the amount of extra output produced by another unit of labor, holding other inputs fixed—is $MP_L = \Delta q / \Delta L$. Thus, the extra labor we need to produce one more unit of output, $\Delta L / \Delta q$, is $1/MP_L$, so the firm's marginal cost is

$$MC = \frac{w}{MP_L}. \tag{6.1}$$

Equation 6.1 says that the marginal cost equals the wage divided by the marginal product of labor. If the firm is producing 5 units of output, it takes 4 extra hours of labor to produce 1 more unit of output in Figure 6.2, so the marginal product of an hour of labor is $\frac{1}{4}$ unit of output. Given a wage of $10 an hour, the marginal cost of the sixth unit is $10 divided by $\frac{1}{4}$, or $40.

Equation 6.1 shows that the marginal product of labor and marginal cost move in opposite directions as output changes. At low levels of labor, the marginal product of labor commonly rises with additional labor because extra workers help the original workers and they can collectively make better use of the firm's equipment. As the marginal product of labor rises, the marginal cost falls.

Eventually, however, as the number of workers increases, workers must share the fixed amount of equipment and may get in each other's way. As more workers are added, the marginal product of each additional worker begins to fall and the marginal cost of each additional unit of product rises. As a result, the marginal cost curve slopes upward because of diminishing marginal returns to labor. Thus, the marginal cost first falls and then rises.

The Average Cost Curves. Because they determine the shape of the variable cost curve, diminishing marginal returns to labor also determine the shape of the average variable cost curve. The average variable cost is the variable cost divided by output: $AVC = VC/q$. For the firm we've been examining, whose only variable input is labor, variable cost is wL, so average variable cost is

$$AVC = \frac{VC}{q} = \frac{wL}{q}.$$

Because the average product of labor, AP_L, is q/L, average variable cost is the wage divided by the average product of labor:

$$AVC = \frac{w}{AP_L}. \tag{6.2}$$

In Figure 6.2, at 6 units of output, the average product of labor is $\frac{1}{4} (= q/L = 6/24)$, so the average variable cost is \$40, which is the wage, \$10, divided by the average product of labor, $\frac{1}{4}$.

With a constant wage, the average variable cost moves in the opposite direction of the average product of labor in Equation 6.2. As we discussed in Chapter 5, the average product of labor tends to rise and then fall, so the average cost tends to fall and then rise, as in panel b of Figure 6.1.

The average cost curve is the vertical sum of the average variable cost curve and the average fixed cost curve, as in panel b of Figure 6.1. If the average variable cost curve is U-shaped, adding the strictly falling average fixed cost makes the average cost fall more steeply than the average variable cost curve at low output levels. At high output levels, the average cost and average variable cost curves differ by ever smaller amounts, as the average fixed cost, F/q, approaches zero. Thus, the average cost curve is also U-shaped.

Using Calculus

Calculating Cost Curves

If we know the production function for a product (Chapter 5) and the factor prices, we can use math to derive the various cost functions. Based on the estimates of Flath (2011), the Cobb-Douglas production function of a typical Japanese beer manufacturer (Chapter 5) is

$$q = 1.52L^{0.6}K^{0.4},$$

where labor, L, is measured in hours, K is the number of units of capital, and q is the amount of output.

We assume that the firm's capital is fixed at $\overline{K} = 100$ units in the short run. If the rental rate of a unit of capital is \$8, the fixed cost, F, is \$800, the average fixed cost is

$$AFC = F/q = 800/q,$$

which falls as output increases.

We can use the production function to derive the variable cost. Given that capital is fixed in the short run, the short-run production function is solely a function of labor:

$$q = 1.52L^{0.6}100^{0.4} \approx 9.59L^{0.6}.$$

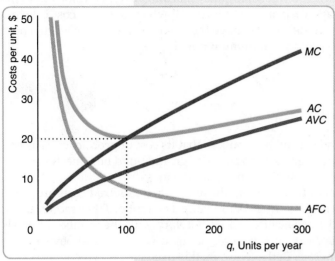

Rearranging this expression, we can write the number of workers, L, needed to produce q units of output as a function solely of output:

$$L(q) = \left(\frac{q}{9.59}\right)^{\frac{1}{0.6}} = \left(\frac{1}{9.59}\right)^{1.67} q^{1.67}$$

$$\approx 0.023q^{1.67}. \tag{6.3}$$

Now that we know how labor and output are related, we can calculate variable cost directly. The only variable input is labor, so if the wage is \$24, the firm's variable cost is

$$VC(q) = wL(q) = 24L(q). \tag{6.4}$$

Substituting for $L(q)$ using Equation 6.3 into the variable cost Equation 6.4, we see how variable cost varies with output:

$$VC(q) = 24L(q)$$

$$= 24(0.023q^{1.67}) \approx 0.55q^{1.67}. \tag{6.5}$$

Using this expression for variable cost, we can construct the other cost measures.

To obtain the equation for marginal cost as a function of output, we differentiate the variable cost, $VC(q)$, with respect to output:

$$MC(q) = \frac{dVC(q)}{dq} \approx \frac{d(0.55q^{1.67})}{dq} = 1.67 \times 0.55q^{0.67} \approx 0.92q^{0.67}.$$

We can also calculate total cost, $C = F + VC$, average cost, $AC = C/q$, and average variable cost, $AVC = VC/q$ using algebra. The figure plots the beer firm's AFC, AVC, AC, and MC curves.

Short-Run Cost Summary

We use cost curves to illustrate three cost level concepts—total cost, fixed cost, and variable cost—and four cost-per-unit cost concepts—average cost, average fixed cost, average variable cost, and marginal cost. Understanding the shapes of these curves and the relationships among them is crucial to the analysis of firm behavior in the rest of this book. Fortunately, we can derive most of what we need to know about the shapes and the relationships between the short-run curves using four basic concepts:

1. In the short run, the cost associated with inputs that cannot be adjusted is fixed, while the cost from inputs that can be adjusted is variable.

2. Given that input prices are constant, the shapes of the variable cost and the cost-per-unit curves are determined by the production function.

3. Where a variable input exhibits diminishing marginal returns, the variable cost and cost curves become relatively steep as output increases, so the average cost, average variable cost, and marginal cost curves rise with output.

4. Because of the relationship between marginal values and average values, both the average cost and average variable cost curves fall when marginal cost is below them and rise when marginal cost is above them, so the marginal cost cuts both these average cost curves at their minimum points.

6.3 Long-Run Costs

In the long run, the firm adjusts all its inputs so that its cost of production is as low as possible. The firm can change its plant size, design and build new machines, and otherwise adjust inputs that were fixed in the short run.

Although firms may incur fixed costs in the long run, these fixed costs are *avoidable* (rather than *sunk*, as they are in the short run). The rent of F per month that a restaurant pays is a fixed cost because it does not vary with the number of meals (output) served. In the short run, this fixed cost is sunk: The firm must pay F even if the restaurant does not operate. In the long run, this fixed cost is avoidable because the restaurant need not renew its rental agreement. The firm does not have to pay this rent if it shuts down. This cost is still a fixed cost, even in the long run, but it is not sunk in the long run.

To simplify our long-run analysis, we use examples with no long-run fixed costs ($F = 0$). Consequently, average cost and average variable cost are identical.

To produce a given quantity of output at minimum cost, our firm uses information about its production function and the price of labor and capital. In the long run when capital is variable, the firm chooses how much labor and capital to use; in the short run when capital is fixed, the firm chooses only how much labor to use. As a consequence, the firm's long-run cost of production is lower than its short-run cost if it has to use the "wrong" level of capital in the short run. In this section, we show how a firm picks the cost-minimizing combination of inputs in the long run.

Input Choice

A firm can produce a given level of output using many different *technically efficient* combinations of inputs, as summarized by an isoquant (Chapter 5). From among the technically efficient combinations of inputs that can be used to produce a given level of output, a firm wants to choose that bundle of inputs with the lowest cost of production, which is the *economically efficient* combination of inputs. To do so, the firm combines information about technology from the isoquant with information about the cost of production.

The Isocost Line. The cost of producing a given level of output depends on the price of labor and capital. The firm hires L hours of labor services at a constant wage of w per hour, so its labor cost is wL. The firm rents K hours of machine services at a constant rental rate of r per hour, so its capital cost is rK. (If the firm owns the capital, r is the implicit rental rate.) The firm's total cost is the sum of its labor and capital costs:

$$C = wL + rK. \tag{6.6}$$

A firm can hire as much labor and capital as it wants at these constant input prices from competitive labor and capital markets.

The firm can use many combinations of labor and capital that cost the same amount. Suppose that the wage rate, w, is $10 an hour and the rental rate of capital, r, is $20. Five of the many combinations of labor and capital that the firm can use that

TABLE 6.2 Bundles of Labor and Capital That Cost the Firm $200

Bundle	Labor, L	Capital, K	Labor Cost, $wL = \$10L$	Capital Cost, $rK = \$20K$	Total Cost, $wL + rK$
a	20	0	$200	$0	$200
b	14	3	$140	$60	$200
c	10	5	$100	$100	$200
d	6	7	$60	$140	$200
e	0	10	$0	$200	$200

cost $200 are listed in Table 6.2. These combinations of labor and capital are plotted on an **isocost line**, which represents all the combinations of inputs that have the same (*iso-*) total cost. Figure 6.3 shows three isocost lines. The $200 isocost line represents all the combinations of labor and capital that the firm can buy for $200, including the combinations *a* through *e* in Table 6.2.

Along an isocost line, cost is fixed at a particular level, $\overline{C}$, so by setting cost at $\overline{C}$ in Equation 6.6, we can write the equation for the $\overline{C}$ isocost line as

$$\overline{C} = wL + rK.$$

Using algebra, we can rewrite this equation to show how much capital the firm can buy if it spends a total of $\overline{C}$ and purchases L units of labor:

$$K = \frac{\overline{C}}{r} - \frac{w}{r}L. \tag{6.7}$$

FIGURE 6.3 A Family of Isocost Lines

An isocost line shows all the combinations of labor and capital that cost the firm the same amount. The greater the total cost, the farther from the origin the isocost lies. All the isocosts have the same slope, $-w/r = -\frac{1}{2}$. The slope shows the rate at which the firm can substitute capital for labor holding total cost constant: For each extra unit of capital it uses, the firm must use two fewer units of labor to hold its cost constant.

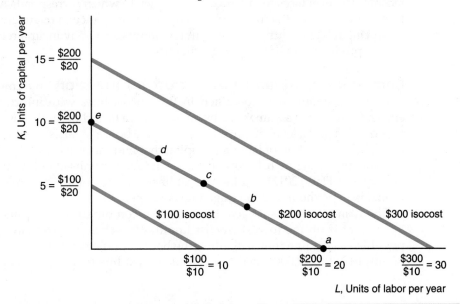

By substituting $\overline{C}$ = \$200, w = \$10, and r = \$20 in Equation 6.7, we find that the \$200 isocost line is $K = 10 - \frac{1}{2}L$. We can use Equation 6.7 to derive three properties of isocost lines.

First, the points at which the isocost lines hit the capital and labor axes depend on the firm's cost, $\overline{C}$, and on the input prices. The $\overline{C}$ isocost line intersects the capital axis where the firm is using only capital. Setting $L = 0$ in Equation 6.7, we find that the firm buys $K = \overline{C}/r$ units of capital. In Figure 6.3, the \$200 isocost line intersects the capital axis at \$200/\$20 = 10 units of capital. Similarly, the intersection of the isocost line with the labor axis is at $\overline{C}/w$, which is the amount of labor the firm hires if it uses only labor. In the figure, the intersection of the \$200 isocost line with the labor axis occurs at $L = 20$, where $K = 10 - \frac{1}{2} \times 20 = 0$.

Second, isocost lines that are farther from the origin have higher costs than those closer to the origin. Because the isocost lines intersect the capital axis at $\overline{C}/r$ and the labor axis at $\overline{C}/w$, an increase in the cost shifts these intersections with the axes proportionately outward. The \$100 isocost line hits the capital axis at 5 and the labor axis at 10, whereas the \$200 isocost line intersects at 10 and 20.

Third, the slope of each isocost line is the same. From Equation 6.7, if the firm increases labor by ΔL, it must decrease capital by

$$\Delta K = -\frac{w}{r} \Delta L.$$

Dividing both sides of this expression by ΔL, we find that the slope of an isocost line, $\Delta K / \Delta L$, is $-w/r$. Thus, the slope of the isocost line depends on the relative prices of the inputs. The slope of the isocost lines in the figure is $-w/r = -\$10/\$20 = \frac{1}{2}$. If the firm uses two more units of labor, $\Delta L = 2$, it must reduce capital by one unit, $\Delta K = -\frac{1}{2}\Delta L = -1$, to keep its total cost constant. Because all isocost lines are based on the same relative prices, they all have the same slope, so they are parallel.

The isocost line plays a similar role in the firm's decision making as the budget line does in consumer decision making. Both an isocost line and a budget line are straight lines whose slopes depend on relative prices. However, they have an important difference. The consumer has a single budget line determined by the consumer's income. The firm faces many isocost lines, each of which corresponds to a different level of expenditure the firm might make. A firm may incur a relatively low cost by producing relatively little output with few inputs, or it may incur a relatively high cost by producing a relatively large quantity.

Combining Cost and Production Information. By combining the information about costs contained in the isocost lines with information about efficient production summarized by an isoquant, a firm chooses the lowest-cost way to produce a given level of output. We illustrate how a Japanese beer manufacturer picks the combination of labor and capital that minimizes its cost of producing 100 units of output. Figure 6.4 shows the isoquant for 100 units of output (based on the estimates of Flath, 2011) and the isocost lines for which the rental rate of a unit of capital is \$8 per hour and the wage rate is \$24 per hour.

The firm minimizes its cost by using the combination of inputs on the isoquant that is on the lowest isocost line that touches the isoquant. The lowest possible isocost line that will allow the beer manufacturer to produce 100 units of output is the \$2,000 isocost line. This isocost line touches the isoquant at the

FIGURE 6.4 Cost Minimization

The beer manufacturer minimizes its cost of producing 100 units of output by producing at x ($L = 50$ and $K = 100$). This cost-minimizing combination of inputs is determined by the tangency between the $q = 100$ isoquant and the lowest isocost line, $2,000, that touches that isoquant. At x, the isocost is tangent to the isoquant, so the slope of the isocost, $-w/r = -3$, equals the slope of the isoquant, which is the negative of the marginal rate of technical substitution. That is, the rate at which the firm can trade capital for labor in the input markets equals the rate at which it can substitute capital for labor in the production process.

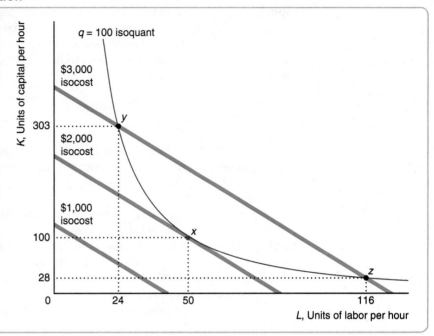

bundle of inputs x, where the firm uses $L = 50$ workers and $K = 100$ units of capital.

How do we know that x is the least costly way to produce 100 units of output? We need to demonstrate that other practical combinations of input produce less than 100 units or produce 100 units at greater cost.

If the firm spent less than $2,000, it could not produce 100 units of output. For example, each combination of inputs on the $1,000 isocost line lies below the isoquant, so the firm cannot produce 100 units of output for $1,000.

The firm can produce 100 units of output using other combinations of inputs beside x; however, using these other bundles of inputs is more expensive. For example, the firm can produce 100 units of output using the combinations y ($L = 24, K = 303$) or z ($L = 116, K = 28$), but both of these combinations cost the firm $3,000.

At the minimum-cost bundle, x, the isoquant is *tangent* to the isocost line: The slopes of the isocost and isoquant are equal and the isocost line touches the isoquant at only one point. Suppose that an isocost line hits the isoquant but is not tangent to it. Then the isocost line must cross the isoquant twice, as the $3,000 isocost line does at points y and z. However, if the isocost line crosses the isoquant twice, then part of the isoquant must lie below the isocost line. Consequently, another lower isocost line also touches the isoquant. Only if the isocost line is tangent to the isoquant—so that it touches the isoquant only once—can we conclude that we are on the lowest possible isocost line.

At the point of tangency, the slope of the isoquant equals the slope of the isocost. As we discussed in Chapter 5, the slope of the isoquant is the firm's *marginal rate of technical substitution*, which tells us how many units of capital the firm can replace with an extra unit of labor while holding output constant given its production function. The slope of the isocost is the negative of the ratio of the wage to the cost of capital, $-w/r$, the rate at which the firm can trade capital for labor in input markets. Thus, at the input bundle where the firm minimizes its cost of producing a given level of output, the isoquant is tangent to the isocost line. Therefore, the firm chooses its inputs so that the marginal rate of technical substitution equals the negative of the relative input prices:

$$MRTS = -\frac{w}{r}. \tag{6.8}$$

To minimize the cost of producing a given level of output, the firm picks the bundle of inputs where the rate at which it can substitute capital for labor in the production process, the *MRTS*, exactly equals the rate at which it can trade capital for labor in input markets, $-w/r$.

The formula for the beer manufacturer's marginal rate of technical substitution is $-1.5K/L$. At the minimum-cost input bundle x, $K = 100$ and $L = 50$, so its *MRTS* is -3, which equals the negative of the ratio of the input prices it faces, $-w/r = -24/8 = -3$. In contrast, at y, the isocost cuts the isoquant so the slopes are not equal. At y, the *MRTS* is -18.9375, which is greater than the ratio of the input price, 3. Because the slopes are not equal at y, the firm can produce the same output at lower cost. As the figure shows, the cost of producing at y is \$3,000, whereas the cost of producing at x is only \$2,000.

We can interpret the condition in Equation 6.8 in another way. We showed in Chapter 5 that the marginal rate of technical substitution equals the negative of the ratio of the marginal product of labor to that of capital: $MRTS = -MP_L/MP_K$. Thus, the cost-minimizing condition in Equation 6.8 (multiplying both sides by -1) is[4]

$$\frac{MP_L}{MP_K} = \frac{w}{r}. \tag{6.9}$$

This expression may be rewritten as

$$\frac{MP_L}{w} = \frac{MP_K}{r}. \tag{6.10}$$

Equation 6.10 states the *last-dollar rule*: Cost is minimized if inputs are chosen so that the last dollar spent on labor adds as much extra output as the last dollar spent on capital.

The beer firm's marginal product of labor is $MP_L = 0.6q/L$, and its marginal product of capital is $MP_K = 0.4q/K$.[5] At Bundle x, the beer firm's marginal product of labor is 1.2 $(= 0.6 \times 100/50)$ and its marginal product of capital is 0.4. The last dollar spent on labor gets the firm

$$\frac{MP_L}{w} = \frac{1.2}{24} = 0.05$$

---

[4]See Appendix 6 at the end of this chapter for a calculus derivation of this cost-minimizing condition.

[5]Because the beer manufacturer's production function is $q = 1.52L^{0.6}K^{0.4}$, the marginal product of labor is $MP_L = \partial q/\partial L = (0.6)1.52L^{(0.6-1)}K^{0.4} = 0.6q/L$, and the marginal product of capital is $MP_K = \partial q/\partial K = (0.4)1.52L^{0.6}K^{(0.4-1)} = 0.4q/K$.

more units of output. The last dollar spent on capital also gets the firm

$$\frac{MP_K}{r} = \frac{0.4}{8} = 0.05$$

more units of output. Thus, spending one more dollar on labor at x gets the firm as much extra output as spending the same amount on capital. Equation 6.10 holds, so the firm is minimizing its cost of producing 100 units of output.

If instead the firm uses more capital and less labor, producing at y, its MP_L is 2.5 ($= 0.6Q/L = 0.6 \times 100/24$) and the MP_K is approximately 0.13 ($\approx 0.4Q/K = 0.4 \times 100/303$). As a result, the last dollar spent on labor yields $MP_L/w \approx 0.1$ more output, whereas the last dollar spent on capital yields only a fourth as much extra output, $MP_K/r \approx 0.017$. At y, if the firm shifts one dollar from capital to labor, the reduction in capital causes output to fall by 0.017 units. Offsetting that reduction, the increase in labor causes output to increase by 0.1 units. Thus, the net gain is 0.083 units of output at the same cost. The firm should shift even more resources from capital to labor—which increases the marginal product of capital and decreases the marginal product of labor—until the firm is operating with the capital-labor bundle x, where Equation 6.10 holds and the last dollar spent on labor increases output just as much as the last dollar spent on capital.

To summarize, a manager can use three equivalent rules to pick the lowest-cost combination of inputs to produce a given level of output when isoquants are smooth: the lowest-isocost rule, the tangency rule (Equation 6.9), and the last-dollar rule (Equation 6.10).

Managerial Implication

Cost Minimization by Trial and Error

How should a manager minimize cost if the manager does not know the firm's production function? The manager should use the last-dollar rule to determine the cost-minimizing combination of inputs through trial and error. The manager should experiment by adjusting each input slightly, holding other inputs constant, to learn how production and cost change and then use that information to choose a cost-minimizing bundle of inputs. (That is, managers don't draw isoquants and isocost lines to make decisions, but they use the insights from such an analysis to obtain the last-dollar rule.)

Factor Price Changes. Once the beer manufacturer determines the lowest-cost combination of inputs to produce a given level of output, it uses that method as long as the input prices remain constant. How should the firm change its behavior if the cost of one of the factors changes? Suppose that the wage falls from $24 to $8 but the rental rate of capital stays constant at $8.

The firm minimizes its new cost by substituting away from the now relatively more expensive input, capital, toward the now relatively less expensive input, labor. The change in the wage does not affect technological efficiency, so it does not affect the isoquant in Figure 6.5. However, because of the wage decrease, the new isocost lines have a flatter slope, $-w/r = -8/8 = -1$, than the original isocost lines, $-w/r = -24/8 = -3$.

The relatively steep original isocost line is tangent to the 100-unit isoquant at Bundle x ($L = 50$, $K = 100$). The new, flatter isocost line is tangent to the isoquant at Bundle v ($L = 77$, $K = 52$). Thus, the firm uses more labor and less capital as

FIGURE 6.5 Effect of a Change in Factor Price

Originally, the wage was $24 and the rental rate of capital was $8, so the lowest isocost line ($2,000) was tangent to the $q = 100$ isoquant at $x(L = 50, K = 100)$. When the wage fell to $8, the isocost lines became flatter: Labor became relatively less expensive than capital. The slope of the isocost lines falls from $-w/r = -24/8 = -3$ to $-8/8 = -1$. The new lowest isocost line ($1,032) is tangent at v ($L = 77, K = 52$). Thus, when the wage falls, the firm uses more labor and less capital to produce a given level of output, and the cost of production falls from $2,000 to $1,032.

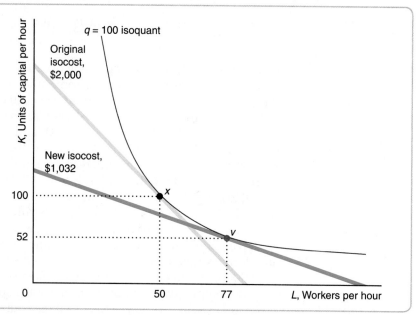

labor becomes relatively less expensive. Moreover, the firm's cost of producing 100 units falls from $2,000 to $1,032 because of the fall in the wage. This example illustrates that a change in the relative prices of inputs affects the mix of inputs that a firm uses.

Mini-Case

The Internet and Outsourcing

To start a children's pajama business, Philip Chigos and Mary Domenico designed their products, chose fabrics, and searched for low-cost workers in China or Mexico from an office in the basement below their San Francisco apartment. Increasingly, such mom-and-pop operations are sending their clothing, jewelry, and programming work to Sri Lanka, China, India, Mexico, and Eastern Europe.

A firm *outsources* if it retains others to provide services that the firm had previously performed itself. Firms have always used outsourcing. For example, a restaurant buys goods such as butter and flour or finished products such as bread and pies from other firms or contracts with another firm to provide cleaning services. A profit-maximizing firm outsources if others can produce a good or service for less than the firm's own cost. Though all domestic firms face the same factor prices, some firms can produce at lower cost than others because they specialize in a good or service.

Many news outlets and politicians have been wringing their hands about outsourcing to other countries. The different factor prices that foreign firms face may allow them to produce at lower cost.

In the past, most small firms could not practically outsource to other countries because of the high transaction costs of finding partners abroad and communicating with them. Now they can use the Internet and other communication technologies—such as e-mail, fax, and phone—to inexpensively communicate with foreign factories, transmit images and design specifications, and track inventory.

Mr. Chigos used the Internet to find potential Chinese and Mexican manufacturers for the pajamas that Ms. Domenico designed. Hiring foreign workers is crucial to their nascent enterprise. Mr. Chigos claims, "We'd love it to say 'Made in the U.S.A.' and use American textiles and production." However, if they did so, their cost would rise four to ten times, and "We didn't want to sell our pajamas for $120." One result of easy access to cheap manufacturing, he said, is that more American entrepreneurs may be able to turn an idea into a product.

The would-be pajama tycoons plan to outsource to U.S. firms as well. They will use a Richmond, California, freight management company to receive the shipments, check the merchandise's quality, and ship it to customers. They will market their clothes on the Internet and through boutique retailers. Indeed, their business will be entirely virtual: They have no manufacturing plant, storefront, or warehouse. As Mr. Chigos notes, "With the technology available today, we'll never touch the product."

Thus, lower communication costs have made foreign outsourcing feasible by lowering transaction costs. Ultimately, however, such outsourcing occurs because the costs of outsourced activities are lower abroad.

If relative factor prices (and hence slopes of isocost lines) are different abroad than at home, the manager of a firm with smooth isoquants should use a different factor mix when producing abroad, as Figure 6.5 illustrates. However, Q&A 6.2 shows that if all foreign prices for capital and labor are proportionally lower than domestic prices so that relative factor prices are the same, the firm should use the same technology as at home.

Q&A 6.2

If it manufactures at home, a firm faces input prices for labor and capital of w and r and produces q units of output using L units of labor and K units of capital. Abroad, the wage and cost of capital are half as much as at home. If the firm manufactures abroad, will it change the amount of labor and capital it uses to produce q? What happens to its cost of producing quantity q?

Answer

1. *Determine whether the change in factor prices affects the slopes of the isoquant or the isocost lines.* The change in input prices does not affect the isoquant, which depends only on technology (the production function). Moreover, cutting the input prices in half does not affect the slope of the isocost lines. The original slope was $-w/r$, and the new slope is $-(w/2)/(r/2) = -w/r$.

2. *Using a rule for cost minimization, determine whether the firm changes its input mix.* A firm minimizes its cost by producing where its isoquant is tangent to the lowest possible isocost line. That is, the firm produces where the slope of its isoquant, *MRTS*, equals the slope of its isocost line, $-w/r$. Because the slopes

of the isoquant and the isocost lines are unchanged after input prices are cut in half, the firm continues to produce using the same amount of labor, *L*, and capital, *K*, as originally.

3. *Calculate the original cost and the new cost and compare them.* The firm's original cost of producing *q* units of output was $wL + rK = C$. Its new cost of producing the same amount of output is $(w/2)L + (r/2)K = C/2$. Thus, its cost of producing *q* falls by half when the input prices are halved. The isocost lines have the same slope as before, but the cost associated with each isocost line is halved.

The Shapes of Long-Run Cost Curves

The shapes of the long-run average cost and marginal cost curves depend on the shape of the long-run total cost curve. The long-run cost curve in panel a of Figure 6.6 corresponds to the long-run average and marginal cost curves in panel b. The long-run cost curve of this firm rises less than in proportion to increases in output at outputs below q^* and then rises more rapidly. The corresponding long-run average cost curve first falls and then rises.

The explanation for why the long-run average cost curve is U-shaped differs from those given for why short-run average cost curves are U-shaped. A key reason why the short-run average cost is initially downward sloping is that the average fixed cost curve is downward sloping: Spreading the fixed cost over more units of output lowers the average fixed cost per unit. In the long run fixed costs are less important than in the short run, and may be absent altogether, as we have assumed in this section. Therefore, we cannot rely on fixed costs to explain the initial downward slope of the long-run average cost curve.

A major reason why the short-run average cost curve slopes upward at higher levels of output is diminishing marginal returns. In the long run, however, all factors can be increased, so diminishing marginal returns do not explain the upward slope of a long-run average cost curve.

As with the short-run curves, the shape of the long-run curves is determined by the production function relationship between output and inputs. In the long run, returns to scale play a major role in determining the shape of the average cost curve and other cost curves. As we discussed in Chapter 5, increasing all inputs in proportion may cause output to increase more than in proportion (increasing returns to scale) at low levels of output, in proportion (constant returns to scale) at intermediate levels of output, and less than in proportion (decreasing returns to scale) at high levels of output. If a production function has this returns-to-scale pattern and the prices of inputs are constant, the long-run average cost curve must be U-shaped.

To illustrate the relationship between returns to scale and long-run average cost, we use the returns-to-scale data given in Table 6.3. The firm produces one unit of output using a unit each of labor and capital. Given a wage and rental cost of capital of $12 per unit, the total cost and average cost of producing this unit are both $24. Doubling both inputs causes output to increase more than in proportion to 3 units, reflecting increasing returns to scale. Because cost only doubles while output triples, the average cost falls. A cost function is said to exhibit **economies of scale** if the average cost of production falls as output expands.

FIGURE 6.6 Long-Run Cost Curves

(a) The long-run cost curve rises less rapidly than output at output levels below q^* and more rapidly at higher output levels. (b) As a consequence, the marginal cost and average cost curves are U-shaped. The marginal cost crosses the average cost at its minimum at q^*.

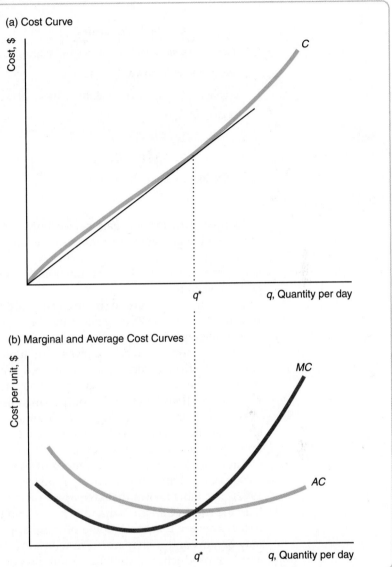

(a) Cost Curve

(b) Marginal and Average Cost Curves

TABLE 6.3 Returns to Scale and Long-Run Costs

Output, Q	Labor, L	Capital, K	Cost, $C = wL + rK$	Average Cost, $AC = C/q$	Returns to Scale
1	1	1	24	24	
3	2	2	48	16	Increasing
6	4	4	96	16	Constant
8	8	8	192	24	Decreasing

$w = r = \$12$ per unit.

TABLE 6.4 Shape of Average Cost Curves in Canadian Manufacturing

Scale Economies	Share of Manufacturing Industries, %	
Economies of scale: Initially downward-sloping *AC*	57	
Everywhere downward-sloping *AC*		18
L-shaped *AC* (downward-sloping, then flat)		31
U-shaped *AC*		8
No economies of scale: Flat *AC*	23	
Diseconomies of scale: Upward-sloping *AC*	14	

Source: Robidoux and Lester (1992).

Doubling the inputs again causes output to double as well—constant returns to scale—so the average cost remains constant. If an increase in output has no effect on average cost—the average cost curve is flat—there are *no economies of scale*. We sometimes refer to such a cost function as exhibiting *constant costs*, because average cost is constant.

Doubling the inputs once more causes only a small increase in output—decreasing returns to scale—so average cost increases. A firm suffers from **diseconomies of scale** if average cost rises when output increases.

Average long-run cost curves can have many different shapes. Perfectly competitive firms typically have U-shaped average cost curves. Average cost curves in noncompetitive markets may be U-shaped, L-shaped (average cost at first falls rapidly and then levels off as output increases), everywhere downward sloping, everywhere upward sloping, or have other shapes. Given fixed input prices, the shape of the average cost curve indicates whether the production process has economies or diseconomies of scale.

Table 6.4 summarizes the shapes of average long-run cost curves of firms in various Canadian manufacturing industries (as estimated by Robidoux and Lester, 1992). The table shows that U-shaped average cost curves are the exception rather than the rule in Canadian manufacturing and that nearly one-third of these average cost curves are L-shaped. Some of these apparently L-shaped average cost curves may be part of a U-shaped curve with long, flat bottoms, where we don't observe any firm producing enough to exhibit diseconomies of scale.

Mini-Case

Economies of Scale in Nuclear Power Plants

Economies of scale can be achieved across an entire company through more efficient management. Over the last decade and a half, the industry consolidated substantially as many U.S. nuclear power plants switched from operating in a regulated to an unregulated market. In the 1970s and 1980s, the typical independent nuclear firm operated a single nuclear power plant. By the late 1990s, the average was three plants. However, the average jumped to six plants in 2000 and is now about nine plants. Indeed, the three largest companies—Entergy, Exelon, and NextEra—operate about one-third of all the nuclear capacity in the United States.

This consolidation improves operating efficiency in several ways. Rather than have a single plant use contract employees to perform infrequent tasks, such as

refueling outages, which take place on average every 18 months, a consolidated nuclear company can hire highly skilled employees and train them to appreciate the idiosyncrasies of the company's reactors. In addition, consolidated firms may have employees and managers share best practices across plants. Gary Leidich, the president of FirstEnergy Nuclear, said that when the company acquired three nuclear plants they went from three separate facilities, "each pretty much doing their own thing" to a corporate organization where managers work together. For example, all the plant operators have a daily 7:30 a.m. conference call to discuss potential problems, and managers at FirstEnergy travel from plant to plant.

These economies of scale due to consolidation result in more efficient plants with substantially fewer outages. Consolidation decreases plant outages from, on average, 21 days per year to 15 days per year. Although this change may not seem substantial, a typical 2,000 megawatt nuclear power plant produces about $100,000 worth of power every hour, so 6 days of extra production increases revenues by over $14 million a year.

According to the estimates of Davis and Wolfram (2012), consolidation increases efficiency (net energy generation relative to plant capacity) and thereby reduces cost per unit of energy produced. The number of extra plants owned by each firm ranges from 0 to 16. According to their estimates, a firm with 16 extra plants would increase efficiency by 7.7 percentage points.

Q&A 6.3

What is the shape of the long-run cost function for a fixed-proportions production function (Chapter 5) in which it takes one unit of labor and one unit of capital to produce one unit of output? What is the shape of the average cost curve? Does it have economies or diseconomies of scale?

Answer

1. *Because no substitution is possible with a fixed-proportion production function, multiply the inputs (= the number of units of output) by their prices, and sum to determine total cost.* The long-run cost of producing q units of output is $C(q) = wL + rK = wq + rq = (w + r)q$. Cost rises in proportion to output. The long-run cost curve is a straight line with a slope of $w + r$.

2. *Divide the total cost function by q to get the average cost function.* The average cost function is $AC(q) = C(q)/q = [(w + r)q]/q = w + r$. Because the average cost for any quantity is $w + r$, the average cost curve is a horizontal straight line at $w + r$. Moreover, because the average cost does not change when the quantity of output changes, the cost function does not have either economies or diseconomies of scale.

Long-Run Average Cost as the Envelope of Short-Run Average Cost Curves

Capital is flexible in the long run but not in the short run. Therefore, the firm has more flexibility in how it produces in the long run than in the short run. Any combination of inputs the firm uses in the short run, the firm could use in the long run. However, the firm may be able to use a different combination of inputs to produce at lower cost in the long run, when it is able to vary its capital input. For this reason, the long-run average cost is always equal to or below the short-run average cost.

Suppose, initially, that the firm in Figure 6.7 has only three possible plant sizes. The firm's short-run average cost curve is $SRAC^1$ for the smallest possible plant. The average cost of producing q_1 units of output using this plant, point a on $SRAC^1$, is $10. If instead the plant used the next larger plant size, its cost of producing q_1 units of output, point b on $SRAC^2$, would be $12. Thus, if the firm knows that it will produce only q_1 units of output, it minimizes its average cost by using the smaller plant size. If it expects to be producing q_2, its average cost is lower on the $SRAC^2$ curve, point e, than on the $SRAC^1$ curve, point d.

In the long run, the firm chooses the plant size that minimizes its cost of production, so it picks the plant size that has the lowest average cost for each possible output level. It opts for the small plant size at q_1, whereas it uses the medium plant size at q_2. Thus, the long-run average cost curve is the solid, scalloped section of the three short-run cost curves.

If many possible plant sizes are possible, the long-run average curve, $LRAC$, is smooth and U-shaped. The $LRAC$ includes one point from each possible short-run average cost curve. This point, however, is not necessarily the minimum point of a short-run curve. For example, the $LRAC$ includes a on $SRAC^1$ and not its minimum point, c. A small plant operating at minimum average cost cannot produce at as low an average cost as a slightly larger plant that is taking advantage of economies of scale.

FIGURE 6.7 Long-Run Average Cost as the Envelope of Short-Run Average Cost Curves

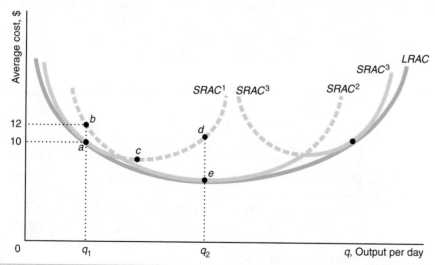

If there are only three possible plant sizes, with short-run average costs $SRAC^1$, $SRAC^2$, and $SRAC^3$, the long-run average cost curve is the solid, scalloped portion of the three short-run curves. $LRAC$ is the smooth and U-shaped long-run average cost curve if there are many possible short-run average cost curves.

**Long-Run Cost
Curves in Beer
Manufacturing
and Oil Pipelines**

Here we illustrate the relationship between long-run and short-run cost curves for our beer manufacturing firm and for oil pipelines.

Beer Manufacturing

The first graph shows the relationship between short-run and long-run average cost curves for the beer manufacturer. Because this production function has constant returns to scale, doubling both inputs doubles output, so the long-run average cost, $LRAC$, is constant. If capital is fixed at 200 units, the firm's short-run average cost curve is $SRAC^1$. If the firm produces 200 units of output, its short-run and long-run average costs are equal. At any other output, its short-run cost is higher than its long-run cost.

The short-run marginal cost curves, $SRMC^1$ and $SRMC^2$, are upward sloping and equal the corresponding U-shaped short-run average cost curves, $SRAC^1$ and $SRAC^2$, only at their minimum points, $20. In contrast, because the long-run average cost is horizontal at $20, the long-run marginal cost curve, $LRMC$, is horizontal at $20. Thus, the long-run marginal cost curve is *not* the envelope of the short-run marginal cost curves.

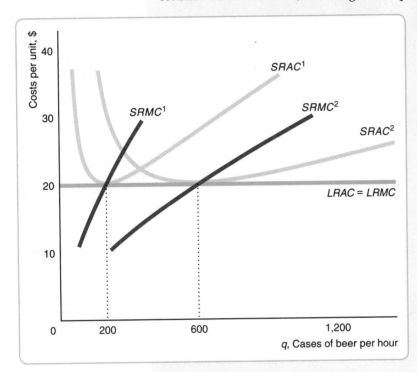

Oil Pipelines

Oil companies use the information in the second graph[6] (next page) to choose what size pipe to use to deliver oil. In the figure, the 8″ $SRAC$ curve is the short-run average cost curve for a pipe with an 8-inch diameter. The long-run average cost curve, $LRAC$, is the envelope of all possible short-run average cost curves. It is more expensive to lay larger pipes than smaller ones, so a firm does not want to install unnecessarily large pipes. However, the average cost of sending a substantial quantity of oil through a single large pipe is lower than that of sending it through two smaller pipes. For example, the average cost per barrel of sending 200,000 barrels per day through two 16-inch pipes is 1.67 (= $50/$30) greater than through a single 26-inch pipe.

Because the company incurs large fixed costs in laying miles and miles of pipelines, and because pipes last for years, it does not vary the size of pipes in the short run. However, in the long run, the oil company installs the ideal pipe size to handle its flow of oil. Indeed, because several oil companies often share

---

[6]Exxon Company, U.S.A., *Competition in the Petroleum Industry*, 1975, p. 30. Reprinted with permission.

interstate pipelines to take advantage of the large economies of scale, very large diameter pipes are typically installed.

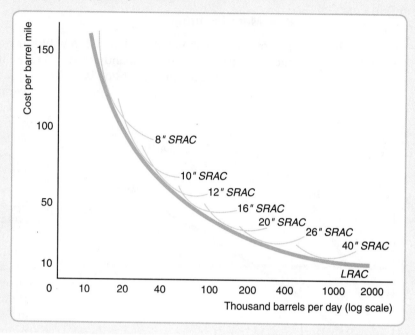

6.4 The Learning Curve

Average cost may fall over time for three reasons. First, operating at a larger scale in the long run may lower average cost due to increasing returns to scale (IRS). Second, technological progress (Chapter 5) may increase productivity and thereby lower average cost. Third, a firm may benefit from **learning by doing**: the productive skills and knowledge that workers and managers gain from experience. Workers who are given a new task may perform it slowly the first few times they try, but their speed increases with practice. Managers may learn how to organize production more efficiently, discover which workers to assign to which tasks, and determine where more inventories are needed and where they can be reduced. Engineers may optimize product designs by experimenting with various production methods. For these and other reasons, the average cost of production tends to fall over time, and the effect is particularly strong with new products.

In some firms, learning by doing is a function of the time elapsed since a particular product or production process was introduced. However, more commonly, learning is a function of *cumulative output*: the total number of units of output produced since the product was introduced. The **learning curve** is the relationship between average costs and cumulative output. The learning curve for Intel central processing units (CPUs) in panel a of Figure 6.8 shows that Intel's average cost fell very rapidly with the first few million units of cumulative output, but then dropped relatively slowly with additional units (Salgado, 2008).

If a firm is operating in the economies of scale section of its average cost curve, expanding output lowers its cost for two reasons. Its average cost falls today because

FIGURE 6.8 Learning by Doing

(a) As Intel produced more cumulative CPUs, the average cost of production fell (Salgado, 2008). (b) In any one period, extra production reduces a firm's average cost due to economies of scale: because $q_1 < q_2 < q_3$, A is higher than B, which is higher than C. Extra production in one period reduces average cost in the future because of learning by doing. To produce q_2 this period costs B on AC^1, but to produce that same output in the next period would cost only b on AC^2. If the firm produces q_3 instead of q_2 in this period, its average cost in the next period is AC^3 instead of AC^2 because of additional learning by doing. Thus, extra output in this period lowers the firm's cost in two ways: It lowers average cost in this period due to economies of scale and lowers average cost for any given output level in the next period due to learning by doing.

(a) Learning Curve for Intel Central Processing Units

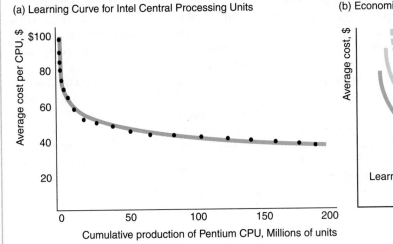

(b) Economies of Scale and Learning by Doing

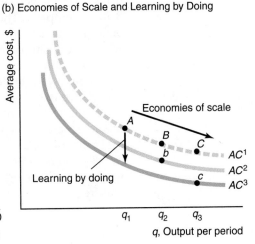

of economies of scale, and for any given level of output, its average cost is lower in the next period due to learning by doing.

In panel b of Figure 6.8, the firm is producing q_1 units of output at point A on average cost curve AC^1 in the first period. We assume that each period is long enough that the firm can vary all factors of production. If the firm expands its output to q_2 in Period 1, its average cost falls to B because of economies of scale. The learning by doing in Period 1 results in a lower average cost, AC^2 in Period 2. If the firm continues to produce q_2 units of output in Period 2, its average cost falls to b on AC^2.

If instead of expanding output to q_2 in Period 1, the firm expands to q_3, its average cost is even lower in Period 1 (C on AC^1) due to even greater economies of scale. Moreover, its average cost curve, AC^3, in Period 2 is even lower due to the extra experience gained from producing more output in Period 1. If the firm continues to produce q_3 in Period 2, its average cost is c on AC^3. Thus all else being the same, if learning by doing depends on cumulative output, firms have an incentive to produce more in any one period than they otherwise would to lower their costs in the future.

Mini-Case	
Learning by Drilling	

Learning by doing can substantially reduce the cost of drilling oil wells. Two types of firms work together to drill oil wells. Oil production companies such as ExxonMobil and Chevron perform the technical design and planning of wells to be drilled. The actual drilling is performed by drilling companies that own and staff drilling rigs. The time it takes to drill a well varies across fields, which vary in terms of the types of rock covering the oil and the depth of the oil.

Kellogg (2011) found that the more experience—the cumulative number of wells that the oil production firm drilled in the field over the past two years—the less time it takes the firm to drill another well. His estimated learning curve shows that drilling time decreases rapidly at first, falling by about 15% after the first 25 wells have been drilled, but that drilling time does not fall much more with additional experience.

This decrease in drilling time is the sum of the benefits from two types of experience. The time it takes to drill a well falls as the production company drills (1) more wells in the field and (2) more wells in that field with a particular drilling company. The second effect occurs because the two firms learn to work better together in a particular field. Because neither firm can apply its learning with a particular partner to its work with another partner, production companies prefer to continue to work with the same drilling rig firms over time.

The reduction in drilling time from a production firm's average stand-alone experience over the past two years is 6.4% or 1.5 fewer days to drill a well. This time savings reduces the cost of drilling a well by about $16,300. The relationship-specific learning from experience due to working with a drilling company for the average duration over two years reduces drilling time per well by 3.8%, or about $9,700 per well. On average, the reduction in drilling time from working with one rig crew regularly is twice as much as from working with rigs that frequently switch from one production firm to another.

6.5 The Costs of Producing Multiple Goods

If a firm produces two or more goods, the cost of one good may depend on the output level of another. Outputs are linked if a single input is used to produce both of them. For example, cattle provide beef and hides, and oil supplies both heating fuel and gasoline. It is less expensive to produce beef and hides together than separately. If the goods are produced together, a single animal yields one unit of beef and one hide. If beef and hides are produced separately (throwing away the unused good), the same amount of output requires two animals and more labor.

A cost function exhibits **economies of scope** if it is less expensive to produce goods jointly than separately (Panzar and Willig, 1977, 1981). All else the same, if a firm has such a cost function, it can lower its total cost by producing its products together (say at one plant) rather than separately (at two plants).

A measure of the degree of economies of *scope* (SC) is

$$SC = \frac{C(q_1, 0) + C(0, q_2) - C(q_1, q_2)}{C(q_1, q_2)},$$

where $C(q_1, 0)$ is the cost of producing q_1 units of the first good by itself, $C(0, q_2)$ is the cost of producing q_2 units of the second good, and $C(q_1, q_2)$ is the cost of producing both goods together. If the cost of producing the two goods separately, $C(q_1, 0) + C(0, q_2)$, is the same as producing them together, $C(q_1, q_2)$, then SC is zero. If it is cheaper to produce the goods jointly, SC is positive. If SC is negative, there are diseconomies of scope, and the two goods should be produced separately.

Mini-Case

Scope

Empirical studies show that some processes have economies of scope, others have none, and some have diseconomies of scope. In Japan, there are substantial economies of scope in producing and transmitting electricity, $SC = 0.2$ (Ida and Kuwahara, 2004), and in broadcasting for television and radio, $SC = 0.12$ (Asai, 2006). Growitsch and Wetzel (2009) found that there are economies of scope from combining passenger and freight services for the majority of 54 railway firms from 27 European countries. Yatchew (2000) concluded that there are scope economies in distributing electricity and other utilities in Ontario, Canada. Kong et al. (2009) found that Chinese airports exhibit substantial economies of scope.

In Switzerland, some utility firms provide gas, electricity, and water, while others provide only one or two of these utilities. Farsi et al. (2008) estimated that most firms have scope economies. The SC ranges between 0.04 and 0.15 for a median-size firm, but scope economies could reach 20% to 30% of total costs for small firms, which may help explain why only some firms provide multiple utilities.

Friedlaender, Winston, and Wang (1983) found that for American automobile manufacturers, it is 25% less expensive ($SC = 0.25$) to produce large cars together with small cars and trucks than to produce large cars separately and small cars and trucks together. However, there are no economies of scope from producing trucks together with small and large cars. Producing trucks separately from cars is efficient.

Cummins et al. (2010) tested whether U.S. insurance firms do better by selling both life-health and property-liability insurance or by specializing, and found that the firms should specialize due to diseconomies of scope. Similarly, Cohen and Paul (2011) estimated that drug treatment centers have diseconomies of scope, so they should specialize in either outpatient or inpatient treatment.

Managerial Solution

Technology Choice at Home Versus Abroad

If a U.S. semiconductor manufacturing firm shifts production from the firm's home plant to one abroad, should it use the same mix of inputs as at home? The firm may choose to use a different technology because the firm's cost of labor relative to capital is lower abroad than in the United States.

If the firm's isoquant is smooth, the firm uses a different bundle of inputs abroad than at home given that the relative factor prices differ (as Figure 6.5 shows). However, semiconductor manufacturers have kinked isoquants. Figure 6.9 shows an isoquant for a semiconductor manufacturing firm that we examined in Chapter 5 in the Mini-Case "A Semiconductor Isoquant." In its U.S. plant, the semiconductor manufacturing firm uses a wafer-handling stepper technology because the C^1 isocost line, which is the lowest isocost line that touches the isoquant, hits the isoquant at that technology.

The firm's cost of both inputs is less abroad than in the United States, and its cost of labor is relatively less than the cost of capital at its foreign plant than at its U.S. plant. The slope of its isocost line is $-w/r$, where w is the wage and r is the rental cost of the manufacturing equipment. The smaller w is relative to r, the less steeply sloped is its isocost curve. Thus, the firm's foreign isocost line is flatter than its domestic C^1 isocost line.

If the firm's isoquant were smooth, the firm would certainly use a different technology at its foreign plant than in its home plant. However, its isoquant has kinks, so a small change in the relative input prices does not necessarily lead to a change in production technology. The firm could face either the C^2 or C^3 isocost curves, both of which are flatter than the C^1 isocost. If the firm faces the C^2 isocost line, which is only slightly flatter than the C^1 isocost, the firm still uses the capital-intensive wafer-handling stepper technology in its foreign plant. However, if the firm faces the much flatter C^3 isocost line, which hits the isoquant at the stepper technology, it switches technologies. (If the isocost line were even flatter, it could hit the isoquant at the aligner technology.)

Even if the wage change is small so that the firm's isocost is C^2 and the firm does not switch technologies abroad, the firm's cost will be lower abroad with the same technology because C^2 is less than C^1. However, if the wage is low enough that it can shift to a more labor-intensive technology, its costs will be even lower: C^3 is less than C^2.

Thus, whether the firm uses a different technology in its foreign plant than in its domestic plant turns on the relative factor prices in the two locations and whether the firm's isoquant is smooth. If the isoquant is smooth, even a slight difference in relative factor prices will induce the firm to shift along the isoquant and use a different technology with a different capital-labor ratio. However, if the isoquant has kinks, the firm will use a different technology only if the relative factor prices differ substantially.

FIGURE 6.9 **Technology Choice**

In the United States, the semi-conductor manufacturer produces using a wafer-handling stepper on isocost C^1. At its plant abroad, the wage is lower, so it faces a flatter isocost curve. If the wage is only slightly lower, so that its isocost is C^2, it produces the same way as at home. However, if the wage is much lower so that the isocost is C^3, it switches to a stepper technology.

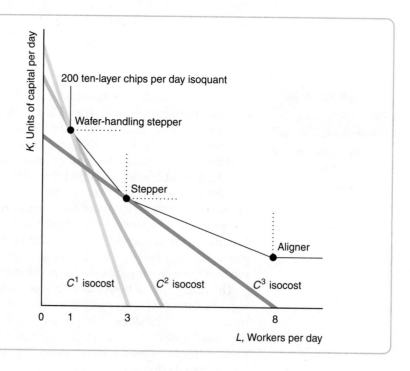

SUMMARY

From all technically efficient production processes, a cost-minimizing firm chooses the one that is economically efficient. The economically efficient production process is the technically efficient process for which the cost of producing a given quantity of output is lowest.

1. **The Nature of Costs.** In making decisions about production, managers need to take into account the opportunity cost of an input, which is the value of the input's best alternative use. For example, if the manager is the owner of the company and does not receive a salary, the amount that the owner could have earned elsewhere—the foregone earnings—is the opportunity cost of the manager's time and is relevant in deciding whether the firm should produce or not. A durable good's opportunity cost depends on its current alternative use. If the past expenditure for a durable good is sunk—that is, it cannot be recovered—then that input has no opportunity cost and the sunk cost should not influence current production decisions.

2. **Short-Run Costs.** In the short run, the firm can adjust some factors, such as labor, while other factors, such as capital, are fixed. Consequently, total cost is the sum of variable costs and fixed costs. Average cost is total cost divided by the number of units of output produced. Similarly, average variable cost is variable cost divided by output. Marginal cost is the amount by which a firm's cost changes if the firm produces one more unit of output. At quantities where the marginal cost curve is below the average cost curve, the average cost curve is downward sloping. Where the marginal cost curve is above the average cost curve, the average cost curve is upward sloping. Thus, the marginal cost curve cuts the average cost curve at its minimum point. Given that input prices are constant, the shapes of the variable cost and the cost-per-unit curves are determined by the production function. If labor is the only variable factor in the short run, the shape of short-run cost curves reflects the marginal product of labor.

3. **Long-Run Costs.** Over a long-run planning horizon, all inputs can be adjusted. In some cases there might be a minimum level of capital necessary for the firm to produce anything at all, implying that there might be fixed costs even in the long run. However, these costs can be avoided if the firm shuts down and are therefore not sunk over a long-run planning horizon. If there are no fixed costs, then average total cost and average variable cost are identical. The firm chooses to use the combination of inputs that minimizes its cost. To produce a given output level, it chooses the lowest isocost line that touches the relevant isoquant, which is tangent to the isoquant. Equivalently, to minimize cost, the firm adjusts inputs until the last dollar spent on any input increases output by as much as the last dollar spent on any other input. If the firm calculates the cost of producing every possible output level given current input prices, it knows its cost function: Cost is a function of the input prices and the output level. If the firm's average cost falls as output expands, it has economies of scale. If its average cost rises as output expands, there are diseconomies of scale.

4. **The Learning Curve.** A firm that introduces a new product or service often benefits from increased productivity as it gains experience and learns how to produce at lower cost, a process called learning by doing. Workers who are given a new task will typically speed up and make fewer mistakes with practice. The learning curve describes the relationship between average cost and cumulative output over time. This curve typically slopes downward, reflecting the decline in cost that arises from learning by doing.

5. **The Costs of Producing Multiple Goods.** If it is less expensive for a firm to produce two goods jointly rather than separately, there are economies of scope. If there are diseconomies of scope, it is less expensive to produce the goods separately. The presence or absence of economies of scope is important in determining the portfolio of products that the firm produces.

QUESTIONS

All exercises are available on MyEconLab; * = *answer at the back of this book;* **C** = *use of calculus may be necessary.*

The Nature of Costs

1.1. Executives at Leonesse Cellars, a premium winery in Southern California, were surprised to learn that shipping wine by sea to some cities in Asia was less expensive than sending it to the East Coast of the United States, so they started shipping to Asia (David Armstrong, "Discount Cargo Rates Ripe for the Taking," *San Francisco Chronicle*, August 28,

2005). Because of the large U.S. trade imbalance with major Asian nations, cargo ships arrive at West Coast seaports fully loaded but return to Asia half to completely empty. Use the concept of opportunity cost to help explain the differential shipping rates.

1.2. Carmen bought a $125 ticket to attend the Outside Lands Music & Arts Festival in San Francisco. Because it stars several of her favorite rock groups, she would have been willing to pay up to $200 to attend the festival. However, her friend Bessie invites Carmen to go with her to the Monterey Bay Aquarium on the same day. That trip would cost $50, but she would be willing to pay up to $100. What is her opportunity cost of going to the festival? (*Hint*: See Q&A 6.1.)

1.3. Many corporations allow CEOs to use the firm's corporate jet for personal travel (see the Mini-Case "Company Jets" in Chapter 7 for more details). The Internal Revenue Service (IRS) requires that the firm report personal use of its corporate jet as taxable executive income, and the Securities and Exchange Commission (SEC) requires that publicly traded corporations report the value of this benefit to shareholders. An important issue is the determination of the value of this benefit. The IRS values a CEO's personal flight at or below the price of a first-class ticket. The SEC values the flight at the "incremental" cost of the flight: the additional costs to the corporation of the flight. The third alternative is the market value of chartering an aircraft. Of the three methods, the first-class ticket is least expensive and the chartered flight is most expensive.

   a. What factors (such as fuel) determine the marginal explicit cost to a corporation of an executive's personal flight? Does any one of the three valuation methods correctly determine the marginal explicit cost?

   b. What is the marginal opportunity cost to the corporation of an executive's personal flight?

*1.4. A firm purchased copper pipes a few years ago at $10 per pipe and stored them, using them only as the need arises. The firm could sell its remaining pipes in the market at the current price of $9. What is the opportunity cost of each pipe and what is the sunk cost?

Short-Run Costs

*2.1. "'There are certain fixed costs when you own a plane,' [Andre] Agassi explained during a break in the action at the Volvo/San Francisco tennis tournament, 'so the more you fly it, the more economic sense it makes. . . . The first flight after I bought it, I took some friends to Palm Springs for lunch.'" (Scott Ostler, "Andre Even Flies Like a Champ," *San Francisco Chronicle*, February 8, 1993, C1.) Discuss whether Agassi's statement is reasonable.

2.2. In the twentieth century, department stores and supermarkets largely replaced smaller specialty stores, as consumers found it more efficient to go to one store rather than many stores. Consumers incur a transaction or search cost to shop, primarily the opportunity cost of their time. This transaction cost consists of a fixed cost of traveling to and from the store and a variable cost that rises with the number of different types of items the consumer tries to find on the shelves. By going to a supermarket that carries meat, fruits and vegetables, and other items, consumers can avoid some of the fixed transaction costs of traveling to a separate butcher shop, produce mart, and so forth. Use math to explain why a shopper's average costs are lower when buying at a single supermarket than from many stores. (*Hint*: Define the goods as the items purchased and brought home.)

2.3. Give the formulas for and plot *AFC*, *MC*, *AVC*, and *AC* if the cost function is

   a. $C = 10 + 10q$,

   b. $C = 10 + q^2$, or

   c. $C = 10 + 10q - 4q^2 + q^3$. **C**

2.4. In 1796, Gottfried Christoph Härtel, a German music publisher, calculated the cost of printing music using an engraved plate technology and used these estimated cost functions to make production decisions. Härtel figured that the fixed cost of printing a musical page—the cost of engraving the plates—was 900 pfennigs. The marginal cost of each additional copy of the page is 5 pfennigs (Scherer, 2001).

   a. Graph the total cost, average total cost, average variable cost, and marginal cost functions.

   b. Is there a cost advantage to having only one music publisher print a given composition? Why?

   c. Härtel used his data to do the following type of analysis. Suppose he expects to sell exactly 300 copies of a composition at 15 pfennigs per page of the composition. What is the greatest amount the publisher is willing to pay the composer per page of the composition?

2.5. Gail works in a flower shop, where she produces 10 floral arrangements per hour. She is paid $10 an hour for the first eight hours she works and $15 an hour for each additional hour she works. What is the firm's cost function? What are its *AC*, *AVC*, and *MC* functions? Draw the *AC*, *AVC*, and *MC* curves.

*2.6. A firm builds shipping crates out of wood. How does the cost of producing a 1-cubic-foot crate (each side is 1-foot square) compare to the cost of building an 8-cubic-foot crate if wood costs $1 a square foot and the firm has no labor or other costs? More generally, how does cost vary with volume?

2.7. The only variable input a janitorial service firm uses to clean offices is workers who are paid a wage, w, of $10 an hour. Each worker can clean four offices in an hour. Use math to determine the variable cost, the average variable cost, and the marginal cost of cleaning one more office. Draw a diagram like Figure 6.1 to show the variable cost, average variable cost, and marginal cost curves.

2.8. A firm has a Cobb-Douglas production function, $q = AL^\alpha K^\beta$, where $\alpha + \beta < 1$. On the basis of this information, what properties does its cost function have? For example, a U.S. chemical firm has a production function of $q = 10L^{0.32}K^{0.56}$ (based on Hsieh, 1995). If it faces factor prices of $w = 10$ and $r = 20$ and its capital is fixed at $\overline{K} = 100$, what are its short-run cost, variable cost, average variable cost, and marginal variable cost functions? Plot these curves.

2.9. Equation 6.5 gives the short run variable cost function for Japanese beer as $VC = 0.55q^{1.67}$. If the fixed cost is 600 and the firm produces 550 units, determine the C, VC, MC, AFC, and AVC. What happens to these costs if the firm increases its output to 600?

Long-Run Costs

3.1. The invention of a new machine serves as a mobile station for receiving and accumulating packed flats of strawberries close to where they are picked, reducing workers' time and burden of carrying full flats of strawberries. According to Rosenberg (2004), a machine-assisted crew of 15 pickers produces as much output, q^*, as that of an unaided crew of 25 workers. In a 6-day, 50-hour workweek, the machine replaces 500 worker-hours. At an hourly wage cost of $10, a machine saves $5,000 per week in labor costs, or $130,000 over a 26-week harvesting season. The cost of machine operation and maintenance expressed as a daily rental is $200, or $1,200 for a six-day week. Thus, the net savings equal $3,800 per week, or $98,800 for 26 weeks.

    a. Draw the q^* isoquant assuming that only two production methods are available (pure labor and labor-machine). Label the isoquant and axes as thoroughly as possible.

    b. Add an isocost line to show which technology the firm chooses (be sure to measure wage and rental costs on a comparable time basis).

    c. Draw the corresponding cost curves (with and without the machine), assuming constant returns to scale, and label the curves and the axes as thoroughly as possible.

*3.2. A bottling company uses two inputs to produce bottles of the soft drink Sludge: bottling machines (K) and workers (L). The isoquants have the usual smooth shape. The machine costs $1,000 per day to run and the workers earn $200 per day. At the current level of production, the marginal product of the machine is an additional 200 bottles per day, and the marginal product of labor is 50 more bottles per day. Is this firm producing at minimum cost? If it is minimizing cost, explain why. If it is not minimizing cost, explain how the firm should change the ratio of inputs it uses to lower its cost. (*Hint*: Examine the conditions for minimizing cost in Equations 6.8, 6.9, and 6.10.)

3.3. Suppose that the government subsidizes the cost of workers by paying for 25% of the wage (the rate offered by the U.S. government in the late 1970s under the New Jobs Tax Credit program). What effect will this subsidy have on the firm's choice of labor and capital to produce a given level of output? What happens if both capital and labor are subsidized at 25%? (*Hint*: See Q&A 6.2.)

*3.4. The all-American baseball is made using cork from Portugal, rubber from Malaysia, yarn from Australia, and leather from France, and it is stitched (108 stitches exactly) by workers in Costa Rica. To assemble a baseball takes one unit each of these inputs. Ultimately, the finished product must be shipped to its final destination—say, Cooperstown, New York. The materials used cost the same anywhere. Labor costs are lower in Costa Rica than in a possible alternative manufacturing site in Georgia, but shipping costs from Costa Rica are higher. What production function is used? What is the cost function? What can you conclude about shipping costs if it is less expensive to produce baseballs in Costa Rica than in Georgia?

3.5. California's State Board of Equalization imposed a higher tax on "alcopops," flavored beers containing more than 0.5% alcohol-based flavorings, such as vanilla extract (Guy L. Smith, "On Regulation of 'Alcopops,'" *San Francisco Chronicle*, April 10, 2009). Such beers are taxed as distilled spirits at $3.30 a gallon rather than as beer at 20¢ a gallon. In response, manufacturers reformulated their beverages so as to avoid the tax. By early 2009, instead of collecting a predicted $38 million a year in new taxes, the state collected only about $9,000. Use an isocost-isoquant diagram to explain the firms' response. (*Hint*: Alcohol-based flavors and other flavors may be close to perfect substitutes.)

3.6. A U.S. electronics firm is considering moving its production to a plant in Mexico. Its estimated production function is $q = L^{0.5}K^{0.5}$ (based on Hsieh, 1995).

The U.S. factor prices are $w = r = 10$. In Mexico, the wage is half that in the United States, but the firm faces the same cost of capital: $w^* = 5$ and $r^* = r = 10$. What are L and K, and what is the cost of producing $q = 100$ units in both countries?

*3.7. What is the long-run cost function for a fixed-proportions production function for which it takes two units of labor and one unit of capital to produce one unit of output as a function of the wage, w, and the price of capital, r? What is the cost function if the production function is $q = L + K$? (*Hint:* See Q&A 6.3.)

3.8. A U-shaped long-run average cost curve is the envelope of U-shaped short-run average cost curves. On what part of the curve (downward sloping, flat, or upward sloping) does a short-run curve touch the long-run curve?

The Learning Curve

4.1. In what types of industry would you expect to see substantial learning by doing? Why?

*4.2. A firm's learning curve, which shows the relationship between average cost and cumulative output (the sum of its output since the firm started producing), is $AC = a + bN^{-r}$; where AC is its average cost; N is its cumulative output; a, b, and r are constants; and $0 < r < 1$.

   a. What is the firm's AC if $r = 0$? What can you say about the firm's ability to learn by doing?

   b. If r exceeds zero, what can you say about the firm's ability to learn by doing? What happens to its AC as its cumulative output, N, gets extremely large? Given this result, what is your interpretation of a?

4.3. In the Mini-Case "Learning by Drilling," an oil drilling firm's average cost when working with production company M depends partly on its own cumulative drilling experience, N, and partly on the cumulative amount of drilling it has done jointly with production company M. Would an average cost curve $AC = a + b_1 N^{-r} + b_2 M^{-s}$ exhibit such learning by doing? Explain. (*Note:* a, b_1, b_2, r, and s are all positive constants.)

The Costs of Producing Multiple Goods

5.1. The United Kingdom started regulating the size of grocery stores in the early 1990s, and today the average size of a typical U.K. grocery store is roughly half the size of a typical U.S. store and two-thirds the size of a typical French store (Haskel and Sadun, 2011). What implications would such a restriction on size have on a store's average costs? Discuss in terms of economies of scale and scope.

5.2. Laura sells mushrooms and strawberries to tourists. If Laura spends the morning collecting only mushrooms, she picks 8 pints; if she spends the morning picking strawberries, she collects 6 pints. If she picks some of each, however, she can harvest more total pints: 6 pints of mushrooms and 4 pints of strawberries. Suppose that Laura's time is valued at $10 an hour. What can you say about her economies of scope? That is, what is the sign of her measure of economies of scope, SC?

*5.3. A refiner produces heating fuel and gasoline from crude oil in virtually fixed proportions. What can you say about economies of scope for such a firm? What is the sign of its measure of economies of scope, SC?

Managerial Problem

6.1. In Figure 6.9, show that there are wage rates and capital rental costs such that the firm is indifferent between using the wafer-handling stepper technology and the stepper technology. How does this wage/cost of capital ratio compare to those in the C^2 and C^3 isocosts?

Spreadsheet Exercises

7.1. The production function for a firm is

$$q = -0.6L^3 + 18L^2K + 10L$$

where q is the amount of output, L is the number of labor hours per week, and K the amount of capital. The wage is $100 and the rental rate is $800 per time period.

   a. Using Excel, calculate the total short-run output, $q(L)$, for $L = 0, 1, 2, \ldots\ 20$, given that capital is fixed in the short run at $\overline{K} = 1$. Also, calculate the average product of labor, AP_L, and the marginal product of labor, MP_L. (You can estimate the MP_L for $L = 2$ as $q(2) - q(1)$, and so on for other levels of L.)

   b. For each quantity of labor in (a), calculate the variable cost, VC; the total cost, C; the average variable cost, AVC; the average cost, AC; and the marginal cost, MC. Using Excel, draw the AVC, AC, and MC curves in a diagram.

   c. For each quantity of labor in (a), calculate w/AP_L and w/MP_L and show that they equal AVC and MC respectively. Explain why these relationships hold.

7.2. A furniture company has opened a small plant that builds tables. Jill, the production manager, knows the fixed cost of the plant, $F = \$78$ per day, and includes the cost of the building, tools, and equipment. Variable costs include labor, energy costs, and wood. Jill wants to know the cost function. She conducts an experiment in which she varies the daily production level over a 10-day period and observes the associated daily cost. The daily output levels assigned are 1, 2, 4, 5, 7, 8, 10, 12, 15, and 16. The associated total costs for these output levels are 125, 161, 181, 202, 207, 222, 230, 275, 390, and 535, respectively.

a. Use the Trendline tool in Excel to estimate a cost function by regressing cost on output (Chapter 3). Try a linear specification $(C = a + bq)$, a quadratic specification $(C = a + bq + dq^2)$, and a cubic specification $(C = a + bq + dq^2 + eq^3)$. Based on the plotted regressions, which specification would you recommend that Jill use? Would it make sense to use the *Set Intercept* option? If so, what value would you choose? (*Hint*: Put output in column A and cost in column B. To obtain quadratic and cubic cost specifications, select the *Polynomial* option from the *Trendline* menu and set *Order* at 2 for the quadratic specification and at 3 for the cubic function.)

b. Generate the corresponding average cost data by dividing the known cost by output for each experimental output level. Estimate an average cost curve using the Trendline tool.

Appendix 6 Long-Run Cost Minimization

We can use calculus to derive the tangency rule, cost-minimization condition, Equation 6.9. The problem the firm faces in the long run is to choose labor, L, and capital, K, to minimize the cost of producing a particular level of output, $\bar{q}$, given a wage of w and a rental rate of capital of r.

The firm's production function is $q = f(L, K)$, so the marginal products of labor and capital are $MP_L(L, K) = \partial f(L, K)/\partial L > 0$ and $MP_K = \partial f(L, K)/\partial K > 0$. The firm's problem is to minimize its cost of production, C, through its choice of labor and capital,

$$\min_{L, K} C = wL + rK,$$

subject to the constraint that a given amount of output, $\bar{q}$, is to be produced:

$$f(L, K) = \bar{q}. \tag{6A.1}$$

Equation 6A.1 is the formula for the $\bar{q}$ isoquant.

We can change this constrained minimization problem into an unconstrained problem by using the Lagrangian technique. The corresponding Lagrangian, $\mathscr{L}$, is

$$\mathscr{L} = wL + rK - \lambda[f(L, K) - \bar{q}],$$

where λ is the Lagrange multiplier.

The first-order conditions are obtained by differentiating $\mathscr{L}$ with respect to L, K, and λ and setting the derivatives equal to zero:

$$\partial\mathscr{L}/\partial L = w - \lambda MP_L(L, K) = 0, \tag{6A.2}$$

$$\partial\mathscr{L}/\partial K = r - \lambda MP_K(L, K) = 0, \tag{6A.3}$$

$$\partial\mathscr{L}/\partial\lambda = f(L, K) - \bar{q} = 0. \tag{6A.4}$$

Using algebra, we can rewrite Equations 6A.2 and 6A.3 as $w = \lambda MP_L(L, K)$ and $r = \lambda MP_K(L, K)$. Taking the ratio of these two expressions, we obtain

$$\frac{MP_L(L, K)}{MP_K(L, K)} = \frac{w}{r}, \tag{6A.5}$$

which is the same as Equation 6.9. This condition states that cost is minimized when the ratio of marginal products is the same as the factor price ratio, w/r.

Firm Organization and Market Structure

7

I won't belong to any organization that would have me as a member.
—Groucho Marx

Many managers, salespeople, and other employees who receive an annual bonus based on the firm's performance this year may have an incentive to take actions that increase the firm's profit this year but reduce profits in future years. Many dramatic examples of such behavior occurred in the last few years leading up to 2007, when banks seemed to go crazy issuing collateralized debt obligations (CDOs).

Banks and other financial firms collected mortgages of varying qualities, sorted them by quality (risk of default) into groups called *tranches*, and sold a CDO for each tranche. A CDO is a promise to pay the mortgage cash flows to the investors who buy the CDO. If the financial firm does not have enough money to cover the amount owed to all investors due to mortgage defaults, then those investors owning CDOs for the lowest tranches are not paid. To offset this greater risk, lower tranches sold for lower prices initially.

Mortgage brokers were rewarded for bringing in large numbers of new mortgages to serve as the basis for new CDOs, and the companies threw accepted lending practices out the window. They provided mortgages to borrowers with bad financial records who put no money down on their houses. In the San Francisco Bay area, 69% of families whose owner-occupied homes were in foreclosure had put down 0% at the time of purchase, and only 10% had made the traditional 20% down payment in the first nine months of 2007. Both home owners and speculators were enticed to take out new mortgages with very low (subprime) initial mortgage rates that adjusted over time.

Perhaps bank managers expected that the price of housing would rise forever, so that defaults would be manageable. However, the housing market tanked in 2007, sending housing prices into a free fall, so refinancing became nearly impossible. As interest rates on adjustable-rate mortgages rose, mortgage defaults skyrocketed, and CDOs lost most of their value.

Merrill-Lynch & Co. provided a prime example of how issuing such CDOs could create serious problems. In the years prior to 2007, Merrill advertised that it was the "#1 global underwriter of CDOs." As an underwriter, Merrill helped banks and other issuers of CDOs sell those CDOs, often purchasing the CDOs from issuers before reselling them to investors. In

We're now tying annual executive bonuses to performance. You owe us $100,000.

193

2006–2007, Merrill was the lead underwriter on 136 CDO deals for $93 billion, from which Merrill made $800 million in underwriting fees. However, Merrill was unable to resell all the CDOs it had purchased, which would not have been a problem if CDO prices had remained stable or rose. When the CDO market started to collapse in mid-2007, Merrill suffered large losses on its holdings of CDOs and its underwriting fees also disappeared.

Because of its managers' reckless practices, Merrill lost over $36 billion in 2007 and 2008, which more than offset all its earnings from 1997 through 2006. Merrill CEO Stanley O'Neal earned "only" $1.2 million in 2007, but over his six previous years as CEO at Merrill he had earned a total of $157.7 million. Neither O'Neal nor Merrill's other managers had to give back any of their prior earnings. Indeed, most Merrill senior managers received large bonuses in 2007.

In 2006, only 18% of Fortune 100 companies had a publicly disclosed *clawback* policy, where the firm could reclaim payments to managers if those managers' earlier actions caused later losses. By 2012, 87% had such a policy. Moreover, Wall Street firms have increasingly shifted bonuses from cash to deferred payments, which reflect the lower stock value if the company does badly later. Does evaluating a manager's performance over a longer time period lead to better management?

Having examined firms' production and cost decisions in earlier chapters, we now turn to some of the firm's other crucial decisions. Owners have to decide what objectives the firm should pursue, and they need to structure incentives to induce managers to pursue these objectives. Managers need to decide which stages of production the firm should perform and which to leave to others. We also consider how market characteristics such as the number of rivals affect a firm's decisions.

Throughout this book, we discuss "how firms behave" or "the firm's decision." Obviously, firms are not conscious entities that make decisions—it is the people within firms who make decisions on behalf of those firms. The main reason we use this short cut is that we do not want to be distracted by discussing which person within the firm makes a particular decision for the firm. However, in this chapter (and in Chapter 15), we examine how owners and managers interact and how laws, transaction costs, market size, individual incentives, and other factors affect decisions owners and managers make.

We start by examining the ownership and governance of firms, which affect the objectives a firm chooses to pursue. Although this book focuses on for-profit firms, the law permits and in some cases requires firms to pursue objectives other than maximizing profit.

Even among for-profit firms, not all firms focus on maximizing profit because managers of the firm, who are not necessarily the firm's owners, may decide to pursue another objective. If the owner of a firm is the manager, or if the manager and the owner have consistent objectives, no problems arise and we can largely ignore whether owners or managers make decisions. However, if their objectives are not aligned and the owner cannot completely control the behavior of the manager, then a conflict may arise.

This conflict is one of many situations where a *principal*, such as an owner, delegates tasks to an *agent*, such as a manager. Such a conflict creates a special type of transaction cost called an *agency cost*. Many features of the firm's organization can be viewed as attempts to minimize the associated agency cost.

In the pursuit of their main goal, such as maximizing profit, owners and managers must make decisions about the nature of the firm, such as whether the firm produces needed inputs internally or buys them. Whether the firm makes or buys an input depends on the relative costs of these two approaches. These costs include agency costs as well as other transaction costs. The size of the market affects transaction and other costs, and thereby affects the make-or-buy decision. We show that as a market grows, firms typically change from producing their own inputs to buying them from others, but, as the market grows even larger, firms may revert to producing the inputs themselves.

The size of the market affects not only individual firms' organizational structure but also the overall structure of the market. A market's structure is described by the number of firms, how easily they can enter or exit the market, their ability to set prices, whether they differentiate their products, and how the firms interact.

Main Topics

In this chapter, we examine five main topics

1. **Ownership and Governance of Firms:** Laws that affect how businesses are organized also affect who makes decisions and the firm's objective, such as whether it tries to maximize profit.

2. **Profit Maximization:** To maximize profit, any firm must make two decisions: how much to produce and whether to produce at all.

3. **Owners' Versus Managers' Objectives:** Differences in objectives between owners and managers affect the success of a firm.

4. **The Make or Buy Decision:** Depending on which approach is most profitable, a firm may engage in many sequential stages of production itself, participate in only a few stages and rely on markets for others, or use contracts or other means to coordinate its activities with those of other firms.

5. **Market Structure:** Markets differ as to the number of firms in the market, the ease of entry of new firms, whether firms produce identical products, how the firms interact, and the ability of firms to set prices.

7.1 Ownership and Governance of Firms

A firm may be owned by a government, by other firms, by private individuals, or by some combination. In the United States and most other countries, laws affect how private firms are owned, how owners may govern them, and whether they pursue profits or not.

Private, Public, and Nonprofit Firms

Atheism is a non-prophet organization. —George Carlin

Firms operate in the private sector, the public sector, or the nonprofit sector. The *private sector*— sometimes referred to as the *for-profit private sector* or *for-profit sector*— consists of firms that are owned by individuals or other nongovernmental entities and whose owners may earn a profit. Most of the firms that we discuss throughout this book—such as Apple, Heinz, and Toyota—belong to the private sector. In almost every country, this sector provides most of that country's gross domestic product (a measure of a country's total output).

The *public sector* consists of firms and other organizations that are owned by governments or government agencies, called *state-owned enterprises*. An example of a public sector firm is the National Railroad Passenger Corporation (Amtrak), which is owned primarily by the U.S. government. The armed forces and the court system are also part of the public sector, as are most schools, colleges, and universities.

The government produces less than a fifth of the total gross domestic product (GDP) in most developed countries, including Switzerland (9%), the United States (11%), Ireland (12%), Canada (13%), Australia (16%), and the United Kingdom (17%).[1] The government's share is higher in a few developed countries that provide many government services—such as Iceland (20%), the Netherlands (21%), and Sweden (22%)—or maintain a relatively large army, such as Israel (24%). The government's share varies substantially in less developed countries, ranging from very low levels like Nigeria (4%) to very high levels like Eritrea (94%). Strikingly, a number of former communist countries such as Albania (20%) and China (28%) now have public sectors of comparable relative size to developed countries and hence rely primarily on the private sector for economic activity.

The *nonprofit sector* consists of organizations that are neither government owned nor intended to earn a profit, but typically pursue social or public interest objectives. Literally, this sector should be called the *nongovernment, not-for-profit sector*, but this term is normally shortened to just the *nonprofit sector*. Well-known examples include Greenpeace, Alcoholics Anonymous, and the Salvation Army, along with many other charitable, educational, health, and religious organizations. According to the 2012 *U.S. Statistical Abstract*, the private sector created 75% of the U.S. gross domestic product, the government sector was responsible for 12%, and nonprofits and households produced the remaining 13%.

Sometimes all three sectors play an important role in the same industry. For example, in the United States, Canada, the United Kingdom, and in many other countries, for-profit, nonprofit, and government-owned hospitals coexist. Similarly, while most schools and other educational institutions are government owned, many are not, including some of the most prominent U.S. universities such as Harvard, Stanford, and the Massachusetts Institute of Technology (MIT). These universities are often referred to as *private* universities. Most private universities are nonprofit organizations. However, some educational institutions, such as the University of Phoenix, are intended to earn profits and are part of the for-profit private sector.

A single enterprise may be partially owned by a government and partially owned by private interests. For example, during the 2007–2009 Great Recession, the U.S. government took a partial ownership position in many firms in the financial and automobile industries. If the government is the dominant owner, it is normal to view the enterprise as part of the public sector. Conversely, if the government has only a small ownership interest in a for-profit enterprise, that enterprise would be viewed as part of the private sector. Organizations or projects with significant government ownership and significant private ownership are sometimes referred to as *mixed enterprises* or *public-private partnerships*.

---

[1]The data in this paragraph are from Alan Heston, Robert Summers, and Bettina Aten, Penn World Table Version 6.2, Center for International Comparisons of Production, Income, and Prices at the University of Pennsylvania, September 2006: **pwt.econ.upenn.edu/php_site/pwt62/pwt62_form .php**. Western governments' shares increased markedly (but presumably temporarily) during the major 2008–2009 recession, when they bought parts or all of a number of private firms to keep them from going bankrupt.

Mini-Case

**Chinese
State-Owned
Enterprises**

Many international corporations are thinking of entering the rapidly growing Chinese market, but they fear that the Chinese government will take actions that favor Chinese state-owned enterprises (SOEs). These fears may go away if China moves away from SOEs, but the role of SOEs in the future is still unclear.

Over the last decade, China has reduced the number of SOEs; however, it has kept the largest ones. Chinese SOEs have always been large relative to private firms. In 1999, SOEs were 36% of Chinese industrial firms, yet they controlled nearly 68% of industrial assets. Since then, the Chinese government has allowed many small SOEs to go private or go bankrupt, while it continues to subsidize large SOEs. By 2011, SOEs were only 5.2% of the firms but still owned 42% of the industrial assets.

Ownership of For-Profit Firms

In this textbook, we focus on the private sector. The private sector has three main types of organizations: the sole proprietorship, the partnership, and the corporation.

Sole proprietorships are firms owned and controlled by a single individual.

Partnerships are businesses jointly owned and controlled by two or more people operating under a partnership agreement.

Corporations are owned by *shareholders*, who own the firm's *shares* (also called *stock*). Each share (or unit of stock) is a unit of ownership in the firm. Therefore, shareholders own the firm in proportion to the number of shares they hold. The shareholders elect a board of directors to represent them. In turn, the board of directors usually hires managers who manage the firm's operations. Some corporations are very small and have a single shareholder. Others are very large and have thousands of shareholders. The legal name of a corporation often includes the term Incorporated (Inc.) or Limited (Ltd) to indicate its corporate status.

Publicly Traded and Closely Held Corporations. Corporations may be either publicly traded or closely held. The term *public* in this context has a different meaning than its use in the term *public sector*. A publicly traded corporation is a corporation whose shares can be readily bought and sold by the general public. The shares of most publicly traded corporations trade on major organized stock exchanges, such as the New York Stock Exchange, the NASDAQ (National Association of Securities Dealers Automated Quotations), the Tokyo Stock Exchange, the Toronto Stock Exchange, or the London Stock Exchange. For example, IBM shares can be readily bought and sold on the New York Stock Exchange.

The stock of a closely held corporation is not available for purchase or sale on an organized exchange. Typically its stock is owned by a small group of individuals. The stock of a closely held corporation is sometimes referred to as *private equity*. The transition from closely held to publicly traded status is often an important step in the evolution of a corporation.

In making the transition from privately held to publicly traded status, the closely held firm will make an *initial public offering* (or IPO) of its shares on an organized stock exchange. This IPO is a way to raise money for the firm. For example, Facebook's IPO in 2012 raised $16 billion for the firm. This ability to raise money by issuing stock is one major advantage of going public. However, a major disadvantage from the point of view of the original owners is that ownership of the firm becomes broadly distributed, possibly causing the original owners to lose control of the firm.

It is also possible for a publicly traded firm to go private and convert to closely held status. Such a change occurs when a small group of shareholders—typically managers of the firm—buy all or most of the shares held by the general public and take the corporation out of any organized exchanges where its stock previously traded. Toys Я Us is one of many well-known companies that went private recently along with many others: Burger King went private in 2010; J. Crew, Warner Music, and the Priory Group (Europe) in 2011; P.F. Chang's, Knology, and Payless ShoeSource in 2012; and American Greeting Corp. in 2013.

Liability. Traditionally, the owners of sole proprietorships and partnerships were fully liable, individually and collectively, for any debts of the firm. In contrast, the owners of a corporation are not personally liable for the firm's debts; they have **limited liability**: The personal assets of the corporate owners cannot be taken to pay a corporation's debts even if it goes into bankruptcy. Because of the limited liability of corporations, the most that shareholders can lose is the amount they paid for their stock, which typically becomes worthless if the corporation goes bankrupt.

Changes in the laws in many countries have allowed a sole proprietorship or a partnership to obtain the advantages of limited liability by becoming a *limited liability company* (LLC).[2] These LLC firms can otherwise do business as usual and need not adopt other aspects of the corporate form such as filing corporate tax returns. The precise regulations that apply to LLCs vary from country to country, and from state to state within the United States. Adopting the LLC form has some costs that many firms are not willing to incur, including registration fees, and firms in some industries are not eligible. Therefore, traditional sole proprietorships and partnerships with unlimited personal liability for the owners remain very common. However, the LLC form has significantly extended the availability of limited liability.[3]

Firm Size. The purpose of limiting the liability of owners of corporations was to allow firms to raise funds and grow larger than was possible when owners risked everything they owned on any firm in which they invested. Consequently, most large firms were (and still are) corporations. According to the 2012 *U.S. Statistical Abstract*, U.S. corporations are responsible for 81% of business receipts and 58% of net business income even though they are only 18% of all nonfarm firms. Nonfarm sole proprietorships are 72% of firms but make only 4% of the sales revenue and earn 15% of net income. Partnerships are 10% of firms, account for 15% of revenue, and make 27% of net income.

As these statistics illustrate, larger firms tend to be corporations and smaller firms are often sole proprietorships. This pattern reflects a natural evolution in the life cycle of the firm, as an entrepreneur may start a small business as a sole proprietorship and then incorporate as the firm's operations expand.

Indeed, successful corporations typically expand, and a relatively small number of corporations account for most of the revenue and income in the U.S. economy.

[2]In the United States, a few states had longstanding provisions for LLCs, but national acceptance and standardization of this form dates from the Uniform Limited Liability Company Act of 1996.

[3]Forming a *limited partnership* has become an alternative method for a partnership to gain the advantages of limited liability. Such firms are owned in whole or in part by *limited partners*, whose financial liability is limited in the sense that they cannot lose more than the amount of their investment. Limited partnerships may also have one or more *general partners* who, like sole proprietors, are personally responsible for the firm's debts.

Eighty-one percent of all corporations earn less than $1 million a year, and they account for only 3% of corporative revenue (*U.S. Statistical Abstract*, 2012). In contrast, less than 1% of all corporations earn over $50 million, but they make 77% of total corporate revenue. In 2012, ExxonMobil was the U.S. corporation with the largest worldwide revenue. Its revenue of $434 billion exceeded the annual GDP of fairly large countries, such as Austria ($301 billion) and Greece ($216 billion).[4]

Firm Governance

In a small private sector firm with a single owner-manager, the governance of the firm is straightforward: the owner-manager makes the important decisions for the firm. In contrast, governance in a large modern publicly traded corporation is more complex.

The shareholders own the corporation. However, most shareholders play no meaningful role in day-to-day decision making or even in long range planning in the firm and therefore do not control the firm in any meaningful sense. Many people own shares in corporations like Microsoft and Sony, but these individuals have no influence on and little knowledge of these firms' day-to-day managerial decisions.

Many of the ownership rights of shareholders are delegated to a board of directors that is elected by the shareholders, often referred to simply as the *board*. The board of a large publicly traded corporation normally includes outside directors, who are not employed as managers by the corporation, and inside directors, such as the chief executive officer (CEO) of the corporation and other senior executives. Current directors of major corporations include former U.S. Vice President Al Gore (Apple), football star Lynn Swann (Heinz), and author and self-help guru Deepak Chopra (Men's Warehouse), among many others.

7.2 Profit Maximization

The managers of all types of firms pursue goals. Managers of government agencies, charitable organizations, and other nonprofit organizations are supposed to take actions that benefit specific groups of people. We assume that most owners of private-sector firms want to maximize their profits, which is the reason why private-sector firms are called *for-profit businesses*. However, managers may not share the owners' objective—particularly if their compensation is not tied closely to the firm's profit.

In this section, we discuss how a firm maximizes its profit. In the next section, we discuss the factors that might lead the manager of a firm to pursue another objective and some of the methods that owners use to ensure that managers try to maximize profit.

Profit

A firm's *profit*, π, is the difference between a firm's revenues, R, and its cost, C:

$$\pi = R - C.$$

If profit is negative, $\pi < 0$, the firm makes a *loss*.

---

[4]*Fortune Magazine* annually provides a list of the largest corporations: **www.forbes.com/sites/scottdecarlo/2012/04/18/the-worlds-biggest-companies**. GDP data are from the IMF for 2011.

Measuring a firm's revenue from the sale of its product is straightforward: Revenue is price times quantity. Measuring cost is more challenging. From the economic point of view, the correct measure of cost is the *opportunity cost*: the value of the best alternative use of any input the firm employs. As discussed in Chapter 6, the full opportunity cost of inputs used might exceed the explicit or out-of-pocket costs recorded in financial accounting statements. The reason that this distinction is important is that a firm may make a serious mistake if it does not measure profit properly because it ignores some relevant opportunity costs.

Two Steps to Maximizing Profit

Because both the firm's revenue and cost vary with its output, q, the firm's profit also varies with output:

$$\pi(q) = R(q) - C(q), \tag{7.1}$$

where $R(q)$ is its revenue function and $C(q)$ is its cost function. A firm decides how much output to sell to maximize its profit, Equation 7.1. To maximize its profit, any firm must answer two questions:

▶ **Output decision:**   If the firm produces, what output level, q, maximizes its profit or minimizes its loss?

▶ **Shutdown decision:**   Is it more profitable to produce q or to shut down and produce no output?

The profit curve in Figure 7.1 illustrates these two basic decisions. This firm makes losses at very low and very high output levels and positive profits at moderate output levels. The profit curve first rises and then falls, reaching a maximum profit of π^* when its output is q^*. As this profit level is positive, the firm chooses to produce output q^* rather than shut down and earn no profit.

Output Rules. A firm can use one of three equivalent rules to choose how much output to produce. These rules are just three different ways of stating essentially the same thing. The most straightforward rule is:

Output Rule 1: The firm sets its output where its profit is maximized.

FIGURE 7.1 Maximizing Profit

By setting its output at q^*, the firm maximizes its profit at π^*, where the profit curve reaches its peak.

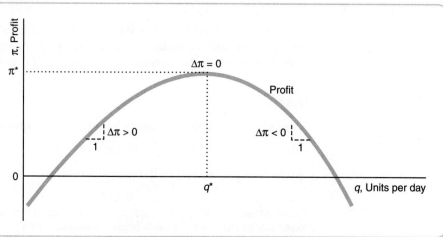

If the firm knows its entire profit curve in Figure 7.1, it sets its output at q^* to maximize its profit at π^*.

Even if the firm does not know the exact shape of its profit curve, it may be able to find the maximum by experimenting. The firm slightly increases its output. If profit increases, the firm increases the output more. The firm keeps increasing output until profit does not change. At that output, the firm is at the peak of the profit curve. If profit falls when the firm first increases its output, the firm tries decreasing its output. It keeps decreasing its output until it reaches the peak of the profit curve.

What the firm is doing is experimentally determining the slope of the profit curve. The slope of the profit curve is the firm's **marginal profit**: the change in the profit the firm gets from selling one more unit of output, $\Delta\pi/\Delta q$, where $\Delta q = 1$. In Figure 7.1, the marginal profit or slope of the profit curve is positive when output is less than q^*, zero when output is q^*, and negative when output is greater than q^*. Thus,

Output Rule 2: A firm sets its output where its marginal profit is zero.

A third way to express this profit-maximizing output rule is in terms of cost and revenue. The marginal profit depends on a firm's *marginal cost* and *marginal revenue*. A firm's **marginal cost (MC)** is the amount by which a firm's cost changes if it produces one more unit of output: $MC = \Delta C/\Delta q$, where ΔC is the change in cost when $\Delta q = 1$. Similarly, a firm's **marginal revenue (MR)** is the change in revenue it gets from selling one more unit of output: $\Delta R/\Delta q$, where ΔR is the change in revenue when $\Delta q = 1$. Provided MR is positive at output q, the firm earns more revenue by selling more units of output, but the firm also incurs an additional cost, $MC(q)$, which must be deducted from $MR(q)$ to determine the net effect on marginal profit. The change in the firm's profit is

$$\text{Marginal profit } (q) = MR(q) - MC(q).$$

Does it pay for a firm to produce one more unit of output? If the marginal revenue from this last unit of output exceeds its marginal cost, $MR(q) > MC(q)$, the firm's marginal profit is positive, $MR(q) - MC(q) > 0$, so it pays to increase output. The firm keeps increasing its output until it is producing q, where its marginal profit$(q) = MR(q) - MC(q) = 0$. There, its marginal revenue equals its marginal cost: $MR(q) = MC(q)$. If the firm produces more output where its marginal cost exceeds its marginal revenue, $MR(q) < MC(q)$, the extra output reduces the firm's profit. Thus, a third, equivalent rule is:

Output Rule 3: A firm sets its output where its marginal revenue equals its marginal cost:

$$MR(q) = MC(q). \tag{7.2}$$

Using Calculus

Maximizing Profit

We can use calculus to derive the condition that marginal revenue must equal marginal cost at the output level that maximizes profit. Using calculus, we define marginal revenue as the derivative of revenue with respect to output:

$$MR(q) = \frac{dR(q)}{dq}.$$

The derivative $dR(q)/dq$ is the limit of $\Delta R(q)/\Delta q$ as Δq gets very small. Our earlier definition of marginal revenue, $\Delta R(q)/\Delta q$ for $\Delta q = 1$, is nearly equivalent to the calculus definition if $\Delta q = 1$ is a "very small" change. Similarly, marginal cost is the derivative of cost with respect to output, $MC(q) = dC(q)/dq$ (Chapter 6).

To maximize profit in Equation 7.1, $\pi(q) = R(q) - C(q)$, the firm operates at the quantity q where the derivative of profit with respect to quantity is zero:

$$\frac{d\pi(q)}{dq} = \frac{dR(q)}{dq} - \frac{dC(q)}{dq} = MR(q) - MC(q) = 0. \tag{7.3}$$

The left side of Equation 7.3, $d\pi/dq$, is the firm's marginal profit. This result shows that marginal profit equals the difference in marginal revenue and marginal cost. Because this profit-maximizing condition requires that $MR(q) - MC(q) = 0$, it follows that the firm maximizes its profit when it chooses output such that $MR(q) = MC(q)$, which is the same condition as in Equation 7.2.

Q&A 7.1

If a firm's revenue function is $R(q) = 120q - 2q^2$ and its cost function is $C(q) = 100 + q^2$, what output level maximizes its profit?

Answer

1. *Determine the marginal revenue and marginal cost by differentiating the revenue and cost functions.* The firm's marginal revenue is $dR(q)/dq = 120 - 4q$. Its marginal cost is $dC(q)/dq = 2q$.

2. *Equate the marginal revenue and marginal cost expressions to determine the output that maximizes profit.* Setting the marginal revenue equal to the marginal cost, we find that $120 - 4q = 2q$. Solving for q, we learn that the profit-maximizing output is $q = 20$.

3. *Alternatively, determine the profit function and then differentiate the profit function to find the maximum.* The profit function is $\pi(q) = R(q) - C(q)$ $= [120q - 2q^2] - [100 + q^2] = 120q - 3q^2 - 100$. Taking the derivative of the profit function with respect to quantity (the marginal profit) and setting it equal to zero, we learn that $d\pi(q)/dq = 120 - 6q = 0$. Consequently, the profit-maximizing output is $q = 20$.

Managerial Implication

Marginal Decision Making

One of the most important implications of economics is that marginal analysis is very valuable to managers. If a manager knows the entire profit function (as in Figure 7.1), then it's easy to choose the profit-maximizing output. However, many managers are uncertain about what profit would be at output levels that differ significantly from the current level.

Such a manager can use marginal reasoning to maximize profit. By experimenting, the manager can determine if increasing output slightly raises profit—that is, the firm's marginal profit is positive (or, equivalently, its marginal revenue is greater than its marginal cost). If so, the manager should continue to increase output until the marginal profit is zero (marginal revenue equals marginal cost). Similarly, if marginal profit is negative, the manager should decrease output until marginal profit is zero.[5]

---

[5]In our examples, this marginal condition ($MR = MC$ or $d\pi/dq = 0$) is met at only one output level, where profit is maximized. However, it is possible to have more than one *local* profit maximum, each of which satisfies the marginal condition. This marginal condition will also be satisfied if there is a positive output level where profit is *minimized*. If the marginal condition holds at more than one quantity, the one with the highest profit is the *global* profit maximum.

Shutdown Rules. Producing the output level q such that $MR(q) = MC(q)$ is a necessary condition to maximize profit if the firm produces a positive output level. However, the firm might make losses even at the best possible positive output (although a smaller loss than at other positive outputs).

Should the firm shut down if its profit is negative? Surprisingly, the answer is "It depends." The general rule, which holds for all types of firms in both the short run and in the long run, is:

Shutdown Rule 1: The firm shuts down only if it can reduce its loss by doing so.

In the short run, the firm has variable costs, such as for labor and materials, and fixed costs, such as from plant and equipment (Chapter 6). If the fixed cost is *sunk*, this expense cannot be avoided by stopping operations—the firm pays this cost whether it shuts down or not. Thus, the sunk fixed cost is irrelevant to the shutdown decision. By shutting down, the firm stops receiving revenue and stops paying the avoidable costs (Chapter 6), but it is still stuck with its fixed cost. Thus, it pays for the firm to shut down only if its revenue is less than its avoidable cost.

Suppose that a firm's weekly revenue is $R = \$2,000$, its variable cost is $VC = \$1,000$, and its fixed cost is $F = \$3,000$, which is the price it paid for a machine that it cannot resell or use for any other purpose. This firm is making a short-run negative profit π (a loss):

$$\pi = R - VC - F = \$2,000 - \$1,000 - \$3,000 = -\$2,000.$$

If the firm shuts down, it still has to pay its fixed cost of $3,000, and hence it loses $3,000, which is a greater loss than the $2,000 it loses if it operates. Because its fixed cost is sunk, the firm should ignore it when making its shutdown decision. Ignoring the fixed cost, the firm sees that its $2,000 revenue exceeds its $1,000 avoidable, variable cost by $1,000, so it does not shut down. The extra $1,000 can be used to offset some of the fixed cost, reducing the firm's loss from $3,000 to $2,000.

However, if its revenue is only $500, it cannot cover its $1,000 avoidable, variable cost and loses an additional $500. When it adds this $500 loss to the $3,000 it must pay in fixed cost, the firm's total loss is $3,500. Because the firm can reduce its loss from $3,500 to $3,000 by ceasing operations, it shuts down. (Remember the shutdown rule: The firm shuts down only if it can reduce its loss by doing so.)

The firm's variable costs are always *avoidable*: the firm only pays the variable costs if it operates. In contrast, the firm's short-run fixed cost is usually *unavoidable*: the firm incurs the fixed cost whether or not it shuts down. Therefore, if the firm shuts down in the short run it incurs a loss equal to its fixed cost because it has no revenue ($R = 0$) or variable cost ($VC = 0$), so its profit is negative: $\pi = R - VC - F = 0 - 0 - F = -F$. If the firm operates and its revenue more than covers its variable cost, $R > VC$, then the firm does better by operating because $\pi = R - VC - F > -F$. Thus, the firm shuts down only if its revenue is less than its avoidable, variable cost: $R < VC$.

In conclusion, the firm compares its revenue to only its avoidable, variable costs when deciding whether to stop operating. If the fixed cost is sunk, the firm pays this cost whether it shuts down or not. The sunk fixed cost is irrelevant to the shutdown decision.

We usually assume that a fixed cost is sunk. However, if a firm can sell its capital for as much as it paid, its fixed cost is avoidable and should be taken into account when the firm is considering whether to shut down. A firm with a fully avoidable fixed cost always shuts down if it makes a short-run loss. If a firm buys a specialized piece of machinery for $1,000 that can be used only in its business but can be sold for scrap metal for $100, then $100 of the fixed cost is avoidable and $900 is sunk. Only the avoidable portion of fixed cost is relevant for the shutdown decision.

In planning for the long run, all costs are avoidable because there are no sunk fixed costs: all capital and other inputs are adjustable in the long run. The firm can eliminate all costs by shutting down. Thus, in the long run, it pays to shut down if the firm faces any loss at all. As a result, we can restate the shutdown rule, which holds for all types of firms in both the short run and the long run, as:

Shutdown Rule 2: The firm shuts down only if its revenue is less than its avoidable cost.

Profit over Time

Through most of this book, we examine a firm whose shareholders want it to maximize its profit in the current period. However, firms are typically interested in maximizing their profit over many periods. Often when one period is just like the others, this distinction in objectives is minor. However, in some situations the difference between maximizing the current period's profit and long-run profit is important.

For example, when Amazon, Netflix, and Groupon launched, each spent large sums of money on advertising, investing in product improvements, providing services below cost, and taking other actions to acquire as many loyal customers as possible. By doing so, they reduced their short-run profit—indeed, often running at a loss—in the hopes of acquiring larger long-run profits.[6] Because money in the future is worth less than money today, the shareholders of a firm may value a stream of profits over time by calculating the *present value*, in which future profits are discounted using the interest rate (Appendix 7).

Managerial Implication **Stock Prices Versus Profit**	Many newspaper articles and business shows focus almost exclusively on the price of a share of the firm's stock rather than on its annual profit. Does it follow that a manager should be more concerned about a firm's stock price than its profit? It makes no difference if the manager's objective is to maximize either measure if the stock price reflects the firm's profit.

The owner of stock in a corporation like Nokia or Starbucks has the right to share in the current and future profits of the firm. Therefore, the stock price reflects both current and future profits. The sum of the value of all outstanding shares in the firm is the stock market valuation of the firm. It is the present value investors place on the flow of current and future profits.

If the firm earns an annual profit of π per year forever, the present value of that profit stream is π/i, where i is the interest rate (Appendix 7, Equation 7A.4). For example, if the firm earns $10 million a year forever and the interest rate is 10%, then the present value is $10/0.10 = $100 million. If shareholders expect this level of profit and interest rate to continue in the future and the firm issued one million shares of stock, then each share would sell for $100.

If the firm's profit were higher, then its present value would also be higher. For example, if the annual profit were known to be $11 million per year forever (instead of $10 million), then the firm's present value would be $110 million and the value of each share would be $110. Thus, maximizing a constant profit flow maximizes the value of the firm and is therefore equivalent to maximizing the stock price.

---

[6]Indeed, Amazon's stock price rose substantially over time, with the price in February 2013 nearly 13 times larger than when it was initially offered in 1997.

However, if a firm's profit flow varies over time, then the link between a firm's profit and its stock price is more complex and the stock price might be more relevant to managers than the current profit. Consider a firm that makes a major investment that causes it to suffer a loss this year but that results in higher profits in the future. If investors understand that the investment will pay off in the long run, the stock price rises after the investment is made. Thus, a manager who is concerned about a firm's long-run profit stream may try to maximize the present value of profit or, equivalently, maximize the firm's stock value, rather than concentrate on the profit this period. However, if investors are not well informed about the firm's profit so that the stock price does not closely track the present value of profits, then maximizing the stock price is not equivalent to maximizing the present value of profits.

7.3 Owners' Versus Managers' Objectives

The executive exists to make sensible exceptions to general rules. —Elting E. Morison

Except for the smallest of firms, one person cannot perform all the tasks necessary to run a firm. In most firms, the owners of the firm have to delegate tasks to managers and other workers. A conflict may arise between owners who want to maximize profit and managers interested in pursuing other goals, such as maximizing their incomes or traveling in a company jet. A conflict between an owner (a principal) and a manager (an agent) may impose costs on the firm—agency costs—that result in lower profit for the firm. However, owners can take steps to minimize these conflicts, and market forces reduce the likelihood that a firm will deviate substantially from trying to maximize profit.

Consistent Objectives

No conflict between owners and managers arises if the owner and the manager have the same objective. To make their objectives more closely aligned, many firms use contingent rewards, so that the manager receives higher pay if the firm does well.

Contingent Rewards. Owners may give managers pay incentives to induce them to work hard and to maximize profit. If good performance by managers is observable, the owner can reward it directly. However, the owners of large corporations—the shareholders—usually cannot observe the performance of individual managers. Owners often provide alternative incentive schemes to managers and others whose productivity is difficult to quantify, especially those who work as part of a team. Such workers may be rewarded if their team or the firm does well in general. Frequently, year-end bonuses are based on the firm's profit or increases in the value of its stock.

A common type of incentive is a lump-sum year-end bonus based on the performance of the firm or a group of workers within the firm. Another incentive is a stock option, which gives managers (and increasingly other workers) the option to buy a certain number of shares of stock in the firm at a prespecified *exercise price* within a specified time period. If the stock's market price exceeds the exercise price during that period, an employee can *exercise the option*—buy the stock—and then sell it at the market price, making an immediate profit. But if the stock's price stays below the exercise price, the option becomes worthless.[7] Steve Jobs, CEO and co-founder of Apple, received a salary of only $1 per year until his retirement in 2011, but he also received stock options worth hundreds of millions of dollars.

Profit Sharing. If profit is easily *observed* by the owner and the manager and *both want to maximize their own earnings*, the agency problems can be avoided by paying the manager a share of the firm's profit. Typically, rather than paying managers a share of the profit directly, their earnings are based on the company's stock price, which rises as the firm's profit increases.

Frydman and Saks (2008) found that large U.S. firms have increasingly linked executive compensation to the firm's financial performance over time. They estimated that by 2005 over 70% of firms provided annual stock options to their top three executives, compared to virtually none in 1950 and about 50% in 1970. On average in 2009, 75% of total compensation of a chief executive at S&P 500 firms came from incentives: bonuses (2%), nonequity incentive plan compensation (19%), option awards (25%), and stock awards (28%).[8]

Such incentive-based compensation is more common in the United States than in most other countries. According to Conyon and Muldoon (2006), U.S. CEO incentives were much stronger than those in the United Kingdom. The share of compensation from salary was only 31% in the United States but 44% in the United Kingdom. Bonuses were comparable: 20% in the United States and 22% in the United Kingdom. The biggest difference was that the stock option share of CEO compensation in the United States, 32%, was nearly three times that in the United Kingdom, 11%.

If the manager is paid a specified fraction of the firm's profit, and both the manager and owners care only about financial returns, then the agency problem is avoided because the objectives of the manager and the owners are aligned. Both parties want to maximize total profit. The output level that maximizes total profit also maximizes any fixed fraction of total profit. In Figure 7.2, the manager (agent) earns one-third of the joint profit of the firm and the shareholders (principals) receive two-thirds. The figure shows that the output level, q^*, maximizes the profits of both the manager and the shareholders.[9] The next Q&A analyzes an alternative compensation scheme.

---

[7]A stock option might have unintended negative consequences if it gives a manager an incentive to increase the firm's short-run stock price at the expense of future stock prices. After all, in the long run, an employee might not even be around and therefore might place excessive emphasis on the short run.

[8]An option award gives the executive the option to buy an amount of stock at a specified price up to a specified date. A stock award grants an executive stock directly. The statistics are from **www.aflcio .org/corporatewatch/paywatch/pay** (viewed February 26, 2013).

[9]To determine where profit is maximized using calculus, we differentiate the profit function, $\pi(q)$, with respect to output, q, and set that derivative, which is marginal profit, equal to zero: $d\pi(q)/dq = 0$. The quantity that maximizes the manager's share of profit, $\frac{1}{3}\pi(q)$, is determined by $d\frac{1}{3}\pi(q)/dq = \frac{1}{3}d\pi(q)/dq = 0$, or $d\pi(q)/dq = 0$. That is, the quantity at which the manager's share of profit reaches a maximum is determined by the same condition as the one that determines that total profit reaches a maximum.

FIGURE 7.2 Profit Sharing

If the manager gets a third of the total profit, $\frac{1}{3}\pi$, then the manager sets output at q^*, which maximizes the manager's share of profit. The firm's owners receive $\frac{2}{3}\pi$, which is the vertical difference between the total profit curve and the agent's earnings at each output. Both total profit and the owner's share of profit are also maximized at q^*.

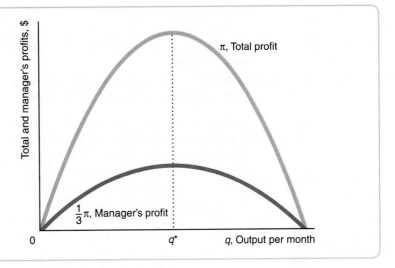

Q&A 7.2

Peter, the owner, makes the same offer to the manager at each of his stores: "At the end of the year, give me $100,000 and you can keep any additional profit." Ann, a manager at one of the stores, gladly agrees, knowing that the total profit at the store will substantially exceed $100,000 if it is well run. If she is interested in maximizing her earnings, will Ann act in a manner that maximizes the store's total profit?

Answer

1. *Draw a diagram showing the total profit curve and use it to derive Ann's profit curve.* The figure shows that the total profit curve is first increasing and then decreasing as output rises. Ann, the manager, receives the total profit minus $100,000, so at every quantity, her profit is $100,000 less than the store's total profit. Thus, her profit curve is the original curve shifted down by $100,000 at every quantity. The figure shows only that part of Ann's profit curve where her profit is positive.

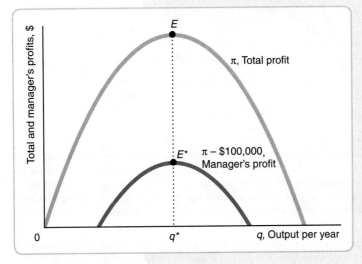

2. *Determine the quantity that maximizes Ann's profit and check whether that quantity also maximizes total profit.* In the figure, Ann's profit is maximized at point E^* where output is q^*. At that quantity, total profit is also maximized at point E. Because the manager's curve is the total profit curve shifted straight down, the quantity that maximizes one curve must maximize the other. Thus, if Ann wants to maximize her earnings, she will work to maximize the store's profit.

Conflicting Objectives

Unfortunately, owners and managers have conflicting objectives in some firms. A manager is especially likely to pursue an objective other than profit if the manager's compensation system rewards the manager for something other than maximizing profit. Moreover, even if the owner offers to share the profit with the manager, a manager who pursues an objective other than purely maximizing personal earnings, such as wanting to avoid working hard, will not maximize profit.

Revenue Objectives. It is not always feasible to tie a manager's compensation to profit, because profit may not be observed by everyone or because the owner or the manager can manipulate the reported profit.[10] For example, if the manager can allocate reported costs to a future year, the manager can increase reported profit this year. Consequently, many firms tie a manager's compensation to an objective other than current profit. As the Mini-Case "Determinants of CEO Compensation" (in Chapter 3) documents, many boards link their chief executive officer's compensation to the size of the firm as measured by sales, the firm's revenue. However, if executive compensation is primarily determined by the firm's revenue, managers prefer to maximize revenue rather than profit.

Figure 7.3 shows the revenue or sales curve as well as the profit curve for a firm.[11] If the owner's agent, the manager, is paid a share of revenue, the manager sets output at $q = 5$, where profit is 5 and revenue is 25. This output level exceeds the output that maximizes profit, $q = 3$, where profit is 9 and revenue is 21.

FIGURE 7.3 Revenue Maximization

If the manager's earnings are in proportion to revenue, the manager wants the firm to produce $q = 5$ units of output. However, profit is maximized where $q = 3$ units are produced.

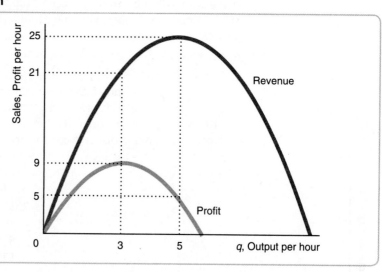

[10]Authors normally receive royalties based on revenue rather than profit. They will not agree to compensation based on profit because they fear that the publisher would be able to reduce reported profit by allocating common costs associated with publishing all books to their particular book. Similarly, top movie stars and directors insist on a percentage of sales rather than profit because studios have been notorious for reporting such implausibly high costs that even blockbuster movies apparently made losses.

[11]In this figure, the firm faces a linear inverse demand curve of $p = 10 - q$ and a cost function of $C = 4q$. Consequently, the firm's revenue is $R = 10q - q^2$ and its profit is $\pi = R - C = 6q - q^2$.

While rewarding a manager solely based on revenue would cause problems, most corporations mix revenue incentives with other incentives, so as to induce the manager to maximize profit. The Mini-Case "Determinants of CEO Compensation" in Chapter 3 shows that a typical CEO's compensation is a weighted average of a measure of revenue, profit, shareholders' returns, and other measures. To the degree that more weight is placed on profit than on revenue, the manager is more likely to set output close to the profit-maximizing output level.

Some boards that reward managers for increasing revenue may do so even though they are interested in maximizing long-run profit. They may believe that the profit measure reflects short-run profit and that long-run profit will be higher if the firm becomes larger in the short run, perhaps due to learning by doing (Chapter 6) or obtaining more loyal customers (as Amazon did).

Q&A 7.3

How does a manager set output to maximize revenue? Describe the role of marginal revenue in your analysis.

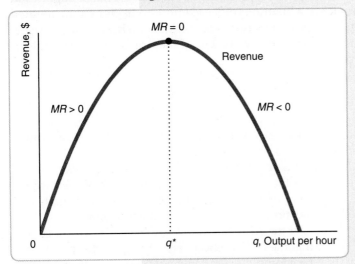

Answer

1. *Draw a diagram showing the sales or revenue curve and identify the quantity at which it reaches a peak.* The figure shows a single-peak revenue curve. This curve reaches its maximum at an output of q^*.

2. *Use marginal revenue to determine when the revenue curve reaches its peak.* The slope of the revenue curve is marginal revenue, MR. Where the curve slopes up, MR is positive. Where it slopes down, MR is negative. Where the revenue curve reaches its maximum, MR is zero.[12] Thus, the manager sets production at q^* to maximize revenue.

Other Objectives. If the manager's utility or well-being depends on personal effort as well as personal earnings, then even receiving a share of profit may not be a sufficient incentive for the manager to maximize the firm's profit. Also, a manager who receives a fixed salary or other compensation that is not tied to the firm's performance and who values leisure may not work hard enough to maximize the firm's profit. If a board reacts by insisting that a certain profit target be achieved, a manager may *satisfice* by merely achieving results that are "good enough" rather than trying to maximize profit.

Another possibility—particularly if executive compensation is not tied closely to profit—is that senior executives may pursue their own values or social objectives instead of maximizing profit. For example, corporations often make large

---

[12]To determine where revenue is maximized using calculus, we differentiate the revenue function, $R(q)$, with respect to output, q, and set that derivative, which is marginal revenue, equal to zero: $MR = dR(q)/dq = 0$.

contributions to sports franchises, hospitals, universities, environmental projects, disadvantaged groups, or other causes. Although it is difficult to argue that such recipients are unworthy, these managers are pursuing social policy with shareholders' money. If shareholders want to donate money for a new football stadium or a new hospital, they can do so directly; thus, they might not want managers making such decisions for them. However, the owners of some firms (such as McDonalds, Unilever, and many others) explicitly authorize a firm's managers to spend limited amounts to pursue particular environmental or other social objectives, even though such actions may reduce the firms' profits.

Although a manager who is solely interested in personal gain may steal from a firm, we hope that relatively few managers are that dishonest. Nonetheless, many managers believe it is appropriate to treat themselves to a variety of *perquisites* (*perks*)—benefits beyond their salary—of dubious value to the firm.

It is perfectly appropriate for a corporation to provide a manager with health or various other benefits. If the firm reduces the manager's salary by the cost of such benefits, then these benefits do not harm the firm's bottom line. A firm might want to provide a flashy perk such as a luxurious office to impress clients or a chauffeured limo that saves a manager's time and increases profit. Nonetheless, some managers unilaterally grant themselves perks that come out of the firm's profit with little or no tangible advantage to the firm.

Mini-Case

Company Jets

Some corporations allow the chief executive officer (CEO) to make personal use of the company's plane—for example, to play golf at a distant course. In 2011, the *Wall Street Journal* reported that, based on a review of the flight records of dozens of corporate jets over a four-year period, more than half of their trips were to or from resort destinations, and usually to locations where executives owned homes.[13]

If the corporation reduces the CEO's earnings so that the CEO is effectively paying for this privilege, providing the aircraft should have no effect on the firm's bottom line or its stock's value. On the other hand, such a perk reduces a firm's profit if managers are directing some of the firm's profit into their own pockets without providing compensating service. Moreover, if workers react adversely to managers' perks, morale may fall and shirking and unethical behavior may increase. If so, we would expect the firm's profit and stock value to fall.

---

[13]These perks are often a large share of an executive's compensation. In a 2012 filing, Facebook reported that Mark Zuckerberg, its CEO, had a compensation package including $483,333 in salary, a $220,500 bonus, and $783,529 in "other compensation," which includes $692,679 for "personal use of aircraft chartered in connection with his comprehensive security program and on which family and friends flew."

According to Yermack (2006), when firms first disclose a CEO's jet plane perquisites, shareholders react very negatively, causing the firm's stock price to fall by 1.1% on average. Moreover, the long-run effect of such disclosures is to reduce average shareholder returns by more than 4% below market benchmarks annually—a large gap that greatly exceeds the cost of resources consumed.

Although perks may be given to reward excellent work by managers, large perks often indicate weak governance by boards. Companies disclosing a plane perk are more likely to take extraordinary accounting write-offs and to report quarterly earnings per share significantly below analyst estimates.

Monitoring and Controlling a Manager's Actions

If the owner's and manager's objectives conflict, the owner may try to monitor or control the manager's behavior. Monitoring is difficult if the owner cannot easily *observe* the actions of the manager and if the profit or other payoff from these actions is subject to *uncertainty*. Moreover, controlling the manager's actions is difficult if the parties cannot write an *enforceable contract*.

If the owner and manager work side by side, monitoring the manager is easy. However, the cost of monitoring the manager's effort is sometimes prohibitively high. Usually the owner does not want to have to shadow the manager all day to ensure that the manager is working hard. Installing a time clock might show that the manager was at work, but it does not show that the manager was working hard. In any case, it is typically difficult to determine if a manager who must engage in a complex set of actions is working well. When direct monitoring of a manager's actions is impractical, the owner may be able to use an indirect method to monitor, as we discuss in Chapter 15.

To minimize agency costs, most corporations set rules that govern the relationship between the board and the senior executives. Senior executives are usually restricted in their ability to carry out activities outside the firm that are related to their duties at the firm. Many are required to disclose to the board various actual or potential conflicts of interest that might arise.

Similarly, most corporations set rules that govern the board of directors to further reduce the likelihood of agency problems between the board and the shareholders. For example, the rules may require the board to have *outside directors*: directors who are not the firm's managers. The rules also specify the nature and frequency of elections to the board and the rights of shareholders to vote on important decisions and to propose various actions at shareholder meetings. Unfortunately, it is difficult to specify or legally enforce what constitutes appropriate effort on the part of the board. Moreover, in most corporations, although board members must be elected by shareholders, new board members are nominated by the existing board. Although some shareholders sue boards, such lawsuits are costly to pursue and rarely solve the associated agency problems.[14]

---

[14]According to Briody (2001), the average payout in shareholder lawsuits that are settled is approximately only 5% of the associated financial loss to shareholders. In addition, many lawsuits are unsuccessful and most alleged or suspected board misconduct never gives rise to lawsuits.

The 2007–2009 financial crisis induced some shareholders to be more vigilant. A new movement to give shareholders' a *say on pay* (SOP) going to upper management gained momentum.[15] For example, Apple's shareholders passed an SOP resolution in 2009. Similarly, in 2009 the Bank of America added four outside directors with banking and finance experience to its board to improve its corporate governance. In 2012, Citigroup shareholders rejected a $15 million pay package for its chief executive, Vikram S. Pandit, on the grounds that it lacked "rigorous goals to incentivize improvement in shareholder value." The compensation package of his successor was smaller and more closely tied to the firm's performance relative to that of other large banks.[16]

The Dodd-Frank Wall Street Reform and Consumer Protection Act of 2010 requires publicly traded companies to have shareholders vote periodically (at least once every three years) on the compensation going to senior executives. The vote is nonbinding, so a negative vote does not necessarily block the compensation. However, failed SOP votes create significant problems for a firm, including negative publicity and greater legal vulnerability to shareholder lawsuits. The U.S. Securities and Exchange Commission released rules on implementing SOP in 2011. However, in the first year of SOP requirements, among the thousands of U.S. public companies, only about 2% of SOP votes had a majority of shareholders vote against the planned compensation packages.

Takeovers and the Market for Corporate Control

Competition is the keen cutting edge of business, always shaving away at costs.
—Henry Ford

Many owners provide adequate monitoring to keep managers on the straight and narrow. However, we generally assume that firms try to maximize profit because of the survivor principle as well as the market for corporate control. According to the *survivor principle*, in highly competitive markets, the only firms that survive are those that are run so as to maximize profit. Firms that fail to maximize profit lose money and go out of business.

Even in less competitive markets, managers can be disciplined through the *market for corporate control*, where outside investors use the stock market to buy enough shares to take over control of an underperforming publicly traded firm. An outsider may profit by seizing control of a company in which the current managers are doing a poor job—undertaking unprofitable projects and spending money on their own comfort and compensation—with little profit going to the shareholders in the form of dividends or capital gains. If the acquiring firm can convince enough shareholders that profit will rise after a takeover, the shareholders can vote out the existing board and management and vote in the one the acquiring firm recommends.

For example, Sophia is the manager of an underperforming company. She knows that a well-known investor or corporate raider (such as Carl Icahn or T. Boone Pickens) has been buying up shares of the firm.[17] She's sure that the raider is planning

---

[15]In 2013, 68% of Swiss voters backed a measure that would give shareholders of publicly traded Swiss firms a binding say on executive pay and limit managerial perquisites and potential conflicts of interest between shareholders and senior executives.

[16]Nathaniel Popper and Jessica Silver-Greenberg, "Citigroup Toughens Executive Bonus Rules," *New York Times*, February 21, 2013.

[17]Unfortunately, some corporate raiders are not interested in turning the company around. Rather, they are engaged in *greenmail*, where they purchasing enough shares that a takeover is plausible so as to force the target firm to buy those shares back at a premium to end the takeover attempt.

a hostile takeover and will replace the current managers with new managers, whom he believes can turn around the underperforming firm. How does Sophia keep her job? If she's like a lot of managers and corporate directors who find themselves in this position, she'll hire the cleverest corporate lawyer she can find to construct takeover defenses.

Common defenses in the United States include a *shareholder rights plan*, which is better known as a *poison pill*.[18] (See Table 7.1 for a list of takeover defense terminology.) A poison pill is a provision that a corporate board adds to its bylaws or charter that makes the firm a less attractive takeover target.

The law on the use of poison pills is evolving, with many countries restricting their use, including the United Kingdom and many other European countries. In Canada, regulatory authorities can remove provisions deemed to be poison pills from takeover bids, and they frequently do.

Poison pills do not always work in preventing a takeover, but they frequently result in some of the resulting profit going to the original managers or boards of directors to induce them not to further fight the takeover. The use of poison pills in

TABLE 7.1 Some Takeover Defense Terms

back-end plan: Provision that gives shareholders the right to cash or debt securities at an above-market price previously defined by the company's board in the event of a hostile takeover.

dead-hand: Provision that allows only the directors who introduce the poison pill to remove it for a fixed period after they have been replaced, thereby delaying a new board's ability to sell the firm.

flip-in: Provision that gives current shareholders of the firm other than the hostile acquirer the right to purchase additional shares of stocks at a discount price after the acquirer obtains a certain percentage of the firm's shares (usually between 20% and 50%).

flip-over: Provision that allows stockholders to buy the acquiring firm's shares at a discount price after a merger or takeover.

golden handcuffs: Employment clauses that require top employees to give back lucrative bonuses or incentives if they leave the firm within a specified period of time. As a poison pill, these clauses cease to hold after a hostile takeover so that the employees may quit immediately after cashing their stock options.

macaroni defense (similar to a flip-over): The issuance of many bonds with the condition they must be redeemed at an above-market price if the company is taken over.

poison pill, porcupine provision, shareholder rights plan, or *shark repellent:* Defensive provisions that corporate boards include in the firm's corporate charter or bylaws that make a takeover less profitable.

poison puts: The issuance of bonds that investors may cash before they mature in the event of a hostile takeover attempt.

---

[18]The use of such a defense was introduced by Martin Lipton, a mergers and acquisitions lawyer, during a takeover battle where T. Boone Pickens was trying to acquire General American Oil in 1982. See **activistinvesting.blogspot.com/2011/01/historial-and-legal-background-of.html** (viewed February 23, 2013).

the United States has declined during the last decade: More than 2,200 corporations had poison pills in 2001 compared to fewer than 900 corporations in early 2011 (Bab and Neenan, 2011). In part, this decline is due to companies increasingly allowing shareholders to vote on poison pills.

Mini-Case	The Yahoo! case illustrates that a successful poison pill defense can seriously hurt shareholders by keeping existing management. Founded in 1994 by Jerry Yang and David Filo, who were then students at Stanford, Yahoo! was a pioneer in providing information services over the Internet. As early as 2001, Yahoo! installed a poison pill. In 2008, Microsoft made an unsolicited takeover bid for Yahoo!, hoping to strengthen its Internet capabilities in its head-to-head battle with Google.
The Yahoo! Poison Pill	

In an afternoon phone call just before it made its bid, Microsoft's chief executive, Steven Ballmer, informed a startled Jerry Yang, the chief executive of Yahoo!, that Microsoft would be making an unfriendly offer. The offer was for $31 (later raised to $33) a share, which was 60% more than the value of Yahoo! shares.

According to a subsequent shareholders' suit against Yahoo!, Mr. Ballmer made it clear that he wanted to keep Yahoo! employees and was allocating $1.5 billion for employee retention. However, Mr. Yang's poison pill would create a "huge incentive for a massive employee walkout in the aftermath of a change in control." The plan gave the 14,000 full-time Yahoo! employees the right to quit their jobs and "pocket generous termination benefits at any time during the two years following a takeover. . . ."

Mr. Ballmer walked away from a Yahoo! deal. One Microsoft executive commented, "They are going to burn the furniture if we go hostile. They are going to destroy the place." Yahoo!'s stock price plunged after Microsoft withdrew the bid. Soon thereafter, Yahoo! faced shareholder lawsuits and an aborted proxy fight led by Carl Icahn. Near the end of 2008, Yahoo!'s value fell as low as $10.9 billion, which was 23% of the $47.5 billion offered by Microsoft. Under pressure from stockholders, Mr. Yang resigned as CEO at the end of 2008.

A sequence of new Yahoo! CEOs failed to restore Yahoo! to its former profitability. From 2009 through early 2013, its stock value ranged between $11.6 billion and $24.1 billion. That is, Microsoft could have bought Yahoo! for between 25% and 50% of what it had offered in 2008. Thus, in the end, the poison pill defense led to a Pyrrhic victory.

7.4 The Make or Buy Decision

Managers make many decisions that affect the horizontal and vertical dimensions of a firm's organization. The *horizontal* dimension refers to the size of the firm in its primary market, while the *vertical* dimension refers to the various stages of the production process in which the firm participates.

To produce a good and sell it to consumers involves many sequential stages of production, marketing, and distribution activities. A manager must decide how many stages the firm will undertake itself. At each stage, a manager chooses whether to carry out the activity within the firm or to pay for it to be done by others. Deciding which stages of the production process to handle internally and which to buy from others is part of what is referred to as *supply chain management*.

Stages of Production

The turkey sandwich you purchase at your local food stand is produced and delivered through the actions of many firms and individuals. Farmers grow wheat and raise turkeys using inputs they purchase from other firms; processors convert these raw inputs into bread and turkey slices; wholesalers transfer these products from the food processors to the food stand; and, finally, employees at the food stand combine various ingredients to make a sandwich, wrap it, and sell it to you.

Figure 7.4 illustrates the sequential or *vertical* stages of a relatively simple production process. At the top of the figure, firms use raw inputs (such as wheat) to produce semiprocessed materials (such as flour). Then the same or other firms use the semiprocessed materials and labor to produce the final good (such as bread). In the last stage, the final consumers buy the product.

In the nineteenth century, production often took place along a river. Early stages of production occurred upstream, and then the partially finished goods were shipped by barge downstream—going with the flow of the river—to other firms that finished the product. These anachronistic river terms are still used to indicate the order of production: *Upstream* refers to earlier stages of production and *downstream* refers to later stages.

Vertical Integration

The number of separate firms involved in producing your turkey sandwich depends on how many steps of the process each firm handles. One possibility is that the food stand carries out many steps itself: making the sandwich, wrapping it, and selling it to you. An alternative is that one firm makes and wraps the sandwich and delivers it to another firm that sells it to you.

FIGURE 7.4 Vertical Organization

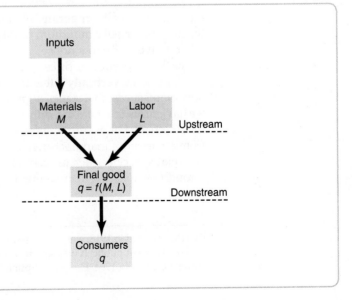

Raw inputs produced upstream are combined using a production process, $q = f(M, L)$, downstream to produce a final good.

A firm that participates in more than one successive stage of the production or distribution of goods or services is **vertically integrated**. A firm may vertically integrate backward and produce its own inputs. For example, after years of buying its unique auto bodies from Fisher Body, General Motors purchased Fisher in a *vertical merger*. Or a firm may vertically integrate forward and buy its former customer. At different times, the car manufacturers General Motors and Ford have owned Hertz, the first car-rental company.[19]

The alternative to a firm producing an input or activity itself is to buy it. Firms may buy inputs from a market (such as buying corn on the Chicago Board of Trade or copper in the London Metal Exchange). Increasingly, many firms reach agreements with other firms to buy services from them on a continuing basis, a practice called *outsourcing*. For example, many U.S. computer manufacturing firms retain firms located in the United States, India, and elsewhere to provide services such as giving technical advice to their customers.

A firm can be partially vertically integrated. It may produce a good but rely on others to market it. Or it may produce some inputs itself and buy others from the market.

Some firms buy from a small number of suppliers or sell through a small number of distributors. These firms often control the actions of the firms with whom they deal by writing contracts that restrict the actions of those other firms. These contractual *vertical restraints* approximate the outcome from vertically merging. Such tight relationships between firms are referred to as *quasi-vertical integration*.

For example, a franchisor and a franchisee have a close relationship that is governed by a contract. Some franchisors such as McDonald's sell a proven method of doing business to individual franchisees, who are owners of McDonald's outlets. A fast-food franchisor may dictate the types of raw products its franchisees buy, the franchisees' cooking methods, the restaurants' appearance, and the franchisees' advertising.

Similarly, a manufacturer that contracts with a distributor to sell its product may place vertical restrictions on the distributor's actions beyond requiring it to pay the wholesale price for the product. These vertical restrictions are determined through contractual negotiations between the manufacturer and the distributor. The manufacturer imposes these restrictions to approximate the outcome that would occur if the firms vertically integrated. Examples of restrictions include requirements that the distributor sell a minimum number of units, that distributors not locate near each other, that distributors not sell competing products, and that distributors charge no lower than a particular price.

All firms are vertically integrated to some degree, but they differ substantially as to how many successive stages of production they perform internally. At one extreme, we have firms that perform only one major task and rely on markets and outsourcing for all others. For example, some retailers, such as computer retailers, buy products from a variety of manufacturers or markets, sell them to final consumers, and have any related service such as technical support for customers provided by other firms through outsourcing arrangements.

---

[19]Hertz, founded in 1918, was purchased by General Motors in 1926, which subsequently sold it. In 1954, Hertz went public. It was sold to a Ford Motor subsidiary in 1987 and became a fully owned Ford subsidiary in 1994. Hertz went public again in 2006.

At the other extreme, we have firms that perform most stages of the production process. The leading broiler chicken producers, such as Tyson, Purdue, and Foster Farms, have integrated or quasi-vertically integrated (through the use of contracts) into virtually every production stage except the final stage of distribution to consumers.

The vertically integrated firms provide supplies to breeder farms that produce eggs. The breeder farms send eggs to a hatchery and the hatched chicks are sent to grow-out farms, where the birds grow to market weight. From there, the chickens are sent to the processing plant to be slaughtered and packed (either frozen or chilled). Packed chicken is then shipped to another company-owned plant for further processing into products such as frozen nuggets and chicken dinners. Finally, the products are sold to other firms such as fast-food restaurants and grocery stores for sale to final consumers (Martinez, 1999). By vertically integrating, these firms are able to take advantage of very large economies of scale at virtually every stage of the production process.

However, no firm is completely integrated: It would have to run the entire economy. Even Foster Farms buys some inputs, such as its equipment, from outside markets. As Carl Sagan observed, "If you want to make an apple pie from scratch, you must first create the universe."

Profitability and the Supply Chain Decision

Firms decide whether to vertically integrate, quasi-vertically integrate, or buy goods and services from markets or other firms depending on which approach is the most profitable.[20] Although at first glance this profitability rule seems very simple, it has a number of tricky aspects. First, the firm has to take into account all relevant costs, including some that are not easy to quantify such as transaction costs. Second, the firm must ensure a steady and timely supply of needed inputs to its production process. Third, the firm may vertically integrate, even if doing so raises its cost of doing business, so as to avoid government regulations.[21]

As a consequence of these complexities, firms in the same industry may reach different decisions about the optimal level of integration. We observe that such firms handle the supply chain in different ways. In the auto industry, Toyota is known as a leader in successful outsourcing and is less vertically integrated than its rivals such as General Motors and Ford.

Firms in some markets differ in how much they integrate because their managers have different strengths or the firms face different costs (such as costs that vary across countries). However, some of these firms could be making a mistake by being more or less integrated than other firms, which will lower their profits and possibly drive them out of business.

---

[20]For a more detailed analysis of the pros and cons of vertical integration, see Perry (1989) and Carlton and Perloff (2005). Two classic articles on vertical integration are Coase (1937) and Williamson (1975).

[21]Firms may also vertically integrate for reasons related to market power, allowing the firm to charge higher prices than it otherwise would or to reduce prices it would otherwise pay for its inputs. We discuss market power issues in later chapters.

Mini-Case

Vertical Integration at American Apparel

The high-fashion garment industry in the United States is noted for outsourcing and for a complex and highly decentralized supply chain. Major clothing brands typically outsource sewing and various other specialized manufacturing functions to subcontractors in a variety of low-wage countries. Bucking this trend is American Apparel, a fast-growing Los Angeles garment maker. As noted by Warren (2005), "American Apparel's greatest . . . innovation may come in the form of its vertical integration, in which every aspect of the business . . . occurs in some portion of the million square feet of American Apparel's Los Angeles space."

Founder and CEO Dov Charney, originally from Montreal, argues that "controlling all the variables in-house leads to greater efficiency, better wages and more flexibility. . . ." Charney takes vertical integration to an extreme. In 2013 the firm's website claimed that "By concentrating our entire manufacturing and distribution operations within a few square miles, American Apparel . . . saves time, money, and unnecessary fuel expenditures." Not only does American Apparel design its clothing and handle its own sewing, it also has its own knitting facility and dyeing operation to produce much of the cloth it uses and it carries out the wholesaling and retailing functions.

American Apparel also does its own marketing and advertising. Most of the models used in its provocative advertisements are ordinary employees and many of the photos used in advertising campaigns are taken by CEO Charney. Indeed, its advertising cites its extreme vertical integration as a selling point. American Apparel even runs its own medical clinic onsite in Los Angeles. This extremely high level of vertical integration saves on transportation costs, allows for close cooperation between designers, production managers and marketers and, supporters argue, leads to a loyal, dedicated, and knowledgeable workforce. However, it may raise their costs of producing clothing. Time will tell if American Apparel's alternative approach is sound.

Transaction Costs. Probably the most important reason to integrate is to reduce *transaction costs*, especially the costs of writing and enforcing contracts. A firm that vertically integrates avoids many transaction costs, but its managerial costs rise as the firm becomes larger and more complex.

For example, a manufacturing firm may decide to vertically integrate forward (downstream) into distributing its own products or it may rely on independent firms to distribute its products. The decision depends on whether the cost of monitoring employees at distribution outlets exceeds the cost of using independent firms. However, even if the independent firms can perform the service at a lower cost per unit, the manufacturer may choose to vertically integrate if the expense from trying to prevent opportunistic behavior by these firms is high. The manufacturer cannot perfectly observe the sales effort of the distributors and realizes that they may try to take advantage. That is, when firms agree to a future transaction, each firm may try to interpret the terms of a contract to its advantage, especially when terms are vague or missing.

Opportunistic behavior is particularly likely when a firm deals with only one other firm: a classic principal-agent problem. If an electronic game manufacturer can buy computer chips from only one firm, it is at the mercy of that chip supplier. The supplier could take advantage of the situation by increasing its price substantially just before the holiday buying season. The game manufacturer may vertically integrate—manufacturing the chip itself—to avoid such opportunistic behavior.

Another potential source of transaction costs is a need for coordination. American Apparel felt that the costs of coordinating various aspects of clothing production are high enough to justify vertical integration.

Security and Flexibility of Supply. A common reason for vertical integration is to ensure supply of important inputs. Having inputs available on a timely basis is very important in many if not most industries. Costs would skyrocket if a car manufacturer had to stop assembling cars while waiting for a part. Backward (upstream) integration to produce the part itself may help to ensure timely arrival of parts. Alternatively, this problem may be eliminated through quasi-vertical integration, in which the buyer and seller agree to a contract whereby the supplier is rewarded for prompt delivery and penalized for delays. Toyota and other Japanese manufacturers pioneered the *just-in-time* system of having suppliers deliver inputs at the time needed to process them, thus minimizing inventory costs and avoiding bottlenecks.

Similarly, it is often important that a firm be able to vary its production quickly. If the demand curve shifts to the left during a recession, a firm may want to cut output, and hence temporarily reduce its use of essential inputs. By vertically integrating, firms may gain greater flexibility. PepsiCo Inc. offered to buy its two largest bottlers, Pepsi Bottling Group and PepsiAmericas, because, as PepsiCo Chairwoman and Chief Executive Officer Indra Nooyi said, "We could unlock significant cost synergies, improve the speed of decision making and increase our strategic flexibility."[22]

Mini-Case	Backward vertical integration is common in the aluminum industry to ensure a steady supply and to avoid being subject to opportunistic behavior. Aluminum production has four main stages: mining, refining, smelting, and fabricating. After mining bauxite, a firm mixes it with caustic soda to refine it into alumina. In the smelting stage, the firm uses electrolysis to produce primary aluminum metal from alumina. Finally, that firm or other firms fabricate the metal into foil, wire, cookware, airplane parts, and many other products.
Aluminum	

A few firms engage in the upstream activities of mining and refining bauxite. Bauxite mines and refineries require large capital investments and face substantial barriers to entry. Only 132 alumina refineries operate worldwide as of 2013, and these are owned by a much smaller number of entities. Moreover, bauxite is expensive to ship, so the market for bauxite is regional. Thus, a mine or a refiner has few if any other firms with which it can deal.

To guarantee a steady supply, some refineries quasi-vertically integrate by signing 20- to 25-year contracts with mines. Because these firms cannot foresee all possible contingencies during such long periods, one trading party can inflict substantial costs on the other by refusing to deal with it (say, when prices are unusually high or low). These firms have no alternative uses for bauxite and the plants that mine and refine it.

---

[22]"PepsiCo bids to buy its bottlers," *Marketwatch*, April 20, 2009, **www.marketwatch.com/story/pepsico-bids-buy-bottlers-reports**.

To avoid the potential for such opportunistic behavior, many of the major producers of aluminum—Alcan Aluminium Ltd. (Canada), Alcoa (Aluminum Company of America), Chalco (China), Comalco (Australia, New Zealand, and Wales), and Pechiney (France)—vertically integrated in bauxite mining, alumina refining, and aluminum smelting. Vertically integrated firms mine and refine virtually all of the world's bauxite and alumina.

Avoiding Government Intervention. Firms may also vertically integrate to avoid government price controls, taxes, and regulations. A vertically integrated firm avoids *price controls* by selling to itself. For example, the U.S. government has set a maximum price for steel products on several occasions since World War II. Under such price controls, steel producers did not want to sell as much steel as before the controls took effect. Consequently, they rationed steel, selling their long-time customers only a fraction of what they sold before the controls went into effect.

Because transactions within a company were unaffected by price controls, a buyer who really desired more steel could purchase a steel company and obtain all the steel it wanted (and at least one firm did so). Thus, purchasing a steel company allowed firms to avoid price controls. Were it not for the high transaction costs, firms could completely avoid price controls by vertically integrating.

More commonly, firms integrate to lower their taxes. Tax rates vary by country, state, and type of product. A vertically integrated firm can shift profit from one of its operations to another simply by changing the *transfer price* at which it sells its internally produced materials from one division to another. By shifting profits from a high-tax state or country to a low-tax state or country, a firm can increase its after-tax profits. The Internal Revenue Service tries to restrict such behavior by requiring that firms use market prices for internal transfers where possible.

Government regulations create additional incentives for a firm to integrate vertically (or horizontally) when the profits of only one division of a firm are regulated. When the government restricts the profit that a local telephone company earns on local services but not its profit on other services, such as selling telephones in competition with other suppliers, the telephone company tries to shift profits from its regulated division to its unregulated division.

Market Size and the Life Cycle of a Firm

Why do workers commonly engage in highly specialized activities? The answer is that it is generally more efficient to divide production processes into several small steps in which workers specialize, with each worker becoming skilled in a certain activity.

Adam Smith, writing in Scotland at the time of the American Revolution, gave an example of a pin factory in *The Wealth of Nations* to illustrate that the division of labor can have important advantages in the "very trifling manufacture" of pins:

> [A] workman not educated to this business . . . nor acquainted with the use of machinery employed in it . . . could scarce, perhaps, with his utmost industry, make one pin a day, and certainly could not make twenty. But in the way in which this business is now carried on, not only the whole work is a peculiar trade, but it is divided into a number of branches, of which the greater part are likewise peculiar trades. One man draws out the wire, another straightens it, a third cuts it, a fourth points it, a fifth grinds it to the top for receiving the head; to make the head requires two or three distinct operations; to put it on, is a peculiar business, to whiten the pins is another; it is even a trade by itself to put them into the paper; and the important business of making a pin is, in this manner, divided into about eighteen distinct operations, which, in some manufactories, are all performed by distinct hands, though in others the same man will sometimes perform two or three of them. I have seen a small manufactory of this kind where ten men only were employed, and where some of them consequently performed two or three distinct operations. . . . [T]hey could, when they exerted themselves, make among them about twelve pounds of pins in a day [or] upward of forty-eight thousand pins in a day.

Using this insight about specialization, Henry Ford became the largest and probably the most profitable automobile manufacturer in the early 1900s by developing mass production techniques. He adapted the conveyor belt and assembly line so that he could produce a standardized, inexpensive car in a series of tasks in which individual workers specialized. By doing so, he achieved cost savings despite paying wages that were considerably above average.

Despite the advantages of specialization, many workers and many firms do not specialize. Why? According to Adam Smith, the answer is that "the division of labor is limited by the extent of the market." That is, a firm can take advantage of specialization and economies of scale only if it produces a sufficiently large amount of output, which it produces only if enough consumers are willing to buy it.

Stigler (1951) and Williamson (1975) showed that Adam Smith's insight provides a theory of the life cycle of firms. They explain why firms rely on markets during certain periods, while during other periods, they vertically integrate. The key insight is that the degree of integration depends on the size of the market. If demand for a product at the current price is low so that the collective output of all the firms in the industry is small, each firm must undertake all the activities associated with producing the final output itself.

Why don't some firms specialize in making one of several inputs that they then sell to another firm to assemble the final product? The answer is that when the industry is small, it does not pay for a firm to specialize in one activity even given increasing returns to scale. A specialized firm may have a large setup or fixed cost. If the specialized firm produces large quantities of output, the average fixed cost per unit is small. In contrast, the average fixed cost is large in a small industry. Therefore, if specialized firms are to earn a profit, the sum of the specialized firms' prices must be higher than the cost of a firm that produces everything for itself.

As the industry expands, it may become profitable for a firm to specialize, because the per-unit transaction costs fall. That is, as the industry grows, firms *vertically disintegrate*. When the industry was small, each firm produced all successive steps of the production process, so that all firms were *vertically integrated*. In the larger industry, each firm does not handle every stage of production itself but rather buys services or products from specialized firms.

As an industry matures further, new products often develop and reduce much of the demand for the original product, so that the industry shrinks in size. As a result, firms again vertically integrate.

7.5 Market Structure

When making their horizontal and vertical decisions, managers need to take account of the behavior of actual and potential rival firms, which affect the profit function the manager's firm faces. So far, we have implicitly ignored the role of other firms. However, a firm's manager must take into account how its profit is affected by rival firms' output levels, the prices rivals set, or whether additional firms are likely to enter the market if the firm makes a large profit.

How rivals behave depends on the organization of the industry in which the firms operate. A firm will behave differently if it is one of a very large number of firms rather than the only firm in the market. The behavior of firms depends on the **market structure**: the number of firms in the market, the ease with which firms can enter and leave the market, and the ability of firms to differentiate their products from those of their rivals.

The Four Main Market Structures

Most industries fit into one of four common market structures: perfect competition, monopoly, oligopoly, and monopolistic competition.

Perfect Competition. When most people talk about *competitive firms*, they mean firms that are rivals for the same customers. By this interpretation, any market that has more than one firm is competitive. However, economists often use the term *competitive* to refer to markets that satisfy the conditions for perfect competition (Chapter 2) or that closely approximate perfect competition.

Economists say that a market is perfectly competitive if each firm in the market is a *price taker*: a firm that cannot significantly affect the market price for its output or the prices at which it buys its inputs. Firms are likely to be price takers in markets where all firms in the market sell identical products, firms can freely enter and exit the market in the long run, all buyers and sellers know the prices charged by firms, and transaction costs are low. If any one of the 26,000 tomato producers in the United States were to stop producing or to double its production, the market price of tomatoes would not change appreciably. Similarly, by stopping production or doubling its production, a producer would have little or no effect on the price for fertilizer, labor, or other inputs.

Because firms can enter freely, firms enter whenever they see an opportunity to make an economic profit. This entry continues until the economic profit of the last firm to enter—the *marginal firm*—is zero.

Monopoly. A *monopoly* is the only supplier of a good for which there is no close substitute. In 1937, Alcoa controlled the entire markets for bauxite, alumina, and primary aluminum. Today, the postal service in most countries and many local public utilities such as cable television companies are local monopolies. Patents give monopoly rights to sell inventions, such as particular pharmaceuticals. A firm may be a monopoly if its costs are substantially below those of other potential firms.

A monopoly can *set* its price—it is not a price taker like a competitive firm. A monopoly's output is the market output, and the demand curve a monopoly faces is the market demand curve. Because the market demand curve is downward sloping, the monopoly—unlike a competitive firm—doesn't lose all its sales if it raises its price. As a consequence, the monopoly typically charges relatively high prices—much higher than the price set in a perfectly competitive market.

Oligopoly. An *oligopoly* is a market with only a few firms and with substantial barriers to entry, which prevent other firms from entering. A barrier to entry could be a government licensing law that limits the number of firms or patents that prevent other firms from using low-cost technologies. Nintendo, Microsoft, and Sony are oligopolistic firms that dominate the video game market. Only a handful of firms control the automobile, television, and aircraft manufacturing markets.

Because relatively few firms compete in an oligopolistic market, each can influence the price. One reason why oligopolies are price setters is because many oligopolies differentiate their products from those of their rivals. Because consumers perceive differences between a Honda Accord and a Toyota Camry, Toyota can raise the price of its Camry above the price of an Accord without losing all its sales. Some customers who prefer the Camry to the Accord will buy a Camry even if it costs more than an Accord.

Moreover, because an oligopoly has few firms, the actions of each firm affect its rivals. An oligopoly firm that ignores or inaccurately predicts its rivals' behavior is likely to lose profit. For example, as Toyota produces more cars, the price Honda can get for its cars falls. If Honda underestimates how many cars Toyota will produce, Honda may produce too many automobiles and lose money.

The need to consider the strategies of rival firms makes analyzing an oligopoly firm's profit-maximization decision more difficult than that of a monopoly or a competitive firm. A monopoly has no rivals, and a perfectly competitive firm ignores the behavior of individual rivals—it considers only the market price and its own costs in choosing its profit-maximizing output.

Oligopolistic firms may act independently or may coordinate their actions. A group of firms that explicitly agree (collude) to coordinate their activities is called a *cartel*. These firms may agree on how much each firm will sell or on a common price. By cooperating and behaving like a monopoly, the members of a cartel seek to collectively earn the monopoly profit—the maximum possible profit. In most developed countries, cartels are illegal. If oligopolistic firms do not collude, they earn lower profits than a monopoly, but usually earn higher profits than do firms in a competitive industry.

Monopolistic Competition. *Monopolistic competition* is a market structure in which firms are price setters but entry is easy. As in a monopoly or oligopoly, there are few enough firms that each can affect the price. Indeed, monopolistically competitive firms often differentiate their products, which facilitates their ability to be price setters. However, as in competition, firms can freely enter, so the marginal firm earns zero economic profit.

Comparison of Market Structures

Table 7.2 summarizes the major features of these four market structures. The first row notes that perfectly competitive firms are price takers, whereas monopolies, oligopolies, and monopolistically competitive firms are price setters. Typically, monopolies charge higher prices than oligopolies and monopolistically competitive firms, while competitive firms charge lower prices.

In both competitive and monopolistically competitive markets, entry occurs until no new firm can profitably enter, so the marginal firm earns zero economic profit. Monopolistically competitive markets typically have fewer firms than perfectly competitive markets do. Barriers to entry in a market result in a monopoly with one firm or an oligopoly with few firms. Monopolies and oligopolies may earn positive economic profits.

Oligopolistic and monopolistically competitive firms must pay attention to rival firms' behavior, in contrast to monopolistic or competitive firms. A monopoly has no rivals. A competitive firm ignores the behavior of individual rivals in choosing its output because the market price tells the firm everything it needs to know about its competitors. Oligopolistic and monopolistically competitive firms may produce differentiated products in contrast to monopolies and competitive firms.

Road Map to the Rest of the Book

In Chapters 8 through 13, we examine the market outcomes under perfect competition, monopoly, oligopoly, and monopolistic competition. We start by examining competitive and monopoly firms, which can ignore the behavior of other firms. Then we turn to oligopolies and other markets where firms need to develop strategies to compete with rival firms. In these chapters, we maintain the assumption that

TABLE 7.2 Properties of Monopoly, Oligopoly, Monopolistic Competition, and Perfect Competition

	Monopoly	Oligopoly	Monopolistic Competition	Perfect Competition
1. Ability to set price	Price setter	Price setter	Price setter	Price taker
2. Price level	Very high	High	High	Low
3. Entry conditions	No entry	Limited entry	Free entry	Free entry
4. Number of firms	1	Few	Few or many	Many
5. Long-run profit	≥ 0	≥ 0	0	0
6. Strategy dependent on individual rival firms' behavior	No (has no rivals)	Yes	Yes	No (cares only about market price)
7. Products	Single product	May be differentiated	May be differentiated	Undifferentiated
8. Example	Producer of patented drug	Automobile manufacturers	Plumbers in a small town	Apple farmers

firms seek to maximize profits. In contrast, in Chapters 14 through 16 we return to the realistic issues introduced in this chapter concerning uncertainty, unequal information, and government regulation, which lead to agency problems. In Chapter 17, many of the issues raised in this chapter, such as outsourcing, are considered in a global context.

Managerial Solution

Clawing Back Bonuses

Does evaluating a manager's performance over a longer time period lead to better management? The answer depends on whether the reward a manager receives in the short run induces the manager to sacrifice long-run profit for short-run gains.

Managers prefer to be paid sooner rather than later because money today is worth more than the same amount later. Thus, if a manager can move a major sale from January of next year to December of this year, the firm's total profits over the two years are unchanged, but the manager's performance-based bonus is paid this year rather than next year. Most boards are probably not very concerned with such shifts over time as they are unlikely to lower long-run profits.

Of more concern are managers who increase this year's profit even though doing so lowers profit in later years. Many firms pay a bonus on a positive profit but do not impose fines or penalties (negative bonuses) in bad years. Suppose that a particular policy results in a large profit this year but an even larger loss next year. If the manager gets a bonus based on each year's profit, the manager receives a large bonus this year and no bonus next year. However, if the bonus is calculated over two years, the manager would receive no bonus in either year. A firm could achieve a similar effect by allowing for a bonus given in one year to be *clawed back* if the firm does badly in the subsequent year. Without such clawbacks the manager has a greater incentive to adopt this policy of increasing profit in one year at the cost of lower profit the next.

In an extreme case, a manager engages in reckless behavior that increases this year's profit but bankrupts the firm next year. The manager plans to grab this year's bonus and then disappear. There were many such examples of bad management leading up to the 2007–2009 financial meltdown involving mortgage and financial instruments, such as CDOs, based on mortgages. As described in the Managerial Problem, bad CDO decisions at Merrill Lynch cost its shareholders billions of dollars, while senior managers kept the bonuses despite the negative effects of their decisions on shareholders. One solution to bad managerial incentives is to base bonuses on more than one year. Starting in 2012, Morgan Stanley paid bonuses to high-income employees over a three-year period. Similarly, Apple stock options and related benefits are paid every two years rather than every year.

To illustrate why paying over time provides a better incentive structure, we examine the case of Angelo, who is an executive in a company that provides auto loans for a two-year period. Initially, he receives 10% of the amount of the loans he makes in the first year. He can loan to two groups of customers. Customers in one group have excellent financial histories and repay their loans on time. Loans to this group produce revenue of $10 million this year, so that over the two-year period, the firm nets $9 million after paying Angelo. Customers in the other group are much more likely to default. That group produces $30 million in revenue this year, but their defaults in the second year cost the firm $40 million. After paying Angelo $3 million in the first year, the firm suffers a $13 million loss over the two years (ignoring discounting).

Because Angelo prefers receiving $4 million by loaning to both groups to $1 million from loaning to only the good risks, he may expose the firm to devastating losses in the second year. He may be happy earning a gigantic amount in the first year even if he's fired in the second year. This management problem can be avoided if his compensation is based on profit over a two-year period, where he has less incentive to loan to the bad risks.

SUMMARY

1. **Ownership and Governance of Firms.** For-profit firms are normally organized as sole proprietorships, partnerships, or corporations. Owners may manage small companies (particularly sole proprietorships and partnerships) themselves, but owners of larger firms (particularly corporations) typically hire managers to run such firms. Government-owned firms and nonprofit firms normally have objectives other than profit maximization.

2. **Profit Maximization.** Most firms maximize economic profit, which is revenue minus economic cost (opportunity cost). A firm earning zero economic profit is making as much as it could if its resources were devoted to their best alternative uses. To maximize profit, a firm must make two decisions. First, the firm determines the quantity at which its profit is highest. Profit is maximized when marginal profit is zero or, equivalently, when marginal revenue equals marginal cost. Second, the firm decides whether to produce at all. It shuts down if doing so reduces a loss (negative profit) it would otherwise suffer.

3. **Owners' Versus Managers' Objectives.** Owners and managers may have conflicting objectives. For example, an owner may want to maximize the firm's profit, while the manager is interested in maximizing personal earnings. Such conflicts are an example of a principle-agent problem or agency problem, where the principal (owner) hires an agent (manager) to perform an action, and the agent acts in his or her own best interest. The owner can use a variety of means including monitoring, contingent rewards, and corporation rules to influence or control the manager's behavior.

Market pressures also make it difficult for a firm to deviate substantially from profit-maximizing behavior.

4. **The Make or Buy Decision.** A firm may engage in many sequential stages of production itself, perform only a few stages itself and rely on markets for others, or use contracts or other means to coordinate its activities with those of other firms, depending on which approach is most profitable. A firm may vertically integrate (participate in more than one successive stage of the production or distribution of goods or services), quasi-vertically integrate (use contracts or other means to control firms with which it has vertical relations), or buy from others depending on which is more profitable. Key incentives to vertically integrate include lowering transaction costs, ensuring a steady supply, and avoiding government restrictions.

5. **Market Structure.** A firm's profit depends in large part on the market structure, which reflects the number of firms in the market, the ease with which firms can enter and leave the market, and the ability of firms to differentiate their products from those of their rivals. The major market structures are perfect competition, monopoly, oligopoly, and monopolistic competition. Competitive firms are price takers, whereas others are price setters. Oligopolies and monopolistically competitive firms, unlike competitive firms and monopolies, must take account of rivals' strategies and may differentiate their products. Competitive and monopolistically competitive firms are in markets where entry by potential rivals is easy, so economic profit is driven to zero.

QUESTIONS

*All exercises are available on MyEconLab; * = answer at the back of this book; C = use of calculus may be necessary.*

1. Ownership and Governance of Firms

1.1. What types of firms would not normally maximize profit?

*1.2. Describe three important consequences of "going public" by selling shares in an initial public offering.

1.3. What types of firm organization allow owners of a firm to obtain the advantages of limited liability?

2. Profit Maximization

2.1. A firm has three different production facilities, all of which produce the same product. While reviewing the firm's cost data, Jasmin, a manager, discovers that one of the plants has a higher average cost than the other plants and suggests closing that plant. Another manager, Joshua, notes that the high-cost plant has high fixed costs but that the marginal cost in that plant is lower than in the other plants. He says that the high-cost plant should not be shut down but should expand its operations. Who is right?

*2.2. A firm has revenue given by $R(q) = 100q - 3q^2$ and its cost function is $C(q) = 100 + 10q$. What is the profit-maximizing level of output? What profit does the firm earn at this output level? (*Hint*: See Q&A 7.1.) **C**

2.3. Should a firm ever produce if it is losing money (making a negative economic profit)? Why or why not?

*2.4. Should a firm shut down if its weekly revenue is $1,000, its variable cost is $500, and its fixed cost is $800, of which $600 is avoidable if it shuts down? Why?

2.5. A firm has to pay a tax equal to 25% of its revenue. Give a condition that determines the output level at which it maximizes its after-tax profit. (*Hint*: See "Using Calculus: Maximizing Profit" and Q&A 7.1.) **C**

2.6. At the time of its initial public offering (initial sale of stock), Groupon, an Internet company that provides discount coupons, used unusual measures of its business performance (Michael J. de la Merced, "Abracadabra! Magic Trumps Math at Web Start-Ups," **dealbook.nytimes.com**, June 17, 2011). One such measure used by Groupon was *acsoi* (pronounced "ack-soy" or, alternatively, "ack-swa") for "adjusted consolidated segment operating income." Acsoi is operating profit before subtracting the year's online marketing and acquisition expenses. The firm's profit was negative, but its acsoi was positive. Groupon argued that acsoi marketing and acquisition expenses were an investment that would build future business and whose costs

should therefore be amortized (spread out over time). If shareholders care about the stock price or the present value of the company, is acsoi an appropriate measure?

2.7. A firm that owns and manages rental properties is considering buying a building that would cost $800,000 this year, but would yield an annual revenue stream of $50,000 per year for the foreseeable future. For what range of interest rates would this purchase increase the present value of the firm?

3. Owners' Versus Managers' Objectives

3.1. In Q&A 7.2, suppose that Ann's compensation, Y, is half of the firm's profit minus $30,000: $Y = \pi/2 - 30,000$. Will she still seek to maximize the firm's profit?

3.2. A firm's revenue varies with its output: $R(q)$. Its manager's income, Y, equals $aR(q)$, where $0 < a < 1$ is the manager's share of the firm's revenue. Use calculus to prove that maximizing $aR(q)$ implies the same output level, q, as maximizing $R(q)$. What does this result imply about the manager's incentive to maximize the firm's profit, $\pi(q) = R(q) - C(q)$? Would it be better for shareholders if the manager received a share of profit rather than a share of revenue? (*Hint*: See Q&A 7.2 and Q&A 7.3.) **C**

3.3. Three firms have identical revenue and profit functions with the same general shape as those in Figure 7.3. Firm 1 is a private sector firm operated by an owner-manager who wishes to maximize profit. Firm 2 is managed by an income-maximizing manager whose pay is proportional to the firm's revenue. Firm 3 is a government-owned firm that has been instructed to maximize the amount of employment, L, subject to the constraint that revenue must not be negative. To increase q, L must increase. Which of these firms produces the most, which the least, and which is in the middle? Show the output level of each firm in a diagram.

*3.4. Each of the three firms in Question 3.3 has a revenue function $R(q) = 100q - 2q^2$ and a cost function $C(q) = 100 + 20q$. Determine how much output each firm chooses. **C**

3.5. Michael, the CEO of a successful firm, enjoys both income, Y, and perquisites, S (such as a nice office and expensive office furniture). Michael's utility function (Chapter 4) is $U(S, Y)$ with normal (convex to the origin) indifference curves. Michael receives a base salary of M. He is able to determine the level of perquisites provided by the firm up to a maximum allowable budget of B. However, any of this budget not spent on perquisites is given to Michael as a bonus over and above his base salary. Illustrate Michael's utility maximization problem in a diagram in which you show his indifference curves and his budget line.

3.6. Inside directors of a firm are also executives of the firm, and they normally receive compensation that includes some form of profit sharing. Outside directors are not employees of the firm. They normally receive some compensation but do not have profit-sharing arrangements. Outside directors are often charged with determining salaries of senior executives. From the shareholders' point of view, why would it be desirable for outside directors to have this responsibility?

3.7. Why are steps taken by corporate management to avoid takeovers often not in shareholders' best interests?

3.8. How does the market for corporate control encourage firms to maximize profits?

3.9. An acquiring firm, A, seeks to buy a target firm, T. The acquiring firm has better managers. The value of the target firm, if acquired by A, is $100 million. The value of the target firm under its current management is only $80 million. However, the managers of T can impose a poison pill that would reduce the value of firm T to the acquirer by amount P without providing any benefit to shareholders of T. What is the minimum value of P that would prevent A from acquiring T? What is the cost of this poison pill to shareholders of the two firms?

4. The Make or Buy Decision

*4.1. In 2012, the Campbell Soup Company acquired Bolthouse Farms for $1.55 billion. This acquisition increased the level of vertical integration in Campbell, as Bolthouse Farms owned and operated extensive farming operations where it produced many food items used in Campbell's products. Suppose that the value of produce provided by these farms after the acquisition would be $75 million per year for Campbell and that, in addition, Campbell could save $10 million per year in costs it would otherwise spend in searching for and negotiating over equivalent produce. However, the transaction cost of the acquisition (lawyers' fees, relocating

some production facilities, paying severance to unnecessary employees, etc.) required a one-time payment of $50 million. If the interest rate used to discount future earnings is 5%, what is the gain to Campbell's from the acquisition?

4.2. Katie's Quilts is a small retailer of quilts and other bed linen products. Katie currently purchases quilts from a large producer for $100 each and sells them in her store at a price that does not change with the number of quilts that she sells. Katie is considering vertically integrating by making her own quilts. If the fixed cost of vertically integrating is $10,000 and she can produce quilts at $50 per quilt, her total cost of producing quilts, q, herself is $C = 10,000 + 50q$. How many quilts does Katie need to sell for vertical integration to be a profitable decision?

4.3. A producer of ballpoint pens has been purchasing ink from an ink supplier and is considering acquiring the ink supplier. Would the pen company be more or less likely to vertically integrate by buying the ink manufacturer if the government taxes ink?

4.4. When the western part of the United States was sparsely populated, many small towns had a single schoolhouse in which one teacher taught all subjects to students of all ages. Nowadays, in large cities, teachers are often highly specialized, teaching a single subject, such as mathematics, to just one grade level. Explain why this change occurred by making reference to Adam Smith's famous description of a pin factory.

5. Market Structure

5.1. Which market structure best describes (a) airplane manufacturing, (b) electricians in a small town, (c) farms that grow tomatoes, and (d) cable television in a city? Why?

6. Managerial Problem

6.1. Consider the following change to Angelo's situation in the Managerial Solution. Now Angelo can provide loans to only one of the two groups. If he loans to the safer group, he gets his 10% in Year 1 and faces the same choice in Year 2 with two new groups of borrowers. If he loans to the risker group, he gets 10% but will be fired in the second year and earns nothing when the risky loans start to go bad. If Angelo wants to maximize his earnings over the two years (ignoring discounting), what will he do in each year? Would his firm gain by using a system of deferred compensation?

7. Spreadsheet Exercises

7.1. A firm's revenue function is $R(q) = 90q - 2q^2$. Its cost function is $C(q) = 104 + 6q + 1.5q^2$.

  a. Using Excel, calculate the levels of revenue, total cost, and profit for the firm for $q = 0, 1, 2, \ldots, 24$. Determine the profit-maximizing output and the maximum profit for the firm.

  b. Using Excel's Charting tool, draw the graph of the profit curve and determine the profit-maximizing level of output.

  c. The firm's marginal revenue function is $MR = 90 - 4q$ and the marginal cost function is $MC = 6 + 3q$. Using Excel, calculate MR and MC for $q = 0, 1, 2, \ldots, 24$. Verify that the "$MR = MC$" rule determines the same profit-maximizing output as you found in part (a).

7.2. A firm has the same revenue and cost function as in Spreadsheet Exercise 7.1.

  a. The shareholders of the firm hire a manager on a profit-sharing basis whose payment, M, is 25% of the firm's profit: $M = 0.25(R - C)$. The shareholders receive the remaining 75%, so their income is $S = 0.75(R - C)$. Add columns for M and S to the spreadsheet in part a of Exercise 7.1 and calculate the manager's payment and the shareholders' income for $q = 0, 1, 2, \ldots, 20$. Determine the amount of output that the manager will produce if the manager's objective is to maximize his or her own compensation. Is this outcome consistent with the shareholders' profit-maximizing objective?

  b. Now suppose that the manager receives compensation equal to 10% of revenue, so that the return to the owners is $S = 0.9R - C$. Use Excel to determine the return to the manager and the return to the owners for $q = 0, 1, 2, \ldots, 20$. Are the incentives of the shareholders and the manager aligned in this case?

Appendix 7   Interest Rates, Present Value, and Future Value

To make decisions based on cash flows such as costs and revenues over time, managers compare current and future cash flows using interest rates.

The interest rate, i, connects the value of money you invest today, the *present value*, PV, and the amount that you will be repaid later, the *future value*, FV. For example, if you put $100 in the bank today, your present value is $100. If the annual interest rate is $i = 5\% = 0.05$, then a year from now the bank will return your original $100 and give you an additional interest payment of $5 = 0.05 \times 100$, so that your future value is $105 one year from now. More generally, if you invest PV today at an interest rate of i, one year from now you will receive

$$FV = PV(1 + i).$$

If you leave this future value, $PV(1 + i)$ in the bank for a second year to earn more interest, you'll receive $PV(1 + i)(1 + i) = PV(1 + i)^2$ at the end of the second year. That is, in the second year, you are earning interest on both your original investment and the interest payment from the first year. After t years, the future value is

$$FV = PV(1 + i)^t. \tag{7A.1}$$

Dividing both sides of Equation 7A.1 by $(1 + i)^t$, we can express the present value in terms of the future value:

$$PV = \frac{FV}{(1 + i)^t}. \tag{7A.2}$$

For example, if the interest rate is 5% and you will receive a payment of $105 with certainty one year from now, your present value of this future payment is $PV = 105/(1.05) = 100$.

Because the future payment of $105 has a present value of only $100, we say that the future payment is *discounted* when compared with the present. At high interest rates, money in the future is virtually worthless today. Using Equation 7A.2, we can calculate that a $100 payment 25 years from now is worth only slightly more than $1 today at a 20% interest rate: $PV = 100/(1.2)^{25} \approx 100/95.4 \approx \$1.05$.

Sometimes we want to calculate the present value of a stream of payments, such as the firm's annual profits over the next 15 years. We can generalize the relationships we have already developed to determine the present value of the stream of payments by calculating the present value of each future payment and then summing them.

Suppose an investor has a share that pays $10 in dividends at the end of each year for three years and nothing thereafter. If the interest rate is 10%, the present value of this series of payments is

$$PV = \frac{\$10}{1.1} + \frac{\$10}{1.1^2} + \frac{\$10}{1.1^3} \approx \$24.87.$$

More generally, a stream of payments of f per year for t years given interest rate i has a present value of

$$PV = f\left[\frac{1}{(1 + i)^1} + \frac{1}{(1 + i)^2} + \cdots + \frac{1}{(1 + i)^t}\right].\tag{7A.3}$$

If these dividend payments are made at the end of each year forever, Equation 7A.3 can be simplified. If you invest PV at i forever, you can receive a future payment of $f = PV \times i$ each year forever. Dividing both sides of this equation by i, we find that

$$PV = \frac{f}{i}.\tag{7A.4}$$

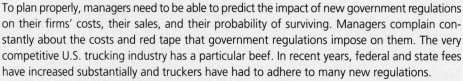

8 Competitive Firms and Markets

The love of money is the root of all virtue. —George Bernard Shaw

To plan properly, managers need to be able to predict the impact of new government regulations on their firms' costs, their sales, and their probability of surviving. Managers complain constantly about the costs and red tape that government regulations impose on them. The very competitive U.S. trucking industry has a particular beef. In recent years, federal and state fees have increased substantially and truckers have had to adhere to many new regulations.

The Federal Motor Carrier Safety Administration (FMCSA) along with state transportation agencies in 41 states (as of 2013) administer interstate trucking licenses through the Unified Carrier Registration Agreement. Before going into the interstate trucking business, a firm needs a U.S. Department of Transportation number and must participate in the New Entrant Safety Assurance Process, which raised the standard of compliance for passing the new entrant safety audit starting in 2009. To pass the new entrant safety audit, a carrier must now meet 16 safety regulations and be in compliance with the Americans with Disabilities Act and certain household goods-related requirements. A trucker must also maintain minimum insurance coverage, pay registration fees, and follow policies that differ across states before the FMCSA will issue the actual authorities (grant permission to operate). The registration process is so complex and time-consuming that firms pay substantial amounts to brokers who expedite the application process and take care of state licensing requirements.

According to its website in 2013, the FMCSA has 27 types of driver regulations, 16 types of vehicle regulations, 42 types of company regulations, 4 types of hazardous materials regulations, and 14 types of other regulatory guidance. Of course, they may have added some additional rules while we wrote this last sentence.[1]

For a large truck, the annual federal interstate registration fee can exceed $8,000. During the 2007–2009 financial crisis, many states raised their annual fee from a few hundred to several thousand dollars per truck. In 2012, Congress debated requiring that each truck install an electronic onboard recorder, which would document its travel time and distance and cost $1,500. There are many additional fees and costly regulations that a trucker or firm must meet to operate. These largely lump-sum costs—which are not related to the number of miles driven—have increased substantially in recent years.

---

[1]Indeed, the first time we checked after writing that sentence, we found that they had added a new rule forbidding truckers from texting while driving. (Of course, many of these rules and regulations help protect society and truckers in particular.)

What effect do these new fixed costs have on the trucking industry's market price and quantity? Are individual firms providing more or fewer trucking services? Does the number of firms in the market rise or fall? (As we'll discuss at the end of the chapter, the answer to one of these questions is surprising.)

To answer questions like these, we need to combine our understanding of demand curves with knowledge about firm and market supply curves to predict industry price, quantity, and profits. We start our analysis of firm behavior by addressing the fundamental question "How much should a firm produce?" To pick a level of output that maximizes its profit, a firm must consider its cost function and how much it can sell at a given price. The amount the firm thinks it can sell depends on the market demand of consumers and on its beliefs about how other firms in the market will behave. As described in Chapter 7, how a firm should approach such issues depends on the market's structure. We identified four primary market structures—monopoly, oligopoly, monopolistic competition, and perfect competition—that differ based on such attributes as the number of firms in the market, the control firms have over market prices, the ease with which firms can enter and leave the market, and the ability of firms to differentiate their products from those of their rivals.

This chapter focuses on *perfect competition*, a market structure in which there are so many buyers and sellers that each market participant is a *price taker*, who cannot affect the market's equilibrium price. Perfect competition is an important market structure for two main reasons. First, a significant part of the economy—including much of agriculture, finance, construction, real estate, wholesale and retail trade, and many service industries—is highly competitive and is well-described by the model of perfect competition. Second, a competitive market is the only market structure that maximizes a commonly used measure of economic well-being (*total surplus*) and thus serves as a baseline against which to compare the economic outcomes of other market structures.

Main Topics	
In this chapter, we examine four main topics	1. **Perfect Competition:** In a perfectly competitive market, each firm is a price taker, which means the firm faces a horizontal demand curve for its product.
	2. **Competition in the Short Run:** Short-run marginal costs determine a profit-maximizing, competitive firm's short-run supply curve and the market supply curve, which, when combined with the market demand curve, determines the competitive equilibrium.
	3. **Competition in the Long Run:** Firm supply, market supply, and the competitive equilibrium may be different in the long run than in the short run because firms can vary inputs that were fixed in the short run.
	4. **Perfect Competition Maximizes Economic Well-Being:** Perfect competition maximizes a widely used measure of economic well-being for society.

8.1 Perfect Competition

Perfect competition is a market structure in which buyers and sellers are price takers. A price-taking firm cannot affect the market price for the product it sells. A firm is a price taker if it faces a demand curve for its product that is horizontal at the market price. That is, it can sell as much as it wants at the market price, so it has no incentive to lower its price to gain more sales. If it raises its price even slightly, it can sell nothing. Thus, the firm sells its product at the market price. In this section, we discuss how the characteristics of a perfectly competitive market lead to price taking and how much a market can deviate from these characteristics and still be regarded as a competitive market.

Characteristics of a Perfectly Competitive Market

Perfectly competitive markets have five characteristics that force firms to be price takers:

1. The market consists of many small buyers and sellers.
2. All firms produce identical products.
3. All market participants have full information about price and product characteristics.
4. Transaction costs are negligible.
5. Firms can freely enter and exit the market in the long run.

Large Numbers of Buyers and Sellers. If the sellers in a market are small and numerous, no single firm can raise or lower the market price. The more firms in a market, the less any one firm's output affects the market output and hence the market price.

For example, the 107,000 U.S. soybean farmers are price takers. If a typical grower were to drop out of the market, market supply would fall by only $1/107,000 = 0.00093\%$, so the market price would not be noticeably affected. Each soybean farm can sell as much output as it can produce at the prevailing market equilibrium price, so each farm faces a demand curve that is a horizontal line at the market price.

Similarly, perfect competition requires that buyers be price takers as well. In contrast, if firms sell to only a single buyer—such as producers of weapons that are allowed to sell to only the government—then the buyer can set the price and the market is not perfectly competitive.

Identical Products. Firms in a perfectly competitive market sell *identical* or *homogeneous* products. Consumers do not ask which farm grew a particular Granny Smith apple because they view all Granny Smith apples as essentially identical products. If the products of all firms are identical, it is difficult for any single firm to raise its price above the going price charged by other firms.

In contrast, in the automobile market—which is not perfectly competitive—the characteristics of a Ferrari and a Honda Civic differ substantially. These products are *differentiated* or *heterogeneous*. Competition from Civics is not in itself a very strong force preventing Ferrari from raising its price.

Full Information. If buyers know that different firms are producing identical products and they know the prices charged by all firms, no single firm can unilaterally raise its price above the market equilibrium price. If it tried to do so, consumers would buy the identical product from another firm. However, if consumers are unaware that products are identical or they don't know the prices charged by other firms, a single firm may be able to raise its price and still make sales.

Negligible Transaction Costs. Perfectly competitive markets have very low transaction costs. Buyers and sellers do not have to spend much time and money finding each other or hiring lawyers to write contracts to make a trade. If transaction costs are low, it is easy for a customer to buy from a rival firm if the customer's usual supplier raises its price.

In contrast, if transaction costs are high, customers may absorb a price increase from their traditional supplier to avoid incurring a substantial transaction cost in finding and contracting with a new supplier. Because some consumers prefer to buy a carton of milk at a local convenience store rather than travel several extra miles to a supermarket, the convenience store can charge slightly more than the supermarket without losing all its customers.

In some perfectly competitive markets, many buyers and sellers are brought together in a single room or online so that transaction costs are virtually zero. Transaction costs are very low at FloraHolland's daily plant and cut flower auctions in the Netherlands, which attract 7,000 suppliers and 4,500 buyers from around the world. There are about 125,000 auction transactions every day, with 12 billion cut flowers and 1.3 billion plants trading in a year.

Free Entry and Exit. The ability of firms to enter and exit a market freely in the long run leads to a large number of firms in a market and promotes price taking. Suppose a firm could raise its price and make a higher profit. If other firms could not enter the market, this firm would not be a price taker. However, if other firms can quickly and easily enter the market, the higher profit encourages entry by new firms until the price is driven back to the original level. Free exit is also important: If firms can freely enter a market but cannot quickly exit if prices decline, they are reluctant to enter the market in response to a possibly temporary profit opportunity.[2]

Perfect Competition in the Chicago Mercantile Exchange. The Chicago Mercantile Exchange, where buyers and sellers can trade wheat and other commodities, has the various characteristics of perfect competition including a very large number of many buyers and sellers who are price takers. Anyone can be a buyer or a seller. Indeed, a trader might buy wheat in the morning and sell it in the afternoon. They trade virtually *identical products*. Buyers and sellers have *full information* about products and prices, which is posted for everyone to see. Market participants waste no time finding someone who wants to trade and they can easily place buy or sell orders in person, over the telephone, or electronically without paperwork, so *transaction costs are negligible*. Finally, *buyers and sellers can easily enter this market and trade wheat*. These characteristics lead to an abundance of buyers and sellers and to price-taking behavior by these market participants.

Deviations from Perfect Competition

Many markets possess some but not all the characteristics of perfect competition, but they are still highly competitive so that buyers and sellers are, for all practical purposes, price takers. For example, a government may limit entry into a market, but if there are still many buyers and sellers, they may still be price takers. Many cities use zoning laws to limit the number of certain types of stores or motels, yet these cities still have a large number of these firms. Other cities impose moderately large transaction costs on entrants by requiring them to buy licenses, post bonds,

---

[2]For example, some governments, particularly in Europe, require firms to give workers six months' warning before they can exit the market.

and deal with a slow moving city bureaucracy, yet a significant number of firms enter the market. Similarly, even if only some customers have full information, that may be sufficient to prevent firms from deviating significantly from price taking. For example, tourists do not know the prices at various stores, but locals do and use their knowledge to prevent one store from charging unusually high prices.

Economists use the terms *competition* and *competitive* more restrictively than do others. To an economist, a competitive firm is a price taker. In contrast, when most people talk about competitive firms, they mean that firms are rivals for the same customers. Even in an oligopolistic market (Chapter 7) with only a few firms, the firms compete for the same customers so they are competitive in this broader sense. From now on, we will use the terms *competition* and *competitive* to refer to all markets in which no buyer or seller can significantly affect the market price—they are price takers—even if the market is not perfectly competitive.

8.2 Competition in the Short Run

In this section, we examine the profit-maximizing behavior of competitive firms, derive their supply curves, and determine the competitive equilibrium in the short run. In the next section, we examine the same issues in the long run.

The *short run* is a period short enough that at least one input cannot be varied (Chapter 5). Because a firm cannot quickly build a new plant or make other large capital expenditures, a new firm cannot enter a market in the short run. Similarly, a firm cannot fully exit in the short run. It can choose not to produce—to shut down— but it is stuck with some fixed inputs such as a plant or other capital that it cannot quickly sell or assign to other uses. In the long run, all inputs can be varied so firms can enter and fully exit the industry.

We treat the short run and the long run separately for two reasons. First, profit-maximizing firms may choose to operate at a loss in the short run, whereas they do not do so in the long run. Second, a firm's long-run supply curve typically differs from its short-run supply curve.

Economists usually assume that *all* firms—not just competitive firms—want to maximize their profits. This assumption is reasonable for at least two reasons (Chapter 7). First, many owners and managers of firms say that their objective is to maximize profits. Second, firms—especially competitive firms—that do not maximize profit are likely to lose money and be driven out of business. As we showed in Chapter 7, all firms—not just competitive firms—use a two-step decision-making process to determine how to maximize profit:

1. **How much to produce.** A firm first determines the output that maximizes its profit or minimizes its loss.
2. **Whether to produce.** Given that it has determined its profit-maximizing output, the firm decides whether to produce this quantity or shut down, producing no output.

How Much to Produce

As Chapter 7 shows, any operating firm—not just a competitive firm—maximizes its profit or minimizes its loss by setting its output where its marginal profit is zero or, equivalently, where its marginal revenue equals its marginal cost: $MR(q) = MC(q)$.[3] A competitive firm can easily determine its marginal revenue. Because it faces a horizontal demand curve, a competitive firm can sell as many units of output as it wants at the market price, p. Thus, a competitive firm's revenue, $R = pq$, increases by p if it sells one more unit of output, so its marginal revenue is p. For example, if the firm faces a market price of $1 per unit, its revenue is $5 if it sells 5 units and $6 if it sells 6 units, so its marginal revenue for the sixth unit is $1 = $6 − $5, which is the market price.[4] Thus, because a competitive firm's marginal revenue equals the market price, *a profit-maximizing competitive firm produces the amount of output, q, at which the market price, p, equals its marginal cost, MC:*

$$p = MC(q). \tag{8.1}$$

To illustrate how a competitive firm maximizes its profit, we examine a representative firm in the highly competitive Canadian lime manufacturing industry. Lime is a nonmetallic mineral used in mortars, plasters, cements, bleaching powders, steel, paper, glass, and other products. The lime plant's estimated average cost curve, AC, first falls and then rises in panel a of Figure 8.1.[5] As always, the marginal cost curve, MC, intersects the average cost curve at its minimum point.

If the market price of lime is $p = $8 per metric ton, the competitive firm faces a horizontal demand curve (marginal revenue curve) at $8. The MC curve crosses the firm's demand curve (or price or marginal revenue curve) at point e, where the firm's output is 284 units (where a unit is a thousand metric tons).

Thus at a market price of $8, the competitive firm maximizes its profit by producing 284 units. If the firm produced fewer than 284 units, the market price would be above its marginal cost. As a result, the firm could increase its profit by expanding output because the firm earns more on the next ton, $p = $8, than it costs to produce it, $MC < $8. If the firm were to produce more than 284 units, the market price would be below its marginal cost, $MC > $8, and the firm could increase its profit by reducing its output. Thus, the competitive firm maximizes its profit by producing that output at which its marginal cost equals its marginal revenue, which is the market price.[6]

At that 284 units, the firm's profit is $\pi = $426,000, which is the shaded rectangle in panel a. The length of the rectangle is the number of units sold, $q = 284,000$ (or 284

---

[3]As explained in Chapter 7, if $MR > MC$, then a small increase in quantity causes revenue to rise by more than cost, so maximizing profit requires an increase in output. If $MR < MC$, then maximizing profit requires a decrease in quantity as the reduction in cost exceeds the reduction in revenue. Only if $MR = MC$ is the firm maximizing profit.

[4]We can use calculus to derive this result. Because $R(q) = pq$, $MR(q) = dR(q)/dq = d(pq)/dq = p$.

[5]The figure is based on Robidoux and Lester's (1988) estimated variable cost function. In the figure, we assume that the minimum of the average variable cost curve is $5 at 50,000 metric tons of output. Based on information from Statistics Canada, we set the fixed cost so that the average cost is $6 at 140,000 tons.

[6]The firm chooses its output level to maximize its *total profit* rather than its *average profit* per ton. If the firm were to produce 140 units, where its average cost is minimized at $6, the firm would maximize its average profit at $2, but its total profit would be only $280,000. Although the firm gives up 50¢ in profit per ton when it produces 284 units instead of 140 units, it more than makes up for that lost profit per ton by selling an extra 144 units. At $1.50 profit per ton, the firm's total profit is $426,000, which is $146,000 higher than it is at 140 units.

FIGURE 8.1 How a Competitive Firm Maximizes Profit

(a) A competitive lime manufacturing firm maximizes its profit at $\pi^* = \$426{,}000$ where its marginal revenue, MR, which is the market price, $p = \$8$, equals its marginal cost, MC. (b) The corresponding profit curve reaches its peak at 284 units of lime. Estimated cost curves are based on Robidoux and Lester (1988).

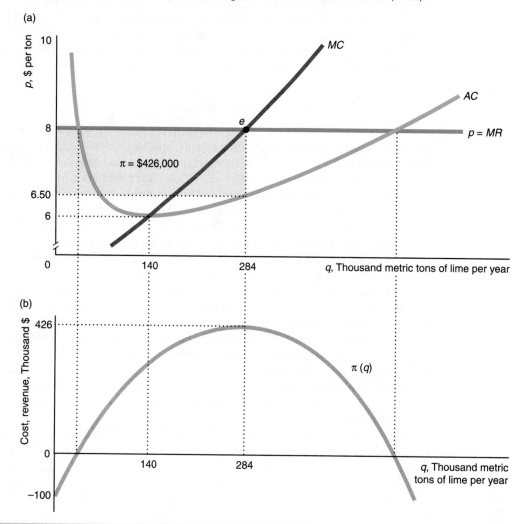

units). The height of the rectangle is the firm's average profit per unit. Because the firm's profit is its revenue, $R(q) = pq$, minus its cost, $\pi(q) = R(q) - C(q)$, its average profit per unit is the difference between the market price (or average revenue), $p = R(q)/q = pq/q$, and its average cost, $AC = C(q)/q$:

$$\frac{\pi(q)}{q} = \frac{R(q) - C(q)}{q} = \frac{R(q)}{q} - \frac{C(q)}{q} = p - AC. \qquad (8.2)$$

At 284 units, the lime firm's average profit per unit is $\$1.50 = p - AC(284) = \$8 - \$6.50$, and the firm's profit is $\pi = \$1.50 \times 284{,}000 = \$426{,}000$. Panel b shows that this profit is the maximum possible profit because it is the peak of the profit curve.

Q&A 8.1

If a competitive firm's cost increases due to an increase in the price of a factor of production or a tax, the firm's manager can quickly determine by how much to adjust output by calculating how the firm's marginal cost has changed and applying the profit-maximization rule. Suppose that the Canadian province of Manitoba imposes a specific (per-unit) tax of t per ton of lime produced in the province. There is only one lime-producing firm in Manitoba, so the tax affects only that firm and hence has virtually no effect on the market price. If the tax is imposed, how should the Manitoba firm change its output level to maximize its profit, and how does its maximum profit change?

Answer

1. *Show how the tax shifts the marginal cost and average cost curves.* The firm's before-tax marginal cost curve is MC^1 and its before-tax average cost curve is AC^1. Because the specific tax adds t to the per-unit cost, it shifts the after-tax marginal cost curve up to $MC^2 = MC^1 + t$ and the after-tax average cost curve to $AC^2 = AC^1 + t$.

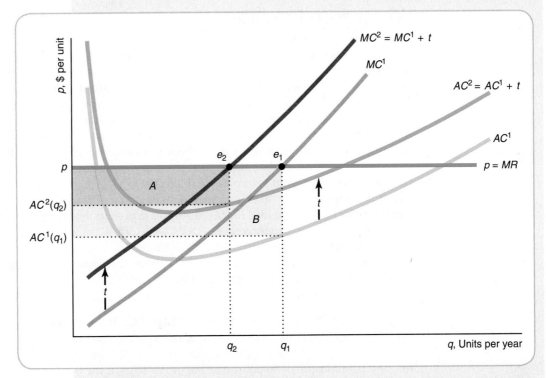

2. *Determine the before-tax and after-tax equilibria and the amount by which the firm adjusts its output.* Where the before-tax marginal cost curve, MC^1, hits the horizontal demand curve, p, at e_1, the profit-maximizing quantity is q_1. The after-tax marginal cost curve, MC^2, intersects the demand curve, p, at e_2, where the profit-maximizing quantity is q_2. Thus, in response to the tax, the firm produces $q_1 - q_2$ fewer units of output.

3. *Show how the profit changes after the tax.* Because the market price is constant but the firm's average cost curve shifts upward, the firm's profit at every output level falls. The firm sells fewer units (because of the increase in MC) and makes less profit per unit (because of the increase in AC). The after-tax profit is area $A = \pi_2 = [p - AC^2(q_2)]q_2$, and the before-tax profit is area $A + B = \pi_1 = [p - AC^1(q_1)]q_1$, so profit falls by area B due to the tax.

Using Calculus

Profit Maximization with a Specific Tax

We can use calculus to solve the problem in Q&A 8.1. The competitive firm's profit after the specific tax t is imposed is

$$\pi = pq - [C(q) + tq],$$

where $C(q)$ is the firm's before-tax cost and $C(q) + tq$ is its after-tax cost. We obtain a necessary condition for the firm to maximize its after-tax profit by taking the first derivative of profit with respect to quantity and setting it equal to zero:

$$\frac{d\pi}{dq} = \frac{d(pq)}{dq} - \frac{d[C(q) + tq]}{dq} = p - \left[\frac{dC(q)}{dq} + t\right] = p - [MC + t] = 0.$$

Thus, the competitive firm maximizes its profit by choosing q such that its after-tax marginal cost, $MC + t$, equals the market price.

Whether to Produce

Once a firm determines the output level that maximizes its profit or minimizes its loss, it must decide whether to produce that output level or to shut down and produce nothing. This decision is easy for the lime firm in Figure 8.1 because, at the output that maximizes its profit, it makes a positive profit. However, the question remains whether a firm should shut down if it is making a loss in the short run.

In Chapter 7, we showed that all firms—not just competitive firms—use the same shutdown rule: The firm shuts down only if it can reduce its loss by doing so. Equivalently, the firm shuts down only if its revenue is less than its avoidable variable cost (VC): $R < VC$. If the firm shuts down, it does not incur the variable cost, so its only loss is its unavoidable fixed cost (F).

For a competitive firm, this rule is $R = pq < VC$. Dividing both sides of this inequality by output, we find that *a competitive firm shuts down only if the market price is less than its average variable cost:* $p < AVC = VC/q$.

We illustrate the logic behind this rule using our lime firm example. We look at three cases where the market price is (1) above the minimum average cost (AC), (2) less than the minimum average cost but at least equal to or above the minimum average variable cost, or (3) below the minimum average variable cost.

The Market Price Is Above Minimum AC.
If the market price is above the firm's average cost at the quantity that it's producing, the firm makes a profit and so it operates. In panel a of Figure 8.1, the competitive lime firm's average cost curve reaches its minimum of $6 per ton at 140 units. Thus, if the market price is above $6, the firm makes a profit of $p - AC$ on each unit it sells and operates. In the figure, the market price is $8, and the firm makes a profit of $426,000.

The Market Price Is Between the Minimum AC and the Minimum AVC.
The tricky case is when the market price is less than the minimum average cost but at least as great as the minimum average variable cost. If the price is in this range, the firm makes a loss, but it reduces its loss by operating rather than shutting down.

Figure 8.2 (which reproduces the marginal and average cost curves from panel a of Figure 8.1 and adds the average variable cost curve) illustrates this case for the lime firm. The lime firm's average cost curve reaches a minimum of $6 at 140 units, while its average variable cost curve hits its minimum of $5 at 50 units. If the market price is between $5 and $6, the lime firm loses money (its profit is negative) because the price is less than its AC, but the firm does not shut down.

FIGURE 8.2 The Short-Run Shutdown Decision

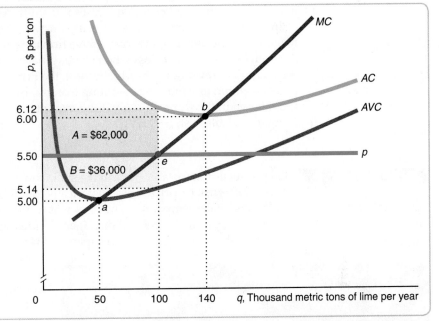

The competitive lime manufacturing plant operates if price is above the minimum of the average variable cost curve, point *a*, at $5. With a market price of $5.50, the firm produces 100 units because that price is above $AVC(100) = \$5.14$, so the firm more than covers its out-of-pocket, variable costs. At that price, the firm makes a loss of area $A = \$62,000$ because the price is less than the average cost of $6.12. If it shuts down, its loss is its fixed cost, area $A + B = \$98,000$. Thus, the firm does not shut down.

For example, if the market price is $5.50, the firm minimizes its loss by producing 100 units where the marginal cost curve crosses the price line. At 100 units, the average cost is $6.12, so the firm's loss is $-62¢ = p - AC(100) = \$5.50 - \$6.12$ on each unit that it sells.

Why does the firm produce given that it is making a loss? The reason is that the firm reduces its loss by operating rather than shutting down because its revenue exceeds its variable cost—or equivalently, the market price exceeds its average variable cost.

If the firm shuts down in the short run, it incurs a loss equal to its fixed cost of $98,000, which is the sum of rectangles A and B.[7] If the firm operates and produces $q = 100$ units, its average variable cost is $AVC = \$5.14$, which is less than the market price of $p = \$5.50$ per ton. It makes $36¢ = p - AVC = \$5.50 - \$5.14$ more on each ton than its average variable cost. The difference between the firm's revenue and its variable cost, $R - VC$, is the rectangle $B = \$36,000$, which has a length of 100 thousand tons and a height of 36¢. Thus, if the firm operates, it loses only $62,000 (rectangle A), which is less than its loss if it shuts down, $98,000. The firm makes a smaller loss by operating than by shutting down because its revenue more than covers its variable cost and hence helps to reduce the loss from the fixed cost.

The Market Price Is Less than the Minimum AVC.

If the market price dips below the minimum of the average variable cost, $5 in Figure 8.2, then the firm should shut down in the short run. At any price less than the minimum average variable cost, the firm's revenue is less than its variable cost, so it makes a greater

---

[7]From Chapter 6, we know that the average cost is the sum of the average variable cost and the average fixed cost, $AC = AVC + F/q$. Thus, the gap between the average cost and the average variable cost curves at any given output is $AC - AVC = F/q$. Consequently, the height of the rectangle $A + B$ is $AC(100) - AVC(100) = F/100$, and the length of the rectangle is 100 units, so the area of the rectangle is F, or $\$98,000 = \$62,000 + \$36,000$.

loss by operating than by shutting down because it loses money on each unit sold in addition to the fixed cost that it loses if it shuts down.

In summary, a competitive firm uses a two-step decision-making process to maximize its profit. First, the competitive firm determines the output that maximizes its profit or minimizes its loss when its marginal cost equals the market price (which is its marginal revenue): $p = MC$. Second, the firm chooses to produce that quantity unless it would lose more by operating than by shutting down. The competitive firm shuts down in the short run only if the market price is less than the minimum of its average variable cost, $p < AVC$.

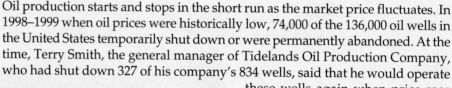

Mini-Case

Oil, Oil Sands, and Oil Shale Shutdowns

Oil production starts and stops in the short run as the market price fluctuates. In 1998–1999 when oil prices were historically low, 74,000 of the 136,000 oil wells in the United States temporarily shut down or were permanently abandoned. At the time, Terry Smith, the general manager of Tidelands Oil Production Company, who had shut down 327 of his company's 834 wells, said that he would operate these wells again when price rose above $10 a barrel—his minimum average variable cost.

Getting oil from oil wells is relatively easy. It is harder and more costly to obtain oil from other sources, so firms that use those alternative sources have a higher minimum average variable cost—higher shutdown points—and hence shut down at a higher price than companies that pump oil from wells.

It might surprise you to know that Canada has the third-largest known oil reserves in the world, 175 billion barrels, trailing only Saudi Arabia and Venezuela and far exceeding Iraq in fourth place. Yet you rarely hear about Canada's vast oil reserves because 97% of those reserves are in oil sands, which cover an area the size of Florida.

Oil sands are a mixture of heavy petroleum (bitumen), water, and sandstone. Extracting oil from oil sands is expensive and causes significant pollution in the production process. To liberate four barrels of crude oil from the sands, a processor must burn the equivalent of a fifth barrel. With the technology available in 2013, two tons of oil sands yielded only a single barrel (42 gallons) of oil.

The first large oil sands mining began in the 1960s, but because oil prices were often less than the $25-per-barrel average variable cost of recovering oil from the sands at that time, production was frequently shut down. In recent years, however, technological improvements in the production process have lowered the average variable cost to $18 a barrel. That, coupled with higher oil prices, has led to continuous oil sands production without shutdowns. As of 2013, more than 50 oil companies had operations in the Canadian oil sands, including major international producers such as Exxon, BP (formerly British Petroleum), and

Royal Dutch Shell, major Canadian producers such as Suncor and Husky, and companies from China, Japan, and South Korea.

The huge amounts of oil hidden in oil sands may be dwarfed by those found in oil shale, which is sedimentary rock containing oil. According to current estimates, oil shale deposits in Colorado and neighboring areas in Utah and Wyoming contain 800 billion recoverable barrels, the equivalent of 40 years of U.S. oil consumption. The United States has between 1 and 2 trillion recoverable barrels from oil shale, which is at least four times Saudi Arabia's proven reserves of crude oil, which are in underground pools.

A federal task force report concluded that the United States will be able to produce 3 million barrels of oil a day from oil shale and sands by 2035. Shell Oil reports that its average variable cost of extracting oil from shale is $30 a barrel in Colorado. In recent years, the lowest price for world oil was $39 a barrel on December 12, 2008. Since then prices have risen significantly, reaching $100 per barrel in early 2011 and remaining close to or above that level through early 2013. Therefore, oil shale production has become profitable and extraction is occurring.

The Short-Run Firm Supply Curve

We just demonstrated how a competitive firm chooses its output for a given market price in a way that maximizes its profit or minimizes its losses. By repeating this analysis at different possible market prices, we can show how the amount the competitive firm supplies varies with the market price.

As the market price increases from $p_1 = \$5$ to $p_2 = \$6$ to $p_3 = \$7$ to $p_4 = \$8$, the lime firm increases its output from 50 to 140 to 215 to 285 units per year, as Figure 8.3 shows. The profit-maximizing output at each market price is determined

FIGURE 8.3 How the Profit-Maximizing Quantity Varies with Price

As the market price increases, the lime manufacturing firm produces more output. The change in the price traces out the marginal cost (MC) curve of the firm. The firm's short-run supply (S) curve is the MC curve above the minimum of its AVC curve (at e_1).

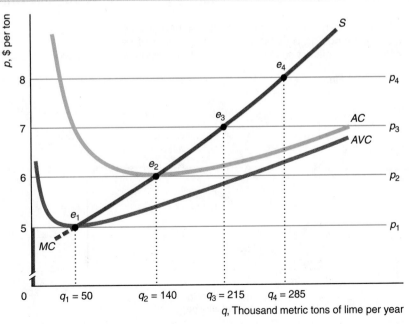

by the intersection of the relevant demand curve—market price line—and the firm's marginal cost curve, as equilibria e_1 through e_4 illustrate. That is, as the market price increases, the equilibria trace out the marginal cost curve. However, if the price falls below the firm's minimum average variable cost at $5, the firm shuts down. Thus, the competitive firm's short-run supply curve is its marginal cost curve above its minimum average variable cost.

The firm's short-run supply curve, S, is a solid red line in the figure. At prices above $5, the short-run supply curve is the same as the marginal cost curve. The supply is zero when price is less than the minimum of the AVC curve of $5. (From now on, to keep the graphs as simple as possible, we will not show the supply curve at prices below the minimum AVC.)

The Short-Run Market Supply Curve

The market supply curve is the horizontal sum of the supply curves of all the individual firms in the market. In the short run, the maximum number of firms in a market, n, is fixed because new firms need time to enter the market. If all the firms in a competitive market are identical, each firm's costs are identical, so their supply curves are identical, and the market supply at any price is n times the supply of an individual firm. If the firms have different costs functions, their supply curves and shutdown points differ. Consequently, the market supply curve reflects a different number of firms operating at various prices even in the short run. We examine competitive markets first with firms that have identical costs and then with firms that have different costs.

Short-Run Market Supply with Identical Firms. To illustrate how to construct a short-run market supply curve, we suppose, for graphical simplicity, that the lime manufacturing market has $n = 5$ competitive firms with identical cost curves. Panel a of Figure 8.4 plots the short-run supply curve, S^1, of a typical

FIGURE 8.4 Short-Run Market Supply with Five Identical Lime Firms

(a) The short-run supply curve, S^1, for a typical lime manufacturing firm is its MC above the minimum of its AVC. (b) The market supply curve, S^5, is the horizontal sum of the supply curves of each of the five identical firms. The curve S^4 shows what the market supply curve would be if there were only four firms in the market.

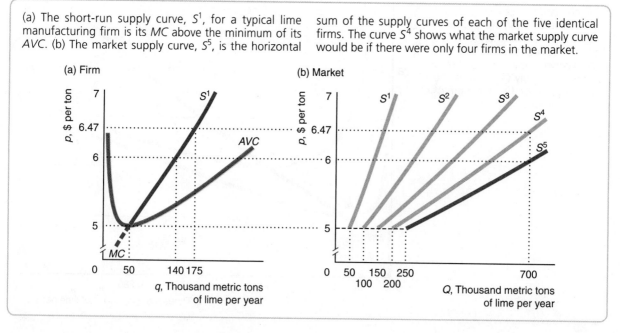

firm—the MC curve above the minimum AVC—where the horizontal axis shows the firm's output, q, per year. Panel b illustrates the competitive market supply curve, the dark line S^5, where the horizontal axis is market output, Q, per year. The price axis is the same in the two panels.

If the market price is less than $5 per ton, no firm supplies any output, so the market supply is zero. At $5, each firm is willing to supply $q = 50$ units, as in panel a. Consequently, the market supply is $Q = 5q = 250$ units in panel b. At $6 per ton, each firm supplies 140 units, so the market supply is 700 (= 5 × 140) units.

Suppose, however, that there were fewer than five firms in the short run. The light-color lines in panel b show the market supply curves for various other numbers of firms. The market supply curve is S^1 if there is one price-taking firm, S^2 with two firms, S^3 with three firms, and S^4 with four firms. The market supply curve flattens as the number of firms in the market increases because the market supply curve is the horizontal sum of more and more upward-sloping firm supply curves.[8] Thus, *the more identical firms producing at a given price, the flatter the short-run market supply curve at that price.*

The flatter the supply curve is at a given quantity, the more elastic is the supply curve. As a result, the more firms in the market, the less the price has to increase for the short-run market supply to increase substantially. Consumers pay $6 per ton to obtain 700 units of lime if there are five firms, but they must pay $6.47 per ton to obtain that much with only four firms. As the number of firms grows very large, the market supply curve approaches a horizontal line at $5.

Short-Run Market Supply with Firms That Differ.
If the firms in a competitive market have different minimum average variable costs, not all firms produce at every price, a situation that affects the shape of the short-run market supply curve. Suppose that the only two firms in the lime market are our typical lime firm with a supply curve of S^1 and another firm with a higher marginal and minimum average cost and the supply curve of S^2 in Figure 8.5. The first firm produces if the market price is at least $5, whereas the second firm does not produce unless the price is $6 or more. At $5, the first firm produces 50 units, so the quantity on the market supply curve, S, is 50 units. Between $5 and $6, only the first firm produces, so the market supply, S, is the same as the first firm's supply, S^1. At and above $6, both firms produce, so the market supply curve is the horizontal summation of their two individual supply curves. For example, at $7, the first firm produces 215 units, and the second firm supplies 100 units, so the market supply is 315 units.

As with the identical firms, where both firms are producing, the market supply curve is flatter than that of either firm. Because the second firm does not produce at as low a price as the first firm, the short-run market supply curve has a steeper slope (less elastic supply) at relatively low prices than it would if the firms were identical.

When the firms differ, only the low-cost firm supplies goods at relatively low prices. As the price rises, the other, higher-cost firm starts supplying, creating a stair-like market supply curve. The more suppliers there are with differing costs, the more steps there are in the market supply curve. As price rises and more firms supply the good, the market supply curve flattens, so it takes a smaller increase in price

---

[8]In the figure, if the price rises by $\Delta p = 47$¢ from $6 to $6.47 per ton, each firm increases its output by $\Delta q = 35$ tons, so the slope (measured in cents per ton) of its supply curve over that range is $\Delta p / \Delta q = 47/35 \approx 1.34$. With two firms, $\Delta q = 70$, so the slope is $47/70 \approx 0.67$. Similarly, the slope is $47/105 \approx 0.45$ with three firms, 0.33 with four firms, and 0.27 with five firms. Although not shown in the figure, the slope is 0.13 with 10 firms and 0.013 with 100 firms.

FIGURE 8.5 Short-Run Market Supply with Two Different Lime Firms

The supply curve S^1 is the same as for the typical lime firm in Figure 8.3. A second firm has an MC that lies to the left of the original firm's cost curve and a higher minimum of its AVC. Thus, its supply curve, S^2, lies above and to the left of the original firm's supply curve, S^1. The market supply curve, S, is the horizontal sum of the two supply curves. When price is $6 or higher, both firms produce, and the market supply curve is flatter than the supply curve of either individual firm.

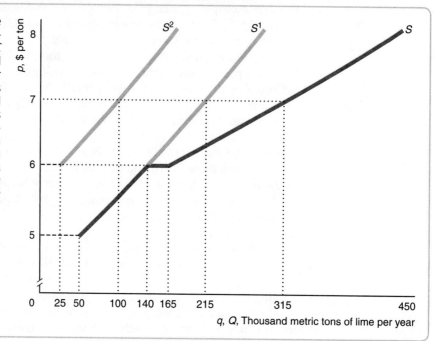

to increase supply by a given amount. Stated the other way, the more firms differ in costs, the steeper the market supply curve at low prices. Differences in costs are one explanation for why some market supply curves are upward sloping.

Short-Run Competitive Equilibrium

By combining the short-run market supply curve and the market demand curve, we can determine the short-run competitive equilibrium. We first show how to determine the equilibrium in the lime market, and we then examine how the equilibrium changes when firms are taxed.

Suppose that there are five identical firms in the short-run equilibrium in the lime manufacturing industry. Panel a of Figure 8.6 shows the short-run cost curves and the supply curve, S^1, for a typical firm, and panel b shows the corresponding short-run competitive market supply curve, S.

In panel b, the initial demand curve D^1 intersects the market supply curve at E_1, the market equilibrium. The equilibrium quantity is $Q_1 = 1{,}075$ units of lime per year, and the equilibrium market price is $7.

In panel a, each competitive firm faces a horizontal demand curve at the equilibrium price of $7. Each price-taking firm chooses its output where its marginal cost curve intersects the horizontal demand curve at e_1. Because each firm is maximizing its profit at e_1, no firm wants to change its behavior, so e_1 is the firm's equilibrium. In panel a, each firm makes a short-run profit of area $A + B = \$172{,}000$, which is the average profit per ton, $p - AC = \$7 - \$6.20 = 80¢$, times the firm's output, $q_1 = 215$ units. The equilibrium market output, Q_1, is the number of firms, n, times the equilibrium output of each firm: $Q_1 = nq_1 = 5 \times 215$ units $= 1{,}075$ units (panel b).

Now suppose that the demand curve shifts to D^2. The new market equilibrium is E_2, where the price is only $5. At that price, each firm produces $q = 50$ units, and

FIGURE 8.6 Short-Run Competitive Equilibrium in the Lime Market

(a) The short-run supply curve is the marginal cost above minimum average variable cost of $5. At a price of $5, each firm makes a short-run loss of $(p - AC)q = (\$5 - \$6.97) \times 50,000 = -\$98,500$, area $A + C$. At a price of $7, the short-run profit of a typical lime firm is $(p - AC)q = (\$7 - \$6.20) \times 215,000 = \$172,000$, area $A + B$. (b) If there are five firms in the lime market in the short run, so the market supply is S, and the market demand curve is D^1, then the short-run equilibrium is E_1, the market price is $7, and market output is $Q_1 = 1,075$ units. If the demand curve shifts to D^2, the market equilibrium is $p = \$5$ and $Q_2 = 250$ units.

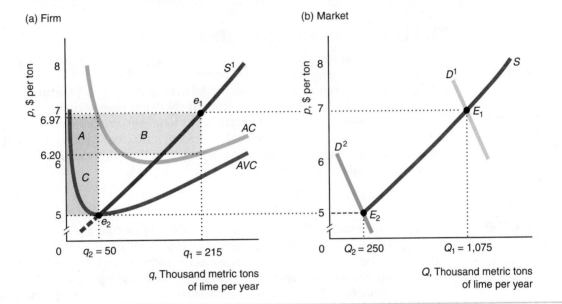

(a) Firm

(b) Market

market output is $Q = 250$ units. In panel a, each firm loses $98,500, area $A + C$, because it earns $(p - AC) = (\$5 - \$6.97) = -\$1.97$ per unit and it sells $q_2 = 50$ units. However, such a firm does not shut down because price equals the firm's average variable cost, so the firm is covering its out-of-pocket expenses.

8.3 Competition in the Long Run

I think there is a world market for about five computers. —Thomas J. Watson, IBM chairman, 1943

In the long run, competitive firms can vary inputs that were fixed in the short run and firms can enter and exit the industry freely, so the long-run firm and market supply curves differ from the short-run curves. After briefly looking at how a firm determines its long-run supply curve to maximize its profit, we examine the relationship between short-run and long-run market supply curves and competitive equilibria.

Long-Run Competitive Profit Maximization

The firm's two profit-maximizing decisions—how much to produce and whether to produce at all—are simpler in the long run than in the short run because, in the long run, all costs are avoidable.

The firm chooses the quantity that maximizes its profit using the same rules as in the short run. The firm picks the quantity that maximizes long-run profit, the difference between revenue and long-run cost. Equivalently, it operates where long-run marginal profit is zero—where marginal revenue (price) equals long-run marginal cost.

After determining the output level, q^*, that maximizes its profit or minimizes its loss, the firm decides whether to produce or shut down. The firm shuts down if its revenue is less than its avoidable cost. Because all costs are avoidable in the long run, the firm shuts down if it would make an economic loss by operating.

The Long-Run Firm Supply Curve

A firm's long-run supply curve is its long-run marginal cost curve above the minimum of its long-run average cost curve (because all costs are avoidable in the long run). The firm is free to choose its capital in the long run, so the firm's long-run supply curve may differ substantially from its short-run supply curve.

The firm chooses a plant size to maximize its long-run economic profit in light of its beliefs about the future. If its forecast is wrong, it may be stuck with a plant that is too small or too large for its level of production in the short run. The firm acts to correct this mistake in plant size in the long run.

Mini-Case

The Size of Ethanol Processing Plants

When a large number of firms initially built ethanol processing plants, they built relatively small ones. When the ethanol market took off in the first half decade of the twenty-first century, with the price reaching a peak of $4.23 a gallon in June 2006, many firms built larger plants or greatly increased their plant size. Then, with the more recent collapse of that market—the price fell below $3 and often below $1.50 from 2007 through 2012—many firms either closed their plants or reduced their size. The capacity of plants under construction or expansion went from 3,644 million gallons per year in 2005 to 5,635 in 2007, but since then the size has fallen to 1,432 in 2010 and 522 in 2011.

The Long-Run Market Supply Curve

The competitive market supply curve is the horizontal sum of the supply curves of the individual firms in both the short run and the long run. Because the maximum number of firms in the market is fixed in the short run, we add the supply curves of a known number of firms to obtain the short-run market supply curve. The only way for the market to supply more output in the short run is for existing firms to produce more.

However, in the long run, firms can enter or leave the market. Thus, before we can add all the relevant firm supply curves to obtain the long-run market supply curve, we need to determine how many firms are in the market at each possible market price.

We now look in detail at how market entry affects long-run market supply. To isolate the role of entry, we derive the long-run market supply curve, assuming that the price of inputs remains constant as market output increases.

Entry and Exit.   The number of firms in a market in the long run is determined by the *entry* and *exit* of firms. In the long run, each firm decides whether to enter or exit depending on whether it can make a long-run profit.

In some markets, firms face significant costs to enter, such as large start-up costs, or barriers to entry, such as a government restriction. For example, many city governments limit the number of cabs, creating an insurmountable barrier that prevents additional taxis from entering. Similarly, patent protection prevents new firms from producing the patented product until the patent expires.

However, in perfectly competitive markets, firms can enter and exit freely in the long run, which is referred to as *free entry and exit*. For example, many construction firms that provide only labor services enter and exit a market several times a year. In the United States, an estimated 198,000 new firms began operations and 187,000 firms exited in the third quarter of 2011.[9] The annual rates of entry and exit of such firms are both about 10% of the total number of firms per year.

In such markets, a shift of the market demand curve to the right attracts firms to enter. For example, if there were no government regulations, the market for taxicabs would have free entry and exit. Car owners could enter or exit the market quickly. If the demand curve for cab rides shifted to the right, the market price would rise, and existing cab drivers would make unusually high profits in the short run. Seeing these profits, other car owners would enter the market, causing the market supply curve to shift to the right and the market price to fall. Entry would continue until he last firm to enter—the *marginal firm*—makes zero long-run profit.

Similarly, if the demand curve shifts to the left so that the market price drops, firms suffer losses. Firms with minimum average costs above the new, lower market price exit the market. Firms continue to leave the market until the next firm considering leaving, the marginal firm, is again earning a zero long-run profit.

Thus, in a market with free entry and exit:

▶ A firm enters the market if it can make a long-run profit, $\pi > 0$.

▶ A firm exits the market to avoid a long-run loss, $\pi < 0$.

If firms in a market are making zero long-run profit, they are indifferent between staying in the market and exiting. We presume that if they are already in the market, they stay in the market when they are making zero long-run profit.

Mini-Case	American fast-food restaurants are flooding into Russia. When McDonald's opened its first restaurant in Pushkin Square in 1990, workers greeted gigantic lines of customers. Today, it has 279 restaurants in Russia. For years, McDonald's faced little western competition, despite the popularity of western fast food. The average bill at a Russian fast-food outlet is $8.92 compared to $6.50 in the United States (even though Russian incomes are about one-sixth U.S. incomes).
Fast-Food Firms' Entry in Russia	

Belatedly recognizing the profit opportunities, other chains are flooding into Russia. Burger King opened 22 restaurants in just two years, Carl's Jr. has 17 restaurants in just two cities, Wendy's has 2 restaurants and plans to have 180 throughout Russia by 2020, Subway has about 200 shops under several franchisees, and Yum Brands (which owns KFC, Pizza Hut, and Taco Bell) has about 350 restaurants in Russia.

Moscow is particularly ripe for entry by pizza restaurants. With a population of 13 million, it has only about 300 pizza restaurants. In contrast, Manhattan, with a population only about a tenth as large (1.6 million) has 4,000 pizza joints.

---

[9]**www.bls.gov/news.release/cewbd.t08.htm** (viewed March 1, 2013).

Christopher Wynne, an American who is fluent in Russian and gained Russian expertise researching arms proliferation, left his original career to open pizza restaurants in Russia. He bought 51% of the Papa John's Russian franchise. Although he competes with the U.S. chains Sbarro and Domino's and a Russian chain, Pizza Fabrika, among others, he says, "I could succeed in my sleep there is so much opportunity here." In 2011, Mr. Wynne opened his twenty-fifth Papa John's outlet in Russia, doubling the number from the previous year. Nineteen are in Moscow.

Each restaurant costs about $400,000 to open, but a restaurant can start earning an operating profit in three months. Mr. Wynne will continue opening outlets until the marginal restaurant earns zero economic profit.

Long-Run Market Supply with Identical Firms and Free Entry. The long-run market supply curve is flat at the minimum of long-run average cost if firms can freely enter and exit the market, an unlimited number of firms have identical costs, and input prices are constant. This result follows from our reasoning about the short-run supply curve, in which we showed that the market supply curve becomes flatter as more firms enter the market. With a large number of firms in the market in the long run, the market supply curve is effectively flat.

The long-run supply curve of a typical vegetable oil mill, S^1 in panel a of Figure 8.7, is the long-run marginal cost curve above a minimum long-run average cost of $10. Because each firm shuts down if the market price is below $10, the long-run market supply curve is zero at a price below $10. If the price rises above $10, firms are making positive profits, so new firms enter, expanding market output until profits are driven

FIGURE 8.7 Long-Run Firm and Market Supply with Identical Vegetable Oil Firms

(a) The long-run supply curve of a typical vegetable oil mill, S^1, is the long-run marginal cost curve above the minimum average cost of $10. (b) The long-run market supply curve is horizontal at the minimum of the long-run minimum average cost of a typical firm. Each firm produces 150 units, so market output is 150n, where n is the number of firms.

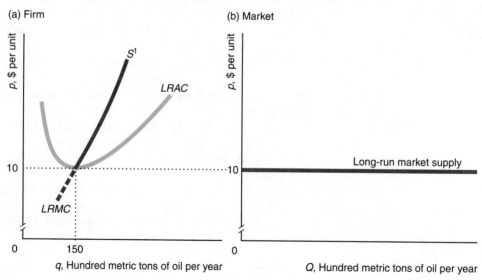

to zero, where price is again $10. The long-run market supply curve in panel b is a horizontal line at the minimum long-run average cost of the typical firm, $10. At a price of $10, each firm produces $q = 150$ units (where one unit equals 100 metric tons). Thus, the total output produced by n firms in the market is $Q = nq = n \times 150$ units. Extra market output is obtained by new firms entering the market.

In summary, the long-run market supply curve is horizontal if the market has free entry and exit, an unlimited number of firms have identical costs, and input prices are constant. As we show next, when these strong assumptions do not hold, the long-run market supply curve typically slopes upward but may slope downward. We examine two reasons why a long-run market supply curve is not flat: limited entry and differences in cost functions across firms. In addition, although we do not demonstrate this result, there is a third reason why long-run supply curves may slope up (or down), which is that input prices rise (or fall) when output increases.

Long-Run Market Supply When Entry Is Limited. If the number of firms in a market is limited in the long run, the market supply curve slopes upward. The number of firms is limited if the government restricts that number, if all firms need a scarce resource, or if entry is costly. An example of a scarce resource is the limited number of lots on which a luxury beachfront hotel can be built in Miami. High entry costs restrict the number of firms in a market because firms enter only if the long-run economic profit is greater than the cost of entering.

The only way to get more output if the number of firms is limited is for existing firms to produce more. Because individual firms' supply curves slope upward, the long-run market supply curve is also upward sloping. The reasoning is the same as in the short run, as panel b of Figure 8.4 illustrates, given that no more than five firms can enter. The market supply curve is the upward-sloping S^5 curve, which is the horizontal sum of the five firms' upward-sloping marginal cost curves above minimum average cost.

Long-Run Market Supply When Firms Differ. A second reason why some long-run market supply curves slope upward is that firms differ. Firms with relatively low minimum long-run average costs are willing to enter the market at lower prices than others, resulting in an upward-sloping long-run market supply curve (similar to the short-run example in Figure 8.5).

Suppose that a market has a number of low-cost firms and other higher-cost firms. If lower-cost firms can produce as much output as the market wants, only low-cost firms produce, and the long-run market supply curve is horizontal at the minimum of the low-cost firm's average cost curve. The long-run supply curve is upward sloping *only* if lower-cost firms cannot produce as much output as the market demands because each of these firms has a limited capacity and the number of these firms is limited.

Mini-Case	Many countries produce cotton. Production costs differ among countries because of differences in the quality of land, rainfall, costs of irrigation, costs of labor, and other factors.
Upward-Sloping Long-Run Supply Curve for Cotton	The length of each step-like segment of the long-run supply curve of cotton in the graph is the quantity produced by the labeled country. The amount that

the low-cost countries can produce is limited, so we observe production by the higher-cost countries if the market price is sufficiently high.

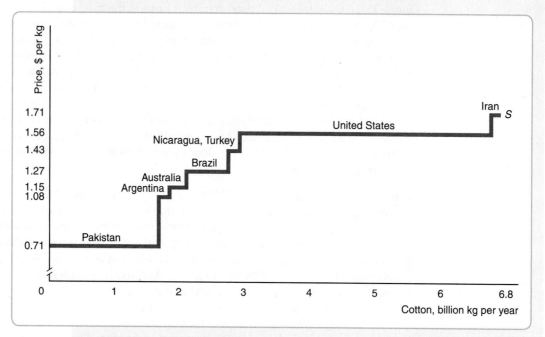

The height of each segment of the supply curve is the typical minimum average cost of production in that country. The average cost of production in Pakistan is less than half that in Iran. The supply curve has a step-like appearance because we are assuming that average cost is constant within a given country, up to capacity.

As the market price rises, the number of countries producing rises. At market prices below $1.08 per kilogram, only Pakistan produces. If the market price is below $1.50, the United States and Iran do not produce. If the price increases to $1.56, the United States supplies a large amount of cotton. In this range of the supply curve, supply is elastic. For Iran to produce, the price has to rise to $1.71. Price increases in that range result in only a relatively small increase in supply. Thus, the supply curve is relatively inelastic at prices above $1.56.

Long-Run Competitive Equilibrium

The intersection of the long-run market supply and demand curves determines the long-run competitive equilibrium. With identical firms, constant input prices, and free entry and exit, the long-run competitive market supply is horizontal at minimum long-run average cost, so the equilibrium price equals long-run average cost. A shift in the demand curve affects only the equilibrium quantity and not the equilibrium price, which remains constant at the minimum of long-run average cost.

The market supply curve is different in the short run than in the long run, so the long-run competitive equilibrium differs from the short-run equilibrium. The relationship between the short- and long-run equilibria depends on where the market demand curve crosses the short- and long-run market supply curves. Figure 8.8

FIGURE 8.8 The Short-Run and Long-Run Equilibria for Vegetable Oil

(a) A typical vegetable oil mill produces where its MR or price equals its MC, so it is willing to produce 150 units of oil at a price of $10, or 165 units at $11. (b) The short-run market supply curve, S^{SR}, is the horizontal sum of 20 individual firms' short-run marginal cost curves above minimum average variable cost, $7. The long-run market supply curve, S^{LR}, is horizontal at the minimum average cost, $10. If the demand curve is D^1, in the short-run equilibrium, F_1, 20 firms sell 2,000 units of oil at $7. In the long-run equilibrium, E_1, 10 firms sell 1,500 units at $10. If demand is D^2, the short-run equilibrium is F_2 ($11, 3,300 units, 20 firms) and the long-run equilibrium is E_2 ($10, 3,600 units, 24 firms).

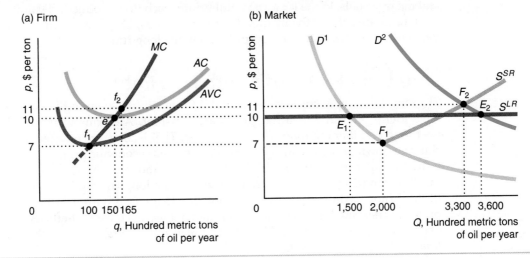

illustrates this point using the short- and long-run supply curves for the vegetable oil mill market.

The short-run firm supply curve for a typical firm in panel a is the marginal cost above the minimum of the average variable cost, $7. At a price of $7, each firm produces 100 units, so the 20 firms in the market in the short run collectively supply 2,000 ($= 20 \times 100$) units of oil in panel b. At higher prices, the short-run market supply curve slopes upward because it is the horizontal summation of the firm's upward-sloping marginal cost curves.

We assume that the firms use the same size plant in the short and long run so that the minimum average cost is $10 in both the short and long run. Because all firms have the same costs and can enter freely, the long-run market supply curve is flat at the minimum average cost, $10, in panel b. At prices between $7 and $10, firms supply goods at a loss in the short run but not in the long run.

If the market demand curve is D^1, the short-run market equilibrium, F_1, is below and to the right of the long-run market equilibrium, E_1. This relationship is reversed if the market demand curve is D^2.[10]

In the short run, if the demand is as low as D^1, the market price in the short-run equilibrium, F_1, is $7. At that price, each of the 20 firms produces 100 units, at f_1 in panel a. The firms lose money because the price of $7 is below average cost at 100 units. These losses drive some of the firms out of the market in the long run, so market output falls and the market price rises. In the long-run equilibrium, E_1, price

---

[10]Using data from Statistics Canada, we estimate that the elasticity of demand for vegetable oil is -0.8. Both D^1 and D^2 are constant -0.8 elasticity demand curves, but the demand at any price on D^2 is 2.4 times that on D^1.

is $10, and each firm produces 150 units, e, and breaks even. As the market demands only 1,500 units, only 10 (= 1,500/150) firms produce, so half the firms that produced in the short run exit the market.[11] Thus, with the D^1 demand curve, price rises and output falls in the long run.

If demand expands to D^2, in the short run, each of the 20 firms expands its output to 165 units, f_2, and the price rises to $11, where the firms make profits: The price of $11 is above the average cost at 165 units. These profits attract entry in the long run, and the price falls. In the long-run equilibrium, each firm produces 150 units, e, and 3,600 units are sold by the market, E_2, by 24 (= 3,600/150) firms. Thus, with the D^2 demand curve, price falls and output rises in the long run.

Zero Long-Run Profit with Free Entry

The long-run supply curve is horizontal if firms are free to enter the market, firms have identical cost, and input prices are constant. All firms in the market are operating at minimum long-run average cost. That is, they are indifferent between shutting down or not because they are earning zero economic profit.

In a competitive market with identical firms and free entry, if most firms are profit-maximizing, profits are driven to zero at the long-run equilibrium. Any firm that does not maximize profit—that is, any firm that sets its output so that the market price does not equal its marginal cost or does not use the most cost-efficient methods of production—loses money. Thus, *to survive in a competitive market in the long run, a firm must maximize its profit.*

8.4 Competition Maximizes Economic Well-Being

Why do we study competition in a book on managerial economics? There are two main reasons. First, many sectors of the economy are highly competitive including agriculture, parts of the construction industry, many labor markets, and much retail and wholesale trade. Second, and perhaps more important, perfect competition serves as an ideal or benchmark for other industries. This benchmark is widely used by economists and widely misused by politicians.

Most U.S. politicians have at one point or another in their careers stated (with a hand over their heart), "I believe in the free market." While we're not about to bash free markets, we find this statement to be, at best, mysterious. What do the politicians mean by "believe in" and "free market?" Hopefully they realize that whether a free market is desirable is a scientific question rather than one of belief. Possibly when they say they "believe in," they are making some claim that free markets are desirable for some unspecified reason. By "free market," they might mean a market without government regulation or intervention.

We believe that this statement is a bad summary of what is probably the most important theoretical result in economics: *a perfectly competitive market maximizes an important measure of economic well-being.* Adam Smith, the father of modern economics, in his book *An Inquiry into the Nature and Causes of the Wealth of Nations* in 1776, was

---

[11]How do we know which firms leave? If the firms are identical, the theory says nothing about which ones leave and which ones stay. The firms that leave make zero economic profit, and those that stay make zero economic profit, so firms are indifferent as to whether they stay or exit.

the first to observe that firms and consumers acting independently in their own self interest generate a desirable outcome. This insight is sometimes called the *invisible hand theorem*.[12]

Because a competitive market is desirable, government intervention in a perfectly competitive market reduces a society's economic well-being. However, government intervention may increase economic well-being in markets that are not perfectly competitive, such as in a monopolized market. In other words, freedom from government intervention does not guarantee that society's well-being is maximized in markets that are not perfectly competitive. In the rest of this section, we first describe widely accepted measures of consumer well-being, *consumer surplus*, and producer well-being, *producer surplus* (a concept close to that of profit). Next, we define a measure of a society's economic well-being, *total surplus*, as the sum of the consumer and producer measures of well-being. Then, we demonstrate why perfect competition maximizes total surplus. Finally, we discuss why a government action that causes a deviation from the perfectly competitive equilibrium reduces total surplus.

Consumer Surplus

The monetary difference between what a consumer is willing to pay for the quantity of the good purchased and what the consumer actually pays is called **consumer surplus (CS)**. Consumer surplus is a dollar-value measure of the extra economic benefit the consumer receives from a transaction over and above the good's price. By measuring how much more a consumer is willing to pay than the consumer actually paid, we know how much the consumer gained from this transaction. For example, if Jane is willing to pay up to $500 for a ticket to a U2 concert, but only has to pay $150, her consumer surplus is $350.

We use this monetary measure to answer questions such as "What effect does a price increase have on consumers' well-being?" or "How much does a government quota on the number of items each consumer may buy hurt consumers?" or "What is the harm to consumers from one firm monopolizing a market?"[13]

Measuring Consumer Surplus Using a Demand Curve. Because consumer surplus is the difference between what a consumer is willing to pay for a unit of a good and the price of that good, it is a measure of what the consumer gains from trade: from exchanging money for the good. We can use the information stored in a demand curve and the market price to determine consumer surplus. The

---

[12]The term *invisible hand* was coined by Smith. He expressed the basic theorem as ". . . every individual . . . intends only his own security; and by directing that industry in such a manner as its produce may be of the greatest value, he intends only his own gain, and he is in this, as in many other cases, led by an invisible hand to promote an end which was no part of his intention. . . . By pursuing his own interest he frequently promotes that of the society more effectually than when he really intends to promote it."

[13]If we knew a consumer's utility function (Chapter 4), we could directly answer the question of how an economic event, such as a price change, affects a consumer's well-being. However, we do not know individual utility functions. Even if we did, we could not compare the utility levels of different individuals. If Mei says that she got 1,000 utils (units of utility) from watching a movie, while Alan reports that he got 872 utils, we would not know if Mei enjoyed the movie more than Alan. She might just be using a different subjective scale. Because of these and other difficulties in comparing consumers' utilities, we use a monetary measure.

demand curve reflects a consumer's *marginal willingness to pay*: the maximum amount a consumer will spend for an extra unit. The consumer's marginal willingness to pay is the *marginal value* the consumer places on the last unit of output.

For example, David's demand curve for magazines per week, panel a of Figure 8.9, indicates his marginal willingness to buy various numbers of magazines. David places a marginal value of $5 on the first magazine. As a result, if the price of a magazine is $5, David buys one magazine, point *a* on the demand curve. His marginal willingness to buy a second magazine is $4, so if the price falls to $4, he buys two magazines, *b*. His marginal willingness to buy three magazines is $3, so if the price of magazines is $3, he buys three magazines, *c*.

David's consumer surplus from each additional magazine is his marginal willingness to pay minus what he pays to obtain the magazine. His marginal willingness to pay for the first magazine, $5, is area $CS_1 + E_1$. If the price is $3, his expenditure to obtain the magazine is area $E_1 = \$3$. Thus, his consumer surplus on the first magazine is area $CS_1 = (CS_1 + E_1) - E_1 = \$5 - \$3 = \$2$. Because his marginal willingness to pay for the second magazine is $4, his consumer surplus for the second magazine is the smaller area $CS_2 = \$1$. His marginal willingness to pay for the third magazine is $3, which equals what he must pay to obtain it, so his consumer surplus is zero, $CS_3 = \$0$. He is indifferent between buying and not buying the third magazine.

FIGURE 8.9 Consumer Surplus

(a) David's demand curve for magazines has a step-like shape. When the price is $3, he buys three magazines, point c. David's marginal value for the first magazine is $5, areas $CS_1 + E_1$, and his expenditure is $3, area E_1, so his consumer surplus is $CS_1 = \$2$. His consumer surplus is $1 for the second magazine, area CS_2, and is $0 for the third (he is indifferent between buying and not buying it). Thus, his total consumer surplus is the shaded area $CS_1 + CS_2 + CS_3 = \$3$. (b) Steven's willingness to pay for trading cards is the height of his smooth demand curve. At price p_1, Steven's expenditure is $E (= p_1 q_1)$, his consumer surplus is CS, and the total value he places on consuming q_1 trading cards per year is $CS + E$.

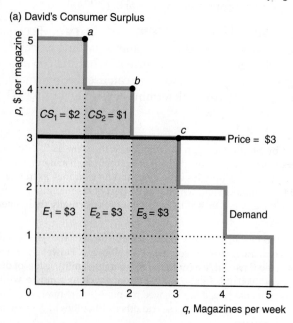

(a) David's Consumer Surplus

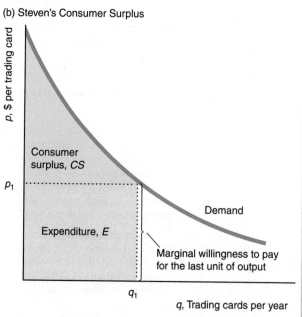

(b) Steven's Consumer Surplus

At a price of $3, David buys three magazines. His total consumer surplus from the three magazines he buys is the sum of the consumer surplus he gets from each of these magazines: $CS_1 + CS_2 + CS_3 = \$2 + \$1 + \$0 = \$3$. This total consumer surplus of $3 is the extra amount that David is willing to spend for the right to buy three magazines at $3 each. Thus, *an individual's consumer surplus is the area under the demand curve and above the market price up to the quantity the consumer buys.*

David is unwilling to buy a fourth magazine unless the price drops to $2 or less. If David's mother gives him a fourth magazine as a gift, the marginal value that David puts on that fourth magazine, $2, is less than what it cost his mother, $3.

We can determine consumer surplus for smooth demand curves in the same way as with David's unusual stair-like demand curve. Steven has a smooth demand curve for baseball trading cards, panel b of Figure 8.9. The height of this demand curve measures his willingness to pay for one more card. This willingness varies with the number of cards he buys in a year. The total value he places on obtaining q_1 cards per year is the area under the demand curve up to q_1, the areas CS and E. Area E is his actual expenditure on q_1 cards. Because the price is p_1, his expenditure is $p_1 q_1$. Steven's consumer surplus from consuming q_1 trading cards is the value of consuming those cards, areas CS and E, minus his actual expenditures E to obtain them, or CS. Thus, his consumer surplus, CS, is the area under the demand curve and above the horizontal line at the price p_1 up to the quantity he buys, q_1.

Just as we measure the consumer surplus for an individual using that individual's demand curve, we measure the consumer surplus of all consumers in a market using the market demand curve. *Market consumer surplus is the area under the market demand curve above the market price up to the quantity consumers buy.*

To summarize, consumer surplus is a practical and convenient measure of consumers' economic benefits from market transactions. There are two advantages to using consumer surplus rather than utility to discuss economic benefits. First, the dollar-denominated consumer surplus of several individuals can be easily compared or combined, whereas the utility of various individuals cannot be easily compared or combined. Second, it is relatively easy to measure consumer surplus, whereas it is difficult to get a meaningful measure of utility directly. To calculate consumer surplus, all we have to do is measure the area under a demand curve.

Managerial Implication

Willingness to Pay on eBay

If a product is sold on eBay, a manager can use the information that eBay reports to quickly estimate the market demand curve for the product. People differ in their willingness to pay for a given item. We can determine individuals' willingness to pay for a 238 A.D. Roman coin, a sesterce (originally equivalent in value to two and a half asses) of Emperor Balbinus, by how much they bid in an eBay auction.

On its website, eBay correctly argues (Chapter 12) that the best strategy for bidders is to bid their willingness to pay: the maximum value that they place on the item. If bidders follow this strategy, from what eBay reports, we know the maximum bid of each person except the winner because eBay uses a *second-price auction*, where the winner pays the second-highest amount bid (plus an increment).[14] In the figure, bids are arranged from highest to lowest. Because each bar on the graph indicates the bid for one coin, the figure shows how many units could have been sold to this group of bidders at various prices (assuming each bidder wants only one coin). That is, it is the market demand curve.

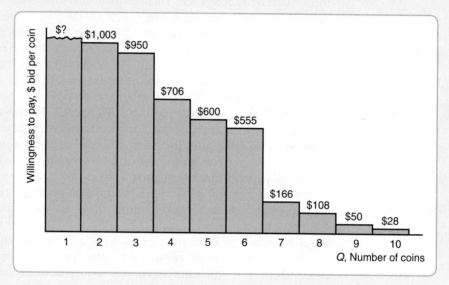

Effects of a Price Change on Consumer Surplus.

If the supply curve shifts upward or a government imposes a new sales tax, the equilibrium price rises, causing the consumer surplus to fall. We illustrate the effect of a price increase on market consumer surplus using estimated supply and demand curves for sweetheart and hybrid tea roses sold in the United States.[15] We then discuss which markets are likely to have the greatest loss of consumer surplus due to a price increase.

Suppose that the introduction of a new tax causes the wholesale price of roses to rise from the original equilibrium price of 30¢ to 32¢ per rose stem, a movement along the demand curve in Figure 8.10. The consumer surplus at the initial price of 30¢ is area $A + B + C = \$173.74$ million per year.[16] At a higher price of 32¢, the consumer surplus falls to area $A = \$149.64$ million. Thus, the loss in consumer surplus from the increase in price is $B + C = \$24.1$ million per year.

Producer Surplus

A supplier's gain from participating in the market is measured by **producer surplus (PS)**, which is the difference between the amount a good sells for and the minimum amount necessary for the producers to be willing to produce the good.

---

[14]The increment depends on the size of the bid. It is $1 for bids between $25 and $100 and $25 for bids between $1,000 and $2,499.99.

[15]We estimated this model using data from the *Statistical Abstract of United States, Floriculture Crops, Floriculture and Environmental Horticulture Products*, and **usda.mannlib.cornell.edu**. The prices are in real 1991 dollars.

[16]The height of triangle A is 25.8¢ $= 57.8$¢ $- 32$¢ per stem and the base is 1.16 billion stems per year, so its area is $\frac{1}{2} \times \$0.258 \times 1.16$ billion $= \$149.64$ million per year. Rectangle B is $\$0.02 \times 1.16$ billion $= \$23.2$ million. Triangle C is $\frac{1}{2} \times \$0.02 \times 0.09$ billion $= \$0.9$ million.

FIGURE 8.10 Fall in Consumer Surplus from Roses as Price Rises

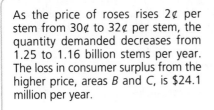

As the price of roses rises 2¢ per stem from 30¢ to 32¢ per stem, the quantity demanded decreases from 1.25 to 1.16 billion stems per year. The loss in consumer surplus from the higher price, areas *B* and *C*, is $24.1 million per year.

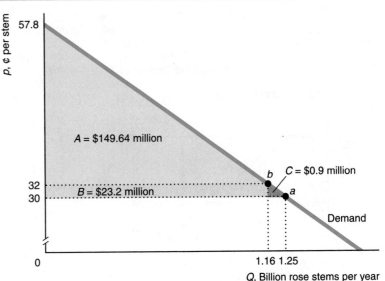

The minimum amount a firm must receive to be willing to produce is the firm's avoidable production cost. Therefore, producer surplus is a measure of what the firm gains from trade.

Measuring Producer Surplus Using a Supply Curve. To determine a competitive firm's producer surplus, we use its supply curve: its marginal cost curve above its minimum average variable cost. The firm's supply curve in panel a of Figure 8.11 looks like a staircase. The marginal cost of producing the first unit is $MC_1 = \$1$, which is the area under the marginal cost curve between 0 and 1. The marginal cost of producing the second unit is $MC_2 = \$2$, and so on. The variable cost, VC, of producing four units is the sum of the marginal costs for the first four units:

$$VC = MC_1 + MC_2 + MC_3 + MC_4 = \$1 + \$2 + \$3 + \$4 = \$10.$$

If the market price, p, is $4, the firm's revenue from the sale of the first unit exceeds its cost by $PS_1 = p - MC_1 = \$4 - \$1 = \$3$, which is its producer surplus on the first unit. The firm's producer surplus is $2 on the second unit and $1 on the third unit. On the fourth unit, the price equals marginal cost, so the firm just breaks even. As a result, the firm's total producer surplus, PS, from selling four units at $4 each is the sum of its producer surplus on these four units:

$$PS = PS_1 + PS_2 + PS_3 + PS_4 = \$3 + \$2 + \$1 + \$0 = \$6.$$

Graphically, the total producer surplus is the area above the supply curve and below the market price up to the quantity actually produced. This same reasoning holds when the firm's supply curve is smooth.

A firm's producer surplus is revenue, R, minus variable cost, VC:

$$PS = R - VC.$$

In panel a of Figure 8.11, revenue is $4 \times 4 = \$16$ and variable cost is $10, so the firm's producer surplus is $6.

FIGURE 8.11 Producer Surplus

(a) The firm's producer surplus, $6, is the area below the market price, $4, and above the marginal cost (supply curve) up to the quantity sold, 4. The area under the marginal cost curve up to the number of units actually produced is the variable cost of production. (b) The market producer surplus is the area above the supply curve and below the line at the market price, p^*, up to the quantity produced, Q^*. The area below the supply curve and to the left of the quantity produced by the market, Q^*, is the variable cost of producing that level of output.

(a) A Firm's Producer Surplus

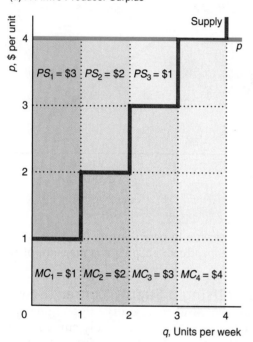

(b) A Market's Producer Surplus

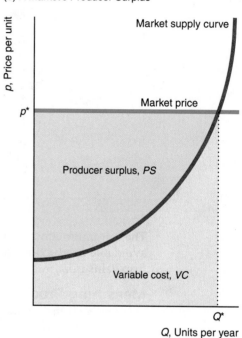

Q & A 8.2

If a firm has unavoidable fixed costs of F, how is its producer surplus related to its profit?

Answer

1. *Express the formula for profit in terms of variable and fixed cost.* A firm's profit is its revenue minus its total cost, C, which equals variable cost plus fixed cost, F:

$$\pi = R - C = R - (VC + F).$$

2. *Take the difference between producer surplus and profit.* The difference is

$$PS - \pi = (R - VC) - (R - VC - F) = F.$$

Thus, the difference between a firm's producer surplus and profit is the fixed cost, F. If the fixed cost is zero (as often occurs in the long run), producer surplus equals profit.

Using Producer Surplus. Even in the short run, we can use producer surplus to study the effects of a shock that affects the variable cost of production, such as a change in the price of a substitute or a variable input. Such shocks change profit by exactly the same amount as they change producer surplus because fixed costs do not change.

A major advantage of producer surplus is that we can use it to measure the effect of a shock on *all* the firms in a market without having to measure the profit of each firm in the market separately. We can calculate market producer surplus using the market supply curve in the same way as we calculate a firm's producer surplus using its supply curve. The market producer surplus in panel b of Figure 8.11 is the area above the supply curve and below the market price, p^*, up to the quantity sold, Q^*. The market supply curve is the horizontal sum of the marginal cost curves of each of the firms. As a result, the variable cost for all the firms in the market of producing Q is the area under the supply curve between 0 and the market output, Q^*.

Q&A 8.3

We estimated the supply curve for roses, which is the upward-sloping line in the following figure. How much producer surplus is lost if the price of roses falls from 30¢ to 21¢ per stem (so that the quantity sold falls from 1.25 billion to 1.16 billion rose stems per year)?

Answer

1. *Draw the supply curve, and show the change in producer surplus caused by the price change.* The figure shows the estimated supply curve for roses. Point *a* indicates the quantity supplied at the original price, 30¢, and point *b* reflects the quantity supplied at the lower price, 21¢. The loss in producer surplus is the sum of rectangle *D* and triangle *E*.

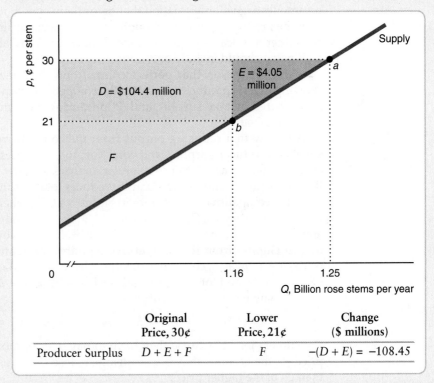

	Original Price, 30¢	Lower Price, 21¢	Change ($ millions)
Producer Surplus	$D + E + F$	F	$-(D + E) = -108.45$

2. *Calculate the lost producer surplus by adding the areas of rectangle D and triangle E.* The height of rectangle D is the difference between the original and the new price, 9¢, and its base is 1.16 billion stems per year, so the area of D (not all of which is shown in the figure because of the break in the quantity axis) is $0.09

per stem × 1.16 billion stems per year = \$104.4 million per year. The height of triangle E is also 9¢, and its length is 90 million stems per year, so its area is $\frac{1}{2}$ × \$0.09 per stem × 90 million stems per year = \$4.05 million per year. Thus, the loss in producer surplus from the drop in price is \$108.45 million per year.

Competition Maximizes Total Surplus

One of the most important results in economics is that perfect competition maximizes the sum of consumer surplus and producer surplus, which we call **total surplus (TS):**[17]

$$TS = CS + PS.$$

Total surplus is a measure of the total benefit to all market participants from market transactions, which are market participants' gains from trade. Total surplus implicitly weights the gains to consumers and producers equally. By using this measure to assess policies that affect market transactions, we are making a value judgment that the well-being of consumers and that of producers are equally important.

While most economists and many other people accept total surplus as a reasonable objective for society to try to maximize, not everyone agrees. Groups of producers commonly argue for legislation that helps them even if it hurts consumers by more than the producers gain—as though only producer surplus matters. Similarly, some consumer advocates argue that we should care only about consumers, so social well-being should include only consumer surplus.

A demonstration that perfect competition maximizes total surplus requires showing that (1) producing less than the competitive output lowers economic benefit as measured by total surplus, and (2) producing more than the competitive output lowers total surplus.

We show that reducing output from the competitive level reduces consumer surplus, producer surplus, and total surplus. (In Question 4.3 at the end of the chapter, you are asked to use a similar analysis to show that producing more than the competitive equilibrium quantity reduces total surplus.)

At the competitive equilibrium in Figure 8.12, E_1, where output is Q_1 and price is p_1, consumer surplus, CS_1, equals areas $A + B + C$, producer surplus, PS_1, is $D + E$, and the total surplus is $TS_1 = A + B + C + D + E$. Now suppose that we reduce output slightly from the competitive equilibrium quantity Q_1 to Q_2. As a result, price rises to p_2 at e_2, consumer surplus falls to $CS_2 = A$, producer surplus drops to $PS_2 = B + D$, and total surplus falls to $TS_2 = A + B + D$.

The change in consumer surplus is

$$\Delta CS = CS_2 - CS_1 = A - (A + B + C) = -B - C.$$

Consumers lose B because they have to pay $p_2 - p_1$ more than at the competitive price for the Q_2 units they buy. Consumers lose C because they buy only Q_2 rather than Q_1 at the higher price.

---

[17]Many economists call this sum *welfare*. We do not use that term because it has many different meanings in common speech.

FIGURE 8.12 Reducing Output from the Competitive Level Lowers Total Surplus

Reducing output from the competitive level, Q_1, to Q_2 causes price to increase from p_1 to p_2. Consumers suffer: Consumer surplus is now A, a fall of $\Delta CS = -B - C$. Producers may gain or lose: Producer surplus is now $B + D$, a change of $\Delta PS = B - E$. Overall, total surplus falls by $\Delta TS = -C - E$, which is a deadweight loss (*DWL*) to society.

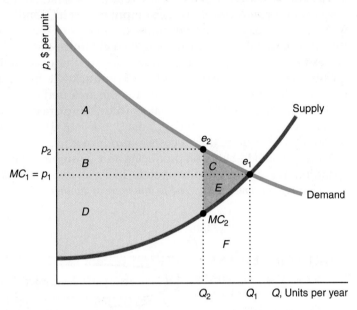

	Competitive Output, Q_1 (1)	Smaller Output, Q_2 (2)	Change (2) – (1)
Consumer Surplus, CS	$A + B + C$	A	$-B - C = \Delta CS$
Producer Surplus, PS	$D + E$	$B + D$	$B - E = \Delta PS$
Total Surplus, $TS = CS + PS$	$A + B + C + D + E$	$A + B + D$	$-C - E = \Delta TS = DWL$

The change in producer surplus is

$$\Delta PS = PS_2 - PS_1 = (B + D) - (D + E) = B - E.$$

Producers gain B because they now sell Q_2 units at p_2 rather than p_1. They lose E because they sell $Q_2 - Q_1$ fewer units.

The change in total surplus, $\Delta TS = TS_2 - TS_1$, is[18]

$$\Delta TS = \Delta CS + \Delta PS = (-B - C) + (B - E) = -C - E.$$

The area B is a transfer from consumers to producers—the extra amount consumers pay for the Q_2 units goes to the sellers—so it does not affect total surplus. Total surplus drops because the consumer loss of C and the producer

---

[18]The change in total surplus is $\Delta TS = TS_2 - TS_1 = (CS_2 + PS_2) - (CS_1 + PS_1) = (CS_2 - CS_1) + (PS_2 - PS_1) = \Delta CS + \Delta PS$.

loss of E benefit no one. This drop in total surplus, $\Delta TS = -C - E$, is a **deadweight loss (DWL)**: the net reduction in total surplus from a loss of surplus by one group that is not offset by a gain to another group from an action that alters a market equilibrium.

The deadweight loss results because consumers value extra output by more than the marginal cost of producing it. At each output between Q_2 and Q_1, consumers' marginal willingness to pay for another unit—the height of the demand curve—is greater than the marginal cost of producing the next unit—the height of the supply curve. For example, at e_2, consumers value the next unit of output at p_2, which is much greater than the marginal cost, MC_2, of producing it. Increasing output from Q_2 to Q_1 raises firms' variable cost by area F, the area under the marginal cost (supply) curve between Q_2 and Q_1. Consumers value this extra output by the area under the demand curve between Q_2 and Q_1, area $C + E + F$. Thus, consumers value the extra output by $C + E$ more than it costs to produce it.

Society would be better off producing and consuming extra units of this good than spending this amount on other goods. In short, *the deadweight loss is the opportunity cost of giving up some of this good to buy more of another good.*

The Deadweight Loss of Christmas Presents

Just how much did Nicholas enjoy the expensive lime green woolen socks with the dancing purple teddy bears that his Aunt Fern gave him last Christmas? Often the cost of a gift exceeds the value that the recipient places on it.

Until the advent of gift cards, only 10% to 15% of holiday gifts were monetary. A gift of cash typically gives at least as much pleasure to the recipient as a gift that costs the same but can't be exchanged for cash. (So what if giving cash is tacky?) Of course, it's possible that a gift can give more pleasure to the recipient than it cost the giver—but how often does that happen to you?

An *efficient gift* is one that the recipient values as much as the gift costs the giver, or more. The difference between the price of the gift and its value to the recipient is a deadweight loss to society. Joel Waldfogel (1993, 2009) asked Yale undergraduates just how large this deadweight loss is. He estimated that the deadweight loss is between 10% and 33% of the value of gifts. Waldfogel (2005) found that consumers value their own purchases at 10% to 18% more,

per dollar spent, than items received as gifts.[19] Indeed, only 65% of holiday shoppers said they didn't return a single gift after Christmas 2010.

Waldfogel found that gifts from friends and "significant others" are most efficient, while noncash gifts from members of the extended family are least efficient (one-third of the value is lost).[20] Luckily, grandparents, aunts, and uncles are most likely to give cash.

Given holiday expenditures of about $66 billion in 2007 in the United States, Waldfogel concluded that a conservative estimate of the deadweight loss of Christmas, Hanukkah, and other holidays with gift-giving rituals is about $12 billion. (And that's not counting about 2.8 billion hours spent shopping.)

The question remains why people don't give cash instead of presents. Indeed, 61% of Americans gave a gift card as a Christmas present. (A gift card is the equivalent of cash, though some can only be used in a particular store.) More than $110 billion in gift cards were purchased in 2012 in the United States. If the reason others don't give cash or gift cards is that they get pleasure from picking the "perfect" gift, the deadweight loss that adjusts for the pleasure of the giver is lower than these calculations suggest. (Bah, humbug!)

Effects of Government Intervention

I don't make jokes. I just watch the government and report the facts. —Will Rogers

A government policy that limits trade in a competitive market reduces total surplus. For example, in some markets the government imposes a *price ceiling*, which sets a limit on the highest price that a firm can legally charge. If the government sets the ceiling below the precontrol competitive price, consumers want to buy more than the precontrol equilibrium quantity but firms supply less than that quantity. (For example, see Chapter 2's Mini-Case "Disastrous Price Controls.") Thus, due to the price ceiling, consumers can buy the good at a lower price but cannot buy as much of it as they'd like. Because less is sold than at the precontrol equilibrium, there is deadweight loss: Consumers value the good more than the marginal cost of producing extra units. Producer surplus must fall because firms receive a lower price and sell fewer units.

---

[19]Gift recipients may exhibit an endowment effect (Chapter 4), in which their willingness to pay (WTP) for the gift is less than what they would have to be offered to give up the gift, their willingness to accept (WTA). Bauer and Schmidt (2008) asked students at the Ruhr University in Germany their WTP and WTA for three recently received Christmas gifts. On average over all students and gifts, the average WTP was 11% percent below the market price and the WTA was 18% above the market price.

[20]People may deal with a disappointing present by "regifting" it. Some families have been passing the same fruitcake among family members for decades. According to one survey, 33% of women and 19% of men admitted that they pass on an unwanted gift (and 28% of respondents said that they would not admit it if asked whether they had done so).

Q&A 8.4

What is the effect on the equilibrium and consumer, producer, and total surplus if the government sets a price ceiling, $\bar{p}$, below the unregulated competitive equilibrium price?

Answer

1. *Show the initial unregulated equilibrium.* The intersection of the demand curve and the supply curve determines the unregulated, competitive equilibrium e_1, where the equilibrium quantity is Q_1.

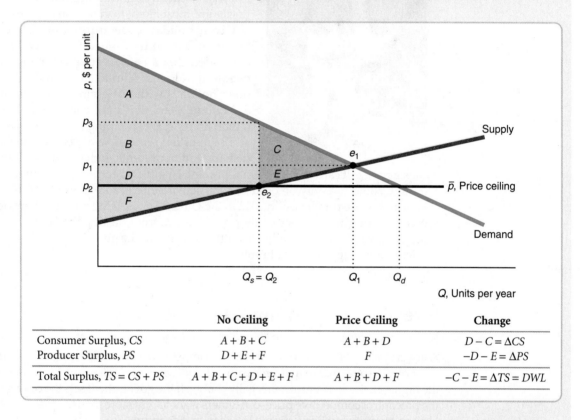

	No Ceiling	Price Ceiling	Change
Consumer Surplus, CS	$A + B + C$	$A + B + D$	$D - C = \Delta CS$
Producer Surplus, PS	$D + E + F$	F	$-D - E = \Delta PS$
Total Surplus, $TS = CS + PS$	$A + B + C + D + E + F$	$A + B + D + F$	$-C - E = \Delta TS = DWL$

2. *Show how the equilibrium changes with the price ceiling.* Because the price ceiling, $\bar{p}$, is set below the equilibrium price of p_1, the ceiling binds. At this lower price, consumer demand increases to Q_d while the quantity firms are willing to supply falls to Q_s, so only $Q_s = Q_2$ units are sold at the new equilibrium, e_2. Thus, the price control causes the equilibrium quantity and price to fall, but consumers have excess demand of $Q_d - Q_s$.

3. *Describe the effects on consumer, producer, and total surplus.* Because consumers are able to buy Q_s units at a lower price than before the controls, they gain area D. Consumers lose consumer surplus of C, however, because they can purchase only Q_s instead of Q_1 units of output. Thus, consumers gain net consumer surplus of $D - C$. Because they sell fewer units at a lower price, firms lose producer surplus $-D - E$. Part of this loss, D, is transferred to consumers because of lower prices, but the rest, E, is a loss to society. The deadweight loss to society is at least $\Delta TS = \Delta CS + \Delta PS = -C - E$.

Comment: This measure of the deadweight loss may *underestimate* the true loss. Because consumers want to buy more units than are sold, they may spend time searching for a store that has units for sale. This unsuccessful search activity is wasteful and hence a deadweight loss to society. (Note that less of this wasteful search does not occur if the good is known to be efficiently but inequitably distributed to people according to some discriminatory criterion such as race, gender, being in the military, or being attractive.) Another possible inefficiency is that consumers who buy the good may value it less than those who are unable to find a unit to purchase. For example, someone might purchase the good who values it at p_2, while someone who values it at p_3 cannot find any to buy.

Managerial Solution	We return to the Managerial Problems at the beginning of the chapter about the effects of higher annual fees and other lump-sum costs on the trucking market price and quantity, the output of individual firms, and the number of trucking firms (assuming that the demand curve remains constant). Because firms may enter and exit this industry in the long run, such higher lump-sum costs can have a counterintuitive effect on the competitive equilibrium.

The Rising Cost of Keeping On Truckin'

All trucks of a certain size are essentially identical, and trucks can easily enter and exit the industry (government regulations aside). Panel a of the figure shows a typical firm's cost curves and panel b shows the market equilibrium.

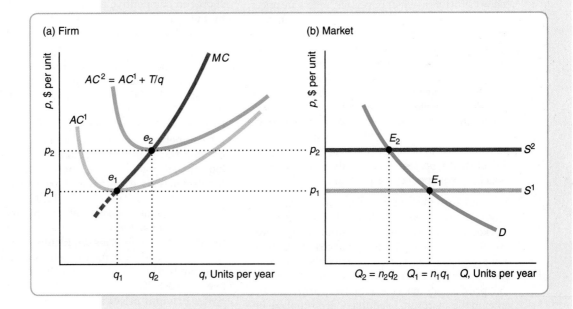

The new, higher fees and other lump-sum costs raise the fixed cost of operating by T. In panel a, a lump-sum, franchise tax shifts the typical firm's average cost curve upward from AC^1 to $AC^2 = AC^1 + T/q$, but does not affect the marginal cost. As a result, the minimum average cost rises from e_1 to e_2.

Given that an unlimited number of identical truckers are willing to operate in this market, the long-run market supply is horizontal at minimum average cost. Thus, the market supply curve shifts upward in panel b by the same amount as the minimum average cost increases. Given a downward-sloping market demand curve D, the new equilibrium, E_2, has a lower quantity, $Q_2 < Q_1$, and higher price, $p_2 > p_1$, than the original equilibrium, E_1.

As the market price rises, the quantity that a firm produces rises from q_1 to q_2 in panel a. Because the marginal cost curve is upward sloping at the original equilibrium, when the average cost curve shifts up due to the higher fixed cost, the new minimum point on the average cost curve corresponds to a larger output than in the original equilibrium. Thus, any trucking firm still operating in the market produces at a larger volume.

Because the market quantity falls but each firm remaining in the market produces more, the number of firms in the market must fall. At the initial equilibrium, the number of firms was $n_1 = Q_1/q_1$. The new equilibrium number of firms, $n_2 = Q_2/q_2$, must be smaller than n_1 because $Q_2 < Q_1$ and $q_2 > q_1$. Therefore, an increase in fixed cost causes the market price to rise and the total quantity and number of trucking firms to fall, as most people would have expected. However, it also has the surprising effect that it causes output per firm to increase for the firms that continue to produce.

SUMMARY

1. **Perfect Competition.** Perfect competition is a market structure in which buyers and sellers are price takers. Each firm faces a horizontal demand curve. A firm's demand curve is horizontal because perfectly competitive markets have five characteristics: there are a very large number of small buyers and sellers, firms produce identical (homogeneous) products, buyers have full information about product prices and characteristics, transaction costs are negligible, and there is free entry and exit in the long run. Many markets are highly competitive—firms are very close to being price takers—even if they do not strictly possess all five of the characteristics associated with perfect competition.

2. **Competition in the Short Run.** To maximize its profit, a competitive firm (like a firm in any other market structure) chooses its output level where marginal revenue equals marginal cost. Because a competitive firm is a price taker, its marginal revenue equals the market price, so it sets its output so that price equals marginal cost. New firms cannot enter in the short run. In addition, firms that are in the industry have some fixed inputs that cannot be changed and whose costs cannot be avoided. In this sense firms cannot exit the industry in the short run. However, a profit-maximizing firm shuts down and produces no output if the market price is less than its minimum average variable cost. Thus, a competitive firm's short-run supply curve is its marginal cost curve above its minimum average variable cost. The short-run market supply curve is the sum of the supply curves of the fixed

number of firms producing in the short run. The short-run competitive equilibrium is determined by the intersection of the market demand curve and the short-run market supply curve.

3. **Competition in the Long Run.** In the long run, a competitive firm sets its output where the market price equals its long-run marginal cost. It shuts down if the market price is less than the minimum of its long-run average cost, because all costs are avoidable in the long run. Consequently, the competitive firm's long-run supply curve is its long-run marginal cost above its minimum long-run average cost. The long-run supply curve of a firm may have a different slope than the short-run curve because it can vary its fixed inputs in the long run. The long-run market supply curve is the horizontal sum of the supply curves of all the firms in the market. If all firms are identical, entry and exit are easy, and input prices are constant, then the long-run market supply curve is flat at minimum average cost. If firms differ, entry is difficult or costly, or input prices increase with output, the long-run market supply curve has an upward slope. The long-run market equilibrium price and quantity may be different from the short-run price and quantity.

4. **Competition Maximizes Economic Well-Being.** Perfect competition maximizes a commonly used measure of economic well-being, total surplus. Total surplus is the monetary value of the gain from trade. It is the sum of consumer surplus and producer surplus. Consumer surplus

is the economic benefit or well-being obtained by a consumer in excess of the price paid. It equals the area under the consumer's demand curve above the market price up to the quantity that the consumer buys. Producer surplus is the amount producers are paid over and above the minimum amount needed to induce them to produce a given output level. A firm's producer surplus is its revenue minus the variable cost of production. Thus, if a firm has no fixed costs, as often occurs in the long run, a firm's producer surplus is the same as profit. In the short run, a firm's producer surplus is greater than profit by an amount equal to unavoidable fixed cost. Producer surplus is the area below the price and above the supply curve up to the quantity that the firm sells.

QUESTIONS

*All exercises are available on MyEconLab; * = answer at the back of this book; C = use of calculus may be necessary.*

1. Perfect Competition

1.1. A large city has nearly 500 restaurants, with new ones entering regularly as the population grows. The city decides to limit the number of restaurant licenses to 500. Which characteristics of this market are consistent with perfect competition and which are not? Is this restaurant market likely to be nearly perfectly competitive? Why?

*1.2. Why would high transaction costs or imperfect information tend to prevent price-taking behavior?

2. Competition in the Short Run

2.1. Mercedes-Benz of San Francisco advertises on the radio that it has been owned and operated by the same family in the same location for 50 years (as of 2012). It then makes two claims: first, that it has lower overhead than other nearby auto dealers because it has owned this land for 50 years, and second, it charges a lower price for its cars because of its lower overhead. Discuss the logic of these claims.

*2.2. Many marginal cost curves are U-shaped. As a result, it is possible that the MC curve hits the demand or price line at two output levels. Which is the profit-maximizing output? Why?

2.3. Initially, the market price was $p = 20$, and the competitive firm's minimum average variable cost was 18, while its minimum average cost was 21. Should it shut down? Why? Now this firm's average variable cost increases by 3 at every quantity, while other firms in the market are unaffected. What happens to its average cost? Should this firm shut down? Why?

2.4. Should a firm shut down if its revenue is $R = \$1,000$ per week,

   a. its variable cost is $VC = \$500$, and its sunk fixed cost is $F = \$600$?

   b. its variable cost is $VC = \$1,001$, and its sunk fixed cost $F = \$500$?

   c. its variable cost is $VC = \$500$, and its fixed cost is 800, of which 600 is avoidable if it shuts down?

*2.5. The cost function for Acme Laundry is $C(q) = 10 + 10q + q^2$, so its marginal cost function is $MC = 10 + 2q$, where q is tons of laundry cleaned. Derive the firm's average cost and average variable cost curves. What q should the firm choose so as to maximize its profit if the market price is p? How much does it produce if the competitive market price is $p = 50$?

2.6. Beta Laundry's cost function is $C(q) = 30 + 20q + q^2$.

   a. What quantity maximizes the firm's profit if the market price is p? How much does it produce if $p = 60$?

   b. If the government imposes a specific tax of $t = 2$, what quantity maximizes its after-tax profit? Does it operate or shut down? (*Hint:* See Q&A 8.1.) **C**

2.7. If the pre-tax cost function for John's Shoe Repair is $C(q) = 100 + 10q - q^2 + \frac{1}{3}q^3$, and it faces a specific tax of $t = 10$, what is its profit-maximizing condition if the market price is p? Can you solve for a single, profit-maximizing q in terms of p? (*Hint:* See Q&A 8.1.) **C**

2.8. If a specific subsidy (negative tax) of s is given to only one competitive firm, how should that firm change its output level to maximize its profit, and how does its maximum profit change? Use a graph to illustrate your answer. (*Hint:* See Q&A 8.1.)

2.9. According to the "Oil, Oil Sands, and Oil Shale Shutdowns" Mini-Case, the minimum average variable cost of processing oil sands dropped from $25 a barrel in the 1960s to $18 due to technological advances. In a figure, show how this change affects the supply curve of a typical competitive firm and the supply curve of all the firms producing oil from oil sands.

2.10. Fierce storms in October 2004 caused TomatoFest Organic Heirlooms Farm to end its tomato harvest two weeks early. According to Gary Ibsen, a partner in this small business (Carolyn Said, "Tomatoes in

Trouble," *San Francisco Chronicle*, October 29, 2004, C1, C2), TomatoFest lost about 20,000 pounds of tomatoes that would have sold for about $38,000; however, because he did not have to hire pickers and rent trucks during these two weeks, his net loss was about $20,000. In calculating the revenue loss, he used the post-storm price, which was double the pre-storm price.

a. Draw a diagram for a typical firm next to one for the market to show what happened as a result of the storm. Assume that TomatoFest's experience was typical of that of many small tomato farms.

b. Did TomatoFest suffer an economic loss? What extra information (if any) do you need to answer this question? How do you define "economic loss" in this situation?

2.11. The Internet is affecting holiday shipping. In years past, the busiest shipping period was Thanksgiving week. Now as people have become comfortable with e-commerce, they purchase later in the year and are more likely to have gifts shipped (rather than purchasing locally). FedEx, along with Amazon and other e-commerce firms, hires extra workers during this period, and many regular workers log substantial overtime hours.

a. Are the marginal and average costs of Internet retailers likely to rise or fall with this extra business? (Discuss economies of scale and the slopes of marginal and average cost curves.)

b. Use side-by-side firm-market diagrams to show the effects on the number of firms, equilibrium price and output, and profits of such a seasonal shift in demand for e-retailers in both the short run and the long run. Explain your reasoning.

2.12. What is the effect on the short-run equilibrium of a specific subsidy of s per unit that is given to all n firms in a market?

3. Competition in the Long Run

3.1. As of 2013, customers at California grocery and drug stores must pay an extra 10¢ for every paper bag that the store provides (the store keeps this fee). Does such a charge affect the marginal cost of any particular good? If so, by how much? Is this fee likely to affect the overall amount that consumers pay for groceries?

*3.2. What is the short-run and long-run effect on firm and market equilibrium of the U.S. law requiring a firm to give its workers six months' notice before it can shut down its plant?

3.3. The "Upward-Sloping Long-Run Supply Curve for Cotton" Mini-Case shows a supply curve for cotton. Discuss the equilibrium if the world demand curve crosses this supply curve in either (a) a flat section labeled Brazil or (b) the following vertical section. What do cotton farms in the United States do?

3.4. Chinese art factories are flooding the world's generic art market (Keith Bradsher, "Own Original Chinese Copies of Real Western Art!" *New York Times*, July 15, 2005). The value of bulk shipments of Chinese paintings to the United States nearly tripled from slightly over $10 million in 1996 to $30.5 million in 2004 (and early 2005 sales were up 50% from the corresponding period in 2004). A typical artist earns less than $200 a month, plus modest room and board, or $360 a month without food and housing. Using a step-like supply function (similar to the one in the "Upward-Sloping Long-Run Supply Curve for Cotton" Mini-Case), show how the entry of the Chinese affects the world supply curve and how this change affects the equilibrium (including who produces art). Explain.

3.5. The 2010 oil spill in the Gulf of Mexico caused the oil firm BP and the U.S. government to greatly increase purchases of boat services, various oil-absorbing materials, and other goods and services to minimize damage from the spill. Use side-by-side firm and market diagrams to show the effects (number of firms, price, output, profits) of such a shift in demand in one such industry, such as boat services, in both the short run and the long run. Explain how your answer depends on whether the shift in demand is expected to be temporary or permanent.

3.6. In late 2004 and early 2005, the price of raw coffee beans jumped as much as 50% from the previous year. In response, the price of roasted coffee rose about 14%. Similarly, in 2012, the price of raw beans fell by a third, yet the price of roasted coffee fell by only a few percentage points. Why did the roasted coffee price change less than in proportion to the rise in the cost of raw beans?

3.7. In 2009, the voters of Oakland, California, passed a measure to tax medical cannabis (marijuana), effectively legalizing it. In 2010, the City Council adopted regulations permitting industrial-scale marijuana farms with no size limits but requiring each to pay a $211,000 per year fee.[21] One proposal called for

---

[21]Matthai Kuruvila, "Oakland Allows Industrial-Scale Marijuana Farms," *San Francisco Chronicle*, July 21, 2010, and Malia Wollan, "Oakland, Seeking Financial Lift, Approves Giant Marijuana Farms," *New York Times*, July 21, 2010.

a 100,000 square feet farm, the size of two football fields. Prior to this legalization, only individuals could grow marijuana. These small farmers complained bitterly, arguing that the large firms would drive them out of the industry they helped to build due to economies of scale. Draw a figure to illustrate the situation. Under what conditions (such as relative costs, position of the demand curve, number of low-cost firms) will the smaller, higher-cost growers be driven out of business? (In 2012, the federal government brought an end to this business in Oakland. However, Colorado and Washington state passed laws permitting marijuana sales as of 2013.)

4. Competition Maximizes Economic Well-Being

*4.1. If the inverse demand function for toasters is $p = 60 - Q$, what is the consumer surplus when the price is 30?

4.2. For a firm, how does the concept of *producer surplus* differ from that of *profit* if it has no fixed costs? (*Hint:* See Q&A 8.2.)

*4.3. Using a graph similar to Figure 8.12, show that increasing output beyond the competitive level decreases total surplus because the cost of producing this extra output exceeds the value consumers place on it.

4.4. If the supply function is $Q = 10 + p$, what is the producer surplus if price is 20? (*Hint:* See Q&A 8.3.)

4.5. Use an indifference curve (Chapter 4) diagram (gift goods on one axis and all other goods on the other) to illustrate that a consumer is better off receiving cash rather than a gift. Relate your analysis to the Mini-Case "The Deadweight Loss of Christmas Presents."

4.6. The government sets a minimum wage above the current equilibrium wage. What effect does the minimum wage have on the market equilibrium? What are its effects on consumer surplus, producer surplus, and total surplus? Who are the consumers and who are the producers? (*Hint:* See Q&A 8.4.)

4.7. Suppose that the demand curve for wheat is $Q = 100 - 10p$ and the supply curve is $Q = 10p$. The government imposes a price ceiling of $p = 3$. (*Hint:* See Q&A 8.4.)

   a. Describe how the equilibrium changes.

   b. What effect does this price ceiling have on consumer surplus, producer surplus, and deadweight loss?

5. Managerial Problem

5.1. The North American Free Trade Agreement provides for two-way, long-haul trucking across the U.S.-Mexican border. U.S. truckers have objected, arguing that the Mexican trucks don't have to meet the same environmental and safety standards as U.S. trucks. They are concerned that the combination of these lower fixed costs and lower Mexican wages will result in Mexican drivers taking business from them. Their complaints have delayed implementation of this agreement (except for a small pilot program during the Bush administration, which was ended during the Obama administration). What would be the short-run and long-run effects of allowing entry of Mexican drivers on market price and quantity and on the number of U.S. truckers?

5.2. In the Managerial Solution, would it make a difference to the analysis whether the lump-sum costs such as registration fees are collected annually or only once when the firm starts operation? How would each of these franchise taxes affect the firm's long-run supply curve? Explain your answer.

5.3. Give an answer to the Managerial Problem for the short run rather than for the long run. (*Hint:* The answer depends on where the demand curve intersects the original short-run supply curve.)

5.4. In a perfectly competitive market, all firms are identical, there is free entry and exit, and an unlimited number of potential entrants. Now, the government starts collecting a specific tax t. What is the effect on the long-run equilibrium market quantity, market price, and the quantity for an individual firm?

6. Spreadsheet Exercises

6.1. A competitive firm's cost of producing q units of output is $C = 18 + 4q + q^2$. Its corresponding marginal cost is $MC = 2q + 4$.

   a. The firm faces a market price $p = \$24$. Create a spreadsheet with $q = 0, 1, 2, \ldots, 15$, where the columns are q, R, C, VC, AVC, MC, and profit. Determine the profit-maximizing output for the firm and the corresponding profit. Should the firm produce this level of output or should it shut down? Explain.

   b. Suppose the competitive price declines to $p = \$12$. Repeat the calculations of part a. Should the firm shut down?

6.2. In a competitive market, the market demand curve is $Q = 28 - 2p$ and the market supply curve is $Q_s = -8 + 2p$. Use a spreadsheet to answer the following questions.

    a. Determine the quantity demanded and quantity supplied for $p = \$4, 5, 6, \ldots, 14$. Determine the equilibrium quantity and price.

    b. For prices $p = \$4, 5, 6, \ldots, 14$, determine the consumer surplus. How does an increase in price affect the consumer surplus?

    c. For prices $p = \$4, 5, 6, \ldots, 14$, determine the producer surplus. How does an increase in price affect the producer surplus?

    d. Suppose the government limits the quantity traded in the market to 6 units. Calculate the resulting deadweight loss.

Monopoly

9

Monopoly: one parrot.

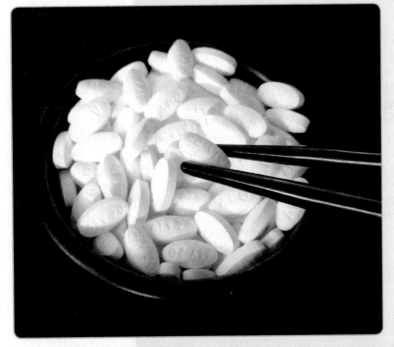

A firm that creates a new drug may receive a patent that gives it the right to be the monopoly or sole producer of the drug for up to 20 years. As a result, the firm can charge a price much greater than its marginal cost of production. For example, one of the world's best-selling drugs, the heart medication Plavix, sold for about $7 per pill but can be produced for about 3¢ per pill.

Prices for drugs used to treat rare diseases are often very high. Drugs used for certain rare types of anemia cost patients about $5,000 per year. As high as this price is, it pales in comparison with the price of over $400,000 per year for Soliris, a drug used to treat a rare blood disorder.[1]

Recently, firms have increased their prices substantially for specialty drugs in response to perceived changes in willingness to pay by consumers and their insurance companies. In 2008, the price of a crucial antiseizure drug, H.P. Acthar Gel, which is used to treat children with a rare and severe form of epilepsy, increased from $1,600 to $23,000 per vial. Two courses of Acthar treatment for a severely ill 3-year-old girl, Reegan Schwartz, cost her father's health plan about $226,000. Steve Cartt, an executive vice president at the drug's manufacturer, Questcor, explained that this price increase was based on a review of the prices of other specialty drugs and estimates of how much of the price insurers and employers would be willing to bear.

In 2013, 107 U.S. drug patents expired, including major products such as Cymbalta and OxyContin. When a patent for a highly profitable drug expires, many firms enter the market

---

[1]When asked to defend such prices, executives of pharmaceutical companies emphasize the high costs of drug development—in the hundreds of millions of dollars—that must be recouped from a relatively small number of patients with a given rare condition.

and sell generic (equivalent) versions of the brand-name drug.[2] Generics account for nearly 70% of all U.S. prescriptions and half of Canadian prescriptions.

Congress, when it passed laws permitting generic drugs to quickly enter a market after a patent expires, expected that patent expiration would subsequently lead to sharp declines in drug prices. If consumers view the generic product and the brand-name product as perfect substitutes, both goods will sell for the same price, and entry by many firms will drive the price down to the competitive level. Even if consumers view the goods as imperfect substitutes, one might expect the price of the brand-name drug to fall.

However, the prices of many brand-name drugs have increased after their patents expired and generics entered the market. The generic drugs are relatively inexpensive, but the brand-name drugs often continue to enjoy a significant market share and sell for high prices. Even after the patent for what was then the world's largest selling drug, Lipitor, expired in 2011, it continued to sell for high prices despite competition from generics selling at much lower prices. Indeed, Regan (2008), who studied the effects of generic entry on post-patent price competition for 18 prescription drugs, found an average 2% increase in brand-name prices. Studies based on older data have found up to a 7% average increase. Why do some brand-name prices rise after the entry of generic drugs?

W hy can a firm with a patent-based monopoly charge a high price? Why might a brand-name pharmaceutical's price rise after its patent expires? To answer these questions, we need to understand the decision-making process for a **monopoly**: the sole supplier of a good that has no close substitute.[3]

Monopolies have been common since ancient times. In the fifth century B.C., the Greek philosopher Thales gained control of most of the olive presses during a year of exceptionally productive harvests. The ancient Egyptian pharaohs controlled the sale of food. In England, until Parliament limited the practice in 1624, kings granted monopoly rights called royal charters to court favorites. Particularly valuable royal charters went to companies that controlled trade with North America, the Hudson Bay Company, and with India, the British East India Company.

In modern times, government actions continue to play an important role in creating monopolies. For example, governments grant patents that allow the inventor of a new product to be the sole supplier of that product for up to 20 years. Similarly, until 1999, the U.S. government gave one company the right to be the sole registrar of Internet domain names. Many public utilities are government-owned or government-protected monopolies.[4]

---

[2]Under the 1984 Hatch-Waxman Act, the U.S. government allows a firm to sell a generic product after a brand-name drug's patent expires if the generic-drug firm can prove that its product delivers the same amount of active ingredient or drug to the body in the same way as the brand-name product. Sometimes the same firm manufactures both a brand-name drug and an identical generic drug, so the two have identical ingredients. Generics produced by other firms usually differ in appearance and name from the original product and may have different nonactive ingredients but the same active ingredients.

[3]Analogously, a *monopsony* is the only *buyer* of a good in a given market.

[4]Whether the law views a firm as a monopoly depends on how broadly the market is defined. Is the market limited to a particular drug or the pharmaceutical industry as a whole? The manufacturer of the drug is a monopoly in the former case, but just one of many firms in the latter case. Thus, defining a market is critical in legal cases. A market definition depends on whether other products are good substitutes for those in that market.

Unlike a competitive firm, which is a price taker (Chapter 8), a monopoly can *set* its price. A monopoly's output is the market output, and the demand curve a monopoly faces is the market demand curve. Because the market demand curve is downward sloping, the monopoly (unlike a competitive firm) doesn't lose all its sales if it raises its price. As a consequence, a profit-maximizing monopoly sets its price above marginal cost, the price that would prevail in a competitive market. Consumers buy less at this relatively high monopoly price than they would at the competitive price.

9.1 Monopoly Profit Maximization

All firms, including competitive firms and monopolies, maximize their profits by setting quantity such that *marginal revenue equals marginal cost* (Chapter 7). Chapter 6 demonstrates how to derive a marginal cost curve. We now derive the monopoly's marginal revenue curve and then use the marginal revenue and marginal cost curves to examine how the manager of a monopoly sets quantity to maximize profit.

Marginal Revenue

A firm's marginal revenue curve depends on its demand curve. We will show that a monopoly's marginal revenue curve lies below its demand curve at any positive quantity because its demand curve is downward sloping.

Marginal Revenue and Price. A firm's demand curve shows the price, p, it receives for selling a given quantity, q. The price is the *average revenue* the firm receives, so a firm's revenue is $R = pq$.

A firm's *marginal revenue*, MR, is the change in its revenue from selling one more unit. A firm that earns ΔR more revenue when it sells Δq extra units of output has a marginal revenue of

$$MR = \frac{\Delta R}{\Delta q}.$$

If the firm sells exactly one more unit ($\Delta q = 1$), then its marginal revenue, MR, is $\Delta R (= \Delta R/1)$.

The marginal revenue of a monopoly differs from that of a competitive firm because the monopoly faces a downward-sloping demand curve, unlike the competitive firm. The competitive firm in panel a of Figure 9.1 faces a horizontal demand curve at the market price, p_1. Because its demand curve is horizontal, the competitive firm can sell another unit of output without reducing its price. As a result, the marginal revenue it receives from selling the last unit of output is the market price.

Initially, the competitive firm sells q units of output at the market price of p_1, so its revenue, R_1, is area A, which is a rectangle that is $p_1 \times q$. If the firm sells one more unit, its revenue is $R_2 = A + B$, where area B is $p_1 \times 1 = p_1$. The competitive firm's marginal revenue equals the market price:

$$\Delta R = R_2 - R_1 = (A + B) - A = B = p_1.$$

A monopoly faces a downward-sloping market demand curve, as in panel b of Figure 9.1. (So far we have used q to represent the output of a single firm and Q to represent the combined market output of all firms in a market. Because a monopoly

FIGURE 9.1 Average and Marginal Revenue

The demand curve shows the average revenue or price per unit of output sold. (a) The competitive firm's marginal revenue, area B, equals the market price, p_1. (b) The monopoly's marginal revenue is less than the price p_2 by area C, the revenue lost due to a lower price on the Q units originally sold.

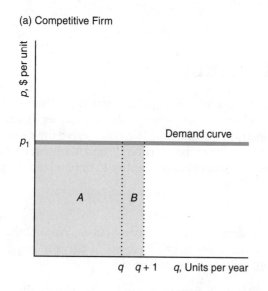

(a) Competitive Firm

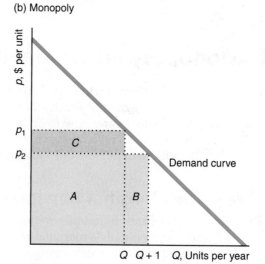

(b) Monopoly

	Initial Revenue, R_1	Revenue with One More Unit, R_2	Marginal Revenue, $R_2 - R_1$
Competition	A	$A + B$	$B = p_1$
Monopoly	$A + C$	$A + B$	$B - C = p_2 - C$

is the only firm in the market, q and Q are identical, so we use Q to describe both the firm's output and market output.

The monopoly, which initially sells Q units at p_1, can sell one extra unit only if it lowers its price to p_2 on *all* units. The monopoly's initial revenue, $p_1 \times Q$, is $R_1 = A + C$. When it sells the extra unit, its revenue, $p_2 \times (Q + 1)$, is $R_2 = A + B$. Thus, its marginal revenue is

$$\Delta R = R_2 - R_1 = (A + B) - (A + C) = B - C.$$

The monopoly sells the extra unit of output at the new price, p_2, so its extra revenue is $B = p_2 \times 1 = p_2$. The monopoly loses the difference between the new price and the original price, $\Delta p = (p_2 - p_1)$, on the Q units it originally sold: $C = \Delta p \times Q$. Therefore the monopoly's marginal revenue, $B - C = p_2 - C$, is less than the price it charges by an amount equal to area C.

Because the competitive firm in panel a can sell as many units as it wants at the market price, it does not have to cut its price to sell an extra unit, so it does not have to give up revenue such as Area C in panel b. It is the downward slope of the monopoly's demand curve that causes its marginal revenue to be less than its price. For a monopoly to sell one more unit in a given period it must lower the price on all the units it sells that period, so its marginal revenue is less than the price obtained for the extra unit. The marginal revenue is this new price minus the loss in revenue arising from charging a lower price for all other units sold.

The Marginal Revenue Curve. Thus, *the monopoly's marginal revenue curve lies below a downward-sloping demand curve* at every positive quantity. The relationship between the marginal revenue and demand curves depends on the shape of the demand curve.

For linear demand curves, the marginal revenue curve is a straight line that starts at the same point on the vertical (price) axis as the demand curve but has twice the slope. Therefore, the marginal revenue curve hits the horizontal (quantity) axis at half the quantity at which the demand curve hits the quantity axis. In Figure 9.2, the demand curve has a slope of -1 and hits the horizontal axis at 24 units, while the marginal revenue curve has a slope of -2 and hits the horizontal axis at 12 units.

We now derive an equation for the monopoly's marginal revenue curve. For a monopoly to increase its output by one unit, the monopoly lowers its price per unit by an amount indicated by the demand curve, as panel b of Figure 9.1 illustrates. Specifically, output demanded rises by one unit if price falls by the slope of the demand curve, $\Delta p / \Delta Q$. By lowering its price, the monopoly loses $(\Delta p / \Delta Q) \times Q$ on the units it originally sold at the higher price (area C), but it earns an additional p on the extra output it now sells (area B). Thus, the monopoly's marginal revenue is

$$MR = p + \frac{\Delta p}{\Delta Q} Q. \tag{9.1}$$

Because the slope of the monopoly's demand curve, $\Delta p / \Delta Q$, is negative, the last term in Equation 9.1, $(\Delta p / \Delta Q)Q$, is negative. Equation 9.1 confirms that the price is greater than the marginal revenue, which equals p plus a negative term and must therefore be less than the price.

We now use Equation 9.1 to derive the marginal revenue curve when the monopoly faces the linear inverse demand function (Chapter 3)

$$p = 24 - Q, \tag{9.2}$$

FIGURE 9.2 Elasticity of Demand and Total, Average, and Marginal Revenue

The demand curve (or average revenue curve), $p = 24 - Q$, lies above the marginal revenue curve, $MR = 24 - 2Q$. Where the marginal revenue equals zero, $Q = 12$, the elasticity of demand is $\varepsilon = -1$. For larger quantities, the marginal revenue is negative, so the MR curve is below the horizontal axis.

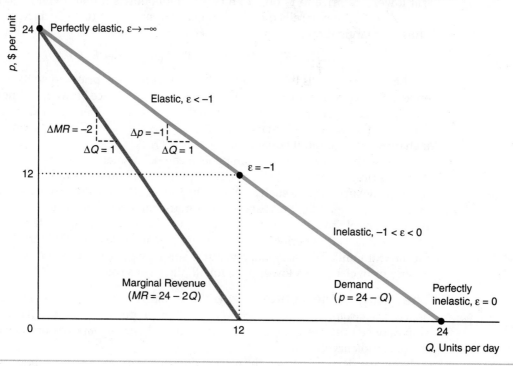

that Figure 9.2 illustrates. Equation 9.2 shows that the price consumers are willing to pay falls \$1 if quantity increases by one unit. More generally, if quantity increases by ΔQ, price falls by $\Delta p = -\Delta Q$. Thus, the slope of the demand curve is $\Delta p / \Delta Q = -1$.

We obtain the marginal revenue function for this monopoly by substituting into Equation 9.1 the actual slope of the demand function, $\Delta p / \Delta Q = -1$, and replacing p with $24 - Q$ (using Equation 9.2):

$$MR = p + \frac{\Delta p}{\Delta Q}Q = (24 - Q) + (-1)Q = 24 - 2Q. \tag{9.3}$$

Figure 9.2 shows a plot of Equation 9.3. The slope of this marginal revenue curve is $\Delta MR / \Delta Q = -2$, so the marginal revenue curve is twice as steep as the demand curve.

Using Calculus

Deriving a Monopoly's Marginal Revenue Function

Using calculus, if a firm's revenue function is $R(Q)$, then its marginal revenue function is defined as

$$MR(Q) = \frac{dR(Q)}{dQ}.$$

For our example, where the inverse demand function is $p = 24 - Q$, the revenue function is

$$R(Q) = (24 - Q)Q = 24Q - Q^2. \tag{9.4}$$

By differentiating Equation 9.4 with respect to Q, we obtain the marginal revenue function, $MR(Q) = dR(Q)/dQ = 24 - 2Q$, which is the same as Equation 9.3.

Q&A 9.1

Given a general linear inverse demand curve $p(Q) = a - bQ$, where a and b are positive constants, use calculus to show that the marginal revenue curve is twice as steeply sloped as the inverse demand curve.

Answer

1. *Differentiate a general inverse linear demand curve with respect to Q to determine its slope.* The derivative of the linear inverse demand function with respect to Q is

$$\frac{dp(Q)}{dQ} = \frac{d(a - bQ)}{dQ} = -b.$$

2. *Differentiate the monopoly's revenue function with respect to Q to obtain the marginal revenue function, then differentiate the marginal revenue function with respect to Q to determine its slope.* The monopoly's revenue function is $R(Q) = p(Q)Q = (a - bQ)Q = aQ - bQ^2$. Differentiating the revenue function with respect to quantity, we find that the marginal revenue function is linear,

$$MR(Q) = dR(Q)/dQ = a - 2bQ.$$

Thus, the slope of the marginal revenue curve,

$$\frac{dMR(Q)}{dQ} = -2b,$$

is twice that of the inverse demand curve, $dp/dQ = -b$.

Comment: Note that the vertical axis intercept is a for both the inverse demand and MR curves. Thus, if the demand curve is linear, its marginal revenue curve is twice as steep and intercepts the horizontal axis at half the quantity as does the demand curve.

Marginal Revenue and Price Elasticity of Demand. The marginal revenue at any given quantity depends on the demand curve's height (the price) and shape. The shape of the demand curve at a particular quantity is described by the price elasticity of demand (Chapter 3), $\varepsilon = (\Delta Q/Q)/(\Delta p/p) < 0$, which tells us the percentage by which quantity demanded falls as the price increases by 1%.

At a given quantity, the marginal revenue equals the price times a term involving the elasticity of demand (Chapter 3):[5]

$$MR = p\left(1 + \frac{1}{\varepsilon}\right). \tag{9.5}$$

---

[5]By multiplying the last term in Equation 9.1 by p/p ($=1$) and using algebra, we can rewrite the expression as

$$MR = p + p\frac{\Delta p}{\Delta Q}\frac{Q}{p} = p\left[1 + \frac{1}{(\Delta Q/\Delta p)(p/Q)}\right].$$

The last term in this expression is $1/\varepsilon$, because $\varepsilon = (\Delta Q/\Delta p)(p/Q)$.

According to Equation 9.5, marginal revenue is closer to price as demand becomes more elastic. Where the demand curve hits the price axis ($Q = 0$), the demand curve is perfectly elastic, so the marginal revenue equals price: $MR = p$.[6] Where the demand elasticity is unitary, $\varepsilon = -1$, marginal revenue is zero: $MR = p[1 + 1/(-1)] = 0$. Marginal revenue is negative where the demand curve is inelastic, $-1 < \varepsilon \le 0$.

With the demand function in Equation 9.2, $\Delta Q / \Delta p = -1$, so the elasticity of demand is $\varepsilon = (\Delta Q / \Delta p)(p/Q) = -p/Q$. Table 9.1 shows the relationship among quantity, price, marginal revenue, and elasticity of demand for this linear example. As Q approaches 24, ε approaches 0, and marginal revenue is negative. As Q approaches zero, the demand becomes increasingly elastic, and marginal revenue approaches the price.

Choosing Price or Quantity

Any firm maximizes its profit by operating where its marginal revenue equals its marginal cost. Unlike a competitive firm, a monopoly can adjust its price, so it has a choice of setting its price *or* its quantity to maximize its profit. (A competitive firm sets its quantity to maximize profit because it cannot affect market price.)

TABLE 9.1 Quantity, Price, Marginal Revenue, and Elasticity for the Linear Inverse Demand Function $p = 24 - Q$

Quantity, Q	Price, p	Marginal Revenue, MR	Elasticity of Demand, $\varepsilon = -p/Q$	
0	24	24	$-\infty$	↑
1	23	22	-23	
2	22	20	-11	more elastic
3	21	18	-7	
4	20	16	-5	
5	19	14	-3.8	
6	18	12	-3	
7	17	10	-2.43	
8	16	8	-2	
9	15	6	-1.67	
10	14	4	-1.4	
11	13	2	-1.18	
12	**12**	**0**	-1	
13	11	-2	-0.85	
⋮	⋮	⋮	⋮	less elastic
23	1	-22	-0.043	
24	0	-24	0	↓

---

[6] As ε approaches $-\infty$ (perfectly elastic demand), the $1/\varepsilon$ term approaches zero, so $MR = p(1 + 1/\varepsilon)$ approaches p.

Whether the monopoly sets its price or its quantity, the other variable is determined by the market demand curve. Because the demand curve slopes down, the monopoly faces a trade-off between a higher price and a lower quantity or a lower price and a higher quantity. A profit-maximizing monopoly chooses the point on the demand curve that maximizes its profit. Unfortunately for the monopoly, it cannot set both its quantity and its price, such as a point that lies above its demand curve. If it could do so, the monopoly would choose an extremely high price and an extremely large output and would earn a very high profit. However, the monopoly cannot choose a point that lies above the demand curve.

If the monopoly sets its price, the demand curve determines how much output it sells. If the monopoly picks an output level, the demand curve determines the price. Because the monopoly wants to operate at the price and output at which its profit is maximized, it chooses the same profit-maximizing solution whether it sets the price or output. Thus, setting price and setting quantity are equivalent for a monopoly. In the following discussion, we assume that the monopoly sets quantity.

Two Steps to Maximizing Profit

All profit-maximizing firms, including monopolies, use a two-step analysis to determine the output level that maximizes their profit (Chapter 7). First, the firm determines the output, Q^*, at which it makes the highest possible profit (or minimizes its loss). Second, the firm decides whether to produce Q^* or shut down.

Profit-Maximizing Output. In Chapter 7, we saw that profit is maximized where *marginal profit equals zero*. Equivalently, because *marginal profit equals marginal revenue minus marginal cost* (Chapter 7), marginal profit is zero where *marginal revenue equals marginal cost*.

To illustrate how a monopoly chooses its output to maximize its profit, we use the same linear demand and marginal revenue curves as above and add a linear marginal cost curve in panel a of Figure 9.3. Panel b shows the corresponding profit curve.

The marginal revenue curve, *MR*, intersects the marginal cost curve, *MC*, at 6 units in panel a. The corresponding price, 18, is the height of the demand curve, point *e*, at 6 units. The profit, π, is the gold rectangle. The height of this rectangle is the average profit per unit, $p - AC = 18 - 8 = 10$. The length of the rectangle is 6 units. Thus, the area of the rectangle is the average profit per unit times the number of units, which is the profit, $\pi = 60$.

The profit at 6 units is the maximum possible profit: The profit curve in panel b reaches its peak, 60, at 6 units. At the peak of the profit curve, the marginal profit is zero, which is consistent with the marginal revenue equaling the marginal cost.

Why does the monopoly maximize its profit by producing where its marginal revenue equals its marginal cost? At smaller quantities, the monopoly's marginal revenue is greater than its marginal cost, so its marginal profit is positive—the profit curve is upward sloping. By increasing its output, the monopoly raises its profit. Similarly, at quantities greater than 6 units, the monopoly's marginal cost is greater than its marginal revenue, so its marginal profit is negative, and the monopoly can increase its profit by reducing its output.

As Figure 9.2 illustrates, the marginal revenue curve is positive where the elasticity of demand is elastic, is zero at the quantity where the demand curve has a unitary

FIGURE 9.3 Maximizing Profit

(a) At $Q = 6$, where marginal revenue, MR, equals marginal cost, MC, profit is maximized. The rectangle shows that the profit is $60, where the height of the rectangle is the average profit per unit, $p - AC = \$18 - \$8 = \$10$, and the length is the number of units, 6. (b) Profit is maximized at $Q = 6$ (where marginal revenue equals marginal cost).

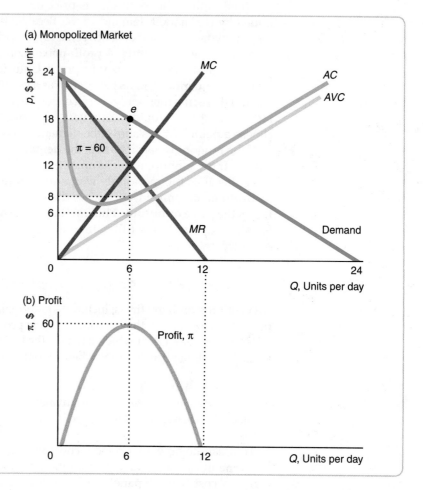

elasticity, and is negative at larger quantities where the demand curve is inelastic. Because the marginal cost curve is never negative, the marginal revenue curve can only intersect the marginal cost curve where the marginal revenue curve is positive, in the range in which the demand curve is elastic. That is, *a monopoly's profit is maximized in the elastic portion of the demand curve.* In our example, profit is maximized at $Q = 6$, where the elasticity of demand is -3. *A profit-maximizing monopoly never operates in the inelastic portion of its demand curve.*

The Shutdown Decision. A monopoly shuts down to avoid making a loss in the short run if its price is below its average variable cost at its profit-maximizing (or loss-minimizing) quantity (Chapter 7). In the long run, the monopoly shuts down if the price is less than its average cost.

In the short-run example in Figure 9.3, the average variable cost, $AVC = 6$, is less than the price, $p = 18$, at the profit-maximizing output, $Q = 6$, so the firm chooses to produce. Price is also above average cost at $Q = 6$, so the average profit per unit, $p - AC$ is positive (the height of the gold profit rectangle), so the monopoly makes a positive profit.

Using Calculus

Solving for the Profit-Maximizing Output

We can also solve for the profit-maximizing quantity mathematically. We already know the demand and marginal revenue functions for this monopoly. We need to determine its cost curves.

The monopoly's cost is a function of its output, $C(Q)$. In Figure 9.3, we assume that the monopoly faces a short-run cost function of

$$C(Q) = 12 + Q^2, \tag{9.6}$$

where Q^2 is the monopoly's variable cost as a function of output and 12 is its fixed cost. Given this cost function, Equation 9.6, the monopoly's marginal cost function is

$$\frac{dC(Q)}{dQ} = MC(Q) = 2Q. \tag{9.7}$$

This marginal cost curve in panel a is a straight line through the origin with a slope of 2. The average variable cost is $AVC = Q^2/Q = Q$, so it is a straight line through the origin with a slope of 1. The average cost is $AC = C/Q = (12 + Q^2)/Q = 12/Q + Q$, which is U-shaped.

Using Equations 9.4 and 9.6, we can write the monopoly's profit as

$$\pi(Q) = R(Q) - C(Q) = (24Q - Q^2) - (12 + Q^2).$$

By setting the derivative of this profit function with respect to Q equal to zero, we have an equation that determines the profit-maximizing output:

$$\frac{d\pi(Q)}{dQ} = \frac{dR(Q)}{dQ} - \frac{dC(Q)}{dQ}$$
$$= MR - MC$$
$$= (24 - 2Q) - 2Q = 0.$$

That is, $MR = 24 - 2Q = 2Q = MC$. To determine the profit-maximizing output, we solve this equation and find that $Q = 6$. Substituting $Q = 6$ into the inverse demand function (Equation 9.2), we learn that the profit-maximizing price is

$$p = 24 - Q = 24 - 6 = 18.$$

Should the monopoly operate at $Q = 6$? At that quantity, average variable cost is $AVC = Q^2/Q = 6$, which is less than the price, so the firm does not shut down. The average cost is $AC = (6 + 12/6) = 8$, which is less than the price, so the firm makes a profit.

Effects of a Shift of the Demand Curve

Shifts in the demand curve or marginal cost curve affect the profit-maximizing monopoly price and quantity and can have a wider variety of effects with a monopoly than with a competitive market. In a competitive market, the effect of a shift in demand on a competitive firm's output depends only on the shape of the marginal cost curve. In contrast, the effect of a shift in demand on a monopoly's output depends on the shapes of both the marginal cost curve and the demand curve.

As we saw in Chapter 8, a competitive firm's marginal cost curve tells us everything we need to know about the amount that the firm is willing to supply at any given market price. The competitive firm's supply curve is its upward-sloping marginal cost curve above its minimum average variable cost. A competitive firm's supply behavior does not depend on the shape of the market demand curve because it always faces a horizontal demand curve at the market price. Thus, if we know a competitive firm's marginal cost curve, we can predict how much that firm will produce at any given market price.

In contrast, a monopoly's output decision depends on the shapes of its marginal cost curve and its demand curve. Unlike a competitive firm, *a monopoly does not have a supply curve.* Knowing the monopoly's marginal cost curve is not enough for us to predict how much a monopoly will sell at any given price.

Figure 9.4 illustrates that the relationship between price and quantity is unique in a competitive market but not in a monopolistic market. If the market is competitive, the initial equilibrium is e_1 in panel a, where the original demand curve D^1 intersects the supply curve, MC, which is the sum of the marginal cost curves of a large number of competitive firms. When the demand curve shifts to D^2, the new competitive equilibrium, e_2, has a higher price and quantity. A shift of the demand curve maps out competitive equilibria along the marginal cost curve, so every equilibrium quantity has a single corresponding equilibrium price.

For the monopoly in panel b, as the demand curve shifts from D^1 to D^2, the profit-maximizing monopoly outcome shifts from E_1 to E_2, so the price rises but the quantity stays constant, $Q_1 = Q_2$. Thus, *a given quantity can correspond to more than one profit-maximizing price*, depending on the position of the demand curve. A shift in

FIGURE 9.4 Effects of a Shift of the Demand Curve

(a) A shift of the demand curve from D^1 to D^2 causes the competitive equilibrium to move from e_1 to e_2 along the supply curve (which is the horizontal sum of the marginal cost curves of all the competitive firms). Because the competitive equilibrium lies on the supply curve, each quantity (such as Q_1 and Q_2) corresponds to only one possible equilibrium price. (b) With a monopoly, this same shift of demand causes the monopoly optimum to change from E_1 to E_2. The monopoly quantity stays the same, but the monopoly price rises. Thus, a shift in demand does not map out a unique relationship between price and quantity in a monopolized market. The same quantity, $Q_1 = Q_2$, is associated with two different prices, p_1 and p_2.

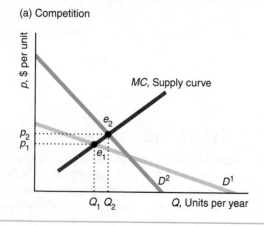

(a) Competition

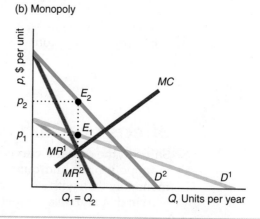

(b) Monopoly

the demand curve may cause the profit-maximizing price to stay constant while the quantity changes. More commonly, both the profit-maximizing price and quantity would change.

9.2 Market Power

A monopoly has **market power**, which is the ability to significantly affect the market price. In contrast, no single competitive firm can significantly affect the market price.

A profit-maximizing monopoly charges a price that exceeds its marginal cost. The extent to which the monopoly price exceeds marginal cost depends on the shape of the demand curve.

Market Power and the Shape of the Demand Curve

If the monopoly faces a highly elastic—nearly flat—demand curve at the profit-maximizing quantity, it would lose substantial sales if it raised its price by even a small amount. Conversely, if the demand curve is not very elastic (relatively steep) at that quantity, the monopoly would lose fewer sales from raising its price by the same amount.

We can derive the relationship between markup of price over marginal cost and the elasticity of demand at the profit-maximizing quantity using the expression for marginal revenue in Equation 9.5 and the firm's profit-maximizing condition that marginal revenue equals marginal cost:

$$MR = p\left(1 + \frac{1}{\varepsilon}\right) = MC. \tag{9.8}$$

By rearranging terms, we see that a profit-maximizing manager chooses quantity such that

$$\frac{p}{MC} = \frac{1}{1 + (1/\varepsilon)}. \tag{9.9}$$

In our linear demand example in panel a of Figure 9.3, the elasticity of demand is $\varepsilon = -3$ at the monopoly optimum where $Q = 6$. As a result, the ratio of price to marginal cost is $p/MC = 1/[1 + 1/(-3)] = 1.5$, or $p = 1.5MC$. The profit-maximizing price, $18, in panel a is 1.5 times the marginal cost of $12.

Table 9.2 illustrates how the ratio of price to marginal cost varies with the elasticity of demand. When the elasticity is -1.01, only slightly elastic, the monopoly's profit-maximizing price is 101 times larger than its marginal cost: $p/MC = 1/[1 + 1/(-1.01)] \approx 101$. As the elasticity of demand approaches negative infinity (becomes perfectly elastic), the ratio of price to marginal cost shrinks to $p/MC = 1.$[7] Thus, even in the absence of rivals, the shape of the demand curve constrains the monopolist's ability to exercise market power.

---

[7]As the elasticity approaches negative infinity, $1/\varepsilon$ approaches zero, so $1/(1 + 1/\varepsilon)$ approaches $1/1 = 1$.

TABLE 9.2 Elasticity of Demand, Price, and Marginal Cost

Elasticity of Demand, ε	Price/Marginal Cost Ratio, $p/MC = 1/[1 + (1/ε)]$	Lerner Index, $(p - MC)/p = -1/ε$
−1.01	101	0.99
−1.1	11	0.91
−2	2	0.5
−3	1.5	0.33
−5	1.25	0.2
−10	1.11	0.1
−100	1.01	0.01
−∞	1	0

(↑ less elastic, more elastic ↓)

Managerial Implication

Checking Whether the Firm Is Maximizing Profit

A manager can use this last result to determine whether the firm is maximizing its profit. Typically a monopoly knows its costs accurately, but is somewhat uncertain about the demand curve it faces and hence what price (or quantity) to set. Many private firms—such as ACNielsen, IRI, and IMS Health—and industry groups collect data on quantities and prices in a wide variety of industries including automobiles, foods and beverages, drugs, and many services. Firms can use these data to estimate the firm's demand curve (Chapter 3). More commonly, firms hire consulting firms (often the same firms that collect data) to estimate the elasticity of demand facing their firm.

A manager can use the estimated elasticity of demand to check whether the firm is maximizing profit. If the p/MC ratio does not approximately equal $1/(1 + 1/ε)$, as required by Equation 9.9, then the manager knows that the firm is not setting its price to maximize its profit. Of course, the manager can also check whether the firm is maximizing profit by varying its price or quantity. However, often such experiments may be more costly than using statistical techniques to estimate the elasticity of demand.

Mini-Case

Cable Cars and Profit Maximization

Since San Francisco's cable car system started operating in 1873, it has been one of the city's main tourist attractions. In 2005, the cash-strapped Municipal Railway raised the one-way fare by two-thirds from $3 to $5. Not surprisingly, the number of riders dropped substantially, and many in the city called for a rate reduction.

The rate increase prompted many locals to switch to buses or other forms of transportation, but most tourists have a relatively inelastic demand curve for cable car rides. Frank Bernstein of Arizona, who visited San Francisco with his wife, two children, and mother-in-law, said they would not visit San Francisco without riding a cable car: "That's what you do when you're here." But the round-trip $50 cost for his family to ride a cable car from the Powell Street turnaround to Fisherman's Wharf and back "is a lot of money for our family. We'll do it once, but we won't do it again."

If the city ran the cable car system like a profit-maximizing monopoly, the decision to raise fares would be clear. The 67% rate hike resulted in a 23% increase in revenue to $9,045,792 in the 2005–2006 fiscal year. Given that the revenue increased when the price rose, the city must have been operating in the inelastic portion of its demand curve ($\varepsilon > -1$), where $MR = p(1 + 1/\varepsilon) < 0$ prior to the fare increase.[8] With fewer riders, costs stayed constant (they would have fallen if the city had decided to run fewer than its traditional 40 cars), so the city's profit increased given the increase in revenue. Presumably the profit-maximizing price is even higher in the elastic portion of the demand curve.

However, the city may not be interested in maximizing its profit on the cable cars. At the time, then-Mayor Gavin Newsom said that having fewer riders "was my biggest fear when we raised the fare. I think we're right at the cusp of losing visitors who come to San Francisco and want to enjoy a ride on a cable car." The mayor said that he believed keeping the price of a cable car ride relatively low helps attract tourists to the city, thereby benefiting many local businesses. Newsom observed, "Cable cars are so fundamental to the lifeblood of the city, and they represent so much more than the revenue they bring in." The mayor decided to continue to run the cable cars at a price below the profit-maximizing level. The fare stayed at $5 for six years, then rose to $6 in 2011 and has stayed there through at least the first half of 2013.

The Lerner Index

Another way to show how the elasticity of demand affects a monopoly's price relative to its marginal cost is to look at the firm's **Lerner Index** (or *price markup*)—the ratio of the difference between price and marginal cost to the price: $(p - MC)/p$. This index can be calculated for any firm, whether or not the firm is a monopoly. The Lerner Index is zero for a competitive firm because a competitive firm produces where marginal cost equals price. The Lerner Index measures a firm's market power: the larger the difference between price and marginal cost, the larger the Lerner Index.

If the firm is maximizing its profit, we can express the Lerner Index in terms of the elasticity of demand by rearranging Equation 9.9:

$$\frac{p - MC}{p} = -\frac{1}{\varepsilon}. \tag{9.10}$$

[8]The marginal revenue is the slope of the revenue function. Thus, if a reduction in quantity causes the revenue to increase, the marginal revenue must be negative. As Figure 9.2 illustrates, marginal revenue is negative in the inelastic portion of the demand curve.

The Lerner Index ranges between 0 and 1 for a profit-maximizing monopoly.[9] Equation 9.10 confirms that a competitive firm has a Lerner Index of zero because its demand curve is perfectly elastic.[10] As Table 9.2 illustrates, the Lerner Index for a monopoly increases as the demand becomes less elastic. If $\varepsilon = -5$, the monopoly's markup (Lerner Index) is $1/5 = 0.2$; if $\varepsilon = -2$, the markup is $1/2 = 0.5$; and if $\varepsilon = -1.01$, the markup is 0.99. Monopolies that face demand curves that are only slightly elastic set prices that are multiples of their marginal cost and have Lerner Indexes close to 1.

Mini-Case

Apple's iPad

Apple started selling the iPad on April 3, 2010. The iPad was not the first tablet. Indeed, it wasn't Apple's first tablet: Apple sold another tablet, the Newton, from 1993–1998. But it was the most elegant one, and the first one large numbers of consumers wanted to own. Users interact with the iPad using Apple's multi-touch, finger-sensitive touchscreen (rather than a pressure-triggered stylus that most previous tablets used) and a virtual onscreen keyboard (rather than a physical one). Most importantly, the iPad offered an intuitive interface and was very well integrated with Apple's iTunes, eBooks, and various application programs.

People loved the original iPad. Even at $499 for the basic model, Apple had a virtual monopoly in its first year. According to the research firm IDC, Apple's share of the 2010 tablet market was 87%. Moreover, the other tablets available in 2010 were not viewed by most consumers as close substitutes. Apple reported that it sold 25 million iPads worldwide in its first full year, 2010–2011. According to one estimate, the basic iPad's marginal cost was $MC = \$220$, so its Lerner Index was $(p - MC)/p = (499 - 220)/499 = 0.56$.

Within a year of the iPad's introduction, over a hundred iPad want-to-be tablets were launched. To maintain its dominance, Apple replaced the original iPad with the feature-rich iPad 2 in 2011, added the enhanced iPad 3 in 2012, and cut the price of the iPad 2 by $100 in 2012. According to court documents Apple filed in 2012, its Lerner Index fell to between 0.23 and 0.32.

Industry experts believe that Apple can produce tablets at far lower cost than most if not all of its competitors. Apple has formed strategic partnerships with other companies to buy large supplies of components, securing a lower price from suppliers than its competitors. Using its own patents, Apple avoids paying as many licensing fees as do other firms.

Copycat competitors with 10" screens have gained some market share from Apple. More basic tablets with smaller 7" screens that are little more than e-readers have sold a substantial number of units, so that the iPad's share of the total tablet market was 68% in the first quarter of 2012.

---

[9]For the Lerner Index to be above 1 in Equation 9.10, ε would have to be a negative fraction, indicating that the demand curve was inelastic at the monopoly's output choice. However, as we've already seen, a profit-maximizing monopoly never operates in the inelastic portion of its demand curve.

[10]As the elasticity of demand approaches negative infinity, the Lerner Index, $-1/\varepsilon$, approaches zero.

Q&A 9.2	When the iPad was introduced, Apple's constant marginal cost of producing this iPad was about \$220. We estimate that Apple's inverse demand function for the iPad was $p = 770 - 11Q$, where Q is the millions of iPads purchased.[11] What was Apple's marginal revenue function? What were its profit-maximizing price and quantity? Given that the Lerner Index for the iPad was $(p - MC)/p = 0.56$ (see the "Apple's iPad" Mini-Case), what was the elasticity of demand at the profit-maximizing level?

Answer

1. *Derive Apple's marginal revenue function using the information about its demand function.* Given that Apple's inverse demand function was linear, $p = 770 - 11Q$, its marginal revenue function has the same intercept and twice the slope: $MR = 770 - 22Q$.[12]

2. *Derive Apple's profit-maximizing quantity and price by equating the marginal revenue and marginal cost functions and solving.* Apple maximized its profit where $MR = MC$:

$$770 - 22Q = 220.$$

Solving this equation for the profit-maximizing output, we find that $Q = 25$ million iPads. By substituting this quantity into the inverse demand function, we determine that the profit-maximizing price was $p = \$495$ per unit.

3. *Use Equation 9.10 to infer Apple's demand elasticity based on its Lerner Index.* We can write Equation 9.10 as $(p - MC)/p = 0.56 = -1/\varepsilon$. Solving this last equality for ε, we find that $\varepsilon \approx -1.79$. (Of course, we could also calculate the demand elasticity by using the demand function.)

Sources of Market Power

What factors cause a monopoly to face a relatively elastic demand curve and hence have little market power? Ultimately, the elasticity of demand of the market demand curve depends on consumers' tastes and options. The more consumers want a good—the more willing they are to pay "virtually anything" for it—the less elastic is the demand curve.

Other things equal, the demand curve a firm (not necessarily a monopoly) faces becomes more elastic as (1) *better substitutes* for the firm's product are introduced, (2) *more firms* enter the market selling the same product, or (3) firms that provide the same service *locate closer* to this firm. The demand curves for Xerox, the U.S. Postal Service, and McDonald's have become more elastic in recent decades for these three reasons.

When Xerox started selling its plain-paper copier, no other firm sold a close substitute. Other companies' machines produced copies on special heat-sensitive paper

---

[11]See the Sources for "Pricing Apple's iPad" for details on these estimates.

[12]Alternatively, we can use calculus to derive the marginal revenue curve. Multiplying the inverse demand function by Q to obtain Apple's revenue function, $R = 770Q - 11Q^2$. Then, we derive the marginal revenue function by differentiating the revenue with respect to quantity: $MR = dR/dQ = 770 - 22Q$.

*Of course you could get it done for less
if I weren't the only plumber in town.*

that yellowed quickly. As other firms developed plain-paper copiers, the demand curve that Xerox faced became more elastic.

In the past, the U.S. Postal Service (USPS) had a monopoly in overnight delivery services. Now FedEx, United Parcel Service, and many other firms compete with the USPS in providing overnight deliveries. Because of these increases in competition, the USPS's share of business and personal correspondence fell from 77% in 1988 to 59% in 1996. Its total mail volume fell 40% from 2006 to 2010. Its overnight market fell to 15% by 2010.[13] Compared to when it was a monopoly, the USPS's demand curves for first-class mail and package delivery have shifted downward and become more elastic.

As you drive down a highway, you may notice that McDonald's restaurants are located miles apart. The purpose of this spacing is to reduce the likelihood that two McDonald's outlets will compete for the same customer. Although McDonald's can prevent its own restaurants from competing with each other, it cannot prevent Wendy's or Burger King from locating near its restaurants. As other fast-food restaurants open near a McDonald's, that restaurant faces a more elastic demand. What happens as a profit-maximizing monopoly faces more elastic demand? It has to lower its price.

9.3 Market Failure Due to Monopoly Pricing

Unlike perfect competition, which achieves *economic efficiency*—that is, maximizes total surplus, *TS* (= consumer surplus + producer surplus = *CS* + *PS*)—a profit-maximizing monopoly is economically inefficient because it wastes potential surplus, resulting in a deadweight loss. The inefficiency of monopoly pricing is an example of a **market failure**: a non-optimal allocation of goods and services such that a market does not achieve economic efficiency. Market failure often occurs because the price differs from the marginal cost, as with a monopoly. This economic inefficiency creates a rationale for governments to intervene, as we discuss in Chapter 16.

Total surplus (Chapter 8) is lower under monopoly than under competition. That is, monopoly destroys some of the potential gains from trade. Chapter 8 showed that competition maximizes total surplus because price equals marginal cost. By setting its price above its marginal cost, a monopoly causes consumers to buy less than the competitive level of the good, so society suffers a deadweight loss.

If the monopoly were to act like a competitive market, it would produce where the marginal cost curve cuts the demand curve—the output where price equals marginal

---

[13]Peter Passell, "Battered by Its Rivals," *New York Times*, May 15, 1997, C1; Grace Wyler, "11 Things You Should Know about the U.S. Postal Service Before It Goes Bankrupt," *Business Insider*, May 31, 2011; "The U.S. Postal Service Nears Collapse," *BloombergBusinessweek*, May 26, 2011; **www.economicfreedom.org/2012/12/12/stamping-out-waste**.

cost. For example, using the demand curve given by Equation 9.2 and the marginal cost curve given by Equation 9.7,

$$p = 24 - Q = 2Q = MC.$$

Solving this equation, we find that the competitive quantity, Q_c, would be 8 units and the price would be $16, as Figure 9.5 shows. At this competitive price, consumer surplus is area $A + B + C$ and producer surplus is $D + E$.

If instead the firm acts like a profit-maximizing monopoly and operates where its marginal revenue equals its marginal cost, the monopoly output Q_m is only 6 units and the monopoly price is $18. Consumer surplus is only A. Part of the lost consumer surplus, B, goes to the monopoly, but the rest, C, is lost. The benefit of being a monopoly is that it allows the firm to extract some consumer surplus from consumers and convert it to profit.

By charging the monopoly price of $18 instead of the competitive price of $16, the monopoly receives $2 more per unit and earns an extra profit of area $B = $12 on the

FIGURE 9.5 Deadweight Loss of Monopoly

A competitive market would produce $Q_c = 8$ at $p_c = $16, where the demand curve intersects the marginal cost (supply) curve. A monopoly produces only $Q_m = 6$ at $p_m = $18, where the marginal revenue curve intersects the marginal cost curve. Under monopoly, consumer surplus is A, producer surplus is $B + D$, and the inefficiency or deadweight loss of monopoly is $-C - E$.

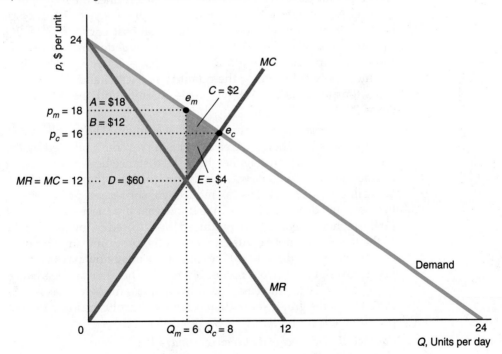

	Competition	Monopoly	Change
Consumer Surplus, CS	$A + B + C$	A	$-B - C = \Delta CS$
Producer Surplus, PS	$D + E$	$B + D$	$B - E = \Delta PS$
Total Surplus, $TS = CS + PS$	$A + B + C + D + E$	$A + B + D$	$-C - E = \Delta TS = DWL$

$Q_m = 6$ units it sells. The monopoly loses area E, however, because it sells less than the competitive output. Consequently, the monopoly's producer surplus increases by $B - E$ over the competitive level. Monopoly pricing increases producer surplus relative to competition.

Total surplus is less under monopoly than under competition. The deadweight loss of monopoly is $-C - E$, which represents the potential surplus that is wasted because less than the competitive output is produced. The deadweight loss is due to the gap between price and marginal cost at the monopoly output. At $Q_m = 6$, the price, \$18, is above the marginal cost, \$12, so consumers are willing to pay more for the last unit of output than it costs to produce it.

Q&A 9.3

In the linear example in panel a of Figure 9.3, how does charging the monopoly a specific tax of $\tau = \$8$ per unit affect the profit-maximizing price and quantity and the well-being of consumers, the monopoly, and society (where total surplus includes the tax revenue)? What is the tax incidence on consumers (the increase in the price they pay as a fraction of the tax)?

Answer

1. *Determine how imposing the tax affects the monopoly price and quantity.* In the accompanying graph, the intersection of the marginal revenue curve, MR, and the before-tax marginal cost curve, MC^1, determines the monopoly quantity, $Q_1 = 6$. At the before-tax solution, e_1, the price is $p_1 = 18$. The specific tax causes the monopoly's before-tax marginal cost curve, $MC^1 = 2Q$, to shift upward by 8 to $MC^2 = MC^1 + 8 = 2Q + 8$. After the tax is applied, the monopoly operates where $MR = 24 - 2Q = 2Q + 8 = MC^2$. In the after-tax monopoly solution, e_2, the quantity is $Q_2 = 4$ and the price is $p_2 = 20$. Thus, output falls by $\Delta Q = 6 - 4 = 2$ units and the price increases by $\Delta p = 20 - 18 = 2$.

2. *Calculate the change in the various surplus measures.* The graph shows how the surplus measures change. Area G is the tax revenue collected by the government, $\tau Q = 32$, because its height is the distance between the two marginal cost curves, $\tau = 8$, and its width is the output the monopoly produces after the tax is imposed, $Q = 4$. The tax reduces consumer and producer surplus and increases the deadweight loss. We know that producer surplus falls because (a) the monopoly could have produced this reduced output level in the absence of the tax but did not because it was not the profit-maximizing output, so its before-tax profit falls, and (b) the monopoly must now pay taxes. The before-tax deadweight loss from monopoly is $-F$. The after-tax deadweight loss is $-C - E - F$, so the increase in deadweight loss due to the tax is $-C - E$. The table below the graph shows that consumer surplus changes by $-B - C$ and producer surplus by $B - E - G$.

3. *Calculate the incidence of the tax on consumers.* Because the tax goes from 0 to 8, the change in the tax is $\Delta \tau = 8$. Because the change in the price that the consumer pays is $\Delta p = 2$, the share of the tax paid by consumers is $\Delta p / \Delta \tau = 2/8 = \frac{1}{4}$. Thus, the monopoly absorbs \$6 of the tax and passes on only \$2.

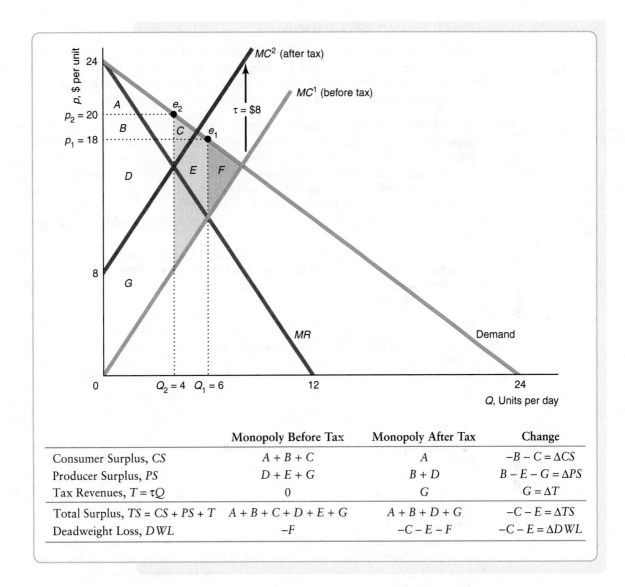

	Monopoly Before Tax	Monopoly After Tax	Change
Consumer Surplus, CS	$A + B + C$	A	$-B - C = \Delta CS$
Producer Surplus, PS	$D + E + G$	$B + D$	$B - E - G = \Delta PS$
Tax Revenues, $T = \tau Q$	0	G	$G = \Delta T$
Total Surplus, $TS = CS + PS + T$	$A + B + C + D + E + G$	$A + B + D + G$	$-C - E = \Delta TS$
Deadweight Loss, DWL	$-F$	$-C - E - F$	$-C - E = \Delta DWL$

9.4 Causes of Monopoly

Why are some markets monopolized? The two most important reasons are cost considerations and government policy.[14]

---

[14]In later chapters, we discuss other means by which monopolies are created. One method is the merger of several firms into a single firm. This method creates a monopoly if new firms fail to enter the market. A second method is for a monopoly to use strategies that discourage other firms from entering the market. A third possibility is that firms coordinate their activities and set their prices as a monopoly would. Firms that act collectively in this way are called a *cartel* rather than a monopoly.

Cost-Based Monopoly

Certain cost structures may facilitate the creation of a monopoly. One possibility is that a firm may have substantially lower costs than potential rivals. A second possibility is that the firms in an industry have cost functions such that one firm can produce any given output at a lower cost than two or more firms can.

Cost Advantages. If a low-cost firm profitably sells at a price so low that other potential competitors with higher costs would lose money, no other firms enter the market. Thus, the low-cost firm is a monopoly. A firm can have a cost advantage over potential rivals for several reasons. It may have a superior technology or a better way of organizing production.[15] For example, Henry Ford's methods of organizing production using assembly lines and standardization allowed him to produce cars at substantially lower cost than rival firms until they copied his organizational techniques.

If a firm controls an essential facility or a scarce resource that is needed to produce a particular output, no other firm can produce at all—at least not at a reasonable cost. For example, a firm that owns the only quarry in a region is the only firm that can profitably sell gravel to local construction firms.

Natural Monopoly. A market has a **natural monopoly** if one firm can produce the total output of the market at lower cost than two or more firms could. A firm can be a natural monopoly even if it does not have a cost advantage over rivals provided that average cost is lower if only one firm operates. Specifically, if the cost for any firm to produce q is $C(q)$, the condition for a natural monopoly is

$$C(Q) < C(q_1) + C(q_2) + \cdots + C(q_n), \tag{9.11}$$

where $Q = q_1 + q_2 + \cdots + q_n$ is the sum of the output of any n firms where $n \geq 2$ firms.

If a firm has economies of scale at all levels of output, its average cost curve falls as output increases for any observed level of output. If all potential firms have the same strictly declining average cost curve, this market is a natural monopoly, as we now illustrate.[16]

A company that supplies water to homes incurs a high fixed cost, F, to build a plant and connect houses to the plant. The firm's marginal cost, m, of supplying water is constant, so its marginal cost curve is horizontal and its average cost, $AC = m + F/Q$, declines as output rises.

Figure 9.6 shows such marginal and average cost curves where $m = 10$ and $F = 60$. If the market output is 12 units per day, one firm produces that output

---

[15]When a firm develops a better production method that provides it with a cost advantage, it is important for the firm to either keep the information secret or obtain a patent, whereby the government protects it from having its innovation imitated. Thus, both secrecy and patents facilitate cost-based monopolies.

[16]A firm may be a natural monopoly even if its cost curve does not fall at all levels of output. If a U-shaped average cost curve reaches its minimum at 100 units of output, it may be less costly for only one firm to produce an output of 101 units even though average cost is rising at that output. Thus, a cost function with economies of scale everywhere is a sufficient but not a necessary condition for a natural monopoly.

FIGURE 9.6 Natural Monopoly

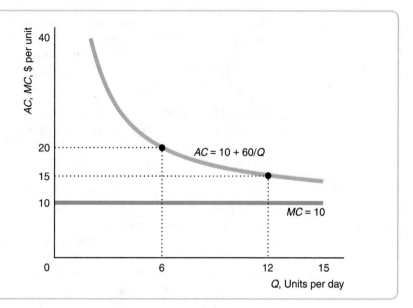

This natural monopoly has a strictly declining average cost, $AC = 10 + 60/Q$.

$AC = 10 + 60/Q$

$MC = 10$

at an average cost of 15, or a total cost of 180 ($= 15 \times 12$). If two firms each produce 6 units, the average cost is 20 and the cost of producing the market output is 240 ($= 20 \times 12$), which is greater than the cost with a single firm.

If the two firms divided total production in any other way, their cost of production would still exceed the cost of a single firm (as the following question asks you to prove). The reason is that the marginal cost per unit is the same no matter how many firms produce, but each additional firm adds a fixed cost, which raises the cost of producing a given quantity. If only one firm provides water, the cost of building a second plant and a second set of pipes is avoided.

In an industry with a natural monopoly cost structure, having just one firm is the cheapest way to produce any given output level. Governments often use a natural monopoly argument to justify their granting the right to be a monopoly to *public utilities*, which provide essential goods or services such as water, gas, electric power, or mail delivery.

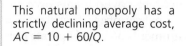

Q&A 9.4

A firm that delivers Q units of water to households has a total cost of $C(Q) = mQ + F$. If any entrant would have the same cost, does this market have a natural monopoly?

Answer

Determine whether costs rise if two firms produce a given quantity. Let q_1 be the output of Firm 1 and q_2 be the output of Firm 2. The combined cost of these two firms producing $Q = q_1 + q_2$ is

$$C(q_1) + C(q_2) = (mq_1 + F) + (mq_2 + F) = m(q_1 + q_2) + 2F = mQ + 2F.$$

If a single firm produces Q, its cost is $C(Q) = mQ + F$. Thus, the cost of producing any given Q is greater with two firms than with one firm (the condition in Equation 9.11), so this market is a natural monopoly.

Government Creation of Monopoly

Governments have created many monopolies. Sometimes governments own and manage such monopolies. In the United States, as in most countries, first class mail delivery is a government monopoly. Many local governments own and operate public utility monopolies that provide garbage collection, electricity, water, gas, phone services, and other utilities.

Barriers to Entry. Frequently governments create monopolies by preventing competing firms from entering a market occupied by an existing incumbent firm. Several countries, such as China, maintain a tobacco monopoly. Similarly, most governments grant patents that limit entry and allow the patent-holding firm to earn a monopoly profit from an invention—a reward for developing the new product that acts as an incentive for research and development.

By preventing other firms from entering a market, governments create monopolies. Typically, governments create monopolies either by making it difficult for new firms to obtain a license to operate or by explicitly granting a monopoly right to one firm, thereby excluding other firms. By auctioning a monopoly right to a private firm, a government can capture the future value of monopoly earnings.[17]

Frequently, firms need government licenses to operate. If one initial incumbent has a license and governments make it difficult for new firms to obtain licenses, the incumbent firm may maintain its monopoly for a substantial period. Until recently, many U.S. cities required that new hospitals or other inpatient facilities demonstrate the need for a new facility to obtain a certificate of need, which allowed them to enter the market.

Government grants of monopoly rights have been common for public utilities. Instead of running a public utility itself, a government might give a private sector company the monopoly rights to operate the utility. A government may capture some of the monopoly profits by charging the firm in some way for its monopoly rights. In many countries or other political jurisdictions, such a system is an inducement to bribery as public officials may be bribed by firms seeking monopoly privileges.

Governments around the world have privatized many state-owned monopolies in the past several decades. By selling cable television, garbage collection, phone service, towing, and other monopolies to private firms, a government can capture the value of future monopoly earnings today. However, for political or other reasons, governments frequently sell at a lower price that does not capture all future profits.

Patents. If an innovating firm cannot prevent imitation by keeping its discoveries secret, it may try to obtain government protection to prevent other firms from duplicating its discovery and entering the market. Most countries provide such protection through patents. A **patent** is an exclusive right granted to the inventor of a new and useful product, process, substance, or design for a specified length of time. The length of a patent varies across countries, although it is now 20 years in the United States and in most other countries.

This right allows the patent holder to be the exclusive seller or user of the new invention.[18] Patents often give rise to monopoly, but not always. For example,

[17]Alternatively, a government could auction the rights to the firm that offers to charge the lowest price, so as to maximize total surplus.

[18]Owners of patents may sell or grant the right to use a patented process or produce a patented product to other firms. This practice is called *licensing*.

although a patent may grant a firm the exclusive right to use a particular process in producing a product, other firms may be able to produce the same product using different processes. In Chapter 16, we discuss the reasons why governments grant patents.

Mini-Case	

Botox

Ophthalmologist Dr. Alan Scott turned the deadly poison botulinum toxin into a miracle drug to treat two eye conditions: strabismus, which affects about 4% of children, and blepharospasm, an uncontrollable closure of the eyes. Blepharospasm left about 25,000 Americans functionally blind before Scott's discovery. His patented drug, Botox, is sold by Allergan, Inc.

Dr. Scott has been amused to see several of the unintended beneficiaries of his research at the Academy Awards. Even before it was explicitly approved for cosmetic use, many doctors were injecting Botox into the facial muscles of actors, models, and others to smooth out their wrinkles. (The drug paralyzes the muscles, so those injected with it also lose the ability to frown—and, some would say, to act.) The treatment is only temporary, lasting up to 120 days, so repeated injections are necessary. Allergan had expected to sell $400 million worth of Botox in 2002. However, in April of that year, the U.S. Food and Drug Administration approved the use of Botox for cosmetic purposes, a ruling that allows the company to advertise the drug widely.

Allergan had Botox sales of $800 million in 2004 and about $1.8 billion in 2012. Allergan has a near-monopoly in the treatment of wrinkles, although plastic surgery and collagen, Restylane, hyaluronic acids, and other filler injections provide limited competition. Between 2002 and 2004, the number of facelifts dropped 3% to about 114,000 according to the American Society of Plastic Surgeons, while the number of Botox injections skyrocketed 166% to nearly 3 million.

Dr. Scott says that he can produce a vial of Botox in his lab for about $25. Allergan then sells the potion to doctors for about $400. Assuming that the firm is setting its price to maximize its short-run profit, we can rearrange Equation 9.10 to determine the elasticity of demand for Botox:

$$\varepsilon = -\frac{p}{p - MC} = -\frac{400}{400 - 25} \approx -1.067.$$

Thus, the demand that Allergan faces is only slightly elastic: A 1% increase in price causes quantity to fall by only a little more than 1%.

If we assume that the demand curve is linear and that the elasticity of demand is -1.067 at the 2002 monopoly optimum, e_m (one million vials sold at $400 each, producing revenue of $400 million), then Allergan's inverse demand function is

$$p = 775 - 375Q.$$

This demand curve (see graph) has a slope of -375 and hits the price axis at $775 and the quantity axis at about 2.07 million vials per year. The corresponding marginal revenue curve,

$$MR = 775 - 750Q,$$

intersects the price axis at $775 and has twice the slope, -750, as the demand curve.

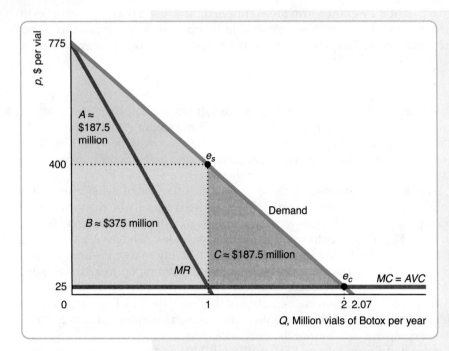

At the point where the *MR* and *MC* curves intersect, *MR* = *MC*. Therefore,

$$775 - 750Q = 25.$$

We can then solve for the profit-maximizing quantity of 1 million vials per year and the associated price of $400 per vial.

Were the company to sell Botox at a price equal to its marginal cost of $25 (as a competitive industry would), consumer surplus would equal areas *A* + *B* + *C* = $750 million per year. At the higher monopoly price of $400, the consumer surplus is *A* = $187.5 million. Compared to the competitive solution, e_c, buyers lose consumer surplus of *B* + *C* = $562.5 million per year. Part of this loss, *B* = $375 million per year, is transferred from consumers to Allergan. The rest, *C* = $187.5 million per year, is the deadweight loss from monopoly pricing. Allergan's profit is its producer surplus, *B*, minus its fixed costs.

9.5 Advertising

You can fool all the people all the time if the advertising is right and the budget is big enough. —Joseph E. Levine (film producer)

In addition to setting prices or quantities and choosing investments, firms engage in many other strategic actions to boost their profits. One of the most important is advertising. By advertising, a monopoly can shift its demand curve, which may allow it to sell more units at a higher price. In contrast, a competitive firm has no incentive to advertise as it can sell as many units as it wants at the going price without advertising.

Advertising is only one way to promote a product. Other promotional activities include providing free samples and using sales agents. Some promotional tactics are subtle. For example, grocery stores place sugary breakfast cereals on lower shelves so that they are at children's eye level. According to a survey of 27 supermarkets nationwide by the Center for Science in the Public Interest, the average position of 10 child-appealing brands (44% sugar) was on the next-to-bottom shelf, while the average position of 10 adult brands (10% sugar) was on the next-to-top shelf.

A monopoly advertises to raise its profit. A successful advertising campaign shifts the market demand curve by changing consumers' tastes or informing them about new products. The monopoly may be able to change the tastes of some consumers by telling them that a famous athlete or performer uses the product. Children and teenagers are frequently the targets of such advertising. If the advertising convinces some consumers that they can't live without the product, the monopoly's demand curve may shift outward and become less elastic at the new equilibrium, at which the firm charges a higher price for its product.

If a firm informs potential consumers about a new use for the product, the demand curve shifts to the right. For example, a 1927 Heinz advertisement suggested that putting its baked beans on toast was a good way to eat beans for breakfast as well as dinner. By so doing, it created a British national dish and shifted the demand curve for its product to the right.

Deciding Whether to Advertise

I have always believed that writing advertisements is the second most profitable form of writing. The first, of course, is ransom notes. . . . —Philip Dusenberry (advertising executive)

Even if advertising succeeds in shifting demand, it may not pay for the firm to advertise. If advertising shifts demand outward or makes it less elastic, the firm's *gross profit*, ignoring the cost of advertising, must rise. The firm undertakes this advertising campaign, however, only if it expects its *net profit* (gross profit minus the cost of advertising) to increase.

We illustrate a monopoly's decision making about advertising in Figure 9.7. If the monopoly does not advertise, it faces the demand curve D^1. If it advertises, its demand curve shifts from D^1 to D^2.

The monopoly's marginal cost, MC, is constant and equals its average cost, AC. Before advertising, the monopoly chooses its output, Q_1, where its marginal cost hits its marginal revenue curve, MR^1, that corresponds to demand curve, D^1. The profit-maximizing equilibrium is e_1, and the monopoly charges a price of p_1. The monopoly's profit, π_1, is a box whose height is the difference between the price and the average cost and whose length is the quantity, Q_1.

After its advertising campaign shifts its demand curve to D^2, the monopoly chooses a higher quantity, Q_2 ($>Q_1$), where the MR^2 and MC curves intersect. In this new equilibrium, e_2, the monopoly charges p_2. Despite this higher price, the monopoly sells more units after advertising because of the outward shift of its demand curve.

As a consequence, the monopoly's gross profit rises. Its new gross profit is the rectangle $\pi_1 + B$, where the height of the rectangle is the new price minus the average cost, and the length is the quantity, Q_2. Thus, the benefit, B, to the monopoly from advertising at this level is the increase in its gross profit. If its cost of advertising is less than B, its net profit rises, and it pays for the monopoly to advertise at this level rather than not to advertise at all.

How Much to Advertise

The man who stops advertising to save money is like the man who stops the clock to save time.

How much should a monopoly advertise to maximize its net profit? The rule for setting the profit-maximizing amount of advertising is the same as that for setting the profit-maximizing amount of output: Set advertising or quantity where the marginal benefit (the extra gross profit from one more unit of advertising or the marginal revenue from one more unit of output) equals its marginal cost.

FIGURE 9.7 Advertising

If the monopoly does not advertise, its demand curve is D^1. At its actual level of advertising, its demand curve is D^2. Advertising increases the monopoly's gross profit (ignoring the cost of advertising) from π_1 to $\pi_2 = \pi_1 + B$.

Thus, if the cost of advertising is less than the benefits from advertising, B, the monopoly's net profit (gross profit minus the cost of advertising) rises.

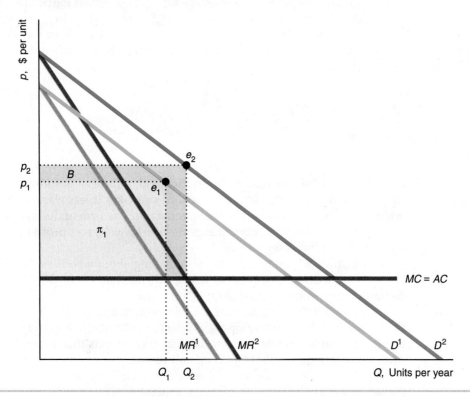

Consider what happens if the monopoly raises or lowers its advertising expenditures by $1, which is its marginal cost of an additional unit of advertising. If a monopoly spends one more dollar on advertising—its marginal cost of advertising—and its gross profit rises by more than $1, its net profit rises, so the extra advertising pays. A profit-maximizing monopoly keeps increasing its advertising until the last dollar of advertising raises its gross profit by exactly $1. If it were to advertise more, its profit would fall.

Using Calculus

Optimal Advertising

We can derive this marginal rule for optimal advertising using calculus. A monopoly's inverse demand function is $p = p(Q, A)$, which says that the price it must charge to clear the market depends on the number of units it chooses to sell, Q, and on the level of its advertising, A. As a result, the firm's revenue function is $R(Q, A) = p(Q, A)Q$. The firm's cost function is $C(Q) + A$, where $C(Q)$ is the cost of manufacturing Q units and A is the cost of advertising, because each unit of advertising costs $1 (by choosing the units of measure appropriately). The monopoly's profit is

$$\pi(Q, A) = R(Q, A) - C(Q) - A. \tag{9.12}$$

The monopoly maximizes its profit by choosing Q and A. Its first-order conditions to maximize its profit are found by partially differentiating the profit function in Equation 9.12 with respect to Q and A in turn:

$$\frac{\partial \pi(Q, A)}{\partial Q} = \frac{\partial R(Q, A)}{\partial Q} - \frac{dC(Q)}{dQ} = 0, \tag{9.13}$$

$$\frac{\partial \pi(Q, A)}{\partial A} = \frac{\partial R(Q, A)}{\partial A} - 1 = 0. \tag{9.14}$$

The profit-maximizing output and advertising levels are the Q and A that simultaneously satisfy Equations 9.13 and 9.14. Equation 9.13 says that the monopoly should set its output so that the marginal revenue from one more unit of output, $\partial R/\partial Q$, equals the marginal cost, dC/dQ, which is the same condition that we previously derived before considering advertising. According to Equation 9.14, the monopoly should advertise to the point where its marginal revenue or marginal benefit from the last unit of advertising, $\partial R/\partial A$, equals the marginal cost of the last unit of advertising, $\$1$.

Q&A 9.5

A monopoly's inverse demand function is $p = 800 - 4Q + 0.2A^{0.5}$, where Q is its quantity, p is its price, and A is the level of advertising. Its marginal cost of production is 2, and its cost of a unit of advertising is 1. What are the firm's profit-maximizing price, quantity, and level of advertising?

Answer

1. *Write the firm's profit function using its inverse demand function.* The monopoly's profit is

$$\begin{aligned} \pi &= (800 - 4Q + 0.2A^{0.5})Q - 2Q - A \\ &= 798Q - 4Q^2 + 0.2A^{0.5}Q - A. \end{aligned} \tag{9.15}$$

2. *Set the partial derivatives of the profit function in Equation 9.15 with respect to Q and A to zero to obtain the equations that determine the profit-maximizing levels, as in Equations 9.13 and 9.14.* The first-order conditions are

$$\frac{\partial \pi}{\partial Q} = 798 - 8Q + 0.2A^{0.5} = 0, \tag{9.16}$$

$$\frac{\partial \pi}{\partial A} = 0.1A^{-0.5}Q - 1 = 0. \tag{9.17}$$

3. *Solve Equations 9.16 and 9.17 for the profit-maximizing levels of Q and A.* We can rearrange Equation 9.17 to show that $A^{0.5} = 0.1Q$. Substituting this expression into the Equation 9.16, we find that $798 - 8Q + 0.02Q = 0$, or $Q = 100$. Thus, $A^{0.5} = 0.1Q = 10$, so $A = 100$.

Mini-Case

Super Bowl Commercials

Super Bowl commercials are the most expensive commercials on U.S. television. A 30-second spot during the Super Bowl averaged over $3.8 million in 2013. A high price for these commercials is not surprising because the cost of commercials generally increases with the number of viewers (*eyeballs* in industry jargon), and the Super Bowl is the most widely watched show, with over 108 million viewers in 2013. What is surprising is that Super Bowl advertising costs 2.5 times as much per viewer as other TV commercials.

However, a Super Bowl commercial is much more likely to influence viewers than commercials on other shows. The Super Bowl is not only a premier sports event; it showcases the most memorable commercials of the year, such as Apple's classic 1984 Macintosh ad, which is still discussed today. Indeed, many Super Bowl viewers are not even football fans—they watch to see these superior ads. Moreover, Super Bowl commercials receive extra exposure because these ads often *go viral* on the Internet.

Given that Super Bowl ads are more likely to be remembered by viewers, are these commercials worth the extra price? Obviously many advertisers believe so, as their demand for these ads has bid up the price. Kim (2011) found that immediately after a Super Bowl commercial airs, the advertising firm's stock value rises. Thus, investors apparently believe that Super Bowl commercials raise a firm's profits despite the high cost of the commercial. Ho et al. (2009) found that, for the typical movie with a substantial advertising budget, a Super Bowl commercial advertising the movie raises theater revenues by more than the same expenditure on other television advertising. They also concluded that movie firms' advertising during the Super Bowl was at (or close to) the profit-maximizing amount.

9.6 Networks, Dynamics, and Behavioral Economics

We have examined how a monopoly behaves in the current period, ignoring the future. For many markets, such an analysis is appropriate as each period can be treated separately. However, in some markets, decisions today affect demand or cost in a future period, creating a need for a *dynamic* analysis, in which managers explicitly consider relationships between different periods.

In such markets, the monopoly may maximize its long-run profit by making a decision today that does not maximize its short-run profit. For example, frequently a firm introduces a new product—such as a new type of candy bar—by initially charging a low price or giving away free samples to generate word-of-mouth publicity or to let customers learn about its quality in hopes of getting their future business. We now consider an important reason why consumers' demand in the future may depend on a monopoly's actions in the present.

Network Externalities

The number of customers a firm has today may affect the demand curve it faces in the future. A good has a **network externality** if one person's demand depends on the consumption of the good by others.[19] If a good has a *positive* network externality, its value to a consumer grows as the number of units sold increases.

---

[19]In Chapter 16, we discuss the more general case of an *externality*, which occurs when a person's well-being or a firm's production capability is directly affected by the actions of other consumers or firms rather than indirectly through changes in prices. The following discussion on network externalities is based on Leibenstein (1950), Rohlfs (1974), Katz and Shapiro (1994), Economides (1996), Shapiro and Varian (1999), and Rohlfs (2001).

When a firm introduces a new good with a network externality, it faces a chicken-and-egg problem: It can't get Max to buy the good unless Sofia will buy it, but it can't get Sofia to buy it unless Max will. The firm wants its customers to coordinate or to make their purchase decisions simultaneously.

The telephone provides a classic example of a positive network externality. When the phone was introduced, potential adopters had no reason to get phone service unless their family and friends did. Why buy a phone if there's no one to call? For Bell's phone network to succeed, it had to achieve a *critical mass* of users—enough adopters that others wanted to join. Had it failed to achieve this critical mass, demand would have withered and the network would have died. Similarly, the market for fax machines grew very slowly until a critical mass was achieved where many firms had them.

Direct Size Effects. Many industries exhibit positive network externalities where the customer gets a *direct* benefit from a larger network. The larger an automated teller machine (ATM) network, such as the Plus network, the greater the odds that you will find an ATM when you want one, so the more likely it is that you will want to use that network. The more people who use a particular computer program, the more attractive it is to someone who wants to exchange files with other users.

Indirect Effects. In some markets, positive network externalities are indirect and stem from complementary goods that are offered when a product has a critical mass of users. The more applications (apps) available for a smart phone, the more people want to buy that smart phone. However, many of these extra apps will be written only if a critical mass of customers buys the smart phone. Similarly, the more people who drive diesel-powered cars, the more likely it is that gas stations will sell diesel fuel; and the more stations that sell the fuel, the more likely it is that someone will want to drive a diesel car. As a final example, once a critical mass of customers had broadband Internet service, more services provided downloadable music and movies and more high-definition Web pages become available. Once those popular apps appeared, more people signed up for broadband service.

Network Externalities and Behavioral Economics

The direct effect of network externalities depends on the size of the network, because customers want to interact with each other. However, sometimes consumers' behavior depends on beliefs or tastes that can be explained by psychological and sociological theories, which economists study in *behavioral economics* (Chapter 4).

One such explanation for a direct network externality effect is based on consumer attitudes toward other consumers. Harvey Leibenstein (1950) suggested that consumers sometimes want a good because "everyone else has it." A fad or other popularity-based explanation for a positive network externality is called a **bandwagon effect**: A person places greater value on a good as more and more other people possess it.[20] The success of the iPad today may be partially due to its early popularity.

The opposite, negative network externality is called a **snob effect**: A person places greater value on a good as fewer and fewer other people possess it. Some people prefer an original painting by an unknown artist to a lithograph by a star because no

---

[20]*Jargon alert*: Some economists use *bandwagon effect* to mean any positive network externality—not just those that are based on popularity.

one else can possess that painting. (As Yogi Berra is reported to have said, "Nobody goes there anymore; it's too crowded.")

Network Externalities as an Explanation for Monopolies

Because of the need for a critical mass of customers in a market with a positive network externality, we sometimes see only one large firm surviving. Visa's ad campaign tells consumers that Visa cards are accepted "everywhere you want to be," including places that "don't take American Express." One could view its ad campaign as an attempt to convince consumers that its card has a critical mass and therefore that everyone should carry it.

The Windows operating system largely dominates the market—not because it is technically superior to Apple's operating system or Linux—but because it has a critical mass of users. Consequently, a developer can earn more producing software that works with Windows than with other operating systems, and the larger number of software programs makes Windows increasingly attractive to users.

But having obtained a monopoly, a firm does not necessarily keep it. History is filled with examples where one product knocks off another: "The king is dead; long live the king." Google replaced Yahoo! as the predominant search engine. Microsoft's Explorer displaced Netscape as the big-dog browser, followed in turn by Google Chrome. Levi Strauss is no longer the fashion leader among the jeans set.

Mini-Case

Critical Mass and eBay

In recent years, many people have argued that natural monopolies emerge after brief periods of Internet competition. A typical Web business requires a large up-front fixed cost—primarily for development and promotion—but has a relatively low marginal cost. Thus, Internet start-ups typically have downward-sloping average cost-per-user curves. Which of the actual or potential firms with decreasing average costs will dominate and become a natural monopoly?[21]

In the early years, eBay's online auction site, which started in 1995, faced competition from a variety of other Internet sites, including one created in 1998 by then mighty Yahoo!. At the time, many commentators correctly predicted that whichever auction site first achieved a critical mass of users would drive the other sites out of business. Indeed, most of these alternative sites died or faded into obscurity. For example, Yahoo! Auctions closed its U.K. and Irish sites in 2002, its Australian site in 2003, its U.S. and Canadian sites in 2007, and its Singapore site in 2008 (however, as of early 2013 its Hong Kong, Taiwanese, and Japanese sites continue to operate).

Apparently the convenience of having one site where virtually all buyers and sellers congregate is valuable to consumers. Such a site lowers buyers' search

---

[21]If Internet sites provide differentiated products (Chapter 11), then several sites may coexist even though average costs are strictly decreasing. In 2007, commentators were predicting the emergence of natural monopolies in social networks such as MySpace, which has since lost its dominance. However, whether a single social network can dominate for long is debatable given frequent innovations. Even if MySpace or Facebook temporarily dominates other similar sites, it may eventually lose ground to Web businesses with new models, such as Twitter.

costs and allows the creation of useful reputation systems for providing user feedback (Brown and Morgan, 2006). These benefits attract more buyers, thereby raising the prices that sellers can expect to receive, which in turn attracts more sellers. Brown and Morgan (2010) found that, prior to the demise of the U.S. Yahoo! Auction site, the same type of items attracted an average of two additional bidders on eBay and, consequently, the prices on eBay were consistently 20% to 70% percent higher than Yahoo! prices—making eBay more attractive than Yahoo! to sellers.

Managerial Implication

Introductory Prices

Managers should consider initially selling a new product at a low introductory price to obtain a critical mass. By doing so, the manager maximizes long-run profit but not short-run profit.

Suppose that a monopoly sells its good—say, root-beer-scented jeans—for only two periods (after that, the demand goes to zero as a new craze hits the market). If the monopoly sells less than a critical quantity of output, Q, in the first period, then its second-period demand curve lies close to the price axis. However, if the good is a success in the first period—at least Q units are sold—the second-period demand curve shifts substantially to the right.

If the monopoly maximizes its short-run profit in the first period, it charges p^* and sells Q^* units, which is fewer than Q. To sell Q units, it would have to lower its first-period price below p^*, which would reduce its first-period profit from π^* to π.

In the second period, the monopoly maximizes its profit given its second-period demand curve. If the monopoly sold only Q^* units in the first period, it earns a relatively low second-period profit of π_l. However, if it sells Q units in the first period, it makes a relatively high second-period profit, π_h.

Should the monopoly charge a low introductory price in the first period? Its objective is to maximize its long-run profit: the sum of its profit in the two periods.[22] If the firm has a critical mass in the second period, its extra profit is $\pi_h - \pi_l$. To obtain this critical mass by charging a low introductory price in the first period, it lowers its first-period profit by $\pi^* - \pi$. Thus, a manager should charge a low introductory price in the first period if the first-period loss is less than the extra profit in the second period. This policy is apparently profitable for many firms: A 2012 Google search found 103 million Web pages touting an introductory price.

Managerial Solution

Brand-Name and Generic Drugs

When generic drugs enter the market after the patent on a brand-name drug expires, the demand curve facing the brand-name firm shifts toward the origin (to the left). Why do the managers of many brand-name drug companies raise their prices after generic rivals enter the market? The reason is that the demand curve not only shifts to the left but it rotates so that it is less elastic at the original price.

---

[22]Firms place lower value on profit in the future than profit today (Chapter 7). However, for simplicity, we assume that the monopoly places equal value on profit in either period.

The price the brand-name firm sets depends on the elasticity of demand. When the firm has a patent monopoly, it faces demand curve D^1 in the figure. Its monopoly optimum, e_1, is determined by the intersection of the corresponding marginal revenue curve MR^1 and the marginal cost curve. (Because it is twice as steeply sloped as the demand curve, MR^1 intersects the MC curve at Q_1, while the demand curve D^1 intersects the MC curve at $2Q^1$.) The monopoly sells the Q_1 units at a price of p_1.

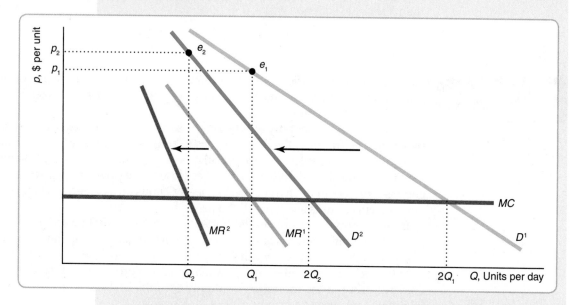

After the generic drugs enter the market, the linear demand curve facing the original patent holder shifts left to D^2 and becomes steeper and less elastic at the original price. The firm now maximizes its profit at e_2, where the quantity, Q_2, is smaller than Q_1 because D^2 lies to the left of D^1. However, the new price p_2 is higher than the initial price p_1 because the D^2 demand curve is less elastic at the new optimum quantity Q_2 than is the D^1 curve at Q_1.

Why might the demand curve rotate and become less elastic at the initial price? One explanation is that the brand-name firm has two types of consumers with different elasticities of demand who differ in their willingness to switch to a generic. One group of consumers is relatively price-sensitive and will switch to the lower-priced generics. However, the brand-name drug remains the monopoly supplier to the remaining brand-loyal customers whose demand is less elastic than that of the price-sensitive consumers. These loyal customers prefer the brand-name drug because they are more comfortable with a familiar product, worry that new products may be substandard, or fear that differences in the inactive ingredients might affect them.

Older customers are less likely to switch brands than younger people. A survey of the American Association of Retired Persons found that people aged 65 and older were 15% less likely than people aged 45 to 64 to request generic versions of a drug from their doctor or pharmacist. Similarly, patients with generous insurance plans may be more likely to pay for expensive drugs (if their insurer permits) than customers without insurance.

SUMMARY

1. **Monopoly Profit Maximization.** Like any firm, a monopoly—a single seller—maximizes its profit by setting its output so that its marginal revenue equals its marginal cost. The monopoly makes a positive profit if its average cost is less than the price at the profit-maximizing output.

2. **Market Power.** Market power is the ability of a firm to significantly affect the market price. The extent of a firm's market power depends on the shape of the demand curve. The more elastic the demand curve at the point where the firm is producing, the lower the markup of price over marginal cost.

3. **Market Failure Due to Monopoly Pricing.** Because a monopoly's price is above its marginal cost, too little output is produced, and society suffers a deadweight loss. The monopoly makes higher profit than it would if it acted as a price taker. Consumers are worse off, buying less output at a higher price.

4. **Causes of Monopoly.** A firm may be a monopoly if it has lower operating costs than rivals, due to reasons such as from superior knowledge or control of a key input. A market may also have a *natural monopoly* if one firm can produce the market output at lower average cost than can a larger number of firms (even if all firms have the same cost function). Many, if not most, monopolies are created by governments, which prevent other firms from entering the markets. One important barrier to entry is a patent, which gives the inventor of a new product or process the exclusive right to sell the product or use the process for 20 years in most countries.

5. **Advertising.** A monopoly advertises or engages in other promotional activity to shift its demand curve to the right or make it less elastic so as to raise its profit net of its advertising expenses.

6. **Networks, Dynamics, and Behavioral Economics.** If a good has a positive network externality so that its value to a consumer grows as the number of units sold increases, then current sales affect a monopoly's future demand curve. A monopoly may maximize its profit over time by setting a low introductory price in the first period in which it sells the good and then later raising its price as its product's popularity ensures large future sales at a higher price. Consequently, the monopoly is not maximizing its short-run profit in the first period but is maximizing the sum of its profits over all periods. Behavioral economics provides an explanation for some network externalities, such as bandwagon effects and snob effects.

QUESTIONS

All exercises are available on MyEconLab; * *= answer at the back of this book;* **C** *= use of calculus may be necessary.*

1. Monopoly Profit Maximization

1.1. If the inverse demand function is $p = 300 - 3Q$, what is the marginal revenue function? Draw the demand and marginal revenue curves. At what quantities do the demand and marginal revenue lines hit the quantity axis? (*Hint*: See Q&A 9.1.)

1.2. If the inverse demand curve a monopoly faces is $p = 10Q^{-0.5}$, what is the firm's marginal revenue curve? **C** (*Hint*: See Q&A 9.1.)

*1.3. If the inverse demand function is $p = 500 - 10Q$, what is the elasticity of demand and revenue at $Q = 10$?

1.4. Does it affect a monopoly's profit if it chooses price or quantity (assuming it chooses them optimally)? Why can't a monopoly choose both price *and* quantity?

1.5. For the monopoly in Figure 9.3 at what quantity is its revenue maximized? (*Hint*: At the quantity where the revenue function reaches its peak, the slope of the revenue function is zero. That is, $MR = 0$.) Why is revenue maximized at a larger quantity than profit? Modify panel b of Figure 9.3 to show the revenue curve.

1.6. Are major-league baseball clubs profit-maximizing monopolies? Some observers of this market have contended that baseball club owners want to maximize attendance or revenue. Alexander (2001) says that one test of whether a firm is a profit-maximizing monopoly is to check whether the firm is operating in the elastic portion of its demand curve (which he finds is true). Why is that a relevant test? What would the elasticity be if a baseball club were maximizing revenue?

1.7. Using a graph, show under what condition the monopoly operates—does not shut down—in the long run. Discuss your result in terms of the demand curve and the average cost curve at the profit-maximizing quantity.

1.8. Why might a monopoly operate in any part (downward sloping, flat, upward sloping) of its long-run average cost curve, but a competitive firm will operate only at the bottom or in the upward-sloping section?

1.9. AT&T Inc., the large U.S. phone company and the one-time monopoly, left the payphone business at the beginning of 2009 because people were switching to wireless phones. U.S. consumers owning cellphones reached 80% by 2007 and 86% by 2012 according to the Pew Research Center. Consequently, the number of payphones fell from 2.6 million at the peak in 1998 to 1 million in 2006 (Crayton Harrison, "AT&T to Disconnect Pay-Phone Business After 129 Years," **Bloomberg.com**, December 3, 2007). (Where will Clark Kent go to change into Superman now?) Use graphs to explain why a monopoly exits a market when its demand curve shifts to the left.

*1.10. The inverse demand function a monopoly faces is $p = 100 - Q$. The firm's cost curve is $C(Q) = 10 + 5Q$. What is the profit-maximizing solution? How does your answer change if $C(Q) = 100 + 5Q$?

1.11. The inverse demand function a monopoly faces is $p = 10Q^{-0.5}$ (*Hint*: See Question 1.2). The firm's cost curve is $C(Q) = 5Q$. What is the profit-maximizing solution? **C**

1.12. Show that after a shift in the demand curve, a monopoly's price may remain constant but its output may rise.

2. Market Power

2.1. Why is the ratio of the monopoly's price to its marginal cost, p/MC, larger if the demand curve is less elastic at the optimum quantity? Can the demand curve be inelastic at that quantity?

2.2. When will a monopoly set its price equal to its marginal cost?

2.3. At the profit-maximizing quantity in Figure 9.2, what is the elasticity of demand? What is the Lerner Index? (*Hint*: Can you determine the answers to these questions using only the price and marginal cost information from the figure?)

2.4. The U.S. Postal Service (USPS) has a constitutionally guaranteed monopoly on first-class mail. In 2012, it charged 44¢ for a stamp, which was not the profit-maximizing price—the USPS's goal, allegedly, is to break even rather than to turn a profit. Following the postal services in Australia, Britain, Canada, Switzerland, and Ireland, the USPS allowed Stamps.com to sell a sheet of twenty 44¢ stamps with a photo of your dog, your mommy, or whatever image you want for $18.99 (that's

94.95¢ per stamp, or a 216% markup). Stamps.com keeps the extra beyond the 44¢ it pays the USPS. What is the firm's Lerner Index? If Stamps.com is a profit-maximizing monopoly, what elasticity of demand does it face for a customized stamp?

2.5. According to the California Nurses Association, Tenet Healthcare hospitals marked up drugs substantially. At Tenet's Sierra Vista Regional Medical Center, drug prices were 1,840.80% of the hospital's costs (Chuck Squatriglia and Tyche Hendricks, "Tenet Hiked Drug Prices, Study Finds More Than Double U.S. Average," *San Francisco Chronicle*, November 24, 2002: A1, A10). Assuming Tenet was maximizing its profit, what was the elasticity of demand that Tenet believed it faced? What was its Lerner Index for drugs?

2.6. Using the information in Q&A 9.2, calculate the elasticity of demand faced by Apple at the profit maximizing price and quantity using the inverse demand function.

*2.7. In 2009, the price of Amazon's Kindle 2 was $359, while iSuppli estimated that its marginal cost was $159. What was Amazon's Lerner Index? What elasticity of demand did it face if it was engaging in short-run profit maximization?

2.8. When the iPod was introduced, Apple's constant marginal cost of producing its top-of-the-line iPod was $200 (iSuppli), its fixed cost was approximately $736 million, and we estimate that its inverse demand function was $p = 600 - 25Q$, where Q is units measured in millions. What was Apple's average cost function? Assuming that Apple was maximizing its short-run monopoly profit, what was its marginal revenue function? What were its profit-maximizing price and quantity, profit, and Lerner Index? What was the elasticity of demand at the profit-maximizing level? Show Apple's profit-maximizing solution in a figure. (*Hint*: See Q&A 9.2.)

3. Market Failure Due to Monopoly Pricing

3.1. A monopoly has a constant marginal cost of production of $1 per unit and a fixed cost of $10. Draw the firm's MC, AVC, and AC curves. Add a downward-sloping demand curve, and show the profit-maximizing quantity and price. Indicate the profit as an area on your diagram. Show the deadweight loss.

3.2. A monopoly has an inverse demand function given by $p = 120 - Q$ and a constant marginal cost of 10. Calculate the deadweight loss if the monopoly charges the profit-maximizing price.

3.3. What is the effect of a lump-sum tax (which is like an additional fixed cost) on a monopoly? (*Hint*: Consider the possibility that the firm may shut down, and see Q&A 9.3.)

3.4. If the inverse demand function is $p = 120 - Q$ and the marginal cost is constant at 10, how does charging the monopoly a specific tax of $\tau = 10$ per unit affect price and quantity and the welfare of consumers, the monopoly, and society (where society's welfare includes the tax revenue)? What is the incidence of the tax on consumers? (*Hint*: See Q&A 9.3.)

*3.5. Show mathematically that a monopoly may raise the price to consumers by more than a specific tax imposed on it. (*Hint*: Consider a monopoly facing a constant-elasticity demand curve and a constant marginal cost, *m*.) **C**

4. Causes of Monopoly

*4.1. Can a firm be a natural monopoly if it has a U-shaped average cost curve? Why or why not? (*Hint*: See Q&A 9.4.)

4.2. Can a firm operating in the upward-sloping portion of its average cost curve be a natural monopoly? Explain. (*Hint*: See Q&A 9.4.)

4.3. Once the copyright runs out on a book or music, it can legally be placed on the Internet for anyone to download. In 1998 the U.S. Congress extended the copyright law to 95 years after the original publication. But the copyright holds for only 50 years in Australia and 70 years in the European Union. Thus, an Australian website could post *Gone With the Wind*, a 1936 novel, or Elvis Presley's 1954 single "That's All Right," while a U.S. site could not. Obviously, this legal nicety won't stop U.S. fans from downloading from Australian or European sites. Discuss how limiting the length of a copyright would affect the pricing used by the publisher of a novel.

4.4. In the "Botox" Mini-Case, consumer surplus, triangle *A*, equals the deadweight loss, triangle *C*. Show that this equality is a result of the linear demand and constant marginal cost assumptions.

4.5. Based on the information in the "Botox" Mini-Case, what would happen to the equilibrium price and quantity if the government had set a price ceiling of $200 per vial of Botox? What welfare effects would such a policy have?

5. Advertising

5.1. Using a graph, explain why a firm might not want to spend money on advertising, even if such an expenditure would shift the firm's demand curve to the right.

*5.2. A monopoly's inverse demand function is $p = 100 - Q + (5A - A^2)/Q$, where Q is its quantity, p is its price, and A is the level of advertising. Its marginal cost of production is constant at 10, and its cost of a unit of advertising is 1. What are the firm's profit-maximizing price, quantity, and level of advertising? (*Hint*: See Q&A 9.5.) **C**

5.3. A monopoly's inverse demand function is $p = Q^{-0.25}A^{0.5}$, where Q is its quantity, p is its price, and A is the level of advertising. Its constant marginal and average cost of production is 6, and its cost of a unit of advertising is 0.25. What are the firm's profit-maximizing price, quantity, and level of advertising? (*Hint*: See Q&A 9.5.) **C**

5.4. Why are newsstand prices higher than subscription prices for an issue of a magazine?

5.5. Canada subsidizes Canadian magazines to offset the invasion of foreign (primarily U.S.) magazines, which take 90% of the country's sales. The Canada Magazine Fund provides a lump-sum subsidy to various magazines to "maintain a Canadian presence against the overwhelming presence of foreign magazines." Eligibility is based on high levels of investment in Canadian editorial content and reliance on advertising revenues. What effect will a lump-sum subsidy have on the number of subscriptions sold?

5.6. Use a diagram similar to Figure 9.7 to illustrate the effect of social media on the demand for Super Bowl commercials. (*Hint*: See the "Super Bowl Commercials" Mini-Case.)

6. Networks, Dynamics, and Behavioral Economics

6.1. A monopoly chocolate manufacturer faces two types of consumers. The larger group, the hoi polloi, loves desserts and has a relatively flat, linear demand curve for chocolate. The smaller group, the snobs, is interested in buying chocolate only if the hoi polloi do not buy it. Given that the hoi polloi do not buy the chocolate, the snobs have a relatively steep, linear demand curve. Show the monopoly's possible outcomes—high price, low quantity; low price, high quantity—and explain the condition under which the monopoly chooses to cater to the snobs rather than to the hoi polloi.

*6.2. A monopoly produces a good with a network externality at a constant marginal and average cost of 2. In the first period, its inverse demand function is $p = 10 - Q$. In the second period, its demand is $p = 10 - Q$ unless it sells at least $Q = 8$ units in the first period. If it meets or exceeds this target, then the demand curve rotates out by α (it sells α times as many units for any given price), so that its inverse demand curve is $p = 10 - Q/\alpha$. The monopoly knows that it can sell no output after the second period. The monopoly's objective is to maximize the sum of its profits over the two periods. In the first period, should the monopoly set the output that maximizes its profit in that period? How does your answer depend on α? **C**

7. Managerial Problem

7.1. Under what circumstances will a drug company charge more for its drug after its patent expires?

7.2. Does the Managerial Solution change if the entry of the generic causes a parallel shift to the left of the patent monopoly's linear demand curve?

7.3. Proposals to reduce patent length for drugs are sometimes made, but some critics argue that such a change would result in even higher prices during the patent period as companies would need to recover drug development costs more quickly. Is this argument valid if drug companies maximize profit?

8. Spreadsheet Exercises

8.1. A monopoly faces the inverse demand function: $p = 100 - 2Q$, with the corresponding marginal revenue function, $MR = 100 - 4Q$. The firm's total cost of production is $C = 50 + 10Q + 3Q^2$, with a corresponding marginal cost of $MC = 10 + 6Q$.

a. Create a spreadsheet for $Q = 1, 2, 3, \ldots, 15$. Using the $MR = MC$ rule, determine the profit-maximizing output and price for the firm and the consequent level of profit.

b. Calculate the Lerner Index of monopoly power for each output level and verify its relationship with the value of the price elasticity of demand (ε) at the profit-maximizing level of output.

c. Now suppose that a specific tax of 20 per unit is imposed on the monopoly. What is the effect on the monopoly's profit-maximizing price?

8.2. A firm's demand function is $Q = 110 - p + 2A^{0.5}$, where A is the amount of advertising undertaken by the firm and the price of advertising is one. The firm's cost of production is $C = 50 + 10Q + 2Q^2$. The government imposes a binding price control at $135. Use Excel to determine the profit-maximizing level of advertising. Try advertising levels that vary in hundreds from 0 to $1,000. Select the most profitable range and try smaller increments within that range. What is the firm's profit-maximizing advertising level and quantity?

Pricing with Market Power

10

Everything is worth what its purchaser will pay for it. —Publilius Syrus (first century B.C.)

Because many retail managers use *sales*—temporarily setting the price below the usual price—some customers pay lower prices than others over time. Grocery stores are particularly likely to put products on sale frequently. In large U.S. supermarkets, a soft drink brand is on sale 94% of the time. Either Coke or Pepsi is on sale half the weeks in a year.

Heinz Ketchup controls up to 60% of the U.S. ketchup market, 70% of the Canadian market, and nearly 80% of the U.K. market. In 2012, Heinz sold over 650 million bottles of ketchup in more than 140 countries and had annual sales of more than $1.5 billion. When Heinz goes on sale, *switchers*—ketchup customers who normally buy whichever brand is least expensive—purchase Heinz rather than the low-price generic ketchup. How can Heinz's managers design a pattern of sales that maximizes Heinz's profit by obtaining extra sales from switchers without losing substantial sums by selling to its loyal customers at a discount price? Under what conditions does it pay for Heinz to have a policy of periodic sales?

Sales are not the only means that firms use to charge customers different prices. Why are airline fares often substantially less if you book in advance? Why do the spiritualists who live at the Wonewoc Spiritualist Camp give readings for $40 for half an hour, but charge seniors only $35 on Wednesdays?[1] Why are some goods, including computers and software, combined and sold as a bundle? To answer these questions, we need to examine how monopolies and other noncompetitive firms set prices.

In Chapter 9, we examined how a monopoly maximizes its profit when it uses **uniform pricing**: charging the same price for every unit sold of a particular good. However, a monopoly can increase its profit if it can use **nonuniform pricing**, where a firm charges consumers different prices for the same product or charges a single customer a price that depends on the number of units the customer buys. In this

---

[1] **www.msnbc.msn.com/id/20377308/wid/11915829**, August 29, 2007.

chapter, we analyze nonuniform pricing for monopolies, but similar principles apply to any firm with market power.

As we saw in Chapter 9, a monopoly that sets a uniform price sells only to customers who value the good enough to buy it at the monopoly price, and those customers receive some consumer surplus. The monopoly does not sell the good to other customers who value the good at less than the single price, even if those consumers would be willing to pay more than the marginal cost of production. These lost sales cause *deadweight loss*, which is the foregone value of these potential sales in excess of the cost of producing the good.

A firm with market power can earn a higher profit using nonuniform pricing than by setting a uniform price for two reasons. First, the firm captures some or all of the single-price consumer surplus. Second, the firm converts at least some of the single-price deadweight loss into profit by charging a price below the uniform price to some customers who would not purchase at the single-price level. A monopoly that uses nonuniform pricing can lower the price to these otherwise excluded consumers without lowering the price to consumers who are willing to pay higher prices.

In this chapter, we examine several types of nonuniform pricing including price discrimination, two-part pricing, bundling, and peak-load pricing. The most common form of nonuniform pricing is **price discrimination**: charging consumers different prices for the same good based on individual characteristics of consumers, membership in an identifiable subgroup of consumers, or on the quantity purchased by the consumers. For example, for a full-year combination print and online subscription, the *Wall Street Journal* charges $99.95 to students, who are price sensitive, and $155 to other subscribers, who are less price sensitive.

Some firms with market power use other forms of nonuniform pricing to increase profits. A firm may use *two-part pricing*, where it charges a customer one fee for the right to buy the good and an additional fee for each unit purchased. For example, members of health or golf clubs typically pay an annual fee to belong to the club and then pay an additional amount each time they use the facilities. Similarly, cable television companies often charge a monthly fee for basic service and an additional fee for recent movies.

Another type of nonuniform pricing is called *bundling*, where several products are sold together as a package. For example, many restaurants provide full-course dinners for a fixed price that is less than the sum of the prices charged if the items (appetizer, main dish, and dessert) are ordered separately (à la carte).

Finally, some firms use *peak-load pricing*: charging higher prices in periods of peak demand than at other times. For example, ticket prices for flights from cold northern cities to Hawaii are higher in the winter months when demand is higher than in the summer.

Main Topics

In this chapter, we examine seven main topics

1. **Conditions for Price Discrimination:** A firm can increase its profit using price discrimination if it has market power, if customers differ in their willingness to pay, if the firm can identify which customers are more price sensitive than others, and if it can prevent customers who pay low prices from reselling to those who pay high prices.

2. **Perfect Price Discrimination:** If a firm can charge the maximum each customer is willing to pay for each unit of output, the firm captures all potential consumer surplus.

3. **Group Price Discrimination:** A firm that lacks the ability to charge each individual a different price may be able to charge different prices to various groups of customers that differ in their willingness to pay for the good.

4. **Nonlinear Price Discrimination:** A firm may set different prices for large purchases than for small ones, discriminating among consumers by inducing them to self-select the effective price they pay based on the quantity they buy.

5. **Two-Part Pricing:** By charging consumers a fee for the right to buy a good and then allowing them to purchase as much as they wish at an additional per-unit fee, a firm earns a higher profit than with uniform pricing.

6. **Bundling:** By selling a combination of different products in a package or bundle, a firm earns a higher profit than by selling the goods or services separately.

7. **Peak-Load Pricing:** By charging higher prices during periods of peak demand and lower prices at other times, a firm increases its profit.

10.1 Conditions for Price Discrimination

We start by studying the most common form of nonuniform pricing, *price discrimination*, where a firm charges various consumers different prices for a good.[2]

Why Price Discrimination Pays

For almost any good or service, some consumers are willing to pay more than others. A firm that sets a single price faces a trade-off between charging consumers with a high willingness to pay a high price and charging a low enough price to sell to some customers with a lower willingness to pay. As a result, a single-price firm sets an intermediate price. By price discriminating, a firm can partially or entirely avoid this trade-off.

As with any kind of nonuniform pricing, price discrimination increases profit above the uniform pricing level through two channels. Price discrimination can extract additional consumer surplus from consumers who place a high value on the good and can simultaneously sell to new customers who would not be willing to pay the profit-maximizing uniform price. We use a pair of extreme examples to illustrate these two benefits of price discrimination to firms—capturing more of the consumer surplus and selling to more customers.

Suppose that the only movie theater in town has two types of patrons: college students and senior citizens. College students see the Saturday night movie if the price is $20 or less, and senior citizens attend if the price is $10 or less. Thus, college students have a willingness to pay of $20 and senior citizens have a willingness to pay of $10. For simplicity, we assume that the theater incurs no cost when showing the movie, so profit is the same as revenue. We also assume that the theater is large enough to hold all potential customers, so the marginal cost of admitting one more customer is zero. Table 10.1 shows how pricing affects the theater's profit.

---

[2]Price discrimination is legal in the United States unless it harms competition between firms, as specified in the Robinson-Patman Act.

TABLE 10.1 Theater Profits Based on the Pricing Method Used

(a) No Extra Customers from Price Discrimination

Pricing	Profit from 10 College Students	Profit from 20 Senior Citizens	Total Profit
Uniform, $10	$100	$200	$300
Uniform, $20	$200	$0	$200
Price discrimination*	$200	$200	$400

(b) Extra Customers from Price Discrimination

Pricing	Profit from 10 College Students	Profit from 5 Senior Citizens	Total Profit
Uniform, $10	$100	$50	$150
Uniform, $20	$200	$0	$200
Price discrimination*	$200	$50	$250

*The theater price discriminates by charging college students $20 and senior citizens $10.
Notes: College students go to the theater if they are charged no more than $20. Senior citizens are willing to pay up to $10. The theater's marginal cost for an extra customer is zero.

In panel a, the theater potentially has 10 college student and 20 senior citizen customers. If the theater charges everyone $10, its profit is $300 because all 30 potential customers buy a ticket. If it charges $20, the senior citizens do not go to the movie, so the theater makes only $200, receiving $20 each from the 10 college students. Thus, if the theater charges everyone the same price, it maximizes its profit by setting the price at $10. The theater does not want to charge less than $10 because the same number of people go to the movie as go when $10 is charged. Charging between $10 and $20 is less profitable than charging $20 because no extra seniors go and the college students are willing to pay $20. Charging more than $20 results in no customers.

If the price is $10, the seniors have no consumer surplus: They pay exactly what seeing the movie is worth to them. Seeing the movie is worth $20 to the college students so, if the price is only $10, each has a consumer surplus of $10, and their combined consumer surplus is $100.

If the theater can price discriminate by charging senior citizens $10 and college students $20, its profit increases to $400. Its profit rises because the theater makes $200 from the seniors (the same amount as when it was selling all tickets for $10) but gets an extra $100 from the college students ($10 more from each of the 10 students). By price discriminating, the theater sells the same number of seats but makes more money from the college students, capturing all the consumer surplus they had under uniform pricing. Neither group of customers has any consumer surplus if the theater price discriminates.

In panel b, the theater potentially has 10 college student and 5 senior citizen customers. If the theater must charge a single price, it charges $20. Only college students see the movie, so the theater's profit is $200. (If it charges $10, both students and seniors go to the theater, but its profit is only $150.) If the theater can price discriminate and charge seniors $10 and college students $20, its profit increases to $250. Here the gain from price discrimination comes from selling more tickets (those sold to seniors) and not from making more money on the same number of tickets, as in panel a. The theater earns as much from the students as before and makes more from the seniors, and neither group enjoys any consumer surplus.

These examples illustrate the two channels through which price discrimination can increase profit: charging some existing customers more or selling extra units. Leslie (1997) found that Broadway theaters in New York increase their profits 5% by price discriminating rather than using uniform prices.

In the examples just considered, the movie theater's ability to increase its profits by price discrimination arises from its ability to segment the market into two groups, students and senior citizens, with different levels of willingness to pay.

Mini-Case

Disneyland Pricing

Disneyland, in southern California, is a well-run operation that rarely misses a trick when it comes to increasing its profit. (Indeed, Disneyland mints money: When you enter the park, you can exchange U.S. currency for Disney dollars, which can be spent only in the park.)[3]

In 2012, Disneyland charged out-of-state adults $199 for a 3-day park hopper ticket, which admits one to Disneyland and Disney's California Adventure Park, but charged residents of southern California only $154. This policy of charging locals a discounted price makes sense if visitors are willing to pay more than locals and if Disneyland can prevent locals from selling discounted tickets to nonlocals. Imagine a Midwesterner who's never been to Disneyland and wants to visit. Travel accounts for most of the trip's cost, so an extra few dollars for entrance to the park makes little percentage difference in the total cost of the visit and hence does not greatly affect that person's decision whether to go. In contrast, for a local who has been to Disneyland many times and for whom the entrance price is a larger share of the total cost, a slightly higher entrance fee might prevent a visit.[4]

Charging both groups the same price is not in Disney's best interest. If Disney were to charge the higher price to everyone, many locals wouldn't visit the park. If Disney were to use the lower price for everyone, it would be charging nonresidents much less than they are willing to pay. Thus price discrimination increases Disney's profit.

Which Firms Can Price Discriminate

Not all firms can price discriminate. For a firm to price discriminate successfully, three conditions must be met.

First, a firm must have market power. Without market power, a firm cannot charge any consumer more than the competitive price. A monopoly, an oligopoly firm, or a monopolistically competitive firm might be able to price discriminate. However, a

---

[3]According to **www.babycenter.com**, it costs $411,214 to raise a child from cradle through college. Parents can cut that total in half, however: They don't *have* to take their kids to Disneyland.

[4]In 2012, a Southern Californian couple, Jeff Reitz and Tonya Mickesh, were out of work, so they decided to cheer themselves up by using their annual passes to visit Disneyland 366 days that year (a leap year).

perfectly competitive firm cannot price discriminate because it must sell its product at the given market price.

Second, for a firm to profitably discriminate, groups of consumers or individual consumers must have demand curves that differ, and the firm must be able to identify how its consumers' demand curves differ. The movie theater knows that college students and senior citizens differ in their willingness to pay for a ticket, and Disneyland knows that tourists and local residents differ in their willingness to pay for admission. In both cases, the firms can identify members of these two groups by using driver's licenses or other forms of identification. Similarly, if a firm knows that each individual's demand curve slopes downward, it may charge each customer a higher price for the first unit of a good than for subsequent units.

Third, a firm must be able to prevent or limit resale. The price-discriminating firm must be able to prevent consumers who buy the good at low prices from reselling the good to customers who would otherwise pay high prices. Price discrimination doesn't work if resale is easy because the firm would be able to make only low-price sales. A movie theater can charge different prices for different groups of customers because those customers normally enter the theater as soon as they buy their tickets, and therefore they do not have time to resell them. For events that sell tickets in advance, other methods can be used to prevent resale, such as having different colors for children's tickets and adults' tickets.

The first two conditions—market power and the ability to identify groups with different price sensitivities—are present in many markets. Usually, the biggest obstacle to price discrimination is a firm's inability to prevent resale.

Managerial Implication

Preventing Resale

In some industries, preventing resale is easier than in others. In industries where resale is initially easy, managers can act to make resale more costly.

Resale is difficult or impossible for most services. If a plumber charges you less than your neighbor for fixing a clogged water pipe, you cannot make a deal with your neighbor to resell this service. Even for physical goods, resale is difficult when transaction costs are high. The higher the transaction costs a consumer must incur to resell a good, the less likely resale becomes. Suppose that you are able to buy a 50-pound bag of cement (which, in addition to being heavy, is also dusty) for $1 less than the usual price. Would you take the time and trouble to buy the cement and seek a buyer willing to pay an extra dollar, or would the transaction costs be prohibitive? The more valuable a product is and the more widely consumed it is, the more likely it is that transaction costs are low enough to allow resale.

Some firms act to raise transaction costs or otherwise make resale difficult. If your college requires that someone with a student ticket to a sporting event show a student identification card containing a photo, it will be difficult to resell your low-price tickets to nonstudents who pay higher prices. When students at some universities buy computers at lower-than-usual prices, they must sign a contract that forbids resale of the computer. Disney prevents resale by locals who can buy a ticket at a lower price by checking driver's licenses and requiring that the ticket be used for same-day entrance.

Governments frequently aid price discrimination by preventing resale. Government *tariffs* (taxes on imports) limit resale by making it expensive to buy a branded good in a low-price country and resell it in a high-price country. For example, under U.S. trade laws, certain brand-name perfumes may not be sold in the United States except by their manufacturers. Similarly, if the countries have very different safety rules, a product sold in one country might not be legally sold in another.

However, such a resale is legal for many products. Imported goods that go through legal, but unofficial channels that are unauthorized by the original manufacturer are said to sell in a *gray market* or *parallel market*. To make such a transaction unattractive Nikon provides a warranty that is only good in the country in which the good is supposed to be sold. Similarly, Canon sells a Rebel DSLR camera in the United States, but calls it the EOS DSLR elsewhere.

Mini-Case

Preventing Resale of Designer Bags

During the holiday season, stores often limit how many of the hottest items— such as this year's best-selling toy—a customer can buy. But it may surprise you that websites of luxury-goods retailers such as Saks Fifth Avenue, Neiman Marcus, and Bergdorf Goodman limit how many designer handbags a person can buy: "Due to popular demand, a customer may order no more than three units of this item every 30 days."

Why wouldn't manufacturers and stores want to sell as many units as possible? How many customers can even afford more than three Prada Visone Hobo handbags at $4,950 each? The simple explanation is that the restriction has nothing to do with "popular demand." Instead, it's designed to prevent resale so as to enable manufacturers to price discriminate internationally. The handbag manufacturers pressure the U.S. retailers to limit sales to prevent anyone from buying large numbers of bags and reselling them in Europe or Asia where the same items in Prada and Gucci stores often cost 20% to 40% more. For example, the Prada Nappa Antique Tote sells for $1,280 at Saks Fifth Avenue in New York City, but sells for $1,570 on Prada's Swiss website. A weak U.S. dollar makes such international resale even more attractive, which explains why Prada's online site allows shipments only to selected countries, expressly forbids resale, and limits purchases.

Not All Price Differences Are Price Discrimination

Not every seller who charges consumers different prices is price discriminating. A firm price discriminates by charging different prices for units of a good that cost the same to produce. In contrast, newsstand prices and subscription prices for magazines differ in large part because of the higher cost of selling at a newsstand rather than the lower cost of mailing magazines directly to consumers.

The 2013 price for 51 weekly issues of the *Economist* magazine for a year is $356 if you buy it at the newsstand, $160 for a standard print subscription, and $96 for a college student subscription. The difference between the newsstand cost and the standard subscription cost reflects, at least in part, the higher cost of selling magazines at a newsstand versus mailing them directly to customers, so this price difference does not reflect pure price discrimination. In contrast, the price difference between the standard subscription rate and the college student rate does reflect pure price discrimination because the two subscriptions are identical in every respect except the price.

Types of Price Discrimination

Traditionally, economists focus on three types of price discrimination: perfect price discrimination, group price discrimination, and nonlinear price discrimination. With **perfect price discrimination**—also called *first-degree price discrimination*—the firm sells each unit at the maximum amount any customer is willing to pay. Under perfect price discrimination, price differs across consumers, and a given consumer may pay higher prices for some units than for others.

With **group price discrimination**—also called *third-degree price discrimination*—the firm charges each group of customers a different price, but it does not charge different prices within the group. The price that a firm charges a consumer depends on that consumer's membership in a particular group. Thus not all customers pay different prices—the firm sets different prices only for a few groups of customers. Group price discrimination is the most common type of price discrimination.

A firm engages in **nonlinear price discrimination** (also called *second-degree price discrimination*) when it charges a different price for large purchases than for small quantities, so that the price paid varies according to the quantity purchased. With pure nonlinear price discrimination, all customers who buy a given quantity pay the same price; however, firms can combine nonlinear price discrimination with group price discrimination, setting different nonlinear price schedules for different groups of consumers.

10.2 Perfect Price Discrimination

A firm with market power that knows exactly how much each customer is willing to pay for each unit of its good and that can prevent resale, can charge each person his or her **reservation price**: the maximum amount a person is willing to pay for a unit of output. Such an all-knowing firm can *perfectly price discriminate*. By selling each unit of its output to the customer who values it the most at the maximum price that person is willing to pay, the perfectly price-discriminating monopoly captures all possible consumer surplus.

Perfect price discrimination is rare because firms do not have perfect information about their customers. Nevertheless, it is useful to examine perfect price discrimination because it is the most efficient form of price discrimination and provides a benchmark against which we can compare other types of nonuniform pricing.

We now show how a firm with full information about consumer reservation prices can use that information to perfectly price discriminate. Next, we compare the market outcomes (price, quantity, surplus) of a perfectly price-discriminating monopoly to those of perfectly competitive and uniform-price monopoly firms.

How a Firm Perfectly Price Discriminates

A firm with market power that can prevent resale and has full information about its customers' willingness-to-pay price discriminates by selling each unit at its reservation price—the maximum amount any consumer would pay for it. The maximum price for any unit of output is given by the height of the demand curve at that output level. In the demand curve facing a monopoly in Figure 10.1, the first customer is willing to pay $6 for a unit, the next is willing to pay $5, and so forth. A perfectly price-discriminating firm sells its first unit of output for $6. Having sold the first unit, the firm can get at most $5 for its second unit. The firm must drop its price by $1 for each successive unit it sells.

FIGURE 10.1 Perfect Price Discrimination

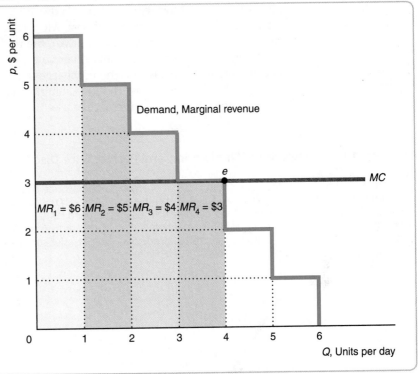

The monopoly can charge $6 for the first unit, $5 for the second, and $4 for the third, as the demand curve shows. Its marginal revenue is $MR_1 = \$6$ for the first unit, $MR_2 = \$5$ for the second unit, and $MR_3 = \$4$ for the third unit. Thus, the demand curve is also the marginal revenue curve. Because the firm's marginal and average cost is $3 per unit, it is unwilling to sell at a price below $3, so it sells 4 units, point e, and breaks even on the last unit.

A perfectly price-discriminating firm's marginal revenue is the same as its price. As the figure shows, the firm's marginal revenue is $MR_1 = \$6$ on the first unit, $MR_2 = \$5$ on the second unit, and $MR_3 = \$4$ on the third unit. As a result, *if it can perfectly price discriminate, a firm's marginal revenue curve is the same as its demand curve.*

This firm has a constant marginal cost of $3 per unit. It pays for the firm to produce the first unit because the firm sells that unit for $6, so its marginal revenue exceeds its marginal cost by $3. Similarly, the firm sells the second unit for $5 and the third unit for $4. The firm breaks even when it sells the fourth unit for $3. The firm is unwilling to sell more than four units because its marginal cost would exceed its marginal revenue on all successive units. Thus, like any profit-maximizing firm, a perfectly price-discriminating firm produces at point e, where its marginal revenue curve intersects its marginal cost curve.

This perfectly price-discriminating firm earns revenues of $MR_1 + MR_2 + MR_3 + MR_4 = \$6 + \$5 + \$4 + \$3 = \$18$, which is the area under its marginal revenue curve up to the number of units, four, it sells. If the firm has no fixed cost, its cost of producing four units is $12 = \$3 \times 4$, so its profit is $6.

Perfect Price Discrimination Is Efficient but Harms Some Consumers

Perfect price discrimination is efficient: It maximizes the sum of consumer surplus and producer surplus. Therefore, both perfect competition and perfect price discrimination maximize total surplus. However, *with perfect price discrimination, the entire surplus goes to the firm, whereas under competition consumers obtain some surplus.*

If the market illustrated in Figure 10.2 is competitive, the intersection of the demand curve and the marginal cost curve, MC, determines the competitive equilibrium at e_c, where price is p_c and quantity is Q_c. Consumer surplus is $A + B + C$, producer surplus is $D + E$, and society suffers no deadweight loss. The market is efficient because the price, p_c, equals the marginal cost, MC_c. With a single-price monopoly (which charges all its customers the same price), the intersection of the MC curve and the single-price monopoly's marginal revenue curve, MR_s, determines the output, Q_s.[5] The monopoly operates at e_s, where it charges p_s. The deadweight loss from monopoly is $C + E$. This efficiency loss is due to charging a price, p_s, above marginal cost, MC_s, so less is sold than in a competitive market.

FIGURE 10.2 Competitive, Single-Price, and Perfect Price Discrimination Outcomes

In the competitive market equilibrium, e_c, price is p_c, quantity is Q_c, consumer surplus is $A + B + C$, producer surplus is $D + E$, and society has no deadweight loss. In the single-price monopoly equilibrium, e_s, price is p_s, quantity is Q_s, consumer surplus falls to A, producer surplus is $B + D$, and deadweight loss is $C + E$. In the perfect price discrimination equilibrium, the monopoly sells each unit at the customer's reservation price on the demand curve. It sells $Q_d(= Q_c)$ units, where the last unit is sold at its marginal cost. Customers have no consumer surplus, but society has no deadweight loss.

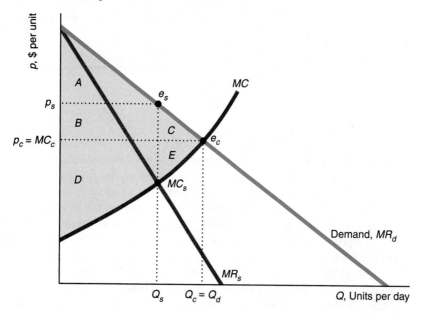

		Monopoly	
	Competition	Single Price	Perfect Price Discrimination
Consumer Surplus, CS	$A + B + C$	A	0
Producer Surplus, PS	$D + E$	$B + D$	$A + B + C + D + E$
Total Surplus, $TS = CS + PS$	$A + B + C + D + E$	$A + B + D$	$A + B + C + D + E$
Deadweight Loss	0	$C + E$	0

---

[5]We assume that if we convert a monopoly into a competitive industry, the industry's marginal cost curve—the lowest cost at which an additional unit can be produced by any firm—is the same as the monopoly MC curve. The industry MC curve is the industry supply curve (Chapter 8).

A perfectly price-discriminating firm sells each unit at its reservation price, which is the height of the demand curve. As a result, the firm's price-discrimination marginal revenue curve, MR_d, is the same as its demand curve. It sells the Q_d unit for p_c, where its marginal revenue curve, MR_d, intersects the marginal cost curve, MC, so it just covers its marginal cost on the last unit. The firm is unwilling to sell additional units because its marginal revenue would be less than the marginal cost of producing them.

A perfectly price-discriminating firm's producer surplus from the Q_d units it sells is the area below its demand curve and above its marginal cost curve, $A + B + C + D + E$. Its profit is the producer surplus minus its fixed cost, if any. Consumers receive no consumer surplus because each consumer pays his or her reservation price. The perfectly price-discriminating firm's profit-maximizing solution has *no deadweight loss* because the last unit is sold at a price, p_c, that equals the marginal cost, MC_c, as in a competitive market. Thus, both a perfect price discrimination outcome and a competitive equilibrium are efficient.

The perfect price discrimination solution differs from the competitive equilibrium in two important ways. First, in the competitive equilibrium, everyone is charged a price equal to the equilibrium marginal cost, $p_c = MC_c$; however, in the perfect price discrimination equilibrium, only the last unit is sold at that price. The other units are sold at customers' reservation prices, which are greater than p_c. Second, consumers receive some net benefit (consumer surplus, $A + B + C$) in a competitive market, whereas a perfectly price-discriminating monopoly captures all the surplus or potential gains from trade. Thus, perfect price discrimination does not reduce efficiency—both output and total surplus are the same as under competition—but it does redistribute income away from consumers. Consumers are much better off under competition.

Is a single-price or perfectly price-discriminating monopoly better for consumers? The perfect price discrimination equilibrium is more efficient than the single-price monopoly equilibrium because more output is produced. A single-price monopoly, however, takes less consumer surplus from consumers than a perfectly price-discriminating monopoly. Consumers who put a very high value on the good are better off under single-price monopoly, where they have consumer surplus, than with perfect price discrimination, where they have none. Consumers with lower reservation prices who purchase from the perfectly price-discriminating monopoly but not from the single-price monopoly have no consumer surplus in either case. All the social gain from the extra output goes to the seller under perfect price discrimination. Consumer surplus is greatest with competition, lower with single-price monopoly, and eliminated by perfect price discrimination.

Mini-Case	To show how perfect price discrimination differs from competition and single-price monopoly, we revisit the Mini-Case on Allergan's Botox from Chapter 9. The graph shows our estimated linear demand curve for Botox and a constant marginal cost (and average variable cost) of $25 per vial. If the market were competitive (so that price equals marginal cost at e_c), consumer surplus would be the triangle $A + B + C = \$750$ million per year, and there would have been no producer surplus or deadweight loss. In the (actual) single-price monopoly equilibrium, e_s, the Botox vials sell for $400 each, and one million vials are sold. The corresponding consumer surplus is triangle $A = \$187.5$ million per year, producer surplus is rectangle $B = \$375$ million, and the deadweight loss is triangle $C = \$187.5$ million.
Botox Revisited	

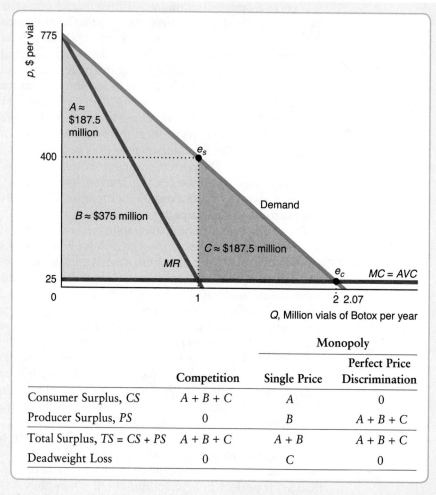

	Competition	Monopoly	
		Single Price	Perfect Price Discrimination
Consumer Surplus, CS	$A + B + C$	A	0
Producer Surplus, PS	0	B	$A + B + C$
Total Surplus, $TS = CS + PS$	$A + B + C$	$A + B$	$A + B + C$
Deadweight Loss	0	C	0

If Allergan could perfectly price discriminate, its producer surplus would double to $A + B + C = \$750$ million per year, and consumers would obtain no consumer surplus. The marginal consumer would pay a price equal to the marginal cost of $25, just as in a competitive market.

Both Allergan and society suffer from Allergan's inability to perfectly price discriminate. The profit of the single-price monopoly is $375 million per year, which is lower than what it could earn if it used perfect price discrimination, $A + B + C = \$750$ million per year. Similarly, society's total surplus under single-price monopoly is lower than under perfect price discrimination by the deadweight loss, C, of $187.5 million per year.

Q&A 10.1

How does total surplus change if the movie theater described in Table 10.1 goes from charging a single price to perfectly price discriminating?

Answer

1. *Calculate total surplus for panel a (a) if the theater sets a single price, (b) if it perfectly price discriminates, and (c) compare them.* (a) If the theater sets the profit-maximizing single price of $10, it sells 30 tickets and makes a profit of $300. The 20 senior citizen customers are paying their reservation price, so they

have no consumer surplus. The 10 college students have reservation prices of $20, so they have consumer surplus of $10 each for a total of $100. Thus, total surplus is $400: the sum of the producer surplus (which equals profit in this case) of $300, and the consumer surplus of $100. (b) If the firm perfectly price discriminates, it charges seniors $10 and college students $20. Because the theater is charging all customers their reservation prices, they have no consumer surplus. The firm's profit rises to $400. (c) Thus, *total surplus is the same ($400) under both pricing systems and output stays the same.*

2. *Calculate total surplus for panel b (a) if the theater sets a single price, (b) if it perfectly price discriminates, and (c) compare them.* (a) If the theater sets the profit-maximizing single price of $20, only college students attend and they receive no consumer surplus. The theater's profit (producer surplus) is $200, so total surplus is $200. (b) With perfect price discrimination, consumers have no consumer surplus, but profit increases to $250, so total surplus rises to $250. (c) Thus, *total surplus is greater with perfect price discrimination and output is greater.* (The result that total surplus increases if and only if output rises holds generally.)

Individual Price Discrimination

Perfect price discrimination is rarely fully achieved in practice because firms lack full information about individuals' reservation prices. For example, a coffee shop would have to know that Yi Lin is willing to pay $4 for her first cup of coffee, $3 for her second, and so on and then actually charge these amounts. We use the term *individual price discrimination* to refer to a situation in which a firm charges individual-specific prices to different consumers, which may or may not exactly equal consumers' reservation prices. Even if firms cannot achieve perfect price discrimination, imperfect individual price discrimination can increase their profits significantly.

Some firms do a good job of estimating each person's reservation price. At most car dealerships, a salesperson negotiates with potential buyers. During the discussions, the salesperson tries to determine each individual's reservation price from the buyer's comments and appearance. Is the potential buyer a local? Is the buyer wearing expensive clothing? Does the buyer claim to own other expensive cars? The salesperson uses this information to estimate the buyer's reservation price and offers to sell the car at that price. As a result, prices vary across consumers for a given car. Similarly, the managers of the Suez Canal set tolls on an individual ship-by-ship basis, taking into account many factors such as weather and each ship's alternative routes.

Private colleges request and receive financial information from students, which allows the schools to apply individual price discrimination. The schools give partial scholarships as a means of reducing tuition to relatively poor students who presumably have lower willingness to pay than wealthier students.

Transaction costs are a major reason why these firms do not perfectly price discriminate: It is often too difficult or costly to gather information about each customer's reservation price for each unit of the product. However, recent advances in computer technologies have lowered these transaction costs, causing hotels, car and truck rental companies, cruise lines, airlines and other firms to increasingly use individual price discrimination, as the following Mini-Case illustrates.

Selling over the Internet facilitates price discrimination. Managers often use the term *dynamic pricing* instead of price discrimination. Dynamic pricing refers to a situation in which the firm can easily and quickly change the price it charges across customers or over time as market conditions change. Basically, the firm tries to charge customers the maximum that each is willing to pay for the product under current conditions. Thus, dynamic pricing based on willingness to pay is the same as price discrimination.

Amazon, a giant among e-commerce vendors, collects an enormous amount of information about its millions of customers' tastes and willingness to buy. If you've shopped at Amazon, you've probably noticed that its website now greets you by name (thanks to a *cookie* it leaves on your computer, which provides information about you to Amazon).

A few years ago, Amazon decided to use this information to engage in dynamic pricing, where the price it charged a customer for a product would depend on that customer's actions in the recent past—including what the customer bought, the prices they paid, the type of shipping purchased (high speed or regular)—and personal data such as where the customer lives. Several Amazon customers discovered this practice. One man reported on the website **DVDTalk.com** that he had bought Julie Taylor's "Titus" for $24.49. The next week, he returned to Amazon and saw that the price had jumped to $26.24. As an experiment, he removed the cookie that identified him, and found that the price dropped to $22.74.

Presumably, Amazon reasoned that a returning customer was less likely to compare prices across websites than was a new customer, and was pricing accordingly. Other DVDTalk visitors reported that regular Amazon customers were charged 3% to 5% more than new customers.

Amazon announced that its pricing variations stopped after it received these complaints. It claimed that the variations were random and designed only to determine price elasticities. A spokesperson explained, "This was a pure and simple price test. This was not dynamic pricing. We don't do that and have no plans ever to do that." However, an Amazon customer service representative called it dynamic pricing in an e-mail to a DVDTalk member, noting that dynamic pricing was a common practice among firms. However, Amazon does seem to have stopped the practice. An academic study found only random fluctuations in prices that did not appear to be tied to individuals' purchasing behavior.

10.3 Group Price Discrimination

Most firms have no practical way to estimate the reservation price for each of their customers. But many of these firms know which groups of customers are likely to have higher reservation prices on average than others. A firm engages in *group price discrimination* by dividing potential customers into two or more groups and setting different prices for each group. Consumer groups may differ by age (such as adults and children), by location (such as by country), or in other ways. All units of the good sold to customers within a group are sold at a single price. As with individual price discrimination, to engage in group price discrimination, a firm must have market power, be able to identify groups with different reservation prices, and prevent resale.

For example, first-run movie theaters with market power charge seniors a lower ticket price than they charge younger adults because typically the elderly are unwilling to pay as much to see a movie. By admitting seniors immediately after they prove their age and buy tickets, the theater prevents resale.

Group Price Discrimination with Two Groups

How does a firm set its prices if it sells to two (or more) groups of consumers with different demand curves and if resale between the two groups is impossible? We explain the process in the following example which looks at a firm that sells to groups of consumers in different countries.

A copyright gives Warner Brothers the legal monopoly to produce and sell the *Harry Potter and the Deathly Hallows, Part 2* DVD. Warner engaged in group price discrimination by charging different prices in various countries. It can ignore the problem of resale between the countries because the DVDs have incompatible formats.

A Graphical Approach. If it can prevent customers in the low cost country from reselling the movie in the other country and if it has a constant marginal cost, then a firm that uses group price discrimination can maximize its overall profit by acting like a traditional monopoly in each country separately. Resale is not a problem between the United States and the United Kingdom because these countries use different DVD formats. The marginal cost of production—primarily the cost of replicating a DVD— is constant, m, which is about $1 per unit.

How should Warner Brothers set its prices p_A and p_B—or, equivalently, Q_A and Q_B— so that it maximizes its combined profit? Because its marginal cost is the same for both sets of customers, we can use our understanding of a single-price monopoly's behavior to answer this question. A group-price-discriminating monopoly with a constant marginal cost maximizes its total profit by maximizing its profit from each group separately. Warner Brothers sets its quantities so that the marginal revenue for each group equals the common marginal cost, m, which is about $1 per unit.

The DVD was released during the holiday season of 2011 and sold Q_A = 5.8 million copies to American consumers at p_A = $29 and Q_B = 2.0 million copies to British consumers at p_B = $39 (£25).[6] We estimate that Warner Brothers has a constant marginal cost of m = $1 in both countries. Figure 10.3 shows our estimates of the linear demand curves in the two countries. In panel a, Warner maximizes its U.S. profit by selling Q_A = 5.8 million DVDs, where its marginal revenue equals its marginal cost $MR^A = m = 1$ (Chapter 9), and charging p_A = $29. Similarly in panel b, Warner maximizes its U.K. profit by selling Q_B = 2.0 million DVDs where $MR^B = m$ = $1, and charging p_B = $39.

Thus, the price-discriminating firm maximizes its profit by operating where its marginal revenue for each country equals its common marginal cost, m = $1, so the marginal revenues in the two countries are equal:

$$MR^A = m = MR^B. \tag{10.1}$$

---

[6]Sources of information and data for this section (viewed July 10, 2012) include Amazon websites for each country, **warnerbros.com**, the UK Film Council, **www.the-numbers.com/dvd/charts/annual/2011.php**, and **www.bbc.co.uk/newsbeat/16444062**, January 6, 2012. We assume that the demand curves in each country are linear.

FIGURE 10.3 **Group Pricing of the *Harry Potter* DVD**

Warner Brothers, the monopoly producer of the *Harry Potter and the Deathly Hallows, Part 2* DVD, charges more in the United Kingdom, p_B = $39 (£25), than in the United States, p_A = $29, because demand is more elastic in the United States. Warner Brothers sets the quantity independently in each country, where its relevant marginal revenue equals its common, constant marginal cost, m = $1. As a result, it maximizes its profit by equating the two marginal revenues: MR^A = 1 = MR^B.

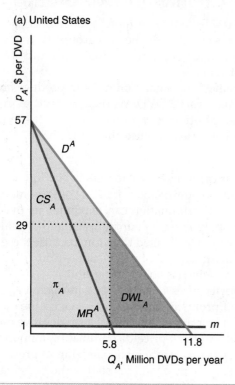

(a) United States

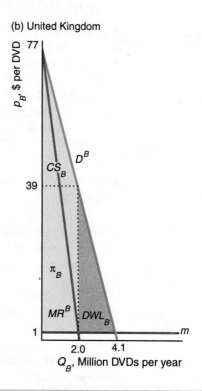

(b) United Kingdom

Using Calculus

Maximizing Profit for a Group Discriminating Monopoly

We can also derive these results using calculus. The group discriminating monopoly's total profit, π, is the sum of its American profit, π_A, and its British profit, π_B:

$$\pi(Q_A, Q_B) = \pi_A(Q_A) + \pi_B(Q_B) = [R_A(Q_A) - mQ_A] + [R_B(Q_B) - mQ_B],$$

where $R_A(Q_A) = p_A(Q_A)Q_A$, is the revenue function for Country A, $p_A(Q_A)$ is the inverse demand function for Country A, and $R_B(Q_B)$ is similarly defined. Again, because of the constant marginal cost of production, the firm's profit in either country depends only on the quantity that it sells in that country.[7]

To find the Q_A and Q_B that maximize Warner's total profit, we can maximize its profit in each country separately as we did in the graphical approach. However, here we solve for the optimal quantities simultaneously (which we would have to do if the marginal cost were not constant). We differentiate the monopoly's

---

[7]For a more general cost function, $C(Q_A, Q_B)$, Warner's profit in each country would depend on the amount it sold in both countries.

profit function with respect to each quantity, holding the other quantity fixed, and set these derivatives equal to zero:

$$\frac{\partial \pi(Q_A, Q_B)}{\partial Q_A} = \frac{dR_A(Q_A)}{dQ_A} - m = 0, \tag{10.2}$$

$$\frac{\partial \pi(Q_A, Q_B)}{\partial Q_B} = \frac{dR_B(Q_B)}{dQ_B} - m = 0. \tag{10.3}$$

According to Equation 10.2, the monopoly sets the marginal revenue in Country A, $MR^A = dR_A/dQ_A$, equal to its constant marginal cost, m. Similarly, Equation 10.3 says the marginal revenue in Country B, $MR^B = dR_B/dQ_B$, equals the marginal cost, m. Consequently, Equation 10.1 holds: $MR^A = m = MR^B$.

Prices and Elasticities. We can use Equation 10.1, $MR^A = m = MR^B$, to determine how the prices in the two countries vary with the price elasticities of demand at the profit-maximizing outputs. Each country's marginal revenue is a function of its price and the price elasticity of demand (Chapter 9). The U.S. marginal revenue is $MR^A = p_A(1 + 1/\varepsilon_A)$, where ε_A is the price elasticity of demand for U.S. consumers, and the U.K. marginal revenue is $MR^B = p_B(1 + 1/\varepsilon_B)$, where ε_B is the price elasticity of demand for British consumers.

Rewriting Equation 10.1 using these expressions for marginal revenue, we find that

$$MR^A = p_A\left(1 + \frac{1}{\varepsilon_A}\right) = m = p_B\left(1 + \frac{1}{\varepsilon_B}\right) = MR^B. \tag{10.4}$$

Given that $m = \$1$, $p_A = \$29$, and $p_B = \$39$ in Equation 10.4, Warner Brothers must believe that $\varepsilon_A = p_A/[m - p_A] = 29/[-28] \approx -1.0357$ and $\varepsilon_B = p_B/[m - p_B] = 39/[-38] \approx -1.0263$.[8]

By rearranging Equation 10.4, we learn that the ratio of prices in the two countries can be written as a function of the demand elasticities in those countries:

$$\frac{p_B}{p_A} = \frac{1 + 1/\varepsilon_A}{1 + 1/\varepsilon_B}. \tag{10.5}$$

Substituting the prices and the demand elasticities into Equation 10.5, we determine that

$$\frac{p_B}{p_A} = \frac{\$39}{\$29} \approx 1.345 \approx \frac{1 + 1/(-1.0357)}{1 + 1/(-1.0263)} = \frac{1 + 1/\varepsilon_A}{1 + 1/\varepsilon_B}.$$

Thus, Warner Brothers apparently believed that the British demand curve was less elastic at its profit-maximizing prices than the U.S. demand curve, as $\varepsilon_B \approx -1.0263$

---

[8]We obtain the expression that $\varepsilon_i = p_i/(m - p_i)$ by rearranging the expression in Equation 10.4: $p_i(1 + 1/\varepsilon_i) = m$.

is closer to zero than is $\varepsilon_A \approx -1.0357$. Consequently, Warner charged British consumers 34% more than U.S. customers.[9]

Mini-Case

**Reselling
Textbooks**

When Supap Kirtsaeng, a Thai math student, was an undergraduate at Cornell University and later a Ph.D. student at the University of Southern California, he found a way to pay for his education. He had his friends and relatives ship him textbooks that they bought in Thailand, which he resold to U.S. college students on eBay and elsewhere, netting hundreds of thousands of dollars.

Why was reselling these books profitable? U.S. textbooks sell at much lower prices in foreign markets. Many of these books differ from their U.S. versions only by having a soft cover with an "international edition" label.

John Wiley & Sons, a publisher, sued Mr. Kirtsaeng for copyright infringement. The company claimed that by importing and selling its books, Mr. Kirtsaeng infringed the company's copyright. It asserted that the *first-sale* doctrine—which allows people who buy something to use or resell it however they want—did not apply to goods produced specifically for sale overseas.

The U.S. Court of Appeals for the 2nd Circuit in New York agreed with Wiley and upheld a $600,000 judgment against Mr. Kirtsaeng. However, in 2013, the U.S. Supreme Court reversed that ruling by a six-to-three vote, concluding that the first-sale rule holds generally. This decision applies to records, movies, art, software, and other goods as well as books that are covered under copyright law.[10]

Thus, unless Congress changes the copyright law, publishers will find it more difficult to maintain price differentials across countries. A possible consequence of this ruling is that low-income foreign students will no longer be able to afford textbooks because the foreign price will rise. The U.S. and foreign price will differ by only the transaction cost of reselling the books. If those transaction costs are negligible, a single price will be charged throughout the world.

Alternatively, publishers may prevent resale. One possibility is that they will differentiate U.S. and foreign textbooks substantially to prevent reselling; however, doing so is expensive and time-consuming. Once electronic textbooks become common, students will likely rent the books for the term and be unable to resell them.

Q&A 10.2

A monopoly book publisher with a constant marginal cost (and average cost) of $MC = 1$ sells a novel in only two countries and faces a linear inverse demand curve of $p_1 = 6 - \frac{1}{2}Q_1$ in Country 1 and $p_2 = 9 - Q_2$ in Country 2. What price would a profit-maximizing monopoly charge in each country with and without a ban against shipments between the countries?

---

[9]By mid-2012, Amazon dropped the price for this DVD at its sites around the world, but maintained its price differentials. Amazon's U.S. price fell to $7, while its U.K. price dropped to $9.50, which still reflected about the same British markup: 36%.

[10]However, the Supreme Court held in 2010 that Omega could prevent Costco from selling its watches produced outside the United States, citing a tiny trademark on each watch, so that they came under the jurisdiction of trademark laws, which provide owners more protection than do copyright laws.

Answer

If resale across borders is banned so that price discrimination is possible:

1. *Determine the profit-maximizing price that the monopoly sets in each country by setting the relevant marginal revenue equal to the marginal cost.* If the monopoly can price discriminate, it sets a monopoly price independently in each country. The marginal revenue curve is twice as steeply sloped as is the linear inverse demand function (see Q&A 9.1), so the marginal revenue function in Country 1 is $MR_1 = 6 - Q_1$, as panel a of the figure shows. The monopoly maximizes its profit where its marginal revenue function equals its marginal cost,

$$MR_1 = 6 - Q_1 = 1 = MC.$$

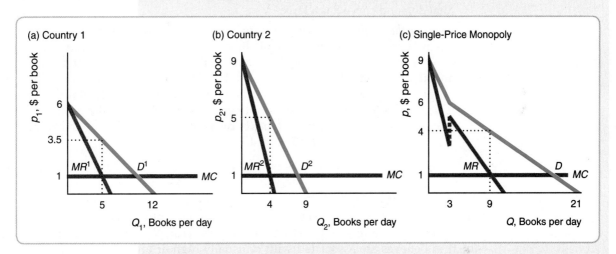

(a) Country 1

(b) Country 2

(c) Single-Price Monopoly

Solving, we find that its profit-maximizing output is $Q_1 = 5$. Substituting this expression back into the monopoly's inverse demand function, we learn that its profit-maximizing price is $p_1 = 3.5$, as panel a illustrates. In Country 2, the inverse demand function is $p_2 = 9 - Q_2$, so the monopoly chooses Q_2 such that $MR_2 = 9 - 2Q_2 = 1 = MC$. Thus, it maximizes its profit in Country 2 where $Q_2 = 4$ and $p_2 = 5$, as panel b shows.

If imports are permitted so that price discrimination is impossible:

2. *Derive the total demand curve.* If the monopoly cannot price discriminate, it charges the same price, p, in both countries. The monopoly faces the total demand curve in panel c, which is the horizontal sum of the demand curves for each of the two countries in panels a and b (Chapter 2). If the price is between 6 and 9, the quantity demanded is positive in only Country 2, so the total demand curve (panel c) is the same as Country 2's demand curve (panel b). If the price is less than 6 where both countries demand a positive quantity, the total demand curve (panel c) is the horizontal sum of the two individual countries' demand curves (panels a and b).[11] As panel c shows, the total demand

---

[11]Rearranging the inverse demand functions, we find that the Country 1 demand function is $Q_1 = 12 - p_1$ and the Country 2 demand function is $Q_2 = 9 - p_2$. As a result for price below 6, the total demand function is $Q = (12 - 2p) + (9 - p) = 21 - 3p$, where $Q = Q_1 + Q_2$ is the total quantity that the monopoly sells in both countries.

curve has a kink at $p = 6$, because the quantity demanded in Country 1 is positive only below this price.

3. *Determine the marginal revenue curve corresponding to the total demand curve.* Because the total demand curve has a kink at $p = 6$, the corresponding marginal revenue curve has two sections. At prices above 6, the marginal revenue curve is the same as that of Country 2 in panel b. At prices below 6, where the total demand curve is the horizontal sum of the two countries' demand curves, the marginal revenue curve has twice the slope of the linear total inverse demand curve. The inverse total demand function is $p = 7 - \frac{1}{3}Q$, and the marginal revenue function is $MR = 7\frac{2}{3}Q$.[12] Panel c shows that the marginal revenue curve *jumps*—is discontinuous—at the quantity where the total demand curve has a kink.

4. *Solve for the single-price monopoly solution.* The monopoly maximizes its profit where its marginal revenue equals its marginal cost. From inspecting panel c, we learn that the intersection occurs in the section where both countries are buying the good: $MR = 7 - \frac{2}{3}Q = 1 = MC$. Thus, the profit-maximizing output is $Q = 9$. Substituting that quantity into the inverse total demand function, we find that the monopoly charges $p = 4$. Thus, the price of the nondiscriminating monopoly, 4, lies between the two prices it would charge if it could price discriminate: $3.50 < 4 < 5$.

Identifying Groups

Firms use two main approaches to divide customers into groups. One method is to divide buyers into groups based on *observable characteristics* of consumers that the firm believes are associated with unusually high or low reservation prices or demand elasticities. For example, movie theaters price discriminate using the age of customers, charging higher prices for adults than for children. Similarly, some firms charge customers in one country higher prices than those in another country. In 2012, Windows 8 Pro upgrade sold for $95 in the United States, £97 ($125) in the United Kingdom, C$160 ($156) in Canada, €54 ($70) in France, and ¥7,290 ($77) in Japan. Most of these differences are much greater than can be explained by shipping costs and reflect group price discrimination.

Another approach is to identify and divide consumers on the basis of their *actions*: The firm allows consumers to self-select the group to which they belong. For example, customers may be identified by their willingness to spend time to buy a good at a lower price or to order goods and services in advance of delivery.

Firms use differences in the value customers place on their time to discriminate by using queues (making people wait in line) and other time-intensive methods of selling goods. Store managers who believe that high-wage people are unwilling to "waste their time shopping" may have sales that require consumers to visit the store and pick up the good themselves while consumers who order over the phone or online pay a higher price. This type of price discrimination increases profit if people who put a high value on their time also have less elastic demand for the good.

---

[12]From the previous footnote, we know that the total demand function for prices less than 6 is $Q = 21 - 3p$. Rearranging this expression, we find that the inverse demand function is $p = 7 - \frac{1}{3}Q$. Because the marginal revenue function has twice as steep a slope, it is $MR = 7 - \frac{2}{3}Q$.

Early adopters of a new product are often very enthusiastic and will pay premium prices. Firms can take advantage of early adopters by charging a high initial price for a new product and then lowering the price after the initial sales are made.

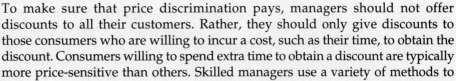

Managerial Implication

Discounts

To make sure that price discrimination pays, managers should not offer discounts to all their customers. Rather, they should only give discounts to those consumers who are willing to incur a cost, such as their time, to obtain the discount. Consumers willing to spend extra time to obtain a discount are typically more price-sensitive than others. Skilled managers use a variety of methods to induce customers to self-identify as being price sensitive by incurring a cost.

Coupons

Many firms use discount coupons to price discriminate. Through this device, firms divide customers into two groups: those who clip coupons and those who do not. People who are willing to spend their time clipping coupons buy cereals and other goods at lower prices than those who value their time more. A 2009 study by the Promotion Marketing Association Coupon Council found that consumers who spend 20 minutes per week clipping and organizing coupons could save up to $1,000 on an average annual grocery bill of $5,000 or more. More than three-quarters of U.S. consumers redeem coupons at least occasionally. In 2011, coupons with a face value of $470 billion were distributed by consumer package goods marketers to U.S. consumers. Of these, 3.5 billion coupons were redeemed for $4.6 billion.

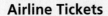
You've got to prove you really want a discount!

The introduction of digital (for example, **EverSave.com** and **zavers.com**) coupons has made it easier for firms to target appropriate groups, but has lowered consumers' costs of using coupons, which means that a larger share of people use them. According to eMarketer, 47% of U.S. adults used online coupons in 2012. Digital coupons are more likely to be redeemed (15%–20%) than are paper coupons (less than 1%).

Airline Tickets

By choosing between two different types of tickets, airline customers indicate whether they are likely to be business travelers or vacationers. Airlines give customers a choice between high-price tickets with no strings attached and low-price fares that must be purchased long in advance.

Airlines know that many business travelers have little advance warning before they book a flight and have relatively inelastic demand curves. In contrast, vacation travelers can usually plan in advance and have relatively high elasticities of demand for air travel. The airlines' rules ensure that vacationers with relatively elastic demand obtain low fares while most business travelers with relatively inelastic demand buy high-price tickets (often more than four times higher than the plan-ahead rate).

Reverse Auctions

Priceline.com and other online merchants use a name-your-own-price or reverse auction to identify price-sensitive customers. A customer enters a relatively low-price bid for a good, such as a grocery product, or a service, such as a concert ticket. Then the merchant decides whether to accept that bid or not. To keep their less price-sensitive customers from using those methods, airlines force successful Priceline bidders to be flexible: to fly at off hours, to make one or more connections, and to accept any type of aircraft. As Jay Walker, Priceline's founder explained, "The manufacturers would rather not give you a discount, of course, but if you prove that you're willing to switch brands, they're willing to pay to keep you."

Rebates

Why do many firms offer a rebate of, say, $5 instead of reducing the price on their product by $5? The reason is that a consumer must incur an extra, time-consuming step to receive the rebate. Thus, only those consumers who are price sensitive or place a low value on their time will actually apply for the rebate. According to a 2009 *Consumer Reports* survey, 47% of customers always or often apply for a rebate, 23% sometimes apply, 25% never apply, and 5% responded that the question was not applicable to them.

Effects of Group Price Discrimination on Total Surplus

Group price discrimination results in inefficient production and consumption. As a result, total surplus under group price discrimination is lower than that under competition or perfect price discrimination. However, total surplus may be lower or higher with group price discrimination than with a single-price monopoly.

Group Price Discrimination Versus Competition. Consumer surplus is greater and more output is produced with perfect competition than with group price discrimination. In Figure 10.3, consumer surplus with group price discrimination is CS_A for American consumers, shown in panel a and CS_B for British consumers, shown in panel b. Under competition, consumer surplus is the area below the demand curve and above the marginal cost curve: $CS_A + \pi_A + DWL_A$ in panel a and $CS_B + \pi_B + DWL_B$ in panel b.

Thus, group price discrimination transfers some of the competitive consumer surplus, π_A and π_B, to the firm as additional profit and causes deadweight loss, DWL_A and DWL_B, which is reduced consumer surplus that is simply lost or wasted. The deadweight loss is due to the price-discriminating firm charging prices above marginal cost, which results in reduced production from the optimal competitive level.

Group Price Discrimination Versus Single-Price Monopoly. From theory alone, we cannot tell whether total surplus is higher if the monopoly uses group price discrimination or if it sets a single price. Both approaches include a price above marginal cost, so too little is produced relative to competition. If a firm changes from uniform pricing to group price discrimination, it may attract additional price-sensitive customers by charging them low prices, which may cause its total sales to increase.

The closer the firm comes to perfect price discrimination using group price discrimination (by, for example, dividing its customers into many groups rather than just two), the more output it produces, and the less production inefficiency—the greater the total surplus. However, total surplus falls if the firm switches to group price discrimination and total output falls.[13]

10.4 Nonlinear Price Discrimination

Many firms are unable to determine which of their customers have the highest reservation prices. However, such firms may know that most customers are willing to pay more for the first unit than for successive units—that is, a typical customer's demand curve is downward sloping. Such a firm can price discriminate by letting the price each customer pays vary with the number of units the customer buys. That is, the firm uses *nonlinear price discrimination* (second-degree price discrimination). Here, the price varies with quantity but each customer faces the same nonlinear pricing schedule.[14] To use nonlinear pricing, a firm must have market power and be able to prevent customers who buy at a low price from reselling to those who would otherwise pay a high price.

A 64-ounce bottle of V8 vegetable juice sells for $4.39 or 6.8¢ an ounce, while a 12-ounce bottle sells for $2.79 or 23¢ an ounce. This difference in the price per ounce reflects nonlinear price discrimination unless the price difference is due to cost differences. This quantity discount results in customers who make large purchases paying less per unit than those who make small purchases.

Another nonlinear pricing strategy is *block pricing*. Many utilities use block pricing schedules, by which they charge one price per unit for the first few units (a *block*) purchased and a different price per unit for subsequent blocks. Both declining-block and increasing-block pricing are commonly used by gas, electric, water, and other utilities.

The block-pricing monopoly in Figure 10.4 faces a linear demand curve for each identical customer. The demand curve hits the vertical axis at $90 and the horizontal axis at 90 units. The monopoly has a constant marginal and average cost of $m = \$30$. Panel a shows how this monopoly maximizes its profit if it can engage in nonlinear price discrimination by setting two prices. The firm uses declining block prices to maximize its profit. The firm charges a price of $70 on any quantity between 1 and 20—the first block—and $50 on any units beyond the first 20—the second block. (The points that determine the blocks, $70 and 20 units and $50 and 40 units, lie on the demand curve.) Given each consumer's demand curve, a consumer decides to buy 40 units and pays $1,400 (= $70 × 20) for the first block and $1,000 (= $50 × 20)

---

[13]An additional source of inefficiency is time spent by consumers trying to resell the product to high-willingness-to-pay customers or searching for low prices. These activities do not occur if everyone knows the firm sets a uniform price.

[14]The term *nonlinear* is used because a consumer's expenditure is a nonlinear function of the quantity purchased. A consumer's expenditure, E, is a linear function of quantity, q, only if the price, p, is constant: $E = pq$. If the price varies with quantity, then the expenditure is not linear in quantity.

FIGURE 10.4 Block Pricing

If this monopoly engages in block pricing with quantity discounting, it makes a larger profit than it does if it sets a single price, and total surplus is greater. (a) With block pricing, its profit is $B = \$1,200$, total surplus is $A + B + C = \$1,600$, and the deadweight loss is $D = \$200$. (b) If the monopoly sets a single price (so that its marginal revenue equals its marginal cost), the monopoly's profit is $F = \$900$, total surplus is $E + F = \$1,350$, and the deadweight loss is $G = \$450$.

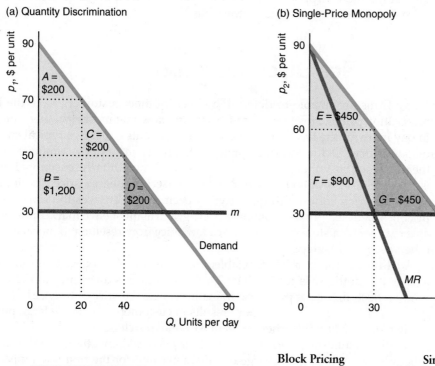

(a) Quantity Discrimination

(b) Single-Price Monopoly

	Block Pricing	Single Price
Consumer Surplus, CS	$A + C = \$400$	$E = \$450$
Producer Surplus or Profit, $PS = \pi$	$B = \$1,200$	$F = \$900$
Total Surplus, $TS = CS + PS$	$A + B + C = \$1,600$	$E + F = \$1,350$
Deadweight Loss, DWL	$D = \$200$	$G = \$450$

for the second block. The consumer gains consumer surplus equal to A on the first block and C on the second block, for a total of $A + C$. The discriminating monopoly's profit or producer surplus is area B. Society suffers a deadweight loss of D because price, $50, is above marginal cost, $30, on the last unit purchased.

In panel b, the firm can set only a single price. It produces where its marginal revenue equals its marginal cost, and sells 30 units at $60 per unit. By using nonlinear price discrimination instead of setting a single price, the utility sells more units, 40 instead of 30, and makes a larger profit, $B = \$1,200$ instead of $F = \$900$. With quantity discounting, consumer surplus is lower, $A + C = \$400$ instead of $E = \$450$; total surplus (consumer surplus plus producer surplus) is higher, $A + B + C = \$1,600$ instead of $E + F = \$1,350$; and deadweight loss is lower, $D = \$200$ instead of $G = \$450$. Thus, in this example, the firm is better off with nonlinear price discrimination, but consumers as a group suffer. Society as a whole—the combination of the firm and consumers—benefits.

The more block prices that a firm can set, the closer the firm gets to perfect price discrimination, where it captures all the potential consumer surplus, and its profit or producer surplus equals total surplus. Moreover, because the last unit is sold at a price equal to marginal cost, total surplus is maximized and society suffers no deadweight loss.

10.5 Two-Part Pricing

We now turn to another form of nonuniform pricing, *two-part pricing*. It is similar to nonlinear price discrimination in that the average price per unit paid by a consumer varies with the number of units purchased by that consumer.

With **two-part pricing**, the firm charges each consumer a lump-sum *access fee* for the right to buy as many units of the good as the consumer wants at a per-unit *price*.[15] Thus, a consumer's overall expenditure for amount q consists of two parts: an access fee, A and a per-unit price, p. Therefore, expenditure is $E = A + pq$.[16] Because of the access fee, the average amount per unit that consumers pay is greater if they buy a small number of units than if they buy a larger number.

Two-part pricing is commonly used.[17] Many fitness clubs charge a yearly access fee and a price per session. Many warehouse stores require that customers buy an annual membership before being allowed to buy goods at relatively low prices. Some car rental firms charge a rental or access fee for the day and an additional price per mile driven. To buy season tickets to the Dallas Cowboys football games in the lower seating areas (at a price from $590 to $1,250), a fan first must pay between $16,000 to $150,000 for a *personal seat license* (PSL), giving the fan the right to buy season tickets for the next 30 years.

To profit from two-part pricing, a firm must have market power and must successfully prevent resale. In addition, a firm must know how individual demand curves vary across its customers. We start by examining a firm's two-part pricing problem in the extreme case in which all customers have the same demand curve. We then consider what happens when the demand curves of individual customers differ.

Two-Part Pricing with Identical Consumers

If all its customers are identical, a firm that knows its customers' demand curve can set a two-part price that has the same two important properties that perfect price discrimination has. First, the efficient quantity is sold because the price of the last unit equals marginal cost. Second, all potential consumer surplus is transferred from consumers to the firm.

---

[15]The prices used in two-part pricing are often referred to as *two-part tariffs*.

[16]The average price varies with quantity with two-part pricing and nonlinear price discrimination. However, the expenditure in two-part pricing, $E = A + pq$, is linear in quantity, unlike with nonlinear price discrimination.

[17]For example, *venting* stores are springing up in shopping malls in China. A customer pays to enter, and then pays for each second-hand mobile phone, television set, or other product that the customer smashes. (**english.people.com.cn/90001/90782/90872/6915069.html**, viewed April 17, 2013.)

To illustrate these points we consider a monopoly that has a constant marginal cost of $MC = 10$ and no fixed cost, so its average cost is also constant at 10. All of the monopoly's customers have the same demand curve, $Q = 80 - p$. Panel a of Figure 10.5 shows the demand curve, D^1, of one such customer, Valerie.

Total surplus is maximized if the monopoly sets its price, p, equal to its constant marginal cost of 10. The firm breaks even on each unit sold and has no producer surplus. Valerie buys $q = 70$ units. Her consumer surplus is area $A = 2,450 (= \frac{1}{2} \times [80 - 10] \times 70)$.

However, if the firm also charges an access fee of 2,450, it captures this 2,450 as its producer surplus or its profit per customer, and leaves Valerie with no consumer surplus. The firm's total profit is 2,450 times the number of identical customers.

The firm maximizes its profit by setting its price equal to its marginal cost and charging an access fee that captures the entire potential consumer surplus. If the firm were to charge a price above its marginal cost of 10, it would sell fewer units and make a smaller profit. In panel b of Figure 10.5, the firm charges $p = 20$. At that higher price, Valerie buys only 60 units, which is less than the 70 units that she buys at a price of 10 in panel a. The firm's profit from selling these 60 units is $B_1 = (20 - 10) \times 60 = 600$. For Valerie to agree to buy any units, the monopoly has to lower its access fee to 1,800 ($= \frac{1}{2} \times 60 \times 60$), the new potential consumer surplus, area A_1. The firm's total profit from Valerie is $A_1 + B_1 = 1,800 + 600 = 2,400$. This amount is less than the 2,450 ($= A$ in panel a) profit the firm earns if it sets price equal to marginal cost, 10, and charges the higher access fee. Area A in panel a equals $A_1 + B_1 + C_1$ in panel b. By charging a price above marginal cost, the firm loses C_1, which is the deadweight loss due to selling fewer units.

FIGURE 10.5 Two-Part Pricing with Identical Consumers

(a) Because all customers have the same individual demand curve as Valerie, D^1, the monopoly captures the entire potential consumer surplus using two-part pricing. The monopoly charges a per-unit fee price, p, equal to the marginal cost of 10, and an access fee, $A = 2,450$, which is the blue triangle under the demand curve and above the per-unit price of $p = 10$. (b) Were the monopoly to set a price at 20, which is above its marginal cost,

it would earn less. It makes a profit of $B_1 = 600$ from the 10 it earns on the 60 units that Valerie buys at this higher price. However, the largest access fee the firm can make now is $A_1 = 1,800$, so its total profit is 2,400, which is less than the 2,450 it makes if it sets its price equal to marginal cost. The difference is a deadweight loss of $C_1 = 50$, which is due to fewer units being sold at the higher price.

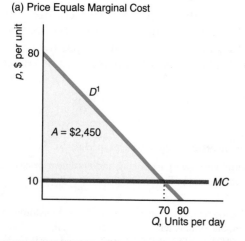

(a) Price Equals Marginal Cost

$A = \$2,450$

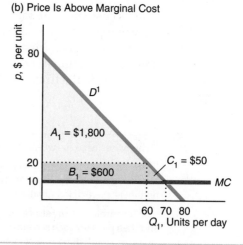

(b) Price Is Above Marginal Cost

$A_1 = \$1,800$

$C_1 = \$50$

$B_1 = \$600$

Similarly, if the firm were to charge a price below its marginal cost, it would also earn less profit. It would sell too many units and make a loss on each unit that it could not fully recapture by a higher access fee.

Two-Part Pricing with Differing Consumers

Two-part pricing is more complex if consumers have different demand curves. Suppose that the monopoly has two customers, Valerie, Consumer 1, and Neal, Consumer 2. Valerie's demand curve, $Q_1 = 80 - p$, is D^1 in panel a of Figure 10.6 (which is the same as panel b of Figure 10.5), and Neal's demand curve, $Q_2 = 100 - p$, is D^2 in panel b. The monopoly's marginal cost, MC, and average cost are constant at 10 per unit.

If the firm knows each customer's demand curve, can prevent resale, and can charge its customers different prices and access fees, it can capture all the potential consumer surplus. The monopoly sets its price for both customers at $p = MC = 10$ and sets its access fee equal to each customer's potential consumer surplus. At $p = 10$, Valerie buys 70 units (panel a), and Neal buys 90 units (panel b). If no access fees were charged, Valerie's consumer surplus would equal the triangle below her demand curve and above the 10 price line, $A_1 + B_1 + C_1$, which is 2,450 ($= \frac{1}{2} \times 70 \times 70$). Similarly, Neal's consumer surplus would be 4,050 ($= \frac{1}{2} \times 90 \times 90$), which is the triangle $A_2 + B_2 + C_2$. Thus, the monopoly charges an access fee of 2,450 to Valerie

FIGURE 10.6 Two-Part Pricing with Different Consumers

The monopoly faces two consumers. Valerie's demand curve is D^1 in panel a, and Neal's demand curve is D^2 in panel b. If the monopoly can set different prices and access fees for its two customers, it charges both a per-unit price of $p = 10$, which equals its marginal cost, and it charges an access fee of 2,450 ($= A_1 + B_1 + C_1$) to Valerie and 4,050 ($= A_2 + B_2 + C_2$) to Neal. If the monopoly cannot charge its customers different prices, it sets its per-unit price at $p = 20$, where Valerie purchases 60 and Neal buys 80 units. The firm charges both the same access fee of 1,800 $= A_1$, which is Valerie's potential consumer surplus. The highest access fee that the firm could charge and have Neal buy is 3,200, but at that level, Valerie would not buy. By charging a price above its marginal cost, the firm captures $B_1 = 600$ from Valerie and $B_2 = 800$ from Neal. Thus, its total profit is 5,000 ($= [2 \times 1,800] + 600 + 800$), which is less than the 6,500 ($= 2,450 + 4,050$) it makes if it can charge separate access fees to each customer.

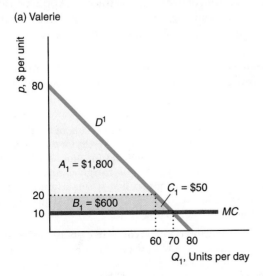

(a) Valerie

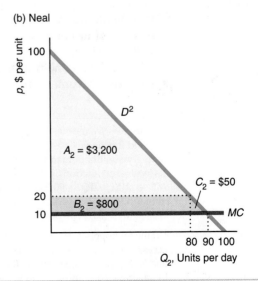

(b) Neal

and 4,050 to Neal, so that the customers receive no consumer surplus. The firm's total profit is 2,450 + 4,050 = 6,500. The monopoly maximizes its total profit by capturing the maximum potential consumer surplus from both customers.

Now suppose that the firm cannot charge its customers different prices or different access fees. The firm maximizes its profit by setting a price of 20, which exceeds its marginal cost, and collecting an access fee equal to Valerie's potential consumer surplus, $A_1 = 1,800$. Although this access fee captures all of Valerie's potential consumer surplus, it is less than Neal's potential consumer surplus, $3,200 = A_2$. Were the firm to charge an access fee of 3,200, it would sell only to Neal and make less money.

At $p = 20$, Valerie buys 60 units, and Neal buys 80 units. Because the firm's average cost is 10, the firm makes $20 - 10 = 10$ per unit, so it earns $B_1 = 600 (= 10 \times 60)$ from Valerie and $B_2 = 800 (= 10 \times 80)$ from Neal for a total $= 1,400$. Adding that to what it makes from the access fees, 3,600, the monopoly's total profit is $5,000 (= [2 \times 1,800] + 600 + 800)$. Valerie receives no consumer surplus, but Neal enjoys a consumer surplus of $1,400 (= 3,200 - 1,800)$.

This 5,000 profit obtained from pure two-part pricing is less than the 6,500 that it could obtain if it could set different access fees for each customer. On the other hand, its profit from pure two-part pricing exceeds the 3,200 profit that the firm could earn from uniform monopoly pricing.[18]

Why does the firm charge a price above marginal cost when using two-part pricing in this case? By raising the price, the firm lowers the amount it can earn from the access fee but increases the amount it can earn from the per-unit price. The amount the firm earns from Valerie because of the higher price is less than the amount it loses from her reduced access fee. However, the situation with Neal is reversed. The gain the firm gets from charging Neal the higher price exceeds the loss from Neal's smaller access fee. Further, the net gain the firm obtains from Neal exceeds the net loss it takes on Valerie, so it is better off overall.[19] Thus, a price above marginal cost increases profit in this case.

Mini-Case

Available for a Song

Prior to 2009, Apple's iTunes music store, the giant of music downloading, used *uniform pricing*, where it sold songs at 99¢ each. However, some of its competitors, such as Amazon MP3, did not use uniform pricing. Some record labels told Apple that they would not renew their contracts if Apple continued to use uniform pricing. Apparently responding to this pressure and the success of some of its competitors, Apple switched in 2009 to selling each song at one of three prices.

Did Apple's one-price-for-all-songs policy cost it substantial potential profit? How do consumer surplus and deadweight loss vary with pricing methods

---

[18]A single-price monopoly faces an aggregate demand function of the sum of the two individual demand functions: $Q = q_1 + q_2 = (80 - p) + (100 - p)$ or $Q = 180 - 2p$, for p less than 80, where both consumers demand a positive quantity. Its inverse demand function is $p(Q) = 90 - \frac{1}{2}Q$. Its revenue function is $R(Q) = p(Q) \times Q = 90Q - \frac{1}{2}Q^2$, so its marginal revenue function is $MR = dR(Q)/dQ = 90 - Q$. To maximize its profit given that it sets a uniform price, the monopoly equates its MR and its MC, so that $90 - Q = 10$, or $Q = 80$. At that quantity, the price is $p = 90 - (80/2) = 50$. The firm's profit is $\pi = (p - AC)Q = (50 - 10) \times 80 = 3,200$.

[19]If the monopoly charges a price of $10 per unit, this price just covers its costs. Its profit-maximizing access fee is $2,450, which is the sum of areas A_1, B_1, and C_1 in panel a of Figure 10.6. Both Valerie and Neal pay this access fee, so the firm earns a profit of $4,900, which is less than the $5,000 it earns by raising its per unit price to $20 and charging an access fee of $1,800.

such as a single price, song-specific prices, price discrimination, and two-part pricing? To answer such questions, Shiller and Waldfogel (2011) surveyed nearly 1,000 students and determined each person's willingness to pay for each of 50 popular songs. Then they used this information to calculate optimal pricing under various pricing schemes.

First, under uniform pricing, the same price is charged for every song. Second, under variable pricing, each song sells at its individual profit-maximizing price. Third, Apple could use two-part pricing, charging a monthly or annual fee for access and then a fixed price for each download.

If we know the demand curve and the marginal cost, we can determine the consumer surplus (CS), the producer surplus (PS), or profit, and the deadweight loss (DWL) from each pricing regime. By dividing each of these surplus measures by the total available surplus—the area under the demand curve and above the marginal cost curve—we can determine the shares of CS, PS, and DWL. The following table shows Shiller and Waldfogel's estimates of the percentage shares of CS, PS, and DWL under each of the three pricing methods:

Pricing	PS	CS	DWL
Uniform	28	42	29
Variable	29	45	26
Two-part pricing	37	43	20

If these students have tastes similar to those of the general market, then Apple raised its profit by switching from uniform pricing to variable pricing (see the PS column in the table). However, these results suggest that it could do even better using two-part pricing. Deadweight loss decreases under both of the alternatives to uniform pricing. Consumers do best with variable pricing, but two-part pricing is also better for consumers than uniform pricing.

10.6 Bundling

Firms with market power often pursue a pricing strategy called **bundling**: selling multiple goods or services for a single price. Indeed, most goods are bundles of many separate parts. Cars come assembled. Left and right shoes are sold together as a pair and include laces. Usually this bundling is done for efficiency because combining goods in a bundle reduces the transaction costs incurred by consumers or the production costs associated with the product. For example, we buy shirts with buttons already attached. Rather than buying shirts without buttons, and then buying buttons, consumers prefer to buy assembled shirts, eliminating the need to make two separate purchases and then sew on buttons. It is also cheaper for the firm to sew on buttons in the factory rather than to distribute two separate products (shirts and buttons) to the marketplace.

However, firms sometimes bundle even when they gain no production advantages and transaction costs are small. Bundling of such products allows firms to increase their profit by taking advantage of differences in consumers' willingness to pay. For example, a computer firm may sell a package including a computer and a printer for a single price even if it has no cost savings from selling these products together.

There are two common types of bundling. Some firms engage in *pure bundling*, in which only a package deal is offered, as when a cable company sells a bundle of Internet, phone, and television services for a single price but does not allow customers to purchase the individual services separately. Other firms use *mixed bundling*, in which the goods are available on a stand-alone basis in addition to being available as part of a bundle, such as a cable company that allows consumers to buy the bundle or the individual services they want.

Pure Bundling

Microsoft Works is a pure bundle. The primary components of this bundle are a word processing program and a spreadsheet program. These programs have fewer features than Microsoft's flagship Word and Excel programs and are not sold individually but only as a bundle.

Whether it pays for Microsoft to sell a bundle or sell the programs separately depends on how reservation prices for the components vary across customers. We use an example of a firm selling word processing and spreadsheet programs to illustrate two cases, one in which pure bundling produces a higher profit than selling the components separately, and one in which pure bundling is not profitable.

The marginal cost of producing an extra copy of either type of software is essentially zero. We assume that the fixed cost is negligible so that the firm's revenue equals its profit. The firm must charge all customers the same price—it cannot price discriminate.

The firm has two customers, Alisha and Bob. The first two columns of Table 10.2 show the reservation prices for each consumer for the two products. Alisha's reservation price for the word processing program, $120, is greater than Bob's, $90; however, Alisha's reservation price for the spreadsheet program, $50, is less than Bob's, $70. The reservation prices are *negatively correlated:* The customer who has the higher reservation price for one product has the lower reservation price for the other product. The third column of the table shows each consumer's reservation price for the bundle, which is the sum of the reservation prices for the two underlying products.

If the firm sells the two products separately, it maximizes its profit by charging $90 for the word processor and selling to both consumers, so that its profit is $180, rather than charging $120 and selling only to Alisha. If it charges between $90 and $120, it still only sells to Alisha and earns less than if it charges $120. Similarly, the firm maximizes its profit by selling the spreadsheet program for $50 to both consumers, earning $100, rather than charging $70 and selling to only Bob. The firm's total profit from selling the programs separately is $280 (= $180 + $100).

TABLE 10.2 Negatively Correlated Reservation Prices

	Word Processor	Spreadsheet	Bundle
Alisha	$120	$50	$170
Bob	$90	$70	$160
Profit-maximizing price	$90	$50	$160
Units sold	2	2	2

If the firm sells the two products in a bundle, it maximizes its profit by charging $160, selling to both customers, and earning $320. This is a better outcome than charging $170 and selling only to Alisha. Pure bundling is more profitable for the firm because it earns $320 from selling the bundle and only $280 from selling the programs separately.

Pure bundling is more profitable because the firm captures more of the consumers' potential consumer surplus—their reservation prices. With separate prices, Alisha has consumer surplus of $30 (= $120 − $90) from the word processing program and none from the spreadsheet program. Bob receives no consumer surplus from the word processing program and $20 from the spreadsheet program. Thus, the total consumer surplus is $50. With pure bundling, Alisha gets $10 of consumer surplus and Bob gets none, so the total is only $10. Thus, the pure bundling approach captures $40 more potential consumer surplus than does pricing separately.

Whether pure bundling increases the firm's profit depends on the reservation prices. Table 10.3 shows the reservation prices for two different consumers, Carol and Dmitri. Carol has higher reservation prices for both products than does Dmitri. These reservation prices are *positively correlated*: A higher reservation price for one product is associated with a higher reservation price for the other product.

If the programs are sold separately, the firm charges $90 for the word processor, sells to both consumers, and earns $180. However, it makes more charging $90 for the spreadsheet program and selling only to Carol, than it does charging $40 for the spreadsheet, selling to both consumers, and earning $80. The firm's total profit if it prices separately is $270 (= $180 + $90).

If the firm uses pure bundling, it maximizes its profit by charging $130 for the bundle, selling to both customers, and making $260. Because the firm earns more selling the programs separately, $270, than when it bundles them, $260, pure bundling is not profitable in this example. Even if Dmitri placed a higher value on the spreadsheet, as long as reservation prices are positively correlated, pure bundling cannot increase the profit.

Mixed Bundling

Restaurants, computer software firms, and many other companies commonly use mixed bundling—allowing consumers to buy the pure bundle or to buy any of the bundle's components separately. For example, Microsoft not only sells the bundle Microsoft Office, which includes Microsoft Word, Microsoft Excel, and various other programs, but it also sells the various programs individually. The following example illustrates that mixed bundling may be more profitable than pure bundling

TABLE 10.3 Positively Correlated Reservation Prices

	Word Processor	Spreadsheet	Bundle
Carol	$100	$90	$190
Dmitri	$90	$40	$130
Profit-maximizing price	$90	$90	$130
Units sold	2	1	2

or only selling components separately because it captures more of the potential consumer surplus.

A firm that sells word processing and spreadsheet programs has four potential customers with the reservation prices in Table 10.4. Again, the firm's cost of production is zero, so maximizing its profit is equivalent to maximizing its revenue.

Aaron, a writer, places high value on the word processing program but has relatively little use for a spreadsheet program. Dorothy, an accountant, has the opposite pattern of preferences—placing a high value on having the spreadsheet program but little value on a word processing program. Brigitte and Charles have intermediate reservation prices. These reservation prices are negatively correlated: Customers with a relatively high reservation price for one product have relatively low reservation prices for the other program. To determine its best pricing strategy, the firm calculates its profit by pricing the components separately, using pure bundling, and engaging in mixed bundling.

If the firm prices each program separately, it maximizes its profit by charging $90 for each product and selling each to three out of the four potential customers. It sells the word processing program to Aaron, Brigitte, and Charles. It sells the spreadsheet program to Brigitte, Charles, and Dorothy. Thus, it makes $270 (= 3 × $90) from each program or $540 total, which exceeds what it could earn by setting any other price per program.[20]

However, the firm can make a higher profit by engaging in pure bundling. It can charge $150 for the bundle, sell to all four consumers, and earn $600, which is $60 more than the $540 it makes from selling the programs separately.

With mixed bundling, the firm obtains an even larger profit. It charges $200 for the bundle and $120 for each product separately. The firm earns $400 from Brigitte and Charles, who buy the bundle. Aaron buys only the word processing program for $120, and Dorothy buys only the spreadsheet for another $120, so that the firm makes $240 from its individual program sales. Thus its profit is $640 (= $400 + $240) from mixed bundling, which exceeds the $600 from pure bundling, and the $540 from individual sales. We could construct other examples with different numbers where selling the programs separately would dominate (such as where reservation prices are positively correlated as in Table 10.3) or where the pure bundle does best (as in Table 10.2).

TABLE 10.4 Reservation Prices and Mixed Bundling

	Word Processor	Spreadsheet	Bundle
Aaron	$120	$30	$150
Brigitte	$110	$90	$200
Charles	$90	$110	$200
Dorothy	$30	$120	$150

[20]If it sets a price of a program as low as $30, it sells both programs to all four customers, but makes only $240. If it charges $110 it sells each program to two customers and earns $440. If it charges $120, it makes a single sale of each program, so it earns $240.

Q&A 10.3

Package deals are common in vacation travel. Online travel services such as Expedia, Orbitz, and Travelocity allow travelers to find many attractive package deals that combine a round-trip airfare and a hotel stay or to book airline flights and hotels individually. At some locations, the package price is much less than the sum of the prices for a flight and a hotel room, whereas at other locations, the package provides little savings. Paradise Vacations has two destinations, Hawaii and Cleveland, to which it sends its customers who live in Seattle. The table shows reservation prices for a weekend holiday for the two destinations for three customers. We assume that both hotels and aircraft have excess capacity so that the marginal cost of one more customer is zero.

	Hawaii			Cleveland		
	Flight	**Hotel**	**Bundle**	**Flight**	**Hotel**	**Bundle**
Allen	$400	$50	$450	$400	$50	$450
Barbara	$350	$350	$700	$300	$300	$600
Colin	$50	$400	$450	$50	$400	$450

What are the profit-maximizing pricing strategies for the two destinations? Which destination yields the bigger package deal discount under mixed bundling?

Answer

1. *Determine the best stand-alone prices, bundle price, and mixed bundling prices for Hawaii.* If the firm prices the flight and the hotel separately, its profit-maximizing prices are $350 for each. The firm sells two units of each product (Allen and Barbara buy flights, and Barbara and Colin rent hotel rooms) and earns $1,400. The best bundle price is $450, which, although all three customers buy, generates a profit of only $1,350. Therefore, pricing the components separately produces a higher profit than does the bundle. However, mixed bundling produces the highest profit. The firm charges $700 for the bundle and $400 for each stand-alone product, earning a total of $1,500 by selling one bundle to Barbara, one flight to Allen, and one hotel stay to Colin.

2. *Determine the best stand-alone prices, bundle price, and mixed bundling prices for Cleveland.* With individual pricing, the firm charges $300 for each product, selling two units of each, and makes a profit of $1,200. Bundling is more profitable. At a bundle price of $450, all customers buy the bundle, generating a profit of $1,350. Mixed bundling is better still. By charging $600 for the bundle and $400 for each item, the firm's profit is $1,400.

3. *Under mixed bundling, compare the bundle price and combined individual prices for Hawaii and Cleveland.* For Hawaii with mixed bundling pricing, the cost of a flight and a hotel stay is $800 if purchased separately while the bundle price is $700, for a $100 saving. In Cleveland, the sum of the individual prices is $800 and the bundle price is only $600, for a $200 savings.

Comments: Hawaii has a relatively low bundling discount because Barbara places a very high value on the bundle compared to other customers who are primarily interested in just one of the products. The firm can charge almost as much for the bundle as for the individual prices and still sell to Barbara. For the Cleveland market, Barbara requires a bigger discount for the bundle compared to the sum of the individual prices.

Requirement Tie-In Sales

One form of bundling—called a *requirement tie-in*—requires customers who buy one product from a firm to make all concurrent and subsequent purchases of a related product from that firm. This requirement allows the firm to identify heavier users and charge them more per unit. For example, if a printer manufacturer can require that consumers buy their ink cartridges only from the manufacturer, then that firm can capture most of the consumers' surplus. Heavy users of the printer, who presumably have a less elastic demand for it, pay the firm more than light users because of the high cost of the ink cartridges.

Unfortunately for such a printer manufacturer, the Magnuson-Moss Warranty Improvement Act of 1975 forbids them from requiring consumers to use their ink cartridges as a condition of the warranty. More broadly, the Act prevents any manufacturer from using such tie-in provisions as a condition of warranty.

Managerial Implication **Ties That Bind**	Managers can increase profit by promoting consumer loyalty. Despite the Magnuson-Moss Act, such loyalty can be induced through warranty provisions. Printer firms such as Hewlett-Packard (HP) write their warranties to strongly encourage consumers to use only their cartridges and not to refill them:

> . . . [I]f printer failure or damage is attributable to the use of a non-HP or refilled cartridge or an expired ink cartridge, HP will charge its standard time and materials charges to service the printer for the particular failure or damage.

Moreover, the company's literature stresses that

> HP recommends that you use original HP cartridges. Original HP cartridges are designed and tested with HP printers to help you easily produce great results, time after time.

Are these warranty restrictions and advertising claims sufficient to induce most consumers to buy cartridges only from HP? Apparently so. HP sells its Deskjet D1660 printer for only $29.99. That is, HP is virtually giving away an impressive machine that will print up to 20 pages per minute in black and white and 16 pages per minute in color in up to 4800 × 1200 optimized dots per inch (dpi) in color. However, HP charges $31.99 for its black and color combination cartridge, which it rates for at most 200 pages in black or 165 in color. If most customers bought inexpensive cartridges or refills from other firms, HP would not sell its printer at a rock-bottom price. Thus, HP demonstrates that the benefits of requirement tie-in sales can be achieved through careful wording of warranties and advertising.

10.7 Peak-Load Pricing

Rooms in Florida's resort hotels that can be rented for $100 or $200 per night in the hot, humid summer months often rent for twice as much in the winter months of January and February when snowbirds from northern states and Canada flock to Florida's warm, sunny beaches. Similarly, in many areas, electricity costs more during business hours than at night. Such pricing strategies are examples of

peak-load pricing: charging higher prices during periods of peak demand than in other periods.

Peak-load pricing is commonly used when firms face a production capacity constraint. For example, a hotel's capacity constraint is the maximum number of rooms, $\overline{Q}$, that it can rent. As Figure 10.7 illustrates, the hotel's marginal cost—primarily the cost of cleaning and maintaining the room—is constant at m up to capacity, where no additional room can be provided at any finite cost in the short run. That is, the marginal cost curve is horizontal at m up to capacity $\overline{Q}$, where it becomes vertical.

During the low season, the hotel's demand curve is D^L and its marginal revenue curve is MR^L. The hotel maximizes its profit by operating where its marginal revenue equals its marginal cost. Its marginal revenue curve hits the marginal cost curve in its horizontal section at Q_L. The corresponding price is p_L. Thus, during the off-season, the hotel's price is above its marginal cost, and it does not rent all available rooms, so the hotel has excess capacity.

The high- or peak-season demand curve D^H lies to the right of the low-season demand curve, D^L. The peak-season marginal revenue curve, MR^H, hits the marginal

FIGURE 10.7 Peak-Load Pricing

A resort has $\overline{Q}$ rooms, which is its capacity constraint. Its marginal cost of providing a room is m up to $\overline{Q}$ and then becomes infinite because the hotel cannot provide more than $\overline{Q}$ rooms. During the low season, the demand curve is D^L and the associated marginal revenue curve is MR^L. The firm maximizes its profit by renting the number of rooms where its marginal revenue curve crosses its marginal cost curve in the horizontal region and sets its price at p_L and rents Q_L rooms as shown by point e_L. The hotel has excess capacity because $Q_L < \overline{Q}$. During the peak season, the demand curve is D^H. The firm maximizes its profit by setting price, p_H, so that the quantity demanded is just equal to the available capacity, because its marginal revenue curve, MR^H, crosses the marginal cost curve in the vertical section. The price is p_H, and the hotel has no excess capacity.

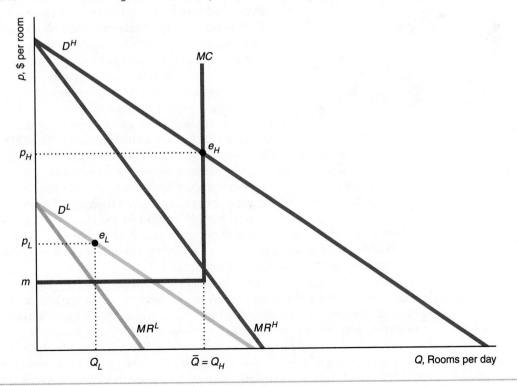

cost curve where it is vertical at $\overline{Q}$. Here, the firm maximizes its profit by charging a price p_H such that the quantity demanded, Q_H, equals the available capacity, $\overline{Q}$. Thus, in the peak period, the hotel charges a price, p_H, that limits the quantity demanded to the available capacity.

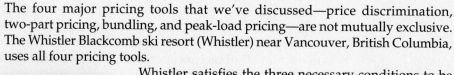

Mini-Case

Downhill Pricing

The four major pricing tools that we've discussed—price discrimination, two-part pricing, bundling, and peak-load pricing—are not mutually exclusive. The Whistler Blackcomb ski resort (Whistler) near Vancouver, British Columbia, uses all four pricing tools.

Whistler satisfies the three necessary conditions to be able to apply these nonuniform pricing tools. First, it has considerable market power as one of North America's top ski resorts. Second, it is able to obtain extensive information about each of its customers. When a consumer buys a ski pass, that transaction goes into a database, typically linked to a credit card or a driver's license. Whistler is then able to keep track of that person's skiing habits and other expenditures at the resort over time. And third, Whistler is able to prevent resale or the sharing of discount tickets, such as season passes and various other multiday passes, by putting the person's photo on the pass.

Whistler engages in individual price discrimination based on individuals' skiing history. Because Whistler tracks individual skiing frequency and links that information to the person's address, Whistler is able to send skiers customized promotional letters, offering them special promotions such as a discounted lesson or a special discount on a daily pass.

Whistler also uses nonlinear price discrimination, offering multiday passes at lower prices per day than single-day passes and offering tickets to large groups at discount prices. Skiers can obtain a one-day pass, three-day, five-day, and other multiday passes, as well as a season pass.

In addition, Whistler uses group price discrimination. Prices vary dramatically by age. For the 2012–2013 season, season passes cost $525 for children under 13, $739 for children 13–18, $1,795 for adults 19–64, $969 for seniors 65–74, and only $225 for super seniors over 75. Groups of 15 or more people can buy a discounted group ticket.

Skiers can obtain lower prices if they are willing to take the time to find tickets sold by certain local vendors at a significant discount. For example, an adult skier can buy a daily pass for $96 instead of the usual $102 at 7-Eleven convenience stores in nearby Vancouver. Thus, Whistler further segments the market on the basis of value of time—charging lower prices for skiers who are willing to invest time in getting discount tickets.

Whistler also uses two-part pricing. Local residents can buy special passes for an access fee that allows them to pay lower daily prices for the season. Whistler also bundles skiing with other products. For example, skiers can buy a daily pass, a lesson, and rental equipment as a package deal for considerably less than the combined stand-alone prices. In addition, Whistler engages in peak-load pricing by varying fees over the week and the season: Skiing on weekdays is cheaper than on weekends. Whistler, like Disney, treats nonuniform pricing as a science.

Managerial Solution

Sale Prices

By putting Heinz ketchup on sale periodically, Heinz's managers can price discriminate. How often should Heinz put its ketchup on sale? Under what conditions does it pay for Heinz to have sales? To answer these questions, we study a simplified market in which Heinz competes with one other ketchup brand, which we refer to as generic ketchup.[21] Every n days, the typical consumer buys either Heinz or generic ketchup. (The number of days between purchases is determined by the storage space in consumers' homes and how frequently they use ketchup.)

Switchers are price sensitive and buy the least expensive ketchup. They pay attention to price information and always know when Heinz is on sale.

Heinz's managers consider holding periodic sales to capture switchers' purchases. The generic is sold at a competitive price equal to its marginal cost of production of $2.01 per unit. Suppose that Heinz's marginal cost is $MC = \$1$ per unit (due to its large scale) and that, if it only sold to its loyal customers, it would charge a monopoly price of $p = \$3$. Heinz's managers face a trade-off. If Heinz is infrequently on sale for less than the generic price, Heinz sells little to switchers. On the other hand, if Heinz is frequently on sale, it loses money on its sales to loyal customers.

We start by supposing that Heinz's managers decide to charge a low sales price, $2, once every n days. For the other $n - 1$ days, Heinz sells at the regular, nonsale (monopoly) price of $3, which is the monopoly price given the demand curve of the loyal customers. During a sale, the switchers buy enough Heinz to last them for n days until it's on sale again. Consequently, the switchers never buy the generic product. (Some other customers are loyal to the generic, so they buy it even when Heinz is on sale.)

If the loyal customers find that Heinz is on sale, which happens $1/n$ of all days, they buy n days' worth at the sale price. Otherwise, they are willing to pay the regular (monopoly) price. If the other loyal customers were aware of this promotion pattern, they could get on a schedule such that they always bought on sale too, thereby making this strategy non-profit maximizing. However, their shopping schedules are determined independently: They buy many goods and are not willing to distort their shopping patterns solely to buy this one good on sale.[22]

Could Heinz make more money by altering its promotion pattern? It does not want to place its good on sale more frequently because it would earn less from its loyal customers without making more sales to switchers. If it pays to hold sales at all, it does not want to have a sale less frequently because it would sell fewer units to switchers. During a promotion, Heinz wants to charge the highest price it can and yet still attract switchers, which is $2. If it sets a lower price, the quantity sold is unchanged, so its profit falls. If Heinz sets a sale price higher than $2, it loses all switchers.

Does it pay for Heinz to have sales? Whether it pays depends on the number of switchers, S, relative to the number of brand-loyal customers, B. If each customer buys one unit per day, then Heinz's profit per day if it sells only to loyals is $\pi = (p - MC)B = (3 - 1)B = 2B$, where $p = 3$ is Heinz's regular price and

---

[21]The rest of the U.S. market consists primarily of Hunt's Ketchup (15%) and generic or house brands (22%). In the following discussion, we assume that customers who are loyal to Hunt's or generic ketchup are unaffected by Heinz sales, and hence ignore those customers.

[22]We make this assumption for simplicity. In the real world, firms achieve a similar result by having random sales or by placing ads announcing sales where the ads are seen by primarily the switchers.

$MC = 1$ is its marginal and average cost. If Heinz uses the sale pricing scheme, its average profit per day is

$$\pi^* = 2B(n - 1)/n + B/n + S/n,$$

where the first term is the profit it makes, $2 per unit, selling B units to loyal customers for the fraction of days that Heinz is not on sale, $(n - 1)/n$, and the second term is the profit it makes, $1 per unit, selling B units to the loyal customers. The third term is the profit from switching. Each switcher buys n units on the sale day and no units on other days, so the average is $1/n$ per day for each of the S switchers.

Thus, it pays to put Heinz ketchup on sale if $\pi < \pi^*$, or $2B < 2B(n - 1)/n + (B + S)(1/n)$. Using algebra, we can simplify this expression to $B < S$. Thus, if switchers outnumber loyal customers, then having sales is more profitable than selling at a uniform price to only loyal customers.

SUMMARY

1. **Conditions for Price Discrimination.** A firm can price discriminate if it has market power, knows which consumers or groups of consumers are willing to pay more than others for the product, and can prevent customers who pay low prices from reselling to those who are willing to pay high prices. A firm earns a higher profit from price discrimination than from uniform pricing because (a) the firm captures additional consumer surplus from customers who are willing to pay more than the uniform price and (b) the firm sells to some people who would not buy at the uniform price.

2. **Perfect Price Discrimination.** To perfectly price discriminate, a firm charges each customer the maximum each is willing to pay for each unit of output. The firm captures all potential consumer surplus and sells the efficient (competitive) level of output. Compared to perfect competition, total surplus is the same, consumers as a whole are worse off, and firms are better off under perfect price discrimination. Perfect price discrimination is rare, but seeking to approach perfect price discrimination using individual-specific prices is quite common.

3. **Group Price Discrimination.** A firm that is not able to perfectly price discriminate can still increase its profit relative to uniform pricing if it can identify different subgroups of consumers with different demand curves. At the profit-maximizing prices, the firm charges groups of consumers prices in proportion to their elasticities of demand, with the group of consumers with the least elastic demand paying the highest price. Total surplus is less under group price discrimination than under competition or perfect price discrimination but may be greater or less than that under uniform monopoly pricing.

4. **Nonlinear Price Discrimination.** Some firms charge customers different prices depending on how many units they purchase. A common pattern of such prices involves quantity discounts, so that the per-unit price for consumers who buy larger quantities would be less than the per-unit price for consumers who buy smaller quantities.

5. **Two-Part Pricing.** By charging consumers an access fee for the right to buy a good and a separate fee per unit, firms may earn higher profits than from uniform pricing. In an extreme case, a firm that knew its customers' demand curves and could charge a different access fee to every customer could use two-part prices to capture all potential consumer surplus. More realistically, even a firm that does not know each customer's demand curve or that cannot vary the access fee across customers can still use two-part pricing to earn a higher profit than it could earn using a single (uniform) price.

6. **Bundling.** Some firms increase their profits by selling products as bundles, often called package deals. Some firms use pure bundling, in which only the bundle is offered for sale. Others use mixed bundling, in which both the bundle and the individual goods are offered for sale. Bundling is likely to be a profitable pricing strategy when consumers have reservation prices that are

negatively correlated—when consumers who have a relatively high willingness to pay for one good have a relatively low willingness to pay for the other good.

7. **Peak-Load Pricing.** Some firms charge higher prices during periods of high demand than during periods of low demand. Such pricing strategies are commonly used by firms that have capacity constraints. During the peak period, the firm sets a high price to limit demand to its available capacity. During the off-peak period, the firm's profit-maximizing price leaves excess capacity.

QUESTIONS

*All exercises are available on MyEconLab; * = answer at the back of this book; C = use of calculus may be necessary.*

1. Conditions for Price Discrimination

1.1. In the examples in Table 10.1, if the movie theater does not price discriminate, it charges either the highest price the college students are willing to pay or the one that the senior citizens are willing to pay. Why doesn't it charge an intermediate price? (*Hint*: Discuss how the demand curves of these two groups are unusual.)

1.2. As of 2013, the pharmaceutical companies Abbott Laboratories, AstraZeneca, Aventis Pharmaceuticals, Bristol-Myers Squibb Company, Eli Lilly, GlaxoSmithKline, Janssen, Johnson & Johnson, Novartis, and Pfizer provided low-income, elderly people with a card guaranteeing them discounts on many prescription medicines. Why would these firms do that?

1.3. A monopoly currently sells its product at a single price. What conditions must be met so that it can profitably price discriminate?

*1.4. Many colleges provide students from low-income families with scholarships, subsidized loans, and other programs so that they pay lower tuitions than students from high-income families. Explain why universities behave this way.

1.5. College students could once buy an IBM or other PC computer at a substantial discount through a campus buying program. The discounts largely disappeared in the late 1990s, when PC companies dropped their prices. "The industry's margins just got too thin to allow for those [college discounts]," said the president of Educause, a group that promotes and surveys using technology on campus (David LaGesse, "A PC Choice: Dorm or Quad?" *U.S. News & World Report*, May 5, 2003, 64). Using the concepts and terminology discussed in this chapter, explain why shrinking profit margins are associated with the reduction or elimination of student discounts. Currently, Apple offers college students discounts on computers, often bundled with a printer, an iPod, or other Apple product. Why is Apple more likely to offer discounts to students than other computer companies?

*1.6. Disneyland price discriminates by charging lower entry fees for children than adults and for local residents than for other visitors. Why does it not have a resale problem?

1.7. A jean manufacturer would find it profitable to charge higher prices in Europe than in the United States if it could prevent resale between the two countries. What techniques can it use to discourage resale?

1.8. On July 12, 2012, Hertz charged $126.12 to rent a Nissan Altima for one day in New York City, but only $55.49 a day in Miami. Is this price discrimination? Explain.

2. Perfect Price Discrimination

2.1. Using the information in the "Botox Revisited" Mini-Case, determine how much Allergan loses by being a single-price monopoly rather than a perfectly price-discriminating monopoly. Explain your answer.

*2.2. If a monopoly faces an inverse demand function of $p = 90 - Q$, has a constant marginal and average cost of 30, and can perfectly price discriminate, what is its profit? What are the consumer surplus, total surplus, and deadweight loss? How would these results change if the firm were a single-price monopoly?

2.3. How would the answers to Q&A 10.1 and Table 10.1 change if seniors' reservation price was $5?

2.4. As described in the "Dynamic Pricing at Amazon" Mini-Case, some Amazon customers contended that Amazon used a dynamic pricing approach where the price offered depended on a customer's past purchases. What type of price discrimination is this?

2.5. To promote her platinum-selling CD *Feels Like Home* in 2005, singer Norah Jones toured the country for live performances. However, she sold an average of only two-thirds of the tickets available for each show, T^* (Robert Levine, "The Trick of Making a Hot Ticket Pay," *New York Times*, June 6, 2005, C1, C4).

a. Suppose that the local promoter is the monopoly provider of each concert. Each concert hall has a fixed number of seats. Assume that the promoter's cost is independent of the number of people who attend the concert (Ms. Jones received a guaranteed payment). Graph the promoter's marginal cost curve for the concert hall, where the number of tickets sold is on the horizontal axis (be sure to show T^*).

b. If the monopoly can charge a single market price, does the concert's failure to sell out prove that the monopoly set too high a price? Explain.

c. Would your answer in part b be the same if the monopoly can perfectly price discriminate? Use a graph to explain.

2.6. A firm is a natural monopoly (Chapter 9). Its marginal cost curve is flat, and its average cost curve is downward sloping (because it has a fixed cost). The firm can perfectly price discriminate.

a. In a graph, show how much the monopoly produces, Q^*.

b. Can it profitably produce where its price equals its marginal cost?

c. Show that a monopoly might shut down if it can only set a single price but will operate if it can perfectly price discriminate.

3. Group Price Discrimination

3.1. A firm charges different prices to two groups. Would the firm ever operate where it was suffering a loss from its sales to the low-price group? Explain.

*3.2. A monopoly sells its good in the U.S. and Japanese markets. The American inverse demand function is $p_A = 100 - Q_A$, and the Japanese inverse demand function is $p_J = 80 - 2Q_J$, where both prices, p_A and p_J, are measured in dollars. The firm's marginal cost of production is $m = 20$ in both countries. If the firm can prevent resale, what price will it charge in both markets? (*Hint*: The monopoly determines its optimal (monopoly) price in each country separately because customers cannot resell the good.)

*3.3. A patent gave Sony a legal monopoly to produce a robot dog called Aibo ("eye-BO"). The Chihuahua-size pooch robot can sit, beg, chase balls, dance, and play an electronic tune. When Sony started selling the toy, it announced that it would sell 3,000 Aibo robots in Japan for about $2,000 each and a limited litter of 2,000 in the United States for $2,500 each. Suppose that Sony's marginal cost of producing Aibo robots was $500. Its inverse demand function was $p_J = 3,500 - \frac{1}{2}Q_J$ in Japan and

$p_A = 4,500 - Q_A$ in the United States. Solve for the equilibrium prices and quantities (assuming that U.S. customers cannot buy robots from Japan). Show how the profit-maximizing price ratio depends on the elasticities of demand in the two countries. What were the deadweight losses in each country, and in which was the loss from monopoly pricing greater?

3.4. A monopoly sells its good in the United States, where the elasticity of demand is -2, and in Japan, where the elasticity of demand is -5. Its marginal cost is $10. At what price does the monopoly sell its good in each country if resale is impossible?

3.5. In Q&A 10.2, calculate the firm's profit with and without a ban against shipments between the two countries.

3.6. How would the analysis in Q&A 10.2 change if $MC = 7$?

3.7. Does a monopoly's ability to price discriminate between two groups of consumers depend on its marginal cost curve? Why or why not? [Consider two cases: (a) the marginal cost is so high that the monopoly is uninterested in selling to one group; and (b) the marginal cost is low enough that the monopoly wants to sell to both groups.]

3.8. A monopoly has a marginal cost of zero and faces two groups of consumers. At first, the monopoly could not prevent resale, so it maximized its profit by charging everyone the same price, $p = \$5$. No one from the first group chose to purchase. Now the monopoly can prevent resale, so it decides to price discriminate. Will total output expand? Why or why not? What happens to profit and consumer surplus?

*3.9. Spenser's Superior Stoves advertises a one-day sale on electric stoves. The ad specifies that no phone orders are accepted and that the purchaser must transport the stove. Why does the firm include these restrictions?

3.10. According to a report from the Foundation for Taxpayer and Consumer Rights, gasoline costs twice as much in Europe as in the United States because taxes are higher in Europe. However, the amount per gallon net of taxes that U.S. consumers pay is higher than that paid by Europeans (24¢ per gallon net of taxes). The report concludes that "U.S. motorists are essentially subsidizing European drivers, who pay more for taxes but substantially less into oil company profits" (Tom Doggett, "US Drivers Subsidize European Pump Prices," *Reuters*, August 31, 2006). Given that oil companies have market power and can price discriminate across countries, is it reasonable to conclude that U.S. consumers are subsidizing Europeans? Explain your answer.

4. Nonlinear Price Discrimination

*4.1. Are all the (identical) customers of the nonlinear price-discriminating monopoly in panel a of Figure 10.4 worse off than they would be if the firm set a single (uniform) price (panel b)? What if the consumers were not identical?

4.2. In panel b of Figure 10.4, the single-price monopoly faces a demand curve of $p = 90 - Q$ and a constant marginal (and average) cost of $m = 30$. Find the profit-maximizing quantity (or price) using math (Chapter 9). Determine the profit, consumer surplus, total surplus, and deadweight loss.

4.3. Assume that the quantity-discriminating monopoly in panel a of Figure 10.4 can set three prices, depending on the quantity a consumer purchases. The firm's profit is

$$\pi = p_1 Q_1 + p_2 (Q_2 - Q_1) + p_3 (Q_3 - Q_2) - m Q_3,$$

where p_1 is the high price charged on the first Q_1 units (first block), p_2 is a lower price charged on the next $Q_2 - Q_1$ units, p_3 is the lowest price charged on the $Q_3 - Q_2$ remaining units, Q_3 is the total number of units actually purchased, and $m = \$30$ is the firm's constant marginal and average cost. Use calculus to determine the profit-maximizing p_1, p_2, and p_3. **C**

4.4. In the nonlinear price discrimination analysis in panel a of Figure 10.4, suppose that the monopoly can make consumers a take-it-or-leave-it offer.

a. Suppose the monopoly sets a price, p^*, and a minimum quantity, Q^*, that a consumer must pay to be able to purchase any units at all. What price and minimum quantity should it set to achieve the same outcome as it would if it perfectly price discriminated?

b. Now suppose the monopolist charges a price of $90 for the first 30 units and a price of $30 for all subsequent units, but requires that a consumer must buy at least 30 units to be allowed to buy any. Compare this outcome to the one in part a and to the perfectly price-discriminating outcome.

4.5. Grocery store chains often set consumer-specific prices by issuing frequent-buyer cards to willing customers and collecting information about their purchases. Grocery chains can use that data to offer customized discount coupons to individuals.

a. Which type of price discrimination—perfect, group, or nonlinear—are these personalized discounts?

b. How should a grocery store use past-purchase data to set individualized prices to maximize its profit? (*Hint*: Refer to a customer's price elasticity of demand.)

5. Two-Part Pricing

5.1. Using math, show why, under two-part pricing, customers who purchase fewer units pay more on average per unit than do customers who buy more units.

5.2. Knoebels Amusement Park in Elysburg, Pennsylvania, charges an access fee, A, to enter its Crystal Pool. It also charges p per trip down the pool's water slides. Suppose that 400 teenagers visit the park, each of whom has a demand function of $q_1 = 5 - p$, and that 400 seniors also visit, each of whom has a demand function of $q_2 = 4 - p$. Knoebels' objective is to set A and p so as to maximize its profit given that it has no (non-sunk) cost and must charge both groups the same prices. What are the optimal A and p?

*5.3. Joe has just moved to a small town with only one golf course, the Northlands Golf Club. His inverse demand function is $p = 120 - 2q$, where q is the number of rounds of golf that he plays per year. The manager of the Northlands Club negotiates separately with each person who joins the club and can therefore charge individual prices. This manager has a good idea of what Joe's demand curve is and offers Joe a special deal, where Joe pays an annual membership fee and can play as many rounds as he wants at $20, which is the marginal cost his round imposes on the Club. What membership fee would maximize profit for the Club? The manager could have charged Joe a single price per round. How much extra profit does the club earn by using two-part pricing?

5.4. Joe in Question 5.3 marries Susan, who is also an enthusiastic golfer. Susan wants to join the Northlands Club. The manager believes that Susan's inverse demand function is $p = 100 - 2q$. The manager has a policy of offering each member of a married couple the same two-part prices, so he offers them both a new deal. What two-part pricing deal maximizes the club's profit? Will this new pricing have a higher or lower access fee and per-unit fee than in Joe's original deal? How much more would the club make if it charged Susan and Joe separate prices?

5.5. As described in the Mini-Case "Available for a Song," Shiller and Waldfogel (2011) estimated that if iTunes used two-part pricing charging an annual access fee and a low price per song, it would raise its profit by about 30% relative to what it would earn using uniform pricing or variable pricing. Assume that iTunes uses two-part pricing and assume that the marginal cost of an additional download is zero. How should iTunes set its profit-maximizing price per song if all consumers are identical? Illustrate profit-maximizing two-part pricing in a diagram for the identical consumer case. Explain why the actual profit-maximizing price per song is positive.

6. Bundling

6.1. A monopoly sells two products, of which any given consumer wants to buy only one (and places no value on the other good). If the monopoly can prevent resale, can it increase its profit by bundling the goods, forcing consumers to buy both goods?

*6.2. A computer hardware firm sells both laptop computers and printers. It has a large inventory of laptops and printers that it wants to sell, so it has no variable production cost. Through the magic of focus groups, their pricing team determines that they have an equal number of three types of customers, and that these customers' reservation prices are

	Laptop	Printer	Bundle
Customer Type A	$800	$100	$900
Customer Type B	$1,000	$50	$1,050
Customer Type C	$600	$150	$750

a. If the firm were to charge only individual prices (not use the bundle price), what prices should it set for its laptops and printers to maximize profit? Assuming for simplicity that the firm has only one customer of each type, how much does it earn in total?

b. After conducting a costly study, an outside consultant suggests that the company could make more money from its customers if it sold laptops and printers together as a bundle instead of separately. Is the consultant right? Assuming again that the firm has one customer of each type, how much does the firm earn in total from pure bundling?

c. Why does bundling pay or not pay? (*Hint*: See Q&A 10.3.)

6.3. Why do Honda service departments emphasize to customers the importance of using "genuine Honda parts" when servicing and tuning Honda cars and motorcycles? Is Honda likely to be as successful as Hewlett-Packard in the Managerial Implication "Ties That Bind"?

7. Peak-Load Pricing

7.1. The inverse demand curve facing a resort hotel is $p = 300 - Q$ during the high season and $p = 100 - Q$ during the low season. The resort's marginal cost is $50 per night in cleaning costs

for the room and general maintenance and administration. The resort has 100 rooms. What is the resort's profit-maximizing peak-load pricing strategy? Illustrate the solution in a diagram.

*7.2. Paradise Cruises has a monopoly in renting luxury yachts for sailing in the Caribbean Sea. In winter its monthly inverse demand function is $p = 200 - q$. In summer the inverse demand function is $p = 200 - 2q$. Paradise has a total of 50 yachts available for rental on a monthly basis.

a. Which season is the peak season. Why?

b. What are the profit-maximizing prices in both seasons?

7.3. Based on the information in Question 7.2, determine the profit-maximizing uniform price. Does Paradise Cruises earn a higher profit under peak-load pricing or uniform pricing? Compare consumer surplus under these two pricing methods.

8. Managerial Problem

8.1. Each week, a department store places a different item of clothing on sale. Give an explanation based on price discrimination for why the store conducts such regular sales.

9. Spreadsheet Exercises

9.1. The manager of an amusement park is considering what price to charge Anil, who is planning a birthday party for his young daughter and her friends. Anil's willingness to pay for rides for the party is $p = 25 - 0.5Q$, where p is the ticket price per ride and Q is the number of rides. The amusement park has a marginal cost of $5 for each additional ride. Its fixed cost for handling the party is $20.

Create a spreadsheet with quantity, price, consumer surplus, revenue, marginal revenue, cost, marginal cost, and profit as column headings. Fill in the spreadsheet's cells for $Q = 5$ up to $Q = 50$ (in increments of 5 units). If the manager uses uniform pricing, what is the profit-maximizing ticket price per ride, the number of rides, and the profit earned by the park?

9.2. Modify your spreadsheet from Exercise 9.1 given that the manager uses two-part pricing.

a. Suppose that the manager charges an entry fee for the entire party of young girls in addition to a price per ride. Calculate the optimal entry fee that it can charge while charging the same monopoly price as in Exercise 9.1. Calculate the total profit earned by the park.

b. Now suppose the manger uses two-part pricing with a per-ride price equal to marginal cost and a profit-maximizing entry fee. Determine the price per ride, the number of rides, and the total profit (including profit from ticket sales and the entry fee) in this case.

9.3. A restaurant faces very high demand for its signature mousse desserts in the evening but is less busy during the day. Its manager estimates that (inverse) demand curves are $p_e = 20 - Q_e$ in the evening and $p_d = 11 - Q_d$ during the day, where e and d denote evening and daytime. The marginal cost of producing its dessert, MC_1, is \$3. Any morning, the restaurant can bring in additional tables and convert its storage space to seating to increase capacity for that day. Creating enough extra capacity to provide one more dessert in the evening or the day costs \$5, which is the restaurant's marginal capacity cost, MC_2.

a. Create a spreadsheet with the column headings Q_e, p_e, MR_e, Q_d, p_d, MR_d, MC_1, MC_2, and $MC_T = MC_1 + MC_2$.

b. Determine the optimal prices for the dessert that the restaurant should charge during the evening hours and during the day, the associated quantities sold, and the total daily profit.

11 Oligopoly and Monopolistic Competition

Anyone can win unless there happens to be a second entry. —George Ade

Managerial Problem

Gaining an Edge from Government Aircraft Subsidies

A manager can use a cost advantage over a rival firm to increase profit. Consequently, managers of aircraft manufacturing firms lobby their governments for subsidies and then use these subsidies to increase their profit.

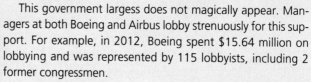

Airbus SAS, based in Europe, and the Boeing Co., based in the United States, are the only two major manufacturers of large commercial jet aircraft. France, Germany, Spain, and the United Kingdom subsidize Airbus, which competes in the wide-body aircraft market with Boeing. The U.S. government decries the European subsidies to Airbus despite giving lucrative military contracts to Boeing, which the Europeans view as implicit subsidies.

This government largess does not magically appear. Managers at both Boeing and Airbus lobby strenuously for this support. For example, in 2012, Boeing spent $15.64 million on lobbying and was represented by 115 lobbyists, including 2 former congressmen.

The United States and the European Union have repeatedly charged each other before the World Trade Organization (WTO) with subsidizing their respective aircraft manufacturers. In 2010, the WTO ruled that Airbus received improper subsidies for its A380 superjumbo jet and several other aircraft, hurting Boeing, as the United States charged in 2005. In 2012, the WTO ruled that Boeing and Airbus both received improper subsidies. Yet the cycle of subsidies, charges, agreements, and new subsidies continues. . . .

If only Boeing or Airbus receives a government subsidy, how should its managers use the subsidy to gain a competitive advantage? What effect does that subsidy have on prices and quantities? What happens if both governments subsidize their firms? Should Boeing and Airbus managers lobby for government subsidies that result in a subsidy war?

In Chapter 7, we discussed the common market structures: perfect competition, monopoly, oligopoly, and monopolistic competition. In this chapter, we focus on oligopolistic and monopolistically competitive markets, which have more than the one firm of a monopoly but fewer firms than in a perfectly competitive market.

An **oligopoly** has few sellers and barriers to entry. Because relatively few firms compete in such a market, each can influence the market price, and hence its actions affect rival firms. As with a monopoly, an oligopolistic firm has market power and is therefore able to profitably set a price above marginal cost.

Many manufacturing, transportation, financial, and other markets with relatively few firms are either oligopolistic or monopolistically competitive. For example, the worldwide video game market is oligopolistic and is dominated by three firms: Nintendo, Microsoft, and Sony. As one of these three firms changes its price or its product's features, the other firms must either respond or lose a substantial amount of business.

The need to consider the behavior of rivals makes the profit-maximization decision for an oligopolistic firm more difficult than for a competitive firm or a monopoly. A competitive firm ignores the behavior of individual rivals and considers only the market price and its own costs in choosing its profit-maximizing output (Chapter 8). A monopoly has no rivals (Chapter 9) and considers only how its choice of quantity or price affects its profit.

Oligopolistic firms may act independently or may coordinate their actions. In this chapter, we focus primarily on independent or *noncooperative* oligopolies. However, a group of firms in the same industry may seek to cooperate. If they coordinate setting prices or quantities, they are said to *collude* and the group of firms is often called a **cartel**. If the colluding firms can cooperate and behave like a monopoly, the members of the cartel collectively earn the monopoly profit. Even if the cartel cannot achieve the full monopoly outcome, it can often collude sufficiently to at least provide its members with higher profits than the firms could earn through independent actions. In the United States and most other developed economies, such cartels are generally illegal.

If oligopolistic firms do not collude, they normally earn less profit than a monopoly could. However, because oligopolistic markets have relatively few firms, oligopolistic firms that act independently may earn positive economic profits in the long run, unlike competitive firms.

In an oligopolistic market, limitations on entry keep the number of firms small. In a market with no limits on entry, firms enter the market until profits are driven to zero. In perfectly competitive markets, enough entry occurs that each firm faces a horizontal demand curve and is a price taker.

However, free entry does not necessarily lead to perfect competition. Even if the entry of many firms drives the last firm's economic profit to zero (Chapter 7), each firm's demand curve may be downward sloping, particularly if each firm differentiates its product from those of its rivals. Given that firms face downward-sloping demand curves, they charge a price above their marginal costs. Such a market is therefore not perfectly competitive and is called monopolistic competition.

Monopolistic competition is a market structure in which firms have market power, but free entry occurs in the long run until no additional firm can enter and earn a positive long-run profit. If all firms have identical costs and produce identical products, all firms earn zero long-run economic profits.

As we saw in Chapter 9, the monopoly outcome is the same whether a monopoly sets price or quantity. In contrast, under oligopoly or monopolistic competition, outcomes can differ depending on whether firms choose to set prices or quantities.

Main Topics In this chapter, we examine four main topics	1. **Cartels:** If firms successfully coordinate their actions, they can seek to raise prices and profits toward monopoly levels. 2. **Cournot Oligopoly:** One important model of oligopoly is the Cournot model, in which firms simultaneously and independently set their quantities.

> 3. **Bertrand Oligopoly:** Another type of oligopoly is described by the Bertrand model, in which firms simultaneously and independently set their prices.
>
> 4. **Monopolistic Competition:** When firms can freely enter the market but face downward-sloping demand curves in equilibrium, firms charge prices above marginal cost but make no economic profit in the long run.

11.1 Cartels

Oligopolistic firms have an incentive to form cartels in which they collude in setting prices or quantities so as to increase their profits. The Organization of Petroleum Exporting Countries (OPEC) is a well-known example of an international cartel; however, many cartels operate within a single country.

Why Cartels Succeed or Fail

Typically, each member of a cartel agrees to reduce its output from the level it would produce if it acted independently. As a result, the market price rises and the firms earn higher profits. If the firms reduce market output to the monopoly level, they achieve the highest possible collective profit. As Adam Smith observed more than two centuries ago, "People of the same trade seldom meet together, even for merriment and diversion, but the conversation ends in a conspiracy against the public, or some contrivance to raise prices."

Luckily for consumers, cartels often fail because of government policies that forbid cartels or because members of the cartel "cheat" on the cartel agreement. Each member has an incentive to cheat because it can raise its profit if it increases its output while other cartel members stick to the agreement.

Why Cartels Form. A cartel forms if members of the cartel believe that they can raise their profits by coordinating their actions. But if a firm maximizes its profit when acting independently, why should joining a cartel increase its profit? The answer involves a subtle argument. When a firm acts independently, it considers how increasing its output affects its own profit only. The firm does not care that when it increases its output, it lowers the profits of other firms. A cartel, in contrast, takes into account how changes in any one firm's output affect the profits of all members of the cartel. Therefore, the aggregate profit of a cartel can exceed the combined profits of the same firms acting independently.

Although cartels are most common in oligopolistic markets, occasionally we see cartels formed in what would otherwise be highly competitive markets with many firms. If a competitive firm lowers its output, it raises the market price very slightly—so slightly that the firm ignores the effect not only on other firms' profits but also on its own. If all the identical competitive firms in an industry lower their output by this same amount, however, the market price will change noticeably. Recognizing this effect of collective action, a cartel chooses to produce a smaller market output than is produced by a competitive market.

Figure 11.1 illustrates the difference between a competitive market and a cartel. This oligopolistic market has n firms, and no further entry is possible. Panel a shows the marginal and average cost curves of a typical perfectly competitive firm. If all firms are price takers, the market supply curve, S in panel b, is the horizontal sum of the individual marginal cost curves above minimum average cost. At the competitive

FIGURE 11.1 Comparing Competition with a Cartel

(a) The marginal cost and average cost of one of the n firms in the market are shown. A competitive firm produces q_c units of output, whereas a cartel member produces $q_m < q_c$. At the cartel price, p_m, each cartel member has an incentive to increase its output from q_m to q^* (where the dotted line at p_m intersects the MC curve). (b) The competitive equilibrium, e_c, has more output and a lower price than the cartel equilibrium, e_m.

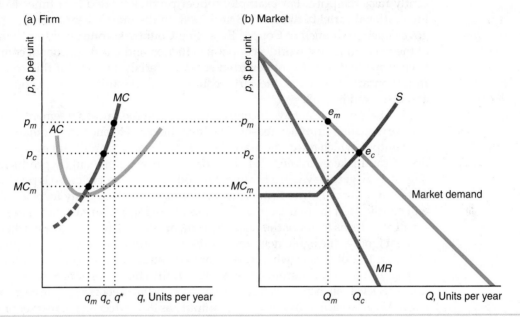

price, p_c, each price-taking firm produces q_c units of output (which is determined by the intersection in panel a of MC and the dotted line at p_c).[1] The market output is $Q_c = nq_c$ (where S intersects the market demand curve in panel b).

Now suppose that the firms form a cartel. Should they reduce their output? At the competitive output, the cartel's marginal cost in panel b (which is S, the sum of the individual firms' marginal cost curves) is greater than its marginal revenue, so the cartel's profit rises if it reduces output. The cartel's collective profit rises until output is reduced by enough that its marginal revenue equals its marginal cost at Q_m, the monopoly output. If the profit of the cartel increases, the profit of each of the n members of the cartel also increases. To achieve the cartel output level, each firm must reduce its output to $q_m = Q_m/n$, as panel a shows.

Why must the firms form a cartel to achieve these higher profits? A competitive firm produces q_c, where its marginal cost equals the market price. If only one firm reduces its output, it loses profit because it sells fewer units at essentially the same price. By getting all the firms to lower their output together, the cartel raises the market price and hence individual firms' profits. The less elastic the market demand curve that the potential cartel faces, holding everything else constant, the higher the price the cartel sets and the greater the benefit from forming a cartel. In regimes where cartels are legal, such possibilities are attractive to producers. Even where cartels are not legal, if the penalty for forming an illegal cartel is relatively low, producers still face an incentive to succumb to the lure of extra profits and join.

---

[1]As drawn, the competitive price exceeds the minimum average cost. These competitive firms earn a profit because the number of firms is fixed.

Why Cartels Fail. In most developed countries, cartels are generally illegal (as we discuss at greater length in Chapter 16), firms in the cartel may incur fines, and the owners or managers of these firms may be subject to individual fines and jail terms.[2] Further, many cartels fail even without legal intervention.

Some cartels fail because they do not control enough of the market to significantly raise the price. For example, copper producers tried four times to form an international cartel between 1918 and 1988. In the most recent attempt, the Intergovernmental Council of Copper Exporting Countries, controlled less than a third of the noncommunist world's copper production and faced additional competition from firms that recycle copper from scrap materials. Because of this competition from noncartel members, the cartel could not successfully increase copper prices and dissolved in 1988.

Members of a cartel have incentives to cheat on the cartel agreement. The owner of a participating firm may reason, "I joined the cartel to encourage others to reduce their output, which raises the market price and increases profits for everyone. However, I can make even more if I cheat on the cartel agreement by producing extra output. I can get away with cheating if the other firms can't tell who is producing the extra output because my firm is just one of many firms and my increase in output will hardly affect the market price." By this reasoning, it is in each firm's best interest for all *other* firms to honor the cartel agreement—thus driving up the market price—while it ignores the agreement and makes extra profitable sales at the high price.

Figure 11.1 illustrates why firms want to cheat. At the cartel output, q_m in panel a, each cartel member's marginal cost is MC_m. A firm that does not restrict its output to the cartel level can increase its profit. It can earn the market price, p_m, on each extra unit it sells because each individual firm's output has little effect on the market price. That is, the firm can act like a price taker, so its marginal revenue equals the market price. The firm maximizes its profit by selling q^* units, which is determined by the intersection of its marginal cost curve and the dotted line at p_m. Because its marginal revenue is above its marginal cost for all the extra units it sells (those between q_m and q^*), it makes extra money by violating the cartel agreement. As more and more firms leave the cartel, the cartel price falls. Eventually, if enough firms quit, the cartel collapses.

Mini-Case	Being thin, rich, and beautiful doesn't make you immune to exploitation. In 2004, some of the world's most successful models charged 10 of New York's top modeling agencies—including Wilhelmina, Ford, Next, IMG, and Elite—with operating a cartel that cut their commissions by millions of dollars. Such collusion between firms is illegal under U.S. law.
A Catwalk Cartel	

Carolyn Fears—a 5'11" redheaded former model who had earned up to $200,000 a year—initiated the suit when she learned that her agency not only charged her a 20% commission every time she was booked, but also extracted a 20% commission from her employers. Her class-action lawsuit (a lawsuit representing a group of people—here, models) alleged that the agencies collectively fixed commissions for Claudia Schiffer, Heidi Klum, Gisele Bundchen, and thousands of other models over many years.

---

[2]With rare exceptions, it is illegal for firms to collude over prices, quantities, market areas, or the equivalent. However, in most jurisdictions, firms are allowed to coordinate R&D efforts or technical standards if they wish.

The agencies had formed an industry group, International Model Managers Association, Inc. (IMMA), which held repeated meetings. Monique Pillard, an executive at Elite Model Management, fired off a memo concerning one IMMA meeting, in which she "made a point . . . that we are all committing suicide, if we do not stick together. Pauline's agreed with me but as usual, Bill Weinberg [of Wilhelmina] cautioned me about price fixing. . . . Ha! Ha! Ha! . . . the usual (expletive)." As the trial judge, Harold Baer, Jr., observed, while "Wilhelmina objects to the outward discussion of price fixing, it is plausible from Pillard's reaction that Wilhelmina's objection was to the dissemination of information, not to the underlying price-fixing agreement."

The models argued that the association was little more than a front for helping agency heads keep track of each other's pricing policies. Documents show that, shortly after association meetings, the agencies uniformly raised their commission rates from 10% to 15% and then to 20%. For example, at a meeting before the last increase, an Elite executive gave his competitors a heads-up—but had not informed his clients—that Elite planned to raise its commissions to 20%. He said that at Elite, "we were also favorable to letting everyone know as much as possible about our pricing policies."

In 2007, the models won their court case, having sued successfully under U.S. laws that prohibit price-fixing cartels. They received payments from the firms. For example, IMG paid the models $11 million. In 2011, the Competition Commission of Singapore fined a cartel consisting of 10 modeling agencies for price-fixing in a case remarkably similar to the U.S. case.

Maintaining Cartels

A thing worth having is a thing worth cheating for. —W. C. Fields

To keep firms from violating a cartel agreement, it is important for the cartel to be able to detect cheating and punish violators. Further, the members of the cartel need to keep their illegal behavior sufficiently hidden from customers and government agencies to avoid prosecution.

Detection and Enforcement. Cartels use various techniques to detect cheating. Some cartels, for example, give members the right to inspect each other's accounts. Cartels may also divide the market by region or by customers, making it more likely that a firm that steals another firm's customers is detected, as in the case of a two-country mercury cartel (1928–1972) that allocated the Americas to Spain and Europe to Italy. Another option is for a cartel to turn to industry organizations that collect data on market share by firm. A cheating cartel's market share would rise, tipping off the other firms that it cheated.

You perhaps have seen "low price" ads in which local retail stores guarantee to meet or beat the prices of any competitors. These ads may in fact be a way for the firm to induce its customers to report cheating by other firms on an explicit or implicit cartel agreement (Salop, 1986).

Various methods are used to enforce cartel agreements. For example, GE and Westinghouse, the two major sellers of large steam-turbine generators, included "most-favored-customer" clauses in their contracts. These contracts stated that the seller would not offer a lower price to any other current or future buyer without offering the same price decrease to the firms that signed these contracts. This type of rebate clause creates a penalty for cheating on the cartel: If either company cheats by cutting prices, it has to lower prices to all previous buyers as well. Threats of violence are another means of enforcing a cartel agreement.[3]

Government Support. Sometimes governments help create and enforce cartels, exempting them from antitrust and competition laws. By successfully lobbying the U.S. Congress for a special exemption, professional baseball teams have not been subject to most U.S. antitrust laws since 1922. As a result, they can use the courts to help enforce certain aspects of their cartel agreement.

The international airline market provides an example where governments first created a cartel and then later acted to end it. In 1944, 52 countries signed the Convention on International Civil Aviation, which established rules ("freedoms") that enabled airlines to fly between countries. International airfares were negotiated through bilateral governmental agreements rather than determined by the market, and airlines were given exemption from cartel laws, which allowed them to discuss prices through the International Air Transport Association (IATA). In the late 1970s, the United States deregulated its airline industry. Soon thereafter, European countries started to deregulate, allowing nongovernment-owned airlines to enter the market. Countries negotiated bilateral *open skies* agreements that weakened IATA's price-fixing role.[4]

Barriers to Entry. Barriers to entry that limit the number of firms help the cartel detect and punish cheating. The fewer the firms in a market, the more likely it is that other firms will know if a given firm cheats and the easier it is to impose penalties. Cartels with a large number of firms are relatively rare, except those involving professional associations.

When new firms enter their market, cartels frequently fail. For example, when only Italy and Spain sold mercury, they were able to establish and maintain a stable cartel. When a larger group of countries joined them, their attempts to cartelize the world mercury market repeatedly failed (MacKie-Mason and Pindyck, 1986).

11.2 Cournot Oligopoly

How do the great number of oligopolistic firms that do not collude interact? Although there is only one model of competition and one model of monopoly, there are many models of noncooperative oligopolistic behavior with many possible equilibrium prices and quantities.

Which oligopoly model is appropriate in a particular market depends on the characteristics of the market, including the type of *actions* firms take (such as whether firms set prices or quantities), whether firms act simultaneously or sequentially, and the time horizon (the number of periods) over which firms compete. In this chapter and in Chapter 12, we examine oligopoly models in which firms act simultaneously and compete in a single period. In Chapter 13, we examine oligopoly models in which firms may act sequentially and compete over many periods. In this chapter, we assume that firms set only prices or quantities, whereas in Chapters 12 and 13,

---

[3]See MyEconLab Chapter Resources, Chapter 11, "Bad Bakers."

[4]The European Court of Justice struck down the central provisions of aviation treaties among the United States and eight other countries in 2002.

we consider other decisions by firms such as how much to advertise and whether to enter a market. To keep the analysis as clear as possible, we initially assume that firms produce identical products, but we later show how these models can incorporate product differentiation.

We begin our study of oligopoly models with the two best-known oligopoly models, the *Cournot model* and the *Bertrand model*. In both models, firms act simultaneously and independently. In the Cournot model, firms choose quantities: how much they produce. In contrast, in the Bertrand model firms set prices. Because each firm acts independently and before it knows how its rivals will act, each firm must choose its output level or price based on how it expects its rivals to behave.

To compare market outcomes under the various oligopoly models, we need to be able to characterize the oligopoly equilibrium. In Chapter 2, we defined an *equilibrium* for the supply-demand model as a situation in which neither firms nor consumers want to change their behavior. John Nash, a Nobel Prize-winning economist and mathematician, defined a related equilibrium concept (Nash, 1951) that has wide applicability to oligopolistic markets and many other situations.

We give a general definition of a Nash equilibrium in Chapter 12. In this chapter we use a special case of that definition that is appropriate for the Cournot model, in which the firm's strategy is the quantity it produces, and for the Bertrand model, in which the firm's strategy is its price. A set of strategies chosen by the oligopolistic firms is a *Nash equilibrium* if, holding the strategies of all other firms constant, no firm can obtain a higher profit by choosing a different strategy. For example, in a Cournot oligopoly, a Nash equilibrium is a set of output levels chosen by the firms such that no firm wants to change its output level if its rivals' output levels remain constant.

The Cournot model is the oldest and still one of the most widely used oligopoly models. It was introduced by the French economist and mathematician Antoine-Augustin Cournot in 1838. The simplest version of the Cournot model relies on four assumptions.

1. The market has a small number of firms, and no other firms can enter;
2. the firms set their quantities independently and simultaneously;
3. the firms have identical costs; and
4. the firms sell identical products.

All of these assumptions are relaxed either later in this chapter or in the next two chapters.

Because the firms set quantities, the price adjusts as needed until the market clears in the sense that the amount purchased by consumers equals the amount offered for sale by sellers. Therefore, each firm's quantity decision affects the profit of the other firm, because an increase in one firm's quantity drives down market price, reducing the revenues received by the other firm. Thus, the firms' profits are interdependent.

Airlines

To illustrate the basic idea of the Cournot model, we examine a real market in which American Airlines and United Airlines compete for customers on flights between Chicago and Los Angeles.[5] An oligopoly with two firms is referred to as a *duopoly*.

---

[5]This example is based on Brander and Zhang (1990). In calculating the airlines' profits, we assume that Brander and Zhang's estimate of the firms' constant marginal cost is the same as the firms' relevant long-run average cost.

The total number of passengers flown by these two firms, Q, is the sum of the number of passengers flown on American, q_A, and those flown on United, q_U.

How many passengers does each airline choose to carry? To answer this question, we determine the Nash equilibrium for this model in which the firms choose quantities. It is called a **Nash-Cournot equilibrium** (or **Cournot-Nash equilibrium** or **Cournot equilibrium**): a set of quantities chosen by the firms such that, holding the quantities of all other firms constant, no firm can obtain a higher profit by choosing a different quantity.

A Graphical Approach. The strategy that each firm uses depends on the demand curve it faces and its marginal cost. American Airlines' profit-maximizing output depends on how many passengers it believes United will fly. Figure 11.2 illustrates two possibilities.

If American were a monopoly, it wouldn't have to worry about United's strategy. American's demand would be the market demand curve, D in panel a. The figure shows the estimated total demand curve for the Chicago–Los Angeles route,

$$Q = 339 - p, \qquad (11.1)$$

where price, p, is the dollar cost of a one-way flight, and the total quantity of the two airlines combined, Q, is measured in thousands of passengers flying one way per quarter.

To maximize its profit, American would set its output so that its marginal revenue curve, MR, intersected its marginal cost curve, MC, which is constant at $147 per passenger. Panel a shows that the monopoly output is 96 units (thousands of passengers) per quarter and the monopoly price is $243 per passenger (one way).

FIGURE 11.2 **American Airlines' Profit-Maximizing Output**

(a) If American is a monopoly, it picks its profit-maximizing output, $q_A = 96$ units (thousand passengers) per quarter, so that its marginal revenue, MR, equals its marginal cost, MC. (b) If American believes that United will fly $q_U = 64$ units per quarter, its residual demand curve, D^r, is the market demand curve, D, minus q_U. American maximizes its profit at $q_A = 64$, where its marginal revenue, MR^r, equals MC.

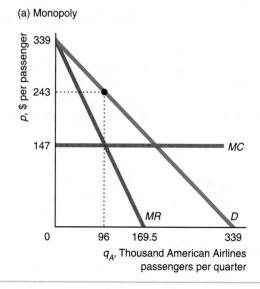

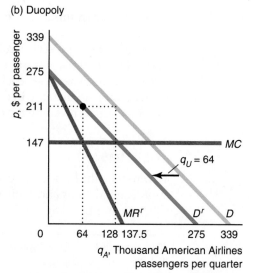

Because American competes with United, American must consider United's behavior when choosing its profit-maximizing output. American's demand is not the entire market demand. Rather, American is concerned with its *residual demand curve*: the market demand that is not met by other sellers at any given price. In general, if the market demand function is $D(p)$, and the supply of other firms is $S^o(p)$, then the residual demand function, $D^r(p)$, is

$$D^r(p) = D(p) - S^o(p).$$

Thus, if United flies q_U passengers regardless of the price, American transports only the residual demand, $Q = D(p)$, minus the q_U passengers, so $q_A = Q - q_U$.

Suppose that American believes that United will fly $q_U = 64$. Panel b shows that American's residual demand curve, D^r, is the market demand curve, D, moved to the left by $q_U = 64$. For example, if the price is \$211, the total number of passengers who want to fly can be determined from market demand Equation 11.1 as $Q = 339 - 211 = 128$. If United transports $q_U = 64$, American flies $Q - q_U = 128 - 64 = 64 = q_A$.

What is American's *best response* (its profit-maximizing output) if its managers believe that United will fly q_U passengers? American can think of itself as having a monopoly with respect to the people who don't fly on United, which its residual demand curve, D^r, shows. To maximize its profit, American sets its output so that its marginal revenue corresponding to this residual demand, MR^r, equals its marginal cost. Panel b shows that if $q_U = 64$, American's best response is $q_A = 64$.

By shifting its residual demand curve appropriately, American can calculate its best response to any given q_U using this type of analysis. Figure 11.3 plots American Airlines' *best-response curve*, which shows how many tickets American sells for each possible q_U.[6] In the figure, the horizontal axis shows American's quantity, q_A, and

FIGURE 11.3 Best-Response Curves for American and United Airlines

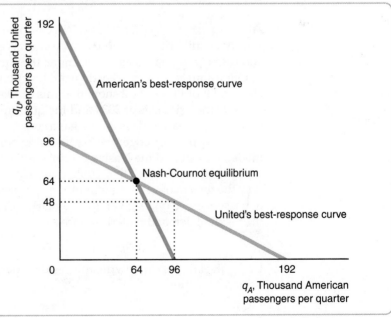

The best-response curves show the output each firm picks to maximize its profit, given its belief about its rival's output. The Nash-Cournot equilibrium occurs at the intersection of the best-response curves.

---

[6]A *best-response curve* is sometimes called a *reaction curve* or *reaction function*.

the vertical axis shows United's quantity, q_U. As the best-response curve shows, American sells the monopoly number of tickets, $q_A = 96$, if American thinks United will fly no passengers, $q_U = 0$. The negative slope of the best-response curve shows that American sells fewer tickets, the more people American thinks that United will fly. American sells $q_A = 64$ if it thinks q_U will be 64. American shuts down, $q_A = 0$, if it thinks q_U will be 192 or more, because operating wouldn't be profitable.

Similarly, United's best-response curve shows how many tickets United sells if it thinks American will sell q_A. For example, United sells $q_U = 0$ if it thinks American will sell $q_A = 192$, $q_U = 48$ if $q_A = 96$, $q_U = 64$ if $q_A = 64$, and $q_U = 96$ if $q_A = 0$.

A firm wants to change its behavior if it is selling a quantity that is not on its best-response curve. The only one pair of outputs where both firms are on their best-response curves, $q_A = q_U = 64$, is determined by the intersection of the firms' best-response curves. If American expects United to sell $q_U = 64$, American wants to sell $q_A = 64$. Because this point is on its best-response curve, American doesn't want to change its output from 64. Similarly, if United expects American to sell $q_A = 64$, United doesn't want to change q_U from 64. Thus, this pair of outputs is a Nash-Cournot equilibrium: Given its correct belief about its rival's output, each firm is maximizing its profit, and neither firm wants to change its output because neither firm regrets the choice it has made.

Any pair of outputs other than the pair at an intersection of the best-response functions is *not* a Nash-Cournot equilibrium. If either firm is producing an output level that is not on its best-response curve, it could increase its profit by changing its output. For example, the output pair $q_A = 96$ and $q_U = 0$ is not a Nash-Cournot equilibrium. American is perfectly happy producing the monopoly output if United doesn't operate at all: American is on its best-response curve. However, United would not be happy with this outcome because it is not on United's best-response curve. As its best-response curve shows, if it knows that American will sell $q_A = 96$, United wants to sell $q_U = 48$. Only at $q_A = q_U = 64$ does neither firm want to change its behavior.

An Algebraic Approach. We can also use algebra to solve for the Nash-Cournot equilibrium for these two airlines. We use estimates of the market demand and firms' marginal costs to determine the equilibrium.

Our estimate of the market demand function, Equation 11.1, is $Q = 339 - p$. Panels a and b of Figure 11.2 show that this market demand curve, D, is a straight line that hits the price axis at $339 and the quantity axis at 339 units (thousands of passengers) per quarter. Each airline has a constant marginal cost, MC, and average cost, AC, of $147 per passenger per flight. Using only this information and our economic model, we can find the Nash-Cournot equilibrium for the two airlines.

If American believes that United will fly q_U passengers, American expects to fly only the total market demand minus q_U passengers. At a price of p, the total number of passengers, $Q(p)$, is given by the market demand function, Equation 11.1. Thus, the residual demand American faces is

$$q_A = Q(p) - q_U = (339 - p) - q_U.$$

Using algebra, we can rewrite this residual demand function as the inverse residual demand function:

$$p = 339 - q_A - q_U. \tag{11.2}$$

The plot of this inverse residual demand function is the linear residual demand curve D^r in panel b of Figure 11.2. It is parallel to the market demand, D, and lies 64 units to the left of D, which is the quantity that United sells, $q_U = 64$.

If a demand curve is linear, the corresponding marginal revenue curve is linear and is twice as steep (Chapter 9). The slope of the residual demand curve, Equation 11.2, is $\Delta p / \Delta q_A = -1$, so the slope of the corresponding marginal revenue curve, MR^r in panel b in Figure 11.2, is -2. Therefore, the marginal revenue function is

$$MR^r = 339 - 2q_A - q_U. \tag{11.3}$$

American Airlines' best response—its profit-maximizing output, given q_U—is the output that equates its marginal revenue, Equation 11.3, and its marginal cost:

$$MR^r = 339 - 2q_A - q_U = 147 = MC. \tag{11.4}$$

By rearranging Equation 11.4, we can write American's best-response output, q_A, as a function of q_U:

$$q_A = 96 - \tfrac{1}{2}q_U. \tag{11.5}$$

Figure 11.3 shows American's best-response function, Equation 11.5. According to this best-response function, $q_A = 96$ if $q_U = 0$ and $q_A = 64$ if $q_U = 64$. By the same reasoning, United's best-response function is

$$q_U = 96 - \tfrac{1}{2}q_A. \tag{11.6}$$

A Nash-Cournot equilibrium is a pair of quantities, q_A and q_U, such that Equations 11.5 and 11.6 both hold: Each firm is on its best-response curve. This statement is equivalent to saying that the Nash-Cournot equilibrium is a point at which the best-response curves cross.

One way to determine the Nash-Cournot equilibrium is to substitute Equation 11.6 into Equation 11.5,

$$q_A = 96 - \tfrac{1}{2}\left(96 - \tfrac{1}{2}q_A\right), \tag{11.7}$$

and solve for q_A. Doing so, we find that $q_A = 64$ is the Nash-Cournot equilibrium quantity for American. Substituting $q_A = 64$ into Equation 11.6, we find that $q_U = 64$ is the Nash-Cournot equilibrium quantity for United.[7] As a result, the total output in the Nash-Cournot equilibrium is $Q = q_A + q_U = 128$. Setting $Q = 128$ in the market demand Equation 11.1, we learn that the Nash-Cournot equilibrium price is $211.

Using Calculus

Deriving a Cournot Firm's Marginal Revenue

The inverse demand function (Equation 11.2), $p = 339 - q_A - q_U$, shows how the price varies with the outputs of the two firms. If we multiply both sides of that equation by American's quantity, we obtain American's revenue, R_A, function:

$$R_A = pq_A = (339 - q_A - q_U)q_A = 339q_A - q_A^2 - q_A q_U.$$

To derive American's marginal revenue curve, we differentiate R_A with respect to q_A. American views q_U as a variable that is not under its control but is determined "externally" by United. Therefore, we treat q_U as a constant when differentiating. By doing so, we obtain the same expression for American's marginal revenue function as in Equation 11.3:

$$MR^r = \frac{dR_A}{dq_A} = 339 - 2q_A - q_U.$$

---

[7]The Nash-Cournot equilibrium outputs of United and American are the same because they have identical costs. As we show later in this chapter, if firms' costs differ, their equilibrium quantities differ.

The Number of Firms

Our airlines example illustrates that, if two Cournot firms set output independently, the price to consumers is lower than the monopoly (or cartel) price. The price to consumers is even lower if more than two Cournot firms produce independently, as we now show.

As before, we work with the airlines' inverse market demand function $p = 339 - Q$. We now consider what would happen for n firms, where n is two or more. Firm 1 produces output q_1, Firm 2 produces output q_2, and so on. Thus, $Q = q_1 + q_2 + \cdots + q_n$. As earlier, each firm has a marginal cost of \$147.

As Appendix 11A shows, the duopoly best-response function in Equation 11.6 generalizes to

$$q_1 = 96 - \tfrac{1}{2}(q_2 + q_3 + \cdots + q_n), \tag{11.8}$$

for n firms and $q_1 = q_2 = \cdots = q_n$ in the Cournot equilibrium. Denoting the common output as q, we can rewrite Equation 11.8 as $q = 96 - \tfrac{1}{2}[n - 1]q$, so the output of any given firm is

$$q = \frac{192}{n + 1}. \tag{11.9}$$

For example, if $n = 2$, $q = q_1 = q_2 = 192/3 = 64$, which is the same result for a duopoly that we derived in the previous section.

Using Equation 11.9, we can calculate that total output, $Q = n \times q$, is

$$Q = nq = \frac{192n}{n + 1}. \tag{11.10}$$

If $n = 2$ in Equation 11.10, then $Q = (192 \times 2)/3 = 128$, and the corresponding price from the inverse demand equation is $p = 339 - Q = 211$, as we derived earlier. If $n = 3$, then $Q = (192 \times 3)/4 = 144$, and $p = 195$. As the number of firms n grows, total output Q rises, approaching 192 as n gets very large, and the price approaches \$147, which is the marginal cost. That is, the Nash-Cournot equilibrium approaches the competitive outcome as the number of firms grows very large.

At the other extreme where $n = 1$, total output is $Q = 192/2 = 96$, the monopoly output, and the corresponding monopoly price is \$243. Thus as the number of firms varies, the Cournot model can capture outcomes that range from monopoly ($n = 1$) through duopoly ($n = 2$) all the way to perfect competition (n is very large).

Mini-Case	The markup of price over marginal cost is much greater on routes in which one airline carries most of the passengers than on other routes. Unfortunately for passengers, a single firm was the only carrier or the dominant carrier on 58% of all U.S. domestic routes (Weiher et al., 2002).
Air Ticket Prices and Rivalry	The first column of the table identifies the market structure for U.S. air routes. The last column shows the share of routes. A single firm (monopoly) served 18% of all routes. Duopolies controlled 19% of the routes, three-firm markets were 16%, four-firm markets were 13%, and five or more firms flew on 35% of the routes.

Although nearly two-thirds of all routes had three or more carriers, one or two firms dominated virtually all routes. We call a carrier a *dominant firm* if it has at least 60% of ticket sales by value but is not a monopoly. We call two carriers a *dominant pair* if they collectively have at least 60% of the market but neither firm is a dominant firm and three or more firms fly this route. All but 0.1% of routes had a monopoly (18%), a dominant firm (40%), or a dominant pair (42%).

The first row of the table shows that the price was slightly more than double (2.1 times) marginal cost on average across all U.S. routes and market structures. (This average price included "free" frequent flier tickets and other below-cost tickets.) The price was 3.3 times marginal cost for monopolies and 3.1 times marginal cost for dominant firms. In contrast, over the sample period, the average price was only 1.2 times marginal cost for dominant pairs.

The markup of price over marginal cost depends much more on whether a single firm or a pair of firms dominate the market than on the total number of firms in the market. If there was a dominant pair, the price was between 1.3 times marginal cost for a four-firm route and 1.4 times marginal cost for a route with five or more firms. With a dominant firm, price was 2.3 times marginal cost on duopoly routes, 1.9 times on three-firm routes, 2.2 times on four-firm routes, and 3.5 times on routes with five or more firms.

Type of Market	p/MC	Share of All Routes (%)
All market types	2.1	100
Dominant firm	3.1	40
Dominant pair	1.2	42
One firm (monopoly)	3.3	18
Two firms (duopoly)	2.2	19
Dominant firm	2.3	14
No dominant firm	1.5	5
Three firms	1.8	16
Dominant firm	1.9	9
No dominant firm	1.3	7
Four firms	1.8	13
Dominant firm	2.2	6
Dominant pair	1.3	7
No dominant firm or pair	2.1	~0
Five or more firms	1.3	35
Dominant firm	3.5	11
Dominant pair	1.4	23
No dominant firm or pair	1.1	0.1

Thus, preventing a single firm from dominating a route may substantially lower prices. Even if two firms dominate the market, the markup of price over marginal cost is substantially lower than if a single firm dominates.

Nonidentical Firms

We initially assumed that the firms are identical in the sense that they face the same cost functions and produce identical products. However, costs often vary across firms, and firms often differentiate the products they produce from those of their rivals. We'll now investigate how these differences affect the Nash-Cournot equilibrium output of firms.

Unequal Costs. As we've seen, in the Cournot model, a firm determines its best-response function by equating its marginal revenue to its marginal cost. If one firm's marginal costs rises or falls, then the firm's best-response function shifts. In the new Nash-Cournot equilibrium, the relatively low-cost firm produces more and each higher cost firm produces less. However, as long as the products are not differentiated, all firms in the market charge the same price.

We can illustrate the effect of unequal costs using our earlier duopoly airlines example. Suppose that American Airlines' marginal cost remains at $147, but United's marginal cost drops to $99. The Cournot model still applies, but we have relaxed the assumption that the firms have identical costs. How does the Nash-Cournot equilibrium change? Your intuition probably tells you that United's output increases relative to that of American. We can show this result in a diagram.

Nothing changes for American, so its best-response function is unchanged. United's best response to any given American output is the output at which its marginal revenue corresponding to its residual demand, MR^r, equals its new, lower marginal cost. Because United's marginal cost curve falls, United wants to produce more than before for any given level of American's output.

Panel a of Figure 11.4 illustrates this reasoning. United's MR^r curve is unaffected, but its marginal cost curve shifts down from MC^1 to MC^2. Suppose we fix American's output at 64 units. Consequently, United's residual demand, D^r, lies 64 units to the left of the market demand, D. United's corresponding MR^r curve intersects its original marginal cost curve, $MC^1 = \$147$, at 64 and its new marginal cost, $MC^2 = \$99$, at 88. Thus, if we hold American's output constant at 64, United produces more as its marginal cost falls.

Because this reasoning applies for any level of output American picks, United's best-response function in panel b shifts outward as its marginal cost falls. United's best response to any given quantity that American sells is to sell more than at its previous, higher cost. As a result, the Nash-Cournot equilibrium shifts from the original e_1, at which both firms sold 64, to e_2, at which United sells 96 and American sells 48.

Using the market demand function, Equation 11.1, we find that the market price falls from $211 to $195, benefiting consumers. United's profit increases from $4.1 million to $9.2 million, while American's profit falls to $2.3 million.[8] Thus, United gains and American loses from the fall in United's marginal cost. As price falls, consumers also benefit from this cost reduction.

Differentiated Products. By differentiating its product from those of a rival, an oligopolistic firm can shift its demand curve to the right and make it less elastic. The less elastic the demand curve, the more the firm can charge. Loosely speaking, consumers are willing to pay more for a product that they perceive as being superior.

---

[8]In the original case with identical costs, each firm's profit per passenger is price minus average cost, $p - AC$, so the firm's profit is $\pi = (p - AC)q$, where q is the number of passengers the firm flies. The price is $211 and the average cost is $147, so the Cournot profit per firm is $\pi = (211 - 147) \times 64$ units per quarter = $4.1 million per quarter in the original symmetric case.

FIGURE 11.4 Effect of a Drop in One Firm's Marginal Cost on a Nash-Cournot Equilibrium

(a) United's marginal cost falls from $MC^1 = \$147$ to $MC^2 = \$99$. If American produces $q_a = 64$, United's best response is to increase its output from $q_U = 64$ to 88 given its lower marginal cost. (b) If both airlines' marginal cost is $\$147$, the Nash-Cournot equilibrium is e_1. After

United's marginal cost falls to $\$99$, its best-response function shifts outward. It now sells more tickets in response to any given American output than previously. At the new Nash-Cournot equilibrium, e_2, United sells $q_U = 96$, while American sells only $q_A = 48$.

(a) United's Residual Demand

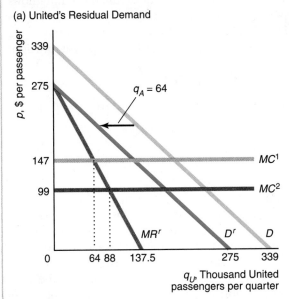

(b) Best-Response Curves

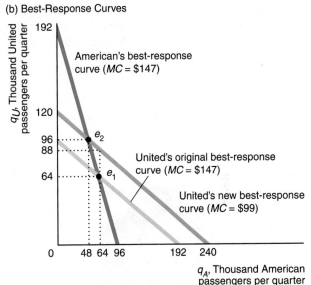

Q&A 11.1

Derive United Airlines' best-response function if its marginal cost falls to $\$99$ per unit. Given that American's marginal cost does not change, what is the new Nash-Cournot equilibrium?

Answer

1. *Determine United's marginal revenue function corresponding to its residual demand curve.* Luckily, we already know that. The shift in its marginal cost curve does not affect United's residual demand curve, hence its marginal revenue function is the same as before: $MR^r = 339 - 2q_U - q_A$. (The same expression as American's marginal revenue function in Equation 11.3, where the A and U subscripts are reversed.)

2. *Equate United's marginal revenue function and its marginal cost to determine its best-response function.* For a given level of American's output, q_A, United chooses its output, q_U, to equate its marginal revenue and its marginal cost, m:

$$MR^r = 339 - 2q_U - q_A = 99 = m.$$

We can use algebra to rearrange this expression for its best-response function to express q_U as a function of q_A:

$$q_U = 120 - \tfrac{1}{2}q_A. \tag{11.11}$$

This equation corresponds to the green best-response curve in panel b of Figure 11.4.

3. *Find the new Nash-Cournot equilibrium pair of quantities by solving the two best-response functions for q_A and q_U.* Because American Airlines' marginal cost is unchanged, its best-response function is the same as in Equation 11.5, $q_A = 96 - \frac{1}{2}q_U$. The intersection of the two best-response functions, Equations 11.11 and 11.5, is that pair of quantities such that both of the best-response functions are true. We can solve for that pair by substituting the expression for q_A from American's best-response function into United's best-response function:

$$q_U = 120 - \tfrac{1}{2}q_A = 120 - \tfrac{1}{2}\left(96 - \tfrac{1}{2}q_U\right).$$

Solving, we find that $q_U = 96$. Substituting $q_U = 96$ into either best-response function, we find that $q_A = 48$.

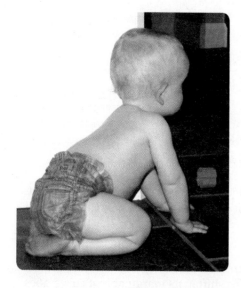

One way to differentiate a product is to give it unique, desirable attributes, such as the Lexus car that was the first to park itself. In 2010, Kimberly-Clark introduced a new Huggies disposable diaper with a printed denim pattern, including seams and back pockets, which sent their sales up 15%. Alternatively, a firm can differentiate its product by advertising, using colorful labels, and engaging in other promotional activities to convince consumers that its product is superior in some (possibly unspecified) way even though it is virtually identical to its rivals' products physically or chemically. Bayer charges more for its chemically identical aspirin than other brands because Bayer has convinced consumers that its product is safer or superior in some other way. Clorox's bottle may be superior to its rivals, but the bleach inside is chemically identical to that from rival brands costing much less.

Because differentiation makes demand curves less elastic, price markups over marginal cost are usually higher when products are differentiated than when they're identical. We know that consumer surplus falls as the gap between price and marginal cost rises for a given good. Does it follow that differentiating products lowers total surplus? Not necessarily. Although differentiation leads to higher prices, which harm consumers, differentiation is desirable in its own right. Consumers value having a choice, and some may greatly prefer a new brand to existing ones.

If consumers think products differ, the Cournot quantities and prices may differ across firms. Each firm faces a different inverse demand function and hence charges a different price. For example, suppose that Firm 1's inverse demand function is $p_1 = a - b_1q_1 - b_2q_2$, where $b_1 > b_2$ if consumers believe that Good 1 is different from Good 2 and $b_1 = b_2 = b$ if the goods are identical. Given that consumers view the products as differentiated and Firm 2 faces a similar inverse demand function, we replace the single market demand with these individual demand functions in the Cournot model. Q&A 11.2 shows how to solve for the Nash-Cournot equilibrium in an actual market with differentiated products.

Q&A 11.2

Assume that Intel and Advanced Micro Devices (AMD) are the only two firms that produce central processing units (CPUs), which are the brains of personal computers. Both because the products differ physically and because Intel's advertising "Intel Inside" campaign has convinced some consumers of its superiority, consumers view the CPUs as imperfect substitutes. Consequently, the two firms' estimated inverse demand functions differ:

$$p_A = 197 - 15.1q_A - 0.3q_I, \tag{11.12}$$

$$p_I = 490 - 10q_I - 6q_A. \tag{11.13}$$

where price is dollars per CPU, quantity is in millions of CPUs, the subscript I indicates Intel, and the subscript A represents AMD.[9] We assume that each firm faces a constant marginal cost of $m = \$40$ per unit and hed cost. Solve for the Nash-Cournot equilibrium quantities and prices.

Answer

1. *Using our rules for determining the marginal revenue for linear demand functions, calculate each firm's marginal revenue function.* For a linear demand curve, we know that the marginal revenue curve is twice as steeply sloped as is the demand curve. Thus, the marginal revenue functions that correspond to the inverse demand Equations 11.12 and 11.13 are:

$$MR^A = 197 - 30.2q_A - 0.3q_I, \tag{11.14}$$

$$MR^I = 490 - 20q_I - 6q_A. \tag{11.15}$$

2. *Equate the marginal revenue functions to the marginal cost to determine the best-response functions.* We determine AMD's best response function by equating MR^A from Equation 11.14 to its marginal cost of $m = \$40$,

$$MR^A = 197 - 30.2q_A - 0.3q_I = 40 = m,$$

and solving for q_A to obtain AMD's best-response function:

$$q_A = \frac{157 - 0.3\, q_I}{30.2}. \tag{11.16}$$

Similarly, Intel's best-response function is

$$q_I = \frac{450 - 6q_A}{20}. \tag{11.17}$$

3. *Use the best-response functions to solve for the Nash-Cournot equilibrium.* By simultaneously solving the system of best-response functions 11.16 and 11.17, we find that the Nash-Cournot equilibrium quantities are $q_A = 15{,}025/3{,}011 \approx 5$ million CPUs, and $q_I = 63{,}240/3{,}011 \approx 21$ million CPUs. Substituting these values into the inverse demand functions 11.12 and 11.13, we obtain the corresponding prices: $p_A = \$115.20$ and $p_I = \$250$ per CPU.

---

[9]We thank Hugo Salgado for estimating these inverse demand functions for us and for providing evidence that this market is well described by a Nash-Cournot equilibrium.

A manager can often increase a firm's profit by differentiating its product so that it can charge a higher price. A skillful manager may find it easier and less expensive to differentiate a product using marketing rather than by physically differentiating the product.

One product that is difficult to differentiate is water. Water can be carbonated or flavored, but doing so caters to only a subset of the $11 billion U.S. bottled water market. How can a skillful manager differentiate its uncarbonated, unflavored water?

Both Coke and Pepsi have successfully differentiated their brands through marketing. Pepsico's top-selling bottled water, Aquafina, has a colorful blue label and a logo showing the sun rising over the mountains. From that logo, consumers may infer that the water comes from some bubbling spring high in an unspoiled wilderness. If so, they're wrong. Pepsi's best-selling bottled water comes from the same place as tap water: public-water sources. Pepsi also claims that it adds value by filtering the water using a state-of-the-art "HydRO-7 purification system," implying that such filtering (which removes natural minerals) is desirable. Similarly, Coke's marketing distinguishes its Dasani bottled water, even though it too is basically bottled public water.

In a recent "blind" taste test reported in *Slate*, no one could distinguish between Aquafina and Dasani, and both are equally clean and safe. However, many consumers, responding to perceived differences created by marketing, strongly prefer one or the other of these brands and pay a premium for these products.

Mergers

In a merger, the assets and operations of two or more firms are combined into one firm. Mergers are very common. The primary reason for mergers is to increase profit, which can occur for several reasons. A merger may provide cost advantages by allowing the new firm to realize increased economies of scale, lowering average cost by operating at a larger scale. Or, a merger may produce economies of scope, where the new firm achieves a reduction in cost from carrying out related activities under common management. Mergers between vertically related firms, such as between a firm and a supplier or a customer, may lower cost by allowing for a more efficient organization of the supply chain.

Another important reason for mergers is to reduce competition. If the only two rivals in an industry combine forces through a merger, they become a monopoly and gain market power, which raises the total market profit. Even when only some firms in a market merge, their market power—their ability to set price above marginal cost profitably—may increase. Mergers between competitors are called *horizontal mergers*. Because of concerns about concentrating market power, most countries have antitrust or competition laws that subject mergers and acquisitions to legal scrutiny to insure that competition is not excessively harmed by such combinations. These authorities are particularly wary of mergers that create a monopoly. Competition authorities are more likely to approve a merger, the smaller the expected market power of the resulting merged firm. (We address the law on mergers in Chapter 16.)

Above, we showed that the Cournot market equilibrium price falls as the number of firms increases. We now examine what happens if a merger reduces the number of firms. The result depends in part on whether the benefit of the merger arises entirely from competition reductions, or whether it arises in part from a cost advantage.

We can illustrate the effects of a merger using the equations from our airline example. Suppose that the market initially has three identical firms, Firm 1, Firm 2, and Firm 3. Would any two of these firms have an incentive to merge? As before, the market inverse demand curve is $p = 339 - Q$, and the marginal cost is constant at $147 per passenger. In the Nash-Cournot equilibrium, each of the three firms flies 48 (thousand) passengers per quarter, charges a price of $195 per passenger, and earns a profit of $2.3 million [$\approx$ ($195 − $147) × 48,000].

Now, Firm 1 and Firm 2 merge, and the resulting firm has the same cost function as did the original firms. Given that the merged firm acts as a single Cournot firm, we now have a duopoly Cournot market.[10] We know from above that the duopoly—the merged firm and Firm 3—each fly 64 (thousand) passengers and earn $4.1 million. If the owners of the original Firms 1 and 2 share the $4.1 million, each gets $2.05 million, which is less than the $2.3 million that they would receive as independent firms. Thus, the merger does not pay for the merging firms, though the other firm profits handsomely (Salant, Switzer, and Reynolds, 1983).

However, if the merger results in even a modest cost advantage, the merger may be worthwhile. If the merged firm were able to realize cost advantages sufficient to reduce the marginal cost for the merged firm from the initial $147 to $138, the merged firm would earn $4.9 million, so the shareholders of Firms 1 and 2 would each earn $2,450 million, which is substantially more than they would earn without the merger.[11] Thus, in general, the reduction in the number of firms may raise price insufficiently to make a merger profitable unless merging provides another benefit such as reducing costs.

---

[10]It is possible that the merged firm does not act just like a single Cournot firm. For example, merged firms may maintain separate brands corresponding to the premerger brand names. After the 2012 merger of the Chilean airline LAN SA and Brazil's TAM SA, to form the LATAM Airlines Group, the two airlines continued to operate independently as separate subsidiaries of LATAM.

[11]Let the merged firm be called Firm M and its quantity be q_M. By equating the merged firm's marginal revenue to its new marginal cost, 138, we obtain its best-response function: $339 - 2q_M - q_3 = 138$. We obtain the best-response function for Firm 3 by equating its marginal revenue to 147, its original marginal cost: $339 - q_M - 2q_3 = 147$. We need to solve these two best-response function equations simultaneously to determine the Nash-Cournot equilibrium quantities q_M and q_3. The solution is $q_M = 70$, $q_3 = 61$. Thus in equilibrium, $Q = 70 + 61 = 131$, and $p = 339 - 131 = 208$. The profit of the merged firm is $(p - 138)q_M = (208 - 138)70 = 4,900$, or $4.9 million. Firm 3's profit is $(p - 147)q_3 = (208 - 147)61 = 3,731$, or $3.731 million.

A firm acquires or merges with another firm by paying cash for it or by allocating shares in the new company to the former owners. Although the terms *acquisition* and *merger* have no legal distinction, typically the term *acquisition* is used if a relatively large pre-existing firm (the *acquirer*) buys a smaller firm (the *target*), and the acquirer continues to exist in more or less unchanged form as a legal entity while the target disappears.

For example, Microsoft has made many acquisitions in recent years. In the three-year period 2008 through 2010, Microsoft acquired 24 different software companies. Obtaining new software and services through acquisitions has long been part of Microsoft's product development strategy, and such software is now embodied in products such as Explorer, Windows, Word, and Excel.

In 2011, Microsoft's most significant acquisition was Skype, which allowed Microsoft to work more closely with Facebook and to integrate video calling with Skype. Microsoft then expanded into "Cloud" computing, purchasing StorSimple (a cloud-storage equipment vendor) in 2012 and MetricsHub (cloud-monitoring software) in 2013.

The term *merger* is typically used if two (or more) combining firms are relatively similar in size or prominence, especially if the continuing firm that acquires the merged assets is a new legal entity. For example, in 2011, British Airways Plc (BA) and Iberia Lineas Aereas de Espana SA merged and started selling stock in the new, resulting firm, International Airlines Group (IAG). Shareholders of both original companies were given shares in the new company and senior managers from both original companies shared senior positions in the new company. The former head of BA heads IAG, the Iberia chairman chairs the new company, and BA's former chairman serves as his deputy.

An acquirer might use either cash or stock to carry out an acquisition. Microsoft typically makes a cash payment to owners of the target company, so the ownership structure of Microsoft is unaffected by the transaction. In the IAG merger, BA shareholders received 56% of the newly merged company and Iberia's shareholders got 44%. It is also possible for a mixture of cash and stock to be used.

11.3 Bertrand Oligopoly

We have examined how oligopolistic firms set quantities to try to maximize their profits. However, many oligopolistic firms set prices instead of quantities and then allow consumers to decide how much to buy at those prices. The market equilibrium in an oligopoly may be different if firms set prices rather than quantities.

In monopolistic and competitive markets, the issue of whether firms set quantities or prices does not arise. Competitive firms have no choice: They cannot affect price and hence can choose only quantity (Chapter 8). The monopoly equilibrium is the same whether the monopoly sets price or quantity (Chapter 9).

In 1883, the French mathematician Joseph Bertrand argued that oligopolies often set prices and then consumers decide how many units to buy. The resulting Nash equilibrium is called a **Nash-Bertrand equilibrium** (or **Bertrand-Nash equilibrium** or **Bertrand equilibrium**): a set of prices such that no firm can obtain a higher profit by choosing a different price if the other firms continue to charge these prices.

Our analysis in this section shows that the price and quantity in a Nash-Bertrand equilibrium are different from those in a Nash-Cournot equilibrium. In addition, the properties of the Nash-Bertrand equilibrium depend on whether firms are producing identical or differentiated products.

Identical Products

We start by examining a price-setting oligopoly in which firms have identical costs and produce identical goods. Because the goods are identical, in any Nash-Bertrand equilibrium, the firms must charge the same price, or no one will buy from the high-price firm. The surprising result of this analysis is that the Nash-Bertrand equilibrium price equals the marginal cost, as in the price-taking equilibrium.

Best-Response Curves. Suppose that each of the two price-setting oligopolistic firms in a market produces an identical product and faces a constant marginal and average cost of $5 per unit. What is Firm 1's best response—what price should it set—if Firm 2 sets a price of $p_2 = \$10$? If Firm 1 charges more than $10, it makes no sales because consumers will buy from Firm 2. Firm 1 makes a profit of $5 on each unit it sells if it also charges $10 per unit. If the market demand is 200 units and both firms charge the same price, we would expect Firm 1 to make half the sales, so its profit is $500.

If Firm 1 slightly undercuts its rival's price by charging $9.99, Firm 1 captures the entire market because the products are identical. Firm 1 makes a profit of $4.99 per unit and a total profit of $998. Thus, Firm 1's profit is higher if it slightly undercuts its rival's price. By similar reasoning, if Firm 2 charges $8, Firm 1 again maximizes its profit by charging slightly less than $8.

Now imagine that Firm 2 charges $p_2 = \$5$. If Firm 1 charges more than $5, it makes no sales. The firms split the market and make zero profit if Firm 1 charges $5. If Firm 1 undercuts its rival, it captures the entire market, but it makes a loss on each unit. Thus, Firm 1 will undercut only if its rival's price is higher than Firm 1's marginal and average cost of $5. By similar reasoning, if Firm 2 charges less than $5, Firm 1 chooses not to produce.

Figure 11.5 shows that Firm 1 will not participate in the market if Firm 2 charges less than $5. Firm 1's best response is $5 if Firm 2 charges $5. If Firm 2 charges prices above $5, Firm 1's best response is to undercut Firm 2's price slightly. Above $5, Firm 1's best-response curve is above the 45° line by the smallest amount possible. (The distance of the best-response curve from the 45° line is exaggerated in the figure for clarity.) By the same reasoning, Firm 2's best-response curve starts at $5 and lies slightly below the 45° line.

The two best-response curves intersect only at e, where each firm charges $5. It does not pay for either firm to change its price as long as the other charges $5, so e is a Nash-Bertrand equilibrium. In this equilibrium, each firm makes zero profit.

Rhymes with Orange © 2013 Hillary Price. Distributed by King Features. Reprinted with permission.

FIGURE 11.5 **Nash-Bertrand Equilibrium with Identical Products**

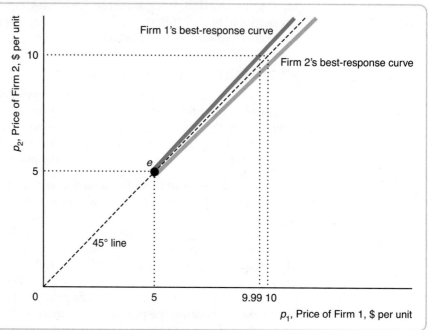

With identical products and constant marginal and average costs of $5, Firm 1's best-response curve starts at $5 and then lies slightly above the 45° line. That is, Firm 1 undercuts its rival's price as long as its price remains above $5. The best-response curves intersect at *e*, the Bertrand or Nash equilibrium, where both firms charge $5.

Thus, *the Nash-Bertrand equilibrium when firms produce identical products is the same as the price-taking, competitive equilibrium.*

Bertrand Versus Cournot. This Nash-Bertrand equilibrium differs substantially from the Nash-Cournot equilibrium. When firms produce identical products and have a constant marginal cost, firms receive positive profits and the price is above marginal cost in the Nash-Cournot equilibrium, whereas firms earn zero profits and price equals marginal cost in the Nash-Bertrand equilibrium.

When firms' products are identical, the Cournot model seems more realistic than the Bertrand model. The Bertrand model appears inconsistent with actual oligopolistic markets in at least two ways. First, the Bertrand model's "competitive" equilibrium price is implausible. In a market with few firms, why would the firms compete so vigorously that they would make no profit, as in the Nash-Bertrand equilibrium? In contrast, the Nash-Cournot equilibrium price with a small number of firms lies between the competitive price and the monopoly price. Because oligopolies typically charge a higher price than competitive firms, the Nash-Cournot equilibrium is more plausible.

Second, the Nash-Bertrand equilibrium price, which depends only on cost, is insensitive to demand conditions and the number of firms. In contrast, the Nash-Cournot equilibrium price depends on demand conditions and the number of firms as well as on cost. Consequently, economists are much more likely to use the Cournot model than the Bertrand model to study homogeneous goods markets.

Differentiated Products

If firms in most markets produced homogeneous goods, the Bertrand model would probably have been forgotten. However, markets with differentiated goods—automobiles, stereos, computers, toothpastes, and spaghetti sauces—are extremely common, as is price setting by firms in such markets. In differentiated-goods markets, the Nash-Bertrand equilibrium is plausible because the two "problems" of the homogeneous-goods model disappear: Firms set prices above marginal cost, and prices are sensitive to demand conditions and the number of firms.

We can use the Bertrand model with differentiated products to analyze the cola market. Figure 11.6 shows the firms' best-response curves. Quantities are in millions of cases (a case consists of 24 twelve-ounce cans) per quarter, and prices (to retailers) and costs are in real 1982 dollars per 10 cases. The best-response curves in the figure were derived (Appendix 11B) from demand functions estimated by Gasmi, Laffont, and Vuong (1992).[12] Coke and Pepsi produce similar but not identical products, so many consumers prefer one of these products to the other. If the price of Pepsi were to fall slightly relative to that of Coke, some consumers who prefer Coke to Pepsi would not switch. Thus, neither firm has to match exactly a price cut by its rival. As a result, neither firm's best-response curve lies along a 45° line through the origin (as in Figure 11.5). Because the firms choose prices, the axes measure prices. The Bertrand best-response curves have different slopes than the Cournot best-response curves in Figure 11.3. The Cournot curves—which plot relationships between quantities—slope downward, showing that a firm produces less the more its rival produces.

The Nash-Bertrand equilibrium, *e* in Figure 11.6, occurs where each firm's price is $13 per unit. In this Nash equilibrium, each firm sets its best-response price *given the price the other firm is charging*. Neither firm wants to change its price because neither firm can increase its profit by so doing.

FIGURE 11.6 Nash-Bertrand Equilibrium with Differentiated Products

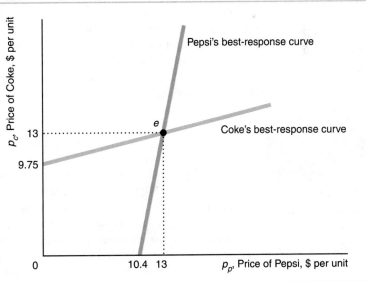

Both Coke and Pepsi, which set prices, have upward-sloping best-response curves. These best-response curves of Coke and Pepsi intersect at *e*, the Nash-Bertrand equilibrium, where each sets a price of $13 per unit.

---

[12]Their estimated model allows the firms to set both prices and advertising. We assume that the firms' advertising is held constant. The Coke equations are the authors' estimates (with slight rounding). The Pepsi equation is rescaled so that the equilibrium prices of Coke and Pepsi are equal.

11.4 Monopolistic Competition

We now turn to monopolistic competition, which is a market structure that has the price setting characteristics of monopoly or oligopoly and the free entry characteristic of perfect competition. Monopolistically competitive firms have market power because they face downward-sloping demand curves, as do oligopolistic firms, but the firms earn zero profit due to free entry, as do perfectly competitive firms.

We have seen that each oligopolistic firm may earn an economic profit because the number of firms is limited due to entry barriers. What would happen without a barrier to entry? Firms seeking profits would enter the market until the last firm to enter earns zero long-run economic profit. The resulting market structure may be either perfectly competitive or monopolistically competitive. In both perfect competition and monopolistic competition, firms earn zero profits. The key difference is that each perfectly competitive firm faces a horizontal residual demand curve and charges a price equal to marginal cost, whereas each monopolistically competitive firm faces a downward-sloping demand curve and can charge a price above marginal cost without losing all of its customers.

Monopolistically competitive firms face downward-sloping demand curves because the market is small or because the firms differentiate their products. Even if the firms produce identical products, if the market demand curve is close to origin, the market may be able to support only a few firms, so the residual demand curve facing a single firm is downward sloping. For example, in a small town the market may be large enough to support only a few plumbing firms, each of which provides a similar service.

If firms differentiate their products, each firm can retain those customers who particularly like that firm's product even if its price is higher than those of its rivals. Gourmet food trucks serve differentiated food in monopolistically competitive markets. Nouveau food trucks like Chairman Bao, Curry Up Now, and Liba Falafel sell high-quality lunches in San Francisco's blighted mid-Market area, which has few traditional, high-quality lunch restaurants. Because some customers prefer Chinese food to Indian food, Chairman Bao could raise its price without losing all its customers to Curry Up Now. As a consequence, each of these trucks faces a downward-sloping demand curve.

Managerial Implication

Managing in the Monopolistically Competitive Food Truck Market

Young entrepreneurs who want to own their own businesses should consider monopolistically competitive markets, as entry costs are often low and a cleverly differentiated product can often succeed. One of the hottest food phenomena in the United States is gourmet food trucks, which started in major West Coast cities such as Los Angeles, Portland, and Seattle. Now, flocks of food trucks ply their business in previously underserved areas of town in cities across the country. The mobile restaurant business has been exploding. As William Bender, a food service consultant in Santa Clara, California, said, "The limited menu approach, high quality, and low operating costs have opened up an entirely new sector."

Even top restaurant chefs have entered this business. Celebrity Los Angeles chef Ludovic Lefebvre created LudoTruck, a mobile fried chicken outlet. San Francisco's Chez Spencer has a "French takeaway," Spencer on the Go, that serves bistro food such as foie gras torchon and toast for $12.

The cost of entry is very low, ranging from $50,000 to lease the equipment and pay ancillary expenses, to $250,000 or more for a deluxe truck and top-of-the-line cooking and refrigeration facilities. Potential entrants can learn about the business at **mobilefoodnews.com**, which reports on local laws, where to buy equipment and obtain insurance, and a host of other topics.

Opening a new restaurant is very risky. If demand is less than anticipated, the firm loses its (large) fixed cost. However, if the manger of a food truck's first guess as to where to locate is wrong, it is easy to drive to another neighborhood.

How do firms identify profit opportunities? "Lunch is our consistent bread-and-butter market," said Matthew Cohen, proprietor of Off the Grid, a food truck promoter and location finder in the San Francisco Bay Area. When lines in front of his trucks grow longer at lunch time, he sets up additional trucks. Having started with about a dozen trucks in June 2010, Cohen planned to expand to at least 70 by the end of 2011 and had over 100 vendors in 2013.

Rather than drive around the city searching for customers, managers should use Internet sites and social media to attract customers to their locations. Fans can find the location of trucks in cities around the country at **Mobimunch.com**. In mid-2012, Off the Grid had more than 19,000 followers on Twitter and more than 33,000 followers on Facebook. According to Cohen, "It's our primary means of marketing. It tells customers where trucks are going to be and when. You can't underestimate what social media has done for the business." He usually charges his clients a base fee of $50 and 10% of sales revenue for his help in successfully locating and attracting customers.

Equilibrium

To examine the monopolistically competitive equilibrium, we initially assume that firms have identical cost functions and produce identical products. Two conditions hold in a long-run monopolistically competitive equilibrium: *marginal revenue equals marginal cost* because firms set output to maximize profit, and *price equals average cost*—that is, profit is zero—because firms enter until no further profitable entry is possible.

Figure 11.7 shows a long-run monopolistically competitive market equilibrium for a representative firm, which faces firm-specific demand curve D. To maximize its profit, the firm sets its output, q, where its marginal revenue curve corresponding to D intersects its marginal cost curve: $MR = MC$. At that quantity, the firm's average cost curve, AC, is tangent to its demand curve. Because the height of the demand curve is the price, at the tangency point price equals average cost, $p = AC$, and the firm makes zero profit.

Why do we know that $p = AC$ in the monopolistically competitive equilibrium? The entry and exit responses of firms ensure this result. If the average cost is less than price at the quantity where $MR = MC$, firms in the market make positive profits and new firms enter. If average cost is above price, firms lose money, and firms exit until the marginal firm breaks even, which occurs where $p = AC$.

In most cities, fast-food restaurants are an example of such a monopolistically competitive industry. These restaurants differentiate their food, so each may face a downward-sloping demand curve. However, restaurants can easily enter and exit the market, so the marginal firm earns zero economic profit. As you've probably observed, most restaurants have empty seats much of the time and hence are operating below full capacity. The following Q&A provides an explanation for this phenomenon.

FIGURE 11.7 **Monopolistic Competition**

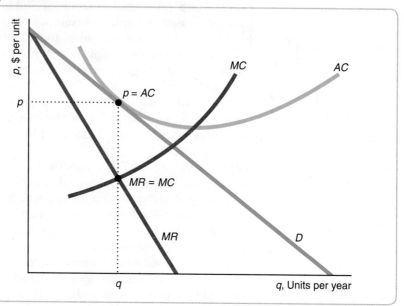

A monopolistically competitive firm, facing the firm-specific demand curve D, sets its output where its marginal revenue equals its marginal cost: $MR = MC$. Because firms can enter this market, the profit of the firm is driven to zero, so price equals the firm's average cost: $p = AC$.

Q&A 11.3

Show that a monopolistically competitive firm maximizes its profit where it is operating at less than *full capacity* or *minimum efficient scale*, which is the smallest quantity at which the average cost curve reaches its minimum (the bottom of a U-shaped average cost curve). The firm's minimum efficient scale is the quantity at which the firm no longer benefits from economies of scale.

Answer

Use the properties of the demand curve to show that a monopolistically competitive firm operates in the increasing-returns to scale section of its average cost curve (the downward-sloping section) in the long-run equilibrium. In the long-run equilibrium, a monopolistically competitive firm operates where its downward-sloping demand curve is tangent to its average cost curve, as Figure 11.7 illustrates. Because its demand curve is downward sloping, its average cost curve must also be downward sloping in the equilibrium. Thus, the firm chooses to operate at less than full capacity in equilibrium.

Profitable Monopolistically Competitive Firms

If all firms in a monopolistically competitive market produce identical products and have identical costs, then each firm earns zero economic profit in the long run. Thus, all firms in the industry are on the margin of exiting the market because even a slight decline in profitability would generate losses. However, it is possible—indeed likely—that monopolistically competitive firms differ from each other in their profitability because they have different cost functions or because they produce differentiated products. If so, low-cost firms or firms with superior products may earn positive economic profits in the long run.

Mini-Case

Zoning Laws as a Barrier to Entry by Hotel Chains

In the United States, local governments restrict land use through zoning. The difficulty of getting permission (generally from many agencies) to build a new commercial structure is a barrier to entry, which limits the number of firms in a monopolistically competitive market. Suzuki (2013) examined the effect of Texas municipalities' zoning laws on chain hotels, such as Best Western, Comfort Inn, Holiday Inn, La Quinta Inn, Quality Inn, and Ramada.

According to his estimates, construction costs are large even in the absence of zoning regulations. Construction costs are $2.4 million for a new Best Western hotel and $4.5 million for a new La Quinta hotel. Going from a lenient to a stringent zoning policy increases a hotel's variable cost by 21% and its sunk entry cost by 19%. The average number of hotels in a small market falls from 2.3 under a lenient policy to 1.9 with a stringent policy due to the higher entry cost. As a consequence, a stringent policy reduces the number of rooms by 15%, which increases the revenue per room by 7%. The change from the most lenient policy to the most stringent policy decreases producer surplus by $1.5 million and consumer surplus by $1 million. Thus, more stringent zoning laws raise entry costs and thereby reduce the number of hotels and rooms, which causes the price to rise and lowers total surplus.

Therefore, owners of existing hotels often strongly support making zoning laws more stringent. These oligopolistic firms want to continue to earn positive economic profits, rather than see these profits driven to zero in a monopolistically competitive market with free entry.

Managerial Solution

Gaining an Edge from Government Aircraft Subsidies

If only Boeing or Airbus receives a government subsidy, how should its managers use the subsidy to gain a competitive advantage? What effect does that subsidy have on prices and quantities? What happens if both firms receive subsidies? Should Boeing and Airbus managers lobby for government subsidies that result in a subsidy war?

To keep our answers to these questions as simple as possible, we assume that Airbus and Boeing compete in a Cournot model in which they produce identical products with identical costs and they face a linear demand curve.[13] A government per-unit subsidy to only one firm would cause its marginal cost to be lower than its rival's.

To maximize profit, a firm in a Cournot market should respond by increasing its output for any expected output level by its rival. That is, its best-response curve shifts out. In panel a of Figure 11.4, we saw how the equilibrium changes if United Airline's marginal cost falls while American's stays constant. As its marginal cost drops, United wants to produce more for any given output of its rival, so that its best-response function shifts out, away from the origin in panel b.

The market equilibrium shifts from e_1 to e_2 in panel b, so that United's Nash-Cournot equilibrium output increases and American's falls. Because total output rises, the equilibrium price falls. United benefits at the expense of

---

[13]We would reach the same conclusions were we to use a Cournot or Bertrand model with differentiated products.

CHAPTER 11 Oligopoly and Monopolistic Competition

American. Indeed, United's profit rises by $5.1 million, which exceeds the actual cost saving of $4.6 million. That is, United's managers used the cost savings to gain a competitive advantage.

The same analysis applies to the aircraft market. If Airbus is subsidized and Boeing is not, Airbus should produce more given any expected output from Boeing. Its equilibrium quantity and profit rise while Boeing's quantity and profit fall. The gain in profit to Airbus exceeds the subsidy from the government.

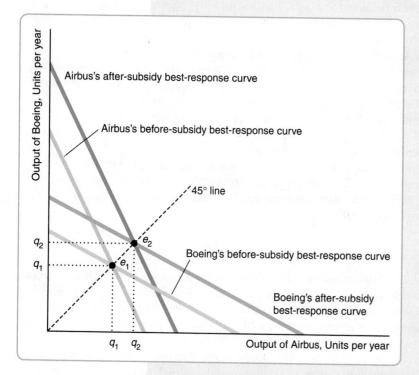

Now suppose that both firms receive subsidies. The figure here shows an initial Nash-Cournot equilibrium, e_1, where both firms produce q_1 units of output. If both governments give identical subsidies that lower the marginal costs of both firms, then both firms' best-response functions shift out. In the new, subsidized equilibrium, e_2, both firms produce $q_2 > q_1$ units of output, so total equilibrium output increases, which causes the equilibrium price to fall.

The market equilibrium moves further away from the maximum profit (monopoly) equilibrium toward the competitive price and quantity. Therefore, the subsidies lead to lower profits (excluding the subsidies), though the firms benefit from the subsidies directly. Each government is essentially subsidizing final consumers in other countries without giving its own firm a strategic advantage over its rival. Thus, both governments lose. It would be in both countries' best interests not to engage in a subsidy war.

Indeed, in 1992, the various involved governments signed a U.S.–EU agreement on trade in civil aircraft that limited government subsidies, including a maximum direct subsidy limit of 33% of development costs and various limits on variable costs.[14]

Does it follow that the managers at these firms should stop lobbying for subsidies? No. These firms still benefit from subsidies. Moreover, either firm would be at a competitive disadvantage if its rival received a subsidy and it did not.

---

[14]Irwin and Pavcnik (2004) found that aircraft prices increased by about 3.7% after the 1992 agreement. This price hike is consistent with a 5% increase in firms' marginal costs after the subsidy cuts.

SUMMARY

1. **Cartels.** If firms successfully collude, they can seek to produce the monopoly output and collectively earn the monopoly level of profit. Although their collective profits rise if all firms collude, each individual firm has an incentive to cheat on the cartel arrangement so as to raise its own profit even higher. For cartel prices to remain high, cartel members must be able to detect and prevent cheating, and noncartel firms must not be able to supply very much output. When antitrust laws or competition policies prevent firms from colluding, firms may try to merge.

2. **Cournot Oligopoly.** If oligopolistic firms act independently, market output and firms' profits lie between the competitive and monopoly levels. In a Cournot model, each oligopolistic firm sets its output at the same time. In the Nash-Cournot equilibrium, each firm produces its best-response output—the output that maximizes its profit—given the output its rival produces. As the number of Cournot firms increases, the Nash-Cournot equilibrium price, quantity, and profits approach the price-taking (perfectly competitive) levels.

3. **Bertrand Oligopoly.** In many oligopolies, firms set prices instead of quantities. If the product is homogeneous and firms set prices, the Nash-Bertrand equilibrium price equals marginal cost and is therefore lower than the Nash-Cournot equilibrium price. If the products are differentiated, the Nash-Bertrand equilibrium price is above marginal cost. Typically, the markup of price over marginal cost is greater the more the goods are differentiated.

4. **Monopolistic Competition.** In monopolistic competition, free entry drives profits to zero for the marginal firm. If firms have identical costs and produce a homogeneous good, all firms earn zero profits. However, even with free entry, firms face downward-sloping demand curves and are therefore able to charge prices that exceed marginal cost. One important reason why demand curves slope downward is that firms may sell differentiated products. However, it is possible that even with homogeneous products the number of firms is small enough that firms face downward-sloping firm-specific demand curves.

QUESTIONS

*All exercises are available on MyEconLab; * = answer at the back of this book; **C** = use of calculus may be necessary.*

1. Cartels

1.1. In most "normal" years (years in which the market has not been disrupted by Middle East wars), at each Organization of Petroleum Exporting Countries (OPEC) meeting, Saudi Arabia, the largest oil producer, argues that the cartel should cut production. The Saudis complain that most OPEC countries (including Saudi Arabia) produce more oil than they are allotted under their cartel agreement. Use a graph and words to explain why cartel members would produce more than the allotted amount despite their understanding that overproduction will drive down the price of their product.

1.2. Many retail stores offer to match or beat the price offered by a rival store. Explain why firms that belong to a cartel might make this offer.

1.3. What are the main factors that increase the likelihood of a cartel being successful?

*1.4. A market has an inverse demand curve $p = 100 - 2Q$ and four firms, each of which has a constant marginal cost of $MC = 20$. If the firms form a profit-maximizing cartel and agree to operate subject to the constraint that each firm will produce the same output level, how much does each firm produce?

2. Cournot Oligopoly

2.1. According to Robert Guy Matthews, "Fixed Costs Chafe at Steel Mills," *Wall Street Journal*, June 10, 2009, stainless steel manufacturers increased prices even though the market demand curve had shifted to the left. In a letter to its customers, one of these companies announced that "Unlike mill increases announced in recent years, this is obviously not driven by increasing global demand, but rather by fixed costs being proportioned across significantly lower demand." If the firms are oligopolistic, produce a homogeneous good, face a linear market demand curve and have linear costs, and the market outcome is a Nash-Cournot equilibrium, does the firm's explanation as to why the market equilibrium price is rising make sense? What is a better explanation?

*2.2. What is the homogeneous-good duopoly's Nash-Cournot equilibrium if the market demand function is $Q = 1,000 - 1,000p$ and each firm's marginal cost is $0.28 per unit? (*Hint*: Start by determining the inverse market demand function.)

2.3. Duopoly quantity-setting firms face the market demand

$$p = 150 - q_1 - q_2.$$

Each firm has a marginal cost of $60 per unit. What is the Nash-Cournot equilibrium?

*2.4. Your college is considering renting space in the student union to one or two commercial textbook stores. The rent the college can charge per square foot of space depends on the firms' profit (excluding rent) and hence on whether the market has a monopoly or a Cournot duopoly. Which number of stores is better for the college in terms of rent? Which is better for students? Why?

2.5. The state of Connecticut sets a maximum fee that bail-bond businesses can charge for posting a given-size bond (Ayres and Waldfogel, 1994). The bail-bond fee is set at virtually the maximum amount allowed by law in cities with only one active firm (Plainville, 99% of the maximum; Stamford, 99%; and Wallingford, 99%). The price is as high in cities with a duopoly (Ansonia, 99.6%; Meriden, 98%; and New London, 98%). In cities with 3 or more firms, however, the price falls well below the maximum permitted price. The fees are only 54% of the maximum in Norwalk with 3 firms, 64% in New Haven with 8 firms, and 78% in Bridgeport with 10 firms. Give possible explanations based on the Cournot model for this pattern.

2.6. In 2012, Southwest Airlines reported that its "cost per available seat mile" was 13.0¢ compared to 13.8¢ for United Airlines. Assuming that Southwest and United compete on a single route, use a graph to show that their equilibrium quantities differ. (*Hint:* See Q&A 11.1.)

2.7. In a homogeneous-good Cournot model where each of the n firms has a constant marginal cost m and the market demand curve is $p = a - bQ$, show that the Nash-Cournot equilibrium output of a typical firm is $q = \dfrac{a - m}{(n + 1)b}$. Show that industry output, $Q (= nq)$, equals the monopoly level if $n = 1$ and approaches the competitive level as n gets very large. **C**

2.8. How does the Nash-Cournot equilibrium change in the airline example if United Airlines' marginal cost is $100 and American's is $200? (*Hint:* See Q&A 11.1.)

2.9. A homogeneous-good duopoly faces an inverse market demand of $p = 120 - Q$. Firm 1 has a constant marginal cost of $MC^1 = 20$. Firm 2's constant marginal cost is $MC^2 = 30$. Calculate the output of each firm, market output, and price for

(a) a Nash-Cournot equilibrium or (b) a collusive equilibrium at the monopoly price.

*2.10. Why does differentiating its product allow an oligopoly to charge a higher price?

2.11. Firms 1 and 2 produce differentiated goods. Firm 1's inverse demand function is $p_1 = 260 - 2q_1 - q_2$, while Firm 2's inverse demand function is $p_2 = 260 - 2q_2 - q_1$. Each firm has a constant marginal cost of 20. What is the Nash-Cournot equilibrium in this market? (*Hint:* See Q&A 11.2.)

2.12. In a Nash-Cournot equilibrium, does an oligopolistic firm produce at less than full capacity, at full capacity, or more than full capacity? Explain.

2.13. In 2008, cruise ship lines announced they were increasing prices from $7 to $9 per person per day because of increased fuel costs. According to one analyst, fuel costs for Carnival Corporation's 84-ship fleet jumped $900 million to $2 billion in 2008 and its cost per passenger per day jumped from $10 to $33. Assuming that these firms are oligopolistic and the outcome is a Nash-Cournot equilibrium, why did prices rise less than in proportion to per-passenger-per-day cost?

*2.14. To examine the trade-off between efficiency and market power from a merger, consider a market with two firms that sell identical products. Firm 1 has a constant marginal cost of 1, and Firm 2 has a constant marginal cost of 2. The inverse market demand function is $p = 15 - Q$.

   a. Solve for the Nash-Cournot equilibrium price, quantities, profits, consumer surplus, and deadweight loss.

   b. If the firms merge and produce at the lower marginal cost of 1, how do the equilibrium values change?

   c. Discuss the change in efficiency (average cost of producing the output) and total surplus—consumer surplus, producer surplus (or profit), and deadweight loss.

3. Bertrand Oligopoly

3.1. If firms produce identical products and have the same constant marginal cost, m, explain why the Nash-Bertrand equilibrium price and market quantity are the same regardless of whether there are two or more firms.

*3.2. Will price be lower if duopoly firms set price or if they set quantity? Under what conditions can you give a definitive answer to this question?

3.3. In an initial Nash-Bertrand equilibrium, two firms with differentiated products charge the same equilibrium prices. A consumer testing agency praises the product of one firm, causing its demand curve to shift to the right as new customers start buying the product. (The demand curve of the other product is not substantially affected.) Use a graph to illustrate how this new information affects the Nash-Bertrand equilibrium. What happens to the equilibrium prices of the two firms?

*3.4. Suppose that identical duopoly firms have constant marginal costs of $10 per unit. Firm 1 faces a demand function of $q_1 = 100 - 2p_1 + p_2$, where q_1 is Firm 1's output, p_1 is Firm 1's price, and p_2 is Firm 2's price. Similarly, the demand function Firm 2 faces is $q_2 = 100 - 2p_2 + p_1$. Solve for the Nash-Bertrand equilibrium. (*Hint*: See Appendix 11B.) **C**

3.5. Solve for the Nash-Bertrand equilibrium for the firms described in Question 3.4 if Firm 1's marginal cost is $30 per unit and Firm 2's marginal cost is $10 per unit. **C**

4. Monopolistic Competition

4.1. In a monopolistically competitive market, the government applies a specific tax of $1 per unit of output. What happens to the profit of a typical firm in this market? Does the number of firms in the market rise or fall? Why?

*4.2. What is the effect on prices and the number of firms under monopolistic competition if a government subsidy is introduced that reduces the fixed cost of each firm in the industry?

4.3. Q&A 11.3 shows that a monopolistically competitive firm maximizes its profit where it is operating at less than full capacity. Does this result depend upon whether firms produce identical or differentiated products? Why?

4.4. Under monopolistic competition with identical firms, is it possible for a firm to produce at the minimum of its average cost curve?

5. Managerial Problem

*5.1. An incumbent firm, Firm 1, faces a potential entrant, Firm 2, that has a lower marginal cost. The market demand curve is $p = 120 - q_1 - q_2$. Firm 1 has a constant marginal cost of $20, while Firm 2's is $10, and they have no fixed costs.

a. What are the Nash-Cournot equilibrium price, quantities, and profits without government intervention?

b. To block entry, the incumbent appeals to the government to require that the entrant incur extra costs. What happens to the Nash-Cournot equilibrium if the legal requirement causes the marginal cost of the second firm to rise to that of the first firm, $20?

5.2. Given the demand and cost conditions of Question 5.1, suppose that the legal intervention imposed by the government leaves the marginal cost unchanged but imposes a fixed cost. What is the minimal fixed cost that will prevent entry?

6. Spreadsheet Exercises

6.1. The inverse market demand curve for a duopoly market is $p = 14 - Q = 14 - q_1 - q_2$, where Q is the market output, and q_1 and q_2 are the outputs of Firms 1 and 2 respectively. Each firm has a constant marginal cost of 2 and a fixed cost of 4. Consequently, the Nash-Cournot best-response curve for Firm 1 is $q_1 = 6 - q_2/2$.

a. Create a spreadsheet with columns titled q_2, BR_1, Q, p, and $Profit_1$. In the first column, list possible quantities for Firm 2, q_2, ranging from 0 to 12 in increments of 2. The column headed BR_1 shows the profit-maximizing output (best response) for Firm 1 given Firm 2's output in the first column. The Q column sums the values in the q_2 and BR_1 columns. The p column lists the price that corresponds to Q. The $Profit_1$ column shows the profit of Firm 1, taking account of its marginal and fixed costs. After filling in the spreadsheet, use the scatterplot option in Excel to draw the best-response curve for Firm 1.

b. What is the monopoly output and profit for Firm 1? (That is, how much does Firm 1 produce if Firm 2 does not produce?) If Firm 1 expects Firm 2 to produce 10 units of output, would it operate in the long run (given that it can avoid incurring its fixed costs by shutting down)? Will it operate in the short run (when its fixed cost cannot be avoided)?

6.2. Use the data from Exercise 6.1. The best-response curve for Firm 2 is $q_2 = 6 - q_1/2$, which can be written as $q_1 = 12 - 2q_2$.

a. Create a spreadsheet with columns denoted BR_2, q_1, Q, p, and $Profit_2$. Set the output of Firm 1 in the second column from 0 to 6 in increments of one unit. Fill in the spreadsheet and use the scatterplot option to draw the best-response curve for Firm 2.

b. Create a new spreadsheet showing the best-response curves for Firm 1 and Firm 2 on the same diagram, with q_2 on the horizontal axis and q_1 on the vertical axis. What is the Nash-Cournot equilibrium price, quantity (for each firm), and profit (for each firm)?

Appendix 11   Cournot Oligopoly with Many Firms

This appendix generalizes the airlines Cournot example in Section 11.2 to allow for n firms, where n is any positive whole number. The market inverse demand function is $p = 339 - q = 339 - q_1 - q_2 - \cdots - q_n$.

Consequently, Firm 1's revenue function is

$$R_1 = pq_1 = (339 - [q_1 + q_2 + \cdots + q_n])q_1$$
$$= 339q_1 - q_1^2 - [q_2 + q_3 + \cdots + q_n]q_1.$$

By differentiating revenue with respect to q_1 while treating the other outputs as constants, we obtain Firm 1's marginal revenue function:

$$MR_1 = 339 - 2q_1 - [q_2 + q_3 + \cdots + q_n].$$

To find the profit-maximizing output for Firm 1, we equate the firm's marginal revenue with its marginal cost of 147. Solving for q_1, we obtain the best-response function for Firm 1 in Equation 11.8:

$$q_1 = 96 - \tfrac{1}{2}(q_2 + q_3 + \cdots + q_n).$$

Equation 11.8 shows how much output Firm 1 should produce to maximize its profit given the output levels of the other firms. Because all n firms are identical, each has an analogous best-response function, which can be determined in the same way. For example, the best-response function for Firm 2 is

$$q_2 = 96 - \tfrac{1}{2}(q_1 + q_3 + \cdots + q_n).$$

That is, each firm's best-response function equates the firm's own output to 192 minus $\tfrac{1}{2}$ times the combined output of all the other firms.

In the Nash-Cournot equilibrium, all n best response functions are satisfied at the same time. That is, $q_1, q_2, \ldots, q_n$ are set such that the equalities in all n best-response functions hold. Rather than simultaneously solve all the equations, we can take a shortcut. Because all the firms are identical and the best-response functions are linear, each will produce the same output, q, in the Nash-Cournot equilibrium: $q = q_1 = q_2 = \cdots = q_n$. Substituting q for each firm's output in Equation 11.8, we find that $q = 96 - \tfrac{1}{2}(n - 1)q$. Adding the last term on the right side of the equation to both sides of the equation, we learn that $q + \tfrac{1}{2}(n - 1)q = 96$, or $\tfrac{1}{2}(n + 1)q = 96$, so

$$q = \frac{192}{n + 1},$$

as Equation 11.9 shows.

Appendix 11B Nash-Bertrand Equilibrium

We can use math to determine the cola market Nash-Bertrand equilibrium discussed in the chapter. First, we determine the best-response functions each firm faces. Then we equate the best-response functions to determine the equilibrium prices for the two firms.

Coke's best-response function tells us the price Coke charges that maximizes its profit as a function of the price Pepsi charges. We use the demand curve for Coke to derive the best-response function.

The reason Coke's price depends on Pepsi's price is that the quantity of Coke demanded, q_c, depends on the price of Coke, p_c, and the price of Pepsi, p_p. Coke's demand curve is

$$q_c = 58 - 4p_c + 2p_p. \tag{11B.1}$$

Partially differentiating Equation 11B.1 with respect to p_c (that is, holding the price of Pepsi fixed), we find that the change in quantity for every dollar change in price is $\partial q_c / \partial p_c = -4$, so a \$1-per-unit increase in the price of Coke causes the quantity of Coke demanded to fall by 4 units. Similarly, the demand for Coke rises by 2 units if the price of Pepsi rises by \$1, while the price of Coke remains constant: $\partial q_c / \partial p_p = 2$.

If Coke faces a constant marginal and average cost of \$5 per unit, its profit is

$$\pi_c = (p_c - 5)q_c = (p_c - 5)(58 - 4p_c + 2p_p), \tag{11B.2}$$

where $p_c - 5$ is Coke's profit per unit. To determine Coke's profit-maximizing price (holding Pepsi's price fixed), we set the partial derivative of the profit function, Equation 11B.2, with respect to the price of Coke equal to zero,

$$\frac{\partial \pi_c}{\partial p_c} = q_c + (p_c - 5)\frac{\partial q_c}{\partial p_c} = q_c - 4(p_c - 5) = 0, \tag{11B.3}$$

and, using Equation 11B.1, we solve for p_c as a function of p_p to find Coke's best-response function:

$$p_c = 7.25 + 0.25p_p + (0.5 \times 5). \tag{11B.4}$$

Equation 11B.4 shows that Coke's best-response price is 25¢ higher for every extra dollar that Pepsi charges and 50¢ higher for every extra dollar of Coke's marginal cost.

If Coke's average and marginal cost of production is \$5 per unit, its best-response function is

$$p_c = 9.75 + 0.25p_p, \tag{11B.5}$$

as Figure 11.6 shows. If $p_p = \$13$, then Coke's best response is to set $p_c = \$13$.

Pepsi's demand curve is

$$q_p = 63.2 - 4p_p + 1.6p_c. \tag{11B.6}$$

Using the same approach, we find that Pepsi's best-response function is

$$p_p = 10.4 + 0.2p_c. \tag{11B.7}$$

The intersection of Coke's and Pepsi's best-response functions (Equations 11B.5 and 11B.7) determines the Nash equilibrium. By substituting Pepsi's best-response function for p_p from Equation 11B.7 in Coke's best-response function, Equation 11B.5, we find that

$$p_c = 9.75 + 0.25(10.4 + 0.2p_c).$$

Solving this equation for p_c, we determine that the equilibrium price of Coke is $13. Substituting $p_c = \$13$ into Equation 11B.6, we discover that the equilibrium price of Pepsi is also $13.

Game Theory and Business Strategy

12

A camper awakens to the growl of a hungry bear and sees his friend putting on a pair of running shoes. "You can't outrun a bear," scoffs the camper. His friend coolly replies, "I don't have to. I only have to outrun you!"

Managerial Problem

Dying to Work

In part because of the differing amounts that firms invest in safety, jobs in some firms are more dangerous than in others. In 2010, a blast at a refinery in Washington state killed 7 workers, 11 workers died when BP's Deepwater Horizon oil rig exploded in the Gulf of Mexico, 29 coal miners died in a disaster at Massey Energy's West Virginia mine explosion, and 33 Chilean miners were trapped half a mile underground for 69 days in another mine disaster. In 2011, workers with inadequate protection were sent to deal with the nuclear crisis at Japan's Fukushima Daiichi power plant, resulting in worldwide condemnation. In China, 1,384 coal miners died in 2012. At least 1,129 workers died when an apparel factory collapsed in Bangladesh in 2013.

Managers at each firm must decide how much to invest in worker safety. Such investments affect its own reputation for safety, but may also affect how safe workers believe they are at other firms in the industry. The recent U.S. disasters resulted in renewed calls by unions for greater U.S. government intervention to protect workers, which would affect all firms.

One justification that is often given for government intervention is that firms have more information than workers about job safety at their plants. Prospective employees often do not know the injury rates at individual firms but may know the *average* injury rate over an entire industry, in part because such data are reported by governments.

Injury rates vary dramatically by industry. U.S. government statistics released in 2012 tell us that the financial services industry has only 1.3 fatal injuries per 100,000 workers each year, while the rate in construction is 9.8, for police is 18.1, and for mining is 19.8. Some occupations are particularly dangerous. Fishing has a fatal injury rate of 152.9 per 100,000 workers; logging, 93.5; agriculture, 42.5; and driving a truck, 23.0. On the other hand, safe occupations include sales, 2.0, and educational services, 0.9 (although students sometimes risk dying of boredom).[1]

If people are rational and fear danger, they agree to work in a dangerous job only if that job pays a sufficiently higher wage than less-risky alternative jobs. Economists have found that workers receive *compensating wage differentials* in industries and occupations that government statistics show are relatively risky.

However, if workers are unaware of the greater risks at certain firms within an industry, they may not receive compensating wage differentials from more dangerous employers within that industry. Workers are likely to have a sense of the risks associated with an industry: Everyone knows that mining is relatively risky—but they do not know which mining companies are particularly risky before a major accident occurs. For example, in the decade before Massey Energy was acquired by Alpha Natural Resources in 2011, 54 coal miners were killed in Massey mines, a much higher rate than at other mines, yet there's no evidence that these workers received higher pay than workers at other mining firms.[2]

Because workers do not know which firms are safer than others, each firm bears the full cost of its safety investments but does not get the full benefits. If workers are aware of the average risk in an industry, all firms benefit from one firm's safety investment because that investment improves the industry average. Thus, other firms share the benefit from one firm's investment in safety. Consequently, managers, when making the important strategic decision of how much their firms should invest in safety, must take this spillover effect into account.

Does such a situation cause firms to underinvest in safety? Can government intervention overcome such safety problems?

In deciding how much to invest in safety, firms take into account the safety investments of rivals. In deciding how to price its products or how much to advertise, Procter & Gamble considers the pricing and advertising of its main rivals, Johnson & Johnson and Unilever. When a small number of firms interact, they know that their actions significantly affect each other's profit, so their actions depend on how they think their rivals will act.

An oligopolistic firm that ignores or inaccurately predicts the behavior of rivals is unlikely to do well. If Ford underestimates how many cars Toyota and Honda will produce, Ford may produce too many vehicles and lose money. These firms are aware of this strategic interdependence, recognizing that the plans and decisions of any one firm might significantly affect the profits of the other firms. To better understand managerial decisions within an oligopoly, we employ **game theory**: a set of tools used by economists and others to analyze strategic decision making.

Game theory has many practical applications. It is particularly useful for analyzing how oligopolistic firms set prices, quantities, and advertising levels. In addition, economists use game theory to analyze bargaining between unions and

---

[1]Government statistics also tell us that males have an accident rate, 6.0, that is an order of magnitude greater than females, 0.7. Some of this difference is due to different occupations and some to different attitudes toward risk. How many women are injured after saying, "Hey! Watch this!"?

[2]The U.S. Mine Safety and Health Administration issued Massey 124 safety-related citations in 2010 prior to the April 2010 accident at Massey's Upper Big Branch mine in West Virginia that killed 29 workers. Massey had 515 violations in 2009. Mine Safety and Health Administration safety officials concluded in 2011 that the 2010 explosion that took 29 lives could have been prevented by Massey. The former head of security at the mine was prosecuted and convicted of two felonies and ultimately sentenced to 36 months in prison.

management or between the buyer and seller of a car; interactions between polluters and those harmed by pollution, transactions between the buyers and sellers of homes, negotiations between parties with different amounts of information (such as between car owners and auto mechanics), bidding in auctions, and many other economic interactions. Game theory is also used by political scientists and military planners to plan for avoiding or fighting wars, by biologists to analyze evolutionary biology and ecology, and by philosophers, computer scientists, and many others.

In this chapter, we analyze how oligopolistic firms interact within a *game*. A **game** is an interaction between players (such as individuals or firms) in which players use strategies. A **strategy** is a battle plan that specifies the *actions* or *moves* that a player will make. For example, a firm may use a simple business strategy where it produces 100 units of output regardless of what any rival does. In such a case the strategy consists of a single action—producing 100 units of output. However, some strategies consist of a combination of actions or moves, possibly contingent on what a rival does. For example, a firm might decide to produce a small quantity as long as its rival produced a small amount in the previous period, and a large quantity otherwise.

The **payoffs** of a game are the benefits received by players from the game's outcome, such as profits for firms, or incomes or utilities for individuals. A *payoff function* specifies each player's payoff as a function of the strategies chosen by all players. We normally assume that players seek to maximize their payoffs. In essence, this assumption simply defines what we mean by payoffs. Payoffs include all relevant benefits experienced by the players. Therefore, rational players should try to obtain the highest payoffs they can.

The **rules of the game** include the *timing* of players' moves (such as whether one player moves first), the various actions that are possible at a particular point in the game, and possibly other specific aspects of how the game is played. A full description of a game normally includes a statement of the players, the rules of the game (including the possible actions or strategies), and the payoff function, along with a statement regarding the information available to the players.

When analyzing a game, we usually have three objectives: to accurately describe and understand the game, to predict the likely outcome of the game, and to offer advice to managers as to how best to play the game.

This chapter focuses on how firms interact strategically in a single period, while the next chapter looks at strategic interactions in games that last for more than one period. The single-period game is called a **static game**, in which each player acts only once and the players act simultaneously (or, at least each player acts without knowing rivals' actions). For example, each of two rival firms might make simultaneous one-time-only decisions on where to locate its new factory. In the next chapter, we examine *dynamic games*, in which players move either sequentially or repeatedly.

In analyzing a game, it is crucial that we know how much information participants have. We start by assuming that all the relevant information is *common knowledge* to the players and then we relax that assumption. **Common knowledge** is a piece of information known by all players, and it is known by all players to be known by all players, and it is known to be known to be known, and so forth. We initially assume that players have **complete information**, a situation in which the strategies and payoffs of the game are *common knowledge*.

The information possessed by firms affects the outcome of a game. The outcome of a game in which a particular piece of information is known by all firms may differ from the outcome when some firm is uninformed. A firm may suffer a worse outcome if it does not know the possible payoffs of other firms. Similarly, a firm may do worse if it has limited ability to make calculations, as when its cost of making many calculations is prohibitively high or its managers have limited analytical abilities. Such limitations are referred to as *bounded rationality*.

In this chapter, we use game theory to analyze two important mechanisms that are often used to determine transaction prices—bargaining and auctions. Both bargaining and auctions may be affected by the nature of the information available to players.

Main Topics

In this chapter, we examine five main topics

1. **Oligopoly Games:** Economists use game theory to analyze firms' behavior in oligopolistic markets.

2. **Types of Nash Equilibria:** The outcome of a static game can be categorized by the type of strategies that firms use and by the number and characteristics of possible Nash equilibria.

3. **Information and Rationality:** What firms know about a game, such as other firms' payoffs, and whether firms have limited (or *bounded*) rationality, affect the strategies that they use and the outcome of the game.

4. **Bargaining:** The strategies that parties to a contract, such as a union and a firm, use while bargaining determine product prices, wages, or other features of a contract.

5. **Auctions:** An auction is a game in which bidders usually have incomplete information about the value that other bidders place on the auctioned good or service.

12.1 Oligopoly Games

We start with an example of two firms that can each take one of only two possible actions. Our example is a simplified version of the real-world competition between United and American Airlines that we described in Chapter 11. Later in this chapter, and in Chapter 13, we relax our simplifying assumptions.

The game has the following characteristics. The two *players* or firms are United and American Airlines. They play a *static game*—they compete only once. The *rules* of the game specify the possible actions or strategies that the firms can take and when they can take them. Each firm has only two possible *actions*: Each can fly either 48 thousand or 64 thousand passengers per quarter between Chicago and Los Angeles. Other than announcing their output levels, the firms cannot communicate, so that they cannot make side-deals or otherwise coordinate their actions. Each firm's *strategy* is to take one of the two actions, choosing either a low output (48 thousand passengers per quarter) or a high output (64 thousand).[3] The firms announce their actions or strategies *simultaneously*. The firms have *complete information*: they know all the possible strategies and the corresponding payoff (profit) to each firm. However, their information is imperfect in one important respect: Because they choose their output levels simultaneously, neither airline knows what action its rival will take when it makes its output decision.

---

[3]A strategy lists what actions to take under various circumstances. In this static game, there is no distinction between an action and a strategy. However, in multiperiod games (Chapter 13), a strategy specifies the set of actions to be taken over time, and an action chosen at a particular time may depend on the actions taken by its rivals in earlier periods.

TABLE 12.1 Dominant Strategies in a Quantity Setting, Prisoners' Dilemma Game

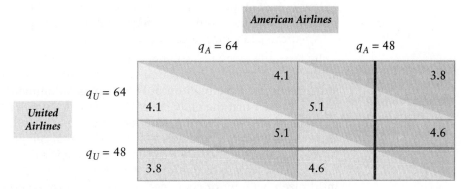

		American Airlines	
		$q_A = 64$	$q_A = 48$
United Airlines	$q_U = 64$	4.1 / 4.1	3.8 / 5.1
	$q_U = 48$	5.1 / 3.8	4.6 / 4.6

Note: Quantities are in thousands of passengers per quarter; (rounded) profits are in millions of dollars per quarter. The payoff to American Airlines is in the upper right corner of each cell and the payoff to United Airlines is in the lower left.

We summarize this static game using the *payoff matrix* or *profit matrix* in Table 12.1. This payoff matrix shows the profits for each of the four possible strategic (output) combinations that the firms may choose. For example, if American chooses a large quantity, $q_A = 64$ (thousand) per quarter, and United chooses a small quantity, $q_U = 48$, the firms' profits are in the cell in the lower-left corner of the profit matrix. That cell shows that American's profit is 5.1 ($5.1 million) per quarter in the upper-right corner, and United's profit is 3.8 ($3.8 million) per quarter in the lower-left corner. We now have a full description of the game, including a statement of the players, the rules, a list of the allowable strategies, the payoffs, and the available information.

Dominant Strategies

If one is available, a rational player always uses a **dominant strategy**: a strategy that produces a higher payoff than any other strategy the player can use no matter what its rivals do. If American Airlines has a dominant strategy, then no action that United Airlines could take would make American prefer a different strategy. If American and United each have and use a dominant strategy, then those dominant strategies determine the outcome of the game.

Both firms have a dominant strategy in the airline game illustrated in Table 12.1. American's managers can determine its dominant strategy using the following reasoning:

▶ *If United chooses the high-output strategy ($q_U = 64$), American's high-output strategy maximizes its profit:* If United chooses high output, American's profit is $4.1 million (the top-right number in the upper-left cell) if it also chooses high output ($q_A = 64$), but is only $3.8 million (the top-right number in the upper-right cell) if it chooses low output ($q_A = 48$). Thus, American is better off choosing high output if United chooses its high-output strategy.

▶ *If United chooses the low-output strategy ($q_U = 48$), American's high-output strategy maximizes its profit:* If United uses its low-output strategy, American's profit is $5.1 million with its high-output strategy and only $4.6 million with its low-output strategy. Therefore, high output is better for American in this case as well.

▶ *Thus, the high-output strategy is American's dominant strategy*: Whichever strategy United uses, American's profit is higher if it uses its high-output strategy. The low-output strategy is a *dominated strategy*. We show that American won't use its dominated low-output strategy by drawing a vertical, dark-red line through American's low-output cells in Table 12.1.

By the same type of reasoning, United's high-output strategy is also a dominant strategy. We draw a horizontal, light-red line through United's low-output strategy. Because the high-output strategy is a dominant strategy for both firms, we can predict that the outcome of this game is the pair of high-output strategies, $q_A = q_U = 64$. We show the resulting outcome—the cell in Table 12.1 where both firms use high-output strategies—by coloring that cell green. Because both players have a dominant strategy, we can call the outcome a *dominant strategy solution*.

A striking feature of this game is that the players choose strategies that do not maximize their joint or combined profit. Each firm could earn $4.6 million if each chose low output ($q_A = q_U = 48$) rather than the $4.1 million they actually earn by setting $q_A = q_U = 64$. In this type of game—called a **prisoners' dilemma** game—all players have dominant strategies that lead to a payoff that is inferior to what they could achieve if they cooperated. Given the rules of the game that the players must act independently and simultaneously, their individual incentives cause them to choose strategies that do not maximize their joint profits.

The prisoners' dilemma takes its name from a classic cops-and-robbers example. The police arrest Larry and Duncan and put them in separate rooms so that they cannot talk to each other. An assistant district attorney (DA) tells Larry, "We have enough evidence to convict you both of a minor crime for which you will each serve a year in prison. If you confess and give evidence against your partner while he stays silent, we can convict him of a major crime for which he will serve five years and you will be set free. If you both confess, you will each get two years."

Meanwhile, another assistant DA is making Duncan an identical offer. By the same reasoning as in the airline example, we expect both Larry and Duncan to confess because confessing is a dominant strategy for each of them. From Larry's point of view, confessing is always better no matter what Duncan does. If Duncan confesses, then by confessing also, Larry gets two years instead of five. If Duncan does not confess, then by confessing Larry goes free instead of serving a year. Either way, confessing is better for Larry. The same reasoning applies to Duncan. Therefore, the dominant strategy solution is for both to confess and get two years in jail, even though they would be better off, getting just one year in jail, if they both kept quiet.

Best Responses

Many games do not have a dominant strategy solution. For these games, we use a more general approach. For any given set of strategies chosen by rivals, a player wants to use its **best response**: the strategy that maximizes a player's payoff given its beliefs about its rivals' strategies. We illustrated this idea in Chapter 11 when we derived the best-response curves for an oligopolistic firm.

A dominant strategy is a strategy that is a best response to *all possible* strategies that a rival might use. Thus, a dominant strategy is a best response. However, even if a dominant strategy does not exist, each firm can determine its best response to *any possible* strategies chosen by its rivals.

The idea that players use best responses is the basis for the Nash equilibrium, a solution concept for games formally introduced by John Nash (1951). A set of strategies is a **Nash equilibrium** if, when all other players use these strategies, no player can obtain a higher payoff by choosing a different strategy. An appealing property of the Nash equilibrium is that it is self-enforcing: If each player uses a Nash equilibrium strategy, then no player would want to deviate by choosing another strategy. In other words, no player regrets the strategy choice it made when it finds out the strategies chosen by the other players. Each player would say, "Given the strategies chosen by my rivals, I made the best possible choice—I chose my best response."

The Nash equilibrium is the primary solution concept used by economists in analyzing games. It allows us to find solutions to more games than just those with a dominant strategy solution. If a game has a dominant strategy solution, then that solution must also be a Nash equilibrium. However, a Nash equilibrium can be found for many games that do not have dominant strategy solutions.

To illustrate these points, we examine a more complex simultaneous-move game in which American and United can each produce an output of 96, 64, or 48 (thousand passengers per quarter). This game has nine possible output combinations, as the 3×3 profit matrix in Table 12.2 shows. Neither American nor United has a single, dominant strategy, but we can find a Nash equilibrium by using a two-step procedure. First, we determine each firm's best response to any given strategy of the other firm. Second, we check whether any pairs of strategies (cells in the profit matrix) are best responses for both firms. Each such pair of strategies is a Nash equilibrium.

We start by determining American's best response for each one of United's possible actions. If United chooses $q_U = 96$ (thousand passengers per quarter), the first row of the table, then American's profit is $0 if it sets $q_A = 96$ (the first column), $2.0 (million) if it chooses $q_A = 64$ (the second column), and $2.3 if it selects $q_A = 48$ (third column). Thus, American's best-response if United sets $q_U = 96$ is to select $q_A = 48$. We indicate American's best response by coloring the upper triangle in the last (third column) cell in this row dark green. Similarly, if United sets $q_U = 64$ (second row), American's best response is to set $q_A = 64$, where it earns $4.1 million, so we color the upper triangle in middle cell (second column) of the second row

TABLE 12.2 Best Responses in a Quantity Setting, Prisoners' Dilemma Game

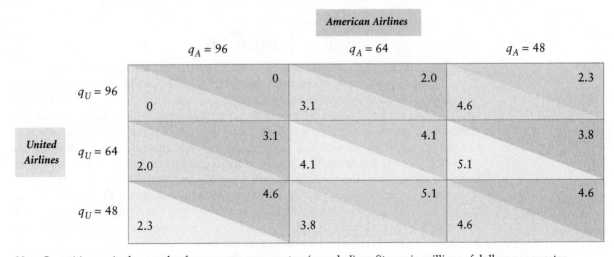

Note: Quantities are in thousands of passengers per quarter; (rounded) profits are in millions of dollars per quarter.

dark green. Finally, if United sets $q_U = 48$ (third row), American's best response is $q_A = 64$, where it earns $5.1 million, so we color the upper triangle in the middle cell of the third row dark green.

We can use the same type of reasoning to determine United's best responses to each of American's strategies. If American chooses $q_A = 96$ (first column), then United maximizes its profit at $2.3 million by setting $q_U = 48$, which we indicate by coloring the lower triangle light green in the lower left cell of the table. Similarly, we show that United's best response is $q_U = 64$, if American sets $q_A = 64$ or 48, which we show by coloring the relevant lower left triangles light green.

We now look for a Nash equilibrium, which is a pair of strategies where both firms are using a best-response strategy so that neither firm would want to change its strategy. In only one cell are both the upper and lower triangles green: $q_A = q_U = 64$. Given that its rival uses this strategy, neither firm wants to deviate from its strategy. For example, if United continued to set $q_U = 64$, but American raised its quantity to 96, American's profit would fall from $4.1 to $3.8. Or, if American lowered its quantity to 48, its profit would fall to $3.1. Thus, American does not want to change its strategy.

Because no other cell has a pair of strategies that are best responses (green lower and upper triangles), at least one of the firms would want to change its strategy in each of these other cells. For example, at $q_A = q_U = 48$, either firm could raise its profit from $4.6 to $5.1 million by increasing its output to 64. At $q_A = 48$ and $q_U = 64$, American can raise its profit from $3.8 to $4.1 million by increasing its quantity to $q_A = 64$. Similarly, United would want to increase its output when $q_A = 64$ and $q_U = 48$. None of the other strategy combinations is a Nash equilibrium because at least one firm would want to deviate. Thus, we were able to find the single Nash equilibrium to this game by determining each firm's best responses.

In these airline examples, we have assumed that the firms can only pick between a small number of output levels. However, we can use game theory to find the Nash equilibrium in games in which the firms can choose any output level. We showed such a generalization for the airline example in Chapter 11. In Figure 11.3, we determined the best-response curves for each of these airlines, found that these best-response curves intersected only once, and identified the set of outputs at that intersection as the Nash-Cournot equilibrium. Indeed, that equilibrium is the same as the equilibria in Tables 12.1 and 12.2.

Failure to Maximize Joint Profits

The dominant-strategy analysis in Table 12.1 and the best-response analysis in Table 12.2 show that noncooperative firms may not reach the joint-profit maximizing outcome. Whether players achieve the outcome that maximizes joint profit depends on the profit matrix. Table 12.3 shows an advertising game in which each firm can choose to advertise or not, with two possible profit matrices. In the first game, the rival doesn't benefit from advertising, and the Nash equilibrium does not maximize the collective profit to the firms. In contrast, in the second game, where the rival benefits from the advertising, the collective profit is maximized in the Nash equilibrium.

In the game in panel a, a firm's advertising does not bring new customers into the market but only has the effect of stealing business from the rival firm. Because each firm must decide whether or not to advertise at the same time, neither firm knows the strategy of its rival when it chooses its strategy.

TABLE 12.3 Advertising Games: Prisoners' Dilemma or Joint-Profit Maximizing Outcome?

(a) Advertising Only Takes Customers from Rivals

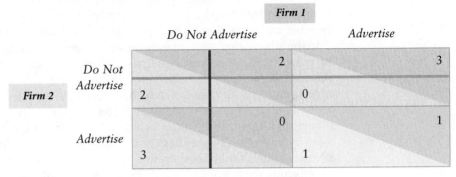

(b) Advertising Attracts New Customers to the Market

If neither firm advertises, then each firm makes a profit of 2 (say, $2 million), as the upper left cell of the profit matrix in panel a shows. If Firm 1 advertises but Firm 2 does not, then Firm 1 takes business from Firm 2 and raises its profit to 3, while the profit of Firm 2 is reduced to 0. The gain to Firm 1 is less than the loss to Firm 2 because the revenue that is transferred from Firm 2 to Firm 1 as customers shift is partially offset by the cost of Firm 2's advertising. If both firms advertise, then each firm gets a profit of 1, as the cell on the lower right shows.

Advertising is a dominant strategy for both firms.[4] We use red lines to show that the firms do not use the dominated do-not-advertise strategies. Advertising for both firms is also a Nash equilibrium, because each firm is choosing its best response to the other firm's strategy, as indicated by the green shading in the lower right cell.

In this Nash equilibrium, each firm earns 1, which is less than the 2 it would make if neither firm advertised. Thus, *the sum of the firms' profits is not maximized in this simultaneous-choice one-period game.*

---

[4]Firm 1 goes through the following reasoning. "If my rival does not advertise, I get 2 if I do not advertise and I get 3 if I do advertise, so advertising would be better. If my rival does advertise, I get 0 if I do not advertise and I get 1 if I do advertise, so advertising is still better." Regardless of what Firm 2 does, advertising is better for Firm 1, so advertising is a dominant strategy for Firm 1. Firm 2 faces a symmetric problem and would also conclude that advertising is a dominant strategy.

Many people are surprised the first time they see this result. Why don't the firms cooperate, refrain from advertising, and earn 2 instead of 1? This game is an example of prisoners' dilemma: The game has a dominant strategy solution in which the players receive lower profits than they would get if the firms could cooperate. Each firm makes more money by advertising than by not advertising regardless of the strategy used by the other firm, even though their joint profit is maximized if neither advertises.

In the advertising game in panel b, advertising by a firm brings new customers to the market and consequently helps both firms. That is, each firm's advertising has a market expansion effect. If neither firm advertises, both earn 2. If only one firm advertises, its profit rises to 4, which is more than the 3 that the other firm makes. If both advertise, they are collectively better off than if only one advertises or neither advertises. Again, advertising is a dominant strategy for a firm because it earns more by advertising regardless of the strategy the other firm uses and is therefore a Nash equilibrium. However, this game is not a prisoners' dilemma. In this Nash equilibrium, the firms' combined profits are maximized, which is the same outcome that would arise if the firms could cooperate. Thus, whether a Nash equilibrium maximizes the combined profit for the players depends on the properties of the game that are summarized in the profit matrix.

Mini-Case

Strategic Advertising

Firms with market power, such as oligopolies, often advertise.[5] The largest advertiser in the United States is Procter & Gamble, the producer of Crest toothpaste, Pampers diapers, and many other household products. In 2012, Procter & Gamble spent $9.3 billion on worldwide advertising. The next largest U.S. advertisers are General Motors, Verizon, Comcast, and AT&T. The largest advertisers based outside the United States are Unilever (United Kingdom, packaged household goods including Dove soap and Lipton foods), L'Oreal (France, cosmetics), Nestle (Switzerland, foods), and Toyota (Japan, motor vehicles).

In oligopolistic markets, firms consider the likely actions of their rivals when deciding how much to advertise. How much a firm should spend on advertising depends critically on whether the advertising helps or harms its rival.

For example, when a firm advertises to inform consumers about a new use for its product, its advertising may cause the quantity demanded for its own *and* rival brands to rise, as happened with toothpaste ads. Before World War I, only 26% of Americans brushed their teeth. By 1926, in part because of ads like those in Ipana's "pink toothbrush" campaign, which detailed the perils of bleeding gums, the share of Americans who brushed rose to 40%. Ipana's advertising helped all manufacturers of toothbrushes and toothpaste.

Alternatively, a firm's advertising might increase demand for its product by taking customers away from other firms. A firm can raise its profit if it can convince consumers that its product is superior to other brands. From the 1930s through the early 1970s, secret ingredients were a mainstay of consumer advertising. These ingredients were given names combining letters

---

[5]Under perfect competition, there is no reason for an individual firm to advertise as a firm can sell all it wishes at the going market price.

and numbers to suggest that they were cooked up in laboratories rather than by Madison Avenue. Dial soap boasted that it contained AT-7. Rinso detergent had solium, Comet included Chlorinol, and Bufferin had di-alminate. Among the toothpastes, Colgate had Gardol, Gleem had GL-70, Crest had fluoristan, and Ipana had hexachlorophene and Durenamel. More recently, natural ingredients have played this role.

Empirical evidence indicates that the impact of a firm's advertising on other firms varies across industries. The cola market is an example of the extreme case in which a firm's advertising brings few new customers into the market and primarily serves to steal business from rivals. Gasmi, Laffont, and Vuong (1992) reported that Coke or Pepsi's gain from advertising comes at the expense of its rivals; however, cola advertising has almost no effect on total market demand, as in panel a of Table 12.3. Similarly, celebrity endorsements (an important form of advertising) increase the sales of endorsed books but reduce sales of other books (Garthwaite, 2012). At the other extreme is cigarette advertising. Roberts and Samuelson (1988) found that cigarette advertising increases the size of the market but does not change market shares substantially, as in panel b.[6] Intermediate results include Canadian fast-foods, where advertising primarily increases general demand but has a small effect on market share (Richards and Padilla, 2009).

Q&A 12.1

Suppose Procter & Gamble (PG) and Johnson & Johnson (JNJ) are simultaneously considering new advertising campaigns. Each firm may choose a high, medium, or low level of advertising. The profit matrix is:

		PG High	PG Medium	PG Low
JNJ	High	1, 1	3, 2	5, 3
JNJ	Medium	2, 3	4, 4	6, 5
JNJ	Low	3, 5	5, 6	7, 5

What are each firm's best responses to each of its rival's strategies? Does either firm have a dominant strategy? What is the Nash equilibrium in this game?

---

[6]However, the Centers for Disease Control and Prevention's evidence suggests that advertising may shift the brand loyalty of youths.

Answer

1. *Show JNJ's best response for each possible strategy of PG.* The light green triangles are JNJ's best responses to each action by PG. If PG chooses a high level of advertising (the first column), JNJ's best response is low, because its profit is 1 if it chooses high, 2 if it chooses medium, and 3 if it chooses low, so we color the lower triangle light green in the last cell in this column. Similarly, low is the best response of JNJ to either medium or low advertising by PG, so the lower triangle is light green in every cell in the bottom row.

2. *Show PG's best response for each possible strategy of JNJ.* The dark green triangles are PG's best responses to each action by JNJ. If JNJ chooses a high level of advertising (the first row), JNJ's best response is low so we color the upper triangle dark green in the cell in the last column of this row. Similarly, low is PG's best response if JNJ picks medium, so the upper triangle is dark green in the cell in the last column of the second row. However, if JNJ uses low, then PG's best response is medium, so the upper triangle is dark green in the middle cell of the last row.

3. *By inspection, determine if either firm has a dominant strategy.* JNJ has a dominant strategy because it chooses low regardless of the strategy that PG selects. However, PG does not have a dominant strategy as its best response depends on the strategy selected by JNJ.

4. *Use the best responses to determine the Nash equilibrium.* In only one cell are the strategies a best response for both firms (that is, all green). It is the one where JNJ selects low and PG picks medium: the middle cell in the bottom row. Thus, that pair of strategies is the Nash equilibrium. We can also determine the Nash equilibrium another way. PG knows that JNJ has a dominant strategy of low. Given that JNJ chooses low, we know that PG's best response is medium; thus, that pair of strategies is the Nash equilibrium.

Comment: In this game, the lowest combined profit occurs when both firms use a high level of advertising and the highest combined profit corresponds to both firms choosing a low level of advertising. This pattern is consistent with a market in which advertising attracts relatively few new customers, and the business-stealing effect of advertising is more important than the market expansion effect. As a consequence, if firms use advertising to fight over existing consumers, joint profit falls.

12.2 Types of Nash Equilibria

The games described in Tables 12.1, 12.2, and 12.3 each have a unique Nash equilibrium: for only one combination of strategies is each firm's strategy a best response to its rival's strategy. The Cournot and Bertrand models of Chapter 11 are other examples of games with unique Nash equilibria. We now consider two other situations. First, we examine games that have multiple Nash equilibria. Second, we consider games in which the firms' strategies require them to choose randomly between possible actions.

Multiple Equilibria

Many oligopoly games have more than one Nash equilibrium. When there are multiple Nash equilibria, we may be able to use additional criteria to predict the likely outcome. The scheduling or coordination game between two television networks that is summarized in Table 12.4 has multiple Nash equilibria.

This profit table shows that each network's profit depends on whether new reality TV shows —one for each network—air on Wednesday or Thursday. Neither network can change its decision once the networks simultaneously announce their schedules. Thus, each network must choose its schedule before it knows its rival's choice. The number of people who watch reality shows is enough for only one show to be profitable on a given night. If both shows appear on Wednesday or if both appear on Thursday, they share the reality market for that night and each network loses 10 (say, $10 million). However, if the shows appear on different nights, then each network earns a profit of 10.

Neither network has a dominant strategy. For each network, its best choice depends on the choice of its rival. If Network 1 opts for Wednesday, then Network 2 prefers Thursday, but if Network 1 chooses Thursday, then Network 2 prefers Wednesday.

To determine the Nash equilibria for this game, we first determine each firm's best responses. If Network 2 were to choose Wednesday, then Network 1 loses 10 if it chooses Wednesday and earns 10 if it chooses Thursday. Thus, Network 1's best response is Thursday, which we indicate by coloring the upper triangle dark green in the upper right cell. Similarly, Network 1's best response is Wednesday, if Network 2 picks Thursday, which we show by coloring the upper triangle dark green in the lower left cell. Similarly, we color the lower triangles light green for Network 2's best responses.

The Nash equilibria are the two cells that are entirely green, showing that those pairs of strategies are best responses for both firms. These Nash equilibria have one firm broadcast on Wednesday and the other on Thursday. Neither firm would want to deviate from these Nash equilibria because doing so would cause it to lose money.

Thus, this game has two Nash equilibria. We might reasonably predict that the networks would show the two new shows on different nights, but we do not have any basis for forecasting which night each network chooses.

Cheap Talk. How can the networks avoid a disaster in this scheduling game? One possibility is that a network communicates with its rival before choosing its strategy if doing so is allowed by the rules of the game.

TABLE 12.4 Network Scheduling: A Coordination Game

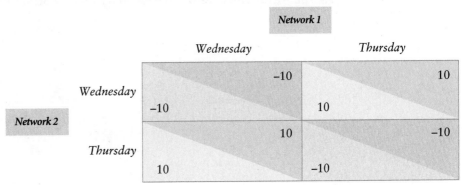

The firms engage in *cheap talk* (or *pre-play communication*) if they communicate before the game starts but the communication does not directly affect the payoffs of the game. Cheap talk does not mean that firms can agree in advance on their strategies. In a real-world, noncooperative game such as this one, firms may not legally make binding agreements of this type. A firm might make a cheap-talk claim, but then do something different. Therefore, in many games, allowing cheap talk has no effect: "Talk is cheap." Managers can say anything but, until decisions are actually made, claims made by firms may lack credibility.

In this game, however, players have an incentive to be truthful so the cheap talk is credible. Each network wants the other to know its actual choice and therefore has an incentive to truthfully reveal its intentions and follow through accordingly. For example, if Network 1 announces in advance that it will broadcast on Wednesday, Network 2 will choose Thursday and both networks will benefit from communicating. Games with multiple Nash equilibria where players can credibly coordinate to select one of these equilibria are referred to as *coordination games*.

The Pareto Criterion. Not all games with multiple Nash equilibria can be resolved with pre-play communication. Cheap talk may be prohibited by antitrust laws. Even where it is allowed, cheap talk lacks credibility if players have an incentive to lie. A variety of other criteria have been suggested to predict a single Nash equilibrium in a game with multiple equilibria. For example, it is possible that one of the Nash equilibria provides a higher payoff to all players than the other Nash equilibria. If so, we expect firms acting independently to choose strategies that lead to that outcome even without communicating.

Table 12.5 shows a variant of the scheduling game in Table 12.4. Table 12.5 has two Nash equilibria in which the networks choose different nights. Neither network would want to switch nights and go head-to-head with its rival. However, both firms receive higher profits if Network 1's show airs on Thursday and Network 2 chooses Wednesday because of other programming in place on those nights.

We might expect that, even without cheap talk, the networks might opt for the Nash equilibrium with the higher profits because each network expects its rival to have a similar understanding of the situation. This criterion—selecting a solution that is better for all parties—is called the *Pareto Criterion*. Of course, each firm may prefer to engage in cheap talk to make sure that the other network understands the situation. Unfortunately, we cannot always use cheap talk or the Pareto Criterion to predict the outcome in a game with multiple equilibria.

TABLE 12.5 The Pareto Criterion in a Network Scheduling Coordination Game

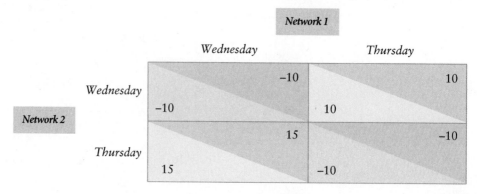

Mini-Case

Timing Radio Ads

A contemporary music radio station can time its commercial breaks so that they occur at the same time or at different times than those of its rival stations. If the breaks are not coordinated, many listeners switch stations at a commercial break. This switching behavior lowers the value of commercials to advertisers, so that they pay the stations less.

Sweeting (2006, 2009) found that stations often have commercial breaks at the same time. During commuting hours, "drive time" listeners are likely to switch stations during commercials. Sweeting estimated that the length of time that commercial breaks occur simultaneously across stations increases by 6% during drive time. Such coordination increases the number of commercials heard by in-car listeners, and Sweeting estimates that such coordination raises annual industry advertising revenues by roughly $90 million.

Mixed-Strategy Equilibria

So far, we have assumed that each firm uses a **pure strategy**, which specifies the action that a player will take in every possible situation in a game. We now consider

How business decisions are made.

games in which a firm uses a **mixed strategy**, in which a player chooses among possible pure strategies according to probabilities that the player sets. That is, a pure strategy is a rule telling the player with certainty what action to take at each decision point in a game, whereas a mixed strategy is a rule telling the player which dice to throw, coin to flip, or other method to use to randomly choose among possible pure strategies.

In static games—the focus of this chapter—a strategy is a single action, such as choosing a particular output level. Thus, for example, in our original airlines example of Table 12.1, an airline manager could use a mixed strategy by assigning a 50% probability to both the low output and the high output as if choosing randomly between them by flipping a coin.[7]

A pure strategy can be viewed as a special case of a mixed strategy in which a player assigns a probability of one to a single pure strategy and a probability of zero to all other possible pure strategies. A mixed strategy that assigns positive probabilities to two or more actions is sometimes called a *non-pure* mixed strategy. Unless we state otherwise, from now on, when we refer to a mixed strategy, we mean a non-pure mixed strategy.

Some games have no pure-strategy Nash equilibrium, but have a mixed-strategy Nash equilibrium. Others have both pure-strategy and mixed-strategy Nash equilibria.[8]

---

[7]In the more complex dynamic games that we examine in the next chapter, a strategy may be a sequence of actions, so a mixed strategy would apply probabilities to particular alternative action sequences.

[8]Nash (1950) proved that every game with a finite number of players and strategies has at least one pure-strategy or mixed-strategy Nash equilibrium.

Mixed-Strategy Only Nash Equilibria. The following design competition game has no pure-strategy Nash equilibrium, but it has a mixed-strategy Nash equilibrium. A firm that wants a new building conducts a design competition between two architectural firms. The terms of the competition specify the location and size of the structure, the maximum allowable construction budget, and various design requirements. The architectural firms compete for the contract by creating preliminary designs.

An established architectural firm competes with a relatively new, upstart firm. There are only two possible major types of design: a traditional design and a modern design. If both firms adopt the same type of design, then the established firm wins the contract in view of its stronger reputation and longer track record. However, if the firms adopt different designs, the upstart wins the contract.

Table 12.6 is the profit matrix, where the contract winner receives a net benefit of 20 ($20 thousand) and the loser incurs the cost of its initial design, 2 ($2 thousand). As before, we indicate each firm's best response by coloring the appropriate triangle green (dark green for the established firm and light green for the upstart firm). The table shows that the upstart's best response is a modern design if the established firm uses a traditional design, and the upstart's best response is a traditional design if the established firm uses a modern approach.

No cell in the table is a Nash equilibrium because in no cell of this profit matrix are both triangles green. For each cell, one firm or the other says, "I regret my choice. Given the choice made by my rival, I should have made a different choice." If both firms pick the same style, the upstart firm regrets its choice. Similarly, if they pick different styles, the established firm regrets its choice.

Thus, if both firms use pure strategies, this game has no Nash equilibrium. However, this design game has a mixed-strategy Nash equilibrium in which each firm chooses the traditional design with probability $\frac{1}{2}$. (Appendix 12 shows how to calculate the probabilities in the mixed strategy.)

Because the probability that a firm chooses a given style is $\frac{1}{2}$, the probability that both firms independently choose a given pair of styles (a cell) is $\frac{1}{2} \times \frac{1}{2} = \frac{1}{4}$. That is, each of the four cells in Table 12.6 is equally likely to be chosen and hence has a one-fourth chance of being chosen. In two cells (the upper left and lower right), the established firm earns 20, so it has a $\frac{1}{2}$ probability of earning 20. Similarly, it has a $\frac{1}{2}$ probability of losing 2 (lower left and upper right cells). Thus, the established firm's expected profit—the firm's profit in each possible outcome times the probability of that outcome—is $(20 \times \frac{1}{2}) + ([-2] \times \frac{1}{2}) = 9$.

TABLE 12.6 Mixed Strategies in a Design Competition

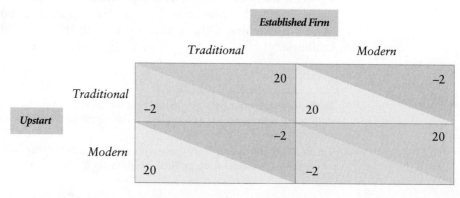

Given that the established firm uses this mixed strategy—in effect flipping a coin to choose between its two possible actions—the upstart firm cannot achieve a higher expected profit by using a pure strategy rather than using the same mixed strategy. If the upstart uses the pure strategy of choosing the traditional style or the pure strategy of the modern style, it has a $\frac{1}{2}$ chance of earning 20 and a $\frac{1}{2}$ probability of losing 2, so it has the same expected profit as if it uses the mixed strategy.[9] That is, each firm chooses the traditional style with a probability of one half in the mixed-strategy, Nash equilibrium.

Why would each of these firms use a mixed strategy of $\frac{1}{2}$? If the upstart knows that the established firm will use the pure strategy of choosing the traditional style, then the upstart chooses the modern style with certainty (a pure strategy), knowing that it will win. If the upstart knows that the established firm is more likely to choose the traditional style (that is, the probability is greater than $\frac{1}{2}$), the upstart would pick the modern style with certainty knowing that its chance of winning is more than a half. Similarly, if the upstart knows that the established firm is very likely to use the modern style (its probability of choosing the traditional style is less than a half), the upstart would choose the traditional style with certainty, and win with a probability greater than a half. Only if both firms are using a mixed strategy of $\frac{1}{2}$ is each maximizing its expected profit given the strategy of its rival.

Both Pure and Mixed-Strategy Equilibria. Some games have both pure-strategy and mixed-strategy Nash equilibria. The following entry game has two pure-strategy Nash equilibria and a mixed-strategy Nash equilibrium.

Two firms are considering opening gas stations at a highway rest stop that currently has no gas station. There's enough physical space for at most two gas stations. The profit matrix in Table 12.7 shows that there is enough demand for only one station to operate profitably. If both firms enter, each loses 2 (say, $200,000). Neither firm has a dominant strategy. Each firm's best action depends on what the other firm does.

The two Nash equilibria in pure strategies are Firm 1 *enters* and Firm 2 *does not enter*, or Firm 2 *enters* and Firm 1 *does not enter*. The equilibrium in which only Firm 1 enters is a Nash equilibrium because neither firm would regret its choice. Given that Firm 2 did not enter, Firm 1 would not regret its decision to enter. If it changed its behavior, it would go from earning 1 to earning nothing. Similarly, given that Firm 1 enters, Firm 2 does not regret staying out because entering would have cost it 2 instead of being able to walk away without any losses. However, the outcome where only Firm 2 enters is also a Nash equilibrium by the same type of reasoning.

How do the players know which outcome will arise? They *don't* know. Without an enforceable collusive agreement, even pre-play communication is unlikely to help. These pure-strategy Nash equilibria might seem unappealing because they call for identical firms to use different strategies.[10]

---

[9]Some economists don't like stories where managers literally flip coins or use another randomization device to choose strategies, arguing that we rarely see such behavior. Rather, managers almost always come up with some substantive reason to choose one action over another rather than resorting to a coin or a dice or some other device. Regardless, as long as their choice appears to be probabilistic to their rivals, they are effectively using a mixed strategy.

[10]This entry game, in which both firms lose if both enter, is called a *hawk-dove game*, because there is an aggressive and a passive strategy. It is also called a *game of chicken*. Movies sometimes show a game of chicken where two guys suffering from testosterone poisoning drive toward each other in the middle of a road. As they approach the impact point, each has the option of continuing to drive down the middle of the road or to swerve. Both believe that if only one driver swerves, that driver loses face and the other gains in self-esteem. If neither swerves, they are maimed or killed. If both swerve, no harm is done to either. Bertrand Russell observed that nuclear brinksmanship is essentially a game of chicken.

TABLE 12.7 Nash Equilibria in an Entry Game

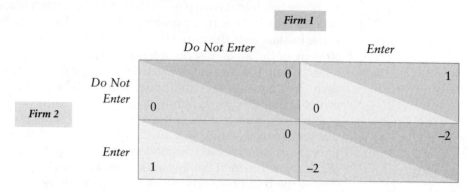

	Firm 1	
	Do Not Enter	Enter
Firm 2 Do Not Enter	0 / 0	1 / 0
Enter	0 / 1	−2 / −2

This entry game also has a mixed-strategy Nash equilibrium in which each firm enters with $\frac{1}{3}$ probability. No firm could raise its expected profit by changing its strategy. The game therefore has three Nash equilibria in total: two pure-strategy Nash equilibria and one additional mixed-strategy Nash equilibrium.

Mini-Case

Competing E-Book Formats

A key strategy decision for a manufacturer of an e-book is which format to use. Currently, not all e-book readers use the same format for books.[11] The current best-selling product, Amazon's Kindle (and its applications for the iPhone and for Windows PCs), uses Amazon's proprietary AZW format. Amazon does not support the open-standard EPUB format, which is used by the Kindle's competitors such as Barnes & Noble's NOOK, Sony's Reader, and Apple's iPad. Amazon provides applications that allow consumers to read AZW books on the iPhone (and slightly less successfully on the iPad) as well as on Windows PCs but not on the other readers. Because e-book readers' formats differ, e-book publishers must incur additional expenses in producing books in the various formats or sell books that can be read on only some readers, which affects consumers' costs and the practicality of using a given reader.

---

[11]However, all readers can display Adobe PDF files, which are used for documents and books in the public domain.

Q&A 12.2

Amazon faces the Other group, which consists of e-book manufacturers other than Amazon, in a game in which the players choose a format, as the profit matrix shows.[12] What are the pure-strategy Nash equilibria if the firms choose their formats simultaneously and are free to choose either format? Determine the mixed-strategy equilibrium, if any.

Answer

1. *Determine the pure-strategy Nash equilibria if the firms decide simultaneously.* We add green triangles to the relevant cells in the profit matrix to indicate each firm's best responses to its rival's strategy. There are two pure-strategy Nash equilibria in which Amazon and the other manufacturers both choose the same format. If both choose the AZW standard, neither Amazon nor the Other group would change its strategy if it knew that its rival was using the AZW format. The Other group's profit falls from 1 to -1 if it changes its strategy from the AZW to the ePub format, whereas Amazon's profit falls from 3 to -1 if it makes that change. Similarly, no firm would change its strategy from the ePub format if it believed that its rival would use the ePub format. Thus, if the firms must choose the formats simultaneously, the only pure-strategy Nash equilibria are where they use the same format; however, each prefers its own format, where its profit is 3 rather than 1.

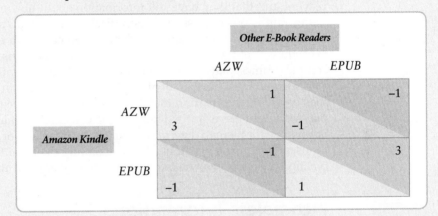

2. *Show that this game has a mixed-strategy Nash equilibrium by calculating the relevant probabilities.* This game has a mixed-strategy equilibrium in which Amazon selects the AZW standard with a probability of $\frac{2}{3}$ and the Other group selects AZW with probability $\frac{1}{3}$.[13]

---

[12]This game is of the same form as the game called *the battle of the sexes*. In that game, the husband likes to go to the mountains on vacation, and the wife prefers the ocean, but they both prefer to take their vacations together.

[13]If the Other group chooses the AZW standard with a probability of θ_O, Amazon's expected profit is $(3 \times \theta_O) + (-1 \times [1 - \theta_O]) = 4\theta_O - 1$ if it chooses the AZW standard and $(-1 \times \theta_O) + (1 \times [1 - \theta_O]) = 1 - 2\theta_O$ if it chooses the ePub standard. For Amazon to be indifferent between these two actions, its expected profits must be equal: $4\theta_O - 1 = 1 - 2\theta_O$. That is, if $\theta_O = \frac{1}{3}$, Amazon is indifferent between choosing either standard. Similarly, if Amazon selects the AZW standard with a probability of $\theta_A = \frac{2}{3}$, the Other group is indifferent between choosing either of the two standards.

Comments: Depending on the profits in the game, there are other possible outcomes: only one format and one group of firms survives in the Nash equilibrium, or the firms adopt a single format (like the universally used MP3 and MP4 standards for digital music players). The real-world competition among e-book reader manufacturers has two additional complications. First, AZW is the proprietary format of Amazon, so the other firms would have to pay Amazon to use it, if Amazon would even permit them to do so. Second, Amazon, which entered the market first, chose its e-book format before other, later entrants into this market. In Chapter 13, we examine how this game changes given that Amazon acted first.

12.3 Information and Rationality

All that I have to say has already crossed your mind," said [Moriarty]. "Then possibly my answer has crossed yours," I replied. —Sherlock Holmes (Sir Arthur Conan Doyle)

Game theory focuses our attention on the crucial role that information plays in a firm's decision-making process. In some situations it makes sense to assume that players have full information about the profits and possible strategies of other players, and that they have full information about how much other players know. For example, our discussion of American and United Airlines assumes that both airlines have the same costs and demand functions, so that each knows virtually everything that the other firm knows. In other situations, particularly in relatively complex games, players may not have complete information about their rival.

We usually assume that all players will act rationally in the sense that they use all their available information to determine their best strategies. However, sometimes players might have limited powers of calculation, making it difficult or even impossible for them to determine their best strategies. For example, if all firms have thousands of possible actions, then calculating the payoffs for every possible combination of actions may be too time-consuming or difficult to be feasible.

Incomplete Information

In the United and American Airlines game in Table 12.1, we assume that each airline has complete information about its rival and knows all the possible strategies and profits. However, in other games, firms may have incomplete information about their rivals. For example, each firm's profit could be *private information* rather than *common knowledge*.

To illustrate how having incomplete information affects a game's outcome, we consider an investment game, in which two firms are considering investing in complementary products that "go together." For example, Google considered whether to invest in a new operating system, Chrome OS, for laptops and netbooks, while Samsung considered whether to design and build a new laptop, a Chromebook, that would use this operating system.[14] The firms made their decisions simultaneously, announcing the availability of the first Chromebook and the new operating system in 2011.

---

[14]J. R. Raphael, "Google's Chrome OS and Samsung's Chromebook," **computerworld.com**, June 15, 2011.

TABLE 12.8 Complementary Investment Game

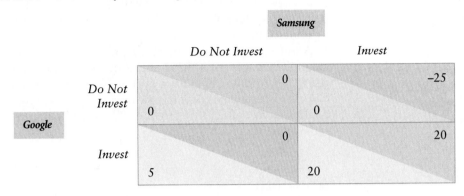

	Samsung	
	Do Not Invest	*Invest*
Google — *Do Not Invest*	0 / 0	0 / −25
Google — *Invest*	5 / 0	20 / 20

Table 12.8 illustrates a simplified version of the game they played (with hypothetical profits). If neither firm invests, each earns nothing (upper left cell). However, there is an asymmetry regarding the returns if only one firm invests. We assume that the new operating system is of value by itself, even without a new laptop by Samsung, as other firms could produce such a laptop (and, indeed, a number of other firms later entered this laptop market as well, including Google in 2013). Consequently, Google receives a benefit of 5 (say, $50 million) if Samsung does not invest in a new laptop and Samsung earns 0 (lower left cell). Because the new, specialized laptop is completely useless without the new operating system, if Samsung invests and Google does not (upper right cell), Samsung incurs a large loss, −25, and Google earns 0. If both firms invest (lower right cell), each receives a profit of 20.

We start by assuming that each firm has complete information about each other's profit—the information in the profit matrix in Table 12.8. This game has a unique Nash equilibrium in which both firms invest. For each firm, investment is the best response to the other firm's decision to invest.

However, what happens if the firms' profits are not common knowledge? In particular, if Samsung does not know Google's possible profits it may not realize that it is in Google's best interest to invest regardless of Samsung's action—that investing is a dominant strategy for Google. Consequently, Samsung might worry that Google will not invest. Given its limited information, Samsung may not invest. If all goes well and Google decides to invest in developing the Chrome operating system, Samsung makes a significant profit. But if all does not go well and Google fails to invest, then Samsung suffers a big loss. Thus, if Samsung thinks it is likely that Google will not invest, Samsung may decide not to invest. In this game, Samsung and Google fail to coordinate their strategies due to incomplete information.

Managerial Implication

Solving Coordination Problems

Managers can use several methods to solve coordination problems, including problems caused by incomplete information. One approach is through merger or acquisition. For example, Google, which developed the Android operating system for mobile phones, faced a coordination problem with Motorola Mobility, a mobile phone manufacturer, and resolved the problem by acquiring Motorola Mobility in 2012, allowing for information-sharing between the former Motorola unit and Google.

A similar, but less extreme approach than merger or acquisition is to form a joint venture. For example, Google and Motorola could have jointly invested in a cooperative project for ongoing development of mobile phones and their operating system. Google often invests with other firms through its Google Ventures unit.

Another approach is for one firm to *subcontract* or "hire" the other. For example, Google could have subcontracted Motorola to build mobile phones using the Android operating system, or Motorola could have subcontracted Google to design and develop the operating system for its phones. Or the firms could sign a contract that provides that a firm will pay the other a penalty if it fails to invest.

Rationality

We normally assume that economic agents are rational in the sense that they consistently choose actions that are in their best interests given the information they have. Rational players choose payoff-maximizing strategies. In the game in Table 12.8, if Google is rational, it invests because its profit is higher if it invests, no matter what Samsung does.

Bounded Rationality. Actual business games are usually much more complex than the one in Table 12.8. For example, AT&T, Verizon, and MetroPCS, among other companies, use complicated strategies in the mobile phone market. Each firm's managers set prices on a variety of products, choose how much to advertise, select locations for cell towers, consider mergers with other companies, contract with cell phone manufacturers (such as to be able to carry Apple's iPhone), and decide simultaneously on many other actions.

Perhaps a manager with infinite powers of calculation could consider all possible combinations of actions by all firms and calculate the resulting profit to each firm and select the optimal strategy. However, even the very best managers do not always choose the optimal strategy. It does not seem reasonable to dismiss such managers as irrational just because they cannot find a fully optimal strategy. Instead, managers with limited powers of calculation or logical inference are described as having *bounded rationality*. Such managers try to maximize profits but, due to their cognitive limitations, do not always succeed.

In a wide range of strategic games, especially business strategy games, it is important to consider how sophisticated or rational one's rivals are. The best strategy against a highly sophisticated rival might differ from the best strategy against a rival with a limited ability to obtain and analyze information.

Maximin Strategies. In very complex games, a manager with bounded rationality may use a *rule of thumb* approach, perhaps using a rule that has worked in the past in choosing a strategy. For example, some players with bounded rationality use a *maximin* strategy, which maximizes the minimum payoff. This approach is designed to ensure the best possible payoff if your rival takes the action that is worst for you.

In Table 12.8, Samsung gets zero if it does not invest. If it does invest it might lose 25 or earn 20. Thus, Firm 2's lowest (or minimum) profit is 0 if it does not invest and is −25 if it does invest. The maximum of these two values is 0, which arises if the firm does not invest. Therefore, not investing is Samsung's maximin strategy in this game. If Samsung fears that Google is subject to bounded rationality and might be unable to determine that it should invest, playing a maximin strategy might be attractive to Samsung. If all players adopt a maximin strategy, then we call the outcome a maximin solution. The maximin solution for the game in Table 12.8 is for Google to invest and for Samsung not to invest.

Managerial Implication Using Game Theory to Make Business Decisions	While many actual business games are too complex to analyze as completely as we've analyzed the relatively simple games in this chapter, knowledge of these games provides insights that a manager can use in designing business strategies. When making strategic decisions, managers should consider five principles based on game theory: 1. *Dominance.* A manager who has a dominant strategy—a strategy that is always best no matter what rivals do—should use it. 2. *Best Response.* A manager who does not have a dominant strategy should determine the best responses to the strategies that rivals might use. 3. *Point of View.* A manager should consider possible strategies from the rival's vantage point, try to predict which strategy the rival will choose, and select the best response to that strategy. 4. *Coordination.* When doing so increases profit, a manager should coordinate with other firms through pre-play communication (cheap talk) or by using legal contracts. 5. *Randomize.* A manager may be able to earn a higher profit by keeping rivals guessing by using a mixed strategy.

12.4 Bargaining

Most consumer items are sold in *posted price* markets. Customers go to a supermarket or a department store, check out the posted prices, and decide what to buy. Rarely do customers in a supermarket bargain over the price of milk or bid on milk in an auction. However, in other markets, bargaining and auctions are used.[15]

Bargaining is common between a manager and employees over wages and working conditions. When workers are represented by a labor union, the bargaining process is referred to as *collective bargaining*. Bargaining between employers and specific employees is common even for many nonunionized workers. Bargaining is also important in the legal system. For example, one party (the plaintiff) might sue another (the defendant) but be willing to bargain with the defendant over the actual payment to avoid the cost and uncertainty of a trial.

Bargaining often arises in vertical business relationships. For example, a manufacturer may bargain with suppliers of specialized inputs to the production process or with downstream distributors or retailers of the produced product. Bargaining is also important in our personal lives. Car buyers bargain with car dealers. Married couples and roommates bargain over responsibility for household chores. Teenagers bargain with their parents over how much time they must spend on homework, how late they can stay out, and when they can drive their parents' cars.

---

[15]An important factor in choosing which market mechanism to use is the size of transaction costs relative to the value of the item being sold. In a supermarket, it is not worth the time it would take for customers to bargain with sales clerks over the price of milk or to participate in an auction.

Bargaining Games

Game theory can be used to explain bargaining strategies. We can think of a **bargaining game** as any situation in which two or more parties with different interests or objectives negotiate voluntarily over the terms of some interaction, such as the transfer of a good from one party to another. For example, the owner of a house might negotiate with a potential buyer over the price of the house and over other aspects of the transaction, such as the date when the house changes hands and any repairs to be made by the seller.

To keep our analysis as simple as possible, we focus on bargaining games between two players. John Nash presented the earliest formal analysis of two-person bargaining games. He proposed a solution for bargaining games, which is called the *Nash bargaining solution*. The Nash bargaining solution is not the same as the *Nash equilibrium* that we have previously discussed. The Nash equilibrium is the solution to a noncooperative game, such as the Cournot game where firms choose output levels. In that game, firms do *not* bargain over output levels, reflecting the legal reality that such bargaining is illegal.

The Nash Bargaining Solution

In two classic papers, Nash (1950, 1953) proposed a solution for two-player cooperative bargaining games. The Nash bargaining solution satisfies several properties. Most importantly, the Nash bargaining solution to a cooperative game is *efficient* in the sense that there is no alternative outcome that would be better for both parties or strictly better for one party and no worse for the other. Basically the two parties are trying to reach an agreement to divide profits or some other payoff. For example, two roommates could bargain about how to divide a pie between them.

Some of the noncooperative games that we have studied could be converted to cooperative bargaining games by allowing the players to sign binding agreements. For example, Table 12.1 shows the profit matrix for an oligopoly game between American Airlines and United Airlines, where each firm must produce an output of either 48 or 64 (thousand passengers per quarter). We showed that, if the game is a static, noncooperative game, the firms face a prisoners' dilemma in which each produces the higher output and each firm earns 4.1 ($4.1 million) in the noncooperative Nash equilibrium.

Suppose that the federal antitrust laws change, so that the rules of the game allow the two firms to bargain over their output levels and to reach a binding agreement. Given that the firms can bargain, we would not expect the firms to choose the high-output outcome because both firms would be better off with an alternative outcome in which each produces the lower output. The Nash bargaining solution, which requires efficiency for the players, rules out the high-output result.

To find the Nash bargaining solution, we first need to determine what happens if the firms cannot reach an agreement. The *disagreement point* or *threat point* is the outcome that arises if no agreement is reached. The profit to a firm at the disagreement point is d. If a proposed agreement is reached, the firm receives a profit of π. Thus, if an agreement is reached, the player earns a *net surplus* that equals the difference between what that player receives under the proposed agreement and what it receives at the disagreement point, $\pi - d$.

The Nash bargaining solution is the outcome in which each firm receives a non-negative surplus (a firm would not agree to an outcome in which it loses money) and in which the product of the net surplus of the two firms (called the *Nash product*, *NP*) is maximized. For the airlines, the Nash bargaining solution maximizes

$$NP = (\pi_A - d_A) \times (\pi_U - d_U), \tag{12.1}$$

where the subscript A refers to American Airlines and U to United Airlines.

In this game, the natural disagreement point is the noncooperative outcome: If no agreement is reached, each firm chooses the high output. Thus, $d_A = d_U = 4.1$.

We can evaluate the Nash product for each of the four possible outcomes for this game. In the upper left cell in Table 12.1, in which each firm produces the large output, the Nash product is zero and each firm has zero net surplus. This cell represents the disagreement point. In the lower left cell and in the upper right cell one of the firms earns a negative net surplus—which is less than at the disagreement point—so the Nash product is negative. Only in the lower right cell, where each firm produces the small output and earns 4.6, is the Nash product positive: $NP = (4.6 - 4.1) \times (4.6 - 4.1) = 0.25$. Thus, the outcome in the lower right cell maximizes the Nash product and is the Nash bargaining solution to this bargaining game.

If the firms could bargain about how they set their output levels in an oligopoly game, they could presumably reach an outcome that they view as *efficient* in the sense that it maximizes the Nash product, *NP*. Such an agreement creates a cartel and raises the firms' profits. The gain to firms from such a cartel agreement is more than offset by lost surplus for consumers (Chapter 11). Consequently, such agreements are illegal in most developed countries under antitrust or competition laws. Although the Nash bargaining solution is not a full theory of bargaining, it is a good predictor in certain situations—especially if contractual obligations arising from bargaining are legally enforceable and if the two parties have full information.

Q&A 12.3

Jane is interested in buying a car from a used car dealer. Her maximum willingness to pay for the car is 12 ($12,000). Bo, the dealer, is willing to sell the car as long as he receives at least 10. Thus, there is a potential surplus or gain from trade of 2. Jane and the dealer bargain over the transaction price, *p*. If they cannot agree on a price, then the transaction does not occur, and neither party receives any surplus. What is the Nash bargaining solution to this game?

Answer

1. *Calculate the Nash product.* If Jane buys the car for price p, her net surplus is $12 - p$. If Bo sells the car for price p, he gets p but must part with a car worth 10 to him, so his net surplus is $p - 10$. Thus, the Nash product is

$$NP = (12 - p)(p - 10).$$

2. *Solve for the p that maximizes the Nash product.* NP is positive if p is more than 10 and less than 12, but it is zero if $p = 10$ or $p = 12$, and it is negative if p is less than 10 or greater than 12. Therefore, the solution must be between 10 and 12. By plotting NP or by using calculus, we can determine that the p that maximizes NP is 11.

Comment: This Nash bargaining solution produces the plausible result that the two parties split the available surplus or gains from trade. Jane values the car at 12, pays 11, and is left with surplus of 1. Bo receives 11, values the car at 10, so he earns a net surplus of 1. A person's bargaining position is weaker the more that person stands to lose if they cannot reach an agreement. In Question 4.1 at the end of the chapter, you are asked to show that if Bo can get only 9 elsewhere, the Nash bargaining solution changes in Jane's favor.

Using Calculus

Maximizing the Nash Product

We can use calculus to solve for the price, p, that maximizes the Nash product, NP. In our example, $NP = (12 - p)(p - 10) = 22p - p^2 - 120$. To find the maximum, we set the derivative of NP with respect to p equal to zero:

$$\frac{dNP}{dp} = 22 - 2p = 0.$$

Using algebra, we can rewrite this expression as $2p = 22$ or $p = 11$, which is the price that maximizes the NP.

Mini-Case

Nash Bargaining over Coffee

In Britain, France, Germany, the United States, and other developed countries, many managers believe that big-box retail chains are increasingly squeezing manufacturer margins due to the consolidation of the retail sector and the rapid growth of big-box store brands. To examine this belief, Draganska, Klapper, and Villas-Boas (2010) investigated how grocery store chains and ground coffee manufacturers bargain over the wholesale price that the manufacturers charge the retailers.[16]

Draganska et al., considered two ways in which the Nash bargaining solution might vary with the party's characteristics. First, a firm's bargaining position depends on that firm's disagreement point, d_R for the retailer or d_M for the manufacturer. Second, Draganska et al., estimated a commonly used generalization of the Nash product, where $NP = (\pi_R - d_R)^a(\pi_M - d_M)^{1-a}$, where a indicates the bargaining power of the parties. The larger a is, the more bargaining power that the retailer has and the less the manufacturer has.

They estimated how d_R, d_M, and a vary with the characteristics of the firms, using data from Germany's six largest supermarket chains—Edeka, Markant, Metro, Rewe, Spar, and Tengelmann—which account for 80% of the German grocery market, and its seven largest ground coffee manufacturers—Dallmayr, Eduscho, Idee, Jacobs, Melitta, Onko, and Tchibo—which control more than 95% of the ground coffee market.

They found that bargaining power lies mainly with manufacturers: on average, the manufacturer gets more than half of the profits ($a < 0.5$). The larger the manufacturer size, the greater the manufacturer's bargaining power and hence the larger the manufacturer's share of profit. Similarly, larger retailers have more bargaining power. In addition, retailers that position their store brands close to national brands reduce the wholesale margins by nearly a quarter (24%).

Inefficiency in Bargaining

The Nash bargaining solution presumes that the parties achieve an efficient outcome where neither party could be made better off without harming the other party. However, in the real world, bargaining frequently yields inefficient outcomes.

---

[16]Bargaining not only affects how profits are split between manufacturers and retailers—the share of the pie—but it determines the prices paid by consumers and hence total profits—the size of the pie. For example, if a brand's high wholesale price drives up the retail price, consumers may substitute other brands or go to another retailer.

One common type of inefficiency occurs because the bargaining process takes time, which delays the start of the benefit flow and therefore reduces the value of benefits overall. That is, it makes the pie to be divided smaller than it need be. An extreme example of a loss due to delaying reaching an agreement is a strike. When a union is on strike, workers do not receive wages from the firm, and the firm cannot produce and sell its product efficiently, if at all.

Strikes may occur because of irrational behavior or limited information. Union-management negotiations may become so acrimonious that the parties act irrationally, leading to a costly strike. More commonly, negotiators fail to quickly reach an agreement due to bounded rationality or incomplete information about the other side's payoffs. The parties are doing the best they can but are unable to determine the best possible strategies and therefore they make mistakes. A union may strike or the employer may shut down operations to convince the other party that failing to reach an agreement has high costs.

12.5 Auctions

We now turn to another important type of game, called an **auction**: a sale in which a good or service is sold to the highest bidder. In auctions, players normally devise bidding strategies without knowing other players' payoff functions.

A substantial amount of exchange takes place through auctions. Government contracts are typically awarded using procurement auctions. In recent years, governments have auctioned portions of the airwaves for radio stations, mobile phones, and wireless Internet access and have used auctions to set up electricity and transport markets. Other goods commonly sold at auction are natural resources such as timber and drilling rights for oil, as well as houses, cars, agricultural produce, horses, antiques, and art. On the Internet, many goods can be purchased on auction websites such as eBay. In this section, we first consider the various types of auctions and then investigate how the rules of the auction influence buyers' strategies.

Elements of Auctions

Before deciding what strategy to use when bidding in an auction, a bidder (or player) needs to know the rules of the game. Auctions have three key components: the number of units being sold, the format of the bidding, and the value that potential bidders place on the good.

Number of Units. Auctions can be used to sell one or many units of a good. In 2004, Google auctioned its initial public offering of many identical shares of stock at one time. In many other auctions, a single good—such as an original painting—is sold. For simplicity in this discussion, we concentrate on auctions where a single, indivisible item is sold.

Format of Bidding. How auctions are conducted varies greatly. However, most approaches are variants of the *English auction*, the *Dutch auction*, or the *sealed-bid auction*.

▶ **English auction**. Most people have seen an *English* or *ascending-bid auction*, at least on TV or in the movies. The auctioneer starts the bidding at the lowest price that is acceptable to the seller and then repeatedly encourages potential buyers to bid more than the previous highest bidder. The auction ends when no one is willing to bid more than the current highest bid: "Going, going, gone!" The good is sold to the last bidder for the highest bid. Sotheby's and Christie's use English auctions to sell art and antiques.

▶ **Dutch auction.** A *Dutch auction* or *descending-bid auction* ends dramatically with the first bid. The seller starts by asking if anyone wants to buy at a relatively high price. The seller reduces the price by given increments until someone accepts the offered price and buys at that price. Variants of Dutch auctions are often used to sell multiple goods at once, such as in Google's initial public offering auction and the U.S. Treasury's sales of Treasury bills.

▶ **Sealed-bid auction.** In a *sealed-bid auction*, everyone submits a bid simultaneously without seeing anyone else's bid (for example, by submitting each bid in a sealed envelope), and the highest bidder wins. The price the winner pays depends on whether it is a first-price auction or a second-price auction. In a *first-price auction*, the winner pays its own, highest bid. Governments often use this type of auction. In a *second-price auction*, the winner pays the amount bid by the second-highest bidder. Many computer auction houses use a variant of the second-price auction.

For example, you bid on eBay by specifying the maximum amount you are willing to bid. If your maximum is greater than the maximum bid of other participants, eBay's computer places a bid on your behalf that is a small increment above the maximum bid of the second-highest bidder. This system differs from the traditional sealed-bid auction in that people can continue to bid until the official end-time of the auction, and potential bidders know the current bid price (but not the maximum that the highest bidder is willing to pay). Thus, eBay has some of the characteristics of an English auction.

Value. Auctioned goods are normally described as having a *private value* or a *common value*. Typically, this distinction turns on whether the good is unique.

▶ **Private value.** If each potential bidder places a different personal value on the good, we say that the good has a *private value*. Individual bidders know how much the good is worth to them but not how much other bidders value it. One example is an original work of art about which people differ greatly as to how much they value it.

▶ **Common value.** Many auctions involve a good that has the same fundamental value to everyone, but no buyer knows exactly what that *common value* is. For example, in a timber auction, firms bid on all the trees in a given area. All firms know what the current price of lumber is; however, they do not know exactly the volume of lumber contained in the trees.

In many actual auctions, both private value and common value are present. For example, in the tree auction, bidding firms may differ not only in their estimates of the amount of lumber in the trees (common value), but also in their costs of harvesting (private value).

Bidding Strategies in Private-Value Auctions

A potential buyer's optimal strategy depends on the number of units, the format, and the type of values in an auction. In order to be specific, we examine auctions in which each bidder places a different private value on a single, indivisible good.

Second-Price Auction Strategies. According to eBay, if you choose to bid on an item in its second-price auction, you should "enter the maximum amount you are willing to spend."[17] Is eBay's advice correct?

In a traditional sealed-bid, second-price auction, bidding your highest value *weakly dominates* (is at least as good as) all other bidding strategies: The strategy of bidding your maximum value leaves you *as well off* as, *or better off* than, bidding any other value. The amount that you bid affects whether you win, but it does not affect how much you pay if you win, which equals the second-highest bid.

Suppose that you value a folk art carving at $100. If the highest amount that any other participant is willing to bid is $85 and you place a bid greater than $85, you will buy the carving for $85 and receive $15 (= $100 − $85) of consumer surplus. Other bidders pay nothing and gain no consumer surplus.

Should you ever bid more than your value? Suppose that you bid $120. There are three possibilities. First, if the highest bid of your rivals is greater than $120, then you do not buy the good and receive no consumer surplus. If you had instead bid your valuation of the carving, $100, you still would have lost the auction and received no consumer surplus. Thus, bidding higher than $100 does not benefit you.

Second, if the highest alternative bid is less than $100, then you win and receive the same consumer surplus that you would have received had you bid $100. Again, bidding higher does not affect the outcome.

Third, if the highest bid by a rival is between $100 and $120—say, $110—then bidding more than your maximum value causes you to win, but you purchase the good for more than you value it, so you receive negative consumer surplus: −$10 (= $100 − $110). In contrast, if you had bid your maximum value, you would not have won, and your consumer surplus would have been zero—which is better than losing $10. Thus, bidding more than your maximum value can never make you better off than bidding your maximum value. Instead, you may actually be worse off.

Should you ever bid less than your maximum value, say, $90? No, because you only lower the odds of winning without affecting the price that you pay if you do win. If the highest alternative bid is less than $90 you win the auction and pay the same price whether you bid $100 or $90, so there is no effect in this case. If the alternative bid exceeds $100, you do not win the auction whether you bid $100 or $90, so again there is no difference. However, if the highest alternative bid lies between $90 and $100, you will lose the auction by bidding $90 and will give up the positive consumer surplus you would have gained if you had bid your true value of $100 and won the auction. You are therefore worse off by underbidding in this case.

Thus, you do as well or better by bidding your value than by over- or underbidding. This argument does not turn on whether or not you know other bidders' valuation. If you know your own value but not other bidders' values, bidding your value is your best strategy. If everyone follows this strategy, the person who places the highest value on the good will win and will pay the second-highest value.

Mini-Case	We've seen that bidding one's value is the dominant strategy in a sealed-bid, second-price auction. Economics professors conducting experimental sealed-bid, second-price auctions under "laboratory" settings using college students as subjects have been surprised to observe many overbids—bids that
Experienced Bidders	

---

[17]**pages.ebay.com/education/gettingstarted/researching.html** (viewed March 30, 2013).

exceed the bidder's value—and few underbids. Garratt et al. (2012) provided an explanation. The students participating in these experiments had little prior experience bidding in auctions. Would experienced bidders use better strategies?

Garratt et al. repeated the experiment using people with extensive experience in eBay auctions. Auctions on eBay are second-price auctions that occur over time rather than sealed-bid auctions. The researchers found that even these experienced bidders did not always bid their values. However, unlike the inexperienced subjects, these bidders did not exhibit a systematic bias: They were just as likely to underbid as to overbid.

English Auction Strategy. Suppose instead that the seller uses an English auction to sell the carving to bidders with various private values. Your best strategy is to raise the current highest bid as long as your bid is less than the value you place on the good, $100. If the current bid is $85, you should increase your bid by the smallest permitted amount, say, $86, which is less than your value. If no one raises the bid further, you win and receive a positive surplus of $14. By the same reasoning, it always pays to increase your bid up to $100, where you receive zero surplus if you win.

However, it never pays to bid more than $100. The best outcome that you can hope for is to lose and receive zero surplus. Were you to win, you would have negative surplus.

If all participants bid up to their value, the winner will pay slightly more than the value of the second-highest bidder. Thus, the outcome is essentially the same as in the sealed-bid, second-price auction.

Equivalence of Auction Outcomes. For Dutch or first-price sealed-bid auctions, one can show that participants *shave* their bids to less than their value. The intuition for this result is based on your lack of knowledge about the values of the other bidders. Reducing your bid reduces the probability that you win but increases your consumer surplus if you win. Your optimal bid, which balances these two effects, is lower than your actual value. Your bid depends on your beliefs about the strategies of your rivals. It can be shown that the best strategy is to bid an amount that is equal to or slightly greater than what you expect will be the second-highest bid, given that your value is the highest.

Thus, the expected outcome is the same under each format for private-value auctions: The winner is the person with the highest value, and the winner pays roughly the second-highest value. According to the Revenue Equivalence Theorem (Klemperer, 2004), under certain plausible conditions we would expect the same revenue from any auction in which the winner is the person who places the highest value on the good.

When you query Google, paid advertising appears next to your search results. The ads that appear vary with your search term. By making searches for unusual topics easy and fast, Google helps firms reach difficult-to-find potential customers with targeted ads. For example, a lawyer specializing in toxic mold lawsuits can place an ad that is seen only by people who search for "toxic mold lawyer." Such focused advertising has higher profit per view than traditional print and broadcast ads that reach much larger, nontargeted groups ("wasted eyeballs") and avoids the problem of finding addresses for direct mailing.

Google uses auctions to price these ads. Advertisers are willing to bid more to be listed first on Google's page. Goldfarb and Tucker (2011) found that how much lawyers will pay for context-based ads depends on the difficulty of making a match. Lawyers will pay more to advertise when there are fewer self-identified potential customers—fewer people searching for a particular phrase.

They also found that lawyers bid more when there are fewer customers, and hence the need to target ads is greater. Some states have anti-ambulance-chaser regulations, which prohibit personal injury lawyers from directly contacting potential clients by mail, phone, or e-mail for a few months after an accident. In those states, the extra amount bid for ads linked to personal injury keywords rather than for other keywords such as "tax lawyer" is 5% to 7% more than in unregulated states.

By taking advantage of advertisers' desire to reach small, difficult-to-find segments of the population and by varying the price according to advertisers' willingness to pay, Google is using individual price discrimination (Chapter 11).

The Winner's Curse

Unlike in private-value auctions, in common-value auctions, a phenomenon called **the winner's curse** occurs in which the auction winner's bid exceeds the common-value item's value. The overbidding occurs when there is uncertainty about the true value of the good.[18]

When the government auctions off timber on a plot of land, potential bidders may differ in their estimates of how many board feet of lumber are available on that land. Typically, bidders' estimates of the value are distributed randomly around the true value. If these people place bids close to their estimates, then the highest bid is likely to be made by a bidder with a very optimistic estimate, and the bid itself is likely to exceed the true value. The "winner" ends up paying too much, which is the winner's curse.

Rational bidders adjust their bids to avoid the winner's curse. Each bidder reasons that "I can reduce the likelihood of falling prey to the winner's curse by *shading* or reducing my bid below my estimate. I know that if I win, I am probably overestimating the value of the good. The amount by which I should shade my bid depends on the number of other bidders, because the more bidders, the more likely that the winning bid is an overestimate."

Although rational managers should avoid the winner's curse, economists have observed the winner's curse in many situations. An important example is the takeover market: the market for corporate acquisitions.[19]

One possible reason for the winner's curse is that bidders have bounded rationality. It is difficult to calculate the correct adjustment that should be made to

---

[18]Mike Shor has a clever website, **www.gametheory.net/mike/applets/winnercurse**, which demonstrates the winner's curse. You are asked, "How much should you offer for a company of uncertain valuation?" You can try various bidding strategies to see which works best.

[19]See Thaler (1994) for many examples of the winner's curse, including a discussion of corporate takeovers.

a bid to offset the winner's curse. Even if most bidders correctly adjust, all it takes to generate a winner's curse is one optimistic bidder who does not adjust properly.

Managerial Implication

Auction Design

Managers who sell assets using auctions need to understand how an auction's design affects bidders' behavior. Because intelligent bidders shade their bids, sellers of common-value goods can do better with an English auction than with a sealed-bid auction. In an English auction, bidders may revise their views about the object's value as they watch others bid.

Many sellers have learned this lesson. For example, online auction sites such as eBay do not use sealed bid auctions but use English auctions or other types of auctions instead. This lesson is one that many governments have failed to learn. They continue to rely heavily on sealed-bid auctions even though it is likely they would earn more money if they used an English auction to sell lumber, rights to airwaves, and other property.

Managerial Solution

Dying to Work

In the Managerial Problem questions at the beginning of the chapter, we asked whether a firm underinvests in safety if the firm knows how dangerous a job is but potential employees do not. Can the government intervene to improve this situation?

Consider an industry with two firms that are simultaneously deciding whether to make costly safety investments such as sprinkler systems in a plant or escape tunnels in a mine. Unlike the firms, potential employees do not know how safe it is to work at each firm. They only know how risky it is to work in this industry. If only Firm 1 invests, workers in the industry do not know that safety has improved at only Firm 1's plant. Because the government's accident statistics for the industry fall, workers realize that it is safer to work in the industry, so both firms pay lower wages.

The profit table shows how the firms' profits depend on their safety investments. Firm 1 has a dominant strategy. If Firm 2 invests (compare profits in the cells in the right column), Firm 1's *no investment* strategy has a higher profit, 250, than its *investment* strategy, 225. Similarly, if Firm 2 does not invest (compare the cells in the left column), Firm 1's profit is higher if it doesn't invest, 200, than if it does. Thus, not investing is the dominant strategy and investing is the dominated strategy, as is indicated by the horizontal red line through the investing strategy. Because the game is symmetric, the same reasoning shows that not investing is the dominant strategy for Firm 2 as well.

Because both firms have a dominant strategy of not investing, that combination of dominant strategies (the upper left cell) is the Nash

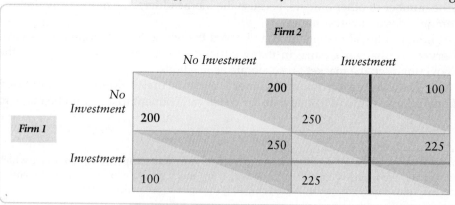

equilibrium. Both firms receive an equilibrium profit of 200. If both firms invest in safety (the lower right cell), each earns 225, which is more than they earn in the Nash equilibrium. However, investment by both firms is not an equilibrium, because each firm can increase its profit from 225 to 250 by not investing if the other firm invests.

The firms are engaged in a prisoners' dilemma game. *Because each firm bears the full cost of its safety investments but derives only some of the benefits, the firms underinvest in safety.*

This prisoners' dilemma outcome results because workers cannot tell which firm is safer. If workers know how safe each firm is, only a firm that invests in safety would be able to pay a lower wage, which would change the profits and increase the likelihood that firms invest in safety. Thus, if the government or a union were to collect and provide workers with firm-specific safety information, the firms might opt to invest. However, for the government or a union to provide this information, their cost of gathering the necessary information has to be relatively low.

SUMMARY

1. **Oligopoly Games.** Interactions between firms can often be analyzed and understood using a set of tools known as game theory. Such interactions or games are particularly important in oligopolies where a small number of firms compete and hence each firm's action affects the profits of other firms. A game in which players act simultaneously and act only once is called a static game. Games with repeated or sequential actions are called dynamic games and are analyzed in the next chapter. A combination of player strategies is a Nash equilibrium if, given that all other players use these strategies, no one player can obtain a higher profit by independently choosing a different strategy. In many games, we can find Nash equilibria by eliminating dominated strategies or by examining all firms' best responses to the actions of other firms.

2. **Types of Nash Equilibria.** If each player has a dominant strategy—a strategy that is best no matter what the rivals do—we expect that strategy to be played. If all players have a dominant strategy and play it, the outcome is called a dominant strategy solution. Such a solution is the only possible Nash equilibrium. A game without dominant strategies may also have a unique Nash equilibrium, but some games have multiple Nash equilibria, in which case additional considerations can sometimes be used to predict the likely outcome. For example, if one Nash equilibrium is better for all players than another, the Pareto criterion selects that preferred equilibrium. Some games have no Nash equilibria in pure strategies, where each firm chooses a particular strategy with certainty. In games with no pure-strategy Nash equilibria and in games with multiple pure-strategy Nash equilibria, there may be mixed-strategy Nash equilibria, where players randomize over two or more pure strategies.

3. **Information and Rationality.** In some games, players have complete information about the payoffs and possible strategies of other players. However, participants in games may sometimes lack important information and, in particular, might be uninformed about their rivals' payoffs or strategies. We typically assume that players are rational and can therefore determine their best strategies based on the information they have. Players that have imperfect powers of calculation and might therefore be unable to calculate optimal strategies are said to have *bounded rationality.*

4. **Bargaining.** An important business activity is bargaining: Buyers and sellers negotiate the price of a good such as a house or a car, and employers and unions engage in collective bargaining over wages and work rules. One possible outcome of bargaining games is the Nash bargaining solution, in which the product of the parties' net surplus from bargaining is maximized.

5. **Auctions.** Auctions are games of incomplete information if bidders do not know the valuation others place on a good. Buyers' optimal strategies depend on the characteristics of an auction. Under fairly general conditions, if the auction rules result

in a win by the person placing the highest value on a good that various bidders value differently, the expected price is the same in all auctions. For example, the expected price in various types of private-value auctions is the value of the good to the person who values it second-highest. In auctions where everyone values the good the same, though they may differ in their estimates of that value, the successful bidder may suffer from the winner's curse—paying too much—unless bidders shade their bids to compensate for their over-optimistic estimation of the good's value.

QUESTIONS

*All exercises are available on MyEconLab; * = answer at the back of this book; C = use of calculus may be necessary.*

1. Oligopoly Games

*1.1. Show the profit matrix and explain the reasoning in the prisoners' dilemma example where Larry and Duncan, possible criminals, will get one year in prison if neither talks, two years in jail if both talk, and if one talks that one goes free while the other gets five years. (*Note*: The payoffs are negative because they represent years in jail, which is a negative payoff.)

1.2. Two firms compete by advertising. Given the payoff matrix to this advertising game, identify each firm's best response to its rival's possible actions. Does either firm have a dominant strategy? What is the Nash equilibrium?

		Firm 1	
		Do Not Advertise	Advertise
Firm 2	Do Not Advertise	1 / 2	0 / 0
	Advertise	2 / 4	1 / 3

1.3. Two firms face the following profit matrix:

		Firm 1	
		Low Price	High Price
Firm 2	Low Price	0 / 2	2 / 1
	High Price	6 / 0	7 / 6

Is it true that, given these profits, Firm 2 wants to match Firm 1's price, but Firm 1 does not want to match Firm 2's price? Does either firm have a dominant strategy? What is the Nash equilibrium in this game? Explain.

*1.4. Suppose that Toyota and GM are considering entering a market for electric automobiles and that their profits (in millions of dollars) from entering or staying out of the market are

		GM	
		Enter	Do Not Enter
Toyota	Enter	-40 / 10	0 / 250
	Do Not Enter	200 / 0	0 / 0

If the firms make their decisions simultaneously, do either or both firms enter? How would your answer change if the U.S. government committed to paying GM a lump-sum subsidy of $50 million on the condition that it would produce this new type of car?

1.5. Firm 1 and Firm 2 manufacture blankets. They compete in quality. Given their payoff matrix, identify each firm's best response to its rival's actions. What is the Nash equilibrium? (*Hint*: See Q&A 12.1.)

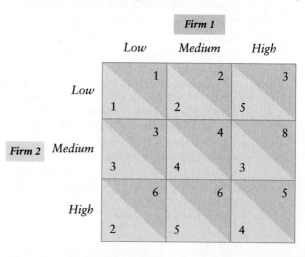

		Firm 1		
		Low	Medium	High
Firm 2	Low	1 / 1	2 / 2	3 / 5
	Medium	3 / 3	4 / 4	8 / 3
	High	6 / 2	6 / 5	5 / 4

1.6. Modify Question 1.5 so that if Firm 1 chooses High and Firm 2 chooses Low (the upper right corner), Firm 1 receives 1 rather than 3. How does that change your answer?

2. Types of Nash Equilibria

2.1. Assume the network scheduling profit matrix is

How many pure-strategy Nash equilibria does this game have? Explain.

*2.2. Given the network profit matrix in Question 2.1, can cheap talk help the networks settle on a single equilibrium? Why or why not?

2.3. Given the network profit matrix in Question 2.2, can the Pareto criterion help the networks settle on a single equilibrium? Explain.

2.4. Two firms face the following profit matrix:

Given these profits, Firm 2 wants to match Firm 1's price, but Firm 1 does not want to match Firm 2's price. Does either firm have a dominant strategy? Does this game have a unique, pure-strategy Nash equilibrium? Identify all pure- and mixed-strategy Nash equilibria.

2.5. Suppose that you and a friend play a "matching pennies" game in which each of you uncovers a penny. If both pennies show heads or both show tails, you keep both. If one shows heads and the other shows tails, your friend keeps them. Show the payoff matrix. What, if any, is the pure-strategy Nash equilibrium to this game? Is there a mixed-strategy Nash equilibrium? If so, what is it? (*Hint*: See the Appendix 12 to see how to solve for a mixed strategy equilibrium.)

2.6. Takashi Hashiyama, president of the Japanese electronics firm Maspro Denkoh Corporation, was torn between having Christie's or Sotheby's auction the company's $20 million art collection, which included a van Gogh, a Cézanne, and an early Picasso (Carol Vogel, "Rock, Paper, Payoff," *New York Times*, April 29, 2005, A1, A24). He resolved the issue by having the two auction houses' representatives compete in the playground game of rock-paper-scissors. A rock (fist) breaks scissors (two fingers sticking out), scissors cut paper (flat hand), and paper smothers rock. At stake were several million dollars in commissions. Christie's won: scissors beat paper.

a. Show the profit or payoff matrix for this rock-paper-scissors game where the payoff is -1 if you lose, 0 if you tie, and 1 if you win.

b. Sotheby's expert in Impressionist and modern art said, "[T]his is a game of chance, so we didn't really give it much thought. We had no strategy in mind." In contrast, the president of Christie's in Japan researched the psychology of the game and consulted with the 11-year-old twin daughters of the director of the Impressionist and modern art department. One of these girls said, "Everybody knows you always start with scissors. Rock is way too obvious, and scissors beats paper." The other opined, "Since they were beginners, scissors was definitely the safest." Evaluate these comments on strategy. What strategy would you recommend if you knew that your rival was consulting with 11-year-old girls? In general, what pure or mixed strategy would you have recommended, and why?

2.7. The recent recession hit young people particularly hard. In June 2010, 15.3% of 20- to 24-year-old Americans were unemployed, compared to 8.2% for older workers. As a result, more adult children moved back to live with their parents or asked for financial help than in previous years. The share of 25- to 34-year-olds living in multigenerational households rose from 11% in 1980 to 20% in 2008. A recent survey finds that 41% of parents provide financial support to their 23- to 28-year-old offspring. Indeed, parents give 10% of their income on average to their adult children. Mimi wants to support her son Jeff if he looks for work but not otherwise. Jeff (unlike most young people) wants to try to find a job only if his mother will not support his life of indolence. Their payoff matrix is

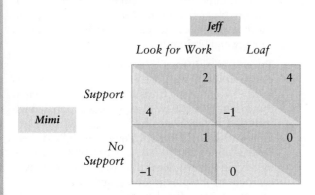

If Jeff and Mimi choose actions simultaneously, what are the pure- or mixed-strategy equilibria?

2.8. Lori employs Max. She wants him to work hard rather than to loaf. She considers offering him a bonus or not giving him one. All else the same, Max prefers to loaf.

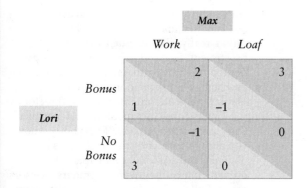

If they choose actions simultaneously, what are their strategies? Why does this game have a different type of equilibrium than the game in Question 2.7?

*2.9. Show that the mixed-strategy equilibrium for the game in Table 12.7 has both firms enter with probability $\frac{1}{3}$.

2.10. How would the analysis in Q&A 12.2 change if the payoffs to both firms are 3 in the upper left corner of the profit matrix (where both firms choose the Amazon standard) and the payoffs to both firms are 2 in the lower right corner, where both firms use the ePub standard?

3. Information and Rationality

*3.1. Suppose we have the following payoff matrix for a complementary investment game. The number in the lower left corner is the payoff to Wild and Crazy Guys (WCG). The other number is the payoff to Blues Brothers Investments (BB).

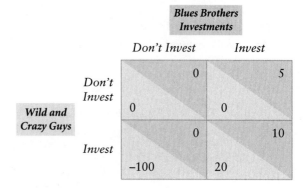

a. Is there a dominant strategy for either player?

b. What is the Nash equilibrium?

c. What is the maximin solution?

d. How would the reputation of Blues Brothers affect the likely outcome?

3.2. How do your answers to Question 3.1 change if everything in the profit matrix remains the same except that Blues Brothers loses 5 (payoff is −5) if it invests and WCG doesn't invest (the upper right cell in the matrix)?

3.3. Traditionally, the Harrison Resort Hotel sponsors an annual festival, making a significant investment in marketing to attract tourists to its hotel. Julie, the manager of nearby Lakeshore Flowers, normally orders extra merchandise in preparation for the festival. However, Harrison was recently bought by a large chain, so its management has changed. Julie is not sure that the new manager knows that investing in marketing will benefit Harrison.

	Harrison Hotel	
	Don't Invest	Invest
Don't Invest	0 / 0	0 / 5
Invest	0 / −20	10 / 6

a. What is the Nash equilibrium in this game?

b. What can Julie do to make sure that Harrison's new manager does what's best for the resort (and also best for her)?

4. Bargaining

4.1. In the used car bargaining problem in Q&A 12.3, if Bo can get only 9 elsewhere, does the Nash bargaining solution change in Jane's favor? Why?

*4.2. Oculus and Maxygen are small drug companies. Oculus has obtained a patent on a new antibiotic that is effective against an emerging superbug—a bacteria that is resistant to traditional antibiotics. Unfortunately, the Oculus drug has severe side effects, making the drug unsuitable except for patients who are desperate. Ownership of this drug is worth $10 (million) to Oculus under the current situation. Maxygen has a patent on another drug that is of no therapeutic value in itself, so the drug generates no current income for Maxygen. However, when combined in a particular way with the Oculus drug, it dramatically reduces the negative side effects. The value of the two drugs together is estimated at $50 (million). Maxygen is negotiating to sell its patent to Oculus. What price would be implied by the Nash bargaining solution? (*Hint*: See Q&A 12.3.) **C**

4.3. Situations of the type described in Question 4.2 are fairly common in the drug business and sales of patent rights are common. However, sometimes negotiations over such sales take a long time and sometimes negotiations are unsuccessful. Why would such wasteful outcomes occur?

5. Auctions

5.1. Charity events often use silent auctions. A donated item, such as a date with a movie star, is put up for bid. (See **www.ecorazzi.com/2008/02/22/ebay-and-oxfam-help-you-win-a-date-with-colin-firth** for a description of auctions for celebrity dates with Colin Firth and Scarlett Johansson.) In a silent auction, bidders write down bids and submit them. Some silent auctions use secret bids, which are submitted in sealed envelopes and kept confidential. Other silent auctions are open: the bidder writes down a bid on a bulletin board that everyone present can see. Which kind of auction would you expect to raise more revenue for the charity?

5.2. At the end of performances of his Broadway play "Cyrano de Bergerac," Kevin Kline, who starred as Cyrano, the cavalier poet with a huge nose, auctioned his prosthetic proboscis, which he and his co-star, Jennifer Garner, autographed (Mitchell, Dan, "This Time, Santa Has Been Too Naughty," *New York Times*, December 9, 2007) to benefit Broadway Cares in its fight against AIDS. An English auction was used. One night, a television producer grabbed the nose for $1,400, while the next night it fetched $1,600. On other nights it sold for $3,000 and $900. Why did the value fluctuate substantially from

night to night? Which bidder's bid determined the sales price? How was the auction price affected by the audience's knowledge that the proceeds would go to charity? Why?

5.3. Suppose that Firm 1, Firm 2, and Firm 3 are the only three firms interested in the lot at the corner of First Street and Glendon Way. The lot is being auctioned by a second-price sealed-bid auction. Suppose Firm 1 values the lot at $20,000, Firm 2 at $18,500, and Firm 3 at $16,800. Each bidding firm's surplus is $v_i - p$ if it wins the auction and 0 if it loses. The values are private. What is each bidder's optimal bid? Which firm wins the auction, and what price does that firm pay?

6. Managerial Problem

6.1. In the Managerial Solution safety game, could cheap talk lead both firms to invest in safety? Why or why not? What is the minimum fine that the government could levy on firms that do not invest in safety that would lead to a Nash equilibrium in which both firms invest?

7. Spreadsheet Exercises

7.1. General Mills and Kellogg's major rivals in the breakfast cereal market, decide simultaneously on their advertising strategies. Each has five options, *A* through *E*. The following table shows their net profits (in millions of dollars) for various advertising strategy combinations. In each cell, the first entry is the profit for Kellogg's and the second is the profit for General Mills.

		General Mills				
		A	*B*	*C*	*D*	*E*
	A	23, 22	37, 18	42, 11	21, 20	25, 15
	B	11, 24	30, 20	27, 29	25, 22	27, 27
Kellogg's	*C*	32, 18	28, 22	30, 20	37, 18	34, 16
	D	19, 20	41, 26	38, 24	32, 25	28, 23
	E	21, 31	33, 17	25, 22	30, 19	23, 28

a. Use Excel to create a spreadsheet showing only the payoff to Kellogg's arising from each strategy combination. For each possible strategy for General Mills (that is, for each column), determine the best response for Kellogg's. (*Hint*: Use the MAX function to find the maximum value for each column.) Does Kellogg's have a dominant strategy?

b. In the same spreadsheet, create a new block of entries showing the payoff to General Mills for each strategy combination. For each possible strategy of Kellogg's identify General Mills' highest possible payoff and corresponding best strategy.

c. Determine the Nash equilibrium for this game. Is it a dominant-strategy equilibrium?

7.2. Atlas Construction wants to buy some custom equipment from Vulcan Manufacturing. Atlas's maximum willingness to pay for the equipment is $320 (thousand). Vulcan is willing to sell the equipment as long as it gets at least $260 (thousand). The two companies bargain over the price, p. The net benefit to Atlas is $320 - p$ and the net benefit to Vulcan is $p - 260$. The Nash product is the product of these two benefits.

a. Use Excel to create a spreadsheet with columns for the price, the benefit to Atlas, the benefit to Vulcan, and the Nash product. Let the price go from 260 to 320 in increments of 10 and find the price that maximizes the Nash product.

b. Now suppose that Atlas' maximum willingness to pay is only 300. What is the price that arises from Nash bargaining now? Explain why the price would change in this way.

Appendix 12   Determining a Mixed Strategy

We use the example in Table 12.6, the design competition, to illustrate how a firm picks the probabilities it uses in a mixed strategy. Each firm maximizes its expected profit by using a mixed strategy such that its rival is indifferent between choosing either of the two styles. If its rival were not indifferent, the firm could do better by picking a different mixed strategy, as we now illustrate.

Consider the upstart firm's choice between the two actions (styles) if it knows that the probability that the established firm chooses the traditional style is θ. The upstart firm's expected payoff is $[\theta \times (-2)] + [(1 - \theta) \times 20] = 20 - 22\theta$ if it picks the traditional style and $[\theta \times 20] + [(1 - \theta) \times (-2)] = -2 + 22\theta$ if it picks the modern style. The upstart is indifferent between these two choices (pure strategies) if the two expected payoffs are equal: $20 - 22\theta = -2 + 22\theta$, or $22 = 44\theta$, or $\theta = \frac{1}{2}$.

Thus, given that the established firm used the mixed strategy $\theta = \frac{1}{2}$, the upstart is indifferent between using either pure strategy or the same mixed strategy, $\theta = \frac{1}{2}$. The upstart has no incentive to deviate from using a probability of $\frac{1}{2}$ for each style, as no other combination of probabilities would increase its expected payoff. The established firm is in the same position. Therefore, if each firm picks a probability of $\frac{1}{2}$, the result is a Nash equilibrium. Each firm is doing the best it can given its rival's strategy.

If the established firm picked any other θ, the upstart would choose one style with certainty. For example, if θ were greater than $\frac{1}{2}$, the upstart would pick the modern style and would win most (θ) of the time. Therefore, the established firm would not be happy with its choice, so $\theta > \frac{1}{2}$ is inconsistent with a mixed-strategy Nash equilibrium.

13 Strategies over Time

In solving a problem of this sort, the grand thing is to be able to reason backward.
—Sherlock Holmes (Sir Arthur Conan Doyle)

Intel and Advanced Micro Devices (AMD) dominate the central processing unit (CPU) market for personal computers, making 95% of total sales. Intel uses aggressive advertising—its very successful *Intel Inside* campaign—and charges relatively high prices, while AMD uses little advertising and relies on lower prices. Even though their products are comparable in quality, Intel controls more than three-quarters of the market.

Consumers are willing to pay a large premium for the Intel brand, according to Salgado's (2008) estimated demand functions. He found that if Intel increased its advertising by 10% (holding prices constant), the total market demand would increase by 1%, while Intel's relative share would rise by more than 3%. Demand for AMD products would therefore fall. Salgado's work indicates that the two firms' shares would be roughly equal if they advertised an equal amount (regardless of the level).

From the start of the personal computer era, Intel has been the 800-pound gorilla in the CPU market. Intel was founded in 1968 and created the first commercial microprocessor chip in 1971. With the growth of the personal computer (PC) market, microchips became Intel's primary business. Intel engages in a variety of strategic actions to dissuade AMD and other firms from taking its customers, including both aggressive advertising and lawsuits to protect its intellectual property. In 1991, Intel launched the "Intel Inside" marketing and branding campaign. Intel offered to share costs for any manufacturer's PC print ads if they included the Intel logo. Not only did these funds reduce the computer manufacturers' costs, but the logo was intended to assure consumers that their computers were powered by the latest technology. Within 6 months, 300 computer manufacturers had agreed to support the program. After the manufacturers' ads started to appear, Intel advertised around the world to explain the logo to consumers. The Intel Inside campaign was one of the first successful attempts at *ingredient branding*.

Advanced Micro Devices was founded in 1969, but didn't compete in the microchip market until 1975 when it started selling a reverse-engineered clone of the Intel 8080 microprocessor. In 1982, AMD and Intel signed a contract allowing AMD to be a licensed second-source manufacturer of Intel's 8086 and 8088 processors because IBM would use these chips in its PCs only if it had two sources for the chips.

Why have Intel's managers chosen to advertise aggressively while AMD engages in relatively little advertising? At the end of the chapter, we discuss one possible explanation: Intel was able to act first and thereby gain an advantage.

The business strategy games we studied in Chapters 11 and 12 are *static* games, in which firms make simultaneous decisions and in which each firm has just a single action to take, such as producing a particular output level, charging a particular price, or choosing a particular level of advertising.

However, many interactions between firms have a *dynamic* character, because firms act at different times. In a **dynamic game**, players move either repeatedly or sequentially. Therefore, dynamic games may be repeated games or sequential games.

In a *repeated game*, a basic component game or *constituent game* is repeated, perhaps many times. Firms choose from the same set of possible actions again and again. An example of a repeated game is a Cournot oligopoly game played period after period.

In a *sequential game*, one player moves before another moves, possibly making alternating moves, as in chess or tic-tac-toe. A game is also sequential if players have a sequence of different decisions to make, even if moves are made simultaneously with a rival. For example, two firms might play a game in which they initially simultaneously choose how much capital to invest and then later simultaneously decide how much output to produce.

In this chapter, we start with repeated games. We show that the strategies in these repeated games are more complex than the strategies employed when the constituent game is played only once. In a repeated game, moves made in one period can affect choices made in subsequent periods. Consequently, the equilibrium in a given period of a repeated game may differ from the equilibrium of a corresponding static game. In particular, we show that collusive behavior may be more likely in a repeated-game oligopoly than in a "one-shot" or static oligopoly setting.

Next, we turn to sequential games. We analyze an oligopoly model in which one firm (the leader) chooses an output level before its rival (the follower). We also examine sequential games in which managers must decide whether their firm should act to prevent potential rivals from entering the market, and in which managers must decide whether to introduce a new product. We show that the leader may gain an advantage over its rival because moving first allows it to *commit* to a particular output level and force the rival to react. Finally, we consider what happens if players are not fully rational.

Main Topics

In this chapter, we examine six main topics

1. **Repeated Games:** If a static game is repeated over many periods, firms may use more complex strategies than in the static one-period game because a firm's action in one period may affect its rivals' actions in subsequent periods.

2. **Sequential Games:** If one firm acts before its rival, it may gain an advantage by converting what would be an empty threat to its rival into a credible, observable action.

3. **Deterring Entry:** Whether a firm acts to prevent potential rivals from entering a market turns critically on whether the firm, by acting before its rivals, can commit to an action that deters entry and whether it pays for the firm to take that action.

4. **Cost Strategies:** A firm that can act first may gain a cost advantage over its rivals by making a capital investment that lowers its marginal cost of production, increasing its rate of learning by doing, or by taking other actions that raise its rivals' marginal cost by more than its own.

5. **Disadvantages of Moving First:** A firm that moves first may suffer if it makes an investment that makes it vulnerable to being exploited by another firm, or by entering a market too hastily so that later entrants have a better product.

6. **Behavioral Game Theory:** Some managers follow simple rules or make biased decisions based on psychological factors rather than deriving a fully rational strategy.

13.1 Repeated Games

In the previous chapter, we analyzed static games, in which firms compete only once. We now consider how firms change their strategies and how the game's equilibrium changes if a static game is repeated. The static constituent game might be played just once, repeated a finite (and prespecified) number of times, or repeated indefinitely.[1]

Strategies and Actions in Dynamic Games

In both static and dynamic games, managers need to be able to describe and understand the game and predict the likely outcome so they can determine their best strategies. To understand either a static or a dynamic game, a manager needs to know the players, the rules, the information that each firm has, and the payoffs or profits. However, a major difference between static and dynamic games is that dynamic games require us to distinguish between strategies and actions.

An *action* is a single move that a player makes at a specified time, such as choosing an output level or a price. A *strategy* is a battle plan that specifies the full set of actions that a player will make throughout the game and may involve actions that are conditional on prior actions of other players or on additional information available at a given time.

In a static game, an action and a strategy are identical. The game lasts for only one period, so the action taken in that period represents the full battle plan or strategy. For example, if two firms play a static game in which their only two possible actions are to set a high price or a low price, then the firms' only possible strategies are the same as the actions: set either a high price or a low price.

In contrast, in a repeated or sequential game, actions and strategies differ. If a static game in which the firms choose either a high price or a low price is played

---

[1]When we say that a game goes on indefinitely, we mean that the players do not anticipate a definite end point. Each period, the players believe that the game may be repeated in the next period.

repeatedly period after period, a firm's strategy determines its action in each period. One possible strategy is for the firm to set the low price in each period. However, it could use a more complex strategy, such as one in which its action in a given period depends on its rival's actions in previous periods. For example, a firm could set a high price in the first period and then, in subsequent periods, it could set its price at the same level that its rival chose in the previous period.

Cooperation in a Repeated Prisoner's Dilemma Game

Because firms may use more complex strategies in repeated games than in static games, the outcomes may differ. To illustrate this difference, we return to the real-world competition between American and United Airlines in which they compete for customers on the Chicago–Los Angeles route, which we examined in Chapter 12. Table 13.1 is the profit matrix for the airlines' static, one-period prisoners' dilemma game in which each firm's only possible actions are to produce a large output (fly 64 thousand passengers per quarter) or a small output (fly 48 thousand passengers per quarter).[2]

In Chapter 12, we noted that in the static game in Table 13.1 each firm has the dominant strategy of selecting the larger output. In the Nash equilibrium in which both firms use their dominant strategy, each firm receives a profit of $4.1 million, which is less than the $4.6 million that they would earn if they both produced the smaller output. Thus, our analysis of this static game demonstrates that a firm's best strategy is to pick an action that does not result in the collusive or cartel outcome.

This result is surprising because we know that some real-world firms collude (Chapter 11). Why does our analysis differ from reality? The problem does not lie with the logic behind our analysis of the prisoners' dilemma. Rather, the explanation is that we have been assuming that the game is played only once. In real-world markets, interactions between firms are often repeated. We now show that the cooperative or cartel outcome is more likely if the airlines' single-period prisoners' dilemma game in Table 13.1 is repeated indefinitely, quarter after quarter.

TABLE 13.1 An Airlines Prisoners' Dilemma Game with Two Actions

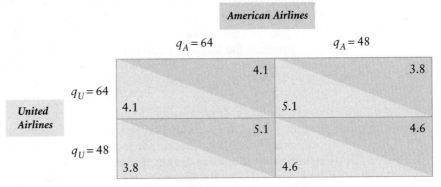

Note: Quantities are in thousands of passengers per quarter; (rounded) profits are in millions of dollars per quarter.

[2]Table 13.1 reproduces the profit matrix in Table 12.1, and is based on the estimates of Brander and Zhang (1990).

In a single-period game, each firm must choose its action *before* observing the rival's action. Therefore, a firm's choice cannot be influenced by its rival's action. It chooses its best response given what it *expects* the rival to do. When the same game is played repeatedly, United may use a strategy in which its action in the current period depends on American's observed actions in previous periods. American may use a similar strategy.

For example, in this repeated game each airline may use a strategy where it *threatens to punish* its rival in later periods by producing a high level of output if its rival produces a high level of output in an early period. In particular, suppose that American tells United in a pre-play communication (Chapter 12) that it will produce the smaller collusive or cooperative quantity in the first period, but that it will use the following two-part strategy to determine its output in subsequent periods:

▶ If United produces the smaller, cooperative quantity in all periods through period t, then American will produce the smaller, cooperative quantity in period $t + 1$.

▶ However, following the first period t, in which United produces the larger quantity, American will produce the larger quantity in period $t + 1$ and in all subsequent periods.

If United believes that American will follow this strategy, United knows that it will make $4.6 million each period if it produces the smaller quantity. Although United can make a higher profit, $5.1 million, in period t by producing the larger quantity, by doing so it lowers its potential profit to $4.1 million in each following period even if it continues to produce the high quantity. Thus, United gains half a million dollars relative to the cooperative payoff ($0.5 = $5.1 − $4.6) in the period when it first defects from the cooperative output, but it loses half a million dollars relative to cooperation (−$0.5 = $4.1 − $4.6) in each subsequent period. After only two punishment periods, the loss would be much larger in magnitude than the initial gain.

United's best policy is to produce the lower quantity in each period unless it cares greatly about current profit and little about future profits. If United values future profits nearly as much as current profits, the one-period gain from deviating from the collusive output level will not compensate for the losses from reduced profits in future periods, which is the punishment American will impose.[3]

Thus, if United believes that American will follow its announced strategy, it should produce the lower output level. But should United believe American? While United cannot be certain of American's future strategy, it is at least reasonable for United to take this threat by American seriously because American's best response is to produce the larger quantity if it believes it can't trust United to produce the smaller quantity. Thus, if firms play the same game *indefinitely*, they should find it easier to reach the lower (and more profitable) output level.

American's strategy is an example of a **trigger strategy**, a strategy in which a rival's defection from a collusive outcome triggers a punishment. In this case, the trigger strategy is extreme because a single defection calls for a firm to permanently punish its rival by producing the high output in all subsequent periods. However, if both firms adopt this trigger strategy, the outcome is a Nash equilibrium in which both firms choose the low output and obtain the collusive profit in every period: Defection and punishment need not occur. Less extreme trigger strategies can also

---

[3]Presumably a firm discounts future gains or losses (Chapter 7) because a dollar today is worth more than a dollar in the future. However, the effect of such discounting over a period as short as a few quarters is small.

be used. For example, a strategy that involved just two periods of punishment for a defection would still be likely to make defection unattractive in this example.

If the low-output strategy is so lucrative for everyone, why don't firms always cooperate when engaging in such indefinitely repeated games? One reason is that the cooperative outcome is not the only possible Nash equilibrium. This game has another Nash equilibrium in which each firm chooses the high output every period. If United believes that American will produce the high output in every period, then its best response is to produce the high output every period. This same reasoning also applies to American. Each firm's belief about its rival will be confirmed by experience and neither firm will have an incentive to change its strategy.

Firms would prefer the cooperative outcome and would probably achieve it in a game as straightforward as this one. However, such cooperation may not be possible in real markets because of antitrust and competition laws or because of limited information. For example, if a firm cannot observe its rival's sales directly, it may try to infer its rival's behavior from observing the demand for its own product. In such a game, the firm may not be able to tell if a dip in the demand for its product is due to its rival producing more or from a reduction in market demand. Appropriate punishments would become more difficult to devise and implicit agreement among firms would become more difficult to enforce.

The trigger strategy that we've been discussing is only one of many possible punishment strategies. Another is the **tit-for-tat strategy**, a strategy for repeated prisoners' dilemma games that involves cooperation in the first round and then copying the rival's previous action in each subsequent round. Thus, producing high output in one period would induce punishment (high output by the rival) in the next. In our airline example, the level of punishment in this tit-for-tat strategy might not be enough to induce cooperation, depending on how much firms discount future gains and losses relative to those in the current period. However, it might work well in other games, as the next Mini-Case illustrates.

Mini-Case	Although we focus primarily on business games, game theory is commonly applied in other areas as well, including military situations. One striking example of the tit-for-tat strategy arose in trench warfare in World War I, as Axelrod (2006) described.
Tit-for-Tat Strategies in Trench Warfare	

Although we focus primarily on business games, game theory is commonly applied in other areas as well, including military situations. One striking example of the tit-for-tat strategy arose in trench warfare in World War I, as Axelrod (2006) described.

No war is pleasant, but the violence in World War I was particularly awful, especially along the 500-mile Western Front in France and Belgium where Germany and its allies fought against the United Kingdom, France, and their allies. Soldiers on the two sides spent most of their time engaged in trench warfare: hiding in trenches, then occasionally standing up and taking shots at the enemy while hoping not to be shot. However, soldiers were sometimes ordered to charge soldiers in the opposing trenches. These actions usually resulted in a terrible loss of life while moving the front only a short distance.

Newcomers to the front were often surprised to discover that soldiers would apparently shoot over the heads of enemy soldiers, deliberately failing to take shots that had a high probability of killing the enemy. A British staff officer on a tour of the trenches remarked that he was "astonished to observe German soldiers walking about within rifle range behind their own line. Our men appeared to take no notice." The newcomers quickly discovered that a tit-for-tat strategy was being played, often referred to as a "live and let live" strategy.

Axelrod pointed out that the soldiers on the Western Front were engaged in a repeated prisoners' dilemma game. Soldiers needed to shoot their weapons, because the generals and other staff officers behind the lines expected to hear shooting when they approached the front. Given that soldiers had to shoot, they had two possible actions: shoot to kill or shoot to miss.

If the game was played only once—a one-day battle—then shooting to kill was a dominant strategy. Regardless of what the enemy did, preventing enemy soldiers from shooting at you by killing or disabling them offered you a better chance of survival than wasting shots. However, the game was played repeatedly, day after day, month after month, often in the same location. In this repeated game, a strategy that led to cooperation—not shooting to kill—was feasible.

Initially, if one side happened to unleash an unusually intense and damaging barrage of fire, the other side was likely to respond with an intense barrage of its own. Soon it became apparent that the way to avoid an intense barrage was not to initiate one. Adopting a "shoot to miss" strategy could induce the other side to do the same thing. Hence, when an enthusiastic new recruit started shooting aggressively at the enemy, experienced soldiers would yell at him to stop before he got everyone killed, as the enemy would fire back.

Implicit Versus Explicit Collusion

In most modern economies, explicit collusion among the firms in an industry is illegal. Firms are prohibited from meeting and agreeing to restrict their outputs or to set high prices. However, antitrust or competition laws do not strictly prohibit choosing the cooperative (cartel) quantity or price as long as no *explicit* agreement is reached.

Thus, if the firms never meet and openly discuss their behavior, they can produce at the collusive level with little chance of running afoul of the law.[4] Firms may be able to engage in such *implicit collusion* or *tacit collusion* using trigger, tit-for-tat, or other similar strategies. For example, if one firm lowers its output in the current period in the hopes that other firms will follow its lead in the next period, it may have stayed within the law as long as it doesn't explicitly communicate with the other firms. Nonetheless, tacit collusion lowers society's total surplus just as explicit collusion does.

Finitely Repeated Games

We have just seen that if firms repeat a prisoners' dilemma game, such as the one in Table 13.1, for an indefinite number of periods, they may achieve a cooperative (low-output) equilibrium. However, if the firms know that the game will be repeated only a finite number of times, T, then cooperation (both firms choosing the low output) is not a Nash equilibrium.

In the final period of the game, T, the firms know that they're not going to play again, so they are essentially playing a static prisoners' dilemma game in this last

---

[4]U.S. antitrust authorities may prosecute *tacit collusion plus*, where the *plus* indicates some communication that facilitated collusion between firms occurred, even if the communication stopped short of explicit talks about restricting output or setting high prices.

period. They know they can "cheat"—produce a large quantity—without fear of punishment. Thus, producing a large output in the final period is a dominant strategy for both firms.

As a result, the last period in which they might achieve the cooperative outcome is period $T - 1$. In period $T - 1$, each firm reasons that it will get punished in the final period in any case. No additional punishment can be imposed. Nothing the firm does in period $T - 1$ will influence what happens in period T. Therefore, the firms view the game in period $T - 1$ as they view a static prisoners' dilemma game. They have no incentive to produce the low output in period $T - 1$, because they cannot avoid subsequent punishment in period T. Thus, the dominant strategy for each firm in period $T - 1$ is to produce the large output, because that output maximizes the firm's return in period $T - 1$, regardless of what the rival does. Thus, period $T - 1$ is also a punishment period.

By the same reasoning, the firms will cheat in period $T - 2$ because they know that they will both cheat in period $T - 1$ anyway. Repeating this reasoning, we conclude that they will cheat in periods $T - 3$, $T - 4$, and so forth, all the way back to the first period. That is, any attempt by the firms to cooperate *unravels* at the very start of the game! The only Nash equilibrium is for the static, high-output equilibrium to occur in every period. Thus, maintaining an agreement to produce the small quantity (or to cooperate in any prisoners' dilemma game) will be more difficult if the game has a known stopping point and if players have complete foresight.[5]

13.2 Sequential Games

In a static Cournot game (Chapter 12), before the firms (simultaneously) choose their output levels, Firm 1 could threaten Firm 2 that it will produce a very large output. If Firm 2 believed that threat, it would be in Firm 2's best interest to reduce its output below the Cournot level, ceding an advantage to Firm 1. However, Firm 2 is unlikely to believe this threat as Firm 1 has not made any commitment to produce the large quantity and therefore might not do it. And Firm 2 could make the same threat, or at least could threaten to produce the Cournot quantity. Firm 1 should not be able to gain a strategic advantage over Firm 2 because they are in symmetric positions.

On the other hand, if Firm 1 produces a large quantity before Firm 2 can act, Firm 1's action is a commitment. The threat to produce a large output acquires credibility once the output is actually produced and observed by the rival. The follower has no choice but to accept that Firm 1 has produced a large output, so the follower chooses to produce less than it otherwise would. Such a game, where one firm moves before the other, is an example of a sequential game.

More generally, a sequential game can have many stages or decision points, such as a game where the players alternate moves indefinitely. In this section, we examine a sequential oligopoly game in which one firm acts before its rival does.

---

[5]However, cooperation can potentially be supported by trigger strategies if the game always has a chance of continuing to the next period. For example, suppose that one firm has a 20% chance of going out of business in any period. Sooner or later the firm will go out of business, but the rival can never be sure that the current period is the firm's last period and must always be concerned about the possibility of being punished in the next period if it deviates from the collusive output this period. As long as the time horizon is indefinite, a cooperative outcome is a possibility for suitable payoff functions.

Stackelberg Oligopoly

In Chapters 11 and 12, we examined oligopoly models, such as the Cournot model, in which firms act simultaneously. Suppose, however, that the rules of the game change so that one of the firms, the *leader*, can set its output in the first stage of the game, but that its rival, the *follower*, cannot choose its output until the second stage of the game. Having one firm act before the other arises naturally if one firm enters the market first. Would the firm that acts first have an advantage?

Heinrich von Stackelberg showed how to modify the Cournot model to answer this question. The Stackelberg model is similar to the Cournot model except that, instead of being a static game, it is a sequential game. We examine a duopoly, with one leader and one follower. (A Stackelberg model can also have one leader and several followers.) The leader realizes that once it sets its output, the rival firm will make its best response to the leader's output decision. That is, the leader predicts what the follower will do before the follower acts. Using this knowledge, the leader chooses its output level to manipulate the follower, thereby benefiting at the follower's expense.

We illustrate this two-stage, sequential-move oligopoly game by changing the airline example in Chapters 11 and 12 to allow American Airlines to commit to a quantity before United chooses its quantity. We simplify the problem by assuming initially that each airline has only three actions: to fly 96, 64, or 48 thousand passengers per quarter. Table 13.2 shows the corresponding profits (the same information as in the profit matrix in Table 12.2). However, this matrix does not show the sequential nature of this new game.

Instead, we can illustrate this sequential game using an *extensive form* diagram (sometimes called a *game tree* or *decision tree*), which is a branched diagram that shows the sequence of moves each player makes. A complete **extensive form** representation shows the players, the sequence of moves, the actions players can take at each move, the information that each player has about previous moves, and the payoff function over all possible strategy combinations. In this section, we assume that players know the payoff function and that, when a player is called upon to make a move, that player knows and can recall the moves that each player has made up to that point.

TABLE 13.2 An Airlines Prisoners' Dilemma Game with Three Actions

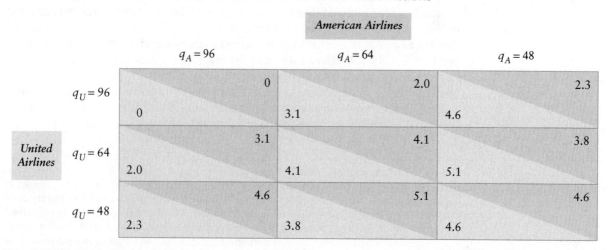

		American Airlines		
		$q_A = 96$	$q_A = 64$	$q_A = 48$
United Airlines	$q_U = 96$	0 / 0	2.0 / 3.1	2.3 / 4.6
	$q_U = 64$	3.1 / 2.0	4.1 / 4.1	3.8 / 5.1
	$q_U = 48$	4.6 / 2.3	5.1 / 3.8	4.6 / 4.6

Note: Quantities are in thousands of passengers per quarter; (rounded) profits are in millions of dollars per quarter.

FIGURE 13.1 Airlines' Stackelberg Game Tree

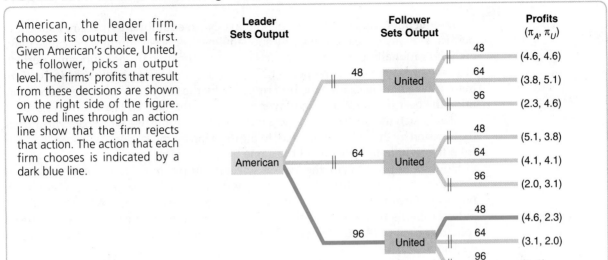

American, the leader firm, chooses its output level first. Given American's choice, United, the follower, picks an output level. The firms' profits that result from these decisions are shown on the right side of the figure. Two red lines through an action line show that the firm rejects that action. The action that each firm chooses is indicated by a dark blue line.

Leader Sets Output	Follower Sets Output		Profits (π_A, π_U)
	United	48	(4.6, 4.6)
		64	(3.8, 5.1)
		96	(2.3, 4.6)
American	United	48	(5.1, 3.8)
		64	(4.1, 4.1)
		96	(2.0, 3.1)
	United	48	(4.6, 2.3)
		64	(3.1, 2.0)
		96	(0, 0)

The extensive-form diagram in Figure 13.1 shows the order of the airlines' moves, each firm's possible actions at the time of its move, and the resulting profits at the end of the game (using the same profit information as in Table 13.2). In the figure, each box is a point at which the firm named in the box makes a move. The lines extending from the box provide a complete list of the possible actions that the player can make at this particular point in the game. On the left side of the figure, American, the *leader* firm, starts by picking one of the three output levels. In the middle of the figure, United, the *follower* firm, chooses one of the three quantities after learning the output level chosen by American. The right side of the figure shows the profits that American and United earn, given that they sequentially took the actions to reach this final branch. For instance, if American selects 64 and then United chooses 96, American earns $2.0 million profit per quarter and United earns $3.1 million.

Within this game are *subgames*. At a given stage, a **subgame** consists of all the subsequent actions that players can take (given the actions already taken) and the corresponding payoffs. The game in Figure 13.1 has four subgames. Three of these subgames arise in the second stage: United makes a decision given which of the three possible first-stage actions American takes. In addition, the entire game is a subgame because it is the set of subsequent decisions arising at the beginning of the game. Subgames other than the entire game are sometimes referred to as *proper* subgames or *strict* subgames.

To predict the outcome of this sequential game between airlines, we introduce a stronger version of the Nash equilibrium concept—a subgame-perfect Nash equilibrium. A set of strategies forms a **subgame-perfect Nash equilibrium** if the players' strategies form a Nash equilibrium in every subgame (including the overall game).

In Chapter 12, we saw that the static, simultaneous-move version of this game results in a Nash equilibrium in which each firm chooses an output level of 64 thousand passengers per quarter. A static game lacks a strict subgame because players move only once and they move at the same time. The only subgame is the overall game. Therefore, any Nash equilibrium in a static game must be subgame perfect.

In sequential games, it is possible to have Nash equilibria that are not subgame perfect. However, we focus on only subgame-perfect Nash equilibria because players who rationally plan ahead will reject outcomes that are not subgame perfect. We can solve for a subgame-perfect Nash equilibrium using **backward induction**, in which we first determine the best response by the last player to move, then determine the best response for the player who made the next-to-last move, and so on until we reach the first move of the game. In our example, we work backward from the decision by the follower, United, to the decision by the leader, American, moving from the right to the left side of the game tree.

How should American, the leader, select its output in the first stage? American determines what United, the follower, will do in the second stage, given each possible output choice by American in the first stage. Thus, American anticipates United's reaction to each output level American might choose. Using its conclusions about United's second-stage reaction, American makes its first-stage decision.

In this game, United, the follower, does not have a dominant strategy. The amount it chooses to produce depends on the quantity that American chose in the first stage. If American chooses 96, then United's profit is $2.3 million if it picks 48, $2.0 million if it chooses 64, and $0 if it selects 96. Thus, if American chooses 96, United's best response is 48 with a profit of $2.3 million. The pair of red vertical lines through the other two action lines show that United will not choose those actions.

Using the same reasoning, American determines how United will respond to each of American's possible actions, as the right side of the figure illustrates. American predicts that

▶ If American chooses 48, United will pick 64, so American's profit will be $3.8 million.

▶ If American chooses 64, United will pick 64, so American's profit will be $4.1 million.

▶ If American chooses 96, United will pick 48, so American's profit will be $4.6 million.

Thus, to maximize its profit, American chooses 96 in the first stage. United's strategy is to make its best response to American's first-stage action: United selects 64 if American chooses 48 or 64, and chooses 48 if American chooses 96. Thus, United responds in the second stage by selecting 48. Therefore, in the subgame-perfect Nash equilibrium, American chooses 96 in the first stage and United chooses 48 in the second stage. In this equilibrium, neither firm wants to change its strategy. Given that American Airlines sets its output at 96, United maximizes its profit by setting $q_U = 48$. Similarly, given how United will respond to each possible American output level, American cannot make more profit than if it chooses 96.

The subgame-perfect Nash equilibrium in this sequential game is different from the Nash equilibrium in the static simultaneous-move game based on Table 13.2 (Chapter 12). In that game both airlines produce 64 and both earn the same profit level, $4.1 million. In the sequential version, American produces 96 and United produces 48, and American makes twice as much profit, $4.6 million, as does United, $2.3 million.

In the real world, firms can choose any output they want—they're not restricted to only three possible output levels. As in the limited-choice game, the Stackelberg leader with an unlimited choice of output levels uses backward induction—starting at the end of the game and working toward the beginning. That is, before the leader chooses which action to take, the leader considers what action the follower will take given each possible action of the leader, as we show mathematically in Appendix 13.

Come here! Don't make me run after you!

Credible Threats

Why do the simultaneous-move and sequential-move output games have different outcomes? Given the option to act first, American chooses a large output level to make it in United's best interest to pick a relatively small output level, 48. American benefits from moving first and choosing a large quantity.

In the simultaneous-move game, United will not believe a threat by American that it will produce a large quantity. For a firm's announced strategy to be a **credible threat**, rivals must believe that the firm's strategy is rational in the sense that it is in the firm's best interest to use it.[6] If American produced the leader's level of output and United produced the Cournot level, American's profit would be lower than if it too produced the Cournot level. Because American cannot be sure that United will believe its threat and reduce its output in the simultaneous-move game, American produces only the Cournot output level. In contrast, in the sequential-move game, because American moves first, its commitment to produce a large quantity is credible.

The intuition for why commitment makes a threat credible is similar to that of "burning bridges." If a general burns the bridge behind an army so that the troops can only advance and not retreat, the army becomes a more fearsome foe. An army facing a choice of winning a battle or dying is likely to fight more aggressively than one that can retreat if things are not going well. Similarly, by limiting its future options, a firm can make itself stronger.[7]

---

[6]You may have been in a restaurant where an exasperated parent tries to control a difficult child with extreme threats like "If you don't behave, you'll have to sit in the car while we eat dinner" or "If you don't behave, I'll never let you watch TV again!" The kid, of course, does not view such threats as credible and continues to terrorize the restaurant—proving that the kid is a better game theorist than the parent.

[7]Some psychologists use the idea of commitment to treat behavioral problems. A psychologist may advise an author with writer's block to set up an irreversible procedure whereby if the author's book is not finished by a certain date, the author's check for $10,000 will be sent to a political candidate the author detests. Such an irreversible commitment helps the author get the project done by raising the cost of failure.

Q&A 13.1

Consider the game described in the Mini-Case "Competing E-Book Formats" in Chapter 12 and analyzed in Q&A 12.2 where Amazon and other e-book firms choose between the e-book formats AZW (the Amazon Kindle's standard) and EPUB (a widely used alternative standard). In Q&A 12.2, we assumed that Amazon and the Other group of e-book manufacturers simultaneously chose their formats. However, because it entered the market first, Amazon chose its e-book standard before the Other firms did. Using the numbers in Q&A 12.2, which is reproduced here, show the game tree. What is the Nash equilibrium if firms are free to choose whichever standard they want?

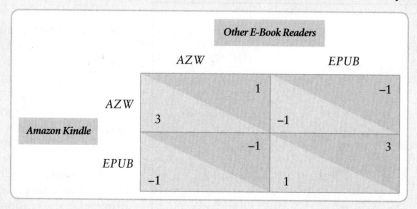

Answer

1. *Draw the extensive-form diagram given that Amazon moves before the Other group of manufacturers using the numbers from the profit table.*

2. *Solve backward to determine the Nash equilibrium.*   The figure shows that if Amazon initially chooses the AZW format, then the Other group would also choose the AZW format because its profit, $\pi_O = 1$, would be higher than if it chose EPUB, $\pi_O = -1$, as indicated by the red double lines through the EPUB option. Similarly, if Amazon initially chooses the EPUB format, so would the Other group. Because Amazon's profit is greater if it chooses the AZW format, $\pi_A = 3$, than if it picks the EPUB format, $\pi_A = 1$, it prefers the AZW format. Thus, with a first-mover advantage, Amazon chooses the AZW format, which the Other group would accept.[8]

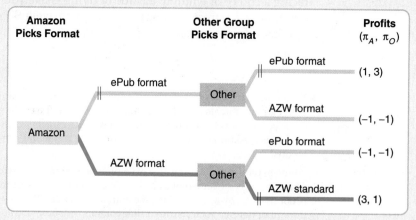

---

[8]Amazon's standard is proprietary so that firms cannot adopt it without paying a license fee. Amazon would like its standard to dominate the market *and* wants others to pay to use it. Our example simplifies the analysis by assuming that the license fee is zero.

13.3 Deterring Entry

The Stackelberg game demonstrates that the leader firm can benefit from moving before the follower firm. In some markets, by moving first, a manger can act strategically to prevent potential rivals from entering the market. How can an *incumbent*, monopoly firm deter a (potential) *rival* from entering that market? Does it pay for the incumbent to take the actions that will deter entry?

The incumbent may prevent entry if it can make a creditable threat. However, a manager cannot deter entry merely by telling a potential rival, "Don't enter! This market ain't big enough for the two of us." The potential rival would merely laugh and suggest that the manager's firm exit if it doesn't want to share the market. The following examples demonstrate how, by acting first, a firm can make a credible threat that deters entry. We use both sequential games and repeated games to illustrate how firms deter entry.

Exclusion Contracts

A mall has a single shoe store, the incumbent firm. The incumbent may pay the mall's owner an amount b to add a clause to its rental agreement that guarantees the incumbent the *exclusive right* to be the only shoe store in the mall. If this payment is made, the landlord agrees to rent the remaining space only to a restaurant, a toy store, or some other business that does not sell shoes. Should the shoe store pay?

The game tree, Figure 13.2, shows the two stages of the game involving the incumbent and its potential rival, another shoe store. In the first stage, the incumbent decides whether to pay b to prevent entry. In the second stage, the potential rival decides whether to enter. If it enters, it incurs a fixed fee of F to build its store in the mall.

The right side of the figure shows the incumbent's and the potential rival's profits (π_i, π_r) for each of the three possible outcomes. The outcome at the top of the figure shows that if the incumbent does not buy exclusivity and the potential rival does not enter, the incumbent earns the "monopoly" profit of $\pi_i = 10$ ($10 thousand) per month and its potential rival earns nothing, $\pi_r = 0$. The middle outcome shows that if the incumbent does not pay the exclusivity fee and the potential rival enters, the incumbent earns a duopoly profit of $\pi_i = 4$ and the rival earns the duopoly profit less its fixed cost, F, of entering, $\pi_r = 4 - F$. In the bottom outcome, the incumbent

FIGURE 13.2 Paying to Prevent Entry

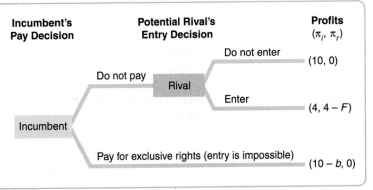

If the potential rival stays out of the mall, it makes no profit, $\pi_r = 0$, and the incumbent firm makes the monopoly profit, $\pi_i = 10$. If the potential rival enters, the incumbent earns the duopoly profit of 4 and the rival makes $4 - F$, where F is its fixed cost of entry. If the duopoly profit, 4, is less than F, entry does not occur. Otherwise, entry occurs unless the incumbent acts to deter entry by paying for exclusive rights to be the only shoe store in the mall. The incumbent pays the landlord only if $10 - b > 4$.

Incumbent's Pay Decision

Potential Rival's Entry Decision

Profits (π_i, π_r)

Do not pay → Rival

Do not enter → (10, 0)

Enter → (4, 4 − F)

Incumbent

Pay for exclusive rights (entry is impossible) → (10 − b, 0)

pays b for the exclusivity right so that it earns the monopoly profit less the exclusivity fee, $\pi_i = 10 - b$, and its potential rival earns nothing, $\pi_r = 0$.

To solve for the subgame-perfect Nash equilibrium, we work backward, starting with the last decision, the potential rival's entry decision. The top portion of the game tree shows what happens if the incumbent does not pay the landlord to prevent entry. The potential rival enters if it earns more from entering, $\pi_r = 4 - F$, than if it stays out of the market, $\pi_r = 0$. That is, the potential rival enters if $F \leq 4$. In the bottom portion of the game tree, where the incumbent pays b for an exclusive contract that prevents entry, the potential rival has no possible action.

Which of the three possible outcomes occurs depends on the parameters b (the incumbent's exclusivity fee) and F (the potential rival's fixed cost of entering the market):

▶ **Blockaded entry** $(F > 4)$: The potential rival chooses not to enter even if the incumbent does not pay to have an exclusive contract, so $\pi_r = 0$. The incumbent avoids spending b and still earns the monopoly profit, $\pi_i = 10$.

▶ **Deterred entry** $(F \leq 4, b \leq 6)$: Because $F \leq 4$, entry will occur unless the incumbent pays the exclusivity fee. The incumbent chooses to pay the exclusivity fee, b, because its profit from doing so, $\pi_i = 10 - b \geq 4$, is at least as large as what it earns if it permits entry and earns the duopoly profit, $\pi_i = 4$. Because the rival does not enter, it earns nothing: $\pi_r = 0$.

▶ **Accommodated entry** $(F \leq 4, b > 6)$: Entry will occur unless the incumbent pays the fee because the rival's fixed costs are less than or equal to 4. The incumbent does not pay for an exclusive contract. The exclusivity fee is so high that the incumbent earns more by allowing entry, $\pi_i = 4$, than it earns if it pays for exclusivity, $\pi_i = 10 - b < 4$. Thus, the incumbent earns the duopoly profit, $\pi_i = 4$, and the rival makes $\pi_r = 4 - F$.

In short, the incumbent does not pay for an exclusive contract if the potential rival's cost of entry is prohibitively high $(F > 4)$ or if the cost of the exclusive contract is too high $(b > 6)$.

Mini-Case	If managers cannot deter entry, they may try to delay entry. For example, pharmaceutical companies pay large amounts to delay entry of generic competitors that follows the expiration of a drug patent.

Pay-for-Delay Agreements

If managers cannot deter entry, they may try to delay entry. For example, pharmaceutical companies pay large amounts to delay entry of generic competitors that follows the expiration of a drug patent.

Patents have expired or will expire soon on many blockbuster drugs, including Cymbalta and OxyContin in 2013, Nexium and Celebrex in 2014, and Neulasta and Abilify in 2015. From these six drugs alone, the manufacturers earned more than $20 billion per year, much of which could be eliminated by generic competition.

After a U.S. pharmaceutical patent expires, the company that was the first to file with the U.S. Food and Drug Administration (FDA) to produce a generic version of the medication has a 180-day exclusivity period in which it is the only new firm that may sell a generic version of the drug. During that period, the former patent holder may also sell its drug under a generic name as well as its original brand name. For a valuable drug, after the six-month period elapses, many generics enter the market, typically siphoning off 90% of sales because generic prices average 30% of brand-name prices. It can be very valuable for a drug company to prevent the first firm from entering during that six-month period so that it can continue to charge a monopoly price.

Drug companies with expired patents have used a variety of *pay-for-delay* schemes to slow the entry of generics. In a 2011 report, the U.S. Federal Trade Commission (FTC) charged that some drug makers had either paid generic firms directly or promised not to introduce their own generic versions if a potential rival delayed its entry into the market.

According to the FTC, in the most recent year for which they had data, 28 agreements included some type of compensation by the original firm in exchange for delaying entry. In 15 agreements, the incumbent agreed not to market its own brand-name generic drug. "Instead of saying, 'Here's $200 million, go away,' they're saying they could penalize them $200 million, but they won't, so go away," said Jon Leibowitz, the chairman of the FTC. Mr. Leibowitz considers such arrangements to be illegal sweetheart deals that cost consumers and government health programs $3.5 billion a year due to reduced competition. The industry contends that these Pay-For-Delay deals are legal business decisions. In 2013, the U.S. Supreme Court decided that such cases should be decided individually based on whether the agreement harms consumers.

Limit Pricing

A firm is **limit pricing** if it sets its price (or, equivalently, its output) so that another firm cannot enter the market profitably. For example, the incumbent could set a price below the potential rival's marginal cost so entry would be unprofitable if that price were maintained after entry. Or the incumbent could produce so much output that the price is very low and too few customers remain for the potential rival to make a profit. However, to successfully limit price, a firm must be able to credibly threaten to choose a price (or output) that will cause an entrant to make losses if entry occurs. Such credibility requires the incumbent to have an advantage over its rivals, as the following example illustrates.

An incumbent could threaten a potential rival that, if entry occurs, it will charge a price so low that the entrant will make a loss. This threat will only work if the threat is credible. It is not credible if the two firms have identical costs and market demand is adequate to support both firms. In that case, if entry occurs, it is in the incumbent's best interest to charge the duopoly price and make a profit rather than charge such a low price that everyone loses money. In such a case, the potential rival ignores the threat and enters.

For the threat of limit pricing to be credible, the incumbent must have an advantage over its rival. For example, if the incumbent's costs are lower than those of the potential rival, the incumbent can charge a price so low that the rival would lose money while the incumbent earns a higher profit than if it allows entry.

Another example is an extreme form of the Stackelberg oligopoly example. The Stackelberg leader acts first and produces a large quantity so that the follower produces a smaller quantity. Depending on the demand curve and the firms' costs, it may be even more profitable for the leader to produce such a large quantity that the follower cannot earn a profit. That is, the leader makes limit pricing credible by committing to provide a very large output level.

On November 30, 2011, the main patent for Lipitor—a drug that treats high cholesterol—expired, allowing generic drug manufacturers to enter this market. That was a tragedy for its manufacturer, Pfizer, because Lipitor was the world's best-selling drug ever, with $106 billion in sales over the previous decade and $10.8 billion in sales in 2010.

Ranbaxy Laboratories of India, as the first firm to file with the FDA to produce generic Lipitor, gained the exclusive rights to produce generic Lipitor from December 2011 through May 2012. Pfizer realized that delaying the entry of generic Lipitor firms for even a few months would pay handsomely.

Pfizer used many methods to delay entry including limit pricing. Pfizer issued a statement saying that "Our intent is to offer Lipitor to payers and patients at or below the cost of the generic during the 180-day period." Pfizer also subsidized patients' private insurance for Lipitor, lowering their out-of-pocket costs at or below the level they pay for generic drugs. One top Pfizer official said that the company would adjust its discounts to beat any tit-for-tat reduction in generic pricing during the first six months.

Pfizer ended its extreme discount program after the first six months. Once other firms entered and generic drugs flooded the market, driving down prices, these subsidies would have been more costly. After ending its limit pricing program, Pfizer reverted to high prices for the customers who remain loyal to brand-name Lipitor. (See the Managerial Problem "Brand-Name and Generic Drugs" in Chapter 9.)

In the first stage of a game between an incumbent and a potential rival, the incumbent builds its plant using either an inflexible technology that allows it to produce only a (large) fixed quantity, or a flexible technology that allows it to produce small or large quantities. In the second stage, the potential rival decides whether to enter. With the inflexible technology, the incumbent makes so much output that its threat to limit price is credible, as the following game tree illustrates. What strategy (technology) maximizes the incumbent's profit?

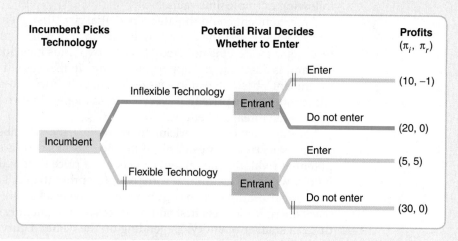

| Incumbent Picks Technology | Potential Rival Decides Whether to Enter | Profits (π_i, π_r) |

Answer

1. *Work backward by determining the potential rival's best strategy conditional on each possible action by the incumbent.* This game has two proper subgames. The upper right subgame shows the profits if the potential rival enters or if it does not enter given that the incumbent uses the inflexible technology. The potential rival loses money ($\pi_r = -1$) if it enters, but breaks even ($\pi_r = 0$) if it doesn't, so it does not enter. In the lower right subgame, the potential rival decides whether to enter given that the incumbent is using the flexible technology. Here, the potential rival prefers to enter and earn a profit of $\pi_r = 5$ rather than stay out and earn nothing.

2. *Given the responses by the potential rival to each of the incumbent's strategies, determine the incumbent's best strategy.* If the incumbent uses the flexible technology, entry occurs, and the incumbent earns $\pi_i = 5$. However, if the incumbent uses the inflexible technology, the other firm does not enter, and the incumbent's profit is $\pi_i = 20$. Thus, the incumbent chooses the inflexible technology.

Comment: The incumbent would earn even a higher profit with the flexible technology if no entry occurs. However, if the incumbent chooses the flexible technology, its rival will enter, so the incumbent is better off committing to the inflexible technology.

Entry Deterrence in a Repeated Game

An entry game can be repeated over time or over space. A successful, profitable firm is likely to face repeated threats of entry by potential rivals over time. A grocery chain with a monopoly in many small towns faces potential entry by other firms in some or all of these towns.

Figure 13.3 shows the constituent entry game—the game in only one town—that the grocery chain faces. If the incumbent retains its monopoly position, its profit is 10 ($10 million). If it accommodates entry, both firms receive 3 and if the incumbent fights, it gets only 1, while the rival loses 1. The incumbent must decide whether to

FIGURE 13.3 A Constituent Game of a Repeated Entry Game

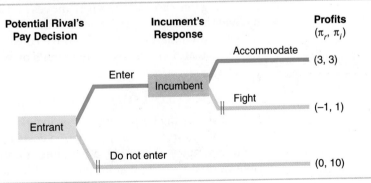

This game tree shows the constituent game in one town that is repeated in many towns. If the potential rival does not enter, the incumbent grocery chain retains its monopoly. If entry occurs, the incumbent decides whether to fight (price aggressively) or accommodate the rival (set a high price). It does not pay for the incumbent to fight once entry occurs, so its rival enters.

engage in a price war with the rival or whether to accommodate the rival by keeping its price high (or its output low) and sharing the market.

Given the profits in this constituent game, if this game is played only once and if the profits are common knowledge, then the only subgame-perfect Nash equilibrium is for entry to occur and for the incumbent to accommodate entry. The potential rival reasons that, if it enters, then the incumbent can choose to fight and get 1 or accommodate entry and gain 3. The potential rival realizes that the incumbent maximizes its profit by accommodating entry. Thus, entry occurs, because the rival earns 3 by entering and nothing by staying out of the market.

Does the equilibrium change if the game is repeated many times in different locations and possibly at different times? Suppose the incumbent firm faces a potential rival in one town and knows that other potential rivals may later enter in other towns. Because what it does in the current game may affect future entry, the manager of the chain may conclude that engaging in an unprofitable price war when the first entry occurs is a good idea if doing so is likely to deter many future rivals.

If the incumbent is known to be a rational profit maximizer and if its profits are common knowledge, the chain will not intimidate future potential rivals merely by fighting once, because the potential rivals realize that fighting each time is not in the chain's best interest.

However, fighting may be a good strategy for the chain if the chain's profits are not common knowledge so that potential rivals have incomplete information. If the chain fights with the first entrant, potential rivals may (falsely) conclude that the chain's profits are such that fighting is its best strategy even if the game is played only once. If potential rivals conclude that the incumbent will always fight, they won't enter because they know they would lose money in a price war.

In such a repeated game, although fighting the first rival is not profitable, the incumbent does so to develop a reputation for being a tough competitor. Thus, fighting the first rival is part of a rational long-run strategy and can be part of a subgame-perfect Nash equilibrium in which entry is successfully deterred.[9]

13.4 Cost Strategies

A firm may be able to gain a cost advantage over a rival by moving first. Our analysis of the Cournot model in Chapter 11 shows that a firm with a lower marginal cost produces more and earns a higher profit than does its high cost rival. We start by examining two cases where a firm moves first to gain a marginal cost advantage over its rivals by using a capital investment or increasing the rate of learning by doing to lower its own marginal cost. Then we consider a firm's strategic action that raises its rivals' marginal cost by more than its own.

Investing to Lower Marginal Cost

It is not surprising that a firm invests in new equipment that lowers its marginal cost if the savings from lower production costs more than offset the cost of the investment. Perhaps surprisingly, a firm might invest in new equipment where the cost savings do not justify that investment, if the investment deters entry.

---

[9]This game-theoretic argument is presented formally in Kreps and Wilson (1982) and Milgrom and Roberts (1982).

For example, suppose a monopoly considers installing robots on its assembly line that would lower its marginal cost of production. However, if the incumbent remains a monopoly, this investment does not pay because the investment expense exceeds the extra profit from the lower marginal cost. Nonetheless, the incumbent may make the investment under certain conditions.

If the market conditions are such that entry is blockaded—no firm will enter even if the incumbent produces the monopoly output—the incumbent does not make the investment. Suppose, however, that entry will occur if the monopoly does not invest. Because the investment lowers the incumbent's marginal cost, the potential rival realizes that the incumbent will produce more output than it otherwise would—it floods the market with extra output and lowers the market price. Faced with this credible threat, the potential rival does not enter because it realizes that it will lose money by entering. As a result, the incumbent may make the investment so as to discourage entry. Figure 13.4 shows the corresponding game tree. The incumbent decides whether to invest in the first stage, and the potential rival decides whether to enter in the second stage.

To solve for the subgame-perfect Nash equilibrium, we work backward from the potential rival's entry decision in the second stage of the game. We start by looking at the potential rival's decision in the proper subgame at the top of the tree given that the incumbent does not invest in the first stage. The potential rival's profit is $\pi_r = 0$ if it stays out of the market and $\pi_r = 4$ (million dollars) if it enters. Thus, the rival chooses to enter because $4 > 0$. We draw a pair of red parallel lines on the path labeled "Do not enter" to indicate that the rival rejects that choice given that the incumbent does not invest in the first stage.

Next, we look at the proper subgame in the lower part of the game tree in which the incumbent invests in the first stage. Here, the potential rival chooses not to enter because $\pi_r = -1$ if it enters and 0 if it stays out of the market.

We now turn to the incumbent's decision in the first stage. By working backward, the incumbent knows that if it does not invest, the potential rival enters, so that the

FIGURE 13.4 Investing to Prevent Entry

First, the incumbent monopoly decides whether to invest in capital that reduces its marginal cost of production, which will induce it to produce more, all else the same. Second, the potential rival decides whether to enter the market. If the incumbent does not invest, it pays for the rival to enter: $\pi_r = 4 > 0$. If the incumbent does invest, the rival knows entry will be unprofitable: $\pi_r = -1 < 0$. The incumbent chooses to invest because its profit if it invests, $\pi_i = 8$, is greater than its payoff if it does not invest, $\pi_i = 4$.

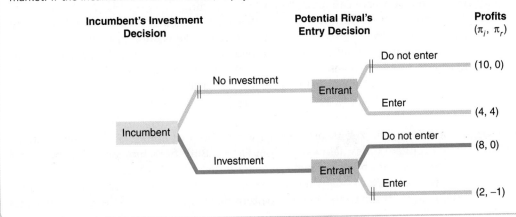

incumbent's profit is $\pi_i = 4$. Alternatively, if it invests, the potential rival stays out of the market, and the incumbent's profit is $\pi_i = 8$. Because $8 > 4$, the incumbent makes the investment.

The incumbent's profit, $\pi_i = 8$, is lower than the profit, $\pi_i = 10$, that it would have earned if it did not make the investment *and* the potential rival stayed out of the market. Nevertheless, the incumbent benefits from this "unprofitable" investment because it deters the entry that would otherwise occur.

Learning by Doing

What we have to learn to do, we learn by doing. —Aristotle

In aircraft and computer chip manufacturing and in some other industries, the more cumulative output a firm has produced, the lower its marginal cost, as its workers and managers learn by doing (Chapter 6). Consequently, the first firm in a market may want to produce more than the quantity that maximizes its short-run profit, so that its future marginal cost will be lower than that of a late-entering rival.

Indeed, Benkard (2004) demonstrated that an aircraft manufacturer may price below current marginal cost in the short run, because of its steep learning curve. The price of the Lockheed L-1011 was below the static marginal cost for essentially its entire 14-year production run. Salgado (2008) found that AMD's cost of manufacturing computer chips was about 12% higher than Intel's cost because AMD had less learning by doing as it had produced fewer units.

Raising Rivals' Costs

A firm may benefit from using a strategy that raises its own cost but raises its rivals' costs by more. As the Cournot example in Chapter 11 illustrates, a firm can benefit from being the lower cost firm.

Firms can use many methods to raise rivals' costs. An incumbent firm may lobby the government for more industry regulations that raise costs, as long as the legislation *grandfathers* existing firms' plants. For example, the incumbent may want all new plants to install expensive pollution-control equipment that raises production costs, provided that its existing plants are exempted.

An incumbent can take many actions that make it costly for its consumers to switch to a rival's product in the future. It may impose a *switching fee*: a charge that customers must pay to take their business elsewhere. By designing software for its computer, phone, or other electronic device so that it won't work on a rival's equipment, an incumbent can raise the cost of switching.

Alternatively, a firm may patent its software, so that it can prevent rivals from using its software on their equipment. Before U.S. legislation prevented this practice, a phone company would prevent customers from transferring their phone numbers to a rival provider, so as to reduce the chance of a consumer switching providers. These practices raise the cost to latecomers of attracting new customers.

Q&A 13.3   In a duopoly market, to produce a given amount of output, Firm 1 uses relatively more capital but less labor than does Firm 2. Both firms hire labor from the same labor union, which sets the same wage for both firms. Firm 1 is about to bargain with the union. Whatever wage it negotiates, Firm 2 has to pay the same wage. Because this industry is suffering from a downturn in demand, the union is willing to accept the current wage. However, if Firm 1 agrees to a higher wage, its cost of production will rise by less than Firm 2's cost. The game tree shows the profits corresponding to the various actions by the firms. Firm 1's profit is *A* if it chooses the high wage and Firm 2 chooses the low output level. Under what condition should Firm 1 offer to pay a high wage?

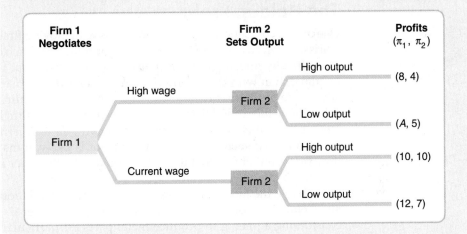

Answer

1. *Determine Firm 2's action conditional on the wage by comparing its profits at each output.* We start by solving backward, as usual. If Firm 1 keeps the current wage (the bottom half of the figure), then Firm 2 will pick a high output level and earn a profit of 10 ($10 million), rather than a low output level and earn only 7. If Firm 1 agrees to the high wage, Firm 2 makes a larger profit from producing the low output level, 5, than the high output level, 4, so it produces the low level.

2. *Determine which wage Firm 1 chooses by comparing the profits from different wage choices.* If Firm 1 chooses the current wage, Firm 2 produces the high output, so Firm 1 earns 10. Alternatively, if Firm 1 agrees to the high wage, Firm 2 produces the low output, so Firm 1 earns *A*. Consequently, Firm 1 chooses the current wage if $A < 10$ and agrees to the high wage otherwise.

Mini-Case

Auto Union Negotiations

The United Auto Workers (UAW), the union that provides labor to the U.S. auto industry, negotiates contracts with the Big 3 automakers when the old contract expires, which occurs roughly every three or four years. Traditionally, the UAW initially negotiates with only one auto firm—the *target* firm—while implicitly threatening that, if the parties fail to come to terms, the UAW will strike only that one company, putting it at a competitive disadvantage. (If the UAW had called a strike during the 2011 negotiations, Ford would have been the target company.) The resulting agreement or *pattern contract* that the firm and the union sign is virtually always adopted by its rivals, so as to avoid strikes of their own. As a consequence, if the target firm makes large wage concessions, it essentially inflicts those high wages on its rivals.

13.5 Disadvantages of Moving First

Moving first is not always an advantage. We discuss two possible drawbacks to moving first: the holdup problem and acting too quickly.

The Holdup Problem

One of the most serious potential problems with moving first is the holdup problem. It arises when two firms want to contract or trade with each other but one firm must move first by making a *specific* investment: an investment that can only be used in its transaction with the second firm. A *holdup problem* arises if the other firm takes advantage of the first firm. If the first firm does not anticipate this opportunistic behavior by the second firm and it occurs, then the first firm loses much of its investment, so that it is at a disadvantage by moving first. Alternatively, if the first firm anticipates that such opportunistic behavior is likely, it may not make the specific investment out of fear that it will be exploited by the other firm with the result that both firms lose the potential benefits from interacting.

Probably the most famous example concerns negotiations between Fisher Body and General Motors (GM) nearly a century ago (Klein et al., 1978). Fisher Body was considering agreeing to produce metal parts for particular GM cars. To do so for each GM part, it needed to create specific dies (molds used to make parts) that a machine press uses to manufacture a part. Fisher worried that these dies were such *specific investments*, with no alternative use, that they would serve as *hostages*—something that Fisher could lose if GM later lowered the amount it would pay for Fisher parts.[10]

We formally analyze a holdup game using a recent example of nationalization. Nationalization occurs when a government seizes property owned by a foreign firm. We focus on Venezuela, but nationalization is common with both Argentina and Indonesia nationalizing property in the first half of 2012.

ExxonMobil, an oil company, is the first mover in a game with the Venezuelan government. It considers making a large investment to obtain rights and build facilities to drill for and refine oil in either Venezuela or in some other country. If Venezuela honors their deal, ExxonMobil believes that it can earn 20 ($20 billion) in Venezuela or 10 elsewhere. If the investment is made, the Venezuelan government, the second-mover, has a hostage: the oil company's investment, which cannot be moved elsewhere. The government can nationalize part of the oil field operations. The game tree in Figure 13.5 indicates that if the Venezuelan government does not nationalize, ExxonMobil's profit is $\pi_X = 20$. However, with a (partial) nationalization, its profit falls to $\pi_X = 8$. The difference, 12, goes to the Venezuelan government, so π_V increases from 20 to 32.

If the company does not anticipate a nationalization problem, it makes the investment because it prefers a profit of 20 to the 10 it would earn elsewhere. If nationalization occurs, the company loses 12. However, if before the oil company invests, it

---

[10]A reverse holdup problem could also have occurred. If GM committed to allowing Fisher to be its only supplier of parts, then Fisher could demand higher prices for these parts and GM would have little recourse in the short run. To keep our formal analysis relatively simple, we concentrate on situations where only the firm that acts first is at risk of being exploited.

FIGURE 13.5 Venezuela–ExxonMobil Holdup Problem

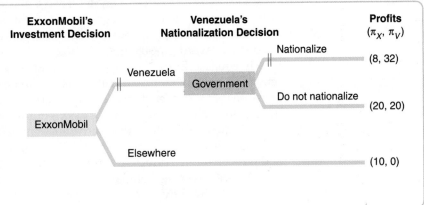

If ExxonMobil invests in Venezuela's oil fields, it runs the risk that Venezuela will later partially nationalize the firm. Given that ExxonMobil invests, Venezuela's profit is higher if it nationalizes, $\pi_V = 32$, than if it does not, $\pi_V = 32$. If Exxon realizes that Venezuela will nationalize, it does not invest in Venezuela because, after nationalization, its Venezuelan profit, $\pi_X = 8$, is less than what it can earn elsewhere, $\pi_X = 10$.

concludes that the Venezuelan government is likely to nationalize its investment, the company invests elsewhere because $\pi_X = 10$ is more than the $\pi_X = 8$ that the company earns after the partial nationalization. Thus, an investment that would benefit both the company and Venezuela would not be made.

Mini-Case

Venezuelan Nationalization

In the 1990s, private oil companies were permitted to invest in a joint venture agreement with Venezuela's state-owned oil company Petroleos de Venezuela S.A. (PDVSA), which had a minority share. Mobil (now ExxonMobil), Chevron-Texaco (now Chevron), Statoil, ConocoPhillips, and BP invested in the Orinoco Oil Belt in eastern Venezuela, which is thought to contain the world's largest reserves of extra-heavy oil. Their plants convert the heavy crude to lighter crude oil.

When these companies first invested in Venezuela, they were given various promises about how they would be treated. However, soon thereafter, Hugo Chavez was elected president and he started nationalizing investments by oil companies and other businesses. In 2007, President Chavez announced that Venezuela was partially nationalizing the Orinoco Oil Belt, substantially reducing foreign oil companies' ownership shares, with PDVSA gaining a minimum of 60% of the shares and hence majority control. Chavez claimed that foreign oil companies were still welcome in Venezuela, but not as majority stakeholders: "The owner will be PDVSA and the business will be in the hands of Venezuelans."

After complaints from ExxonMobil and ConocoPhillips, the Venezuelan government ultimately agreed to go to an international arbitration panel to determine the amount of compensation the two oil companies would receive. In 2012, Exxon was awarded $908 million for one nationalization, an amount approximately equal to Exxon's investment in that project. However, Venezuela paid only $255 million after deducting what it claimed were debts owed by Exxon. Decisions were expected on the Conoco claim and the rest of the Exxon claims in late 2013. The companies were asking for about $8 billion while Venezuela has indicated it expected to pay no more than $2.5 billion.

Nationalization is a shortsighted policy that can destroy a nation's reputation and prevent foreign direct investment. For example, since Fidel Castro nationalized American-owned companies in Cuba without compensation in 1960, Cuba has suffered from over half a century of sanctions and no U.S. foreign investment. However, some firms have made investments in Venezuelan oil since the partial nationalizations.

Managerial Implication

Avoiding Holdups

Managers should seek ways to avoid losing money due to holdups. Five frequently used approaches are contracts, vertical integration, quasi-vertical integration, reputation building, and multiple or open sourcing.

Many managers use contracts to prevent holdup problems. The second-mover firm contractually guarantees the first-mover firm that it will not be exploited. To alleviate the fears of Fisher Body that GM would later drop its price or stop buying from Fisher, GM signed a 10-year exclusive cost-plus contract stipulating that Fisher Body would be the exclusive supplier for GM.

By vertically integrating (Chapter 7)—that is, becoming one firm—two firms can eliminate the possibility of a holdup problem. After a number of years under the contract, unanticipated holdup problems occurred between GM and Fisher Body. To eliminate them, GM bought Fisher Body, vertically integrating with its parts supplier.

A "mild form" of vertical integration is quasi-vertical integration, which is a contracting solution that mimics vertical integration. The biggest danger to Fisher Body was that it would invest in expensive dies and machines that could be used only to produce parts for GM cars. To avoid this danger before the two firms merged, GM partially or *quasi-vertically integrated* with Fisher Body, by paying for and owning the specific physical asset (the dies) rather than buying all of Fisher. As a consequence, Fisher and GM were both protected against holdups. If something went wrong in their relationship, Fisher could transfer GM's dies back to GM and both firms could walk away unharmed.[11]

Establishing a reputation for straight dealing can also prevent holdup problems. If GM goes many years without behaving opportunistically, then new suppliers are unlikely to worry about having their specific investments held as hostages by GM.

---

[11]Monteverde and Teece (1982) looked at hundreds of parts that GM and Ford bought from suppliers. They found that the more specialized the die (the less likely it produces a part that can be used by another firm), the more likely an automobile company was to own it or to vertically integrate with the supplier.

Managers use multiple sources or open sources for software to avoid holdup problems. For example, a firm that uses proprietary software may want to upgrade its computer in a few years, but to do so it needs the software firm to modify its code. Thus, the firm using the software is at the mercy of the software firm. By using open-source software, where it can modify the code itself if need be, the user firm is not subject to a holdup problem. Some firms prefer to use the open-source Linux computer operating system rather than proprietary Windows and Mac operating systems.

Moving Too Quickly

Typically, introducing the first product in a market gives a firm an important advantage. Consumers become loyal to that product so that later entrants find it difficult to take market share from the leader firm. However, the disadvantages of entering early are that the cost of entering quickly is higher, the odds of miscalculating demand are greater, and later rivals may build on the pioneer's research to produce a superior product.

For example, as the first of a new class of anti-ulcer drugs, Tagamet was extremely successful when it was introduced. However, the second entrant, Zantac, rapidly took the lion's share of the market. Zantac worked similarly to Tagamet but had fewer side effects, could be taken less frequently, and was promoted more effectively when it was introduced.

Mini-Case

Advantages and Disadvantages of Moving First

We have seen how a firm that enters the market first gains an advantage over potential rivals by moving first. The first-mover firm may prevent entry by committing to a large plant, raising costs to potential rivals, or getting an early start on learning by doing. Denstadli et al. (2005) found that early Norwegian discount supermarket entrants benefited from long-lasting consumer perceptions that they had superior attributes to later entrants.

However, first movers do not always gain an advantage. Toshiba, the main proponent of HD DVD, spent large sums of money to be the first to sell a next-generation DVD in 2006. It sold its initial HD-DVD player for $499 even though it apparently contained nearly $700 worth of components, presumably to reinforce its first-to-market advantage by permeating the market with HD-DVD units. In 2007, the backers of HD DVD reportedly paid Paramount and DreamWorks a combined $150 million to adopt their format. However, when most content producers sided with Blu-ray, Toshiba stopped producing HD-DVD players in February 2008, conceding the market to Blu-ray.

Nonetheless, such examples of domination by second entrants are unusual. Urban, Carter, and Gaskin (1986) examined 129 successful consumer products and found that the second entrant gained, on average, only three-quarters of the market share of the pioneer and that later entrants captured even smaller shares.

Similarly, Usero and Fernández (2009) found that the first entrants in European mobile phone markets maintained their market share advantage over time. In the early 1990s, most European governments licensed only a single firm, which was typically a state-owned monopoly (though France, Sweden, and the United Kingdom each had two mobile firms in 1990). After mobile phones took off, other firms were allowed to enter. According to Usero and Fernández, followers were unlikely to erode the first-mover's market share advantage by taking more aggressive market actions such as innovation and marketing, but they were able to gain market share through nonmarket actions such as litigation and complaints.

13.6 Behavioral Game Theory

We normally assume that managers are rational in the sense that they optimize using all available information. However, they may be subject to psychological biases and may have limited powers of calculation that cause them to act irrationally. Such possibilities are the domain of behavioral economics (Chapters 4 and 9), which seeks to augment the rational economic model so as to better understand and predict economic decision making.

Ultimatum Games

One example of nonprofit maximizing behavior occurs in *ultimatum games*. Businesspeople often face an *ultimatum*, where one person (the *proposer*) makes a "take it or leave it" offer to another (the *responder*). No matter how long the parties have negotiated, once an ultimatum is issued, the responder has to accept or reject the offer with no opportunity to make a counter-offer. An ultimatum can be viewed as a sequential game in which the proposer moves first and the responder moves second.

Mini-Case

GM's Ultimatum

In 2009, General Motors (GM) was struggling financially and wanted to shut down about one-fourth of its dealerships in the United States and Canada. Because GM was concerned that dealer opposition could cause delays and impose other costs, it offered dealers slated for closure an ultimatum: They would receive a (small) payment from GM if they did not oppose the restructuring plan.

Dealers could accept the ultimatum and get something, or they could reject the offer, oppose the reorganization, and receive nothing. Although it may have been irrational, some dealers rejected the ultimatum and loudly complained that GM was "high-handed, oppressive, and patently unfair." In 2011, some terminated Canadian dealerships filed a class-action suit against GM of Canada. The case was still moving forward at a glacial pace in 2013, using up resources as it proceeds.

An Experiment. The possibility that someone might turn down an offer even at some personal cost is important in business negotiations. To gain insight into real decisions, Camerer (2003) conducted an ultimatum experiment.

A group of student participants are seated in a computer lab. Each person is designated as either a proposer or a responder. Using the computers, each proposer is matched (anonymously) with one responder. The game is based on dividing $10. Each proposer makes an ultimatum offer to the responder of a particular amount. A responder who accepts receives the amount offered and the proposer gets the rest of the $10. If the responder rejects the offer, both players get nothing.

To find the rational, subgame-perfect solution, we use backward induction. In the second stage, the responder should accept if the offer x is positive. Thus in the first stage, the proposer should offer the lowest possible positive amount.

However, such rational behavior is not a good predictor of actual outcomes. The lowest possible offer is almost never made and, when it is made, it is usually rejected. Thus, a proposer who makes the mistake of expecting the responder to be fully rational is likely to receive nothing. The most common range for offers is between $3 and $4—far more than the "rational" minimum offer. Offers of under $2 are relatively rare and, when they do occur, are turned down about half the time.

One concern about such experiments is that the payoffs are small enough that not all participants take the game seriously. However, when the total amount to be divided was increased to $100, the results were essentially unchanged: The typical offer remained between 30% and 40% of the total. If anything, responders are even more likely to turn down lowball offers when the stakes are higher.

Reciprocity. Some responders who reject lowball offers feel the proposer is being greedy and would prefer to make a small sacrifice rather than reward such behavior. Some responders are angered by low offers, some feel insulted, and some feel that they should oppose "unfair" behavior. Most proposers anticipate such feelings and offer a significant amount to the responder, but almost always less than 50%.

Apparently, most people accept that the advantage of moving first should provide some extra benefit to proposers, but not too much. Moreover, they believe in *reciprocity*. If others treat us well, we want to return the favor. If they treat us badly, we want to "get even" and will retaliate if the cost does not seem excessive.[12] Thus, if a proposer makes a low offer, many responders are willing to give up something to punish the proposer.

Analysis of ultimatum games is useful partly because ultimatums arise in real business interactions. More important, however, the behavioral norms illustrated by the ultimatum game are of general significance—even in nonultimatum situations. For example, in dealing with workers, good managers often take account of reciprocity by providing benefits over and above the minimum needed, rather than squeezing every cent they can from workers. Such an approach makes sense if workers who feel exploited might quit or go on strike even when it is against their economic interest. Conversely, workers who feel well treated often develop a sense of loyalty that causes them to work harder than needed—such as staying late to get a job finished—rather than doing only the minimum amount required.

Eckel and Grossman (1996) found that men are more likely than women to punish if the personal cost is high in an ultimatum game. They speculate that this difference may explain gender patterns in wages and unemployment during downturns, where men are more likely to rigidly insist on a given wage than more flexible women. Visser and Roelofs (2011) are able to explain gender effects based on a few personality traits.[13]

---

[12]Reciprocity is central to many ethical systems as with, for example, the Golden Rule: "Do unto others as you would have them do unto you," and the Code of Hammurabi: "An eye for an eye and a tooth for a tooth."

[13]The personality traits considered were "extraversion, agreeableness, conscientiousness, emotional stability, and intellect/imagination." After controlling for these personality traits, they find no other differences between men and women. That is, gender matters only to the extent that these personality attributes differ by gender.

Levels of Reasoning

John Maynard Keynes (1936) observed that investment decisions are often based on "animal spirits" rather than rational calculation. He questioned whether investors are able to rationally assess the value of a stock by recognizing that its value is based primarily on what *other people* think the stock is worth.

Keynes suggested that deciding which stock to buy is like predicting the outcome of a beauty contest. Your prediction should not be based on what *you* think of the contestants; it should be based on what you think *other people* will think. Keynes questioned whether most people are able to rationally assess the likely opinions of others—in stock markets, beauty contests, and other situations.

Modern experimental economists have devoted considerable attention to testing whether decision makers do rationally infer the likely assessments and actions of others in strategic games. One game that has been used for such experiments is called the *beauty contest game* in recognition of Keynes's original example.

The *Financial Times* (FT) of London with the help of economist Richard Thaler held a relatively straightforward beauty contest game (Bosch-Domènech et al., 2002). The FT invited readers to choose an integer between 0 and 100. The submission closest to two-thirds of the average of all numbers submitted would win. If 10, 20, 30, 40, and 50 are the five numbers submitted, the average is 30. As two-thirds of this average is 20, the person who chose 20 would win. Thus, the objective is to predict the average and pick a number that is two-thirds of that amount.

The Nash equilibrium to this game is for everyone to choose zero! The average would then be 0, and two-thirds of 0 is 0, so everyone would be correct and would share the prize for winning. No one would have an incentive to defect by choosing a higher number, as someone who did so would lose rather than have a winning number.[14] Further, this common choice of zero is the *only* possible Nash equilibrium.[15]

Thus if all players are fully rational, they should choose zero. However, only about 5% of the nearly 1,500 people who participated chose zero. The average in the FT experiment was 18.9 and the winning submission was 13. Some people chose randomly, not thinking about what other people might do. This approach is called *level-0 strategic reasoning*. A more sophisticated participant might expect others to choose randomly so that the average would be roughly 50, and should therefore choose the integer closest to two-thirds of 50, which is 33. In fact, a large group did choose 33, exhibiting level-1 reasoning.

A still more sophisticated person may anticipate that others would use level-1 reasoning to choose 33, and therefore choose two-thirds of this amount, which is 22. Many people did choose 22, exhibiting level-2 reasoning. Similarly, a player who expects others to use level-2 reasoning should expect an average of 22 and should therefore choose 15, which is level-3 reasoning, and so on. The end point of this thought process is to select 0, the (fully rational) Nash equilibrium.

---

[14]Suppose the game has five players. If one person were to defect from the Nash equilibrium and choose 1 instead of 0, then the average would be $\frac{1}{5}$ and two-thirds of the average is $\frac{2}{15}$. Those who chose 0 would be closer to $\frac{2}{15}$ than the defector. The same type of reasoning applies for any positive number and for any number of players greater than two.

[15]If any positive number is submitted, then the average must exceed zero and at least one person must be above two-thirds of the average as it is impossible for everyone to be below the average. But a choice above two-thirds of the average cannot be a best response, as the person could do better by choosing two-thirds of the average instead.

This experiment has been repeated many times. The overall average is usually about 22, implying a winning number of about 15. Therefore, on average, participants seem to exhibit level-2 reasoning. To win the game it is therefore usually necessary to go through three layers of reasoning—not more and not less—so as to be one step ahead of most other players.

A manager who underestimates the capability of rivals for strategic thinking (similar to assuming others will use level-0 reasoning in the beauty contest game) will make mistakes. However, a manager who overestimates the strategic sophistication of others will also make mistakes. The best results are obtained by having a good sense of exactly how sophisticated others are and staying one step ahead.

A dramatic example of CEOs anticipating rivals' strategies is provided by the telecommunications industry. The U.S. Telecommunications Act of 1996 allowed new firms to enter local telephone markets. Goldfarb and Xiao (2011) found that some CEOs consistently made the mistake of entering markets that became excessively crowded while others consistently entered markets that did not attract excessive entry, apparently anticipating the behavior of rivals. The more successful CEOs were those who were more experienced, more likely to have studied economics or business in university, and had stronger records of academic achievement.

Managerial Implication

Taking Advantage of Limited Strategic Thinking

Managers should consider the level of strategic sophistication of customers (and rivals). For example, successful managers of Hollywood movie studios anticipate limited strategic thinking by moviegoers. Normally Hollywood studios release movies for prescreening by critics before general release to generate buzz through positive reviews. This technique works well for good movies, but has the opposite effect for movies that get poor reviews.

If a studio is not confident about a movie's quality it can use a *cold opening*, releasing the movie with no prescreenings for movie critics. A fully rational moviegoer understands this tactic and is less likely to go to movies with cold opens. Thus, if everyone were rational, studios wouldn't use cold openings.

However, Brown et al. (2012) found that while some moviegoers instantly understand the system, some never catch on to this pattern. As a result, cold opens generate more revenue and more profit on average than comparable not-very-good movies that are prescreened. And, on average, moviegoers are disappointed by cold opens relative to other movies. Thus, a manager is well-advised not to overestimate the reasoning ability of the general movie-going public.

Managerial Solution

Intel and AMD's Advertising Strategies

As we've seen, when one firm in a market acts before another, the first mover may gain an advantage large enough to discourage the second firm from entering the market. In a less extreme case, the original firm may gain a smaller advantage so that the second firm enters, but it produces less than the original firm (as in a Stackelberg model). We can use this insight to provide a possible explanation for the Managerial Problem: In the market for CPUs for personal computers, why does Intel advertise substantially while AMD does not?

The game tree indicates a plausible explanation. Intel decides on how much to invest in its advertising campaign before AMD can act. AMD then decides whether to advertise heavily. We solve for the subgame-perfect Nash equilibrium by working backward. For the profits in this game, if Intel were to have a minimal advertising campaign, AMD makes more if it advertises a lot ($\pi_A = 8$) than if it too has a low level of advertising ($\pi_A = 2$). If Intel advertises heavily, AMD makes more with a low-level advertising campaign ($\pi_A = 4$) than with a high-level campaign ($\pi_A = 3$). Given how it expects AMD to behave, Intel intensively advertises because doing so produces a higher profit ($\pi_I = 8$) than does the lower level of advertising ($\pi_I = 4$).

Thus, because Intel acts first and can commit to advertising aggressively, it can place AMD in a position where it makes more with a low-key advertising campaign. Of course, the results might vary if the profits in the game tree differ, but this example provides a plausible explanation for why the firms use different strategies.

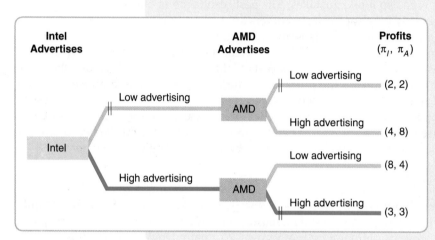

Intel Advertises	AMD Advertises	Profits (π_I, π_A)

Low advertising → (2, 2)
High advertising → (4, 8)
Low advertising → (8, 4)
High advertising → (3, 3)

SUMMARY

1. **Repeated Games.** In some dynamic games, a constituent game (a static game) is repeated over subsequent periods, such as when firms make price or quantity decisions every quarter. Therefore, a firm may use a strategy in which it makes a particular move contingent on its rival's actions in previous periods. By using contingent strategies, such as a tit-for-tat strategy or another trigger strategy, it is often easier for firms to maximize their joint payoff—achieve a collusive solution—in a repeated game than in a single-period game.

2. **Sequential Games.** In other dynamic games, firms move sequentially, with one player acting before another. By moving first, a firm is able to make a *commitment* or *credible threat*. As a consequence, the first mover may receive a higher profit than if the firms act simultaneously. For example, in the Stackelberg oligopoly model, one firm is a *leader* in a sequential game and therefore chooses its output level before rival firms (followers) choose theirs. Applying backward induction, the leader anticipates a follower's reaction and chooses its best output accordingly in the first stage. This first-stage output is a commitment that allows the

leader to gain a first-mover advantage. The leader produces more output and earns higher profits than does a follower firm with the same costs.

3. **Deterring Entry.** An incumbent firm may be able to maintain its monopoly by acting first to deter entry. Some incumbents can sign exclusive contracts that prevent entry, but they do so only if entry is likely and it pays to prevent it. Other incumbents engage in limit pricing where they set a low price or, equivalently, produce a large quantity of output so that a rival cannot profitably enter. The incumbent can feasibly do so only if it has an advantage over the potential rival. If the incumbent can act first, it may be able to commit to producing a large enough output or low enough price after entry that the rival would make losses, thereby deterring entry. If an incumbent faces entry in many markets, it may act to deter the first several entry attempts even if it doesn't pay in those markets so as to gain a reputation for toughness that may deter entry in other markets.

4. **Cost Strategies.** A firm that can act first to lower its marginal cost relative to its rivals may gain a strategic advantage. This strategic advantage from

having a relatively low cost may be large enough that it pays a firm to invest in capital to lower its marginal cost even if the investment cost exceeds the potential production cost savings. Because firms in many industries can lower their marginal cost of production through learning by doing, the first firm in the industry may produce more than the short-run profit-maximizing output so as to lower its future costs and gain an advantage over latecomers. Similarly, firms sometimes lobby legislatures to impose standards that raise costs throughout the industry if they raise rivals' costs by more than its own.

5. **Disadvantages of Moving First.** Although moving first is usually an advantage, exceptions exist. If one firm must make a specific investment to transact with another firm, the investment may

become a hostage. The second firm can hold up the investing firm, for example, by lowering its payment to the investing firm. When firms fear such holdup problems, some desirable transactions never occur. If the first entrant in a market enters so hastily that it incurs excessive costs or doesn't refine its product adequately, it may not compete well with later entrants with superior products.

6. **Behavioral Game Theory.** Managers in strategic games may not use fully rational strategies because of psychological bias, lack of reasoning ability, or a belief that other managers will not use fully rational strategies. The ultimatum and beauty contest games illustrate that managers should take account of the limited powers of calculation and insight of rivals and should not necessarily assume that all rivals are fully rational.

QUESTIONS

*All exercises are available on MyEconLab; * = answer at the back of this book; C = use of calculus may be necessary.*

1. Repeated Games

*1.1. Two firms are planning to sell 10 or 20 units of their goods and face the following profit matrix:

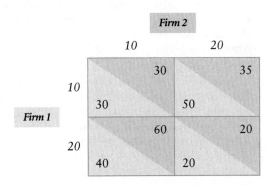

a. What is the Nash equilibrium if both firms make their decisions simultaneously? (*Hint*: See Chapter 12.) What strategy does each firm use?

b. Draw the game tree if Firm 1 can decide first. What is the outcome? Why?

c. Draw the game tree if Firm 2 can decide first. What is the outcome? Why?

*1.2. In the repeated-game airline example illustrated in Table 13.1, what happens if the players know the game will last only five periods? What happens if the game is played forever but the managers of one or both firms care only about current profit?

1.3. In a repeated game, how does the outcome differ if firms know that the game will be (a) repeated indefinitely, (b) repeated a known, finite number of times, and (c) repeated a finite number of times but the firms are always unsure whether the current period will be the last?

1.4. A small tourist town has two Italian restaurants, Romano's and Giardino's. Normally both restaurants prosper with no advertising. Romano's could take some of Giardino's customers by running radio ads and Giardino's could do the same thing. The one-month profit matrix (showing payoffs in thousands of dollars) is:

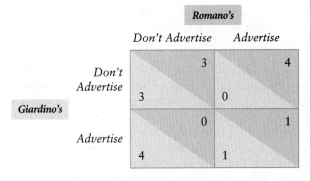

a. What is the Nash equilibrium in the static (one-month) game?

b. If the game is repeated indefinitely, can the use of tit-for-tat strategies result in a Nash equilibrium?

c. Does the game have multiple equilibria if it is repeated indefinitely?

d. Would pre-play communication (Chapter 12) or the Pareto criterion (Chapter 12) have implications for the repeated game equilibrium?

2. Sequential Games

2.1. Solve for the Stackelberg subgame-perfect Nash equilibrium for the following game tree. What is the joint-profit maximizing outcome? Why is that not the outcome of this game? (*Hint*: See Q&A 13.1.)

2.2. The market demand function is $Q = 1,000 - 1,000p$. Each firm has a marginal cost of $m = 0.28$ (28¢ per unit). Firm 1, the leader, acts before Firm 2, the follower. Solve for the Stackelberg equilibrium quantities, prices, and profits. (*Hint*: See Appendix 13.) Compare your solution to the Nash-Cournot equilibrium. **C**

2.3. Suppose the demand function is $Q = 200 - 2p$. Firm A, the leader, acts before Firm B, the follower. Both firms have a constant marginal cost of 10. Draw a diagram with Firm A's output on the horizontal axis. Show the best-response function of Firm B. On the diagram, identify the Nash-Cournot solution, the Stackelberg solution, and the cartel solution.

2.4. Levi Strauss and Wrangler are planning new-generation jeans and must decide on the colors for their products. The possible colors are white, black, and violet. The payoff to each firm depends on the color it chooses and the color chosen by its rival, as the profit matrix shows:

a. Given that the firms move simultaneously, identify any dominant strategies in this game and find any Nash equilibria.

b. Now suppose the firms move sequentially, with Wrangler moving first. Draw a game tree and identify any subgame-perfect Nash equilibria in this sequential-move game.

*2.5. In the sequential-move game described in part b of the previous question, Levi Strauss engages in pre-play communication (cheap talk). Levi Strauss tells Wrangler that it will match Wrangler's color choice if Wrangler chooses black and violet, but that if Wrangler opts for white, Levi Strauss will choose violet. Why would Levi Strauss want Wrangler to believe this claim? Should Wrangler believe it?

2.6. A thug wants the contents of a safe and is threatening the owner, the only person who knows the code, to open the safe. "I will kill you if you don't open the safe, and let you live if you do." Should the owner believe the threat and open the safe? The table shows the value that each person places on the various possible outcomes.

	Thug	Safe's Owner
Open the safe, thug does not kill	4	3
Open the safe, thug kills	2	1
Do not open, thug kills	1	2
Do not open, thug does not kill	3	4

Similar games appear in many films, including *Die Hard*, *Crimson Tide*, and *The Maltese Falcon*.

a. Draw the game tree. Who moves first?

b. What is the equilibrium?

c. Does the safe's owner believe the thug's threat?

d. Does the safe's owner open the safe?

3. Deterring Entry

3.1. A gas station at a rest stop along the highway can pay the owner of the rest stop $40,000 to prevent a second station from opening. Without entry, the incumbent gas station's profit is $\pi_i = \$100,000$. With entry, its duopoly profit would be $45,000 and the entrant would earn a profit of $30,000. Will the incumbent pay for exclusivity? Will entry occur? Use a game-tree diagram to answer these questions.

3.2. The more an incumbent firm produces in the first period, the lower its marginal cost in the second period. If a potential rival expects the incumbent to produce a large quantity in the second period, it does not enter. Draw a game tree to illustrate why an incumbent would produce more in the first period than the single-period profit-maximizing level. Now change the payoffs in the tree to show a situation in which the firm does not increase production in the first period.

*3.3. An incumbent can commit to producing a large quantity of output before the potential rival decides whether to enter. The incumbent chooses whether to commit to produce a small quantity, q_i, or a large quantity. The rival then decides whether to enter. If the incumbent commits to the small output level and the rival does not enter, the rival makes $0 and the incumbent makes $900. If it does enter, the rival makes $125 and the incumbent earns $450. If the incumbent commits to producing the large quantity, and the potential rival stays out of the market, the potential rival makes $0 and the incumbent makes $800. If the rival enters, it loses $20, and the incumbent earns only $400. Show the game tree. What is the subgame-perfect Nash equilibrium? (*Hint*: See Q&A 13.2.)

*3.4. Xavier and Ying are partners in a course project. Xavier is the project leader and is the first to decide how many hours, x, to put into the project. After observing the amount of time that Xavier contributes, Ying decides how many hours, y, to devote. The mark obtained by the project is $10(x + y)^{0.5}$. Ying's utility function is $U = 10(x + y)^{0.5} - y$. How many hours does Ying work if Xavier works 15 hours? If Xavier does not want Ying to work on the project at all, how many hours should he work? **C**

3.5. Walmart has a reputation for using a variety of legal means to prevent unionization of its stores by frustrating union organizers (Lichtenstein, 2008). Why would it make sense for Walmart to spend more trying to deter unionization at a given store than it would save by preventing unionization at that one store? (*Hint*: Walmart has thousands of stores in the United States alone and thousands more in other countries. Would the theory of repeated games apply?)

4. Cost Strategies

4.1. A monopoly manufacturing plant currently uses many workers to pack its product into boxes. It can replace these workers with an expensive set of robotic arms. Although the robotic arms raise the monopoly's fixed cost substantially, they lower its marginal cost because it no longer has to hire as many workers. Buying the robotic arms raises its total cost: The monopoly can't sell enough boxes to make the machine pay for itself, given the market demand curve. Suppose the incumbent does not invest. If its rival does not enter, it earns $0 and the incumbent earns $900. If the rival enters, it earns $300 and the incumbent earns $400. Now suppose that the incumbent does invest. If the rival does not enter, it earns $0 and the incumbent earns $500. If the rival enters, the rival loses $36 and the incumbent makes $132. Show the game tree. Should the monopoly buy the machine anyway?

*4.2. Before entry, the incumbent earns a monopoly profit of $\pi_m = \$10$ (million). If entry occurs, the incumbent and rival each earn the duopoly profit, $\pi_d = \$3$. Suppose that the incumbent can induce the government to require all firms to install pollution-control devices that cost each firm $4. Show the game tree. Should the incumbent urge the government to require pollution-control devices? Why or why not?

4.3. Use a game tree to illustrate why an aircraft manufacturer may price below the current marginal cost in the short run if it has a steep learning curve. (*Hint*: Show that learning by doing lowers its cost in the second period.)

4.4. In Q&A 13.3, suppose that $A = 12$ but that profits under the current wage and high output are 14 for Firm 1 and 11 for Firm 2. Which wage would Firm 1 choose?

5. Disadvantages of Moving First

5.1. In the Venezuela–ExxonMobil Holdup Problem in Figure 13.5, suppose that the parties could initially agree to a binding contract that Venezuela would pay ExxonMobil x dollars if it nationalizes the oil fields. How large does x have to be for ExxonMobil to invest in Venezuela?

*5.2. Ford invites Clarion to set up a plant at Ford's industrial complex in Brazil, where Clarion will build navigation systems for installation in the Ford cars produced there. If Clarion builds the plant, it would have no buyers for the plant's output except Ford. If Clarion does not build the plant, neither firm benefits. If Clarion does build the plant, Ford considers paying three possible prices for the systems: $p_1 < p_2 < p_3$. Price p_1 is below Clarion's average variable cost, which implies that Clarion would produce nothing. Therefore, Clarion would be out of pocket for the cost of the plant, 100 (million), and Ford would get nothing. If Ford pays price p_2, Clarion would more than cover its variable costs but still lose 90 and Ford would gain 140. At price p_3, both firms would gain 25. Draw the game tree. What is the subgame-perfect Nash equilibrium? Specify a contract that would solve the potential holdup problem. Illustrate your solution in a new game tree and explain why it works.

5.3. Show a game tree where the firm that moves second has a higher profit than one who moves first in the subgame-perfect Nash equilibrium.

6. Behavioral Game Theory

6.1. Draw a game tree that represents the ultimatum game in which the proposer is a first mover who decides how much to offer a responder and the responder then decides to accept or reject the offer. The total amount available is $50 if agreement is reached, but both players get nothing if the responder rejects the offer. Offers must be in whole dollars. What is the subgame-perfect Nash equilibrium? What would you expect to happen in practice?

6.2. A prisoners' dilemma game is played for a fixed number of periods. The fully rational solution is for each player to defect in each period. However, in experiments with students, players often cooperate for a significant number of periods if the total number of repetitions is fairly large (such as 10 of 20). Why? (*Hint*: Consider reciprocity and players' limited reasoning ability.)

*6.3. A new government lottery has been announced. Each person who buys a ticket submits an integer number between 0 and 100. The winner is the person whose submission is closest to $\frac{2}{3}$ of the average of all submissions. If ties occur, the prize will be shared. If Chloe expects other players to select numbers randomly, what number should she choose? If you expect all other players to exhibit the same depth

of reasoning as Chloe, what number would you choose?

7. Managerial Problem

7.1. In the game between Intel and AMD in the Managerial Solution, suppose that each firm earns a profit of 9 if both firms advertise. Use a game tree to determine the new subgame-perfect Nash equilibrium outcome.

7.2. What are the Nash equilibria if both Intel and AMD act simultaneously in the game in the Managerial Solution?

8. Spreadsheet Exercises

8.1. The local cement market is a duopoly with City Cement and Mountain Cement producing quantities q_c and q_m. Cement is a homogeneous product with the inverse demand function $p = 20 - Q$, where $Q = q_c + q_m$. Each firm has a marginal cost of $4 and a fixed cost of $6. City Cement is a Stackelberg leader that sets output first. Mountain Cement acts as a follower. Mountain's best response to any output of City's is $q_m = 8 - q_c/2$.

a. Create a spreadsheet with columns for q_c, q_m, Q, p, and the revenue and profit of each firm. Let q_c take on the values of 0 to 16 in increments of 2 and use the spreadsheet to determine the other values in the table. Assuming that Mountain cannot avoid its fixed costs by shutting down, what output level will City Cement choose?

b. Now use the spreadsheet to determine the monopoly output by setting $q_m = 0$ no matter what output City produces. What is the monopoly price and output? How do these amounts compare with the industry price and output for the Stackelberg model?

8.2. Using the same data as in Spreadsheet Exercise 8.1, assume that City Cement is an incumbent monopoly and Mountain Cement is a potential entrant. City chooses an output level and then Mountain decides whether or not to enter the industry. Mountain can avoid paying fixed costs if it decides not to enter. Create a modified version of the spreadsheet used for Exercise 8.1 to determine what output City should produce now to maximize profit. Is entry blockaded, deterred, or accommodated? (*Hint*: Mountain does not enter if it will earn a negative profit. If it does not enter, its output is 0.) How would your answer change if fixed costs were 2 instead of 6?

Appendix 13   A Mathematical Approach to Stackelberg Oligopoly

We suppose that American Airlines is a Stackelberg leader and United Airlines is a follower in the Chicago–Los Angeles market that we discussed in Chapters 11 and 12. The residual demand function facing American Airlines is the market demand function (Equation 11.1), $Q = 339 - p$, minus the best-response function of United Airlines (Equation 11.6), $q_U = 96 - 0.5q_A$:

$$q_A(p) = Q(p) - q_U(q_A) = 339 - p - [96 - 0.5q_A] = 243 - p + 0.5q_A. \quad (13A.1)$$

Using algebra, we can rewrite Equation 13A.1 as the inverse residual demand function:

$$p = 243 - 0.5q_A. \quad (13A.2)$$

American Airlines, the Stackelberg leader, acts like a monopoly with respect to its residual demand. We know that its marginal revenue (MR_A) function has the same intercept as the inverse residual demand function, Equation 13A.2, and twice the slope: $MR_A = 243 - q_A$.[16] To maximize its profit, American Airlines picks its output so as to equate its marginal revenue to its marginal cost (MC) of 47:

$$MR_A = 243 - q_A = 147 = MC. \quad (13A.3)$$

Using algebra to solve Equation 13A.3 for American Airlines' output, we find that $q_A = 96$. Substituting $q_A = 96$ into United Airlines' best-response function, we learn that United Airlines sells half as many seats as American Airlines: $q_U = 96 - 0.5q_A = 48$. Thus, total output is $Q = q_A + q_U = 96 + 48 = 144$. Substituting $Q = 144$, total output, into the market demand function, we determine that the equilibrium market price is $195.

---

[16]American's revenue function is $R(q_A) = p(q_A)q_A = (243 - 0.5q_A)q_A = 243 - 0.5q_A^2$. Consequently, the marginal revenue function is $MR(q_A) = dR(q_A)/dq_A = 243 - q_A$.

14 Managerial Decision Making Under Uncertainty

We must believe in luck. For how else can we explain the success of those we don't like? —Jean Cocteau

On April 20, 2010, a massive explosion occurred on the Transocean Deepwater Horizon oil rig, which was leased by the oil company BP. The explosion itself killed 11 workers and seriously injured 17 others. In addition, many of the 90,000 workers who participated in the cleanup suffered significant health problems from exposure to various toxins. Safeguards in the well to automatically cap the oil well in case of an accident did not work as expected. Consequently, a massive oil spill of roughly 200 million gallons (according to federal authorities) of oil polluted

the Gulf of Mexico before the well was finally capped. This catastrophic 2010 oil spill in the Gulf of Mexico inflicted gigantic costs for cleaning up Louisiana and other Gulf states and inflicted very large losses on the Gulf fishing and tourism industries.

A bad outcome does not necessarily imply that bad decisions were made. BP could have taken reasonable safety precautions and merely been unlucky. However, government agencies concluded that the explosion and the resulting massive oil leak were largely due to a failure to take appropriate safety and other precautions by BP and its subcontractors.[1] In 2012, BP pled guilty to 11 counts of seaman's manslaughter and was fined a record $4 billion in penalties. In addition, BP was liable for much more due to cleanup costs, civil lawsuits, and other fines and penalties.

There are two explanations for the BP managers' decisions. First, they may have ignored or underestimated the chance of these expensive calamities, improperly reasoning that such

---

[1] According to a *New York Times* column, years before its Deepwater Horizon rig blew, BP was developing a reputation as an oil company that took safety risks to save money. Politicians and regulators pointed to a 2005 Texas refinery explosion that killed 15 workers and a corroded pipeline in Alaska that poured oil into Prudhoe Bay in 2006. Congressman Joe Barton chastised BP managers for their "seeming indifference to safety and environmental issues."

major disasters had not happened to them before and would therefore never happen in the future (or at least that the chances were miniscule).

Second, they may have assumed that they would not bear the full costs of the catastrophe even if it did occur because governments would either partially bail them out or the courts would limit their liability. They had good reason for making this assumption. In 1990, Congress passed a law that limited liability beyond cleanup costs at $75 million for a rig spill, a tiny fraction of the harm in this case. In the face of international condemnation for the massive Gulf spill, BP agreed to waive this cap and estimated that it would ultimately pay $42 billion for the cleanup and fines. (However, based on court decisions in 2013, it may owe substantially more.) These losses are substantial compared to its profit of $9 billion and shareholders' equity of $73 billion in 2012.

BP made a calculated choice about the risks that a catastrophic oil spill would happen, presumably taking the $75 million cap on liability into account in making their decisions. How does a cap on liability affect a firm's willingness to make a risky investment or to invest less than the optimal amount in safety? How does a cap affect the amount of risk that the firm and others in society bear? How does a cap affect the amount of insurance against the costs of an oil spill that a firm buys?

L ife is full of uncertainty. Will you get a good summer job? Will you be in a car accident? Will the shares of stock you've bought increase in value? Will you avoid earthquakes and floods? Managers in all types of business confront a wide variety of risks, including the danger of fire and theft, exchange rate fluctuations, economic downturns, and adverse scientific findings about their products. Some managers dread having to make risky decisions, because if the outcome is bad, they may be fired or have their pay cut.

In this chapter, we extend our analyses of decision making by individuals and firms to include uncertainty. We look at how uncertainty affects consumption decisions made by individuals and business decisions made by firms.

When making decisions about investments and other matters, consumers and managers consider the possible *outcomes* under various circumstances, or *states of nature*. For example, a pharmaceutical firm's drug may either be approved or rejected by a regulatory authority, so the two states of nature are *approve* or *reject*. Associated with each of these states of nature is an outcome: the value of the pharmaceutical firm's stock will be $100 per share if the drug is approved and only $75 if the drug is rejected.

Although we cannot know with certainty what the future outcome will be, we may know that some outcomes are more likely than others. Often an uncertain situation—one in which no single outcome is certain to occur—can be quantified in the sense that we can assign a probability to each possible outcome. For example, if we toss a coin, we can assign a probability of 50% to each of the two possible outcomes: heads or tails. Sometimes quantifiable uncertainty is referred to as *risk*. However, many people do not distinguish between the terms risk and uncertainty. Henceforth, we use these terms interchangeably. All of the examples in this chapter concern quantifiable uncertainty.[2]

---

[2]Uncertainty is unquantifiable when we do not know enough to assign meaningful probabilities to different outcomes or if we do not even know what the possible outcomes are. If asked "Who will be the U.S. President in 10 years?" most of us do not even know the likely contenders, let alone the probabilities.

Consumers and firms modify their decisions about consumption and investment as the degree of risk varies. Indeed, most people are willing to spend money to reduce risk by buying insurance or taking preventive measures. Moreover, most people will choose a riskier investment over a less risky one only if they expect a higher return from the riskier investment.

Main Topic	
In this chapter, we examine five main topics	1. **Assessing Risk:** Probability, expected value, and variance are important concepts that are used to assess the degree of risk and the likely profit from a risky undertaking.
	2. **Attitudes Toward Risk:** Whether managers or consumers choose a risky option over a nonrisky alternative depends on their attitudes toward risk and on the expected payoffs of each option.
	3. **Reducing Risk:** People often try to reduce their overall risk by choosing safe rather than risky options, taking actions to reduce the likelihood of bad outcomes, obtaining insurance, pooling risks by combining offsetting risks, and in other ways.
	4. **Investing Under Uncertainty:** Whether people make an investment depends on the riskiness of the payoff, the expected return, attitudes toward risk, the interest rate, and whether it is profitable to alter the likelihood of a good outcome.
	5. **Behavioral Economics and Uncertainty:** Because some people do not choose among risky options in the way that traditional economic theory predicts, it is important for managers to consider models that incorporate psychological factors.

14.1 Assessing Risk

In America anyone can be president. That's one of the risks you take. —Adlai Stevenson

Gregg, a promoter, is considering whether to schedule an outdoor concert on July 4th. Booking the concert is a gamble: He stands to make a tidy profit if the weather is good, but he'll lose a substantial amount if it rains.

To analyze this decision Gregg needs a way to describe and quantify risk. A particular *event*—such as holding an outdoor concert—has a number of possible *outcomes*—here, either it rains or it does not rain. When deciding whether to schedule the concert, Gregg quantifies how risky each outcome is using a *probability* and then uses these probabilities to determine what he can expect to earn.

Probability

A *probability* is a number between 0 and 1 that indicates the likelihood that a particular outcome will occur. If an outcome cannot occur, it has a probability of 0. If the outcome is sure to happen, it has a probability of 1. If it rains one time in four on July 4th, the probability of rain is $\frac{1}{4}$ or 25%.

These weather outcomes are *mutually exclusive*. Only one of these outcomes can occur: either it rains or it does not rain. This list of outcomes is also *exhaustive*, as no other outcomes are possible. If outcomes are mutually exclusive and exhaustive, exactly one of these outcomes will occur, and the probabilities must add up to 100%.

How can Gregg estimate the probability of rain on July 4th? Usually the best approach is to use the *frequency*, which tells us how often an uncertain event occurred in the past. Otherwise, one has to use a *subjective probability*, which is an estimate of the probability that may be based on other information, such as informal "best guesses" of experienced weather forecasters.

Frequency. The probability is the actual chance that an outcome will occur. Managers do not know the true probability so they have to estimate it. Because Gregg (or the weather department) knows how often it rained on July 4th over many years, he can use that information to estimate the probability that it will rain this year. He calculates θ (theta), the frequency that it rained, by dividing n, the number of years that it rained on July 4th, by N, the total number of years for which he has data:

$$\theta = \frac{n}{N}.$$

Gregg then uses θ, the frequency, as his estimate of the true probability that it will rain this year.

Subjective Probability. Unfortunately, often we lack a history of repeated events that allows us to calculate frequencies. For example, the disastrous magnitude-9 earthquake that struck Japan in 2011, with an accompanying tsunami and nuclear reactor crisis, was unprecedented in modern history.

Where events occur very infrequently, we cannot use a frequency calculation to predict a probability. We use whatever information we have to form a *subjective probability*, which is a best estimate of the likelihood that the outcome will occur—that is, our best, informed guess.

The subjective probability can combine frequencies and all other available information—even information that is not based on scientific observation. If Gregg is planning a concert months in advance, his best estimate of the probability of rain is based on the frequency of rain in the past. However, as the event approaches, a weather forecaster can give him a better estimate that takes into account atmospheric conditions and other information in addition to the historical frequency. Because the forecaster's probability estimate uses personal judgment in addition to an observed frequency, it is a subjective probability.

Probability Distributions. A *probability distribution* relates the probability of occurrence to each possible outcome. Panel a of Figure 14.1 shows a probability distribution over five possible outcomes: zero to four days of rain per month in a relatively dry city. The probability that it rains no days during the month is 10%, as is the probability of exactly four days of rain. The chance of two rainy days is 40%, and the chance of one or three rainy days is 20% each. The probability that it rains five or more days in a month is 0%. These weather outcomes are mutually exclusive and exhaustive, so exactly one of these outcomes will occur, and the probabilities must add up to 100%. For simplicity in the following examples, we concentrate mainly on situations with only two possible outcomes.

Expected Value

One of the common denominators I have found is that expectations rise above that which is expected. —George W. Bush

Gregg's earnings from his outdoor concert will depend on the weather. If it doesn't rain, his profit or value from the concert is $V = 15$ ($15,000). If it rains, he'll have to

FIGURE 14.1 **Probability Distributions**

The probability distribution shows the probability of occurrence for each of the mutually exclusive outcomes. Panel a shows five possible mutually exclusive outcomes. The probability that it rains exactly two days per month is 40%. The probability that it rains more than four days per month is 0%. The probability distributions in panels a and b have the same expected value or mean. The variance is smaller in panel b, where the probability distribution is more concentrated around the mean than the distribution in panel a.

(a) Less Certain

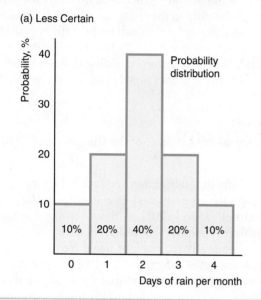

(b) More Certain

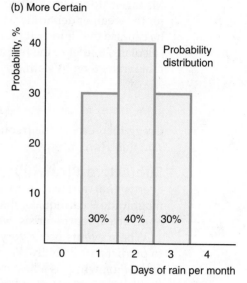

cancel the concert and he will lose the money, $V = -5$ ($5,000), that he must pay the band. Although Gregg does not know what the weather will be with certainty, he knows that the weather department forecasts a 50% chance of rain.

Gregg may use the *mean* or the *average* of the values from both outcomes as a summary statistic of the likely payoff from booking this concert. The amount Gregg expects to earn is called his *expected value* (here, his *expected profit*). The **expected value**, EV, is the weighted average of the values of the outcomes, where each possible outcome is weighted by its probability. That is, the expected value is the sum of the product of the probability and the value of each outcome:[3]

$$EV = [Pr(\text{no rain}) \times \text{Value(no rain)}] + [Pr(\text{rain}) \times \text{Value(rain)}]$$

$$= \left[\tfrac{1}{2} \times 15\right] + \left[\tfrac{1}{2} \times (-5)\right] = 5,$$

where Pr is the probability of an outcome, so $Pr(\text{rain})$ is the "probability that rain occurs."

The expected value is the amount Gregg would earn on average if the event were repeated many times. If he puts on such concerts on the same date over many years and the weather follows historical patterns, he will earn 15 at half of the concerts (those without rain), and he will get soaked for −5 at the other half of the concerts, when it rains. Thus, he'll earn an average of 5 per concert over a long period of time.

---

[3]The expectation operator, E, tells us to take the weighted average of all possible values, where the weights are the probabilities that a particular value will be observed. If there are n possible outcomes, the value of outcome i is V_i, and the probability of that outcome is Pr_i, then the expected value is $EV = Pr_1 V_1 + Pr_2 V_2 + \cdots + Pr_n V_n$.

Q&A 14.1

Suppose that Gregg could obtain perfect information so that he can accurately predict whether it will rain far enough before the concert that he could book the band only if needed. How much would he expect to earn, knowing that he will eventually have this perfect information? How much does he gain by having this perfect information?

Answer

1. *Determine how much Gregg would earn if he had perfect information in each state of nature.* If Gregg knew with certainty that it would rain at the time of the concert, he would not book the band, so he would make no loss or profit: $V = 0$. If Gregg knew that it would not rain, he would hold the concert and make 15.

2. *Determine how much Gregg would expect to earn before he learns with certainty what the weather will be.* Gregg knows that he'll make 15 with a 50% probability $\left(= \frac{1}{2}\right)$ and 0 with a 50% probability, so his expected value, given that he'll receive perfect information in time to act on it, is

$$\left(\tfrac{1}{2} \times 15\right) + \left(\tfrac{1}{2} \times 0\right) = 7.5.$$

3. *Calculate his gain from perfect information as the difference between his expected earnings with perfect information and his expected earnings with imperfect information.* Gregg's gain from perfect information is the difference between the expected earnings with perfect information, 7.5, and the expected earnings without perfect information, 5. Thus, Gregg expects to earn 2.50 ($= 7.50 - 5$) more with perfect information than with imperfect information.[4]

Variance and Standard Deviation

From the expected value, Gregg knows how much he is likely to earn on average if he books many similar concerts. However, he cannot tell from the expected value how risky the concert is. If Gregg's earnings are the same whether it rains or not, he faces no risk and the actual return he receives is the expected value. If the possible outcomes differ from one another, he faces risk.

We can measure the risk Gregg faces in various ways. The most common approach is to use a measure based on how much the values of the possible outcomes differ from the expected value, EV. If it does not rain, the *difference* between Gregg's actual earnings, 15, and his expected earnings, 5, is 10. The difference if it does rain is $-5 - 5 = -10$. It is convenient to combine the two differences—one difference for each state of nature (possible outcome)—into a single measure of risk.

One such measure of risk is the *variance*, which measures the spread of the probability distribution. For example, the probability distributions in the two panels in Figure 14.1 have the same mean (two days of rain) but different variances. The variance in panel a, where the probability distribution ranges from zero to four days of rain per month, is greater than the variance in panel b, where the probability distribution ranges from one to three days of rain per month.

---

[4]This answer can be reached directly. Perfect weather information is valuable to Gregg because he can avoid hiring the band when it rains. (Having information has no value if it cannot be used.) The value of this information is his expected savings from not hiring the band when it rains: $\frac{1}{2} \times 5 = 2.50$.

TABLE 14.1 Variance and Standard Deviation: Measures of Risk

Outcome	Probability	Value	Deviation = Value − 5	Deviation^2	Deviation^2 × Probability
No rain	$\frac{1}{2}$	15	10	100	50
Rain	$\frac{1}{2}$	−5	−10	100	50
				Variance	100
				Standard Deviation	10

Note: Deviation = Value − EV.

Formally, the variance is the probability-weighted average of the squares of the differences between the observed outcome and the expected value.[5] The variance of the value Gregg obtains from the outdoor concert is

$$\text{Variance} = [Pr(\text{no rain}) \times (\text{Value(no rain)} - EV)^2]$$
$$+ [Pr(\text{rain}) \times (\text{Value(rain)} - EV)^2]$$

$$= \left[\tfrac{1}{2} \times (15 - 5)^2\right] + \left[\tfrac{1}{2} \times (-5 - 5)^2\right]$$

$$= \left[\tfrac{1}{2} \times (10)^2\right] + \left[\tfrac{1}{2} \times (-10)^2\right] = 100.$$

Table 14.1 shows how to calculate the variance of the profit from this concert step by step. The first column lists the two outcomes: rain and no rain. The next column gives the probability that each outcome will occur. The third column shows the value or profit of each outcome. The next column calculates the difference between the values in the third column and the expected value, $EV = 5$. The following column squares these differences, and the last column multiplies these squared differences by the probabilities in the second column. The sum of these probability-weighted differences, 100, is the variance.

Instead of describing risk using the variance, economists and businesspeople often report the *standard deviation*, which is the square root of the variance. The usual symbol for the standard deviation is σ (sigma), so the symbol for variance is σ^2. For the outdoor concert, the variance is $\sigma^2 = 100$ and the standard deviation is $\sigma = 10$.

Managerial Implication

Summarizing Risk

Making managerial decisions in the presence of uncertainty is challenging. Managers can make better decisions by listing the possible outcomes, assigning probabilities to each, and calculating expected values and variances that serve as summary measures of the uncertainty they face. These measures can be used to evaluate the profit potential of risky investments and to determine the degree of risk arising from such investments.

---

[5]If there are n possible outcomes with an expected value of EV, the value of outcome i is V_i, and the probability of that outcome is Pr_i, then the variance is

$$Pr_1(V_1 - EV)^2 + Pr_2(V_2 - EV)^2 + \cdots + Pr_n(V_n - EV)^2.$$

The variance puts more weight on large deviations from the expected value than on smaller ones.

14.2 Attitudes Toward Risk

Given the risks Gregg faces if he schedules a concert, will Gregg stage the concert? To answer this question, we need to know Gregg's attitude toward risk.

Expected Utility

If Gregg did not care about risk, then he would promote either an indoor or an outdoor concert based on which option had a higher expected value (profit) regardless of any difference in risk. However, like most people, Gregg cares about risk as well as expected value. Indeed, most people are *risk averse*—they dislike risk.

They will choose a riskier option over a less risky option only if the expected value of the riskier option is sufficiently higher than that of the less risky one.

We need a formal means to judge the trade-off between expected value and risk—to determine if the expected value of the riskier option is sufficiently higher to justify the greater risk. The most commonly used method is to extend the model of utility maximization. In Chapter 4, we noted that one can describe an individual's preferences over various bundles of goods by using a utility function. John von Neumann and Oskar Morgenstern (1944) extended the standard utility-maximizing model to include risk.[6] This approach can be used to show how people's taste for risk affects their choices among options that differ in both expected value and risk, such as career choices, the types of contracts to accept, where to build plants, whether to buy insurance, and which stocks to buy.

In this reformulation, we assume that the individual knows the value of each possible outcome and the probability that it will occur. A rational person maximizes *expected utility*. Expected utility is the probability-weighted average of the utility from each possible outcome. For example, Gregg's expected utility, EU, from promoting the outdoor concert is

$$EU = [Pr(\text{no rain}) \times U(\text{Value(no rain)})] + [Pr(\text{rain}) \times U(\text{Value(rain)})]$$

$$= \left[\tfrac{1}{2} \times U(15)\right] + \left[\tfrac{1}{2} \times U(-5)\right],$$

where his utility function, U, is a function of his earnings. For example, $U(15)$ is the amount of utility Gregg gets from earnings or wealth of 15.[7]

---

[6]This approach to handling choice under uncertainty is the most commonly used method. Schoemaker (1982) discusses the logic underlying this approach, the evidence for it, and several variants. Machina (1989) discusses a number of alternative methods. Here we treat utility as a cardinal measure rather than an ordinal measure.

[7]People have preferences over the goods they consume. However, for simplicity, we'll say that a person receives utility from earnings or wealth, which can be spent on consumption goods.

In short, the expected utility calculation is similar to the expected value calculation. Both are weighted averages in which the weights are the probabilities that correspond to the various possible outcomes. The mathematical difference is that the expected value is the probability-weighted average of the monetary value, whereas the expected utility is the probability-weighted average of the utility from the monetary value. The key economic difference is that the expected utility captures the trade-off between risk and value, whereas the expected value considers only value.

If we know how an individual's utility increases with wealth, we can determine how that person reacts to risky situations. We refer to a risky situation as a *bet*. Thus, for example, if Gregg schedules his concert outdoors, he is betting that it will not rain. We can classify people based on their willingness to make a **fair bet**: a bet with an expected value of zero. An example of a fair bet is one in which you pay a dollar if a flipped coin comes up heads and receive a dollar if it comes up tails. Because you expect to win half the time and lose half the time, the expected value of this bet is zero:

$$\left[\tfrac{1}{2} \times (-1)\right] + \left[\tfrac{1}{2} \times 1\right] = 0.$$

In contrast, a bet in which you pay \$2 if you lose the coin flip and receive \$4 if you win is an unfair bet that favors you, with an expected value of

$$\left[\tfrac{1}{2} \times (-2)\right] + \left[\tfrac{1}{2} \times 4\right] = 1.$$

Someone who is unwilling to make a fair bet is **risk averse**. A person who is indifferent about making a fair bet is **risk neutral**. A person who is **risk preferring** is always willing to make a fair bet.[8]

Risk Aversion

We can use our expected utility model to examine how Irma, who is risk averse, makes a choice under uncertainty. Figure 14.2 shows Irma's utility function. The utility function is concave to the wealth axis, indicating that Irma's utility rises with wealth but at a diminishing rate. She has *diminishing marginal utility of wealth*: The extra pleasure from each extra dollar of wealth is smaller than the extra pleasure from the previous dollar. An individual whose utility function is concave to the wealth axis is risk averse. More precisely, a person with a concave utility function would be unwilling to take a fair bet, as we now illustrate.

Unwillingness to Take a Fair Bet. Suppose that Irma has an initial wealth of 40 and has two options. One option is to do nothing and keep the 40, so that her utility is $U(40) = 120$ (the height of point d in Figure 14.2) with certainty. Her other option is to buy a share (a unit of stock) in a start-up company. Her wealth will be 70 if the start-up is a big success and 10 otherwise. Irma's subjective probability is 50% that the firm will be a big success. Her expected value of wealth remains

$$40 = \left(\tfrac{1}{2} \times 10\right) + \left(\tfrac{1}{2} \times 70\right).$$

Thus, buying the stock is a fair bet because she has the same expected wealth whether she purchases the stock or not.

If Irma were risk neutral so that she only cared about her expected value and didn't care about risk, she would be indifferent between buying the stock or

---

[8]The terms *risk loving* and *risk seeking* are sometimes used as synonyms for risk preferring.

FIGURE 14.2 Risk Aversion

Initially, Irma's wealth is 40, so her utility is $U(40) = 120$, at point d. If she buys the stock and it's worth 70, her utility is $U(70) = 140$ at point c. If she buys the stock and it's worth only 10, she is at point a, where $U(10) = 70$. If her subjective probability that the stock will be worth 70 is 50%, the expected value of the stock is $40 = (0.5 \times 10) + (0.5 \times 70)$ and her expected utility from buying the stock is $0.5U(10) + 0.5U(70) = 105$, at point b, which is the midpoint of the line between the good outcome, point c, and the bad outcome, point a. Thus, her expected utility from buying the stock, 105, is less than her utility from having a certain wealth of 40, $U(40) = 120$, so she does not buy the stock. In contrast, if Irma's subjective probability that the stock will be worth 70 is 90%, her expected utility from buying the stock is $0.1U(10) + 0.9U(70) = 133$, point f, which is more than her utility with a certain wealth of 40, $U(40) = 120$, at d, so she buys the stock.

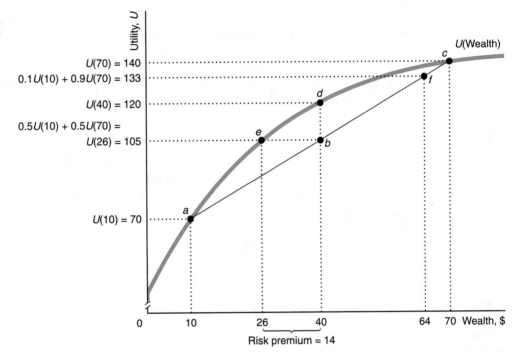

not. However, because Irma is risk averse, Irma prefers not buying the stock because both options have the same expected wealth and buying the stock carries more risk.

We can show that her expected utility is lower if she buys the stock than if she does not. If she buys the stock, her utility if the stock does well is $U(70) = 140$, at point c. If it doesn't do well, her utility is $U(10) = 70$, at point a. Thus, her expected utility from buying the stock is

$$\left[\tfrac{1}{2} \times U(10) \right] + \left[\tfrac{1}{2} \times U(70) \right] = \left[\tfrac{1}{2} \times 70 \right] + \left[\tfrac{1}{2} \times 140 \right] = 105.$$

Her expected utility is the height of point b, which is the midpoint of a line between points a and c. Because Irma's utility function is concave, her utility from certain wealth, 120 at point d, is greater than her expected utility from the risky activity, 105 at point b. As a result, she does not buy the stock. Buying the stock, which is a fair bet, increases the risk she faces without changing her expected wealth. Thus, Irma, because her utility function is concave, prefers not to take a fair bet and is therefore risk averse. *A person whose utility function is concave picks the less risky choice if both choices have the same expected value.*

A risk-averse person chooses a riskier option only if it has a sufficiently higher expected value. Given her wealth of $40, if Irma were much more confident that the stock would be valuable, her expected value would rise and she'd buy the stock, as Q&A 14.2 shows.

Q&A 14.2

Suppose that Irma's subjective probability is 90% that the stock will be valuable. What is her expected wealth if she buys the stock? What is her expected utility? Does she buy the stock?

Answer

1. *Calculate Irma's expected wealth.* Her expected value or wealth is 10% times her wealth if the stock bombs plus 90% times her wealth if the stock does well:

$$(0.1 \times 10) + (0.9 \times 70) = 64.$$

In Figure 14.2, 64 is the distance along the wealth axis corresponding to point f.

2. *Calculate Irma's expected utility.* Her expected utility is the probability-weighted average of her utility under the two outcomes:

$$[0.1 \times U(10)] + [0.9 \times U(70)] = [0.1 \times 70] + [0.9 \times 140] = 133.$$

Her expected utility is the height on the utility axis of point f. Point f is nine-tenths of the distance along the line connecting point a to point c.

3. *Compare Irma's expected utility to her certain utility if she does not buy the stock.* Irma's expected utility from buying the stock, 133 (at point f), is greater than her certain utility, 120 (at point d), if she does not. Thus, if Irma is this confident that the stock will do well, she buys it. Although the risk is greater from buying than from not buying, her expected wealth is sufficiently higher (64 instead of 40) that it's worth it to her to take the chance.

Using Calculus

Diminishing Marginal Utility of Wealth

Irma's utility from W wealth is $U(W)$. She has positive marginal utility from extra wealth, $dU(W)/dW > 0$. That is, the slope of her utility function is positive.

Because Irma's utility function is concave in Figure 14.2, Irma is risk averse. This concavity is also equivalent to saying that her utility increases with wealth at a diminishing rate: $d^2U(W)/dW^2 < 0$. Therefore, if we know an individual's utility function, we can infer that person is risk averse if the second derivative of the utility function is negative.

The Risk Premium. The *risk premium* is the maximum amount that a decision maker would pay to avoid taking a risk. Equivalently, the risk premium is the minimum extra compensation (premium) that a decision maker would require to willingly incur a risk.

We can use Figure 14.2, where Irma owns the stock that has a 50% chance of being worth 70 and a 50% chance of being worth 10, to determine her risk premium. The risk premium is the difference between her expected wealth from the risky stock and the amount of wealth, called the *certainty equivalent*, that if held with certainty, would yield the same utility as this uncertain prospect.

Irma's expected wealth from holding the stock is 40, and the corresponding expected utility is 105. The certainty equivalent income is 26, because Irma's utility is 105 if she has 26 with certainty: $U(26) = 105$, which is the same as her expected utility from owning the stock. Thus, she would be indifferent between keeping the stock or selling it for a price of 26. Thus her risk premium, the difference between the expected value of the uncertain prospect and the certainty equivalent, is $40 - 26 = 14$, as the figure shows.

Mini-Case

Stocks' Risk Premium

The value of most stocks is more variable over time than are bonds. Because stocks are riskier than bonds, for both to be sold in the market to risk-averse investors, the rates of return on investing in stocks must exceed those on bonds over the period that the investor plans to hold these investments. This greater return is an investor's risk premium for stocks.

For example, a U.S. government bond is essentially free of any risk that the U.S. government will default. As Figure 14.2 illustrates, an investor will buy a stock only if it provides a risk premium over a risk-free U.S. government bond. That is, the investor buys the stock only if the amount by which the expected return on the stock exceeds the rate of return on the bond.

In 2012, the stocks in the Standard and Poor's index of 500 leading stocks, the S&P 500, had a return of 15.8%, which substantially exceeded the 3.0% return on 10-year U.S. treasury bonds. However, stocks do not always outperform safe government bonds. In some years, such as 2011, stocks have performed worse than bonds.

Nonetheless, stocks have had a higher rate of return over longer periods. For the 50-year period 1963–2012, the average annual return was 11.1% for S&P 500 stocks and 7.2% on long-term bonds.[9]

Risk Neutrality

Someone who is risk neutral is indifferent about taking a fair bet. Such a person has a constant marginal utility of wealth: Each extra dollar of wealth raises utility by the same amount as the previous dollar. With a constant marginal utility of wealth, the utility function is a straight line in a graph of utility against wealth. As a consequence, a risk-neutral person's utility depends only on wealth and not on risk.

Suppose that Irma is risk neutral and has the straight-line utility function in panel a of Figure 14.3. She would be indifferent between buying the stock and receiving 40 with certainty if her subjective probability is 50% that it will do well. Her expected utility from buying the stock is the average of her utility at points a (10) and c (70):

$$\left[\tfrac{1}{2} \times U(10)\right] + \left[\tfrac{1}{2} \times U(70)\right] = \left[\tfrac{1}{2} \times 70\right] + \left[\tfrac{1}{2} \times 140\right] = 105.$$

Her expected utility exactly equals her utility with certain wealth of 40 (at point b) because the line connecting points a and c lies on the utility function and point b is the midpoint of that line.

Here Irma is indifferent between buying and receiving 40 with certainty, a fair bet, because she doesn't care how much risk she faces. Because the expected wealth from both options is 40, she is indifferent between them.

In general, *a risk-neutral person chooses the option with the highest expected value, because maximizing expected value maximizes utility.* A risk-neutral person chooses the

---

[9]Adjusting for inflation, which averaged 4.2% per year over this period, the average annual real rates of return were 6.9% on the S&P 500 and 3.0% on long-term U.S. government bonds.

FIGURE 14.3 Risk Neutrality and Risk Preference

(a) If Irma's utility function can be graphed as a straight line, she is risk neutral and is indifferent as to whether or not to make a fair bet. Her expected utility from buying the stock, 105 at *b*, is the same as from a certain wealth of 40 at *b*. (b) If the plot of Irma's utility function is convex to the horizontal axis, Irma has increasing marginal utility of wealth and is risk preferring. She buys the stock because her expected utility from buying the stock, 105 at *b*, is higher than her utility from a certain wealth of 40, 82 at *d*.

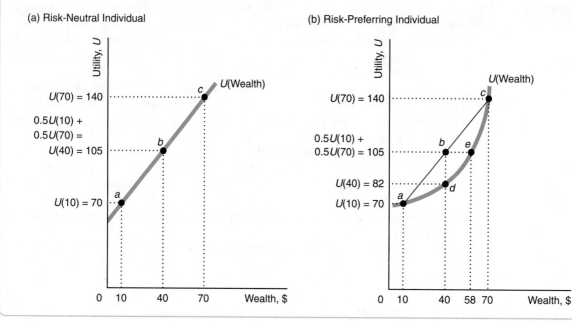

(a) Risk-Neutral Individual

(b) Risk-Preferring Individual

riskier option if it has even a slightly higher expected value than the less risky option. Equivalently, the risk premium for a risk-neutral person is zero.

Risk Preference

An individual with an increasing marginal utility of wealth is risk preferring and is therefore happy take a fair bet. If Irma has the utility function in panel b of Figure 14.3, she is risk preferring. Her expected utility from buying the stock, 105 at *b*, is higher than her certain utility if she does not buy the stock, 82 at *d*. Therefore, she buys the stock.

A risk-preferring person is willing to pay for the right to make a fair bet (a negative risk premium). As the figure shows, Irma's expected utility from buying the stock is the same as the utility from a certain wealth of 58. Given her initial wealth of 40, if you offer her the opportunity to buy the stock or offer to give her 18, she is indifferent. With any payment smaller than 18, she prefers to buy the stock.

Mini-Case	*Horse sense is the thing a horse has which keeps it from betting on people.*

—W. C. Fields

Gambling

Most people say that they don't like bearing risk. Consistent with such statements, most consumers purchase insurance such as car insurance, homeowner's insurance, medical insurance, and other forms of insurance that reduce the risks they face. But many of these same people gamble.

Christiansen Capital Advisors estimates that U.S. gambling industry revenues were $89 billion in 2009 and global Internet gambling was $24.5 billion in 2010. Over half of the countries in the world have lotteries. According to eLottery, worldwide sales were about $245 billion in 2010. Market research firm **Ystat.com** estimates online gambling growth of about 10% per year from 2010 through 2016.

Not only do many people gamble, but they make unfair bets, in which the expected value of the gamble is negative. That is, if they play the game repeatedly, they are likely to lose money in the long run. For example, the British government keeps half of the total amount bet on its lottery. Americans lose at least $50 billion or 7% of all legal bets.

Why do people take unfair bets? Some people gamble because they are risk preferring or because they have a compulsion to gamble.[10] However, neither of these observations is likely to explain noncompulsive gambling by most people who exhibit risk-averse behavior in the other aspects of their lives (such as buying insurance). Risk-averse people may make unfair bets because they get pleasure from participating in the game or because they falsely believe that the gamble favors them.

The first explanation is that gambling provides entertainment as well as risk. Risk-averse people insure their property, such as their homes, because they do not want to bear the risk of theft, flooding, and fire. However, these same people may play poker or bet on horse races because they get enough pleasure from playing those games to put up with the financial risk and the expected loss.

Many people definitely like games of chance. One survey found that 65% of Americans say that they engage in games of chance even when the games involve no money or only trivial sums. That is, they play because they enjoy the games. The anticipation of possibly winning and the satisfaction and excitement arising from a win generate greater benefits than the negative feelings associated with a loss.

Instead or in addition, people may gamble because they make mistakes.[11] Either people do not know the true probabilities or cannot properly calculate expected values, so they do not realize that they are participating in an unfair bet. And some gamblers are simply overconfident: they over-estimate their likelihood of winning.

---

[10]Friedman and Savage (1948) suggest that some gamblers are risk averse with respect to small gambles but risk preferring for large ones, such as a lottery.

[11]Economists, who know how to calculate expected values and derive most of their excitement from economic models, are apparently less likely to gamble than are other people. A number of years ago, an association of economists met in Reno, Nevada. Reno hotels charge low room rates on the assumption that they'll make plenty from guests' gambling losses. However, the economists gambled so little that they were asked pointedly not to return.

Risk Attitudes of Managers

Some shareholders want managers to be risk neutral and to maximize expected profit. However, for a variety of reasons, managers may make either risk-averse or risk-preferring decisions even if shareholders prefer risk-neutral decisions.

First, managers may act in their own interests. (See Chapters 7 and 15 for a discussion of the principal-agent problem.) If a manager is risk averse when making personal decisions, the manager may also avoid risk when making decisions for the firm. For example, if a manager is worried about being fired if the firm has large losses, the manager may act to avoid the possibility of such losses, even if doing so lowers the firm's expected profit. That is, the manager is willing for the firm to pay a risk premium (reduced expected profit) to avoid bearing an extreme risk of losing a lot of money. Alternatively, a manager may prefer risk if the manager's compensation is based on the firm's short-run profit and the manager can walk away in the event of a very bad outcome.

It is also possible that shareholders might want managers to behave in a risk-averse manner. For example, if bankruptcy would impose large costs on individual shareholders, they might prefer that managers try to avoid the very bad outcome of bankruptcy even at the expense of reduced expected profit.

14.3 Reducing Risk

If most accidents occur in the home, why not live elsewhere?

Risk-averse people want to eliminate or reduce the risks they face. Risk-neutral people avoid unfair bets that are stacked against them, and even risk-preferring people avoid very unfair bets. Individuals can avoid optional risky activities, but often they can't escape risk altogether. Property owners, for instance, always face the possibility that their property will be damaged or stolen. However, they may be able to reduce the probability that bad events (such as earthquakes, tornadoes, fires, floods, and thefts) happen to them.

But dear! Flying is safer than driving.

The simplest way to avoid risk is to abstain from optional risky activities. No one forces you to bet on the lottery, go into a high-risk occupation, or buy stock in a start-up biotech firm. If one brand of a product you use comes with a warranty and an otherwise comparable brand does not, you lower your risk by buying the product with the warranty.

Even when you can't avoid risk altogether, you can take precautions to reduce the probability of bad events or the magnitude of any loss that might occur. For example, by maintaining your car as the manufacturer recommends, you reduce the probability that it will break down. By locking the door to your home, you lower the chance that your television will be stolen. Installing fire alarms and indoor sprinkler systems lessens the likelihood that your house will burn down. By reducing your risk, these actions raise the expected value of your asset.

In this section, we look at the three most common ways in which people and firms avoid or limit the risks they face: obtaining information, diversification, and insurance.

Obtaining Information

Collecting accurate information before acting is one of the most important ways in which people can reduce risk and increase expected value and expected utility, as Q&A 14.1 illustrated. Armed with information, you might avoid a risky choice or might be able to take actions that reduce the probability of a disaster or the size of the loss.

Before deciding where to locate a new plant, a prudent manager collects information about various locations concerning local crime rates, fire risks, and other potential hazards. Similarly, a bond fund manager tries to determine risk associated with various bonds before buying them.

Mini-Case

Bond Ratings

Investors obtain information about the riskiness of bonds by checking reports on their riskiness, such as the Moody's and Standard & Poor's ratings in the table. Even though the 2007–2009 financial crisis cast much doubt on the reliability of these ratings, they are still widely used by investors.

These letter-grade ratings reflect whether a bond's issuer has made timely payments in the past, whether the issuer is in danger of becoming bankrupt, and other problems. *Investment grade* bonds (Moody's Baa through Aaa or Standard and Poor's BBB– through AAA) are said to be suitable for purchase by an institutional money manager, such as a pension fund manager, who is legally obligated to be a *prudent investor*—one who does not take great risks. Lower-ranked bonds (Moody C through Ba and Standard and Poor D through BB+) are riskier and thus must offer higher rates of return as inducements for people to buy them. The lowest ranked, junk bonds are generally issued by new firms that have little or no financial history or by established firms that have had their bond ratings downgraded because they've suffered severe financial problems.

Bond Ratings[12]

Moody's		Standard and Poor's	
Descriptor	Grade	Descriptor	Grade
Investment Grade			
Highest quality/minimal credit risk	Aaa	Extremely strong capacity to meet financial commitments	AAA
High quality/very low credit risk	Aa	Very strong capacity to meet financial commitments	AA
Upper medium quality/low credit risk	A	Strong capacity to meet financial commitments	A
Medium grade/moderate credit risk	Baa	Adequate capacity to meet financial commitments	BBB
		Lowest investment grade	BBB–

---

[12]The labels in the table are descriptive. See the companies **www.moodys.com** and **www.standardandpoors.com** for more precise definitions.

Moody's		Standard and Poor's	
Descriptor	**Grade**	**Descriptor**	**Grade**
High Yield or Junk Bonds			
Speculative elements/subject to substantial credit risk	Ba	Speculative, major ongoing uncertainties	BB+, BB
Speculative/high credit risk	B	Vulnerable but has current capacity to meet commitments	B
Poor quality/very high credit risk	Caa	Vulnerable, dependent on favorable conditions	CCC
Highly speculative/default likely	Ca	Highly vulnerable	CC, C
Lowest quality/in default or default imminent	C	In default	D

Diversification

Although it may sound paradoxical, individuals and firms often reduce their overall risk by making many risky investments instead of only one. This practice is called *risk pooling* or *diversification* and is reflected in the commonly given advice: "Don't put all your eggs in one basket."

Correlation and Diversification. The extent to which diversification reduces risk depends on the degree to which the payoffs of various investments are correlated or move in the same direction.[13] If two investments are positively correlated, one performs well when the other performs well. If two investments are negatively correlated, when one performs well, the other performs badly. If the performances of two investments move *independently*—do not move together in a predictable way—their payoffs are uncorrelated.

   Diversification can eliminate risk if the returns to two investments are perfectly negatively correlated. Suppose that two firms are competing for a government contract and have an equal chance of winning it. Because only one firm can win, if one wins the other must lose. You can buy a share of stock in either firm for $20. The stock of the firm that wins the contract will be worth $40, whereas the stock of the loser will be worth $10. Investments in these stocks have a perfect negative correlation. If one stock turns out to have the high value, 40, the other must have the low value, 10, and vice versa.

---

[13]A measure of the *correlation* between two random variables x and y is

$$\rho = E\left(\frac{(x - \bar{x})}{\sigma_x} \frac{(y - \bar{y})}{\sigma_y}\right),$$

where the E(·) means "take the expectation" of the term in parentheses, $\bar{x}$ and $\bar{y}$ are the means (expected values), and σ_x and σ_y are the standard deviations of x and y. This correlation can vary between -1 and 1. If $\rho = 1$, these random variables are perfectly positively correlated; if $\rho = -1$, they have a perfect negative correlation; and if $\rho = 0$, they are uncorrelated.

If you buy two shares of the same company, your shares are going to be worth either 80 or 20 after the contract is awarded. Thus, their expected value is

$$EV = \left(\tfrac{1}{2} \times 80\right) + \left(\tfrac{1}{2} \times 20\right) = 50$$

with a variance of

$$\sigma^2 = \left[\tfrac{1}{2} \times (80 - 50)^2\right] + \left[\tfrac{1}{2} \times (20 - 50)^2\right] = 900.$$

However, if you buy one share of each, your two shares will be worth $50 no matter which firm wins, and the variance is zero—the risk has been completely eliminated by investing in these negatively correlated stocks.

For diversification to reduce risk, it is not necessary for the investments to have a perfect negative correlation. Indeed, it is not even necessary for the investments to have a negative correlation. Diversification reduces risk even if the two investments are uncorrelated or imperfectly positively correlated, although the risk reduction is not as dramatic as in the case of perfect negative correlation, where the risk can be completely eliminated.

Suppose, for example, that each of the two firms has a 50% chance of getting a government contract, but whether one firm gets a contract does *not* affect whether the other firm wins one. Thus, the stock values of the two firms are uncorrelated and each firm's stock price has an equal probability of being 40 or 10. The probability that both firms win contracts and have a stock price of 40 is $\tfrac{1}{4}$, the chance that one is worth 40 and the other is worth 10 is $\tfrac{1}{2}$, and the chance that each is worth 10 is $\tfrac{1}{4}$. If you buy one share of each firm, the expected value of these two shares is

$$EV = \left(\tfrac{1}{4} \times 80\right) + \left(\tfrac{1}{2} \times 50\right) + \left(\tfrac{1}{4} \times 20\right) = 50,$$

and the variance is

$$\sigma^2 = \left[\tfrac{1}{4} \times (80 - 50)^2\right] + \left[\tfrac{1}{2} \times (50 - 50)^2\right] + \left[\tfrac{1}{4} \times (20 - 50)^2\right] = 450.$$

This expected value is the same as from buying two shares of one firm, but the variance is only half as large. Thus, diversification lowers risk when the values are uncorrelated.

Diversification can reduce risk even if the investments are positively correlated provided that the correlation is not perfect. *Diversification does not reduce risk if two investments have a perfect positive correlation.* For example, if the government awards contracts only to both firms or to neither firm, the risks are perfectly positively correlated. The expected value of the stocks and the variance are the same whether you buy two shares of one firm or one share of each firm.

Diversification Through Mutual Funds. Because the stock price of any given firm is not perfectly correlated with the stock price of other firms, an investor or a manager can reduce risk by buying the stocks of many companies rather than the stock of just one firm. One way to effectively own shares in a number of companies at once is by buying shares in a *mutual fund* of stocks. A mutual fund share is issued by a company that buys stocks in many other companies.

For example, a mutual fund may be based on the *Standard & Poor's Composite Index of 500 Stocks* (S&P 500), which is a value-weighted average of 500 large firms' stocks.[14] The S&P 500 companies constitute only about 7% of all the publicly traded firms in the United States, but they represent approximately 80% of the total value of the U.S.

---

[14]The weights are the market values of the firms, so larger firms get more weight in the index.

stock market. A number of "total market" funds have been introduced, such as the *Wilshire 5000 Index Portfolio*, which initially covered 5,000 stocks but now includes many more, as Wilshire seeks to include nearly all U.S. publicly traded stocks and adds new stocks as they are issued. Other mutual funds are based on bonds or on a mixture of stocks, bonds, and other types of investments.

Mutual funds allow investors to reduce the risk associated with uncorrelated price movements across stocks. Suppose that two companies look very similar on the basis of everything you know about them. You have no reason to think that the stock in one firm will increase more in value or be riskier than the stock of the other firm. However, luck may cause one stock to do better than the other. You can reduce this type of random, firm-specific risk by diversifying and buying stock in both firms.

However, a stock mutual fund has a *market-wide risk*, a risk that is common to the overall market, which arises because the prices of almost all stocks tend to rise when the economy is expanding and to fall when the economy is contracting. You cannot avoid the systematic risks associated with shifts in the economy that have a similar effect on most stocks even if you buy a diversified stock mutual fund.

Managerial Implication

Diversifying Retirement Funds

Risk-averse managers and other employees should diversify their own retirement funds and other savings. However, many managers fail to appropriately diversify their own portfolios by keeping a large portion of their wealth tied up in their employer's stock. One reason for this large share is that many managers receive company stock from their employers as bonuses or to match their pension contributions. In addition, some managers invest voluntarily in company stock as a sign of loyalty.

An important example is the investment firm Bear Stearns, where employees owned one-third of the company's stock. The firm faced bankruptcy in early 2008. Claiming that the firm was too big to be allowed to fail, the U.S. government bailed it out. Under the rescue plan, JPMorgan Chase offered $10 a share to buy Bear Stearns in 2008, which was only a tenth of the stock's value in December 2007. Consequently, not only did many Bear Stearns employees face losing their livelihoods, they also had lost most of their wealth.

In 2007, at the beginning of the recent financial crisis, nearly two of every five employees participating in 401(k) retirement plans in large firms held 20% or more of their money in employer stock.[15] About one-sixth of participants invested 50% or more. On average, these funds held 16% in company stock.

It is very risky for workers to hold such a high percentage of their employer's stock. If a Bear Stearns employee's 401(k) had invested $100,000 in a Standard & Poor's 500-stock index fund at the end of 2007, its value would have fallen to $90,760 by the end of the first quarter of 2008. However, if that employee shifted 16% into Bear Stearns stock, the investment would have fallen to slightly less than $77,838. Even worse, if all the funds had been in Bear Stearns stock, the 401(k) would only have been worth $10,000.

Consequently, many investment advisors recommend investing no more than 5% in employer stock. However, many employees have failed to learn the lesson

---

[15]A 401(k) plan is a retirement program run by a firm for its employees under Section 401 (paragraph k) of the Internal Revenue Code. Employees defer paying taxes on investment returns provided they do not start withdrawing income until after age $59\frac{1}{2}$.

of Bear Stearns and do not follow this advice. For example, in 2011 Morgan Stanley employees held 24% of their retirement assets in company stock at the beginning of the year. The stock price dropped 44% in 2011, imposing a loss of $570 million on these retirement funds. Even by 2013, the average share of 401(k) funds invested in company stock was still over 13%. As managers and other employees are at risk of losing their jobs if their employer does poorly, they should consider diversifying their risk by making investments that are independent of their employer.

Insurance

Individuals and organizations can also avoid or reduce risk by purchasing insurance. As we've already seen, a risk-averse person is willing to pay money—a risk premium—to avoid risk. The demand for risk reduction is met by insurance companies, which bear the risk for anyone who buys an insurance policy. Many risk-averse individuals and firms buy insurance, leading to an industry of enormous size: Global insurance revenues exceeded $4.59 trillion in 2011, approximately 6% of world GDP.[16]

Determining the Amount of Insurance to Buy. Many individuals and firms buy insurance to shift some or all of the risk they face to an insurance company. A risk-averse person or firm pays a premium to the insurance company, and the insurance company transfers money to the policyholder if a bad outcome occurs, such as becoming ill, having an accident, or suffering a property loss due to theft or fire.

Because Scott is risk averse, he wants to insure his store, which is worth 500. The probability that his store will burn next year is 20%. If a fire occurs, the store will be worth nothing.

With no insurance, the expected value of his store is

$$EV = (0.2 \times 0) + (0.8 \times 500) = 400.$$

Scott faces a good deal of risk. The variance of the value of his store is

$$\sigma^2 = \left[0.2 \times (0 - 400)^2 \right] + \left[0.8 \times (500 - 400)^2 \right] = 40,000.$$

Suppose that an insurance company offers **fair insurance**: a contract between an insurer and a policyholder in which the expected value of the contract to the policyholder is zero. That is, the insurance is a fair bet. With fair insurance, for every dollar that Scott pays the insurance company, the *insurance premium*, the company will pay Scott $5 to cover the damage if the fire occurs, so that he has one dollar less if the fire does not occur, but $4 (= $5 – $1) more if it does occur.[17]

Because Scott is risk averse and the insurance is fair, he wants to *fully insure* by buying enough insurance to eliminate his risk altogether. That is, he wants to buy the amount of fair insurance that will leave him equally well off in both states of nature. He pays a premium of x so that he has $500 - x$ if the fire does not occur, and

---

[16]**www.plunkettresearch.com/insurance-risk-management-market-research/industry-overview** (viewed April 8, 2013).

[17]Following standard practice in the insurance industry, we use the term *insurance premium* (or just *premium*) in this section to refer to the amount *actually paid* for insurance. The *insurance premium* is different from a *risk premium*, which is a person's *willingness to pay* to avoid risk.

has $4x$ if the fire occurs, such that $500 - x = 4x$, or $x = 100$.[18] If a fire does not occur, he pays a premium of 100 and has a store worth 500 for a net value of 400. If a fire does occur, Scott pays 100 but receives 500 from the insurance company for a net value of 400. Thus, Scott's wealth is 400 in either case.

Although Scott's expected value with full and fair insurance is the same as his expected value without insurance, the variance he faces drops from 40,000 without insurance to 0 with insurance. Scott is better off with full fair insurance because he has the same expected value and faces no risk. A risk-averse person always wants full insurance if the insurance is fair.

Sometimes insurance companies put limits on the amount of insurance offered. For example, the insurance company could offer Scott fair insurance but only up to a maximum gross payment of, for example, 400 rather than 500. Given this limit, Scott would buy the maximum amount of fair insurance that he could.

Q&A 14.3

The local government collects a property tax of 20 on Scott's store. If the tax is collected whether or not the store burns, how much fair insurance does Scott buy? If the tax is collected only if the store does not burn, how much fair insurance does Scott buy?

Answer

1. *Determine the after-tax expected value of the store without insurance.* If the tax is always collected, the store is worth $480 = 500 - 20$ if it does not burn and -20 if it does burn. Thus, the expected value of the store is

$$380 = [0.2 \times (-20)] + [0.8 \times 480].$$

If the tax is collected only if the fire does not occur, the expected value of the store is

$$384 = [0.2 \times 0] + [0.8 \times 480].$$

2. *Calculate the amount of fair insurance Scott buys if the tax is always collected.* Because Scott is risk averse, he wants to be fully insured so that the after-tax value of his store is the same in both states of nature. If the tax is always collected, Scott pays the insurance company 100. If no fire occurs, his net wealth is $500 - 100 - 20 = 380$. If a fire occurs, the insurance company pays 500, or a net payment of 400 above the cost of the insurance, and Scott pays 20 in taxes, leaving him with 380 once again. That is, he buys the same amount of insurance as he would without any taxes. The tax has no effect on his insurance decision because he owes the tax regardless of the state of nature.

3. *Calculate the amount of fair insurance Scott buys if the tax is collected only if no fire occurs.* If the tax is collected only if no fire occurs, Scott pays the insurance company 96 and receives 480 if a fire occurs. With no fire, Scott's wealth is $500 - 96 - 20 = 384$. If a fire occurs, the insurance company pays 480, so Scott's wealth is $480 - 96 = 384$. Thus, he has the same after-tax wealth in both states of nature.

Comment: Because the tax system is partially insuring Scott by dropping the tax in the bad state of nature, he purchases less private insurance, 480, than the 500 he buys if the tax is collected in both states of nature.

---

[18]The expected value of Scott's insurance contract is $[0.8 \times (-100)] + [0.2 \times 400] = 0$, which shows that the insurance is fair.

Fairness and Insurance. We have been examining situations where the insurance is fair so that the customer's insurance contract has an expected value of zero. However, an insurance company could not stay in business if it offered fair insurance. With fair insurance, the insurance company's expected payments would equal the premiums that the insurance company collects. Because the insurance company has operating expenses—costs of maintaining offices, printing forms, hiring sales agents, and so forth—an insurance firm providing fair insurance would lose money. Insurance companies' rates must be high enough to cover their operating expenses. Thus, we expect that real-world insurance companies offer unfair insurance, charging a premium that exceeds the fair-insurance premium. However, it is important to realize that when we say insurance companies offer unfair insurance, we are not implying that insurance companies are behaving unethically. We only mean that the expected payout to policyholders is less than the premiums paid by policyholders.

In the previous section, we showed that a risk-averse consumer who is offered fair insurance fully insures so that the consumer is equally well off in all states of nature. If insurance companies charge a premium that exceeds the fair-insurance price, these same individuals will buy less insurance so that they are not fully insured.[19]

How much can insurance companies charge for insurance? A monopoly insurance company could charge an amount up to the risk premium a person is willing to pay to avoid risk. For example, in Figure 14.2, Irma's risk premium is 14. She would be willing to pay up to $14 for an insurance policy that would compensate her if her stock did not perform well. The more risk averse an individual is, the more a monopoly insurance company can charge. If many insurance companies compete for business, the price of an insurance policy is less than the maximum that risk-averse individuals are willing to pay—but still high enough that the firms can cover their operating expenses.

Insurance and Diversifiable Risks. Why is an insurance company willing to sell policies and take on risk? By pooling the risks of many people, the insurance company can lower its risk much below that of any individual. If the probability that one car is stolen is independent of whether other cars are stolen, the risk to an insurance company of insuring one person against theft is much greater than the average risk of insuring many people.

Insurance companies generally try to protect themselves from insolvency (going bankrupt) by selling policies only for risks that they can adequately diversify. If the risks from disasters to its policyholders are highly positively correlated, an insurance company is not well diversified just by holding many policies. A war affects all policyholders, so the outcomes that they face are perfectly correlated. Because wars are *nondiversifiable risks*, insurance companies normally do not offer policies insuring against wars.

Mini-Case

Limited Insurance for Natural Disasters

In recent years, many insurance companies have started viewing some major natural disasters as nondiversifiable risks because such catastrophic events cause many insured people to suffer losses at the same time. As more homes have been built in areas where damage from storms or earthquakes is likely, the size of the potential losses to insurers from nondiversifiable risks has grown.

---

[19]As Q&A 14.3 shows, tax laws may offset the problem of unfair insurance, so that some insurance may be fair or more than fair after tax.

Insurers paid out $12.5 billion in claims to residential homeowners after the 1994 Los Angeles earthquake. Farmers Insurance Group reported that it paid out three times more for the Los Angeles earthquake than it had collected in earthquake premiums over the previous 30 years.

According to some estimates, Hurricane Katrina in 2005 caused $100 to $200 billion worth of damage and major loss of life. Private insurers paid out $41 billion, or between 20.5% and 41% of the total damages.

Japan's 2011 magnitude-9 earthquake and the associated tsunami was the most costly in history, with estimated damages of more than $200 billion (with some estimates as high as $350 billion). However, the insurance industry paid only $35 billion, or about 17%, because of Japan's low levels of earthquake insurance protection.

The United States suffered 90% of the $160 billion of global natural disaster damages in 2012, compared to 65% in a typical year. Much of the 2012 U.S. losses were due to drought damage to Midwestern crops and Superstorm Sandy, a massive Atlantic storm that flooded shorelines in the Northeast and even parts of New York City, causing an estimated $65 billion of losses.

Insurance companies now refuse to offer hurricane or earthquake insurance in many parts of the world for these relatively nondiversifiable risks. When Nationwide Insurance Company announced that it was sharply curtailing sales of new policies along the Gulf of Mexico and the eastern seaboard from Texas to Maine, a company official explained, "Prudence requires us to diligently manage our exposure to catastrophic losses."

The U.S. government has stepped in to partially replace private insurers. Since 2008, the Flood Insurance and Mitigation Administration, which is part of the Federal Emergency Management Agency, has provided flood insurance under the National Flood Insurance Program. It has insured over 5.6 million Americans against floods associated with hurricanes, tropical storms, heavy rains, and other conditions. However, Congress has not provided consistent funding for this program, which lapsed at least four times in 2010 alone. Thus, consumers may not be able to count on federal flood insurance always being available.[20]

In some high-risk areas, state-run insurance pools—such as the Florida Joint Underwriting Association and the California Earthquake Authority—provide households with insurance. However, not only do these policies provide less protection, but their rates are often three times more expensive than previously available commercial insurance, and they provide compensation only for damages beyond a specified level, called the *deductible*.

---

[20]One argument against programs that subsidize insurance is that they provide incentives to engage in excessively risky behavior, such as building or buying homes in areas that have a high probability of being flooded.

14.4 Investing Under Uncertainty

We now investigate how uncertainty affects investment decisions. In particular, we examine how attitudes toward risk affect willingness to invest and how investors pay to alter their probabilities of success.

In the following examples, the owner of a monopoly decides whether to open a new retail outlet. Because the firm is a monopoly, the return from the investment (the profit from the new store) does not depend on the actions of other firms. As a result, the owner of the monopoly faces no strategic considerations. The owner knows the cost of the investment but is unsure about how many people will patronize the new store; hence, the store's future profit is uncertain. Because the investment has an uncertain payoff, the owner must take risk into account when deciding to invest in the new store.

We first consider the decision of Chris, a risk-neutral owner. Because she is risk neutral, she invests if the expected value of the firm rises due to the investment. Any action that increases her expected value must also increase her expected utility because she is indifferent to risk. In contrast, in the next example, Ken is risk averse, so he might not make an investment that increases his firm's expected value if the investment is very risky. That is, maximizing expected value does not necessarily maximize his expected utility.

Risk-Neutral Investing

Chris, the risk-neutral owner of the monopoly, uses a *decision tree* (panel a of Figure 14.4) to decide whether to invest. The rectangle, called a *decision node*, indicates that she must make a decision about whether to invest or not. The circle, a *chance*

FIGURE 14.4 Investment Decision Trees with Uncertainty

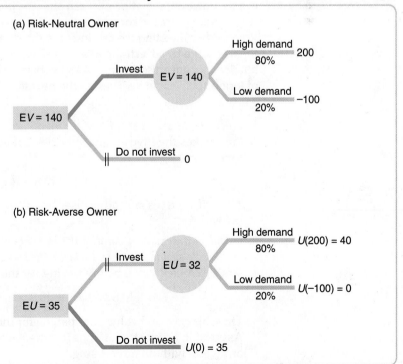

Chris and Ken, each the owner of a monopoly, must decide whether to invest in a new store. (a) The expected value of the investment is 140, so it pays for Chris, who is risk neutral, to invest. (b) Ken is so risk averse that he does not invest even though the expected value of the investment is positive. His expected utility falls if he makes this risky investment.

(a) Risk-Neutral Owner

$EV = 140$

Invest — $EV = 140$ — High demand 80% — 200 / Low demand 20% — -100

Do not invest — 0

(b) Risk-Averse Owner

$EU = 35$

Invest — $EU = 32$ — High demand 80% — $U(200) = 40$ / Low demand 20% — $U(-100) = 0$

Do not invest — $U(0) = 35$

node, denotes that a random process determines the outcome (consistent with the given probabilities). If Chris does not open the new store, she makes $0. If she does open the new store, she expects to make $200 (thousand) with 80% probability and to lose $100 (thousand) with 20% probability. The expected value from a new store (see the circle in panel a) is

$$EV = [0.2 \times (-100)] + [0.8 \times 200] = 140.$$

Because Chris is risk neutral, she prefers an expected value of 140 to a certain one of 0, so she invests. Thus, her expected value in the rectangle is 140.

Risk-Averse Investing

Let's compare Chris' decision-making process to that of Ken's, a risk-averse owner of a monopoly who faces the same investment decision. Ken invests in the new store if his expected utility from investing is greater than his certain utility from not investing. Panel b of Figure 14.4 shows his decision tree, which is based on a particular risk-averse utility function. The circle shows that Ken's expected utility from the investment is

$$EU = [0.2 \times U(-100)] + [0.8 \times U(200)]$$
$$= (0.2 \times 0) + (0.8 \times 40) = 32.$$

Ken's certain utility from not investing is $U(0) = 35$, which is greater than 32. Thus, Ken does not invest. As a result, his expected utility in the rectangle is 35 (his certain utility from not investing).

Q&A 14.4

We have been assuming that nature dictates the probabilities of various possible events. However, sometimes we can alter the probabilities at some expense. Gautam, who is risk neutral, is considering whether to invest in a new store, as Figure 14.5 shows. After investing, he can increase the probability that demand will be high at the new store by advertising at a cost of $50 (thousand). If he makes the investment but does not advertise, he has a 40% probability of making 100 and a 60% probability of losing 100. Should he invest in the new store?

Answer

1. *Calculate the expected value of the investment if Gautam does not advertise.* If Gautam makes the investment but does not advertise, the expected value of his investment is

$$[0.4 \times 100] + [0.6 \times (-100)] = -20.$$

Thus, if he does not advertise, he expects to lose money if he makes this investment.

2. *Calculate the expected value of the investment if. Gautam advertises and determine whether he should invest and whether he should advertise.* With advertising, Gautam's expected value before paying for the advertisements is

$$[0.8 \times 100] + [0.2 \times (-100)] = 60.$$

Thus, his expected value after paying for the advertisements is 10 (= 60 − 50). As a result, he is better off if he invests *and* advertises than if he does not invest or invests without advertising.

FIGURE 14.5 An Investment Decision Tree with Uncertainty and Advertising

By advertising, Gautam, the risk-neutral owner of a monopoly, can alter the probability of high demand. The expected value of the investment is −20 without advertising and 60 with advertising. Because the cost of advertising is 50, the expected value of investing and advertising is 10 (= 60 − 50). Thus, Gautam invests and advertises.

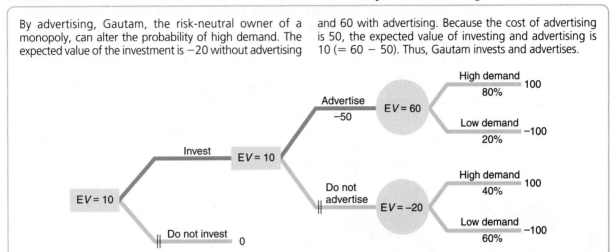

14.5 Behavioral Economics and Uncertainty

In the expected utility model, as in the standard utility model, we assume that people make rational choices (Chapter 4). However, many individuals make choices that are inconsistent with the predictions of the expected utility model. Economists and psychologists explain some of these departures from the predictions of the expected utility model using *behavioral economics*: the use of insights from psychology and research on human cognition and emotional biases to augment the rational economic model in an attempt to better predict economic decision making. (We discussed other applications of behavioral economics in Chapters 4, 9, and 13.)

Biased Assessment of Probabilities

People often have mistaken beliefs about the probability that an event will occur. These biases in estimating probabilities come from several sources, including false beliefs about causality and overconfidence.

The Gambler's Fallacy. Many people fall victim to the *gambler's fallacy*: the false belief that past events affect current, independent outcomes.[21] For example, suppose that you flip a fair coin and it comes up heads six times in a row. What are the odds that you'll get a tail on the next flip? Because past flips do not affect this one, the chance of a tail remains 50%, yet many people believe that a head is much more likely because they are on a "run." Others hold the opposite but equally false view that the chance of a tail is high because a tail is "due."

Suppose that you have an urn containing three black balls and two red ones. If you draw a ball without looking, your probability of getting a black ball is $\frac{3}{5} = 60\%$.

---

[21]The false belief that one event affects another independent event is captured by the joke about a man who brings a bomb on board a plane whenever he flies because he believes that "The chances of having one bomb on a plane are very small, so the chance of having two bombs on a plane is near zero!"

If you replace the ball and draw again, the chance of a picking a black ball remains the same. However, if you draw a black ball and do not replace it, the probability of drawing a black ball again falls to $\frac{2}{4} = 50\%$. Thus, the belief that a tail is due after several heads are tossed in a row is analogous to falsely believing that you are drawing without replacement when you are actually drawing with replacement.

Overconfidence. Another common explanation for why some people make bets that the rest of us avoid is that these gamblers are overconfident. For example, Golec and Tamarkin (1995) found that football bettors tend to make low-probability bets because they greatly overestimate their probabilities of winning certain types

of exotic football bets (an *exotic bet* depends on the outcome of more than one game). In one survey, gamblers estimated their chance of winning a particular bet at 45% when the objective probability was 20%.

Few groups exhibit more overconfidence than male high school athletes. Many U.S. high school basketball and football players believe they will get an athletic scholarship to attend college, but less than 5% receive one. Of this elite group, about 25% expect to become professional athletes, but only about 1.5% succeed.[22]

Mini-Case	Do newspaper stories, television, and movies cause people to overestimate relatively rare events and underestimate relatively common ones? Newspapers are more likely to publish "man bites dog" stories than the more common "dog bites man" reports.[23]
Biased Estimates	

If you have seen the movie *Jaws*, you can't help but think about sharks before wading into the ocean. In 2012, newspapers around the world reported that a mother saved her daughter from a shark attack off a Florida beach and an Australian man suffered a major gash in his leg from a shark. Do you worry about shark attacks? You really shouldn't.

Only 8 people were killed by sharks in U.S. waters from 2003 through 2012: an average of 0.8 a year. An American's chance of dying from a shark attack is 1 in 3.7 million, but is 1 in 80 thousand from lightning (about 43 times as likely), 1 in 14 thousand from sun or heat exposure, 1 in 218 from a fall, 1 in 84 from a car accident, 1 in 63 from flu, 1 in 38 from hospital infection, 1 in 24 from a stroke, 1 in 7 from cancer, and 1 in 5 from a heart attack.

Benjamin et al. (2001) reported that, when asked to estimate the frequency of deaths from various causes for the entire population, people overestimate the number of deaths from infrequent causes and underestimate those from more common causes. In contrast, if they are asked to estimate the number of deaths among their own age group from a variety of causes, their estimates are almost completely unbiased. That is not to say that people know the true probabilities—only that their mistakes are not systematic.

---

[22]See **www.ncaa.org/wps/wcm/connect/public/Test/Issues/Recruiting/Probability+of+Going+Pro** and Rossi and Armstrong (1989).

[23]For example, Indian papers reported on a man bites snake story, noting that Neeranjan Bhaskar has eaten more than 4,000 snakes (*Calcutta Telegraph*, August 1, 2005) and the even stranger "Cobra Dies after Biting Priest of Snake Temple!" (*Express India*, July 11, 2005).

Violations of Expected Utility Theory

Economists and psychologists have shown that some people's choices violate the basic assumptions of expected utility theory. One important class of violations arises because people change their choices in response to inessential changes in how choices are described or *framed*, even when the underlying probabilities and events do not change. Another class of violations arises because of a bias toward certainty.

Framing. Many people reverse their preferences when a problem is presented or *framed* in different but equivalent ways. Tversky and Kahneman (1981) posed the problem that the United States expects an unusual disease (e.g., avian flu) to kill 600 people. The government is considering two alternative programs to combat the disease. The "exact scientific estimates" of the consequences of these programs are:

- If Program A is adopted, 200 out of 600 people will be saved.
- If Program B is adopted, the probabilities are $\frac{1}{3}$ that 600 people will be saved and $\frac{2}{3}$ that no one will be saved.

When college students were asked to choose, 72% opted for the certain gains of Program A over the possibly larger but riskier gains of Program B.

A second group of students was asked to choose between an alternative pair of programs, and were told:

- If Program C is adopted, 400 out of 600 people will die.
- If Program D is adopted, the probabilities are $\frac{1}{3}$ that no one will die, and $\frac{2}{3}$ that 600 people will die.

When faced with this choice, 78% chose the potentially larger but uncertain losses of Program D over the certain losses of Program C. These results are surprising if people maximize their expected utility: Program A is identical to Program C and Program B is the same as Program D in the sense that these pairs have identical expected outcomes. Expected utility theory predicts consistent choices for the two pairs of programs, but many people make inconsistent choices, preferring Programs A and D. (Even after rereading the options and having the inconsistency problem explained, most of us still feel drawn toward Programs A and D.)

In many similar experiments, researchers have repeatedly observed this pattern, called the *reflection effect*: attitudes toward risk are reversed (reflected) for gains versus losses. People are often risk averse when making choices involving gains, but they are often risk preferring when making choices involving losses.

The Certainty Effect. Many people put excessive weight on outcomes that they consider to be certain relative to risky outcomes. This *certainty effect* (or *Allais effect*, after the French economist who first noticed it) can be illustrated using an example from Kahneman and Tversky (1979). First, a group of subjects was asked to choose between two options:

- **Option A.** You receive $4,000 with probability 80% and $0 with probability 20%.
- **Option B.** You receive $3,000 with certainty.

The vast majority, 80%, chose the certain outcome, B.

Then, the subjects were given another set of options:

- **Option C.** You receive $4,000 with probability 20% and $0 with probability 80%.
- **Option D.** You receive $3,000 with probability 25% and $0 with probability 75%.

Now, 65% prefer C.

Kahneman and Tversky found that over half the respondents violated expected utility theory by choosing B in the first experiment and C in the second one. If $U(0) = 0$, then choosing B over A implies that the expected utility from B is greater than the expected utility from A, so that $U(3,000) > 0.8U(4,000)$, or $U(3,000)/U(4,000) > 0.8$. Choosing C over D implies that $0.2U(4,000) > 0.25U(3,000)$, or $U(3,000)/U(4,000) < 0.8 (= 0.2/0.25)$. Thus, these choices are inconsistent with each other, and hence inconsistent with expected utility theory. The certainty of option B seems to give it extra attractiveness over and above what is implied by expected utility theory.

Expected utility theory is based on gambles with known probabilities, whereas most real-world situations involve unknown or subjective probabilities. Ellsberg (1961) pointed out that expected utility theory cannot account for an ambiguous situation in which many people are reluctant to put substantial decision weight on any outcome. He illustrated the problem in a "paradox." Each of two urns contains 100 balls that are either red or black. You know with certainty that the first urn has 50 red and 50 black balls. You do not know the ratio of red to black balls in the second urn. Most of us would agree that the known probability of drawing a red from the first urn, 50%, equals the subjective probability of drawing a red from the second urn. That is, not knowing how many red and black balls are in the second urn, we have no reason to believe that the probability of drawing a red is greater or less than 50%. Yet, most people would prefer to bet that a red ball will be drawn from the first urn rather than from the second urn.

Prospect Theory

Kahneman and Tversky's (1979) *prospect theory*, an alternative theory of decision making under uncertainty, can explain some of the choices people make that are inconsistent with expected utility theory. According to *prospect theory*, people are concerned about gains and losses—the changes in wealth—rather than the level of wealth, as in expected utility theory. People start with a reference point—a base level of wealth—and think about alternative outcomes as gains or losses relative to that reference level.

Comparing Expected Utility and Prospect Theories. We can illustrate the differences in the two theories by comparing how people would act under the two theories when facing the same situation. Both Muzhe and Rui have initial wealth W. They may choose a gamble where they get A dollars with probability θ or B dollars with probability $1 - \theta$. For example, A might be negative, reflecting a loss, and B might be a positive, indicating a gain.

Muzhe wants to maximize his expected utility. If he does not gamble, his utility is $U(W)$. To calculate his expected utility if he gambles, Muzhe uses the probabilities θ and $1 - \theta$ to weight the utilities from the two possible outcomes:

$$EU = \theta U(W + A) + (1 - \theta)U(W + B),$$

where $U(W + A)$ is the utility he gets from his after-gambling wealth if A occurs and $U(W + B)$ is the utility if he receives B. He chooses to gamble if his expected utility from gambling exceeds his certain utility from his initial wealth: $EU > U(W)$.

In contrast, Rui's decisions are consistent with prospect theory. Rui compares the gamble to her current reference point, which is her initial situation where she has W with certainty. The value she places on her reference point is $V(0)$, where 0 indicates that she has neither a gain nor a loss with this certain outcome. The negative value that she places on losing is $V(A)$, and the positive value from winning is $V(B)$.

To determine the value from taking the gamble, Rui does not calculate the expectation using the probabilities θ and 1 − θ, as she would with expected utility theory. Rather, she uses *decision weights* w(θ) and w(1 − θ), where the w function assigns a weight that differs from θ. If people assign disproportionately high weights to rare events (see the Mini-Case "Biased Estimates"), the weight w(θ) exceeds θ for low values of θ and is less than θ for high values of θ.

Rui gambles if the value from not gambling, V(0), is less than her evaluation of the gamble, which is the weighted average of her values in the two cases:

$$V(0) < [w(\theta) \times V(A)] + [w(1 - \theta) \times V(B)].$$

Thus, prospect theory differs from expected utility theory in both how outcomes are valued and weighted.

Properties of Prospect Theory.

To resolve various mysteries about how people choose, prospect theory proposes a value function, V, that has an S-shape, as in Figure 14.6. This curve has three properties. First, the curve passes through the reference point at the origin, because gains and losses are determined relative to the initial situation.

Second, both sections of the curve are concave to the horizontal, outcome axis. Because of this curvature, Rui is less sensitive to a given change in the outcome for large gains or losses than for small ones. For example, she cares more about whether she has a loss of $1 rather than $2 than she does about a loss of $1,001 rather than $1,002.

Third, the curve is asymmetric with respect to gains and losses. People treat gains and losses differently, in contrast to the predictions of expected utility theory. The S-curve in the figure shows that people suffer more from a loss than they benefit from a comparable size gain. That is, the value function reflects *loss aversion*: people dislike making losses more than they like making gains. Given the subjective weights, valuations based on gains and losses, and the shape of the value curve, prospect theory can resolve some of the behavioral mysteries of choice under uncertainty. Because the S-shaped curve shows that people treat gains and losses differently, it can explain the reflection effect in the disease experiment described earlier in this section, where people make different choices when identical outcomes are stated in terms of lives saved instead of lives lost.

FIGURE 14.6 The Prospect Theory Value Function

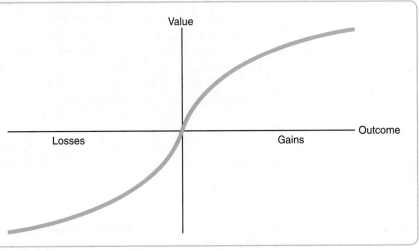

The prospect theory value function has an S-shape. It passes through the reference point at the origin, because gains and losses are measured relative to the reference point. Because the curve is asymmetric with respect to gains and losses, people treat gains and losses differently. This S-curve shows a bigger impact to a loss than to a comparably sized gain, reflecting loss aversion.

Managerial Solution

Risk and Limited Liability

As the Managerial Problem at the beginning of this chapter noted, firms such BP and Transocean that have deep-water oil rigs may face limited liability for a major spill. Although it is possible that BP and Transocean underestimated the true probabilities of disaster prior to the 2010 spill, a cap on the firms' liability may have also influenced these firms' behavior and led to the disaster. In particular, we now address the three questions raised in the Managerial Problem: How does a cap on liability affect a firm's willingness to make a risky investment or to invest less than the optimal amount in safety? How does a cap affect the amount of risk borne by the firm and by the rest of society? How does a cap affect the amount of insurance that a firm buys?

To illustrate the basic ideas, suppose that an oil rig firm expects to earn $1 billion in the absence of a spill on its new rig and to lose $39 billion if a spill occurs. The probability of a spill is θ. We start by considering whether the firm invests in a new rig (the analysis would be similar if it were deciding to invest in a given safety feature for a rig).

If the firm is risk neutral, then it invests in the new rig only if the expected return is positive, $[(1 - \theta) \times 1] + [\theta \times (-39)] > 0$, or if $\theta < 1/40 = 2.5\%$.[24] If the firm is risk averse, this *threshold probability*—the highest probability at which the firm is willing to invest—is less than 2.5%.

Now suppose that the firm's liability is capped at $19 billion. If the firm is risk neutral, it invests in the new rig if $[(1 - \theta) \times 1] + [\theta \times (-19)] > 0$, or if $\theta < 1/20 = 5\%$. Similarly, if the firm is risk averse, the threshold probability is higher than it would be without the limit on liability.

A limit on liability increases society's total risk if it encourages the drilling company to drill when it would not otherwise. If the drilling company is risk neutral, the probability of a spill is $\theta = 3\%$, and the firm bears the full liability for the damages from a spill, then the company's expected earnings are $[0.97 \times 1] + [0.03 \times (-39)] = -0.2 < 0$, so it would not drill. However, if its liability is capped at $19 billion, then its expected gain from drilling is $[0.97 \times 1] + [0.03 \times (-19)] = 0.4 > 0$, so it would drill. Because the firm is more likely to drill because of the liability cap, the cap causes the rest of society's total risk to increase. Moreover, the rest of society bears the risk from the $20 billion ($39 billion $-$ $19 billion) for which it is now responsible if a spill occurs.

If the firm is risk averse, it wants to buy fair insurance to cover its risk. To illustrate the effect of the cap on its decision as to how much insurance the firm buys, we now assume that the probability of a disaster is $\theta = 1\%$. Without either a liability cap or insurance, the firm's expected gain is $[0.99 \times 1] + [0.01 \times (-39)] = \$0.6$ billion. If an insurance company would provide fair insurance, the drilling firm could buy $100 of insurance for each $1 spent. Given that the drilling company is risk averse, it fully insures, so that if a spill occurs, the insurance company pays $39 billion. To buy this much insurance, the drilling company pays $0.39 billion, so that the expected value of the insurance contract is $-0.39 + [0.01 \times 39] = \$0$. With the insurance, the company earns $[0.99 \times 1] - 0.39 = \$0.6$ billion whether or not a spill occurs.

---

[24]The firm compares the expected return to that of the second-best investment opportunity, which we assume is zero for simplicity.

If the drilling company's liability is capped at $19 billion, it buys $19 billion worth of insurance for $0.19 billion, so that its expected gain in either state of nature is $1 - 0.19 = \$0.81$ billion. That is, the drilling company's expected profit increases by $0.2 billion due to the limit on its liability. This amount is a transfer from the rest of society to the firm, because society will be responsible for the extra $20 billion in damages if the spill occurs.[25]

SUMMARY

1. **Assessing Risk.** A probability measures the likelihood that a particular state of nature occurs. People may use historical frequencies, if available, to calculate probabilities. Lacking detailed information, people may form subjective estimates of a probability on the basis of available information. The expected value is the probability-weighted average of the values in each state of nature. One widely used measure of risk is the variance (or the standard deviation, which is the square root of the variance). The variance is the probability-weighted average of the squared difference between the value in each state of nature and the expected value.

2. **Attitudes Toward Risk.** Whether people choose a risky option over a nonrisky one depends on their attitudes toward risk and the expected payoffs of the various options. Most people are *risk averse* and will choose a riskier option only if its expected value is sufficiently higher than that of a less risky option. *Risk-neutral* people choose whichever option has the higher rate of return because they do not care about risk. *Risk-preferring* people may choose the riskier option even if it has a lower rate of return because they like risk and are willing to give up some expected return to take on more risk. An individual's utility function reflects that person's attitude toward risk. Expected utility is the probability-weighted average of the utility from the outcomes in the various states of nature. According to expected utility theory, decision makers choose the option that provides the highest expected utility.

3. **Reducing Risk.** People try to reduce the risk they face in several ways. They avoid some risks

altogether and, when risks cannot be completely avoided, take actions that lower the probabilities of bad events. They might also take actions that reduce the harm from bad events when they do occur. By collecting information before acting, investors can make better choices. People can further reduce risk by diversifying over a range of investments. Unless returns to the different investments are perfectly positively correlated, diversification reduces risk. Insurance companies offer policies for risks that they can diversify by pooling risks across many individuals. Insurance is called fair insurance if the expected return to the policyholder is zero: the expected payout equals the premium paid. Risk-averse people fully insure if they are offered fair insurance. Because insurance companies must earn enough income to cover their full operating costs, including paying salaries to workers, they offer insurance that is less than fair. Risk-averse people often buy some insurance even if it is unfair, but they typically buy less than full insurance. When buying unfair insurance, policyholders exchange the risk of a large loss for the certainty of a smaller loss (paying the premium).

4. **Investing Under Uncertainty.** Whether a person makes an investment depends on the uncertainty of the payoff, the expected return, the individual's attitudes toward risk, the interest rate, and the cost of altering the probabilities of various outcomes. For a risk-neutral person, an investment pays if the expected value is positive. A risk-averse person invests only if that person's expected utility is higher after investing. Thus, risk-averse people make risky investments if the investments pay sufficiently higher rates of return than do safer

---

[25]Why would governments adopt such limits on liability? One possible answer is rent seeking, where firms induce legislatures to pass laws that favor the firms (Chapter 9). However, proponents of the policy argue that there are social benefits to oil drilling not captured by the companies (including having a secure energy supply) and that private insurance companies would not be large enough to diversify over such large risks. In effect, the government acts as the insurer of last resort.

investments. People pay to alter the probabilities of various outcomes from an investment if doing so raises their expected utility.

5. **Behavioral Economics and Uncertainty.** Economists and psychologists have identified behavior under uncertainty that is inconsistent with expected utility theory. These choices may be due to biased estimates of probabilities or different objectives than maximizing expected utility. For example, some people care more about losses than about gains. One alternative theory that is consistent with many of these puzzling choices is prospect theory, which allows individuals to be risk averse over gains but risk preferring over losses.

QUESTIONS

All exercises are available on MyEconLab; * = *answer at the back of this book.*

1. Assessing Risk

1.1. Mme. Giselle's boutique in Cleveland, Ohio, is planning to sell a Parisian frock. If the public view it as being the latest style, the frocks will be worth $10,000. However, if they are viewed as passé, they will be worth only $2,000. If the probability that they are stylish is 20%, what is the expected value of the frocks?

*1.2. Asa buys a painting. He believes that the artist will become famous and the painting will be worth $1,000 with a 20% probably, the painting will be destroyed by fire or some other disaster with a 10% probability, and otherwise the painting will be worth $500. What is the expected value of the painting?

1.3. The EZ Construction Company is offered a $20,000 contract to build a new deck for a house. The company's profit if it does not have to sink piers (vertical supports) down to bedrock will be $4,000. However, if it does have to sink the piers, it will lose $1,000. The probability it will have to put in the piers is 25%. What is the expected value of this contract? Now, EZ learns that it can obtain a seismic study of the property that would specify whether piers have to be sunk before EZ must accept or reject this contract. By how much would the seismic study increase EZ's expected value? What is the most that it will pay for such a study? (*Hint:* See Q&A 14.1.)

*1.4. By next year, a stock you own has a 25% chance of being worth $400 and a 75% probability of being worth $200. What are the expected value and the variance?

1.5. What is the difference—if any—between an individual gambling at a casino and gambling by buying a stock? What is the difference for society?

1.6. To discourage people from breaking laws against speeding, society can increase the probability that someone exceeding the speed limit will be caught and punished, or it can increase the size of the fine for speeding. Explain why either method can be used to discourage speeding. Which approach is a government likely to prefer, and why?

2. Attitudes Toward Risk

2.1. Ryan offers to bet Kristin that if a six-sided die comes up with one or two dots showing, he will pay her $3, but if it comes up with any other number of dots, she'll owe him $2. Is that a fair bet for Kristin?

2.2. Would risk-neutral people ever buy insurance that was not fair (that was biased against them)? Explain.

2.3. Maoyong's utility function with respect to wealth is $U(W) = \ln W$ (where "ln W" means the natural logarithm of W). Plot his utility function and use your figure to determine whether Maoyong is risk averse. (*Comment:* You can also use calculus to see if he is risk averse by taking the second derivative of the utility function.)

2.4. Suppose that Laura has a utility function of $U(W) = W^{0.5}$ and an initial wealth of $W = \$100$. How much of a risk premium would she want to participate in a gamble that has a 50% probability of raising her wealth to $120 and a 50% probability of lowering her wealth to $80?

*2.5. Hugo has a concave utility function of $U(W) = W^{0.5}$. His only asset is shares in an Internet start-up company. Tomorrow he will learn the stock's value. He believes that it is worth $144 with probability $\frac{2}{3}$ and $225 with probability $\frac{1}{3}$. What is his expected utility? What risk premium would he pay to avoid bearing this risk? (*Hint:* See Q&A 14.2 and the discussion of the risk premium in Figure 14.2.)

2.6. Given the information in Q&A 14.2, Irma prefers to buy the stock. Show graphically how high her certain wealth would have to be for her to choose not to buy the stock.

2.7. Suppose that an individual is risk averse and has to choose between $100 with certainty and a risky option with two equally likely outcomes: $100 − x and $100 + x. Use a graph (or math) to show that this person's risk premium is smaller, the smaller x is (the less variable the gamble is).

2.8. Joanna is considering three possible jobs. The following table shows the possible incomes she might get in each job.

	Outcome A		Outcome B	
	Probability	Earnings	Probability	Earnings
Job 1	0.5	20	0.5	40
Job 2	0.3	15	0.7	45
Job 3	1	30		

For each job, calculate the expected value, the variance, and the standard deviation. If Joanna is averse to risk (as measured by variance), what can you predict about her job choice? What if she is risk neutral?

2.9. Catalina just inherited a vineyard from a distant relative. In good years (when there is no rain or frost during harvest season), she earns $100,000 from the sale of grapes from the vineyard. If the weather is poor, she loses $20,000. Catalilna's estimate of the probability of good weather is 60%.

   a. Calculate the expected value and the variance of Catalina's income from the vineyard.

   b. Catalina is risk averse. Ethan, a grape buyer, offers Catalina a guaranteed payment of $70,000 each year in exchange for her entire harvest. Will she accept this offer? Explain.

   c. Why might Ethan make such an offer?

3. Reducing Risk

3.1. Malee, who is risk averse, has two pieces of jewelry, each worth $1,000. She plans to send them to her sister's firm in Thailand to be sold there. She is concerned about the safety of shipping them. She believes that the probability that any box shipped will not reach its destination is θ. Is her expected utility higher if she sends the articles together or in two separate shipments?

3.2. Lucy, the manager of the medical test firm, Dubrow Labs, worries about being sued for botched results from blood tests. If it isn't sued, the firm expects to earn a profit of 100, but if it is successfully sued, its profit will be only 10. Lucy believes the probability of a successful suit is 5%. If fair insurance is available and Lucy is risk averse, how much insurance will she buy?

*3.3. Consider a household that possesses $160,000 worth of valuables such as jewelry. This household faces a 0.2 probability of burglary, in which case it loses $70,000 worth of the valuables. Suppose it can buy an insurance policy for $15,000 that would fully reimburse the amount of loss from burglary. The household's utility is given by $U(X) = 4X^{0.5}$

   a. Should the household buy this insurance policy?

   b. What is the actuarially fair price for the insurance policy?

   c. What is the most the household is willing to pay for this insurance policy that fully covers it against the loss?

3.4. An insurance agent (interviewed in Jonathan Clements, "Dare to Live Dangerously: Passing on Some Insurance Can Pay Off," *Wall Street Journal*, July 23, 2005, D1) states, "On paper, it never makes sense to have a policy with low deductibles or carry collision on an old car." But the agent notes that raising deductibles and dropping collision coverage can be a tough decision for people with a low income or little savings. (Collision insurance is the coverage on a policyholder's own car for accidents where another driver is not at fault.)

   a. Suppose that the loss is $4,000 if an old car is in an accident. During the six-month coverage period, the probability that the insured person is found at fault in an accident is $\frac{1}{36}$. Suppose that the price of the coverage is $150. Should a wealthy person purchase the coverage? Should a poor person purchase the coverage? Do your answers depend on the policyholder's degree of risk aversion? Does the policyholder's degree of risk aversion depend on his or her wealth?

   b. The agent advises wealthy people not to purchase insurance to protect against possible small losses. Why?

3.5. After Hurricane Katrina in 2005, the government offered subsidies to people whose houses were destroyed. How does the expectation that subsidies will be offered again for future major disasters affect the probability that risk-averse people will buy insurance and the amount they buy? (*Hint*: Use a utility function for a risk-averse person to illustrate your answer. See Q&A 14.3.)

4. Investing Under Uncertainty

*4.1. Andy and Kim live together. Andy may invest $10,000 (possibly by taking on an extra job to earn the additional money) in Kim's MBA education this year. This investment will raise the current value of Kim's earnings by $24,000. If they stay together, they will share the benefit from the additional earnings. However, the probability is $\frac{1}{2}$ that they will split up in the future. If they were married and then split, Andy would get half of Kim's additional earnings. If they were living together without any legal ties and they split, then Andy would get nothing. Suppose that Andy is risk neutral. Will Andy invest in Kim's education? Does your answer depend on the couple's legal status?

4.2. Use a decision tree to illustrate how a risk-neutral plaintiff in a lawsuit decides whether to settle a claim or go to trial. The defendants offer $50,000 to settle now. If the plaintiff does not settle, the plaintiff believes that the probability of winning at trial is 60%. If the plaintiff wins, the amount awarded is X. How large can X be before the plaintiff refuses to settle? How does the plaintiff's attitude toward risk affect this decision?

4.3. DVD retailers choose how many copies of a movie to purchase from a studio and to stock. The retailers have the right to return all unsold copies to the studio for a full refund, but the retailer pays the shipping costs for returned copies. A small mom-and-pop retailer will sell 1, 2, 3, or 4 copies with probabilities 0.2, 0.3, 0.3, and 0.2, respectively. Suppose that the retail market price of the DVD is $15 and that the retailer must pay the studio $8 for each copy. The studio's marginal cost is $1. The retailer's marginal profit is $7 for selling each copy, and the studio's marginal profit is $7 for each nonreturned copy sold to the retailer. The cost of shipping each DVD back to the studio is $2. The studio and retailer are risk neutral.

   a. How many copies of the DVD will the retailer order from the studio? What is the studio's expected profit-maximizing number of copies for the retailer to order?

   b. Alternatively, suppose that the studio pays the shipping costs to return unsold DVDs. How many copies would the retailer order?

   c. Does the number of copies the retailer orders depend on which party pays the shipping costs? Why?

4.4. Use a decision tree to illustrate how a risk-averse kidney patient would make a decision about whether to have a transplant operation. The patient currently uses a dialysis machine, which lowers her utility. If the operation is successful, her utility will return to its level before the onset of her kidney problems. However, she faces a 5% probability that she will die if she has the operation. (If it will help, make up utility numbers to illustrate your answer.)

4.5. Robert Green repeatedly and painstakingly applied herbicides to kill weeds that would harm his sugar beet crops in 2007. However, in 2008, he planted beets genetically engineered to withstand Monsanto's Roundup herbicide. Roundup destroys weeds but leaves the crop unharmed, thereby saving a farmer thousands of dollars in tractor fuel and labor (Andrew Pollack, "Round 2 for Biotech Beets," *New York Times*, November 27, 2007). However, this policy is risky. In the past when beet breeders announced they were going to use Roundup-resistant seeds, sugar-using food companies like Hershey and Mars objected, fearing consumer resistance. Now, though, sensing that consumer concerns have subsided, many processors have cleared their growers to plant the Roundup-resistant beets. A Kellogg spokeswoman said her company was willing to use such beets, but Hershey and Mars declined to comment. Thus, a farmer like Mr. Green faces risks by switching to Roundup Ready beets. Use a decision tree to illustrate the analysis that a farmer in this situation needs to do.

4.6. In Q&A 14.4, advertising increases the probability of high demand to 80%. If all the other information in the Q&A stays the same, what is the minimum probability of high demand resulting from advertising such that Gautam decides to invest and advertise?

5. Behavioral Economics and Uncertainty

5.1. First answer the following two questions about your preferences:

   a. You are given $5,000 and offered a choice between receiving an extra $2,500 with certainty or flipping a coin and getting $5,000 more if heads or $0 if tails. Which option do you prefer?

   b. You are given $10,000 if you will make the following choice: return $2,500 or flip a coin and return $5,000 if heads and $0 if tails. Which option do you prefer?

   Most people choose the certain $2,500 in the first case but flip the coin in the second. Explain why this behavior is not consistent. What do you conclude about how people make decisions concerning uncertain events?

5.2. Evan is risk seeking with respect to gains and risk averse with respect to losses. Louisa is risk seeking with respect to losses and risk averse with respect to gains. Illustrate both utility functions. Which person's attitudes toward risk are consistent with prospect theory? Which of these people would you expect to be susceptible to framing effects?

*5.3. Joe lost a substantial amount gambling at a racetrack today. On the last race of the day, he decides to make a large enough bet on a longshot so that, if he wins, he will make up for his earlier losses and break even on the day. His friend Sue, who won more than she lost on the day, makes just a small final bet so that she will end up ahead for the day even if she loses the last race. This is typical race track behavior for winners and losers. Would you explain this behavior using overconfidence bias, prospect theory, or some other principle of behavioral economics?

6. Managerial Problem

6.1. Global Gas International offers to subcontract the Halidurton Heavy Construction Corporation to build an oil pipeline from Canada to New Orleans for $500 million. The probability that the oil pipeline will leak causing environmental damage is θ. If so, the legal liabilities will be $600 million.

  a. If Halidurton is risk neutral and liable for the damages from a leak, what is the θ such that it is indifferent between accepting or rejecting the contract?

  b. If Halidurton is risk averse and fair insurance is offered, how much insurance would it buy?

  c. If Global Gas International will partially indemnify Halidurton so that the largest damages that Halidurton would have to pay is $200 million, what is the θ that leaves it indifferent about accepting the contract?

  d. If partially indemnified, how much fair insurance will Halidurton buy?

7. Spreadsheet Exercises

7.1. Aman, Bo, and Celia are considering an investment opportunity such that each person's final wealth (the return net of the investment) will be $W_1 = \$25$ thousand with probability 0.6 or $W_2 = \$100$ thousand with probability 0.4.

  a. Calculate the expected value of wealth $E(W)$.

  b. Aman's utility function is $U(W) = W$, while Bo's is $U(W) = W^{0.5}$ and Celia's is $U(W) = W^2$. For each person, calculate the expected utility of wealth, $EU(W)$, the certainty equivalent wealth, CE, and the risk premium, RP. (*Hint*: If

an individual's utility function is, say, $U = W^x$, then the wealth corresponding to that utility level is $W = U^{1/x}$, so the certainty equivalent wealth is $CE = EU^{1/x}$.)

  c. Determine each person's attitude toward risk by his or her risk premium.

7.2. An investor is considering five possible investment strategies. The investor cares only about the expected payoff and possibly the variance of each strategy. The following table shows the payoffs under bad luck and good luck and the associated probabilities.

Strategy	Bad Luck Payoff	Probability of Bad Luck	Good Luck Payoff	Probability of Good Luck
A	4	0.6	9	0.4
B	5	0.3	5	0.7
C	2	0.5	12	0.5
D	4	0.8	11	0.2
E	3	0.7	10	0.3

  a. Using a spreadsheet, determine the expected value and variance for each strategy.

  b. Which strategy would be chosen by a risk-neutral investor? A risk-preferring investor?

  c. If we know only that the investor is risk averse, can we rule out any strategies?

15 Asymmetric Information

The buyer needs a hundred eyes, the seller not one. —George Herbert (1651)

A major cause of the worldwide financial crisis of 2007–2009 was that managers and other employees of banks, insurance companies, and other firms took excessive risks. Looking back on the events that led to the financial meltdown, Goldman Sachs Chief Executive Lloyd Blankfein admitted that Wall Street firms, caught up in the pursuit of profits, had ignored risks, and that these firms needed to dramatically change compensation practices. As he noted, "Decisions on compensation and other actions taken and not taken, particularly at banks that rapidly lost a lot of shareholder value, look self-serving and greedy in hindsight."

During the mortgage market meltdown that started in 2007, record numbers of mortgage holders defaulted on their loans and their homes went into foreclosure, where the lender took ownership. Foreclosures went from 100,000 a month nationally in summer 2006 to 250,000 in 2007, 300,000 in 2008, and 350,000 in 2009 and 2010, before falling to 225,000 in 2011 and 200,000 in 2012.

Prior to the crash, many banks and other mortgage-initiating firms started providing riskier mortgages in four ways. First, many mortgage-initiating firms stopped requiring down payments for *subprime* mortgage loans, which are loans made to people who are not prime (low-risk) borrowers. In the San Francisco Bay Area, 69% of families whose owner-occupied homes were in foreclosure had put down 0% at the time of purchase, and only 10% made the traditional 20% down payment in the first nine months of 2007.

Second, firms loaned to speculators who were more likely to walk away from a loan than would someone who lived in the mortgaged house. Speculators were a serious problem in Miami and Las Vegas. In Las Vegas during the first half of 2007, absentee investors owned 74% of single-family homes in foreclosure. (Nationwide, nonowner-occupied homes accounted for 13% of prime defaults and 11% of subprime defaults.)

Third, mortgages used adjustable rates that started very low and increased rapidly over time. Because the implications of these escalator clauses were not made clear to borrowers, many poor people suddenly found themselves unable to make their mortgage payments.

Fourth, many mortgage-originating firms such as banks failed to check borrowers' creditworthiness properly. Of the properties repossessed in the San Francisco Bay Area, one in six was owned by people who had two or more past foreclosures, and some had five or more.

Why did executives at these banks take risks that resulted in so much lost shareholder value? We examine how a manager's incentives can lead to excessive risk taking in Q&A 15.3. How can a firm compensate its corporate executives so as to prevent them from undertaking irresponsible and potentially devastating actions? In the Managerial Solution, we examine how a manager's incentives can be changed to reduce excessive risk taking.

In previous chapters, we focused on situations in which all firms and consumers have *symmetric information*: Everyone is equally knowledgeable or equally ignorant about prices, product quality, and other factors relevant to a transaction. In perfectly competitive markets, everyone knows all the relevant facts about a potential transaction. In the insurance examples discussed in Chapter 14, the companies that sell insurance and the people who buy it are equally uncertain about future events. In contrast, in this chapter, we consider situations in which people have **asymmetric information**: One party to a transaction has relevant information that another party does not have.

We concentrate on two types of asymmetric information: *hidden characteristics* and *hidden actions*. A **hidden characteristic** is a fact about a person or thing that is known to one party but unknown to others. For example, the owner of a property may possess extensive information about the mineral composition of the land that is unknown to a mining company that is considering buying the land.

Another type of informational asymmetry, a **hidden action**, occurs when one party to a transaction cannot observe important *actions* taken by another party. For example, senior managers may take actions that are not observed by shareholders, such as using a company jet for personal use or making hidden financial decisions that create excessive risk for shareholders.

A more-informed party may exploit the less-informed party, engaging in *opportunistic behavior*: taking economic advantage of someone when circumstances permit. Two problems of opportunistic behavior arise from asymmetric information. One—*adverse selection*—is due to hidden characteristics, while the other—*moral hazard*—is associated with hidden actions.

The problem of **adverse selection** arises when one party to a transaction possesses information about a hidden characteristic that is unknown to other parties and takes economic advantage of this information. For example, if a roadside vendor sells a box of oranges to a passing motorist and only the vendor knows that the oranges are of low quality, the vendor may allege that the oranges are of high quality and charge a premium price for them. That is, the seller seeks to benefit from an informational asymmetry due to a hidden characteristic, the quality of the oranges. If potential buyers worry about such opportunistic behavior, they may be willing to pay only low prices or may forego purchasing the oranges entirely.

The primary problem arising from hidden action is **moral hazard**, which occurs when an informed party takes an action that the other party cannot observe and that hurts the less-informed party. If you pay a mechanic by the hour to fix your car, and you do not actually watch the repairs, then the time spent by the mechanic on your car is a hidden action.[1] A moral hazard occurs if the mechanic bills you for excessive hours.

---

[1]A lawyer dies in an accident and goes to heaven. A host of angels greet him with a banner that reads, "Welcome Oldest Man!" The lawyer is puzzled: "Why do you think I'm the oldest man who ever lived? I was only 47 when I died." One of the angels replied, "You can't fool us; you were at least 152 when you died. We saw how many hours you billed!"

This chapter concentrates on identifying the various problems that arise due to asymmetric information. In particular, adverse selection often leads to markets in which some desirable transactions do not take place or even the market as a whole cannot exist. Moral hazard often results from contracts that give one party an incentive to act such that joint profits are reduced or a relatively risk-averse party bears excessive risk. In this chapter, we discuss how these problems can be reduced or eliminated by government actions, properly designed contracts, outside firms that provide information, and other means.

Main Topics	1. **Adverse Selection:** Adverse selection may prevent desirable transactions from occurring, possibly eliminating a market entirely.
In this chapter, we examine five main topics	2. **Reducing Adverse Selection:** Adverse selection problems are reduced if exploiting knowledge of hidden characteristics can be prevented by law or if information about hidden characteristics can be obtained by uninformed parties.
	3. **Moral Hazard:** Moral hazard leads to inefficient market outcomes by reducing the combined profits of participants or by causing relatively risk-averse individuals to bear excessive risk.
	4. **Using Contracts to Reduce Moral Hazard:** Moral hazard problems can often be reduced or eliminated by using contracts that provide the optimal incentives for all parties to a transaction.
	5. **Using Monitoring to Reduce Moral Hazard:** Moral hazard problems can be limited or eliminated through monitoring and using contracts to impose penalties for undesirable actions.

15.1 Adverse Selection

One of the most important problems associated with adverse selection is that if consumers lack relevant information, they may not engage in transactions to avoid being exploited by better-informed sellers. As a result, not all desirable transactions occur, and potential consumer and producer surplus is lost. Indeed, in the extreme case, adverse selection may prevent a market from operating at all. We illustrate this idea using two important examples of adverse selection problems: insurance and products of varying quality.

Adverse Selection in Insurance Markets

Hidden characteristics and adverse selection are very important in the insurance industry. If a health insurance company provided fair insurance by charging everyone a rate for insurance equal to the average cost of health care for the entire population, then the company would lose money due to adverse selection. Unhealthy people—people who expect to incur health care costs that are higher than average—would view this insurance as a good deal and many would buy it. In contrast, unless they were very risk averse, healthy people would not buy it because the premiums would exceed their expected health care costs. Given that a disproportionately large share of unhealthy people would buy the insurance, the market for health insurance would exhibit adverse selection, and the insurance company's average cost of medical care for covered people would exceed the population's average.

Adverse selection results in an inefficient market outcome because the sum of producer and consumer surplus is not maximized. The loss of potential surplus occurs because some potentially beneficial sales of insurance to relatively healthy individuals do not occur. These consumers would be willing to buy insurance at a lower rate that was closer to the fair rate for them given their superior health. The insurance company would be willing to offer such low rates only if it could be sure that these individuals were relatively healthy.

Products of Unknown Quality

Anagram for General Motors: Or Great Lemons

Adverse selection often arises because sellers of a product have better information about the product's quality—a hidden characteristic—than do buyers. Cars that appear to be identical on the outside often differ substantially in the number of repairs they will need. Some cars, often called *lemons*, have a variety of problems that become apparent to the owner only after buying the car and driving it for a while. The seller of a used car usually knows whether a car is a lemon.

If buyers have the same information as sellers, no adverse selection problem arises. However, if sellers have more information than buyers, adverse selection may drive high-quality products out of the market (Akerlof, 1970). Why? Used car buyers worry that a used car might be a lemon. As a result they will not pay as high a price as they would if they knew the car was of good quality. They will only buy if the price is low enough to reflect the possibility of getting a lemon. Given that sellers of excellent used cars do not want to sell their cars for that low a price, they do not enter the market. Adverse selection has driven the high-quality cars out of the market, leaving only the lemons.

In the following example, we assume that sellers cannot alter the quality of their used cars and that the number of potential used car buyers is large. All are willing to pay $4,000 for a lemon and $8,000 for a good used car: The demand curve for lemons, D^L, is horizontal at $4,000 in panel a of Figure 15.1, and the demand curve for good cars, D^G, is horizontal at $8,000 in panel b.

Although the number of potential buyers is virtually unlimited, only 1,000 owners of lemons and 1,000 owners of good cars are willing to sell. The *reservation price* of lemon owners—the lowest price at which they will sell their cars—is $3,000. Consequently, the supply curve for lemons, S^L in panel a, is horizontal at $3,000 up to 1,000 cars, where it becomes vertical (no more cars are for sale at any price). The reservation price of owners of high-quality used cars is v, which is less than $8,000. Panel b shows two possible values of v. If $v = \$5,000$, the supply curve for good cars, S^1, is horizontal at $5,000 up to 1,000 cars and then becomes vertical. If $v = \$7,000$, the supply curve is S^2.

Market Equilibrium with Symmetric Information. If both sellers and buyers know the quality of all the used cars before any sales take place (they have full, symmetric information), all 2,000 cars are sold, and the good cars sell for more than lemons. In panel a of Figure 15.1, the intersection of the lemons demand curve D^L and the lemons supply curve S^L determines the equilibrium at e in the lemons market, where 1,000 lemons sell for $4,000 each. Regardless of whether the supply curve for good cars is S^1 or S^2 in panel b, the equilibrium in the good-car market is E, where 1,000 good cars sell for $8,000 each.

FIGURE 15.1 Markets for Lemons and Good Cars

If everyone has full information, the equilibrium in the lemons market is e (1,000 cars sold for $4,000 each), and the equilibrium in the good-car market is E (1,000 cars sold for $8,000 each). If buyers can't tell quality before buying but assume that equal numbers of the two types of cars are for sale, their demand in both markets is D*, which is horizontal at $6,000. If the good-car owners' reservation price is $5,000, the supply curve for good cars is S¹, and 1,000 good cars (point F) and 1,000 lemons (point f) sell for $6,000 each. If their reservation price is $7,000, the supply curve is S². No good cars are sold; 1,000 lemons sell for $4,000 each (point e).

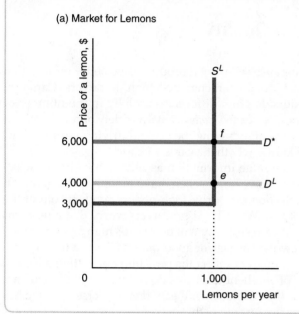

(a) Market for Lemons

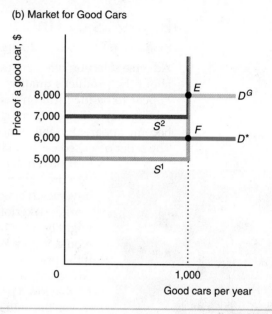

(b) Market for Good Cars

All the cars are sold if everyone has the same information. As a result, *this market is efficient because the goods go to the people who value them the most.* All current owners, who value the cars less than the potential buyers, sell their cars.

It does not matter whether all buyers and sellers have full information or all lack information—it's the equality (or symmetry) of information that matters. However, *the amount of information they have affects the price at which the cars sell.* With full information, good cars sell for $8,000 and lemons for $4,000.

If information is symmetric and buyers and sellers are equally ignorant (they don't know if a car is good or a lemon), both types of cars sell for the same price. A buyer has an equal chance of buying a lemon or a good car. The expected value of a used car is

$$\$6,000 = \left(\tfrac{1}{2} \times \$4,000\right) + \left(\tfrac{1}{2} \times \$8,000\right).$$

A risk-neutral buyer would pay $6,000 for a car of unknown quality.[2] Because sellers cannot distinguish between the cars either, sellers accept this amount and sell all the cars.[3] Thus, this market is efficient because the cars go to people who value them more than their original owners.

If only lemons were sold, they would sell for $4,000. The presence of good-quality cars raises the price received by sellers of lemons to $6,000. Similarly, if only good

---

[2] A risk-neutral person cares about only the expected value and does not worry about uncertainty (Chapter 14).

[3] Risk-neutral sellers place an expected value of $\left(\tfrac{1}{2} \times \$3,000\right) + \tfrac{1}{2}v = \$1,500 + \tfrac{1}{2}v$ on a car of unknown quality. If $v = \$7,000$, this expected value is $\$1,500 + \$3,500 = \$5,000$. If $v = \$5,000$, the expected value is only $4,000. In either case, sellers would be happy to sell their cars for $6,000.

cars were sold, they would sell for $8,000. The presence of lemons lowers the price that sellers of good cars receive to $6,000. Thus, effectively, sellers of good-quality cars are subsidizing sellers of lemons.

Market Equilibrium with Asymmetric Information.

If sellers know the quality but buyers do not, this market may be inefficient: The better-quality cars may not be sold even though buyers value good cars more than sellers do. The equilibrium in this market depends on whether the value that the owners of good cars place on their cars, v, is greater or less than the expected value of buyers, $6,000. The two possible equilibria are: All cars sell at the average price, or only lemons sell at a price equal to the value that buyers place on lemons.

Initially, we assume that the sellers of good cars value their cars at $v = \$5,000$, which is less than the buyers' expected value of the cars ($6,000), so that transactions occur. The equilibrium in the good-car market is determined by the intersection of S^1 and D^* at F in panel b of Figure 15.1, where 1,000 good cars sell at $6,000. Similarly, owners of lemons, who value their cars at only $3,000, are happy to sell them for $6,000 each. The new equilibrium in the lemons market is f.

Thus, all cars sell at the same price. In this case *asymmetric information does not cause an efficiency problem, but it does have equity implications*. Sellers of lemons benefit and sellers of good cars suffer from consumers' inability to distinguish quality. Consumers who buy the good cars get a bargain, and buyers of lemons are left with a sour taste in their mouths.

Now suppose that the sellers of good cars place a value of $v = \$7,000$ on their cars and thus are unwilling to sell them for $6,000. As a result, the *lemons drive good cars out of the market*. Buyers realize that they can buy only lemons at any price less than $7,000. Consequently, in equilibrium, the 1,000 lemons sell for the expected (and actual) price of $4,000, and no good cars change hands. This equilibrium is inefficient because high-quality cars remain in the hands of people who value them less than potential buyers do.

In summary, if buyers have less information about product quality than sellers do, the result might be a lemons problem in which high-quality cars do not sell even though potential buyers value the cars more than their current owners do. If so, asymmetric information causes an otherwise perfectly competitive market to lose its desirable efficiency properties. The lemons problem does not occur if the information is symmetric. If buyers and sellers of used cars know the quality of the cars, each car sells for its true value in a perfectly competitive market. If, as with new cars, neither buyers nor sellers can identify lemons, both good cars and lemons sell at a price equal to the expected value rather than at their (unknown) true values.

Q&A 15.1

Suppose that everyone in our used car example is risk neutral, and potential car buyers value lemons at $4,000 and good used cars at $8,000. The reservation price of lemon owners is $3,000 and the reservation price of owners of high-quality used cars is $7,000. The share of current owners who have lemons is $\frac{1}{5}$ (in contrast to our previous example, where the share was $\frac{1}{2}$). Describe the equilibrium.

Answer

1. *Determine how much buyers are willing to pay if all cars are sold.* Because buyers are risk neutral, if they believe that the probability of getting a lemon is $\frac{1}{5}$, the most they are willing to pay for a car of unknown quality is

$$p = \left[\$8,000 \times \left(1 - \tfrac{1}{5}\right) \right] + \left(4,000 \times \tfrac{1}{5}\right) = \$7,200. \qquad (15.1)$$

2. *Determine whether sellers will sell their cars and describe the equilibrium.* All owners will sell if the market price equals or exceeds their reservation price, $7,000. Using Equation 15.1, we know that the market (equilibrium) price is $7,200 if all cars are sold. Thus, all sellers will choose to sell their cars and the equilibrium price will be $7,200.

Varying Quality Under Asymmetric Information.

Most firms can adjust their product's quality. If consumers cannot identify high-quality goods before purchase, they pay the same for all goods regardless of quality. Because the price that firms receive for top-quality goods is the same as they receive for low-quality items, they do not produce top-quality goods. Such an outcome is inefficient if consumers are willing to pay sufficiently more for top-quality goods.

Q&A 15.2

It costs $10 to produce a low-quality wallet and $20 to produce a high-quality wallet. Consumers cannot distinguish between the products before purchase, they do not make repeat purchases, and they value the wallets at the cost of production. The five firms in the market produce 100 wallets each. Each firm produces only high-quality or only low-quality wallets. Consumers pay the expected value of a wallet. Do any of the firms produce high-quality wallets?

Answer

Show that it does not pay for one firm to make high-quality wallets if the other firms make low-quality wallets due to asymmetric information. If all five firms make a low-quality wallet, consumers pay $10 per wallet. If one firm makes a high-quality wallet and all the others make low-quality wallets (so the probability that a consumer buys a high-quality wallet is $\frac{1}{5}$), the expected value per wallet to consumers is

$$(\$10 \times \tfrac{4}{5}) + (\$20 \times \tfrac{1}{5}) = \$12.$$

Thus, if one firm raises the quality of its product, all firms benefit because the wallets sell for $12 instead of $10. The high-quality firm receives only a fraction of the total benefit from raising quality. It gets $2 extra per high-quality wallet sold, which is less than the extra $10 it costs to make the better wallet. The other $8 is shared by the other firms. The high-quality firm would incur all the expenses of raising quality, $10 extra per wallet, and reap only a fraction, $2, of the benefits. Therefore, it opts not to produce the high-quality wallets. *Due to asymmetric information, the firms do not produce high-quality goods even though consumers are willing to pay for the extra quality.*

Mini-Case

Reducing Consumers' Information

Because firms may benefit from having better information than consumers, some managers take actions that reduce consumers' information. For example, because consumers are willing to pay more for higher quality products, a firm may benefit if consumers falsely believe that identical products differ in quality.

By intentionally increasing consumer uncertainty, a firm may be better able to profit from ignorant consumers and earn a higher profit (Salop, 1977). One way in which firms confuse consumers is to create *noise* by selling virtually the same product under various brand names. A *noisy monopoly* may be able to sell a product under its own brand name at a relatively high price and supply grocery stores (such as Safeway) or discount stores (such as Walmart) with a virtually identical product that is sold at a lower price under a *private label*, which is a house or store brand. For example, a single processor produces name-brand Prego spaghetti sauce and private-label house brand spaghetti sauces for various grocery stores.

For decades, outside firms have manufactured products that Sears, Roebuck & Company sells under its house brand names, Kenmore, Die-Hard, and Craftsman. Amana refrigerators are sold under their own brand name and under the Kenmore brand name. Similarly, Whirlpool sells its own washers and driers, but Sears also markets these products under the Kenmore name. Sears also places its label on Caloric, Frigidaire, GE, Gibson, Jenn-Air, and Toshiba products.[4]

If some consumers know that two products are identical while others believe that their qualities differ, a firm may have an opportunity to engage in a special type of price discrimination (Chapter 10). For example, a food manufacturer may take advantage of less-informed customers by charging a higher price for the allegedly superior national brand while informed customers buy a less expensive but equally good private-label brand.

Brand proliferation pays if the cost of producing multiple brands is relatively low and the share of consumers who are willing to buy the higher-price product is relatively large. Otherwise, the firm makes a higher profit by selling a single product at a moderate price than by selling one brand at a low price and another at a high price.

Over time, as consumers have become familiar with private-label brands and recognized their quality, the advantage from maintaining multiple brands has diminished. Indeed, private-label products are rapidly gaining market share. According to the Private Label Manufacturers Association's 2012 *International Private Label Yearbook*, the private-label share of relevant products was 53% of the market in Switzerland, 49% in Spain, and over 40% in the United Kingdom and Germany. Private-label goods are not as popular in North America, but their share is growing and has reached 20% in both the United States and Canada.

15.2 Reducing Adverse Selection

Because adverse selection results from one party exploiting asymmetric information about a hidden characteristic, the two main methods for solving adverse selection problems are to *restrict the ability of the informed party to take advantage of hidden information* and to *equalize information* among the parties. Responses to adverse selection problems increase welfare in some markets, but may do more harm than good in others.

Restricting Opportunistic Behavior

Which type of restriction works best to curb opportunistic behavior depends on the nature of the adverse selection problem. For insurance problems, adverse selection may be prevented by mandating universal insurance coverage. With varying product quality, laws to prevent opportunism are commonly used.

---

[4]Want to know which firm made the product you bought at Sears? Go to **www.applianceaid.com/searscodes.html**.

Universal Coverage. Health insurance markets have adverse selection because low-risk consumers do not buy insurance at prices that reflect the average risk. Such adverse selection can be eliminated by providing insurance to everyone or by mandating that everyone buy insurance. Canada, the United Kingdom, and many other countries provide basic health insurance to all residents, financed by a combination of mandatory premiums and taxes. In 2012, the U.S. Supreme Court confirmed the constitutionality of the *individual mandate* in the 2010 Patient Protection and Affordable Care Act, which requires virtually all Americans to have health care coverage.

Similarly, firms often provide mandatory health insurance to all employees as a benefit, rather than paying a higher wage and letting employees decide whether to buy such insurance on their own. By doing so, firms reduce adverse selection problems for their insurance carriers: Both healthy and unhealthy people are covered. As a result, firms can buy medical insurance for their workers at a lower cost per person than workers could obtain on their own.

Laws to Prevent Opportunism. Product quality and product safety are often hidden characteristics that are known to manufacturers but are not observed by consumers. Manufacturers have an incentive to behave opportunistically by selling low-quality products or unsafe products to consumers at excessive prices. However, product liability laws protect consumers from being stuck with nonfunctional or dangerous products.

Moreover, many U.S. state supreme courts have concluded that products are sold with an implicit understanding that they will safely perform their intended function. If they do not, consumers can sue the seller even in the absence of product liability laws. If consumers can rely on explicit or implicit product liability laws to force a manufacturer to make good on defective products, they need not worry about adverse selection. Similarly, truth-in-advertising laws and food labeling requirements are both efforts to discourage opportunistic behavior by preventing misleading claims about product characteristics.

Equalizing Information

Adverse selection problems can be reduced or eliminated by providing information to all parties. Either informed or uninformed parties can act to eliminate or reduce informational asymmetries. Three methods for reducing informational asymmetries are:

1. An uninformed party (such as an insurance company) can use **screening** to infer the information possessed by informed parties.

2. An informed party (such as person seeking to buy health insurance) can use **signaling** to send information to a less-informed party.

3. A third party (such as a firm or a government agency) not directly involved in the transaction may collect information and sell it or give it to the uninformed party.

Screening. Insurance companies reduce adverse selection problems by screening potential customers based on their health records or requiring them to undergo medical exams. A life insurance company uses such information to better estimate the probability that it will have to pay off on a policy. The firm can then decide not to insure high-risk individuals or can charge high-risk people higher premiums.

It is costly to collect information on the health of a person or whether that individual has dangerous habits such as smoking, drinking, or skydiving. As a

Congratulations! You qualify for our auto insurance.

result, insurance companies collect information only up to the point at which the marginal benefit from the extra information they gather equals the marginal cost of obtaining it. Over time, insurance companies have increasingly concluded that it pays to collect information about whether individuals exercise, have a family history of dying young, or engage in potentially life-threatening activities. If the individuals but not the insurance companies know about these characteristics, adverse selection occurs.

Consumers can use screening techniques too. For example, they can screen used cars by test-driving them, or by having an objective, trustworthy mechanic examine the car. They can also pay a company such as CARFAX to check the history of the repairs on a vehicle they are considering purchasing.

As long as the consumers' costs of securing information are less than the private benefits, they obtain the information, transactions occur, and markets function smoothly. However, if the costs exceed the benefits, they do not gather the information, mutually beneficial transactions are not made, and the market is inefficient.

In some markets, consumers rely on a firm's *reputation*, which they learn from other consumers or from observation. Consumers can avoid the adverse selection problem by buying only from firms that have reputations for providing high-quality goods. For example, consumers know that a used car dealer that expects repeat purchases has a strong incentive not to sell defective products.

Generally, in markets in which the same consumers and firms trade regularly, a reputation is easy to establish. In markets in which consumers buy a good only once, such as in tourist areas, firms cannot establish reputations as easily and we might expect adverse selection to be a more significant problem. Remember this warning the next time you are tempted to buy an "authentic, genuine designer" watch or purse from a street vendor.

Signaling. An informed party may signal the uninformed party to eliminate adverse selection. However, signals solve the adverse selection problem only when the recipients view them as credible. Smart consumers may place little confidence in a firm's unsubstantiated claims. Would you believe that a used car runs well just because an ad tells you so?

If only high-quality firms find it worthwhile to send a signal, then a signal is credible. Producers of high-quality goods often try to signal to consumers that their products are of better quality than those of their rivals. If consumers believe their signals, these firms can charge higher prices for their goods. But if the signals are to be effective, they must be credible. A firm may, for example, distribute a favorable report on its product by an independent testing agency to try to convince buyers that its product is of high quality. Because low-quality firms cannot obtain such a report from a reliable independent testing agency, consumers believe this signal.

An applicant for life insurance could have a physical examination and then present an insurance company with a written statement from the doctor as a signal of good health. If only people who believe that they can show that they are better than others want to send a signal, insurance companies may rely upon it. However, an insurance company may not trust such a signal if it is easy for people to find unscrupulous doctors who will report falsely that they are in good health. Here screening by the insurance company using its own doctors may work better because the information is more credible.

Education can also serve as a signal. No doubt you've been told that one good reason to go to college is to get a good job. Going to college may get you a better job because you obtain valuable training. However, another possibility is that a college degree may land you a good job because it serves as a signal to employers about your ability. If high-ability people are more likely to go to college than low-ability people, schooling signals ability to employers.

Managerial Implication

Using Brand Names and Warranties as Signals

Honesty is the best policy—when there is money in it. —Mark Twain

Managers can often sell more if they successfully send potential customers a signal that the quality of their product is high. Some agricultural firms brand their produce (such as Dole pineapples and Chiquita bananas), while rivals sell their produce without labels. Many shoppers assume that branding makes sense for a firm only if its product quality is superior to that of unbranded products.

A warranty may serve as both a signal and a guarantee. It is less expensive for the manufacturer of a reliable product to offer a warranty than it is for a firm that produces low-quality products. Consequently, if one firm offers a warranty and another does not, then a consumer may infer that the firm with the warranty produces a superior product. Of course, sleazy firms may try to imitate high-quality firms by offering a warranty that they do not intend to honor.

Top manufacturers of consumer durables such as cars and refrigerators usually offer warranties. In recent years, some leading auto manufacturers have started offering warranties comparable to those of new cars on their pre-owned cars to signal quality.

Mini-Case

Changing a Firm's Name

A firm's good name is one of its most valuable assets. If the firm has sold high-quality goods or provided superior service in the past, then its reputation serves as a signal to consumers that they can expect the same excellence in the future. Consequently, good managers work hard to maintain the firm's reputation so that its name remains a signal of quality.

What should a firm do if its good or service has been below par in the past so that it is poison to consumers? A manager of such a firm can spend a great deal of money trying to improve its reputation. However, a less expensive approach may be to change the firm's name, because having no reputation is better than having a bad one. In a more extreme case, the firm may exit the market. For example, Cabral and Hortacsu (2010) reported that sellers on eBay are likely to stop selling on the site after receiving their first negative feedback.

McDevitt (2011) found that the more complaints that the Better Business Bureau received about a plumbing firm in Illinois, the more likely that firm was to change its name or exit the industry.[5] Firms that extensively advertised were more likely to change their names than to exit. Finally, all else the same, firms

---

[5]Controlling for other factors, a firm with a record of complaints one standard deviation above the mean was 133% more likely to change its name or exit.

in smaller cities outside of Chicago were 49% less likely to change their names than firms within metro Chicago. Presumably it is more difficult to shake a bad reputation just by changing names in a small town than in a large city.

Because shady operators can simply change the names of their businesses, some consumer advocates have called for making name changes more difficult. The U.S. Government Accountability Office found that at least 9% percent of motor coach carriers that were ordered "out of service" by the Federal Motor Carrier Safety Administration for violating safety standards merely changed their names, undermining the effectiveness of such regulatory bodies.

Third-Party Information. In some markets, consumer groups, nonprofit organizations, and government agencies provide buyers with information about the quality of different goods and services. If this information is credible, it can reduce adverse selection by enabling consumers to avoid buying low-quality goods or to lower the price of poorer quality products.

For an outside organization to provide believable information, it must convince consumers that it is trustworthy. Consumers Union, which publishes the product evaluation guide *Consumer Reports*, tries to establish its trustworthiness by refusing to accept advertising or other payments from firms.

Auditing is another important example of third-party assessment, in which an independent accounting firm assesses the financial statements of a firm or other organization. Sometimes a firm obtains an audit voluntarily to enhance its reputation (a signal). Sometimes audits are required as a condition of being listed on a particular exchange or of participating in a particular transaction, and sometimes audits are required by law (screening).

Many local governments require that home sellers disclose all important facts about the home to potential buyers such as the age of the home and any known defects in the electrical work or plumbing. By doing so, these governments protect buyers against adverse selection due to undisclosed defects.

Governments, consumer groups, industry groups, and others also provide information by establishing *standards*, which are metrics or scales for evaluating the quality of a particular product. For example, the R-value of insulation tells how effectively insulation works. Consumers learn of a brand's quality through **certification**: a report that a particular product meets or exceeds a given standard level.

Many industry groups set their own standards and get an outside group or firm, such as Underwriters Laboratories (UL) or Factory Mutual Engineering Corporation (FMEC), to certify that their products meet specified standard levels. For example, by setting standards for the size of the thread on a screw, we ensure that screws work in products regardless of brand.

When standard and certification programs inexpensively and completely inform consumers about the relative quality of all goods in a market and do not restrict the goods available, the programs are socially desirable. However, some of these programs have harmful effects for two reasons.

First, standard and certification programs that provide imprecise information may mislead consumers. Some standards use only a high- versus low-quality rating even though quality varies continuously. Such standards encourage the manufacture of products that have either the lowest possible quality (and cost of production) or the minimum quality level necessary to obtain the top rating.

Second, if standard and certification programs restrict salable goods and services to those that are certified, such programs may also have anticompetitive effects. Many governments license only professionals and craftspeople who meet some minimum standards. People without a license are not allowed to practice their profession or craft. In most states, dozens, if not hundreds, of categories of professionals, craftspeople, and others are licensed, including public school teachers, electricians, plumbers, dentists, psychologists, contractors, and beauticians. (See the Mini-Case "Occupational Licensing" in Chapter 2.)

Licenses or certifications that restrict entry raise the average quality in the industry by eliminating low-quality goods and services. They drive up prices to consumers for two reasons. First, the number of people providing services is reduced because the restrictions eliminate some potential suppliers. Second, consumers are unable to obtain lower-quality and less-expensive goods or services. As a result, welfare may go up or down, depending on whether the increased-quality effect or the higher-price effect dominates. Whether such restrictions can be set properly and cost-effectively by government agencies is widely debated.

Mini-Case	
Adverse Selection on eBay Motors	Because consumers can't see a good before buying it over the Internet, it's easy for a shady seller to misrepresent its quality. In the worst-case lemons-market scenario, low-quality goods drive out high-quality goods. We'd expect adverse selection to be particularly bad on eBay Motors, the largest used car marketplace in the United States, where nearly 50,000 cars are sold each month. Three-quarters of the cars are sold to out-of-state buyers, so most people cannot examine the car before bidding.

Sellers' reputations and warranties are of limited help. Although eBay posts reviews from past customers, most sellers have limited records except for dealers, who sell only 30% of the cars. Usually only dealers offer warranties, and then on only some cars.

However, enforceable contracts and sellers' signals reduce adverse selection on eBay Motors. The disclosures on eBay's Web page create an enforceable contract. If the car doesn't live up to the claims, buyers can refuse to pay on delivery. In addition, outright lies are fraudulent and may be prosecuted. (In contrast, in most private sales between individuals, buyers do not have an enforceable contract.)

Each Web page contains some standard, mandatory information such as car make, model, and mileage. But most sellers signal by voluntarily disclosing additional information ("the car has no rust, scratches, or dents") and post photos, graphics, and videos. The typical Web page has 17 photos.

Sellers disclose more information for high-quality cars than for lemons. All else the same, a seller who posts 10 photos rather than 9 sells a car for 1.54% more, about $171 on average (Lewis, 2011).

15.3 Moral Hazard

We now turn from adverse selection problems caused by hidden characteristics to moral hazard problems that result from hidden actions. Examples include renters driving rental cars off-road, workers loafing when the boss is not watching, and lawyers acting in their own interests instead of those of their clients.

We start by examining moral hazard problems that occur in insurance markets and in principle-agent relationships. Later, we discuss means of reducing or eliminating these moral hazard problems.

Moral Hazard in Insurance Markets

The term *moral hazard* was introduced into common usage by the insurance industry. Many types of insurance are highly vulnerable to hidden actions by insured parties that result in moral hazard problems.

For example, Ralph, the owner of a clothing store, purchased a large quantity of designer jeans and stored the jeans in a warehouse. Following standard practice, he insured the merchandise for its original purchase price against such hazards as fire or theft. Unfortunately for Ralph, these jeans have become unfashionable and are not selling. Because he faces a significant financial loss, he burns down the warehouse and makes an insurance claim.[6] The hidden action is that of setting the warehouse on fire. Because most people view such an action as unethical or *immoral* (as well as being illegal), we use the term *moral* hazard.

A somewhat less extreme example of moral hazard arises when medical insurance covers the expense of doctor visits. If one of the benefits of the medical insurance is that insured people do not have to pay for visits to their doctors, some insured people make "excessive" visits to the doctor—more than if they had to pay for the visits themselves. Some people visit a doctor in part because they are hypochondriacs or are lonely and want some company.

Such behavior is not illegal and may not seem unethical. However, because it is costly, insurance companies take actions to reduce the number of visits. For example, they may cap the number of visits to, say, three per year. Or the insurance company may require its customers to make a copayment, which is part of the cost of each visit to a doctor, often about $20 to $30 per visit.[7]

Moral Hazard in Principal-Agent Relationships

Moral hazard problems in business are frequent when responsibilities are delegated by a *principal* who contracts with an *agent* to take an *action* that benefits the principal. If an agent's actions are hidden, moral hazard may result. Moral hazard in a principal-agent relationship is referred to as a *principal-agent problem* or *agency problem*.

If information is symmetric so that actions cannot be hidden, principal-agent relationships do not give rise to a moral hazard problem. When a building contractor (the principal) subcontracts with a house painter (the agent) and both work on the same building site, the contractor can directly observe how hard and how well the painter is working. Due to this close monitoring, the painter cannot engage in any hidden action, such as taking an hour-long coffee break or running personal errands during work hours. Consequently, no inefficiency arises from this principal-agent relationship.

---

[6]Insurance frauds are common. A wide range of examples are described by the Coalition Against Insurance Fraud at **www.insurancefraud.org**.

[7]The lower the copayment, the more likely a patient visits a doctor, which increases the chance of early detection and treatment of health problems. Because early detection reduces the long-run cost, the insurance company has to balance this advantage against the moral hazard problem of excessive visits.

However, if agents' actions are hidden from principals, moral hazard may result. For example, if a business owner (the principal) hires an employee (the agent) to work at a remote site and cannot observe whether the employee is working hard, then the employee may *shirk* by not providing all the services the employee is paid to provide. Chapter 7 provides examples of this type of moral hazard in which managers (agents) act in their own best interest rather than that of the owners (principals) by not working hard or by spending the firm's assets on personal benefits (perquisites or perks). These hidden actions benefit the mangers but reduce the collective earnings of the managers and the owners.

We consider an example where the payoffs to the owner of a firm (the principal) and the manager (the agent) depend on the agent's actions and the *state of nature*, such as weather (which affects demand) or input prices (which affect costs). The principal and the agent care about how payoffs are allocated and how the risk is shared.

Ideally, the principal and agent agree to an **efficient contract**: an agreement in which neither party can be made better off without harming the other party. If the parties to the contract are risk neutral, efficiency requires that the combined profit of the principal and agent be maximized. If one party is more risk averse than the other, efficiency requires that the less risk-averse party bear more of the risk (Chapter 14). In our example, the outcome is efficient if the agent works extra hard so that the total profit that the parties share is as large as possible and if the agent, who is the only risk-averse party, bears none of the risk.

Reducing Moral Hazard Using Efficient Contracts.
Paul, the principal, owns many ice cream parlors across North America. He contracts with Amy, the agent, to manage his Miami shop. Her duties include supervising workers, purchasing supplies, and performing other necessary actions.

The shop's daily earnings depend on the local demand conditions and on how hard Amy works. Demand for ice cream varies with the weather, and is high half the time, and low otherwise.

Amy puts forth either normal or extra effort. She views herself as an honest person and would never steal from Paul. She is always at the shop during regular business hours and puts in at least a normal amount of effort, even if Paul cannot check on her. She politely, but impersonally, asks everyone who enters the shop, "May I help you?"

Nonetheless, Amy might not be working as hard as possible. She could put forth extra effort by enthusiastically greeting regular customers by name, serving customers rapidly, spending extra hours checking with nearby businesses to see if they would be interested in joint promotions, and improving the appearance of the shop. However, extra work is tiring and prevents Amy from spending time at the beach with friends, reading novels, watching "Dancing with the Stars," and engaging in other activities that she enjoys. She values her personal cost of this extra effort at $40 per day.

For any given level of demand, the shop sells more ice cream if Amy puts forth extra effort. The shop also sells more for a given level of Amy's effort if demand is high. Table 15.1 shows the profit of the ice cream shop before Amy is paid—the combined payoff to Paul and Amy—for the four possible combinations of effort and demand. If the demand is high and Amy puts in little effort, or if the demand is low and she works hard, the firm's daily profit is 300. The profit is 500 if the demand is high and Amy works hard but is only 100 if the demand is low and she applies only normal effort.

TABLE 15.1 Ice Cream Shop Profits

		Demand	
		Low	*High*
	Normal	100	300
Amy's Effort			
	Extra	300	500

Because Paul owns many ice cream parlors across North America, he can pool the returns from all these stores and is risk neutral. Amy, like most people, is risk averse. Thus, risk bearing is efficient if Paul bears all of the risk and Amy bears none of it (Chapter 14).

Symmetric Information. Moral hazard is not a problem if Paul lives in Miami and can directly supervise Amy. They could agree to a contract that specifies Amy receives 200 per day if she works extra hard, but loses her job if she doesn't. Because Amy's cost of working extra hard is 40, she nets 160 (= 200 − 40) if she works hard, which is better than being fired and getting nothing. Even though the shop's profit varies with demand, Amy bears no risk: She receives 200 regardless of demand conditions.

Paul is the *residual claimant*: He receives the *residual profit*, which is the amount left over from the store's profit after Amy's wage is paid. Because Amy works hard (as she does not want to get fired), Paul's residual profit varies only with demand. If demand is low, the shop earns 300, he pays Amy 200 and retains 100. If demand is high, the shop earns 500, so Paul keeps 300, after paying Amy 200. Paul's expected profit is the probability of low demand, 50% (or $\frac{1}{2}$), times 100, plus the probability of high demand, 50%, times 300, or

$$\left(\tfrac{1}{2} \times 100\right) + \left(\tfrac{1}{2} \times 300\right) = 200.$$

Under this contract, Paul bears all the risk from the shop's uncertain earnings. The variance of Paul's earnings is large relative to his expected profit: $\frac{1}{2}(100 − 200)^2 + \frac{1}{2}(300 − 200)^2 = 10,000.$[8]

This result is summarized in the first row of Table 15.2, which is labelled *perfect monitoring*. Is this contract efficient? The last two columns show that it is because Paul, the risk-neutral party, bears all the risk, and their combined earnings are as high as possible because Amy works extra hard.

Asymmetric Information. Paul grows tired of warm weather and moves from Miami to Toronto, Canada, where he can no longer observe Amy's effort. Because Amy's effort is now a hidden action to Paul, he faces a moral hazard problem.

---

[8]The variance (Chapter 14) is the probability of low demand, 50%, times the square of the difference between the payoff under low demand, 100, and the expected payoff, 200, plus the probability of high demand, 50%, times the square of the difference between the payoff under high demand, 300, and the expected payoff.

TABLE 15.2 Ice Cream Shop Outcomes

Contract	Expected Payoffs				Efficiency	
	Paul	Amy[a]	Paul + Amy	Amy's Variance	Risk Bearing[b]	Joint Payoff[c]
Symmetric Information						
Perfect monitoring	200	160	360	0	yes	yes
Asymmetric Information						
Fixed wage of 100	100	100	200	0	yes	no
Licensing fee of 200	200	160	360	10,000	no	yes
State-contingent fee of 100 or 300	200	160	360	0	yes	yes
50% profit share	200	160	360	2,500	no	yes
Wage and bonus of 200; Amy is risk neutral	200	160	360	10,000	yes	yes
Wage and bonus of 200; Amy is very risk averse	100	100	200	0	yes	no

[a]If Amy puts in extra work, her payoff is net of 40, which is the value she places on having to work harder.
[b]Because Amy is risk averse and Paul is risk neutral, risk bearing is efficient only if Paul bears all the risk, so that Amy's variance is zero.
[c]Production is efficient if Amy puts in extra work, so that the shop's expected payoff is 400 rather than 200.

When Paul could monitor Amy's effort, he could make her wage contingent on hard work. Now, he pays her a wage that does not vary with her (hidden) effort. Initially, let's assume that Paul and Amy's contract specifies that Paul pays Amy a daily wage of 100 regardless of how much profit the shop earns. Such a contract is called a *fixed-fee contract*, because one party pays the other a constant payment or fee.

Because Amy receives the same amount no matter how hard she works, Amy chooses not to work hard, which is a moral hazard problem. If she works normally, she incurs no additional personal cost from extra effort and receives 100. On the other hand, if she provides extra effort, she receives a wage of 100 but incurs a personal cost of 40, so her net return is only 60.

Because Amy provides normal effort, the shop earns 100 with low demand, which is just enough to pay Amy with nothing left over for Paul, and the shop earns 300 with high demand, so Paul nets 200. Thus Paul faces an uncertain profit with an expected value of $(\frac{1}{2} \times 0) + (\frac{1}{2} \times 200) = 100$. The variance of Paul's earnings remains high: $\frac{1}{2}(0 - 100)^2 + \frac{1}{2}(200 - 100)^2 = 10,000$.

This situation is summarized in the second row of Table 15.2, which is labelled *fixed wage*. Paul bears all the risk, so risk bearing is again efficient. However, their combined earnings are less than in the previous example with symmetric information. Amy now makes 100. Paul has an expected value of 100, which is all he cares about because he is risk neutral. Both were better off with symmetric information: Amy netted 160 and Paul expected to earn 200. Because the moral hazard substantially reduces the shop's expected earnings, having Paul pay Amy a fixed wage is not the best way to compensate her. In the next section, we examine how well-designed contracts can reduce inefficiency due to moral hazard.

Selfless or Selfish Doctors?

Patients (principals) rely on doctors (agents) for good medical advice. Do doctors selflessly act only in their patient's best interests, or do they take advantage of their superior knowledge to exploit patients or the companies that insure them?

Lu (2012) conducted an experiment to investigate doctors' behavior at top Beijing hospitals, in which the doctors were unaware that they were part of an experiment. In the experiment, a doctor knew whether a patient had insurance or not. The doctor also knew if the patient planned to buy any prescribed drugs at the hospital, where the doctor received a share of the patient's payment for drugs, or at an outside drugstore, where the doctors received no compensation from the prescriptions. Many doctors were asked to recommend treatment for a particular patient under these four possibilities: insurance–buy at the hospital, insurance–buy elsewhere, no insurance–buy at the hospital, and no insurance–buy elsewhere.

If a doctor is concerned about a patient's overall well-being and takes the patient's ability to pay into account, the doctor may prescribe more for patients with insurance, even if the doctor does not receive compensation for extra prescriptions. If *the doctor is primarily interested in earning as much as possible*, the doctor is likely to prescribe excessively for patients who are insured and who buy the drugs at the hospital. This excessive prescribing is a hidden action that creates a moral hazard.

Lu (2012) found that doctors prescribed similarly whether or not a patient had insurance if the doctors received no compensation for prescriptions. However, if the doctors were compensated for prescriptions, they prescribed drugs that cost 43% more on average for insured patients than for uninsured patients. Moreover, many of these extra, very expensive drugs were unjustified by the patient's medical condition. Thus, many of these doctors appeared to be motivated largely by self-interest rather than purely out of concern for their patients.

Traditionally the Las Vegas Home Bank made only *prime* loans—providing mortgages just to people who were very likely to repay the loans. However, Leonardo, a senior executive at the bank, is considering offering *subprime* loans—mortgages to speculators and other less creditworthy borrowers. If he makes only prime loans, the bank will earn $160 million. If he also makes subprime loans, the bank will make a very high profit, $800 million, if the economy is good so that few people default. However, if the economy is bad, the large number of defaults will cause the bank to lose $320 million.

The probability that the economy is bad is 75%. Leonardo will receive 1% of the bank's profit if it is positive. He believes that if the bank loses money, he can walk away from his job without repercussions but with no compensation. Leonardo and the bank's shareholders are risk neutral. Does Leonardo provide subprime loans if all he cares about is maximizing his personal expected earnings? What would the bank's stockholders prefer that Leonardo do (given that they know the risks involved)?

Answer

1. *Compare the bank's expected return on the two types of mortgages.* If the bank makes both prime and subprime loans, its expected return is $(0.25 \times 800) + (0.75 \times [-320]) = -40$ million dollars, an expected loss. That is substantially less than the certain profit of $160 million the bank makes if it provides only prime mortgages.

2. *Compare the manager's expected profits on the two investments.* Leonardo earns 1% of $160 million, or $1.6 million, if he provides only prime loans. If he makes prime and subprime loans, he earns 1% of $800 million, or $8 million, with a probability of 25%, and gets no compensation with a probability of 75%. Thus, he expects to earn $(0.25 \times 8) + (0.75 \times 0) = 2$ million dollars. Because Leonardo is risk neutral and does not care about the shareholders' returns, he makes both types of loans.

3. *Compare the shareholders' expected profits on the two types of mortgages.* If the bank provides only prime mortgages, the bank's shareholders earn 99% of the profit from the prime mortgages, or $0.99 \times \$160$ million $= \$158.4$ million. If the bank makes both prime and subprime loans, shareholders earn 99% of the $800 million, $792 million, if the economy is good. But in a bad economy, the shareholders bear the full loss, $320 million. The expected return to shareholders is $(0.25 \times 792) + (0.75 \times [-320]) = -42$ million dollars, an expected loss. Thus, the shareholders would prefer that the bank make only prime loans.

Comment: Given that Leonardo has the wrong incentives (and ignores his responsibility to shareholders), he takes a hidden action—choosing to provide subprime loans—that is not in the shareholders' best interest. This type of moral hazard was one of the major causes of the 2007–2009 financial crisis. One possible solution to the problem of managers' and shareholders' diverging interests is to change the manager's compensation scheme, as we discuss in the Managerial Solution.

15.4 Using Contracts to Reduce Moral Hazard

A verbal contract isn't worth the paper it's written on. —Samuel Goldwyn

A skillfully designed contract that provides the agent with strong incentives to act so that the outcome of any transaction is efficient may reduce or eliminate moral hazard problems. In this section, we illustrate how several types of contracts can increase efficiency in the Paul and Amy ice cream shop example. These contracts provide greater incentives for Amy, the agent, to work hard, but often require her to bear some risk even though she is more risk averse than Paul, the principal.

Fixed-Fee Contracts

We initially considered a fixed-fee contract in which Paul (the principal) pays Amy (the agent) a fixed wage, with the result that Paul bears all of the risk and Amy bears none. Alternatively, Amy could pay Paul a fixed amount so that she receives the residual profit: the profit left over after Paul has been paid his fixed return. Amy is, in effect, paying a *license fee* to operate Paul's ice cream shop.[9] With such a contract, Paul bears no risk as he receives a fixed fee, while Amy bears all the risk.[10]

---

[9]In the Sherlock Holmes mystery *A Study in Scarlet*, Jefferson Hope says, "I applied at a cab-owner's office, and soon got employment. I was to bring a certain sum a week to the owner, and whatever was over that I might keep for myself."

[10]In some businesses, both types of fixed-fee contracts are used. For example, in some hair salons, hairdressers rent a chair from the owner for a fixed fee and bear all the risk associated with variations in demand, while other hairdressers are paid an hourly rate, with the owner getting the residual profit from their activities.

As Amy receives the residual profit under such a licensing contract, she receives all the increase in expected profit from her extra effort. She is therefore motivated to work hard.

To illustrate why, we suppose that Amy pays Paul a fixed licensing fee of 200 per day and keeps any residual profit. (Our analysis depends *only* on Amy paying Paul a fixed fee and *not* on the exact amount that she pays.) If she does not work hard, she makes 100 ($= 300 - 200$) with high demand, but suffers a loss, -100 ($= 100 - 200$), if demand is low. Her expected gain if she does not work hard is $0 = (\frac{1}{2} \times [-100]) + (\frac{1}{2} \times 100)$. If she works hard, she nets 60 ($= 300 - 200 - 40$) with low demand and 260 ($= 500 - 200 - 40$) with high demand, so that her expected net payoff is $160 = (\frac{1}{2} \times 60) + (\frac{1}{2} \times 260)$. Thus, her expected gain from working hard is 160.

Her variance in earnings is $10{,}000 = \frac{1}{2}(-100 - 0)^2 + \frac{1}{2}(100 - 0)^2$ with low demand, which is the same as the variance with high demand, $10{,}000 = \frac{1}{2}(60 - 160)^2 + \frac{1}{2}(260 - 160)^2$. Thus, because her risk is the same with both levels of effort but her expected net earnings are higher if she puts forth high effort, it is in her best interest to work hard.

Consequently, Amy's and Paul's total expected earnings are higher if Amy pays a fixed fee to Paul than if Paul pays a fixed fee to Amy, because Amy works harder if she is the residual claimant and therefore reaps all the benefits of working harder. As the third row (*licensing fee*) of Table 15.2 shows, when Amy pays Paul a license fee, the shop's expected earnings are 400 because Amy works hard. Paul makes 200 with certainty, and Amy expects a net gain of 160 after deducting her cost, 40, of providing high effort. Therefore, the expected sum of their payoffs is 360. In contrast, if Paul pays Amy a fixed wage (second row), Amy earns 100 and Paul expects to earn 100 for an expected total payoff of 200.

Although Amy paying Paul rather than the other way around increases their total earnings, it makes the risk-averse person, Amy, bear all the risk, while Paul, the risk-neutral person, bears no risk. Therefore, although this contract maximizes combined expected earnings, it does not provide for efficient risk bearing.

Which contract is better depends on how risk averse Amy is. If Amy is nearly risk neutral, the fixed payment to Paul is superior, because both parties have higher expected earnings and Amy is not very concerned about the risk. However, if Amy is extremely risk averse, she may prefer receiving a fixed wage even if that means giving up significant expected earnings.[11]

Contingent Contracts

Many contracts specify that the parties receive payoffs that are contingent on some other variable, such as the action taken by the agent, the state of nature, or the firm's profit, output, or revenue. For example, when Paul could monitor Amy's effort, he offered her a contract that made her payoff contingent on her effort. She was paid only if she provided extra effort and lost her job otherwise. Such a contract would be efficient, but is not feasible if Paul cannot monitor Amy's effort. However, contingent contracts may be used even when monitoring is not feasible.

State-Contingent Contracts. In a *state-contingent contract*, one party's payoff is contingent on *only* the state of nature. For example, suppose Amy pays Paul a license fee of 100 if demand is low and a license fee of 300 if demand is high and

---

[11]Amy might be more risk averse if, for example, she has no savings and would find it difficult to support herself during periods of low demand if she were the residual claimant.

keeps any additional earnings. As the residual claimant, Amy has an incentive to provide high effort. With low demand the shop earns 300, Amy pays Paul 100, and Amy's residual profit is $160 = 300 - 100 - 40$, where 40 is the cost of her extra effort. With high demand, the shop earns 500, Amy pays Paul 300, and Amy's residual profit is $160 = 500 - 300 - 40$.

Paul's expected payoff is $200 = (\frac{1}{2} \times 100) + (\frac{1}{2} \times 300)$, as the fourth row of Table 15.2 shows. Because Amy earns 160 in both states of nature, she bears no risk, while Paul bears all the risk. This result is efficient because Paul is risk neutral and Amy is risk averse. This state-contingent contract is fully efficient even if Paul cannot monitor Amy's effort. However, it does require that both parties observe and agree on the state of nature, which may not be possible.

Profit-Sharing Contracts. Even if the principal cannot observe the state of nature or the agent's actions, the principal may be able to design a contingent contract that reduces the moral hazard problem by making payments contingent on an outcome, such as profit or output. One common contingent contract is a *profit-sharing contract*, in which the payoff to each party is a fraction of the observable total profit.

Suppose that Paul and Amy agree to split the earnings of the ice cream shop equally. Does making Amy's pay contingent on the firm's earnings induce Amy to work hard?

If Amy works normally, the shop earns 100 if the demand is low and Amy receives half, or 50. If demand is high, the shop earns 300, so Amy's share is 150 $(= \frac{1}{2} \times 300)$. Thus, Amy's expected value from normal effort is $100 = (\frac{1}{2} \times 50) + (\frac{1}{2} \times 150)$. The variance of her earnings is $2,500 = \frac{1}{2}(50 - 100)^2 + \frac{1}{2}(150 - 100)^2$.

If Amy provides extra effort, the shop earns 300 if the demand is low, and Amy receives 150, but she incurs a personal cost of 40 for providing high effort, so her net return is 110. If the demand is high, the shop's profit is 500, so that Amy nets $210 (= 250 - 40)$. Thus, her expected return from high effort is $160 = (\frac{1}{2} \times 110) + (\frac{1}{2} \times 210)$. The variance of her earnings is $2,500 = \frac{1}{2}(110 - 160)^2 + \frac{1}{2}(210 - 160)^2$, which is the same as with normal effort. Because extra effort provides Amy with higher expected earnings without increasing her risk, she provides extra effort.

Given that Amy works hard, Paul makes 150 $(= \frac{1}{2} \times 300)$ if demand is low and 250 $(= \frac{1}{2} \times 500)$ if demand is high. His expected profit is $200 = (\frac{1}{2} \times 150) + (\frac{1}{2} \times 250)$, as the profit-sharing row of Table 15.2 shows. Paul prefers this profit-sharing contract to a fixed-fee contract where he pays Amy a fixed wage of 100 and makes an expected profit of 100.

However, Amy chooses to work harder only if she gets a large enough share of the profit to offset her personal cost from doing the extra work. If Amy gets less than 20% of the profit, she chooses not to work hard and earns less than she would from the wage of 100.[12] Thus, profit sharing may reduce or eliminate the moral hazard problem, especially if the agent's share of the profit is large, but may not do so if the agent's share is small.

Bonuses and Options. To induce an agent to work hard, a principal may offer the agent a *bonus*: an extra payment if a performance target is hit. For example, Paul

---

[12]If θ is Amy's share, then her expected earnings with normal effort is $(\frac{1}{2} \times 100\theta) + (\frac{1}{2} \times 300\theta) = 200\theta$, and her expected net earnings from extra effort is $(\frac{1}{2} \times 300\theta) + (\frac{1}{2} \times 500\theta) - 40 = 400\theta - 40$. She chooses not to put in extra effort if what she expects to earn from normal effort exceeds that from extra effort: $200\theta > 400\theta - 40$, or $\theta < 20\%$.

could offer Amy a base wage of 100 and a bonus of 200 if the shop's earnings (before paying Amy) exceed 300.

If Amy provides normal effort, the shop does not earn enough to trigger the bonus, so Amy receives 100 in both states of nature. If Amy provides extra effort but the demand is low, the shop earns 300, so Amy receives her wage of 100 and incurs a cost of 40, so her net benefit is 60. However, if she works hard and the demand is high, the shop earns 500, the bonus is triggered, and Amy gets her wage of 100 plus the bonus of 200. After subtracting her cost of extra effort, 40, she nets 260. Thus, Amy's expected return with extra effort is $160 = (\frac{1}{2} \times 60) + (\frac{1}{2} \times 260)$, which exceeds the 100 she earns with normal effort.

However, the variance in her net earnings with extra effort is $10,000 = \frac{1}{2}(60 - 160)^2 + \frac{1}{2}(260 - 160)^2$. Thus, whether Amy chooses to work extra hard depends on how risk averse she is. If she is nearly risk neutral, she works extra hard. However, if she is very risk averse, she puts in only normal effort, receives a modest but predictable wage, and avoids the risk of sometimes earning very little.

The next to last row of Table 15.2 shows the outcome of a bonus contract if Amy is risk neutral. If Amy is risk neutral or nearly risk neutral, she chooses to work hard. If demand is low, the bonus is not triggered, so Paul pays Amy only her base salary of 100 and keeps the residual amount of 200. With high demand, Paul pays Amy 300—the base of 100 plus the bonus of 200—and keeps the residual of 200 (= 500 − 300). Paul expects to earn $200 = (\frac{1}{2} \times 200) + (\frac{1}{2} \times 200)$. Indeed, he earns 200 regardless of demand conditions, so he bears no risk. Thus, if Amy is risk neutral, the bonus leads to efficient payoffs and efficient risk bearing even though Amy bears all the risk. (If Amy were nearly but not quite risk neutral, she would still choose to work hard, but would dislike bearing all the risk.)

The last row in Table 15.2 shows the outcome of a bonus contract if Amy is extremely risk averse. Now, she'd rather have 100 with certainty than take a chance on sometimes netting only 60 after incurring the cost of high effort, so she works only normal hours. Consequently, the total payoffs are low and hence not efficient, but risk is shared efficiently, with Paul bearing all the risk. Thus, this bonus may—but does not necessarily—induce Amy to work hard.

Many senior executives receive part of their salary in the form of an *option*, which is a type of bonus (Chapter 7). An option gives the holder the right to buy up to a certain number of shares of the company at a given price (the *exercise price*) during a specified time interval. An option provides a benefit to the executive if the firm's stock price exceeds the exercise price and is therefore a bonus based on the stock price.

Piece Rates and Commissions. Another common type of contingent contract is a *piece-rate contract*, in which the agent receives a payment for each unit of output the agent produces. Under such a contract, Amy is paid for every serving of ice cream she sells rather than by the hour, which gives her an incentive to work hard, but she bears the risk from fluctuations in demand, which she does not control.

Similarly, under a revenue-sharing contract, the agent receives some share of revenues earned. For people who work in sales, such payments are called *commissions*. For example, a salesperson in a clothing store might receive a commission of 5% of the revenue for each item sold. As with profit sharing, piece rates and commissions provide an incentive for agents to provide more effort than they would with a fixed-rate contract. As with a bonus, this incentive is not necessarily strong enough to offset the agent's cost of extra effort and the agent bears some risk.

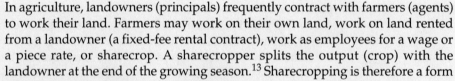

Mini-Case

Contracts and Productivity in Agriculture

In agriculture, landowners (principals) frequently contract with farmers (agents) to work their land. Farmers may work on their own land, work on land rented from a landowner (a fixed-fee rental contract), work as employees for a wage or a piece rate, or sharecrop. A sharecropper splits the output (crop) with the landowner at the end of the growing season.[13] Sharecropping is therefore a form of profit sharing or revenue sharing.

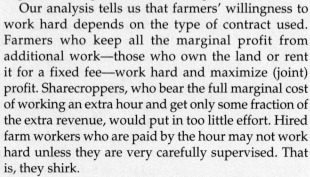

Our analysis tells us that farmers' willingness to work hard depends on the type of contract used. Farmers who keep all the marginal profit from additional work—those who own the land or rent it for a fixed fee—work hard and maximize (joint) profit. Sharecroppers, who bear the full marginal cost of working an extra hour and get only some fraction of the extra revenue, would put in too little effort. Hired farm workers who are paid by the hour may not work hard unless they are very carefully supervised. That is, they shirk.

Foster and Rosenzweig (1994) tested these predictions using data on Philippine farmers. Foster and Rosenzweig could not directly monitor farmers' work effort—any more than most landowners can. Rather, they ingeniously measured the effort indirectly. They contended that the harder people work, the more they eat and the more they use up body mass, holding calorie intake constant.

Foster and Rosenzweig estimated the effect of each compensation method on a measure of relative body mass (weight divided by height squared) and on consumption (after adjusting for gender, age, type of activity, and other factors). They found that people who work for themselves or are paid by the piece use up 10% more body mass, holding calorie consumption constant, than workers paid by the hour, and 13% more than sharecroppers. Foster and Rosenzweig also discovered that piece-rate workers consume 25% more calories per day and that people who work on their own farm consume 16% more than workers paid by the hour. Thus, these farm workers respond strongly to contractual incentives.

Q&A 15.4

Gary's demand for doctor visits depends on his health. Half the time his health is good and his demand is D^1 in the figure. When his health is poor, his demand is D^2. Gary is risk averse. Without medical insurance, he pays $50 a visit. With full insurance, he pays a fixed fee at the beginning of the year, and the insurance company pays the full cost of any visit. Alternatively, with a contingent contract, Gary pays a smaller premium at the beginning of the year, and the insurance company covers only $20 per visit, with Gary paying the remaining $30. How likely is a moral hazard problem to occur with each of these contracts? What is Gary's risk (the variance of his medical costs) with no insurance and with each of the two types of insurance? Compare the contracts in terms of the trade-offs between risk and moral hazard.

---

[13]If a farmer is someone who is out standing in his field, a sharecropper is someone who is out standing in someone else's field.

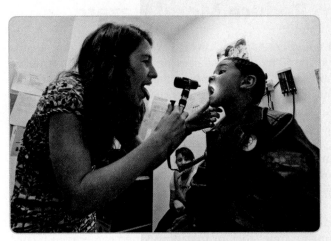

Answer

1. *Describe the moral hazard for each demand curve for each contract.* Given that Gary's health is good, if he does not have insurance, Gary pays the doctor $50 a visit and goes to the doctor once, at point a_1 in the figure. In contrast, with full insurance where he pays nothing per visit, he visits the doctor 6 times, at c_1. Similarly, if his health is poor, he goes to the doctor five times, a_2, without insurance, and 10 times, c_2, with full insurance. Thus, regardless of his health, he makes five extra visits a year with full insurance. These extra visits are the moral hazard.

   With a contingent contract, Gary pays $30 a visit. He makes three visits if his health is good (at point b_1)—only two more than at a_1. If his health is poor, he makes seven visits, once again two more than if he were paying the full fee (at point a_1). Thus, with a contingent contract, he makes only two extra visits, so the moral hazard problem is reduced.

2. *Calculate the variance of Gary's medical expenses for no insurance and for the two insurance contracts.* Without insurance, his average number of visits is $3 = (\frac{1}{2} \times 1) + (\frac{1}{2} \times 5)$, so his average annual medical cost is $150. Thus, the variance of his medical expenses without insurance is

$$\sigma_n^2 = \tfrac{1}{2}[(1 \times \$50) - \$150]^2 + \tfrac{1}{2}[(5 \times 50) - \$150]^2$$
$$= \tfrac{1}{2}(\$50 - \$150)^2 + \tfrac{1}{2}(\$250 - \$150)^2$$
$$= \$10,000.$$

If he has full insurance, he makes a single fixed payment each year, so his payments do not vary with his health: His variance is $\sigma_f^2 = 0$. Finally, with partial insurance, he averages five visits with an average cost of $150, so his variance is

$$\sigma_p^2 = \tfrac{1}{2}(\$90 - \$150)^2 + \tfrac{1}{2}(\$210 - \$150)^2$$
$$= \$3,600.$$

Thus, $\sigma_n^2 > \sigma_p^2 > \sigma_f^2$.

3. *Discuss the trade-offs.* Because Gary is risk averse, efficiency in risk bearing requires the insurance company to bear all the risk, as with full insurance. However, full insurance results in the largest moral hazard. Without insurance, there is no moral hazard, but Gary bears all the risk. This contingent contract is a compromise in which both the moral hazard and the degree of risk lie between the extremes.

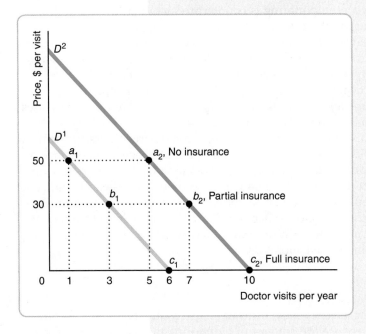

15.5 Using Monitoring to Reduce Moral Hazard

Often when a firm cannot use piece rates or reward workers contingent on the firm's success, the employer pays fixed-fee salaries or hourly wages. As we've seen, employees who are paid a fixed salary have little incentive to work hard if the employer cannot observe shirking. And if an employer pays employees by the hour but cannot observe how many hours they work, employees may inflate the number of hours they report working. A firm can reduce such shirking by intensively supervising or monitoring its workers. Monitoring eliminates or at least reduces the asymmetric information problem: Both the employee and the employer know how hard the employee works. If the cost of monitoring workers is low enough, it pays to prevent shirking by carefully monitoring and firing employees who do not work hard.

Firms have experimented with various means of lowering the cost of monitoring. Requiring employees to punch a time clock or installing video cameras to record employee work effort are examples of firms' attempts to use capital to monitor job performance. Similarly, by installing assembly lines that force employees to work at a pace dictated by the firm, employers can control employees' work rate.

According to a survey by the American Management Association, nearly two-thirds of employers record employees' voice mail, e-mail, or phone calls; review their computer files; or videotape workers. A quarter of the firms that use surveillance don't tell their employees. The most common types of surveillance are tallying phone numbers called and recording the duration of the calls (37%), videotaping employees' work (16%), storing and reviewing e-mail (15%), storing and reviewing computer files (14%), and taping and reviewing phone conversations (10%). Monitoring and surveillance are most common in the financial sector, in which 81% of firms use these techniques. Rather than watching all employees all the time, companies usually monitor selected workers using spot checks.

For some jobs, however, monitoring is counterproductive or not cost effective. Monitoring may lower employees' morale, which in turn reduces productivity. Many years ago, Northwest Airlines took the doors off bathroom stalls to prevent workers from staying too long in the stalls. When new management eliminated this policy (and made many other changes as well), productivity increased.

It is usually impractical for firms to monitor how hard salespeople work if they spend most of their time away from the main office. As telecommuting increases, monitoring workers may become increasingly difficult.

A firm's board of directors is supposed to represent shareholders (principals) by monitoring senior executives (agents) to ensure that executive decisions are made in the shareholders' interests. Bad executives may try to hide their actions from directors or select directors who won't "rat" on them. González, Schmid, and Yermack (2013) studied firms in which senior executives were engaging in illegal price-fixing, exposing the firm and its shareholders to significant legal liability. They found that senior executives in such firms were more inclined to recruit directors who were likely to be inattentive monitors.

Hostages

When direct monitoring is very costly, firms often use contracts containing various financial incentives to reduce the amount of monitoring that is necessary. Each of these incentives—bonding, deferred payments, and efficiency wages (unusually high wages)—acts as a *hostage* for good behavior (Williamson, 1983). Workers who are caught shirking or engaging in other undesirable acts not only lose their jobs but give up the hostage too. The more valuable the hostage, the less monitoring the firm needs to use to deter bad behavior.

Bonding. One way to ensure agents behave well is to require them to deposit funds guaranteeing their good behavior, just as a landlord requires tenants to post security deposits to ensure that they will not damage an apartment. For example, an employer (principal) may require an employee (agent) to provide a *performance bond*, an amount of money that will be given to the principal if the agent fails to complete certain duties or achieve certain goals. Typically, the agent posts (leaves) this bond with the principal or another party, such as an insurance company, before starting the job.

Many couriers who transport valuable shipments (such as jewels) or guards who watch over them have to post bonds against theft and other forms of moral hazard. Similarly, bonds may be used to keep employees from quitting immediately after receiving costly training. Two major problems are inherent in posting bonds. First, to capture a bond, an unscrupulous employer might falsely accuse an employee of stealing or of failing to meet the required performance standard. An employee who fears such employer opportunism might be unwilling to post a bond. One possible solution to this problem is for the firm to develop a reputation for not behaving in this manner. Another possible approach is for the firm to make the grounds for forfeiture of the bond objective and thus verifiable by others.

A second problem with bonds is that workers may not have enough wealth to post them. Because of such problems, bonds are more common in contracts between firms than in those between an employer and employees. Moreover, firms have fewer problems than typical employees do in raising funds to post bonds.

Construction contractors frequently post bonds to guarantee that they will satisfactorily finish their work by a given date. It is easy to verify whether the contract has been completed on time, so the principal is unlikely to engage in opportunistic behavior.

Deferred Payments. Effectively, firms can post bonds for their employees through the use of deferred payments. For example, a firm pays new workers a low wage for some initial period of employment. Then, over time, workers who are caught shirking are fired, and those good workers who remain receive higher wages. In another form of deferred wages, the firm provides a retirement pension that rewards only workers who stay with the firm for a sufficiently long period of time (or who reach a certain age). Workers who are terminated early forfeit this benefit, so they have an incentive to work hard to avoid early termination. Deferred payments serve the same function as bonds. They raise the cost of being fired, so less monitoring is necessary to deter shirking.

Reduced shirking leads to greater output. If the employer and the employee share the extra output in the form of higher profit and lifetime earnings, both the firm and workers prefer the deferred-payment scheme that lowers incentives to shirk.

A drawback of the deferred-payment approach is that, like posting bonds, it can encourage employers to engage in opportunistic behavior. For example, an employer might fire nonshirking senior workers to avoid paying their higher wages or pensions and then replace them with less expensive junior workers. However, if the firm can establish a reputation for not firing senior workers unjustifiably, the deferred-payment system can help prevent shirking.

Managerial Implication

Efficiency Wages

Managers can often reduce employee shirking by paying an *efficiency wage*: an unusually high wage above the worker's opportunity cost (the amount the worker can get elsewhere). If a worker who is fired for shirking can immediately go to another firm and earn the same wage, the worker risks nothing by shirking. But an efficiency wage acts as a hostage. A high wage raises the cost of getting fired, so it discourages shirking.[14] If the saving from reducing shirking exceeds the cost of the higher wage, then paying an efficiency wage is profitable.

After-the-Fact Monitoring

So far we've concentrated on monitoring by employers looking for undesirable behavior as it occurs. However, it is often easier to detect the effects of shirking or other undesirable actions after the actions occur. For example, an employer can check the amount that an employee produces or the quality of the work after it is completed. If shirking or other unwanted behavior is detected after the fact, the offending employee may be fired or otherwise disciplined. This punishment discourages shirking in the future.

If an insurance company determines after the fact that an insurance claim resulted from intentional behavior rather than chance, the firm may refuse to pay. Insurance companies may refuse to pay damages for a traffic accident if the insured driver was drunk at the time. House insurance companies disallow claims due to explosions resulting from illegal activities such as making methamphetamine, and claims by arsonists who torch their own homes or businesses are rejected. Life insurance companies may refuse to pay benefits to the family of someone who commits suicide soon after buying the policy (as in the play *Death of a Salesman*).

Mini-Case

Abusing Leased Cars

Because drivers of fleet automobiles such as rental cars and leased cars do not own them, they do not bear all the costs caused by neglecting or abusing the vehicles, resulting in a moral hazard problem. These vehicles are driven harder and farther and depreciate faster than owner-operated vehicles. According to the Research and Innovation Technology Administration in 2012, new vehicle leases were 26% of new vehicle sales.

Using data from sales at used car auctions, Dunham (2003), after controlling for mileage, found that fleet vehicles (not including taxis or police cars) depreciate 10% to 13% more rapidly than owner-driven vehicles.[15] The average auction

---

[14]See Yellen (1984), Stiglitz (1987), and Shapiro and Stiglitz (1984). There are other explanations for why efficiency wages lead to higher productivity. Some economists claim that in less-developed countries, employers pay an efficiency wage—more than they need to hire workers—to ensure that workers can afford to eat well enough so that they can work hard. Other economists (Akerlof, 1982) and management experts contend that the higher wage acts like a gift, making workers feel beholden or loyal to the firm, so less (or no) monitoring is needed.

[15]According to National Public Radio's *Car Talk*—one of the world's most reliable sources of information—police cars have very few miles on them, but their engines are quickly shot because cops spend untold hours sitting in their cruisers in front of donut shops with the engine running and the air conditioner on high.

price for a Pontiac 6000 was $5,200 for a fleet car and $6,500 for a nonfleet car. This $1,300 difference, which was one-fourth of the fleet car's price, reflects the increased depreciation of fleet cars.

To deal with this moral hazard, an automobile-leasing firm commonly writes contracts—open-ended leases—in which the driver's final payment for the vehicle depends on the selling price of the car. In this way, the contract makes the leasing driver responsible for at least some of the harm done to the car, to encourage the lessee to take greater care of the vehicle. Given the difference in auction prices, however, such leases apparently are not the full solution to this moral hazard problem.

Managerial Solution

Limiting Managerial Incentives

In the aftermath of the financial crisis of 2007–2009, most economists and government officials concluded that banks and many other firms in the financial sector had taken on excessive risks. In Q&A 15.3, we answered the first question in our Managerial Problem as to why managers take excessive risks by showing that they have an incentive to take a hidden, risky action if they're compensated for success and not substantially penalized for failure.

We now return to the second question in the Managerial Problem: How can a firm compensate its corporate executives so as to prevent them from undertaking irresponsible and potentially damaging actions? One approach is to provide incentives that penalize them relatively more for failure.

We can illustrate this idea by modifying Q&A 15.3. As before, Leonardo, a senior executive at the Las Vegas Home Bank, either offers only low-risk prime mortgages or a combination of prime and riskier subprime mortgages. If he provides only prime mortgages, the bank's profit is $160 million with certainty. If he sells both prime and subprime mortgages, the bank earns $800 million with a 25% probability or loses $320 million with a 75% probability, because subprime loans carry a high risk of default.

Before, Leonardo received 1% of the bank's profit if it was positive and nothing if it was negative. Under his new contract, Leonardo receives a salary of $1.15 million a year and 0.25% of the bank's profit. If the bank suffers a loss, Leonardo is fired, so that he loses his salary and receives no bonus.

This new compensation scheme gives him the same earnings if he makes only prime loans. However, now he stands to lose his salary if he chooses to also make the riskier, subprime loans and the firm loses money.

Given Leonardo's original compensation scheme—1% of the bank's profit—he chooses the riskier approach: He has a 25% chance of earning $8 million, so that he expects to earn $2 million. Because that exceeds his earnings of $1.6 million if he sells only prime mortgages, he decides to provide subprime loans as well, so the firm has a negative expected profit. (See Q&A 15.3.)

With the new compensation plan of $1.15 million salary plus 0.25% of positive profits, if Leonardo provides only prime loans, he makes $1.15 million + 0.25% of $180 million = 1.6 million, which is the same as he previously made. If he also makes subprime loans, he expects to earn nothing three-quarters of the time, and $1.15 million salary plus 0.25% of $800 million (= $2 million) one-quarter of the time. As a result, his expected earnings are

$(0.75 \times 0) + (0.25 \times [1.15 + 2]) = 0.7875$ million dollars. As he expects to earn more than twice as much from providing only prime loans, he no longer wants to offer subprime mortgages.

Thus, with this new compensation scheme, the bank shareholders avoid the original moral hazard problem. Leonardo's hidden action—whether he offers subprime loans—no longer exposes them to excessive risk.

Before the 2007–2009 financial crisis, contracts creating this excessive risk-taking moral hazard were very common, partly because the people designing the contracts—firms' senior executives—were the beneficiaries of the generous incentives. If shareholders had understood these contracts and had had symmetric information, they would have objected, but few shareholders had the time, the ability, or sufficient information to scrutinize executive compensation contracts.

SUMMARY

1. **Adverse Selection.** Adverse selection arises when one party to a transaction possesses information about a hidden characteristic that is unknown to other parties and the informed party exploits this advantage. Due to adverse selection not all desirable transactions take place. As a result, low-quality items tend to be overrepresented in transactions, as with the lemons problem associated with used cars and many other products. Bad products may drive good products out of the market. Adverse selection creates problems in insurance markets because people with low risk do not buy insurance, which drives up the price for high-risk people.

2. **Reducing Adverse Selection.** Methods of dealing with the adverse selection problem include laws limiting the ability of informed parties to exploit their private information, consumer screening (such as by using experts or relying on firms' reputations), the provision of information by third parties such as government agencies or consumer groups, and signaling by firms (including establishing brand names and providing guarantees or warranties).

3. **Moral Hazard.** If one party to a transaction can act in a way that is hidden from the other party, a moral hazard problem may occur in which the informed person exploits the ignorance of the other by means of this hidden action. Moral hazard problems are common in insurance markets and in principal-agent relationships when the agent, such as an employee, takes actions that the principal, such as the manager, cannot observe. For

example, if the manager cannot observe how hard an employee works, the employee may shirk. Ideally, a contract or agreement between the parties is efficient, maximizing the total profit of the parties and sharing risk optimally.

4. **Using Contracts to Reduce Moral Hazard.** Moral hazard problems can often be reduced or eliminated by using an appropriately designed contract that aligns the parties' interests. Often such contracts reflect a trade-off between maximizing total profit and efficient risk bearing. Commonly observed contracts used to address potential moral hazard incorporate outcome-based contingent rewards such as profit sharing, bonuses, commissions, and piece-rate payments.

5. **Using Monitoring to Reduce Moral Hazard.** A direct approach to limiting moral hazard problems is for a principal to monitor the agent to prevent the agent's action from being hidden. A moral hazard problem can often be reduced or eliminated by monitoring coupled with a contract that penalizes bad behavior. Less monitoring is necessary as the employee's interest in keeping the job increases. The employer may require the employee to post a large bond that is forfeited if the employee is caught shirking, stealing, or otherwise misbehaving. If an employee cannot afford to post a bond, the employer may use deferred payments or efficiency wages—unusually high wages—to make it worthwhile for the employee to keep the job.

QUESTIONS

*All exercises are available on MyEconLab; * = answer at the back of this book.*

1. Adverse Selection

1.1. According to the Federal Trade Commission, millions of U.S. consumers have been recent victims of weight-loss frauds, ranging from a tea that promised to help you shed the pounds to fraudulent clinical trials and fat-dissolving injections. Do these frauds illustrate adverse selection or moral hazard?

*1.2. The state of California set up its own earthquake insurance program for homeowners. The rates vary by ZIP Code, depending on the proximity of the nearest fault line. However, critics claim that the people who set the rates ignored soil type. Some houses rest on bedrock; others sit on unstable soil. What are the implications of such rate setting for possible adverse selection?

*1.3. A firm spends a great deal of money on advertising to inform consumers of the brand name of its mushrooms. Should consumers conclude that its mushrooms are likely to be of higher quality than unbranded mushrooms? Why or why not?

1.4. You want to determine whether the market for single-engine airplanes has a lemons problem. Can you use any of the following information to help answer this question? If so, how?

 a. Repair rates for original-owner planes versus planes that have been resold

 b. The fraction of planes resold in each year after purchase

1.5. If you buy a new car and try to sell it in the first year—indeed, in the first few weeks after you buy it—the price that you get is substantially less than the original price. Use your knowledge about signaling and Akerlof's lemons model to explain why this price is low.

1.6. Use Akerlof's lemons model to explain why restaurants that cater to tourists are likely to serve low-quality meals. Tourists will not return to this area, and they have no information about the relative quality of the food at various restaurants, but they can determine the relative price by looking at menus posted outside each restaurant.

1.7. Suppose that everyone in the used car example in the text is risk neutral, potential car buyers value lemons at $4,000 and good used cars at $8,000, the reservation price of lemon owners is $3,000, and the reservation price of owners of high-quality used cars is $7,000. The share of current owners who have lemons is θ [in the example in the text,

$\theta = \frac{1}{2} = 1000/(1000 + 1000)$]. For what values of θ do all the potential sellers sell their used cars? Describe the equilibrium. (*Hint*: See Q&A 15.1.)

*1.8. Many buyers value high-quality used cars at the full-information market price of p_1 and lemons at p_2. A limited number of potential sellers value high-quality cars at $v_1 \le p_1$ and lemons at $v_2 \le p_2$. Everyone is risk neutral. The share of lemons among all the used cars that might potentially be sold is θ. Under what conditions are all cars sold? When are only lemons sold? Under what, if any, conditions are no cars sold?

1.9. It costs $12 to produce a low-quality stapler and $16 to produce a high-quality stapler. Consumers cannot distinguish good staplers from poor staplers when they make their purchases. Consumers value staplers at their cost of production and are risk neutral. The three firms in the market produce low-quality staplers at a price of $12. A fourth firm is considering entering the market. Given that each firm produces and sells the same quantity of staplers, will the fourth firm be able to produce high-quality staplers without making losses? How does your answer change if consumers are willing to pay $36 for high-quality staplers? (*Hint*: See Q&A 15.2.)

1.10. Suppose that half the population is healthy and the other half is unhealthy. If an insured healthy person gets sick, the full cost to the insurance company is $1,000. If an insured unhealthy person gets sick, the cost to the insurance company is $10,000. In a given year, any one person (healthy or unhealthy) has a 40% chance of getting sick. People know whether they are healthy but the insurance company does not. The insurance company offers complete, actuarially fair insurance at the same price to everyone. The insurance company covers all medical expenses of its policyholders, and its expected profit is zero.

 a. If everyone purchases insurance, what is the price of the insurance?

 b. If only unhealthy people purchase insurance, what is the price of the insurance?

 c. If each person has the option of buying insurance, explain why adverse selection might be expected unless healthy people are highly risk averse.

2. Reducing Adverse Selection

2.1. In the world of French high cuisine, a three-star rating from the Michelin Red Guide is a widely accepted indicator of gastronomic excellence. French consumers consider Gault Milleau, another restaurant guide, not as authoritative as the Michelin guide because Gault Milleau, unlike Michelin, accepts advertising and its critics accept free meals.

a. Why are guides' ratings important to restaurant owners and chefs? Discuss the effect of a restaurant's rating on the demand for the restaurant.

b. Why do advertising and free meals taint the credibility of Gault Milleau? Discuss the moral hazard problem of Gault Milleau's ratings.

c. If advertising and free meals taint the credibility of Gault Milleau, why does the guide accept advertising and free meals?

2.2. Certain universities give written evaluations of student performance rather than letter grades. One rationale is that eliminating the letter-grade system reduces the pressure on students, thus enabling them to do better in school. Why might this policy help or hurt students?

*2.3. Employers often have a hard time predicting the quality of job applicants. Can education be used as a signal by workers to indicate that they have high ability?

2.4. Some sellers offer to buy back a good later at some prespecified price. Why would a firm make such a commitment?

3. Moral Hazard

*3.1. Sometimes a group of hungry students will go to a restaurant and agree to share the bill at the end regardless of who orders what. What is the implication of this fee-sharing arrangement on the size of the overall bill? Why?

3.2. In 2012, a California environmental group found that 14 plum and ginger candies imported from Asia contained 4 to 96 times the level of lead allowed under California law (Lee, Stephanie M., "Lead Found in Asian Candies," *San Francisco Chronicle*, August 14, 2012). Some observers predicted that U.S. consumers would face significant price increases if U.S. law were changed to require third-party testing by manufacturers and sellers. Suppose instead that candies could be reliably labeled "tested" or "untested," and untested candy sold at a discount. Would consumers buy cheaper, untested goods or would they fear a moral hazard problem? Discuss.

*3.3. A promoter arranges for many different restaurants to set up booths to sell Cajun-Creole food at a fair. Appropriate music and other entertainment are provided. Restaurants agree to pay a share of their earnings to the promoter, but the promoter cannot

monitor how much business each restaurant does. However, the promoter requires that customers can buy food using only "Cajun Cash," which is scrip with the same denominations as actual cash sold by the promoter at the fair. How does Cajun Cash solve a potential moral hazard problem that might arise between the promoter and the restaurants?

3.4. The state of California set up its own earthquake insurance program. Because the state agency in charge has few staff members, it pays private insurance carriers to handle claims for earthquake damage. These insurance firms receive 9% of each approved claim. Is this compensation scheme likely to lead to opportunistic behavior by insurance companies? What would be a better way to handle the compensation?

3.5. A bank can make one of two types of loans. It can loan money to local firms, and have a 75% probability of earning $100 million and a 25% probability of earning $80 million. Alternatively, it can loan money to oil speculators, and have a 25% probability of earning $400 million and a 75% probability of losing $160 million (due to loan defaults by the speculators). Sarah, the manager of the bank, makes the lending decisions, and receives 1% of the bank's earnings. She believes that if the bank loses money, she can walk away from her job without repercussions, although she will not receive any compensation. Sarah and the bank's shareholders are risk neutral. How does Sarah invest the bank's money if all she cares about is maximizing her personal expected earnings? How would the stockholders prefer that Sarah invest the bank's money? (See Q&A 15.3.)

4. Using Contracts to Reduce Moral Hazard

4.1. Traditionally, doctors have been paid on a fee-for-service basis. Now doctors are increasingly paid on a capitated basis (they get paid for treating a patient for a year, regardless of how much treatment is required), though a patient may still have to pay a small fee each visit. In this arrangement, doctors form a group and sign a capitation contract whereby they take turns seeing a given patient. What are the implications of this change in compensation for moral hazard and for risk bearing?

4.2. According to a flyer from Schwab *Advisor-Source*, "Most personal investment managers base their fees on a percentage of assets managed. We believe this is in your best interest because your manager is paid for investment management, not solely on the basis of trading commissions charged to your account. You can be assured your manager's investment decisions are guided by one primary goal—increasing your assets." Is this policy in a customer's best interest? Why?

*4.3. Zhihua and Pu are partners in a store in which they do all the work. They split the store's *business profit* equally (ignoring the opportunity cost of their own time in calculating this profit). Does their business profit-sharing contract give them an incentive to maximize their joint economic profit if neither can force the other to work? (*Hint*: Imagine Zhihua's thought process late one Saturday night when he is alone in the store, debating whether to keep the store open a little later or to go out on the town.)

*4.4. Priscilla hires Arnie to manage her store. Arnie's effort is given in the left column of the table. Each cell shows the net profit to Priscilla (ignoring Arnie's cost of effort).

	Low Demand	High Demand
Low Effort	20	40
Medium Effort	40	80
High Effort	80	100

Arnie's personal cost of effort is 0 at low effort, 10 at medium effort, and 30 at high effort. It is equally likely that demand will be low or high. Arnie and Priscilla are risk-neutral.

They consider two possible contracts: (1) *fixed fee*: Arnie receives a fixed wage of 10; and (2) *profit sharing*: Arnie receives 50% of the firm's net income but no wage.

a. What happens if they use the fixed-fee contract?

b. What happens if they use the profit-sharing contract?

c. Which contract does each prefer?

4.5. In the situation described in Question 4.4, how do your answers change if Arnie's first contract changes so that he receives a basic fixed wage of 10 and, in addition, a bonus equal to 80% of any net income?

4.6. Suppose that an author of popular science fiction novels is paid a royalty of α share of the revenue from sales, where the revenue is $R = pq$, p is the competitive market price for such novels, and q is the number of copies of this novel sold. The publisher's cost of printing and distributing the book is $C(q)$. Determine the output level that maximizes the publisher's profit. Compare it to the outcome that maximizes the sum of the payment to the author plus the firm's profit. Answer using both math and a graph.

4.7. Suppose now that the publisher in Question 4.6 faces a downward-sloping demand curve. The revenue is $R(Q)$, and the publisher's cost of printing and distributing the book is $C(Q)$. Compare the equilibria for the following compensation methods in which the author receives the same total compensation from each method:

a. The author is paid a lump sum, +.

b. The author is paid α share of the revenue.

c. The author receives a lump-sum payment and a share of the revenue.

Why do you think that authors are usually paid a share of revenue?

4.8. A health insurance company tries to prevent the moral hazard of "excessive" dentist visits by limiting the visits per person per year to a specific number. How does such a restriction affect moral hazard and risk bearing? (*Hint*: See Q&A 15.4.)

4.9. Louisa is an avid cyclist who is currently working on her business degree. She normally rides an $800 bike to class. If Louisa locks her bike carefully—locks both wheels—the chance of theft for the term is 5%, but this careful locking procedure is time consuming. If she is less careful—just quickly locks the frame to a bike rack—the chance of theft is 20%. Louisa is risk averse and is considering buying theft insurance for her bike. Louisa may purchase one of two types of insurance. With full insurance, Louisa pays the premium and gets the full, $800 value of the bike if it is stolen. Alternatively, with partial insurance, Louisa receives only 75% of the bike's value, $600, if the bike is stolen. Which contract is more likely to induce moral hazard problems? To break even on consumers like Louisa, what price would the risk-neutral insurance company have to charge for full insurance? If we observe Louisa buying partial insurance, what can we say about the trade-off between moral hazard and efficient risk bearing? (*Hint*: See Q&A 15.3.)

5. Using Monitoring to Reduce Moral Hazard

5.1. Many law firms consist of partners who share profits. On being made a partner, a lawyer must post a bond, a large payment to the firm that will be forfeited on bad behavior. How would such an arrangement reduce moral hazard problems?

*5.2. Explain why full employment may be inconsistent with no shirking based on the efficiency wage model.

5.3. Starting in 2008, Medicare would not cover the cost of certain surgical mistakes, certain types of hospital-acquired infections, or other "preventable" mistakes (Liz Marlantes, "Medicare Won't Cover Hospital

Mistakes: New Rules Aimed at Promoting Better Hospital Care and Safety," *ABC News*, August 19, 2007). Hospitals have to cover these costs and cannot bill the patient. These changes were designed to provide hospitals with a stronger incentive to prevent those mistakes, particularly infections. The Centers for Disease Control and Prevention estimates that 2 million patients are annually infected in hospitals, costing society more than $27 billion. Nearly 100,000 of those infections are fatal. Many of these infections could be prevented if hospitals more rigorously follow basic infection control procedures, including having doctors and nurses wash their hands between every patient. Is Medicare's policy designed to deal with adverse selection or moral hazard? Is it likely to help? Explain.

5.4. When rental cars are sold on the used car market, they are sold for lower prices than cars of the same model and year that were owned by individual owners. Does this price difference reflect adverse selection or moral hazard? Could car rental companies reduce this problem by carefully inspecting rental cars for damage when renters return such cars? Why do car companies normally perform only a cursory inspection?

6. Managerial Problem

6.1. In the Managerial Solution, show that shareholders' expected earnings are higher with the new compensation scheme than with the original one.

6.2. Curtis manages an electronics store in Wichita, Kansas. He considers carrying either cameras from Nikon Americas that come with a U.S. warranty or *gray market* Nikon cameras from a European supplier, which are the same cameras but their warranties are only good in Europe. The gray market cameras have a lower wholesale price. Curtis earns 10% of the store's profit (and no wage). If the store loses money, he leaves with nothing. He believes that if he sells the Nikon Americas cameras, the store's profit will be $400,000. The profit on the gray market cameras is more uncertain—will locals be willing to buy a less expensive camera without a warranty? If he goes with the gray market camera, he believes that there's a 50% chance that the store's profit will be $1,000,000 and a 50% probability that the store will lose $300,000. Curtis and the store's owner are both risk neutral. Which camera does Curtis choose to sell? What choice would the owner prefer (if she were fully informed)? Construct an alternative compensation plan involving a salary such that Curtis will earn as much from selling Nikon Americas cameras and that will dissuade him from selling black market cameras if doing so lowers the owner's expected earnings.

7. Spreadsheet Exercises

7.1. In a used car market all potential buyers and sellers are risk neutral. The buyers value the good-quality used cars at $10,000 and the lemons at $4,000, while the reservation price of the lemon owners is $2,000. The probability that a car potentially available for sale in the market is a lemon is θ.

a. For $\theta = 0.1$ to $\theta = 0.9$ in increments of 0.1, calculate the price that the buyers will be willing to pay if all cars are sold. (*Hint*: Put the values of θ in column A and put the associated buyers' expected value of a car in column B, assuming that all cars are sold.)

b. For which values of θ will all cars be sold if sellers of good-quality cars have a reservation price of $7,600?

c. How does your answer to (b) change if sellers of good used cars have a reservation price of $8,500?

*7.2. Anika is hired by the owner of a kitchen supply store to manage the store. Anika and the owner are both risk neutral. The probability of weak demand is 0.2 and the probability of strong demand is 0.8. Each cell in the following table shows the store's profit from a specific combination of demand and Anika's managerial effort. Anika's cost of effort is *not* subtracted from these profits. This effort cost is 2 for low effort, 10 for medium, and 32 for high.

	Weak Demand	Strong Demand
Low Effort	40	60
Medium Effort	60	100
High Effort	100	140

Create a spreadsheet containing this information. Add a column showing Anika's cost of effort and also add columns for the expected payoff to Anika and the owner.

a. Fill in the expected payoffs to both parties if Anika is compensated with a profit-sharing contract providing her with 50% of the profits (and the owner gets the other 50%). Which effort level does Anika choose?

b. Now suppose that Anika's contract provides her with a base salary of 30 and 100% of any profits exceeding 100. Which effort level does she choose?

c. Which of the two contracts in (a) and (b) would Anika prefer? Which would the owner prefer?

Government and Business

16

If it moves, tax it. If it still moves, regulate it. If it stops moving, subsidize it.
—Ronald Reagan

Managerial Problem

Licensing Inventions

Government patents grant *intellectual property* rights to inventors of new products or processes. The owner of such a property right has an exclusive right to produce an invention covered by a patent but may sell the patent or license its use to others. Selling and licensing intellectual property rights is big business. Payments for the use of intellectual property across international borders reached $239 billion in 2011. Industrial processes and computer software account for over 70% of all royalty receipts and payments for intellectual property in the United States.

In 2011, patent filings (applications for patents) reached 2.14 million worldwide, and nearly 1 million patents were granted. IBM received 6,478 new patents in 2012 alone, and generates an estimated $1 billion per year by licensing its patents. Not all inventions lend themselves to licensing. U.S. firms typically license less than 10% of their patents to other firms.

Consider a competitive market in which all firms use the same technology, but one firm invents a new, lower-cost process. Should that firm patent its invention or keep it a trade secret? If the innovating firm manufactures the good itself, under what conditions can it charge the monopoly price? If the innovating firm obtains a patent, will the firm earn more if it produces itself or if it licenses its new process to other firms?

Surprisingly, those robo-arms increase productivity substantially.

Because governments intervene in markets in many ways, almost all managers have to respond to a range of government policies. In our earlier chapters, we often touched on various government interventions in the economy such as taxes and price ceilings and floors. In this chapter, we examine many additional government policies that affect business, especially those designed to address market failures.

We start by discussing rules that a government might use to decide whether to intervene in a market. This discussion is *normative* or *prescriptive* because it suggests or prescribes what governments *should do* (a value judgment). In other parts of the chapter, we examine *positive* questions concerning what governments *actually do* and how managers respond, issues that can be examined objectively or scientifically.

We examine government responses to market failures from noncompetitive market structures and those that arise when the rights to a resource are not clearly defined. We describe two basic approaches to dealing with market failures due to *noncompetitive market structures*. A preventative approach is to regulate the behavior of firms with market power to avoid a market failure. A remedial approach is to correct serious market power problems *after* they emerge and to punish firms that fail to obey legal requirements regarding the creation and exploitation of market power.

We then look at market failures that arise due to *incomplete property rights*, which lead to such problems as pollution. We consider government policies that directly regulate the related problem and those that assign and enforce property rights.

Main Topics

In this chapter, we examine six main topics

1. **Market Failure and Government Policy:** The failure of some markets to achieve economic efficiency provides an important rationale for government policies.

2. **Regulation of Imperfectly Competitive Markets:** Governments often directly control price or other variables to eliminate or reduce market failures arising from market power.

3. **Antitrust Law and Competition Policy:** When markets are not perfectly competitive, authorities may use antitrust laws or competition policies to promote competition and reduce market failures due to firms exercising market power.

4. **Externalities:** One type of market failure resulting from a lack of clearly defined property rights is externalities, which are the costs or benefits that production or consumption activities impose on others through nonmarket channels.

5. **Open-Access, Club, and Public Goods:** Open-access, club, and public goods are special types of goods which may give rise to market failures that governments often address.

6. **Intellectual Property:** Inventors, writers, and other innovators under-produce unless they capture sufficient value from their innovations, which can be provided by intellectual property rights such as patents and copyrights.

16.1 Market Failure and Government Policy

A perfectly competitive market achieves economic efficiency: It maximizes total surplus, the sum of consumer and producer surplus (Chapter 8). This property is one of the strongest arguments for relying on competitive markets without government intervention. However, most markets fall short of perfect competition, and some exhibit a significant market failure, which substantially reduces economic efficiency and results in deadweight losses. Thus, one important rationale for government policy is to reduce or eliminate market failure. By eliminating a market failure, society can recapture the associated deadweight loss.

In addition to wanting to reduce deadweight loss, society may care about who benefits from a government policy and who is harmed. However, for some policies, no one loses.

The Pareto Principle

Economist Vilfredo Pareto argued that society should favor a change that benefits some people without harming anyone else, a belief called the **Pareto principle**. According to this principle, if everyone shares in the extra surplus when a government policy eliminates a market failure, then this change is socially desirable. Even if only some people gain, as long as no one is harmed, the Pareto principle is satisfied.

A **Pareto improvement** is a change, such as a reallocation of goods or productive inputs, that helps at least one person without harming anyone else. When two collectors of baseball cards trade cards, both are better off and no one else is harmed by this exchange. Thus, this exchange is a Pareto improvement.

The Pareto principle cannot always be used to compare allocations. Some changes that eliminate a market failure benefit one group while harming another. For example, a monopoly creates a market failure by charging a price above marginal cost, causing a deadweight loss to society (Chapter 9). If the government breaks up the monopoly and replaces it with a competitive industry, the price falls and the deadweight loss from monopoly is eliminated. For example, during World War II, the U.S. government ended Alcoa's aluminum monopoly to aid the war effort by increasing production. This change benefited consumers, but harmed the owners of the monopoly.

However, the government could modify such a policy to create a Pareto improvement by compensating the former owners. Because consumers gain more than the owners of the monopoly lose (Chapter 9), the government could tax away some of the gain to consumers and use it to fully compensate the owners of the former monopoly. This redistribution of income might be difficult to achieve politically, but this example illustrates that Pareto improvements are possible in principle when a market failure creates a deadweight loss.

Once all possible Pareto improvements have occurred, the outcome is **Pareto efficient**: any possible change would harm at least one person. A perfectly competitive market is Pareto efficient. Any possible reallocation that benefits someone without harming others occurs through voluntary exchange in a competitive market, so any additional reallocation must harm someone. When assessing market transactions, Pareto efficiency implies economic efficiency: the maximization of surplus.[1]

---

[1]Pareto efficiency is a more general concept than economic efficiency, which is based on maximization of total surplus. If a market exhibits Pareto efficiency, the market is efficient: it maximizes total surplus. Unlike the surplus concept, the Pareto concept can also be used in nonmarket situations. For example, if two people are happier after they marry, and no one else is harmed, then that marriage is a Pareto improvement, even if we cannot reasonably define a related price or measure of consumer and producer surplus.

Cost-Benefit Analysis

When a policy benefits some people while harming others, we cannot use the Pareto principle to evaluate its desirability. Instead, we can evaluate a policy using an alternative value judgment based on the **cost-benefit principle**: a change is desirable if its benefits exceed the costs. To do so, we may need to make interpersonal comparisons in which a gain of one dollar of surplus to one person has the same weight as a one dollar loss of surplus to anyone else. That is, if one person gains $1,000 in surplus and another loses $500, society has a net gain of $500 and the cost-benefit test is satisfied. Thus, the cost-benefit principle supports policies that increase total surplus.

Any policy that generates a Pareto improvement satisfies the cost-benefit principle. If some people gain from a policy and no one suffers a loss, then the aggregate benefit is positive. However, the converse is not true. Many policies that pass the cost-benefit test by generating net benefits are not Pareto improvements because they produce both winners and losers.

While the vast majority of people would probably support eliminating a monopoly even though the monopoly's owners suffer a loss, other policies that create winners and losers are more contentious. Consider a new tax policy that reduces the tax burden on people with incomes over $1 million a year by $50 billion, while increasing the tax burden on those earning less than $50,000 per year by $49 billion. In addition to producing a relatively small net benefit, this policy would have a large effect on the distribution of after-tax income, generating large gains for people who are already very well off and imposing a very large burden on people of modest means. Many people would oppose such a change, viewing it as unfair and inequitable.

As a practical matter, policies that have large net benefits and only small distributional effects tend to generate broad support. Policies whose distributional effects are large relative to the net benefits are likely to be more contentious, especially if the distributional effect is *regressive*, making the distribution of income less equal.

16.2 Regulation of Imperfectly Competitive Markets

A government can take one of three approaches to eliminating a market failure caused by imperfectly competitive pricing, such as by a monopoly. The most direct approach is for the government to own the monopoly and set relatively low prices. For example, many governments own and operate electric power and water utilities.

A second approach is to change the market structure, as when the U.S. government increased the number of aluminum manufacturers during World War II, ending Alcoa's monopoly. We address other attempts to change the nature of competition in a market using antitrust or competition laws in the next section.

A third approach is to regulate the industry to prevent firms from setting excessively high prices, which we examine now. We show how regulations can correct market structure problems and then discuss why some regulators do not regulate effectively.

Regulating to Correct a Market Failure

Today, the most commonly used approach to regulating monopoly pricing is to impose a price ceiling, called a *price cap*. For example, price cap regulation is used for telecommunications monopolies in 33 U.S. states and in many other countries, including Australia, Canada, Denmark, France, Germany, Mexico, Sweden, and the United Kingdom (Sappington and Weisman, 2010).[2]

Optimal Price Regulation. A government can eliminate the deadweight loss of monopoly by imposing a price cap equal to the price that would prevail in a competitive market, as we now illustrate. Given the demand and marginal cost curves in Figure 16.1, an unregulated monopoly maximizes its profit at e_m, where marginal revenue equals marginal cost: $MR = MC$. The monopoly sells 6 units at a price of $18 per unit, and society suffers a deadweight loss, $-C - E$ (Chapter 9). The optimal price cap is $16, which is the competitive price.

Because the price cap prevents the monopoly from charging a price greater than $16, the monopoly's regulated demand curve is horizontal at $16 up to 8 units. At larger output levels, the monopoly's regulated demand curve is the market demand curve: The monopoly can lower its price to sell extra units because it charges less than the maximum price of $16. The regulated marginal revenue curve, MR^r, corresponding to the regulated demand curve, is horizontal where the regulated demand curve is horizontal up to 8 units and equals the original marginal revenue curve, MR, at larger quantities.

To maximize its profit, the regulated monopoly sets its output at 8 units, where MR^r equals its marginal cost, MC, and charges the maximum permitted price, $16. The regulated firm still makes a profit because we assume that its average cost is less $16 at 8 units. The regulated monopoly optimum, e_o, occurs where the MC curve intersects the market demand curve. Thus, setting a price ceiling where the MC curve and market demand curve intersect eliminates the deadweight loss of monopoly.

We know this outcome is economically efficient because it is the same as the competitive market equilibrium. It occurs where the marginal cost equals price so that total surplus is maximized (Chapter 8). As the table accompanying Figure 16.1 shows, the deadweight loss from unregulated monopoly, $-C - E$, is eliminated by this economically efficient regulation.

Non-Optimal Price Regulation Due to Poor Information. Well-intentioned government regulators often fail to regulate monopolies optimally because of limited information about the monopoly's demand and cost curves. As a consequence, the regulators may mistakenly set the price cap above or below the competitive level.

If regulators rely on the monopoly or on industry experts for information, they may be misled. For example, a regulated monopoly might deliberately overstate its costs so that regulators impose a price cap that is too high.

---

[2]Price regulation is also used in some oligopolistic markets. Although we concentrate here on regulating a monopoly, similar principles apply to markets with oligopolistic firms.

FIGURE 16.1 Optimal Price Regulation

If the government sets a price ceiling at $16, where the monopoly's marginal cost curve hits the demand curve, the new demand curve the monopoly faces has a kink at 8 units, and the corresponding marginal revenue curve, MR^r, "jumps" at that quantity. The regulated monopoly sets its output where $MR^r = MC$, selling the same quantity, 8 units, at the same price, $16, as a competitive industry would. The regulation eliminates the monopoly deadweight loss, $C + E$. Consumer surplus, $A + B + C$, and producer surplus, $D + E$, are the same as under competition.

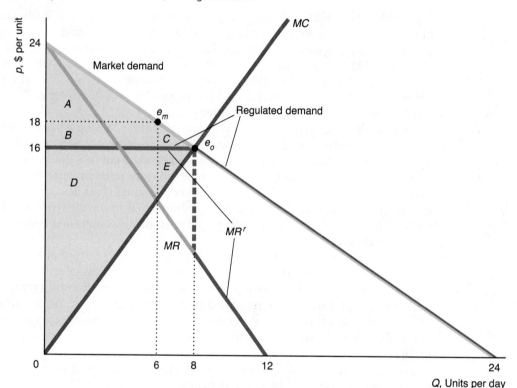

	Monopoly Without Regulation	Monopoly with Optimal Regulation	Change
Consumer Surplus, CS	A	$A + B + C$	$B + C = \Delta CS$
Producer Surplus, PS	$B + D$	$D + E$	$E - B = \Delta PS$
Total Surplus, $TS = CS + PS$	$A + B + D$	$A + B + C + D + E$	$C + E = \Delta TS$
Deadweight Loss, DWL	$-C - E$	0	$C + E = \Delta DWL$

If the government sets the price ceiling below the optimal price but high enough that the firm does not shut down, a deadweight loss results. The regulated firm chooses to sell less than consumers want at the regulated price, creating excess demand. Consumers who are lucky enough to buy the good are better off because they can buy goods at a lower price than with optimal regulation. However, other potential customers are frustrated because the monopoly will not sell them the good. Some of those frustrated consumers are willing to pay more than marginal cost and their inability to buy the good is a loss of potential surplus or inefficiency, as Q&A 16.1 shows.

Q&A 16.1

A government regulates a monopoly by setting a maximum price, p_2, that is below the economically efficient level, p_1, but above the monopoly's minimum average cost, as the figure shows. How do the price, the quantity sold, the quantity demanded, and the total surplus under this regulation compare to those under optimal regulation?

Answer

1. *Describe the optimally regulated outcome.* With optimal regulation, e_1, the price is set at p_1, where the market demand curve intersects the monopoly's marginal cost curve on the accompanying graph. The optimally regulated monopoly sells Q_1 units.

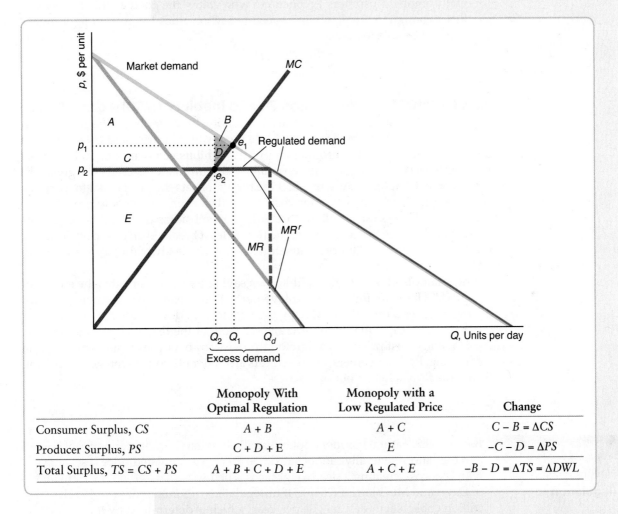

	Monopoly With Optimal Regulation	Monopoly with a Low Regulated Price	Change
Consumer Surplus, CS	$A + B$	$A + C$	$C - B = \Delta CS$
Producer Surplus, PS	$C + D + E$	E	$-C - D = \Delta PS$
Total Surplus, $TS = CS + PS$	$A + B + C + D + E$	$A + C + E$	$-B - D = \Delta TS = \Delta DWL$

2. *Describe the outcome when the government regulates the price at p_2.* Where the market demand is above p_2, the regulated demand curve for the monopoly is horizontal at p_2 (up to Q_d). The corresponding regulated marginal revenue curve, MR^r, is horizontal where the regulated demand curve is horizontal. At the kink in the regulated demand curve where it starts sloping down, the MR^r drops, as the dashed line shows, to the original, downward sloping marginal revenue line, MR. The monopoly maximizes its profit by selling Q_2 units at p_2.

The new regulated monopoly optimum is e_2, where MR^r intersects MC. The firm does not shut down when regulated as long as its average variable cost at Q_2 is less than p_2.

3. *Compare the outcomes.* The quantity that the monopoly sells falls from Q_1 to Q_2 when the government lowers its price ceiling from p_1 to p_2. At that low price, consumers want to buy Q_d, so excess demand equals $Q_d - Q_2$. Compared to optimal regulation, total surplus is lower by at least $B + D$.

Comment: The total surplus loss is even greater if unlucky consumers waste time trying to buy the good unsuccessfully or if goods are not allocated optimally among consumers. A consumer who values the good at only p_2 may be lucky enough to buy it, while a consumer who values the good at p_1 or more may not be able to obtain it.

Non-Optimal Price Regulation Due to Inability to Subsidize. Because regulators generally cannot subsidize a monopoly, they cannot set the price as low as the marginal cost if the firm would lose money at that price and choose to shut down. For example, if the production process exhibits economies of scale over all relevant levels of output, average cost falls with output and exceeds marginal cost everywhere (Chapter 9). As a result, if the regulator sets the price equal to marginal cost, the price is less than average cost, so the firm cannot profitably produce and shuts down. Unless the regulators are willing to subsidize the firm, the regulators must raise the price to a level where the firm at least breaks even or society loses the product altogether. If the firm shuts down, society's deadweight loss is the loss in total (potential) surplus.

This example illustrates the well-known saying that "the perfect is the enemy of the good." Here, attempting to achieve perfection—using efficient marginal cost pricing—causes a problem by forcing the firm to shut down. A better regulation is to set the price cap equal to the average cost so that the firm continues to operate. Here, average-cost pricing is a Pareto improvement over (unsubsidized) marginal cost pricing. Both consumers and producers are better off under average cost pricing than if the firm is forced out of business.

Mini-Case	
Natural Gas Regulation	Because U.S. natural gas monopolies usually have significant economies of scale and regulators generally cannot subsidize them, the regulated price is set above marginal cost, creating a deadweight loss. The figure is based on the estimates of Davis and Muehlegger (2010).[3] If unregulated, this monopoly would sell 12.1 trillion cubic feet of natural gas per year, which is determined by the intersection of its marginal revenue and marginal cost curves. It would charge the

---

[3]We use their most conservative estimate: the one that produces the smallest deadweight loss. We approximate their demand curve with a linear one that has the same price elasticity of demand of -0.2 at point b. This figure represents the aggregation of state-level monopolies to the national level.

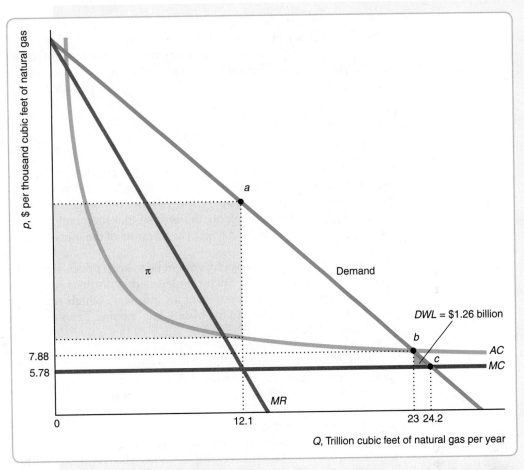

corresponding price on the demand curve at point *a*. Its profit is the rectangle labeled π, with a length equal to the quantity, 12.1 trillion cubic feet, and a height equal to the difference between the price at *a* and the corresponding average cost.

To eliminate deadweight loss, the government should set the price ceiling equal to the marginal cost of $5.78 per thousand cubic feet of natural gas so that the monopoly behaves like a price taker. The price ceiling or marginal cost curve hits the demand curve at *c*, where the quantity is 24.2 trillion cubic feet per year—double the unregulated quantity. At that quantity, the regulated utility would lose money. The average cost at that quantity is $7.78 (slightly less than the average cost of $7.88 at a quantity of 23 trillion cubic feet). The regulated price, $5.78, is less than the average cost at that quantity of $7.78, so it would lose $2 on each thousand cubic feet it sells, or $48.4 billion in total. Thus, it would be willing to sell this quantity at this price only if the government subsidizes it.

Typically, it is politically infeasible for a government regulatory agency to subsidize a monopoly. On average, the natural gas regulatory agencies set the price at $7.88 per thousand cubic feet, where the demand curve intersects the average cost curve and the monopoly breaks even, point *b*. The monopoly sells 23 trillion cubic feet per year. The corresponding price, $7.88, is 36% above marginal cost, $5.78. Consequently, society incurs a deadweight loss of $1.26 billion annually, which is the gray triangle in the figure. This deadweight loss is much smaller than it would be if the monopoly were unregulated.

Regulatory Capture

So far, we've discussed situations in which the regulators try to achieve efficient regulation but may not succeed because they lack complete information or because they cannot subsidize a monopoly. However, some regulators do not try to achieve efficiency, particularly if they are *captured* so that they regulate in the manner that the industry wants. That is, they put the interests of the industry ahead of the public interest.

A captured regulator's objective might be to keep prices high rather than to lower them to competitive levels. Such regulators may impose *entry restrictions* to keep potential competitors from entering an industry, which raises the price and the profits of existing firms, as in the Mini-Case "Zoning Laws as a Barrier to Entry by Hotel Chains" (Chapter 11).

In some countries, it is common for firms to capture regulators by directly bribing them. In developed countries, such as the United States, direct bribery is not common, but regulators may be captured by more subtle means. For example, many U.S. regulators worked in the industry before they became regulators and hence are sympathetic to those firms.[4] Other regulators want to obtain good jobs in the industry after they leave the regulatory agency, so they act so as not to offend potential employers. A regulated firm that invests resources (such as explicit bribes or taking regulators to dinner) is **rent seeking**: devoting effort and expenditures to gain a rent or profit from government actions.

Applying the Cost-Benefit Principle to Regulation

Imperfect competition that results in the price exceeding the marginal cost causes a market failure. Therefore, most imperfectly competitive markets—everything from restaurants to jet aircraft—suffer from market failure.

Would regulating each of these markets increase total surplus? No, because a regulation would not pass a cost-benefit test in some markets. Regulation has its own costs. It may be difficult or costly for regulators to gather the information they need, regulators may make honest mistakes, or regulators may be captured by the industry. And firms in the industry may engage in costly rent-seeking activities. Price regulation, or regulation of any type, passes a cost-benefit test only when the market failure is large enough so that the benefits from significantly reducing it exceed the cost associated with regulation.

---

[4]Overall, 40% of state oil and gas regulators have industry connections. Indeed, five of nine members of the Arkansas regulatory commission own drilling companies and two others are officers of such companies (Mike Soraghan, "40% of State Drilling Regulators Have Industry Ties," *Greenwire*, December 19, 2011.)

16.3 Antitrust Law and Competition Policy

Rather than regulate firms that set high prices, a government may forbid firms from collectively setting high prices—that is, acting like a cartel (Chapter 11). These laws are called *antitrust laws* in the United States and *competition policies* in many other countries.

In the late nineteenth century, cartels, which were then called *trusts*, were legal and were common in the United States. Oil, railroad, sugar, and tobacco trusts raised prices substantially above competitive levels.[5] In response to the trusts' high prices, the U.S. Congress passed the Sherman Antitrust Act in 1890 and the Federal Trade Commission Act of 1914, which prohibited firms from *explicitly* agreeing to take actions that reduce competition.[6] In particular, cartels that are formed for the purpose of jointly setting price are strictly prohibited. In legal jargon, price-fixing is a *per se* violation: It is strictly against the law and firms have no possible mitigating justifications. By imposing penalties on firms caught colluding, government agencies seek to discourage cartels from forming.

The Antitrust Division of the Department of Justice (DOJ) and the Federal Trade Commission (FTC) divide the responsibility for U.S. antitrust policy. The Antitrust Division states that its mission is "to promote economic competition through . . . promoting free and fair competition in the marketplace." The FTC's objective is "to prevent unfair methods of competition in commerce" and "to administer . . . other consumer protection laws." Both U.S. agencies can use criminal and civil law to attack cartels, price-fixing, and other anticompetitive actions.

Recently, the U.S. Department of Justice, quoting the Supreme Court that collusion is the "supreme evil of antitrust," stated that prosecuting cartels was its "top enforcement priority." However, cartels persist despite these laws for three reasons. First, some international cartels and cartels within certain countries operate legally. The Organization of Petroleum Exporting Countries (OPEC) is an international cartel that was formed in 1960 by five major oil-exporting countries: Iran, Iraq, Kuwait, Saudi Arabia, and Venezuela.[7] In 1971, OPEC members agreed to take an active role in setting oil prices.

Second, some illegal cartels operate believing that they can avoid detection or that the punishment will be insignificant. At least until recently, they were often correct. For example, in a cartel case involving the $9 billion U.S. carpet industry, a firm with $150 in million annual sales agreed with the DOJ to plead guilty and pay a fine of $150,000. It is difficult to imagine that a fine of one-tenth of 1% of annual sales significantly deters cartel behavior.

Even larger fines fail to discourage repeated collusion. In 1996, Archer Daniels Midland (ADM) paid to settle three civil price-fixing-related cases: $35 million in a

---

[5]Nineteenth-century and early twentieth-century *robber barons* who made fortunes due to these cartels include John Jacob Astor (real estate, fur), Andrew Carnegie (railroads, steel), Henry Clay Frick (steel), Jay Gould (finance, railroads), Mark Hopkins (railroads), J. P. Morgan (banking), John D. Rockefeller (oil), Leland Stanford (railroads), and Cornelius Vanderbilt (railroads, shipping).

[6]Some cartels are not prohibited by U.S. laws. A bizarre Supreme Court decision largely exempted Major League Baseball from antitrust laws (**www.slate.com/id/2068290**). Unions are explicitly exempt from antitrust laws. Workers are allowed to act collectively to raise wages. A historical justification for exempting labor unions was that the workers faced employers that could exercise monopsony power.

[7]As of 2013, OPEC had 12 member countries, including the 5 original members.

case involving citric acid (used in many consumer products), $30 million to share-holders as compensation for lost stock value after the citric acid price-fixing scandal became public, and $25 million in a lysine (an animal feed additive) case. ADM paid a $100 million fine in a federal criminal case for fixing the price of lysine and citric acid in 1996, but only eight years later, ADM settled a fructose corn syrup price-fixing case for $400 million.

Third, some firms are able to coordinate their activities without explicitly colluding and thereby running afoul of competition laws. To determine guilt, U.S. antitrust laws use evidence of conspiracy (such as explicit agreements) rather than the economic effect of the suspected cartel. Charging monopoly-level prices is not necessarily illegal—only the "bad behavior" of explicitly agreeing to raise prices is against the law. As a result, some groups of firms charge monopoly-level prices without violating competition laws. These firms may *tacitly collude* without meeting by signaling to each other through their actions. If one firm raises its price and keeps it high only if other firms follow its lead, it is not necessarily violating the law if the firms did not explicitly communicate.

For example, shortly before Thanksgiving in 2012, United Airlines announced a fare increase. However, when rivals failed to match this increase, United rolled back its fares the next day. Shortly thereafter, the president of US Airways observed that if Southwest Airlines, the firm that carries the most passengers, fails to match an increase by other airlines, rivals cancel the increase.[8]

Canada is normally credited with the modern world's first antitrust statute, enacted in 1889, one year before the U.S. Sherman Act. Canada's current Competition Act regulates most business conduct, and contains both criminal and civil provisions that are designed to prevent anticompetitive practices and that are enforced by the Competition Bureau. As under U.S. law, price-fixing cartels are *per se* illegal and are subject to civil and criminal punishment. Australia and New Zealand have laws on cartels that are similar to those in Canada and the United States.

In the past, the German, Japanese, and British governments permitted some cartels to operate because these governments felt doing so would promote economic efficiency. However, in recent years, most developed countries have followed Canada and the United States in strictly prohibiting cartels. The European Union's competition policy under the Treaty of the European Community (EC Treaty or Treaty of Rome) in 1957 gives the European Union and member states substantial civil powers to prevent actions that hinder competition, including formation of cartels. Price-fixing is *per se* illegal.

We can't legally discuss price. However, look at how many sugar cubes I can stack!

The DOJ, the FTC, the Canadian Competition Bureau, and the European Union authorities have become increasingly aggressive, prosecuting many more cases and

---

[8]Charisse Jones, "United Airlines Hikes Fares; Will Rivals Follow?" *USA Today*, October 11, 2012; "US Airways President Talks about Southwest Fares," *Businessweek*, October 24, 2012.

increasing fines dramatically. Following the lead of the United States, which imposes both civil and criminal penalties, the British government introduced legislation in 2002 to criminalize certain cartel-related conduct. In 2004, Japan started pursuing antitrust cases more aggressively.

In 1993, the DOJ introduced the Corporate Leniency Program, guaranteeing that cartel whistle-blowers will receive immunity from federal prosecution. As a consequence, the DOJ has caught, prosecuted, and fined several gigantic cartels. In 2002, European authorities adopted a similar policy.

In addition to making price-fixing strictly illegal, these competition laws restrict mergers between firms and ban abusive behavior by firms that dominate a market. In addition, such laws limit various vertical relationships between firms (relationships governing how firms deal with their suppliers and their customers in the supply chain).[9]

Increasingly, antitrust authorities from around the world are cooperating. Cooperation agreements exist between authorities in Canada, Mexico, Europe, Australia, New Zealand, and the United States, among others. Such cooperation is critical given the increasingly global scope of the firms engaged in collusion and other anticompetitive activities.

Mergers

If antitrust or competition laws prevent firms from colluding, firms could try to achieve the same end by merging to form a monopoly. To prevent this potential problem, most antitrust and competition laws restrict the ability of firms to merge if the net effect is to harm society.

Proposed U.S. mergers beyond a certain size must be reported to U.S. authorities and may be evaluated by either the DOJ or the FTC. These agencies block mergers that they believe harm society. However, firms can appeal this decision to the federal courts. Most other developed countries also have similar merger review procedures.

Would banning any possible merger increase economic efficiency? No, because some mergers reduce production costs substantially. Formerly separate firms may become more efficient because of greater scale, the sharing of trade secrets, or the closure of duplicative retail outlets. For example, when Chase and Chemical banks merged, they closed or combined seven Manhattan branches that were located within two blocks of other branches.

Whether a merger helps or harms society depends on which of its two offsetting effects—reducing competition and increasing efficiency—is larger. Consider two extreme cases. In one, the merger of the only two firms in the market does not lower costs, but it increases monopoly power, so the newly merged firm substantially raises prices to consumers. Here, the merger hurts society. At the other extreme, two of a large number of firms in the market merge, with substantial cost savings, but with no noticeable increase in market power or market price. Here, the merger benefits society.

The contentious cases lie in the middle, where market power increases significantly *and* costs decrease. However, if the price falls after the merger because the cost reduction effect dominates the increased market power effect, the merger is desirable.

---

[9]The FTC has a broader range of other responsibilities that include *consumer protection*, such as preventing misleading advertising, which we do not discuss here.

Since the 1990s, the hospital market has consolidated substantially through mergers, with an average of nearly 60 mergers per year in major metropolitan areas. When two hospitals merge, eliminating duplication can produce substantial efficiency gains, which may result in lower prices. However, the merger may reduce competition and raise price. Which effect dominates is an empirical question.

Using a sample of U.S. hospitals, Dafny (2009) found that local hospital prices rise by about 40% on average after a merger, with the (apparently large) cost savings going to the hospitals rather than to the patients. However, the price effects of hospital mergers vary substantially across hospitals. Haas-Wilson and Garmon (2011) studied a merger of two hospitals in Evanston, Illinois, and found that one hospital raised its prices by 20% but the other's prices remained constant. Tenn (2011) examined the Summit-Sutter mergers in Berkeley and Oakland, California, and found that Summit's prices increased between 28% and 44%. Brand et al. (2012) looked very carefully at one proposed hospital merger in Virginia and argued that it would raise prices by 4%.

Predatory Actions

Antitrust policy also seeks to prevent other actions that harm society such as predatory pricing. A firm engages in *predatory pricing* if it charges a price below marginal (or average) cost so as to drive its rivals out of business and then raise its price.

Presumably if the firm that engages in predation has deep pockets and its rivals do not, it can absorb short-run losses until its rivals leave the market. However, the firm does not benefit from predatory behavior if its rivals or other firms reenter the market as soon as it raises its price. Thus, for a firm to benefit from engaging in predation, something must prevent firms from reentering the market when the predatory firm eventually raises its price. In 1993, the U.S. Supreme Court agreed with this reasoning in *Brooke Group Ltd. v. Brown and Williamson Tobacco Corp*. Since then, the federal government has brought few predation cases and has won none.

Vertical Relationships

Laws that forbid price-fixing and predatory practices and limit mergers are directed at *horizontal* interactions between firms that compete directly in a given industry. Antitrust policy also addresses vertical interactions between a firm and its customers or suppliers. Vertical actions that competition authorities investigate include resale price maintenance, refusal to deal, exclusive dealing, and price discrimination.

Resale Price Maintenance. A manufacturer engages in *resale price maintenance* (RPM) if it requires the retailers that sell its product to charge a price no lower than a price it specifies. (Price ceilings are also possible, but not frequently observed.) The rule on RPM does not apply if the prices are only *suggested* and not required by the manufacturer.

At one time, RPM was *per se* illegal in the United States. That is, this practice was strictly banned with no appeal to mitigating circumstances. However, in 2007, the

U.S. Supreme Court changed to a *rule of reason* (or cost-benefit) approach where an RPM rule is illegal only if it is shown to have a net negative effect on competition.

This legal decision is consistent with an argument made by many economists. Usually, a manufacturer wants its dealers to add as small a markup as possible to its wholesale price to keep the price low to final consumers so that many units are purchased. That is, both the manufacturer and consumers prefer low markups by dealers. However, for some products, the amount sold depends on promotional or informational activities by retailers as well as price, as when a camera store salesperson demonstrates a camera's features to potential customers. If discounters, such as Internet firms, can sell the camera at lower prices without providing such services, few camera stores can afford to provide these services. A store that did try to provide this service would find that many customers would come into their store to learn about the product but then would purchase the camera from a discount store. Therefore, the manufacturer wants all dealers to charge a relatively high price to encourage the provision of these valuable information services.

Today, restrictions on dealers' prices or other activities are usually legal if the manufacturer acts unilaterally. However, if the manufacturer tries to coordinate its actions with other manufacturers, then RPM and related restrictions are viewed as an attempt to create a cartel.

Refusal to Deal. Some firms are *integrated*, selling both the final product in the *downstream market* and the key input to this product in the *upstream market*. An integrated aluminum firm not only produces and sells aluminum, but it also produces bauxite, the main input required to make aluminum. If such a firm is *dominant*—has a very large share—in both markets, and it refuses to sell the input to other downstream rivals, it may be charged with a *refusal to deal*. The law is still evolving in this area. In general, a firm does not have an obligation to sell to another firm. However, if a dominant firm such as a monopoly refuses to sell to one firm what it sells to others, it needs to provide a sound business reason for its actions other than an attempt to destroy competition.

U.S. courts are more likely to find a firm (or a group of firms) guilty of illegally refusing to deal if the firm has an **essential facility**: a scarce resource that a rival needs to use to survive. The classic example is a century-old case in which all the railroad bridges into St. Louis were owned by a group of railroads. The U.S. Supreme Court was concerned that these railroad companies could keep rivals from serving St. Louis. The Court ruled that the owning group had to provide access to rival railroads on reasonable terms.

Exclusive Dealing. A concept similar to refusal to deal is *exclusive dealing*, which arises when a firm will sell its product only to customers who agree to buy from that firm and not from its rivals. Or the relationship can be reversed: An upstream firm could be forced to sell to only one buyer and not to the buyer's rivals. (Chapter 13 discusses the theory of exclusive dealing.)

Exclusive contracts can promote efficiency and competition in the market by guaranteeing a source of supply, lowering transaction costs, or creating dealer loyalty. The courts have found that exclusive dealing contracts between a manufacturer and its dealers are lawful if they increase competition between this manufacturer and its rivals. However, exclusive contracts are illegal if a monopoly uses them to prevent new firms from entering the market and, more generally, if competition is significantly damaged.

Mini-Case

An Exclusive Contract for a Key Ingredient

The FTC and the attorneys general of 33 states settled a lawsuit against drug producer Mylan Labs and its suppliers, Profarmaco and Gyma Laboratories, for $100 million and an agreement to terminate their ten-year exclusive contract. (A subsequent private suit cost the defendants another $77 million in 2010.) Under the agreement between MyLan and its suppliers, the suppliers would provide essential ingredients for two drugs used for Alzheimer patients to only Mylan and not to Mylan's competitors. In exchange, Mylan Labs would pay a percentage of profit from the drug to the suppliers. The suit claimed that, by cornering the market for the active ingredients, Mylan was able to raise the price of its drug Clorazepate by more than 3,000% (from about 2¢ a tablet to over 75¢) and increase the price of its drug Lorazepam by more than 2,000% (from about 1¢ a tablet to over 37¢).

Price Discrimination. Under the U.S. Robinson-Patman Act of 1936, *price discrimination* (Chapter 10) is legal unless it harms competition. For example, price discrimination is probably illegal if a manufacturer sells a good at a lower price to only one of several downstream firms, which may allow the favored customer to drive its rivals out of business.

A firm accused of a Robinson-Patman Act violation has two possible defenses. A price concession offered to one firm but not to its rivals can be justified if it is due to cost differences, such as a volume discount to a larger firm, or because it was offered in good faith to meet a competitor's price.

16.4 Externalities

An **externality** occurs when a person's well-being or a firm's production capability is directly affected by the actions of other consumers or firms rather than indirectly through changes in prices. The effect is *external* in the sense that it occurs outside a market and hence has no associated price. A firm whose production process lets off fumes that harm its neighbors is creating an externality for which no market exists. In contrast, the firm is not causing an externality when it harms a rival by selling extra output that lowers the market price.

Externalities may either help or harm others. An externality that harms someone is called a *negative externality*. You are harmed if your neighbors keep you awake by playing loud music late at night. A chemical plant creates a negative externality when it dumps its waste into the water, reducing the profits of a firm that rents boats on the lake and the utility of visitors to the lake. A *positive externality* benefits others. By installing attractive shrubs and outdoor sculpture around its building, a firm provides a positive externality to its neighbors.

A single action may confer positive externalities on some people and negative externalities on others. The smell of perfume pleases some people, but causes an unpleasant allergic reaction in others. Some people think that their wind chimes please their neighbors, whereas anyone with an ounce of sense would realize that those chimes drive us crazy! It was reported that efforts to clean up the air in Los Angeles, while helping people breathe more easily, caused harmful ultraviolet (UV) radiation levels to increase more rapidly as cleaner air filtered out less of the sun's UV emissions.

Spam—unsolicited bulk e-mail messages—inflicts a major negative externality on businesses and individuals around the world by forcing people to waste time removing it, by inducing people to unintentionally reveal private information, and in other ways. A spammer targets people who might be interested in the information provided in the spam message. This target group is relatively small compared to the vast majority of recipients who do not want the message and who incur the costs of reading and removing it. (Moreover, many spam messages are scams.) In 2012, 30 billion spam messages were sent daily, constituting 69% of global e-mail traffic according to Symantec.

Firms incur large costs to delete spam by installing spam filters and using employees' labor. A study at a German university found that the working time losses caused by spam were approximately 1,200 minutes or $2\frac{1}{2}$ days per employee per year (Caliendo et al., 2012).

The worldwide cost of spam is enormous. Various estimates of the cost range from $20 billion to $50 billion per year.

The Inefficiency of Competition with Externalities

Competitive firms and consumers do not have to pay for the harm caused by negative externalities, so they create excessive amounts. Similarly, if producers are not compensated for the benefits of a positive externality, too little of such externalities is produced.

Externalities create a market failure, causing economic inefficiency. To illustrate why externalities cause such inefficiency, we examine a competitive market in which firms produce paper and emit by-products of the production process—such as air and water pollution—that harm people who live near paper mills. (The paper industry is a major industrial source of water pollution.)

To make the point as clearly as possible, we assume initially that each additional ton of paper produced increases these harmful emissions and that the only way to decrease the volume of emissions is to reduce the amount of paper manufactured. No alternative technologies that reduce pollution are available, and it is not possible to locate plants where the emissions harm no one.

Paper firms do not have to pay for the harm from the pollution they cause. As a result, each firm's **private cost** includes its direct costs of production (such as the cost of inputs) but does not include costs imposed on others. The true **social cost** consists of all the costs incurred by society, including the private costs of firms and individuals and the harm from externalities.

We use a supply-and-demand diagram for the paper market in Figure 16.2 to illustrate that *a competitive market produces excessive pollution because the firms' private cost is less than the social cost*. In the competitive equilibrium, the firms consider only their private costs in making decisions and ignore the harm of the pollution externality they inflict on others. The market supply curve is the aggregate *private marginal cost* curve, MC^p, which is the horizontal sum of the private marginal cost curves of each of the paper manufacturing firms.

The competitive equilibrium, e_c, is determined by the intersection of the market supply curve and the market demand curve for paper. The competitive equilibrium quantity is $Q_c = 105$ tons per day, and the competitive equilibrium price is $p_c = \$240$ per ton.

FIGURE 16.2 Welfare Effects of Pollution in a Competitive Market

The competitive equilibrium, e_c, is determined by the intersection of the demand curve and the competitive supply or private marginal cost curve, MC^p, which ignores the cost of pollution. The social optimum, e_s, is at the intersection of the demand curve and the social marginal cost curve, $MC^s = MC^p + MC^x$, where MC^x is the marginal cost of the pollution. Private producer surplus is based on the MC^p curve, and social producer surplus is based on the MC^s curve.

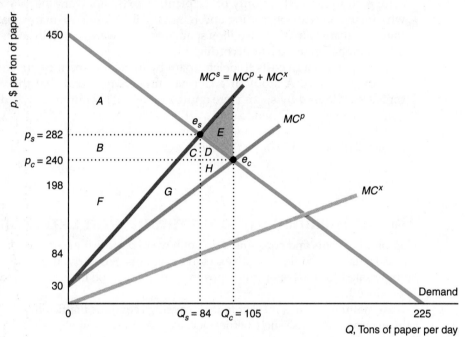

	Social Optimum	Private	Change
Consumer Surplus, CS	A	$A + B + C + D$	$B + C + D$
Private Producer Surplus, PS_p	$B + C + F + G$	$F + G + H$	$H - B - C$
Externality Cost, C_x	$C + G$	$C + D + E + G + H$	$D + E + H$
Social Producer Surplus, $PS_s = PS_p - C_x$	$B + F$	$F - C - D - E$	$-B - C - D - E$
Total Surplus, $TS = CS + PS_s$	$A + B + F$	$A + B + F - E$	$-E = DWL$

The firms' *private producer surplus* is the producer surplus of the paper mills based on their *private marginal cost* curve: the area $F + G + H$, which is below the market price and above MC^p up to the competitive equilibrium quantity, 105. The competitive equilibrium maximizes the sum of consumer surplus and private producer surplus. In the absence of an externality, the sum of consumer surplus and private producer surplus equals total surplus, so competition maximizes total surplus.

When we introduced surplus measures in Chapter 8, we considered examples in which the total surplus associated with a particular market consisted of the sum of producer surplus and consumer surplus. However, externalities impose additional costs that are not captured by total surplus if the producer surplus is calculated using the supply curves based only on firms' private costs. To properly measure total surplus, we need to calculate producer surplus based on the full social costs.

Because the paper market produces pollution, the competitive equilibrium does *not* maximize the correct measure of total surplus, which takes into account the harm from the externality. Competitive firms produce too much pollution because they do not have to pay for the externality harm. This market failure results from competitive forces that equalize the price and *private marginal cost* rather than the *social marginal cost*, which includes both the private costs of production and the external damage.

For a given amount of paper production, the full cost of one more ton of paper to society, the *social marginal cost* (MC^s), is the cost of manufacturing one more ton of paper to the paper firms plus the additional external damage to people in the community from producing this last ton of paper. Thus, the height of the social marginal cost curve, MC^s, at any given quantity equals the vertical sum of the height of the MC^p curve (the private marginal cost of producing another ton of paper) plus the height of the MC^x curve (the marginal external damage) at that quantity.

The social marginal cost curve intersects the demand curve at the socially efficient quantity, $Q_s = 84$. At smaller quantities, the price—the value consumers place on the last unit of the good sold—is higher than the full social marginal cost. The gain to consumers of paper exceeds the cost of producing an extra unit of output (and hence an extra unit of pollution). At larger quantities, the price is below the social marginal cost, so the gain to consumers is less than the cost of producing an extra unit.

Total surplus is maximized where price equals social marginal cost. At this output level no deadweight loss occurs so the result is Pareto efficient. Total surplus equals $A + B + F$: the area between the demand curve and the MC^s curve up to the optimal quantity, 84 tons of paper.

Total surplus at the competitive equilibrium, e_c, is lower: $A + B + F - E$, the areas between the demand curve and the MC^s curve up to 105 tons of paper. The area between these curves from 84 to 105, $-E$, is a deadweight loss because the social cost exceeds the value that consumers place on these last 21 tons of paper. *A deadweight loss results because the competitive market equates price with private marginal cost instead of with social marginal cost.*

Total surplus is higher at the efficient output level than at the competitive equilibrium because the gain from reducing pollution from the competitive to the efficient level more than offsets the loss to consumers and producers of the paper. The cost of the pollution to people who live near the factories is the area under the MC^x curve between zero and the quantity produced. By construction, this area is the same as the area between the MC^p and the MC^s curves. The total damage from the pollution is $-C - D - E - G - H$ at the competitive equilibrium and only $-C - G$ at the efficient outcome. Consequently, the extra pollution damage from producing the competitive output rather than the efficient quantity is $-D - E - H$. The main beneficiaries from producing at the competitive output level rather than at the efficient level are the paper buyers, who pay $240 rather than $282 for a ton of paper. Their consumer surplus rises from A to $A + B + C + D$.

The figure illustrates two main results with respect to negative externalities. First, *if production generates negative externalities, then a competitive market produces excessive negative externalities.* Because the price of the pollution to the firms is zero, which is less than the marginal cost that the last unit of pollution imposes on society, an unregulated competitive market produces more pollution than is socially optimal.

Second, *the optimal amount of pollution is greater than zero*. Even though pollution is harmful and we'd like to have none of it, we cannot wipe it out without eliminating virtually all production and consumption. Making paper, dishwashers, and televisions creates air and water pollution. Fertilizers used in farming pollute the water supply. Delivery people pollute the air by driving to your home.

Reducing Externalities

Because competitive markets produce excessive negative externalities, government intervention may provide a social gain. More than 60 years ago, in 1952, London suffered from a particularly thick "peasouper" fog—pollution so dense that people had trouble finding their way home—for five days. This pollution-based fog killed an estimated 4,000 to 12,000 people and caused perhaps 100,000 more to experience significant illness. Those dark days prompted the British government to pass its first Clean Air Act, in 1956. Both the United States and Canada passed a Clean Air Act in 1970.

The Clean Air Act (CAA) of 1970 and the Clean Air Act Amendments of 1990 greatly improved U.S. air quality. Between 1980 and 2010, the national average atmospheric concentration of sulfur dioxide (SO_2) plummeted 83%, carbon monoxide (CO) fell 82%, nitrogen dioxide (NO_2) tumbled 52%, and ozone dropped 28%. From 1990 to 2010, particulate matter (PM10) in the air decreased by 38%.[10]

The U.S. Environmental Protection Agency (EPA) believes that the CAA saves over 160,000 lives a year, averts more than 100,000 hospital visits, prevents millions of cases of respiratory problems, and avoids 13 million lost workdays. The EPA (2011) estimated the costs of complying with the Clean Air Act were $53 billion, but the benefits were $1.3 trillion in 2010. Thus, benefits outweighed costs by nearly 25 to 1.

Politicians around the world disagree about how and whether to control pollution. In 2012 at the United Nations (U.N.) Rio+20 meeting, 120 heads of state and 50,000 environmentalists, social activists, and business leaders met to encourage sustainable, green growth in poor countries. They argued and accomplished little. Clearly, pollution control will be a major cause of disagreement throughout the world for the foreseeable future.

If a government has sufficient knowledge about pollution damage, the demand curve, costs, and the production technology, it can force a competitive market to produce the social optimum. The government can control pollution directly by restricting the amount of pollution that firms may produce or by taxing them for pollution they create. A governmental limit on the amount of air or water pollution that may be released is called an *emissions standard*. A tax on air pollution is called an *emissions fee*, and a tax on discharges into the air or waterways is an *effluent charge*.

Frequently, however, a government controls pollution indirectly, through quantity restrictions or taxes on outputs or inputs. Whether the government restricts or taxes outputs or inputs may depend on the nature of the production process. It is generally more efficient to regulate pollution directly rather than to regulate output. Direct regulation of pollution encourages firms to adopt efficient new technologies to control pollution (a possibility we ignore in our paper mill example).

One alternative to direct government taxation or regulation is for the government or the courts to clearly assign property rights giving one party the right to pollute or the other party the right to be free from pollution. If clear property rights can be established, pollution can be priced and the externality problem can be reduced or eliminated.

---

[10]According to **www.epa.gov/air/airtrends** (viewed August 1, 2012).

Emissions Standards.

We use the paper mill example in Figure 16.2 to illustrate how a government may use an *emissions standard* to reduce pollution. Here the government can maximize total surplus by forcing the paper mills to produce no more than 84 units of paper per day. (Because output and pollution move together in this example, regulating either reduces pollution in the same way.)

Unfortunately, the government usually does not know enough to regulate optimally. For example, to set quantity restrictions on output optimally, the government must know how the marginal social cost curve, the demand for paper curve, and pollution vary with output. The ease with which the government can monitor output and pollution may determine whether it sets an output restriction or a pollution standard.

Even if the government knows enough to set the optimal regulation, it must enforce this regulation to achieve the desired outcome. Though the EPA sets federal pollution standards for major pollutants, obtaining compliance is not easy. The EPA posts online a (long) list of areas that do not meet regulatory standards. In December 2012, for example, the large Los Angeles-South Coast Air Basin was listed in the "extreme" category for noncompliance with the ground-level ozone standard and in the "serious" category for carbon monoxide.[11]

Mini-Case

Pulp and Paper Mill Pollution and Regulation

Pulp and paper mills are major sources of air and water pollution. Air pollution is generated primarily during the pulping process, in which the plant separates the wood fibers from the rest of the tree using various chemical and mechanical methods. Additional pollution occurs during the paper-making process if the paper is chemically treated to produce smoother surfaces.

For simplicity in our example, we assumed that the amount of pollution emitted varied only with output. However, in reality, firms may use less-polluting production technologies (such as pollution-abatement equipment) or may change the input mix to lower the amount of pollution for a given level of output.

Gray and Shimshack (2011) summarized many studies on regulating paper mill pollution and concluded that effective regulation can reduce pollution markedly. A 10% increase in pollution-reducing capital lowers emissions for a given amount of paper by 6.9% (Shadbegian and Gray, 2003). Each dollar spent on extra capital stock provides an annual return of about 75¢ in pollution reduction benefits. An additional fine for violating pollution laws induces about a two-thirds reduction in the statewide water pollution violation rate of pulp and paper mills in the year following the fine (Shimshack and Ward, 2005). Inclusion on a public list of noncompliant pulp and paper mills in British Columbia, Canada, produced incentives for pollution control that were similar to a regulatory fine (Foulon et al., 2002).

---

[11]See **www.epa.gov/airquality/greenbook/** for details on noncompliance with EPA standards, and go to **www.scorecard.org** to learn about environmental risks in your area.

FIGURE 16.3 Using Taxes to Control Pollution

Placing a tax on the firms equal to the harm from the pollution, $t(Q) = MC^x$, causes them to internalize the externality, so their private marginal cost is the same as the social marginal cost, MC^x. As a result, the competitive after-tax equilibrium is the same as the social optimum, e_s. Alternatively, applying a specific tax of $\tau = \$84$ per ton of paper, which is the marginal harm from the gunk at $Q_s = 84$, also results in the social optimum.

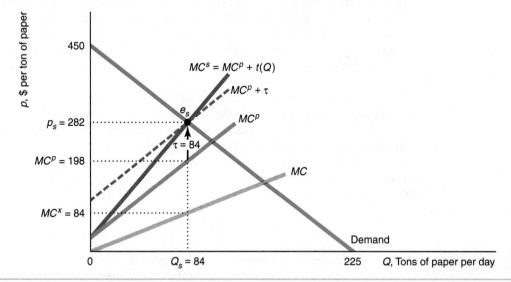

Emission Fees. The government may impose costs on polluters by taxing their output or the amount of pollution produced. (Similarly, a law could make a polluter liable for damages in a court.) In our paper mill example, taxing output works as well as taxing the pollution directly because the relationship between output and pollution is fixed. However, if firms can vary the output-pollution relationship by varying inputs or adding pollution-control devices, then it is more efficient for the government to tax pollution than output.

In our paper mill example, if the government knows the marginal cost of the emissions, MC^x, it can set the output tax, $t(Q)$, which varies with output, Q, equal to this marginal cost curve: $t(Q) = MC^x$. Figure 16.3 illustrates the manufacturers' after-tax marginal cost, $MC^s = MC^p + t(Q)$.

The output tax causes a manufacturer to *internalize the externality*—to bear the cost of the harm that the firm inflicts on others. The after-tax private marginal cost or supply curve is the same as the social marginal cost curve. As a result, the after-tax competitive equilibrium is efficient.

Usually, the government sets a specific tax rather than a tax that varies with the amount of pollution, as MC^x does. As Q&A 16.2 shows, applying an appropriate specific tax results in the socially efficient level of production.

Q&A 16.2

For the market with pollution in Figure 16.3, what constant, specific tax, τ, on output could the government set to maximize total surplus?

Answer *Set the specific tax equal to the marginal harm of pollution at the optimal quantity.* At the optimal quantity, $Q_s = 84$, the marginal harm from the emissions is $84, as Figure 16.3 shows. If the specific tax is $\tau = \$84$, the after-tax private marginal cost (after-tax competitive supply curve), $MC^p + \tau$, equals the social marginal cost at the optimal quantity, where total surplus is maximized. As a consequence, the after-tax competitive supply curve intersects the demand curve at the optimal quantity. By paying this specific tax, the firms internalize the cost of the externality at the optimum quantity. All that is required for optimal production is that the tax equals the marginal cost of pollution at the optimum quantity; it need not equal the marginal cost of pollution at other quantities.

Mini-Case

Why Tax Drivers

Driving causes many externalities including pollution, congestion, and accidents. Taking account of pollution from producing fuel and driving, Hill et al. (2009) estimated that burning one gallon of gasoline (including all downstream effects) causes a carbon dioxide-related climate change cost of 37¢ and a health-related cost of conventional pollutants associated with fine particulate matter of 34¢.

Edlin and Karaca-Mandic (2006) measured the accident externality from additional cars by the increase in the cost of insurance. These externalities are big in states with a high concentration of traffic but not in states with low densities. In California, with lots of cars per mile, an extra driver raises the total statewide insurance costs of other drivers by between $1,725 and $3,239 per year, and a 1% increase in driving raises insurance costs 3.3% to 5.4%. While the state could build more roads to lower traffic density and hence accidents, it's cheaper to tax the externality. A tax equal to the marginal externality cost would raise $66 billion annually in California—more than the $57 billion raised by all existing state taxes—and over $220 billion nationally.

An alternative to a tax per driver is a tax per mile or gallon of gas. Each 10% increase in the gasoline tax results in a 0.6% decrease in the traffic fatality rate (Grabowski and Morrissey, 2006).

Vehicles are inefficiently heavy because owners of heavier cars ignore the greater risk of death that they impose on other drivers and pedestrians in accidents (Anderson and Auffhammer, 2011). Raising the weight of a vehicle that hits you by 1,000 pounds increases your chance of dying by 47%. The higher externality risk due to the greater weight of vehicles since 1989 is 27¢ per gallon of gasoline and the total fatality externality roughly equals a gas tax of $1.08 per gallon.

In addition, a driver imposes delays on other drivers during congested periods. Parry et al. (2007) concluded that this cost is roughly equivalent to $1.05 per gallon of gas on average across the United States.

To reduce the negative externalities of driving, governments have taxed gasoline, cars, and the carbon embodied in gasoline. However, such taxes have generally been much lower than the marginal cost of the externality and have not been adequately sensitive to vehicle weight or time of day. The Netherlands is debating introducing a tax on the distance driven (a pay-as-you-drive tax) that is more clearly targeted at preventing congestion and accidents.

Assigning Property Rights. Instead of controlling externalities directly through emission fees or emission standards, the government may take an indirect approach by assigning a property right. If no one holds a property right for a good or a bad, the good or bad is unlikely to have a price. If you had a property right to be free from air pollution, you could get the courts to prevent a factory next door from emitting smoke. Or you could sell your right, permitting the factory to emit.

If you did not have this property right, no one would be willing to pay you a positive price for this right.

The Coase Theorem

According to the Coase Theorem (Coase, 1960), a polluter and its victim can achieve the optimal levels of pollution if property rights are clearly defined and they can bargain effectively. The Coase Theorem is not a practical solution to most pollution problems. Rather, it demonstrates that a lack of clearly defined property rights is the root of the externality problem.

To illustrate the Coase Theorem, we consider two adjacent firms, the Fixit Auto Body Shop and the Secret Garden Tea House. Fixit causes noise pollution, which hurts business at the Secret Garden, as Table 16.1 illustrates. If the auto body shop works on more cars per hour, its profit increases, but the resulting extra noise reduces the tea house's profit. The last column shows the total profit of the two firms. Having the auto body shop work on one car at a time maximizes their joint profit. Anything else is inefficient.

Initially, because property rights are not clearly defined, Fixit won't negotiate with the Secret Garden. After all, why would Fixit reduce its output and the associated noise if the Secret Garden has no legal right to be free of noise? Thus, Fixit works on two cars per hour, which maximizes its profit at 400. The resulting excessive noise drives the Secret Garden out of business, so the joint profit is 400.

Now, suppose that the courts grant the Secret Garden the right to silence. If it forces Fixit Auto Body to shut down, the Secret Garden makes 400 and their joint profit is 400. However, if Fixit works on one car at a time, its gain is 300, while the Secret Garden loses only 200. The firms should be able to reach an agreement where Fixit pays the tea house between 200 and 300 for the right to work on one car. Under such an agreement, their joint profit is maximized at 500.

Why doesn't Fixit buy the rights to work on two cars instead of one? Its gain of 100 from working on a second car is less than the tea house's loss of 200, so the firms cannot rationally reach a deal to let Fixit work on the second car.

Alternatively, suppose that the court says that Fixit has the right to make as much noise as it wants. Unless the tea house pays Fixit to reduce the noise, it has to shut down. The gain to the tea house of 200 from Fixit working on only one car rather than two is greater than the 100 loss to Fixit. They should be able to reach a deal where the tea house pays Fixit between 100 and 200, Fixit works on only one car, and the two firms maximize their joint profit at 500.

This example illustrates the three key implications of the Coase Theorem:

1. If property rights are not clearly assigned, one firm pollutes excessively and the firms earn less than the maximum possible joint profit.

TABLE 16.1 Daily Profits Vary with Production and Noise

Fixit's Output, Cars per Hour	Profit, $		
	Auto Body Shop	Tea House	Total
0	0	400	400
1	300	200	500
2	400	0	400

2. Clearly assigning the property rights maximizes joint profit, regardless of who gets the rights.

3. However, who gets the property rights affects how they split the joint profit. The property rights are valuable. The party with the property rights is compensated by the other party.

To achieve the efficient outcome, the two sides must bargain successfully with each other. However, the parties may not be able to bargain successfully if transaction costs are so high that it doesn't pay for the two sides to meet or if either side lacks information about the costs or benefits of reducing pollution. Because these impediments are common, Coasian bargaining is likely to occur in relatively few situations. However, even if bargaining is not feasible, the allocation of property rights may affect the amount of pollution. For example, if the tea house has the right to be free of noise pollution, it can shut down the auto body shop.

Managerial Implication

Buying a Town

When the Environmental Protection Agency (EPA) stated that the James Gavin American Electric Power was violating the Clean Air Act by polluting Cheshire, Ohio, the EPA effectively gave the residents the right to be free from pollution. To avoid the higher cost of litigation and installing new equipment and other actions to reduce pollution

at its plant, the company bought the town for $20 million, inducing the residents to pack up and leave. Thus, once clear property rights are established, a manager may find it less expensive to purchase those rights from others rather than incur endless litigation and pollution-reduction costs.

16.5 Open-Access, Club, and Public Goods

Previous chapters focused on *private goods*, which have the properties of rivalry and exclusion. A **rival good** is used up as it is consumed. If Jane eats an orange, that orange is gone so no one else can consume it. **Exclusion** means that others can be prevented from consuming the good. If Jane owns an orange, she can easily prevent others from consuming that orange. Thus, an orange is subject to rivalry and exclusion.

If a good lacks rivalry, everyone can consume the same good, such as clean air or national defense or the light from a streetlight. If a market charges a positive price for that good, a market failure occurs because the marginal cost of providing the good to one more person is zero.

If the good lacks exclusion, such as clean air—you can't stop anyone else from breathing the clean air—then no one has a property right to the good. Consequently, a market failure may occur if people who don't have to pay for the good exploit it excessively, as when they pollute the air. If the market failure is severe, as it often is for open-access common property and for public goods, governments may play an important role in provision or control of the good. Streetlights, for example, are normally provided by (local) governments.

We can classify goods by whether they exhibit rivalry and exclusion. Table 16.2 outlines the four possibilities: private good (rivalry and exclusion), open-access common property (rivalry, no exclusion), club good (no rivalry, exclusion), and public good (no rivalry, no exclusion).

Open-Access Common Property

An **open-access common property** is a resource that is nonexclusive but rival, such as an open-access fishery. Anyone can fish in an open-access fishery so it is nonexclusive, but a fish is rival. If one person catches a fish, that fish (and its future offspring) are not available for anyone else.

Open-access common property leads to the overexploitation of the resource due to incomplete property rights. In an open-access ocean fishery, everyone has equal rights to a fish until it is caught, at which point it becomes private property. Each fisher wants to catch a given fish before others so as to gain the property right to that fish, even if that means catching fish while they are still young and small. The lack of clearly defined property rights leads to overfishing.

Like polluting manufacturers, fishing boat owners look at only their private costs. In calculating these costs, they include the cost of boats, other equipment, a crew, and supplies. They do not include the cost that they impose on future generations by decreasing the stock of fish today, which reduces the number of fish in the sea next year. The fewer fish, the harder it is to catch any, so reducing the population today raises the cost of catching fish for others, both now and in the future.

The social cost of catching a fish is the private cost plus the *externality cost* from reduced current and future populations of fish. Thus, the market failure arising from open-access common property is a negative externality.

Other important examples of open-access common property are petroleum, water, and other fluids and gases that are often extracted from a *common pool*. Owners of wells drawing from a common pool compete to remove the substance most rapidly, thereby gaining ownership of the good. This competition creates an externality by lowering fluid pressure, which makes further pumping more difficult. Iraq justified its invasion of Kuwait, which led to the Persian Gulf War in 1991, partly on the grounds that Kuwait was overexploiting common pools of oil underlying both countries. In 2011, the State of Alaska proposed leasing land next to the Arctic National Wildlife Refuge (ANWR), which would allow the leasing companies to drill and potentially drain oil from ANWR.

TABLE 16.2 Rivalry and Exclusion

	Exclusion	No Exclusion
Rivalry	*Private good*: apple, pencil, computer, car	*Open-access common property*: fishery, freeway
No Rivalry	*Club good*: cable television, concert, tennis club	*Public good*: national defense, clean air, lighthouse

If many people try to access a single website at one time, congestion may slow traffic to a crawl. In addition, e-mail messages can be sent freely, as the Internet allows open access, even though each message imposes a handling cost on its recipients. This negative externality leads to excessive amounts of unwanted or junk e-mail.

If you own a car, you have a property right to drive that car, but public roads and freeways are common property. Because you lack an exclusive property right to the highway on which you drive, you cannot exclude others from driving on the highway and must share it with them. Each driver, however, claims a temporary property right in a portion of the highway by occupying it, thereby preventing others from occupying the same space. Competition for space on the highway leads to congestion, a negative externality that slows up every driver.

Government Regulation of Common Property.
Overuse of an open-access common resource occurs because individuals do not bear the full social cost—they ignore the externality they impose on other users. The government can restrict access to these common areas. A typical approach is to grant access on a first-come, first-served basis, such as at some popular national parks.

Alternatively, the government can impose a tax or fee to use the resource so that only those users who value the resource more than that fee gain access. Governments often charge an entrance fee to a park or a museum. Tolls are commonly used on highways and bridges. By applying a tax or fee equal to the externality harm that each individual imposes on others (such as the value of increased congestion on a highway), a government forces each person to internalize the externality. Unfortunately, many governments subsidize fishing efforts rather than taxing or restricting fishing, which leads to even more fishing.

Mini-Case	In 2010 toll to cross the Bay Bridge from Oakland into San Francisco rose from $4 to $6 during weekday rush hours (5:00 to 10:00 A.M. and 3:00 to 7:00 P.M.), and the cost of using the formerly free carpool lanes rose to $2.50. This fee for carpool lanes reduced traffic in those lanes by 30% compared to the previous year. Overall traffic was down roughly 9% during the first few days after the toll changed. The effect on the Bay Bridge's traffic flow during the busiest hours was dramatic: rush hour traffic moved twice as quickly as in the previous year. The managers of the bridge were delighted by the substantially increased toll revenue and decreased congestion.
For Whom the Bridge Tolls	

Assigning Property Rights.
An alternative approach to resolving the commons problem is to assign private property rights. Converting open-access common property to private property removes the incentive to overuse it.

If fisheries are not open access but are privately owned, as with fish farms or privately owned lakes, the owners have clearly defined property rights and therefore do not face an externality. Each owner is careful not to overfish so as to maintain adequate numbers of fish to breed for the future. Similarly, in many developing countries, common agricultural land has been broken up into smaller private farms to avoid excess exploitation of the resource.

Club Goods

A **club good** is a good that is nonrival but is subject to exclusion. Some club goods are provided through true clubs, such as swimming clubs or golf clubs. These clubs exclude people who do not pay membership fees, but the services they provide, swimming or golfing, are nonrival: An extra person can swim or golf without reducing the enjoyment of others until these facilities become congested as capacity is reached.

However, the most significant club goods are not offered through actual clubs. An important example is cable television. Any available channels can be provided to additional consumers at almost no additional cost to the cable company once the cable is in place. The service lacks rivalry as adding one more viewer for a given channel in no way impairs the viewing experience of other viewers. However, people can be easily excluded. Only people who pay for the service receive the signal and can view the channel. Unlike with swimming pools or golf courses, extra consumers can subscribe to cable television channels almost without limit.

Because club goods are nonrival, the goods can be provided to additional consumers at (virtually) zero marginal cost. A cable company can add extra consumers at virtually no additional marginal cost without harming existing customers. If a positive price is charged for the channel, a market failure occurs because the price exceeds the marginal cost of providing the good. If some cable subscribers are willing to pay a positive amount for the channel, but less than the current price, then failure to provide the channel to those people is a deadweight loss to society.

Although club goods create a market failure, government intervention is rare because it is difficult for the government to help. As with regulation, an attempt to eliminate deadweight loss by forcing a cable television company to charge a price equal to its near-zero marginal cost would be self-defeating, as the service would not be produced and even more total surplus would be lost. A government could cap the cable TV price at average cost, which would reduce but not eliminate the deadweight loss.

Mini-Case

Piracy

One of the most important examples of a good that is not rival but does allow for exclusion is computer software, such as Microsoft Word. Software is nonrival. At almost no extra cost, Microsoft can provide a copy of the software program to another consumer. Because Microsoft charges a (high) positive price, a market failure results in which too few units are sold.

However, if Microsoft cannot enforce its property right by preventing *pirating* of its software (use of software without paying for it), an even greater market failure may result: It may stop producing the product altogether. In countries where the cost of excluding nonpaying users is high, computer software is pirated and widely shared, which reduces the profitability of producing and selling software. In its 2012 report, the Business Software Alliance (BSA) estimated that the share of software that was pirated was over 90% in some developing countries such as Georgia, Zimbabwe, and Bangladesh; between 22% and 30% for most EU countries, Australia, Canada, Japan, and New Zealand; and 19% in the United States.

Public Goods

A **public good** is nonrival and nonexclusive. Clean air is a public good. One person's enjoyment of clean air does not stop other people from enjoying clean air as well, so clean air is nonrival. In addition, if we clean up the air, we cannot prevent others who live nearby from benefiting, so clean air is nonexclusive.

A public good is a special type of externality. If a firm reduces the amount of pollution it produces, thereby cleaning the air, it provides a nonpriced benefit to its neighbors: a positive externality.

Free Riding. Unfortunately, public goods tend to be under-supplied by markets. As with other externality problems, the under-provision of a public good is due to a lack of clearly defined property rights. Because people who do not pay for the good cannot be excluded from consuming it, the provider of a public good cannot exercise property rights over the services provided by the public good. This problem is often described as the **free-rider problem**: a situation in which people benefit from the actions of others without paying. That is, they benefit from a positive externality. Consequently, it is very difficult for firms to profitably provide a public good because few people want to pay for the good no matter how valuable it is to them.

To illustrate why public goods are under-provided by markets, we first examine why the demand curve for a public good is different from that for a private good. The social marginal benefit of a private good is the same as the marginal benefit to the individual who consumes that good. The market demand or social marginal benefit curve for private goods is the *horizontal* sum of the demand curves of each individual (Chapter 2).

In contrast, the social marginal benefit of a public good is the sum of the marginal benefit to each person who consumes the good. Because a public good lacks rivalry, many people can get pleasure from the same unit of output. As a consequence, the *social demand curve* or *willingness-to-pay curve* for a public good is the *vertical* sum of the demand curves of each individual.

We illustrate this vertical summing by deriving the demand for guard services by stores in a mall that want to discourage theft. Guards patrolling the mall provide a service without rivalry: All the stores in the mall are simultaneously protected. Each store's demand for guards reflects its marginal benefit from a reduction in thefts due to the guards. The demand curve for the television store, which stands to lose a lot if thieves strike, is D^1 in Figure 16.4. The ice-cream parlor, which is at less risk from a theft, demands fewer guards at any given price, D^2.

FIGURE 16.4 Inadequate Provision of a Public Good

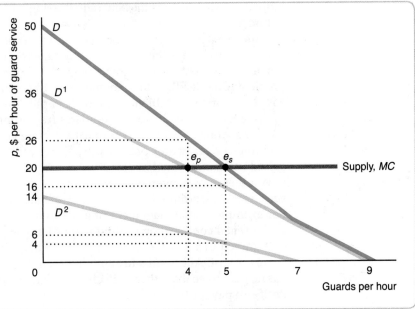

Security guards protect both tenants of the mall. If each guard costs $20 per hour, the television store, with demand D^1, is willing to hire four guards per hour. The ice-cream parlor, with demand D^2, is not willing to hire any guards. Thus, if everyone acts independently, the equilibrium is e_p. The social demand for this public good is the vertical sum of the individual demand curves, D. Thus, the social optimum is e_s, at which five guards are hired.

Because a guard patrolling the mall protects both stores at once, the marginal benefit to society of an additional guard is the sum of the benefit to each store. The social marginal benefit of a fifth guard, $20, is the sum of the marginal benefit to the television store, $16 (the height of D^1 at five guards per hour), and the marginal benefit to the ice-cream store, $4 (the height of D^2 at five guards per hour). Thus, the social demand is the vertical sum of the individual demand curves.

A competitive market supplies as many guards as the stores want at $20 per hour per guard. At that price, the ice-cream store would not hire any guards on its own. The television store would hire four. If the stores act independently, four guards are hired at the private equilibrium, e_p. The sum of the marginal benefit to the two stores from four guards is $26, which is greater than the $20 marginal cost of an additional guard. If a fifth guard is hired, the social marginal benefit, $20, equals the marginal cost of the last guard. Therefore, the social equilibrium, e_s, has five guards.

The ice-cream store can get guard services without paying because the guard service is a public good. Acting alone, the television store hires fewer guards than are socially optimal because it ignores the positive externality provided to the ice-cream store, which the television store does not capture. Thus, the competitive market for guard services provides too little of this public good. In more extreme cases, no public good is provided.

Reducing Free Riding. One solution to the under-provision of a public good due to free riding is for the government to provide it. Societies rely on governments to provide public defense, roads, and many other common goods.

In addition, governmental or other collective actions can reduce free riding. Methods that may be used include social pressure, mergers, privatization, and compulsion.

Social pressure may reduce or eliminate free riding, especially for a small group. Such pressure may cause most firms in a mall to contribute "voluntarily" to hire security guards.

A direct way to eliminate free riding by firms is for them to *merge* into a single firm and thereby internalize the positive externality. The sum of the benefit to the individual stores equals the benefit to the single firm, so an optimal decision is made to hire guards.

If the independent stores sign a contract that commits them to share the cost of the guards, they achieve the practical advantage from a merger. However, the question remains why they would agree to sign the contract, given the prisoners' dilemma problem (Chapter 12). One explanation is that firms are more likely to cooperate in a repeated prisoners' dilemma game (Chapter 13).

Privatization—exclusion—eliminates free riding. A good that would be a public good if anyone could use it becomes a private good if access to it is restricted. An example is clean water provided by water utilities, which can be monitored and priced using individual meters.

Another way to overcome free riding is through *mandates*. Some outside entity such as the government may mandate (dictate) a solution to a free-riding problem. For example, the management of a mall with many firms may require tenants to sign a rental contract committing them to pay fees to hire security guards that are determined through tenants' votes. If the majority votes to hire guards, all must share the cost. Although a firm might be unwilling to pay for the guard service if it has no guarantee that others will also pay, it may vote to assess everyone—including itself—to pay for the service.

16.6 Intellectual Property

Our lives are made much better by inventions, music, art, literature, and even textbooks. The rate of innovation has been much more rapid in the past two centuries than at any other time in human history. One major reason for the increased rate of invention

is that society developed mechanisms to assign property rights to knowledge, making it *intellectual property*. Without property rights, potential innovators have weaker incentives to innovate due to the public good nature of knowledge.

For example, when a chip manufacturer develops a new microchip, one particular chip is rival and exclusive. However, without intellectual property rights, the knowledge of how to make the chip is a public good. This knowledge is nonrival: if one person uses that knowledge, it does not prevent others from also using it. Moreover, it is nonexclusive if another company can buy a chip, reverse engineer it, and copy it.

Almost all of the cost of producing a new drug is the development cost of discovering the new medicine and verifying its efficacy and safety. If other firms can free ride on this knowledge and produce the same medicine, the innovator would have little chance of recovering its development cost. The free riders only have to pay the small production cost of the pills. Thus, this free-rider problem would greatly reduce private sector incentives to develop new drugs.

The innovation problem, as with other public good and externality problems, is due to a failure of property rights. If an innovator is able to treat the new knowledge embodied in an invention or other innovation as *intellectual property* and can prevent others from using it, then the ability of potential users to free ride is greatly diminished and the incentive to innovate is enhanced. Intellectual property can be created and protected in several ways, including by patents (which cover inventions) and copyrights (which protect original works such as books and music).[12]

Patents

The inventor of a new product can apply for a patent, which provides the intellectual property right underlying a new invention. The patent grants the inventor or the inventor's designate— often a firm—exclusive rights over the invention for 20 years in the United States and in most other countries.[13] Patents can be obtained for new

---

[12]Trademarks can also be protected, which allows a firm to protect its investment in building a favorable reputation for its brand.

[13]Traditionally, U.S. patents lasted 17 years from the date they were *granted*, but the United States agreed in 1995 to an international agreement that standardized patent lengths and the rule as to when a patent starts. U.S. patents now last for 20 years after the date the inventor *files* for patent protection. The length of protection can be shorter under the new rules, because it sometimes takes more than three years after filing to obtain final approval of a patent. According to the U.S. Patent and Trademark Office, the average time between the date a successful patent application is filed and the date the patent is granted is about two years (**www.uspto.gov**).

and useful machines, new compositions of material (such as pharmaceuticals), new production processes, and improvements in any of these areas.

The owner of a patent may choose to be the sole producer of the product, license others to produce the good for a fee, or sell the patent. In essence, the patent is a piece of intellectual property that can be treated like any other type of property.

Advantages and Disadvantages of Patents.

The patent system greatly reduces the free-rider problem. Because of the patent system, other companies cannot legally free ride on the drug discovery process or on other innovative activities that receive patent protection. Supporters of the patent system argue that most new drugs developed in the last 50 years would not have been developed without patent protection. As those drugs have provided enormous and frequently life-saving benefits to many people, the loss of total surplus from such a market failure would have been very large.

Patents apply to a wide range of potential innovations in all areas of the economy. In the United States, the patent process is administered by the U.S. Patent and Trademark Office (USPTO). Other countries have similar patent agencies, many of which cooperate closely with the USPTO under the terms of an international patent treaty called the Patent Cooperation Treaty. Inventors can apply for patents in many jurisdictions relatively easily using a common application process.

The key disadvantage of the patent system is that a patent creates monopoly power. As the Botox example in Chapter 9 illustrates, the holder of a patent on a new drug may have considerable monopoly power and may charge a monopoly price that is substantially greater than its marginal cost. Thus, in implementing a patent system, society reduces the social cost from reduced innovation due to the free-rider problem but incurs the deadweight loss of monopoly pricing. Patent policy also causes other problems, such as patent holders using litigation or other methods to block others from building on their discoveries to create new inventions.

Q&A 16.3

In a competitive market, the inverse demand curve is $p = 100 - Q$ and the supply curve is horizontal at 70. One firm believes that, if it invests 1,000 in research and development, it can develop a new production process that will lower its marginal cost from 70 to 20, and that it will be able to obtain a patent for its invention. Would this profit-maximizing firm undertake the innovation (assuming that the market lasts one period)? Does consumer surplus increase? Would consumers be better off or worse off if this firm could not obtain patent protection?

Answer

1. *Solve for the monopoly outcome and show that this monopoly pricing is feasible because no competitive firm can afford to undercut its price.* If the firm is a monopoly, its marginal revenue function is $MR = 100 - 2Q$ (Chapter 9).[14] It would produce where $MR = MC$ or $100 - 2Q = 20$, or $Q = 40$. The price at that quantity is $p = 100 - 40 = 60$. This outcome is feasible because the monopoly price is less than the price that any competitive firm can afford to charge.

---

[14]Its revenue is $R = pQ = (100 - Q)Q = 100Q - Q^2$. Differentiating, we find that the marginal revenue is $MR = dR/dQ = 100 - 2Q$. See Chapter 9 for a non-calculus approach to finding the marginal revenue of a linear demand curve.

2. *Calculate the firm's profit net of its investment to determine if the investment is profitable.* The firm's profit including the investment cost is $\pi = pQ - 20Q - 1{,}000 = (60 \times 40) - (20 \times 40) - 1{,}000 = 2{,}400 - 800 - 1{,}000 = 600$. Thus, it pays to innovate and become a monopoly.

3. *Determine if consumer surplus increases by comparing price before and after the invention.* The competitive price is 70, while the patent monopoly price is 60, so consumers benefit from the invention despite the exercise of monopoly power because the cost of production has fallen substantially. That is, the consumer surplus increases.[15]

Alternatives to Patents. Some alternatives to patents encourage research while avoiding the creation of monopoly power by making the knowledge from the discoveries public or *open source*. One important alternative is for the government to fund research by firms and universities. In 2009, the U.S. Congress allocated $2.4 billion to encourage development of plug-in vehicles and advanced batteries. Between 2004 and 2011, the U.S. Energy Department along with state agencies granted $348 million in loans, grants, and tax exemptions to research centers, fuel producers, and refiners to develop biofuels for jetliners.

Another method is to offer a prize for a discovery. Napoleon's prize for finding a way that the army could safely transport food great distances led to the invention of canning. More recent prizes have been offered to develop new light-weight batteries for military use (U.S. government), energy-saving refrigerators (industry organization), new rockets capable of moon exploration (Google), and new meat substitutes (People for the Ethical Treatment of Animals).

Managerial Implication

Trade Secrets

Managers do not necessarily patent new inventions to prevent free riding. Sometimes the best way to protect intellectual property is to keep it secret. A *trade secret* is a form of intellectual property, though it remains the exclusive property of the inventor only as long as it remains secret.

In the United States, the United Kingdom, and many other countries, government policy supports trade secrets by allowing firms to enter into enforceable contracts with employees that prevent employees from revealing trade secrets to others. Coca-Cola's formula is one of the world's most famous trade secrets. Not only has Coca-Cola kept the formula secret, but it has used the existence of the secret formula as a marketing tool.

Cohen et al. (2000) surveyed 1,478 R&D labs at U.S. manufacturing firms. Firms reported protecting their inventions through the use of patents, secrecy, lead time advantages, and other mechanisms. When asked whether a method was effective in protecting a product innovation, 51% mentioned secrecy compared to only 35% for patents. Secrecy was most frequently mentioned in miscellaneous chemicals

---

[15]At the competitive equilibrium where $p = 70$ and $Q = 30$, the consumer surplus is a triangle with a height of $30 = 100 - p = 100 - 70$ and a base of $Q = 30$, so $CS = \frac{1}{2} \times 30 \times 30 = 450$. Under the patent monopoly, the consumer surplus is the triangle with a height of $40 = 100 - 60$ and a base of 40, so $CS = \frac{1}{2} \times 40 \times 40 = 800$.

(71%), textiles (64%), and petroleum (62%). Thus, many managers believe that secrecy is one of the best ways to protect intellectual property. In Britain, only 22% of firms use formal intellectual property protection such as patents, while 32% use trade secrets (Hall et al., 2012).

Copyright Protection

Copyrights provide intellectual property rights to creative arts, such as music, literature, and visual images. The principles underlying copyright protection are generally the same as for patents. For example, the composer of a popular song faces the same free-rider problem that the inventor of a new drug faces. The song is essentially a public good: One person can listen to it without preventing others from also listening, and it is very difficult to stop people from copying songs.

The owner of the copyright to a song has an intellectual property right. According to U.S. law, the owner can prevent anyone else from playing or listening to that song without paying for that right. Without such protection, it would be difficult for an artist to earn a return from songwriting efforts. It is true that many people would produce music anyway "for love, not money." However, the incentive for highly talented artists to produce music would be much reduced, and they might be diverted to areas where they could expect compensation, such as creating advertising jingles.

Managerial Solution

Licensing Inventions

We now return to the three questions we posed at the beginning of the chapter. Should a firm patent its invention or keep it a trade secret? If the innovating firm produces the product itself, under what conditions can it charge the monopoly price for its product? Given that it obtains a patent, will the innovating firm earn more if it produces itself or licenses its new process to other firms?

A firm may use trade secrets instead of patenting for at least three reasons. First, it is costly to apply for a patent. Second, patents have a finite life, whereas a firm may be able to maintain a secret indefinitely (as Coca-Cola has done with its famous formula). Third, another firm may use the information in a patent to invent around the patent: create another invention that is sufficiently different that it does not violate the patent. Nonetheless, many firms opt for a patent because of the extra protection it provides, especially if the firm wants to license its invention.

We illustrate the answer to the next two questions using an example. Initially, a competitive market has many firms that produce at a constant marginal and average cost m, so that the competitive market supply curve is horizontal at m. As the figure shows, at the competitive equilibrium, e_c, the market price, p^*, equals m, and the quantity is Q^*.

A firm invents a new process that lowers the cost of production by 20% to $0.8m$. If the firm manufactures the good itself, under what conditions can it charge the monopoly price for its product?

If it were an unconstrained monopoly, the innovating firm would sell Q_m units at price p_m. This outcome is determined by the intersection of its red marginal cost line at $0.8m$ and the light purple marginal revenue curve (which corresponds to the light blue market demand curve). However, the competitive supply curve at m constrains the monopoly exactly as would a government price cap set at m: It

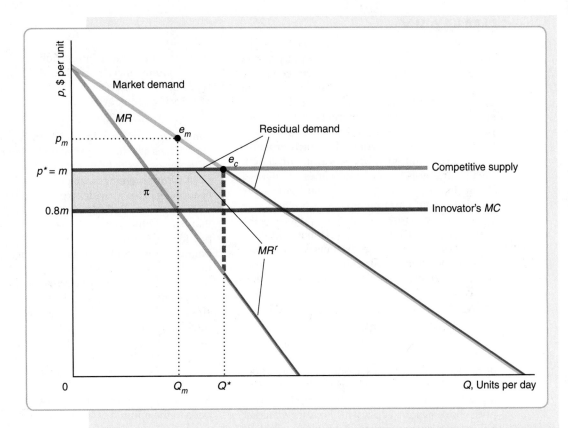

prevents the innovating firm from charging a price above m. Thus, the innovating firm can charge the unconstrained monopoly price only if p_m is less than m. Because m is less than p_m in the figure, this firm charges a price less than p_m.

Given that the competitive supply curve is horizontal at m, the residual demand curve facing the innovating firm is the dark blue line that is horizontal at m until it hits the market demand curve, and then it equals the market demand curve at prices below m. Consequently, the firm's dark purple residual marginal revenue curve, MR^r, is horizontal at m up to Q^*, and then, at larger quantities, it equals the light purple marginal revenue curve that corresponds to the downward-sloping market demand curve.

The innovating firm's marginal cost curve at $0.8m$ cuts MR^r in the (dashed) vertical section at Q^*. Thus, the firm's profit-maximizing output is Q^*. The firm charges a price that is slightly less than m so that it undercuts the competitive firms and makes all the sales. Thus, this equilibrium has (virtually) the same price and quantity as the competitive equilibrium. However, one firm sells the entire quantity and makes a profit virtually equal to $\pi = (m - 0.8m)Q^* = 0.2mQ^*$, which equals the gold rectangle in the figure.

Should the firm manufacture the good itself or license its process? The competitive firms are willing to pay a license fee up to $0.2m$ for the ability to produce at a marginal cost of $0.8m$. If they had to pay more than that, their costs would rise above their current cost of m. Given that the innovating firm sets this maximum possible license fee at $0.2m$, the competitive firms' supply curve is unchanged and the competitive equilibrium remains the same. The licensing firm's total license payments equal $\pi = 0.2mQ^*$. That is, the firm makes the same profit whether it produces itself or licenses its process.

SUMMARY

1. **Market Failure and Government Policy.** A perfectly competitive market achieves economic efficiency—it maximizes total surplus—so government intervention can only reduce total surplus. In contrast, in markets that are not perfectly competitive, market failures occur—total surplus is not maximized—which provides an important rationale for government action. Ideally, the government intervenes to make a Pareto improvement: a change that helps some people without harming anyone. An alternative approach to choosing government policies is the cost-benefit principle: the government imposes a policy if it results in a net benefit to society because the winners gain more than others lose. If the government can require that gainers compensate losers, then such policies provide a Pareto improvement.

2. **Regulation of Imperfectly Competitive Markets.** Governments often use direct controls on price or other variables to eliminate or reduce market failures arising from monopoly power or other sources. For example, to prevent a profit-maximizing monopoly from charging a price above marginal cost, which creates a market failure, the government can set a price ceiling. If the maximum price allowed equals the marginal cost, the market failure and associated deadweight loss are eliminated, provided the firm stays in business. If the price ceiling is set at a higher level, but below the unregulated monopoly price, the harm of the market failure is reduced but not eliminated. Well-intentioned regulators may not achieve economic efficiency because they have inadequate information about demand or marginal cost. However, other regulators are captured by the regulated industry—for example, they might be bribed—and hence work to enrich the industry rather than benefit society.

3. **Antitrust Law and Competition Policy.** Rather than regulate a noncompetitive market, governments may use antitrust laws or competition policy to promote competition and to prevent a market failure from occurring. The most important competition policies are those that forbid price-fixing and other cartel behavior. Merger policies try to prevent harmful mergers, such as those that increase market power by more than any offsetting benefits from lower costs. Other policies seek to prevent predatory actions where a dominant firm drops its price to drive out other firms and then raises the price. Several policies limit certain vertical interactions such as resale price maintenance, refusal to deal, and certain types of price discrimination that have the effect of reducing competition.

4. **Externalities.** An externality occurs when a consumer's well-being or a firm's production capabilities are directly affected by the actions of other consumers or firms rather than being affected only through changes in prices. Maintaining a beautiful garden provides a positive externality to your neighbors. Pollution is a negative externality that harms others. Because manufacturers do not pay for the externalities they create by producing pollution, their private costs of production are less than the full social costs that include the private costs and the externality cost. As a consequence, competitive markets produce more than the efficient output due to a negative externality, causing a market failure. If the government has sufficient information about demand, production cost, and the harm from the externality, it can use taxes or quotas to reduce or even eliminate the associated inefficiency or deadweight loss. Alternatively, assigning property rights sometimes leads to the optimal reduction in an externality.

5. **Open-Access, Club, and Public Goods.** Private goods are subject to rivalry—if one person consumes a unit of the good it cannot be consumed by others—and to exclusion—others can be prevented from consuming the good. Some goods lack one or both of these properties. Open-access common property, such as a fishery, is nonexclusive, but is subject to rivalry. This lack of exclusion causes overfishing because users of the fishery do not take into account the costs they impose on others (foregone fish) when they go fishing. A club good is nonrival but exclusive. For example, a swimming club lacks rivalry up to capacity but can exclude nonmembers. If a firm charges a positive price for such a good despite having extra capacity, a market failure results because the marginal cost of providing the good to one more person is zero, which is less than the price. A public good such as public defense is both nonrival and nonexclusive. The lack of exclusion causes a free-rider problem in a market: People use the good without paying for it. Therefore, potential suppliers of such goods are not adequately compensated and under-provide the good. Because private markets tend to under-provide nonprivate goods, governments often produce or subsidize such goods.

6. **Intellectual Property.** In the absence of government intervention, innovation is a public good. The resulting knowledge is nonrival and lacks exclusion. The information about the new invention has a free-rider problem: People who did not pay to develop the new product can copy the product and produce it. Thus, people may put little effort into inventing as they cannot be fully compensated. To avoid this problem, governments provide patents (and copyrights for the arts) that give the creator intellectual property rights to the invention for 20 years. While patents encourage invention, they create monopoly power. Alternatively, governments can subsidize research or provide other incentives to promote research. Some innovators rely on trade secrets rather than patents to protect their intellectual property.

QUESTIONS

All exercises are available on MyEconLab; * = answer at the back of this book; C = use of calculus may be necessary.

1. Market Failure and Government Policy

*1.1. If a policy change causes a Pareto improvement, is the outcome necessarily Pareto efficient? If a situation is Pareto efficient, are Pareto improvements possible? If a change occurs that causes a Pareto efficient outcome, is the change necessarily a Pareto improvement? Explain.

1.2. Does a Pareto improvement necessarily pass the cost-benefit test? Is the converse true? Explain.

1.3. A town council is considering building a new bridge over a small river that runs through the town to reduce congestion on the existing bridge and reduce commuting times. Each of 1,000 commuters who must cross the bridge would experience a benefit of $15 per day from saving commuting time. The bridge would be financed through increased property taxes that amount to $1 per day for each of the 10,000 households in the town. Would the bridge pass a cost-benefit test? Would building the bridge be a Pareto improvement (relative to not having a bridge)? Could using tolls instead of taxes to finance the bridge yield a Pareto improvement? Would using tolls be Pareto efficient? (Assume that the marginal cost of using the new bridge for an extra trip is zero and assume the demand for trips across the bridge is downward sloping.)

1.4. Describe the market failures analyzed in Chapter 9 (monopoly) and Chapter 15 (asymmetric information).

2. Regulation of Imperfectly Competitive Markets

2.1. Illustrate and describe the effects on output and welfare if the government regulates a monopoly so that it may not charge a price above $\bar{p}$, which lies between the unregulated monopoly price and the economically efficient price (determined by the intersection of the firm's marginal cost and the market demand curve). (*Hint*: See Q&A 16.1)

*2.2. A monopoly drug company produces a lifesaving medicine at a constant cost of $10 per dose. The demand for this medicine is perfectly inelastic at prices less than or equal to the $100 (per day) income of the 100 patients who need to take this drug daily. At a higher price, nothing is bought. Show the equilibrium price and quantity, and the consumer and producer surplus, in a diagram. Now the government imposes a price ceiling of $30. Show how the equilibrium, consumer surplus, and producer surplus change. What is the deadweight loss, if any, from this price control?

2.3. The price of wholesale milk dropped by 30.3% when the Pennsylvania Milk Marketing Board lowered the regulated price. The price to consumers fell by substantially less than 30.3% in Philadelphia. Why? (*Hint*: Show that a monopoly will not necessarily lower its price by the same percentage as its constant marginal cost drops.)

3. Antitrust Law and Competition Policy

*3.1. Suppose that the only two firms in an industry face the market (inverse) demand curve $p = 100 - Q$. Each has constant marginal cost equal to 10 and no fixed costs. Initially, the two firms compete as Cournot rivals (Chapter 11) and each produces an output of 30. Why might these firms want to merge to form a monopoly? What reason would antitrust authorities have for opposing the merger? (*Hint*: Calculate price, profits, and total surplus before and after the merger.) C

3.2. In Question 3.1, now suppose that each firm has fixed costs, F, of 300. Merging would imply that the monopoly firm would pay fixed costs of 300. How would your answer change?

3.3. A maker of specialty soaps supplies a unique soap made from a cactus extract to the only two retailers in a small town. The producer sells the soap to the retailers at the marginal cost of production of the soap, $1 per bar, and receives 20% of the profit earned when the retailers sell the soap to customers. Would the producer prefer that the retailers compete with each other on price or to specify the retail selling price of the soap to both retailers?

3.4. Why would an upstream producer of some product ever refuse to sell to downstream buyers who wish to buy the product at the going price?

4. Externalities

4.1. According to a study in the *New England Journal of Medicine*, your friendships or "social networks" are more likely than your genes to make you overweight (Jennifer Levitz, "Can Your Friends Make You Fat?" *Wall Street Journal*, July 26, 2007, D1). If it is true that people who have overweight friends are more likely to be overweight, is that an example of a negative externality? Why? (*Hints*: Is this relationship a causal one, or do heavier people choose heavier friends?)

4.2. When *Star Wars Episode III: Revenge of the Sith* opened at 12:01 A.M., Thursday, May 19, 2005, the most fanatical *Star Wars* fans paid $50 million for tickets to stay up until 3:00 to 4:00 A.M. Businesses around the country, especially those tied to high-tech industries, suffered reduced productivity due to absent (suffering from Darth Vader flu) or groggy workers on Thursday and Friday. By one estimate, fan loyalty cost U.S. employers as much as $627 million (Josie Roberts, *Pittsburgh Tribune-Review*, May 19, 2005). On the other hand, this sum is chicken feed compared to the estimated $890 million loss during NCAA March Madness: 16 days of the virtually nonstop college basketball games (James Paton, "Hooky and Hoops—March Rituals," *Rocky Mountain News*, March 19, 2005, 3C). Are these examples of a negative externality? Explain.

*4.3. Why is zero pollution not the best solution for society? Can we have too little pollution? Why or why not?

4.4. A number of countries have either banned incandescent light bulbs already or have begun phasing out such lighting in favor of more fuel-efficient compact fluorescent bulbs. These restrictions are intended to promote energy conservation and therefore to reduce greenhouse gas emissions and global warming. What alternative approaches could be used to achieve the same goals? What are the advantages and disadvantages of a ban relative to the alternatives?

4.5. The State of Connecticut announced that commercial fleet operators would get a tax break if they converted vehicles from ozone-producing gasoline to what the state said were cleaner fuels such as natural gas and electricity. For every dollar spent on the conversion of their fleets or building alternative fueling stations, operators could deduct 50¢ from their corporate tax. Is this approach likely to be a cost-effective way to control pollution?

4.6. Let $H = \bar{E} - E$ be the amount that emissions, E, are reduced from the competitive level, $\bar{E}$. The benefit of reducing emissions is $B(H) = AH^\alpha$. The cost is $C(H) = H^\beta$. If the benefit is increasing but at a diminishing rate in H, and the cost is rising at an increasing rate, what are the possible ranges of values for A, α, and B? **C**

4.7. In the model in Question 4.6, use calculus to determine the optimal level of H. **C**

*4.8. Suppose that the inverse demand curve for paper is $p = 200 - Q$, the private marginal cost (unregulated competitive market supply) is $MC^p = 80 + Q$, and the marginal external harm from emissions is $MC^x = Q$. Determine the unregulated competitive equilibrium and the social optimum (where total surplus is maximized). What specific tax (per unit of output) would achieve the social optimum? (*Hint*: See Q&A 16.2.)

4.9. In the model in Question 4.8, what is the unregulated monopoly equilibrium? How would you optimally regulate the monopoly to maximize total surplus? What is the resulting equilibrium?

4.10. Suppose that the only way to reduce pollution from paper production is to reduce output. The government imposes a tax equal to the marginal harm from the pollution on the monopoly producer. Show that the tax may or may not raise welfare.

4.11. To the dismay of business travelers, airlines now discretely cater to families with young children who fly in first class (Katherine Rosman, "Frequent Criers," *Wall Street Journal*, May 20, 2005, W1). Suppose the family's value is $4,500 from traveling in first class and $1,500 from traveling in coach. The total price of first-class tickets for the family is $4,000. Thus, the family's net value of traveling in first class is $500 = $4,500 − $4,000. Because the total price of coach tickets for the family is $1,200, the family's net value of traveling in coach is $300 = $1,500 − $1,200. A seasoned and weary business traveler who prefers to travel first class observes that the family is about to purchase first-class tickets. The business traveler quickly considers whether to offer to pay the family to fly in coach instead.

   a. Suppose that the business traveler knows the value that the family places on coach and first-class travel. What is the minimum price the traveler can offer the family not to travel in first class?

   b. Suppose the business traveler values peace and quiet at $600. Can the business traveler and the family reach a mutually agreeable price for the family to move to coach?

c. If instead the business traveler values peace and quiet at $200, can the business traveler and the family reach a mutually agreeable price for the family to move to coach?

4.12. Many jurisdictions strictly limit sales of hard liquor (liquor with a significantly higher alcohol content than wine) in an effort to limit the associated negative externalities. (De Melo et. al., 2013). One approach is to impose a high tax on sales of such products. Another approach is to require sellers to obtain licenses and to limit the number of licenses to the socially desirable number. Often these licenses are sold to the highest bidder. Frequently, the price of such licenses is set at a low enough level that extensive excess demand for licenses occurs at that price.

a. Under what circumstances would auctioning licenses be equivalent to a tax?

b. Why might regulators or politicians favor underpricing of liquor licenses? (*Hint*: Such licenses often end up in the hands of political donors or of friends and associates of donors.)

5. Open-Access, Club, and Public Goods

5.1. Are heavily used bridges, such as the Brooklyn Bridge and the Golden Gate Bridge, commons? If so, what can be done to mitigate congestion problems?

5.2. To prevent overfishing, could regulators set a tax on fish or on boats? Explain and illustrate with a graph.

*5.3. Are broadcast television and cable television public goods? Is exclusion possible? If either is a public good, why is it privately provided?

5.4. Do publishers sell the socially optimal number of managerial economics textbooks? Discuss in terms of public goods, rivalry, and exclusion.

5.5. Guards patrolling a mall protect the mall's two stores. The television store's demand curve for guards is strictly greater at all prices than that of the ice-cream parlor. The marginal cost of a guard is $20 per hour. Use a diagram to show the equilibrium, and compare that to the socially optimal equilibrium. Now suppose that the mall's owner will provide a $s per hour subsidy per guard. Show in your graph the optimal s that leads to the socially optimal outcome for the two stores.

5.6. In 2009, when the world was worried about the danger of the H1N1 influenza virus (swine flu), Representative Rosa DeLauro and Senator Edward Kennedy proposed the Healthy Families Act in Congress to guarantee paid sick days to all workers (Ellen Wu and Rajiv Bhatia, "A Case for Paid Sick Days," *San Francisco Chronicle*, May 15, 2009). Although the Centers for Disease Control and Prevention urges ill people to stay home from work or school to keep from infecting others, many workers—especially those who do not receive paid sick days—ignore this advice. Evaluate the efficiency and welfare implications of the proposed law taking account of externalities.

5.7. Receiving flu shots provides private benefits to recipients. However, pandemic influenza spreads between cities through the international airline network and between cities and rural areas through ground transport. Thus, it may be in the self-interest of rich countries to pay for flu shots in poor countries (Bobashev et al., 2011). Discuss this issue using the concepts of externalities, public goods, and free riders.

5.8. You and your roommate have a stack of dirty dishes in the sink. Either of you would wash the dishes if the decision were up to you; however, neither will do it in the expectation (hope?) that the other will deal with the mess. Explain how this example illustrates the problem of public goods and free riding.

5.9. Potentially, 240 automobile drivers per minute may use the EZPass lanes of the Interstate 78 toll bridge over the Delaware River that connects Easton, Pennsylvania, and Phillipsburg, New Jersey. Congestion occurs if that many autos cross even with a 5 mph speed restriction through the E-ZPass sensors. We can divide the drivers of these cars into four groups: A, B, C, and D. Each group has 60 drivers. Each driver in Group i has the following value of crossing the bridge: v_i if 60 or fewer autos cross, $v_i - 1$ if between 61 and 120 autos cross, $v_i - 2$ if between 121 and 180 cross, and $v_i - 3$ if more than 180 cross. Suppose that $v_A = \$4$, $v_B = \$3$, $v_C = \$2$, and $v_D = \$1$. The marginal cost of crossing the bridge, not including the marginal cost of congestion, is zero.

a. If the price of crossing equals a driver's marginal private cost—the price in a competitive market—how many cars per minute will cross? Which groups will cross?

b. In the social optimum, which groups of drivers will cross? That is, which collection of groups crossing will maximize the sum of the drivers' utilities?

5.10. Under federal laws, firms in many agricultural industries can force all industry members to contribute to collective activities such as industry advertising if the majority agrees. Under the Beef Promotion and Research Act, all beef producers must pay a $1-per-head fee on cattle sold in the United States. This fee raises $80 million annually, which finances research, educational programs on mad cow disease, and collective advertising such as the 2012 campaign, "Stay Home. Grill Out." Explain the logic of this law using the concepts of free riding and public goods. Supporters of this collective advertising estimate that producers receive $5.67 in additional marginal revenue for every dollar they contribute. If so, does this result suggest that there was a public good problem? Is the industry advertising optimally? (Chapter 9)

6. Intellectual Property

6.1. Woz Enterprises specializes in electrical components. The market for one particular component is perfectly competitive and in long-run equilibrium. Marginal cost is constant at 30. Woz can develop a much cheaper process for producing this component, lowering its marginal cost to 10. The R&D cost of developing the new process would be F, and Woz would be able to obtain a patent for it and become a monopoly supplier of this component. Demand for the product over the relevant period is given by $p = 50 - 2Q$. Show the R&D investment would be worthwhile (raise profit) for Woz if $F = 150$ but not if $F = 250$. What is the critical value for F that determines whether R&D is worthwhile for Woz? (*Hint*: See Q&A 16.3.)

*6.2. In Question 6.1, assume that the R&D cost is 150. Are consumers made better off by the action taken by Woz? Does total surplus rise?

6.3. In Question 6.1 with an R&D cost of 150, suppose that the government waits until Woz works out the new process and then changes patent rules, requiring Woz to charge a price no greater than 12. Does Woz stay in business? What happens to consumer surplus and to total surplus? Why don't governments impose such price controls on patented processes and products?

6.4. For trade secrets to effectively protect intellectual property, it is important that the innovation cannot be easily *reverse engineered*, a process by which a firm can take a rival's product and determine how it was produced. Patents are important when reverse engineering is easy. In the chemical business, firms try to develop lower-cost processes for producing chemical products, but the chemical product itself does not change. Therefore, examining the product does not reveal the new process, so reverse engineering is not feasible. With a computer chip, on the other hand, the innovation is embodied in the chip, so rivals can copy the chip. Which industry would you expect to rely more on trade secrets? Explain briefly.

7. Managerial Problem

7.1. In the Managerial Solution example, who benefits and who loses from the invention? Does the innovating firm capture the full value of its innovation?

8. Spreadsheet Exercises

8.1. A competitive fertilizer market has many small firms. The inverse demand function for fertilizer is $p = 40 - 2Q$, where Q is a ton of fertilizer and p is the price per ton of fertilizer. The market supply curve—the sum of the private marginal cost curves of all the firms—is $MC^p = Q + 4$. The fertilizer industry is a major source of water pollution and the marginal external damage, MC^x, caused by the industry to the communities near the fertilizer firms is $6 per ton of fertilizer produced.

a. Create a spreadsheet with column headings for output Q, price p, private marginal cost MC^p, marginal cost of pollution MC^x, and social marginal cost $MC^s = MC^p + MC^x$. Fill in the spreadsheet for $Q = 1, 2, 3, \ldots 20$.

b. Determine the equilibrium output and price in the competitive fertilizer market if firms do not have to pay for the pollution they create.

c. Determine the socially optimal amount of fertilizer.

d. What per unit tax can be imposed by the government to generate the socially optimal amount of output?

8.2. In a perfectly competitive market, the inverse demand function is $p = 50 - Q$. Market supply, Q^s, is perfectly elastic at a price of 40, because each firm has a constant marginal cost $MC = 40$.

a. Create a spreadsheet with column headings Q, p, MC, and CS (consumer surplus). Fill in the spreadsheet for $Q = 1, 2, 3, \ldots 25$. Calculate the competitive market's equilibrium output and price.

b. One firm invests 200 in a successful R&D project that allows it to lower its marginal cost of production from 40 to 10. The firm gets a patent for its new process. Create a new spreadsheet showing the situation under this patent monopoly, with no competitive firms. The column headings are Q, p, MR, MC, CS, and Profit (including the investment of 200). Calculate the patent monopoly's profit-maximizing output, price, and profit. Did the R&D investment pay?

c. How does consumer surplus change if the market changes from competition to a patent monopoly?

Global Business

17

Traditionally, most of Australia's imports come from overseas.
—Keppel Enderbery, former Australian cabinet minister (allegedly)

Business is now global. Virtually every country in the world exports and imports goods and services and invests in assets in other countries. Most major corporations actively trade and invest internationally.

The United States is the world's largest exporter of wheat. In 2012, its exports were about 21% of world exports even though U.S. production was only about 9% of the world's total. Wheat exporting is so important that Cargill, Inc., the U.S. agribusiness giant, and CHS, the largest U.S. farm co-op, have a major joint venture, Temco LLC, which built an export facility in the Pacific Northwest to ship wheat to Asia.

Rolls-Royce Motors, the maker of the world's most famous luxury cars, sold 3,575 of its British-built cars worldwide in 2012, a small number compared to the millions sold by General Motors, Toyota, and other large producers. Nonetheless, Rolls-Royce's sales revenue is large because it charges astronomical prices. The 2012 Rolls-Royce convertible, the Phantom Drophead Coupé, listed for $450,000 in the United States and for £332,000 in Great Britain.

Managers of these firms must make crucial pricing decisions when an exchange rate changes. An *exchange rate* is the number of units of one currency it takes to buy a unit of another currency. For example, in 2012 the exchange rate between the U.S. dollar ($) and the Japanese yen (¥) averaged about 80, so that one dollar bought 80 yen.

How do firms' prices change around the world when exchange rates change? In particular, is the responsiveness of prices to exchange rates greater for highly competitive wheat or for Rolls-Royce automobiles, which are not sold in a competitive market?

Not long ago international business issues were of only modest significance in countries such as the United States, China, and India, which had large domestic markets and engaged in little trade. However, international trade has increased dramatically in recent years. From 1990 to 2011, exports rose from 19% of the world's total output as measured by gross domestic product (GDP) to 32%.[1] The increase was even more dramatic for China and India, the world's two most populous countries. Chinese exports as a percentage of its GDP more than doubled

---

[1]Data in this paragraph and the next are from the United Nations: **www.unctad.org** and **unctadstat.unctad.org**.

from 14% to 30% during that period, and Indian exports more than tripled, going from less than 7% to 24%. Even in the United States, which has long been well integrated into the world economy, the share of trade increased significantly, going from 9.3% of its GDP in 1990 to 13.9% in 2011—an increase of more than one-third in the trade share of GDP.

Simply quoting trade as a share of GDP fails to adequately portray the remarkable increase in trade that has occurred in much of the world, especially in countries where GDP has been growing rapidly. The real value of exports (measured in 2011 U.S. dollars) flowing from China increased from $90 billion in 1988 to $1,898 billion ($1.898 trillion) in 2011. For every one freighter filled with containers of goods headed from China to the rest of the world in 1988, there were approximately 21 such freighters in 2011!

Effectively, the world has grown smaller, with countries becoming more interconnected and more interdependent than ever. This increasing integration of the world economy is due in large part to improvements in communications technology, which have reduced the effect of distance, and to policy changes that have allowed for freer trade and investment flows between countries.

The increased integration of the world economy creates both opportunities and challenges for businesses. Gaining increased access to foreign markets is an important means of expanding demand for many firms. A more integrated global economy also provides managers with the opportunity to use an international supply chain, obtaining materials, components, and other inputs to production from many countries. For example, IBM uses inputs from about 20,000 suppliers in close to 100 different countries in producing its products and sells its output in almost all of the world's more than 190 countries.[2] However, increasing competition from foreign rivals is a potential problem for managers, as is the difficulty of dealing with a range of different legal and policy environments from country to country.

In this chapter, we start by considering why countries and firms engage in international trade by exporting and importing goods and services, then address the role of exchange rates in international trade. Next, we examine how international trade policy affects managerial decisions regarding trade flows. We then turn to trade and investment by *multinational enterprises* (MNEs), which are firms that control productive assets in more than one country. We show how managers of an MNE must take international differences in law and economic policy into account. For example, we show how an MNE reacts to differential corporate tax rates in the countries where it operates. Finally, we discuss a very contentious issue: international outsourcing. In many developed countries, labor unions and other groups have protested when a firm lays off domestic employees and shifts production to foreign countries where labor costs are lower.

Main Topics

In this chapter, we examine five main topics

1. **Reasons for International Trade:** Nations trade for many reasons, the most important of which is *comparative advantage*: a country exports goods it can produce at relatively low cost and imports goods that are relatively costly to produce domestically.

2. **Exchange Rates:** A change in the exchange rate affects trade in goods and services and leads to adjustments that bring prices in different countries closer together.

[2]See **www.ibm.com/ibm/responsibility/2011/bin/downloads/IBM_Corp_Responsibility _Report_2011.pdf** (viewed April 29, 2013).

3. **International Trade Policies:** Governments have traditionally restricted imports by setting *tariffs*, which are taxes on imports, and *quotas*, which directly limit the quantity of imports, and often use subsidies to encourage exports.

4. **Multinational Enterprises:** Multinational enterprises are responsible for the majority of the world's international trade and investment and are greatly affected by variations in tax rates across nations and changes in exchange rates.

5. **Outsourcing:** Firms shift from domestic production of needed inputs to buying them from foreign firms to lower their costs, but the resulting shifts in employment patterns have generated criticism by domestic workers who lose their jobs.

17.1 Reasons for International Trade

Everyone consumes many imported products. A typical American breakfast might include bread made from Canadian wheat, jam imported from England, fruit from Mexico, and tea from India or coffee from Brazil—along with perhaps some corn flakes produced in the United States.

Why do we rely on other countries for these goods that we consume? Why doesn't each country produce everything it needs domestically?

Trade between countries occurs for many reasons. The most important is that international trade allows countries to specialize in producing goods and services for which they have a **comparative advantage**: the ability to produce a good or service at lower opportunity cost than other countries.

Comparative Advantage

Number of chopsticks made every day by Georgia Chopsticks in Americus, Georgia, for use in China: 2,100,000. —Harper's Index 2012

According to the principle of comparative advantage, a country exports goods it can produce at relatively low cost and imports goods that are relatively costly to produce domestically. For example, Sweden and Spain benefit from such trade. Sweden has a climate and geography that enable it to produce forest products such as timber, pulp, and paper. Spain has a climate well suited to producing many types of fruit. Neither country is good at producing the other country's product. Thus, it is not surprising that Sweden exports forest products to Spain while Spain exports fruit to Sweden and that both countries benefit from such trade.

Gains from Trade Between Countries. We use an example to illustrate why participants gain from trade. Suppose that the United States and Japan initially do not trade and each country is in competitive equilibrium, in which the prices of goods equal their marginal costs of production. The United States produces and sells a bag of rice for $1 and a silk scarf for $10. Japan produces and sells a bag of rice for ¥200 and a scarf for ¥1,000. If the United States were to reduce the number of silk scarves it produces by one, it could afford to produce 10 extra bags of rice. In contrast, Japan could produce one more scarf at the cost of only five bags of rice. Therefore, the two countries could produce the same number of scarves and have five extra bags of rice if they reallocated their resources. In the absence of transportation costs, both countries could gain if the United States shipped rice to Japan and Japan shipped scarves to the United States.

The reason for this gain is that the United States has a comparative advantage in producing rice and Japan has a comparative advantage in producing scarves. The cost of producing a scarf is 10 bags of rice in the United States and only 5 in Japan, so it is relatively inexpensive to produce a scarf in Japan. Similarly, the cost of producing a bag of rice is one-tenth of a scarf in the United States and one-fifth of a scarf in Japan, so it is relatively inexpensive to produce a bag of rice in the United States.

Gains from Intra-firm Trade. This basic idea of comparative advantage also works for *intra-firm trade*—where a single firm is on both sides of an international transaction—exporting the output from its operation in one country to an affiliated business unit in another country. About one-third of world trade is intra-firm trade.[3]

We illustrate the gains from intra-firm trade with an example concerning General Electric (GE), a major producer of kitchen appliances and many other products, which has production facilities in many countries, including Hungary and Romania. Suppose that GE is considering how to organize its production of refrigerators in Eastern Europe. To produce a refrigerator, GE must manufacture the basic parts or components and assemble those components into a finished product. A production employee might work in either component production or assembly.

We assume that Hungarian workers are more productive at both component production and assembly than workers in Romania. (This difference in productivity might reflect factors such as the quality of equipment and training.) That is, a Hungarian worker has *absolute advantage* over a Romanian worker: With the same amount of effort, the Hungarian worker can produce more of both outputs than can the Romanian. As Table 17.1 shows, a Hungarian worker can produce enough components (parts) for four refrigerators per day or can assemble four refrigerators in a day. A Romanian worker can produce enough parts for two refrigerators per day or can assemble one refrigerator per day.

However, both plants have a comparative advantage. If a Romanian worker assembles one refrigerator, that worker does not have the time to produce two sets of parts, so the opportunity cost of assembling a refrigerator is the value of the labor it takes to produce two sets of parts. In contrast, if a Hungarian assembles one refrigerator, the opportunity cost is that the worker does not produce one set of parts. Thus, the cost to GE of having a Romanian working in assembly is twice that of a Hungarian. Therefore, the Hungarian plant should specialize in assembling refrigerators. Similarly, it is more efficient to have the Romanian plant produce parts, because producing a set of parts has an opportunity cost of assembling one refrigerator in Hungary, but only half a refrigerator in Romania.

Suppose that GE has 120 workers in its Hungarian plant and 240 in its Romanian plant. If GE cannot lay off any workers in the short run, how should GE allocate activities in Hungary and Romania to maximize total output?

One approach is for each plant to act independently, producing complete refrigerators by manufacturing the parts and then assembling them. Under this plan, the Hungarian plant allocates 60 workers to parts and 60 to assembly. Because a component worker

TABLE 17.1 Output per Worker per Day

	Components	Assembly
Hungary	4	4
Romania	2	1

[3]**www.oecd.org/dataoecd/6/18/2752923.pdf** (viewed August 30, 2011).

TABLE 17.2 Total Production of Refrigerators

	Refrigerators per day
No trade: Plants work independently	400
Trade: Plants specialize	
Romania specializes in components, Hungary in assembly	480
Romania specializes in assembly, Hungary in components	360

produces 4 sets of parts per day, these workers produce $4 \times 60 = 240$ sets of parts. The 60 Hungarian assembly workers can assemble all 240 sets of parts because each worker can assemble 4 refrigerators per day. This allocation of workers to tasks yields 240 refrigerators per day in Hungary. Any other allocation would yield less output.

In Romania, 80 workers work on parts and 160 on assembly, yielding an output of 160 refrigerators per day. Thus, the two plants working independently can produce 400 refrigerators per day—240 in Hungary and 160 in Romania—as the first row of Table 17.2 shows.

A better alternative is to have Romania specialize in producing parts and Hungary specialize in production. If all 240 workers in Romania produced parts, they could manufacture enough for 480 refrigerators each day. If these parts were then sent to Hungary, the 120 Hungarian workers could assemble all 480 refrigerators in a day, as the second line of Table 17.2 shows.[4] This allocation of labor, involving specialization and trade, maximizes output. The gain from trade is 80 refrigerators.

If instead GE has its Romanian plant specialize in assembly, only 360 refrigerators would be produced (third row of Table 17.2), as Q&A 17.1 explains. Such an outcome is worse than no trade as 40 fewer refrigerators are produced. As summarized in Table 17.2, the best outcome is for the Romanian plant to produce parts and for the Hungarian plant to assemble these parts into refrigerators. This allocation of resources produces the most output because each plant specializes in the activity in which it has a comparative advantage.

Q&A 17.1

In our GE example, if the Romanian plant specializes in assembly and the Hungarian plant in producing components, what is the largest number of refrigerators that GE can produce per day?

Answer

1. *Determine how many Hungarian workers must produce components to keep the 240 Romanian workers fully occupied assembling refrigerators and how many refrigerators are produced.* The Romanian workers can assemble 240 refrigerators a day. To keep all the Romanian workers busy, only 60 Hungarian workers are needed to make 240 sets of parts each day.

2. *Explain how the remaining 60 Hungarian workers must be allocated to produce the most additional refrigerators and determine how many refrigerators they make.* The remaining 60 Hungarian workers can produce the largest number of refrigerators by having 30 workers each producing 4 sets of components a day and 30 assembling 4 refrigerators per day, thereby producing an additional 120 refrigerators.

---

[4]We assume the cost of transporting components or assembled products is small enough so that we do not need to consider it explicitly.

3. *Determine GE's total production with this allocation of workers and compare to GE's other two options.* Because 240 refrigerators are assembled in the Romanian plant and 120 more refrigerators are completely produced in the Hungarian plant, this approach yields a total of only 360 refrigerators. This quantity is less than the 400 GE produces if the plants do not trade or the 480 they produce if they trade and the Romanian plant specializes in components and the Hungarian plant in assembly.

Managerial Implication

Paul Allen's Comparative Advantage

The principle of comparative advantage is important for managers, such as Paul Allen, who co-founded Microsoft with Bill Gates. In the early years when the company was relatively small, Allen spent much of his time programming and wrote advanced microprocessor simulators. However, as the company grew, he became more involved in management and stopped programming. He was so good at managing Microsoft, the opportunity cost of having Allen spend his time programming became too high. Even if he was the best programmer in the company, Allen's comparative advantage was in dealing with managerial issues, so having him specialize in that activity increased Microsoft's profits and Allen's income. The managerial lesson is that a manager should assign workers to their areas of greatest *comparative* advantage and not focus just on their absolute advantages.

Increasing Returns to Scale

Trade occurs for many reasons in addition to comparative advantage. One of the other major motives for trade is to take advantage of increasing returns to scale (Chapter 5). With an increasing returns to scale (IRS) production function, doubling all the inputs more than doubles output. Thus, all else the same, having one IRS plant produce a given amount of output is less costly than spreading the production over two IRS plants.

In our GE refrigerator example, the production process exhibits constant returns to scale. Production involves only one input, labor. Doubling the number of workers doubles the output. We showed that with constant returns to scale, GE benefits from trade due to comparative advantage.

Suppose instead that GE's production function exhibits increasing returns to scale, so that doubling labor triples output. Initially, GE has two plants in Hungary, each with 50 workers. The workers in both plants are equally productive in all activities. Operating independently, each plant can produce 200 refrigerators, so total production is 400 refrigerators. GE could increase its output by closing one plant and shifting all its workers to the remaining plant, where the 100 workers could produce 600 refrigerators due to increasing returns to scale.

Indeed, if GE increases its labor force at this one plant even more, its production will grow more than in proportion, so that its cost per refrigerator would drop further. If GE can only sell its refrigerators in Hungary, the limited demand for refrigerators there would cap the number of refrigerators it wants to produce at this plant. However, if GE can export refrigerators to other countries, it can increase production at this one plant and lower its cost of production. Thus, increasing returns to scale provides an incentive to trade by selling in other countries.

Country Size. Relatively small countries in particular may benefit from taking advantage of returns to scale. Consider Canada, whose population and gross domestic product (GDP) are about one-tenth that of the United States. If Canada were unable to trade with other countries, its relatively small market would prevent it from cost-effectively producing and consuming commercial jet aircraft, which are produced with substantial increasing returns to scale.

However, if a Canadian producer can export its products all over the world, it can take advantage of increasing returns to scale by producing a large quantity of jet aircraft. For example, by taking advantage of international trade, Bombardier Aerospace, a Canadian firm, has become the world's third-largest commercial jet producer, specializing in light jets, including the business jets favored by senior executives and rock stars. Canada exports these light commercial jets and imports large commercial jets produced by the two major producers, the United States' Boeing Company and Europe's Airbus S.A.S. All the countries involved gain from trade due to increasing returns to scale.

Product Variety. Increasing returns to scale play an even greater role in a market with substantial product variety, such as toys, than in a market with a homogeneous product, such as DRAM memory chips for computers. The more varieties in a market, the fewer the units of any one variety a firm can sell. Thus, without international trade, it is very difficult for the manufacturer of a highly differentiated product to benefit from returns to scale.

The toy industry produces an incredible variety of products, and adds new varieties every year (usually in time for the winter holiday season). Toy producers could lower their average cost by producing fewer toy varieties and using longer production runs for the toys they do produce, so that they could spread the design, setup, and marketing fixed costs over more units of output. However, children love variety and new toys. Even a single category of toys, such as dolls or trucks, has hundreds of different varieties. Because children demand variety, a manufacturer that decides to sell only one product year after year so as to lower its average cost will quickly find that it can sell very few units and will likely go out of business.

How can a toy manufacturer produce differentiated toys and yet take advantage of increasing returns to scale? The only practical way is to sell its product to children in many countries instead of only in its home country.

Mini-Case

Barbie Doll Varieties

Barbie, produced by the U.S.-based Mattel, Inc., is perhaps the world's best-known toy. While other toy fads come and go, Barbie has had remarkable staying power. She was introduced in 1959 and is still a hot product. Although Barbie was invented and first produced in the United States, Mattel has produced Barbie dolls in many other countries, including Indonesia, China, Malaysia, Thailand, and Mexico. In 2011, Barbie was the top toy *import* into the United States for the winter holiday season, and was the most popular toy overall for girls during the 2012 holidays.

One key to Barbie's success is product variety. Mattel's Barbie website lists over one hundred dolls and closely related products. Most products are variations on the original Barbie doll. Mattel also produces many versions of her various friends, including Ken, her on-again, off-again boyfriend.[5]

[5]In 2004, Mattel sent out a news release indicating that Barbie and Ken had decided to "spend some time apart" after being together for 43 years, although they would "remain the best of friends" (**investor. shareholder.com/mattel/releasedetail.cfm?ReleaseID=128705**). In 2011, they got back together.

Barbie dolls come in many different price ranges. The basic dolls are pink-label dolls, but some are also silver-label dolls, gold-label, platinum-label, and black-label dolls in sequentially higher price ranges. Each label has many different versions, and every year many new versions are introduced while older versions are retired and become collectibles that often increase in value over time. Well over two thousand Barbie doll varieties have been produced since Barbie first appeared. Because of the great variety of Barbie dolls, many consumers have large collections, often numbering in the hundreds. Many Barbie collectors are in their 30s, 40s, and 50s, and the higher-priced dolls are targeted primarily at adults.

This success-based-on-variety model is made possible by international trade. Each variety requires a significant fixed cost in product design and manufacturing setup, so the manufacturer must produce a huge number of each variety of doll to benefit from increasing returns to scale. Due to international trade, a single factory in Indonesia can produce gigantic quantities of a particular variety of Barbie for the entire world market and take advantage of scale economies. A factory in China can do the same thing for a different version of Barbie.

17.2 Exchange Rates

How willing people are to trade one type of currency for another affects trade in goods and services. An **exchange rate** is the price of one currency (such as the euro) in terms of another currency (such as the dollar). Most countries or groups of countries have a unique currency, which can be traded or exchanged for the currencies of other countries. The euro (€) is the currency of 23 European countries that belong to the Eurozone.[6] It can be traded for U.S. dollars ($), Japanese yen (¥), British pounds (£), or many other currencies. In early 2013, one euro could be exchanged for $1.30 in U.S. currency. That is, the exchange rate between the dollar and the euro was 1.3.

Determining the Exchange Rate

Because currency is exchanged in a competitive market, we can use a supply-and-demand model to determine the exchange rate or price of one currency in terms of another. In Figure 17.1, the quantity on the horizontal axis is the number of euros that Americans want to buy using dollars. As X increases, the price of a euro in terms of dollars increases, or equivalently, the price of the dollar in terms of euros falls. The price on the vertical axis is the exchange rate, X, which is the number of dollars it takes to buy one euro.

The initial demand curve for euros in the United States is D^1. The demand curve slopes down because the quantity of euros demanded by Americans increases as

---

[6]The euro was created by the European Union (EU) and is the currency of 17 of the 27 EU countries, including France, Germany, and Italy. The EU country with the largest GNP that is not using the euro is the United Kingdom, which still uses its traditional currency, the pound (£). Non-EU countries using the euro include Andorra, Kosovo, Monaco, Montenegro, San Marino, and the Vatican City.

FIGURE 17.1 Supply and Demand Curves Determine the Exchange Rate

The interaction between supply and demand curves determines the exchange rate or price of one currency in terms of another. If U.S. consumers and firms want more euros at any given exchange rate so that the U.S. demand curve for euros shifts to the right from D^1 to D^2 while the supply curve of euros remains unchanged, then the equilibrium exchange rate rises from X_1 to X_2.

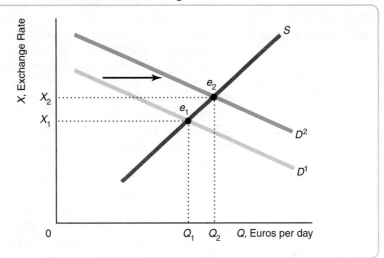

the exchange rate falls: the euro costs fewer dollars. The supply curve of euros, S, slopes up because Europeans are willing to trade more euros as the exchange rate increases.

The intersection of the supply and demand curves determines the initial equilibrium: the number of euros exchanged, Q_1, and the exchange rate, X_1, which was 1.3 in early 2013. If U.S. consumers and firms want more euros at any given exchange rate, so that the demand curve for euros shifts to the right to D^2, then the equilibrium quantity increases to Q_2 and the equilibrium exchange rate rises to X_2. That is, the price of a euro in U.S. dollars increases.

Many factors affect the supply and demand for a particular currency, including financial and macroeconomic conditions. For example, if investment opportunities increase in the United States relative to those in Europe, the exchange rate for the euro falls.

Exchange Rates and the Pattern of Trade

If the exchange rate for the euro falls, U.S. consumers and firms increase their demand for European goods as they can now buy more goods for a given number of dollars. Similarly, the demand of European consumers and firms for U.S. goods falls. Thus, a change in exchange rates affects the incentives to trade between countries.

The Brazilian currency is the real, denoted BRL. Suppose that initially one U.S. dollar is worth one Brazilian real. A volleyball sells for $10 in the United States and 10 BRL in Brazil. Now suppose that the exchange rate changes so that $1 is worth 2 BRL. If transaction and shipping costs are negligible, Brazilian retailers can increase their profits by selling the product in the United States for $10 (worth 20 BRL), rather than in Brazil for 10 BRL. As the quantity sold in the United States increases, the U.S. price of the ball falls if the U.S. demand curve slopes down. Similarly, as the number of balls sold in Brazil falls, the price in Brazil rises.

This process, called *arbitrage*, equates the prices of the ball in the two countries in the absence of transaction costs. If the transaction cost is t, arbitrage moves the price in one country to within t of the price in the other country because further arbitrage is unprofitable.

Managerial Implication

Limiting Arbitrage and Gray Markets

Managers can often increase profits by engaging in international price discrimination (Chapter 10): charging higher prices in countries where consumers have a greater willingness to pay. However, for international price discrimination to be profitable, firms must limit resale or arbitrage across countries. Managers have to be particularly concerned about increased arbitrage opportunities as exchange rates change.

If arbitrageurs can buy the good in the low-price country and sell it at a higher price in other countries without incurring transaction costs, their actions eliminate the price differential. Arbitrage will not completely eliminate price differentials if arbitrageurs incur transaction costs. If the price differential between countries for some product is $5 while the transaction cost (including transportation) is $10 per unit, then no arbitrage occurs. Thus, a price difference of $10 or less could persist.

For many goods, the Internet has greatly facilitated arbitrage. A student in the United States can save money by buying textbooks from Amazon's sites in lower-price countries. People around the world use eBay to trade a wide variety of goods from one country to another. The Internet has reduced but not eliminated international price differences in such products.

One way that a firm's managers try to prevent arbitrage is to permit only authorized dealers to handle their products. Any authorized dealer that imports the product from another country instead of buying it from the manufacturer could lose its authorization.

Foreign goods shipped to the high price country and sold outside of authorized channels of distribution are called *gray market* goods. Although Apple's iPad was the top-selling tablet in China in 2011, nearly half (49%) of these tablets were purchased overseas and then resold by nonauthorized, local vendors in China's gray market. Initially, the 3G iPad 2 with 64GB storage sold for $829 in the United States but 6,288 yuan or $990 in China, which allowed arbitrageurs to undercut Apple's price in China while still making a profit. Thus, by selling only through authorized dealers, Apple has not succeeded in preventing arbitrage in China, although Apple's actions may have reduced the extent of the arbitrage.

Managers use a variety of other techniques to successfully prevent gray markets. Managers of perfume firms have called upon governments to enforce their rights under patent, trademark, and copyright laws to prevent arbitrageurs from importing their products. A 2011 ruling in favor of the French cosmetics manufacturer L'Oreal held that European Union trademark law applies to sales on eBay, and that eBay must help identify gray market sellers who do not comply.

One technique that most camera and electronic equipment manufacturers use is to provide a country-specific warranty. A gray market camera purchased in the United States that was imported from Europe comes with a warranty that is good only in Europe and hence less attractive to U.S. customers. Of course, arbitrageurs responded. Today, many stores offer nonmanufacturer warranties on gray market cameras and electronic equipment. The main lesson for managers in firms selling branded products internationally is that investments in preventing or reducing arbitrage are often profitable.

Managing Exchange Rate Risk

Managing risk (Chapter 14) is particularly important for firms doing business in multiple countries because exchange rate movements increase risk, as we now illustrate. Martin, the manager of a small U.S. producer of medical equipment, signs a contract to provide custom equipment to a hospital in India for 60 million Indian rupees (INR), to be paid in 6 months when the equipment is delivered. At the current exchange rate, 50 rupees can be exchanged for one U.S. dollar, so the equipment would cost the Indian firm 1.2 (= 60/50) million if paid today.

Martin is very worried about the risk from a change in the exchange rate. Martin's firm is going to incur $1.1 million in expenses to build and ship the equipment. Thus, at the current exchange rate, his firm stands to make a profit of $100,000. However, if the exchange rate falls to 60 rupees per dollar in 6 months, Martin's firm will receive only $1 (= 60/60) million and suffer a loss of $100,000, which may be enough to bankrupt the firm.

Of course, if the exchange rate moves in the other direction, Martin's firm will earn additional profit. If the rupee appreciates to INR 48 per dollar, Martin's firm will earn $1.25 (= 60/48) million, and make a profit of $150,000. Nonetheless, this exchange rate risk, which may lead to bankruptcy, is unacceptable to Martin.

Martin has a couple of options. First, he could try to insist that payment be made in U.S. dollars so that the Indian firm bears the exchange rate risk.

Second, Martin can *hedge* the risk by purchasing a *forward contract* or a *futures contract*. Such a contract is an agreement to exchange one currency for another in the future at a specified rate. For example, Martin could contract to exchange INR 60 million for $1.2 million in 6 months. Such a contract is called a forward contract if it is a private agreement with another party, such as a bank. The bank would charge a fee for the contract, say $10,000. Effectively, the bank is selling Martin an insurance policy for $10,000.

Futures contracts are similar, except that they are standardized contracts, often called *Forex* contracts, that sell on organized exchanges. The Chicago Mercantile Exchange is the major trading venue for such contracts in the United States.

17.3 International Trade Policies

Although firms and consumers in one country want to trade with people in other countries, governments often prevent free trade between nations. A government may prevent trade so as to protect domestic suppliers from competition by foreign firms. For example, a government may ban trade or set a *quota* that limits the amount of a good that can be imported. Alternatively, a government may tax imports or exports to raise government revenue. Commonly, governments collect an import *tariff* (sometimes called a *duty*), which is a tax on only imported items.

Historically, governments have concentrated on restricting imports rather than limiting or encouraging exports. Consequently, we focus on the effects of a country's trade policies that restrict imports based on prices, government revenue, and total surplus in a competitive, domestic market.

Quotas and Tariffs in Competitive Markets

Quotas and tariffs are usually applied to imports by the government of the importing country. A government chooses one of four import policies:

▶ **Allow free trade:** Foreign firms may sell in the importing country without restrictions.

▶ **Ban all imports:** The government sets a quota of zero on imports.

▶ **Set a tariff:** The government imposes a tariff on imported goods.

▶ **Set a positive quota:** The government limits imports to $\overline{Q}$.

Quotas, including bans, change the supply curve. As we showed in our analysis of taxes in Chapter 2, we can think of a tariff or tax as either shifting the supply curve up or shifting the demand curve down.

To illustrate the effects of these various policies, we examine the U.S. market for crude oil. For simplicity, we assume that transportation costs are zero and that the United States is small enough to be a price taker in world markets. We further assume that the supply curve of oil is horizontal at the *world price p**, which is the market-clearing price in the world market. Given these assumptions, the importing country, the United States, can buy as much crude oil as it wants at p^* per unit.

Free Trade Versus a Ban on Imports.   Preventing imports into the domestic market raises the price. In Figure 17.2, the estimated U.S. domestic supply curve,

FIGURE 17.2 The Loss from Eliminating Free Trade

Because the world supply curve is horizontal at the world price of $93, the total U.S. supply curve of crude oil is S^1 without free trade. The free-trade equilibrium is e_1. With a ban on imports, the equilibrium e_2 occurs where the domestic supply curve, $S^a = S^2$, intersects D. The ban increases producer surplus by $B \approx \$1.09$ billion per day and decreases consumer surplus by $B + C \approx 1.58$ billion per day, so the deadweight loss is $C = \$481$ million per day or $176 billion per year.

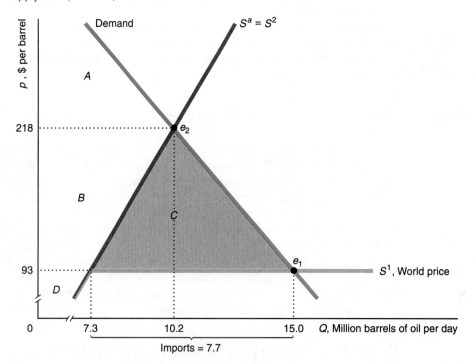

U.S.	Free Trade	U.S. Import Ban	Change ($ billions)
Consumer Surplus, CS	$A + B + C$	A	$-B - C = \Delta CS = -1.58$
Producer Surplus, PS	D	$B + D$	$B = \Delta PS = 1.09$
Total Surplus, $TS = CS + PS$	$A + B + C + D$	$A + B + D$	$-C = \Delta TS = DWL = -0.48$

S^a, is upward sloping, and the foreign supply curve is horizontal at the world price, which averaged \$93 per barrel during the week of April 26, 2013.[7] The total U.S. supply curve, S^1, is the horizontal sum of the domestic supply curve and the foreign supply curve. Thus, S^1 is the same as the upward-sloping domestic supply curve for prices below \$93 and is horizontal at \$93. With free trade, the United States imports crude oil if its domestic price in the absence of imports would exceed the world price.

The free-trade equilibrium, e_1, is determined by the intersection of S^1 and the demand curve, where the U.S. price equals the world price, \$93, and the quantity is 15 million barrels per day. At the equilibrium price, domestic supply is 7.3, so imports are 7.7 ($= 15 - 7.3$). U.S. consumer surplus is $A + B + C$, U.S. producer surplus is D, and the U.S. total surplus is $A + B + C + D$. Throughout our discussion of trade, we ignore welfare effects in other countries.

If imports are banned, the total U.S. supply curve, S^2, is the American domestic supply curve, S^a. The equilibrium is at e_2, where S^2 intersects the demand curve. The new equilibrium price is \$218, and the new equilibrium quantity, 10.2 million barrels per day, is produced domestically. Consumer surplus is A, producer surplus is $B + D$, and total surplus is $A + B + D$.

The ban helps U.S. crude oil producers but harms consumers. Because of the higher price, domestic firms gain producer surplus of $\Delta PS = B \approx \$1.09$ billion per day. The change in consumers' surplus is $\Delta CS = -B - C \approx -\$1.58$ billion per day. Consumers lose \$1.45 ($= 1.58/1.09$) for every \$1 that producers gain from a ban.

Does the ban help the United States? No. The deadweight loss is the change in total surplus, ΔTS: the sum of the gain to producers and the loss to consumers, $\Delta TS = \Delta PS + \Delta CS \approx -\$481$ million per day or $-\$176$ billion per year. This deadweight loss is 44% ($= 0.481/1.09$) of the gain to producers.

Free Trade Versus a Tariff. Two common types of tariffs are *specific tariffs*—τ dollars per unit—and *ad valorem tariffs*—α percent of the sales price. In the modern era, tariffs have been applied throughout the world, most commonly to agricultural products.[8] For most of the post-World War II period, the United States has had a tariff on oil to raise government revenue or to reduce U.S. dependence on foreign oil.

You may be asking yourself, "Why should we study tariffs if we've already looked at taxes (Chapter 2)? Isn't a tariff just another tax?" Good point! Tariffs are just taxes. If the only goods sold were imported, the effect of a tariff in the importing country would be the same as we showed for a sales tax. We study tariffs separately because an import tariff is applied only to imported goods, so it affects domestic and foreign producers differently.

Because tariffs are applied to only imported goods, they do not raise as much tax revenue or affect equilibrium quantities as much as taxes applied to all goods in a market. For example, De Melo and Tarr (1992) calculated that almost five times more tax revenue would be generated by a 15% additional *ad valorem* tax on all petroleum products than by a 25% additional import tariff on oil and gas.

---

[7]We derived these linear demand and supply curves using data for the week of April 26, 2013, and supply and demand elasticity estimates from Baumeister and Peersman (forthcoming).

[8]After World War II, most trading nations signed the General Agreement on Tariffs and Trade (GATT), which limited their ability to subsidize exports or limit imports using quotas and tariffs. The rules prohibited most export subsidies and import quotas, except when imports threatened "market disruption" (a term that was left undefined). Modifications of the GATT and agreements negotiated by its successor, the World Trade Organization, have reduced or eliminated many tariffs.

To illustrate the effect of a tariff, suppose that the government imposes a specific tariff of $\tau = \$40$ per barrel of crude oil. Given this tariff, firms will not import oil into the United States unless the U.S. price is at least $40 above the world price, $93. The tariff creates a wedge between the world price and the U.S. price. This tariff causes the total supply curve to shift from S^1 to S^3 in Figure 17.3. As the world supply

FIGURE 17.3 Effects of a Tariff or a Quota

A tariff of $\tau = \$40$ per barrel of oil imported or a quota of 5.2 million barrels per day drives the U.S. price of crude oil to $133, which is $40 more than the world price. Under the tariff, the equilibrium, e_3, is determined by the intersection of the S_3 total U.S. supply curve and the D demand curve. Under the quota, e_3 is determined by a quantity wedge of 5.2 million barrels per day between the quantity demanded, 13.3 million barrels per day, and the quantity supplied by domestic firms, 8.1 million barrels per day, at a price of $133 per barrel. Compared to free trade, producers gain area B and consumers lose areas $B + C + D + E$ from either a tariff or a quota. If the government gives the quota rights to foreign producers, the deadweight loss is $C + D + E$. With a tariff, the government's tariff revenue increases by D, so the deadweight loss is only $C + E$.

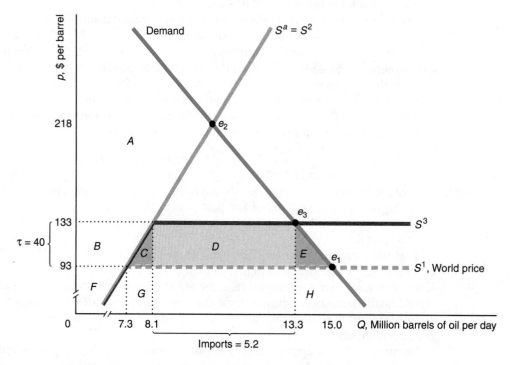

U.S.	Free Trade	U.S. Tariff or Quota	Change ($ millions)
Consumer Surplus, CS	$A + B + C + D + E$	A	$-B - C - D - E = -566$
Producer Surplus, PS	F	$B + F$	$B = 308$
Tariff Revenues, T	0	D (tariff)	$D = 208$ (tariff)
		0 (quota)	0 (quota)
Total Surplus from a Tariff, $TS = CS + PS + T$	$A + B + C + D + E + F$	$A + B + D + F$	$-C - E = DWL = -50$
Total Surplus from a Quota, $TS = CS + PS$	$A + B + C + D + E + F$	$A + B + F$	$-C - D - E = DWL = -258$

curve for oil is horizontal at a price of $93, adding a $40 tariff shifts this supply curve upward so that it is horizontal at $133. That is, the rest of the world will supply an unlimited amount of oil at $133 inclusive of the tariff. As a result, the total U.S. supply curve with the tariff, S^3, equals the domestic supply curve for prices below $133 and is horizontal at $133.

The new equilibrium, e_3, occurs where S^3 intersects the demand curve. At this equilibrium, price is $133 and quantity is 13.3 million barrels of oil per day. At this higher price, domestic firms supply 8.1 million barrels of oil per day, so imports are $5.2 (= 13.3 - 8.1)$ million barrels of oil per day.

The tariff *protects* American producers from foreign competition. The larger the tariff, the less crude oil that is imported, hence the higher the price that domestic firms can charge. (With a large enough tariff, nothing is imported, and the price rises to the no-trade level, $218.) With a tariff of $40, domestic firms' producer surplus increases by area $B \approx \$308$ million per day.

Because of the $40 price increase, consumer surplus falls by $B + C + D + E \approx \$566$ million per day. The government receives tariff revenues, T, equal to area $D \approx \$208$ million per day.

The deadweight loss is $C + E = \$50$ million per day, or $18.3 billion per year.[9] Because the tariff doesn't completely eliminate imports, the loss of total surplus is smaller than it is if all imports are banned.

We can interpret the two components of this deadweight loss. First, C is the loss from domestic firms producing 8.1 million barrels per day instead of 7.3 million barrels per day. Domestic firms produce this extra output because the tariff drives up the price from $93 to $133. The cost of producing this extra 0.8 million barrels of oil per day domestically is $C + G$. Had Americans bought this oil at the world price, the cost would have been only G. Thus, C is the extra cost from producing the additional 0.8 million barrels of oil per day domestically instead of importing it.

Second, E is a *consumption distortion loss* from American consumers buying too little oil, 13.3 instead of 15 million barrels per day, because of the tariff-induced price increase. American consumers value this extra output as $E + H$, the area under their demand curve between 13.3 and 15, whereas the value in international markets is only H. Thus, E is the difference between the value at world prices and the value American consumers place on this extra 1.7 million barrels per day.

Free Trade Versus a Quota. The effect of a positive quota is similar to that of a tariff. If the government limits imports to 5.2 million barrels per day, the quota is binding because 7.7 million barrels per day were imported under free trade (see Figure 17.2). In Figure 17.3, if the price equals $133, the gap between the quantity demanded, 13.3 million barrels per day, and the quantity supplied by domestic firms, 8.1 million barrels per day, is 5.2 million barrels per day. Thus, a quota on imports of 5.2 million barrels per day leads to the same equilibrium, e_3, as a tariff of $40.

With a quota, the gain to domestic producers, B, and the loss to consumers, $C + E$, are the same as with a tariff. The key difference between a tariff and a quota concerns who gets D. With a tariff, the government receives tariff revenue equal to area D. With a quota, the government does not receive any revenue. Instead, if the government gives the rights to sell the quota to foreign producers, they earn an extra arbitrage profit of D because they buy the oil quota, 5.2 million barrels

---

[9]If the foreign supply is horizontal, welfare in the importing country *must* fall. However, if the foreign supply is upward sloping, welfare in the importing country may rise.

per day, at the world price, $93, but sell it for $133. Thus, the deadweight loss is $C + E = \$50$ million per day with a tariff but $C + D + E = \$258$ million per day with a quota.

Therefore, the importing country fares better using a tariff than setting a quota that reduces imports by the same amount if the quota rights are given away to foreigners. However, if the government sells the quota rights to either foreign producers or domestic importers for $40 per barrels, the tariff and the quota have the same effect on government revenue and deadweight loss.

Q&A 17.2

How does a quota set by the United States on foreign sugar imports affect the total American supply curve for sugar given the domestic supply curve, S^d in panel a of the graph, and the foreign supply curve, S^f in panel b?

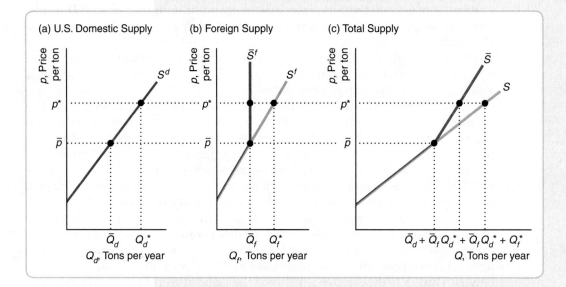

Answer

1. *Determine the U.S. supply curve without the quota.* The *no-quota* total supply curve, S in panel c, is the horizontal sum of the U.S. domestic supply curve, S^d, and the no-quota foreign supply curve, S^f.

2. *Show the effect of the quota on foreign supply.* At prices below $\bar{p}$, foreign suppliers want to supply quantities less than the quota, $\bar{Q}_f$, as panel b shows. As a result, the foreign supply curve under the quota, $\bar{S}^f$, is the same as the no-quota foreign supply curve, S^f, for prices less than $\bar{p}$. At prices above $\bar{p}$, foreign suppliers want to supply more but are limited to $\bar{Q}_f$. Thus, the foreign supply curve with a quota, $\bar{S}^f$, is vertical at $\bar{Q}_f$ for prices above $\bar{p}$.

3. *Determine the U.S. total supply curve with the quota.* The total supply curve with the quota, is the horizontal sum of S^d and $\bar{S}^f$. At any price above the total supply equals the quota plus the domestic supply. For example, at p^*, the domestic supply is Q_d^* and the foreign supply is $\bar{Q}_f$, so the total supply is $Q_d^* + \bar{Q}_f$. Above $\bar{p}$, S is the domestic supply curve shifted $\bar{Q}$ units to the right. As a result, the portion of S above $\bar{p}$ has the same slope as S^d.

4. *Compare the U.S. total supply curves with and without the quota.* At prices less than or equal to $\bar{p}$, the same quantity is supplied with and without the quota, so S is the same as S. At prices above $\bar{p}$, less is supplied with the quota than without one, so S is steeper than S, indicating that a given increase in price raises the quantity supplied by less with a quota than without one.

Mini-Case	When is a van not a van? Give up? The answer is "When there's a chicken tax." Still unclear? Welcome to the Alice-in-Wonderland world of trade wars.
Managerial Responses to the Chicken Tax Trade War	Several times a month, Ford Motor Co. ships brand new, shiny Transit Connect wagons from its factory in Turkey to the United States, where virtually all are delivered to a brick warehouse. There, 65 workers rip out rear windows, rear seats, and rear seatbelts and send the fabric, steel parts, and glass to be recycled.

Why? Because by shipping light trucks with seats, Ford can tell the U.S. Customs that it is importing *wagons*, which primarily transport people, instead of *commercial vans*, which primarily transport goods. The reason Ford cares about the definition is that the import tariff on a van is 25%, but it is only 2.5% on a wagon. Thus, by adding and then removing seats and windows at a cost of hundreds of dollars per van, Ford saves thousands in tariffs.

Ford is legally circumventing a half-century-old tariff that arose during a trade dispute. In the early 1960s, after European countries placed high tariffs on chickens imported from the United States to protect domestic producers, the United States retaliated with an import tax on foreign-made trucks and commercial vans. Ironically, in contrast to Ford's sneaky import strategy, the Japanese-based firms Toyota, Nissan, and Honda avoid the tariff by constructing their vans in the United States. (In 2011, the United States accused China of violating trade rules by imposing chicken tariffs. Stay tuned for more unintended consequences.)

Rent Seeking

Given that tariffs and quotas hurt the importing country, why do the Japanese, U.S., and other governments impose tariffs, quotas, or other trade barriers? One reason is that domestic producers stand to make large gains from such government actions; hence, it pays for them to organize and lobby the government to enact these trade policies. Although consumers as a whole suffer large losses, the loss to any one consumer is usually small. Moreover, consumers rarely organize to lobby the government about trade issues. Thus in most countries, producers are often able to convince (cajole, influence, or bribe) legislators or government officials to aid them, even though consumers suffer more-than-offsetting losses.

If domestic producers can talk the government into a tariff, quota, or other policy that reduces imports, they gain extra producer surplus, such as area B in Figures 17.2 and 17.3. Economists call efforts and expenditures to gain a rent or a profit from government actions **rent seeking**. If producers or other interest groups bribe legislators to influence policy, the bribe is a transfer of income and hence does not directly increase deadweight loss. However, if this rent-seeking behavior—such as hiring lobbyists and engaging in advertising to influence legislators—uses up resources, the deadweight loss from tariffs and quotas understates the true loss to society. The domestic producers may spend an amount up to the gain in producer surplus to influence the government.[10]

Lopez and Pagoulatos (1994) estimated the deadweight loss and the additional losses due to rent-seeking activities in the United States in food and tobacco products. They estimated that the deadweight loss was $17.8 billion (in 2013 dollars), which was 2.6% of the domestic consumption expenditure on these products. The largest deadweight losses were in dairy products and sugar manufacturing, which primarily use import quotas to raise domestic prices. The overall gain in producer surplus was $64.4 billion. In addition, the government gained $2.6 billion in tariff revenues, and these revenues do count in total domestic surplus. Thus, gainers gained $67.0 billion. However, the loss to consumers was $84.8 billion, yielding a deadweight loss of $84.8 − $67.0 = $17.8 billion.

Noncompetitive Reasons for Trade Policy

A government intervenes in international trade for many reasons beyond raising revenues from tariffs or from selling quotas. Often, trade policy is used to create or eliminate market failures that result from noncompetitive markets. First, the government may use trade policy to create market power and capture some of the extra profit. Second, the government may use strategic trade policies to help its domestic industry compete more effectively with foreign firms when selling in a world market. Third, it may use contingent protection policies to prevent predation by foreign firms or to protect domestic firms from foreign competition.

Creating Market Power. A government can exploit monopoly power by using tariffs or quotas, even if the underlying industry is highly competitive. By restricting supply in a competitive market, the government can drive the price to the monopoly level.

The Philippines supplied four-fifths of the world's coconut oil, so it was large enough to affect the world price of coconut oil. However, because its growers, refiners, and exporters operated in competitive markets, the world price was a competitive price. To create market power, the government imposed a tariff or tax on copra (the part of the coconut used to create coconut oil). Doing so not only increased the world price, but it allowed the government to capture the increased profit as tariff revenue. The government could have achieved the same outcome by limiting exports using quotas that it would sell to the highest bidder.

Strategic Trade Policy.[11] A government's trade policy can increase the share of the profits in imperfectly competitive industries that goes to its domestic industry. To illustrate this idea, we consider a vaccine market that is large enough to support one producer but not two—a market with a natural monopoly. Each disease requires a different vaccine, and each vaccine is costly to develop. Many vaccines in a given region are produced and sold by a monopoly supplier (Danzon and Pereira, 2011).

---

[10]Tullock (1967) and Posner (1975) made this argument. Fisher (1985) and Varian (1989) contended that the expenditure is typically less than the producer surplus.

[11]This section uses game theory (Chapter 12); however, the rest of this chapter does not assume knowledge of this material. The following analysis is based on Brander and Spencer (1985) and Krugman (1987).

TABLE 17.3 Drug Entry Game

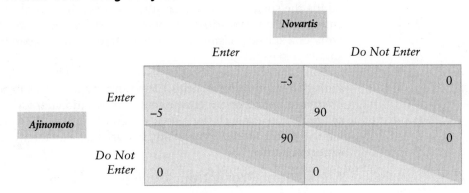

		Novartis	
		Enter	Do Not Enter
Ajinomoto	Enter	−5 / −5	0 / 90
	Do Not Enter	90 / 0	0 / 0

Ajinomoto (a major Japanese vaccine producer) and Novartis (a Swiss producer) choose whether to enter and produce a particular vaccine for the U.S. market. Table 17.3 shows their profits from the resulting entry game (Chapter 12).

If both firms enter, both lose, making a profit of −5. Therefore, if its rival enters, a firm prefers to stay out of the market. If Novartis enters and Ajinomoto does not, then Novartis earns 90 and Ajinomoto earns nothing. If Ajinomoto also enters, its profit is −5, so it regrets entering. Similarly, if Ajinomoto enters, then Novartis prefers not to enter. Neither firm has a dominant strategy. However, using the game theory analysis from Chapter 12, we see that this game has two pure strategy Nash equilibria: Novartis enters while Ajinomoto stays out or Ajinomoto enters and Novartis stays out.[12]

Can a government act to increase the profit of its domestic firm? If only the Japanese government acts by offering a subsidy of 10 to Ajinomoto if it enters, then the profit matrix changes to Table 17.4. This subsidy makes entering a dominant strategy for Ajinomoto. If Novartis enters, Ajinomoto earns 5, which is greater than the zero profit it earns if it does not enter. If Novartis does not enter, Ajinomoto's profit is 100 if it enters and 0 otherwise. Thus, Ajinomoto should enter regardless of what Novartis does. Knowing that Ajinomoto wants to enter, Novartis decides not to enter, because to do so would cause it to lose 5. Thus, the subsidy results in a Nash equilibrium in which Ajinomoto enters and earns 100, and Novartis stays out.

TABLE 17.4 Drug Entry Game with a Subsidy to Ajinomoto of 10

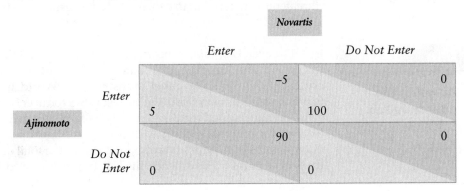

		Novartis	
		Enter	Do Not Enter
Ajinomoto	Enter	−5 / 5	0 / 100
	Do Not Enter	90 / 0	0 / 0

---

[12]The game also has a mixed-strategy equilibrium, in which each firm chooses to enter with a positive probability less than one (Chapter 12).

As a consequence, Japan obtains a net surplus of 90 (= Ajinomoto's profit of 100 minus the subsidy of 10). This surplus is much more than Japan gets if Novartis enters and Ajinomoto does not, or if both firms enter—both of which are possibilities without a subsidy. Using this strategic trade policy, Japan has shifted an uncertain situation in its favor.

Both strategic trade policy tools and the trade policies that create market power are *beggar-thy-neighbor* policies. One country gains at the expense of other countries. Therefore, an important component of international trade agreements is to prevent or limit the use of such trade policies. Consequently, the trade agreements underlying the World Trade Organization specify that signatory countries agree not to use export subsidies.

Contingent Protection. *Contingent protection* is a trade policy that protects domestic producers from certain actions by foreign firms or governments. The World Trade Organization allows member countries to impose contingent protection using antidumping laws and countervailing duty policies.

Many countries have contingent protection laws against *dumping*, which occurs if a foreign producer sells a product at a price that is below the price that it sets in its home country or at a price that is lower than its cost of production. Under its antidumping law, the United States imposes a tariff (or *duty*) on the dumped good.

A common justification for this law is to prevent a foreign firm from engaging in predation (Chapter 16), keeping its U.S. price low until it drives U.S. firms out of the industry and then raising its U.S. price. Such a story is implausible unless something prevents firms from entering the market after the price rises. Apparently the primary use of antidumping laws is to protect domestic industries from lower-price foreign competition and to prevent foreign firms from price discriminating when such discrimination would favor domestic consumers.

Under a *countervailing duty policy*, a government may impose a duty if an imported good is subsidized by a foreign government through direct cash payments, credits against taxes, below-market rate loans, or in other ways. For example, in 2012, the U.S. Department of Commerce imposed both antidumping and countervailing duties on imports of high-pressure steel cylinders from China in response to a complaint by the Norris Cylinder Company of Texas. The antidumping duties ranged across Chinese suppliers from 6.6% to 31.2%. In addition, the countervailing duties, intended to offset government subsidies in China, were set at 15.8% of the import price. These duties resulted from a legal determination that the price of the Chinese firms' cylinders was low due to dumping and subsidies, thereby materially injuring, or threatening material injury to, the U.S. domestic industry.[13]

Mini-Case

Dumping and Countervailing Duties for Solar Panels

In 2011, seven U.S. solar panel makers asked the U.S. Department of Commerce to conduct antidumping and countervailing duties investigations of China's crystalline silicon solar panel industry. SolarWorld Industries America Inc. (a branch of a German firm), the largest U.S. producer of crystalline silicon solar cells and panels, filed the petition on behalf of this group of U.S. manufacturers. SolarWorld contended that the Chinese government provided its industry with massive subsidies, which were about 20 times the total of U.S. solar subsidies in the past year. As a consequence, the U.S. firms contended, Chinese firms flooded

[13]This decision is described on the U.S. Department of Commerce website at **ia.ita.doc.gov/download/factsheets/factsheet-prc-hpsc-adcvd-final-20120501.pdf**.

the U.S. market with silicon products that sold at low prices, which drove U.S. firms out of business. According to Gordon Brinser, president of the U.S. Solar-World branch, "Our domestic industry is under siege. Let's be clear, China has a plan for our market: to gut it and own it."

These U.S. firms were concerned because Chinese exports of crystalline silicon solar cells and panels to the United States increased by more than 350% from 2008 to 2010, while worldwide panel prices tumbled 40% during that period. Seven U.S. manufacturers shut down or downsized from 2010 to mid-2011.

Not all U.S. firms supported this request. "Growth is a result of declining prices," said Arno Harris, CEO of Recurrent Energy. "We're not going to shift a bunch of jobs to the U.S. by putting in tariffs. All we're going to do is shrink the market and slow the growth." He went on to say that "One manufacturer who can't compete with today's solar panel prices is basically looking to put in place trade barriers to make the U.S. a safe market for their own more expensive solar panels." Indeed, although the firms represented in the SolarWorld suit lost money and many had to close, other solar firms did well enough that the U.S. solar industry was a net exporter to China in 2010. Harris concluded that "It's not in any way in the interest of American consumers . . . and it's certainly not in the interest of slowing global climate change."

In 2012, the U.S. International Trade Commission (ITC) ruled that Chinese solar manufacturers had received illegal subsidies from its government and sold products in the United States at prices 18.32% to 249.96% below the fair market value. The ITC imposed tariffs that ranged from 24% to 255% on Chinese solar modules. However, the tariffs apply only to solar modules and panels made with Chinese-origin cells, so Chinese companies can avoid the tariffs by assembling the modules in China using cells from other countries.

Trade Liberalization and the World Trading System

The World Trade Organization (WTO), an organization of most of the world's trading nations, coordinates international trade and limits trade policies that create distortions, such as tariffs and quotas used to create market power. The WTO was created by several international agreements. The most important of these agreements is the General Agreement on Tariffs and Trade (GATT). The GATT was originally drafted and signed in 1947, partly in reaction to the costly trade wars of the 1930s and partly to reestablish commercial relations among the nations that were disrupted during World War II. The WTO was established in 1995, although it was, in essence, a formalization of the administrative structure that had developed around the GATT.

The most important aspect of the GATT and the WTO has been to promote trade liberalization, which allows firms and consumers to benefit from trade. The WTO imposes various requirements on member countries that facilitate international trade, including limits on tariffs and quotas. Over time, countries gradually accepted the WTO free-trade principles. Only 23 nations signed the first GATT agreement in 1947. At present, over 150 countries are members of the WTO and signatories to the GATT. These countries are responsible for almost all of the world's trade. Most of the other countries in the world have *observer* status in the WTO and hope to become full members.

Reducing trade barriers, particularly tariffs and quotas, has been the most significant achievement of the GATT and the WTO. When the GATT was first created, many countries had prohibitive trade barriers, which prevented any trade with a wide range of potential trading partners. The immediate contribution of the GATT during its early years was to enable any trade at all between many countries. However, even as late as the 1980s, tariffs, quotas, and other trade barriers were still significant impediments to trade. Since then, trade barriers have continued to fall. From 1986 through 2009 the world average tariff rate fell from 26.3% to 8.6%. In high-income countries, the average tariff fell from about 10% to under 3%.[14]

Countries that belong to the WTO are allowed to establish *preferential trading arrangements* between groups of WTO member countries, including free trade agreements that eliminate tariffs and quotas altogether. The United States participates in the North American Free Trade Agreement (NAFTA) with Canada and Mexico, and the Dominican Republic-Central America-United States Free Trade Agreement (CAFTA-DR) with Costa Rica, El Salvador, Guatemala, Honduras, Nicaragua, and Dominican Republic. In addition, the United States has bilateral free trade agreements with Australia, Bahrain, Chile, Colombia, Israel, Jordan, Morocco, Oman, Panama, Peru, Singapore, and South Korea.

Not surprisingly, trade liberalization has increased the amount of international trade. However, perhaps less obviously, trade liberalization has made it easier for firms to use inputs from many different countries to produce their final products. General Motors, Westinghouse, Sony, and other companies can manufacture parts in one country and assemble them in another because tariffs and other trade barriers are low or nonexistent. High tariffs would make such supply chain arrangements much less attractive. Thus, a major effect of trade liberalization has been to increase the globalization of supply chains. Many efforts have been made to assess the costs and benefits of trade liberalization. Virtually all such studies find that these trading nations gain significantly from liberalization (Feenstra, 2010). Trade liberalization has been a major driving force behind the recent dramatic improvements in the standard of living in China, India, and other developing countries.

Trade Liberalization Problems

Critics of freer trade raise concerns about a variety of negative effects, particularly relating to environmental standards and to wages and labor standards. Freer trade might exacerbate environmental problems caused by environmental externalities or open-access common property (Chapter 16). Because most developing countries have weaker environmental laws than do the United States and other high-income countries, critics predict that freer trade will cause these developing countries to become *pollution havens*: Firms based in developed countries will move their manufacturing to these developing countries, save money due to avoiding the cost of environmental regulation, and then export their products to their home countries. Such issues were important when Mexico joined Canada and the United States in the North American Free Trade Agreement (NAFTA) in 1994, which removed tariffs on goods traded by these countries. Many U.S. companies moved operations across the Mexican border, including major auto producers such as Ford and General Motors and major producers of electrical equipment such as Honeywell and General Electric.[15]

---

[14]These tariffs are unweighted averages (**go.worldbank.org/LGOXFTV550**).

[15]Proponents of NAFTA noted that it incorporated specific agreements on environmental regulation that were intended to improve environmental policy in Mexico. They also argued that because NAFTA would raise incomes in Mexico, Mexico would be more likely to institute greater environmental protections.

Analysis of the Mexican experience following its entry into NAFTA indicates neither a notable increase in environmental problems, nor a notable decrease (Gallagher, 2004; Lipford and Yandle, 2011). Some areas close to the U.S. border experienced an increase in pollution problems, but improvements occurred in other areas.

Critics of freer trade similarly argue that U.S. firms might move operations to developing countries with low wages and weak labor standards. However, these cases differ in a critical manner. The pollution haven problem is based on market failure, and liberalizing trade and investment can make this market failure worse—reducing total surplus in the global economy. Low wages do not, in themselves, imply a market failure. Freer trade should be faulted only if it results in lower wages or labor standards in developing nations. So far, little evidence exists showing such a negative effect (Salem and Rozental, 2012).

17.4 Multinational Enterprises

The managers of companies that produce in many countries must decide how much to trade and what prices to use when trading internationally between their units. These decisions turn critically on differences in tax laws across countries.

Most of the world's largest companies are *multinational enterprises* (MNEs): enterprises that control productive assets in more than one country.[16] The largest 500 multinational enterprises account for nearly 70% of world trade.[17]

Multinationals normally have a parent company and a number of foreign affiliates. According to the definitions used by international agencies including the United Nation Conference on Trade and Development (UNCTAD) and the International Monetary Fund (IMF), any company in which the parent has an ownership share of 10% or more is regarded as an *affiliate*. An affiliate in which the parent has an ownership share of 50% or more is called a *subsidiary*. Many subsidiaries are wholly owned by the parent.

Toyota is one of the world's largest MNEs. The parent Toyota Motor Corporation is based in Japan and has subsidiaries throughout the world, including in the United States. Typically, a multinational enterprise is not a single corporation. Rather, the parent company is a corporation and each subsidiary is itself a corporation, with its own CEO and senior managers. The only shareholder of a wholly owned subsidiary is the parent corporation. Thus, a multinational enterprise, such as Toyota, is an interlocking network of corporations connected through ownership.

The management of each subsidiary normally has discretion over business decisions such as how much to produce, what prices to charge, and how much and where to advertise. Each subsidiary is normally treated as an independent profit center: The managers of each subsidiary seek to maximize the profits of their subsidiary and do not consider the profits of other subsidiaries. However, the parent corporation may intervene in business decisions of subsidiaries to achieve better performance for its bottom line, even if that imposes costs on particular subsidiaries.

Very few firms start as multinational enterprises. A start-up firm typically initially focuses only on its domestic market. After it is well established, it may export its

[16]MNEs are sometimes called transnational corporations (TNCs) or multinational corporations (MNCs).

[17]www.gatt.org/trastat_e.html (viewed November 12, 2012).

products. After its exports become numerous enough, the firm may decide that it is more cost-effective to produce its good or services in another country, and it becomes a multinational enterprise.

Becoming a Multinational

A firm becomes a multinational through foreign direct investment (FDI). The two types of FDI are *greenfield investments* and the purchase of foreign assets.

A *greenfield investment* creates a new production facility in a foreign country, such as in an undeveloped, green field. For example, Brazil-based Vale S.A., one of the world's largest mining companies, opened a new iron-ore mine in Oman in 2011.[18] The mine was initially developed in the form of a wholly owned subsidiary, Oman Vale, which was a legally distinct company that was fully owned by the parent Vale S.A.

The other type of FDI is the acquisition of existing productive assets such as a plant or a firm. When a foreign firm acquires 10% or more of a domestic company's voting stock, the purchase is categorized as a direct investment, and is sufficient to classify the parent company as a multinational in official statistics. For example, Vale purchased Inco, a large Canadian mining company, in 2006. Inco became a wholly owned subsidiary of Vale and was ultimately renamed Vale Canada Limited.

Traditionally, a major motive for a firm to acquire or build foreign productive assets is to lower its cost of supplying that foreign market by producing in that market rather than exporting to it. Toyota originally built plants in the United States to produce for the American market largely because it was less expensive than shipping cars from Japan. Producing locally allows the company to reduce transport costs and avoid tariffs or quotas on imported goods.

However, as tariffs and transportation costs have fallen in recent years, and international communication has become easier, a second motive has become relatively more important: comparative advantage in the supply chain. Increasingly, multinationals have found it efficient to produce various components or other inputs to production around the world, selecting the best location for each component.

Mini-Case	
What's an American Car?	U.S. car manufacturers and labor unions regularly lobby the U.S. government for trade policies that favor their cars over imports. However, one might ask which firms are the true all-American manufacturers.

U.S. car manufacturers and labor unions regularly lobby the U.S. government for trade policies that favor their cars over imports. However, one might ask which firms are the true all-American manufacturers.

Annually, **cars.com** posts its American-Made Index, which rates vehicles by how American they are in terms of the source of the car's parts and whether the car is assembled in the United States. To be included in the index, the car must be assembled in the United States using more than 75% domestic parts.

In 2012, the most-American car was the Toyota Camry, which is assembled in Georgetown, Kentucky, and Lafayette, Indiana. It is followed by the Ford F-150 and the Honda Accord. Toyota and Honda manufactured four out of the top five and half of the top ten cars and trucks, even though both of these multinational corporations are based in Japan. General Motors, which is based

---

[18]S.A. is a particular type of corporation in some countries. The terms that correspond to this abbreviation vary across languages but usually mean anonymous company, anonymous partnership, or share company.

in the United States, had three on the list, while the other major U.S. producers, Ford and Chrysler, had only one each. Of the 113 best-selling vehicles in the United States—which accounted for 89% of all the cars sold—more than 80% had less than 75% of their parts produced domestically or were assembled abroad.

For all manufacturers, the share of U.S. parts in their vehicles varies annually in response to changes in relative prices, disruption of supply lines due to natural disasters (such as in Japan after the major 2011 earthquake and tsunami), and other factors. The U.S. content of the Ford F-100 was 60% in 2011, but 75% in 2012. The redesigned 2012 Ford Focus, which is supposed to be a poster car for Ford's global One Ford strategy, had only 40% domestic parts. Moreover, many of the main U.S. models, such as Chrysler's minivans, the Ford Fusion, and the Chevy Camaro, are assembled in Canada or Mexico, in large part due to the North American Free Trade Agreement, which eliminates tariffs when the assembled vehicles are shipped to the United States.

International Transfer Pricing

An MNE can gain many tax and other advantages by having its subsidiary in one country sell its goods or services to a subsidiary in another country. Typically, a MNE lets its subsidiaries make most decisions independently. However, the parent firm may lose profit if it lets one subsidiary set a very high **transfer price**: the price used for an intra-firm transfer of goods or services.

Toyota provides an example of such intra-firm transfers. Toyota Motor Engineering & Manufacturing North America (TEMA), a subsidiary of the parent firm, Toyota Motor Corporation, produces most Toyota motor vehicles sold in the United States. The cars are marketed and sold primarily by Toyota Motor Sales, U.S.A., Inc. (TMS), another subsidiary of the parent Toyota Motor Corporation. TEMA sells cars to TMS, which in turn sells and distributes them to Toyota dealerships. The price at which TEMA sells cars to TMS is a domestic transfer price.

Toyota subsidiaries also engage in international transfer pricing. For example, Toyota Motor Manufacturing Canada Inc. (TMMC) is another Toyota subsidiary, based in Canada, which sells vehicles to TMS for sales in the United States using an international transfer price.

We illustrate the key issues in international transfer pricing by examining how TMMC sets its transfer price to TMS for a Toyota Rav4 electric crossover SUV, which was jointly developed with Tesla Motors and is produced by only TMMC as of 2012.[19] For simplicity, we assume that the electric RAV4 is essentially a monopoly product (the only such vehicle in its class).

Profit-Maximizing Transfer Pricing. How should TMMC set its transfer price? We consider two possibilities. First, we ask how TMS would set its monopoly price if it were a vertically integrated firm (Chapter 7) that both manufactured and sold cars. Second, we examine how TMS would price the car if TMMC sets a monopoly transfer price to TMS, which then sets a monopoly price to final consumers.

---

[19]However, the drive train for the electric RAV4 will be built in a Tesla plant in California: **wheels.blogs .nytimes.com/2011/08/05/tesla-powered-toyota-rav4-e-v-to-be-built-in-canada-not-california**.

If TMS were vertically integrated—if it produced the RAV4 instead of obtaining it from TMMC—it would apply a monopoly markup M based on the demand curve of its U.S. customers to its marginal cost of producing a car, m, to obtain its profit-maximizing monopoly price, $p_1 = M \times m$.[20] We know that the markup M exceeds 1 because a profit-maximizing monopoly sets its price above its marginal cost.

However, the two subsidiaries are not vertically integrated. They act independently. Because TMMC is the monopoly supplier of the electric RAV4 to TMS, TMMC maximizes its profit by setting a monopoly transfer price for the cars it manufactures and sells to TMS. TMMC applies a markup of M^* to its marginal cost, m, setting its transfer price to TMS at $p^* = M^* \times m$. TMS views this transfer price, p^*, as its marginal cost (rather than m). TMS applies its markup, M, to its marginal cost p^* to determine the final price to consumers: $p_2 = M \times p^* = M \times M^* \times m$. Thus, the final price reflects a double markup, $M \times M^*$, instead of the single markup, M, if the companies were vertically integrated. Because both markups are larger than one, the double markup price, p_2, is greater than the price of the vertically integrated company with a single markup, p_1. As a result, TMS sells fewer cars at a higher price than if it were a vertically integrated firm. Because p_1 is the profit-maximizing monopoly price, charging a higher-than-monopoly price reduces the parent company's total profit.

For this reason, the parent company would not want TMMC to set a monopoly transfer price. The transfer price that maximizes combined profits of TMMC and TMS equals TMMC's marginal cost of production. This price maximizes combined returns to the two subsidiaries.

However, Toyota might have a tax-based incentive to use a different transfer price—one that does not equal marginal cost. Using an alternative transfer price can help Toyota avoid taxes.[21]

Q&A 17.3

Reebok Vietnam (RV) is a subsidiary of the German multinational corporation Adidas. RV makes shoes in Vietnam and sells some of these shoes to Adidas Japan (AJ), another Adidas subsidiary, at the transfer price p^*. AJ sells the shoes to Japanese consumers. For simplicity, we assume AJ has a monopoly in Japan. Suppose that the inverse demand function in Japan for Reebok shoes is $p = 100 - Q$, where Q is measured in tens of thousands of pairs per month and p is the price per pair of shoes. RV's cost of production is $C^R = 20Q$, so its marginal cost of producing shoes is $20 per pair in Vietnam. If the parent Adidas Corporation directs RV and AJ to maximize their combined profit, what are the price, quantity, and resulting profit? What happens if, instead, RV sets its transfer price at $p^* = 60$?

---

[20]Equation 9.5 shows that the monopoly's marginal revenue is $MR = p(1 + 1/\varepsilon)$, where ε is the elasticity of demand. Thus, as Equation 9.8 shows, the monopoly sets $MR = p(1 + 1/\varepsilon) = m$. Therefore, its profit-maximizing monopoly price is $p = m/(1 + 1/\varepsilon)$. That is, its markup is $M = 1/(1 + 1/\varepsilon)$. For simplicity in this section, we assume that ε is constant, so that M is a constant. It does not change even if a change in m causes the firm to move to a different point on its demand curve. If ε is not constant (such as with a linear demand curve), M varies as m varies. We use a linear demand curve Q&A 17.3.

[21]Toyota might also want to make sure that TMMC does not incur a loss, which occurs if TMMC incurs fixed costs such that a transfer price equal to marginal cost does not cover its total costs. Car production has high fixed costs (plant, equipment, and managerial staff).

Answer

1. *Determine the profit-maximizing quantity and price for shoes if RV and AJ act like a single profit-maximizing firm, and calculate the profit.* Because the demand curve is linear, the marginal revenue curve has the same intercept and twice the slope of the inverse demand curve: $MR = 100 - 2Q$. To maximize its profit, Adidas operates where its marginal cost, 20, equals its MR:

$$MR = 100 - 2Q = 20 = MC.$$

By solving this equation for Q, we find that the firm's optimal $Q = 40$. Substituting that quantity into the inverse demand function, we learn that Adidas sets a price in Japan of $p = 100 - 40 = 60$. Its profit, π, is the difference between its revenue and cost: $\pi = R - C = (60 \times 40) - (20 \times 40) = 1,600$.

2. *Determine AJ's profit-maximizing quantity and price for shoes and the profits of RV and AJ if RV sets a transfer price of $p^* = 60$.* The transfer price is AJ's new marginal cost. It operates where its marginal revenue equals its marginal cost: $MR = 100 - 2Q = 60$. Thus, the quantity that maximizes AJ's profit is $Q = 20$. Substituting that quantity into the inverse demand function, we find that AJ's price is $p = 80$. AJ's profit is $\pi^J = R^J - C^J = pQ - (p^* \times Q) = (p - p^*)Q = (80 - 60) \times 20 = 400$. RV's profit is $\pi^R = R^R - C^R = (p^* \times Q) - 20Q = (60 \times 20) - (20 \times 20) = 800$. The sum of the profits of AJ and RV is $400 + 800 = 1,200$. This sum is considerably less than the profit of 1,600 that they earn if they act like a single firm.

Comment: The transfer price $p^* = 60$ maximizes RV's profit given that the subsidiaries act independently.[22]

Tax Avoidance. If corporate tax rates differ across countries, Toyota prefers to earn most of its profit in the low-tax country. The transfer price determines the allocation of profits between TMMC and TMS. As the price increases from marginal cost toward the monopoly price, TMMC's profit rises and TMS's profit falls.

If the Canadian corporate income tax, which is paid by TMMC, is 20%, while the U.S. corporate tax rate, which is paid by TMS, is 30%, then Toyota prefers to earn its profits in Canada rather than in the United States.[23] Accordingly, the Toyota parent prefers a relatively high transfer price.

---

[22]Because AJ views the transfer price p^* as its marginal cost, it sets its marginal revenue equal to p^*: $MR = 100 - 2Q = p^*$ or $Q = 50 - 0.5p^*$. That is, for any transfer price p^*, AJ will purchase $Q = 50 - 0.5p^*$ from RV. This relationship is the demand function facing RV. It is referred to as a *derived demand* because it is derived from the downstream consumer demand for shoes. RV's corresponding marginal revenue function is $MR = 100 - 4Q$, which it equates to its marginal cost of 20: $100 - 4Q = 20$. Thus, it maximizes its profit when $Q = 20$. Substituting this quantity into RV's derived demand function, we know that $20 = 50 - 0.5p^*$, so $p^* = (50 - 20)/0.5 = 60$. Thus, RV's profit-maximizing transfer price is $p^* = 60$.

[23]Corporate tax rates in the United States vary from state to state. The actual amount paid depends on a host of special deductions and other tax code provisions. Consequently, U.S. firms often locate offices in low-tax states to avoid domestic taxes. For example, although Apple's corporate headquarters are in California, it set up a small office in Nevada to collect and invest its profits because California's corporate tax is 8.84% and Nevada's is zero.

Suppose that TMMC initially produces a vehicle at a marginal cost of $30,000 and transfers that vehicle to TMS at a transfer price of $30,000, so that TMMC earns no profit in Canada. TMS resells the vehicle to an independent locally owned American dealership at a (wholesale) price of $32,000, so that its before-tax profit margin on this car is $2,000. Given that the U.S. corporate tax rate is 30%, TMS pays 30% of its profit on the vehicle—$600 to the U.S. tax authorities—yielding an after-tax profit of $1,400 (= $2,000 − $600), which goes to the parent, Toyota.

Now suppose that the transfer price on the vehicle is raised to $32,000. TMMC earns a before-tax profit of $2,000, on which it pays taxes of $400 at the Canadian rate of 20% per vehicle, yielding a net profit of $1,600. TMS earns no profit and therefore pays no U.S. corporate income tax on this vehicle. Toyota now earns an after-tax profit of $1,600 on this vehicle instead of the $1,400 it earned with the lower transfer price in place.

Thus, the higher transfer price has the effect of shifting profit from the U.S. to the Canadian subsidiary, where the profit is taxed at a lower rate. As the parent Toyota Motor Corporation is the owner of both TMMC and TSM, it benefits from this increased transfer price, other things equal.

But other things are not equal. A trade-off exists between the tax advantage of high transfer prices and the inefficiency of having a transfer price above marginal cost. The after-tax profit per vehicle transferred rises with the higher transfer price, but TMS imports fewer vehicles. If the marginal benefit of raising the transfer price from avoiding taxes exceeds the marginal cost from a non-optimal price signal to a subsidiary, the firm should raise the transfer price. The profit-maximizing transfer price would be where the marginal cost and marginal benefit of increases in the transfer price were just equal.

An MNE might be able to avoid this distortion. For example, it could use a marginal cost transfer price as the *real* price between the subsidiaries, but tell the tax authorities that the price was higher so as to reduce its tax liability. However, such a practice is not legal.

Tax authorities pay careful attention to transfer pricing to restrain the ability of companies to reduce tax liabilities. Specific rules vary from country to country, but the general rule is that transfer prices must reflect normal pricing practices that apply in the absence of tax incentives. Presumably because of an inability to determine a single "correct" transfer price, tax authorities set a reasonable range. Within that range, companies have some ability to use transfer price variations to reduce taxes. Such a practice is called *tax avoidance:* a legal way of reducing taxes. Illegal methods of reducing tax payments, such as keeping fraudulent financial records, are called *tax evasion.*

Mini-Case

Profit Repatriation

A U.S. parent firm that uses transfer pricing to avoid paying taxes in the United States may face a serious problem that much of its profit is overseas. If it brings the money back to the United States, it would normally have to pay taxes on this transfer as the United States, unlike most other countries, taxes its multinational corporations on their repatriated foreign earnings (earnings brought back to the United States). U.S. companies can avoid these taxes as long as the profits remain overseas.

Sophisticated managers use transfer pricing (and other accounting maneuvers) to shift profits to low-tax countries and then invest these profits offshore.

JPMorgan Chase estimated that 519 U.S. MNEs held $1.375 trillion outside the United States in 2011. Tech companies in particular keep massive profits abroad. As of late 2012 Microsoft had $54 billion (86%), and Cisco Systems had $42.5 billion (87%). A 2013 U.S. Senate subcommittee hearing revealed that Apple held $102 billion overseas to avoid paying taxes.

Large U.S. corporations have been intensively lobbying for a repatriation holiday, where the federal income tax owed on returned profits would fall from the usual 35% to 5.25% for one year. These firms argue that the tax break would stimulate the economy by inducing multinational corporations to inject $1 trillion or more into the economy, creating hundreds of thousands of jobs.

Many doubt this claim because the same repatriation tax incentive, the American Jobs Creation Act of 2004, did not result in significant domestic investment. In 2005, 800 firms repatriated $312 billion back to the United States, paid $16 billion in taxes, but returned 92% of the repatriated money to shareholders in dividends and stock buybacks rather than use this money to expand domestic operations. Indeed, 15 of the largest MNEs repatriated 60% of the returning money, and many of these firms laid off domestic workers, closed plants, and shifted even more of their profits and resources abroad, presumably waiting to cash in again on the next repatriation holiday. Merck, the pharmaceutical giant, retrieved $15.9 billion in profits but cut its workforce and reduced capital spending in the United States over the next three years. Similarly, Hewlett-Packard repatriated $14.5 billion, and then announced that it was eliminating 14,000 domestic jobs.

17.5 Outsourcing

Probably no international trade issue has been more controversial than *international outsourcing*, where a firm buys goods and services from foreign suppliers that the firm would otherwise provide internally. In extreme cases, a manager who outsources abroad to reduce costs may face a boycott by consumers, which can hurt the firm's bottom line.

Less controversial and more common is domestic outsourcing. For example, a restaurant may outsource its cleaning needs to a company that provides janitorial services rather than hire its own cleaning staff. No firm produces all its own inputs and provides all the necessary services to sell its product. All firms outsource to some degree.

International outsourcing used to be rare. However, trade liberalization under the World Trade Organization and other international agreements has made it much easier for firms to outsource internationally. Manufacturing firms import inputs rather than producing them in their home countries, and call centers in India and other nations provide phone support service for many U.S. firms.

Multinational enterprises often engage in foreign outsourcing by shifting production of a needed input from a subsidiary in one country to another country. For example, Toyota's wholly owned U.S. production subsidiary imports some parts from Toyota affiliates in China rather than produce them domestically. However, a firm does not need to be a multinational enterprise to engage in foreign outsourcing.

Some firms with purely domestic production operations import inputs that they previously produced themselves.

When a firm starts outsourcing abroad, it lays off domestic workers who produced a needed input and imports that input from another country instead, where new workers are hired. Many U.S. groups are incensed by this outsourcing of U.S. jobs, particularly workers in the service sector. By some reports, U.S. financial services firms save $2 billion per year by outsourcing to India, giving this sector a strong incentive to outsource.

The U.S. government does not systematically report the number of jobs outsourced overseas. It is widely believed that most international outsourcing is by information technology firms. Deloitte's 2012 survey of large corporations reported that 76% of information technology firms outsourced, but that only 11% of firms in sales or marketing support did.[24] Of the information technology firms, 51% were outsourcing offshore.

According to former WTO director Supachai Panitchpakdi, new jobs more than offset the jobs lost to international outsourcing. By one estimate (see Mankiw and Swagel, 2006), every dollar of outsourcing results in an increase of U.S. income of $1.12 to $1.14. Ultimately, outsourcing is a consequence of comparative advantage—particular tasks get shifted to locations where they have the lowest opportunity cost.

While the debate rages in the United States about jobs moving to India and other foreign countries, Europeans are protesting that high-paying R&D jobs are being outsourced to the United States from Europe. Indeed, *insourcing*, where foreign companies buy U.S. services—particularly legal services—has grown increasingly common.

Most economics textbooks dealing with international trade emphasize that trade, including outsourcing, leads to more efficient market outcomes due to comparative advantage. Does it follow that people who attack free trade and outsourcing are simply ignorant or venal? No. Once a nation starts trading, it reduces the production of some goods and services so that it can concentrate on those in which it has a comparative advantage. As a consequence, some people gain and some people lose from free trade. Firms in noncompetitive sectors may lose sunk capital. Their workers may suffer from at least temporary unemployment. The gains in the other sectors are large enough to compensate the losers. However, if society fails to compensate them, they will be adamantly (and reasonably) opposed to free trade.

As the *Doonesbury* cartoon illustrates, we can see the gains from trade in services by imagining that domestic workers rather than firms outsource. Suppose that you are hired to design a Web page for $25 an hour. You know that Ivan, a very competent, reliable Russian worker, can do the job as well as you can, and he is willing to work for $10 an hour. You can subcontract with Ivan, pocket $15 an hour, and, with your free time, take on an additional job or enjoy your extra leisure. Clearly, you would favor this plan. However, if your firm fired you and outsourced your job to Ivan, you would be outraged over your loss. This example illustrates that much of the debate on outsourcing jobs concerns who reaps the benefits and who suffers the losses rather than whether or not society has a net gain. As with any desirable trade, the winners can in principle compensate the losers so that everyone benefits, although such compensation often does not take place.

[24]See www.deloitte.com/assets/Dcom-UnitedStates/Local%20Assets/Documents/IMOs/Shared%20Services/us_sdt_2012GlobalOutsourcingandInsourcingSurveyExecutiveSummary_050112.pdf.

Doonesbury © 2003 G. B. Trudeau. Reprinted with permission of Universal Uclick. All rights reserved.

Rather than giving up the benefits of free trade, both domestic proponents and opponents of free trade are now calling for more compensation for the losers. The U.S. Trade Adjustment Assistance program provides up to $220 million to train workers who lost their jobs due to foreign competition for new jobs. However, the United States spends only 0.5% of its gross domestic product to assist displaced workers, compared to 0.9% in the United Kingdom, 3.1% in Germany, and 3.7% in Denmark (Farrell, 2006).

Managerial Solution

Responding to Exchange Rates

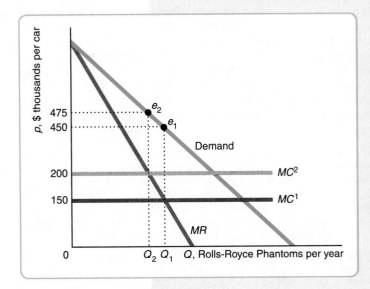

How does the price of wheat or a Rolls-Royce change in response to a change in exchange rates? Does the change depend on the competitiveness of the market?

Earlier in the chapter, we discussed why arbitrage causes a price to react completely to exchange rate changes. Wheat is a nearly perfectly competitive market. Japan receives 15% of U.S. exports. If the U.S. supply curve of wheat is horizontal at a dollar price of p in the United States and the exchange rate is 75 yen per dollar, then arbitrage forces the yen price in Japan to be $75p$. If the exchange rate goes to 80 yen to the dollar, the U.S. price remains constant and the Japanese price shifts in proportion to $80p$. Consequently, the yen-denominated price and the dollar-denominated price are equivalent.

It is not much of a stretch to think of Rolls-Royce as a monopoly. Obviously no one "needs" a Rolls-Royce, but it is perhaps the world's best-known luxury product and is a must for people who want "the best of everything."

New vehicles are sold in Britain and the United States at only a handful of authorized dealers. Given the desire for warranty protection among customers and the high cost of shipping a Rolls across the Atlantic Ocean, the company does not worry excessively about resale or international arbitrage. As a consequence, the U.S. and the U.K. prices may differ.

The figure shows the U.S. demand curve for a Phantom Coupé. Rolls-Royce acts like a monopoly, equating its marginal revenue, MR, to its marginal cost, $MC^1 = \$150$ thousand, to determine its profit-maximizing quantity, Q_1. At that quantity, the dollar-denominated price is $\$450$ thousand.[25] This price is equivalent to £300 thousand at an exchange rate of 1.5 dollars to a pound. This U.S. price is less than the British price, which was £332 thousand in 2012.

Now suppose that the dollar becomes less valuable relative to the pound so that the exchange rate changes to 2 dollars to a pound. The change in the exchange rate causes the U.S. marginal cost to rise by a third ($= [2 - 1.5]/1.5$) to $MC^2 = \$200$ thousand. In the figure, this increase in the marginal cost causes the profit-maximizing U.S. price to rise to $\$475$ thousand, or £237.5 thousand.[26] Thus, when the exchange rate increases by a third, the dollar-denominated price increases by only 5.6% ($\approx [475 - 450]/450$) and the pound-denominated price falls by 20.8% ($\approx [237.5 - 300]/300$).

In the competitive wheat example and in the Rolls-Royce example, the price in the exporting country remains constant in response to a change in the exchange rate. In the wheat market, the foreign (Japanese) price adjusted fully to a change in the exchange rate. In contrast, in the noncompetitive Rolls-Royce example, the foreign, U.S. price only partially adjusted to a change in the exchange rate. Indeed, if the Rolls were manufactured in the United States as well as in Britain (as is the case for a Rolls-Royce jet engine), then the exchange rate change would have no effect on the U.S. price.

SUMMARY

1. **Reasons for International Trade.** One key reason for international trade is comparative advantage. If producers in Country A can produce relatively more of Good 1 than Good 2 from a given amount of input, while producers in Country B are relatively better at producing Good 2, both countries can benefit from trading. A second important reason for trade is increasing returns to scale. Rather than producing everything at a small scale in a single country, producers can take advantage of increasing returns to scale by producing a large quantity of some good in one country and exporting much of the output to other countries. Increasing returns to scale are particularly important in industries where product variety is important. Allowing each country to produce and export a few varieties while its consumers enjoy a wide range of variety based on production in many countries underlies much of the trade we see.

2. **Exchange Rates.** An exchange rate is the price of one currency, such as the euro, in terms of another currency, such as the dollar. An increase in an

---

[25]This figure is based on the assumption that the U.S. inverse demand function (in thousands of dollars) is $p = 750 - Q$. Thus, the marginal revenue function is $MR = 750 - 2Q$. Given that the marginal cost is $MC = 150$, then profit is maximized where $MR = 750 - 2Q = 150 = MC$, or $Q = 300$. Substituting this quantity into the inverse demand function, we find that the price is $p = \$450$ thousand. At the exchange rate $R_1 = 1.5$, the price in pounds is $p^* = $ £300 thousand.

[26]Continuing our example from the last footnote, if the exchange rate increases to 2 dollars to the pound, the dollar-denominated marginal cost increases to $MC = 200$. Thus, the profit-maximizing solution is determined by $MR = 750 - 2Q = 200 = MC$, so $Q = 275$ and $p = \$475$ thousand.

exchange rate can cause large changes in which goods and services are traded and at what prices. After an exchange rate changes, arbitrage causes the prices across countries for a given good to move closer together. The possibility of exchange rate fluctuations creates additional risk for firms engaged in international trade and investment. Such risks can be reduced by using forward or futures contracts.

3. **International Trade Policies.** Governments intervene in the movement of goods across borders. The most important types of intervention are tariffs—taxes on imports (or, rarely, on exports), and quotas, which limit the quantity of a good that can be imported (or exported). Tariffs produce government revenue, as do quotas if the government sells them to importers or exporters. Governments sometimes intervene to create market power for domestic exporters or to help domestic firms compete with foreign firms in world markets. Trade policy is also often used to protect domestic firms from certain contingencies, such as dumping (selling at unreasonably low prices) by foreign firms.

4. **Multinational Enterprises.** Multinational enterprises are firms that own production facilities in more than one country. Such enterprises are responsible for the majority of the world's international trade and investment flows. Most firms that become multinationals initially produce in a single country and then expand into other countries by purchasing productive assets in those countries or by building new production facilities in those countries (greenfield investments). Trade between units of a multinational enterprise is significantly affected by variations in tax rates across nations. These firms may reduce their taxes by adjusting the transfer price that one unit charges another for a good shipped internationally.

5. **Outsourcing.** A firm outsources if it buys an input from another firm rather than producing it internally. Although most outsourcing occurs within a single country, global outsourcing is increasing and is controversial. Critics complain that sending work overseas causes a loss of domestic jobs. Firms outsource to lower their production costs. International outsourcing reflects comparative advantage.

QUESTIONS

*All exercises are available on MyEconLab; * = answer at the back of this book.*

1. Reasons for International Trade

*1.1. Suppose that auto workers in South Korea can produce components used to make cars at the rate of six sets of components per worker per day and can assemble cars at the rate of four cars per worker per day. In North Korea auto workers can produce components at the rate of one set of components per day and can assemble cars at the rate of three cars per worker per day. What is the opportunity cost of car assembly in terms of component production in each country? If one economy exports components and the other exports assembled cars, which economy will export cars according to the theory of comparative advantage?

1.2. Trade between North and South Korea was legalized in 1988, but is currently very limited. Assume, however, that Hyundai has 200 workers in a plant in North Korea just across the boundary with South Korea, where a "partner" plant with 200 workers is located. Using the numbers from Question 1.1, how much output can be produced if each plant carries out component production and assembly independently and no trade occurs? How much output can be produced if specialization according to comparative advantage occurs and how should labor be allocated in each plant? (*Hint*: See Q&A 17.1.)

1.3. ABC Software, a small software producer, decides to renovate its premises. Instead of hiring an outside contractor and tradespeople, the firm decides to use its employees—secretaries, programmers, sales staff, and others—to do most of the work. The firm makes all its employees try painting and carpentry and other tasks needed for the renovation and selects the people with the strongest skills in those areas to take time off from their regular tasks and work on the renovation. Is this strategy a good one? Why or why not?

1.4. Carrot Patch Dolls, a small doll producer in Malaysia, is considering producing a new doll variety. Production of this doll type requires an initial setup cost, followed by constant variable cost. The cost function of producing variety i is $C = 12{,}000 + 2Q_i$, where Q_i is the quantity of variety i. The demand function for this particular variety in Malaysia is $Q_i = 4000 - 1000p$. Carrot Patch seeks to maximize its profit and will not produce the doll if it would make a loss ($p < AC$) by doing so. If Carrot Patch cannot sell the doll outside Malaysia, does it pay to produce this variety? What decision does it make if Carrot Patch is able to sell the doll in Singapore as well as Malaysia, where the demand curve is exactly the same as in Malaysia?

2. Exchange Rates

2.1. Suppose that one euro can be exchanged for 1.3 U.S. dollars and that one U.S. dollar can be exchanged for 80 Japanese yen. If these currencies can be traded freely with low transaction costs, what exchange rate would you expect between euros and the Japanese yen? Describe the transactions that would occur if the euro-yen exchange rate is higher than this amount (more yen per euro). (*Hint*: Is arbitrage relevant?)

*2.2. Figure 17.1 shows the effect on the exchange rate (U.S. dollars per euro) on the demand for euros by U.S. residents. What would happen if the U.S. government tried to establish a fixed exchange rate at X_2 after demand shifted out to D^2?

2.3. Explain why gray markets reduce the ability of multinational firms to price discriminate.

3. International Trade Policies

3.1. In the first quarter of 2012, the world price for raw sugar, 24¢ per pound, was about 70% of the U.S. price, 34¢ per pound, because of quotas and tariffs on sugar imports. As a consequence, American-made corn sweeteners can be profitably sold domestically. A decade ago, the U.S. Commerce Department estimated that the quotas and price support reduced American welfare by about $3 billion a year, so, each dollar of profit of a domestic manufacturer such as Archer Daniels Midland costs Americans about $10. Use graphs to show the effects of a quota on sugar in both the sugar and corn sweetener markets. (*Hint*: See Q&A 17.2.)

3.2. How would the shape of the total supply curve in Q&A 17.1 change if the U.S. domestic supply curve hit the vertical axis at a price above $\bar{p}$?

3.3. Canada has 20% of the world's known freshwater resources, yet many Canadians believe that the country has little or none to spare. Over the years, U.S. and Canadian firms have struck deals to export bulk shipments of water to drought-afflicted U.S. cities and towns. Provincial leaders have blocked these deals in British Columbia and Ontario. Use graphs to show the likely outcome of such an export

ban on the price and quantity of water used in Canada and in the United States if markets for water are competitive. Show the effects on consumer and producer surplus in both countries. Show that if the importing country faces an upward-sloping foreign supply curve (excess supply curve), a tariff may raise welfare in the importing country.

3.4. Given that the world supply curve is horizontal at the world price for a given good, can a subsidy on imports raise welfare in the importing country? Explain your answer.

3.5. After Mexico signed the North American Free Trade Agreement (NAFTA) in 1994, corn imports from the United States doubled within a year, and today U.S. imports make up nearly one-third of the corn consumed in Mexico. According to the charity Oxfam in 2003, the price of Mexican corn fell more than 70% after NAFTA took effect. Part of the reason for this flow south of the border was that the U.S. government subsidizes corn production to the tune of $10 billion a year. According to Oxfam, the 2002 U.S. cost of production was $3.08 per bushel, but the export price was $2.69 per bushel, with the difference reflecting an export subsidy of 39¢ per bushel. The U.S. exported 5.3 metric tons. Use graphs to show the effect of such a subsidy on the welfare of various groups and on government expenditures in the United States and Mexico.

3.6. During the Napoleonic Wars, Britain blockaded North America, seizing U.S. vessels and cargo and impressing sailors. At President Thomas Jefferson's request, Congress imposed a nearly complete—perhaps 80%—embargo on international commerce from December 1807 to March 1809. Just before the embargo, exports were about 13% of the U.S. gross national product (GNP). Due to the embargo, U.S. consumers could not find acceptable substitutes for manufactured goods from Europe, and producers could not sell farm produce and other goods for as much as in Europe. According to Irwin (2005), the welfare cost of the embargo was at least 8% of the GNP in 1807. Use graphs to show the effects of the embargo on a market for an exported good and one for an imported good. Show the change in equilibria and the welfare effects on consumers and firms.

3.7. A government is considering a quota and a tariff, both of which will reduce imports by the same amount. Why might the government prefer one of these policies to the other?

*3.8. In Table 17.3, suppose that the payoff if both firms enter is positive, 5 rather than −5, while the other payoffs remain the same. Now, what is the effect of a subsidy of 10 to Novartis?

3.9. Why do antidumping policies limit the ability of firms to carry out international price discrimination?

4. Multinational Enterprises

4.1. As a result of the North American Free Trade Agreement, many iconic "American" cars are not assembled in the United States. Explain why. Provide some examples of U.S. cars that are assembled outside of the United States. (*Hint*: See the "What's an American Car?" Mini-Case.)

*4.2. The Timex Group, a large multinational watchmaker, has its headquarters in the Netherlands. It has subsidiaries in many countries, including the Timex Group USA and TMX Philippines, Inc. One particular type of specialty watch is produced in the Philippines for export to the Timex Group USA. Suppose the inverse demand function for this watch in the United States is $p = 90 - 2Q$, where p is measured in dollars and Q is measured in thousands of watches per week. These watches are produced at a constant marginal cost of $10 per watch by TMX Philippines. Timex USA treats the transfer price charged by TMX Philippines as its marginal cost. If these two subsidiaries are instructed to maximize combined profits, what are the price, quantity, and transfer price? Could TMX Philippines raise its own profit by charging a higher price? (*Hint*: See Q&A 17.3.)

4.3. In Question 4.2, what transfer price would maximize the profit of TMX Philippines? (*Hint*: For any given transfer price, the Timex Group USA will demand some quantity of watches. This relationship determines the demand facing TMX Philippines.)

4.4. In Question 4.2, suppose that the Philippines has a lower corporate tax rate than the United States. How would that lower tax rate affect the transfer price that maximizes the overall profit of the Timex Group?

5. Outsourcing

5.1. Outsourcing of services by American firms has contributed significantly to wage growth in India. Explain why using a graph of the Indian labor market.

5.2. Suppose Hewlett-Packard is considering outsourcing its telephone-based technical support functions for its printers to India. The hourly cost of a tech support person in the United States is $50 per hour. In India workers are paid in rupees but, at the current exchange rate, cost the equivalent of $20 per hour. However, calls serviced in India require paying for long-distance telephone service. Initially the telephone costs were about $35 per hour. However, a switch to voice over Internet protocol (VOIP) technology reduced the telephone cost to $25 per hour.

Explain how the technological change affects the decision of where to base service. How much would the Indian currency (the rupee) have to rise in value (in percentage terms) for Hewlett-Packard to keep the service activity in the United States even after telephone time falls in price?

6. Managerial Problem

6.1. Chanel perfume is sold in France and in the United States. Assume initially that one euro is worth $1.30 and that a 100 ml bottle of perfume sells for $80 in the United States. If Chanel does not price discriminate internationally, what is the price that would be paid for this perfume in France? Now suppose that Chanel decides to price discriminate and finds that it would maximize its profit by lowering its price in the United States to $70 and raising its price by 25% in France. Explain why. Next, explain what happens if the value of the euro rises by 25% in terms of the dollar.

7. Spreadsheet Exercises

7.1. Suppose the demand function for U.S dollars by holders of Japanese yen is $Q_{d1} = 1000 - 5x$, where Q is the amount of U.S. dollars per day and x is the exchange rate (yen per dollar). The supply function of U.S. dollars available to be exchanged into Japanese yen is $Q_{s1} = 100 + 4x$.

   a. Create a spreadsheet with columns for the exchange rate, x, the quantity demanded, and the quantity supplied. Let the exchange rate range from 50 to 150 in increments of 10. Determine the equilibrium exchange rate using the spreadsheet.

   b. Now suppose that the U.S. Federal Reserve announces a long-run low interest rate policy that causes the foreign demand for U.S. dollars to fall. The new demand function is $Q_{d2} = 850 - 4x$. The Japanese investors begin to liquidate their holdings of U.S. assets, increasing the supply of U.S. dollars to $Q_{s2} = 130 + 4x$. Add additional columns for Q_{d2} and Q_{s2} to the spreadsheet from part a and determine the new dollar-yen exchange rate.

   c. Use the Excel charting tool to draw the graphs of the demand and supply curves for U.S. dollars to illustrate the change in the equilibrium exchange rate.

7.2. The domestic demand and supply functions for a particular type of latex paint are $Q_d = 14 - 0.5p$ and $Q_s = -4 + p$, respectively. The price is measured in dollars per gallon and the quantities are measured in millions of gallons. The world price for the paint is $p^* = \$8$, at which the foreign producers are willing to sell unlimited quantities.

a. Suppose paint is freely traded. Create a spreadsheet with columns for price (p), domestic demand (D), domestic supply (S), imports (M), consumer surplus (CS), producer surplus (PS), and total surplus (TS). Let price go from $4 to $28 in increments of $1. Fill in the spreadsheet.

b. Determine the domestic price, domestic consumption, domestic production, and the amount of imports in the free-trade equilibrium. Also calculate the consumer surplus, producer surplus, and the total surplus using the spreadsheet.

c. Now, the government bans importing paint. Determine the domestic price, domestic consumption, domestic production, consumer surplus, producer surplus, total surplus, and the deadweight loss.

d. Next, instead of banning imports, the domestic government imposes an import quota of 3 million gallons. Determine the domestic price, domestic consumption, domestic production, consumer surplus, producer surplus, surplus, and the deadweight loss under such a quota.

Answers to Selected Questions

I know the answer! The answer lies within the heart of all mankind! The answer is twelve? I think I'm in the wrong building. —Charles Schultz

Chapter 2

1.1 Draw the graph with quantity on the horizontal axis and price on the vertical axis. The avocado demand function (Equation 2.2) shows that, for any given price, quantity demanded increases as income increases. Therefore, an increase in income causes the demand curve to shift to the right. A movement along the demand curve is caused by a change in price, holding income and other relevant variables constant.

1.4 (a) The inverse demand function for town residents is $p = 200 - 0.5Q_r$. (b) At a price of $300, college students will buy some firewood, but other town residents will not. Other town residents will demand a quantity of zero at any price of $200 or more. (c) The total demand curve has a price intercept of $400 and coincides with the college students' demand curve for prices from $400 to $200. At a price of $200 it has a kink, and for prices of $200 or below it is the horizontal sum of student demand and other demand and follows the equation $Q = 600 - 2p$.

2.2 A movement along the supply curve occurs only when the price of the good changes. Therefore, a change in the price of fertilizer would not cause a movement along the supply curve. A change in a variable that affects quantity demanded other than the good's own price would cause the entire supply curve to shift. In this example, fertilizer is such a variable. For any given price of avocados, the quantity supplied would be lower if the price of fertilizer is higher. Thus, a change in the price of fertilizer shifts the entire supply curve.

2.3 The supply function for avocados (Equation 2.5) is $Q = 58 + 15p - 20p_f$. The change in quantity supplied is therefore $\Delta Q = Q_2 - Q_1 = (50 + 15p_2) - (50 + 15p_1) = 15(p_2 - p_1) = 15\Delta p$. It follows that the change in price needed to cause $\Delta Q = 60$ is $\Delta p = 60/15 = 4$.

3.1 When the graph is drawn, the intercept of the supply curve on the vertical axis is 6 and the curve slopes up from there. The demand curve has a vertical axis intercept at 4 and slopes down from there. Therefore, the demand and supply curves do not intersect each other at any positive price and quantity. The equilibrium in this case is at a quantity of 0. There is no market price for this good as no trades take place.

4.3 Outsourcing of skilled jobs to India increases the demand for skilled workers in India. Therefore, the (downward-sloping) demand curve for skilled workers in India shifts outward. If the supply curve is upward sloping and stays in the same place, the shift in demand will cause the equilibrium price—the wage—to increase.

4.10 In Japan, the supply curve for beef shifted in, putting upward pressure on price. The demand curve may have shifted in as well, putting downward pressure on price, but not enough to fully offset the supply effect so price rose overall. In the United States, initially the demand curve shifted in and the supply curve shifted out (as less could be exported). Therefore price fell. The inward shift in demand put downward pressure on quantity, but the outward shift in supply put upward pressure on quantity. The supply effect more than offset the demand effect on quantity.

4.12 If the price of petroleum rises, the cost of producing plastic rises, causing the supply curve for plastic to shift in. As plastic is a substitute for aluminum, the demand for aluminum shifts out. An increase in the price of petroleum also increases the cost of producing electricity, which in turn increases the cost of producing aluminum, causing the supply curve for aluminum to shift in. Therefore, the demand for aluminum shifts out and the supply shifts in. The price of aluminum must rise and the quantity sold could rise, fall, or remain unchanged depending on the relative size of the demand effect and the supply effect.

5.2 If the law had passed, a price ceiling would have been imposed, presumably at a level below the intersection of the supply and demand curves. At this price there would be an excess demand for gasoline, resulting in a shortage of gasoline and likely giving rise to lines at gas stations.

Chapter 3

1.3 The point price elasticity ε is given by $\varepsilon = (\Delta Q/\Delta p)(p/Q) = -2p/Q = -2(10/80) = -0.25$.

1.7 The price elasticity of demand ε is the percentage change in quantity demanded divided by the percentage change in price, which in this case is $-3.8/10 = -0.38$. As this elasticity has an absolute value of less than one, demand is inelastic.

1.9 The elasticity of demand $\varepsilon = (\Delta Q/\Delta p)(p/Q) = (-9.5)(45)/1{,}275 \approx -0.34$. That is, for every 1% fall in the price, a third of a percent more coconut oil is demanded. The cross-price elasticity of demand for coconut oil with respect to the price of palm oil is $(\Delta Q/\Delta p_p)(p_p/Q) = (16.2)(31)/1{,}275 \approx 0.39$.

2.3 The predicted quantity is $Q = 130 - 3.5p = 130 - 3.5(2.0) = 123$. The residual is $129 - 123 = 6$. There are several possible relevant unobserved variables, including the temperature and the price of substitute goods (such as ice cream).

3.3 The estimated demand function is $Q = 53.857 - 1.438p$, where p is measured in thousands of dollars. If p rises by \$1 (thousand), then Q falls by 1.438. At a price of \$20 (thousand), the predicted demand from the focus group is $Q = 53.857 - 1.438(20) = 25.097$. The elasticity of demand at this price is $-(1.438)(20/25.097) \approx -1.146$.

4.3 Linear demand has the form $Q = a - bp$. Revenue, which is price times quantity, has the form $R = pQ = p(a - bp) = ap - bp^2$. Thus, revenue is a *quadratic* function of price, *not* a linear function. Using a linear functional form for the regression would be a mistake. A quadratic functional form should be used.

6.2 The R^2 is 0.96 (rounded to two decimal places). The coefficient estimates are 1,024 and −413 (rounded to whole numbers), the standard errors are 33.8 and 32.7 (rounded to one decimal place), and the t-statistics are 30.3 and −12.6 (rounded to one decimal place). Thus, using the 95% confidence criterion, we would reject the hypothesis that the price coefficient is zero.

Chapter 4

1.2 With the neutral product (bread) on the vertical axis, the indifference curves are parallel, vertical lines.

2.1 William's indifference curves are right angles (as in panel b of Figure 4.4). His utility function is $U = \min(H, W)$, where *min* means the minimum of the two arguments, H is the number of units of hot dogs, and W is the number of units of mustard.

2.4 Andy's marginal utility of apples per dollar is $\frac{3}{2} = 1.5$. The marginal utility per dollar for kumquats is $\frac{5}{4} = 1.2$. That is, a dollar spent on apples gives Andy more extra utility than a dollar spent on kumquats. He therefore maximizes his utility by spending all his money on apples and buying $\frac{40}{2} = 20$ pounds of apples.

3.4 Suppose that Dale purchases opera and ice hockey tickets at prices p_1 and p_2. If her original income is Y_1, the intercept of the budget line on the opera axis (where she buys only opera tickets) is Y_1/p_1. Similarly, the intercept is Y_1/p_2 on the hockey axis. A 25% income tax lowers after-tax income to 75% of its original level, $0.75Y_1$. As a result, the budget line shifts inward toward the origin. The intercepts on the opera and hockey axes are $0.75Y_1/p_1$ and $0.75Y_1/p_2$, respectively. The slope is unchanged. The opportunity set is reduced by the area between the original budget line and the new budget line.

4.2 (a) Setting $MU_R/p_R = MU_C/p_C$ yields $20RC/10 = 10R^2/5$ or $2C = 2R$. Therefore, $R = C$. We then substitute $R = C$ into the budget equation to obtain $10C + 5C = 90$ or $C = 6$ (and $R = 6$). The diagram looks like Figure 4.8 with only the middle indifference curve shown and with R and C on the axes. (b) Using the same method as in part a, the new solution is $R = 6, C = 3$. In this case the budget line from part a has the same intercept on the R axis but the intercept on the C axis falls by half, so the budget line pivots inward.

4.4 If the U.S. price of gasoline changes from being below the Canadian price to going above, then a utility-maximizing Canadian who lives equally close to gas stations on both sides of the border would shift from buying gas in the United States to buying gas in Canada. In the diagram, the two goods on the axes are Canadian gas and U.S. gas. They are perfect substitutes, so the indifference curves are straight lines. The consumer will consume on one axis or the other depending on which price is lower.

6.2 The answer relates to *salience* and *bounded rationality*. A consumer's demand for a product might change when the product price is quoted inclusive of taxes because the taxes and the associated higher price become more salient (more obvious) to the consumer. Some consumers might therefore ignore a tax that is not quoted in the price but would take account of it if it is quoted, or they might not calculate the effect of the tax if doing calculations is difficult for them (bounded rationality). These *salience* and *bounded rationality* effects would imply that a job would attract fewer applicants if the salary were quoted after deducting income tax.

Chapter 5

1.2 No, it is not possible for $q = 10$, $L = 3$, and $K = 6$ to be a point on this production function. Holding output and other inputs fixed, a production function shows the minimum amount needed of a given factor. As only 5 units of capital are needed to produce 10 units of output given that 3 units of labor are used, using 6 units of capital would imply excess capital. Such an input combination cannot be on the production function.

2.1 One worker produces one unit of output, two workers produce two units of output, and n workers produce n units of output. Thus, the total product of labor equals the number of workers: $q = L$. The total product of labor curve is a straight line with a slope of 1. Because we are told that each extra worker produces one more unit of output, we know that the marginal product of labor, $\Delta q / \Delta L$, is 1. By dividing both sides of the production function, $q = L$, by L, we find that the average product of labor, q/L, is 1.

2.3 The production function is $q = L^{0.75}K^{0.25}$. (a) As a result, the average product of labor, holding capital fixed at $\overline{K}$, is $AP_L = q/L = L^{-0.25}\overline{K}^{0.25} = (\overline{K}/L)^{0.25}$. (b) The marginal product of labor is $MP_L = dq/dL = \frac{3}{4}(\overline{K}/L)^{0.25}$. (c) The marginal product curve intersects the average product at the maximum of the average product curve. If the marginal product exceeds the average product, the average product curve must be rising. If marginal product is less than average product, the marginal product curve must be falling.

3.3 (a) The isoquants are right angles as the firm must have one disk and one hour of recording time (capital) to make a recording. Increasing one input

without increasing the other results in no increase in output. (b) The *MRTS* is 0 along the horizontal portion of an isoquant and is negative infinity along the vertical portion. It is undefined at the corner point. (c) If labor is less than capital, then the total product curve is increasing in the labor input up to the point where labor equals capital, after which it is constant. The average product of labor is positive and constant if labor is less than capital and declining if labor exceeds capital. The marginal product of labor is one if labor is less than capital and drops to zero if labor exceeds or equals capital.

3.6 The isoquants are straight lines. The marginal product of B is one. If we put B on the vertical axis, the *MRTS* (the slope of the isoquant) is $-\frac{1}{2}$.

3.7 Using Equation 5.3, we know that the marginal rate of technical substitution is $MRTS = -MP_L/MP_K = -\frac{2}{3}$.

4.2 This production function is Cobb-Douglas. Even though it has three inputs instead of two, the same logic applies. Thus, we can calculate the returns to scale as the sum of the exponents: $0.27 + 0.16 + 0.61 = 1.04$. Therefore, this production function has nearly constant returns to scale. The marginal product of materials is $\partial q/\partial M = 0.61L^{0.27}K^{0.16}M^{-0.39} \approx 0.61q/M$.

4.5 Diminishing marginal returns to each factor imply convex isoquants—isoquants that are bowed in toward the origin. Constant returns to scale imply that the distance between isoquants is proportional to the amount of input used. Thus, diminishing marginal returns relate to the shape of a single isoquant and returns to scale relate to the distance between isoquants.

4.7 We can determine returns to scale for Cobb-Douglas production functions by adding the exponents. If the sum exceeds one, there are increasing returns to scale. If the sum equals one, there are constant returns; if the sum is less than one, we have decreasing returns. In this case Blackberry has increasing returns to scale, U.S. housing has constant returns to scale, and U.K. supermarkets have decreasing returns to scale.

5.1 Given any particular input levels, Firm 2 has a higher marginal product of labor and of capital. For Firm 1, $MP_L = \partial q_1/\partial L = 0.9\partial q_2/\partial L$. Thus, the marginal product for Firm 1 is 90% that of Firm 2 if input levels are the same.

6.2 Not enough information is given to fully answer this question. If we assume that Japanese and American firms have identical production functions and produce using the same ratio of factors during good times, Japanese firms will have a lower average product of labor during recessions because they are less likely to lay off workers. However, it is not clear how Japanese and American firms expand output during good times (e.g., do they hire the same number of extra workers?). As a result, we cannot predict which country has the higher average product of labor.

Chapter 6

1.4 The sunk cost is $1 per pipe. The opportunity cost of each pipe is $9.

2.1 If the plane cannot be resold, its purchase price is a sunk cost, which is unaffected by the number of times the plane is flown. Consequently, the average cost per flight falls with the number of flights, but the total cost of owning and operating the plane rises because of extra consumption of gasoline and maintenance. Thus, the more frequently someone has reason to fly, the more likely that flying one's own plane costs less per flight than a ticket on a commercial airline. However, by making extra ("unnecessary") trips, Mr. Agassi raises his total cost of owning and operating the airplane.

2.6 The total cost of building a 1-cubic-foot crate is $6. It costs four times as much to build an 8-cubic-foot crate, $24. In general, as the height of a cube increases, the total cost of building it rises with the square of the height, but the volume increases with the cube of the height. Thus, the cost per unit of volume falls.

3.2 To minimize costs, the firm should set the marginal product per dollar equal for each factor. For labor, $MP_L/w = 50/200 = 0.25$. For capital, $MP_K/r = 200/1000 = 0.20$. In this case, the firm is not minimizing the cost of Sludge because these ratios are not equal. The firm should use less capital and more labor. (This assumes that the isoquants are smooth, which means the firm can make small adjustments to capital.)

3.4 From the information given and assuming that there are no economies of scale in shipping baseballs, it appears that balls are produced using a constant returns to scale, fixed-proportion production function. The corresponding cost function is $C(q) = [w + s + m]q$, where w is the wage for the time period it takes to stitch one ball, s is the cost of shipping one ball, and m is the price of all material to produce a ball. As the cost of all inputs other than labor and transportation are the same everywhere, the cost difference between Georgia and Costa Rica depends on $w + s$ in both locations. As firms choose to produce in Costa Rica, the extra shipping cost must be less than the labor savings in Costa Rica.

3.7 Let w be the cost of a unit of L and r be the cost of a unit of K. For the fixed-proportions production function, the cost function is $C(q) = (2w + r)q$. For the other (linear) production function, the two inputs are perfect substitutes in the production process so the firm uses only the less expensive of the two inputs. Therefore, the long-run cost function is $C(q) = wq$ if $w \leq r$; otherwise, it is $C(q) = rq$.

4.2 (a) If $r = 0$, the average cost (AC) of producing one unit is $a + b$ (regardless of the value of N). There is no learning by doing in this case. (b) If $r > 0$, then average cost falls as N rises, so learning by doing does occur. As N gets very large, AC approaches a. Therefore, a is the lower limit for average cost—no matter how much learning is done, AC can never fall below a.

5.3 This firm has significant economies of scope, as producing gasoline and heating oil separately would cost approximately twice as much as producing them together. In this case, the measure of economies of scope, SC, is a positive number.

Chapter 7

1.2 One important consequence of going public is that the firm is able to raise money by issuing stock and selling it on a public stock exchange. Another important consequence is that ownership of the firm becomes more broadly distributed as investors purchase the stock. A third possible consequence is that the original owners may lose control of the firm.

2.2 To maximize profit we set $MR = MC$, where $MR = dR/dq = 100 - 6q$ and $MC = dC/dq = 10$. Setting $MR = MC$ yields $100 - 6q = 10$ or $q = 15$ and $\pi = 575$.

2.4 Only $200 of the fixed cost is sunk. The firm should shut down if its revenue is less than the avoidable cost. Avoidable cost in this case is $1,100 and revenue is $1,000. As revenue is less than the avoidable cost, the firm should shut down. Shutdown rule 1: the firm shuts down only if it can reduce its loss by doing so.

3.4 Firm 1 maximizes profit. Setting $MR = MC$ to maximize profit yields $100 - 4q = 20$ or $q = 20$. Firm 2 is run by a manager who maximizes revenue. Setting $MR = 0$ yields $100 - 4q = 0$ or $q = 25$. Firm 3 maximizes the labor input subject to not making a loss, which implies maximizing output subject to not making a loss. At this point revenue will just equal cost: $100q - 2q^2 = 100 + 20q$. This quadratic equation can be rewritten in standard form as $2q^2 - 80q + 100 = 0$. This quadratic equation has two solutions, the larger of which requires more labor and is therefore the correct answer. It is approximately 38.7.

4.1 Campbell gains produce and savings worth $85 million per year. Using an interest rate of 5% and applying Equation 7A.4 implies that the present value of this flow is $85/0.05$ million = $1,700 million or $1.7 billion. The cost of the acquisition is $1.55 billion plus the one-time transaction cost of $50 million or $0.05 billion, yielding a cost of $1.6 billion. The overall gain in value to Campbell is $1.7 - $1.6 = $0.1 billion or $100 million.

Chapter 8

1.2 If the transaction cost of switching to a different seller is high, then some consumers would continue to buy from a seller even if that seller raised its price. The seller would therefore not be a price taker, as it would not lose all its sales by raising its price above the going market level. Also, if buyers do not know the prices available in the market (imperfect information), then a seller might be able to raise prices without losing all its customers, so it would not be a price taker in this case either.

2.2 Suppose that a U-shaped marginal cost curve cuts a competitive firm's demand curve (price line) from above at q_1 and from below at q_2. By increasing output to $q_1 + 1$, the firm earns extra profit because the last unit sells for price p, which is greater than the marginal cost of that last unit. Indeed, the price exceeds the marginal cost of all units between q_1 and q_2, so it is more profitable to produce q_2 than q_1. Thus, the firm should either produce q_2 or shut down (if it is making a loss at q_2).

2.5 Average cost is $AC = C(q)/q = 10/q + 10 + q$. Similarly, average variable cost is $AVC = VC/q = 10 + q$. If the market price is p, the firm maximizes profit by setting $MC = 10 + 2q = p$. Therefore, $q = p/2 - 5$. If $p = 50$, then $q = 50/2 - 5 = 20$.

3.2 This law has no effect on the long-run equilibrium. However, in the short run—within the six-month worker notification period—the cost of labor would be an unavoidable fixed cost instead of an avoidable variable cost. Even if the firm did not earn enough to pay its labor cost it would stay in business in the short run whereas, without the notification law, it would shut down in the short run. The effect of the law in the short run is to make quantity larger and price lower than it would otherwise be and to impose additional losses on the firm that it would otherwise avoid.

4.1 The consumer surplus at a price of 30 is $\frac{1}{2}(30 \times 30) = 450$.

4.3 We can draw a diagram with a downward-sloping industry demand curve and an upward-sloping industry marginal cost curve (which is the industry supply curve). The competitive output occurs where the industry marginal cost curve intersects the demand curve. If output rises above this level, the marginal cost of the extra output exceeds its marginal benefit as given by the demand curve. The area between the marginal cost curve and the demand curve at output levels beyond the competitive level is a deadweight loss that must be subtracted in calculating the total surplus provided by this market. Thus, total surplus falls as output rises above the competitive level.

Chapter 9

1.3 At $Q = 10, p = 500 - 10(10) = 400$. The elasticity is $\varepsilon = -0.1(400)/10 = -4$. Revenue $R = pQ = 10(400) = \$4,000$.

1.10 To obtain the profit-maximizing output we set $MR = MC$. As $MR = 100 - 2Q$ and $MC = 5$, it follows that $100 - 2Q = 5$ or $Q = 47.5$. If the cost function changes to $C = 100 + 5Q$, there is no change in the profit-maximizing output as the marginal cost function does not change. Also, the firm continues to earn positive profits even with the higher level of fixed costs and therefore does not shut down.

2.7 The Lerner Index was $(p-MC)/p = (359-159)/359 \approx 0.557$. If the firm was profit maximizing, it follows that $0.557 = -1/\varepsilon$ or $\varepsilon = -1/0.557 = -1.795$

3.5 Suppose that the monopoly faces a constant-elasticity demand curve with elasticity ε, has constant marginal cost, m, and that the government imposes a specific tax of τ. The monopoly sets its price such that $p = (m + \tau)/(1 + 1/\varepsilon)$. Thus, $dp/d\tau = 1/(1 + 1/\varepsilon) > 1$.

4.1 Yes. If the demand curve intersects the downward-sloping part of the AC curve, then AC is downward sloping over the relevant range and the firm must be a natural monopoly. Also, the firm may still be able to produce the market quantity more cheaply than the aggregation of separate firms' production and therefore be a natural monopoly even if the demand curve cuts the upward-sloping portion of its AC curve, provided that occurs sufficiently close to the minimum of the AC curve.

5.2 To maximize profit the monopoly must set marginal revenue $MR\,(= \partial R/\partial Q)$ equal to marginal cost, MC, and must set the marginal revenue of advertising, $MR_A\,(= \partial Q/\partial A)$, equal to the marginal cost of advertising, which is 1. $R = pQ = 100Q - Q^2 + 5A - A^2$. Setting $MR = MC$ yields $100 - 2Q = 10$ or $Q = 45$. Setting $MR_A = 1$ yields $5 - 2A = 1$ or $A = 2$. The profit-maximizing price is $p = 100 - (45) + (5(2) - (2)2)/(45) = 55.13$.

6.2 If the demand curve is given by $p = 10 - Q$, the marginal revenue curve is $MR = 10 - 2Q$. Thus, the output that maximizes the monopoly's profit is determined by $MR = 10 - 2Q = 2 = MC$, or $Q^* = 4$. At that output level, its price is $p^* = 6$ and its profit is $\pi^* = 16$. If the monopoly chooses to sell 8 units in the first period (it has no incentive to sell more), its price is 2 and it makes no profit. Given that the firm sells 8 units in the first period, its demand curve in the second period is $p = 10 - Q/\alpha$, so its marginal revenue function is $MR = 10 - 2Q/\alpha$. The output that leads to its maximum profit is determined by $MR = 10 - 2Q/\alpha = 2 = MC$, or its output is 4α. Thus, its price is 6 and its profit is 16α. It pays for the firm to set a low price in the first period if the lost profit, 16, is less than the extra profit in the second period, which is $16(\alpha - 1)$. Thus, it pays to set a low price in the first period if $16 < 16(\alpha - 1)$, or $2 < \alpha$.

Chapter 10

1.4 The colleges may be providing scholarships as a form of charity, or they may be price discriminating by lowering the final price to less wealthy families (with presumably higher elasticities of demand). Because wealthier families have lower elasticities (and higher willingness to pay) than poor families, they pay higher prices.

1.6 Disneyland's tickets are clearly identified as being for a child or an adult. Thus, only children are allowed to enter using a child's ticket. Similarly, local residents are required to show identification (such as a driver's license) before being allowed to enter using a local resident ticket. In these ways, resale across groups can be easily prevented.

2.2 Under perfect price discrimination, the firm's profit is the area below the demand curve and above marginal cost. This area is $0.5(60)(60) = 1,800$. The

consumer surplus is zero, as all surplus is extracted by the monopoly. The total surplus is therefore 1800. The deadweight loss is zero as the monopoly produces up to the point where marginal cost cuts the demand curve. For a single-price monopoly, the profit is 900, the consumer surplus is 450, the total surplus is 1,350, and the deadweight loss is 450.

3.2 The marginal revenue function corresponding to a linear inverse demand function has the same intercept and twice as steep a slope. Thus, the American marginal revenue function is $MR_A = 100 - 2Q_A$, and the Japanese one is $MR_J = 80 - 4Q_J$. To determine how many units to sell in the United States, the monopoly sets its American marginal revenue equal to its marginal cost, $MR_A = 100 - 2Q_A = 20$, and solves for the optimal quantity, $Q_A = 40$ units. Similarly, because $MR_J = 80 - 4Q_J = 20$, the optimal quantity is $Q_J = 15$ units in Japan. Substituting $Q_A = 40$ into the American demand function, we find that $p_A = 100 - 40 = \$60$. Similarly, substituting $Q_J = 15$ units into the Japanese demand function, we learn that $p_J = 80 - (2 \times 15) = \$50$. Thus, the price-discriminating monopoly charges 20% more in the United States than in Japan.

We can also show this result using elasticities. From Equation 3.6, we know that the elasticity of demand is $\varepsilon_A = -p_A/Q_A$ in the United States and $\varepsilon_J = -\frac{1}{2}p_J/Q_J$ in Japan. In the equilibrium, $\varepsilon_A = -60/40 = -\frac{3}{2}$ and $\varepsilon_J = -50/(2 \times 15) = -\frac{5}{3}$. As Equation 10.5 shows, the ratio of the prices depends on the relative elasticities of demand: $p_A/p_J = 60/50 = (1 + 1/\varepsilon_J)/(1 + 1/\varepsilon_A) = (1 - \frac{3}{5})/(1 - \frac{2}{3}) = \frac{6}{5}$.

3.3 The two marginal revenue curves are $MR_J = 3,500 - Q_J$ and $MR_A = 4,500 - 2Q_A$. Equating the marginal revenues with the marginal cost of \$500, we find that $Q_J = 3,000$ and $Q_A = 2,000$. Substituting these quantities into the demand curve equations, we learn that $p_J = \$2,000$ and $p_A = \$2,500$. We can use Equation 9.9 to determine the elasticities of demand

$$\varepsilon_J = p/(MC - p) = 2,000/(500 - 2,000) = -\tfrac{4}{3},$$
$$\varepsilon_A = 2,500/(500 - 2,500) = -\tfrac{5}{4}.$$

Thus, using Equation 10.3, we find that

$$\frac{p_J}{p_A} = \frac{2,000}{2,500} = 0.8 = \frac{1 + 1/(-\frac{5}{4})}{1 + 1/(-\frac{4}{3})} = \frac{1 + 1/\varepsilon_A}{1 + 1/\varepsilon_J}.$$

The profit in Japan is $(p_J - m)Q_J = (\$2,000 - \$500) \times 3,000 = \$4.5$ million, and the U.S. profit is \$4 million. The deadweight loss is greater in Japan, \$2.25 million $(\frac{1}{2} \times \$1,500 \times 3,000)$, than in the United States, \$2 million $(\frac{1}{2} \times \$2,000 \times 2,000)$.

3.9 This policy allows the firm to maximize its profit by price discriminating if people who put a lower value on their time (and are therefore willing to drive to the store and move their purchases themselves) have a higher elasticity of demand than people who want to order over the phone and have the goods delivered.

4.1 Figure 10.4 depicts a situation with identical consumers. Each consumer purchases the same fraction of the total output and gets the same fraction of the consumer surplus. As consumer surplus is lower in panel a than in panel b, it follows that all consumers are made worse off by nonlinear price discrimination in this case. However, if consumers were different, it is possible that some consumers would gain under nonlinear price discrimination. Specifically, consumers who purchase a large volume at the lower price might be better off under nonlinear price discrimination than under uniform monopoly pricing.

5.3 Under two-part pricing, the Club would charge a fee per round of $20 and Joe would purchase 50 rounds. In the absence of a membership fee his consumer surplus would be $2,500 (=0.5(100)(50)). The Club can charge this amount as an annual membership fee and thereby convert this consumer surplus to profit. Therefore, the profit-maximizing membership fee is $2,500. Under standard (uniform) monopoly pricing, the Club would charge a price of $70 and Joe would purchase 25 rounds, generating a profit of only $1,250 for the Club. The Club therefore earns an additional $1,250 from two-part pricing.

6.2 (a) If the firm uses individual pricing, the best it can do is to charge $600 for the laptop and $100 for the printer. It will sell laptops to all consumer types and will sell printers only to *Type A* and *Type C* consumers. Assuming just one consumer of each type, the revenue (and profit) would be $1,800 for laptops and $200 for printers, or $2,000 in total. (b) If the firm bundles the two products, it would maximize profit by charging a bundle price of $750 and selling to all three customers for a profit of $2,250, which is $250 more than it earns from pricing the products individually. (c) Bundling pays because reservation prices are negatively correlated.

7.2 (a) Winter is the peak season. Write the equations for the demand curves with q on the left side. Then we have $q^W = 200 - p$ in winter and $q^S = 100 - p/2$ in summer. The difference is $100 - p/2$, which is strictly positive for any price at which output can be sold ($p < 200$). Thus, demand is higher in winter than in summer for any feasible price. (b) In the winter, setting $MR = MC = 0$ yields $q = 100$, but the firm has only 50 yachts. It will therefore maximize profit by choosing the price at which demand

is exactly 50, which is given by $p = 200 - 50 = 150$. In the summer, the firm's profit maximizing output is also 50, but the price needed to sell this output level is $200 - (2 \times 50) = 100$.

Chapter 11

1.4 The profit-maximizing cartel output is the monopoly output. Setting $MR = MC$ yields $100 - 4Q = 20$, so $Q = 20$. There are four firms, so each firm produces $20/4 = 5$.

2.2 The inverse demand function is $p = 1 - 0.001Q$. The first firm's profit is $\pi_1 = [1 - 0.001(q_1 + q_2)]q_1 - 0.28q_1$. Its first-order condition is $d\pi_1/dq_1 = 1 - 0.001(2q_1 + q_2) - 0.28 = 0$. If we rearrange the terms, the first firm's best-response function is $q_1 = 360 - \frac{1}{2}q_2$. Similarly, the second firm's best-response function is $q_2 = 360 - \frac{1}{2}q_1$. By substituting one of these best-response functions into the other, we learn that the Nash-Cournot equilibrium occurs at $q_1 = q_2 = 240$, and the equilibrium price is 52¢.

2.4 The monopoly will make more profit than the duopoly will, so the monopoly is willing to pay the college more rent. Although granting monopoly rights may be attractive to the college because of the higher rent that can be earned, students will suffer (lose consumer surplus) because of the higher prices.

2.10 By differentiating its product, a firm makes the residual demand curve it faces less elastic everywhere. For example, no consumer will buy from that firm if its rival charges less and the goods are homogeneous. In contrast, some consumers who prefer this firm's product to that of its rival will still buy from this firm even if its rival charges less. As the chapter shows, a firm sets a higher price, the lower the elasticity of demand at the equilibrium.

2.14 (a) For the duopoly, $q_1 = 5$, $q_2 = (15 - 4 + 1)/3 = 4$, $p_d = 6$, $\pi_1 = (6 - 1)5 = 25$, and $\pi_2 = (6 - 2)4 = 16$. Total output is $Q_d = 5 + 4 = 9$. Total profit is $\pi_d = 25 + 16 = 41$. Consumer surplus is $CS_d = \frac{1}{2}(15 - 6)9 = 40.5$. At the efficient price (equal to the marginal cost of 1), the output is 14. The deadweight loss is $DWL_d = \frac{1}{2}(6 - 1)(14 - 9) = 12.5$. (b) A monopoly equates its marginal revenue and marginal cost: $MR = 15 - 2Q_m = 1 = MC$. Thus, $Q_m = 7$, $p_m = 8$, and $\pi_m = (8 - 1)7 = 49$. Consumer surplus is $CS_m = \frac{1}{2}(15 - 8)7 = 24.5$. The deadweight loss is $DWL_m = \frac{1}{2}(8 - 1)(14 - 7) = 24.5$. (c) The average cost of production for the duopoly is $[(5 \times 1) + (4 \times 2)]/(5 + 4) = 1.44$, whereas the average cost of production for the monopoly is 1.

The increase in market power effect swamps the efficiency gain, so consumer surplus falls while deadweight loss nearly doubles.

3.2 If duopolies produce identical goods, the equilibrium price is lower if the duopolies set price rather than quantity. If the goods are heterogeneous, we cannot answer this question definitively.

3.4 Firm 1 wants to maximize its profit: $\pi_1 = (p_1 - 10)q_1 = (p_1 - 10)(100 - 2p_1 + p_2)$. Its first-order condition is $d\pi_1/dp_1 = 100 - 4p_1 + p_2 + 20 = 0$, so its best-response function is $p_1 = 30 + \frac{1}{4}p_2$. Similarly, Firm 2's best-response function is $p_2 = 30 + \frac{1}{4}p_1$. Solving for the Nash-Bertrand equilibrium prices yields $p_1 = p_2 = 40$. Each firm produces 60 units.

4.2 Initially, in the short run, the subsidy will lower fixed costs and increase profits for firms in the industry. However, above-normal profits will attract entry into the industry in the long run and the increased competition will force prices down until a new equilibrium is re-established in which marginal firms again earn zero profit. In the new equilibrium, there will be more firms and lower prices.

5.1 (a) The Nash-Cournot equilibrium in the absence of a government intervention is $q_1 = 30, q_2 = 40$, $p = 50, \pi_1 = 900$, and $\pi_2 = 1,600$. (b) The Nash-Cournot equilibrium is now $q_1 = 33.3, q_2 = 33.3$, $p = 53.3, \pi_1 = 1,108.9$, and $\pi_2 = 1,108.9$.

Chapter 12

1.1 If Duncan stays silent, Larry gets 0 if he talks and -1 (a year in jail) if he stays silent. If Duncan confesses, Larry gets -2 if he talks and -5 if he does not. Thus, Larry is better off talking in either case, so talking is his dominant strategy. By the same reasoning, talking is also Duncan's dominant strategy. As a result, the Nash equilibrium is for both to confess.

1.4 We start by checking for dominant strategies. Given the payoff matrix, Toyota always does at least as well by entering the market. If GM enters, Toyota earns 10 by entering and 0 by staying out of the market. If GM does not enter, Toyota earns 250 if it enters and 0 otherwise. Thus, entering is Toyota's dominant strategy. GM does not have a dominant strategy. It wants to enter if Toyota does not enter (earning 200 rather than 0), and it wants to stay out if Toyota enters (earning 0 rather than -40). Because GM knows that Toyota will enter (entering is Toyota's dominant strategy), GM stays out of the market. Toyota's entering and GM's not entering is a Nash

equilibrium. Given the other firm's strategy, neither firm wants to change its strategy.

Next we examine how the subsidy affects the payoff matrix and dominant strategies. The subsidy does not affect Toyota's payoff, so Toyota still has a dominant strategy: It enters the market. With the subsidy, GM's payoffs if it enters increase by 50: GM earns 10 if both enter and 250 if it enters and Toyota does not. With the subsidy, entering is a dominant strategy for GM. Thus, both firms' entering is a Nash equilibrium.

2.2 No, cheap talk (pre-play communication) does not help in this case. Network 2 would prefer the Nash equilibrium in which it schedules the show on Thursday and can indicate its intent to choose Thursday. However, Network 1 prefers the Nash equilibrium in which it schedules the show on Thursday so it can announce the same intention. These announcements are not consistent and would not resolve the problem of settling on one equilibrium.

2.9 We can see whether this outcome is a mixed-strategy equilibrium by checking whether either firm wishes to change its strategy given its rival's strategy. Consider the situation from Firm 1's point of view. If both firms enter with probability $\frac{1}{3}$, then Firm 1 will stay out $\frac{2}{3}$ of the time and get nothing. Both firms will enter $\frac{1}{3}\frac{1}{3} = \frac{1}{9}$ of the time and Firm 1 will get -2. Firm 1 will enter alone $\frac{1}{3}\frac{2}{3} = \frac{2}{9}$ of the time and get 1. The expected payoff to firm 1 is therefore $(\frac{2}{3})(0) + \frac{1}{9}(-2) + (\frac{2}{9})(1) = 0$. Firm 1 can do no better by adopting any other strategy, including entering with certainty or staying out with certainty. It therefore has no incentive to change its strategy. The same is true of Firm 2. Therefore, this combination of mixed strategies is a mixed-strategy equilibrium.

3.1 (a) WCG does not have a dominant strategy. BB does have a dominant strategy. Investing is better for BB no matter what WCG does. (b) The Nash equilibrium is for BB and WCG to both invest. At this outcome each is doing the best it can given the other's strategy. (c) The maximin solution is for BB to invest and WCG not to invest. (d) If Blues Brothers acquires a reputation for always playing a dominant strategy and WCG believes this reputation, then WCG does not need to play a maximin strategy and can use its standard Nash best response instead.

4.2 If the two firms reach agreement, Maxygen sells the patent to Oculus for a price of p. Oculus has a net value of $50 - p$ and Maxygen gets p. If they do not agree, Oculus's value is 10, and Maxygen gets nothing. Therefore, the Nash product is $N = (50 - p - 10)(p - 0) = 40p - p^2$. To maximize the Nash product, we set the derivative of the product with respect to p equal to zero: $dN/dp = 60 - 2p = 0$ or $p = 20$. In the Nash bargaining solution, Maxygen sells the patent for 20 and gets a net gain of 20 relative to the disagreement point. Oculus also gains 20 ($= 50 - 20 - 10$) relative to the disagreement point.

Chapter 13

1.1 (a) In the simultaneous move game there are two Nash equilibria (in pure strategies). One Nash equilibrium is for Firm 1 to sell 10 and Firm 2 to sell 20. The other is for Firm 1 to sell 20 while Firm 2 sells 10. (b) After drawing the game tree, you can use backward induction to see that if Firm 1 sells 10 then Firm 2 will choose 20, while if Firm 1 sells 20 then Firm 1 will sell 10. The first of these possibilities is better for Firm 1. Since Firm 1, the leader, can choose first, it therefore sells 10. Thus, the subgame-perfect Nash equilibrium is for Firm 1 to sell 10 and Firm 2 to sell 20. (c) If Firm 2 is the leader, the subgame-perfect Nash equilibrium is that Firm 2 sells 10 and Firm 1 sells 20.

1.2 In a game that is repeated a finite number of times, the outcome will yield the noncooperative solution if the players are fully rational. This solution is $q_u = 64$ and $q_a = 64$ in each period. Similarly, if one firm cares only about current period profits (and both firms know this), then the same thing happens.

2.2 First we determine the Nash-Cournot equilibrium. The inverse demand function is $p = 1 - 0.001Q$. Firm 1's profit is $\pi_1 = [1 - 0.001(q_1 + q_2)]q_1 - 0.28q_1$. Its first-order condition is $d\pi_1/dq_1 = 1 - 0.001(2q_1 + q_2) - 0.28 = 0$. If we rearrange the terms, Firm 1's best-response function is $q_1 = 360 - \frac{1}{2}q_2$. Similarly, Firm 2's best-response function is $q_2 = 360 - \frac{1}{2}q_1$. By substituting one of these best-response functions into the other, we learn that the Nash-Cournot equilibrium occurs at $q_1 = q_2 = 240$, so the total output is 480 and the equilibrium price is 52¢.

Next we determine the Stackelberg equilibrium. In this case Firm 1 substitutes the best-response function of Firm 2 into Firm 1's profit function: $\pi_1 = [1 - 0.001(q_1 + (360 - \frac{1}{2}q_1)]q_1 - 0.28q_1$. Taking the derivative of this profit function and setting it to zero yields $d\pi_1/dq_1 = 0.36 - 0.001q_1 = 0$ or $q_1 = 360$. Therefore, $q_2 = 360 - \frac{1}{2}(360) = 180$. The total Stackelberg output is $360 + 180 = 540$, which exceeds the Nash-Cournot output of 480. The Stackelberg price is $1 - 0.001(540) = \$0.46$ or 46¢, which is lower than the Nash-Cournot price. Relative to the Nash-Cournot case, profit is higher for the leader and lower for the follower and aggregate profits are lower in the Stackelberg case.

2.5 Levi Strauss would want Wrangler to believe this claim because, if it did, Wrangler would choose white and Levi Strauss would choose violet and earn a profit of 40, the highest possible profit. However, Wrangler should not believe this claim. If, for example, Wrangler chooses violet, then Levi would be better off choosing black rather than also choosing violet. Levi's claim that it would choose violet in this case is not credible.

3.3 Draw the game tree and analyze the game using backward induction (moving from right to left in the diagram). If the incumbent commits to the small quantity, its rival enters and the incumbent earns \$450. If the incumbent commits to the larger quantity, its rival does not enter and the incumbent earns \$800. Clearly, the incumbent should commit to the larger quantity because it earns a larger profit and the potential entrant chooses to stay out of the market. In the subgame-perfect Nash equilibrium, the incumbent produces the large quantity and the potential rival stays out.

3.4 Ying takes x as fixed and maximizes utility with respect to y: $dU/dy = 5(x + y)^{(-0.5)} - 1$. Therefore, $5 = (x + y)^{0.5}$, so $y = 25 - x$. If $x = 15$, it follows that $y = 10$. Ying will work for 10 hours. Xavier can keep Ying from doing any work by working for 25 hours or more.

4.2 Draw the game tree. It is worth more to the monopoly to keep the potential entrant out than it is worth to the potential entrant to enter, as the figure shows. Before the pollution-control device requirement, the entrant would pay up to \$3 to enter, whereas the incumbent would pay up to $\pi_m - \pi_d = \$7$ to exclude the potential entrant. With the device, the incumbent's profit is \$6 if entry does not occur, and it loses \$1 if entry occurs. Because the new firm would lose \$1 if it enters, it does not enter. Thus, the incumbent has an incentive to raise costs by \$4 to both firms. The incumbent's profit is \$6 if it raises costs and only \$3 if it does not.

5.2 The subgame-perfect Nash equilibrium is that Clarion would not build the plant. The problem is that if it did, then Ford would have an incentive to pay only p_2 and Clarion would lose money, an example of the hold-up problem. One possible solution is for Ford to make a contractual commitment before Clarion invests that it will pay p_3.

6.3 If Chloe expects other players to choose randomly, then she would expect the average among those players to be about 50. Her own bid will lower the average slightly, but we will assume that there are enough players so that her effect on the average is too small to affect her optimal bid. She should therefore pick the integer closest to $\frac{2}{3}$ of 50, which would be 33. If you are playing and you think everyone else is like Chloe, then you should bid $\frac{2}{3}$ of 33, which is 22.

Chapter 14

1.2 Assuming that the painting is not insured against fire, its expected value is $550 = (0.2 \times \$1,000) = (0.1 \times \$0) + (0.7 \times \$500)$.

1.4 The expected value of the stock is $(0.25 \times 400) + (0.75 \times 200) = 250$. The variance is $0.25(400 - 250)^2 + 0.75(200 - 250)^2 = 0.25(150)^2 + 0.75(-50)^2 = 5,625 + 1,875 = 7,500$. The standard deviation is 86.6.

2.5 Hugo's expected wealth is $EW = (\frac{2}{3} \times 144) + (\frac{1}{3} \times 225) = 96 + 75 = 171$. His expected utility is $EU = [\frac{2}{3} \times U(144)] + [\frac{1}{3} \times U(225)] = [\frac{2}{3} \times \sqrt{144}] + [\frac{1}{3} \times \sqrt{225}] = [\frac{2}{3} \times 12] + [\frac{1}{3} \times 15] = 13$.
He would pay up to an amount P to avoid bearing the risk, where $U(EW - P)$ equals his expected utility from the risky stock, EU. That is, $U(EW - P) = U(171 - P) = \sqrt{171 - P} = 13 = EU$. Squaring both sides, we find that that $171 - P = 169$, or $P = 2$. That is, Hugo would accept an offer for his stock today of $169 (or more), which reflects a risk premium of $2.

3.3 (a) $EU(\text{NoInsurace}) = (0.2)U(90,000) + (0.8)U(160,000) = 240 + 1,280 = 1,520$. $U(\text{Insurance}) = U(160,000 = 15,000) = 1,523.15$. Because $U(\text{Insurance}) > EU$ (No Insurance), this household should buy the insurance. (b) The actuarially fair price is the expected value of the payout, which is $(0.2)(70,000) = 14,000$. (c) The maximum the household would pay for this insurance is the price that would give it the same utility as not buying the insurance. If this price is p, then $U(160,000 - p) = EU(\text{No Insurance}) = 1,520$. Therefore, $(4)(160,000 - p)^{0.5} = 1,520$ or $160,000 - p = (1,520/4)^2 = 144,400$. It follows that $p = 15,600$.

4.1 If they were married, Andy would receive half the potential earnings whether they stayed married or not. As a result, Andy will receive $12,000 in present-value terms from Kim's additional earnings. Because the returns to the investment exceed the cost, Andy will make this investment (unless a better investment is available). However, if they

stay unmarried and split, Andy's expected return on the investment is the probability of staying together, $\frac{1}{2}$, times Kim's half of the returns if they stay together, $12,000. Thus, Andy's expected return on the investment, $6,000, is less than the cost of the education, so Andy is unwilling to make that investment (regardless of other investment opportunities).

5.3 Either Joe or Sue might suffer from overconfidence, but there is no information in the question to indicate that would be the reason for their different behavior. However, prospect theory would be a good explanation. Under prospect theory, people are risk seeking in the domain of losses, so Joe is willing to take a substantial risk on the last race. Sue is in the domain of gains and is therefore fundamentally risk averse, although a small gamble is still fun for her (see the Mini-Case "Gambling"). But she does not want to take a large risk.

Chapter 15

1.2 Because insurance costs do not vary with soil type, buying insurance is unattractive for houses on good soil and relatively attractive for houses on bad soil. Relatively more homeowners with houses on poor soil buy insurance, so the state insurance agency will have a higher payout rate in the next major earthquake than it would if everyone bought earthquake insurance. This is a form of adverse selection—high-risk consumers will buy the insurance.

1.3 Brand names allow consumers to identify a particular company's product in the future. If a mushroom company expects to remain in business over time, it would be foolish to brand its product if its mushrooms are of inferior quality. Thus, all else the same, we would expect branded mushrooms to be of higher quality than unbranded ones.

1.8 Because buyers are risk neutral, if they believe that the probability of getting a lemon is θ, the most they are willing to pay for a car of unknown quality is $p = p_1(1 - \theta) + p_2\theta$. If p is greater than both v_1 and v_2, all cars are sold. If $v_1 > p > v_2$, only lemons are sold. If p were less than both v_1 and v_2, no cars would be sold. However, we know that $v_2 < p_2$ and $p_2 < p$, so owners of lemons are certainly willing to sell them. (If sellers bear a transaction cost of c and $p < v_2 + c$, no cars are sold.)

2.3 If education is easier to obtain for high-quality workers than for low-quality workers, then high-quality workers may signal their quality to prospective employers by getting higher levels of education than lower quality workers.

3.1 This arrangement would likely increase the size of the overall bill. If there are n students, then each student will incur a cost of only $1/n$ times the cost of any additional item that the student orders. Because the student placing the order will get the entire marginal benefit but will bear only a small part of the marginal cost, an excessive amount would be ordered.

3.3 Presumably, the promoter collects a percentage of the revenue at each restaurant. If customers can pay cash, the restaurants may lie to the promoter as to the amount of food they sold. The scrip makes such opportunistic behavior difficult.

4.3 A partner who works an extra hour bears the full opportunity cost of this extra hour but gets only half the marginal benefit from the extra business profit. The opportunity cost of extra time spent at the store is the partner's best alternative use of time. A partner could earn money working for someone else or use the time to have fun. Because a partner bears the full marginal cost but gets only half the marginal benefit (the extra business profit) from an extra hour of work, each partner works only up to the point at which the marginal cost equals half the marginal benefit. Thus, each has an incentive to put in less effort than the level that maximizes their joint profit, where the marginal cost equals the marginal benefit.

4.4 (a) If Arnie is paid a fixed wage of 10, then Arnie would provide low effort. Any additional effort would be costly to him and would not increase his wage and therefore be a net loss. (b) Under a 50-50 profit-sharing contract Arnie would choose medium effort. With medium effort the expected profit is $0.5(40) + 0.5(80) = 60$. Arnie gets 50% or 30 and subtracts the cost of effort, 10, yielding a net gain of 20. With either low effort or high effort, Arnie's net gain is only 15. (c) Arnie gets 20 under the profit-sharing contract and 10 with a fixed wage, so he prefers profit sharing. Priscilla has an expected value of $30 - 10 = 20$ with a fixed wage and $0.5(60) = 30$ under profit sharing, so she prefers profit sharing also.

5.2 One important factor that deters shirking is that employees may lose their jobs if they are caught shirking. This possibility is a stronger deterrent to shirking if the employee anticipates a period of unemployment after being fired. If the worker can easily move to a new job, as occurs under full employment, then the incentive to avoid shirking is weaker.

Chapter 16

1.1 A Pareto improvement does not necessarily cause Pareto efficiency. If a situation is Pareto efficient, no further Pareto improvements are possible. A change that leads to Pareto efficiency does not necessarily cause a Pareto improvement, as there may be losers as well as winners.

2.2 As demand is perfectly inelastic up to a price of $100 per day, the profit-maximizing monopoly price is $100 and all 100 consumers will purchase a daily dose at this price. There is no consumer surplus. The daily producer surplus (and profit) is $(100 - 10)100 = \$9,000$. If a price ceiling of $30 is imposed, the price falls to $30, quantity remains unchanged at 100, consumer surplus rises to $(100 - 30)100 = \$7,000$, and producer surplus falls to $(30 - 10)100 = \$2,000$. In this case, the price control imposes no deadweight loss.

3.1 Under duopoly each firm produces 30, so total industry output is 60, price is 40, and total profit for the two firms combined is $(40 - 10)60 = 1,800$. If the two firms merge to form a monopoly, industry quantity falls to 45, price rises to 55, and profit rises to $(55 - 10)45 = 2,025$. Thus, merging increases the combined profit of the firms. Antitrust authorities might oppose the merger because consumer surplus falls by more than profit rises, so deadweight loss rises as a result of the merger.

4.3 Zero pollution is not the optimal level of pollution for society. The optimal level of pollution is where the marginal social cost of pollution is equal to the marginal social benefit of pollution. At zero pollution, the marginal social benefit of a little pollution is high while the marginal social cost is low. We can have "too little" pollution.

4.8 The competitive outcome occurs where the supply and demand curves cross, which is where price (inverse demand) equals marginal cost. Therefore, $200 - Q = 80 + Q$ or $Q = 60$. The social optimum occurs where the social marginal benefit given by the inverse demand function equals the social marginal cost, which is the sum of the private marginal cost and the marginal external damage. Therefore, $200 - Q = 80 + 2Q$ and the optimal output level is $Q = 40$. The market will produce this amount of output if a specific tax is set equal to the amount of the external damage at the optimal output level. In this case, the tax should therefore be 40.

5.3 A public good is both nonrival and nonexclusive. Cable television is nonrival but it is exclusive as potential users can be easily excluded. Therefore, cable television is not a public good (it is a club good). Broadcast television is both nonrival and nonexclusive—anyone with a TV and appropriate antenna can receive and view the signals. Therefore, broadcast TV is a public good. However, broadcast TV is provided by private firms because those firms do not need to collect revenue from viewers. Instead, the revenue comes from advertisers who hope to sell products to the viewers. Even so, in the days before cable TV became common, broadcast TV probably was underprovided by private sources and, in many countries, broadcasting was (and is) either provided by government or subsidized by government.

6.2 In this case, price is 30 and output is 10 whether or not Woz develops the new process. Therefore, consumer surplus does not change. However, Woz earns positive producer surplus (and positive profit) from the innovation and total surplus rises.

Chapter 17

1.1 In South Korea, the opportunity cost of car assembly is 1.5 sets of components per assembled car. In North Korea, the opportunity cost of assembly is only one-third of a set of components. The theory of comparative advantage implies that North Korea would export assembled cars as it has a lower opportunity cost of assembly.

2.2 Figure 17.1 shows the supply and demand for euros per day. The exchange rate is the price in U.S. dollars of a euro. If the U.S. government tries to fix the exchange rate at X_1 even after demand for euros shifts out to D^2, there will be an excess demand for euros at that price. Supply and demand would come into balance only if the exchange rate were allowed to rise to the new equilibrium level at X_2.

3.8 If the payoff to each firm is 5 (rather than −5) if both enter, then entering becomes a dominant strategy for each firm, even without a subsidy to Novartis. If a subsidy of 10 is provided to Novartis, both firms enter, Ajinomoto earns 5, and Novartis earns 15.

4.2 To maximize combined profits, TMX Philippines should charge a transfer price equal to the marginal cost of $10. The Timex Group USA then sets its marginal revenue of $90 - 4Q$ equal to the transfer price (its marginal cost) of 10, which yields $90 - 4Q = 10$ or $Q = 20$. Price will be $90 - 40 = 50$. TMX Philippines makes no profit in this case, but it could make positive profits if it raised the transfer price. However, the profit of the Timex Group USA would fall by more than the profit of TMX Philippines would rise.

Definitions

adverse selection: when one party to a transaction possesses information about a hidden characteristic that is unknown to other parties and takes economic advantage of this information, causing low-quality items to be over-represented in transactions. (15)

arc price elasticity: an elasticity that uses the average price and average quantity as the denominator for percentage calculations. (3)

asymmetric information: a situation in which one party to a transaction has relevant information that another party does not have. (15)

auction: a sale in which a good or service is sold to the highest bidder. (12)

average cost (or *average total cost*) (*AC*): the total cost divided by the units of output produced: $AC = C/q$. (6)

average fixed cost (*AFC*): the fixed cost divided by the units of output produced: $AFC = F/q$. (6)

average product of labor (*AP_L*): the ratio of output, q, to the amount of labor, L, used to produce that output: $AP_L = q/L$. (5)

average variable cost (or *variable cost per unit of output*) (*AVC*): the variable cost divided by the units of output produced: $AVC = VC/q$. (6)

backward induction (in a game): first determine the best response by the last player to move, next determine the best response for the player who made the next-to-last move, and then repeat the process back to the first move of the game. (13)

bad: something for which less is preferred to more, such as pollution. (4)

bandwagon effect: the situation in which a person places greater value on a good as more and more other people possess it. (9)

bargaining game: any situation in which two or more parties with different interests or objectives negotiate voluntarily over the terms of some interaction, such as the transfer of a good from one party to another. (12)

behavioral economics: the use of insights from psychology and research on human cognition and emotional biases to augment the rational economic model to better predict economic decision making. (4)

Bertrand equilibrium (or *Nash-Bertrand* or *Bertrand-Nash equilibrium*): a Nash equilibrium in prices; a set of prices such that no firm can obtain a higher profit by choosing a different price if the other firms continue to charge these prices. (11)

best response (in a game): the strategy that maximizes a player's payoff given its beliefs about its rivals' strategies. (12)

bounded rationality: a situation in which people have a limited capacity to anticipate, solve complex problems, or enumerate all options. (4)

budget line (or *budget constraint*): the bundles of goods that can be bought if the entire budget is spent on those goods at given prices. (4)

bundling (or *package deal*): a type of sale in which two or more goods or services are combined and offered at a single price. (10)

cartel: a group of firms that explicitly agree (collude) to coordinate setting prices or quantities. (11)

certification: a report that a particular product meets or exceeds a given standard level. (15)

club good: a good that is nonrival but is subject to exclusion. (16)

common knowledge (in a game): a piece of information known by all players, and is known by all players to be known, and is known to be known to be known, etc. (12)

common property, open-access: resources to which everyone has free access and equal rights to exploit. (16)

comparative advantage (in international trade): the ability to produce a good or service at lower opportunity cost than other countries. (17)

complete information (in a game): a situation in which the strategies and payoffs of the game are common knowledge. (12)

constant returns to scale (*CRS*): the property of a production function whereby when all inputs are increased by the same proportion, output increases by that same proportion. (5)

consumer surplus (*CS*): the monetary difference between what a consumer is willing to pay for the quantity of the good purchased and what the good actually costs. (8)

cost (or *total cost, C*): the sum of a firm's variable cost and fixed cost: $C = VC + F$. (6)

cost-benefit principle: a change is desirable if its benefits exceed the costs. (16)

Cournot equilibrium (or *Nash-Cournot* or *Cournot-Nash equilibrium*): a set of quantities chosen by firms such that, holding the quantities of all other firms constant, no firm can obtain a higher profit by choosing a different quantity. (11)

credible threat: a claim or threat that a player will, under particular circumstances, use a strategy harmful to its rival, and the threat is believable because it is in the player's best interest to use it if those circumstances arise. (13)

cross-price elasticity of demand: the percentage change in the quantity demanded divided by the percentage change in the price of another good. (3)

deadweight loss (DWL): the net reduction in total surplus from a loss of surplus by one group that is not offset by a gain to another group from an action that alters a market equilibrium. (8)

decreasing returns to scale (DRS): the property of a production function whereby output rises less than in proportion to an equal proportional increase in all inputs. (5)

demand curve: a curve showing the quantity of a good demanded at each possible price, holding constant the other factors that influence purchases. (2)

dependent variable: the variable whose variation is to be explained. (3)

diminishing marginal returns (law of): that if a firm keeps increasing an input, holding all other inputs and technology constant, the corresponding increases in output will eventually become smaller (diminish). (5)

diseconomies of scale: the property of a cost function whereby the average cost of production rises when output increases. (6)

dominant strategy: a strategy that produces a higher payoff than any other strategy the player can use no matter what its rivals do. (12)

duopoly: an oligopoly with two firms. (11)

durable good: a product that is usable for a long period, perhaps for many years. (6)

dynamic game: a game in which players move either sequentially or repeatedly. (13)

economically efficient (for a producer): minimizing the cost of producing a specified output level. (6)

economics: the study of decision making in the presence of scarcity. (1)

economies of scale: the property of a cost function whereby the average cost of production falls as output expands. (6)

economies of scope: the situation in which it is less expensive to produce goods jointly than separately. (6)

efficient contract: an agreement in which neither party can be made better off without harming the other party. (15)

efficient production (or *technological efficiency*): the situation in which the current level of output cannot be produced with fewer inputs, given existing knowledge about technology and the organization of production. (5)

elasticity: the percentage change in one variable divided by the associated percentage change in the other variable. (3)

endowment effect: people place a higher value on a good if they own it than they do if they are considering buying it. (4)

equilibrium: a situation in which no participant wants to change his or her behavior. (2)

essential facility: a scarce resource that a rival needs to use to survive. (16)

excess demand: the amount by which the quantity demanded exceeds the quantity supplied at a specified price. (2)

excess supply: the amount by which the quantity supplied is greater than the quantity demanded at a specified price. (2)

exchange rate: the price of one currency (such as the euro) in terms of another currency (such as the U.S. dollar) (17)

exclusion: the property that others can be prevented from consuming a good. (16)

expected value: is derived by taking the value of each possible outcome times the probability of that outcome and adding up those values. (14)

explanatory variables: the factors that are thought to affect the value of a dependent variable. (3)

extensive form (of a game): specifies the n players, the sequence in which they make their moves, the actions they can take at each move, the information that each player has about players' previous moves, and the payoff function over all possible strategies. (13)

externality: a person's well-being or a firm's production capability is directly affected by the actions of other consumers or firms rather than indirectly through changes in prices. (16)

fair bet: a bet with an expected value of zero. (14)

fair insurance: a contract between an insurer and a policyholder in which the expected value of the contract to the policyholder is zero. (14)

fixed cost (F): a production expense that does not vary with output. (6)

fixed input: a factor of production that cannot be varied in the short run. (5)

free-rider problem: a situation in which people benefit from the actions of others without paying. (16)

game: any interaction between players (such as individuals or firms) in which strategic interdependence plays a major role. (12)

game theory: a set of tools used by economists and others to analyze decision-making in situations of strategic interdependence. (12)

good: a commodity for which more is preferred to less, at least at some levels of consumption. (4)

group price discrimination (or *third-degree price discrimination*): a situation in which a firm charges each group of customers a different price. (10)

hidden action: one party to a transaction cannot observe important actions taken by another party. (15)

hidden characteristic: a fact about a person or thing that is known to one party but unknown to others. (15)

income elasticity of demand (or *income elasticity*): the percentage change in the quantity demanded divided by the given percentage change in income. (3)

increasing returns to scale (*IRS*): the property of a production function whereby output rises more than in proportion to an equal proportional increase in all inputs. (5)

indifference curve: the set of all bundles of goods that a consumer views as being equally desirable. (4)

indifference map (or *preference map*): a complete set of indifference curves that summarize a consumer's tastes or preferences. (4)

inferior good: a good for which the quantity demanded falls as income rises. (3)

isocost line: all the combinations of inputs that require the same (*iso-*) total expenditure (*cost*). (6)

isoquant: a curve that shows the efficient combinations of labor and capital that can produce a single (*iso-*) level of output (*quantity*). (5)

Law of Demand: consumers demand more of a good if its price is lower, holding constant the prices of other goods, tastes, and other factors that influence the amount they want to consume. (2)

learning curve: the relationship between average cost and cumulative output. (6)

Lerner Index: the ratio of the difference between price and marginal cost to the price: $(p - MC)/p$. (9)

limit pricing: when a firm sets its price (or, equivalently, its output) so that another firm cannot enter the market profitably. (13)

limited liability (for a corporation): the condition whereby the personal assets of the corporate owners cannot be taken to pay a corporation's debts even if it goes into bankruptcy. (7)

long run: a lengthy enough period of time that all relevant inputs can be varied. (5)

managerial economics: the application of economic analysis to managerial decision making. (1)

marginal cost (*MC*): the amount by which a firm's cost changes if the firm produces one more unit of output. (6)

marginal product of labor (*MP_L*): the change in total output resulting from using an extra unit of labor holding other factors constant. (5)

marginal profit: the change in profit a firm gets from selling one more unit of output. (7)

marginal rate of substitution (*MRS*): the rate at which a consumer can substitute one good for another while remaining on the same indifference curve. (4)

marginal rate of technical substitution (of capital for labor) (*MRTS*): the units of capital the firm can replace with an extra unit of labor while holding output constant. (5)

marginal rate of transformation (*MRT*): the trade-off the market imposes on the consumer in terms of the amount of one good the consumer must give up to purchase more of the other good. (4)

marginal revenue (*MR*): the change in revenue a firm gets from selling one more unit of output. (7)

marginal utility: the extra utility that a consumer gets from consuming one more unit of a good. (4)

market: an exchange mechanism that allows buyers to trade with sellers. (1)

market failure: a non-optimal allocation of resources such that total surplus in a market is not maximized. (9)

market power: the ability of a firm to significantly affect the market price. (9)

market structure: the number of firms in the market, the ease with which firms can enter and leave the market, and the ability of firms to differentiate their products from those of their rivals. (7)

maximin strategy (in a game): a strategy that maximizes the lowest possible payoff the player might receive. (12)

mixed strategy: a player in a game chooses among possible pure strategies according to probabilities it assigns. (12)

model: a description of the relationship between two or more variables. (1)

monopolistic competition: a market structure in which firms have market power, but free entry occurs in the long run until no additional firm can enter and earn a positive long-run profit. (11)

monopoly: the sole supplier of a good that has no close substitute. (9)

moral hazard: an informed party takes advantage of a less-informed party by undertaking actions the other party cannot observe and that results in a poor outcome for the less-informed party. (15)

multivariate regression (or *multiple regression*): regression with two or more explanatory variables. (3)

Nash equilibrium: a set of strategies such that, holding the strategies of all other players constant, no player can obtain a higher payoff by choosing a different strategy. (12)

Nash-Bertrand equilibrium (or *Bertrand* or *Bertrand-Nash equilibrium*): a set of prices such that no firm can obtain a higher profit by choosing a different price if the other firms continue to charge these prices. (11)

Nash-Cournot equilibrium (or *Cournot* or *Cournot-Nash equilibrium*): a set of quantities chosen by firms such that, holding the quantities of all other firms constant, no firm can obtain a higher profit by choosing a different quantity. (11)

natural monopoly: the situation in which one firm can produce the total output of the market at lower cost than two or more firms could. (9)

network externality: the situation where one person's demand for a good depends on the consumption of the good by others. (9)

nonlinear price discrimination (or *second-degree price discrimination*): a firm charges a different price for large quantities than for small quantities with the result that the price paid varies according to the quantity purchased. (10)

nonuniform pricing: charging consumers different prices for the same product, or charging a single customer a price that depends on the number of units the customer buys. (10)

normal good: a good for which the quantity demanded increases as income rises. (3)

normative statement: a belief about whether something is good or bad. (1)

oligopoly: a market structure with only a few firms and limited entry. (11)

open-access common property: resources to which everyone has free access and equal rights to exploit. (16)

opportunity cost (or *economic cost*): the value of the best alternative use of a resource. (6)

opportunity set: all the bundles a consumer can buy, including all the bundles inside the budget constraint and on the budget constraint. (4)

Pareto efficient: an outcome with the property that any change would harm at least one person. (16)

Pareto improvement: a change, such as a reallocation of goods and services between people, that helps at least one person without harming anyone else. (16)

Pareto principle: society should favor any change that benefits some people without harming anyone else. (16)

patent: an exclusive right granted to the inventor of a new and useful product, process, substance, or design for a specified length of time. (9)

payoffs (of a game): players' valuations of the outcome of the game, such as profits for firms or income or utilities for individuals. (12)

peak-load pricing: charging higher prices during periods of peak demand than in other periods. (10)

perfect complements: goods that a consumer wants to consume only in fixed proportions. (4)

perfect price discrimination (or *first-degree price discrimination*): a situation in which a firm sells each unit at the maximum amount any customer is willing to pay for it. (10)

perfect substitutes: goods that are essentially equivalent from the consumer's point of view. (4)

positive statement: a testable hypothesis about matters of fact such as cause-and-effect relationships. (1)

price discrimination: charging consumers different prices for the same good based on individual characteristics of consumers, membership in an identifiable subgroup of consumers, or on the quantity purchased. (10)

price elasticity of demand (or *elasticity of demand, demand elasticity*, ε): the percentage change in the quantity demanded, Q, divided by the percentage change in the price, p. (3)

price elasticity of supply (or *elasticity of supply*, η): the percentage change in the quantity supplied divided by the percentage in price. (3)

prisoners' dilemma: a game in which all players have dominant strategies that lead to a payoff that is inferior to what they could achieve if they cooperated. (12)

private cost: a firm's direct costs of production (such as the cost of inputs), but not including any costs imposed on others. (16)

producer surplus (*PS*): the difference between the amount for which a good sells and the minimum amount necessary for the producers to be willing to produce the good. (8)

production function: the relationship between the quantities of inputs used and the maximum quantity of output that can be produced, given current knowledge about technology and organization. (5)

profit (π): the difference between revenues, R, and costs, $C: \pi = R - C$.

public good: a commodity or service that is both nonrival and nonexclusive. (16)

pure strategy: a specification of the action that a player will take in every possible situation in a game. (12)

quantity demanded: the amount of a good that consumers are *willing* to buy at a given price, holding constant the other factors that influence purchases. (2)

quantity supplied: the amount of a good that firms *want* to sell at a given price, holding constant other factors that influence firms' supply decisions, such as costs and government actions. (2)

random error term (in a regression equation): a term that captures the effects of unobserved influences on the dependent variable that are not included as explanatory variables. (3)

regression analysis: a statistical technique used to estimate the mathematical relationship between a dependent variable, such as quantity demanded, and one or more explanatory variables, such as price and income. (3)

regression specification: includes the choice of the dependent variable, the explanatory variables, and the functional relationship between them (such as linear, quadratic, or exponential (3)

rent seeking: devoting effort and expenditures to gain a rent or a profit from government actions. (16)

reservation price: the maximum amount a person is willing to pay for a unit of output. (10)

risk averse: unwilling to make a fair bet. (14)

risk neutral: indifferent about making a fair bet. (14)

risk preferring: always willing to make a fair bet. (14)

risk premium: the amount that a risk-averse person would pay to avoid taking a risk. (14)

rival good: a good that is used up as it is consumed. (16)

rules of the game: regulations that determine the timing of players' moves and the actions that players can make at each move, and possibly other specific aspects of how the game is played. (12)

screening: an action taken by an uninformed person or party to determine the information possessed by informed people. (15)

short run: a period of time so brief that at least one factor of production cannot be varied practically. (5)

signaling: an action taken by an informed person or party to send information to an uninformed person. (15)

snob effect: the situation in which a person places greater value on a good as fewer and fewer other people possess it. (9)

social cost: all the costs incurred by society, including the private costs of firms and individuals and the harm from externalities. (16)

static game: a game in which each player acts only once and the players act simultaneously (or, at least, each player acts without knowing rivals' actions). (12)

strategy: a battle plan that specifies the actions or moves that a player will make conditional on the information available at each move and for any possible contingency. (12)

subgame: all the subsequent actions that players can take given the actions already taken and the corresponding payoffs. (13)

subgame-perfect Nash equilibrium: players' strategies are a Nash equilibrium in every subgame (including the overall game). (13)

substitution effect: the change in the quantity of a good that a consumer demands when the good's price changes, holding other prices and the consumer's utility constant. (4)

sunk cost: a past expenditure that cannot be recovered. (6)

supply curve: the quantity supplied at each possible price, holding constant the other factors that influence firms' supply decisions. (2)

technological efficiency (or *efficient production*): the property of a production function such that the current level of output cannot be produced with fewer inputs, given existing knowledge about technology and the organization of production. (5)

technological progress: an advance in knowledge that allows more output to be produced with the same level of inputs. (5)

tit-for-tat strategy: in a game, a strategy for repeated prisoners' dilemma games that involves cooperation in the first round and then copying the rival's previous action in each subsequent round. (13)

total cost (or *cost, C*): the sum of a firm's variable cost and fixed cost: $C = VC + F$. (6)

total surplus: the sum of consumer surplus and producer surplus, $TS = CS + PS$. (8)

transaction costs: the expenses, over and above the price of the product, of finding a trading partner and making a trade for the product. (2)

transfer price: the price used for an intra-firm transfer of goods or services. (17)

trigger strategy (*in a game*): a strategy in which a rival's defection from a collusive outcome triggers a punishment. (13)

two-part pricing: a pricing system in which the firm charges each consumer a lump-sum access fee for the right to buy as many units of the good as the consumer wants at a per-unit price. (10)

unbiased: an estimation method that produces an estimated coefficient, $\hat{b}$, that equals the true coefficient, b, on average. (3)

uniform pricing: charging the same price for every unit sold of a particular good. (10)

utility: a set of numerical values that reflect the relative rankings of various bundles of goods. (4)

utility function: the relationship between utility measures and every possible bundle of goods. (4)

variable cost (*VC*): a cost that changes as the quantity of output changes. (6)

variable input: a factor of production whose quantity can be changed readily by the firm during the relevant time period. (5)

vertically integrated: describing a firm that participates in more than one successive stage of the production or distribution of goods or services. (7)

winner's curse: in an auction, the phenomenon when a winner's bid exceeds the common-value item's value. (12)

References

Akerlof, George A., "The Market for 'Lemons': Quality Uncertainty and the Market Mechanism," *Quarterly Journal of Economics*, 84(3), August 1970:488–500.

Akerlof, George A., "Labor Contacts as Partial Gift Exchanges," *Quarterly Journal of Economics*, 97(4), November 1982:543–569.

Alexander, Donald L., "Major League Baseball," *Journal of Sports Economics*, 2(4), November 2001:341–355.

Anderson, Michael, and Maximilian Auffhammer, "Pounds that Kill: The External Costs of Vehicle Weight," NBER Working Paper 17170, June 2011.

Asai, Sumiko, "Scale Economies and Scope Economies in the Japanese Broadcasting Market," *Information Economics and Policy*, 18(3), April 2006:321–331.

Axelrod, Robert, *The Evolution of Cooperation* (Revised ed.). Cambridge, MA: Perseus Books Group, 2006.

Ayres, Ian, and Joel Waldfogel, "A Market Test for Race Discrimination in Bail Setting," *Stanford Law Review*, 46(5), May 1994:987–1047.

Bab, Andrew L., and Sean P. Neenan, "Poison Pills in 2011," *Director Notes*, 3(5), March 2011.

Basker, Emek, "Raising the Barcode Scanner: Technology and Productivity in the Retail Sector," NBER Working Paper 17825, 2012.

Bauer, Thomas K., and Christoph M. Schmidt, "WTP vs. WTA: Christmas Presents and the Endowment Effect," Institute for the Study of Labor Working Paper, 2008.

Baumeister, Christiane, and Gert Peersman, "The Role of Time-Varying Price Elasticities in Accounting for Volatility Changes in the Crude Oil Market," *Journal of Applied Econometrics*, published online June 26, 2012.

Benjamin, Daniel K., William R. Dougan, and David Buschena, *Journal of Risk and Uncertainty*, 22(1), January 2001:35–57.

Benkard, C. Lanier, "A Dynamic Analysis of the Market for Wide-Bodied Commercial Aircraft," *Review of Economic Studies*, 71(3), July 2004:581–611.

Bento, Antonio M., Lawrence H. Goulder, Mark R. Jacobsen, and Roger H. von Haefen, "Distributional and Efficiency Impacts of Increased U.S. Gasoline Taxes," *American Economic Review*, 99(3), June 2009:667–699.

Bobashev, Georgiy, Maureen L. Cropper, Joshua M. Epstein, D. Michael Goedecke, Stephen Hutton, and Mead Over, "Policy Response to Pandemic Influenza: The Value of Collective Action," NBER Working Paper 17195, July 2011.

Borenstein, Severin, and Nancy L. Rose, "Competition and Price Dispersion in the U.S. Airline Industry," *Journal of Political Economy*, 102(4), August 1994:653–683.

Bosch-Domènech, Antoni, José G. Montalvo, Rosemarie Nagel, and Albert Satorra, "One, Two, (Three), Infinity, . . . : Newspaper and Lab Beauty-Contest Experiments," *American Economic Review*, 92(5), December 2002:1687–1701.

Brand, Keith, Gautam Gowrisankaran, Aviv Nevo, and Robert Town, "Mergers When Prices Are Negotiated: Evidence from the Hospital Industry," University of Arizona Working Paper, 2012.

Brander, James A., and Barbara J. Spencer, "Export Subsidies and International Market Share Rivalry," *Journal of International Economics*, 18(2), 1985:83–100.

Brander, James A., and M. Scott Taylor, "The Simple Economics of Easter Island: A Ricardo-Malthus Model of Renewable Resource Use," *American Economic Review*, 88(1), March 1998:119–138.

Brander, James A., and Anming Zhang, "Market Conduct in the Airline Industry: An Empirical Investigation," *RAND Journal of Economics*, 21(4), Winter 1990:567–583.

Brown, Jennifer, and John Morgan, "Reputation in Online Auctions: The Market for Trust," *California Management Review*, 49(1), Fall 2006:61–81.

Brown, Jennifer, and John Morgan, "How Much Is a Dollar Worth? Tipping versus Equilibrium Coexistence on Competing Online Auction Sites," *Journal of Political Economy*, 117(4), August 2010:668–700.

Brunk, Gregory G., "A Test of the Friedman-Savage Gambling Model," *Quarterly Journal of Economics*, 96(2), May 1981:341–348.

Buschena, David E., and Jeffrey M. Perloff, "The Creation of Dominant Firm Market Power in the Coconut Oil Export Market," *American Journal of Agricultural Economics*, 73(4), November 1991:1000–1008.

Cabral, Luis, and Ali Hortacsu, "The Dynamics of Seller Reputation: Evidence from eBay," *Journal of Industrial Economics*, 58(1), March 2010:54–78.

Caliendo, Marco, Michel Clement, Domink Papies, and Sabine Scheel-Kopeinig, "The Cost Impact of Spam Filters: Measuring the Effect of Information System Technologies in Organizations," *Information Systems Research*, 23, September 2012:1068–1080.

Camerer, Colin F., *Behavioral Game Theory: Experiments in Strategic Interaction*. New York: Russell Sage Foundation, 2003.

Camerer, Colin F., George Lowenstein, and Matthew Rabin, eds., *Advances in Behavioral Economics*. New York: Russell Sage Foundation, 2004.

Card, David, "Immigration and Inequality," *American Economic Review*, 99(2), May 2009:1–21.

Card, David, and Alan B. Krueger, *Myth and Measurement: The New Economics of the Minimum Wage*. Princeton, NJ: Princeton University Press, 1995.

Carlton, Dennis W., and Jeffrey M. Perloff, *Modern Industrial Organization*, 4th ed. Boston, MA: Addison-Wesley, 2005.

Carman, Hoy F., and Richard J. Sexton, "The 2007 Freeze: Tallying the Toll Two Months Later," *ARE Update*, 10(4), March/April, 2007.

Chetty, Raj, Adam Looney, and Kory Kroft, "Salience and Taxation: Theory and Evidence," NBER Working Paper 13330, 2007.

Chouinard, Hayley H., David Davis, Jeffrey T. LaFrance, and Jeffrey M. Perloff, "Fat Taxes: Big Money for Small Change," *Forum for Health Economics & Policy*, 10(2), 2007.

Coase, Ronald H., "The Nature of the Firm," *Economica*, 4(16), November 1937:386–405.

Coase, Ronald H., "The Problem of Social Cost," *Journal of Law and Economics*, 3, October 1960:1–44.

Cohen, Jeffrey P., and Catherine Morrison Paul, "Scale and Scope Economies for Drug Abuse Treatment Costs: Evidence for Washington State," *Applied Economics*, January 2011:1–8.

Cohen, Jerry, and Allan S. Gutterman, *Trade Secret Protection and Exploitation 2000 Supplement Edition*, BNA Books, 2000.

Conyon, Martin J., and Mark R. Muldoon, "The Small World of Corporate Boards," *Journal of Business Finance & Accounting*, 33(9–10), November/December 2006:1321–1343.

Cummins, J. David, Mary A. Weiss, Xiaoying Xie, and Hongmin Zi, "Economies of Scope in Financial Services: A DEA Efficiency Analysis of the US Insurance Industry," Journal of Banking & Finance, 34(7), July 2010:1525–1539.

Dafny, Leemore S., "Estimation and Identification of Merger Effects: An Application to Hospital Mergers," *Journal of Law & Economics*, 52, August 2009:523–550.

Danzon, Patricia, and Nuno Pereira, "Vaccine Supply: Effects of Regulation and Competition," NBER Working Paper 17205, July 2011.

Davis, Lucas W., and Erich Muehlegger, "Do Americans Consume Too Little Natural Gas? An Empirical Test of Marginal Cost Pricing," *RAND Journal of Economics*, 41(4), Winter 2010:791–810.

Davis, Lucas W., and Catherine Wolfram, "Deregulation, Consolidation, and Efficiency: Evidence from U.S. Nuclear Power," *American Economic Journal: Applied Economics*, 4(4), October 2012:194–225.

de Mello, Joao, Daniel Mejia, and Lucia Suarez, "The Pharmacological Channel Revisited: Alcohol Sales Restrictions and Crime in Bogotá," March 6, 2013, Documento CEDE No. 2013-20. **ssrn.com/abstract=2262335**.

de Melo, Jaime, and David Tarr, *A General Equilibrium Analysis of U.S. Foreign Trade Policy*. Cambridge, MA: MIT Press, 1992.

DellaVigna, Stefano, "Psychology and Economics: Evidence from the Field," *Journal of Economic Literature*, 47(2), June 2009:315–372.

Denstadli, Jon Martin, Rune Lines, and Kjell Grønhaug, "First Mover Advantages in the Discount Grocery Industry," *European Journal of Marketing*, 39(7–8), 2005:872–884.

Draganska, Michaela, Daniel Klapper, and Sofia B. Villas-Boas, "A Larger Slice or a Larger Pie? An Empirical Investigation of Bargaining Power in the Distribution Channel," *Marketing Science*, 29(1), January–February 2010:57–74.

Duffy-Deno, Kevin T., "Business Demand for Broadband Access Capacity," *Journal of Regulatory Economics*, 24(3),2003:359–372.

Dunham, Wayne R., *Moral Hazard and the Market for Used Automobiles, Review of Industrial Organizations*, 23(1), 2003:65–83.

Eastlack, Joseph, and Ambar G. Rao, "Advertising Experiments at the Campbell Soup Company," *Marketing Science*, 8(1), Winter 1989:57–71.

Eckel, Catherine C., and Philip J. Grossman, "Altruism in Anonymous Dictator Games, *Games and Economic Behavior*, 16, 1996:181–191.

Economides, Nicholas, "The Economics of Networks," *International Journal of Industrial Organization*, 14(6), October 1996:673–699.

Edlin, Aaron S., and Pinar Karaca-Mandic, "The Accident Externality from Driving," *Journal of Political Economy*, 114(5), October 2006:931–955.

Ellsberg, Daniel, "Risk, Ambiguity, and the Savage Axioms," *Quarterly Journal of Economics*, 75(4), November 1961:643–669.

Epple, Dennis, Brett Gordon, and Holger Sieg, "A New Approach to Estimating the Production Function for Housing," *American Economic Review*, 100(3), June 2010:905–924.

Espey, Molly, "Gasoline Demand Revisited: an International Meta-analysis of Elasticities," *Energy Economics*, 20(3), June 1998:273–295.

Exxon Company, U.S.A., *Competition in the Petroleum Industry*. Submission to the U.S. Senate Judiciary Subcommittee on Antitrust and Monopoly, January 21, 1975.

Fabrizio, Kira R., Nancy L. Rose, and Catherine D. Wolfram, "Do Markets Reduce Costs? Assessing the Impact of Regulatory Restructuring on US Electric Generation Efficiency," *American Economic Review*, 97(4), September 2007:1250–1277.

Farrell, Diana, "U.S. Offshoring: Small Steps to Make It Win-Win," *Economist Voice*, March 2006.

Farsi, Mehdi, Aurelio Fetz, and Massimo Filippini, "Economies of Scale and Scope in Multi-Utilities," *Energy Journal*, 29(4), [J. M.1] 2008:123–143.

Feenstra, Robert, *Product Variety and the Gains from International Trade*. Cambridge, MA: MIT Press, 2010.

Fisher, Franklin M., "The Social Cost of Monopoly and Regulation: Posner Reconsidered," *Journal of Political Economy*, 93(2), April 1985:410–416.

Flath, David, "Industrial Concentration, Price-Cost Margins, and Innovation," *Japan and the World Economy*, 23(2), March 2011:129–139.

Foster, Andrew D., and Mark R. Rosenzweig, "A Test for Moral Hazard in the Labor Market: Contractual Arrangements, Effort, and Health," *Review of Economics and Statistics*, 76(2), May 1994:213–227.

Foulon, Jerome, Paul Lanoie, and Benoit Laplante, "Incentives for Pollution Control: Regulation or Information?" *Journal of Environmental Economics and Management*, 44(1), July 2002:169–187.

Friedlaender, Ann F., Clifford Winston, and Kung Wang, "Costs, Technology, and Productivity in the U.S. Automobile Industry," *Bell Journal of Economics and Management Science*, 14(1), Spring 1983:1–20.

Friedman, Milton, and Leonard J. Savage, "The Utility Analysis of Choices Involving Risk," *Journal of Political Economy*, 56(4), August 1948:279–304.

Frydman, Carola, and R. E. Saks, "Executive Compensation: A New View from a Long-Term Perspective, 1936–2005," *Review of Financial Studies*, 23(5), 2008:2099–2138.

Furnham, Adrian, "Understanding the Meaning of Tax: Young Peoples' Knowledge of the Principles of Taxation," *Journal of Socio-Economics*, 34(5), October 2005:703–713.

Gallagher, Kevin, *Free Trade and the Environment: Mexico, NAFTA, and Beyond*. Stanford, CA: Stanford University Press, 2004.

Garratt, Rod, Mark Walker, and John Wooders, "Behavior in Second-Price Auctions by Highly Experienced eBay Buyers and Sellers," *Experimental Economics*, 15(1), March 2012:44–57.

Garrett, Thomas A., "An International Comparison and Analysis of Lotteries and the Distribution of Lottery Expenditures," *International Review of Applied Economics*, 15(20), April 2001:213–227.

Garthwaite, Craig L, "Demand Spillovers, Combative Advertising, and Celebrity Endorsements," NBER Working Paper 17915, March 2012.

Gasmi, Farid, D. Mark Kennet, Jean-Jacques Laffont, and William W. Sharkey, *Cost Proxy Models and Telecommunications Policy*. Cambridge, MA: MIT Press, 2002.

Gasmi, Farid, Jean-Jacques Laffont, and Quang H. Vuong, "Econometric Analysis of Collusive Behavior in a Soft-Drink Market," *Journal of Economics and Management Strategy*, 1(2), Summer 1992, 277–311.

Goldfarb, Avi, and Catherine Tucker, "Search Engine Advertising: Channel Substitution When Pricing Ads to Context," *Management Science*, 57(3), March 2011:458–470.

Goldfarb, Avi, and Mo Xiao, "Who Thinks about Competition? Managerial Ability and Strategic Entry in U.S. Telephone Markets," *American Economic Review*, 10(1), December 2011:3130–3161.

Golec, Joseph, and Maurry Tamarkin, "Do Bettors Prefer Long Shots Because They Are Risk Lovers, or Are They Just Overconfident?" *Journal of Risk and Uncertainty*, 11(1), July 1995:51–64.

González, Tanja, Markus Schmid, and David Yermack, "Smokescreen: How Managers Behave When They Have Something to Hide," NBER Working Paper 18886, March 2013.

Gray, Wayne B., and Jay P. Shimshack, "The Effectiveness of Environmental Monitoring and Enforcement: A Review of the Empirical Evidence," *Review of Environmental Economics and Policy*, 5(1), Winter 2011:1–23.

Growitsch, Christian, and Heike Wetzel, "Testing for Economies of Scope in European Railways: An Efficiency Analysis," *Journal of Transport Economics and Policy*, 43(1), January 2009:1–24.

Haas-Wilson, Deborah, and Christopher Garmon, "Hospital Mergers and Competitive Effects: Two Retrospective Analyses," *International Journal of the Economics of Business*, 18(1), February 2011:37–41.

Hall, Bronwyn H., Christian Helmers, Mark Rogers, and Vania Sena. "The Choice between Formal and Informal Intellectual Property: A Literature Review," NBER Working Papers 17983, National Bureau of Economic Research, 2012.

Haskel, Jonathan, and Raffaella Sadun. "Regulation and UK Retailing Productivity: Evidence from Micro Data," *Economica*, 79, July 2012:425–448.

Helliwell, John, Richard Layard, and Jeffrey D. Sachs, eds., *World Happiness Report*. New York: The Earth Institute, Columbia University, 2012. **www.earth.columbia.edu/articles/view/2960**.

Herod, Roger, "Analyzing the Metrics of Global Mobility Programs," *International HR Journal*, Summer 2008:9–15.

Hill, Jason, S. Polasky, E. Nelson, D. Tilman, H. Huo, L. Ludwig, J. Neumann, H. Zheng, and D. Bonta, "Climate Change and Health Costs of Air Emissions from Biofuels and Gasoline," *Proceedings of the National Academy of Sciences*, 106(6), February 2009:2077–2082.

Ho, Jason, Tirtha Dhar, and Charles Weinberg, "Playoff payoff: Super Bowl advertising for movies," *International Journal of Research in Marketing*, 26(3), September 2009:168–179.

Hsieh, Wen-Jen, "Test of Variable Output and Scale Elasticities for 20 U.S. Manufacturing Industries," *Applied Economics Letters*, 2(8), August 1995:284–287.

Ida, Takanori, and Tetsuya Kuwahara, "Yardstick Cost Comparison and Economies of Scale and Scope in Japan's Electric Power Industry," *Asian Economic Journal*, 18(4), December 2004:423–438.

Irwin, Douglas A., "The Welfare Cost of Autrky: Evidence from the Jeffersonian Trade Embargo, 1807–09," *Review of International Economics*, 13(4), September 2005:631–645.

Irwin, Douglas A., and Nina Pavcnik, "Airbus versus Boeing Revisited: International Competition in the Aircraft Market," *Journal of International Economics*, 64(2), December 2004:223–245.

Kahneman, Daniel, Jack L. Knetsch, and Richard H. Thaler, "Experimental Tests of the Endowment Effect and the Coase Theorem," *Journal of Political Economy*, 98(6), December 1990:1325–1348.

Kahneman, Daniel, and Amos Tversky, "Prospect theory: An analysis of decisions under risk," *Econometrica*, 47(2), March 1979:313–327.

Katz, Michael L., and Carl Shapiro, "Systems Competition and Network Effects," *Journal of Economic Perspectives*, 8(2), 1994:93–115.

Kellogg, Ryan, "Learning by Drilling: Inter-Firm Learning and Relationship Persistence in the Texas Oilpatch," *Quarterly Journal of Economics*, 126(4), 2011:1961–2004.

Keynes, John Maynard, *The General Theory of Employment, Interest and Money*. Basingstoke, Hampshire: Palgrave Macmillan, 1936.

Kim, H. Youn, "Economies of Scale and Scope in Multiproduct Firms: Evidence from U.S. Railroads," *Applied Economics*, 19(6), June 1987:733–741.

Kim, Jin-Woo, *When Are Super Bowl Advertisings Super? An Empirical Analysis of the Economic Impact of Super Bowl Advertising*. Unpublished Ph.D. dissertation, University of Texas, Arlington, 2011. **dspace.uta.edu/handle/10106/6136**.

Klein, Benjamin, Robert G. Crawford, and Armen A. Alchian, "Vertical Integration, Appropriable Rents, and the Competitive Contracting Process," *Journal of Law and Economics*, 21(2), October 1978:297–326.

Klein, Lawrence R., "The Use of the Input-Output Tables to Estimate the Productivity of IT," *Journal of Policy Modeling*, 25(5), July 2003:471–475.

Kleiner, Morris M., and Alan B. Krueger, "Analyzing the Extent and Influence of Occupational Licensing on the Labor Market," *Journal of Labor Economics*, April 2013, 31(2):S173–S202.

Klemperer, Paul, *Auctions: Theory and Practice*. Princeton, NJ: Princeton University Press, 2004.

Knetsch, Jack L., "Preferences and Nonreversibility of Indifference Curves," *Journal of Economic Behavior and Organization*, 17(1), 1992:131–139.

Kong, Clement, Wing Chow, Michael Ka, and Yiu Fung, "Efficiencies and Scope Economies of Chinese Airports in Moving Passengers and Cargo," *Journal of Air Transport Management*, 15(6), November 2009:324–329.

Kotchen, Matthew J., and Nicholas E. Burger, "Should We Drill in the Arctic National Wildlife Refuge? An Economic Perspective," NBER Working Paper 13211, July 2007.

Kreps, David M., and Robert Wilson, "Reputation and Imperfect Information," *Journal of Economic Theory*, 27(2), August 1982:253–279.

Krugman, Paul R., "Is Free Trade Passé?" *Journal of Economic Perspectives*, 1, 1987:131–144.

LaPlante, Benoit, and Paul Rilstone, "Environmental Inspections and Emissions of the Pulp and Paper Industry in Quebec," *Journal of Environmental Economics and Management*, 31(1), July 1996:19–36.

Leibenstein, Harvey, "Bandwagon, Snob, and Veblen Effects in the Theory of Consumers' Demand," *Quarterly Journal of Economics*, 64(2), May 1950:183–207.

Leslie, Phillip J., "A Structural Econometric Analysis of Price Discrimination in Broadway Theatre," working paper, University of California, Los Angeles, November 15, 1997.

Levy, Douglas E., and Ellen Meara, "The Effect of the 1998 Master Settlement Agreement on Prenatal Smoking," NBER Working Paper 11176, March 2005.

Lewis, Gregory, "Asymmetric Information, Adverse Selection and Online Disclosure: The Case of eBay Motors," *American Economic Review*, 101(4), June 2011:1535–1546.

Lichtenstein, Nelson, "How Walmart Fights Unions," *Minnesota Law Review*, 92(5), May 2008:1462–1501.

Lipford, Jody W., and Bruce Yandle, "NAFTA, Environmental Kuznets Curves, and Mexico's Progress," *Global Economic Journal*, 10(4), January 2011.

List, John A., "Does Market Experience Eliminate Market Anomalies?" *Quarterly Journal of Economics*, 118(1), February 2003:41–71.

Lopez, Rigoberto A., and Emilio Pagoulatos, "Rent Seeking and the Welfare Cost of Trade Barriers," *Public Choice*, 79(1–2), April 1994:149–160.

Lu, Fangwen, "Insurance Coverage and Agency Problems in Doctor Prescriptions: Evidence from a Field Experiment in China," Discussion Paper, Renmin University of China, 2012.

Luchansky, Matthew S., and James Monks, "Supply and Demand Elasticities in the U.S. Ethanol Fuel Market," *Energy Economics*, 31(3), 2009:403–410.

MacCrimmon, Kenneth R., and M. Toda, "The Experimental Determination of Indifference Curves," *Review of Economic Studies*, 56(3), July 1969:433–451.

Machina, Mark, "Dynamic Consistency and Non-Expected Utility Models of Choice Under Uncertainty," *Journal of Economic Literature*, 27(4), December 1989:1622–1668.

MacKie-Mason, Jeffrey K., and Robert S. Pindyck, "Cartel Theory and Cartel Experience in International Minerals Markets," in R. L. Gordon, H. D. Jacoby, and M. B. Zimmerman, eds., *Energy: Markets and Regulation: Essays in Honor of M. A. Adelman*. Cambridge, MA: MIT Press, 1986.

Madrian, Brigitte C., and Dennis F. Shea, "The Power of Suggestion: Inertia in 401(k) Participation and Savings Behavior," *Quarterly Journal of Economics*, 116(4), November 2001:1149–1187.

Madrian, Brigitte C., and Dennis F. Shea, "The Power of Suggestion: Inertia in 401(k) Participation and Savings Behavior: Erratum," *Quarterly Journal of Economics*, 117(1), February 2002:377.

Mankiw, Gregory N., and Phillip Swagel, "The Politics and Economics of Offshore Outsourcing," *Journal of Monetary Economics*, 53(5), July 2006:1027–1056.

Manzi, Jim, *Uncontrolled: The Surprising Payoff of Trial-and-Error for Business, Politics, and Society*, New York: Basic Books, 2012.

Martinez, Steve W., "Vertical Coordination in the Pork and Broiler Industries: Implications for Pork and Chicken Products," Food and Rural Economics Division, Economic Research Service, U.S. Department of Agriculture, Agricultural Economic Report No. 777, 1999.

McDevitt, Ryan C., "Names and Reputations: An Empirical Analysis," *American Economic Journal: Microeconomics*, 3(3), August 2011:193–209.

Milgrom, Paul, and John Roberts, "Predation, reputation, and entry deterrence," *Journal of Economic Theory*, 27(2), August 1982:280–312.

Monteverde, Kirk, and David J. Teece, "Appropriable Rents and Quasi-Vertical Integration," *Journal of Law and Economics*, 25(2), October 1982:403–418.

Nash, John F., "Equilibrium Points in *n*-Person Games," *Proceedings of the National Academy of Sciences*, 36, 1950:48–49.

Nash, John F., "Non-Cooperative Games," *Annals of Mathematics*, 54(2), July 1951:286–295.

Nash, John F., "Two-Person Cooperative Games," *Econometrica*, 21(1), April 1953:128–140.

Nataraj, Shanthi, "Do Residential Water Consumers React to Price Increases? Evidence from a Natural Experiment in Santa Cruz," *Agricultural and Resource Economics Update*, 10(3), January/February 2007:9–11.

Nicol, C. J., "Elasticities of Demand for Gasoline in Canada and the United States," *Energy Economics*, 25(2), March 2003:201–214.

Panzar, John C., and Robert D. Willig, "Economies of Scale in Multi-Output Production," *Quarterly Journal of Economics*, 91(3), August 1977:481–493.

Panzar, John C., and Robert D. Willig, "Economies of Scope," *American Economic Review*, 71(2), May 1981:268–272.

Parry, Ian W. H., Margaret Walls, and Winston Harrington, "Automobile Externalities and Policies," Resources for the Future Discussion Paper No. 06-26, January 2007.

Perry, Martin K., "Vertical Integration: Determinants and Effects," in Richard Schmalensee and Robert D. Willig, eds., *Handbook of Industrial Organization*. New York: North Holland, 1989.

Pielke, Roger A., Jr., Joel Gratz, Christopher W. Landsea, Douglas Collins, Mark A. Saunders, and Rade Musulin, "Normalized Hurricane Damages in the United States: 1900–2005." *Natural Hazards Review*, 9(1), February 2008:29–42.

Plott, Charles R., and Kathryn Zeiler, "The Willingness to Pay—Willingness to Accept Gap, the 'Endowment Effect,' Subject Misconceptions, and Experimental Procedures for Eliciting Values," *American Economic Review*, 95(3), June 2005:530–545.

Posner, Richard A., "The Social Cost of Monopoly and Regulation," *Journal of Political Economy*, 83(4), August 1975:807–827.

Rao, Justin M., and David H. Reiley, "The Economics of Spam," *Journal of Economic Perspectives*, 26(3), Fall 2012:87–110.

Regan, Tracy L., "Generic Entry, Price Competition, and Market Segmentation in the Prescription Drug Market," *International Journal of Industrial Organization*, 26(4), July 2008:930–948.

Richards, Timothy J., and Luis Padilla, "Promotion and Fast Food Demand," *American Journal of Agricultural Economics*, 91(1), February 2009:168–183.

Roberts, Mark J., and Larry Samuelson, "An Empirical Analysis of Dynamic Nonprice Competition in an Oligopolistic Industry," *RAND Journal of Economics*, 19(2), Summer 1988:200–220.

Robidoux, Benoît, and John Lester, "Econometric Estimates of Scale Economies in Canadian Manufacturing," Working Paper No. 88-4, Canadian Dept. of Finance, 1988.

Robidoux, Benoît, and John Lester, "Econometric Estimates of Scale Economies in Canadian Manufacturing," *Applied Economics*, 24(1), January 1992:113–122.

Rohlfs, Jeffrey H., "A Theory of Interdependent Demand for a Communications Service," *Bell Journal of Economics and Management Science*, 5(1), Spring 1974:16–37.

Rohlfs, Jeffrey H., *Bandwagon Effects in High-Technology Industries.* Cambridge, MA: MIT Press, 2001.

Rosenberg, Howard R., "Many Fewer Steps for Pickers—A Leap for Harvestkind? Emerging Change in Strawberry Harvest Technology," *Choices*, 1st Quarter 2004:5–11.

Rossi, R. J., and Armstrong, T., Studies of intercollegiate athletics: Summary results from the 1987–88 National Study of Intercollegiate Athletes (Report No. 1), Palo Alto, CA: Center for the Study of Athletics, American Institutes for Research, 1989.

Rousseas, S. W., and A. G. Hart, "Experimental Verification of a Composite Indifference Map," *Journal of Political Economy*, 59(4), August 1951:288–318.

Salant, Stephen W., Sheldon Switzer, and Robert J. Reynolds, "Losses from Horizontal Merger: The Effects of an Exogenous Change in Industry Structure on Cournot-Nash Equilibrium," *Quarterly Journal of Economics*, 98(2), 1983:185–199.

Salem, Samira, and Faina Rozental, "Labor Standards and Trade: A Review of Recent Empirical Evidence," *Journal of International Commerce and Economics*, 4(2), November 2012:63–98.

Salgado, Hugo, "A Dynamic Duopoly Model under Learning by Doing in the Computer CPU Industry," University of California, Berkeley, Ph.D. dissertation, 2008.

Salop, Steven C., "The Noisy Monopolist: Imperfect Information, Price Dispersion, and Price Discrimination," *Review of Economic Studies*, 44(3), October 1977:393–406.

Salop, Steven C., "Practices That (Credibly) Facilitate Oligopoly Coordination," in Joseph E. Stiglitz and G. Frank Mathewson, eds., *New Developments in the Analysis of Market Structure*. Cambridge, MA: MIT Press, 1986.

Sappington, David E. M., and Dennis L. Weisman, "Price Cap Regulation: What Have We Learned from 25 Years of Experience in the Telecommunications Industry?" *Journal of Regulatory Economics*, 38(3), 2010:227–257.

Scherer, F. M., "An Early Application of the Average Total Cost Concept," *Journal of Economic Literature*, 39(3), September 2001:897–901.

Schoemaker, Paul J. H., "The Expected Utility Model: Its Variants, Purposes, Evidence and Limitation," *Journal of Economic Literature*, 20(2), June 1982:529–563.

Shadbegian, Ronald J., and Wayne B. Gray, "What Determines Environmental Performance at Paper Mills? The Roles of Abatement Spending, Regulation and Efficiency," *Topics in Economic Analysis and Policy*, 3(1), 2003.

Shapiro, Carl, and Joseph E. Stiglitz, "Equilibrium Unemployment as a Worker Discipline Device," *American Economic Review*, 74(3), June 1984:434–444.

Shapiro, Carl, and Hal R. Varian, *Information Rules: A Strategic Guide to the Network Economy*. Boston: Harvard Business School Press, 1999.

Shiller, Ben, and Joel Waldfogel, "Music for a Song: An Empirical Look at Uniform Pricing and Its Alternatives," *The Journal of Industrial Economics*, 59(4), December 2011:630–660.

Shimshack, Jay, and Michael B. Ward, "Regulator Reputation, Enforcement, and Environmental Compliance," *Journal of Environmental Economics and Management*, 50(3), November 2005:519–540.

Slade, Margaret E., "Product Rivalry with Multiple Strategic Weapons: An Analysis of Price and Advertising Competition," *Journal of Economics and Management Strategy*," 4(3), Fall 1995:224–276.

Stigler, George J., "The Division of Labor Is Limited by the Extent of the Market," *Journal of Political Economy*, 59(3), June 1951:185–193.

Stiglitz, Joseph E., "The Causes and Consequences of the Dependence of Quality on Price," *Journal of Economic Literature*, 25(1), March 1987:1–48.

Suzuki, Junichi, "Land Use Regulation as a Barrier to Entry: Evidence from the Texas Lodging Industry," *International Economic Review*, 54(2), 2013:495–523.

Sweeting, Andrew, "Coordination, Differentiation and the Timing of Radio Commercials," *Journal of Economics and Management Strategy*, 15(4), Winter 2006:909–942.

Sweeting, Andrew, "The Strategic Timing of Radio Commercials: An Empirical Analysis Using Multiple Equilibria," *RAND Journal of Economics*, 40(4), Winter 2009, 710–742.

Tenn, Steven, "The Price Effects of Hospital Mergers: A Case Study of the Sutter–Summit Transaction," *International Journal of the Economics of Business*, 18(1), February 2011:65–82.

Thaler, Richard H., *The Winner's Curse: Paradoxes and Anomalies of Economic Life*. Princeton, NJ: Princeton University Press, 1994.

Tullock, G., "The Welfare Cost of Tariffs, Monopolies, and Theft," *Western Economic Journal*, 5(3), June 1967:224–232.

Tversky, Amos, and Daniel Kahneman, "The Framing of Decisions and the Psychology of Choice," *Science*, 211(4481), January 1981:453–458.

Urban, Glen L., Theresa Carter, and Steven Gaskin, "Market Share Rewards to Pioneering Brands: An Empirical Analysis and Strategic Implications," *Management Science*, 32(6), June 1986:645–659.

U.S. Environmental Protection Agency, *The Green Book Nonattainment Areas for Criteria Pollutants*, 2012. **www.epa.gov/ airquality/greenbook/**.

U.S. Census Bureau, Statistical Abstract of the United States: 2012 (131st Edition) Washington, DC.

Usero, B., and Z. Fernández., "First come, first served: How market and non-market actions influence pioneer market share," *Journal of Business Research*, 62, 2009:1139–1145.

Varian, Hal R., "Measuring the Deadweight Cost of DUP and Rent-Seeking Activities," *Economics and Politics*, 1(1), Spring 1989:81–95.

Veracietro, Marcelo, Luis, "Firing Costs and Business Cycle Fluctuations," *International Economic Review*, 49(1), 2008:1–39.

Visser, Michael S., and Matthew Roelofs, "Heterogeneous Preferences for Altruism:gender and personality, social status, giving and taking," *Experimental Economics*, 14, 2011:490–506.

von Hippel, F. A., and W. F. von Hipple, "Sex, Drugs and Animal Parts: Will Viagra Save Threatened Species?" *Environmental Conservation*, 29(3), 2002:277–281.

von Hippel, F. A., and W. F. von Hipple, "Is Viagra a Viable Conservation Tool? Response to Hoover, 2003," *Environmental Conservation*, 31(1), 2004:4–6.

von Hippel, William, Frank A. von Hippel, Norma Chan, and Clara Cheng, "Exploring the Use of Viagra in Place of Animal and Plant Potency Products in Traditional Chinese Medicine," *Environmental Conservation*, 32(3), September 2005:235–238.

von Neumann, John, and Oskar Morgenstern, *Theory of Games and Economic Behavior*. Princeton, NJ: Princeton University Press, 1944.

Waldfogel, Joel, "The Deadweight Loss of Christmas," *American Economic Review*, 83(5), December 1993:1328–1336.

Waldfogel, Joel, "Does Consumer Irrationality Trump Consumer Sovereignty?" *Review of Economics and Statistics*, 87(4), November 2005:691–696.

Waldfogel, Joel, *Scroogenomics*. Princeton, NJ: Princeton University Press, 2009.

Weiher, Jesse C., Robin C. Sickles, and Jeffrey M. Perloff, "Market Power in the U.S. Airline Industry," in D. J. Slottje, ed., *Economic Issues in Measuring Market Power, Contributions to Economic Analysis*, Volume 255, Elsevier 2002.

Weinstein, Arnold A., "Transitivity of Preferences: A Comparison Among Age Groups," *Journal of Political Economy*, 76(2), March/April 1968:307–311.

Williamson, Oliver E., *Markets and Hierarchies: Analysis and Antitrust Implications*. New York: Free Press, 1975.

Williamson, Oliver E., "Credible Commitments: Using Hostages to Support Exchange," *American Economic Review*, 73(4), September 1983:519–540.

Wyatt, Edward, "Supreme Court Lets Regulators Sue Over Generic Deals," *New York Times*, June 17, 2013.

Yatchew, Adonis, "Scale Economies in Electricity Distribution: A Semiparametric Analysis," *Journal of Applied Econometrics*, 15(2), March/April 2000:187–210.

Yellen, Janet L., "Efficiency Wage Models of Unemployment," *American Economic Review*, 74(2), May 1984:200–205.

Yermack, David, "Flights of Fancy: Corporate Jets, CEO Perquisites, and Inferior Shareholder Returns," *Journal of Financial Economics*, 80(1), April 2006:211–242.

Sources for Managerial Problems, Mini-Cases, and Managerial Implications

Chapter 1

Mini-Case *Using an Income Threshold Model in China*: "Next in Line: Chinese Consumers," *Economist*, 326 (7795), January 23, 1993:66–67. Jeff Pelline, "U.S. Businesses Pour into China," *San Francisco Chronicle*, May 17, 1994:B1–B2. *China Statistical Yearbook*, 2000. Keith Bradsher, "With First Car, a New Life in China," *New York Times*, April 24, 2008. Bloomberg News, "Foreign Direct Investment in China in 2010 Rises to Record $105.7 Billion," January 17, 2011, **www.bloomberg .com/news/2011-01-18/foreign-direct-investment-in-china-in-2010-rises-to-record-105-7-billion.html**. "China's Auto-Sales Growth Trails U.S. for First Time in at Least 14 Years," Bloomberg News, January 11, 2012, **www.bloomberg.com/ news/2012-01-12/china-s-auto-sales-growth-trails-u-s-for-first-time-in-at-least-14-years.html**. Chris Woodyard, "Ford Investing $600 Million in Chinese Car Factory," *USA Today*, April 9, 2012, **www.worldometers.info/cars**.

Chapter 2

Managerial Problem: Carbon Taxes Chouinard and Perloff (2007). Charles Herman, "Pain in the Gas: Refinery Troubles Push Gas Prices Higher," ABC News, May 15, 2007, **www .abcnews.go.com/print?id=3176143**. Tom Krisher, "Why Honda Is Growing as Detroit Falls Behind," *San Francisco Chronicle*, July 3, 2008. "Cedar Balls and Rum," *The Economist*, June 7, 2011. "Let the World's #1 Automaker Switcheroo Continue!" CNN Money, June 16, 2011, **www.auto123.com/ en/news/car-news/let-the-worlds-1-automaker-switcheroo-continue?artid=132475**. Mike Ramsey, "GM's 2011 Auto Sales Spark Feud Over Count," *Wall Street Journal*, January 20, 2012. Todd Wasserman, "Google's Investment in Renewable Energy Approaches $1 Billion," November 15, 2012, **mashable .com/2012/11/15/googles-renewable-energy-1-billion**. Daniel Cusick, "Warren Buffett Makes Another Solar Power Play, Expanding His Holdings," Climatewire, January 4, 2013,

www.eenews.net/climatewire/2013/01/04/2. The Carbon Tax Center, **www.carbontax.org** (viewed on January 3, 2013).

Mini-Cases *Aggregating the Demand for Broadband Service*: Duffy-Deno (2003).

Genetically Modified Foods: Dick Ahlstrom, "Use of GM Foods Inevitable in EU—Expert," *Irish Times*, July 18, 2008. Steven Sexton, "The Economics of Agricultural Biotechnology: Implications for Biofuel Sustainability," University of California Berkeley, working paper, 2010. Hong Van, "Genetically Modified Food Is Almost Everywhere," *The Saigon Times*, April 21, 2010. David Cronin, "Advantage GM in Europe," Inter Press Service, May 18, 2010. Stefanie Hundsdorfer, "Europe Takes Step Towards Ban on Genetically Modified Crops," Greenpeace, April 13, 2011, **www.greenpeace.org/ international/en/news/Blogs/makingwaves/europe-takes-step-towards-ban-on-genetically-/blog/34239**. **www.isaaa .org/resources/publications/briefs/44/executivesummary**. John Vidal, "Campaigners Clash Over Industry Claims of Rise in GM Crops," *The Guardian*, February 8, 2012. "Genetically Modified Food," **en.wikipedia.org/wiki/Genetically_ modified_food** (viewed on July 7, 2012). "Adoption of Genetically Engineered Crops in the U.S.," U.S. Department of Agriculture, July 12, 2012. **www.ers.usda.gov/data-products/ adoption-of-genetically-engineered-crops-in-the-us.aspx**.

Occupational Licensing: **admissions.calbar.ca.gov/ Examinations/Statistics.aspx** (viewed on December 22, 2012). **www .ncbex.org/assets/media_files/Statistics/2011Statistics.pdf**. Kleiner and Krueger (2013).

Disastrous Price Controls: Ivan Vera, "Zimbabwe: Forex Shortage Spurs Sugar Smuggling," *Harare*, November 10, 2000, **allafrica.com/stories/200011100299.html**. Kumbirai Mafunda, "Zimbabwe: Construction Industry Faces Bleak Future," *Zimbabwe Standard*, May 5, 2002, **allafrica .com/stories/200205080214.html**. Ngoni Chanakira, "Zimbabwe: Makoni Admits Price Controls to Blame for Thriving Black Market," *The Daily News*, May 10, 2002, **allafrica .com/stories/200205100207.html**. "Zim Slaps Price Control on Food," *News24*, June 4, 2005, **www.news24.com/Africa/ Zimbabwe/Zim-slaps-price-control-on-food-20050406-2**. Fanuel Jongwe, "Watchdog Unlikely to Get Teeth into Zimbabwe Inflation," *Mail & Guardian*, November 12, 2006.

Kotchen and Burger (2007). "Zimbabwe Arrests Over Price Curbs," Al Jazeera, July 9, 2007, **www.aljazeera.com/news/africa/2007/07/2008525132038645691.html**. "Robert Mugabe Zimbabwe Poll Ploy Strips White Firms," *The Australian*, March 11, 2008. "Zimbabwe Manufacturing Output Falls 27 Percent," *Harare*, July 24, 2008, **www.monstersandcritics.com/news/business/news/printer_1419238.php**. Brian Latham, "Zimbabwe Abandons Price Controls, Promotes Currency Trading," January 29, 2009, **www.tradeafricablog.com/2009/01/zimbabwe-abandons-price-controls.html**. Godfrey Marawanyika, "Mugabe Defends Sale of Foreign Firms to Locals," Google, February 27, 2010, **www.google.com/hostednews/afp/article/ALeqM5jKPanDRNzEjTbmWRZ48AgI9KesNw**.

Managerial Implication *Taking Advantage of Future Shocks*: Larry Rohter, "Shipping Costs Start to Crimp Globalization," *New York Times*, August 3, 2008. "Global shipping hits record volume as prices fall: UN," *Taipai Times*, December 6, 2012.

Chapter 3

Managerial Problem: Estimating the Effect of an iTunes Price Change "Changes Coming to the iTunes Store," Apple Press Info, January 6, 2009, **www.apple.com/pr/library/2009/01/06itunes.html**. John Paczkowski, "25 Million iPads, 14 Billion Apps: WWDC 2011 by the Numbers," All Things D, June 7, 2011, **allthingsd.com/20110607/25-million-ipads-1-billion-tweets-wwdc-2011-by-the-numbers/**.

Mini-Cases *Substitution May Save Endangered Species*: Von Hippel and von Hippel (2002, 2004). Von Hippel et al. (2005).

Turning Off the Faucet: Nataraj (2007).

The Portland Fish Exchange: "Portland Fish Exchange," **www.pfex.org/** (viewed on July 21, 2012).

Determinants of CEO Compensation: Standard & Poor's Compustat (viewed on March 1, 2012 through **whartonwrds.com/**).

Managerial Implication: Experiments: Jim Manzi, "What Social Science Does—and Doesn't—Know," *City Journal*, Summer 2010, vol. 20, no. 3. Lizzy Van Alstine and Jon Vaver, "Measuring Ad Effectiveness Using Geo Experiments," *Google Research Blogspot*, December 9, 2011, **googleresearch.blogspot.ca/2011/12/measuring-ad-effectiveness-using-geo.html**. Jon Vaver and Jim Koehler, "Measuring Ad Effectiveness Using Geo Experiments," Google Inc., December 9, 2011, **services.google.com/fh/files/blogs/geo_experiments_final_version.pdf**. Manzi (2012).

Chapter 4

Managerial Problem: Paying Employees to Relocate Katherine Rosman, "Expat Life Gets Less Cushy," *Wall Street Journal*, October 26, 2007. Barbara Worthington, "FYI: Relocation," February 1, 2008. Grace W. Weinstein, "The Good and Bad of Moving Overseas," *Financial Times*, May 24 2008. "Applying Negative Cost of Living Indices—Bad Practice or Logical Solution?" Mercer, July 21, 2008, **www.mercer.com/referencecontent.htm?idContent=1312800**. Jane M. Von Bergen, "More U.S. Workers Getting Global Assignments," *Philadelphia Inquirer*, August 4, 2008. Herod (2008). "New Zealand Cities More Affordable for Global Expats—Mercer Worldwide Cost of Living Survey 2009," Mercer, July 7, 2009, **www.mercer.com/summary.htm?idContent=1351425**. "The Most Expensive and Richest Cities in the World," *City Mayors Economics*, August 18, 2011 (viewed on July 14, 2012). "Cost of living comparison between London (United Kingdom) and Seattle (United States)," Expatistan, 2012, **www.expatistan.com/cost-of-iving/comparison/seattle/london** (viewed on July 14, 2012). Mercer Worldwide Survey of International Assignment Policies and Practices Report, 2012, **www.imercer.com/products/2012/WorldwideIAPP.aspx**.

Mini-Cases *You Can't Have Too Much Money*: *Businessweek*, February 28, 2005, p. 13. Stevenson and Wolfers (2008). "Annual Happiness Index Again Finds One-Third of Americans Very Happy," Harris Interactive, June 22, 2011, **www.digitaljournal.com**. Emily Alpert, "Happiness Tops in Denmark, Lowest in Togo, Study Says," *Los Angeles Times*, April 2, 2012. Helliwell et al. (2012).

Rationing: Rawlings Otini, "Dams Full, But Water Rationing Goes On," *Business Daily*, May 17, 2010, **www.marsgroupkenya.com/multimedia/?StoryID=292045**. "Egypt PM Reassures about Water Quota," *Egypt News*, May 25, 2010. "Water Rationing in Pindi from June 1," *Daily Times*, May 28, 2010. Joe Carroll, "Worst Drought in More Than a Century Strikes Texas Oil Boom," Bloomberg News, June 13, 2011, **www.bloomberg.com/news/2011-06-13/worst-drought-in-more-than-a-century-threatens-texas-oil-natural-gas-boom.html**.

Why Americans Buy More E-Books Than Do Germans: Rüdiger Wischenbart et al., Global ebook Market: 2012, O'Reilly, 2012. Caroline Winter, "The Story Behind Germany's Scant E-Book Sales," *Bloomberg Businessweek*, April 19, 2012.

How You Ask the Question Matters: Madrian and Shea (2001, 2002). "Aon Hewitt Study Shows Record-High Participation in Defined Contribution Plans Driven by Automatic Enrollment," AON, May 24, 2011, **aon.mediaroom.com/index.php?s=43&item=2285**. "401(k) Plans in Living Color," Ariel Investments, April 3, 2012, **www.arielinvestments.com/401k-Study-2012**.

Chapter 5

Managerial Problem: Labor Productivity During Recessions Hsieh (1995). Tom Abate, "Licorice Company Looks to Weather the Storm," *San Francisco Chronicle*, September 28, 2008. Veracierto (2008). Timothy Aeppel and Justin Lahart, "Lean Factories Find It Hard to Cut Jobs Even in a Slump," *Wall Street Journal*, March 9, 2009. "Union City Licorice Factory Workers Accept Contract, End Strike," CBS San Francisco, January 11, 2012, **sanfrancisco.cbslocal.com/2012/01/11/**

union-city-licorice-factory-workers-accept-contract-end-strike/.

Mini-Cases *Malthus and the Green Revolution*: Norman Borlaug, "Nobel Lecture," December 11, 1970, **www.nobelprize.org/nobel_prizes/peace/laureates/1970/borlaug-lecture.html**. Gregg Easterbrook, "Forgotten Benefactor of Humanity," *Atlantic Monthly*, January 1997. Brander and Taylor (1998). "Food and Population: FAO Looks Ahead," July 24, 2000, **www.fao.org/NEWS/2000/000704-e.htm**. Alan Barkema, "Ag Biotech: Bold New Promise or Bold New Risk?" *The Main Street Economist*, October 2000, **www.kansascityfed.org/Publicat/mse/MSE_1000.pdf**. "Biotechnology and the Green Revolution: Interview with Norman Borlaug," Action Bioscience, November 2002, **www.actionbioscience.org/biotechnology/borlaug.html**. **www.ers.usda.gov/data-products.aspx** (viewed on May 16, 2012). **www.wfp.org/hunger/stats** (viewed on June 11, 2012). **www.fao.org/economic/ess/ess-fs/ess-fadata/en** (viewed on February 3, 2013).

A Semiconductor Isoquant: Nile Hatch, personal communications. Roy Mallory, personal communications. "PC Processor War Rages On," *Deutsche Presse-Agentur*, September 1, 2002.

Returns to Scale in U.S. Manufacturing: Hsieh (1995).

U.S. Electric Generation Efficiency: Peter Van Doren and Jerry Taylor, "Rethinking Electricity Restructuring," Policy Analysis, Cato Institute, November 30, 2004, **www.cato.org/sites/cato.org/files/pubs/pdf/pa530.pdf**. Mark D. Symes et al., "Integrated 3D-Printed Reactionware for Chemical Synthesis and Analysis," *Nature Chemistry*, April 2012. Deborah Netburn, "Dutch Architect Plans World's First 3-D-Printed Building," *Los Angeles Times*, January 21, 2013.

Tato Nano's Technical and Organizational Innovations: Adil Jal Darukhanawala, "Engineering the Nano," *The Times of India*, January 11, 2008. John Hagel and John Seely Brown, "Learning from Tata's Nano," *Bloomberg Businessweek*, February 27, 2008. "How Green Is My Low-Cost Car? India Revs Up Debate," June 19, 2008, Reuters. Gerard J. Tellis, "A Lesson for Detroit: Tata Nano," *San Francisco Chronicle*, March 31, 2009. "Tata Nano: Not Only a Product Revolution, but also a Breakthrough in Product Distribution," Datamonitor, May 6, 2009, **www.datamonitor.com/store/News/tata_nano_not_only_a_product_revolution_but_also_a_breakthrough_in_product_distribution?productid=71712496-06B8-4CC3-9AA6-0832CE85D4D1**. Lijee Philip and Kala Vijayraghavan, "Smart Selling Helps Tata Nano Sales Drive Past 10k Units Mark in April," *The Economic Times*, May 10, 2011. Nachiket Kelkar, "LCVs, Nano Push Tata Motors May Sales Up 4%," Money Control, June 1, 2012, **www.moneycontrol.com/news/business/lcvs-nano-push-tata-motors-may-sales4_712210.html**.

Managerial Implication *Small Is Beautiful*: Print Me a Stradivarius," *Economist*, February 10, 2011.

Chapter 6

Managerial Problem: Technology Choice at Home Versus Abroad *Semiconductor Industry Association*, **www.sia-online.org** (viewed on February 10, 2013).

Mini-Cases *The Opportunity Cost of an MBA*: Profile of GMAT Candidates, Five Year Summary, GMAT, 2011, **www.gmac.com/market-intelligence-and-research/research-library/gmat-test-taker-data/profile-documents/profile-of-gmat-candidates-2006-07-2010-11.aspx**.

The Internet and Outsourcing: Matt Richtel, "Outsourced All the Way," *New York Times*, June 21, 2005.

Economies of Scale in Nuclear Power Plants: Lucas W. Davis and Catherine Wolfram, "Deregulation, Consolidation, and Efficiency: Evidence from U.S. Nuclear Power," NBER Working Paper 17341, 2011.

Long-Run Cost Curves in Beer Manufacturing and Oil Pipelines: Exxon (1975). Hsieh (1995). Flath (2011).

Learning by Drilling: Kellogg (2011).

Scope: Friedlaender et al. (1983). Kim (1987). Yatchew (2000). Ida and Kuwahara (2004). Asai (2006). Farsi, Fetz, and Filippini (2008). Growitsch and Wetzel (2009). Kong et al. (2009). Cummins et al. (2010). Cohen and Morrison (2011).

Chapter 7

Managerial Problem: Clawing Back Bonuses Advertisement in *Derivatives Week*, 15(44), November 7, 2005, **www.derivativesweek.com/pdf/DW110705.pdf**. Matthew Goldstein, "Why Merrill Lynch Got Burned," *Businessweek*, October 25, 2007. Erin McCormick and Carolyn Said, "Investors Own about One-Fifth of Bay Area Homes in Foreclosure," *San Francisco Chronicle*, December 16, 2007. Dan Frommer, "Everything You Need to Know about Tim Cook, Apple's COO," *San Francisco Chronicle*, January 17, 2011. Louise Story, "Executive Pay," *New York Times*, March 3, 2011. Jessica Silver-Greenberg and Neslon D. Schwartz, "Citigroup's Chief Rebuffed on Pay by Shareholders," *New York Times*, April 17, 2012. Elizabeth G. Olson, "Executive pay clawbacks: Just a shareholder pacifier?" CNN Money, August 16, 2012, **management.fortune.cnn.com/2012/08/16/executive-pay-clawbacks/**. "Morgan Stanley Defers Bonuses for High-Earners," *Chicago Tribune*, January 15, 2013.

Mini-Cases *Chinese State-Owned Enterprises*: Gao Xu, "State-Owned Enterprises in China: How Big Are They?" January 19, 2010, **blogs.worldbank.org/eastasiapacific/state-owned-enterprises-in-china-how-big-are-they**. China Statistical Database, **219.235.129.58** (viewed June 9, 2013).

Company Jets: Yermack (2006). Kim Peterson, "Should CEOs Vacation with the Corporate Jet?" MSN Money, June 16, 2011, **money.msn.com/top-stocks/post.aspx?post=5b680a57-64c2-4ea8-93e4-786b65eb689c**. Rik Myslewski, "Zuckerberg's 2012 Personal Income Tax Bill: $1.5 Billion," *The Register*, February 4, 2012, **www.theregister.co.uk/2012/02/04/zuckerberg_tax_bill**.

The Yahoo! Poison Pill: "Microsoft Withdraws Proposal to Acquire Yahoo," Microsoft News Center, May 3, 2008, **www.microsoft.com/presspass/press/2008/may08/05-03letter.mspx**. Steve Lohr, "Microsoft's Failed Yahoo Bid Risks Online Growth," *New York Times*, May 5, 2008. Dawn Kawamoto, "Icahn to Yahoo: Nix the Poison Pill," CNET News, June 4, 2008, **news.cnet.com/8301-10784_3-9959776-7.html**. Nancy Gohring, "Judge OKs Settlement in Yahoo Shareholder Suit," IDG News Service,

May 9, 2009, **www.macworld.com/article/139291/2009/03/yahoo_settlement.html**. Brian Womack, "Yahoo Discount Means U.S. Web Portal Free in Takeover: Real M&A," *Bloomberg Businessweek*, August 9, 2011. **ycharts.com/companies/YHOO/enterprise_value**.

Vertical Integration at American Apparel: Joseph Warren, "Sexy sustainability for sale?" Sustainable Industries, Dec 5, 2005, **sustainableindustries.com/articles/2005/12/sexy-sustainability-sale**. Jennifer Ordonez, "California Hustlin'," *Newsweek*, Aug 20, 2006.

Aluminum: "History," Kaiser Aluminum, **www.kaiseraluminum.com/about-us/history** (viewed on May 26, 2012). Pu Jan, "Mines, Power Plants in a Chinalco Survival Strategy" January 7, 2011, **english.caixin.com/2011-01-07/100214940.html?p2**. **www.bloomberg.com/markets/companies/metal-aluminum** (viewed on April 7, 2013).

Chapter 8

Managerial Problem: The Rising Cost of Keeping on Truckin' Nicholas Katers, "About Interstate Trucking Authority," eHow, **www.ehow.com/about_4739672_interstate-trucking-authority.html** (viewed on June 16, 2012). "Rules & Regulations," U.S. Department of Transportation, **www.fmcsa.dot.gov/rules-regulations/rules-regulations.htm** (viewed on June 16, 2012). "Unified Carrier Registration," **www.dotauthority.com/ucr.htm?gclid=CKma5tebnqQCFSFZiAodN2bunA** (viewed on June 16, 2012).

Mini-Cases *Oil, Oil Sands, and Oil Shale Shutdowns*: Agis Salpukas, "Low Prices Have Sapped Little Oil Producers," *New York Times*, April 3, 1999. Robert Collier, "Fueling America, Oil's Dirty Future," *San Francisco Chronicle*, May 22, 2005. Robert Collier, "Coaxing Oil from Huge U.S. Shale Deposits," *San Francisco Chronicle*, September 4, 2006. Jon Birger, "Oil Shale May Finally Have Its Moment," *Fortune*, November 1, 2007. Judith Kohler, "Energy Firms Cautious on Oil Shale," OCRegister, November 3, 2007, **www.ocregister.com/news/oil-204519-shale-research.html**. Ben Geman, "Canada Warns U.S. Against Using Energy Law to Bar Fuel from Oil Sands," Greenwire, February 28, 2008, **groups.google.com/forum/#!msg/parklandsupdate/J_sCB8bxBpc/Uho5ZYVlpUUJ**. Robert Kunzig, "Scraping Bottom," *National Geographic Magazine*, March 2009. Oil reserve data are from the BP Statistical Review at **www.bp.com**.

The Size of Ethanol Processing Plants: "Statistics," Renewable Fuels Association, **www.ethanolrfa.org/pages/statistics** (viewed on May 28, 2012).

Fast-Food Firms' Entry in Russia: Andrew E. Kramer, "Russia Becomes a Magnet for U.S. Fast-Food Chains," *New York Times*, August 3, 2011.

Upward-Sloping Long-Run Supply Curve for Cotton: International Cotton Advisory Committee, *Survey of the Cost of Production of Raw Cotton*, September 1992:5. *Cotton: World Statistics*, April 1993:4–5.

The Deadweight Loss of Christmas Presents: Waldfogel (1993, 2005, 2009). Hubert B. Herring, "Help! What Do We Do With All This Stuff? 'Regift,' of Course," *New York Times*,

December 26, 2004. "Branded Gift Cards Popular with Consumers," November 6, 2006. Marshall Loeb, "How to Offload Unwanted Gift Cards," *Market Watch*, July 30, 2007, **articles.marketwatch.com/2007-07-30/finance/30730973_1_gift-cards-sale-or-swap-trade**. Sandra M. Jones, "Gift Cards May Be Losing Their Purchase Power," *Chicago Tribune*, November 13, 2007. Andrea Chang, "A Neat Gift Card Trick," *Los Angeles Times*, December 1, 2007. Alan Krauss, "Gift Cards Go Philanthropic," *New York Times*, December 5, 2007. "Gift Card Appeal Remains Strong and Continues to Grow," May 20, 2008. Eve Mitchell, "Cashing In," *Oakland Tribune*, June 12, 2011, C1. Barbara Farfan, "2011 U.S. Christmas Holiday Retail Data, Statistics, Results, Numbers Roundup Complete U.S. Retail Industry Christmas Holiday Shopping Year-Over-Year Results," December 29, 2011. Miguel Helft, "Meet the Anti-Groupon," CNN Money, April 30, 2012. **tech.fortune.cnn.com/2012/04/30/wrapp/**. Matt Brownell, "Gift Cards," *Forbes*, December 12, 2012.

Chapter 9

Managerial Problem: Brand-Name and Generic Drugs "Thailand Imports Generic Plavix from India," PMLiVE Intelligence Online, August 24, 2007, **www.pmlive.com/pharma_news/thailand_imports_generic_plavix_from_india_8936**. Richard G. Frank, "The Ongoing Regulation of Generic Drugs," *New England Journal of Medicine*, November 15, 2007. Regan (2008). Milt Freudenheim, "Benefit Managers Profit by Specialty Drug Rights," *New York Times*, April 19, 2008. "Canada Generics Set for Double Digit Growth," EmailWire, August 26, 2009, **www.emailwire.com/release/printPR.php?prID=26411**. Ken MacQueen, "The Case for a National Drug Plan," *Maclean's*, June 8, 2011, **www2.macleans.ca/2011/06/08/the-case-for-a-national-drug-plan**. "Top 15 Patent Losses for 2013,"**www.fiercepharma.com/special-reports/top-15-patent-expirations-2013**. **www.q1medicare.com/PartD-BrandNameDrugPatent-ExpirationsRX.php**.

Mini-Cases *Cable Cars and Profit Maximization*: Rachel Gordon, "A Fare Too Steep?" *San Francisco Chronicle*, September 12, 2006. Rachel Gordon, "Cable Car Fares Rising a Buck to $6 on July 1," *San Francisco Chronicle*, June 7, 2011. "Cable Car Fares," *SFMTA*, 2012, **www.sfmta.com/cms/mfares/fareinfo.htm#cable** (viewed on June 4, 2012).

Apple's iPad: Chloe Albanesius, "iSuppli: iPad Could Produce Profits for Apple," *PC Magazine*, February 10, 2010. Arik Hesseldahl, "Apple iPad Components Cost at Least $259," *Businessweek*, April 7, 2010. Don Reisinger, "IDC: Apple iPad Secures 87 Percent Market Share," CNET News **cnet.com**, January 18, 2011. Don Reisinger, "Study: iPad Tallies 89 Percent of Table Traffic," CNET News **cnet.com**, January 24, 2011. Jenna Wortham, "So Far Rivals Can't Beat iPad's Price," *New York Times*, March 6, 2011. "iPad Remains Dominant in 1Q 2012 While Kindle Fire Fizzles," ABI Research, **www.abiresearch.com/press/3919-iPad+Remains+Dominant+in+1Q%E2%80%992012+While+Kindle+Fire+Fizzles**. In Q&A 9.2, the marginal cost estimate (slightly rounded) is from iSuppli. Seth Fiegerman, "Apple Vs. Samsung: Everything You

Need to Know About the (Patent) Trial of the Century," Business Insider, June 30, 2012. **www.businessinsider.com**. We assumed that the company's gross profit margin for 2010 of about 40% (**forbes.com**) held for the iPad and used that to calculate the fixed cost. We derived the linear demand curve by assuming Apple maximizes short-run profit using the information on price, marginal cost, and quantity. The marginal cost estimate is based on iSuppli.

Botox: Mike Weiss, "For S.F. Doctor, Drug Botox Becomes a Real Eye-Opener," *San Francisco Chronicle*, April 14, 2002. Reed Abelson, "F.D.A. Approves Allergan Drug for Fighting Wrinkles," *New York Times*, April 16, 2002. Harriet Tramer, "Docs Detecting How to Boost Botox Profitability," *Crain's Cleveland Business*, March 7, 2005. Natasha Singer, "Botox Plus: New Mixes for Plumping and Padding," *New York Times*, July 14, 2005. Lisa Rapaport, "Allergan Profit Rises on Sales of Botox," Bloomberg News, August 1, 2007, **www.forums.pharma-mkting.com/ showthread.php?t=921**. Natasha Singer, "So Botox Isn't Just Skin Deep," *New York Times*, April 12, 2009. "Nice News for Allergan—Analyst Blog," NASDAQ, June 29, 2012, **community .nasdaq.com/News/2012-06/nice-news-for-allergan-analyst-blog.aspx?storyid=152408**.

Super Bowl Commercials: Ho et al. (2009). Kim (2011). Yinka Adegoke, "Super Bowl Advertisers Seek Buzz on Social Media," Reuters, January 29, 2012. Sharon Terlep and Suzanne Vranica, "GM to Forgo Pricey Super Bowl Ads," *The Wall Street Journal*, May 18, 2012. Lisa de Moraes, "Super Bowl Commercial Prices Spike" *Washington Post*, February 1, 2013. Scott Collins, "TV Ratings Dip for Blackout-Plagued CBS Game" *Los Angeles Times*, February 4, 2013.

Critical Mass and eBay: Ina Steiner, "Yahoo Closes Australian Auction Site," August 7, 2003, **www.auctionbytes .com/cab/abn/y03/m08/i07/s03**. Brown and Morgan (2006, 2009). John Barrett, "MySpace Is a Natural Monopoly," January 17, 2007, **www.ecommercetimes.com/story/55185 .html?welcome=1218648444&wlc=1251740474**. Carol Xiaojuan Ou and Robert M. Davison, "Why eBay Lost to TaoBao in China: The Global Advantage," *Communications of the ACM*, 52(1), January 2009.

Chapter 10

Managerial Problem: Sale Prices Karen Datko, "My Ketchup Taste Test: It's an Upset!" MSN Money, January 14, 2011, **money.msn.com/saving-money-tips/post .aspx?post=80c1a82a-df10-4e84-960b-30ed5ad96a33** Rebecca Smithers, "Heinz Left Playing Tomato Catch-Up after Ketchup Tasting Trouncing," *The Guardian*, May 26, 2011. Andrew Adam Newman, "Ketchup Moves Upmarket, with a Balsamic Tinge," *New York Times*, October 25, 2011.

Mini-Cases *Disneyland Pricing*: *Disneyland Resort*, 2012, **www.Disneyland.com**. "Couple Tries for Year of Daily Disneyland Visits," *San Francisco Chronicle*, July 3, 2012.

Preventing Resale of Designer Bags: Eric Wilson, "Retailers Limit Purchases of Designer Handbags," *New York Times*, January 10, 2008.

Botox Revisited: See Chapter 9, "Botox."

Dynamic Pricing at Amazon: David Streitfeld, "Amazon Pays a Price for Marketing Test," *Los Angeles Times*, October 2, 2000. "Dynamic Pricing Survey Analysis," June 2003, **www.managingchange.com/dynamic/survey/analysis .html**,(viewed on June 7, 2012). David Streitfeld, "Amazon Mystery: Pricing of Books," *Los Angeles Times*, January 2, 2007.

Reselling Textbooks: Adam Liptak, Justices Weigh Case on Imported Textbooks, *New York Times*, October 29, 2012. Ry Rivard, "Libraries Can Lend Foreign Books," *Inside Higher Ed*, March 20, 2013. Robert Barnes, "In Copyright Case, Supreme Court Rules that Goods Made Overseas Can Be Resold Here," *Washington Post*, March 19, 2013. Daniel Fisher, "Supreme Court Upholds Right to Sell Foreign-Published Books," *Forbes*, March 19, 2013.

Available for a Song: "iTunes Store Tops 10 Billion Songs Sold," Apple Press Info, February 25, 2010, **www.apple.com/pr/ library/2010/02/25itunes.html**. (Shiller and Waldfogel (2011).

Downhill Pricing: "2012–2013 Whistler Blackcomb Season Passes and Edge Cards on Sale," *SBC Skier*, March 29, 2012, **www.sbcskier.com/headlines_article?news_id=1405**. "Whistler Blackcomb 2011.12 Season Pass," Whistler Blackcomb, 2012, **www.whistlerblackcomb.com/tickets/seasonpass/index.htm**.

Managerial Implications *Discounts*: Borenstein and Rose (1994). Jenna Wortham, "Coupons You Don't Clip, Sent to Your Cellphone," *New York Times*, August 29, 2009. "Up Front," *Consumer Reports*, September 2009:7. Carmen Musick, "Computer Technology Fueling Coupon Trend," *Times News*, October 31, 2009. "Groupon and the Online Deal Revolution," eMarketer, June 7, 2011, **www.emarketer.com/ Article.aspx?R=1008427**. "Coupon Trends," *JPS*, March 2, 2012, **www.santella.com/Trends.htm**. "NCH Annual Coupon Facts," NCH Marketing, 2012, **www.nchmarketing.com/**.

Ties That Bind: hp.com. **www.consumerchoice.info/ warranty.htm**. **www.mlmlaw.com/library/guides/ftc/ warranties/undermag.htm**.

Chapter 11

Managerial Problem: Gaining an Edge from Government Aircraft Subsidies Irwin and Pavcnik (2004). John Heilpin, "WTO: Boeing Got $5B in Illegal Subsidies," March 12, 2012, **www.manufacturing.net/news/2012/03/wto-boeing-got-5b-in-illegal-subsidies**. **www.opensecrets.org/ lobby/clientsum.php?id=D000000100&year=2012**.

Mini-Cases *A Catwalk Cartel*: "Models File Class Action Law Suit," **abcnews.go.com/GMA/story?id=125935&page=1# .T9gTzBfY8sI**. William Sherman, "Catwalk Rocked by Legal Catfight," *New York Daily News*, March 14, 2004. Warren St. John, "Behind the Catwalk, Suspicion and Suits," *New York Times*, April 18, 2004. *United States District Court Southern District of New York*, July 5, 2007, **graphics8.nytimes.com/ packages/pdf/national/20071126Fears.pdf**. "Singapore—Competition Commission Fines Modelling Agencies for Price Fixing," Conventus Law, December 8, 2011, **conventuslaw.com/ competition-commission-of-singapore-fines-modelling-agencies-for-price-fixing**.

Air Ticket Prices and Rivalry: Weiher et al. (2002).

Acquiring Versus Merging: "BA Iberia Merger Gets Approval from Shareholders," BBC News, November 29, 2010, **www.bbc.co.uk/news/business-11862956**.

Zoning Laws as a Barrier to Entry by Hotel Chains: Suzuki (2013).

Managerial Implications *Differentiating a Product Through Marketing*: Julia Felsenthal, "Water, Water Everywhere: What's the Best-Tasting Kind of Water?" Slate, October 12, 2011, **www.slate.com/articles/business_and_tech/shopping/2011/10/what_s_the_best_tasting_kind_of_water_.html**.

Managing in the Monopolistically Competitive Food Truck Market: Andrew S. Ross, "San Francisco Food Truck Empire Expanding," *San Francisco Chronicle*, February 18, 2011. **www.mobilefoodnews.com** (viewed on June 17, 2012). **offthegridsf.com/about-3** (viewed on March 29, 2013).

Chapter 12

Managerial Problem: Dying to Work "Mining: Probe faults Massey, regulators in Upper Big Branch Disaster," Greenwire, May 19, 2011, **www.eenews.net/gw/2011/05/19**. Kris Maher, "Agency Blames Massey for Fatal Mine Disaster," *Wall Street Journal*, June 29, 2011. "China Accident Inside Coal Mine Kills 21 Workers; 4 Others Still Missing," **www.huffingtonpost.com/2013/03/13/china-mine-accident_n_2865523.html**. Lateef Mungin and Farid Ahmed, "Report: 8 Arrested after Deadly Bangladesh Building Collapse," CNN, April 27, 2013, **www.cnn.com/2013/04/27/world/asia/bangladesh-building-collapse/index.html**. **world.time.com/2013/06/10/bangladesh-factory-collapse-uncertain-future-for-rana-plaza-survivors**, June 10, 2013.

Mini-Cases *Strategic Advertising*: Roberts and Samuelson (1988). Slade (1995). Gasmi et al. (2002). Salgado and Hugo (2008). Timothy J. Richards and Luis Padilla (2009). "Leading Global Advertisers in 2010 by Estimated Revenue," Adbrands.net: Top Global Advertisers, 2010, **www.adbrands.net/top_global_advertisers.htm**. Garthwaite (2012). "Kantar Media Reports U.S. Advertising Expenditures Increased 0.8 Percent in 2011," Kantar Media, March 12, 2012, **www.kantarmedia.com/sites/default/files/press/Kantar_Media_2011__Q4_US_Ad_Spend.pdf**. Procter and Gamble 2012 Annual Report online, **annualreport.pg.com/annualreport2012/index.shtml**.

Timing Radio Ads: Sweeting (2006, 2009).

Nash Bargaining Over Coffee: Draganska et al. (2010).

Experienced Bidders: Garratt et al. (2012).

Google Advertising: Avi Goldfarb and Catherine Tucker (2011).

Chapter 13

Managerial Problem: Intel and AMD's Advertising Strategies Salgado (2008).

Mini-Cases *Tit for Tat Strategies in Trench Warfare*: Axelrod (2006).

Pay-for-Delay Agreements: Matthew Herper, "The Best-Selling Drugs in America," *Forbes*, April 19, 2011. Duff Wilson, "F.T.C.: 28 'Pay-for-Delay' Generic Drug Deals," *New York Times*, October 25, 2011. Edward Wyatt, "Justices to Take Up Generic Drug Case," *New York Times*, December 7, 2012. Katie Thomas and Barry Meier, "Drug Makers Losing a Bid to Foil Generic Painkillers," *New York Times*, January 1, 2013. Wyatt (2013).

Pfizer Uses Limit Pricing to Slow Entry: Melly Alazraki, "The 10 Biggest-Selling Drugs That Are About to Lose Their Patent," *Daily Finance*, February 27, 2011. Duff Wilson, "Facing Generic Lipitor Rivals, Pfizer Battles to Protect Its Cash Cow," *New York Times*, November 29, 2011. Anna Edney and Adi Narayan, "Ranbaxy's Lipitor Copy in U.S. Stores Threatens Pfizer Sales," *Bloomberg Businessweek*, December 1, 2011. Duff Wilson, "Senators Question Deals to Block Generic Lipitor," *New York Times*, December 1, 2011. Drew Armstrong, "Pfizer After Lipitor Slims Down to Push Mini-Blockbusters," *Bloomberg Businessweek*, December 5, 2011. Anna Edney, Adi Narayan, and Drew Armstrong, "Pfizer Lipitor Sales Are Threatened by Ranbaxy Generic Copy," *Bloomberg Businessweek*, December 6, 2011. Jonathan Rockoff, "Goodbye, Lipitor. Pfizer Bids a Farewell," *Wall Street Journal*, May 9, 2012. Allan Rubin and Harold Rubin, "Patents and Prescription Drugs – Part II of a III Part Series," May 23, 2012, **www.therubins.com/legal/patext2.htm**. "Pharmaceutical Sales 2010," *Drug Information Online*.

Auto Union Negotiations: Alisa Priddle, "Ford an Attractive Target for UAW Contract Talks," *Detroit News*, January 28, 2011, **www.cawlocal584.com/news_12.html**. Bernie Woodall, "3-UAW's King Hopes for Early Auto Talks Settlement," Reuters, August 17, 2011.

Venezuelan Nationalization: Gregory Wilpert, "Venezuela Decrees Nationalization of Last Foreign Controlled Oil Fields," February 27, 2007, **venezuelanalysis.com/news/2245**. "Venezuela," U.S. Energy Information Administration, March 2011, **www.eia.gov/countries/cab.cfm?fips=VE**. Patrick MacLeod, "U.S. Energy Information Administration Assessment of the Venezuelan Oil Industry," *Blogspot*, April 4, 2011, **venezuelanoil.blogspot.com/2011/04/us-energy-information-administration.html**. Marianna Parraga and Daniel Wallis, "PDVSA Says Debt Rose 55 Percent to $10.9 Billion at the End of 2010," Reuters, July 27, 2011. **www.petroleumworld.com/storyt11072701.htm**. John Daly, "Venezuela to Compensate American Oil Companies for Nationalization?" July 29, 2011, **oilprice.com/Energy/Energy-General/Venezuela-to-Compensate-American-Oil-Companies-for-Nationalization.html**. Marianna Parraga, "Venezuela sees Exxon, Conoco arbitration rules in late 2013," Reuters, November 8, 2012.

Advantages and Disadvantages of Moving First: Urban et al. (1986). Denstadli et al. (2005). Dylan McGrath, "'Teardown' Finds Toshiba Taking a Loss on HD DVD Player," EE Times, June 23, 2006, **www.eetimes.com/design/other/4004124/-Teardown-finds-Toshiba-taking-a-loss-on-HD-DVD-player**. Dylan McGrath, "Analyst Predicts Stalemate in Next-Gen DVD War," EE Times, June 23, 2006, **www.eetimes.com/electronics-products/other/4085173/Analyst-predicts-stalemate-in-next-gen-DVD-war**. Usero and Fernández (2009).

GM's Ultimatum: Robert Schoenberger, "GM Sends Ulti-matums to All Its 6000 US dealers," *Cleveland Plain Dealer*, June 2, 2009. Tony Van Alphen, "GM Dealers Sue to Keep Doors Open," *Toronto Star*, November 27, 2009. Janet Kur-novich, "GM Canada Sued For $750 Million by Former Deal-ers," May 17, 2011, **insurance-car.co/automotive-insurance/gm-canada-sued-for-750-million-by-former-dealers/**.

Chapter 14

Managerial Problem: Risk and Limited Liability Mark Long and Angel Gonzalez, "Transocean Seeks Limit on Liability," *Wall Street Journal*, May 13, 2010. David Leonhardt, "Spil-lonomics: Underestimating Risk," *New York Times*, May 21, 2010. Andrew Ross Sorkin, "Imagining the Worst in BP's Future," *New York Times*, June 7, 2010. "BP Reports $4.9bn Annual Loss after Oil Spill Costs," BBC News, February 1, 2011, **www.bbc.co.uk/news/business-12331804**. Sabrina Can-field, "BP, Transocean Wrangle Over Insurance," Courthouse News Service, February 28, 2011, **www.courthousenews .com/2011/02/28/34488.htm**. Jef Feeley and Allen Johnson Jr., "BP Wins Final Approval of Guilty Plea Over Gulf Oil Spill," Bloomberg News, January 29, 2013, **www.bloomberg.com/news/2013-01-29/bp-wins-final-approval-of-guilty-plea-over-gulf-oil-spill.html**. Kathy Finn, "Gulf Oil Spill Payouts," **www.huffingtonpost.com/2013/04/05/bp-gulf-oil-spill-payouts_n_3022877.html**. "The Storybook Romance Comes to an End for Barbie and Ken," Mattel, February 12, 2004, **investor .shareholder.com/mattel/releasedetail.cfm?ReleaseID=128705**. **www.bp.com/sectiongenericarticle800.do?categoryId=9048917&contentId=7082602** (viewed on April 12, 2013).

Mini-Cases *Stocks' Risk Premium*: "The Cost of Looking," *Economist*, 328(7828), September 11, 1993:74. Leslie Eaton, "Assessing a Fund's Risk Is Part Math, Part Art," *New York Times*, April 2, 1995. Jagannathan et al. (2000). **www .standardandpoors.com** (viewed on June 25, 2012). **people .stern.nyu.edu/adamodar/New_Home_Page/datafile/histretSP.html** (viewed on April 8, 2013).

Gambling: Friedman and Savage (1948). Brunk (1981). Steve Coll, "Chances Are Brits Have Bet on It," *San Fran-cisco Examiner*, July 10, 1994:4. Meghan Cox Gurdon, "Brit-ish Accuse Their Lottery of Robbing the Poor to Give to the Rich," *San Francisco Chronicle*, November 25, 1995. Andrew Pollack, "In the Gaming Industry, the House Can Have Bad Luck, Too," *New York Times*, July 25, 1999. Garrett (2001). Marsha Walton, "The Business of Gambling," *CNN*, July 6, 2005. **www.elottery.com/markets.html** (viewed on June 26, 2012). **www.reportlinker.com/p0157384-sum-mary/Global-Online-Gaming-Report.html** (viewed on April 8, 2013).

Bond Ratings: "Credit Ratings Definitions & FAQs," 2012, Standard and Poor's **www.standardandpoors.com/ratings/definitions-and-faqs/en/us** (viewed on June 26, 2012). "Rating Symbols and Definitions," *Moody's Investors Services*, **www.moodys.com/researchdocumentcontentpage .aspx?docid=PBC_79004** (viewed on June 26, 2012).

Limited Insurance for Natural Disasters: Joseph B. Treaster, "Insurer Plans to Curb Sales Along Coasts," *New York Times*, October 10, 1996. Joseph B. Treaster, "Why Insurers Shrink from Earthquake Risk," *New York Times*, November 21, 1999. Paul Vitello, "Home Insurers Cancel-ing in East," *New York Times*, October 16, 2007. Pielke et al. (2008). "Tropical Storm Bonnie Dissipates; Still No Plan from Congress on Flood Insurance," Insurance News Net, July 28, 2010, **www.insurancenewsnet.com/article.aspx?id =210913&type=newswires**. Evan Lehmann, "U.S. Hit with 90% of the World's Disaster Costs in 2012," Climatewire, January 4, 2013, **www.eenews.net/stories/1059974314**. "Hurricane Sandy, Drought Cost U.S. $100 Billion," *USA Today*, January 24, 2013

Biased Estimates: Benjamin et al. (2001). "What Should You Really Be Afraid of?—Mortality Risks," 2003, Sophie Ted-manson, "Fisherman Dean Brougham Tells of Lucky Escape After Shark Attack," *The Times*, November 9, 2009. Arthur Hu, "Death Spectrum," April 11, 2011, **www.arthurhu.com/index/health/death.htm#deathrank**. International Shark Attack File, *Ichthyology*, **www.flmnh.ufl.edu/fish/sharks/isaf/graphs.htm** (viewed on June 26, 2012).

Managerial Implication *Diversifying Retirement Funds*: Paul J. Lim, "Don't Paint Nest Eggs in Company Colors," *New York Times*, March 30, 2008. Jilian Mincer, "Company-Stock Ownership Down Amid Fears," Financial Advisor, August 9, 2010, **financialadviserblog.dowjones.com/blog/stay-ahead-of-your-clients/company-stock-ownership-down-amid-fears**. Michael J. Moore, "Wall Streeters Lose $2 Billion in 401(k) Bet on Own Firms," Bloomberg News, July 9, 2012, **www.bloomberg.com/news/2012-07-09/wall-streeters-lose-2-billion-in-401-k-bet-on-own-firms.html**.

Chapter 15

Managerial Problem: Limiting Managerial Incentives Emily Zimmerman, "Foreclosures Down 19% from One Year Ago," Virginia Commonwealth University, Center on Needs Blog, March 12, 2012, **wp.vcu.edu/humanneeds/2012/03/12/1-in-every-399-housing-units-r-2/**. RealtyTrac, 2012, **www .realtytrac.com** (on November 21, 2012).

Mini-Cases *Reducing Consumers' Information*: Salop (1977).

Changing a Firm's Name: Cabral and Hortacsu (2010). McDevitt (2011).

Adverse Selection on eBay Motors: Lewis (2011).

Selfless or Selfish Doctors: Lu (2012).

Contracts and Productivity in Agriculture: Foster and Rosenzweig (1994).

Abusing Leased Cars: Dunham (2003). "Table 1-17: New and Used Passenger Car Sales and Leases," *RITA*, 2011, **www .rita.dot.gov/bts/sites/rita.dot.gov.bts/files/publications/national_transportation_statistics/html/table_01_17.html**. Manuel Quinones, "Probe Faults Massey, Regulators in Upper Big Branch Disaster," Greenwire, May 19, 2011, **www.eenews .net/gw/2011/05/19**.

Chapter 16

Managerial Problem: Licensing Inventions data .worldbank.org/indicator/BX.GSR.ROYL.CD/ countries/1W?display=graph (viewed on April 28, 2013). World Intellectual Property Organization, 2012 World Intellectual Property Indicators, **www.wipo.int/ipstats/en/wipi/**. World Intellectual Property Organization, 2012 World Intellectual Property Report, The Changing Face of Innovation. Steve Lohr, "The 2012 Patent Ranks," *New York Times*, January 10, 2013.

Mini-Cases *Natural Gas Regulation:* Davis and Muehlegger (2009).

Hospital Mergers: Market Power Versus Efficiency: Dafny (2009). Haas-Wilson and Garmon (2011). Tenn (2011). Brand et al. (2012).

An Exclusive Contract for a Key Ingredient: "Memorandum Opinion," *United States District Court*, January 24, 2008, **www .crowell.com/pdf/managedcare/Lorazepam-Clorazepate-Antitrust-Litigation.pdf**. "Lorazepam & Clorazepate Antitrust Litigation," *Find A Case*, January 18, 2011, **tn.findacase.com/ research/wfrmDocViewer.aspx/xq/fac.20110118_0000003.CDC .htm/qx**. "Exclusionary or Predatory Acts: Exclusive Supply or Purchase Agreements," Federal Trade Commission, 2012, **www.ftc.gov/bc/antitrust/exclusive_supply.shtm**.

Negative Externalities from Spam: Marc Caliendo et al., "The Cost Impact of Spam Filters: Measuring the Effect of Information System Technologies in Organizations," *Information Systems Research*, 2011. "Email Attacks: This Time It's Personal," Cisco, June 2011, **www.cisco.com/en/ US/prod/collateral/vpndevc/ps10128/ps10339/ps10354/ targeted_attacks.pdf**. Nicole Henderson, "Symantec Report Finds Spam Accounts for 73 Percent of June Email," *Web Host Industry Review*/June 28, 2011. Rao and Reiley (2012). Dino Grandoni, "Spam Costs You a Lot More Than You'd Think," **www.huffingtonpost.com/2012/08/08/cost-of-spam_n_1757726.html**. Lance Whitney, "Targeted Cyberattacks Jump 42 Percent in 2012, Symantec Says," **news.cnet .com/8301-1009_3-57579847-83/targeted-cyberattacks-jump-42-percent-in-2012-symantec-says**.

Pulp and Paper Mill Pollution and Regulation: LaPlante and Rilstone (1996). Foulon et al. (2002). Shimshack and Ward (2005). Gray and Shimshack (2011).

Why Tax Drivers: Edlin and Karaca-Mandic (2006) Parry et al. (2007) Hill et. al. (2009) Michael Anderson and Auffhammer Maximilian, "Pounds that Kill: The External Costs of Vehicle Weight," NBER Working Paper 17170, 2011.

For Whom the Bridge Tolls: Michael Cabanatuan "New Tolls Don't Gum Up Bay Bridge Commute," *San Francisco Chronicle*, July 2, 2010. Will Kane, "Bay Area Bridge Tolls Take a Toll on Commuters," *San Francisco Chronicle*, July 29, 2010.

Piracy: "2011 Piracy Study," Business Software Alliance, **portal.bsa.org/globalpiracy2011/**.

Managerial Implications *Buying a Town:* Katharine Q. Seelye, "Utility Buys Town It Choked, Lock, Stock and Blue Plume," *New York Times*, May 13, 2002. "Cheshire Ohio," Abandoned, **www.abandonedonline.net/neighborhoods/ cheshire-ohio**.

Trade Secrets: Hall et al. (2012).

Chapter 17

Managerial Problem: Responding to Exchange Rates "Rolls Royce Phantom Drophead Coupe," *Convertible Car Magazine*, 2011. "Rolls-Royce Announces Record Half-Year Sales," Rolls-Royce Motor Cars Press Club, July 7, 2011, "CHS in Talks to Expand US Grain Export Venture," Reuters, August 4, 2011. "Rolls-Royce Convertibles," Aol Autos, 2012, **autos.aol.com/ rolls_royce/convertible**. USDA Economic Research Service, "Wheat Data," **www.ers.usda.gov/data-products/wheat-data .aspx#.UX9KnpUx0ct** (viewed on April 29, 2013).

Mini-Cases *Barbie Doll Varieties:* "The Storybook Romance Comes to an End for Barbie and Ken," Mattel, February 12, 2004. Venessa Wong, "Barbie Wins Contest for No. 1 Holiday Import," *Bloomberg Businessweek*, December 13, 2011. "Santa to Bring High-Tech Gadgets, Familiar Favorites to Children This Holiday Season," National Retail Federation Press Release, November 20, 2012, **www.nrf.com/modules .php?name=News&op=viewlive&sp_id=1459**.

Managerial Responses to the Chicken Tax Trade War: "U.S. Files Complaint Over Chinese Chicken Tariffs," *The New York Times*, September 20, 2011.

Dumping and Countervailing Duties for Solar Panels: Arno Harris, "The 'Blame China' Game," *The National Geographic*, October 14, 2011. "China's Solar Industry and the U.S. Anti-Dumping/ Anti-Subsidy Trade Case," China Global Trade, 2012, **www .chinaglobaltrade.com/sites/default/files/china-global-trade-solar-manufacturing_may2012_0.pdf**. Eric Wesoff, "China Retaliates in Solar Trade War," Greentech Media, July 20, 2012, **www.greentechmedia.com/articles/read/china-retaliates-in-solar-trade-war/**. John McArdle, "Trade Case Combatants Spar Over Impact of Commerce Ruling," Greenwire, October 11, 2012 **www.eenews.net/Greenwire/2012/10/11/1**. Kirsten Korosec, "Case Closed: U.S. Sticks Chinese Solar Makers with Tariffs," Smart Planet, November 7, 2012, **www.smartplanet .com/blog/bulletin/case-closed-us-sticks-chinese-solar-makers-with-tariffs/4910?tag=search-river**.

What's an American Car? Kelsey Mays, "The Cars.com American-Made Index," 2011, **www.cars.com/go/advice/ Story.jsp?section=top&subject=ami&story=amMade0712** (viewed on December 3, 2012).

Profit Repatriation: John Aloysius Farrell, "Senate Committee Finds Most 'Trapped' Offshore Income Is Already in U.S.," The Cutting Edge News, December 18, 2011, **www .thecuttingedgenews.com/index.php?article=53402&pagei d=37&pagename=Page+One**. John Aidan Bryne, "US Tech Investors Hurt by Offshore Cash," *New York Post*, July 29, 2012. Eric Savitz, "Election Fallout: Will Tech Cash Piles Remain Trapped Overseas?" *Forbes*, November 7, 2012. Editorial, "Apple Showdown with Congress Shows Need for Corporate Tax Reform," *Mercury News*, May 23, 2013.

Managerial Implication *Limiting Arbitrage and Gray Markets:* Peter Sayer, "EU Court Says eBay Must Comply with Trademark Rules," *PC World Australia*, July 13, 2011. David Needle, "Unauthorized iPads Make Up Half of All Sales in China," Tab Times, October 11, 2011, **tabtimes.com/news/ittech-other/2011/10/11/ unauthorized-ipads-make-half-all-sales-china**.

Index

Credits

Featured Mini-Cases in This Book